C0-AYF-629

A Garland Series

The Legislative Origins of American Foreign Policy

The Senate Foreign Relations Committee in Executive Session 1913–1933; 1947–1950

Ten Volumes

edited with introductions by
Richard D. Challener
Princeton University

The Legislative Origins of American Foreign Policy

Proceedings of the Committee on Foreign Relations, United States Senate (1913–1933)

1. April 7, 1913, to March 3, 1923
2. December 3, 1923, to March 3, 1933

The Senate Foreign Relations Committee's Historical Series (1947–1950)

3. Legislative Origins of the Truman Doctrine (March–April 1947)
4. Foreign Relief Aid: 1947 (April and November 1947)
5. Foreign Relief Assistance Act of 1948 (February, March, April 1948)
6. The Vandenberg Resolution and the North Atlantic Treaty (May, June 1948; February, March, April, June 1949)
7. Economic Assistance to China and Korea: 1949–50 (March, June, July 1949; January 1950)
8. Reviews of the World Situation: 1949–50
9. Military Assistance Program: 1949 (July, August, September 1949)
10. Extension of the European Recovery Program: 1949 (February-March 1949)

The Senate Foreign Relations Committee's
Historical Series

Foreign Relief Assistance Act of 1948

with an introduction by
Richard D. Challener

Garland Publishing, Inc.
New York & London / 1979

This facsimile has been made from a copy in
the Princeton University Library (KF26.F6.1973g).

Library of Congress Cataloging in Publication Data

United States. Congress. Senate. Committee on Foreign Relations.
Foreign relief assistance act of 1948.

(The Legislative origins of American foreign policy)
Reprint of the 1973 ed. published by U. S. Govt. Print. Off., Washington,
in series: Historical series.
1. Economic assistance, American. 1. Title.
II. Series. III. Series: Historical series (Washington, D.C.).
[KF26.F6 1948] 343'.73'074 78-26586
ISBN 0-8240-3034-6

The volumes in this series are printed on acid-free,
250-year-life paper.

Printed in the United States of America

Introduction

These hearings focus primarily upon the Marshall Plan—officially, the European Recovery Program (ERP)—but the more than five hundred pages of testimony and cross-examination in this volume also include an extended debate over the continuation of aid to Nationalist China and the extension of the Greek-Turkish aid program for another year. The Foreign Relations Committee was compelled to act on these issues because the House of Representatives, contrary to the wishes of the Senate, had not dealt separately with the Marshall Plan, but had put together a three-part package which tied aid to China, Greece, and Turkey into the European Recovery legislation. In addition (as with most volumes in this series) there is an appendix of supporting documentation—more than two hundred pages of legislative chronologies, drafts of the bills in question, staff memoranda, some correspondence with the State Department, and several special reports (among the more important, a secret report by General A.M. Harper on military problems in Greece and a top secret communication from another American general on Turkish defense needs).

The Marshall Plan did not create controversy. Bipartisanship remained in force; the Senators clearly respected and trusted Secretary of State George Marshall; and the coup in Czechoslovakia occurred while the hearings were in progess. Both Republicans and Democrats were extremely pleased with the multilateral dimensions of the European Recovery Program—that is, pleased that the participating nations had met, pledged a joint effort, and made specific commitments to reach certain goals ("I think," said Senator Walter George, "we must lay special emphasis upon the multilateral undertaking or agreement . . . it is absolutely vital, because I think it is the only door through which we can enter into European affairs at all except running the risk of having them slide right back into a simple undertaking between country X over there and ourselves, very much as we are bogged up with Greece at the moment."). At none of these closed sessions did any member of the Truman administration make a major presentation on the overall purposes and objectives of the European Recovery Program. Instead, Lewis Douglas, Ambassador to Great Britain, represented the State Department, and most hearings consisted of a detailed, line-by-line examination of the proposed legislation, with members of the committee suggesting changes or amendments and Douglas responding on behalf of the administration.

This is not to suggest that there was no substantive discussion of real issues. The Senators cared greatly about the power and authority to be conferred upon the administrator and about how the program would be administered (Senator Hickenlooper: "The people in our State [Iowa], who have been erroneously accused of being isolationists—they never have been—will vigorously support a program of real reconstruction in Europe, but not a program of a gargantuan WPA over there. If they get the idea that this money . . . is being wasted . . . with a bunch of altruism instead of practical recovery programs, they are going to kick a lot on it. If it is run in a sound way and with acceptable administration, they are going to support it very definitely."). The Senators worried about creating too much European dependence on petroleum, debated the merits of providing guaranties to encourage American investment in Europe, expressed concern about making excessive demands upon the American economy and its price structure, and, in particular, debated the extent to which the United States, as a "condition precedent" to granting aid, could demand that the European nations meet certain conditions and live up to their pledges. (The committee, on the whole, was quite responsible. The Senators, for example, agreed that while they favored greater European political and economic integration, the United States could not require it. "I do not think," said Senator Barkley, "we can impose upon them political consolidation. I would like to see it come about, of course.")

The committee quizzed Ambassador Douglas at length about the reasons why nations such as Canada and Argentina could not extend credits as the United States was doing. The answer—these were the now remote days when the dollar was the strongest currency in the world—was the dollar gap (Ambassador Douglas: "They are short of dollars now, Senator. The Argentine has imposed restrictions on imports. She cannot convert other European currencies into dollars as she did before the war, so she therefore suffers from a shortage of dollars . . . these countries do not have dollars, and they need dollars to live."). There was extended discussion about writing the legislation in such a way that other European countries, not part of the original Marshall Plan group, could join at a later date. The motivation was in large part political—in Vandenberg's terse words, "I want a textual answer to the Henry Wallace so-and-sos who say this is a closed corporation." Or as the chairman put it on another occasion, "It must be kept open for scenic purposes, if nothing else." (Though the thought that Russia might apply provoked him to remark, "God help us if they ever accepted our invitation.") But it was not all cosmetic. At the outset the committee had hoped for eventual Czech participation, while already more than one Senator was interested in exploring ways whereby Franco's Spain might achieve eligibilty.

The Senators genuinely belived that the United States faced a crisis. At one point, indeed, they involved themselves in a collective *mea culpa* over their inability to transmit their sense of the gravity of the Soviet challenge to the American public. And Chairman Vandenberg not only insisted upon the need for domestic unity but viewed Henry Wallace as the ultimate menace:

> I think the greatest hazard to American peace is Henry Wallace. I mean that literally, and I mean it for this reason. I have, as I have said repeatedly, faced Mr. Molotov a couple of hundred days last year, and I have seen his reaction to things, and when he confronts what he thinks is a united America which has drawn the line and said "That is it," he thinks it over and usually he backs up. But if he has the slightest encouragement to think that the representatives of the United States who were talking to him haven't got a united country behind them, he just has a holiday, and I know of no reason, sitting there in the Politburo in Moscow, when he sees Henry Wallace carry a congressional district, why he should not just laugh and say, "All I have to do is wait."
>
> Then he looks across the country and he sees polls in which sometimes Wallace outruns Truman somewhat. That is the deadliest thing, in my book, that can happen to the United States.

But crisis or not, domestic politics—high as well as low—affected the decisions of the Foreign Relations Committee. It accpeted, first, Vandenberg's argument that the initial appropriation for the Marshall Plan should run for twelve instead of fifteen months, reducing the cost from $6,800 million to $5,300 (The Chairman: "when you get down to the bare bones of the rollcall up here, I venture to say that there are 25 Senators . . . and certainly 200 Members of the House who have got to vote for something less than $6,800 million, and you have to give them something less than that to vote for"). More importantly, the committee responded to the special pleading of Senator Eugene Millikin, Chairman of the Senate Finance Committee, who sought to have as much as possible of the overall appropriation charged to fiscal 1948 (when the Treasury anticipated a surplus) with the carryover funds for 1949 placed in a special trust for use in that year. Everyone realized Millikin's purpose: "The motivating power behind it," Senator Barkley observed, "is probably a new bookkeeping maneuver in connection with a tax reduction." Then, when Millikin appeared before the committee:

> Senator Barkley: As a mattter of fact, Senator—just all of us letting our hair down—this is a device to create a bigger surplus for 1949 as a basis for a larger tax reduction; is it not?
>
> Senator Millikin: That is one of the purposes. . . . It is also to create a larger surplus for ERP. It is also to create larger surpluses for any other projects that may be in the Senate that are considered important.
>
> Senator Barkley: That is a little unusual procedure, in order to create a larger surplus in a given year than actually exists.
>
> Senator Millikin: I come back to the point that it is all out of the same bag, and we are piling up an extraordinary number of projects. . . . I believe that this is a practical way to aid you in the solution of this immediate problem, and I would be less than candid if I did not say that I hope also it would aid us in our tax reduction program.

Millikin's final pitch was bluntly political: "I think it is perfectly obvious, gentlemen, that it will certainly soften the complaints of those who have other things in mind and other projects in which they are interested, that this project is hogging up all of the surplus of the next fiscal year."

But Alben Barkley, representing Kentucky and its tobacco interests, was no less politically motivated: He pushed incessantly for an amendment that would direct the administrator or ERP to use, in the first instance, agricultural products that were in surplus and to use them "in proportion to the surplus of each type and kind that is in existence." Discussion was a mixture of seriousness and Senatorial humor:

> The Chairman: Senator Connally suggested that inasmuch as this was a relief bill, we ought to put our emphasis upon edible tobacco.
>
> So far as the tobacco item is concerned, I think the chief complaint I have had, more than against any one thing is this question: Why do you spend a quarter of a billion dollars for tobacco in order to save the lives of these Europeans and keep them sustained?
>
> Senator George: Keep them from going Communist.
>
> Senator Barkley: It is an incentive payment. The purpose of it is to keep up the morale of the people in the factories and mines.
>
> The Chairman: I understand.
>
> Senator Smith: That is what the movie people say.

Barkley, ever insistent, always blandly asserted that while he might talk about tobacco and tobacco surpluses, the issue at stake was much broader and involved all surplus agricultural products. Still, his purposes, like those of Millikin, were not hidden:

> I am frank to say that the tobacco growers of my State and other states are interested in this thing. They feel that if we are going to buy tobacco, which seems to be essential and which is part of the programs for incentive purposes in Europe, that preference ought to be given to these types which are in surplus.

And later in the debate:

> Those agricultural interests that suggested the amendment wanted to see to it that in the process we work off some of the surplus that is already in existence and incidentally create, probably, a future market for some of our American products if the European countries have a taste for them.

The Foreign Relations Committee behaved better, however, on the issue of leasing or selling surplus American merchant shipping to the European nations for the transport of ERP products abroad. American shipping interests—and, reportedly, important segments of labor—were opposed (The Chairman: "Then we confront the fundamental challenge that has been raised by all branches of organized labor, which has otherwise given us complete support for this legislation, the complaint that this is a blow at the employment of American seamen."). Shipping interests, indeed, had just managed to push through the Senate a bill which flatly prohibited the lease or sale of any American vessels. But Ambassador Douglas insisted that lease or sale would save the American people millions of dollars:

> Shipping about 48 million tons a year will exhaust, in American bottoms, about $480 million. That is the magnitude of the drain in dollars imposed on the European countries by the use of ships flying the American flag. If they have ships flying under their own flags, even though their costs were the same as ours . . . they would be paying the freight in their own currencies and not in ours.

Moreover, Douglas went on, American shippers had made excess profits out of UNRRA shipments:

> If there is no authority in this bill to charter, the American shipping interests will doubtless do precisely what they did after the enactment of UNRRA, increase their rates, and if they increase their rates to the level 1 1/2 or halfway between the present level and the rates which they charged after the enactment of the UNRRA legislation . . . the cost to the United States will be $184 million in addition.

He pleaded for a chartering provision because "it gives the Administrator a club which he can use over the shipping interests to prevent them from doing exactly what they did after UNRRA was passed." In the last analysis the Foreign Relations Committee held most of its guns: it agreed that up to two hundred ships could be leased to European nations, provided that they were dry cargo ships and were taken from the inactive merchant marine.

But what most disturbed the Senators was the House bill that included China—as well as Greece and Turkey—within the European Recovery legislation. Thus, they had to act on these matters as well. Greece and Turkey produced some restiveness (for example, Senator George indicated that he might not have voted for the original Greek-Turkish aid bill in 1947 if he had known then what he knew now). There was a frank presentation from General Marshall about increased guerilla activity in Greece and the failure of the Greek economy to revive as anticipated. But Greek-Turkish aid was never really in question: the commitment had been made a year previously, and Greece was already included in the Marshall Plan.

With China, the committee's attitude and perceptions were strikingly different. The committee—to a man—thought that money spent on Chiang Kai-shek would be wasted. Indeed, had the committee been free to act according to its own inclinations, it might well have rejected further assistance to Nationalist China. Chairman Vandenberg set the tone, early in the discussion, when he described the House bill as something "purely on a sentimental basis." "Yes," interjected Utah's Senator Thomas, "and the theory that Chiang Kai-shek is something of a saint."

Members of the committee did not dispute the adverse reports on Nationalist China furnished by Secretary Marshall, and in early 1948 China was not a divisive political issue between Republicans and Democrats. On the Democratic side, Walter George would characterize any American involvement in China as "an adventure in chaos," and Tom Connally would complain that "China has been a sore spot for years and years, and she is always going to be a sore spot. . . . China is going to be around our necks as long as any of us are around here." But Bourke Hickenlooper, a Republican conservative from Iowa, could be no less scathing in his assessment of Chiang: "Chiang has been in charge . . . in China for 15 or 18 years, and he still hasn't cleaned out the corrupt war lords that are in his own machine. He is still operating on the basis of loot and graft. . . . That is the thing that discourages me about China."

These transcripts demonstrate, clearly and beyond reasonable doubt, that as of early 1948 it was not inevitable that the United States would commit itself to the role of global policeman or rush into the breech to save Chiang's fast-fading fortunes. The committee, for example, did not view communism as a monolithic movement, with Mao simply serving as the advance agent for Stalin and world communism. It accepted the State Department view that while the Soviet Union favored Mao and thought that his successes benefitted the Kremlin, Russia's own aims in the Far East were largely confined to Manchuria (Secretary Marshall: "I do not think the Russians themselves could go very far south into China, because they will get themselves into difficulties which they are anxious to avoid. I think they can get most of the things they want by a Chinese-Communist infiltration in control of a region." Walton Butterworth, Director, Office of Far Eastern Affairs: "I would say at the present time the Kremlin would not like to see a united China, even if that China was a so-called Communist China."). Thus, Senator Connally stated, "I do not believe that all this opposition to him [Chiang] is necessarily, strictly speaking, Communist. I think they are fighting the government that is in. They are just opposed to his long regime, and they don't think they are getting their reforms, and they are not getting their land. . . ." Republican Senator Wiley wondered aloud if the Russians weren't getting into a situation where the Kremlin "won't be able to assimilate what she is trying to chew" and asked George Marshall whether or not he thought "that there is a great deal of fear in this picture that is not realizable in the sense that Russia can't assimilate all these folks." Senator Thomas made this sweeping assertion:

I think we make too much of the notion that the Chinese Communists are actual proxies of the world revolution notion, because it is very, very sure that if the Communists become completely successful in China, it will not be successful in accordance with the Russian notion of what Communism is.

At times the Senators were surprisingly prescient and saw the danger inherent in continuing any assistance to Chiang. "I hate to see us on the horns of this dilemma all over the world," warned Henry Cabot Lodge, "that because we don't like Communists, we have to deal with reactionaries all over the world." Alexander Wiley worried about the future:

If it is true that the common people have in their hearts a feeling for this revolutionary Communist movement, what are we doing about the future of America? If we are going to back up the opposition and the opposition is going down, where do we come out? Heretofore China has been friendly toward us. But if the new dominant group takes over and we have created in them a sense of opposition and of hatred toward us, then it seems to me that we are doing the very thing we say we are afraid of having accomplished if Russia takes over.

If we get one-sixth of the people of the globe . . . feeling that we of this hemisphere are opposing their desire for more light, for more development, then we are injuring the future of our children and grandchildren, and to me this is a serious question. . . . It isn't the exact dollars involved. It is a question of whether maybe we proceeded wrongly heretofore. If we have, we had better straighten out our course and correct it.

More importantly, the committee categorically rejected the idea of any direct American military involvement in China or military commitment to Chiang and the Nationalists. "The day we send troops to China or Russia," Lodge insisted, "this country is through." Later the Massachusetts Republican added, "The only one thing where I don't want to compromise is on the question of sending American military aid to China." When the Senate committee learned that a prominent Army officer had told the House committee that America should provide Chiang with troops and military supplies, its response to that general was negative:

Senator Connally: Mark him off.

Senator Lodge: I am marking him off anyway, but I cite this to show that this idea that you and I have about troops isn't the same as others have.

Senator Wiley: They are cockeyed.

Senator Lodge: You bet they are. I would like to ask General Marshall what does he suggest we put in this bill to make sure it isn't a military bill.

Marshall's reply was that "his entire predeliction is to make sure that we make no military commitments to China, and that nothing we do can be read as an obligation on our part to follow through with military aid."

Yet in the last analysis the committee agreed that it had no choice but to report a separate bill continuing assistance to China. The Senators believed that if the aid proposal was rejected, the Nationalist government would soon collapse—and no Senator wanted to assume that responsibility. Second, as noted, the House had included China in its omnibus relief bill. Like it or not, the Senate committee had to face this political reality:

The Chairman: I think we confront a condition, not a theory, and I don't think it makes much difference what China is or what China is going to be. This is a problem in psychology, in the first place, and it is a problem of parliamentary necessities in the second place.

Senator Lodge: And political skulduggery in the third place.

The Chairman: I don't think this country would stand for our turning our backs on China, and that is what we have done if we don't do something about China. And I am sure Congress wouldn't let you turn your back on China. So you can't turn your back. You have to do something. And your problem is, What can we do?

To Vandenberg, aid to China, then, "is just a gesture . . . a pretty expensive one, but nevertheless, it is probably unavoidable, psychologically":

I come back to the fact that we have just got to coldbloodedly here deal with the fact that we confront a condition and not a theory, and half of it is parliamentary and half of it is Chinese, and I think the House is about as imponderable as China is in dealing with it.

I was about to say though, that it is not confined to the House. We have some key men in the Senate, and the Chairman of the Appropriations Committee is one of them. This is the sine qua non as far as he is concerned.

Senator George: He is for China, is he?

The Chairman: And military aid.

Senator Lodge: What is the opposite of sine qua non? That's what I am.

But the decisive consideration was the European Aid Program. ERP could not pass Congress, the Senators realized, if aid to China was not included somewhere in the package. Hickenlooper stated the problem: "we may be searching around for what is the least thing we can do for China as a gesture, and as a practical thing to save ERP. It is not so much China as it is the European Recovery Program and how can we get out of the mess?"

The entire committee recognized its dilemma:

The Chairman: I don't think we can say "No" at the moment.

Senator Smith: We can't say "No" on aid to China. I think we can say "No" on military operations in China, very definitely.

Senator Lodge: You can't say "No" on aid to China if you want to save ERP. I can say "No" on aid to China by itself. I am being put under pressure.

Senator Hatch: Everybody is being blackmailed into this.

Senator Smith: We all admit that without a struggle.

So once again, and not for the last time, the Nationalist cause survived in the Congress. As a regretful Vandenberg summed it up, "I very much doubt whether we could hope to get ERP through . . . if we failed to take some cognizance of this demand for Chinese legislation."

Richard D. Challener
Princeton University

FOREIGN RELIEF ASSISTANCE ACT OF 1948

HEARINGS

HELD IN

EXECUTIVE SESSION

BEFORE THE

COMMITTEE ON FOREIGN RELATIONS UNITED STATES SENATE

EIGHTIETH CONGRESS

SECOND SESSION

ON

UNITED STATES ASSISTANCE TO EUROPEAN ECONOMIC RECOVERY, AID TO CHINA, CONTINUED ASSISTANCE TO GREECE AND TURKEY, ADDITIONAL MONEY FOR THE INTERNATIONAL CHILDREN'S EMERGENCY FUND, AND THE NOMINATION OF PAUL G. HOFFMAN AS ADMINISTRATOR OF THE ECONOMIC COOPERATION ADMINISTRATION

(Executive Hearings Held on February 9, 10, 11, 12, 13, 17, 24, 26, and 28, and March 15, 17, 20, 22, and 25, and April 7, 1948; Made Public June 11, 1973)

HISTORICAL SERIES

Printed for the use of the Committee on Foreign Relations

U.S. GOVERNMENT PRINTING OFFICE

85-743 WASHINGTON : 1973

COMMITTEE ON FOREIGN RELATIONS

EIGHTIETH CONGRESS, SECOND SESSION

ARTHUR H. VANDENBERG, Michigan, *Chairman*

ARTHUR CAPPER, Kansas
WALLACE H. WHITE, Jr., Maine
ALEXANDER WILEY, Wisconsin
H. ALEXANDER SMITH, New Jersey
BOURKE B. HICKENLOOPER, Iowa
HENRY CABOT LODGE, Jr., Massachusetts
TOM CONNALLY, Texas
WALTER F. GEORGE, Georgia
ROBERT F. WAGNER, New York
ELBERT D. THOMAS, Utah
ALBEN W. BARKLEY, Kentucky
CARL A. HATCH, New Mexico

FRANCIS O. WILCOX, *Chief of Staff*
C. C. O'DAY, *Clerk*

NINETY-THIRD CONGRESS, FIRST SESSION

J. W. FULBRIGHT, Arkansas, *Chairman*

JOHN SPARKMAN, Alabama
MIKE MANSFIELD, Montana
FRANK CHURCH, Idaho
STUART SYMINGTON, Missouri
CLAIBORNE PELL, Rhode Island
GALE W. McGEE, Wyoming
EDMUND S. MUSKIE, Maine
GEORGE S. McGOVERN, South Dakota
HUBERT H. HUMPHREY, Minnesota
GEORGE D. AIKEN, Vermont
CLIFFORD P. CASE, New Jersey
JACOB K. JAVITS, New York
HUGH SCOTT, Pennsylvania
JAMES B. PEARSON, Kansas
CHARLES H. PERCY, Illinois
ROBERT P. GRIFFIN, Michigan

CARL MARCY, *Chief of Staff*
ARTHUR M. KUHL, *Chief Clerk*

CONTENTS

PREFACE

June 1973.

This is one of a historical series of Senate Committee on Foreign Relations hearings held in executive session and relating to important historical topics during the early post-World War II period. The transcripts of these hearings, along with related material from committee files, are published in their complete form.

In executive session on February 6, 1973, the committee decided to publish this series. The transcript regulations of the committee read in relevant part as follows:

> Executive transcripts and other executive records of the Committee shall be released to the National Archives and Records Service for unclassified use in accordance with the policies of that Agency: *Provided*, That no such transcripts or other executive records shall be declassified within a period of 12 years except by majority vote of the Committee and with the permission of surviving members of the Committee at the time such transcripts or records were made and with the permission of the Executive Department, if any, concerned; and *Provided further*, That after 12 years from the date such transcripts or records were made, they shall be declassified unless the Committee by majority vote shall decide otherwise.

In accordance with the committee's regulations, former Senator Henry Cabot Lodge, Jr. has given his permission for this publication and the Department of State has indicated that it has no foreign policy objection to the publication of these hearings.

The hearings which are printed herewith have not been corrected for grammar or mistakes made by verbatim reporters inasmuch as most participants are no longer available.

J. W. FULBRIGHT, *Chairman.*

EUROPEAN RECOVERY PROGRAM*

MONDAY, FEBRUARY 9, 1948

UNITED STATES SENATE,
COMMITTEE ON FOREIGN RELATIONS,
Washington, D.C.

The committee met, pursuant to call, in the committee hearing room, U.S. Capitol, at 10 a.m., Senator Arthur H. Vandenberg, chairman, presiding.

Present: Senators Vandenberg, Capper, Wiley, Smith, Lodge, Connally, George, Thomas of Utah, and Hatch.

Also present: the Honorable Lewis W. Douglas, Ambassador to Great Britain; Paul Nitze, Deputy Director, Office of International Trade Policy, Department of State; Ernest Gross, legal adviser, Department of State; Stephen E. Rice, legislative counsel, U.S. Senate.

The CHAIRMAN. The committee will come to order.

COMMITTEE PROCEDURE

First let me ask the committee. I informally suggested to Ambassador Douglas that I thought it would be a fine thing if he sat through with us, straight through our consideration on this thing, so that he could be available to answer any questions that arise. Is there any objection to having him sit with us? If not, OK.

Senator GEORGE. Let me ask a little bit about the legislative program. Are we going to have a session of the Senate today?

The CHAIRMAN. Yes.

Senator GEORGE. All day, after 12?

The CHAIRMAN. I do not know what the program of the Senate is.

Senator WILEY. Senators Aiken and Lucas will talk, and if they have a session tomorrow, about which I do not know——

Senator GEORGE. You are not still going on with the St. Lawrence thing, are you?

Senator WILEY. Not still. We are going on, though.

Senator GEORGE. Will we be sitting both morning and afternoon?

The CHAIRMAN. Not when the Senate is in session. I am very hopeful that the Senate will recess from today until Thursday. I do not know how the rest of you feel, but I think we ought to get this bill out as reasonably promptly as possible, and I would like to stick to it until we get it out.

Senator SMITH. You are planning to meet this afternoon, are you not?

*The Foreign Relations Committee held hearings on the European Recovery Program in public session throughout January and early February 1948. The transcripts of these hearings were subsequently printed in 3 volumes.

The CHAIRMAN. Not if the Senate is in session.

Senator SMITH. Not even getting consent to meet?

The CHAIRMAN. No, because we have too many people interested in the subject matter. I would be very happy to meet.

Senator SMITH. Can we not recess the Senate, then?

The CHAIRMAN. May we proceed?

DRAFT BILL†

Senator CONNALLY. Let me ask you, Mr. Chairman: Has this bill ever been introduced?

The CHAIRMAN. No, sir. There isn't any bill.

Senator CONNALLY. We have a proposed bill.

The CHAIRMAN. No. This draft is just a working sheet. I have not seen it myself. It was put together by the staff of the committee in collaboration with the experts from the State Department in an effort, first, to put down in black and white the administrative phases as recommended by the Brookings Institution, and then to put into type some of the major suggestions that arose in the course of the hearings.‡

Senator CONNALLY. How is this changed from that? You have just added a little paragraph, is that all?

Dr. WILCOX (Chief of Staff, Foreign Relations Committee). The changes are in italics, the stricken part in lined type. This is the original text presented by the State Department as amended by the suggestions which the staff, in collaboration with Mr. Rice and the State Department have prepared.

Senator LODGE. Does the State Department approve of these new parts?

The CHAIRMAN. Yes.

Dr. WILCOX. Yes.

The CHAIRMAN. Would it be agreeable if we start in on the administrative end of the affair, inasmuch as apparently we are closer to general agreement on that than on anything else, and perhaps if we got that out of the way it would facilitate the rest of our work?

SUGGEST PREAMBLE

Senator THOMAS of Utah. First of all, Mr. Chairman, may I ask this: You remember suggestions were made about inserting a preamble which might declare some of the policies. Nothing has been done about that?

The CHAIRMAN. I think that as this thing has been drawn—I repeat I have not seen it before—instead of attempting to do what you are talking about in a preamble, they have attempted to do it by an expansion of the statement of principles and purposes.

Senator THOMAS of Utah. They have put that right in the body?

The CHAIRMAN. Yes.

---

†For a copy of this draft see pp. 527.

‡ See *Report to the Committee on Foreign Relations, U.S. Senate, on Administration of the United States Aid to a European Recovery Program,* submitted at the request of the Chairman of the committee by The Brookings Institute, January 22, 1948. Committee Print, 80th Cong., 2d Sess.

ESTABLISHMENT OF THE ECONOMIC COOPERATION ADMINISTRATION

Where does the administration start?

Dr. WILCOX. I would suggest that you start on section 4, page 5.

The CHAIRMAN. We are at page 5, line 15:

> SEC. 4. (a) There is hereby established, with its principal office in the District of Columbia, an agency of the Government which shall be known as the Economic Cooperation Administration, hereinafter referred to as the Administration.

Senator CONNALLY. Where you say "an agency of the Government", would it not be better to say "an agency of the United States"?

I am not going to raise any problem about it, but I think it is better.

The CHAIRMAN. Is there any comment on that? We might as well clean them up as we go along.

Senator THOMAS of Utah. I think probably following what is the routine wording. Mr. Chairman, in most of these acts, "Government" is used.

Senator WILEY. If you want to make it clear, make it "an agency of the United States Government."

The CHAIRMAN. What have you to say, Mr. Rice?

Mr. RICE. I do not think it makes any difference from a legal standpoint, whatever you prefer. You do not need it in there at all, as a matter of fact. Quite frequently it is not put in. There is precedent for both ways, "Government" or "U.S." It is just what you prefer personally.

The CHAIRMAN. "The Administration shall be headed . . ."

Senator SMITH. Might I ask this question: Are we entirely happy about the title, "Economic Cooperation Administration"? Is that the best possible title for this set-up? It has been called in the press and everywhere else "The European Rehabilitation Administration."

"ERP" NOT LIKED

The CHAIRMAN. I would like to get away from "ERP."

Senator SMITH. I am just questioning whether this is the best possible title.

The CHAIRMAN. I thought it was "ERA" when you got down to the administration—"The Economic Recovery Administration."

Senator SMITH. Something like that. I though it was, too.

The CHAIRMAN. What have you to say about that, Mr. Ambassador?

Ambassador DOUGLAS. I had not thought about that, offhand. There is some advantage to the use of the word "cooperation" because it rather emphasizes the cooperative features of the undertaking. But "Economic Cooperation Administration," as one mentions it, is clumsy.

Senator SMITH. It has no relation to Europe whatever in the title.

Senator THOMAS of Utah. If you go on with an Asiatic Administration later on, it is better to leave it this way, and it fits right into that scheme, if that is what the State Department is going to follow through with, with what General Marshall said we were going to follow through with.

Ambassador DOUGLAS. The title of the bill is "Economic Cooperation Act of 1948."

Senator SMITH. You would have to change that, too. I am not objecting to this. I just want to highlight the question of whether this is the best thing we can do. We might postpone it, Mr. Chairman, until we have gone into discussion further, and see if something comes to us. I would like to put a question mark on it.

The CHAIRMAN. It is a kind of tough mouthful.

Ambassador DOUGLAS. Yes, it is clumsy.

The CHAIRMAN (reading):

> The Administration shall be headed by an Administrator for Economic Cooperation, hereinafter referred to as the Administrator, who shall be appointed by the President, by and with the advice and consent of the Senate, and who shall receive compensation at the rate of $20,000 per annum. The Administrator shall be responsible to the President and shall have a status in the executive branch of the Government comparable to that of the head of an executive department.

I think that is a good statement of what we are trying to do.

Senator SMITH. That follows the Brookings report, apparently. I was studying that report in the last day or two.

The CHAIRMAN (reading). "Except as otherwise provided in this Act, the administration of the provisions of this Act is hereby vested in the Administrator and his functions shall be performed under the direction and control of the President."

Senator LODGE. When you read it, does that mean it is approved?

The CHAIRMAN. No, no. I am just reading it for the purpose of having you jump in if you do not like it.

ADMINISTRATOR'S SALARY AND EXPENSE ALLOWANCE

Senator LODGE. I wanted to ask a question as to whether $20,000 is considered a high enough salary for this job. If he is the type of man you want to get, he is going to have to have some income of his own if he is going to do this job on $20,000 a year.

The CHAIRMAN. When you fix his compensation at $20,000, does that disallow expense allowances, Mr. Rice?

Mr. RICE. No, it does not disallow them, Senator, but as you know, expense allowances do not amount to very much. I think it is $7 per diem.

Senator SMITH. $7 a day we got on our trip abroad, and it cost us twice that.

The CHAIRMAN. That is implicit in the thing, without any reference.

Senator HATCH. Is this the same salary that Cabinet Members get?

Mr. RICE. It is more. They get $15,000. They have not been raised yet.

Senator CONNALLY. They have been getting $15,000 all the time? We did not raise them when we raised our pay?

Senator HATCH. Mr. Rice says we did not.

Senator GEORGE. He is subject to tax unless you excuse him.

Senator CONNALLY. He is going to stay in Washington. That is where his office is going to be. He ought to have a liberal expense account. He isn't going to be worth anything unless he goes over there pretty often, even if Lew is over there.

The CHAIRMAN. He surely has to be mobile.

Senator CONNALLY. He has to be able to go, and he can not be hemming and hawing on whether he will go on a basis of $7 or $7.85.

Senator LODGE. And when he goes to some capital abroad, he wants to have 35 or 40 fellows in. He has to be able to do it.

Senator CONNALLY. He won't be wise if he has that many.

Senator THOMAS of Utah. I do not think you need any more. You say "his functions shall be performed under the direction and control of the President." Just what cannot a man do under that?

Senator CONNALLY. My view is that we ought to make him a liberal allowance for expenses. We can get to that later.

Senator LODGE. I just wanted to raise the question, to be sure we all thought he got enough.

The CHAIRMAN. We will put a question there.

Senator THOMAS of Utah. When you give him the status of head of an executive branch of the Government, and you give him $5,000 more than Cabinet officers have, we all know that the Cabinet officers get along all right on expense accounts and everything. They have cars, they have chauffeurs, they have a lot of things that the rest of the people do not have in Government.

Senator CONNALLY. He will have one. The first thing any agency we set up does is buy an automobile.

Senator THOMAS of Utah. He will have it unless you put a limitation in that he cannot have it. I know that.

Senator WILEY. I think he will need a steamboat too, won't he?

ECA ADMINISTRATOR'S PARTICIPATION IN CABINET MEETINGS

Senator LODGE. When you say "shall have a status in the executive branch of the Government comparable to that of the head of an executive department," that does not mean he would take part in Cabinet meetings, does it?

The CHAIRMAN. It would if his department was involved.

Mr. RICE. That is under the discretion of the President. This does not require it.

DIRECTION AND CONTROL OF PRESIDENT

Senator CONNALLY. Wait a minute, Mr. Chairman. I may be wrong here; "and his functions shall be performed under the direction and control of the President" means the general control, I suppose, of the President. We do not want to spread that out so that the President has got to approve every little act that he does, and so forth and so on. You say his acts shall be performed "under the direction and control of the President." If you stopped with "direction," it would not be so bad.

The CHAIRMAN. Or if you left out "direction" and just said "control." Mr. Rice, what have you to say about that?

Mr. RICE. That language was inserted for the specific purpose of giving the President complete overall authority. That is what it is usually interpreted, Senator, as from the administrative standpoint. But if you say just one or the other, you do not need both of them, in my opinion.

The CHAIRMAN. Which would you rather have, if you have to take one of them? I think both are a litte too much.

Senator CONNALLY. I think "control" would be better, probably.

Senator THOMAS of Utah. I wish you would note that those are the exact words we gave the Secretary of State in the original bill.

The CHAIRMAN. We are getting away from the original bill.

Senator THOMAS of Utah. Your idea is, as I understand it, Mr. Chairman, to hold the President responsible for this action and for this administration.

Senator SMITH. And you dispose of your foreign policy question by this clause, too.

The CHAIRMAN. I think when you say "shall be performed under the direction," it sounds as though he could not to a thing unless he got a directive. Let's say "under the control of the President." Is there any objection to that?

Senator SMITH. I think that is better.

The CHAIRMAN. All right: "under the control of the President."

Senator CONNALLY. That is a great victory for me!

DEPUTY ADMINISTRATOR FOR ECONOMIC COOPERATION

The CHAIRMAN (reading):

> (b) There shall be in the Administration a Deputy Administrator for Economic Cooperation who shall be appointed by the President, by and with the advice and consent of the Senate, and shall receive compensation at the rate of $17,500 per annum. The Deputy Administrator for Economic Cooperation shall perform such functions as the Administrator shall designate, and shall be Acting Administrator for Economic Cooperation during the absence or disability of the Administrator or in the event of a vacancy in the office of Administrator.

Senator CONNALLY. I would rather have that job than the Administrator's.

Senator SMITH. You are applying for the job?

Senator CONNALLY. I would not have either one of them!

PERFORMANCE OF FUNCTIONS PENDING APPOINTMENT AND QUALIFICATION

The CHAIRMAN (reading):

> (c) The President is authorized, pending the appointment and qualification of the first Administrator or Deputy Administrator for Economic Cooperation appointed hereunder, to provide for the performance of the functions of the Administrator under this Act through such departments, agencies, or establishments of the United States Government as he may direct.

Senator SMITH. Have we approved (b), or are we just going along?

The CHAIRMAN. It is approved unless we object.

I suppose (c) is to cover the gap between April 1 and the time when this Administrator would actually get on the job.

Senator HATCH. Will that not raise some question, though?

The CHAIRMAN. Oh, yes.

POSSIBILITY OF PRESIDENT DELAYING APPOINTMENT

Senator HATCH. He might never appoint one. He could operate it through any department or agency he wanted to. I do not anticipate that any such thing would happen, but I anticipate objections that may come.

Senator GEORGE. I do not like that at all, without limit or direction.

The CHAIRMAN. I agree with you.

Senator HATCH. I think the President, of course, will make the appointment, but he would not have to, under this act.

The CHAIRMAN. What could be an alternative?

Senator LODGE. Within 60 days.

Senator THOMAS of Utah. You could say "The President shall appoint." You get the man before you get the organization, then.

Senator GEORGE. You will have to, anyway.

Senator THOMAS of Utah. I do not think there is any danger in this paragraph.

The CHAIRMAN. You do not think there is any danger in leaving it in?

Senator THOMAS of Utah. No.

The CHAIRMAN. Except the homiletics which it will precipitate.

Senator HATCH. Why don't you say, in section 4, "appointed by the President with 60 days after the effective date of this act"?

Senator CONNALLY. Suppose the Senate does not confirm him for 60 more days?

Senator HATCH. "He shall be appointed by the President within 60 days," to get away from that objection that the President might delay it.

The CHAIRMAN. What would you do about this, Senator George?

Senator GEORGE. I do not know yet, but I do not like it the way it is, hung up in the air like that. I do not think you can put an absolute time on the President's appointment, because he might not be able to get somebody to act, and then he might not be confirmed quickly.

Senator THOMAS of Utah. I still think the way to handle it is to provide that the President make his appointment of the Administrator before he starts operating the act.

The CHAIRMAN. Then what do you do?

Ambassador DOUGLAS. Then you get into very serious trouble, Senator. Let us assume, for example, that the bill does not become a law until the 1st of April. An Administrator could not be appointed and confirmed by the Senate, even if the administration knew whom it was going to nominate to the Senate, much before the 15th of April. No commodities could therefore move during that period, and there are two—at least two—very critical and urgent situations that cannot wait in which we are deeply involved, in which, if commodities do not move prior to the 1st of April, we might very well have bloodshed on our hands. Austria is one of them. The pipeline as of the 1st of April for Austria will be enough to carry through until about the middle of May, but it takes 8 weeks for commodities to move. During that period, that lapse of time in which commodities do not arrive in Austria, the diet in western Austria is apt to fall as low as 500 to 600 calories a day, and the situation there would be very explosive.

Senator HATCH. Mr. Rice has a suggestion here about another section of the bill that might throw a little light on it.

The CHAIRMAN. All right, Mr. Rice.

Mr. RICE. The State Department recommends that in the period of enactment through June 30, 1948—this provision is on page 33; I want to just use it for an analogy—they can send certain relief supplies, notwithstanding various limitations here in the bill, and I was just suggesting to Senator Hatch that you might be able to put that provision in, that the Persident is authorized, but not after June 30, 1948.

The CHAIRMAN. I think that is too broad. You can get the whole thing committed in 90 days.

POSSIBILITY OF DELAYED APPOINTMENT

Senator CONNALLY. How about saying, "Pending appointment and qualification, the temporary Relief Administration"?

The CHAIRMAN. That is only four countries.

Senator GEORGE. That is the State Department, too.

Senator CONNALLY. I am not allergic to the State Department, generally speaking. A lot of them are howling about it. They are doing the best they can, and much better than some of us would do in the circumstances.

Senator LODGE. That is damning them with faint praise!

Ambassador DOUGLAS. Would the word "temporary" make the intention clear?

The CHAIRMAN. That is clear, but it is still very elastic. I am President pro tempore, but it is lasting a long time.

Senator THOMAS of Utah. I do not think you are risking very much with this wording.

The CHAIRMAN. I do not think you are risking anything, other than an awful lot of chatter on the floor upstairs.

Senator LODGE. Supposing you left out the question of qualification, which means confirmation by the Senate, and had a time limit on the appointment. Surely the President could appoint somebody within 60 days, could he not?

Senator GEORGE. He does not appoint except by and with the consent of the Senate.

Senator LODGE. Supposing we said "pending the selection."

Senator GEORGE. Suppose we pass that, until we get along further and see something about it. I think that is somewhat important. I think it is a little more important than we are inclined to think.

The CHAIRMAN. We will put a question mark there.

PERSONNEL, EXPERTS AND CONSULTANTS

At the top of page 7, line 3:

(d) Any department, agency, or establishment of the Government (including, whenever used in this Act, any corporation which is an instrumentality of the United States) performing functions under this Act is authorized to employ, for duty within the continental limits of the United States, such personnel as may be necessary to carry out the provisions and purposes of this Act, and funds available pursuant to Section 13 of this Act shall be available for personal services in the District of Columbia and elsewhere without regard to section 14(a) of the Federal Employees Pay Act of 1946 (60 Stat. 219). Personnel, not to exceed sixty, of the Administration may be compensated without regard to the provisions of the Classification Act of 1923, as amended, of whom not more than ten may be compensated at a rate in excess of $10,000 per annum, but not in excess of $15,000 per annum. Experts and consultants, as authorized by section 15 of the Act of August 2, 1946 (5 U.S.C. 55a), may be employed by the Administration, and may be compensated at rates for individuals not in excess of $50 per diem.

Have we got to spell all that out?

Ambassador DOUGLAS. I think so.

HIRING CORPORATIONS AND FIRMS

Senator LODGE. We had to get legislation through about 2 months ago on this matter of hiring corporations and firms. I wonder if Mr. Rice thinks this language is sufficiently broad to permit that. In case they wanted to employ some firm of accountants or something like that, or an engineering firm, could this do that?

Mr. RICE. I would not think it would be broad enough for that. You are talking about that last sentence now, lines 18 to 22?

Senator LODGE. Yes.

Mr. RICE. That deals with individuals, rates for individuals not in excess of $50 per diem. I think we would have to spell it out a little bit more if you wanted to employ a firm as a firm.

Senator LODGE. Do you think you might ever want to do that?

Ambassador DOUGLAS. I would doubt it, although it is conceivable that in rare instances you might want to.

Senator LODGE. I just raise the point.

The CHAIRMAN. I should think you might very well want to use some big engineering outfit here to do a job for you by way of supervision, which could be done infinitely better by an experienced cohesive team than it could by some individual.

Senator LODGE. To check up on something; to follow through, you know.

Ambassador DOUGLAS. There is an authorization in the act—I think it is section 11(3) on page 18. He is authorized to arrange for the "procurement of and furnishing technical information and assistance." That would be on a temporary and consultant basis, I presume, and I should think that language was broad enough to authorize him to retain a corporation, unless paragraph (d) of section 4 would be considered to be a limitation upon subsection 3 of section 11.

Senator LODGE. I just wanted to raise the point.

Senator CONNALLY. Do you not get away from a lot of personal responsibility when you go out and employ a firm?

Senator HATCH. Mr. Rice does not think it would be a limitation.

Mr. RICE. I think that is just the provision for furnishing assistance to participating countries—vocational school technicians and things of that sort. I do not think it means an outfit that would cause administrative expenses here in Washington. I do not think it is broad enough for that.

Ambassador DOUGLAS. Let us assume, for example, that there was a coal problem in, let us say, the Ruhr, or let us even say in England, and a competent mining engineering firm would be necessary and sought for by the participating country.

Mr. RICE. I agree with that 100 percent. It is broad enough for that. I was thinking of the example that Senator Vandenberg had, a firm here in Washington that would be put more or less on the payroll to do some of the administrative work around here. Maybe I misunderstood you.

The CHAIRMAN. I think there might well be instances where that would be the case. Take the Brookings Institution, which is only a half parallel because it did not cost anything, but it proved to be, I think, very useful to refer to the Brookings Institution in connection with one of our problems. I think there is some analogy in the fact that there might be a kindred corporation somewhere which might well be the most available thing to which to refer.

Ambassador DOUGLAS. There are going to be certain accounting problems, to take a very simple case, that may be quite complicated, and the Administrator might really require a very competent firm of accountants to come in and help him set up his books.

Senator LODGE. Does this bill authorize that?

Ambassador DOUGLAS. I do not think it does.

Senator LODGE. That is the point. I thought of a firm like Haskins & Sells, for instance.

The CHAIRMAN. Mr. Rice, will you have that in mind and see what you can do about it?

Senator SMITH. That would be added to this subsection (d).

The CHAIRMAN. Yes. It would be covered in some way.

USE OF OTHER GOVERNMENT AGENCIES

Senator GEORGE. Is it clear that the Administrator is to call on these agencies and departments and Federal corporations and firms and so forth, and appoint them or designate them, or how is that to be done?

Ambassador DOUGLAS. Do you mean the departments of Government, Senator?

Senator GEORGE. Yes. There may be some other subsequent clause about that.

Ambassador DOUGLAS. There is.

Senator GEORGE. I have not seen it down to now. Of course, the administration of the provisions of the act is hereby vested in the Administrator, subject to the control of the President, but there isn't any very clear-cut and definite indication that the Administrator could himself say, for instance—suppose he wanted to use the RFC; suppose he wanted to use some other agency of the Government—that he himself could do it.

Mr. RICE. That is on page 21, Senator.

Senator GEORGE. I do not know what you have in here hereafter.

Senator CONNALLY. There is a clause somewhere. I read it.

Senator GEORGE. What line?

Mr. RICE. Beginning in line 13.

Senator CONNALLY. He can use that without the consent of the President.

Ambassador DOUGLAS. But with the consent of the head of the Department.

Senator CONNALLY. Yes, I understand that.

The CHAIRMAN. We have a question mark on that for several purposes.

INVESTIGATION OF PERSONNEL

Senator HATCH. Mr. Chairman, there is one question that you are going to have to meet on the floor, and if not on the floor in the House, in connection with personnel—one that I do not like at all. Do you want any provision about investigating the personnel?

Senator CONNALLY. That is in here.

Senator HATCH. Is it in here?

Senator SMITH. I think it is in here.

Dr. WILCOX. At the bottom of page 17.

PERSONNEL EXEMPTION FROM LIMITING PROVISIONS

Senator CONNALLY. What, in short, if Mr. Rice can tell us, are the provisions we are exempting them from under "without regard to section 14(a)"?

Mr. RICE. Section 14(a) of the Federal Employees Pay Act has to do with Government personnel ceilings. These people that would be employed here would not be counted in order to determine how many Government employees you have for the ceiling limitation. That is the first thing.

Senator CONNALLY. Is that all that does?

Mr. RICE. Now, with regard to the personnel, not to exceed 60, if you want that policy, you have to spell it out, because the Classification Act limits them to $10,000.

Senator CONNALLY. On that "experts and consultants," there is no limitation on how many of those are employed, or how long you keep them. There is no limitation on the number of these $50-a-day fellows, and no limit on their time.

Senator GEORGE. There is no limitation. That is all in the good sense of the Administrator. If you are going to give the Administrator enough power to turn around in, fine. But if he has to have the head of every little Department here in Washington agreeing to do something that he wants done and done now, he is going to be a pretty poor sort of Administrator.

The CHAIRMAN. Do you find that in here, Walter?

Senator GEORGE. Yes, on page 21. He cannot do it except by the President's direction, or unless he can get the consent of the heads of these little Departments, and we are classifying even a corporation, a Government corporation, here as including, whenever used in this act, any corporation which is an instrumentality of the United States, as a department or agency or establishment of the Government. But then that is another broader question that I want to come back to myself. I am not raising it now.

The CHAIRMAN. We will come back to it.

Ambassador DOUGLAS. I think there is a limitation on the period of time that a consultant can serve continuously in any fiscal year.

Senator CONNALLY. But you can lay him off for a week's vacation and then rehire him.

Ambassador DOUGLAS. I would suggest that in the administration of the act there be great flexibility in the employment of consultants. It is going to be very difficult to get competent men, and the employment of a consultant is a very useful thing. It is a method by which you can get competents to deal with certain specific questions.

The CHAIRMAN. We are leaving that generally open.

PROMULGATING RULES AND REGULATIONS AND DELEGATING AUTHORITY

Let us go to (e) and see where we are.

(e) The head of any department, agency, or establishment of the Government performing functions under this Act may, from time to time, promulgate such rules and regulations as may be necessary and proper to carry out his functions under this Act, and he may delegate to such officers of his department, agency, or establishment as he may designate the authority to perform any of his functions under this Act.

85-743—73——2

Senator THOMAS of Utah. Mr. Chairman, I think that is probably the most troublesome paragraph in the whole bill, if you get these conflicts between regular departments and the Administrator and the rest. I think that every head of a department can do all you give him here just simply in an ordinary way, without pointing out this invitation that he set up these conflicting rules and regulations. When you realize that the Administrator is functioning here, he is functioning in Europe, he is functioning in all these various countries, he may need the agricultural agency of the State Department to do something, has he got to wait until the State Department draws up rules so that the agricultural attaché may function, and so on and so forth?

Mr. Rice, cannot these heads of the departments do all we allow them to do here by this law in the ordinary running?

Senator GEORGE. I think so, Senator Thomas. The moment that we put additional responsibilities on any branch of the Government, or any agency or any department, then, of course, I think all the general laws that they have to protect themselves and to make rules and regulations governing their own employees certainly apply. You are just expanding their authority, and they certainly have power to act now.

The CHAIRMAN. I think you have made it almost impossible for the Director to even move.

Senator GEORGE. I think this whole concept makes it impossible for the Director to move. If the Administrator is to be an administrator he must have the right to call on the President to give him any agency of Government or any corporation or any other force in the Government organization that he desires, and that is the end of it. Of course that agency has then the authority and power to go ahead and control its own forces, within limits.

Senator SMITH. In case of emergency the President could set down conditions. The President in the last analysis would have power to help the Administrator out of his hole.

Senator GEORGE. Here is some equivocation right in the beginning, that the President may direct it or the heads of the Government departments may consent to it. You are going to hamper your Administrator there. He can't turn about.

Senator SMITH. I agree with you.

Senator GEORGE. He won't be able to do anything.

Senator CONNALLY. Well, but they are set up now under certain statutory limitations and regulations. Their authorities are limited now. Now you are putting on them additional responsibility.

Senator GEORGE. That is right.

Senator CONNALLY. Within the limits of these responsibilities, why would it not be desirable to give him the authority to make these regulations?

Senator THOMAS of Utah. Give the Administrator, yes; but you are giving the head of any Department authority.

Senator CONNALLY. He has it over the things that the statute now puts under his control.

Senator GEORGE. When we enlarge his powers, I think his existing powers go right along with the enlargement.

Senator CONNALLY. I hope so, but I do not see any harm in putting that in. Of course the Director, naturally, in the essence of things, must be in control. He must tell these fellows what he expects them to do. If they do not do it as he says, he can kick them in the pants.

MAKING OF RULES AND REGULATIONS

Senator THOMAS of Utah. What I see in this scheme, Mr. Chairman, I think if this becomes effective, a subordinate of the Agriculture Department might hesitate to take a directive from the Administrator, if we say that the head of any department, agency, or establishment shall make rules and regulations for his actions. You see, it leaves the subordinate in a bad way, if he reads the law, with regard to from whom he should take orders.

I think that if General Marshall were here he could make it very, very plain that you do not have to say that the colonel shall make rules for all his subordinates in carrying out this general order. It is just taken for granted that it is done.

I do not know, Mr. Rice; you are not taking away anything from the man in the way of making rules for cooperating by leaving this out, are you?

Mr. RICE. Senator, this, as I understand it, is more an administrative problem than anything else.

Mr. Gross, would you give the committee the background on that?

Mr. GROSS. That was put in primarily to make sure that the Export-Import Bank, which would be the agent for the Administrator to make the loans, or that the Director, would be free to promulgate appropriate regulations which would not normally be the case under the present authority of the Bank, and it was not intended that it would be purely permissive, so that there would be no question as to the Export-Import Bank's authority to promulgate appropriate regulations.

The CHAIRMAN. If that is the objective, why not tend to it when we reach the Export-Import Bank, instead of putting it in here?

Let's take it out. Does anybody object?

Senator CONNALLY. Yes; I do. It seems to me that the case counsel has suggested would apply with equal force to any other department that the Administrator called upon. Certainly the head of a department now has his general powers to issue regulations and so forth, and if you put these additional burdens or responsibilities on him why, as to those particular things, should he not issue regulations to govern his subordinates and his clerks and everybody else?

Senator THOMAS of Utah. Would he not do it under the ordinary course?

Senator CONNALLY. I do not think he has the authority to do it. He has authority to do it under the functions vested in him under the law. I am not greatly concerned; I think it will work either way. Whether you put them in there or not, he could make the regulations.

AUTHORITY TO DELEGATE FUNCTIONS

Mr. RICE. I think he probably could make the regulations as a question of law, but what you run into are some Comptroller General decisions about delegation, as to whether the head of an agency can delegate certain functions or whether he cannot. This language is put in to make it clear that he can, and his delegation is not subject to those decisions.

In addition to that, if you leave in this policy that the President is authorize to use the departments and agencies pending the confirmation of the nomination of this Administrator, then all the more reason why this should be in during that temporary period, anyhow.

The CHAIRMAN. It looks to me as though this were subject to a terrific barrage of assault, because when you finally get down to the last phrase, "and he may delegate to such officers of his department, agency, or establishment as he may designate the authority to perform any of his functions under this act," you have finally created a floating authority to some unnamed subordinate in all these various departments and agencies, and the opportunity, it seems to me, to completely checkmate the Administrator.

Senator CONNALLY. Mr. Chairman, may I ask this question?

The CHAIRMAN. Yes.

Senator CONNALLY. To my mind, I conceive this simply to be that in every Department affected, it could set up a little division whose particular function would be the administration of this act.

Senator LODGE. I think that is what it intends to do, but I do not think that is as it is written.

Senator CONNALLY. Fix it so it does. Give us a little Harvard language in there.

Senator LODGE. I am not a lawyer.

PERFORMING SERVICES AND PROVIDING FACILITIES ADMINISTRATOR REQUIRES

Ambassador DOUGLAS. There is one question, the ability of the Administrator to require heads of departments to function; and the second is, how the head of a department shall perform the services and make available the facilities which the Administrator, acting on his own or through the President, shall require the head of the department to make available. The question we are now discussing is the latter and not the former.

Senator THOMAS of Utah. That is it. That is where I see the confusion in the actual functioning of the administration.

Senator LODGE. You do not have in mind that the head of any department shall go ahead and promulgate regulations on his own motion? He shall do it at the request of the Administrator. So why not put that in: "May, at the request of the Administrator"?

Senator CONNALLY. You are putting a big burden on the Administrator, to have to investigate the functions each Department performs.

Senator THOMAS of Utah. I still think it is better left out, in spite of what Mr. Rice says.

Senator CONNALLY. When the Administrator calls on the head of a Department he tells him what he wants them to do. Then the head of that Department, under that direction, draws up those regulations to carry out that request. That is in the law, is it not?

Senator GEORGE. The head of the Department would necessarily do it in his own way, and by adapting his forces so as to accomplish it.

IMPORTANCE OF ADMINISTRATOR'S AUTHORITY

Suppose the Administrator said, "We want so many bushels of wheat delivered at certain points, and delivered to certain recipients," and he calls on the Department of Agriculture or the Commodity Credit Corporation or somebody else down there to do it. Then the Administrator ought not to have anything further to do with that. I agree to that, unless the head of the Department could do something to stymie him, and I would not think that that problem would arise. I think he would have full authority to do it once we extend his power, and I think we have to make it explicit here that the President, on the request of the Administrator, shall have full power to order these things done. I guess we have done that somewhere. I think the most important aspect of it is whether the Administrator himself is to have a right to say, without having an interminable fuss every morning and then every night with some agency of Government as to whether or not that agency thinks it is qualified or desirable for it to do what the Administrator wants done. The Administrator has to be a man who will make decisions and see them go through, and there isn't anybody who can do that except the President, in final analysis.

It seems to me the Administrator has a right to call on the President. The President might overrule him, but if he did that very much, the Administrator would quit, if he was a good one.

Senator CONNALLY. Does not the power granted by the Administrator to the Department to do certain things, involve also the power to not do them? He can recall it whenever he gets ready.

Senator GEORGE. Certainly.

Ambassador DOUGLAS. Is the language in the section on page 21 sufficient to carry out what you have in mind: "by utilizing the services and facilities of any department, agency, or establishment of the Government as the President shall direct * * *"?

Senator GEORGE. Yes, and I would stop right there.

Ambassador DOUGLAS. And take out the alternative?

Senator GEORGE. Yes, sir. I would not have him negotiate with the head of a Department.

Senator CONNALLY. That is qualified, though. It says: "or with the consent of the head of any such Department or agency, in the President's discretion." It has to go to the President after all.

Senator GEORGE. The President would talk with the Department, I suppose, before he gave them an order to sign. But if he directed them, that would be the end of it.

Senator CONNALLY. He naturally would want to do that, because he would not want to put on the Department something they bucked at and claimed they could not perform.

Senator GEORGE. Maybe they would not be equipped to do it.

Senator SMITH. Why would you not satisfy (d) with (e) if you said, "The head of the Department may promulgate, subject to the approval of the Administrator, such regulations * * *"?

CONFLICT BETWEEN DEPARTMENTS

I can see danger there, but I am troubled, as you are, with the conflict between Departments. You are going to have the Commerce Department, for instance, having export controls, and you are going to get into a jam with the Administrator probably right off the bat. Why couldn't we say, "make such rules and regulations, subject to the control of the Administrator"? In the last analysis, Mr. Ambassador, I think you would need the Administrator to control the thing.

ADMINISTRATOR'S ALLOCATION AUTHORITY QUESTIONED

Ambassador DOUGLAS. I am just wondering, Senator. Let us take, for example, the authority of the Department of Agriculture to make allocations of foodstuffs for export as between the amount allocated for export, or the amount that will become available for export to participating countries, and the amount that will become available for export to participating countries, and the amount that may become available to other parts of the world. That is an authority which is now vested in the Department of Agriculture. The Department of Agriculture is a purely American Department, and it is looking at the internal economic effects, its effects upon the United States. Would you want the Administrator, who is charged with the responsibility of administering the Economic Cooperation Administration, to have the power to tell the Department of Agriculture how much shall be allocated? I would question that.

The same thing applies in part to steel products in Commerce.

Senator WILEY. You have the same head-on collision.

Ambassador DOUGLAS. And take petroleum in Commerce and Interior. I would question whether the Administrator ought to have that authority.

QUESTION OF EXTENT OF ADMINISTRATOR'S CONTROL

Senator SMITH. That presents the issue of what we are up against, squarely. To what extent are we going to let the Administrator control?

Ambassador DOUGLAS. There are two things that a Department does. No. 1, it has authority to make certain basic decisions, and now it has the authority to determine how those decisions shall be carried out, the execution of them. I wonder whether the Administrator ought to have the authority to be clothed with the power to interrupt or interfere with, or impede, the authority of a Department——

Senator CONNALLY. It is normal operation.

Ambassador Douglas (continuing). Either in the determination of policy or the administration of it.

Senator SMITH. We are contemplating those conflicts, and we are going to let the President decide those conflicts.

Senator CONNALLY. Senator Smith, may I ask you this: I think Mr. Douglas has put his finger upon a very important aspect. All of these Departments have their normal operations under the law.

Senator SMITH. I agree with that. That is why I am troubled with that.

Senator CONNALLY. It seems to me that that makes it appropriate that the head of that Department, in allocating to his subordinates the functions they are to perform, will issue regulations saying, "This foreign business will be over here under a certain division, and we will run that, and you folks go on over here with the rest of your work as you have always done."

Senator SMITH. You have Agriculture allocating foodstuffs, and you might have a case of allocation running head-on into the Administrator's program. In that case, I want to see the President, as boss of the whole show, determine that conflict.

Senator CONNALLY. He has that now. We have already told him he has to: "under the control and direction of the President of the United States."

Senator SMITH. If he has that, then you can take it out here, and just let (e) refer to the delegation of authority: "may delegate to such officers of his department, agency, or establishment as he may designate the authority to perform any of his functions under this act."

Then leave out that making of the rules. If you are right, the President in the last analysis, in the making of the rules, in cases of a jam between the Department and the Administrator, will settle these jams.

Senator CONNALLY. That is true, but wherever we can point out those limitations, we are saving the President a great deal of annoyance, trouble, and intervention.

Senator SMITH. Would you not say that if that was not in here, the Secretary of Agriculture could go ahead and make his ordinary rules for running his show, and the Secretary of Commerce could do the same thing?

Senator CONNALLY. I assume they could, but if they did not agree, they could be running to the President.

NECESSITY OF LANGUAGE IN VIEW OF COMPTROLLER GENERAL'S RULINGS

Ambassador DOUGLAS. I suggest that that is a legal question. If it is true that the Comptroller General's rulings have impeded the authority of the head of a department delegated to carry out certain functions which are related to another department, then I should think language approximating this might be necessary. That is a question of fact. I should think that could be determined.

Senator LODGE. Is that why this paragraph was put in?

Ambassador DOUGLAS. That is what I understand. That is a question of fact, and it could be determined.

Senator SMITH. Does anybody here know the answer to that?

Mr. RICE. I cannot cite you the cases, but I am pretty sure that is why it is put in, Senator. However, we will look it up and get a memorandum on it for you.

Senator CONNALLY. Suppose, without this, they called on the Export-Import Bank. Well, that is contrary to what they would do in their usual practice. Therefore, it seems to me that somebody ought to have authority to issue regulations and controls as to how they shall perform these new duties that they are getting, which they do not have now, and not just turn some subordinate loose and say, "Go to it, boy."

I did not write this language. I am not wedded to it. But it seems to me that something in the nature of this ought to be in the bill.

Senator SMITH. Are we getting confused between the overall inclusion of these agencies to help carry out this policy and the way that it be carried out, if we assume that they are in the picture? I am assuming that the Department of Agriculture, the Export-Import Bank, and so on are in the picture as part of the so-called plan.

Senator CONNALLY. They are.

Senator SMITH. Then the only question we are discussing is the rules as to how that particular agency shall cooperate to carry out these plans. If there is a dispute, without anything in here, I would say the President would have to decide the dispute.

Senator CONNALLY. If you keep on, you are going to make him Administrator.

It seems to me, on this question of hell raising in the Senate, if you leave this out, you cause more debate than you will by leaving it in, because a lot of these fellows now are complaining, "Well, you don't set it out. You don't limit this concern," and so forth.

The CHAIRMAN. But does this not spell it out in the wrong way? That is the difficulty.

Senator CONNALLY. I do not think so.

Senator SMITH. The way we word it here, it gives the head of a department, like the Secretary of Agriculture or Commerce, the opportunity to govern the whole works.

CONFINING LANGUAGE TO IMPLEMENTING DELEGATION OF JOB

The CHAIRMAN. If all we are trying to do is to implement the delegation of a job by the Administrator to a department head, suppose you confine the language to that. Suppose it reads something like this: "The head of any department, agency, or establishment of the Government performing temporary functions assigned to him by the Administrator under this act may, from time to time, promulgate such rules and regulations as may be necessary and proper to carry out such functions."

Senator LODGE. That is right. That gets it in under the Administrator.

Senator THOMAS of Utah. Leave out "necessary and proper" and say "consistent with these added functions."

Senator CONNALLY. I do not think you ought to insert the word "temporary." Some of these agencies will operate so long as the plan is in operation. The whole bill is temporary, but you appoint him once and he is there until you kick him out.

Ambassador DOUGLAS. I wonder whether the insertion of the word "administrative" might not be helpful: "administrative rules and regulations."

Senator GEORGE. I think that is all this particular part of it is intended to apply to, purely the administration, purely the carrying out of his orders. When the Administrator goes to the President and says, "Mr. President, I want the Secretary of Commerce to do so-and-so under this program; I wish you would designate him to do that job," then the question arises whether or not the Secretary of Commerce is to control exports and imports, or whether the Administrator, with respect to that decision, is to be controlling. And when the President gives the green light, then I think this section here is intended to apply.

As to whether it is necessary, I do not see how it could be necessary, only with respect to administrative orders and regulations.

Ambassador DOUGLAS. Maybe the word, "administrative" before the word "rules" would be helpful.

Senator CONNALLY. I have no objection.

The CHAIRMAN. Does that meet your point, Senator George?

Senator GEORGE. I think it does.

DELEGATION TO SUBORDINATE OFFICERS

Now, as to the delegation by the Secretary of Commerce in the case I have just supposed, to some subordinate in his Department, to make these rules and regulations, I see no objection to that, and I imagine that the Comptroller General has raised questions about that. He sometimes gets a bit technical. He has been known to hold up the whole Army and Navy on occasion.

The CHAIRMAN. Mr. Rice, does your point include the last point made by Senator George? Is the delegation to subordinate officers necessary to achieve the end you are after ?

Mr. RICE. In some technical circumstances, that is correct, Senator, because of his decisions over a long period of years. I cannot cite them to you offhand, but I will have them looked up and have a memorandum prepared on it.

The CHAIRMAN. Your word is good enough, without a memorandum. I do not like the idea of shifting this off down to some unidentified person.

Senator GEORGE. No. In the last analysis, the head of a department or agency ought to make them. He ought to sign them, if he does not write them out.

The CHAIRMAN. He could get somebody to write them out, without putting this language in, could he not?

Senator GEORGE. I think so. But there have been decisions made. For instance, I recall some of the decisions where the Comptroller General has said, "Here is something done under the direction of a subordinate, and that subordinate did not have the authority and we can't pay this bill and we can't O.K. these accounts." We frequently amend legislation to try to get around those things, but I should think that could be stated in some other way. You could say, the head of the Department or any one of his authorized assistants or deputies could do this. That still would not give you specific information about him.

Senator CONNALLY. Would not his delegation control there? He delegates. If he went beyond the authority—it seems to me that we ought to have something of this kind, because he has to delegate the details of carrying on this administrative process to somebody. A Cabinet officer can't go around and look after every detail of this whole program.

The CHAIRMAN. Do you think it is a detail, to set up the fundamental rules and regulations?

Senator CONNALLY. These are not fundamental; these are purely administrative, within the Department.

The CHAIRMAN. But they are basic in respect to the actions of the Department.

Senator GEORGE. That is right.

Senator CONNALLY. They are basic under the general delegation of power by the Administrator or the President. Whenever the Administrator calls on a Department to do certain things he would state it, I assume, in writing, and then within the framework, the Department is to go on and carry it out, and the Cabinet officer that is going to do it would certainly not do it himself. He could not possibly see about the details, and he designates some subordinate, the chief of a division or somebody, to perform certain functions.

I assume that will be in writing. He will have to tell them what to do and what they are not supposed to do.

TECHNICAL MEANING OF WORD "OFFICER"

Ambassador DOUGLAS. It raises this question: What is the technical meaning of the word "officer"?

Senator THOMAS of Utah. It is a pretty big one.

Mr. RICE. It includes "employee," I am sure, when used in that sense.

Ambassador DOUGLAS. ". . . may delegate to responsible subordinates of the Department"?

Senator THOMAS of Utah. I think that means the same thing. It is used just generally here, and not limited to those people who are officers of the United States, used in that way.

What Senator Vandenberg is fearful of is that perhaps the head of a Department will delegate to a subordinate too far down the line.

Senator CONNALLY. Does not the use of the word "officer" suggest somebody in a responsible position?

Ambassador DOUGLAS. Yes. That is why I asked the question.

TAKING ORDERS FROM DEPARTMENT HEAD AND NOT ADMINISTRATOR

Senator THOMAS of Utah. This is an invitation for somebody in the Administration somewhere to simply say outright, "I take my orders from the head of my Department and not from the Administrator."

Ambassador DOUGLAS. On the administration of the functions of that Department.

Senator CONNALLY. Why shouldn't he?

Senator THOMAS of Utah. Immediately by so doing you curb the even functioning of these directives.

Senator CONNALLY. The Administrator does not deal with the subordinates. He deals with the head of the Department. If you go over his head and you begin to dictate to some subordinate clerk, then you would have a mess.

Ambassador DOUGLAS. Take the case of the Commodity Credit Corporation. It might be designated, and probably will be, to make certain bulk purchases of certain agricultural products. Does the Administrator, in a case of that order, want to be the person who issues the rules and regulations as to how the bulk commodities will be purchased? I should think that ought to be the Commodity Credit Corporation's function.

Senator THOMAS of Utah. It ought to be done by the Commodity Credit Corporation.

DELEGATION TO SUBORDINATES QUESTIONED

The CHAIRMAN. I do not know what you want to do about it. I have no objection to the language that was suggested, except that I have a very violent hex against this delegation to subordinates, because I have seen how it works, and it works pretty horribly sometimes.

Senator CONNALLY. In essence, though, the delegation is always subordinate to the will of the head of the Department. He can revoke it or modify it. He is the one who is responsible, whatever is done.

The CHAIRMAN. So, I think, he ought to sign the rules and regulations.

Senator CONNALLY. I think he ought to.

The CHAIRMAN. All right. If he is going to sign them, he can ask Joe Doakes to draw them. He does not have to be told in here that Joe Doakes has specific authority for it. I think this is just a delusion which is very aggravating in the experience of a lot of us with the third and fourth echelon officers in a lot of departments.

Ambassador DOUGLAS. That is the point you have in mind.

The CHAIRMAN. Yes, sir.

Senator CONNALLY. We know every department has certain fellows who are experts on certain things.

Senator LODGE. Don't you think some of these Departments have grown so big that the head of them can't even influence them at all?

Senator CONNALLY. That may be. But to illustrate the Commodity Credit thing, if they had to buy all this stuff they would call on the fellows that have been doing that all the time, and if it did not suit the head of the Department he would veto it. He would cut it out. I do not see how else you are going to do it.

Senator HATCH. Is the objection to giving the subordinate power to make rules and regulations?

The CHAIRMAN. Yes

Senator CONNALLY. No.

Senator LODGE. That is lines 2, 3, and 4 you are objecting to?

The CHAIRMAN. Yes. That is all I am talking about.

Senator HATCH. Then give the subordinate power to carry out administrative details.

The CHAIRMAN. I have no objection to that in the world.

Senator CONNALLY. Doesn't this do that? It says:

> The head of any department, agency, or establishment of the Government performing functions under this act may, from time to time, promulgate such rules and regulations as may be necessary and proper to carry out his functions under this act . . .

Senator HATCH. That is the head of the Department. He can do that. That is what they want him to do.

Ambassador DOUGLAS. And could you say "and under his direction, such officers as he may designate, within his Department, agency, or establishment, to perform any of his functions. * * *"?

The CHAIRMAN. I haven't any objection to that. I just do not want basic rules and regulations issued by the 17th assistant vice president of the subsection of so and so.

Senator LODGE. Isn't this a very unusual procedure in public law? Certainly in the Army the head man signs everything. He doesn't write everything, but he signs it.

WHO IS AUTHORIZED TO MAKE REGULATIONS?

Senator CONNALLY. As I read this section, it does not authorize anybody but the head of the Department to make the regulations.

Senator THOMAS of Utah. Look at the last sentence.

Senator GEORGE. He can delegate it, under that language.

Senator CONNALLY. That is true, but the rules and regulations must be made by the head of the department. No subordinate can make them.

The CHAIRMAN. Do you agree with that, Senator George?

Senator GEORGE. No. I think Senator Connally is wrong about that.

Senator CONNALLY. Read the provision.

The head of any department, agency, or establishment of the Government performing functions under this act may, from time to time, promulgate such rules and regulations as may be necessary and proper to carry out his functions under this act,.

Senator GEORGE.

* * * and he may delegate to such officers of his department, agency, or establishment as he may designate the authority to perform any of his functions under this act.

Senator CONNALLY. I think that certainly means within the rules and regulations that he has set up. I am willing to change the language.

FUNCTIONS DESIGNATED TO SUBORDINATES

Mr. RICE. You can cure that very simply; after the word "functions" on page 8, line 4, "perform any of the functions" "other than the function of promulgating rules and regulations."

Ambassador DOUGLAS. Would this do it, after the word act: "* * * and such officers as he may designate shall, under his direction and his rules and regulations, carry out such functions under this act as he may define."?

The CHAIRMAN. I have no objection to that.

Senator GEORGE. That would do it all right, I think. I do not know that that gets you away from the Comptroller General. I reckon it might.

Senator HATCH. Under that, though, he could still designate some subordinate to make rules and regulations.

Ambassador DOUGLAS. No; because this says "under his direction and his rules and regulations."

Senator GEORGE. Or "the rules and regulations promulgated by him".

The CHAIRMAN. Mr. Rice, have you that in mind, and will you take a crack at that?

Mr. RICE. All right, sir.

GENERAL FUNCTIONS OF ADMINISTRATOR

The CHAIRMAN. Page 8, line 5:

General Functions of Administrator.

SEC. 5. (a) The Administrator, under the direction of the president, shall—

(1) review and appraise the requirements of participating countries for assistance under the terms of this Act:

(2) formulate program of United States assistance under this Act for such countries;

(3) provide for the efficient execution of any such programs as may be placed in operation; and

(4) terminate provision of assistance or take other remedial action as provided in section 15 of this Act.

(b) In order to strengthen and make more effective the conduct of the foreign relations of the United States—

(1) the Administrator and the Secretary of State shall keep each other fully and currently informed on all matters, including prospective action, arising within the scope of their respective duties which are relevant to the conduct of the duties of the other;

(2) whenever the Secretary of State believes that any action, proposed action, or failure to act on the part of the Administrator is inconsistent with the foreign-policy objectives of the United States, he shall consult with the Administrator and, if differences of view are not adjusted by consultation, the matter shall be referred to the President for final decision.

That is practically the language of the Atomic Energy Act.

DIFFICULTY RESULTING FROM DIVULGING ASSISTANCE PROGRAMS

Senator CONNALLY. I want to ask about (a)(2), "formulate programs of United States assistance under this act for such countries;". Is it contemplated that that would be a private program, or would he divulge it to the countries? He would have to finally divulge it to them, I suppose, but it seems to me that right there is where we are going to have a difficult time when you put up these programs, and this or that country is going to say, "Well, you are giving this country more than you have me, and you haven't treated me right. You are discriminating", and so forth and so on.

I don't know how you can correct it, after hearing those things.

Ambassador DOUGLAS. I think you just have to face that, Senator.

Senator CONNALLY. I am trying to, now.

Ambassador DOUGLAS. I think that sort of difficulty is probably implicit in the whole program.

Senator CONNALLY. That is true, and you are going to have a whale of a time satisfying them.

INTERNATIONALIZATION OF THE RUHR

Senator THOMAS of Utah. Can you bring about internationalization of the Ruhr under (2)?

Ambassador DOUGLAS. I think that is a separate matter.

Senator THOMAS of Utah. It is a matter outside of this bill entirely. But could you go so far? I am asking for real information on this, because people have dreamed a long time that probably the Ruhr could be internationalized and we would get rid of the troubles there.

Senator CONNALLY. You could not do it under this bill.

Senator SMITH. You would have to have special legislation under that, would you not?

Senator THOMAS of Utah. It is not our function. It would have to be somebody else's function. But at the same time you surely could work out a program, so far as this act is concerned, to act under a basis of internationalization there, could you not?

Ambassador DOUGLAS. He could formulate a program for Germany, whether the Ruhr were internationalized or whether it remained as it was.

Senator THOMAS. In other words, that is broad enough so that such countries plus three or four countries or one country or a complex situation like the internationalization of a part of a country would be covered.

Ambassador DOUGLAS. Were the Ruhr to be placed under some sort of international control, that is one form of internationalization that might take place, and the Administrator certainly would have the authority to formulate a program for Germany which would embrace the Ruhr under international control.

The CHAIRMAN. Dr. Wilcox wants to make a statement regarding the language.

BACKGROUND OF SECTION CONCERNING ADMINISTRATOR'S FUNCTIONS

Dr. WILCOX. I just wanted to say that because of the uncertainty in the hearings as to the specific functions of the Administrator, and because of the uncertainty with regard to the relationship between the Secretary and the Administrator, it was felt desirable to add this section. It is all new language, indicating pretty clearly what the Administrator would do, particularly point 2. There was some question in the hearings as to who would initiate programs, whether they should all be initiated by the Administrator or whether the Secretary of State would be able to initiate a program, and this specific language was thought desirable in order to clarify the uncertainty.

Senator THOMAS of Utah. That applies to the whole thing?

Dr. WILCOX. Yes.

DEALING WITH INTERNATIONALIZED AREAS

Senator THOMAS of Utah. I think it is great, myself. I like all of it. I am wondering whether it is broad enough so that if, when we move on and have a treaty and the Ruhr is internationalized, the Administrator can move into a situation like that under (2).

Senator SMITH. You mean, whether he could deal with it if it were internationalized?

Senator THOMAS of Utah. Yes.

Ambassador DOUGLAS. Yes, I should think so.

Senator THOMAS of Utah. Do you see what I mean?

Ambassador DOUGLAS. Yes.

Senator THOMAS of Utah. The Saar, I suppose, is going to France. Does France take care of the relief provisions of the Saar now, under this act, or does Germany? Do you see what I mean?

Ambassador DOUGLAS. Yes.

Senator THOMAS of Utah. Can we contemplate these various changes which may take place, such as the internationalization of the Ruhr? I use that as illustrative of all of the changes that may happen.

Ambassador DOUGLAS. I am sure it does.

Senator GEORGE. Could not the Administrator lay down almost any condition which the President would approve for aid to a specific country?

Ambassador DOUGLAS. Oh, yes.

Senator GEORGE. Almost any.

Ambassador DOUGLAS. I should think so, Senator.

Senator GEORGE. It is very broad authority. It has to be.

Ambassador DOUGLAS. Yes.

Senator GEORGE. In the first place he is directed, under the President's control, of course, to review and appraise the requirements of each of these countries, and then to formulate programs. That is completed programs, so to speak. It is not just a decision on one particular matter, necessarily, although it might be. It might be just on one phase of it, but a rather comprehensive program. And it seems to me that he could formulate his basic programs upon almost any pertinent condition which the President would think wise.

Ambassador DOUGLAS. Yes.

Senator Thomas of Utah. If such countries, Senator George, can be expanded into territories which are not countries at all, that is all right. But if this is a limitation, so that we can not give relief in something which is not a country, then it is not all right.

Senator LODGE. That is the point.

Senator GEORGE. It is under some country, is it not?

Senator THOMAS of Utah. Not if it is internationalized.

Senator GEORGE. It is not internationalized yet.

Senator LODGE. Would you say, Senator George, that this Bill included Western Germany, the way it reads now?

Senator GEORGE. I should think so.

Senator SMITH. It is not a participating country at the moment.

Senator GEORGE. That is my understanding at the moment.

The CHAIRMAN. Section 3 is very clear.

Senator LODGE. We have not reached that.

CHANGING "SUCH COUNTRIES" SUGGESTED

Senator THOMAS of Utah. Can't we change "such countries", Mr. Chairman, in such a way that there will be no question about a situation of this kind—such countries, such divisions, international groups, trusteeships, or what not that may occur as we move on?

The CHAIRMAN. You probably accomplish your purpose if you say "formulate programs of U.S. assistance under this act;".

Senator THOMAS. Period. That would take care of my part of it.

The CHAIRMAN. Why not? All right.

Senator THOMAS of Utah. I should think it would be stronger that way.

Senator GEORGE. I should think that would be all right, but, of course, "such countries" is inserted in view of (1) where he is to appraise each one of these countries.

QUESTION OF WHETHER SECTION 3 INCLUDES RUHR

Senator LODGE. Does not your question go back to the question of whether section 3 would include the Ruhr?

Senator THOMAS of Utah. Yes.

The CHAIRMAN. In (1), if you said "review and appraise the requirements of participating countries as identified in section 3 * * *."

Senator GEORGE. Does that identify Western Germany?

Senator LODGE. Mr. Nitze points out that on page 21, lines 18 and 19, the words "other international organizations" would include the situation you describe, Senator Thomas.

Ambassador DOUGLAS. No. That is by utilizing the services of or acting in cooperation with. I should think, Senator, that the present language would cover the point you had in mind, particularly if construed in connection with section 3 and with other language in the act which provides that any country which becomes a participating country is also eligible.

Senator CONNALLY. How does it become a participating country, by knocking at the door?

Ambassador DOUGLAS. By assuming the obligations of participating countries.

The CHAIRMAN. By joining the multilateral treaty and making a bilateral treaty.

Senator THOMAS of Utah. Couldn't we put a question mark there, to insert some wording which means "international organizations" or "international territories"?

Ambassador DOUGLAS. You could call it an instrumentality, I suppose.

Senator CONNALLY. Does not the wording here include everything in Germany, including the Ruhr?

Senator GEORGE. I would think it would cover everything which Germany would have if she were an existing state with any sort of jurisdiction.

The CHAIRMAN. In view of the language of the balance of the act, what is the objection to doing what Senator Thomas has suggested, and putting your semicolon after the word "Act"? Then it would read, "formulate programs of U.S. assistance under this Act;".

Senator GEORGE. I do not think there is any special objection. I would not have any. I think that would mean for such countries, or for such areas.

Senator THOMAS of Utah. It means, of course, for those political divisions of the world or territories oragnized under political divisions, but immediately you set up an international division that is not a country. A trusteeship is not a country. A dependent territory is not a country. The internationalization of the Ruhr would not make a country, and I think it would be just a shame, Mr. Chairman, to retard any great political development like that.

The CHAIRMAN. You have to rewrite section 3 to begin with.

Senator THOMAS of Utah. May I suggest this, Mr. Chairman, that we decide to put a semicolon after "Act," subject to the opinion of the drafting officers after they see that if this is tightly construed we may have to deal only with countries, and if they set up a United States of Europe, and you want to deal with them—as so many have said—can you deal with so many countries?

The CHAIRMAN. You have another immediate question; namely, Trieste.

Senator THOMAS of Utah. Yes. Trieste now, and places of that kind.

Then, say you make this customs union that people have talked so much about function as a political entity in the world. You may rather deal with that than with either Belgium or Luxembourg or with Holland.

The CHAIRMAN. Suppose we put a semicolon after the word "Act" and thrash out the rest of it when we get to section 3. Is there any objection to that?

Senator THOMAS of Utah. That will be fine with me.

IMPLICATION OF SETTING UP BILATERAL AGREEMENTS

Senator SMITH. I would like to ask Dr. Wilcox one question, whether in section 5(a) there is the implication of setting up the bilateral agreements, or does that come in other sections of the bill?

Dr. WILCOX. That is in another section.

Senator SMITH. You do not try to imply it here by this?

Dr. WILCOX. No, sir.

The CHAIRMAN. Is there anything else on this section?

WORKING LATIN AMERICA INTO PICTURE

Senator LODGE. I would like to ask—and I do not know whether this is the place to ask the question—whether it is contemplated in this bill that there be a sort of clearinghouse for international trade with which we can work Latin America into this picture on a triangular basis.

The CHAIRMAN. I cannot answer that. The possibility certainly should be available for exploration.

Senator CONNALLY. We are going to do that now. We are going to buy the products of Latin American countries wherever possible and furnish them to Europe.

Senator LODGE. I was wondering whether it is the intention of the executive branch to do that; and second, whether this bill is set up so that it makes that possible.

Senator CONNALLY. I cannot see how anything interferes with it under the bill. You can buy anything wherever you want to.

The CHAIRMAN. Let us look at that when we come to it.

Page 9, line 7, section 6: "Section 4(a) of the Bretton Woods Agreement Act (59 Stat. 512, 513) is hereby amended to read as follows:"

ADMINISTRATOR'S INFORMING SECRETARY OF STATE

Senator SMITH. May I ask one question, Mr. Chairman, under (b) on page 8?

It says, "the Administrator and Secretary of State shall keep each other fully and currently informed on all matters * * * " Does that mean before the Administrator acts he tells the Secretary of State what he is going to do, so the Secretary of State has a chance to act under subparagraph (2), or does he go right ahead?

The CHAIRMAN. It says "all matters, including prospective action * * *."

Senator SMITH. He might say "At 3 o'clock this afternoon I am going to do thus and so," and the Secretary of State, through his Ambassador, might not like that. I am just wondering what the practical outcome is. We have considered right straight through, I think, in these foreign countries, that the representative of the Administrator would be in contact with his Ambassador, with his Minister. He might say, "All right, I am going to see the Minister of Belgium this afternoon at 3 o'clock and make this proposition to him with regard to these tons of coal," and the Ambassador does not want him to do that.

What is your thought on that, Mr. Douglas? Have you had both jobs?

Ambassador DOUGLAS. There is a section, Senator, that deals with the relationship between the Ambassador in a specific country and the head of the Economic Cooperation Administration in that country.

Senator SMITH. Then these provisions here in this section 5 do not refer to the relationship of the representatives abroad with the Ambassador? This just has to do with the immediate relationship of the Administrator and the Secretary of State?

Ambassador DOUGLAS. Yes.

Senator SMITH. It probably is adequate, then, because it does say "including prospective action," but I am wondering how much time you are going to give the Secretary of State, and can you say you are going to put this thing in effect at 3 o'clock.

Ambassador DOUGLAS. If the Administrator went to the Secretary at 2:30 and said, "At 3 o'clock this is what I am going to do," and the Secretary said, "Well now, I think that is a mistake," and the Administrator and the Secretary could not reconcile the difference, then the Administrator, as I understand the language, will refrain from taking the action which he contemplated until it had been submitted to the President and resolved by him.

Senator GEORGE. That is the implication, certainly, in (2), and that was, I believe, the answer that you made during the examination before the full committee.

Ambassador DOUGLAS. Yes, sir.

Senator GEORGE. That very question was presented.

ADDITIONAL OBLIGATION OF SECRETARY OF STATE

I would like to raise this one question. I confess at once that it is very hard to resolve, but in "(1) the Administrator and the Secretary of State . . .", are you putting an additional obligation on the Secretary of State?

Ambassador DOUGLAS. Yes.

Senator GEORGE. "The Administrator and the Secretary of State shall keep each other fully and currently informed on all matters, including prospective action, arising within the scope of their respective duties which are relevant to the conduct of the duties of the other;".

CONFINING INFORMATION REQUIREMENT

If there were any way in the world to confine that to important decisions, to decisions of great consequence in foreign affairs, it ought to be done beyond all doubt.

Senator THOMAS of Utah. I would cut out "on all matters."

Senator CONNALLY. Who is going to say what is important and what is not?

Senator GEORGE. I say there is a difficulty there, but it certainly ought not to embrace every trivial decision or relatively unimportant decision.

Then I do not know whether the Secretary of State should be required to tell this Administrator what he is going to do in some of these countries, unless it is confined to something that embraces the dual duties of the two.

Senator LODGE. Would not those words "which are relevant" take care of what you mean?

Senator GEORGE. They may, but it is very doubtful.

Senator THOMAS of Utah. Wouldn't that be all right, Senator George: "The Administrator and Secretary of State shall keep each other fully and currently informed, including prospective action. . ."?

Senator SMITH. You would have to have "on matters" in there. You can take out the word "all."

Senator THOMAS of Utah. ". . . on matters, including prospective action, arising within the scope of their respective duties. . .". That is a straight limitation without including all of outdoors.

Senator GEORGE. "All" is embracing. That is what disturbs me. I think it is too all embracing.

Now, "arising within the scope of their respective duties which are relevant to the conduct of the duties of the other;" I suppose does mean that the Secretary of State, if he was going to ask the President to declare war, would not have to go to the Administrator and talk about that, because it would be a sort of a stretch of the imagination to say that it fell within the class of dual duties or dual responsibilities.

The CHAIRMAN. I should think the Administrator ought to know about it.

Senator GEORGE. He would know about it the next day.

Ambassador DOUGLAS. The Secretary of State might have information in regard to a certain country that would affect the situation.

Senator GEORGE. He might wish to pursue a certain policy that is only remotely, if at all, affected by the administration of the act.

Ambassador DOUGLAS. It raises the question of who is to determine what is relevant and what is not.

Senator LODGE. As a practical matter, won't it work out this way, that all the messages the Administrator sends to his people will have a copy go to the State Department, and there would be somebody reading those messages and he would fish out those he thought the Secretary ought to see?

Senator THOMAS of Utah. I think it would be improved by leaving out "which are relevant to the conduct of the duties of the other." Those words are an invitation to somebody to be sore if somebody forgets something.

Ambassador DOUGLAS. But there may be certain things which the Secretary of State is doing which the Administrator perhaps should know about.

Senator THOMAS of Utah. Do you not do everything you want to do, Mr. Douglas, when you say "the Administrator and Secretary of State shall keep each other fully and currently informed on matters, including prospective action, arising within the scope of their respective duties"?

Ambassador DOUGLAS. I would not think so, Senator, because the Secretary of State, if the last qualifying clause is left out, would then be required to keep the Administrator informed on all matters that fell within the jurisdiction of his office.

Senator HATCH. I do not want to be technical, but if you say "under this act" the Secretary of State will have to keep the Administrator informed of everything he does.

Ambassador DOUGLAS. Yes.

The CHAIRMAN. The thing will work out. I think it is most interesting to note that there never was a more violent clash of rival interests than we had in the atomic energy situation between civil and military authority, and we set up a kindred formula, and unless I am mistaken, there never once has been an appeal to the President to settle a dispute between them. The whole thing has just worked right out in good shape.

PRECEDENT OF DEMOBILIZATION AND RECONVERSION

Senator GEORGE. In drafting this, was any notice given to the Act of Demobilization and Reconversion? That is a very strong precedent here for setting up an independent agency and giving it specified broad duties and making everybody come under it, and it worked pretty well, to the extent that it has worked at all.

Ambassador DOUGLAS. I cannot answer, Senator. This language here follows almost exactly the language of the Brookings Institution.

Senator GEORGE. And the Brookings Institution had in mind the Demobilization and Reconversion Act. I do say that that was a very accurately drawn act. Every word in it means a great deal.

[Discussion was continued off the record.]

LIMITING SECRETARY OF STATE'S DISCLOSURES TO ADMINISTRATOR

Senator GEORGE. The thing that bothers me about making the Secretary of State disclose everything to the Administrator is this: Certainly he must disclose everything that is pertinent to the administration of this act, and they may do that by, as Senator Lodge suggested, simply exchanging their orders and directives. But it is pretty hard to do that, because some of the things the Secretary of State will be dealing with will be very highly confidential at times, yet the Administrator, if they affect his duties unde rthis act, ought to know about them.

Senator CONNALLY. Why couldn't that be corrected by saying "the conduct of their duties under this act"?

Senator GEORGE. That is what this language is intended to do: "Arising within the scope of their respective duties which are relevant to the conduct of the duties of the other;".

Senator HATCH. Senator George, do you like the word "relevant" in there?

Senator GEORGE. No, sir; I do not.

Senator HATCH. It is an awfully bad word in law.

Senator GEORGE. No, sir. I think the language Senator Connally has suggested might be thought through and might be better, and that would restrict the Secretary of State.

The CHAIRMAN. What is your language?

Senator CONNALLY. I am meditating. If you want to get rid of "relevant" you can say, "The scope of their respective duties which relate to the conduct of the duties of the other under this act."

Senator THOMAS of Utah. You want more than that from the Secretary of State. If the Secretary of State has information that France is going to blow up, the Administrator ought to be told.

Senator CONNALLY. That would be covered.

Senator SMITH. Why could you not say "which affect"?

Ambassador DOUGLAS. Or "which are pertinent to the conduct of their duties under this act"?

Senator GEORGE. I would think that would be satisfactory—"arising within the scope of their respective duties which are pertinent to the conduct of the duties of the other under this act."

Senator CONNALLY. You thereby relieve the Secretary of State from advising him as to everything the State Department is doing, and you limit it to the things which the Department is doing which affect his operations, which is right. There is no sense in feeding him a lot of stuff.

MAKING ADMINISTRATOR'S DECISIONS AND PLANS PUBLIC

Senator GEORGE. We have not got to do it, Mr. Chairman, but I believe that we will face it and it is a very important thing in the administration of this act if it should be finally written into law:

Making public the decisions reached by the Administrator and the plans formulated by him, making them matters of public record. There will be a certain demand for that, and it is going to have a pretty strong backing because it sounds reasonable, you know, and it is a matter we are going to have to think of.

The CHAIRMAN. Would you think that arises at this point?

Senator GEORGE. It arises here. It may run all through. It arises here.

The CHAIRMAN. Let us put that question down.

Senator GEORGE. I just simply suggest that that is one of the stubborn things that we are going to have to face.

Senator CONNALLY. Go back a minute to section 3, page 5. I haven't any real definite ideas about the thing, but it seems to me that is a pretty sloppy way of handling things.

The CHAIRMAN. We have not taken that section up yet.

CHANGE IN INFORMATION SECTION

Senator SMITH. Do I understand that (b) (1) on page 8 has been changed now to eliminate the word "all" in line 21 and to make the end of it read "which are pertinent"?

The CHAIRMAN. It now reads:

> The Administrator and the Secretary of State shall keep each other fully and currently informed on matters, including prospective action, arising within the scope of their respective duties which are pertinent to the duties of the other under this act.

Senator SMITH. Cutting out the word "conduct"?

Senator HATCH. Before we leave this section I want to ask the lawyers: I am always a little bit worried when you go to enumerating powers whether you are excluding some, and whether it would be wise to add a section saying "without limiting powers otherwise conferred, the Administrator shall * * * ".

The CHAIRMAN. Mr. Rice, will you take a look at that?

Mr. RICE. Yes, sir.

Senator CONNALLY.

> * * * arising within the scope of their respective duties which are pertinent to the conduct of the duties of the other under this act.

The CHAIRMAN. I think that is as far as we can go this morning, gentlemen, because we have to go to the floor. Tomorrow I hope we can sit all day.

PARTICIPATING COUNTRIES

Senator CONNALLY. Before we go I want to give them something to think about. It is a section over here. We haven't got to it. It is section 3 on page 5, "Participating Countries." It seems to me that that language is pretty nebulous. We insert "provided it adheres to" and I think it leaves it up to them largely whether they will adhere. Of course that is up to them, whether they sign all these agreements and all that, but it seems to me there ought to be a pretty clear indication there that just anybody who knocks at the door is not going to be admitted. We have the right to say to whom and what, but we never in this bill name the countries, do we?

The CHAIRMAN. We name them right here.

Senator CONNALLY. You say "any country". Indonesia could apply here, under this.

Ambassador DOUGLAS. It is not in Europe. It has to be wholly or partly in Europe.

Senator CONNALLY. "* * * including its colonies and dependencies * * *". Indonesia is a colony of Holland.

Ambassador DOUGLAS. It would be eligible.

Senator CONNALLY. I just want you to be thinking about that. It seems to me that that whole section could be included there.

Senator SMITH. With this rather broad language, how can we talk in terms of dollars until we know who the countries are?

Ambassador DOUGLAS. We know the 16 participating countries.

Senator CONNALLY. But this provides for anybody else.

Senator LODGE. Why do you mention the United Kingdom and not mention France?

Dr. WILCOX. The United Kingdom is not in Europe, strictly speaking.

Senator LODGE. The United Kingdom is not part of Europe?

Ambassador DOUGLAS. No.

Senator LODGE. Is Martha's Vineyard part of America?

Ambassador DOUGLAS. Yes, but that is part of a country.

[Whereupon, at 11:55 a.m., a recess was taken until the following day, Tuesday, February 10, 1948, at 10 a.m.]

EUROPEAN RECOVERY PROGRAM

TUESDAY, FEBRUARY 10, 1948

UNITED STATES SENATE,
COMMITTEE ON FOREIGN RELATIONS,
Washington, D.C.

The committee met, pursuant to call, in the committee hearing room, U.S. Capitol, at 10 a.m., Senator Arthur H. Vandenberg, chairman, presiding.

Present: Senators Vandenberg, Capper, Wiley, Smith, Lodge, George, Thomas of Utah, and Hatch.

Also present: The Honorable Lewis W. Douglas, Ambassador to Great Britain; Mr. Paul Nitze, Deputy Director, Office of International Trade Policy, Department of State; Mr. Ernest Gross, legal adviser, Department of State; Mr. Stephen E. Rice, legislative counsel, U.S. Senate.

The CHAIRMAN. We have a quorum.

We passed over three or four things yesterday with the suggestion that some drafting be done. The drafting has been done. Suppose we briefly revert and see where we are at. This drafting is the joint work of our staff and the legislative counsel, and the State Department.

QUESTION OF TEMPORARY ADMINISTRATOR

First is on page 6, line 24. That involves the question of this temporary Administrator pending the authority of the act itself. It is proposed to insert, after the word "provide" in line 24, "for a period of not to exceed 60 days after the date of enactment of this act". It would then read:

(c) The President is authorized, pending the appointment and qualification of the first Administrator or Deputy Administrator for Economic Cooperation appointed hereunder, to provide, for a period of not to exceed sixty days after the date of enactment of this Act, for the performance of the functions of the Administrator under this Act through such departments, agencies, or establishments of the United States Government as he may direct.

Senator SMITH. That would mean, Mr. Chairman, that if nothing was accomplished within the 60 days we would come to an end?

The CHAIRMAN. Then something goes with it.

Also, on page 7, after the word "direct" at the end of the sentence, insert:

In the event the President nominates an Administrator or Deputy Administrator prior to the expiration of such sixty-day period, the Authority conferred upon him by this subsection shall be extended beyond such sixty-day period, but only until said Administrator qualifies and takes office.

Senator THOMAS of Utah. That means that in case the Senate holds up confirmation, and things of that type, the business doesn't stop. Isn't that right?

Dr. WILCOX. That is right.

Senator SMITH. "Him" is the President, not the Administrator.

Mr. RICE. "Him" is the President.

Senator THOMAS of Utah. That does not destroy in any sense any continuity, Mr. Chairman.

The CHAIRMAN. No. I understand.

Senator HATCH. But if he does not nominate within that time, then the authority would expire.

Senator SMITH. He has to nominate within 60 days.

What happens in case he nominates and conceivably the Administrator is turned down by the Senate?

Ambassador DOUGLAS. Then the power of authority is extended.

Senator SMITH. You could not say "said Administrator" under your construction.

NOMINATION WITHIN THIRTY DAYS SUGGESTED

The CHAIRMAN. 60 days is 2 months. That is one-sixth of a year. That is a long time to wait to start this show if it is as important as we have been led to believe. Why shouldn't he do it in 30 days?

Ambassador DOUGLAS. Whatever period is agreed upon.

The CHAIRMAN. Is there any reason why he should not do it in 30 days, for Heaven's sake?

Ambassador DOUGLAS. I would not think so.

Senator SMITH. If the President has trouble finding somebody, it might take him 20 or 25 days, and we might want a little more than 5 days to check him up.

I have no objection to 30 days, but I can see the reason for putting in that much time.

The CHAIRMAN. What do you say, Senator George?

Senator GEORGE. Thirty days would seem long enough, because he could certainly nominate somebody within 30 days.

The CHAIRMAN. If you cannot get this thing going within 30 days——

Senator GEORGE. I should think the President would almost nominate simultaneous with the signing of the act.

The CHAIRMAN. Let us make this 30 days. We will make it 30 days, and with that change the amendment is approved.

ADDITIONAL CHANGES IN AMENDMENT

Ambassador DOUGLAS. And changing the word "said" to "an".

Mr. RICE. Shouldn't that last "but" clause be changed—"but only to an Administrator or Deputy Administrator * * *".

Senator SMITH. Yes. Then in case he is turned down he carries on until somebody fills the place.

Mr. RICE. And I think you ought to add "an Administrator or Deputy Administrator."

The CHAIRMAN. All right.

HIRING OF EXPERTS AND CONSULTANTS

Then insert on page 7, line 18, beginning with the word "Experts" another change. Strike out down through line 22 and insert in lieu thereof the following. This is to take care of——

Senator LODGE. It is to take care of that situation which we had under the Commission which reorganized the executive branch.

The CHAIRMAN. The new language is "Experts and consultants, or organizations thereof, as authorized by section 15 of the act of August 2, 1946 (5 U.S.C. 55a),". What is that, Mr. Rice?

Mr. RICE. That is an act that permits the executive department to hire consultants and experts and organizations thereof and pay them $50 per diem.

Senator GEORGE. In excess of the regular fixed limit on employees, too, is it not?

Mr. RICE. Senator, I will have to look that up, but that is not important so far as this particular bill is concerned, because we have already exempted them from the personnel ceilings up above there, in lines 11 and 12. That is section 14(a) of the Federal Employees Pay Act.

The CHAIRMAN. So that the new language would read:

> Experts and consultants, as authorized by section 15 of the act of August 2, 1946 (5 U.S.C. 55a), may be employed by the Administration, and individuals so employed may be compensated at rates not in excess of $50 per diem.

Senator LODGE. Where does that leave a firm like Haskins & Sells?

Mr. RICE. It permits them to hire them.

The CHAIRMAN. There is no limit on the organization?

Mr. RICE. You could contract for their services and pay them within the limits of your appropriation, unless you have limiting language in the appropriation.

Senator LODGE. So that under this language they could retain a firm of engineers and pay them whatever is necessary, is that right?

Mr. GROSS. On a contract basis.

Senator LODGE. Does this take care of the situation which was brought up on the floor 2 months ago about a firm not being able to keep its private clients while working for the Government?

Mr. RICE. You are talking now about exempting them from those criminal provisions.

Senator LODGE. Obviously you will never get anybody to work for the Government if they have to give up all their clients.

Mr. RICE. That is a question of policy. Those criminal provisions are applicable unless you put in a provision exempting them.

Senator LODGE. Do you think we should do it, or will we have to have that whole fight all over later?

The CHAIRMAN. It is perfectly obvious that the provision is futile. If everybody who is going to do a 60-day job for ERP has to go out of business everywhere else, we will never get anyone.

Senator LODGE. That is what it seems to me. It seems to me we might clear this all up now, rather than have a hurry call 2 months from now, and have to go back and put it in.

Senator GEORGE. I think we should put that exemption in when we are dealing with these exemptions, and write that in so as to take care of those criminal statutes.

The CHAIRMAN. All right. We will return this for additional revisions.

ADMINISTRATOR'S FUNCTIONS

Now, page 8 line 7. After the word "shall" insert "in addition to all other functions vested in him by this act—". It would then read "section 5(a) the Administrator, under the direction of the President, shall, in addition to all other functions vested in him by this act—".

What is the purpose of that?

Senator HATCH. That is the question I raise, whether the enumeration of these powers might be a limitation.

The CHAIRMAN. Is there any objection to that?

Senator LODGE. I would like to ask whether that ought to be under the control of the President instead of under the direction, in order to harmonize with the change you made yesterday on page 6, line 6.

Senator GEORGE. Then you should say "subject to the control of the President".

The CHAIRMAN. I prefer the word "control" myself. Suppose that we make it read as indicated by both Senator George and Senator Lodge: "The Administrator, under the control of the President, shall, in addition to all other functions vested in him by this act—".

Is there any objection to that? OK.

DELEGATION OF FUNCTIONS BY ADMINISTRATOR

Senator SMITH. Mr. Chairman, on page 8 above that, lines 2 to 4, I have a note here that Mr. Douglas gave a certain revised language. Is that going to be incorporated? That is in lines 2 to 4.

The Chairman. We are coming to it now.

The next amendment, insert on page 8, line 2, beginning with the word "and" the following. Strike out through line 4, the balance of the sentence, and insert in lieu thereof "and he may delegate authority to perform any of such functions to his subordinates, acting under his direction, and under rules and regulations promulgated by him."

I think that meets my point.

Senator SMITH. That meets our discussion yesterday.

The CHAIRMAN. The alternatives on page 8, line 4, after the word "functions" insert "other than the function of promulgating rules and regulations."

Mr. RICE. In other words, he could delegate any of his functions except the function of promulgating regulations.

The CHAIRMAN. Either is satisfactory with me. Which would the committee prefer?

Senator GEORGE. I think the first is probably preferable. You propose to introduce this as a clean bill?

The CHAIRMAN. Oh, yes.

Senator LODGE. We will take the first one, then?

Senator SMITH. I prefer the first one.

The CHAIRMAN. Without objection, the first suggestion will be adopted.

NATIONAL ADVISORY COUNCIL

Now we are over to page 9, line 6 "National Advisory Council."

Sec. 6. Section 4(a) of the Bretton Woods Agreement Act (59 Stat. 512, 513) is hereby amended to read as follows:

"Sec. 4 (a) In order to coordinate the policies and operations of the representatives of the United States on the Fund and the Bank and of all agencies of the Government which make or participate in making foreign loans or which engage in foreign financial, exchange or monetary transactions, there is hereby established the National Advisory Council on International Monetary and Financial problems (hereinafter referred to as the council), consisting of the Secretary of Treasury as Chairman, the Secretary of State, the Secretary of Commerce, the Chairman of the Board of Governors of the Federal Reserve System, the Chairman of the Board of Trustees of the Export-Import Bank of Washington, and during such period as the Economic Cooperation Administration shall continue to exist, the Administrator for Economic Cooperation."

That is the same language, is it, of the existing statute, except that you have added the Administrator, is that right, Mr. Rice?

Mr. Rice. Yes, sir; that is right.

U.S. SPECIAL REPRESENTATIVE FOR EUROPE

The Chairman. Is there any objection? OK. On page 10:

Sec. 7. There shall be a United States Special Representative in Europe who shall (a) be appointed by the President, by and with the advice and consent of the Senate, (b) be entitled to receive the same compensation and allowances as a chief of mission, class 1, within the meaning of the Act of August 13, 1946 (60 Stat. 999), and (c) have the rank of ambassador extraordinary and plenipotentiary. He shall be the chief United States representative to any European organization of participating countries which may be established by the participating countries to further a joint program for European recovery, and shall discharge in Europe such additional responsibilities as may be assigned to him with the approval of the President in furtherance of the purposes of this Act. He may also be designated as the United States representative on the Economic Commission for Europe.

PAYMENT OF SPECIAL REPRESENTATIVE AND ADMINISTRATOR

Does this compensation and allowances pay him more than we are going to pay the Administrator?

Ambassador Douglas. Yes.

The Chairman. Should it?

Senator Smith. It is only expenses more, isn't it?

Ambassador Douglas. No, the salary of an Ambassador is $25,000 and in addition to the salary there are allowances which vary according to post, from $10,000 .

Senator Wiley. How does this fellow fit into the picture in relation to the Administrator? Who is the big shot, if he goes over there with all this extra pay and extra position as an ambassador extraordinary?

The Chairman. We are coming to that a little later. It is spelled out in just a minute.

But the question at this point, it seems to me, is whether you ipso facto have not made the Ambassador, higher, in giving the Ambassador a higher rating than the administrator by the salary you pay him?

Senator Thomas of Utah. You can make the salary of the Administrator $25,000 and change that. You cannot very well give a man the rank of ambassador and not treat him the same as the other ambassadors.

Senator LODGE. Do the other ambassadors get paid more than the Secretary of State now?

The CHAIRMAN. There is a parallel I had not thought of.

AMBASSADOR'S ACCREDITATION TO UNITED KINGDOM

Senator LODGE. I don't think that would make much difference. I would like to ask whether this Ambassador is going to be accredited to the United Kingdom.

Ambassador DOUGLAS. I think that would have to be construed in the light of the language of section 3.

Senator THOMAS of Utah. His representation on the Economic Commission for Europe will cover that, I imagine.

Senator GEORGE. We have to find European countries to include the United Kingdom. We have not dealt with that section, but it is in here.

Senator LODGE. That does not say that. It says that these countries shall participate in the program, but it does not say they are part of Europe.

Mr. RICE. It says they are participating countries, and that says "European organization of participating countries."

Senator LODGE. I think the United Kingdom is in Europe. I looked it up on the Columbia Encyclopaedia, and I quote:

> European Islands include the British Isles.

That is the end of the quotation. I have not looked up Harvard's expression on it. That is Columbia's expression on it.

The CHAIRMAN. Let's thresh that out when we get to section 3.

Tentatively we will pass this, because the guts of the thing comes next.

EQUALIZING SALARIES OF ADMINISTRATOR AND AMBASSADOR RECOMMENDED

Senator SMITH. I would think, Mr. Chairman, you would have to give your administrator at least equal rank with this chap by salary and so forth.

The CHAIRMAN. Cabot Lodge stymied me on that argument when he pointed out that the Secretary of State is paid less than his ambassadors.

Senator SMITH. But the Secretary of State is a Cabinet officer, and of course he has to take the same medicine the other poor Cabinet officers have to take. But here you are creating something new, and in this field, which is the ERP field, you are saying one man gets $20,000 and another man gets $25,000, and I am a little concerned about that.

Senator WILEY. One man can headquarter in America, and the other has to live in that wornout Europe.

Senator SMITH. We are giving him an expense account which offsets that, are we not?

Mr. RICE. Is it not true that the Ambassador gets $17,500 as compensation, and the allowances bring it to $25,000?

Ambassador DOUGLAS. No, the Ambassador gets $25,000, and he does have certain allowances.

[Discussion was continued off the record.]

SPECIAL COMMISSIONS FOR ECONOMIC COOPERATION

The CHAIRMAN. This section stricken out, section 6, is replaced by another section. The substitute is misplaced in the bill by error, and it is section 9, so let us go to section 9 on page 13, line 7:

SEC. 9. (a) There shall be established in each participating country, except any of the zones of occupation of Germany, a special mission for economic cooperation under the direction of a chief who shall be responsible for the performance within such country of operations under this Act. The chief shall be appointed by the Administrator, shall receive his instructions from the Administrator—

This is answering your question, Senator Wiley—

and shall report to the Administrator on the performance of the duties assigned to him. The chief of the special mission shall take rank immediately after the chief of the United States diplomatic mission in such country.

(b) The chief of the special mission shall keep the chief of the United States diplomatic mission fully and currently informed on all matters, including prospective action, arising within the scope of the operations of the special mission and the chief of the diplomatic mission shall keep the chief of the special mission fully and currently informed on all matters relative to the conduct of the duties of the chief of the special mission. The chief of the United States diplomatic mission will be responsible for assuring that the operations of the special mission are consistent with the foreign-policy objectives of the United States in such country and to that end whenever the chief of the United States diplomatic mission believes that any action, proposed action, or failure to act on the part of the special mission is inconsistent with such foreign-policy objectives, he shall so advise the chief of the special mission. If differences of view are not adjusted by consultation, the matter shall be referred to the Secretary of State and the Administrator for decision.

FINAL RESOLUTION OF DIFFERENCES OF VIEW

Senator THOMAS of Utah. Now then, in your step of dispute, it is a bad thing to bring out, but I think it is best to bring it out so that I can follow you. If there is a difference of opinion between the Administrator and the Secretary of State, then can this difference, which happens over in Europe, between the two Ambassadors, be carried to the President of the United Sates for its final determination?

The CHAIRMAN. I would assume so, because I think we have said elsewhere that under such circumstances the President is the umpire.

Senator THOMAS of Utah. He would be the umpire in spite of what it says here:

If differences of view are not adjusted by consultation, the matter shall be referred to the Secretary of State and the Administrator for decision?

Senator LODGE. The Ambassadors would not carry it to the President. The Secretary of State or the Administrator would carry it.

Senator THOMAS of Utah. That is understood by everybody, is it?

Senator SMITH. Isn't that covered by subsection 2 on page 8? I think it is covered by subsection 2 on page 8, because there you have a jam between the Secretary of State and the Administrator.

Senator THOMAS of Utah. If it is not covered, it ought to be put in.

Senator SMITH. I agree with you. If it is not clearly covered by (b) (2) on page 8, it ought to be put in.

Senator GEORGE. I think it is.

Senator THOMAS of Utah. You assume that any difference between the Secretary of State and the Administrator can be carried to the President, and that this does not preclude carrying the European question to him?

Senator GEORGE. No, sir, I do not think it makes any difference as to where the question would arise. It all relates to the same subject matter, and it seems to me it goes there finally for his final decision if they cannot resolve their differences.

The CHAIRMAN. Because the language on page 8 is:

whenever the Secretary of State believes that any action, proposed action, or failure to act on the part of the Administrator is inconsistent with the foreign-policy objectives of the United States, he shall consult with the Administrator and, if differences of view are not adjusted by consultation, the matter shall be referred to the President for final decision.

This would be one of those "whenevers".

Ambassador DOUGLAS. This, Senator, does not refer to the "stumbling" ambassador in Europe, it refers to the relationship between the ambassador accredited to a specific country, and the head of the Economic Cooperation Administration within that country.

Senator THOMAS of Utah. Isn't that the "stumbling" ambassador?

Ambassador DOUGLAS. No, sir, that is something entirely different.

DUTIES OF ROVING AMBASSADOR

Senator WILEY. Where does he fit in? That is not answered at all by this.

The CHAIRMAN. You mean the overall rolling ambassador?

Senator WILEY. One is stumbling, one is rolling.

Ambassador DOUGLAS. His job, according to this language, is to be the representative of the United States on any continuing organization which is established, and he shall discharge in Europe such additional responsibilities as may be assigned to him with the approval of the President in furtherance of the purposes of the act.

Senator LODGE. He does not check with any American Ambassadors over there at all?

Ambassador DOUGLAS. As the language now reads, defining the duties of the roving ambasador, the President may, in addition to the duties expressly stated in the act, assign him other duties.

The Brookings Institution report on that subject is not quite clear, and as I understand it, deliberately not clear. There is a three-way relationship, you see. In one corner of the triangle is the roving ambassador; another corner of the triangle is the head of the diplomatic mission in a specific country. The third corner of the triangle is the head of the Economic Cooperation Administration in each country, and it is a rather complicated thing to work out the relationships in black and white in a statute, it seems to me, between those three points of the triangle.

Dr. WILCOX. I think the Brookings staff did envisage the possibility of this roving ambassador coordinating the activities of the chiefs of special economic missions in the 16 countries.

Ambassador DOUGLAS. Oh, yes. It says very clearly that he shall consult with the heads of the diplomatic missions and the heads of the Economic Cooperation Administration in each one of the countries, and shall call upon them for such advice and help as they may provide.

Senator THOMAS of Utah. If you have this triangular arrangement, why should not the chief stumbling ambassador be the head of his triangle in his country?

Ambassador DOUGLAS. Then one runs into this language, which is of some significance, which defines the relationship between the head of the special economic cooperation mission in each country, and the head of the diplomatic mission in that country, the ambassador in that country. Do you follow that?

NEED FOR ROVING AMBASSADOR QUESTIONED

Senator THOMAS of Utah. Yes, I can follow that, except that when you think of differences between all these people, the more you have of them the more complicated those differences become for smooth administration. I am wondering in my mind whether this has not grown up by thinking we should have an ambassador moving around, and then we discover that probably we don't need him.

Ambassador DOUGLAS. I think you do need him. I think you need him very badly as the representative of the United States on the continuing organization. You need him to coordinate.

The CHAIRMAN. You need him as the watchdog of the multilateral agreement.

ROLE OF ROVING AMBASSADOR

Senator THOMAS of Utah. He is the one that is to encourage all of this international cooperation, isn't he?

Ambassador DOUGLAS. He is the one to encourage it through the participating countries and he may use the head of a diplomatic mission in any particular country to exert pressure within that country. He may do it jointly with the head of the diplomatic mission within that country. He also may use, and doubtless will use, the head of the Economic Cooperation Administration within that country.

Senator THOMAS of Utah. In each country?

Ambassador DOUGLAS. Yes.

Senator THOMAS of Utah. Then there is a proper connection between the individual country's head of the economic mission and this roving ambassador, is there not?

Ambassador DOUGLAS. There is a relationship, but the Brookings Institution thought, if my recollection is correct, that it would be better to leave a definition of the specific relationship to the President rather than to write it into the statute.

Senator THOMAS of Utah. So that the individual representative of the Commission in the individual country will report directly to the representative in that country, and not to this roving man?

Ambassador DOUGLAS. He will do both. He will report directly to the Administrator in Washington.

Senator THOMAS of Utah. The line of authority comes——

Ambassador DOUGLAS. From the Administrator in Washington.

Senator THOMAS of Utah. Through?

Ambassador DOUGLAS. It may come directly.

Senator LODGE. So he is not like the Ambassador to France, under the Secretary of State. He is under the Administrator. He is the only ambassador who is. He is the only ambassador-at-large who is contemplated, to follow through on the multilateral agreements and to encourage the integration of Europe.

Ambassador DOUGLAS. That is right.

Senator THOMAS of Utah. Is he in a position so that he can be a troubleshooter on almost any kind of question? Say he is in Paris now without any particular job and trouble comes up in Norway. Who will send him, the Administrator?

Ambassador DOUGLAS. He will probably consult with and advise with the head of the Economic Cooperation Administration in Norway. He may participate himself in Norway and call upon the Ambassador in Norway.

Senator SMITH. He could go there without being instructed from Washington to go there?

Ambassador DOUGLAS. Of course he can.

Senator THOMAS of Utah. And when he gets into Norway, his relationship with the American Ambassador in Norway is just exactly the same as his relations with the American Ambassador in Paris were?

Ambassador DOUGLAS. Yes.

Senator LODGE. But nothing is set forth in the act as to what his relations are?

Ambassador DOUGLAS. Nothing is set forth in the act. Duties other than defined in the act, or in addition to those defined in the act, are left for the President to prescribe.

RESTRICTIONS ON ROVING AMBASSADOR

Senator THOMAS of Utah. Are we creating a situation which is similar to the situations that have always been created when we have had roving ambassadors? Is this roving ambassador tied down enough so that he cannot interfere with the ordinary diplomatic procedures? I am reading now Mr. Hull's experiences, or the last one.

Ambassador DOUGLAS. I think it depends largely upon the additional powers which the President may assign to him.

Senator WILEY. That is right.

Ambassador DOUGLAS. On the one hand it depends upon those additional powers, and upon the quality of the Ambassador in each individual country.

Senator THOMAS of Utah. In other words, you cannot legislate personality out of existence.

Ambassador DOUGLAS. It is very difficult. I do not know exactly what the reason behind the Brookings report may have been. Speaking to you confidentially, it is the purpose, I think, of the administration, or should be the purpose of any administration, to strengthen the quality of its diplomatic representation. If you restrict too much and subordinate the head of a mission, an ambassador somewhere in some country, really able people may not be disposed to accept the post. You are caught on the horns of a dilemma, and I think probably the relationship just has to work its way out in experience and the designation by the President of such additional responsibilities, having due regard, it seems to me, the essential thing of foreign relations, of improving the quality and the competence of the heads of missions.

U.S. SPECIAL REPRESENTATIVE ONLY NEW DIPLOMAT SENT ABROAD

The CHAIRMAN. Am I right that this is the only new diplomatic agent that goes abroad under ERP?

Ambassador DOUGLAS. If you call him a diplomatic agent, yes.

The CHAIRMAN. Foreign policy agent.

Ambassador DOUGLAS. That is right.

Senator LODGE. That is the U.S. special representative in Europe. He is the only one?

Senator SMITH. And you look upon him as a foreign policy agent, and not as the voice of the economic set-up to run ERP? I had not understood that he was a foreign policy agent.

The CHAIRMAN. I mean, he is the only new diplomat who is sent abroad in connection with this picture. I don't mean to have my language microscoped for sinister hidden meanings.

Senator SMITH. Pardon me, Mr. Chairman. I never think your language needs any mircroscopic analysis. It is always clear as daylight.

Senator WILEY. But he believes it is sinister.

The CHAIRMAN. It seems to me the boys have done a pretty good job of putting this down in black and white.

DIFFERENT FOOTINGS OF ECA MISSIONS AND OVER-ALL ECA

Senator LODGE. Don't you think a question will be asked on the floor as to why we make the chief economic recovery man in each country show his messages to the Ambassador, but the overall economic man abroad does not show anybody anything?

That is certain to be asked, it seems to me. You take care of the ECA mission in each country, but you do not take care of the overall ECA. I do not object to it. I think we should have a clear answer as to why one is set on a different footing from the other.

Senator THOMAS of Utah. I do not think you can ever get the clear answer, Mr. Chairman. We had a situation in the last war when the Surgeon General of the Army was ordered to keep out of hospitals by the commander in the field. We had that to go through with. It is just one of those things.

Senator LODGE. General Kirk?

Senator THOMAS of Utah. Yes. Kirk was not allowed to see what he went over to the Philippines to see.

Ambassador DOUGLAS. There is a probability that questions will be asked on the floor on this subject. Language paraphrasing the last two sentences of the Brookings report might be drafted. Those two sentences read:

> He should keep the Administrator, the Secretary of State, the heads of the Embassies concerned, fully and currently informed of his activities. He should consult with the heads of the special missions and the chiefs of the regular missions, meet with them as necessary, and be entitled to receive their assistance.

Senator LODGE. I am glad to know that. That is all I want to know.

Ambassador DOUGLAS. It is not in the law.

The CHAIRMAN. Why not put it in?

Ambassador DOUGLAS. You can put it in the report. I would not think, offhand, that there would be any objection to paraphrasing that language and inserting it in the section.

Senator LODGE. I think it is just one more sharp bloody angle that you might smooth out, that is all.

85-743—73——4

The CHAIRMAN. Mr. Rice, you grab that, will you, for the next meeting?

Mr. RICE. All right, Senator.

ADMINISTRATIVE ARRANGEMENTS

The CHAIRMAN. Page 14, continuing:

(c) The Secretary of State shall provide such office space, facilities, and other administrative services for the special mission in each participating country as may be agreed between the Secretary of State and the Administrator.

(d) With respect to any of the zones of occupation of Germany, the President shall make appropriate administrative arrangements for the conduct of operations under this Act, in order to enable the Administrator to carry out his responsibility to assure the accomplishment of the purposes of this Act.

REFERENCES TO GERMANY

Is there any other place in this act where we refer to Germany?

Ambassador DOUGLAS. In section 3, in the definition of participating countries, and the first three lines of section 9 on page 13, which excepts any of the zones of occupation of Germany. I think those are the only three places in which specific reference is made to Germany.

Dr. WILCOX. We still have in mind, Mr. Chairman, putting in something in the preamble, or in the statement of findings and purposes with respect to the importance of Western Germany.

The CHAIRMAN. All right.

Well, now, down to there, can we tentatively say, OK?

OMISSION OF WORD "ALL"

Senator SMITH. Just one very small question, Mr. Chairman. On page 13, line 23, the words "on all matters" is there, and I think probably it is all right there, although we took the word "all" out of page 8, line 21.

Senator LODGE. Where do you see that?

Senator SMITH. Line 23, page 13, "currently informed on all matters."

Senator THOMAS of Utah. It is also in line 20.

Senator SMITH. My point would more affect line 20; no, it would affect either one. I ask whether there is any reason to make this conform to the omission of "all" on page 8?

The CHAIRMAN. I rather think that might be a point. That rather underscores too much detail.

Senator SMITH. I think, to be consistent, you could take the word "all" out, as long as you have the word "matters" in.

The CHAIRMAN. Without objection, we will take the word "all" out in both places.

LANGUAGE CONCERNING ESTABLISHMENT OF MISSIONS IN GERMANY

Dr. WILCOX. Before you go ahead, may I just say a word about the last section, the one you have just completed.

The staff raised a question as to why it would not be possible to insert words in this section which would make it possible for the administrator to establish his own missions in Germany as they would be established in the other participating countries. The representatives of the State Department felt that in view of the peculiar nature of the administrative setup in Germany, and the fact that it was not as yet established, and the State Department was taking over on June 30, it would be preferable from their point of view to use broad language such as this. I call that to the attention of the committee because we had quite a little discussion about it when we drafted this.

Senator SMITH. This is a blank check to the President to deal with Germany however things may develop.

Dr. WILCOX. Yes, and it does not authorize the Administrator to establish his own economic missions in Germany. It authorizes the President to do so if he should want to. It is not quite as clear here what kind of arrangement shall be made between the Administrator and his staff on the one hand, and the State Department representatives on the other. I just wanted to call that to the attention of the committee in view of the controversy that took place in our meeting.

Senator SMITH. We will probably get a blast on the floor on that one, anyway. Germany will be a subject of controversy.

The CHAIRMAN. I wonder if there is anything that can be done about that.

Senator SMITH. I think they have handled it pretty well.

Dr. WILCOX. We drafted the language in a way that we thought would be broad enough to cover any contingencies.

Ambassador DOUGLAS. It is broad enough.

Dr. WILCOX. We thought perhaps lines 19 to 21 would cover the Administrator adequately and protect his interest there.

The CHAIRMAN.

> . . . in order to enable the Administrator to carry out his responsibility to assure the accomplishment of the purposes of this Act.

I would not want to see the administrator ignored at this point. He might find it very definitely necessary, I would think, in dealing with Benelux problems to be able to explore his phase of this venture in Western Germany.

Ambassador DOUGLAS. He might do that either through any administrative arrangement that the President might make, or through the roving ambassador, or through the head of a diplomatic mission in any one of the Benelux countries, or all of them.

DIFFICULTY CAUSED BY U.S. ADMINISTRATION OF GERMANY

This is a difficult question because so long as we are occupying Germany we are, in a sense, and in a very real sense, the Administrator of Germany. Certainly the administration of Germany is under our direction and control.

Senator SMITH. And we will be until the ERP is finished, so far as I can see. We will be there for 4 or 5 years.

Ambassador DOUGLAS. That, of course, is a question that is in the lap of the gods.

Senator SMITH. It is in the lap of the gods.

Ambassador DOUGLAS. Now, should one have two administrators in Germany? I would presume that the relationship between the head of a special mission in Germany and the military government, or the government of occupation in Germany would be not unlike the relationship between the head of a special mission in any one country, and the government of the country in which he has been designated.

But whatever the Government of Germany may be, good, bad, or indifferent, I should think it would be clear that the head of the economic mission should not be the administrator of economic affairs within Germany.

Senator THOMAS of Utah. The Secretary of State is going to be responsible for the administration in Germany after June 1, is he not?

Ambassador DOUGLAS. June 30, I think, is the date.

Senator THOMAS of Utah. Whenever it comes. If he is responsible, it seems to me that he should be mentioned here, so that we do not have a conflict there, probably by some such expression as "the President, through the Secretary of State, shall make appropriate administrative * * *."

The CHAIRMAN. Well, that follows.

Senator THOMAS of Utah. It follows and it does not follow. If you get a clash over Germany, then we have a clash quite different from one that you have over anything else.

Senator SMITH. But the Secretary of State, in the case you suggest, sort of corresponds to the head of the government of another country, rather than representing the President in this ERP business.

Senator THOMAS of Utah. To leave him out may make a personality conflict which would be very bad to the German situation.

The CHAIRMAN. Dr. Wilcox tells me that it was left out deliberately because you have a split timetable. You have up until July 1st to deal with the Army and after July 1st to deal with the Secretary of State, and you have to have quite a complicated divided definition if you are going to do what you want to do, Senator Thomas.

Senator THOMAS of Utah. I do not think so, because of the time limit. I do not think that the Army will ever figure in this picture, Senator Vandenberg.

Ambassador DOUGLAS. But it will, since it is the agency of government now clothed with authority in Germany, during the period from the first of April, or whenever this bill becomes law, and June 30th.

Senator THOMAS of Utah. Do you think you are going to jump right into Germany like you are into the other places? I doubt it. You have your 16 nations to take into consideration.

The CHAIRMAN. I do not see how you can have any conflict when the President is the boss and it is so stated.

Senator THOMAS of Utah. I do not think you will have any conflict between the President and the Secretary of State here, or anything of that kind, but you may have conflict between subordinates down the line.

I think what Dr. Wilcox says merely points out that the problem was so blooming hard, therefore we can't say anything about it, but if not saying anything about it produces a problem harder than ever, we are a little bit lax in not foreseeing that situation.

RESPONSIBILITIES OF SECRETARY OF STATE AND ADMINISTRATOR IN GERMANY

As the Ambassador has pointed out, if we are responsible in Germany, the U.S. Government is the real administrator in Germany, so we are dealing with ourselves. We can treat Germany as our own to

a considerable extent. But we have already delegated the power to the Secretary of State to represent the government there. Not to bring him into the picture in some way or other would be rather tough on the subordinate.

The CHAIRMAN. On the other hand, I do not think you can identify the Secretary of State solely as the one responsible for making arrangements for the conduct of operations under this Act. That immediately eliminates the ERP administrator, sets him aside, and makes the Secretary of State monarch of all he surveys, even in respect to responsibilities of the administrator.

Ambassador DOUGLAS. In this area.

The CHAIRMAN. In this area. I think you have to leave it to the President, Senator Thomas. I do not see how you can do anything else.

Senator THOMAS of Utah. Probably the word "appropriate" guards against that thing. It would surely be an inappropriate action for the President to forget the Secretary of State's channel of command there.

Ambassador DOUGLAS. It would be inappropriate, and I would doubt that he would.

Senator THOMAS of Utah. I do not think he will.

STATE DEPARTMENT TAKEOVER FROM ARMY

Ambassador DOUGLAS. Of course there is another consideration, Senator. The Secretary of State has stated publicly that the State Department hopes to take over—I delete the word "hopes"—anticipates taking over the control and administration of Germany on June 30. I am not certain that that date is a firm and fixed date. I think discussions are going on now between the State Department and the Army, are they not, on that subject? It might very well be that the date would be postponed.

Senator THOMAS of Utah. I think, Mr. Chairman, we have brought out enough discussion on this point to take care of anybody on the floor of the Senate questioning the situation.

ADMINISTRATOR'S OPERATING UNDER ARMY OR STATE DEPARTMENT QUESTIONED

Senator GEORGE. I may be a little hazy about it, but I do not see how the administrator is going to operate there under the Army or under the Secretary of State. I do not see how the administrator is going in there and provide food and fertilizer and so forth, and take care of physical needs, and then also undertake the rehabilitation of Germany under the State Department or under the War Department. I do not see how it would work. It can't possibly work.

Ambassador DOUGLAS. There are two representatives of the same government.

Senator GEORGE. Two representatives of the same government, yes. Their duties, their responsibilities, will be so nearly identical in many instances, or so identical, until I just do not see how they can work.

Ambassador DOUGLAS. Not only in the matter of providing for the necessary import, but there is also the important consideration, and the very important one, of the relationship of Germany in the zones of occupation to the other particpating countries.

Senator GEORGE. I think so. I think this is the crux of the thing, it seems to me, so far as Western Europe is concerned. I think a mistake here of conflicting authority would be fatal. I do not see how to resolve it at the moment. I suppose that is why Brookings and the staff had some difficulty with it.

Senator SMITH. Senator George, why doesn't this language leave it sufficiently flexible in the last analysis? The President has to work it out with the Department of the Army and also with the Secretary of State. We are practically saying that we are not settling this; we are leaving it up to the President to work that situation, and we are leaving it flexible.

DEFINITION OF PARTICIPATING COUNTRIES

Senator GEORGE. Yes, sir, but we are putting in an administrator with pretty wide authority. Where is this first thing that we said here, about what the recipient countries consist of? How are they defined?

Ambassador DOUGLAS. Section 3, page 5.

Senator GEORGE. How are they defined?

Ambassador DOUGLAS (reading):

> Any of 3 zones of occupation of Germany.

The CHAIRMAN (reading):

> Any country (including the United Kingdom of Great Britain and Northern Ireland, Iceland, Ireland and any of the zones of occupation of Germany) wholly or partly in Europe, including its colonies and dependencies, is a participating country within the meaning of this Act provided it adheres to, and for so long as it remains an adherent to, a joint program for European recovery designed to accomplish this Act.

COMPLICATION OF WEST GERMAN ZONES

Ambassador DOUGLAS. There is another complication, too, just to add complication to complication. There are three zones in Western Germany. Two of them, within certain limits and within a certain meaning, have been merged. The third one has not been. Whether the three zones will be merged and how they will be completely merged if they are is still a matter to be determined in the future.

SUBORDINATION OF ADMINISTRATOR TO OCCUPYING AUTHORITY

Senator GEORGE. It seems to me, Mr. Chairman, that here you have to subordinate this administrator to the occupying authority, whether it be War or the Secretary of State, and that the administrator will come into any of these zones only upon invitation of that supreme authority. I do not see how else it could possible be worked. As a practical thing, I do not see how it can be worked.

The CHAIRMAN. Then the existing language would be agreeable to you, is that right?

Senator GEORGE. I do not think it is spelled out here enough at all, because you have necessarily a conflict. You have the Administrator, and you have his jurisdiction territorially defined back on page 5 as including these zones. I had not thought about this particular thing.

Senator HATCH. Doesn't this language mean, in effect, that it is a command to the President, not a blank check? It is a specific order that he must make the appropriate arrangements so that the administrator can go into those zones.

Senator GEORGE. That's right. He recognizes the existence of that administrator in having authority there, and that authority of the administrator here, under this act, would not necessarily conflict—it might be worked out in harmony with, but it would have to be under—one authority there. Somebody would have to have the supreme authority to say who controls that area and who invited activities, other activities than would be carried on by War so long as the War Department is in charge there, or by the State Department, assuming they do take control.

(Discussion was continued off the record.)

POSSIBILITY OF PROVISIONAL OR PERMANENT GOVERNMENT

Ambassador DOUGLAS. There is another complication, too. Presumably, the provisions of this act run for 4¼ years.

Senator GEORGE. And you may have a peace treaty in the interim.

Ambassador DOUGLAS. Or, in the absence of a peace treaty, there may be a provisional government established, not a permanent government, but a provisional one. Under a peace treaty there might be a permanent government.

Senator GEORGE. There are a lot of complications here.

Mr. Chairman, could we go over this? This is a problem within itself. It is a part of the whole problem, but it is a definite problem within itself. Could we go over this and on to something else, and let us sleep over this?

INTERPRETATION OF PARAGRAPH

Senator THOMAS of Utah. Before we go over it, let me emphasize what Senator Hatch has said, which immediately makes this paragraph read very, very differently from the way I read it in the first place, and which gives it an awful lot of sense.

Senator Hatch's interpretation of this was that the administrator would not fuss around in Germany until he gets directions from the President. Now, if that is the case, then, of course, this is a very proper paragraph, and it means that the administrator stays out of Germany until the President is ready to have him go in. If that is what it means, I am very much for it.

Senator HATCH. I asked a question; I didn't interpret it. I am puzzled about it.

Senator GEORGE. That may very well be, Senator Thomas, but I also have a way of thinking over these things that perplex me, and this is the heart of it, as I see it. I don't foresee the recovery of Western Europe without something constructive taking place in Germany, and I do not see how you are going to fit this administrator that is created under this act with all his broad general powers in there with any occupying agency or representatives, for the reasons that the Ambassador says, and for various other reasons that do occur. So I think if we could get over this, this is so definitely a separate problem, it seems to me, one that has to be dealt with as an entity within itself, so to speak, or almost so, and if we could go on to something else, maybe our minds might become clear on it, because we could be thinking over it.

The CHAIRMAN. I quite agree, Senator. We will tentatively approve this section down to subsection (d), and we will pass that over with a question mark.

COMPENSATION AND ALLOWANCE OF PERSONNEL OUTSIDE UNITED STATES

Now we are down to the bottom of page 14:

PERSONNEL OUTSIDE UNITED STATES

SEC. 10. (a) For the purpose of performing functions under this Act outside the continental limits of the United States the Administrator may—

(1) without regard to the provisions of the Classification Act of 1923, as amended, employ personnel who shall receive compensation at any of the rates provided for Foreign Service Reserve officers under Section 414 of the Foreign Service Act of 1946 (60 Stat. 999, 1003), or any of the rates provided for Foreign Service Staff officers and employees by section 415 of the Foreign Service Act of 1946 (60 Stat. 999, 1003). Personnel so appointed shall be entitled to receive the allowances and benefits authorized by title IX of the Foreign Service Act of 1946 (60 Stat. 999, 1025), and established under authority of title IX; and.

Will somebody explain all that—Dr. Wilcox or Mr. Rice?

Mr. RICE. They have an expert over there, Senator, from the State Department.

Ambassador DOUGLAS. Mr. Smith.

Mr. DONALD W. SMITH (Foreign Service officer). Senator, the salaries provided for Foreign Service Reserve officers range from $3,300 to $13,500. The salaries for staff employees range from a low of $720 to $10,000. The various allowances referred to in this section come under title IX of the Foreign Service Act of 1946. The allowances are to cover quarters, cost of living, and representation.

Senator WILEY. What is the last?

Mr. SMITH. Representation allowances, entertainment.

Senator SMITH. Am I right in this, that we are simply putting the personnel of the new Administrator in the same compensation and allowance classification of all other Foreign Service officers? Isn't that the gist of it?

Dr. WILCOX. Mr. Douglas made the point during the hearings that one of the great advantages of having these officers inducted into the Foreign Service would be the fact that that they would get a little higher salary. This accomplishes that without actually putting them into the Foreign Service.

Mr. SMITH. This spells out, by reference to the various laws that affect that, what we need in the way of legislation in order to put them in exactly the same classification without being in the Foreign Service.

Senator GEORGE. So far as salaries and allowances are concerned.

Ambassador DOUGLAS. May I interrupt to determine a question of fact?

I understood that in the case of a Minister his basic compensation might be as high as between $16,500 and $17,500.

Mr. SMITH. If he is a chief of mission, yes, sir. The salaries of chiefs of mission range from $15,000 to $25,000.

Ambassador DOUGLAS. Then I testified incorrectly before your committee.

Senator WILEY. That is terrible!

Ambassador DOUGLAS. Yes, it is.

Senator WILEY. It is terrible that you should make a mistake.

Senator SMITH. And you are confessing your sin now to correct the record?

Ambassador DOUGLAS. It is too late to correct the record.

Senator SMITH. Then, as I understand it, the head of the economic mission in, let us say, France, will receive a basic salary of $13,500 and certain allowances. What do his allowances amount to?

Mr. SMITH. In the case of France, they amount to about $4,500 to $6,000.

Ambassador DOUGLAS. He would receive at most in France $19,500 of which $13,500 would be taxable and the balance untaxable.

Mr. SMITH. That is right.

(Discussion was continued off the record.)

10 MEN COMPENSATED UP TO $15,000

The CHAIRMAN. How does all of this dovetail in with the language on page 7 that we are not going to have over 10 men compensated up to $15,000? Is that exclusively at home?

Ambassador DOUGLAS. That is exclusively at home, as I understand it.

The CHAIRMAN. Does it say so?

Ambassador DOUGLAS. Yes, it is limited to the District of Columbia.

The CHAIRMAN. All right. Question withdrawn.

LIMITATION OF SALARIES

Senator SMITH. Do you suggest, Mr. Ambassador, that we leave the sky the limit on these fellows, and let the Administrator pay what he has to?

Ambassador DOUGLAS. I do not know what the answer is.

The CHAIRMAN. The answer is that if you have got to depend upon men for these jobs who take the jobs as jobs, the thing is not going to work. You have to have men who will take the thing as a patriotic assignment, quite regardless of compensation, and whether they are getting $19,000 or $23,000 would not affect their decision to go to it.

Ambassador DOUGLAS. That is probably right.

The CHAIRMAN. You did not hesitate to accept the ambassadorship at a loss.

Ambassador DOUGLAS. No.

The CHAIRMAN. The kinds of men that are going to be required if this thing stands any sort of a chance are the kinds of men to whom a few thousand dollars one way or the other in salary cannot be determinative.

Ambassador DOUGLAS. I think that is right.

The CHAIRMAN. And if you try to put the salary up to a point where they take the job for the sake of the salary, you will probably get less youthful men than if you take them on the other basis.

Ambassador DOUGLAS. It is a question of degree.

RECEIVING COMPENSATION FROM PREVIOUS EMPLOYER QUESTIONED

There is another suggestion, and I think it is a bad one. I do not know what the provisions of law are that may prohibit a person from receiving compensation from his previous employer. In my case, of course, I receive none. I think that is always a dangerous thing to do.

Senator HATCH. We had that all during the war years by the dollar-a-year men, many of whom were paid their salaries by their companies, and they were subject to a lot of criticism.

Ambassador DOUGLAS. It is a dangerous thing to embark on.

EMPLOYING CONSULTANTS OUTSIDE UNITED STATES

Senator LODGE. I would like to ask Mr. Rice, or whoever is a specialist on this, as to the significance of the first three words in line 23, page 14:

> For the purpose of performing functions under this Act outside the continental limits of the United States the Administrator may——

Does that mean no category of persons not enumerated here can be employed outside the continental limits of the United States? I come back again to these consultants. It is altogether possible that they would be sent outside the United States.

Mr. RICE. I do not so interpret that. This deals with the pay they would receive if they work outside the continental limits of the United States.

The CHAIRMAN. Let us be sure of that, because that is a point on which I agree with the Senator from Massachusetts.

Do I understand that there is anything, Mr. Rice, in connection with performing functions under this act outside of the continental limits of the United States which would prohibit the Administrator from contracting with J. G. White and Co., or something of the sort, for the purpose of doing a job?

Mr. RICE. Not that I know of.

The CHAIRMAN. You think he could?

Mr. RICE. I think so.

Mr. Gross, you agree with me?

Mr. GROSS. Yes, I do.

APPOINTMENT OR ASSIGNMENT TO FOREIGN SERVICE

The CHAIRMAN. The Administrator may:

> (2) recommend persons to be appointed or assigned to any class in the Foreign Service Reserve, and the Secretary of State may appoint or assign such persons to any class in the Foreign Service Reserve, for the duration of operations under this Act, without regard to that provision of the Foreign Service Act of 1946 (60 Stat. 999, 1009) which limits appointments to periods of not more than four years; or recommend persons to be appointed as Foreign Service Staff officers and employees and the Secretary of State may appoint, for the duration of operations under this Act, such persons as Foreign Service Staff officers and employees, and a person so appointed from any Government agency without break in service and with the consent of the head of the agency concerned shall, upon the termination of such appointment, be entitled to the same rights as those provided for Foreign Service Reserve officers in section 528 of the Foreign Service Act of 1946 (60 Stat. 1003, 1010). Transfers of Foreign Service Officers, Foreign Service Reserve officers, and Foreign Service Staff officers and employees appointed or assigned pursuant to this subsection and

promotions of Foreign Service Reserve officers and Foreign Service Staff officers and employees appointed or assigned pursuant to this subsection may be effected by the Secretary of State upon the recommendation of the Administrator. The provisions of the Foreign Service Act of 1946 (60 Stat. 999) shall, except as otherwise provided herein, apply fully to all persons appointed or assigned to the Foreign Service system pursuant to the authority contained in this subsection.

Well, that is complete Sanskrit to me. Will somebody kindly make a speech on the subject?

Mr. GROSS. The purpose of this section, Senator Vandenberg, is to give to the Administrator the authority, at his option, either to designate persons, employees under subsection (1) on page 15, which you just read, previously discussed, and those persons would not be in the Foreign Service; or, under this subsection (2) which you have now read, to recommend to the Secretary of State for appointment in the Foreign Service as Foreign Service Reserve officers or Foreign Service Staff officers or employees, within the Foreign Service System, individuals upon his nomination who would thereupon receive the rights and benefits and compensation under the Foreign Service Act. They would become members of the Foreign Service Reserve System.

Now, if I may trace through briefly the various aspects of that: A Foreign Service Reserve officer, so appointed by the Secretary of State on nomination of the Administrator, would not be limited to employment for the 4-year period which the Foreign Service Act provides for appointment in the Foreign Service Reserve. He could be employed for the duration of the operation of this act.

The Foreign Service Reserve officers or Foreign Service Staff officers are employees appointed by the Secretary on nomination of the Administrator under this section and would, if they came from another agency and were released by that agency without a break in service, which is at the discretion of the head of the agency which employs the individual in question, be entitled to reinstatement to that agency upon termination of their employment as Foreign Service Reserve officers.

SIGNIFICANCE OF "WITHOUT BREAK IN SERVICE"

Senator LODGE. Why do you say "without a break in service"?

Mr. GROSS. This is to assure them rights of reinstatement so as to make employment here more attractive to regular employees, civil service employees of the Federal Government, and without this explicit provision in line 25 at the bottom of page 15 through the top 4 or 5 lines on page 16, the purpose of that explicit language would not be effective, which is to assure those employees now engaged in the Government service in other capacities of a right of reinstatement upon the termination of their employment under this act as Foreign Service Reserve officers or Staff officers.

Without that explicit provision, they would not have the right to reinstatement in their own old jobs.

The significance of the language "without break in service" is simply a technical term. The way it is done is to have the head of the employing department signify his intention to allow the employee in question to leave that department without a break in service. That is the technical meaning of the phrase.

Actually, it is a work of art that appears in the Foreign Service Act of 1947.

Senator LODGE. I think if there was a gap of a week it ought not to count against him.

Mr. GROSS. It does not mean he must start his new employment immediately. It means that the head of his old agency must allow him to leave that agency without a so-called break in service.

AUTHORITY OVER APPOINTEES OR ASSIGNEES TO FOREIGN SERVICE RESERVE

The CHAIRMAN. Let us say that the Secretary takes advantage of subsection (2). The Administrator wants a group of persons appointed or assigned to the Foreign Service Reserve. When they are thus assigned, who is their boss, the Secretary of State or the Administrator?

Mr. GROSS. For certain purposes they are under divided authority. With respect to the management, they receive their pay checks and their immediate orders from the Secretary of State. Actually, their working relationships, and this is on the analogy, for example, of the Treasury or the Department of Labor or other employees who come into the Foreign Service Reserve and serve abroad—they actually receive their working instructions from the Department of the Treasury or the Department of Labor, as the case may be. They do, for administrative relations, come under the Foreign Service establishment. That is not in a chain of command since they do not receive any operating instructions. They have a divided authority in the sense that the Department of State administering the Foreign Service Reserve System does provide their housekeeping services and would, except for this next section in the section, also be responsible for their transfers or promotions. That is why we wrote in the language on page 16, lines 6 through 13.

In the ordinary case, and without this provision, the Foreign Service Administration, which is under the Secretary of State, would have authority to assign the individuals and to promote them.

The intention of that sentence, of course, is to give the Administrator the authority to make recommendations for promotion and transfer.

EMPHASIS ON STATE DEPARTMENT SERVICE QUESTIONED

The CHAIRMAN. I would like to ask a very blunt and frank question. I would like to know how seriously important this page and a half of language is to the operation of this show. For better or for worse, for good or for bad reasons, we confront a congressional demand to establish the independence, within reason, of the Administrator, and we have gone to considerable lengths to keep separate him and his responsibility from the State Department, which is no reflection on the State Department except that the State Department in the view of Congress, is not an operating agency for the purposes of this character.

Having labored and sweated to get out of the State Department, we run into a page and a half of language now which any innocent bystander would think tied the whole shooting match back in under the State Department.

Senator LODGE. Not only that, Mr. Chairman, but take the language on page 7, and it looks as though the whole bill was trying to compel the Administrator to get all of his personnel out of the Foreign

Service, and that suggests the question that I asked Ambassador Douglas in public that day, as to whether a man could move in with his own team and bring in his own people, and it seems to me that this section that has just been read, and the language on page 7, make it awfully hard for the Administrator to come in there, to turn around with his own crowd, and do a job.

The CHAIRMAN. It seems to me it puts the whole emphasis on Government service generally, and State Department service specifically.

Ambassador DOUGLAS. I was going to ask the question, whether the word "and" in line 12 of page 15 should not, at least applying to certain parts, be changed to "or", at least in the application of certain parts of the following subsection, so that it is entirely optional with the Administrator.

The CHAIRMAN. That would be some improvement, but still the overwhelming weight of all this language, which nobody on the floor is going to understand, and I am certainly not going to try to make them understand it because I would fail, and the psychology of it, I think, is all wrong in the light of the situation we confront.

How essential is that? That is what I want to know.

Senator SMITH. Would you include (1) as well as (2), or are you just talking about (2)?

The CHAIRMAN. Subsection (1) is all right.

Senator SMITH. You are discussing paragraph (2)?

The CHAIRMAN. Yes.

Ambassador DOUGLAS. Could not under the language of subsection (1) all of the emoluments and privileges be afforded without specific appointment into the Foreign Service Reserve?

Mr. GROSS. There would be certain difficulties and this, of course, is designed to give particularly to junior employees the right of reinstatement, which is important and which would not be available except for some such language as there is in subsection (2).

Ambassador DOUGLAS. Couldn't you attach that language to subsection (1)?

The CHAIRMAN. "Personnel so appointed shall be entitled to receive the allowances and benefits of the Foreign Service." I should think you could put one more sentence in there.

I just think this is just staggering, all this business about the Foreign Service. That is what we are trying to get away from.

Ambassador DOUGLAS. I would suggest, Mr. Chairman, that somebody take a look at this, and see if they cannot incorporate the privileges defined in subsection (2) into subsection (1).

The CHAIRMAN. All right. we will refer this back to the joint authorship.

OBJECTIVE IS TO REINVIGORATE FOREIGN SERVICE

Dr. WILCOX. It is not the purpose of the committee to reconstruct the Foreign Service with this bill, but it was hoped that if this was carried through, and some of these people were brought into the Foreign Service, it would bring into the Foreign Service some new red blood that is badly needed and might help to reinvigorate the Foreign Service.

The CHAIRMAN. That is a fine objective, but we have enough objectives at the moment. If we reach just a few of them it will be nice.

Senator LODGE. One war at a time!

The CHAIRMAN. All right. We will just skip over that for the time being.

CLARIFYING ADMINISTRATOR'S HIRING OPTIONS RECOMMENDED

It must be made perfectly plain, furthermore, that this administrator can hire whom he pleases, regardless of Foreign Service or anything else. The way this reads I do not know; it all just seems to smother you into something.

Senator THOMAS of Utah. You should serve on the Military Affairs Committee for awhile, and get smothered under these ordnances.

Dr. WILCOX. May I ask, for the sake of the drafting committee, is it the wish of the committee not to make it possible to bring people into the Foreign Service at all in case the Administrator might want to do so?

The CHAIRMAN. Not unless you can do it in a couple of sentences.

Ambassador DOUGLAS. This does not make it clear that this is entirely optional.

Senator LODGE. This business of the Foreign Service is a privilege the Administrator can use if he wants to. This looks as though the intent of the act was to force the Administrator to use the Government service as much as possible, and I do not think in this case you want to do that.

Ambassador DOUGLAS. That is why that word "and" I think should be "or."

The CHAIRMAN. "Or" is better than "and." A couple of "ors" would be better than "and."

You get whatever you want to do in section 2 into a couple of sentences stuck on to section (1).

APPOINTMENT OF ALIEN CLERKS AND EMPLOYEES

On page 16, line 19:

> (b) For the purpose of performing functions under this Act outside the continental limits of the United States, the Secretary of State may, at the request of the Administrator, appoint, for the duration of operations under this Act, alien clerks and employees in accordance with applicable provisions of the Foreign Service Act of 1946 (60 Stat. 999).

I guess that has to be in, doesn't it?

Ambassador DOUGLAS. I think so.

The CHAIRMAN. All right.

PUTTING ADMINISTRATOR ON FOREIGN SERVICE BOARD

Now, page 17, "(c) Section 211(a) of the Foreign Service Act of 1946 (60 Stat. 999, 1001) is hereby amended to read as follows:

What is this all about? Do I have to read all this?

Dr. WILCOX. It puts the Administrator on the Foreign Service Board. It amends the act to put the Administrator on the Foreign Service Board along with these other members.

Senator LODGE. Why put him on?

Dr. WILCOX. So he will have some say.

The CHAIRMAN. So he will have some say, just a little.

Senator LODGE. This staggers me.

The CHAIRMAN. I don't think he needs to be there at all.

Dr. WILCOX. He would have a representative.

The CHAIRMAN. The Board of Foreign Service, in my concept, is performing a purely ministerial function to cover in somebody that the Administrator has asked them to cover in, and he does not need to sit on the Board in order to do that, does he?

Dr. WILCOX. I refer that to the expert from the State Department.

Senator LODGE. If the Administrator cannot take a man and put him into the Government service by signing a piece of paper himself, then I completely misunderstand this whole thing. If he has to sit on a board and haggle and compromise and give and take and all that all day long, I don't go for it.

Dr. WILCOX. If you want them in the Foreign Service, you have to make provisions consistent with the Foreign Service Act.

Senator LODGE. If he is going to have $6,800 million to administer, he certainly ought to be able to say, "I want to put Charlie Horseface into the Foreign Service," if he is good enough for that.

Senator SMITH. I am not clear why we have to bring them into the Foreign Service.

The CHAIRMAN. We are going to try to work that out in a couple of sentences on the other page. I certainly do not understand why he has to sit on the Board in order to accomplish this purely ministerial function.

Senator LODGE. He ought to give an order, just the way we put a clerk on our payroll.

The CHAIRMAN. What have you to say, Dr. Wilcox? I give you 2 minutes.

Senator LODGE. Why am I wrong, Dr. Wilcox?

Dr. WILCOX. I do not think you are wrong if you say that the Administrator ought to have the right to put anybody into the Foreign Service without going through any of the normal procedures which are ordinarily followed in inducting people into the Foreign Service. This bill does not make mandatory the use of the Foreign Service. It simply makes optional the use of the Foreign Service.

A lot of people might want to be in the Foreign Service in order to get the advantages that accrue from the Foreign Service.

The CHAIRMAN. Can't you put them in two sentences, unless you are trying to do something else that you aren't telling me about?

Dr. WILCOX. So far as I know, there is nothing hidden in this.

The CHAIRMAN. If I turn over another page and find the Bureau of the Budget in here, I am going to scream.

Dr. WILCOX. We shall be very happy to see if we can cut these four pages down to one paragraph.

The CHAIRMAN. For the moment, my executive peremptory command, this monkey business on page 17 is out.

FBI INVESTIGATION

Now, down to the bottom:

(d) Civilian personnel who are citizens of the United States appointed pursuant to this section to perform functions under this Act shall be appointed subject to investigation by the Federal Bureau of Investigation: *Provided, however,* That they may assume their posts and perform their functions after preliminary investigation and clearance by the Adinistrator or the Secretary of State, as the case may be.

Senator LODGE. What does that mean "appointed subject to investigation"? Does that mean the FBI has a veto power?

Senator HATCH. It certainly does.

Senator LODGE. I think that is way outside of their functions.

Dr. WILCOX. May I say, Mr. Chairman, that the drafting committee left this language as it was, because it is my understanding that the Department of State is negotiating with the FBI in order to arrive at some suitable compromise.

Clearly the language as it is now would permit two or three agencies to investigate, 1 perhaps 2 months after the other, contacting the same people, asking the same questions. It would cause a great deal of confusion and difficulty, so we left that language, pending the compromise with the State Department, that the State Department and FBI may be able to work out.

Senator LODGE. I certainly do not favor giving the FBI veto power in the appointment of people in the State Department or the economic administration. This is one of those things that those three fellows in the House all insist on, and I am through yielding to them.

Senator SMITH. What we said in our bill was a report by the FBI.

Senator LODGE. Let the economic cooperation administrator see the report, and if he wants to go against the FBI, that is his lookout.

The CHAIRMAN. I agree with your point of view. What you want to do, or let us say, what we want to do, is to require an investigation by the FBI with the results submitted to the appointing power for his information.

Senator LODGE. That is right.

Dr. WILCOX. I should add one more. There is a time limit involved here. The normal clearance by the FBI involves some several months, and clearly the administrator could not wait 4 or 5 months in order to get his employees cleared by the FBI. That problem is being studied by the FBI now.

The Chairman. Your proviso covers that, does it not?

> *Provided, however,* That they may assume their posts and perform their function after preliminary investigation and clearance by the Administrator or the Secretary of State, as the case may be.

Does that cover your point?

Dr. WILCOX. Yes, except that it would seem undesirable to have two agencies investigating people, one after the other.

The CHAIRMAN. What language do you recommend? We have to have some language.

Dr. WILCOX. I suggest that the Drafting Committee had waited——

The CHAIRMAN. Time is up. What do we do now?

Dr. WILCOX. We were still waiting for the FBI to come through with a new suggestion on the time limit involved.

Senator SMITH. What was the language we had in our bill? We had something about a report by the FBI.

Mr. GROSS. That is in Public Law 389: "* * * until such person has been investigated as to loyalty and security by the FBI." That was inserted into the Foreign Aid Act, Public Law 389, despite the objections of the Department of State, because of the timelag Dr. Wilcox is talking about. We have tempered that down a little bit by saying "subject to investigation."

We would prefer to have no requirement of this sort at all.

The CHAIRMAN. You have to have it.

INVESTIGATION AND REPORT BY FBI

Mr. GROSS. It is not our intention, of course, to require FBI approval. It is simply completion of investigation. The decision as to hiring or rejection is up to the administrator or the head of the agency concerned.

Senator LODGE. The State Department has its own security check.

Mr. GROSS. Yes, we do.

Senator LODGE. This new official will not have, will he? How about that?

Ambassador DOUGLAS. I had not thought about it.

The CHAIRMAN. That is rather up to him.

What do we do about this? Do we say here, "P.S.: It is understood that negotiations are under way"?

Senator HATCH. You would take out the word "appointed" in line 21, and improve it materially: "shall be subject to investigation by the Federal Bureau of Investigation."

The CHAIRMAN. That is all right with me.

Senator LODGE. "shall be appointed only after investigation."

Senator SMITH. That might cause the delay we are talking about.

Ambassador DOUGLAS. Would it not perhaps be well to say, "Shall be investigated by the Federal Bureau of Investigation"?

The CHAIRMAN. You cannot leave that just hanging there. What do they do after they investigate?

Mr. GROSS. They submit a report.

Senator LODGE. "They shall be appointed after receipt of a report."

Senator GEORGE. The House people will insist on having the investigation before the appointment, or some statement from the FBI.

Senator LODGE. We can say "they shall be appointed after receipt of a report from the FBI."

Senator GEORGE. That means a long delay in a lot of cases, because if the FBI has any doubt about a fellow, or there are any bad marks on his record, it takes a long time.

The CHAIRMAN. The proviso takes care of that, does it not?

Senator GEORGE. It does in a sort of way. I do not know what they would do with him, after they put him in and he worked over there about 8 or 9 months, right next to the Iron Curtain, and they had to turn him loose.

The CHAIRMAN. They ought to shoot him or put him in the Bureau of the Budget.

Suppose we ask Mr. Rice and company to take a look at that, and see what they can recommend.

Senator GEORGE. I think it is rather bad to have that in, but we had the experience of the House brethren, and they will have the same view again.

PUBLIC ADVISORY BOARD AND OTHER ADVISORY COMMITTEES

The CHAIRMAN. Now let us go back to section 8 which we skipped on page 12.

SEC. 8. (a) There is hereby created a Public Advisory Board, hereinafter referred to as the Board which shall advise and consult—

this is the group that stands behind the Administrator——

with the Administrator with respect to general or basic policy matters arising in connection with the Administrator's discharge of his responsibilities. The Board shall consist of the Administrator, who shall be Chairman, and not to exceed twelv additional members to be appointed by the President, by and with the advice and consent of the Senate, and who shall be selected from among citizens of the United States of broad and various experience in matters affecting the public interest, other than officers and employees of the United States (including any agency or instrumentality of the United States (including any agency or instrumentality of the United States) who, as such, regularly receive compensation for current services. Members of the Board other than the Administrator shall receive, out of funds made available for the purposes of this Act, a per diem allowance of $50 per day for each day spent in actual meetings of the Board or at conferences held upon the call of the Administrator, plus necessary travel and other expenses incurred while so engaged.

(b) The Administrator may appoint such other advisory committees as he may determine to be necessary or desirable to effectuate the purposes of the Act.

Senator LODGE. Mr. Chairman.

The CHAIRMAN. The Senator from Massachusetts.

BIPARTISANSHIP AND REQUIRED MEETINGS OF BOARD

Senator LODGE. I know that there are two criticisms that will be made of this on the floor. They do not mean anything to me personally, but I know that they will be made, and they will be made in the House, too. One is that this Board ought to be bipartisan and the other is that it should be required to meet every so often. The reason for that, I think, is to give some assurance to people who think that various economic interests in this country are going to be hurt, and they should have some places where they can go to be heard.

The CHAIRMAN. I do not know of any reason why they should not be met.

Senator LODGE. I do not know whether they should be given some recognition here, or whether we should wait and have our heads batted against the wall on the floor.

Senator THOMAS of Utah. This is the same problem we are bound up against in surplus property, the bringing in of somebody who can take care of the interests back home.

Senator LODGE. The way this thing is set up now, unless there is a 30-day provision in there or something like that, the feeling is that it will never be used, and it is a dead letter.

Senator GEORGE. We had that in the Demobilization and Reconversion Act, and you remember we set up a board of 12, I think, and the demobilizer did not call the board together until Max Gardner got on there, and he insisted that the board was either functions officio or it ought to be called together, so they got them together thereafter. They did some good, I think, after they got them functioning.

This makes the Administrator the Chairman of the Board, and I think seems to contemplate that he shall have them meet periodically.

The CHAIRMAN. In connection with the first suggestion of the Senator from Massachusetts, is there any objection to saying in line 14, "not to exceed 12 additional members to be appointed by the President, not more than 7 of whom shall be members of the same political party"?

Senator GEORGE. I think that is all right. I think you should make it bipartisan. And I think there should be a provision made that, while the Administrator is Chairman of the Board, he may designate a Vice Chairman, or the Board itself may select a Vice Chairman, and that some periodic meetings of that Board should be had for awhile, at least.

The CHAIRMAN. Is there any objection to the language I suggested, implementing the suggestion of the Senator from Massachusetts?

SIZE OF BOARD

Senator THOMAS of Utah. The only objection I have is, is not the Board too large, with 12?

Senator LODGE. Doesn't that depend on who the President finds? If you find 12 men that are absolutely right for it, it would not be fatal. If you had to fill it up, it would be too bad.

Dr. WILCOX. The Administrator might decide seven might be sufficient, but if he decided certain other groups should receive recognition, they could be added.

MAJORITY OF BOARD

The CHAIRMAN. Then we would have to change it to read "not more than a majority of whom shall be members of the same political party."

Senator LODGE. Now there is a third point.

The CHAIRMAN. Let's get your second point in first. When you get up steam you go right past the depot.

Ambassador DOUGLAS. Does that "not more than a majority" do it? A majority might be quite a large one.

The CHAIRMAN. I see what you mean. You mean a majority could be all but one of them.

Ambassador DOUGLAS. I think the intention is perfectly clear.

The CHAIRMAN. No, I think you are all right. That simply shows that you have been raised in a cunning school of politics.

Senator GEORGE. We have that language in a hundred different acts.

Ambassador DOUGLAS. I bow to my tutor.

The CHAIRMAN. Let's take a chance on "majority." I do not think the President will appoint Pauley.

Senator LODGE. Not this year.

Senator GEORGE. He might. Pauley might be a good man.

REQUIRED MEETINGS OF ADVISORY BOARD

The CHAIRMAN. Next, take the second statement. I think we ought to require them to meet at least every 2 weeks. I do not think a month is enough. That just sort of emphasizes the fact that you have a part-time assignment.

Senator THOMAS of Utah. You have to take into consideration, judging from experience, the type of thought that was expressed in the President's message when he sent up here and asked us for an amendment of the Surplus Property Act. It insists that you should have a single administrator, and no advice from anywhere under the sun, and no consultation or anything of that kind. You have that type of thinking down here.

Then the next type is, you do not want an advisory council that is going to retard quick action, and your making them meet every 2 weeks will probably aid in that, but at the same time, if you require them to meet, you emphasize the administrator having to pay attention to his council, all the time.

You have to decide one question, Mr. Chairman. If you want this thing to be done by one man, then let's build it around the one man. If you want to have it done by a council, or after deliberation of some kind, then you ought to make the council important.

Senator LODGE. Supposing you said, Senator Thomas, that the deputy administrator could preside?

Ambassador DOUGLAS. I think that is implicit in the long range. He is clothed with all of the authority and charged with performing the functions of the administrator in the absence of the administrator.

The CHAIRMAN. You are arguing, Senator Thomas, against requireing any stated timetable?

Senator THOMAS of Utah. As the thing reads here, it seems to me that the logic is mixed. Are you in favor of an administrator? Yes, but you must be in favor of a council because you put it in, and then you say it must meet.

Senator LODGE. We are trying to get as many people under this tent as we can.

Senator THOMAS of Utah. You believe, then, in the council idea.

Senator LODGE. I personally do not, but I say there are a lot of fellows in the House and Senate who do.

The CHAIRMAN. I don't either. I don't care for this council, but on the other hand, I don't want this council to be a mere facade. I want it to be around and available for the precise purposes Senator Lodge indicated, a place to go if you think you are being hurt.

Senator THOMAS of Utah. To represent the public interest in this thing.

Ambassador DOUGLAS. Couldn't you do it in this way: Presumably the council will not become involved in administrative matters. The council will give advice on questions of policy, and perform the general functions of the board of directors of a corporation.

Senator LODGE. They will be there to hear complaints and criticisms.

Ambassador DOUGLAS. I was wondering if you could not say that the board shall meet not less frequently than so often, and it may be convened upon the request of, let us say, three members or more. Would that cover it?

Senator LODGE. I tried to put it from the standpoint of Congress. When you say it shall meet at certain stated intervals, and state that it shall be——

ADVISORY BOARD MEETINGS

The CHAIRMAN. I would rather not put anything in, and leave it that way, then put in "six times a year."

Senator LODGE. Once a month is the figure I have gotten from these fellows who have talked to me.

Senator SMITH. You can say "not less than once a month."

I think if you stipulated every 2 weeks that would bring up a lot of objections along the line Senator Thomas mentions.

The CHAIRMAN. All right, but the whole idea collides with Senator Thomas' ideas.

Senator LODGE. The idea of any advisory board at all collides with the idea of any Simon Pure administrator, of course, but we have the Board in here, and we have to handle it in some way.

The CHAIRMAN. What have you to say about it?

Senator GEORGE. I don't think a lot of it, but I think you had better leave your Advisory Board in and fix it that they shall meet not less than some specified time, once a month or something of that kind. I think you have to do that.

The CHAIRMAN. They shall meet at least once a month and oftener if called by the Administrator, or at the request of any three members of the council.

Senator LODGE. That makes the thing look as though it had some reality to it, if you have that language in it.

Senator GEORGE. I think you had better do that.

Mr. RICE. And also if three or more members of the Board request it?

The CHAIRMAN. Yes.

All right, that's that.

Senator LODGE. There is one other point I would like to bring up.

The CHAIRMAN. I got off the train. I thought we had reached the depot.

Senator LODGE. These points I raise are not anything that I am personally hot and bothered about.

The CHAIRMAN. They are very good.

LABOR'S REPRESENTATION ON BOARD SUGGESTED

Senator LODGE. This matter of labor representation is another. There are quite a few people who feel, and I think you do, and I know I do, that a certain type of labor leader is a very effective front man for us in Europe. I keep wondering whether this is the place, or whether subparagraph (b) in this section is the place to put in something about having some people from organized labor on this thing, or whether you have to leave it to the Administrator.

Senator THOMAS of Utah. If you mention organized labor you have to mention something else.

Senator HATCH. Lawyers and veterans.

Senator LODGE. Don't you think it is true that a fellow like Bob Watt was, who could talk their language, does an awful lot of good abroad, and I just bring the matter up for discussion. I am not offering an amendment.

Senator THOMAS of Utah. You could do it in a general way by insisting not only that they be from two parties, but that they be representative of the diverse interests of various interests of the American public. In that way you can leave the President free, but at the same time think for him that he must have a balanced board.

Mr. NITZE. I think that is the intention of the words "broad and varied experience."

Senator THOMAS of Utah. You cannot get unity out of the industrial crowd if you allow two or three of them in. They have to have their lawyers with them.

The CHAIRMAN. I do not believe we can start identifications.

Senator THOMAS of Utah. I think maybe this provision—I say the sentence here—that the President would select these people "with broad and varied experience" is sufficient. Those are the words used here. That would mean a balanced board to me. We used another expression. Mr. Rice would probably have it. What is another wording for "broad and varied" which means you get them from various walks of life?

The CHAIRMAN. Ubiquitous.

Mr. RICE. We have used the expression "in matters affecting the various segments of the public interest, such as labor, and so on."

Senator THOMAS of Utah. That is right. We did have to put the "such as" in, didn't we, after "affecting the various segments of public life"? But I think this would do it, if in the report we say that the board and varied experience means that the President will not have an advisory board made up of all steamship operators, for example. You have to have labor, industry, and the professions.

Senator LODGE. I just wanted to raise the point.

Senator THOMAS of Utah. I think it is very important.

The CHAIRMAN. I think it is important, but I hate to start even trying to spell it out. I would like to really think that we are setting up something here that is dedicated to the public interest as defined in line 17.

All right. In the absence of Senator George—we are going to run until 12:30—is there some noncontroversial thing that we can move to?

EMPLOYMENT OF RETIRED MILITARY PEOPLE PERMITTED

Mr. RICE. Before we get off of section 8, I would like to point out that the language in lines 17, 18, and 19 "other than officers and employees of the United States," excludes the officers and employees of the United States, but it permits the employment of retired military people.

The CHAIRMAN. I do not object to that. It may be necessary.

Mr. RICE. I wanted to point that out because of some appointments that have been made recently.

EXCLUSION OF U.S INSTRUMENTALITY EMPLOYEES

Ambassador DOUGLAS. May I raise a question about the language in lines 18 and 19, "including any agency or instrumentality of the United States"? I understand that the Joint Defense Commission with Canada has been construed as an instrumentality of the United States and that construction has resulted in the resignation of one or two members of that Commission.

Senator THOMAS of Utah. Canadians?

Ambassador DOUGLAS. American members of the Commission.

The CHAIRMAN. Why did they resign? I don't follow that.

Ambassador DOUGLAS. Because one or two of them were lawyers, and under some specific statute they cannot be in the employ of the United States or receive compensation from the United States if they have a case against the United States.

I wonder whether the use of the word "instrumentality" might stand as an interference in the way of selecting a very competent person who you might want to have on this Board.

The CHAIRMAN. You are using the Canadian thing merely as an example?

Ambassador DOUGLAS. As an example, that is right.

Mr. GROSS. The American members of that Board do not regularly receive compensation. The parenthetical clause was put in to exclude the employees of the Federal Reserve Board, TVA, or Government corporations, as to whom there might be some question otherwise.

Ambassador DOUGLAS. If you insert the word "regular" in line 17, before "officers"——

Mr. GROSS. It is in line 19: "who, as such, regularly receive compensation for current services."

Ambassador DOUGLAS. "Regularly" or "continuously". If a Board meets regularly, isn't the compensation regularly received?

Mr. RICE. I believe we can reach the problem you have by doing the same thing for the Board members that was suggested for the experts on page 7, namely, exempt all of them from section 109 of the Criminal Code, and 14(a) of the Contract Settlement Act. That is the usual thing. It usually applies only to attorneys, sometimes to accountants when they have tax claims.

Senator HATCH. I thought you might want someone from TVA or somebody on the Board from some instrumentality of the United States.

Ambassador DOUGLAS. I was not raising that question particularly, Senator. I was raising the other question. I do not know if the point is a valid one.

The CHAIRMAN. Any point you raise is valid, Mr. Ambassador, up to a point.

Is there any necessity for giving further consideration to the Ambassador's prayer? The Chair hears none.

Where can we go from here?

REPORTS TO CONGRESS

Dr. WILCOX. I should suggest page 38, a very short section on Reports to Congress.

Ambassador DOUGLAS. Page 38?

The CHAIRMAN. Page 38, section 19:

> The President from time to time, but not less frequently than once every calendar quarter through June 30, 1952, and once every year thereafter until all funds made available for the purpose of this Act have been expended, shall transmit to the Congress a report of operations under this Act. Reports provided for under this section shall be transmitted to the Secretary of the Senate or the Clerk of the House of Representatives, as the case may be, if the Senate or the House of Representatives, as the case may be, is not in session.

Is that the only provision for reports in this bill?

Dr. WILCOX. I am not sure.

Mr. GROSS. Yes, it is, Senator.

Senator SMITH. How about the Administrator?

The CHAIRMAN. I want some report from the Administrator.

Senator LODGE. This raises the whole question of following through and inspection on it. A lot can be said on that.

Mr. RICE. There is one more report of the joint committee on page 39. You set up your joint committee in the next section, and then over next to that the committee makes the continuous study and report.

Senator HATCH. Isn't this rather odd language here "until all funds have been expended"? Why have you got to spend the funds? It seems to me that that is most unusual language, "until all funds have been expended." You are just going to have to spend all the money, we are saying.

Senator THOMAS of Utah. Why can't you say "until the purposes of the act have been met"?

Senator LODGE. If we get all these foreign assets, we may not have to spend all this money.

The CHAIRMAN. I agree with you completely.

Senator GEORGE. You could say "and once every year thereafter during the life of this act" or something like that.

The CHAIRMAN. But the purpose of this is to go beyond the existence of the act.

Senator THOMAS of Utah. The act lives forever, I guess.

Ambassador DOUGLAS. There is this complication. The funds may not be expended within a period, first: secondly, if certain action is taken by the Administrator in regard to local currency counterparts there may be an accumulation of local currency counterparts that will last for a great many years.

Senator THOMAS of Utah. We hope so. Some of them may blow right up.

Ambassador DOUGLAS. Shouldn't Congress be informed long after the terms of this act have come to an end, or the operations under the act have been terminated? And shouldn't Congress receive a report with regard to this?

The CHAIRMAN. Suppose you say "once a year thereafter, until all functions under this act have been concluded"?

Senator HATCH. That is much better.

The CHAIRMAN. "Until all functions under this act have been concluded."

Senator THOMAS of Utah. I think all you have to do is to say "every year until the purposes of this act have been fulfilled."

Senator GEORGE. "And annually thereafter during the continuance of the act" is all that I think you want to say. That means the functions. But either way you want to put it is all right with me. It does not make a particle of difference to me.

The CHAIRMAN. Mr. Rice, you do that in appropriate language.

Mr. RICE. How about "operations"?

Mr. GROSS. "After all operations under the authority of this act have been completed." That is Public Law 389.

The CHAIRMAN. Let's just put that in.

JOINT COMMITTEE ON FOREIGN ECONOMIC COOPERATION

Well, now, we might as well come on down to the joint congressional committee.

Senator LODGE. It does seem to me we can pass on section 19 finally only after we have passed on section 20.

The CHAIRMAN. We will do that right now, Senator.

SEC. 20. (a) There is hereby established a joint congressional committee to be known as the Joint Committee on Foreign Economic Cooperation (hereinafter referred to as the committee), and to be composed of seven Members of the Senate to be appointed by the President of the Senate, and seven Members of the House

of Representatives to be appointed by the Speaker of the House. A vacancy in the membership of the committee shall be filled in the same manner as the original selection. The President of the Senate and the Speaker of the House, acting jointly, shall appoint a chairman and a vice chairman from among the members of the committee.

(b) It shall be the function of the committee to make a continuous study of the programs of United States economic assistance to foreign countries, and to review the progress achieved in the execution and administration of such programs. The committee shall aid, to the extent it deems advisable, the several standing committees of the Congress having legislative jurisdiction over any part of the programs of United States economic assistance to foreign countries; and it shall make a report to the Senate and the House of Representatives from time to time concerning the results of its studies, together with such recommendations as it may deem desirable. The Administrator shall consult with the committee from time to time with respect to his activities unler this Act.

Senator THOMAS of Utah. Now, Mr. Chairman, may I ask a question there on the last sentence?

The CHAIRMAN. Yes, sir.

COMMITTEE IS FOLLOWTHROUGH COMMITTEE

Senator THOMAS of Utah. If you are not going to give this special committee any legislative functions at all, and you are not, are you, if an amendemnt to this act is proposed, it comes before the Foreign Relations Committee of the Senate, and not before this special committee; does it not?

Senator GEORGE. This simply says "the committee shall aid to the extent it deems advisable the several standing committees of the Congress."

Senator LODGE. This is a followthrough committee; isn't it?

The CHAIRMAN. Yes.

Senator SMITH. This is like the Joint Committee on Labor of the House.

GIVING LEGISLATIVE AUTHORITY TO COMMITTEE

The CHAIRMAN. I would much prefer to give it legislative authority, except for the fact that that would rob the Appropriations Committees of their responsibilities; would it not? Would it?

Senator LODGE. You can't take the Appropriations Committees' powers away from them, no matter what you do.

The CHAIRMAN. Why not?

Senator LODGE. You always have to go to them for a grant of funds.

The CHAIRMAN. Is that true, Mr. Rice?

Mr. RICE. Not under the rules of the Senate. Under the rules of the House, that is true.

Senator LODGE. What other committee in the Senate can make an appropriation?

Mr. RICE. So far as the rules of the Senate, any committee can report out an appropriation bill. They do not report out general appropriations bills, which this would be so considered, because of the great amount of money involved. They just do not do it by reason of precedent.

Senator LODGE. A point of order could not be made on the floor?

Mr. RICE. No, sir. All your private relief bills over in the Senate carry appropriations. They cannot in the House because of the House rules. By reason of custom and precedent, the big appropriation bills have always gone to the Appropriations Committee.

The CHAIRMAN. The Atomic Energy Joint Committee is one of the greatest legislative successes I have ever seen in my 20 years around here. It happens to have fallen under the chairmanship of a Senator who has really dedicated himself to it, and as a result, the work of that Joint Committee, of which I am a member, has been superb, not on account of my membership, but on account of the extraordinary devotion of Senator Hickenlooper to his assignment.

As a result, I think Congress generally has a feeling that the whole subject of atomic energy in its legislative aspect is in safe hands, where there is completely intimate knowledge of what is going on, and a complete comprehension through continued continuity of contact which no standing committee of the Senate or House could possibly have. If it was not a matter clothed with such top secrecy, I could give repeated examples of this superlative importance of the fact that that committee has been elevated to a maximum authority, legislative authority, in respect to the problem given to them.

Now, it seems to me that this thing we are embarking upon is another specialty, very distinctly a specialty, and I would think that if we got the right kind of a joint committee, and the right kind of a chairman, it would be infinitely more competent to deal with the legislative phases of the recovery program than any possible standing committee of the Senate could ever hope to be.

Senator THOMAS of Utah. I agree with you. This is the type of thing we tried to do in the first Neutrality Act, and the State Department said it was unconstitutional. I got it through the Senate, Mr. Chairman, that we would have representatives of Congress functioning along with the administration. The joint committee does not function along with the administration because legally there is a difference, but at the same time it does function because it knows, and it follows through and it watches. And in the Reorganization Act there is that special provision there that all committees follow through in watching the Departments for which they legislate. I brought the question up because I believe so thoroughly in this thing, in this technique, that I wondered if it would not be a good idea, although I did not know what was in here. I would like to see the atomic energy legislative provision put in this.

IS COMMITTEE TO BE HONORARY OR LEGISLATIVE?

The CHAIRMAN. There is a fundamental question for the committee to decide. Is this to be just an honorary committee, or is this to be a legislative committee?

Mr. RICE. Senator, let me point out there that it seems to me that this joint committee will cut across practically every standing committee in the Senate, much more so than the Atomic Energy Committee would do. You have petroleum, you have coal, you have steel, you have agricultural products, you have everything that this committee will study. If you gave it legislative jurisdiction over everything dealing with this foreign relief, then you have export controls, you have the allocation priority powers under title III of the Second War Powers' Act; expenditures in the executive branch of Government. It seems to me it cuts across everything, so that if you gave it over-all legislative jurisdiction with respect to anything that deals with this European recovery program, you might be giving it a great deal more authority than the Atomic Energy Committee had.

The CHAIRMAN. Aside from that you think my idea is a good one?

Senator LODGE. That is a qualified endorsement.

Senator THOMAS of Utah. Also, Mr. Chairman, you must remember that you have a time limit on this thing, but that which is set up in this time limit may bring about a different organization of Europe, may actually bring about a functional economic Western Europe. These are great things that are going on, and I think that if you are going to make any of the dreams come true which are in the minds and in the backs of the heads of practically every witness that has appeared before us, we have got to have some kind of an organization up here keeping up with those dreams in order to at all times meet the situation that may develop.

CONTINUING STAFF TO WORK FOR COMMITTEE

Senator SMITH. Then you would suggest a continuing staff just to work for this committee? We have an analogy in our Joint Labor Committee, for example. We have a regular staff that is watching every development in the labor field, to see what legislation we propose to recommend in that field, but it would go, I think, if we recommended legislation, to the regular Labor Committee to be worked out. Isn't that your conception of that Labor Committee, Senator Thomas? You were on it.

Senator THOMAS of Utah. I did not go on it.

The CHAIRMAN. You do or do not have legislative authority?

Senator SMITH. We do not have any authority. We have a followup authority with a staff that is keeping us posted, so we can say that in this particular field we should have this act. If we go into that, we pass it up to the Labor Committee.

CONSIDERATIONS WITH RESPECT TO IMPACT ON CONGRESS

The CHAIRMAN. There are two considerations with respect to its impact on the Congress. I know the Congress overwhelmingly wants what it calls a watchdog committee. That is universal, and we have to have one.

Now, to that extent we are assisting ourselves by putting it in. I wonder, however, if after Mr. Rice has advised all the chairman of all the standing committees in the House and Senate that we have undermined and gutted them, the net result will not be a liability instead of an asset.

Mr. RICE. Let me give you a specific example that might happen. Suppose the Secretary of Agriculture and the Secretary of Commerce get together and say that not more than 200 million bushels of wheat can be spared to go to Europe under this program. Congress thinks that maybe 500 million should be set aside for that purpose, and somebody introduces a bill that says that not less than 500 million bushels shall be set aside for export in fiscal 1949. Where would the bill go? Should it go to Agriculture or should it go to this joint committee?

Senator THOMAS of Utah. That should go to Agriculture, because it does not say that the 500 million should be spent for this particular purpose.

Mr. RICE. I was assuming that that is what the bill would say.

OVERLAPPING FUNCTIONS IN ALL GENERAL COMMITTEES

Senator THOMAS of Utah. It seems to me, in spite of what Mr. Rice says—and he is generally so straight on everything that I hate to say this—that there is an overlapping of functions in all of the general committees. When the Military Affairs Committee starts working it gets into commerce. It was that committee that put embargoes on commerce and it upset the whole economy of the United States and it stepped on the toes of every committee in Congress. But it did it for a purpose. It did it for the purpose of taking care of our national defense at a time that our national defense had to be taken care of.

I do not think that you can ever get away from the fact that we have only got one country here, and that the committees are all the time functioning in a general way, and not in a particular way. They pass laws for the whole country, and they may be thinking along the line of just commerce, for example, or just military affairs, but when their action is once taken it affects all of these things. You even get over into the atomic energy field when, for instance, we instruct the Bureau of Mines to do something about uranium ore, and already that conflict has come. It has been settled administratively. The President simply ordered the Bureau of Mines to cease functioning until the atomic energy organization made up its mind how to do that. It is going to do it through the Bureau of Mines ultimately, we know that. So those things do not hold.

Then there is a time limit on this bill. It has a particular job to do to bring about a decent peace in Europe, and that time limit protects you from stepping on the toes of other committees.

Senator LODGE. I agree with what Senator Thomas says, that all committees potentially overlap; I can still see there might be human objections on the part of some of these chairmen. But I do not follow your statement that unless the committee has legislative authority it is honorary, purely honorary.

The CHAIRMAN. I will withdraw that. That was just a little license I used to emphasize my point.

Senator LODGE. It seems to me it has a tremendous job to do on the matter of the integration and consolidation of Western Europe, and particularly it can do a tremendous job of followthrough. That is going to be a hard job. It is going to take a lot of organization. It is going to take a high-powered staff. It is going to take a lot of money.

The CHAIRMAN. I would like to hear what Senator George has to say, not only because I respect his wisdom, but also because he has two votes today.

GIVING COMMITTEE LEGISLATIVE POWERS QUESTIONED

Senator GEORGE. Mr. Chairman, we probably have to have this committee, but I don't think very much of it. I think it is going to be a hindrance without a lot of compensating advantages. I do not believe that it should be made a legislative committee, because that cuts across the whole velocity of the Reorganization Act. We do not pay much attention to it, but maybe we should. Maybe we should be trying to develop the Congressional Reorganization Act. The whole philosophy of that is to get away from these special committees and to lodge the jurisdiction in fairly well-defined committees.

Of course, you have overlappings and a whole lot of work to be done on that Reorganization Act in order to ever make it workable.

I do not belive that this committee should be given legislative powers or jurisdiction. Assuming that you were going to have it, and I suppose the demand for it will be overwhelming, as the chairman has said, it is really and essentially a watchdog organization, but one that can hear protests and objections and can go to the administrator and go even to the President. It can tell him things are being done wrong, or are being done right, and they can make recommendations to the regular standing committees that have jurisdiction.

I would hesitate to think that we ought to make it a special committee with legislative power and jurisdiction.

But this bill does here provide for the creation of an additional staff and for a lot of printing and a lot of examinations, and a lot of hearings and all those kinds of things. I have my own doubts about this being a very proper approach to this particular piece of legislation, this particular program.

The Atomic Energy Committee, of course, is altogether a different thing, it seems to me. There was real necessity for the action I think that the Congress took in setting up that committee with the fullest possible authority and power. I don't think that ought to be done in this setup.

The CHAIRMAN. I agree that the analogy is pretty loose between the two.

VOTE CONCERNING COMMITTEE'S HAVING LEGISLATIVE AUTHORITY

Well, those members of the committee who think this committee ought to have legislative authority will hold up their hands.

Those who feel otherwise will hold up their hands.

Senator GEORGE. I do not know how Senator Connally would want to vote on his question, but I think he would be against it.

The CHAIRMAN. All right. We are plowed under, Senator Thomas. "Right forever on the scaffold; wrong forever on the throne."

Is there anything else about this section?

COMMITTEE'S AID TO STANDING COMMITTEES

Senator HATCH. I have a question or two about the language. Take that sentence "The committee shall aid, to the extent it deems advisable, the several standing committees of the Congress having legislative jurisdiction over any part of the programs of U.S. economic assistance to foreign countries. What kind of aid does that contemplate, just how is it going to operate?

The CHAIRMAN. I do not know what that is in there for. What is that "to the extent it deems advisable"? Who put that in, the Bureau of the Budget?

Dr. WILCOX. It must have slipped in. I agree with Senator Hatch.

Senator GEORGE. The committee should assist the standing committees and make reports to them when requested. That is about what they ought to do.

Senator LODGE. They also ought to have the right to submit things on their own motion.

Senator GEORGE. It does provide that they shall make reports to the Congress, and that reports shall go to the appropriate committees.

Senator HATCH. It gives them power to make recommendations generally.

Senator GEORGE. And also says the administrator shall consult with the committee from time to time with respect to his activities.

ADMINISTRATOR'S OBLIGATION TO CONSULT WITH COMMITTEE

Senator HATCH. That is a sentence I wanted to ask about, lines 14 and 15. Just how much obligation does that place on the administrator to consult with the committee?

The CHAIRMAN. I am afraid there is not enough obligation in here. I think this committee is entitled to know everything.

Dr. WILCOX. The drafting committee considered that point at some length, and we all agreed that the joint committee would not want to be burdened with all the communications that came to the Administrator, and there should be some limitation on it, and we thought some general clause on this would probably catch the relationship rather than to be kept fully informed on all matters.

Mr. RICE. In subsection (3) if they do not get what they want they have the power of subpena and they can hold hearings.

Senator HATCH. That is the question in my mind, as to what would be the effect of that.

COMMITTEE'S RIGHT TO INFORMATION

Senator GEORGE. I think this committee should have the right to call on the Administrator. They should be given that full power, otherwise they won't be of much service.

The CHAIRMAN. I think you have to have a pretty positive, affirmative sentence in here on that phase, and I do not find it.

Senator GEORGE. I think the committee itself should have the right to call on the Administrator for such information as it desires at any time and all times, because that is the whole purpose of his committee.

Senator LODGE. Does this language as it now stands enable the joint committee to make a spot-check of any operation it wanted to, and go in and see all the books and every thing? I don't get that.

The CHAIRMAN. I do not think so.

Ambassador DOUGLAS.

> * * * to require by subpoena or otherwise the attendance of such witnesses and the production of such books, papers, and documents * * *.

Senator LODGE. That is more of a formal, conventional hearing. I am in favor of having a man go downtown and have a look at things.

Dr. WILCOX. We thought the language in section (b) would cover that:

> It shall be the function of the committee to make a continuous study of the programs of United States economic assistance to foreign countries, and to review the progress achieved in the execution and administration of such programs.

Senator LODGE. You think that authorizes the spotcheck, do you?

Dr. WILCOX. We thought so.

The CHAIRMAN. Why can't we have a sentence such as we were talking about?

Dr. WILCOX. You can.

The CHAIRMAN. Without objection, you put something like that in, and let's take a look at it.

ENABLING COMMITTEE TO HIRE EXPERTS

Senator LODGE. I agree we ought to also have some language in here such as we have had two other places in this bill, so that this committee can hire experts.

The CHAIRMAN. Isn't that in here, Senator?

Senator LODGE. There isn't the exemption for them.

Senator GEORGE.

The committee is authorized to appoint and fix compensation of such experts, consultants, technicians, and clerical and stenographic assistants as it deems necessary and advisable.

Senator LODGE. And contract for the services of a firm that has other government business?

Mr. RICE. That is not included.

Senator GEORGE. That is not included.

Senator LODGE. They ought to be able to hire J. B. White to make a survey for them.

The CHAIRMAN. They might want to make an auditor something. Mr. Rice, will you, Dr. Wilcox, et al. take a crack at that?

COMMITTEE REPORT IN LIEU OF REPORT BY ADMINISTRATOR

Senator SMITH. May I ask the chairman if he is satisfied with this report by this committee in lieu of a report by the administrator? The President has to, and the committee has to. The administrator does not have to make a report.

The CHAIRMAN. My concept would be that the administrator is making constant reports to the committee and that is the liaison with Congress.

Senator SMITH. That is the kind of report you would expect, not a periodic report to the Congress.

The CHAIRMAN. I think this committee, if it is worth its salt. serves 10 times the function of the report of the administrator.

LIAISON

Senator LODGE. Do you envisage a liaison the way they have it with the military, where the liaison officer is down there all the time, living there, sleeping with them?

The CHAIRMAN. I certainly do. I envisage the same kind of relationship that the Atomic Energy Joint Committee has, even though the parallel is not fully complete. We are represented at almost every meeting of the Atomic Energy Commission. We are represented at meetings of the Military Liaison Committee, and I am simply amazed at the intimacy of command over the situation which Senator Hickenlooper has as a result of his small but extremely expert staff. He, believe it or not, has confronted the Atomic Energy Commission itself with situations that it did not know existed in its own organization. It has just been superlatively useful, and if you could organize this thing in that fashion—I am not talking about snoopers at all; I am talking about intelligent watchdogging——

Senator LODGE. That is the strength of our system of government when it works right, that you have different viewpoints coming in outside of the chain of command, outside of the departmental channel, and I was wondering whether that was what you had in mind, or whether it was the traditional thing where we have an expression, an investigation and subpena everything after the harm has been done. I do not think that is much good.

The CHAIRMAN. It does you no good at all, particularly in a thing of this sort.

Senator LODGE. It seems to me you should have somebody down there knowing what he is doing, and being there to help them.

ADMINISTRATOR'S CONSULTATION WITH COMMITTEE

Senator HATCH. Did you make any decision about that last sentence, about the administrator consulting with the committee?

The CHAIRMAN. Yes, we have told Mr. Rice and Dr. Wilcox to work out an alternative language under which the committee has complete authority to do what it pleases, and to ask him for what it wants.

BIPARTISANISM OF COMMITTEE

Senator HATCH. One other question: This is a bipartisan committee, I presume, but I do not see anything in there to that effect.

The CHAIRMAN. I think you have something there.

> "There is hereby established a joint congressional committee, to be composed of 7 members of the Senate to be appointed by the President of the Senate, not more than 4 to be members of the same political party.'

Senator GEORGE. In both cases.

The CHAIRMAN. All right. We will meet at 2 o'clock. We are doing beautifully.

(Whereupon, at 12:50 p.m. the committee was recessed until 2 p.m. of the same day.)

AFTERNOON SESSION

The committee reconvened at 2 p.m., Senator Arthur H. Vandenberg presiding.

The CHAIRMAN. If all statesmen will come to order, we will proceed.

Let us fix up section 3, page 5. Dr. Wilcox, you had a suggestion at that point to meet some of the dubieties involved.

PARTICIPATING COUNTRIES: ZONES OF OCCUPATION AND TRUSTEESHIPS

Dr. WILCOX. The drafting committee yesterday afternoon thought that the insertion of some such language as this in line 6 might meet the objections certain members of the committee had, so that it would read:

> "Any country (including the United Kingdom of Great Britain and Northern Ireland), Iceland, Ireland, and any of the zones of occupation of Germany), or any areas under international administration or control, wholly or partly in Europe * * *."

That would take care of such zones as those Senator Thomas was
Would you want to say "international or national control?"

Senator THOMAS of Utah. That will cover a trusteeship, all right.

Senator SMITH. That might leave out the French Zone in Germany.
talking about yesterday.

Ambassador DOUGLAS. This says "any of the zones of occupation."

Senator GEORGE. What countries would that take in that are under trusteeship?

Senator THOMAS of Utah. The only trusteeship that is working now that I know of is Trieste, but I imagine there will be some more. I hope that they are going to make a trusteeship out of the Ruhr, or an international control of it in some way.

The CHAIRMAN. Palestine?

Senator SMITH. That is hardly in Europe.

The CHAIRMAN. It is quite a ways over; I will agree to that.

Senator THOMAS of Utah. But we have Turkey in here.

Senator GEORGE. Is Turkey in Europe?

Senator SMITH. Turkey is in both Europe and Asia.

DEFINITION OF PARTICIPATING COUNTRIES

The CHAIRMAN. I must say that is a curious definition:

> Any country (including the United Kingdom of Great Britain and Northern Ireland, Iceland, Ireland, and any of the zones of occupation of Germany) wholly or partly in Europe * * *.

It makes it look as though Great Britain was not in Europe.

Senator THOMAS of Utah. We had an awful time over Iceland at the beginning of the war.

The CHAIRMAN. Great Britain has to be in some continent. What continent is it in?

Senator LODGE. Haven't we always regarded Great Britain as in Europe? The State Department regards it in the western European Division.

The CHAIRMAN. Who is this that says we have to identify the United Kingdom here, Great Britain, and Northern Ireland? That we have to have an Ireland in here once is irritating enough, without having it in here twice.

Senator WILEY. You remember that Hibernian, don't you?

The CHAIRMAN. Who says you have to identify Great Britain as a part of Europe?

Mr. RICE. The State Department.

Ambassador DOUGLAS. I suppose somebody in the State Department has taken that view, geographically.

Senator WILEY. When you are in Great Britain where are you?

Ambassador DOUGLAS. In Great Britain.

Politically, however, there may be a distinction.

Senator THOMAS of Utah. England itself has always felt that Great Britain was not a part of Europe.

The CHAIRMAN. What is it a part of, a sixth continent?

Ambassador DOUGLAS. It is part of a Commonwealth.

The CHAIRMAN. This is a geographical description.

Ambassador DOUGLAS. I am making no case for it. I am just trying to think out loud about—"any country, wholly or partly in Europe * * *." Yes, it is geographical.

85-743—73——6

Senator GEORGE. " * * * including its colonies and dependencies * * * ." It looks to me like all you need to put in here is a description of these zones of occupation and trusteeships and so forth.

Senator SMITH. You have to put in Iceland, don't you?

Senator GEORGE. Yes.

Senator SMITH. You say "Any country, including Iceland * * *."

Senator LODGE. Mr. Stefansson says Iceland is in the American Hemisphere by virtue of its geology and its flora and fauna.

Senator THOMAS of Utah. And you run a line down east of the coast of Greenland, and Iceland is in the Western Hemisphere.

The CHAIRMAN. I would just as soon say "including Iceland," but I would like to get both of those "Irelands" out of there.

Senator GEORGE. Was Iceland a participating country in the 16-Nation agreement?

Senator SMITH. I think it was.

Ambassador DOUGLAS. Yes.

Senator LODGE. That is very clumsy politically, with Ireland in there twice.

Ambassador DOUGLAS. I am told the Irish Minister asked us to change the word "Eire" to Ireland. Why?

Mr. GROSS. He didn't say.

The CHAIRMAN. "Any country (including Iceland)* * * ."

Senator THOMAS of Utah. It would be an improvement on the act, Senator Vandenberg, if we named these 16 countries here, and then included their colonies.

The CHAIRMAN. I suppose the reason for not naming them is that theoretically the act is open.

AID TO CHINA

Senator LODGE. What will happen when we have this aid to China? Are we going to set up a separate administrator for China who is going to compete with this administrator?

The CHAIRMAN. I don't know. He sure isn't in this bill.

Senator LODGE. Ought we not keep this open for him? Somebody is going to have to decide priorities, and you are going to have French Indo-China in here.

Ambassador DOUGLAS. They would come in under relief, not because they were parties to any multilateral agreements arrived at in Paris, but solely for administrative purposes. Isn't that true?

Senator LODGE. I did not hear the first part of that.

Ambassador DOUGLAS. This section deals with the participating countries, those that have entered into multilateral agreements, who have given pledges among themselves. China and other parts of the Orient would not be a party to those multilateral agreements, and while the poor administrator might be called upon to administer the relief for China it should come, I presume, under another title rather than under this title.

Senator LODGE. I can readily see the force of that argument. But don't you think that you are going to have to have one administrator for the whole world? You can't have one for China, one for Latin America, and another for Europe.

The CHAIRMAN. I suspect the China thing does not call for an administrator in any such sense.

Senator LODGE. If there is competition for scarce materials, as there is going to certainly be between the countries of Europe, there is probably going to be competition with China. Somebody is going to have to decide who is going to get the first crack at what.

DEFINITION OF PARTICIPATING COUNTRIES

Senator THOMAS of Utah. I can get rid of Ireland, Mr. Chairman.

The CHAIRMAN. How?

Senator THOMAS of Utah. The 16 countries of Europe cooperating, naming them, and all countries wholly or partly in Europe, including the colonies, plus your international idea, and you haven't gotten into a conflict over geography at all.

The CHAIRMAN. Why not do that?

Senator SMITH. Do you mean name them all?

Senator THOMAS of Utah. Whatever is the proper phrasing. I mean the 16 countries that made——

The CHAIRMAN. The C.E.E.C. (Committee for European Economic Cooperation).

Senator THOMAS of Utah. Yes, and all countries wholly or partly in Europe, including their colonies and dependencies, and then your international expression. Then no country is named.

Senator LODGE. You would have to name Iceland, would you not?

The CHAIRMAN. No, because that is one of the 16. Is there any objection to that on the part of the State Department?

Senator SMITH. Would you say "parties to that * * *"?

Ambassador DOUGLAS. The Committee for European Economic Cooperation.

Senator THOMAS. Did they sign anything, Mr. Ambassador? They did, didn't they?

Ambassador DOUGLAS. Yes.

Senator GEORGE. You have to put in your zones of occupation.

Ambassador DOUGLAS. And you should make specific the Free Territory of Trieste, or either of its zones.

Senator GEORGE. Suppose some of these Balkan States do want to come in.

Ambassador DOUGLAS. They will be required to become a party to the multilateral agreement.

Senator GEORGE. But we would be including them with this?

The CHAIRMAN. Not under Senator Thomas' language.

Senator THOMAS of Utah. It says: "All other countries wholly or partly in Europe," so even Russia could come in.

The CHAIRMAN. It must be kept open for scenic purposes, if nothing else.

I think this can be written the way Senator Thomas is talking about it. This is perfectly awful.

Senator GEORGE. It would take half a day to explain that to the Senate.

The CHAIRMAN. It would take half a day to explain one of them. It would take all day to explain both of them.

Do you understand what we are talking about, Mr. Rice?

Mr. Rice. Yes, sir.

The Chairman. You and the Ambassador collaborate.

Ambassador Douglas. And I do suggest the Free Territory of Trieste.

The Chairman. You just sell your bill of goods to Mr. Rice, now. Where do we go now, Dr. Wilcox?

Dr. Wilcox. There is one other relatively simple one, if you want to catch that before you go into the heart of the bill. It is the one on the United Nations, section 17, page 35.

Senator George. I do not make any suggestion about a change of language, but those words in italics seem to be odd or a little awkward: "Provided it adheres to, and for so long as it remains adherent to, a joint program for European recovery designed to accomplish the purposes of this act."

It is a little bit awkward, is it not?

Dr. Wilcox. Senator, if you look at the language that is stricken, it was thought that the new language is better, because it would provide new adherents even after the act is in effect. It would permit new States to come in with this new language. With the old that would not be very clear, "while it remains an adherent to".

Senator George. I understand it, but it seems to me to be a bit awkward.

The Chairman. See what you can do with it.

USE OF U.N. SERVICES AND FACILITIES

Page 35, line 7:

Sec. 17. (a) The President is authorized to request the cooperation of or the use of the services and facilities of the United Nations, its organs and specialized agencies or other international organizations, in carrying out the purposes of this Act, and may make payments, by advancements or reimbursements, for such purpose, out of funds made available for the purposes of this Act, as may be necessary therefor to the extent that special compensation is usually required for such services and facilities.

(b) The President shall transmit to the Secretary General of the United Nations copies of reports to Congress on the operations conducted under this Act.

(c) Any agreements concluded between the United States and participating countries or groups of such countries in implementation of the purposes of this Act shall be registered with the United Nations if such registration is required by the Charter of the United Nations.

Is there any objection?

Senator Lodge. Is that the only reference to the United Nations in the bill?

Ambassador Douglas. I think it is.

Mr. Nitze. There is one on page 21.

BUILDING UP THE U.N.

Senator Lodge. That does not reach what I want to mention. These boys that I talk with, meeting in secret, keep saying to me:

"Now, the Marshall Plan isn't the way to do it. The thing to do is build up the United Nations and get the nations that agree to band together, and if Russia doesn't want to come in, O.K., we will go along together."

Then you explain to them that before the nations in the United Nations that do not like Russia can band together they have to get off their backs. In other words, the Marshall Plan is the first step in this program. I think the bill is ideologically weak on that point. When you hear these fellows talking, that is the point they always make: "Let's not do the Marshall Plan; let's build up the United Nations." We ought to get the idea into this declaration of purposes or in here somewhere that this is essential to bring up the United Nations. I don't care, personally. I just bring it up as a political point.

Ambassador DOUGLAS. Reference is made in the preamble to the attainment of the objectives of the United Nations.

Senator LODGE. That is not quite what they mean. They mean building up and strengthening the United Nations into an effective organization whether Russia joins or not, which of course is just what this is in a less official way.

Senator GEORGE. Do you suppose the President would be able to utilize the services and facilities of the United Nations to any measurable extent?

The CHAIRMAN. I suppose that Europe Commission was in mind, was it not, Mr. Ambassador?

Ambassador DOUGLAS. That might be used. There is the social and economic council which might be used. Then there is the Coal Committee and there is the Food and Agricultural Organization, which is very important, because that does the allocating among them of the foodstuffs available. FAO makes the allocations among countries, in large measure.

Senator THOMAS of Utah. There are all the expert facilities, too, libraries and things of that kind, carrying on in all the different branches. I think that we would find ourselves dependent on some other institution, if not the United Nations, for worldwide information which they are constantly gathering and keeping up to date with.

Senator GEORGE. We are going to pay for those things, too.

This says, "The President shall transmit to the Secretary General of the United Nations * * *." I would prefer, Mr. Chairman, myself, to say "The President shall cause to be transmitted to the Secretary General * * *." I do not want to put the burden on the President to be writing to the Secretary General of the United Nations.

The CHAIRMAN. The change is made. I will not quarrel with that, so long as you have two votes.

Senator LODGE. On this point that I mention, Mr. Chairman, it occurs to me that on page 3 there, in line 2, some words might be put in to this effect: "strengthening and building up the United Nations into an increasingly effective agency for peace."

The CHAIRMAN. Let's take that when we get to that section of the bill.

Senator LODGE. OK.

The CHAIRMAN. Is there anything else under this section?

Senator GEORGE. We have a lot rubbed out under that section, but I suppose that is taken care of.

The CHAIRMAN. That is another section.

Where do you want to go next, Dr. Wilcox?

NATURE AND METHOD OF ASSISTANCE

Dr. WILCOX. If you want to postpone consideration of the declaration of policy, I suppose you might just as well go into the nature and method of assistance, on page 18.

The CHAIRMAN. Page 18, line 4.

Senator THOMAS of Utah. Isn't this the part that Senator Barkley is so much interested in, Mr. Chairman?

The CHAIRMAN. Is it?

Senator THOMAS of Utah. I don't know. We can read on. Well, let's wait and see. Let's try it.

Senator GEORGE. He probably will get back, Senator, before we finally dispose of it. He will be back on Thursday, I understand.

Senator THOMAS of Utah. If it is understood that we are going to do with this section what we have done to the others, I think we can go to any other part of the bill.

Senator GEORGE. We are to this part of it, are we not, with some exceptions?

The CHAIRMAN. We either have to do this or go to the dollars and cents.

Senator GEORGE. I think we had just as well tackle this.

The CHAIRMAN. All right; line 4:

> SEC. 11. (a) The Administrator may, from time to time, furnish assistance to any participating country by providing for the performance of any of the functions set forth in paragraphs (1) through (5) of this subsection when he deems it to be in furtherance of the purposes of this Act, and upon the terms and conditions set forth in this Act and such additional terms and conditions consistent with the provisions of this Act as he may determine to be necessary and proper.
>
> (1) Procurement from any source, including Government stocks, of any commodity which he determines to be required for the furtherance of the purposes of this Act, and the term commodity as used in this Act shall mean any material, article, merchant vessel, supply, or goods necessary for the purposes of this Act.

Senator GEORGE. There you get up against your merchant vessel, and I honestly confess that I was a little bit impressed with the showing made by these fellows about transferring outright 200 of our ships and chartering 300 additional ships.

The CHAIRMAN. You come to that definitely in just a minute.

INCLUSION OF PUBLICATIONS AND MOVIES SUGGESTED

Senator SMITH. Mr. Chairman, can I raise a question in connection with this section? I have a letter from Mr. Allen Dulles, who is a partner of Foster Dulles, on the question of publications here, and movies, on the ground that they ought to be included in this picture by some such expression as this, after the words "any material, article," and before "merchant vessel," "including copyrighted articles, such as publications and motion pictures."

That raises a question as to whether things of that kind are to be used in connection with this whole program. It came up in the discussion of the "Voice of America" program. They felt they would have to leave it out there for the moment, but it might be appropriate here. I told Mr. Dulles I would be glad to bring it up for discussion. I suggest, for purposes of discussion, that we include "including copyrighted articles, such as publications and motion pictures."

Senator GEORGE. Senator Smith, do we not run into danger when we talk about exporting moving pictures under the Marshall plan? We already have an informational bureau set up under the bill which you were so useful in developing here and getting through the Senate, and I think that you have got to consider public reaction to a thing like that. It is the little things that just overturn you, frequently. It may be all right. I am just suggesting, Mr. Chairman, that it seems to me that we have got to be a bit careful or we run into a situation there where it is not very far from the sublime to the ridiculous, frequently.

MOVIE SITUATION IN ENGLAND

Senator SMITH. I would like to ask the Ambassador how far this thing is a serious matter in England, with the present jam there with regard to movies in England, and the so-called tax of 75 percent of the earnings on the movie business. I had lunch with Mr. Dulles and others a few days ago and he raised the question, and I told him I would bring it up so it would be considered.

Ambassador DOUGLAS. So far as the situation in England is concerned, it is very serious. It is very serious for the American moving picture industry. It is very serious for the theatergoers in England, because the British industry cannot now, and will not be able for a long time, to produce enough films to satisfy the demand. The tax was imposed in an effort to prevent that relatively small seepage of dollars that was being transferred from sterling into dollars on account of a certain portion of the earnings of the American film industry in Britain. It is a confiscatory tax. It is a 75-percent tax levied upon the value of the film, and the value of the film is always to be determined by the amount of income which the film earns. So, in effect, it is an income tax.

No American films have been imported into Britain since shortly after the tax was imposed. It was imposed very suddenly, too. Not only is the tax a bad tax for the reasons that I have given, as well as other reasons; it was also imposed in a very abrupt and, I thought, a very rude manner, because negotiations were being held at the time with a view to trying to solve the British dollar problem insofar as movies were concerned, and suddenly, right in the midst of these negotiations, the tax was levied.

The real answer to the moving picture industry in Britain, and the American moving picture industry, is to relieve the British dollar position on the one hand, and on the other for the American moving picture industry to arrive at some satisfactory settlement of the controversy with the British Treasury. But I would doubt that the importation of movies as such should be included in the language of this legislation.

Senator THOMAS of Utah. If we did include it, could it possibly be interpreted as a retaliatory action on our part against what Great Britain has done?

Senator WILEY. If you wrote that in here you would have to pay 75 percent on the value of the film you wanted to show in Great Britain, then.

Ambassador DOUGLAS. You would under the existing tax law.

QUESTION OF WHETHER TO EXPAND COMMODITY DEFINITION

Senator SMITH. I am not pressing the matter. I brought it up because I told Allen that I would, and just considered whether we ought to include under the definition of commodities copyrighted articles such as publications and motion pictures. That is the issue before us, whether we want to expand this commodity definition here.

Mr. RICE. I would interpret this language to include it without saying so. If you want to exclude it, it seems to me you would have to put in excluding language.

Ambassador DOUGLAS. The question is, should we be expending American dollars to provide an article of this character? Do the movies, stating it differently, fall within a program of European recovery?

Senator LODGE. Cigarettes apparently do.

Ambassador DOUGLAS. But cigarettes fall clearly within the category, it seems to me, of incentive goods. One could say, perhaps, movies do too, but certainly they are not as clearly distinguishable.

Senator LODGE. I do not see any difference, myself.

People like to go to the movies and like to smoke, and they are willing to go to work in order to smoke and go to the movies.

The CHAIRMAN. You won't find the word "tobacco" in the bill anywhere.

Senator LODGE. That is true.

Senator SMITH. Do you think, Mr. Ambassador, that Mr. Rice's suggestion, that by implication that is included under the words "any material" and so forth, or "goods necessary for the purposes of this act" would include what I have in mind?

The CHAIRMAN. It would if the administrator decided that they were incentive goods.

Ambassador DOUGLAS. I suppose so, and particularly if a moving picture or moving pictures were included within the program approved by the administrator and initiated by the participating country.

Senator LODGE. So long as the language does not exclude them, that is all we care about it.

The CHAIRMAN. Are you satisfied with that?

Senator SMITH. I am satisfied. I am especially satisfied with the point that the administrator probably would include these if he felt they were classified as incentive goods.

PETROLEUM PRODUCTS: PROCUREMENT, CONSUMPTION, AND DEMAND

Senator LODGE. I have an amendment at this point, Mr. Chairman, if it is in order to offer it now.

The CHAIRMAN. Section7 (a) (1), at the end of line 18:

> *Provided, however*, That the procurement of petroleum and petroleum products shall, to the maximum extent possible, be made from petroleum sources outside the United States; and provided further that no commodity shall be furnished under the provisions of this Act which, through the use or operation thereof, creates or encourages a substantially increased consumption and demand by the participating countries for petroleum and petroleum products.

Senator LODGE. There are two parts to that. The first part is what we have in the interim aid bill, that petroleum and petroleum products shall, to the maximum extent possible, be procured outside of the

United States. The second part was suggested by the testimony which showed that it was planned to enormously increase the utilization of petroleum and petroleum products in Europe. There is a lot of testimony in the record to that effect, and it seemed to me and it seemed to some of the witnesses, also, that it was not a sound thing to encourage the dependence of Europe on petroleum when they have so much fuel in the form of coal that is readily available.

The CHAIRMAN. Would this proviso eliminate tractors and such?

Senator LODGE. It would not eliminate all of them, no. It would prevent tractors being sent into Europe to a point which would substantially increase the consumption of petroleum; yes, it would.

PLANNED INCREASE IN EUROPEAN PETROLEUM CONSUMPTION

Senator SMITH. It is definitely contemplated in the recovery of Europe that there will be an increase?

Senator LODGE. They are planning to send in 65,000 tractors, and there is testimony showing that there is very grave doubt as to whether that machinery shall be used or can be used on the small compartmented farms in Europe. My feeling is that the plans to increase European consumption of petroleum were made wholly on a commercial basis, not giving sufficient weight to the unfortunate possibilities which can happen in the strategic and military spheres.

The CHAIRMAN. I would not think you could go this far.

Senator LODGE. Do you agree with the plan to double the consumption, I think it is, by 1951 over what they had in 1938? It is something like that. I was quoting from memory I think there is a plan to double the consumption of what she had in 1938.

Ambassador DOUGLAS. Sixty-seven percent.

Senator LODGE. That is a huge increase. I asked questions about it all through the hearings, and I was unable to get a very forthright statement as to why it was done.

Ambassador DOUGLAS. The real reason for it, Senator, is because all over the world petroleum has been becoming, and still is becoming, an important source of energy. The petroleum consumption in Europe, expressed in terms of hard coal equivalent, is very, very much under anything that we have had here, or do have. I can't recollect the figures. In terms of hard coal equivalent before the war the energy derived from petroleum and petroleum products was approximately 10 percent of the total energy, whereas in the United States it was almost 50 percent. By 1952 in Europe it will still be just approximately 11 percent, whereas in the United States it will be about 40 percent. In the United States in 1938 it was about 30 percent. In 1951 in the United States it will be about 40 percent, or 38 percent, whereas in Europe in 1938 it was slightly under 10 percent, and in 1951 it will be just about 11 percent.

Senator LODGE. I do not think the comparison is pertinent at all. We have the petroleum here, and they haven't got it there.

Ambassador DOUGLAS. But there are a great many things Europe does not have that she has to import. Aviation, for instance, would be wholly impossible without petroleum imports. The mechanization of agriculture consumes petroleum products. The installation of the diesel engine, a more efficient source of motive power than the steam engine, has been made in some of the ships, both for inland waterway purposes and for overseas purposes. The diesel engine on the railroads, too, is coming. I don't think we contemplate sending any diesel engines abroad. I am perfectly clear about that.

SERIOUSNESS OF PETROLEUM SITUATION

I recognize how serious the problem situation is. Developments in the Middle East make the situation potentially quite critical. The developments there have already interfered with the development of the petroleum industry.

Senator LODGE. You saw the announcement this morning. The Office of International Trade has shut down on all exports of all oil from the eastern seaboard.

Ambassador DOUGLAS. I read that in the press this morning.

One review of the petroleum requirements has been made, and the requirements have been substantially reduced. I would suggest that if anything should happen to interfere with or interrupt the flow of petroleum from the Middle East, or that seriously impaired the program for the development of petroleum in the Middle East, the whole program must be reviewed again and it must be reviewed continuously. I can understand what your concern is.

Senator LODGE. Have you seen Senator Bridge's bill, which will undoubtedly be attached as an amendment to this, to completely cut off all shipments of petroleum? That will make this look like an afternoon tea.

Ambassador DOUGLAS. I recognize that it will.

EUROPEAN DEPENDENCE ON SOMETHING THEY CAN EASILY GET SUGGESTED

Senator LODGE. The American people simply have got to have enough oil to function. Of course, Europe can't get along with just what it produces itself, but this petroleum thing is in a different category from the normal European import, because petroleum is so strategic. I should think it would be much sounder for us to do this and for them to go ahead and bear down on something they can easily get, instead of being dependent on something that is 3,000 miles away.

Ambassador DOUGLAS. There are two factors that will impede that. I can only give you the facts as they appear to me. They are two factors which impede and make impossible the hydrogenization of coal in the next 4 or 5 years in sufficient quantities to permit the mechanization of agriculture to proceed. The use of the airplane——

Senator LODGE. Why can't they use those things they used during the war?

Ambassador DOUGLAS. They might. Hydrogenization of coal is impeded for two reasons; first, because of the tremendous shortage of coal in Europe, and second because of the shortage of steel. You can't construct hydrogenization plants until you have steel.

Senator LODGE. I was not talking so much about that. You have been in Germany since the war and you saw what Hitler did. He built these enormous high-speed roads all over Germany, and then he ran out of gas and they were wasted. If he had put that amount of energy and work and labor into railroads he might not have been licked. The

Europeans are fascinated by petroleum, and it always gets them into trouble. It always gets them into trouble.

I do not think this is in the category of a normal European import, and I do not think you are doing Europe a good turn by increasing Europe's dependence on petroleum so much.

COAL AS AN ALTERNATIVE TO PETROLEUM

Ambassador DOUGLAS. What is the alternative?

Senator LODGE. It seems to me the alternative is to bear down on coal.

Ambassador DOUGLAS. Senator, in the first place the construction of hydrogenization plants—I presume that everybody concedes that petroleum is necessary for a highly industrialized, complicated, intricate economy, over here to a very much greater extent. We have relied upon petroleum much more than European countries have. But petroleum products are necessary, I think, for a highly industrialized economic system.

Now, if we accept that premise, and somebody may throw some doubt upon it, but if we accept it for the purpose of argument, then from what source may this highly industrialized area derive its petroleum as a source of energy, either from natural sources or synthetic sources? The synthetic sources are clearly impossible and impracticable within any reasonable period of time, first because of the shortage of coal and second because of the shortage of steel.

Therefore, that as an alternative seems to me to be reasonably well out and erased.

Now, if the sources of petroleums are inadequate to supply the United States and the requirements as they have been substantially reduced for Western Europe, then the matter will have to be reviewed again.

There is still one third alternative, and that is to make sure, through the recovery of Western Europe, that untoward and unfortunate events do not take place in the Middle East which will interrupt and interfere with the flow of petroleum in that area.

SIZE OF INCREASES IN PETROLEUM CONSUMPTION QUESTIONED

Senator LODGE. I know they have to have petroleum to operate the kind of mechanized economy they have got to have, but why do they have to have it 67 percent bigger than it was in 1938?

Ambassador DOUGLAS. Our increase over 1938——

Senator LODGE. I don't care about our increase. I do not think that has anything to do with it.

Ambassador DOUGLAS. It is only of significance because it is some measure of the relative importance of petroleum to the two areas. I have forgotten exactly what the increase in this country has been, but it is well over 100 percent, as I recollect it. It is about 100 percent or over 100 percent in this country.

Senator LODGE. I think it is too big in this country, so far as that goes.

Ambassador DOUGLAS. Our developments, of course, have been extraordinary, and 100 percent of the new locomotives on order are diesels.

BRITISH CONVERSION TO PETROLEUM

Senator LODGE. It was said in England that they were going in for oil heating of homes. What on earth justification is there for that?

Ambassador DOUGLAS. Britain was short of coal. They have hundreds of years of reserve in the ground, it is true. They did resort to a modified and very modest conversion program for the substitution of petroleum for coal because it was the only source of heating. A few houses did convert. One or two of the utilities have substituted petroleum for coal, and in terms of the cost per Btu it is about as cheap today—and I think it is probably cheaper—than the cost of British coal. The British coal costs $10.50 a ton.

You are asking why, and I am telling you why.

U.S. SUGGESTION THAT FRENCH CONVERT TO PETROLEUM

In France, when I was there in the summer of 1945, Americans were persuading the French to substitute petroleum for coal.

Senator LODGE. American salesmen?

Ambassador DOUGLAS. No; some of those in authority were talking about their shortage of coal, and they proceeded to make the suggestion.

Senator LODGE. The American Government was urging people to convert? They should have consulted the Secretary of the Navy, who did not have enough oil last summer with which to run the Navy.

Ambassador DOUGLAS. This was in 1945. In this country, as you recollect, during the war, people were interested in substituting petroleum for coal because there was a shortage of coal. These sudden developments occur. I am not suggesting by any manner of means that we export petroleum from the United States to our disadvantage, to our very great disadvantage, for the benefit of Europe, because I think we ought to be cautious in dealing with it because we do not know what the future situation is going to be.

ASSURING PETROLEUM PRODUCTS FOR EVERYBODY

One of the certain ways of assuring petroleum products for ourselves and for everybody else is to provide for the countries of Western Europe. If Western Europe does not recover then the threat to the Middle East becomes a very real one, and certainly we would not be able to rely upon the Middle East with any assurance at all as a source of petroleum.

Senator LODGE. I do not figure anybody can rely on the Middle East.

Ambassador DOUGLAS. It is a very nice question.

AMENDMENT TO SECTION CONCERNING PETROLEUM

The CHAIRMAN. Well, what are we going to do about this?

Senator LODGE. I am not wedded to this wording at all.

Senator SMITH. Why won't you leave out your second proviso?

Senator LODGE. I do not see how we can report out a bill and completely ignore the question of petroleum.

The CHAIRMAN. I think your first proviso is essential:

Provided, however, That the procurement of petroleum and petroleum products shall, to the maximum extent possible, be made from petroleum sources outside the United States.

Without objection, that much of the amendment at least is adopted. Let's go that far.

Then, going further—I see what you are shooting at.

Senator LODGE. You see what I mean, do you not?

Ambassador DOUGLAS. Yes, I see what you mean.

The CHAIRMAN. And the idea that the chap from Missouri had, that we ought to be combing our farms for horse-drawn farm machines, which would be far more competent for their small farm use.

Senator LODGE. You fly over Europe the way I have done, and I am sure the way you have done, and it is all little farms with hedges around them. Those hedges have been there for hundreds of years. It is ideal for animal farming. Russell Brown spoke on this point, you remember—the independent petroleum man.

I am not wedded to this language at all, but I know as well as I am sitting here that Bridges or somebody else is going to come out with a ripsnorting amendment that is going to go sailing through if we do not have something in here.

Ambassador DOUGLAS. I understand exactly what the Senator has in mind.

The CHAIRMAN. We will adopt the first half of this amendment, and suspend judgment on the last half.

Senator LODGE. All right.

PERFORMANCE OF COMMODITY AND OTHER SERVICES

The CHAIRMAN. Now we are down to another highly controversial question on the top of page 19.

Senator SMITH. Have you read (2) and (3)?

The CHAIRMAN. I thought so. All right; I will go through them.

(2) Processing, storing, transporting, and repairing any commodities, or performing any other services with respect to a participating country which he determines to be required for accomplishing the purposes of this Act;

(3) Procurement of and furnishing technical information and assistance.

Senator SMITH. In connection with (3), my friends who are in the business of publishing textbooks say that we are way ahead of the other countries of the world in that connection, and this probably would be broad enough to cover that, would it not—"technical information"?

The CHAIRMAN. I should think so.

Senator SMITH. I would think it would. I would like to note that, in passing.

The CHAIRMAN. If you will introduce me some day to your friends who print these textbooks, I would like to tell them what a loyal advocate you are of their products.

Senator SMITH. I will always be happy, Mr. Chairman, to have you say anything to my friends, but it happens that I happen to know the McGraw-Hill people, and they have been doing a lot of work on the best kind of technical information.

Senator THOMAS of Utah. If it is McGraw-Hill I would be in favor of cutting it out, because they turned down one of my manuscripts.

Senator SMITH. That shows they do not always recognize genius when they see it.

CHARTERING OF EXCESS U.S. MERCHANT VESSELS

The CHAIRMAN. No. (4), at the top of page 19:

(4) Chartering any merchant vessel owned by the United States which the U.S. Maritime Commission certifies as excess to its current requirements.

Now relax.

Senator LODGE. I would like to ask whether we have had a reply from Secretary Forrestal on approving this proposal, which request I asked be made.

Dr. WILCOX. Senator, I am told that the Munitions Control Board is making a study of the general problem, but that the Secretary of Defense has not been asked to prepare any statement with respect to the relationship between our maritime fleet and our national defense.

Senator LODGE. I askéd him to, through you.

Dr. WILCOX. I am sorry if I misunderstood your instructions, but the gentleman who testified that morning said that such a study was being made, and you directed the staff to ask for that study if it were available. If you want the separate job done, we will get it.

Senator LODGE. I want to know whether Forrestal, who is in charge of our national defense, thinks it is all right to let these ships go, in the light of the fact that the merchant marine is an auxiliary to our Navy.

Senator THOMAS of Utah. Does the chartering of a merchant ship mean the transferring?

Senator GEORGE. To all practical purposes, Senator, I think it does. yes. You do not get them back—hardly ever.

Senator THOMAS of Utah. Then this would be one of the sections which both the merchant marine and the man who testified for the CIO, Curran, would object to, would it not?

Senator GEORGE. He very strongly objected, but it was not Curran alone. Others called our attention to it.

The CHAIRMAN. There was Lundeberg, too.

Senator GEORGE. Three or four, and I was impressed, if their statements were true, that every other country is building very rapidly merchant marine ships—every other European country. They all developed those facts. One of them gave us percentages of how many ships were laid down and how many were in course of actual construction and how many in prospect, what they would have a total of in 1951, I think, and it looked like we were losing out in the race. I do not like to see our merchant ships, unless they are surplus for some reason or other, either because we have a surplus or an inferior ship, disposed of to the point where we will fall back below what we ought to have.

Senator SMITH. I agree with that, Senator, but of course here is a way by which we can save an awful lot of actual dollars in this whole show, the extent to which foreign bottoms and foreign currencies pay for the transportation. I agree with you, if we are falling below what we need for our protection, but here is one of the ways by which, as

I understand it—maybe I am wrong—you had in mind that we might save a large amount in the amount we are appropriating for the purpose. Am I wrong in that?

Ambassador DOUGLAS. That is right.

Senator SMITH. How far we ought to go is a matter of judgment, but I do think there is something. Take the Scandinanvian countries. They are all keen to get back into their own shipping business and up to the point where they were before. I don't know that we are jeopardizing ourselves in letting them charter some of our boats and develop this trade. We do not need to spend dollars for that.

SAVINGS FROM CHARTERING AND SELLING SHIPS

Senator GEORGE. What is estimated, would you say, to be involved in giving away 200 ships, or selling them for foreign currency?

Senator SMITH. What do we save in dollars?

Ambassador DOUGLAS. As I understand it, it is $350 million immediately. That $350 million was on account of the chartering of the ships. The total sum over the 4¼ years was something like $650 million. That is over 4¼ years.

Senator GEORGE. I was figuring during the first year.

Ambassador DOUGLAS. During the first year, on account of the chartering of vessels, the saving amounted, as I recollect it, to $140 million. That was less during the initial period on account of the sale of ships because of the 25 percent downpayment that has to be made. Let me look up the exact figures for you.

GETTING RID OF SOMETHING THAT MIGHT BE VITAL, QUESTIONED

Senator GEORGE. I was impressed with that line of testimony. It impressed me that we were just getting rid of something here that might be very, very vital to us.

Ambassador DOUGLAS. The chartering, Senator, of the vessels, is one method. The transfer, sale, is another. You understand that.

Senator GEORGE. Yes.

Ambassador DOUGLAS. We have got back all of the ships chartered by the United Kingdom during the war, except those which they purchased. We have not gotten back the ships chartered to the Soviets, during the war.

The CHAIRMAN. Which is it that the Maritime Commission are complaining about, the charter?

Ambassador DOUGLAS. Both, because they go from under our flag.

Senator SMITH. That is true because the cost of operating is very much more under our flag.

Senator GEORGE. You can make an awfully good case for getting rid of the last boat we have, but I do not believe we should do it.

Senator SMITH. I thought this was a matter dealing with the 4-year program.

Senator GEORGE. I imagine we will meet this on the floor.

The CHAIRMAN. Yes, sir.

(Discussion was continued off the record.)

Senator GEORGE. I am not prepared to say that all the testimony we heard is correct or accurate, but if so, it was impressive.

Senator THOMAS of Utah. Of course, Mr. Chairman, we built up a great merchant marine in the First World War and then we let it get stuck in the mud. Then we went out buying any kind of ship that we could purchase. I think the Ambassador probably bought more than anybody else.

Ambassador DOUGLAS. Some lousy ones, too, if I may say so, but anything that would float.

Senator THOMAS of Utah. Then we did not get started, even, on a merchant marine program until the Second World War was on the horizon. Then we were forced through necessity to build a type of boat which was to be used for war purposes, primarily. There have been some shipping companies, like United Fruit, that stepped out and built new boats to satisfy everybody and to satisfy the merchant fleet idea, but I would hate to see us lose the gains we have made in the building up of our merchant marine by dissipating our ships.

OBJECTIONS TO LEASING SHIPS

Senator SMITH. Do you feel the same about the leasing of ships?

Senator THOMAS of Utah. I do not know just what chartering means. It would be objectionable to the personnel, to the labor on the ships, because a chartered boat changes its flag, and with the change in flag they lose their jobs.

Just think what we have done to build up the personnel of the merchant marine. We gave them practically all the reemployment rights. We gave them some of the educational rights. We have done practically everything for them that we did for the soldier, excepting letting them come in and get the benefits of the soldiers' educational bill. It was necessary to do that. But at the same time, is it not kind of contrary to sensible national policy to dissipate that immediately and find ourselves practically without ships?

UNUSED SHIPPING

Senator SMITH. I was under the impression that this was practically unused shipping that we had set aside because we could not use it, and we are going to greatly expand our shipping, and instead of expanding by building up our marine further, we would have our static, where it is, now.

The CHAIRMAN. This is what puzzles me. My conception of this thing is those sights I see of 50 or 60 vessels all tied up in some back bay, just rotting.

Senator THOMAS of Utah. Take the wooden vessels that burned up in Seattle.

Senator SMITH. Go up the Hudson and see some of them in those bays.

The CHAIRMAN. Is there anything like that going on today?

Senator GEORGE. There are a lot of ships in refuge.

Ambassador DOUGLAS. About 20 million tons.

The CHAIRMAN. What is going to happen to them, just disintegrate?

Senator GEORGE. They will finally disintegrate unless we have some need for them. They are not particularly merchant ships. They were used for all sorts of cargo carrying in the war.

The CHAIRMAN. Would it involve the same argument if those were the kinds of ships that we were passing out under this program?

Senator GEORGE. I do not think so. I do not think it would. Those are specialties and peculiar types, made for special purposes. They are all tied up together there in groups of 6 and 8 and 10.

The CHAIRMAN. Are those any good in this program?

Ambassador DOUGLAS. I do not know the particular ships Senator George is referring to, but my recollection is that there are somewhere in the vicinity of 20 million tons of oceangoing merchant dry-cargo vessels tied up. It is a huge tonnage in the Hudson River.

Senator GEORGE. They have them in the Hudson and down here at Norfolk, and then down in the St. Johns in Florida and all around.

The CHAIRMAN. Would these maritime boys have the same objection to the transfer of those ships?

Ambassador DOUGLAS. I think they probably would, because it might have the effect of reducing the amount of cargo carried in a ship flying the American flag.

TWO PHASES OF CHARTERING PROPOSAL

There are two phases of this proposal. The first is the chartering phase and to charter a ship is to rent a ship. It is not proposed that the chartering shall last beyond the life of the program, so that other than the ships that are lost at sea, or damaged, we will get them all back at the termination of the lease.

Second, in respect to the chartered ships, they must be declared to be in excess of the current requirements by the Maritime Commission.

Senator THOMAS of Utah. That is right.

MONEY SAVED

Ambassador DOUGLAS. And it will save us money. It will save us about $100 million. The dollar cost of shipping cargo to Europe, the drain of dollars on European countries, amounts, as I recollect the figure, to about $1,157 million over the period on coal alone. Shipping about 48 million tons a year will exhaust, in American bottoms, about $430 million. That is the magnitude of the drain of dollars imposed on the European countries by the use of ships flying the American flag. If they have ships flying under their own flags, even though their costs were the same as ours—their costs of operation—they would be paying the freight in their own currency and not in ours.

Senator SMITH. That is just my point in the whole discussion.

Ambassador DOUGLAS. That is the point in your discussion.

As to the sale, the ships pass permanently out of our control and do not come back. The savings on account of the sale of ships will be less during the first year or 15 months, and will increase thereafter. That is so because of the 25 percent down payment that is required under the Merchant Ship Sales Act, with a smaller payment—I think it is 5 percent in each succeeding year—for 15 years after that. The savings after the first year through the sale of ships is greater than are the savings during the first year. In chartering the opposite is the case. The total savings for the first year would amount to about $154 million, I believe, of which $100 million would be on account of the chartering of the vessels and $54 million on account of the proposal that 200 be sold.

The CHAIRMAN. Mr. Ambassador, you know this problem and you know our problems better than we do. Have you any suggestions that would be helpful in at least partially fending off the assault which lurks?

Ambassador DOUGLAS. Repelling the boarders?

LEAVING OUT PARAGRAPH 4 SUGGESTED

Senator THOMAS of Utah. Let me offer you a suggestion before you answer. Would it hurt this bill at all to leave out paragraph 4? Couldn't you do everything under the bill without it that you want to do?

Ambassador DOUGLAS. Yes. It would cost more money.

Senator THOMAS of Utah. Could you not even do what you want to do there under the bill without that paragraph?

Senator GEORGE. In other words, do it and say nothing about it.

Ambassador DOUGLAS. No, sir. I think under paragraph 4 there is today a prohibition in the Merchant Marine Act against doing this.

Senator THOMAS of Utah. There is a prohibition in the Surplus Property Act in which all of the ships that are sold have to be declared surplus by the Maritime Commission instead of by the surplus property administrator. That was put in. But I still think we have disposed of some surplus ships in spite of that.

I am wondering if you merely have to overcome, then, the prohibition against the sale of ships which has been put there as a result of the Surplus Property Act.

Ambassador DOUGLAS. I am not clear that it is the result of the Surplus Property Act. Perhaps, in order to know what the facts are, I had better look this up. I am quite certain, however, that the prohibition against charters is in the Merchant Marine Act. Is that right?

Mr. GROSS. It is in the Ship Sales Act, giving priority to American citizens. If you deleted paragraph 4, the net effect would be to take away the Maritime Commission's right to certify the ships as being excess, which is quite important.

Senator THOMAS of Utah. Probably we could do it "except as to those ships" inserted in your parentheses in your first section.

Ambassador DOUGLAS. Let's see what we can do with this.

The CHAIRMAN. All right.

Ambassador DOUGLAS. (5) is more contentious than (4). That is permanent transfer.

Senator THOMAS of Utah. Of course, the theories that I have been talking about would hold both for (4) and (5).

Ambassador DOUGLAS. That is right.

The CHAIRMAN. Do you think that with a little time you could disguise this?

Senator THOMAS of Utah. I do not mean to disguise it, but the fact remains, if you are going into a prize fight, the shorter you know it is the better you are off.

The CHAIRMAN. That is the theory I am talking about.

Senator LODGE. We will get an expression from Secretary Forrestal too, I hope.

The CHAIRMAN. Are you pointing to me?

Senator LODGE. No; to Dr. Wilcox.

The CHAIRMAN. Dr. Wilcox, you are pointed at.

Dr. WILCOX. We will have it.

ESTABLISHMENT OF CREDITS BY ADMINISTRATOR AND OPERATING PROCEDURES

The CHAIRMAN. Let's move on down to something that a tired mind can have less difficulty with—(b), at the bottom of page 19:

The Administrator may provide for the performance of any of the functions described in subsection (a) of this section—

And then something comes out and this comes in—

(1) by establishing accounts against which, under regulations prescribed by the Administrator—

(i) letters of commitment may be issued in connection with supply programs approved by the Administrator (and such letters of commitment, when issued, shall constitute obligations of applicable appropriations); and

(ii) withdrawals may be made by participating countries, or agencies or organizations representing participating countries, upon presentation of contracts, invoices, or other documentation specified by the Administrator.

Does somebody want to explain that?

Dr. WILCOX. I think Mr. Gross might.

Mr. GROSS. That is intended to permit the administrator to establish credits which can be drawn against by a participating country, or the representative of a participating country, and this is an attempt to make explicit the procedures by which those credits will be operated. This is purely a mechanical section, lines 12 through 16, and that is the way it now operates under Public Law 84. The administrator may issue this so-called letter of commitment, which does obligate whatever amount the letter authorizes to be obligated. The letter of commitment can then be used by a purchaser on behalf of a participating country to purchase commodities which are part of an approved program, a program approved by the administrator.

HOW GOODS WILL BE PURCHASED

Senator LODGE. Does this envisage a purchasing commission by each one of these countries, or purchasing by an American purchasing service, or normal commercial types of transactions, or how? How is this money that we appropriate going to be converted into goods for the utilization of these European nations?

Mr. GROSS. Any one of the alternatives that you mention would be available to a participating country or to the Administrator. The participating country could set up a supply mission or utilize a firm here as its agent, as has been the case with the countries that have received assistance under the interim aid program.

Senator LODGE. Has that worked out well?

Mr. GROSS. Yes, it has. That has been the normal method of making the purchases.

Senator LODGE. In the case of Greek relief, don't we do all the purchasing ourselves?

Mr. GROSS. No, sir; it is a combination. We are authorized to procure, and we do a considerable amount of procuring, through the Federal Bureau of Supply. But the recipient countries themselves are authorized to, and do in fact, conduct their own procurement to a very large extent under the interim aid program.

Senator LODGE. I should think it would be so much better, that unless you are going to have normal commercial transactions, you have the purchasing done by an American purchasing agency. I think you would save a lot of money and avoid a lot of graft, and certainly make it much easier to justify.

Mr. GROSS. I think that will prove to be the case in the bulk items, like wheat. I think direct procurement by participating countries or their agents will probably be machinery or special type items, shopping around for types of commodities or services. But either course is open to the Administrator and it would be entirely in his discretion as to which method of procurement were undertaken.

Ambassador DOUGLAS. Many of these procurement, or practically all of these procurement, devices, are in existence now. They have been used by participating countries in the purchase of commodities out of their own resources and by participating countries that have received no support from us except for the bulk purchases, which have generally been made by the Commodity Credit or by the Federal Bureau of Purchases, I think it is called, of the Treasury.

SUPERVISION OF PURCHASING

Senator LODGE. Suppose you have a foreign purchasing mission in Washington that is going around buying machinery and so on. Isn't the recovery administrator going to supervise him at all, to see that he gets control so that he won't blow it all in?

Ambassador DOUGLAS. The program has to be approved by the Administrator, otherwise his letter of commitment is worthless.

Senator LODGE. I do not mean just the plan; I mean the actual purchase, so that you won't have things happen such as have happened in the past.

Ambassador DOUGLAS. Assuming there is a program which contemplates the purchase of a few tractors, for example, that program would have to be submitted by the participating country to the Administrator—the kind, size, and cost of the tractors would have to be included in the program, and he, presumably, would not approve of that part of the program and issue a commitment until he had that information. But I should think we would get into a very complicated administrative problem ourselves if we tried to do all the purchasing of a vast variety of different commodities for each one of the participating countries.

Senator LODGE. How about supervising the purchasing, though, seeing to it that they get value received? Some of the people I have seen on purchasing missions——

Ambassador DOUGLAS. But the program consists, let us say, among other things, of X tractors of a certain size, of a certain quality, at a certain price. The Administrator would review that program, and if he found that the price was right, the price of that particular type of tractor was right, he would then issue the commitment, and the purchase could not exceed the commitment which had been made, and he would be required to receive the type of tractor which was included within the program.

Senator LODGE. Will there be somebody to see that he got it?

Mr. GROSS. That is controlled by this presentation of the invoice. It is then drawn against the commitment. The invoice is the check.

Senator SMITH. Who negotiates that price, the parties themselves? They negotiate the price?

Mr. NITZE. I think a good case in point is the present procurement of coal. In the case of the French, that is not done by the French Government. It is done by an agency representing the coal consuming industries of France, the dealers of France, as a single agency which represents all of the coal consumers in France, and he negotiates over here for the purchase of coal that is allotted to him by the Department of Commerce. He takes his negotiation and then he submits the contract to the people who are now administering the Foreign Aid program and gets their approval as to the contract. On the submission of the documents showing that the coal has moved and has been delivered, payment is made, so that you get complete control over the program, but it is still between private sellers here and a representative of private purchasers in France.

I think there would be great objection, for instance, on the part of the U.S. coal industry, to a change in that procedure, because that has worked out more efficiently than direct procurement by the Treasury Bureau of Supplies in several instances.

Ambassador DOUGLAS. One has a check first through the Administrator's approval of the program, and second through the documents, the invoices that have to be submitted before the commitment which has been issued to the purchase will be honored.

Senator SMITH. You do not think we are tying down our Administrator too much by these provisions? Suppose he had a little different conception of the setup and there was some language in here that would cramp his style.

FOLLOWTHROUGH ON LOANS

The CHAIRMAN. What does Jack McCloy mean when he testifies that when he makes a loan he hands it out in small quantities and follows it from the cradle to the grave? He follows it all the way to be sure that it is used just as the borrower promised to use it, and that every condition which he has stipulated is being fulfilled? Is there any followthrough of that sort in this bill?

Ambassador DOUGLAS. Yes, there is. Definite language has been drafted. I think I can tell you how the bank does it.

The CHAIRMAN. If you have it in here, never mind.

CHANCES OF GRAFT AND FRAUD

Senator GEORGE. There would not be any way to prevent a certain amount of grafting and fraud here if they wanted to do it; but after all, it depends on the vigilance of the Administrator and how effectively he administers his own regulations, how he may enforce them, because all that happens here, of course, is that there is always one fundamental check on purchases that are made by any outside government, foreign government. When they are using their own money they are interested in getting value. But when we are putting up the money and setting up these credits against which these transactions are all debited and credited, they haven't got that incentive, and you can have a good deal of graft. There is no question about that. There are credits that are to be set up here for transactions within this country, and there are also to be transactions set up in other parts of the world outside of the United States, and there isn't very much way that you could follow up unless you had somebody to go to see that the purchasing agent didn't make a corrupt contract with the seller and that the seller invoiced him properly. There is not much way of doing that, except the experience and ability and effectiveness of the administration itself, which can look at things and say whether these prices are out of line or they are in line and they are regular, and from all the information available, so many of these should cost this and should not cost more, and in that way, of course, to keep a fair check.

Temptation is always very great when one fellow is furnishing the money and also is paying the bills and the other man is just getting the use of it to do a little grafting.

Ambassador DOUGLAS. That experience is true even at home on ourselves.

Senator GEORGE. Yes; we find it to be true, and that is no way to avoid it. I mean, there is no way to a void the opportunity for that kind of thing, because it can be done, and obviously the Administrator, without an Army, could not possibly send out somebody to observe every transaction.

Ambassador DOUGLAS. It would be impossible.

The CHAIRMAN. I think we would all be happier.

Ambassador DOUGLAS. He can have a series of spot checks.

Senator GEORGE. Yes, he can do that. They can do a good deal of it.

Ambassador DOUGLAS. He can use certain instrumentalities of credit by which he can support his own vigilance and observation.

Senator GEORGE. We have had it here. I have seen it in my State, where county after county bought a lot of road machinery. Invoices were always 10 to 15 percent above what the cost of the machines was, yet the money was coming out of public funds.

Senator LODGE. In this case, if something like this comes to light, it will pretty well knock this thing in the head.

Senator GEORGE. It would. Most of it will be hidden. Most of it will be hidden and never come out.

Senator WILEY. You have fellows in Washington now, soliciting the manufacturers and so forth, giving the impression that they will have an "in" on sales and orders and stuff. A letter was brought in to my office the other day. That is why I have been very insistent on trying to get out the best methods and means of procurement, because we have taken the people's money and if we are going to pay out two or three times what the articles are worth to send to Europe, we are not fulfilling a sacred trust.

Senator GEORGE. This is only a permissive course that the Administrator may pursue. He can do anything under subsection (a) that we have been spending some time on. He may, if he wishes to or decides to do it, proceed under this method here. I can see, of course, that there would be chances for graft, but I think that is simply inevitable, because in a large program of this kind you can not safeguard yourself against all possibilities. It comes back to the Administrator and how strong an organizational setup he has.

POSSIBILITY OF CENTRALIZING RESPONSIBILITY FOR EUROPEAN COUNTRIES

Senator LODGE. Mr. Ambassador, is there some way that you can centralize the responsibility in these European countries, having a sort of RFC set up within a European country, and more or less trying to centralize activities there, so as to put the responsibility on Europeans? Or are you going to have to have all this diffusion, with some of it done one way and some another?

Ambassador DOUGLAS. I am again caught on the horns of a delimma. One of the purposes is to try to encourage the revival of normal individual-to-individual transactions

Senator LODGE. That is right.

Ambassador DOUGLAS. That may lead to graft in certain instances. And, as Senator George has said, it will be reduced to the very minimum, even though it may not be entirely wiped out, according to the strength of the Administrator and the quality of his staff.

The alternative is to require the 16 participating countries to modify their purchasing procedures and establish some centralized governmental agencies through which the purchasing is to be done. If you adopt that course, it would be inconsistent with the other purpose, which is to encourage the revival of ordinary, normal commercial transactions.

Senator LODGE. You have seen the suggestion made that the countries establish an RFC of their own and conduct their economic activities under this bill through that. Your point is that would defeat the revival of individual transactions.

Ambassador DOUGLAS. That is right.

The CHAIRMAN. That collides completely with the viewpoint of these rebellious Republicans, who want to put everything on a project-to-project basis, which is the exact opposite.

Senator LODGE That is right.

[Discussion was continued off the record.]

SAFEGUARDS AGAINST GRAFT AND CORRUPTION

The CHAIRMAN. What can we do with the bill, in the light of this discussion——

Senator GEORGE. I do not see, so far as this particular provision of the bill is concerned, that there is very much more that can be done to better it.

Senator SMITH. It is all permissive.

Senator GEORGE. And the Administrator will find it necessary to do this. He will undoubtedly find it necessary to use this. That is the way bankers and others do in this country, as individuals, you know.

Senator LODGE. Senator George, couldn't you say, if there is any crookedness or graft, and they get caught, that the project ceases?

Senator GEORGE. I suppose that undoubtedly the Administrator will say that, Senator, in establishing this. He may do so under such regulations as he wishes to prescribe, and he would certainly try to safeguard against anything of that kind.

Senator THOMAS of Utah. The ordinary code would cover any criminal act, would it not?

Senator LODGE. Not abroad.

It might look nice to have something like that in the bill.

Mr. RICE. Section (5) gives him broad termination powers.

Senator LODGE. I know about the termination powers, but I wanted to spell out that we are opposed to graft.

Senator GEORGE. I have no objection to that, Mr. Chairman.

The CHAIRMAN. Where would that go?

Ambassador DOUGLAS. A new section was drafted which, as I recollect, had to do with termination of assistance.

FOLLOW UP SYSTEM

The CHAIRMAN. It occurs to me that I think we would all be happier with the rest of the things we are doing if we turn to page 34 and go over this new langauge, because it deals with the precise concept that we are discussing. Look at page 34, Senator George.

Senator GEORGE. "Termination of Assistance."

The CHAIRMAN. And the paragraph preceding. Let's take these up.

(e) The Administrator shall encourage the joint organization of the participating countries referred to in subsection (b) of section 14 of this act to ensure that each participating country makes efficient use of the resources of such country, including any commodities, facilities, or services furnished under this act, by observing and reviewing such use through an effective followup system approved by the joint organization.

What is section 14(b)?

Ambassador DOUGLAS. Section 14(b) refers to conditions precedent.

The CHAIRMAN. I do not know why the followup system has to be approved by the joint organization.

Ambassador DOUGLAS. I raised some question about that phrase, "by the joint organization."

The CHAIRMAN. I do not think that makes sense. You are going to audit somebody according to the method that the guy who is going to be audited is satisfied to let you audit him with.

Senator LODGE. I move we strike that out.

Senator SMITH. I thought this had to do with the individual countries.

Ambassador DOUGLAS. That language, as I understand it, was drafted to meet a view expressed by one or two members of the committee that the joint organization itself should undertake to review the use of commodities and resources. Is that historically correct?

Dr. WILCOX. That is right, Mr. Ambassador. It is due to the fact that several members of the committee expressed very deep approval of Mr. McCloy's thought that the followup system ought not only be a part of the joint organization, but it should not be made up of Americans, that it ought to be made up of Europeans themselves who would be agents of the joint organization.

Senator LODGE. It was not ever thought that that would be the only followup system.

Dr. WILCOX. The United States, under the bilateral agreements, would have certain conditions which it would have to check up on, but this particular followup system envisaged here we had thought would be the mechanism of the joint organization.

The CHAIRMAN. Perhaps I am just confusing things by jumping around.

Senator GEORGE. This administrator will undertake to encourage this joint activity, so as to bring about some integration of their efforts, some unification of their efforts.

TERMINATION OF ASSISTANCE

The CHAIRMAN. We can take up "Termination of Assistance," can we not? Let's look at that.

SEC. 15. The Administrator, in determining the form and measure of assistance provided under this Act to any participating country, shall take into account the extent to which such country is complying with its undertakings embodied in its pledges to other participating countries and to its agreement concluded with the United States under section 14. The Administrator shall terminate the provision of assistance under this Act to any participating country whenever he determines that (1) such country is not adhering to its agreement concluded under section 14, and that in the circumstances remedial action other than termination will not more effectively promote the purposes of this Act or (2) because of changed conditions, assistance is no longer consistent with the national interest of the United States.

Senator GEORGE. That is all right, Mr. Chairman, but that rather refers to the entire program with a country, and does not quite reach what Senator Lodge had in mind.

Senator LODGE. This refers to the conditions precedent.

Senator GEORGE. This refers immediately to the credits that are going to be set up, and in the case of any fraud we could very well direct the administrator that he could very well cancel.

Senator LODGE. But not under this section.

The CHAIRMAN. Well, I guess there is nothing to do but go back where we were and keep on plugging. I was getting a little tired of all this arithmetic.

USE OF LETTERS OF COMMITMENT

Ambassador DOUGLAS. The letters of commitment, Senator, that are made permissive under the subsection the committee has just been considering, may not be used for off-shore purchases outside of the continental limits of the United States.

Senator LODGE. Do you mean that proviso beginning on line 5?

Ambassador DOUGLAS. The credits would be set up in the United States. The credits would not be set up outside.

CERTIFICATION FOR PURCHASES OUTSIDE U.S. CONTINENTAL LIMITS

Senator GEORGE. But it is provided that such expenditures for commodities or purchases procured outside the continental limits of the United States under authority of this paragraph may be accounted for exclusively on such certification as the administrator may prescribe.

Senator LODGE. Is it the purpose of that to enable the administrator to get raw materials in Latin America for European use, and have the

Europeans repay the Latin Americans in some commodities, to promote barter between Latin American and Europe?

Ambassador DOUGLAS. No; that is not the purpose of that.

Senator LODGE. That is not in this?

Ambassador DOUGLAS. No, sir.

Senator LODGE. We had a lot of testimony about that clearinghouse idea, and developing triangular trade without dollars passing.

Ambassador DOUGLAS. Except to American manufacturers, as I recollect it. Isn't that right? Am I not right? The dollars were passed out, but they went to the American manufacturers.

GUARANTIES OF INVESTMENTS

The CHAIRMAN [reading].

(2) by utilizing the services and facilities of any department, agency, or establishment of the Government as the President shall direct, or with the consent of the head of such department, agency, or establishment, in the President's discretion, by acting in cooperation with the United Nations or with other international organizations or with agencies of the participating countries, and funds allocated pursuant to this section to any department, agency, or establishment of the Government shall be established in separate appropriation accounts on the books of the Treasury;

(3) by making, under rules and regulations to be prescribed by the Administrator, guaranties to any person of investments in connection with projects approved by the Administrator and the participating country concerned as furthering the purposes of this Act, which guaranties shall terminate not later than fourteen years from the date of enactment of this Act: *Provided*, That—

(i) the guaranty to any person shall not exceed the amount of dollars invested by such person in the project with the approval thereof by the Administrator and shall be limited to the transfer into United States dollars of other currencies or credits in such currencies received by such person as income from the approved investment, as repayment or return thereof, in whole or in part, or as compensation for the sale or disposition of all or any part thereof;

(ii) the total liabilities assumed under such guaranties shall not exceed 5 per centum of the total funds appropriated for the purposes of this Act and any liabilities accruing under such guaranties shall be defrayed out of funds so appropriated; and

(iii) as used in this paragraph, the term "person" means a citizen of the United States or any corporation, partnership, or other association created under the law of the United States or of any State or Territory and substantially beneficially owned by citizens of the United States.

I guess we had better draw a long breath at that point.

This means, as I understand it, that the guaranty is solely a guaranty of convertibility.

Ambassador DOUGLAS. And then only in the event the enterprise is profitable, and only to the extent of the invested capital.

Senator WILEY. What do you mean by that first statement, profitable?

Ambassador DOUGLAS. If it is a losing enterprise, of course, there is nothing to be transferred unless, of course, it is sold.

Senator LODGE. What is the nature of the project for which such a guaranty shall be made?

Ambassador DOUGLAS. It might, for example, take the form of——

The CHAIRMAN. An oil refinery——

Ambassador DOUGLAS [continuing]. To refine Middle Eastern oil, an American enterprise; an American company or individual might undertake to make a capital investment for the purpose of constructing an oil refinery, and might seek a guaranty under this provision of the Act. That guaranty would then apply, and could be invoked only in the event the project was a profitable one, in the event that the investor could not transfer his profits into dollars; and finally, he could invoke the guaranty up to, but not beyond, the amount of capital which he had invested. In other words it is not contemplated, and this guaranty cannot be invoked, for the purpose of transferring profits.

Senator LODGE. The guaranty shall only take effect in the change of dollars for local currencies. That is the only way the guaranty takes effect?

The CHAIRMAN. And then only for the initial investment.

Senator LODGE. Why do you have a 14-year time limit?

Ambassador DOUGLAS. Because it will take 14 years to amortize the capital invested.

Senator LODGE. I was wondering why you could not make it even longer. In this matter of strategic materials, we might want to make a contract for a longer period of time.

Ambassador DOUGLAS. There is no time limitation for a loan made under the bill to be repaid in strategic materials. This was a time limitation upon the ability of a person to invoke this guaranty.

WAY IN WHICH GUARANTY OPERATES

The CHAIRMAN. Mr. Ambassador, where do you get the money 14 years hence to operate this guaranty?

Ambassador DOUGLAS. This guaranty would operate in the following way: Let's assume the investment of $10 million to which this guaranty had been extended. The amount of the guaranty would have to be considered as an expenditure as the bill is presently drawn and if the money is appropriated.

The CHAIRMAN. Is there any charge against the first year's appropriation?

Ambassador DOUGLAS. Yes, sir, the full amount of the guaranty.

The CHAIRMAN. The full amount of the guaranty is set aside?

Senator GEORGE. Would that be setup on the books as soon as it is made?

Ambassador DOUGLAS. So that there is no contingent liability being setup against some future appropriation.

The CHAIRMAN. So that the first thing you do is to set aside 5 percent of your appropriation?

Ambassador DOUGLAS. No, you set aside the amount of the guaranty as it is made, and the total guaranty shall not exceed 5 percent of the total amount appropriated.

Senator WILEY. If we are going to build any power plants in Europe, I presume it would be under some such method as you have suggested. There would be this guaranty there. In other words, under this bill, if we arranged $5 billion this year, there would be $250 million that could be used for guaranty purposes, and immediately that would be considered as an expenditure.

Ambassador DOUGLAS. That is right. The guaranty when made will be considered an obligation. It is set aside so that there is no accumulation of contingent liability.

Senator WILEY. It is considered as an obligation, but at the same time on the books it would appear just the same as if you expended that for something else, so it is really taken out of the $5 billion, which is my figure.

Senator GEORGE. If you finally came back and you did not have to make good the guaranty, it would be a profit and loss transaction.

Ambassador DOUGLAS. That is right, but it would have performed the same dollar service for the participating country as though it had been expended directly by the administrator for the same purpose.

LANGUAGE CONCERNING KINDS AND EXTENT OF ECONOMIC ACTIVITIES SUGGESTED

Senator LODGE. I would like to raise a point there, about having some language in the report which would make it clear that this bill contemplates economic activities of various kinds which will extend over a period of years. I think that is of interest, and I think it improves the attraction of the bill. You have this matter, and then you have the point Senator Wiley spoke of, and then as I understand it, it is the plan of the administrator, is it not, to make arrangements for deliveries of strategic raw materials over a period of years exceeding this act, and it might even be that for the future it is planned that we shall pay for all these strategic raw materials, because you figure them in when you compute the nations' unfavorable trade balance. But in 10 or 15 years they might be able to send us some of that as barter, where it would not be necessary. I think all of that ought to be stated in the report, because I think it opens up some very attractive prospects.

Ambassador DOUGLAS. Specifically, the administrator, under the language of the bill, might make a loan and require the repayment of the loan in strategic raw materials. That would be the same. It would have the same effect as though the debtor had sold us the raw materials, acquired the raw materials and applied the dollars against the loan.

Senator LODGE. There you are. I do not think it is necessary to write what the Ambassador just said in the bill, but I do think it should be stated somewhere in the report that they intend to do it. I think it is good news.

The CHAIRMAN. Do you follow this discussion, Dr. Wilcox?

Dr. WILCOX. Yes, sir, I have duly made note thereof.

CHECK ON GUARANTY

Senator WILEY. This one contemplates, you say, a guaranty virtually of repayment. Mr. X enters into this arrangement with country Y to build an oil plant, or build one of these powerplants. Now we come to the point: What check have you got on that if he wants the guaranty? He wants the Government to guaranty repayment. But it would be easy enough, as was suggested heretofore by Senator George that he knows how these Europeans will take us if we permit them, to check a plant that might cost $50 million, and it goes up to $100 million.

Ambassador DOUGLAS. In the first place the guaranty applies only to an American citizen.

Senator WILEY. He is building the plant and it is his. He is the American citizen.

Ambassador DOUGLAS. It is his. He is not building it for someone else. He is not building it for a Frenchman or an Italian, or a French corporation or Italian corporation. He is building it for his own beneficial interest.

Senator WILEY. That is a condition, then, that he has title?

The CHAIRMAN. He has to sell it first, hasn't he?

Ambassador DOUGLAS. He may sell it later on.

The CHAIRMAN. That is what I mean. But the guaranty is not designed for the purpose of guarantying the type of project which was to be built for the primary purpose of subsequent sale. It was for the encouraging the investment of American dollars in enterprises and projects that are a part of a country's program for the purpose of producing the commodities which might be produced by that project.

CASHING IN ON GUARANTY

Now follow Senator Wiley's example through. When does his friend X cash in on his guaranty, and how does he do it?

Ambassador DOUGLAS. How does the American citizen cash in on his guaranty?

The CHAIRMAN. Yes.

Ambassador DOUGLAS. Let's assume 2 years from now the plant is constructed, it is a profitable enterprise, he is earning francs—this is a plant that has been constructed in France—but he can not transfer his francs back into dollars. He is an American citizen. The beneficial interest is in an American. He then invokes this section. He then says, "I want this guaranty to be honored, and I want the francs I have earned to be transferred back into dollars," and the guaranty would then have to be honored.

The CHAIRMAN. And is that the only type of situation in which he could invoke his guaranty?

Ambassador DOUGLAS. He might sell the project and receive francs for it, and he could then, in the event that he found it unable to transfer the francs into dollars, invoke the guaranty. But in neither case could he invoke the guaranty beyond the amount of the original dollar investment. If he sold the plant at a profit in terms of francs he could not invoke a guaranty for the entire sum which he received. He would only invoke it up to, but not beyond, his original actual dollar investment.

The CHAIRMAN. And if you ever reestablished normal, standard exchange, there would be no use for the guaranty under any circumstances.

GUARANTY APPLIES TO AFRICAN COLONIES

Senator WILEY. Would this apply to the colonies in Africa of any of these 16 countries?

The CHAIRMAN. I think it would.

Ambassador DOUGLAS. Yes, I think it would.

Senator WILEY. One of the plans contemplated now by Britain is opening up a tremendous coal mine in one of her colonies in Africa. In other words, this would be a pretty good way for American financiers, if they thought there was a chance to make some real money, to do so. They might be willing to take the risk. I think it is a good idea.

STRATEGIC MATERIALS CLAUSE

The CHAIRMAN. We will go on to page 23 (c):

(c) (i) The Administrator may provide assistance for any participating country, in the form and under the procedures authorized in subsections (a) and (b), respectively, of this section, through grants or upon payment in cash or on credit terms or on such other terms of payment as he may find appropriate, including payment by the transfer to the United States under such terms and in such quantities as may be agreed to between the Government of the United States and the participating country of materials which are required by the United States as a result of deficiencies or potential deficiencies in its own natural resources—

That is the strategic materials clause, I assume—

In determining whether such assistance shall be through grants or upon terms of payment, and in determining the terms of payment, he shall act in consultation with the National Advisory Council on Monetary and Financial Problems, and the determination whether or not a participating country should be required to make payment for any assistance furnished to such country in furtherance of the purposes of this Act, and the terms of such payment, if required, shall depend upon the capacity of such country to make such payments without jeopardizing the accomplishment of the purposes of this Act.

Senator THOMAS of Utah. Mr. Chairman, may I ask why we have gone through such circumlocution in describing a strategic or critical material, and if we are trying to get out of the range of just the strategic and critical category? This seems pretty general, when we think only in terms of deficiencies, regardless of the material. Personally, I like to expand the strategic and critical notion as far as we can, but there is nothing in the Strategic Materials Act which is based upon the theory of simply deficiencies.

The CHAIRMAN. No; that is right.

Senator THOMAS of Utah. This, of course, is a bit in keeping with Mr. Baruch's notion of expanding it—anything that any nation produces and which we can use—and as a good old Cleveland free-trader, if we can get by with that we can get by with murder with you people up in the New England part of the country.

The CHAIRMAN. Do I get your point, that strategic and critical materials are not necessarily deficits?

Senator THOMAS of Utah. Yes, it is a new definition for strategic materials and critical materials. I think that it is a kind of good definition, Mr. Chairman. I am not objecting to it, but I do want to understand it.

LIMITATION TO DEFICIENT MATERIALS SUGGESTED

Senator LODGE. Don't you think you will save a lot of trouble if you limit yourself to materials that are deficient? When you arrange to bring in materials that are not deficient in this country you run into a lot of trouble.

Senator THOMAS of Utah. I do not know what constitutes deficiency. For instance, you have a deficiency in New England, and you put an embargo on the exportation of oil and things of that kind, but there may not be any deficiency in another part of the United States with regard to those things. The deficiency in New England is probably due to transportation and other things that come into our economic life.

Senator LODGE. This, of course, assumes a deficiency in the United States as a whole, and not New England.

Senator THOMAS of Utah. If it is a deficiency in the United States as a whole, I doubt very much whether we can even bring in nickel, for instance, because we might say, "Well, we have enough for our economy, but we are building stockpiles."

Senator LODGE. "Potential deficiencies" are pretty big words.

STOCKPILING STRATEGIC MATERIALS

Senator THOMAS of Utah. I wonder whether we are trying to tell other countries that we are not building stockpiles of strategic materials, yet every country on earth knows we have been doing that for a long time.

I would like to emphasize the stockpile wording a little bit better than this.

Senator LODGE. There is another place where this occurs in the bill, on page 31, which we ought to look at at the same time.

The CHAIRMAN. Paragraph (5) on page 31, facilitating the sale to the United States for stockpiling purposes.

Senator LODGE. I have an amendment I would like to offer to that one.

The CHAIRMAN. We have not got to that one yet.

Senator GEORGE. Senator Thomas, in that connection is it not considerably broader, and is it not intended to be broader because here the administrator is doing the best he can on any terms and conditions he sees fit to deal on?

Senator THOMAS of Utah. Probably this is an improvement upon just the strategic materials idea.

Senator GEORGE. It would include the strategic materials, but it is considerably broader.

Senator THOMAS of Utah. Copper is strategic, but it is not critical.

PURPOSE OF SECTIONS SO FAR AS EXPENDITURES ARE CONCERNED

Senator WILEY. Does either 23, which you just read, or that on page 31, attempt to place the limitation that, whatever the money is used for must be within the limit of, say, $5 billion a year? In other words, we certainly are going to have the right outside of this to buy whatever material we want to buy from anybody, anywhere. I was just wondering what the purpose was of these two sections so far as expenditures are concerned.

Ambassador DOUGLAS. In the section on 23, which we have been considering, the purpose is to make more clear than was otherwise the intent that if loans were extended to a country which had strategic materials, we could require the repayment of the loan in the strategic materials which that country possessed. There is nothing in the act to prohibit the purchase of strategic materials by appropriating sums to the Federal Purchasing Bureau, I think, or the strategic materials board, whichever it is, beyond anything that may be made available in this act.

The purpose of the language on 23 was, as I said, to clarify the intention and to expressly state the intention.

Senator WILEY. To try to get something for it if you can.

Senator THOMAS of Utah. We can bring in diamonds, for instance, from South Africa, under this provision?

Ambassador DOUGLAS. We can, if we can——

Senator THOMAS of Utah. Prove they are deficient.

Ambassador DOUGLAS. I think the ability to require repayment of a loan would depend upon our ability to negotiate that kind of loan. Diamonds are deficient in this country, because, aside from the great diamond hoax in Utah in 1878—either Utah or Idaho—we have no diamonds. A lot of diamonds had been salted in that instance. It took in some of the most distinguished engineers and geologists in the profession at the time. Aside from that, we have produced no diamonds.

Senator THOMAS of Utah. We are getting a few from Brazil, are we not? Are the Brazilian diamonds hard enough for industrial use?

Ambassador DOUGLAS. I think so. We bought some during the war.

BROADENING SECTION SUGGESTED

Senator LODGE. Would you object to putting a period after "United States"?

Ambassador DOUGLAS. No.

Senator GEORGE. That would make it still broader.

Senator LODGE. I know it would. You run into more trouble politically, but you get what you want more easily.

Ambassador DOUGLAS. You might add, and it would make the language even more circumlocutory than it now is, "and its potential requirements."

Senator THOMAS of Utah. Under this provision it seems to me Arizona could import water.

REFERENCE TO STRATEGIC MATERIALS ACT SUGGESTED

Senator LODGE. Why don't you refer to the Strategic Materials Act, with which you had so much to do, and just say "carry out the provisions of that Act"?

Senator THOMAS of Utah. I think that is better under the provision on page 31, but this is so gloriously general that it satisfies me entirely.

The CHAIRMAN. What are you kicking about?

Senator THOMAS of Utah. I am not kicking; I am just wondering. Every time somebody gets converted I feel so good over it I have to see if it is true.

The CHAIRMAN. You are very generous in not being personal with your observations.

IMPORTING FERTILIZER

Senator THOMAS of Utah. Let's get to something else, to some other material, to see what we can do.

Fertilizer is not a deficiency, but it is a scarce item. We would like to import certain fertilizers, but at the same time not retard the development of the fertilizing industry in America that has been just anxious for generations to be tapped, and still it is deficient.

Senator GEORGE. We do import, Senator. We get Chilean nitrate and we used to get potash before the war from abroad.

Senator THOMAS of Utah. When we get to page 31, let's see if we can't get a reference to the scripture on the subject.

The CHAIRMAN. Are we all right on page 23?

Senator THOMAS of Utah. I am perfectly satisfied.

Senator LODGE. You do not want to deal with the strategic materials question now?

The CHAIRMAN. No, thank you.

WHO IS "GOVERNMENT OF UNITED STATES"?

By the way, "as may be agreed to between the Government of the United States and the participating country." Who is the Government of the United States at that point?

Ambassador DOUGLAS. The Administrator, I think.

MAKING AND ADMINISTERING CREDITS

The CHAIRMAN. Now, over on page 24:

(ii) When it is determined that assistance should be extended under the provisions of this Act on credit terms, the Administrator shall allocate funds for the purpose to the Export-Import Bank of Washington, which shall, notwithstanding the provisions of the Export-Import Bank Act of 1945 (59 Stat. 526), as amended, make and administer the credit as directed, and on terms specified, by the Administrator in consultation with the said National Advisory Council. The Administrator shall make advances to or reimburse the Export-Import Bank of Washington for necessary administrative expenses in connection with such credits. The bank shall deposit into the Treasury of the United States as miscellaneous receipts amounts received by the bank in repayment of principal and interest of any such credits. Credits made by Export-Import Bank of Washington with funds so allocated to it by the Administrator shall not be considered in determining whether the bank has outstanding at any one time loans and guaranties to the extent of the limitation imposed by Section 7 of the Export-Import Bank Act of 1945 (59 Stat. 529), as amended.

Is there anything wrong with that?

Senator WILEY. As I understand this, Mr. Chairman, the whole function here is in two parts. First, the Administrator determines whether or not the loan shall be made and, when it is, the Export-Import Bank then is just the officiating agent to perfect the loan. They have no judgment at all in the matter.

The CHAIRMAN. None whatever.

Senator GEORGE. None whatever. It is purely an administrative matter.

The CHAIRMAN. Is the Administrator bound by the National Advisory Council at this point?

Ambassador DOUGLAS. No, sir. As I read the language, the Administrator consults with the National Advisory Council—lines 9, 10, and 11.

The CHAIRMAN. That is what I am looking at Ambassador Douglas.

* * * make and administer the credit as directed, and on terms specified, by the Administrator in consultation with the said National Advisory Council.

Senator WILEY. This is just the kind of loan on which you would get the Government guaranty.

Ambassador DOUGLAS. No, sir. The Government guaranty would not apply to a thing of this sort.

Senator WILEY. Why not? You said that only applied to individuals, American citizens, corporations, and so forth. This, you think, only applies to foreign countries?

Ambassador DOUGLAS. That is right, sir.

The CHAIRMAN. Well, you have been good boys and girls. Do you want to stop there until tomorrow morning? I am willing, reluctantly.

We are recessed until 10 o'clock in the morning.

[Whereupon, at 4:30 p.m., a recess was taken until 10 a.m. of the following day, Wednesday, February 11, 1948.]

EUROPEAN RECOVERY PROGRAM

WEDNESDAY, FEBRUARY 11, 1948

United States Senate,
Committee on Foreign Relations,
Washington, D.C.

The committee met, pursuant to adjournment, in the Committee Hearing Room, U.S. Capitol, at 10 a.m., Senator Arthur H. Vandenberg, chairman, presiding.

Present: Senators Vandenberg, Capper, Wiley, Smith, Lodge, George, Thomas of Utah, and Hatch.

Also present: The Hon. Lewis W. Douglas, Ambassador to Great Britain; Mr. Paul Nitze, deputy director, Office of International Trade Policy, Department of State; Mr. Ernest Gross, legal adviser, Department of State; Mr. Walter S. Surrey, legal division, Department of State; Mr. Stephen E. Rice, legislative counsel, U.S. Senate.

The Chairman. Mr. Rice, have we any knicknacks for this morning?

Mr. Rice. Yes, sir; we have a bunch of them.

Senator Smith. Mr. Chairman, might I ask you a question? I was called to the long distance telephone yesterday and I apologize for withdrawing so abruptly, but while I was out you disposed of page 23 and I had some correspondence with regard to certain phases of that. I am not prepared to bother the committee with it now, but I would like the privilege of discussing it with the staff, and especially with Steve Rice, and then, if there is something to the suggestion made to me, I will bring them back; otherwise I will not do anything about it.

Again, my friend Allen Dulles is making a suggestion, and he is a brother of the great John Foster Dulles.

The Chairman. I do not think you ought to keep repeating that.

Senator Smith. I am one of these frank fellows who believes in repeating everything he knows.

The Chairman. I am not clear that the implication follows all the way through.

Your caveat will be filed with respect to pages 22 and 23, in spite of the fact that Allen is Foster's brother.

Now let us go back and catch up with our knitting on the things we referred to Steve Rice & Co.

MEANING OF "PARTICIPATING COUNTRY"

On page 5 strike out section 3 and insert in lieu thereof the following:

As used in this Act the term "participating country" means—

(a) any country, together with its colonies and dependencies, which signed the report of the Committee of European Economic Cooperation at Paris on September 22, 1947; and

(b) any other country (including any of the zones of occupation of Germany; any areas under international administration or control; and the Free Territory of Trieste, or either of its zones) wholly or partly in Europe, together with its colonies and dependencies; Provided such country adheres to, and for so long as it remains an adherent to, a joint program for European recovery designed to accomplish the purposes of this act.

I would think that does it.

Senator SMITH. That picks up Iceland and Ireland because they signed; is that correct? They signed in Paris.

The CHAIRMAN. Yes, sir, and it takes three Irelands out of line 5 of the original text.

QUESTION OF WHEN WE START AID TO CHINA

Senator LODGE. If the question is raised—I am not going to raise it, but somebody will raise the question of when we start aid to China; Representative Herter is raising it all the time in the House; he is raising it to me personally all the time—what can we say?

The CHAIRMAN. You have to make a fundamental decision at that point, Senator. Is China coming into this plan, or is it going to be on its own? I do not believe anybody knows what the Chinese plan is.

Ambassador DOUGLAS. And whether China would sign a program of recovery.

Senator GEORGE. And basically whether we want to be diverted from the Western European problem at this time to face that.

Senator SMITH. It is not included in the $6,800 million, is it?

Ambassador DOUGLAS. No.

The CHAIRMAN. I quite agree it is going to be raised.

First, until I see the China plan, I do not know whether it integrates into this sort of program or not. My suspicion would be that it does not. If it does, OK. If it does not, OK. The time and events will disclose the facts, and I do not believe we can do anything about it until we get the facts.

Senator LODGE. That satisfies me all right, but I just wanted to bring up the fact that there are others that are going to bring it up all the time.

The CHAIRMAN. You just want to be able to say "I told you so."

Senator LODGE. You might say it to me.

Senator THOMAS of Utah. There is a place right in this act itself, or in the bill as it has been drawn up, to make this as broad as all outdoors and include the whole world. When you once setup the plan as we have setup the administration, without limitation, it would be foolish for anyone to say that if we moved into another sphere we would act entirely independently of these agencies that are going now. That isn't the way our Government has ever worked on anything. It will be just as sensible for us to say here that since this European Recovery Plan is something we have never done before, in just this way, and since it modifies so greatly our American foreign policy, we hereby declare that all contact with the State Department and past theory and other organizations is severed.

I think you will find when you read it over that on the recovery plan it is broad enough so that if a Chinese plan comes in or a Japanese plan, it may or not fit in, but there is nothing in the law to keep it from fitting in, if we want it to work.

The CHAIRMAN. That is a fact.

Senator THOMAS of Utah. And I think that is the answer.

Senator SMITH. My thought would be that we would pass special legislation for China and then put it into this plan. You are not objecting to this definition of participating countries?

Senator THOMAS of Utah. No, not in the least. That definition is wonderful, after the few remarks made about international organizations and so on. But for us to assume that we have foreclosed any consideration of other plans by this act puts us in a defensive position in which we do not want to be put, because Secretary Marshall, in his very first statement, said that other plans would be forthcoming and they will be forthcoming in the same orderly way that these plans came, and he mentioned China specifically.

Now, we cannot dodge Japan. Everybody knows that we are there and we are there alone, and it is a plan that will have to be worked out, but it can fit into the logic of this situation.

Senator SMITH. The chairman has asked for overall figures of all these programs, so we are on record as having contemplated the inclusion of those in some way in the overall picture, are we not?

Senator THOMAS of Utah. And we have not forgotten Asia. Just look around the committee table, and we know we have not forgotten Asia.

The CHAIRMAN. If the China thing comes to issue appropriately within the jurisdiction of this legislation and in time, we will simply write part II of this bill and there you are.

Senator SMITH. I think that is right.

Senator THOMAS of Utah. I think that is the answer.

SUBSTITUTE LANGUAGE CONCERNING PARTICIPATING COUNTRIES

The CHAIRMAN. Is there any complaint about the language of the substitute?

Senator THOMAS of Utah. I think it is fine.

The CHAIRMAN. How do your two votes stand on this?

Senator GEORGE. I think this is all right, but I am very greatly worried about how the occupation zones of Germany and areas under international administration and control, and the Free Territory of Trieste, and so forth, are going to participate, how they are going to enter into the participation agreement. I do not know who will act for them. I suppose that we might not get to that, or cross that bridge until we get to it. It looks like the definition is all right.

The CHAIRMAN. If the definition is all right, we will put that in the book.

Ambassador DOUGLAS. In the Free Territory of Trieste, when the Governor is appointed, if he is, he may act for that territory, and as such become a party to carry out the purposes of the act. Until he is appointed, then our own military governor in our zone in Trieste may act, and much the same situation will exist in regard to Western Germany, or Germany, when, as and if it is reconstituted; that is to say, the Government of Germany then might become a party to the program in the meantime.

Senator GEORGE. In the meantime is a rather long time at best.

Ambassador DOUGLAS. In the meantime the occupational authorities.

Senator GEORGE. I suppose that would be necessarily true.

Ambassador DOUGLAS. They would have to authenticate participation of Germany in the recovery program for Europe.

Senator GEORGE. And in large measure we would have to agree with ourselves.

Ambassador DOUGLAS. That is right, in large measure. It depends, of course, Senator, upon what happens in the French Zone.

Senator GEORGE. Yes, I know.

EXTENSION OF PRESIDENT'S AUTHORITY

The CHAIRMAN. We will move over to page 6, line 24: after the word "provide" insert "for a period of not to exceed 30 days after the date of enactment of this act", and on page 7, line 2, after the word "direct" insert the following new sentence:

> In the event the President nominates an Administrator or Deputy Administrator prior to the expiration of such thirty-day period, the authority conferred upon him by this subsection shall be extended beyond such thirty-day period, but only until an Administrator or Deputy Administrator qualifies and takes office.

Dr. Wilcox points out that we approved the theory of this amendment yesterday, and this simply puts it into text which I think is satisfactory, unless there is objection.

Senator SMITH. I only raise this question, Mr. Chairman: I think it is reasonably clear what we mean, but I am still bothered by the word "him"—"In the event the President nominates the Administrator, the authority conferred upon him" might be the President or it might be the Administrator. Why couldn't we say "the authority conferred upon the President by this subsection" instead of the word "him", to remove any possible ambiguity as to what we mean by "him"?

Senator GEORGE. I have no objection to it. I think it is clear, Senator, but I have no objection to it.

The CHAIRMAN. The change will be made and the amendment is approved as changed.

QUESTION OF LIAISON WITHIN BENEFICIARY COUNTRY

Page 10, at the end of line 16, insert the following new sentence: "He"—and he is the U.S. special representative abroad, and the question raised was regarding liaison within the beneficiary country; "He," I repeat being the U.S. roving Ambassador, "shall keep the Administrator, the Secretary of State, the chiefs of the U.S. diplomatic missions and the chiefs of the special missions provided for in section 9 of this act, fully and currently informed concerning his activities. He shall consult with the chiefs of all such missions, who shall render such assistance to him as he may require for the performance of his duties under this act."

Senator SMITH. That is slightly different from the text I have, Mr. Chairman.

Dr. WILCOX. This was substituted overnight.

Mr. RICE. The one everybody has is the one we worked up last night in my office, and the State Department reworked it this morning.

The CHAIRMAN. This text I have read has the approval of the State Department, is that correct?

Ambassador DOUGLAS. Yes, sir.

Senator THOMAS of Utah. I still think, in spite of what has been said and in spite of the State Department's approval, that, that adverb "fully" is going to be one of our troublesome things.

Ambassador DOUGLAS. That is the language used in the Brookings Report.

Senator THOMAS of Utah. Even then I think it is a bad one.

The CHAIRMAN. What do you mean, that you want to leave it out?

Senator THOMAS of Utah. Yes, I think any measure of amount of information is just an invitation for somebody who is unhappy to say that he did not "keep me fully informed." It carries strength to say "currently informed with respect to his activities." I do not know how anyone can keep anybody fully informed about anything, and even if you have all of the information you can still use that word as an alibi in case of trouble.

Senator SMITH. You would cut out "fully and"?

The CHAIRMAN. I am sure the State Department would not object to that change.

Senator THOMAS of Utah. I don't think they would.

Mr. GROSS. We have no objection.

The CHAIRMAN. Is there objection to taking "fully and" out?

With that change the amendment, without objection, is approved.

MEETINGS AND MEMBERSHIP OF BOARD

Page 12, line 20: This is the requirement about the meetings of the Board:

> The Board shall meet at least once a month and at other times upon the call of the Administrator, or when three or more additional members of the Board request the Administrator to call a meeting. Not more than a majority of two of the additional members appointed to the Board may belong to the same political party.

Mr. RICE. They are all the people not to exceed 12 additional members. Look at line 13, Senator.

Senator LODGE. I don't know what it means, then.

Senator GEORGE. Additional to the Administrator, who is the Chairman of the Board.

The CHAIRMAN. It is pretty clumsy, when read with the rest of it: "and not to exceed 12 additional members to be appointed by the President."

Ambassador DOUGLAS. Isn't "other" a better word than "additional"?

The CHAIRMAN. I do not know what you need it for at all, because you are talking about members appointed on the Board.

Ambassador DOUGLAS. I was talking about three or more members of the Board. What you mean is other members of the Board, not additional members.

The CHAIRMAN. Obviously, that is better—"other" instead of "additional" in line 5.

Mr. RICE. You will also want to change it in line 13 in the bill, too, I presume, if you change it down there.

Ambassador DOUGLAS. No. The one refers to the calling of the Board, the other refers to additional appointees.

Senator GEORGE. Yes. "The Board shall consist of the Administrator, who shall be chairman, and not to exceed 12 additional members."

It seems that that would be all right.

The CHAIRMAN. I do not know what you need "additional" or "other" for. It is sort of confusing.

Senator LODGE. I do not like the word "additional" in line 13 at all.

The CHAIRMAN. "* * * and at other times upon call of the Administrator or when three or more members of the Board request the Administrator." What do you have to say "additional" or "other" for, either one?

Ambassador DOUGLAS. The use of the word "additional" means, I take it that the Board may consist of 13 members, and if you strike out the word "additional" then the size of the Board cannot exceed 12.

The CHAIRMAN. I do not see what that has to do with it. The Board is already set up and the Administrator is in the Chair and 12 or less additional members. Then the Board shall meet at least once a month, and at other times upon the call of the Administrator, or when three or more members of the Board request the Administrator to call a meeting.

Mr. RICE. Senator, we put "additional" in there at that point so that it would be clear that the Administrator could not be counted in those three.

Senator SMITH. He does not have to have anybody.

Mr. RICE. If he joined with two other members, that would be your three.

The CHAIRMAN. He doesn't have to join with them, because he can call it himself. Let's take out both of those, and make it "when three or more members of the Board request the Administrator to call a meeting."

MEMBERSHIP OF BOARD

Now, this next sentence, it seems to me, is needlessly confusing:

> Not more than a majority of two of the additional members apointed to the Board may belong to the same political party.

Mr. RICE. Suppose you had seven additional members appointed. The language reads "not to exceed 12." That is what causes all the trouble. If it said 12 we would be all right. But when you say not to exceed 12 there may be only 7 members. You wanted a bipartisan outfit, so if there are only seven, then you would have four and three, and that would fall within that rule of not more than two belonging to one. If you had eight additional members, it would be five and three. That would be not more than two.

The CHAIRMAN. You are discussing something else. I am discussing purely the use of this word "additional" in defining members. I do not see why that is in. It is confusing. When you read it you wonder what it means: "Not more than a majority of two of the members appointed to the Board may belong to the same political party."

Mr. RICE. That is all right.

The CHAIRMAN. All right. Let us take out "additional." It requires half an hour's explanation.

With those changes the amendment is approved.

Ambassador DOUGLAS. Mr. Chairman, I think the striking of the word "additional" in line 13 of the Committee Print does have the effect of reducing the board to 12.

The CHAIRMAN. We did not strike that.

Ambassador DOUGLAS. I beg your pardon.

EMPLOYMENT AND APPOINTMENT TO FOREIGN SERVICE

The CHAIRMAN. Section 10: We have the Foreign Service in 2 paragraphs instead of 15 volumes. Section 10, page 14: Strike out all of section 10 down to line 18 on page 16. That is two pages. That is something. Insert in lieu thereof the following:

For the purpose of perfoming functions under this Act, outside the continental limits of the United States, the Administrator may—

(1) employ persons who shall receive compensation at any of the rates provided for the Foreign Service Reserve and Staff by the Foreign Service Act of 1946 (60 Stat. 999), together with allowances and benefits established thereunder;

Ambassador DOUGLAS. Then that should be "or in addition".

The CHAIRMAN [continuing].

(2) recommend the appointment or assignment of persons, and the Secretary of State may appoint or assign such persons, to any class in the Foreign Service Reserve or Staff for the duration of operations under this Act, and the Secretary of State may thereafter assign, transfer, or promote such persons upon the recommendation of the Administrator. Persons so appointed to the Foreign Service Staff shall be entitled to the benefits of Section 528 of the Foreign Service Act of 1946.

Senator LODGE. That gives the Secretary of State the veto of everybody, doesn't it?

Ambassador DOUGLAS. I do not so understand it. The administrator may employ anybody he chooses at any time.

Senator WILEY. Outside or in the service?

Ambassador DOUGLAS. Outside or in the service, and those whom he employs shall be entitled to all the emoluments and privileges——

Senator SMITH. This is a "may;" it is not a "must."

Ambassador DOUGLAS. No, it is not, and the persons so employed may receive all the benefits, emoluments and privileges of those in the Foreign Service; in addition to employing persons under an authority which is unrestricted, he may recommend to the Secretary of State that they also be appointed and covered into the Foreign Service.

The reason I raise the question about the use of the word "may" as to the Secretary's power to appoint upon the recommendation of the administrator, I think there is a case to be made for the use of the word "may" in order to maintain a reasonable amount of orderliness.

Senator LODGE. Anyway the Secretary of State should have the power to decide who is going to the Foreign Service.

Ambassador DOUGLAS. That is right. But that is merely an additional power which the administrator may exercise. It is no limitation upon his power to employ. Do you get that?

Senator LODGE. Yes, that is very clear.

Senator WILEY. Mr. Chairman, I want to get this clear if I can.

First the administrator is the boss of the job, and he does not have to look to anyone form whom he shall employ. He does not have to look to any group in Government, and he does not have to look any place else. All right, that is established.

Now, (1), the word "may" up there—if he does employ he can given them the same emoluments as the chaps in the Foreign Service have, or he can create some other basis of emolument, can't he, as provided in the bill as to compensation and so forth? Or he can throw them into this Foreign Service Reserve outfit, so that they have the privileges of that.

Ambassador DOUGLAS. Yes, he may do both.

Senator WILEY. All right. Then, under (2) he can recommend the appointment or assignment of persons. The Secretary of State may appoint or assign such persons to any class in the Foreign Service Reserve. What is the difference between (1) and (2)?

Ambassador DOUGLAS. Under (1), Senator, the administrator has a complete and unqualified authority to employ anybody he chooses in or out of Government. Persons so employed by him shall receive all of the privileges and emoluments and prerogatives of anybody in the Foreign Service.

Senator SMITH. That is mandatory, that part.

Ambassador DOUGLAS. Yes, and there is no restriction upon his authority to do it.

EMPLOYMENT AND APPOINTMENT POWERS

Senator WILEY. That does not agree with your previous answer to me. You say, once he employs them, they come in under this classification and they get all the emoluments.

Suppose you wanted to employ some without putting them into that Foreign Service business?

Ambassador DOUGLAS. The first one does not require them to be covered into the Foreign Service. It is an unrestricted authority vested in the administrator to employ anyone whom he chooses to employ, and he shall receive the emoluments and privileges, but they need not be covered into the Foreign Service.

Senator WILEY. Oh.

The CHAIRMAN. Wait a minute. I still think that it is not too clear. Do you mean that everbody he employs outside of the United States must be paid at the rates indicated in the Foreign Service and receive the benefits and compensation?

Ambassador DOUGLAS. That is right.

The CHAIRMAN. That is the compulsory pay scale.

Ambassador DOUGLAS. That is right.

Senator GEORGE. But it is at any of the rates for the different classifications.

The CHAIRMAN. It is really a ceiling.

Ambassador DOUGLAS. Yes. It would depend, I presume, upon the classification of the employee.

Now, as to (2), having employed somebody, he may then recommend to the Secretary of State that that person so employed be covered into the Foreign Service.

The CHAIRMAN. Why would he be interested in having him do that under any circumstances?

Ambassador DOUGLAS. He might be interested in doing it in order to preserve the rights and privileges of a government employee. He might employ somebody from within the government. Isn't that correct?

Senator SMITH. They would not lose their continuity.

Ambassador DOUGLAS. And there would not be a break in their employment.

The CHAIRMAN. This might be an additional inducement for employment in some specific instances.

Ambassador DOUGLAS. That is right. That is why I suggested the use of the word "may".

The CHAIRMAN. You strike out "and" and put in "or in addition".

MAKING UP DIFFERENCE IN PAY FROM PRIVATE INDUSTRY

Senator SMITH. As I understand it, under the Selective Service Act it was possible for an employer to make up compensation to somebody who might be drafted into the armed service. I do not see why we should not in this bill make it possible for the employer of some topnotch fellow, who could not afford because of his family requirements, to take one of these positions, to continue his pay to make up the difference. I would like to ask Mr. Rice whether that could not be properly phrased in here, so that if the president of General Motors wanted to lend us the vice president of General Motors for this thing, that pay could be made up without violating any law and without preventing any fellow from taking this compensation.

It seems to me we will get a lot of good men if they do not have to suffer financially by taking these jobs. I think there is a big opening for them. I do not recall the Selective Service provisions.

The CHAIRMAN. Would that be against the law as the situation stands? Could General Motors, under existing law, do that? Would it be impossible for General Motors to loan us a $50,000 vice president and make up the difference in his pay? Is that against the law?

Senator SMITH. I am afraid it would be.

Mr. RICE. I do not think so. I do not want to say categorically.

Senator SMITH. It was done in a lot of cases I know of under the Selective Service Act.

Mr. RICE. I may be wrong about it, Senator. I would like to look it up and be sure. During the war a great many people who went into the service had their salaries continued by their companies. The general prohibition is that you cannot get money from a private firm, corporation, or individual for doing governmental work. As I understand your proposition, General Motors would just continue to keep that man on their payroll because they wanted him to come back, and they would not be paying him because he was doing something under this act.

The CHAIRMAN. It is a sort of retainer.

Senator SMITH. They would probably pay the difference between what the Government pays him and what he got before.

The CHAIRMAN. This is loaded with dynamite.

Senator SMITH. I am raising the question whether we wouldn't be offering an inducement in giving a larger range to get topnotchers by that process.

Ambassador DOUGLAS. Quite irrespective of the law and prohibitions which may be imposed, a person who took an important position at the head of an economic mission in one of the important countries, and who still received compensation from the corporation or outfit for which he had been previously working, might at some time fall under a cloud unless there were specific legislative authority for him to do so.

The CHAIRMAN. He might fall under a cloud anyway, with or without the legislation.

Senator SMITH. If the interests of that corporation became mixed up in it, there would be that danger.

What would be your reaction to this?

Ambassador DOUGLAS. It would give you larger latitude and widen the field of selection, but it raises a question about which personally I have always had some doubt about people in Government service.

Senator SMITH. That can be explored.

The CHAIRMAN. For the time being, we will pass this amendment as amended.

Mr. RICE. Senator, before you get away from it, I think that should be in the conjunctive, and the "and" ought to be in there instead of "or".

Ambassador DOUGLAS. I agree.

Mr. RICE. If you say "and" he can employ them all under (1), all under (2) or he can employ them under both. If you say "or" he has to do one or the other.

The CHAIRMAN. All right; we are back to "and".

APPOINTMENT OF ALIEN CLERKS AND EMPLOYEES

On page 16, that still leaves in one paragraph. The only paragraph left in on page 16 in this major surgery is commencing on line 19:

(b) For the purpose of performing functions under this Act outside the continental limits of the United States, the Secretary of State may, at the request of the Administrator, appoint, for the duration of operations under this act, alien clerks and employees in accordance with applicable provisions of the Foreign Service Act of 1946 (60 Stat. 999).

That is obviously indispensable.

EMPLOYEE INVESTIGATION BY THE FBI

Then, at the bottom of page 17, strike out lines 21 and 22 (this is with regard of the FBI) so it would read:

Civilian personnel who are citizens of the United States appointed pursuant to this section to perform functions under this act shall be appointed subject to investigation by the Federal Bureau of Investigation, which shall make a report thereof to the appointing authority as soon as possible: *Provided, however* . . .

and so forth.

Senator LODGE. I think that is all right. But yesterday I raised the question of the Administrator having his own security service, and it did not seem to strike anybody here as very important. I certainly think we ought to be sure that this bill authorizes him to do that, because if he has any sense of self-preservation at all he is going to have a pretty good security service.

Does the bill authorize him to set up his own, or is he going to use the State Department's?

The CHAIRMAN. I would think there was certainly no prohibition to his setting up anything he pleases of that sort.

Mr. RICE. Yes, sir.

Senator GEORGE. Then you would have the double investigation?

Senator LODGE. That is what we have now. The State Department, for instance, has its own security service.

Senator George. I know, but then they are not required to be investigated by the FBI, are they?

Mr. Gross. Yes.

Senator Lodge. There is a double investigation on State Department, isn't there?

Mr. Gross. Yes, sir.

The Chairman. Then you find your proviso, Senator Lodge: "Provided, however, that they may assume their posts and perform their functions after preliminary investigation and clearance by the Administrator or the Secretary of State, as the case may be."

That would clearly permit the Administrator to do any gumshoeing he wanted to.

Senator Lodge. Well, that is right.

Senator Thomas of Utah. I cannot see it quickly here; I think there is an answer. But why, under (d) on page 17, do we investigate only citizens?

Senator Smith. Citizens among the civilian personnel. Say you would hire a foreign assistant who is working along with these other people. Does he come in uninvestigated?

The Chairman. I would not know how to get away from your question, Senator. I would not know why it should not just read "civilian personnel appointed pursuant to this section."

Ambassador Douglas. The Foreign Service Act of 1946, as I understand it, provides for the investigation of alien personnel, not by the FBI.

Senator Thomas of Utah. But you have just given the Administrator authority to go outside of the Foreign Service law, have you not, in making appointments?

Ambassador Douglas. Under (b) on page 16, the Administrator is authorized to employ aliens.

Senator Thomas of Utah. Without any investigation?

Ambassador Douglas. In accordance with the applicable provisions of the Foreign Service Act of 1946.

Senator Thomas of Utah. Do they all have to be investigated?

Ambassador Douglas. By the State Department?

Senator Thomas of Utah. Therefore there are only two classes, aliens and citizens, and they are both investigated.

Mr. Gross. By the State Department, and the FBI in addition, investigates the citizens who are employed.

Senator Thomas of Utah. So that they will receive the same treatment, then, will they not?

Senator Smith. Aliens won't have the FBI.

Ambassador Douglas. The alien will not be subject to FBI investigation.

Senator Hatch. Does the FBI have any services abroad?

Mr. Gross. No, sir.

Senator Thomas of Utah. They have services abroad, but not this kind of service. They are everywhere, are they not?

Senator Hatch. Was that perhaps the reason you excluded it?

Mr. Gross. The FBI has no jurisdiction to investigate aliens overseas.

Senator Thomas of Utah. My point is an alien in this country who is employed.

Senator HATCH. This does not apply to employees inside the United States.

Ambassador DOUGLAS. This is just employees outside of the United States.

Mr. SURREY. People employed in this country are subject to the general law. That includes investigation by the FBI within the United States.

The CHAIRMAN. OK; that is approved.

ELIMINATION OF INHIBITION ON EMPLOYEES

Now, page 35. This is in response to the suggestion of Senator Lodge, I think, regarding the elimination of that inhibition on employees. It is a new section.

Insert the following new section between lines 5 and 6, reading as follows:

SEC. 17. Service of an individual as a member of the Public Advisory Board (other than the Administrator) created by Section 8(a), as a member of an advisory committee appointed pursuant to section 8(b), as an expert or consultant under section 4(d), as an expert, consultant, or technician under section 20(d), shall not be considered as service or employment bringing such individual within the provisions of sections 109 or 113 of the Criminal Code (U.S.C., 1940 edition, title 18, secs. 198 and 203), or of section 19(e) of the Contract Settlement Act of 1944, or of any other Federal law imposing restrictions, requirements, or penalties in relation to the employment of persons, the performance of services, or the payment or receipt of compensation in connection with any claim, proceeding, or matter involving the United States.

Mr. RICE. This is similar to the provision that was put in the Commission to Investigate the Executive Departments last year that Senator Lodge talked about.

The CHAIRMAN. And this is a correct statement, is it, that the sole effect of this section is to eliminate the requirement which otherwise would prohibit a temporary employee in the classification indicated from having any outside occupation?

Mr. RICE. No, sir; not that. It would permit, if I may say it in the affirmative, these people specified here to take these jobs temporarily and still have their claims against the Government, prosecute claims against the Government—cases of lawyers, claims of tax accountants, maybe some special consultants, like ex-Senator LaFollette, who has claims. It is to permit them to come in and keep these claims. Otherwise, you would not get these people. You suspend the laws which say that no officer or employee of the United States may prosecute a claim against the Government.

The CHAIRMAN. That is obviously essential, isn't it?

Senator LODGE. You can't get off the ground without doing it.

The CHAIRMAN. You found that to be true in the Hoover Commission?

Senator LODGE. That is right, and we had to get a special act through in December, I guess it was, otherwise we could not get the consultant.

Senator WILEY. They did it the day before yesterday in the Senate when we permitted a gentleman appointed assistant district attorney down there in Harry Truman's bailiwick to go on practicing law.

The CHAIRMAN. Is there objection?

Mr. Rice. I might point out, Mr. Chairman, that last year a provision somewhat similar to this was offered for ex-Senator Wheeler to be counsel for the War Investigating Committee, and President Truman vetoed it on the ground that the way it was written it was susceptible of the interpretation that he could prosecute suits for the Government and take away the prerogatives of the Attorney General of the United States. That is why he vetoed it. I did not agree with the interpretation at the time, but we, in writing this thing for Mr. Ackerson last year, had that in mind, and the language that we have used is not susceptible to that objection.

The Chairman. Is there objection?

Senator George. Just one question: Do these technicians and consultants and other individuals falling in any one of these classifications here go on and retain their salaries and regular business, and do this job, notwithstanding, on a per diem basis?

Mr. Rice. Yes, sir; I would think so. That is tied up with that same question we were discussing.

Senator George. That is one phase of it. That is an important part of it. Is it clear that they can do that under the law?

Mr. Rice. I don't think there is any question about that particular case that you give.

Senator George. All right.

The Chairman. The amendment is approved.

Senator Smith. Mr. Chairman, line 6 on my copy changes the word "and" to "or".

Mr. Rice. It should be "or", Senator.

The Chairman. OK. Page 38, beginning with the word "funds" in line 6, strike out through the word "expended" in line 8. That is the thing we agreed upon, and this is the recommended language: In lieu thereof substitute the following: "operations under this act have been completed."

In other words, the President makes his reports until operations under this act have been completed.

I think that reflects our agreement yesterday. Without objection that is approved.

NOT MORE THAN FOUR MEMBERS OF THE SAME PARTY

Page 38, line 21: After the word "House" insert the following new sentence: "In each instance not more than four members shall be members of the same political party." That is in accordance with our agreement yesterday. Without objection that is approved.

Page 39, line 8, beginning with the word "the" or rather, commencing with the word "The" in line 7, insert in lieu thereof the following: "Upon request, the committee shall aid the several standing committees of the Congress having legislative jurisdiction * * * .".

Mr. Rice. Your sentence would read, "Upon request, the committee shall aid the several standing committees of the Congress having legislative jurisdiction. * * * .".

The Chairman. All right, without objection, that is agreed to. We agreed to that yesterday.

On page 39, line 14, after "Administrator" insert a comma and the following: "at the request of the committee". That is completing the same thought.

Senator LODGE. What is that, the Administrator?

The CHAIRMAN. That puts the initiative and control in the committee.

ENOUGH MONEY FOR GOOD PAY

Senator LODGE. Do you think that this language will make it possible, for instance, for this Joint Congressional Committee to employ a man like former Senator LaFollette and have him be the chief liaison man with Administrator, and pay him enough so that he could afford to do it? I just use that as an illustration.

The CHAIRMAN. The committee is authorized to appoint and fix the compensation of such experts, consultants, technicians and clerical and stenographic assistants as it deems necessary and advisable.

Senator LODGE. That would authorize him to have some permanent people abroad, too, would it not?

The CHAIRMAN. Yes, and they must have.

Senator LODGE. If they are going to do the thing at all, they might as well do it right, and they should be ablè to do those things.

Mr. RICE. With regard to the compensation that you pay those people, the way it is written now, "The committee is authorized to appoint and fix compensation," that will be subject to the Classification Act. The last amendment that we have here typed, that you have not gotten to, Mr. Chairman, will permit you to do that without regard to the Classification Act.

Senator THOMAS of Utah. It seems to me if it is our committee it will be subject to the rules of the Reorganization Act.

Mr. RICE. This is a joint committee, set up by law, so it will take precedence over the restrictions of the Reorganization Act.

The CHAIRMAN. This is the new amendment, on page 40, line 5: Strike out lines 5 and 6, and insert in lieu thereof the following: "The committee is authorized to appoint and, with regard to the Classificcation Act of 1923 as amended, fix the compensation of such experts, consultants, technicians," and so forth.

Mr. RICE. "And organizations thereof." That has been added, too.

Senator LODGE. I am just trying to visualize what this might be. Let us suppose the congressional committee decided they wanted to have three top men, one man who would sit alongside the Administrator, another man abroad sitting alongside of the roving Ambassador, and the third man would be the chief man in charge of the committee's staff here in the Capitol. They can go ahead and pay salaries sufficiently high—

NO PAY LIMIT

Mr. RICE. You can pay $50,000. There is no limit under this language, if you can get the money and if there is no restriction placed on the appropriation when you get it.

The CHAIRMAN. I think the answer is, there is no limit except in the appropriation, Senator Lodge.

That concludes the laundry work for the morning.

Now, what page are we on, Dr. Wilcox?

Mr. RICE. Page 24.

PETROLEUM AND MERCHANT MARINE PROVISIONS

Senator LODGE. Mr. Chairman, the State Department has done some laundry work, too, on page 18, on these provisions regarding petroleum and the merchant marine. I do not know whether you are ready to hear that now or not.

Mr. NITZE. It does not include the merchant marine.

Senator LODGE. Just petroleum products. I hand this to you.

The CHAIRMAN. Is this with your blessing?

Senator LODGE. I think so. There is one verb I don't understand.

The CHAIRMAN. This is a substitute for what language?

Senator LODGE. Line 13, page 18.

The CHAIRMAN. To what?

Senator LODGE. Section 11, subsection (1), page 18.

The CHAIRMAN. That is lines 13 to 18. This is what the Administrator may do:

> (1) Procurement from any source, including Government stocks, of any commodity which he determines to be required for the furtherance of the purposes of this act, and the term commodity as used in this act shall mean any material, article, supply, or goods necessary for the purposes of this act.

That is all the present language.

Senator LODGE. They have taken out "merchant vessel."

The CHAIRMAN. Oh. And here is the new language:

> *Provided, however,* That the procurement of petroleum and petroleum products shall, to the maximum extent practicable, be made from petroleum sources outside the United States, and provided further that in furnishing commodities under the provisions of this act, the Administrator shall take fully into account the present and anticipated world shortage of petroleum and its products, and the consequent undesirability of expansion in petroleum consuming equipment where alternate fuel sources are practicable.

I think that is a darned smart job.

Senator LODGE. I think it is, too. I want to ask about the words "take fully into account." Just what does that mean, "take fully into account"? How much of a directive does that give them?

Mr. RICE. I would say it left it in his discretion and sort of passed the buck to him. He would be on the hot seat.

Senator LODGE. Does it put it on to the Administrator that he would be doing something wrong if he encouraged the utilization of petroleum over there? It does put him in that position, does it not?

Mr. RICE. It would certainly do that, I would think, if he encouraged it.

Ambassador DOUGLAS. "Where alternate fuel sources are practicable."

Mr. NITZE. It would not discourage him from aviation, for instance.

Senator LODGE. I would not want to do that.

The CHAIRMAN. I do not know that you can say anything more than that, Senator Lodge.

Senator GEORGE. It means he will just consider that situation, that is all.

Senator SMITH. That is true, of course, of any situation. Your fertilizer situation is in the same class.

Senator GEORGE. Yes. It might very well be applied to all commodities, actually.

85-743—73——9

Senator SMITH. The only point of this, I gather, is to highlight the particular crisis in petroleum.

Senator GEORGE. Because there are alternate fuel sources of supply. They say not.

The CHAIRMAN. Is the rest of this typewritten sheet the same as the present bill?

Senator LODGE. No; it isn't. The rest of it has to do with merchant vessels.

The CHAIRMAN. Let's deal with this one. Is there objection to this?

Without objection, it is agreed to.

Senator THOMAS of Utah. May I ask this one privilege, and that is that I may use it to bathe the bruises on the "Buy American" people who have hounded us for so long. Incidentally, the oil lobby was one of the worst we had.

The CHAIRMAN. You now have a bathing license. (2) is the same, is it not?

Mr. NITZE. The rest of those are not yet cleared.

The CHAIRMAN. Merchant vessels, you mean?

Ambassador DOUGLAS. (2) and (3) already have been approved. (4) and (5) are waiting.

The CHAIRMAN. All right. Now we get down to what page?

Dr. WILCOX. 24.

PROCUREMENT FROM GOVERNMENT AGENCIES

The CHAIRMAN. At the bottom of the page, "Procurement from Government agencies":

> Section 12(a) The Administrator, in the exercise of any authority conferred under section 11 of this Act, may procure (i) commodities owned by any department, agency, or establishment of the Government if the owning agency determines that such commodities are available for such procurement.

Did you grunt then?

Senator GEORGE. If the owning agency is willing, is all that means. Otherwise he can't get them.

The CHAIRMAN [reading].

> And (ii) services from any department, agency, or establishment of the Government which the owning agency determines to be available for such procurement.

You can grunt there, Senator George.

> The Administrator shall reimburse or pay, at replacement cost or, if required by law, at actual cost, or at such other price authorized by law agreed by the Administrator and the owning agency, out of funds available for the purposes of this Act, the owning or disposal agency, as the case may be, for such commodities or services. The amount of any reimbursement or payment to an owning agency for commodities or services so employed shall be credited to current applicable appropriations, funds, or accounts from which there may be procured replacements of similar commodities or such services and facilities: Provided, That where such appropriations, funds, or accounts are not reimburseable except by reason of the foregoing provision and when the head of the owning agency determines that replacement of any commodity employed under authority of this section is not necessary, any funds received in payment therefor shall be covered into the Treasury as miscellaneous receipts.

Well, all that means is, isn't it, that the owning agencies are under an injunction to cooperate if they can. Isn't that about all it means?

Senator GEORGE. That is all.

Ambassador DOUGLAS. That is all.

The CHAIRMAN.

(b) Any commodity procured out of funds made available for the purposes of this Act may, in lieu of being transferred to a participating country, be disposed of for any other purpose authorized by law, whenever in the judgment of the Administrator the interests of the United States will best be served thereby. Funds realized from such disposal shall, upon approval, of the Bureau of the Budget, revert to the respective appropriation or appropriations out of which funds were expended for the procurement of such commodity.

Would there be any objection to using the favorite State Department phrase instead of the Bureau of the Budget, and substitute the words "the little Kremlin"? What does that section mean?

TRIANGULAR TRADE AUTHORIZED

Senator SMITH. Doesn't this authorize triangular trade? Isn't that what it means?

Senator LODGE. Is that the place which I have been looking for everyday?

Mr. GROSS. The most usual example of this is where a commodity is procured and in the hands of the administrator intended for delivery to a participating country under the program but, for example, in the case of a foodstuff which would be subject to spoilage, if for any reason it could not be shipped on time, this authorizes disposal of a commodity of that sort in lieu of shipment in accordance with the original purpose of procurement. That would be the most likely example to arise.

The CHAIRMAN. What has the Bureau of the Budget got to do with it?

Mr. GROSS. That authorizes the Bureau of the Budget to allocate back to the original owning agency the funds which it procured for delivery under this program, so that the original owning agency can replace its stocks. Without this provision the original owning agency would not be able to reimburse itself, so that the Bureau of the Budget is simply introduced here as the most convenient agency for making the determination that the original owning agency of the commodity shall be reimbursed for its expenditures.

The CHAIRMAN. Can't you get a better agency? I mean, an alternative agency. If the Bureau of the Budget finds its name in this bill in some place, they will say, "Look, there we are! Now from here out don't do nothing without coming around and getting our OK."

[Discussion was continued off the record.]

Senator HATCH. Why should not the funds go back to the original appropriation whence they came without any approval by the Bureau of the Budget?

Mr. GROSS. I do not think we would object to that. There is a foreseeable case. The proceeds of the sale of wheat that was liable to spoil should revert to the Department of Agriculture, which procured the wheat.

Senator LODGE. Do you contemplate that on a bulk purchase like wheat the Department of Agriculture shall purchase it and then transfer it to the administrator, or shall the administrator go out and purchase the wheat himself?

Mr. Gross. He will procure through the Department of Agriculture.

Senator Lodge. Will the Department of Agriculture try to buy the wheat at such times and places as not to put the price up?

Mr. Gross. I think Secretary Anderson did testify to that.

ACT ADMINISTERED TO HOLD DOWN COST OF LIVING

Senator Lodge. I think seriously that this act should be administered so as not to increase the cost of living any more in this country than possible.

The Chairman. I think we will have some general directives in that connection before we get through.

Senator Lodge. I am glad to hear that. I am not entirely surprised.

Senator George. I would like to ask this question: In line 2 on page 26, "be disposed of for any other purpose authorized by law,". For what other purpose is the administrator authorized to be dealing in commodities, if he gets out and cannot handle them? He may cancel the program with country A after he has gotten so much wheat, petroleum products, and machinery for country A. For what other purpose can he dispose of those articles?

Senator Smith. Couldn't they send machinery to the Argentine in return for their sending grain to France?

Ambassador Douglas. I do not think this refers to that kind of transaction.

Senator George. This just does not do that. If he gets something that he cannot use, or it is decayed, perishable, and he decides to dispose of it rather than dispose of it to the recipient country, then we are authorizing him to dispose of it for any purpose authorized by law. What other purpose has this administrator got in dealing with that kind of thing, or dealing with those kinds of articles or commodities?

DISPOSITION OF PERISHABLE COMMODITIES

Mr. Gross. He has none, Senator. The purpose of that language in lines 2 and 3 is to limit his right, the administrator's right, to dispose of these perishable commodities for some reason, for some purpose that is authorized by other laws. There are, for example, laws which permit of diversion of commodities for disaster relief purposes; there are laws which authorize the disposition of perishable commodities which could not otherwise be used; there are restrictive methods of disposition of commodities which are provided in other laws. We did not want to give this administrator the right to dispose of these commodities for any purpose whatever. We wanted him to be bound by the provisions of other restricting laws respecting the disposition of Government stocks of commodities.

Mr. Rice. He could sell it for the school lunch program, I presume.

Senator George. I do not want him setting up a school lunch program. He has enough to do anyhow in administering this other program.

The Chairman. The example is withdrawn.

Senator George. Why do you need anything more than this, that in the event the administrator gets anything that he cannot use for the purpose for which he acquired it, if you want to restrict his purpose, why didn't you just let him turn it back to the agency from which he procured it, and get done with it and not have all this trouble about the Bureau of the Budget or anybody else?

Senator THOMAS of Utah. Don't you run into surplus property the minute you buy more than you need? You know what the Army or Navy would do with their surplus property. They would survey it and do all sorts of things to it without the Surplus Property Act. I can't think of an illustration, but say a man did buy 50 trucks that were to be delivered to one place, and he didn't want to deliver them, and they were surplus so far as that need is concerned. This department of the Government would be controlled in regard to the disposal of that surplus the same as any other department of the Government, I think, and now this provision here, "with the approval of the Bureau of the Budget," does permit the equivalent of a revolving fund. When it is sold it goes back for its original purpose without another appropriation. That is the only addition I see.

Senator GEORGE. Yes, but Senator Thomas, this particular provision applies to any commodity procured out of funds made available for the purposes of this act, may "in lieu of being transferred to a participating country." I suppose that would mean all participating countries, "be disposed of for any other purpose authorized by law whenever in the judgment of the administrator or the interests of the United States will best be served thereby."

Senator THOMAS of Utah. Say you ordered 50 trucks for Ireland, and Ireland blew up and you didn't want to send the trucks. You could not send them somewhere else under the law. But if the proceeds from it should go to some other institution or branch or some other place, you ought to allow it, it seems to me.

The CHAIRMAN. Suppose he has purchased a carload of perishable food for relief, and there is a strike in the port and he cannot ship. Does he just have to let the food rot, or can he turn it into some other avenue authorized by law? Isn't that a fair example of what you are talking about?

Senator HATCH. If there were no avenue authorized by law, he would have to let it rot.

Senator THOMAS of Utah. Yes, and no one wants that.

Senator HATCH. Your language is tying it to that.

Senator THOMAS of Utah. I read it the other way, that it gives him an out from letting it rot.

Senator HATCH. The only time he can dispose of it is when there is some other provision authorized by law. Suppose there was not any other authorization.

Senator LODGE. Wouldn't that completely run counter to this idea of triangular trade? Wouldn't this have quite an impact on that?

Ambassador DOUGLAS. I do not see how it would.

The CHAIRMAN. I don't see why.

Senator LODGE. If he can only dispose of these commodities in accordance with existing law for disaster, and so on, and he might want to make a trade with Latin America, he could not do it unless we gave him specific authorization.

Mr. GROSS. I think that is right. Of course he could dispose of it in accordance with, let us say, the interim aid program. He could dispose of it to a country that was eligible to receive assistance under Public Law 389.

AUTHORIZATION FOR TRIANGULAR TRADE

Senator LODGE. Do you think we should have specific authorization in this bill for this triangular trade in order to be on the safe side?

Mr. GROSS. I think it would subvert the purpose of this, which was just a sort of emergency authority to do the unusual if he was confronted with a weather situation, or spoilage, or some disaster condition, where you would have an economic waste, simply because the original purpose of the program had failed of execution in this particular case.

The sense of it is that the administrator may dispose of the commodity without the provisions relating to this Government-owned property.

Senator LODGE. I realize that the scope of this thing is intended to be rather limited, but I confirm my suspicion that perhaps unwittingly it has quite a limiting effect on something that might be developed to quite an extent under this act.

The CHAIRMAN. I think your problem has to be covered in another affirmative section of the bill. I do not think this collides with it.

Senator LODGE. I think unless we put in something affirmative in some other section of the bill, this would collide with it.

SPECIFIC EXAMPLES

Senator WILEY. I would like to ask this expert here, specifically: Let us take a carload, as you suggested, of good food that is liable to spoil. He cannot dispose of it unless there is some channel provided now by law. It seems to me you are trusting a man with about $5 billion or $6 billion here, and he ought to have authority to have some judgment some place so that he would not have to put it just into that channel, if that channel is blocked, so he could at least sell it on the market, dispose of it. To me that would be the commonsense way. This is a big business proposition.

The CHAIRMAN. Is there anything that would prevent him from selling it?

Mr. GROSS. No, sir.

Ambassador DOUGLAS. Except any restriction in existing law.

The CHAIRMAN. Is there any restriction in existing law which would prohibit him from selling a carload of food which is about to deteriorate?

Mr. GROSS. This is intended to give him the same authority the Department of Agriculture now has under existing law, to dispose of commodities which are about to spoil, and which the administrator would not have, except for a specific provision here, since his authority is limited to carrying out these programs.

The CHAIRMAN. Then, under the example I have given you, with this section in, the administrator could dispose of this carload of perishing food by sale, if he pleased, or by any other disposition which the Secretary of Agriculture could pursue under like circumstances.

Mr. GROSS. That is precisely it. It is to give the administrator the same authority to dispose of commodities that the owning agencies have.

The CHAIRMAN. I think this is all right.

Senator THOMAS of Utah. I think it is necessary, if you go back into some of the experiences we have been through, Mr. Chairman.

At the beginning of the last war we embargoed tools that had been bought by Russia before Russia got into the war. It had nothing to do with Russian feeling at all. But we needed those machine tools for our own industry, and we kept them on a wharf in Seattle or Portland or some place like that because there was no way of handling them after we had stopped this shipment, and we had to get special permission because it resulted in something like confiscation.

Then, to go through the agonies of what we went through a year ago last Christmas, in trying to get to the country $4 million worth of ordinary cardboard that was stored outside and being rained on, you could not do it. You had to go through all of the preliminaries that would take up more time, until after the demand was over, and every paperman in this country, every paper manufacturer in this country, urged the release of that stuff to satisfy a demand which they could not supply.

Now, if this will help us in overcoming those situations, it is a wonderful provision. I do not know whether it will or not.

Senator WILEY. Here is the proposition. It says there:

> In lieu of being transferred to participating countries, to be disposed of for any other purposes authorized by law.

I understood from the expert here that that was a limiting phrase, and it had to be disposed of in certain channels. I would cut that out, and give him the absolute authority to dispose of it, whenever in his judgment it was necessary. If there are a lot of laws you have to look up and you have to see whether you can do so-and-so and you have to comply with this technicality, you are just hamstringing him, and the result is you do get all this spoilage. My land, in the Army, in the Far East, it is a disgrace to the American people, the way that stuff has been destroyed, because, probably, of some limiting statute. I can't understand, if you are going to give a man anywhere from $5 billion to $17 billion to handle, why you are not going to give him some authority when he has something on hand where he can save a few dollars by disposing of it. Why shouldn't he have absolute authority to use his own judgment?

Senator THOMAS of Utah. Would that hurt if he were given that authority?

ARBITRARY DISPOSAL BY THE ADMINISTRATION

Mr. GROSS. We wrote this into the bill on the assumption that Congress would want to control the purposes for which the administrator might otherwise arbitrarily dispose.

Senator THOMAS of Utah. All law is beneficial when it is written, but when it is executed it becomes executionary.

The CHAIRMAN. Suppose, if you are going to do that, you put this additional injunction on the administrator: "in lieu of being transferred to a participating country, be disposed of for any other purpose whenever, and in whatever manner, in the judgment of the administrator, the interests of the United States will best be served thereby."?

Senator THOMAS of Utah. Any other purpose not inconsistent with the spirit of this act is what you want, isn't it?

The CHAIRMAN. What do you think about this, Senator George?

Senator GEORGE. I do not know. This has been a very confusing provision to me. If you leave it "dispose of" it probably would be held to mean by the comptroller or somebody else who has jurisdiction that he would have to sell it. I don't think he would be authorized to throw it away or give it away to somebody else other than a participating country.

The CHAIRMAN. But without some such authority, would he not be required to just let it rot?

Senator GEORGE. I do not know about that.

Mr. GROSS. That is what we were afraid of.

Senator GEORGE. You don't put any limitations on that; you just say, whenever he gets anything by the use of this appropriation he may, in lieu of transferring the product or commodity obtained to a participating country, dispose of it for any other purpose authorized by law.

If that is the thing you want to do, it seems to me you had better say, "in lieu of being transferred to a participating country, he shall make whatever disposition of it he may, in his judgment, in the interest of the United States, not inconsistent with this act. * * *".

Then, if you say "not inconsistent with it," you are putting some limitation on it. If it is a perishable product that you anticipate he may get hold of, I can see some reason for it. If it is a nonperishable product, it seems to me he should turn it back to the agency from which he got it, and that obviates all the difficulty then, about revolving funds and whatnot.

I have no special objection. I was confused by this provision "be disposed of for any other purpose authorized by law."

This administrator has not got any authority to administer any law except in this act, and here we would be putting him in the shoes of other disposing agencies.

Mr. GROSS. That is right, sir.

Senator GEORGE. Now, solely for the purpose of preserving and conserving the commodity, I can see that that is all right. But that is not so limited here.

The CHAIRMAN. Why can't this be written as a conservation paragraph?

Senator GEORGE. I think as a conservation paragraph——

AN OVERRIDING CONSERVATION ITEM

The CHAIRMAN. Why can't you put an overriding conservation item in here?

Senator LODGE. And not put him in the business of disaster relief except as a conservation item.

The CHAIRMAN. Will you take a crack at that, Mr. Rice?

Mr. RICE. Do you mean, limit it to commodities of a perishable nature?

The CHAIRMAN. No, just as a conservation measure.

Senator LODGE. To prevent it from being wasted.

Senator THOMAS of Utah. Didn't we read yesterday that warehouses full of UNRRA stuff had just been discovered? Somebody said he did not have the authority.

The CHAIRMAN. Yes, and it irritates the American people beyond words, and it should.

Senator LODGE. It certainly does.

The CHAIRMAN. I do not see any reason in the world why the approval of the Bureau of the Budget is necessary in connection with this transaction.

Mr. RICE. We will leave it out of the redraft, then.

The CHAIRMAN. They have balled this bill up enough as it is.

Senator LODGE. Have they had a hand in this?

The CHAIRMAN. I'll say so.

STRIKING OUT THE WORD "NATURAL"

(c) The Administrator, in furtherance of the purposes of paragraph (5) of subsection (b) of section 14, and in agreement with a participating country, may promote, by means of funds made available for the purposes of this Act, an increase in the production in such participating country of materials which are required by the United States as a result of deficiencies or potential deficiencies in the natural resources of the United States.

That is the contract for strategic materials.

Mr. GROSS. Is there any objection, sir, to striking out the word "natural?"

Senator THOMAS of Utah. I think it ought to be out, Mr. President, because a natural resource has an idea like a great big waterway, and things of that kind. I doubt very much whether brass can ever be a natural resource, but it is surely a resource that becomes efficient at times, and it is something necessary for our economy.

The CHAIRMAN. Is there any objection to striking out "natural"?

Senator LODGE. Let's do it.

Mr. RICE. It should come out in two other places.

RESOURCES OF THE UNITED STATES

Senator THOMAS of Utah. One more question there. When you say "resources of the United States" will that limit this to the resources which the United States actually owns? We do not mean that. We mean the resources within the United States which we need in our economy, don't we? Would any lawyer get after that, Mr. Rice?

Ambassador DOUGLAS. "Within" would be better than "of."

Senator THOMAS of Utah. Yes, "resources within the United States."

The CHAIRMAN. Without objection, "within" instead of "of."

(d) Whenever the Administrator shall determine that sale to a participating country, or to a citizen thereof, of any merchant vessel would be in furtherance of the purposes of this Act, and whenever the President shall so direct, the United States Maritime Commission . . .

—and we had better leave that until we are ready to tackle the whole Maritime Commission, the whole merchant vessel problem.

THE USUAL RFC CLAUSE

This RFC clause on page 27, section 13, is the usual RFC clause, isn't it? This is the same RFC clause that we have been using?

Mr. GROSS. It is in the Foreign Aid Act.
The CHAIRMAN. Is this the same as the Foreign Aid Act?
Mr. GROSS. Yes, sir.

The CHAIRMAN. ——

Section 13(a) Notwithstanding the provisions of any other law, the Reconstruction Finance Corporation is authorized and directed, until such time as an appropriation shall be made pursuant to subsection (c) of this section, to make advances not to exceed in the aggregate $1,000,000,000 to carry out the provisions of this Act, in such manner, at such time and in such amounts as the President shall determine, and no interest shall be charged on advances made by the Treasury to the Reconstruction Finance Corporation for this purpose. The Reconstruction Finance Corporation shall be repaid without interest from appropriations authorized under this Act for advances made by it hereunder.

(b) Such part as the President may determine of the unobligated and unexpended balances of appropriations or other funds available for the purposes of the Foreign Aid Act of 1947 shall be available for the purpose of carrying out the purposes of this Act.

What are calculated to be the unobligated and unexpendable balances?

Ambassador DOUGLAS. By the first of April I think there will be none.

Senator SMITH. That means that that whole Foreign Aid Act show goes over into this?

Ambassador DOUGLAS. If there are any unobligated funds. I think it is zero.

The CHAIRMAN. This applies exclusively to the Interim Aid Act?

Mr. GROSS. Yes.

The CHAIRMAN. "(c)" is the $68 question. We will pass that up. I am prepared to discuss it at any time the committee wishes.

Dr. WILCOX. Have we approved (a) and (b) on page 27?

The CHAIRMAN. Yes.

ACCESSORIAL AND ADMINISTRATIVE FUNDS

(d) Funds made available for the purposes of this Act shall be available for incurring and defraying all necessary expenses incident to carrying out the provisions of this Act, including accessorial and administrative expenses and expenses for compensation, allowances and travel of personnel, including Foreign Service personnel whose services are utilized primarily for the purposes of this Act, and, without regard to the provisions of any other law, for motor vehicles, typewriters and printing and binding.

Senator LODGE. What does "accessorial" mean?

Senator GEORGE. You are going to have to explain that. You had better get another word.

Mr. GROSS. We thought it was going to be deleted in the committee print. In connection with the Interim Aid program, it means repackaging.

The CHAIRMAN. Can we do without it? We will take out "accessorial and."

LOCAL CURRENCY PROCEEDS

(e) The unexpended portions of any deposits which may have been made by any participating country pursuant to Section 6 of the joint resolution providing for relief assistance to the people of countries devastated by war (Public Law 84, Eightieth Congress) and section 5 (b) of the Foreign Aid Act of 1947 (Public Law 389, Eightieth Congress) may be merged with the deposits to be made by such participating country in accordance with section 14 (b) (6) of this Act, and shall be held or used under the same terms and conditions as are provided in section 14 (b) (6) of this Act.

What does that mean?

Mr. GROSS. The local currency proceeds accounts that are to be maintained under the Interim Aid program shall go into the same account.

The CHAIRMAN. The Interim Aid bill said that any balance had to be disposed of with the consent of Congress.

Mr. GROSS. And so does this, and this provision aggregates the proceeds into one account, and they would all be subject to approval of Congress.

The CHAIRMAN. OK.

Senator Thomas, do you have something you want to talk about?

INVITATION FOR USE OF MOTORCARS

Senator THOMAS of Utah. There is an invitation here for trouble to these people who like to make it, in lines 13 and 14. It is an invitation to let them have all the motorcars they want in the administration of this act, and Europe is one of the places that they have always charged that people do such things. Here is an invitation for them to do it more.

Senator HATCH. Why do you pick out motor vehicles and typewriters?

Mr. SURREY. There is not a limitation on the number you can buy, but there is a limitation on the price you can spend for a typewriter or motor vehicle.

Senator THOMAS of Utah. You can change it by putting in "without regard to the price provisions". Will that satisfy you?

Mr. SURREY. I would have to check the provisions of the act.

Senator THOMAS of Utah. I think we have had this question with every relief bill we have had to face since UNRRA.

The CHAIRMAN. What did we do with it?

Senator LODGE. Why should they not buy their cars along with everybody else?

Mr. SURREY. You simply cannot get them.

Senator LODGE. Why can't they buy their typewriters over here?

Mr. SURREY. Because of the same situation. The law was passed in 1920-something, and prices have gone up.

The CHAIRMAN. So this is necessary, is it?

Mr. GROSS. From the price standpoint it is, but if you would like to limit it to price, may we take a look at the law to see if there are any other limitations?

The CHAIRMAN. I certainly would like to get it out.

Senator LODGE. That is a red flag in the face of a bull.

The CHAIRMAN. That is a good stopping point until 2 o'clock this afternoon.

Thank you very much.

[Whereupon, at 11:45 a.m., a recess was taken until 2 p.m. of the same day.]

AFTER RECESS

The hearing was resumed at 2 p.m., Senator Arthur H. Vandenberg, chairman, presiding.

The CHAIRMAN. The committee will come to order.

This morning we were rowing a bit about the language at the top of page 26, which is the "rotten apple" section. The language now proposed is as follows, which I think meets all points of view. This is the new language for (b) starting in line 25 of page 25:

The Administrator, whenever in his judgment the interests of the United States will best be served thereby, may dispose of any commodity procured out of funds made available for the purposes of this Act, in lieu of transferring such commodity to a participating country, by (1) transfer of such commodity to any department, agency, or establishment of the Government for use or disposal by such department, agency, or establishment as authorized by law, or (2) without regard to provisions of law relating to the disposal of Government-owned property, disposal of such commodity when necessary to prevent spoilage or wastage of such commodity or to conserve the usefulness thereof. Funds realized from such disposal or transfer shall revert to the respective appropriation or appropriations out of which the funds were expended for the procurement of such commodity.

Is that agreeable?

Senator GEORGE. Agreeable, Mr. Chairman, by two votes.

Senator SMITH. Ought not the word "disposal" be "disposed" in (2)?

Should it not be "to dispose of such commodity"?

The CHAIRMAN. Who wrote this?

Mr. RICE. We suggest that down in (2) after "of government-owned property" that you strike out "disposal of such commodity" and just before the (1), put the "by" after the "(1)" so it would read that he could dispose of it by transfer and (2) without regard to provisions of law when necessary to prevent spoilage.

Senator GEORGE. Mr. Chairman, I would have said, "When it becomes surplus to the objectives of this act, he can do as he doggoned pleases".

Senator THOMAS of Utah. There again, if you explain the words to me it is all right, but if you are merely going to conserve an automobile, for example, conserve the usefulness thereof, you are not helping this act at all. It is like putting in generators, which we are doing for stockpiles, covering them with cellophane and so on. If someone will tell us what "the usefulness thereof" is. I suppose it means the usefulness of the article or the instrument or the truck, or whatever it is. It seems to me it is like Senator George said, usefulness for the purposes of this act.

Senator GEORGE. I think that is the effect of it, Senator. I would much rather have said, "when it becomes surplus to the objectives of the act," they can do so-and-so, but I am not kicking on this. I think it is all right.

Senator THOMAS of Utah. That is better. Do you think they will dispose of it in some other direction, or will they put it in cold storage?

Senator GEORGE. Not in the case of an automobile. They will use that.

The CHAIRMAN. Do you want to change this, Senator Thomas?

Senator THOMAS of Utah. I do not know how to change it. If it means what Senator George says, all right, but it does not mean that to me at all.

As a boy who has come up in a warehouse and the rest of it, it means to dust it off every day and put it back on the shelf.

The CHAIRMAN. Oh, no. I would not think so. Let the record show that it means what Senator George says it means.

Senator GEORGE. I believe that is what it means, and I think this is all right.

Senator THOMAS of Utah. "Conserve the usefulness thereof."

Ambassador DOUGLAS. It relates to "dispose". He may dispose of any commodity without regard to the provisions of law relating to the disposal of Government-owned property, when necessary * * * to conserve the usefulness thereof."

Senator GEORGE. When it is deteriorating, becoming less valuable, he can do something about it. I think that is all right, Senator Thomas. It looks all right to me.

Senator HATCH. It is a vast improvement.

The CHAIRMAN. All right. It is done.

"BILATERAL AND MULTILATERAL AGREEMENTS"

Now, we are over at the top of page 29, "Bilateral and Multilateral Agreements."

> Section 14(a) The Secretary of State, after consultation with the Administrator, is authorized to conclude, with individual participating countries or any number of such countries or with an organization representing any such countries, agreements in furtherance of the purposes of this Act.

A new section (b):

> As a condition precedent to the performance for any participating country of any of the functions authorized under this Act, such country shall conclude an agreement with the United States providing for the adherence of such country to the purposes of this Act and containing commitments by such country to make reciprocal multilateral pledges to all of the participating countries, including, among others, undertakings by each country to participate in a joint program for European recovery based on self-help and mutual cooperation in which each country undertakes, among other things.

Boy, is that a sentence!

> (1) to use all its efforts to develop its production to reach agreed targets;
>
> (2) to apply all necessary measures leading to the rapid achievement of internal financial, monetary and economic stability;
>
> (3) to cooperate in all possible steps to reduce barriers to the expansion of trade;
>
> (4) to remove progressively obstacles to the free movement of persons within Europe; and
>
> (5) to set up by mutual agreement a joint organization to review progress achieved in the execution of the program and to insure to the fullest extent possible by joint action, the realization of the economic conditions necessary to the effective achievement of the general objectives to which each country has pledged itself.

LANGUAGE TAKEN FROM THE CEEC REPORT

Senator LODGE. May I ask, are those the five rules taken from the CEEC report?

Ambassador DOUGLAS. There were others, but those are the principal ones.

Senator LODGE. These are taken out of the CEEC report? *

---

*For this report see the Committee of European Economic Cooperation, *General Report*, 2 vols. published by the U.S. Department of State, publication 2930 (Washington: Government Printing Office, September 1947).

Ambassador DOUGLAS. That is right, and with the exception of the deletion of a few words, that it their precise language.

Senator LODGE. I think the committee report ought to show that.

Ambassador DOUGLAS. That is why we used the CEEC language.

The CHAIRMAN.

(c) In addition to the provisions to be included pursuant to subsection (b) of this section, such agreement with the United States shall also, where applicable, make appropriate provision for—

(1) promoting industrial and agricultural production in order to enable the participating country to become independent of abnormal outside economic assistance;

(2) taking financial and monetary measures necessary to stabilize its currency, establish or maintain a proper rate of exchange, and generally to restore or maintain confidence in its monetary system.

Senator SMITH. Mr. Chairman, how does that differ from (2) on the top of the page? Why is that necessary, in addition to (2) on the top of the page?

PLEDGES AND UNDERTAKINGS OF PARTICIPATING COUNTRIES

Ambassador DOUGLAS. (b) (1), (2), (3), (4), and (5) refer to the pledges and undertakings which each one of the participating countries gives to the other. (c) Has to do with the provisions of the agreement which each country makes with the United States.

Senator SMITH. Then it makes two agreements with the United States, one an agreement to engage in these multilateral pledges, and second, to make special agreements with the United States.

Ambassador DOUGLAS. As a condition precedent to the performance by the Administrator of any of his functions for and on behalf of any of the participating countries two things must happen: First, these countries must reaffirm and make commitments to make these pledges enumerated in (1), (2), (3), (4), and (5) of (b) and (c), and second, they must enter into a contract with the United States to do (1), (2), (3), (4), and (5) and (6).

Senator SMITH. And some of these are the same things that appear in the first?

Ambassador DOUGLAS. Yes, but they are reworded so as not to use the language of the CEEC.

The CHAIRMAN.

(3) cooperating with other participating countries in facilitating and stimulating an increasing interchange of goods and services among the participating countries and with other countries and cooperating to reduce barriers to trade among themselves and with other countries;

(4) making efficient use, within the framework of a joint program for European recovery, of the resources of such participating country, including any commodities, facilities, or services furnished under this Act.

Senator LODGE. I have an amendment to this.

The CHAIRMAN. We will read it through, first, Senator.

(5) facilitating the sale to the United States for stockpiling purposes, for such period of time as may be agreed to and upon reasonable terms and in reasonable quantities, of materials which are required by the United States as a result of deficiencies or potential deficiencies ni its own natural resources, and which may be available in such participating country after due regard for reasonable requirements for domestic use and commercial export in such country;

(6) placing in a special account a deposit in the currency of such country, in commensurate amounts and under such terms and conditions as may be agreed to between such country and the Government of the United States, when any commodity or service is made available through any means authorized under this Act, and is not furnished to the participating country on terms of payment. Such special account, together with the unexpended portions of any deposits which may have been made by such country pursuant to section 6 of the joint resolution providing for relief assistance to the people of countries devastated by war (Public Law 84, Eightieth Congress) and section 5 (b) of the Foreign Aid Act of 1947, shall be held or used only for such purposes as may be agreed to between such country and the Government of the United States, and under agreement that any unencumbered balance remaining in such account on June 30, 1952, will be disposed of within such country for such purposes as may, subject to the approval by Act or joint resolution of the Congress, be agreed to between such country and the Government of the United States;

(7) publishing in such country and transmitting to the United States, not less frequently than every calendar quarter after the date of the agreement, of full statements of operations under the agrement, including a report of the use of funds, commodities and services received under this Act; and

(8) furnishing promptly, upon request of the United States, any relevant information which would be of assistance to the United States in determining the nature and scope of future operations under this Act.

I guess that is far enough to go. That is to line 3 on page 33.

"FREE MOVEMENT OF PERSONS IN EUROPE"

Senator GEORGE. I have one question. There may be a lot of things, Mr. Chairman, you could say about this, but there is one thing I want to raise now.

That is back on 30, "to remove progressively obstacles to the free movement of persons within Europe."

I don't think that is any of our business. It has something to do with the recovery of Europe, but I do not think it is any of our business. I think it is on an exact parallel or parity with an FEPC here in this country, saying whom somebody should employ and whom he should turn off. I do not agree with that. There are two votes against that. That should come out. It has nothing to do with this recovery program in any sense. That is an interference with the internal affairs of those countries over there that I would not undertake to justify and I don't think you will.

The CHAIRMAN. This is quoted from their proposal, Senator.

Senator GEORGE. I do not care. I don't care anything about it.

The CHAIRMAN. Doesn't that respond to the question that we are interfering? This is their agreement. They are going to agree that they are going to try to do these things themselves at this point.

Senator GEORGE. I understand that, but we say we are conditioning our participation somewhat on these grounds.

Now, if you will say "et al" or something else at the end of it, and say that these are the agreements that other people have made, all right, but that is a direct interference in a most vital particular, and while I would like to see progressively removed the obstacles to the free movement of persons within Europe, I do not believe that is a wise thing to put here as a condition of our participation or continuance of our participation, or of our assistance to Europe. That seems to me to be too remote in the sense at least that we don't want to interfere too much with their own internal affairs.

If it is stated that they have agreed to these things, why that is all right.

Ambassador DOUGLAS. I can tell you, Senator, why the participating countries used that language and incorporated it in their list of pledges.

Some of the countries were suffering from a labor shortage.

Senator GEORGE. I know that. I understand that. But, we are not saying that they agreed to these things, and they are all right by us. We are putting them down as conditions on which we do so-and-so.

I do not think that we should do that. That is just one criticism I had to make of this. Most of the other things seem to me to be reasonable.

The CHAIRMAN. Suppose, Senator George, in the introduction on page 29 you said:

> As a condition precedent to performance for any participating country of any of the functions authorized under this Act, such country shall conclude an agreement with the United States providing for the adherence of such country to the purposes of this Act and containing commitments by such country to make reciprocal multilateral pledges to all of the participating countries pursuant to their own agreement in so-and-so.

Senator GEORGE. "Agreeable," Mr. Chairman, "agreeable to their joint agreement." That is all right. I do not object to that.

But here we are. If there was anything on this earth that would put us in the middle of the whole universe, it is this, "to remove progressively obstacles to the free movement of persons within the area that we are aiding."

I don't think it will do it at all, and I would not undertake it at all under any circumstances.

If it is agreeable to their own conclusions and deliberations, that is all right.

The CHAIRMAN. What do they mean by it, Mr. Ambassador? Are they trying to get away from passport requirements?

Senator GEORGE. Oh, no.

Ambassador DOUGLAS. Oh, no.

Senator WILEY. It would open up the whole D.P. problem in this country, as well as immigration.

Senator GEORGE. It would open up the whole immigration problem all over the world.

Who did this, Mr. Ambassador?

Ambassador DOUGLAS. This was language which was drawn to meet a suggestion made during the hearings.

The CHAIRMAN. By whom, do you remember?

Ambassador DOUGLAS. I think it was perhaps by Senator Lodge.

Dr. WILCOX. There were several requests that the legislation incorporate specific commitments which the CEEC countries had agreed to.

Senator GEORGE. That is all right, if you stated their commitments.

Ambassador DOUGLAS. I had a little apprehension about this language.

Senator GEORGE. Mr. Ambassador, this is more than language, a good deal more than language. I wouldn't raise any question about language.

Ambassador DOUGLAS. Could you say "pursuant to the pledges and undertakings recited in the CEEC report of such-and-such a date, and agreeable to the participating countries?"

Senator GEORGE. I have no objection to them carrying out what they have agreed to.

Senator WILEY. It is all right if you don't tie it in as a condition precedent.

Senator GEORGE. You don't make ourselves a party to saying what they are going to do. The next thing you will be saying is what they are going to cook in the kitchen.

HOLDING THEM TO ACHIEVEMENT OF GOALS

Senator LODGE. What I felt, Senator George, is that we ought to hold them to the achievement of some goals, and I raise the question whether, when we cut down the amounts that they asked for in Paris, we were still going to hold them to the same goals that they set for themselves in Paris. I think that is what led to the idea of putting these goals right into the bill, insofar as they affect an integrated Europe and some attempt to get away from the old anarchy that they have had there that has gotten us into two wars.

Senator GEORGE. I have no objection on earth to saying:

> Whereas, these countries have set these following goals, we commit ourselves from then on to do so-and-so and so-and-so.

But I do not want to do this. There is nothing more vital, when you come down to the last analysis, than saying to a State in Europe, "You have to break down your immigration and all your restrictions about the flow and interflow of populations."

If they want to do it, I think it is fine. I don't want to do it here, and I don't want to be a party to it at all.

Now, some of the others dangerously approach that. If they were all stated as the goals set by these countries, these participating nations, these cooperating nations. OK. But we are not doing this that way. We are committing ourselves here to a proposition of saying who is going to come into what country.

Well, you can't do that, gentlemen, without saying who is coming into your country, and who is not going to come into your own country, and I am not willing to do that.

Ambassador DOUGLAS. Would it meet the specifications if language along the following lines were used:

> Pursuant to the pledges and undertakings recited in the CEEC report on such-and-such a date, and agreeable to the participating nations?

Senator LODGE. Where would you put that?

Senator SMITH. After the word "cooperation" in line 22.

Ambassador DOUGLAS. This is on page 29, line 17 and line 18:

> Containing commitments by such country to make reciprocal multilateral pledges to all of the participating countries, pursuant to or agreeable to the pledges and undertakings recited in the CEEC report on such-and-such a date, and agreeable to the participating countries.

Senator GEORGE. No, sir; that would not suit me at all, Mr. Ambassador.

If it were said that "whereas they said these things, then we will go ahead and do so-and-so," that is a different story. I am not willing to commit myself there. We are committing ourselves by hand, foot, leg, and thigh on everything, you know, in this thing.

85-743—73——10

Senator HATCH. Mr. Chairman, I was just looking here. I think we should take quite a bit of time on this. You start on paragraph (b) on page 29 and say "as a condition precedent."

LANGUAGE BECOMES TOO BINDING

Senator GEORGE. That is right. You are making it so binding, it becomes our obligation. I am not willing to do it at all, and a whole lot of these others are very objectionable, and I do think we are not thinking very clearly. We are dealing with a European civilization that is much older than ours in all these countries, and we are trying to remake them.

Senator LODGE. Does your objection go to the other points, or just to No. 4?

Senator GEORGE. I specifically pointed out No. 4, Senator Lodge.

Senator SMITH. Wouldn't No. 3 have the same principle involved, where we are telling them what to do about their tariff program?

Senator GEORGE. Yes, sir; to some extent, but that is an international program, and it is not international to say to country A, B, or C, who is going to cross our borders? If so, we become the whole thing, and we might as well go all out and sink at once, because you cannot carry any such load as this.

Senator THOMAS of Utah. Senator George, this is just to throw out an idea here. What we are trying to accomplish is to encourage them in fulfilling a pledge they have already made.

Senator GEORGE. I have no objection to that.

I could say "whereas, they have said these things,".

Senator THOMAS of Utah. That is what I mean. Can't we start out by getting rid of the condition precedent, with the idea of encouraging them in meeting their own objective?

Senator GEORGE. That is perfectly all right. The objective is good. I am not fussing about that.

But I do not want to undertake it. We are undertaking plenty under any circumstances, and to undertake the whole broad program of remodeling the earth all at one fell swoop is just a bit beyond us, even in an election year.

Senator THOMAS of Utah. In addition to that I would combine (3) and (4) to help them accomplish their purposes both as to things and as to persons, without emphasizing this staggering fact.

BARRIERS INTERFERING WITH TRADE EXPANSION

There is a question in the minds of a lot of people whether certain barriers are interfering with the expansion of trade.

Senator GEORGE. No, Senator; don't misunderstand me. I am not fussing with the principle. I am fussing with us endorsing a thing and saying that this is a condition precedent to our participation in this program.

Senator THOMAS of Utah. I am in entire agreement with and I think if we rewrite, attempting to make the Administrator do these things to encourage them in the accomplishment of the program which they themselves have laid down, and then make these statements a little bit more general than specific, you will accomplish all the purposes.

Senator GEORGE. I agree with you there, Senator.

Now, when you come to another question about what sort of fiscal policy these nations who are to receive our money shall set up, then I think we have a right to step into that field, but when we step in here and say with respect to the age-old question of immigration, or emigration, that here are the conditions that we lay down, I am afraid we are foolish.

MATTERS INCLUDED IN A DECLARATION OF POLICY

Senator HATCH. Mr. Chairman, may I make a suggestion?

I have been talking to Mr. Rice here. These matters might well be set forth in the declaration of policy.

On page 3 you will find it is the hope of the United States that those countries, through a joint organization, and so forth, might. * * * Might not that be given some consideration?

A PUSH FOR EUROPEAN INTEGRATION

Senator LODGE. That is my verbiage that you are reading there. You flatter me very much. I had thought of making it a condition precedent, and then I had gotten talked out of it, and I had written these words here for the declaration of purpose, and my whole thought was to have this thing give a tremendous push to the idea of an integrated Europe. I was not talking about immigration so much as the removal of customs barriers and general consolidation along the Benelux line.

I think we have to make it very clear that we are not jamming it down their throats.

Senator HATCH. This does jam it down their throats, doesn't it?

Senator LODGE. This language on page 29 and page 30, I think maybe does a little bit. I do not know.

I think we want to make them realize that that is what we hope to see happen, but I think we want to do it tactfully and not do it in such a way as to lay us open to charges of imperialism.

The CHAIRMAN. Somewhere in here there are going to be some things that they agree to do, or else I am going to quit paying taxes.

Senator HATCH. Can you write in legislation "You have to do so-and-so"?

The CHAIRMAN. Yes, certain things.

Senator LODGE. If we took out No. 4, would that make everyone happy?

The CHAIRMAN. For instance, they have agreed to mine so much coal by 1952.

Senator HATCH. I would recite all of those things. I am perfectly willing to.

But to lay it down and say, as a condition precedent to this you have to do so-and-so——

The CHAIRMAN. You have to agree to try to reach your objectives.

Now that does not apply to the thing we are talking about here, because these are mutual objectives within their own relationships.

Senator HATCH. I would like to recite them and make them very strong.

The CHAIRMAN. You left out some of them. Why did you leave some of them out?

Ambassador DOUGLAS. There were some of them that were not particularly applicable.

The CHAIRMAN. You left one that I should think was extremely applicable relative to the modernization of equipment.

Ambassador DOUGLAS. That places us in a position where there might be reposed on us a responsibility to try and up the program. That is what they undertake to do among themselves. But in order to do it completely and adequately and in as short a period of time as possible, a burden falls upon us.

That is the reason that that particular provision was eliminated from specific reference.

Senator LODGE. Suppose you said in line 23, page 29, "Each country undertakes, among other things, to work for the following goals, to which the participating countries agreed at the Paris Conference of September 1947" and then list those things, and state right in the Bill that these things were the things that they agreed to. Do you see what I mean in line 23, page 29?

Ambassador DOUGLAS. It would still be a condition precedent.

Senator LODGE. Oh, yes, but it would be there a condition precedent.

The CHAIRMAN. I certainly think you are entitled as a condition precedent to require that these countries shall pursue the promises they made as the basis upon which we have moved in to respond to them.

Senator GEORGE. I do, too, Mr. Chairman, but to illustrate exactly my position——

The CHAIRMAN. I see your point, and I don't think what I have said collides with what you have said.

Senator GEORGE. No, I don't think it does.

A RESOLUTION TYPE OF THING

Senator THOMAS of Utah. My technique would be to almost go back to the old resolution type of thing and say:

> Since this European organization has made the following declarations, and so on and so forth, the administrator shall, in drawing up his agreements, pursue the objectives in every way.

It has to be a little stronger than that. Do you see the idea? Do you or don't you?

Senator GEORGE. Yes, I do, Senator. I have no objection to that, if you say it is their objective and that our administrator shall see, so far as possible and practicable, that those things are done.

Senator THOMAS of Utah. And to encourage them in the accomplishment of their objective.

Senator GEORGE. I have no objection to that.

But when you get into a debatable area as to what countries shall do, and we lay it down as precedent, it seems to me we are going a bit too far, and I don't understand how we could try to accomplish those things.

Here is a recovery program which has one main objective, to enable these countries to recover and to get on their feet to the point where they can decide these issues for themselves, and with whom they are going to associate and what sort of ideologies they are going to adopt—economic, social, and political.

And the moment we step over and say that we are going to do all these things, "But you have to do so-and-so according to our ideas," I just know we can't sustain it, not in this troubled world.

And if the world has ever been more confused than at this hour, I don't know when.

MAKING CLEAR THE OBJECTIVES

Senator LODGE. What you want to make clear is that these objectives are their objectives.

Senator GEORGE. Their objectives, and our administrator shall advance them as far as he can, shall keep them in mind in the administration of the act, and have them constantly before him.

Senator SMITH. Why don't you just refer in general terms, then, to the undertakings set forth in the CEEC agreement in Paris of a certain date, without specifying these things?

The CHAIRMAN. That is precisely what I was trying to do, Senator Smith.

Senator GEORGE. I think, Senator Smith, you may be entirely right. If you want to emphasize some of them, we could repeat them.

The CHAIRMAN. I do not think it is necessary to do that.

Senator GEORGE. I don't think so.

The CHAIRMAN. Suppose you say:

> As a condition precedent to the performance for any participating country of any of the functions authorized under this Act, such country shall conclude an agreement with the United States providing for the adherence of such country to the purposes of this Act, and containing commitments by such country to make reciprocal multilateral pledges to all of the participating countries to pursue the objectives stated by them in their report in Paris of such-and-such a date.

Senator SMITH. Let that cover (b).

Senator GEORGE. "To pursue the objectives"?

Senator LODGE. To work toward.

Senator GEORGE. But not to necessarily attain the objectives. They do not become conditions precedent.

The CHAIRMAN. Certainly not.

Senator GEORGE. They are to try to do these things. They did not say they were going to do this in this agreement, if you read it carefully.

Senator LODGE. They are not going to, either, don't worry.

Senator GEORGE. No, sir. They haven't any idea of doing it, I am afraid. They can't. They just can't.

The CHAIRMAN. I think the language ought to be a little stronger than "pursue the objectives" but that is the general idea.

Senator GEORGE. I have no objection to that.

The CHAIRMAN. I want them to pursue it honestly.

Senator THOMAS of Utah. I would like to see their own words printed in our law.

Senator GEORGE. I don't object to that. That emphasizes what they have said themselves.

The CHAIRMAN. All right, "to pursue earnestly the objectives stated by them in their agreement of such-and-such a date, as follows:".

Senator GEORGE. I have no objection to that, "to pursue faithfully their objectives."

The CHAIRMAN. Can't that be done, Mr. Ambassador?

Ambassador DOUGLAS. I wonder whether that cures Senator George's objection, because it would still be the following language:

"As a condition precedent * * *.".

The CHAIRMAN. As a condition precedent they agree to pursue.

Senator GEORGE. They just agree that they are going to try to live up to their own agreement.

Ambassador DOUGLAS. Containing commitments by such country to pursue.

The CHAIRMAN. Yes.

Senator GEORGE. Put the burden on them to do it. That is perfectly all right. I have no objection to that.

The CHAIRMAN. And then make the whole thing the way they wrote it.

Senator GEORGE. The way we have it here, we are dictating what they are going to do.

The CHAIRMAN. Put them all in—these, plus a couple more than they did not put in.

Senator GEORGE. Just think of the idea of our Russian friends hitting on No. 4 as we have written it.

Ambassador DOUGLAS. They are going to hit on all of this.

Senator GEORGE. But they hit on some much louder than they do on others: "To remove progressively obstacles to the free movement of persons."

INTERCOURSE BETWEEN EAST AND WEST EUROPE

How soon would you get any sort of intercourse between Eastern and Western Europe, if ever? You could not do it.

You are touching on vital things when you come into things like this.

When you stay in the economic realm and say, "Whereas you have said so-and-so, and whereas we want to extend aid, but we do think that this aid, to be effective, must be conditioned on certain things," that is a different thing, but here we are saying what they are going to do about their emigration and immigration laws, their transport, and all those kinds of things.

I don't think you can do it at all. I think it would be the most unwise thing you could ever put into any Act of this kind, and whatever we put into this, Mr. Chirman, you may be dead sure that sooner or later they are coming back to us and saying, "You said this to us. Now what about you?"

The CHAIRMAN. So far as that section of this amendment, down to the point where we reached the direct agreements with the United States on things we do have a right to talk about, which starts at line 14 on page 30, suppose down to that point we handle the multilateral agreement by approximately the language originally used, as follows, coming down to line 17 on page 29: "and containing commitments by such country to make reciprocal multilateral pledges to all of the participating countries, to faithfully pursue the objectives stated by them in their Paris agreement of blank date as follows:", quoting their own language.

Senator GEORGE. Are you making it a condition precedent?

The CHAIRMAN. It is a condition precedent that they agree to pursue.

Senator THOMAS of Utah. That is, that they work in harmony with what they said they would do.

The CHAIRMAN. Sure, that they simply meant what they said when they said what they said.

Senator LODGE. All we can hope to do anyway in this country is to make them realize that we hope to God they are going to integrate.

You can't say, "You are not going to get a dollar until you get a certain amount of integration."

The CHAIRMAN. Marshall said to them, "You have to something for yourselves."

They said, "We are willing to try to do the following things."

Marshall said, "All right, then we will help you."

All in the world we are saying is, "In response to our invitation you said you would try to do the following things. We are just reminding you as a condition precedent to the first check you get that you said you would try."

Senator HATCH. That is not this item.

Senator LODGE. The chairman's new language does that.

Ambassador DOUGLAS. No, I think it is stronger than that.

I would say, Mr. Chairman, it was stronger than that.

Senator GEORGE. I would say, Mr. Chairman, that in addition to the commitments which these countries have themselves undertaken, we set forth the following.

The CHAIRMAN. I think that is exactly what we are saying here.

Senator GEORGE. Not prescisely. I would say it there. I would say, "In addition to what you have undertaken, we are going to say that certain things must be done," and they may not be the same things at all. They may be more, they may be less. But we are recognizing that what they have said is an important factor in what we are saying.

And we would say that in addition to what these countries themseleves have severally and jointly convenanted, you could enumerate them if you want to for the purpose of emphasis, but then I would provide—and I would rather proceed this way—that such agreements with the United States shall also, where applicable, make appropriate provisions for:

Now, those are our conditions. We are setting forth what we want.

The CHAIRMAN. I still don't understand why we are in disagreement.

Senator GEORGE. We are not especially in disagreement. You and I would understand it, but we are dealing with countries.

The CHAIRMAN. Senator Hatch, why did you say that what I suggested does not do what I thought it does?

LAYING DOWN HARD AND FAST RULES

Senator HATCH. I am not quite sure about it. Senator. The language of this, that is here written, is that we are laying down hard and fast rules, and telling these countries, You have got to do so-and-so.

That is the way I read it, and I think that is wrong, but I am perfectly willing, if you are going to rewrite this and incorporate their own language, to say "Now, in consideration of what you have agreed to do, so-and-so and so-and-so."

Senator LODGE. Then you took out the condition precedent?

Senator GEORGE. You are making it a condition precedent for any participating country for any of the functions authorized under this Act.

"Such country shall conclude an agreement." It is terrible!

Senator HATCH. It is as hard and fast as it can be.

The CHAIRMAN. My God, you are breaking my heart!

Senator HATCH. I know what you are talking about, and I understand perfectly. A lot of people in this country do want to lay out much more stringent terms than this.

Senator LODGE. Unless we give them a friendly lift, they will never do it.

Senator HATCH. I understand what is in the Chairman's mind, and I sympathize with him, but it is a question of what we can do in legislation.

Ambassador DOUGLAS. You can do this, can't you?

The Administrator shall encourage the participating countries to carry out the pledges and undertakings recited in the CEEC reports.

Senator HATCH. I don't like that.

The CHAIRMAN. I don't like that. I think it is very weak.

Ambassador DOUGLAS. It does not meet your point.

The CHAIRMAN. They said they would try to do something. I don't know why we should not say to them, "Listen, Bud, this is what you promised to do."

Senator HATCH. Can we say that? How about it, Mr. Rice?

Mr. RICE. Sure, you can say it.

Senator GEORGE. We can say it. It is not a very wise course.

I am not willing to say it, because I don't want anybody to say it to me.

The CHAIRMAN. You don't want anybody to say to you that you promised to pay your 30-day note and the 30 days is up?

Senator GEORGE. No, the fellow who holds the note will do that, but I do not want any country in Europe, or any combination of countries, to turn around and say, "You must progressively free all movement of persons in and out of the United States."

The CHAIRMAN. Neither do I.

Senator LODGE. And neither do I.

Senator THOMAS of Utah. You would just as soon have them progressively move some out, wouldn't you?

Senator GEORGE. I would not mind that, but they would not like it, so I would not want to say by law that they should be moved out.

I think it is perfectly all right to say in effect that they have agreed to these things, and in addition, we think certain other things should be done. That is all right. That is making it pretty strong on them, but you come close in, now, to the main thing here. I don't care whether you want to face it or not, that you are not going to help "if you are a Communist or a sympathizer with the Communists; if you haven't the ideology and philosophy that we want to put in here."

Now, if we are going to do that, we might as well, in my opinion, abandon this program; that is just my own idea. I would like to do that.

Senator WILEY. Abandon it?

Senator GEORGE. No, I would love to say, "You can't be a Communist and run with that gang and get any aid."

But I think it would be the most unwise policy that this country could ever adopt.

Ambassador DOUGLAS. Certainly it would be unwise to write it into the law.

Senator GEORGE. Certainly. It would be the most unwise thing that could ever happen, and the further we go in saying what these countries shall or shall not do, we just approach that just around the rim, and then your American people are going to turn around and say, "Well, why didn't you say if these fellows didn't abandon Joe Stalin they could not get any aid?"

What is going to be your answer?

You regulated them as to what they should do internally, except down to the point where we understood we were trying to do something, and that is to stop the movement of communism all over the world.

The CHAIRMAN. We have said in the termination section, that the contract can be terminated if such country is not adhering to its agreement included under section 14.

Senator GEORGE. That is right.

The CHAIRMAN. Suppose all of this interest in what Bevin calls the Western Union promptly subsides just as soon as they get their checks. Do we just ignore that? That makes no difference to us?

> You have made some nice speeches to us about how you were going to cooperate and what you were going to try to do with each other. You aren't doing it, but that is all right.

Senator LODGE. We have to have something in here that shows that we expect and hope that they will do these things.

Senator GEORGE. We hope they will. We are saying:

> You must do something in addition to what you said you would do. This is your pious wish and your hope and your purpose, and we are not disposed to question it, but we want certain other things done that can be done.

USING DIFFERENT LANGUAGE

Senator HATCH. I have been talking with the members of the staff here, Dr. Wilcox and Mr. Rice, and I think they can work this out by using a little different language. When you lay down a condition that is very harsh language. Dr. Wilcox said "In order to insure", or something like that. Suppose we give them a chance to work on this a little bit?

Dr. WILCOX. To get away from your condition precedent, simply say—this language isn't quite right—"In order to insure the effective execution of the program contemplated in this Act, these countries shall conclude agreements," and then use Senator Vandenberg's language.

Then you would do away with your rigid condition precedent.

Senator HATCH. It still means the same thing, but you don't point it out and say it does.

Senator GEORGE. That does not quite meet my objection, Dr. Wilcox. I do not want to say to any of the European countries that they shall permit the free movement of persons in and out of their own countries as a condition of this help. If I have to say that, I would vote against this help.

Senator SMITH. You would not object to referring to the agreement entered into in Paris?

Senator GEORGE. I do not object, Senator Smith, to anything they themselves have resolved, but I do not want to make that a condition precedent to this help. I would not go that far, to give a dollar of American money away. I want to make that plain. And there are other things here that I think are wholly impracticable, but they are not very harmful. But when you come to avoid all things like that, you just can not say that that hasn't something to do with everything. That is my own view.

Senator SMITH. Would you be willing to agree to the slight change which Dr. Wilcox makes beginning with (b), and then run down through (b) on page 29, through the clause that I like to see here, that they undertake to participate in a joint program for European recovery based on self-help and mutual cooperation as expressed in the agreement?

Senator GEORGE. I do not object to the fact that implicit in the whole Marshall program we would help somebody who desired to help himself. You can say "Whereas", if you want to. You do not have to do that. You can say "Since they have done so and so", as indicating their desire and willingness to cooperate, and then we go on with what we say are conditions precedent. I don't want to make these things conditions precedent. You can't do it. You haven't any power on earth to do it, and there is not any use to fool yourself that you can do it.

Senator SMITH. Why wouldn't you say, then, as Dr. Wilcox says, "As an aid to carrying out the purposes of this Act," or "In order to insure the successful carrying out of the purposes of this act, each participating country shall conclude an agreement with the United States providing for the adherence of such country to the purposes of the act and containing commitments by such country to make reciprocal multilateral pledges to all of the participating countries, including, among others, undertakings by each country to participate in a joint program for European recovery based on self-help"?

Senator GEORGE. I would not be willing to do that, Senator Smith. I wouldn't do that at all. That means that the countries are going to do this as a condition precedent to doing so and so. I wouldn't do it. Whatever they have done, if we are satisfied to proceed here legislatively on what they have done, let's do it, and let us say that we have some other things to say ourselves. You can say: "You have said so and so." I don't object to saying that. And you can emphasize, if you wish to, what they have said. But we have some other things to say, and we think they are vitally connected with the practical help that will come under this program.

The CHAIRMAN. Now I will add another thought to what you are saying, Senator George, in a different approach: The five things set out here in detail as the schedule of things that are to represent self-help are so totally inadequate and incomplete in respect to the great concept of the Western Union that Bevan was talking about that I think a powerful argument can be made against the recital of any details at this point, lest the recital of the details would exclude an awful lot of things that are also involved and that ought to be achieved.

Now, would it be satisfactory—we are just talking about the multilateral contract—when you get down to the bilateral contract I think you have to hold them to strict accountability, but at this point it would not serve all our purposes if we recited the fact that our participation in this plan is caused by and is contingent upon the continuous effort of the participating countries?

Senator HATCH. To accomplish the following objectives.

EUROPEAN RECOVERY BASED ON SELF-HELP AND COOPERATION

The CHAIRMAN. To accomplish European recovery based on self-help and mutual cooperation as set forth by the participating countries in the Paris agreement of such and such a date, and perhaps you can add even something more to it at that point, to emphasize the fact that unless they are going ahead on their own responsibility to gear themselves into effective unity, we are not going to be interested very long.

Senator HATCH. Senator George, what do you think about that sort of approach?

Senator GEORGE. I just don't want to make it a condition precedent.

Senator HATCH. No, he is not making it a condition precedent.

Senator WILEY. It is a recitation.

Senator GEORGE. I have said that all the time. But I don't want to make it a condition precedent that we are going to demand of other European nations certain things here, and I want to be careful to avoid it because there are some of the things that are here enumerated that I don't think any American would ever agree to, with respect to his own country.

The CHAIRMAN. May I suggest that Mr. Rice and his colleagues undertake to rewrite this particular section on the basis of a recital?

Senator GEORGE. That is all right, if you wish to recite it.

The CHAIRMAN. I don't want to recite it in detail. Let me finish—a recital of the basic fact that we are moving into the situation in response to an agreement for reciprocal self-help which is the basis of everything we are proposing here to do, and we expect a multilateral agreement to be made between them in pursuit of this objective with-with a lot of the major things that are not recited at all.

Senator GEORGE. That is all right. These are the details that they have said, as I understand it—I haven't got it before me——

The CHAIRMAN. The details are totally inadequate. So far as I am concerned they are a lot of things that are utterly minor compared with a lot of the major things that are not recited at all.

Senator GEORGE. And some of them remotely relevant, at least.

SUGGESTED LANGUAGE

Ambassador DOUGLAS. This is what you have in mind:

Inasmuch as the participating countries have made certain pledges and undertakings among themselves, including the participation in a joint program for European recovery based on self-help and mutual cooperation, recited in the Paris Report of September 22, 1947, as a condition precedent to the performance for any participating country of any of the functions authorized under this act, such participating country shall conclude an agreement with the United States providing for the adherence of such country to the purposes of this act and, where applicable, shall make appropriate provision for * * *

and then recite the provisions of the bilateral contract.

Senator GEORGE. You are putting back your condition precedent.

Ambassador DOUGLAS. No, sir.

Senator GEORGE. Who is saying "condition precedent"?

Ambassador DOUGLAS. That refers only to the contract between the United States and the participating country.

Senator GEORGE. That means, "As a condition precedent, we agree to do so and so."

Ambassador DOUGLAS. "As a condition precedent to the performance of any participating country of any of the functions authorized under this act * * *". That is merely the language preliminary to the terms of the bilateral contract.

Senator HATCH. You do not have to use the words "condition precedent." This refers only to the contract they make with us.

Senator GEORGE. You mean what is going to follow after that, as a condition precedent—the following.

Ambassador DOUGLAS. That is right.

The CHAIRMAN. Are you not also going to require, as a condition precedent, whether you say so or not, multilateral agreements between these countries to cooperate for self-help and so forth?

Senator GEORGE. Sure, Mr. Chairman. There is no objection on that point.

Ambassador DOUGLAS. Yes; we recite all these.

The CHAIRMAN. That is the bilateral agreement.

Senator LODGE. The Declaration of Policy that you have in here is just what you have said.

Senator GEORGE. I do not object to what they agree among themselves to do. I do not object to that at all. I just don't want to be stating it here as a hard and fast condition of our participation in this program.

Ambassador DOUGLAS. Then there are certain other——

Senator GEORGE. Except as what we are suggesting really relates to the effectiveness of the program which we undertake, and unmistakably so. It might in our opinion, but it might not in theirs, relate to it at all. In other words, when you get into a debatable area, why do you want to write it into law?

Ambassador DOUGLAS. Then, if I understand you correctly, Senator, you have doubts about some of the general provisions, at least, which it is contemplated should be written into the bilateral contract?

DOUBTS ABOUT CONDITIONS PRECEDENT TO PARTICIPATION

Senator GEORGE. I am talking about the bilateral contract. I have doubts about a good many of the things we are laying down in this act as conditions precedent to our participation. I just don't think those things ought to be done. I don't think they ought to be undertaken, and I don't think it is really the way to approach this subject.

Mr. RICE. Would this be a possible compromise, to recite what Mr. Douglas just recited: "Inasmuch as the participating countries have mutually pledged themselves," and so forth, and so forth, "to a joint program, the Secretary of State, after consultation"—then go back up to subsection (a), "is authorized to conclude these bilateral agreements"?

Senator GEORGE. That is almost saying "As a condition precedent."

Mr. RICE. No, sir. We just recite that they have entered into these things.

Senator GEORGE. Mr. Rice, I know very well that that means exactly what I have said. "Inasmuch as so and so said so and so, we are going to do so and so."

Mr. RICE. Inasmuch as they met at Paris and reached an agreement among themselves for a joint program, then the Secretary of State may conclude a bilateral agreement with each country. Then each bilateral agreement would have these conditions precedent in it that are over on page 30 in subsection (c), not a condition precedent for the multilaterals.

Senator GEORGE. If you are going to do these things, how are you going to escape the criticism that you did not say they must not be Communists if they get our aid? These things are only modified conditions that we are putting on these people. And if you are going to put these on, why can't you just say, "Now, you must not be a disciple of Joe Stalin"?

Senator LODGE. Because they themselves have not agreed to that.

Senator GEORGE. I know, Senator Lodge.

Senator LODGE. That would be forcing something down their throats, whereas if you confine yourself to the things they have agreed to, I think that is what keeps you from getting into that dilemma.

Senator GEORGE. I do not mind reciting what they have agreed to, but I don't want to do it by way of conditions precedent.

The CHAIRMAN. I would rather not recite it, because I don't think they have agreed to do enough.

Senator GEORGE. I don't think they have either, but I don't mind putting it as the Ambassador suggests—inasmuch as they have done so and so, as a condition precedent, this act will provide for the following conditions:

That is all right. That hasn't anything to do with what they have said.

The CHAIRMAN. What reference, then, would you make to the multilateral agreements? We certainly must require a multilateral agreement.

Senator GEORGE. Are we dealing here with multilateral or bilateral?

The CHAIRMAN. At this point we are discussing simply the multilateral.

Senator GEORGE. I would simply start off and put down the things that have to do with the absolute minimum of success that we have to have for the success of this program. That is what I would do.

I don't interfere with their ideologies. That just relates to the things that must be done to make this program effective.

Senator LODGE. What we mean is we hope they are going to do those things, and the progress which they make toward those ends shall be a measure of the assistance they will receive from us. Isn't that what we mean to say?

Ambassador DOUGLAS. You say it in the preamble.

Senator LODGE. We say that in the declaration of policy, and I wonder whether that isn't business enough—beginning in line 16.

Ambassador DOUGLAS. And on line 4 of page 4.

RESPONSIBILITY FOR SAYING "YOU MUST NOT BE COMMUNISTS"

Senator GEORGE. I don't mind that, but I know this, that if you are going to specify what all these countries are going to do over there, you can't escape the responsibility of saying that you must not be Communists, and saying "You must establish what we understand to be a democracy," and then you would have 17,000 definitions of a democracy to see whether they lived up to it or not.

Senator SMITH. I don't quite see that that follows, because what we are asking for is the attainment of certain targets of production. That is the test. That hasn't anything to do with communism. If they can do it through communism or socialism or anything else, we are not going to kick, if they attain their objectives.

[Discussion was continued off the record.]

Senator GEORGE. If we are going to do these intimate things of their own life, and regulate their immigration and emigration and all those kinds of things, how can we stop short of saying, "You can't be a Communist?"

Senator SMITH. I thought the Ambassador had a pretty good statement here, and I thought it met your point without throwing in the Communist argument. We are simply asking them to agree among themselves to carry out what they agreed to in Paris. That is what your plan was.

Ambassador DOUGLAS. It is even milder than that.

Senator GEORGE. I have no objection to the way he put it, if he said, "As a condition precedent, the following * * *"

Ambassador DOUGLAS. The condition precedent referred to the provisions of the bilateral agreement between ourselves and each of the participating countries.

Senator GEORGE. I do not want to commit myself to saying that these countries must do this, either to get aid or not to get it.

The CHAIRMAN. I am still in a fog; I'm sorry.

Senator GEORGE. I do not want to enumerate, because I think when you go to enumerating you weaken your position altogether.

The CHAIRMAN. I don't want to enumerate. But it was my understanding that a multilateral treaty among these 16 participating countries is a condition precedent. What is in that multilateral treaty, so far as we are concerned, is the pursuit of the objectives defined in the Paris agreement by the 16 countries themselves, and we expect them to make a good faith effort to proceeed in the direction of self-help and cooperation.

Senator LODGE. To set up a joint organization which will move in that direction.

The CHAIRMAN. To set up a joint organization to move in that direction. Is there anything wrong about that?

Senator GEORGE. No; there is nothing wrong about that, except you have your chronology a bit mixed. General Marshall made his statement June 5th at Harvard. There hadn't been a Paris Conference. Then they met and they said what they would do. Now then, what do we want to say: "You must do that particular thing," when we don't believe in it, for instance?

The CHAIRMAN. You mean you don't believe in the enumeration?

Senator GEORGE. Certain of them.

The CHAIRMAN. But you certainly agree that there is no use in going into this show at all unless these cooperating countries are going to make an honest to God effort to do business together.

Senator GEORGE. I do believe in that. I think the whole thing ought to be conditioned on their disposition to help themselves. If they are not going to do any work, just quit them.

Senator LODGE. That is just it. Wouldn't you like to see them set up a joint organization?

Senator GEORGE. I have no objection in the world to that, but are we going to make it a condition precedent? If so, you will have the United Nations of Europe on your hands before you have finished.

DIFFERENT LANGUAGE SUGGESTED

Dr. WILCOX. May I ask if the language Senator George started on some time earlier might be enough. It may be too simple, but something comparable to this, Senator George: "In addition to the pledges which the participating countries voluntarily agreed to in their Paris declaration of such and such a date, each of the participating countries agrees to enter into the bilateral agreement," and then proceed to enumerate the pledges that are to be entered into in the bilateral agreement.

The CHAIRMAN. Where is the requirement for a multilateral agreement?

Dr. WILCOX. That would be in here.

The CHAIRMAN. It is not in the language you read.

Senator GEORGE. That is almost satisfactory to me, I think.

Dr. WILCOX. It is, Senator, in that it refers to these undertakings, and one of the undertakings is to cooperate with one another.

The CHAIRMAN. Read what you said again.

Dr. WILCOX. "In addition to the pledges which the participating countries voluntarily agreed to in their Paris declaration of such and such a date."

Senator GEORGE. I would not want to put it that way. That is almost making it a condition precedent. I am telling you the truth. Your Administrator is not going to live up to it. He can't live up to it. How can he see that these things are done before he extends aid? There is no use to expect the impossible.

The CHAIRMAN. I do not think that is required at all, and it is not in my concept of the thing. I am simply talking about the reiteration of a promise to cooperate for self-help as a condition precedent—the promise to cooperate.

Senator GEORGE. I don't care how strong you make that.

The CHAIRMAN. I think we are talking about the same thing.

Senator LODGE. I think it has got to a point now where Dr. Wilcox can write it out.

Senator GEORGE. I think so. How can any Administrator on this earth see that they will apply all these measures leading to the rapid achievement of internal monetary and economic stability as a condition precedent to extending aid?

Senator LODGE. He can't do that.

Senator GEORGE. Certainly he can't. He just can't do it. These are their goals that they are agreeing on.

The CHAIRMAN. That is the point.

Senator GEORGE. These are their objectives, and that is all right, so long as it is left in their realm. But I just don't want to commit myself to it for a whole year.

Senator LODGE. I don't think there is any conflict any more, Mr. Chairman.

The CHAIRMAN. We will leave it, and see what the staff can do with it. Let's see what is in the bilateral section. I will read page 30, line 14:

FROM THE BILATERAL SECTION

(c) In addition to the provisions to be included pursuant to subsection (b) of this section, such agreement with the United States shall also, where applicable, make appropriate provision for——.

Senator LODGE. Mr. Chairman, at that point I would like to point out that the original draft required all of these eight things that follow to be conditions precedent, but in this new draft that is taken out. They shall just make appropriate provision for. I wonder why that change was made. It seems to me these are the conditions that we are going to require, and that these ought to be conditions precedent.

Excuse me; Mr. Surrey says these are conditions precedent too.

The CHAIRMAN.

(1) Promoting industrial and agricultural production in order to enable the participating country to become independent of abnormal outside economic assistance;

(2) Taking financial and monetary measures necessary to stabilize its currency, establish or maintain a proper rate of exchange, and generally to restore or maintain confidence in its monetary system;

(3) Cooperating with other participating countries in facilitating and stimulating an increasing interchange of goods and services among the participating countries and with other countries and cooperating to reduce barriers to trade among themselves and with other countries;

Senator LODGE. Mr. Chairman, at that point is where I have this amendment on foreign assets. That is where that will come. Half of it will come in section 2 and half of it will come here. Would you rather take that all up as a unit later?

The CHAIRMAN. Let's read it through and we will come right back to that, Senator.

Senator LODGE. All right.

The CHAIRMAN.

(4) Making efficient use, within the framework of a joint program for European recovery, of the resources of such participating country, including any commodities, facilities, or services furnished under this Act;

(5) Facilitating the sale to the United States for stock-piling purposes, for such period of time as may be agreed to and upon reasonable terms and in reasonable quantities, of materials which are required by the United States as a

result of deficiencies or potential deficiencies in its own natural resources, and which may be available in such participating country after due regard for reasonable requirements for domestic use and commercial export of such country;

(6) Placing in a special account a deposit in the currency of such country, in commensurate amounts and under such terms and conditions as may be agreed to between such country and the Government of the United States, when any commodity or service is made available through any means authorized under this Act, and is not furnished to the participating country on terms of payment. Such special account, together with the unexpended portions of any deposits which may have been made by such country pursuant to section 6 of the joint resolution providing for relief assistance to the people of countries devastated by war (Public Law 84, Eightieth Congress) and section 5 (b) of the Foreign Aid Act of 1947, shall be held or used only for such purposes as may be agreed to between such country and the Government of the United States, and under agreement that any unencumbered balance remaining in such account on June 30, 1952, will be disposed of within such country for such purposes as may, subject to approval by Act or joint resolution of the Congress, be agreed to between such country and the Government of the United States;

(7) Publishing in such country and transmitting to the United States, not less frequently than every calendar quarter after the date of the agreement, of full statements of operations under the agreement, including a report of the use of funds, commodities and services received under this Act; and

(8) Furnishing promptly, upon request of the United States, any relevant information which would be of assistance to the United States in determining the nature and scope of future operations under this Act.

Does that, Mr. Ambassador, embrace the total bilateral agreement requirements?

Ambassador DOUGLAS. The principles, yes.

Senator SMITH. This is not exclusive of anything else.

Senator GEORGE. Why shouldn't you say, "among other things shall provide," so as not to restrict it merely to these things? Of course these are the main things.

The CHAIRMAN. "Such agreement with the United States shall also, where applicable, make appropriate provision, among other provisions," or something of that sort.

SECTION COMPARED TO THE INTERIM AID ACT

Dr. WILCOX. I should point out at this stage that in the drafting the question was raised as to whether this bill incorporated all of the additions that were in the Interim Aid Act. It does not, as you see. There is no provision comparable to the one with respect to publicity, there is no provision relating to reasonable prices; there is no provision relating to representatives of the press and radio having access to the countries, and there is no provision with respect to labeling.

Senator LODGE. There isn't anything relative to the use of funds to pay off debts, either.

Dr. WILCOX. We left the language as it was in the original State Department draft on this bilateral agreement.

AMBASSADOR DOUGLAS. You made one or two changes.

Dr. WILCOX. Yes, we did make that one with respect to the Congress. I thought we should point that out.

Senator GEORGE. Mr. Chairman, I don't know what may be omitted there, but it does seem to me that the things that are included are all right, except when you come back over here to your stockpiling proposal. Senator Thomas has gone out. That is restricted here, "as a result of deficiencies or potential deficiencies in its own natural resources, and which may be available in such participating country," and so forth.

Senator WILEY. After "participating country" "and colonies."

AN AMENDMENT BY SENATOR LODGE

Senator LODGE. I have an amendment I have offered on that. I have one amendment to section 5, which you have there, facilitating the transfer to the United States by sale, exchange, barter, or otherwise, for stockpiling purposes, and then I go on to line 17 and take Senator Wiley's suggestion: "including its colonies, territories, and possessions."

The purpose of that is that there has been testimony developed by many witnesses who said that it might be possible some day to acquire these materials by barter or exchange or some other way, and this just opens the way to that in case it should be considered desirable.

The CHAIRMAN. What is your comment on that, Mr. Ambassador?

Ambassador DOUGLAS. The first I think is satisfactory. I have some doubt about the need for the insertion of the language "including its colonies, territories, and possessions," because by definition participating countries include its colonies and dependenices.

Senator WILEY. It will do no harm, then.

Ambassador DOUGLAS. It will do no harm.

Senator LODGE. That is where most of the raw materials are.

Ambassador DOUGLAS. By definition a participating country embraces its colonies.

The CHAIRMAN. You have done no harm by it.

Ambassador DOUGLAS. It is no harm to insert it.

The CHAIRMAN. I would think that was a very useful change, because you have enlarged the category of the methods by which you can achieve these results.

Senator LODGE. That's right.

Ambaassdor DOUGLAS. I would not want it inferred from this language that there would immediately be a free transfer to the United States of strategic raw materials.

Senator LODGE. I think that is right, and I think the report should indicate that we do not expect anything like that in the immediate future. It is just a possibility for the remote future, because, as we have agreed, this is a process that may be spread over 10 or 20 years.

Ambassador DOUGLAS. Yes.

Senator LODGE. I think that is right. It ought to be made clear.

The CHAIRMAN. We will make that clear. Without objection, we will make that amendment.

Mr. RICE. I would like to raise one question, if I may.

The CHAIRMAN. Yes, sir.

Mr. RICE. As Mr. Douglas has just said, we have defined participating countries to include colonies and dependencies. If you add, in line 17, after "participating countries," "its colonies and dependencies," and do not put it in these other places—for instances on page 30, "promoting industrial and agricultural production in order to enable the participating country to become independent of abnormal outside economic assistance," can you argue there that you do not mean to include your colonies and dependencies whereas, as a matter of fact, wherever you use the expression "participating country" throughout the act, and in the agreements that will be based upon it, it will mean at all times, every place you have used it, "dependencies and colonies." It is bound to. It would be preferable from a technical standpoint to leave it out in line 17 and then expound on it in the committee report, that that is what the intention is.

Ambassador DOUGLAS. And that throughout the act the use of the word "participating country" means to include its dependencies and colonies.

Senator LODGE. What do you say, Senator Wiley? You are my lawyer on this.

Senator WILEY. That is OK.

The CHAIRMAN. You could certainly cover what you are talking about by just changing the language we adopted for section 3, which now reads "As used in this act, the term 'participating country.' means," and so forth, if you were to say "Wherever used in this act * * *" Then it certainly is clear, isn't it?

Senator LODGE. That's right.

Senator GEORGE. "In this act" means "wherever used."

The CHAIRMAN. You think this is plain as is?

Senator GEORGE. I think so. We have defined it. I don't think we can do any better.

The CHAIRMAN. Is that satisfactory?

Senator LODGE. Quite.

AN AMENDMENT ON FOREIGN ASSETS

I have an amendment on foreign assets, and I have given Dr. Wilcox the copies. In order to deal with this subject, you have to amend the bill in two places. One is here in subsection (4), and the other is in section (2)(b). I have prepared an amendment, and I think it would save time if I were to read a statement I have prepared in this connection.

It is generally agreed, I think, that we must be absolutely sure that all assets owned by foreigners in this country are put into service by the Marshall Plan in so far as this can be intelligently done.

In this connection, former Secretary of War Patterson, testifying on January 22, made a distinction between these two broad classifications of assets in this country. He said:

> One kind is the regular ordinary reserves nationals of a country may have here in the regular course of business * * * the other kind is hoarded, hidden money by nationals of other countries. That kind I believe we should give the nations over there every facility to recover and get behind their own economic rehabilitation.

I suppose in the first he meant Lever Brothers and all those different outfits.

In order to carry out these objectives, the bill is amended to provide:

(1) That it is one of the purposes of the European recovery programs to further efficient use of foreign assets in this country in the recovery program, and that the administrator and Secretary of the Treasury are directed to cooperate fully with foreign governments to carry out this purpose;

(2) That each participating country must agree to make efficient and practical use of these assets.

You will note that the amendments are stated in broad terms on the understanding that the administrator will use his discretion in an "efficient" and "practical" way.

After careful consideration, I concluded that it would not be desirable to attempt legislatively to distinguish between so-called working capital and idle or hoarded capital as these terms are generally understood, but I think if these amendments are adopted the intent of the committee should be made planning the report that the idle or hoarded or unproductive assets are the ones which should be reached.

ILLUSTRATIVE INSTANCES OF ASSETS

I have some instances which illustrate the impossibility of making a distinction between the two types of assets right in the bill. For example, the assets of foreign enterpises held in the United States for use in their ordinary business would generally fall into the category of working capital. But it is well known that some enterprises maintain dollar balances in the United States in excess of their working needs in order to protect such balances against depreciation of the local currency of the country in which the particular enterprise is organized. Foreign steamship companies, for example, may maintain such excessive balances here.

A second instance: Investments by individuals in U.S. Government securities would generally be regarded as not falling within the category of working capital. Yet such securities may be held by foreign insurance companies and used as deposits with State insurance authorities in order to qualify such companies to do business in a particular State.

A third instance: Private residences owned by foreign nationals may be said not to fall within the category of working capital. But such residences may be held by foreign nationals who are in this country on productive business and who find it more economical to own than to rent their residences. Even cash balances may present difficulties of classification. A number of foreign citizens who frequently visit the United States on productive business may maintain cash balances here for the purpose of paying their expenses while in this country and in order to avoid risk of loss in foreign exchange transactions. The question whether or not such balances are excessive would be difficult to determine in statutory provisions.

Finally, a fourth instance: It was also recognized that investments of foreign nationals in securities of American corporations would present difficulties. If such corporations are operating subsidies of foreign enterprises, the investments may properly be classified as working capital. But here again other classes of investments, superficially similar, would more realistically be classified as "hoarded" or "idle."

I think that that shows why it was necessary to write this language in a broad way and flexible way, and give to the Administrator the chance to exercise his discretion. I have shown this language to Mr. Southard and Mr. Friedman of the Treasury Department about 10 or 11 days ago and I have not heard anything from them since. At that time they said that they thought, generally speaking, I was on the beam. I have not heard anything more since.

The CHAIRMAN. Now will you indicate what your amendments precisely do, Senator Lodge?

LODGE AMENDMENT IN TWO PARTS

Senator LODGE. It is in two parts, as I said.

The CHAIRMAN. Let's take the part we are right on.

Senator LODGE. All right; we will take the part we are right on. It is paragraph (4):

"Making efficient" and insert "and practical" "use, within the framework of joint program for European recovery, of the resources of such participating country, including any commodity, facilities, or services furnished under this act", and the new language is "and including further the assets, tangible or intangible, of the citizens of the respective participating countries which are situated within the United States, its territories and possessions and which can be of effective use in the furtherance of such program."

Senator SMITH. Does that mean that the names of people who have investments in the United States must be given to the participating country?

Senator LODGE. If you look at the first part, it means that the Administrator and the Secretary of the Treasury are authorized to cooperate fully in assisting the governments of these participating countries..

Senator SMITH. Then it does mean that they are to give them those names.

Senator LODGE. The French Government has requested the help of our Government in locating the assets of their own nationals, to get them behind this plan.

Senator SMITH. That has been pointed out as the danger of this thing. For years we have had foreign investments in the United States, and whether we should be a watchdog to give to various foreign countries the names of everybody who invests in the United States is a very important question of policy.

Senator LODGE. I think it is a very important question of policy, and I think it is very acutely before us in connection with this whole program.

Senator SMITH. It is also pointed out that the income from the investments in the United States helps the dollar balances over there, and these people have to account for that income, or I suppose they account for it.

Senator LODGE. They do not pay a capital gains tax at all. That is another point we can reach in this. I am thinking of offering an amendment before the Finance Committee to make them subject to the capital gains tax.

Senator SMITH. The Swiss have very large investments in this country, and I have a representation from people representing the Swiss people that they do not feel that this would be just to the ordinary investor, and they also point out that the total amount involved is much less than has been estimated. Have you any idea what might be reached? Some extravagant statements were made that it went up to $13 billion. It is probably less than that.

Senator LODGE. If we realized something out of it we would be that much to the good, whatever we got out of it. It is a matter of justice. You cannot defend putting this burden on to the average American taxpayer of moderate means and letting the well-to-do foreigner go scot-free.

Senator SMITH. Are you sure they are all very wealthy people, or are some of them little investors?

Senator LODGE. They are of all kinds.

AMERICAN NATIONALS SHOULD HELP THEIR OWN NATION

Senator WILEY. Mr. Chairman, I haven't been saying much. I can see a great deal on both sides of this question. But I want to say that I feel, with regard to what Senator Smith says, that on the other hand, if you are going to sell this bill, not only to the House and Senate but to the American people, you had better have some provisions like this in it, that the nationals of the nations ought to be willing to help their own people if we, who are not nationals of those nations, are going to go into our jeans and help them. My mail is running tremendously against the whole proposition, and I am getting letters from business organizations and they want us to make certain findings, to let them get the facts. I am going to bring one of those letters over one of these days. It comes from a small business organization, asking a complete evaluation of the effect upon our own economy now, and a number of other questions.

As I say, if we have a bill of goods on which most of us feel something has to be done, we had better dress up that bill of goods a little bit.

SELLING A BILL OF GOODS HARD

Senator SMITH. I am not arguing with the Senator from Wisconsin on the point that it is hard to sell a bill of goods where we are asking our taxpayers to pay something out, where people of other countries have these other assets, but the case was made, I think, in the presentation of the case, I recall, by the Ambassador from London for not interfering with these foreign investments in this country. In fact, the British called some of them in, did they not, by some process?

Ambassador DOUGLAS. They did during the early part of the war.

Senator SMITH. What is your judgment from your experience there on this particular point? I would be interested ot hear that, because I have heard the argument from the Swiss and the French standpoints, that we should protect these investors from having their governments get all these names.

BRITISH POSITION AGGRAVATED

Ambassador DOUGLAS. Of course the liquidation of the British assets in this country and in other parts of the world is one of the factors that aggravates her position now. Her invisible income before the war was very substantial. One of the items in her invisible income was a return on foreign investments. I was reading Cripps' statement in this morning's press. The deficiency on account of invisible income in the year 1947 was, I think, about £227 million, very close to a billion dollars.

DISTINCTION BETWEEN CAPITAL INVESTED IN UNITED STATES

There is, of course, Senator, a distinction between the type of capital which is invested in this country and which is reported on its own to the governments of the nationals which have invested it in that type of investment in the United States. That particular country, presumably, directly or indirectly, derives some benefit, in whole or in part, from the dollar income. At least the national pays an income tax on it.

There probably is, on the other hand, a certain amount of capital in this country which is flight and hidden capital, not reported to the government of the national who has moved the capital to this country. With respect to that type of flight capital the country of the person that has moved the capital derives no benefit, and perhaps even is unable to impose its taxes, and I presume it was toward the second type of capital that the amendment offered by the Senator is aimed.

I recognize the prejudices that can be aroused by referring to capital in this country, flight capital, of nationals of the 16 participating countries. One of the characteristics of a free enterprise and capitalistic system has been, up to a few years ago, the freedom of an individual to move his capital from one country to another. There have been times in our own history when Americans have moved their capital out. After the Civil War and during the Civil War many of our citizens did.

There have been other occasions in history when capital fled from the United States. There have been periods in history when capital of Europeans has come to the United States or, if not to the United States, to other parts of the world.

There is a general principle—I am talking very personally—involved in playing the part of a discloser, of our Government playing the part of a discloser to another government. There is the principle, too, of requiring a government to confiscate or appropriate or otherwise to acquire the capital of its citizens. It is a principle that jars me a little bit because I think it is inconsistent with my general view of the economic organization of society. As I say, I recognize the difficulties.

There is one thing I would suggest that you avoid doing, and that is, taking any action, or requiring that any action be taken, which would compel the liquidation of those assets.

Senator LODGE. We have not done that. We have been very careful not to do that.

Ambassador DOUGLAS. It would be forced liquidation.

Senator LODGE. The Treasury is opposed to liquidation, and I agreed with Mr. Southard on that on the record. They have seen this, and I think I am correct in saying that they think it is within the general tenor of his remarks.

The CHAIRMAN. The Secretary's letter to me under date of February 2 on this subject reports on the decision of the National Advisory Council, and he says:

> The Council concluded that no action should be taken regarding free assets, because the amounts which are unknown to the governments of recipient countries are probably insignificant, and in any event serious practical difficulties would be involved. The Council also concluded, however, that this Government should assist the recipient countries to obtain control of the blocked assets in the United States of their resident citizens.

Senator SMITH. They would only be blocked as former enemy countries—Italy and some countries like that.

Senator LODGE. They do not want that distinction made in the legislative language, do they? They do not say that.

Senator SMITH. You could not very well distinguish between your participating countries.

Senator LODGE. You can not distinguish in the terms of the bill. You have to give the administrator discretion to do the thing right.

Senator SMITH. If he is operating, he has to give the names to the other countries, and you can't prevent the liquidation of those assets if they want to grab them, whether it is for this purpose or not, once they get the names.

Senator LODGE. He does not have to under the terms of this language, "furthering the efficient utilization." If he does not think it is efficient he would not do it.

EFFECT UPON U.S. FOREIGN INVESTMENTS

Ambassador DOUGLAS. There is this further general consideration that bothers me a little bit. What effect might action of this order and character on our part have upon possible action by foreign countries in regard to the foreign investments of American nationals? Will this type of action establish a precedent which might invoke against American nationals some time in the future?

Senator WILEY. How would that work? Most of those countries, like Germany, just took the assets, didn't they? They didn't hesitate. They went in and took whatever there was of foreigners.

Ambassador DOUGLAS. I don't think so, Senator. I do not know the whole history by any manner of means, and I am speaking only from a recollection that has become rather hazy.

Senator WILEY. If they didn't, it is the only place in the world that Hitler didn't take everything he could lay his hands on, including art treasures, money, and gold.

Ambassador DOUGLAS. I think American investments in Germany still remained intact.

Dr. WILCOX. And the peace treaties with the satellite countries provide for the restitution of property.

Senator SMITH. We have a case now of property taken over by the Bulgarian Government. They violated the Bulgarian peace treaty, in my judgment.

Ambassador DOUGLAS. But we are here dealing with these 16 participating countries.

Senator SMITH. I don't understand this business well enough to know all the answers, I am frank to say. I agree with Senator Lodge that it is pretty hard to say that our taxpayers should be contributing to this thing, where we know there are other assets.

SUGGESTION FROM THE TREASURY DEPARTMENT

Senator LODGE. One of these gentlemen has just handed me a text which the Treasury Department has just sent up. I do not know why they have waited so long and why they sent it to me in this indirect way.

The CHAIRMAN. They suggest, "Make efficient and practical use within the framework of the joint program for European recovery of the resources of such participating country, including any commodities, facilities, or services furnished under this act," and then the new language, "and to the extent practicable, taking measures to locate and control in furtherance of such program assets and earnings therefrom which belong to the citizens of such country, and which are situated within the United States, its territories, and possessions."

Senator LODGE. The only difference in that is that it does not say "tangible or intangible," that I can see. What is the difference?

Mr. GROSS. The essential difference, as I understand the Treasury point of view, is that instead of referring to making efficient and practical use, this requires an undertaking to take measures to locate and control. They seem to attach great importance to the distinction between "use" and "control," on the ground that "use" has at least the implication, and they think perhaps more than an implication, of forced liquidation of assets.

Senator LODGE. I do not want to do that. There is no desire on my part to do that.

Ambassador DOUGLAS. That is right. That is the distinction which the Treasury makes.

The CHAIRMAN. Do I understand this language is satisfactory to the Treasury?

Mr. GROSS. Yes, sir.

The CHAIRMAN. Doesn't that accomplish your purpose?

Senator LODGE. I think it does.

The CHAIRMAN. Particularly if you have language that you can say the Treasury backs up. That is worth more than two or three extra words in your own amendment.

Senator LODGE. Yes, they have been awfully slow in giving me any response at all.

The CHAIRMAN. Did you not see the Secretary's letter of February 2?

Senator LODGE. Yes. I think it is a forward step. There is going to be a demand on the floor to nail that down in the bill.

TREASURY AMENDMENT ADOPTED

The CHAIRMAN. You are satisfied with the Treasury amendment? Is there any objection to the adoption of the Treasury draft? The Chair hears none. It is adopted. That is one cleared up.

Senator SMITH. I think that takes care of the point, because it gives the Administrator discretion to deal with it.

Senator LODGE. My amendment always did give the Administrator discretion.

The CHAIRMAN. You do not need to be afraid of anything so long as you can say John Snyder says it is all right.

Senator LODGE. Now there is the other part of it that goes into section (2) (b).

The CHAIRMAN. Let's wait until we get to that.

Is there anything else pending that has been proposed to be put into these bilateral agreements?

Senator LODGE. I would like to ask one question.

The CHAIRMAN. Was there something in the questions I asked you, Mr. Ambassador?

PROCEEDS OF AID NOT USED TO PAY PRINCIPAL OR INTEREST

Senator LODGE. This is a question raised by Senator Connally, and I think I raised it too, on the matter of putting in a paragraph in which the recipient country would agree not to use any part of the proceeds of any loan, credit, grant, or gift for the making of any payment on account of the principal or interest on any loan which would be made by a participating country to a foreign government. We have that in the Greek bill. How do you feel about putting it into this bill?

The CHAIRMAN. I am afraid the Ambassador did not hear your question. He was looking up something for me.

Senator LODGE. I want to ask you how you would feel about adding a paragraph, which would be paragraph 9, in which the participating country would agree not to use any part of the proceeds of any loan, credit, or grant that it received under this act, for the making of any payment on account of the principal or interest on any loan made or to be made to such participating country by any other foreign government. We have that in the Greek bill now.

Ambassador DOUGLAS. I was not here at the time. That was written in the House, as I recall it.

Senator LODGE. No, it was put in over here.

Senator GEORGE. What do you mean by that?

Senator LODGE. I am not offering it. I am asking the question whether you think it ought to go in, because one of the criticisms of this is that they will get this money and siphon it right through to take care of their own people and to take care of foreign loans that have been made to them. In the case of Greece the argument was made, as I recall it, that unless we put something like that in, the Greeks would take this money and use it to pay off loans Great Britain had made to them.

Ambassador DOUGLAS. Offhand, these countries have an exchange problem, and one of the factors that goes to make up the exchange problem is obligations which they have entered into. To the extent to which their resources, from whatever source derived, are unavailable to service the debt, they default. I don't know how this would affect some of the countries. Would you let me think about it?

Senator LODGE. I am not proposing it. It is something I wrote out. I am not even offering it or pressing it. It is something that is liable to come up; it is one of those things the boys like ot bring up.

Ambassador DOUGLAS. I would like to think about it.

The CHAIRMAN. That is the great charge that my hometown Congressman makes against this bill, that we are going to let Britain pay her debts to somebody else. Of course we are.

Senator LODGE. I am not pressing the thing. I think it is a thing we ought to think about here and now, and get our answers ready.

The CHAIRMAN. If the result of our help did not help her pay her debts it would not be very effective help.

Ambassador DOUGLAS. I should think that this would have the effect of aggravating one of the conditions we are trying to cure.

Senator LODGE. If that is what you really think, let's not do anything about it.

Ambassador DOUGLAS. Offhand, that is my judgment.
Senator SMITH. How does that read?
Ambassador DOUGLAS.

Agreeing not to use any part of the proceeds of any loan, credit, grant, or any other form of assistance, for the making of any payment on account of principal or interest on any loan made or to be made such participating country by any foreign government.

Senator LODGE. I took that out of the Greek aid bill.
Ambassador DOUGLAS. I think we will aggravate a condition we are trying to cure.
Senator SMITH. I can see why straight relief funds should not be used for this purpose, but here where we have these economic issues I think we should be careful.
The CHAIRMAN. Now, Mr. Administrator, I have handed you one or two things that I was asked to submit. Do they go here?
Ambassador DOUGLAS. Yes, Mr. President.
The CHAIRMAN. All right, Mr. Ambassador.

A BETTER PHRASE THAN "PROPER RATE OF EXCHANGE"

Ambassador DOUGLAS. You asked me to see if we could not find a better phrase than "proper rate of exchange" in subsection (2), section (3) on page 30.
The CHAIRMAN. Yes.
Ambassador DOUGLAS. You suggested the possibility of some language which read: "To maintain a rate of exchange which will reflect with reasonable accuracy the relative purchasing powers of the currencies involved."
The CHAIRMAN. That is a request from the rump Republican Convention.
Ambassador DOUGLAS. You spoke to me about it privately. I personally have objection to it because it is an implication, and my implication rests upon the whole Keynesian doctrine of fluctuating exchange in order to make adjustments for variations in internal prices and costs. I myself believe very strongly that internal prices and costs fluctuate around the exchange rate, otherwise I think it is impossible to expect or hope for any sort of stable international currency arrangement. Therefore I personally, in my own mind, would be very reluctant to agree to that language.
"The proper rate of exchange." The use of that phrase does not avoid an interpretation by one of the countries of the phrase not unlike the one which has been suggested. But I do not know what better phrase to use than "a proper rate of exchange."
The CHAIRMAN. How about a "valid rate of exchange"?
Ambassador DOUGLAS. I would accept "valid."
The CHAIRMAN. I do not know what either "proper" or "valid" means, but as for a proper rate of exchange, you might just as well go out and let the moon shine in your mouth.
Ambassador DOUGLAS. If it is good moonshine it might not be objectionable!
The CHAIRMAN. It means nothing, does it?
Ambassador DOUGLAS. A "valid" rate of exchange carries the implication that it is a rate of exchange which can be maintained.
The CHAIRMAN. I think "proper" means just nothing.
Ambassador DOUGLAS. It does not mean much.

The CHAIRMAN. What do you say, Senator George? Is there now any utility in changing that word?

Senator GEORGE. Well, I don't know. The word "proper" doesn't seem to fit there so much, and yet that is about what you mean, I suppose.

The CHAIRMAN. You mean the gentlemanly rate of exchange.

Senator GEORGE. No, you don't mean that.

Senator WILEY. You mean a workable rate of exchange.

Senator GEORGE. No, you mean an accurate rate, one that reflects the real value of the currency involved. That is what you mean. It is more of an accurate rate, but that does not exactly say it.

Ambassador DOUGLAS. "Valid", I think, is a good word.

Senator GEORGE. "Valid" is one you can validate, one that you can sustain. "Valid" does imply that it has the attributes of genuineness.

Senator WILEY. A soundness.

Ambassador DOUGLAS. It has continuity to it.

The CHAIRMAN. Without objection, we will change "proper" to "valid."

Senator GEORGE. The Ambassador, when he gets to be Administrator, will have some trouble with pound, but that is a small matter.

The CHAIRMAN. Did you have another one?

Ambassador DOUGLAS. No, sir; I think that is all there was in this section.

The CHAIRMAN. Does that conclude the bilateral agreements? I think there was something about projects.

Ambassador DOUGLAS. That was in another subparagraph, (6) of section 7. Maybe that is the old section 7.

[Discussion was continued off the record.]

THE POWER OF ALLOCATION

The CHAIRMAN. We have not dealt with any allocations yet.

Ambassador DOUGLAS. No.

The CHAIRMAN. That would be the other print. The rump convention didn't have this print.

Senator GEORGE. We have not done anything back over here, Mr. Chairman, with section (d) on page 14, with reference to these zones.

The CHAIRMAN. No. That has a question mark on it.

Senator LODGE. How about the declaration of purpose?

The CHAIRMAN. We have not done anything about that, yet.

Where is the power of allocation under this bill? Does it stay in the Department of Commerce or does it go over to the Administrator?

Ambassador DOUGLAS. It stays in the Department of Commerce and the Department of Agriculture.

Senator GEORGE. Is it expressly so stated anywhere here, or is it just not dealt with?

Ambassador DOUGLAS. It is just not dealt with.

Senator SMITH. That would be export controls also?

[Discussion was continued off the record.]

Ambassador DOUGLAS. The Department of Agriculture is concerned with the American economy. The Department of Commerce is concerned with the American economy. The Administrator is charged with the responsibility of administering a European recovery program. It seemed to me more prudent to leave the power to allocate in a purely American agency of the Government that is concerned with the internal American economy. The Administrator of the European recovery program, under such circumstances, would then be limited by the authority of purely American agencies of Government insofar as commodities of various sorts and descriptions might become available for export.

On the other hand, if the power to allocate grain, foodstuffs, steel, petroleum, were vested in the Administrator, he would thereby become the arbiter of the economy of the European recovery program and of the internal American economy. I should think, therefore, that it would be better to leave the powers in a purely American agency of the Government—that is, the power to allocate——

The CHAIRMAN. Let me see if I understand it.

Ambassador DOUGLAS [continuing]. Than to put them in the Administrator.

The CHAIRMAN. Does that mean the Secretary of Commerce could checkmate the Administrator?

Ambassador DOUGLAS. The Secretary of Commerce and the Secretary of Agriculture could say, acting together with regard to petroleum, "The American petroleum which will be available for export to the Western European countries must be reduced."

ALLOCATION DECIDED BY THE PRESIDENT

Senator GEORGE. Would there be any way to get the matter up to the President?

Of course, actually it would go up to him.

Ambassador DOUGLAS. Yes. If there were a disagreement, the Administrator would take the matter to him.

Senator GEORGE. That is not written out here.

Ambassador DOUGLAS. No, it isn't.

Senator GEORGE. It is not spelled out in the bill.

Ambassador DOUGLAS. No, it isn't.

Senator GEORGE. That sounds logical and proper, but it is an awfully good way to pass the buck.

Ambassador DOUGLAS. Yes. There are objections that can be raised to it. Yet I should think that in a program of this character, which carries with it implications for the American economy, it would be the course of prudence to retain certain powers over the allocation of materials for export in purely American agencies.

The CHAIRMAN. That is as sound as a nut!

Senator GEORGE. I think that is all right. I do agree it is sound, but it is an awfully fine way for the Administrator to say, "Well, I couldn't carry out the program."

Mr. RICE. That couldn't happen under this, Senator. The President has absolutely direct control over the Export Control Act. He has absolute direct control over the allocation of foods for export. He has absolute control over the Administrator under this Act. So he is right up at the apex of all three of them, as a matter of law.

Ambassador DOUGLAS. But he has delegated those powers to the Department of Agriculture and the Department of Commerce, and if the Administrator disagreed with any person to whom the President had delegated authority, the Administrator would carry the issue, if he were a man of character and conviction, up to the President, and it would become a Cabinet issue, or certainly an issue which the President would decide.

Mr. RICE. I just wanted to point out the legal technical aspect.

Ambassador DOUGLAS. I am sorry that I did not mention what you had pointed out. The fact is that under the authority of the President to delegate, the Secretary of Agriculture does exercise the authority to allocate foodstuffs, and the Department of Commerce, acting in consultation with other departments, exercises the authority over export controls, including petroleum.

Senator WILEY. Mr. Ambassador, I could not agree to any course other than what has just been stated. I agree fully with the Ambassador. Whoever the Administrator is, his job is so tremendous, he is looking at the European situation, he see the needs, and so forth. Now, you have got to have someone over here who is eyeing the local needs, and between the two of them they have to work out this program. If they can't work it out, then the umpire, the President, will do it, but one human being isn't big enough to handle the economy of this country and that of Europe at the same time, and I am sure that the policy outlined is the one for us to follow.

The CHAIRMAN. I think it greatly simplifies our problem.

TERMINATION OF AID

Mr. Ambassador, there was one amendment that you were going to work on dealing with the diversion of relief, or the divergence of assistance from this objective to other objectives.

Ambassador DOUGLAS. The amendment is related to the termination.

The CHAIRMAN. Can we look at it for just a minute?

Ambassador DOUGLAS. Yes, and I found the place for the other amendment; at least I think I have.

Page 34, line 19, "Termination of Assistance."

"After the comma after the word section in section 15, page 34"—that is diverting support provided by the United States for the purposes of this Act.

Senator GEORGE. What is it you propose to do?

Ambassador DOUGLAS (reading):

> Whenever he determines that (1) such country is not adhering to its agreement concluded under this section; is diverting support provided by the United States from the purposes of this Act.

The CHAIRMAN. Is there some kind of conjunctive in there?

Ambassador DOUGLAS (reading). "And that, in the circumstances, remedial action * * *."

The CHAIRMAN. Read it again the way it will read.

Ambassador DOUGLAS (reading):

> Whenever he determines that (1) such country is not adhering to its agreement concluded under Section 14, is diverting such support provided by the Unitd States from the purposes of this Act;

The CHAIRMAN. Yes.

That language will be of great assistance with some of our dissident members, and I think the Ambassador himself is quite agreeable to it, because he has had some experience with diversion.

Ambassador DOUGLAS. Yes. It was a vicarious experience, but an experience, nevertheless.

The CHAIRMAN. And you give me a vicarious "yes" in reply.

Is there objection to that? Without objection, that will be put in, because it helps a lot in connection with the rump convention.

Ambassador DOUGLAS. My legal counsel tells me that the language is not good, but that is the idea.

Senator SMITH. That might be applied, though, to applying it to these debts. Still, it might be assumed that the purposes of this Act included that.

The CHAIRMAN. What was the other one?

Ambassador DOUGLAS. I had another one in section 7, the new section 11. I have not fitted it into this.

Senator LODGE. What page?

Mr. RICE. It starts on page 18.

Ambassador DOUGLAS.

> (a) The Administrator may, from time to time, furnish assistance to any participating country by providing for the performance of any of the functions set forth in paragraphs (1) through (5) of this subsection when he deems it to be in furtherance of the purposes of this Act . . .",

and then it goes "Procurement," "Processing," "Procurement," "Chartering," and "Transfer," and this was the language which I suggested as a new paragraph, subparagraph (6).

The CHAIRMAN. Oh, yes; that's it.

Ambassador DOUGLAS.

> (6) The allocation of commodities or services designed to carry out the purposes of this Act to specific projects, which have been submitted to the Administrator by the participating countries, and have been approved by him.

IDENTIFICATION OF SPECIFIC PROJECTS

The CHAIRMAN. The idea that these gentlemen have is that they wanted somewhere to identify the idea of specific projects as part of this program, which I think is very sound.

Ambassador DOUGLAS. I do not think there is any harm in it. The commodities that may be provided by the extension of aid or in the form of a grant or loan by the United States to a participating country will, in many instances, become merged with the commodities provided or purchased by the same participating country out of its own resources. The identity of one becomes merged with the identity of the other, and you have only a quantitative measure of the articles or commodities that may be used in a specific project.

The CHAIRMAN. This cannot possibly do any harm.

Ambassador DOUGLAS. I do not believe it can do any harm.

The CHAIRMAN. It will do some good upstairs, so if there is no objection, we will put it in.

All right, that is in, Mr. Rice.

Senator SMITH. Mr. Chairman, when are we going to hear the ultimatums of the rump convention, or is it necessary to hear them? Do we hear them by degrees?

The CHAIRMAN. You are getting them all from the horse's mouth, right here. [Discussion off the record.]

The CHAIRMAN. We still have something to finish on page 33. I am going to let you go in just a minute. I just wonder if we can't finish this section.

POWER OF THE ADMINISTRATOR WITHIN 3 MONTHS OF ENACTMENT

Page 33:

(d) Notwithstanding the provision of subsection (b) or (c) of this section, the Administrator, during the three months after the date of enactment of this Act, may perform with respect to any participating country any of the functions authorized under this Act which he may determine to be essential in furtherance of the purposes of this Act, provided that such country (i) has signified its adherence to the purposes of this Act and its intention to conclude an agreement pursuant to subsections (b) and (c) of this section, and (ii) he finds that such country is complying with the applicable provisions of subsection (b) or (c) of this section: Provided, That, notwithstanding the provisions of this subsection, the Administrator may, through June 30, 1948, provide for the transfer of food, medical supplies, fibers, fuel, petroleum and petroleum products, fertilizer, pesticides, and seed to any country of Europe which participated in the Committee of European Economic Cooperation and which undertook pledges to the other participants therein, when the Administrator determines that the transfer of any such supplies to any such country is essential in order to make it possible to carry our the purposes of this Act by alleviating conditions of hunger and cold by preventing serious economic retrogression.

What does that all mean?

Senator SMITH. Isn't that an interim relief program to carry on until we get the new program going?

Ambassador DOUGLAS. Until the Administrator has taken office and has an appropriate staff to carry out the full recovery purposes of the act. There are certain countries that are going to be in desperate shape. In the case of Austria, for example, where we have troops of occupation, all the funds appropriated by the Interim Aid Act will have been obligated and the pipelines will be sufficient to carry food into Austria up to about the middle of May. If no further shipments can be made immediately after the first of April, to Austria, by the 20th of May it is calculated that the ration in the western part of Austria may fall to as low as 500 or 600 calories, and the situation there would be very serious.

Senator GEORGE. Is it going to take 3 months after the act is passed and the Administrator is appointed to get going?

Ambassador DOUGLAS. No, but certainly you cannot appoint the Administrator until the act has become the law.

Senator GEORGE. That is right, of course.

Ambassador DOUGLAS. And the Administrator may have to take a week or 2 or 3 weeks after appointment for confirmation. Then it will take him perhaps a week or 2 to take office and to surround himself with several competent people.

The CHAIRMAN. A week or 2? I would think so. It might even take 10 days.

Ambassador DOUGLAS. It might—or 3 weeks.

The purpose of this language is to permit certain features of the program to progress during the period in which his office is becoming organized.

The CHAIRMAN. What features are those?

Ambassador DOUGLAS. The shipment of food, fertilizers, drugs, and medical supplies.

Senator SMITH. Suppose the debate on the act carries through to May.

The CHAIRMAN. Then you go back to another section. You have another section here.

IF BILL NOT PASSED BY APRIL 1

Ambassador DOUGLAS. The Senator's question is, suppose the debate is extended beyond the first of April. The act is not then a law. The administration will then have to come to Congress for an emergency appropriation.

Senator SMITH. You see, this will go to the House, and there will be a debate even longer in the House.

Senator GEORGE. To fill up that gap if it does not get too long.

Ambassador DOUGLAS. There will be no other alternative.

Senator GEORGE. I do not like for you to state those things in that form. You mean, if we are going to do these things there is no other alternative.

Ambassador DOUGLAS. In the case of Austria, unless we are prepared to face what I have been told may be a very critical situation, even disorder and violence, in an area in which we have troops of occupation, we will have to come forward with a request for further assistance, further aid, further appropriation.

Senator GEORGE. You mean if we do not pass this by April 1.

Ambassador DOUGLAS. In the case of Austria, yes.

Senator GEORGE. And get it all set up?

Ambassador DOUGLAS. At least have the authority to make shipments promptly after the first of April.

Senator GEORGE. You might have some acute situations in this country, but nobody ever states them in the absolute alternative in that way.

Ambassador DOUGLAS. I apologize to you for stating it as an alternative, but I think it is a fact.

Senator GEORGE. It might be. I do not mean to say it is not.

Senator SMITH. Mr. Chairman, I just call attention to the fact, on this page 33, we refer to subsection (b) (2) or (3) many times, and of course that is in abeyance at the moment in the light of our earlier conversation this morning, so if you are getting the approval of this section now, it may be the subject of such changes as Mr. Rice will have to make.

The Chairman. That is correct.

ENCOURAGING JOINT ORGANIZATION OF PARTICIPATING COUNTRIES

There is just one final sentence at the top of page 34:

(e) The Administrator shall encourage the joint organization of the participating countries referred to in subsection (b) of section 14 of this Act to ensure that each participating country makes efficient use of the resources of such country, including any commodities, facilities, or services furnished under this Act, by observing and reviewing such use through an effective follow-up system approved by the joint organization.

I think we have approved of that before.

Senator LODGE. Yes.

The CHAIRMAN. OK.

Senator WILEY. Mr. Chairman, have we got that information called for, the overall program of relief to Turkey, Greece, China, and so on?

Senator GEORGE. No.

Senator WILEY. Then how are we going to discuss the thing unless we know what we are talking about.

Senator GEORGE. We get it in installments.

The CHAIRMAN. You have the overall figures. A copy was sent to your office.

Senator GEORGE. $9,373 million.

Senator WILEY. When was that?

The CHAIRMAN. Last week.

[Whereupon, at 4:40 p.m., the hearing was recessed, to reconvene on the following day, Thursday, February 11, 1948, at 10 a.m.]

EUROPEAN RECOVERY PROGRAM

THURSDAY, FEBRUARY 12, 1948

UNITED STATES SENATE,
COMMITTEE ON FOREIGN RELATIONS,
Washington, D.C.

The committee met, pursuant to adjournment, in the committee hearing room, U.S. Capitol, at 10 a.m., Senator Arthur H. Vandenberg, chairman, presiding.

Present: Senators Vandenberg, Capper, Wiley, Smith, George, Thomas of Utah, Barkley, and Hatch.

Also present: the Honorable Lewis W. Douglas, Ambassador to Great Britain; Mr. Paul Nitze, Deputy Director, Office of International Trade Policy, Department of State; Mr. Ernest Gross, Legal Adviser, Department of State; Mr. Stephen E. Rice, legislative counsel, U.S. Senate.

The CHAIRMAN. The committee will come to order.

OPENING STATEMENT

When we adjourned yesterday we were dealing with the multilateral and bilateral agreements, starting on page 29.

Senator BARKLEY. Mr. Chairman, may I ask a question, on account of my absence. I understand that you already have completed the administrative features.

The CHAIRMAN. That is correct.

Senator BARKLEY. Are they included in this print?

The CHAIRMAN. Not in this print.

Senator BARKLEY. May I have a copy to take it with me tonight?

The CHAIRMAN. This is what I intended to do, if it is agreeable with the committee. I think we can complete by tomorrow night the amending process so far as we are concerned in respect to this first writeup of the bill. When that is completed, I propose that we shall have a new complete committee print made of the bill in the form in which we have agreed upon it. Then I propose to recess until Monday so that everybody can see what it is.

Senator BARKLEY. That is all right. I just wanted to bring the stuff up to date.

Senator SMITH. Then you plan to act on the whole bill probably on Monday or Tuesday?

The CHAIRMAN. I would like to have as many members of the committee here as possible when we act on the bill, either present in person or by proxies committed to a vote.

PROBLEM WITH MULTILATERAL AGREEMENT

The problem yesterday was not with the bilateral agreements. We had completed our consideration of the bilateral agreements. The problem was with the multilateral agreement, and the language beginning on page 29, line 13 on page 30.

The committee will recall that Senator George was particularly disturbed about this method of approach and some of this detail and I shared his view.

We now have a new suggestion as a substitute, as I understand it, for all the language from line 13 on page 29, to line 13 on page 30, and the substitute I think is before you, and I will read it:

The provision of assistance under this Act results from the multilateral pledges of the participating countires to use all their efforts to accomplish a joint recovery program based upon self-help and mutual cooperation as embodied in the report of the Committee of European Economic Cooperation signed in Paris on September 22, 1947, and is contingent upon continuous effort of the participating countries to accomplish such a joint program and the establishment of a continuing organization for that purpose.

In addition to continued mutual cooperation of the participating countries in such a program, each such country shall conclude an agreement with the United States in order for such country to be eligible to receive assistance under the Act. Such agreement shall provide for the adherence of such country to the purposes of this Act, and shall, where applicable, make appropriate provision, among others, for—

and then we pick up the bilateral provisions which we have agreed to already.

Senator SMITH. We omit the details at the top of page 30?

The CHAIRMAN. We omit all the details, which I think is very preferable.

Senator SMITH. Oh, much.

The CHAIRMAN. The only thing I miss in this text is the identification of a multilateral treaty, which is one of the conditions precedent. Is that not missing here in this language?

Ambassador DOUGLAS. I gather that it is in the language: "Provision of assistance under this act results from multilateral pledges of participating countries."

Senator SMITH. That implies past multilateral pledges rather than one set up in the future.

Ambassador DOUGLAS. And is contingent upon the continuous efforts of the participating countries to accomplish such a joint program in the establishment of a continuing organization for such purpose.

Senator SMITH. Then we do not actually care whether they sign a new multilateral agreement or not?

Ambassador DOUGLAS. Yes, I think we do.

Senator THOMAS of Utah. Can't we have a reference to what they have done, in parenthesis?

The CHAIRMAN. I think this will do it, if you will just allow me a second.

Suppose, at the end of line 7, you add the phrase "through a multilateral agreement for this purpose," so that it will then read:

The provision of assistance under this Act results from the multilateral pledges of the participating countries to use all their efforts to accomplish a joint recovery program, based upon self-help and mutual cooperation, as embodied in the

report of the Committee of European Economic Cooperation, signed in Paris on September 22, 1947, and is contingent upon the continued effort of the participating countries to accomplish such a joint program, through a multilateral agreement for this purpose, and through the establishment of a continuing organization for this purpose.

Ambassador DOUGLAS. Would you object to the use of the word "undertaking"—"multilateral undertaking"?

The CHAIRMAN. No, I do not.

Senator THOMAS of Utah. Instead of "agreement"?

The CHAIRMAN. Now I would like to know particularly what Senator George's reaction is to this, because he has a special interest in it.

EMPHASIS UPON MULTILATERAL UNDERTAKING OR AGREEMENT

Senator GEORGE. I think that it is all right. I am willing to go along with that. I think that is all right. I think we must lay special emphasis upon the multilateral undertaking or agreement, or whatever you call it. I suspect some of these Western countries have very great difficulty now in getting back into another conference and formally agreeing to something. They might. Wouldn't you think so?

Ambassador DOUGLAS. I think they will do it as soon as they are confident that support from the United States is forthcoming. They cannot—at least they would find it embarrassing to take the risk if they were doubtful.

Senator GEORGE. I interpret all this language, down to where you start the new sentence, "in addition" as making this multilateral agreement, this multilateral undertaking, a condition precedent to anything that we do under this act.

Senator SMITH. You do not object to that?

Senator GEORGE. No, I do not object to it. But I say it seems to me that that emphasizes that idea.

And I think it absolutely vital, because I think it is the only door through which we can enter into European affairs at all except running the risk of having them slide right back into a simple undertaking between country X over there and ourselves, very much as we are bogged up with Greece at the moment.

The CHAIRMAN. We spent most of the afternoon yesterday debating the subject. It looks to me as though this was a very happy meeting of minds.

Senator GEORGE. You might strengthen your language and clarify it a little bit, but that seems all right. The thought is all right.

Ambassador DOUGLAS. Would it be acceptable if the language which the chairman suggested would read "through multilateral undertakings for this purpose"?

Senator GEORGE. That's all right.

The CHAIRMAN. There is no objection on my part.

Senator GEORGE. They might have to meet frequently.

Ambassador DOUGLAS. They might have to be frequent and in some instances, in regard to some matters, the undertakings might not include the 16 countries, but they might include at first three or four countries.

Senator SMITH. You mean Benelux might add France and Italy?

Ambassador DOUGLAS. That is right.

The CHAIRMAN. That is all right.

Without objection, we will stand on that language.

Senator BARKLEY. May I ask where the language that is agreed to down at the bottom picks up? Is that in line 18?

The CHAIRMAN. That is right.

INFORMATION REQUIRED AS TO USE OF SUPPORT PROVIDED

Ambassador DOUGLAS. Mr. Chairman, may I make a suggestion in regard to page 33, line 2? I make this suggestion because of my own experience.

(Discussion was continued off the record.)

Ambassador DOUGLAS. Subsection (8) which is part of the multilateral agreement now, merely required the participating countries to furnish this country relevant information which would be of assistance to the United States in determining the nature and scope of the future operations under this act. I think it is important for them to be required to give us information as to the use which they have made of the support provided.

The CHAIRMAN. I think everybody would be delighted to do that.

Ambassador DOUGLAS. Therefore I suggest, after the word "operations" in line 2 of page 33, "and of the use of support provided."

The CHAIRMAN. I think that is a very great improvement.

Senator SMITH. But you would stay within this act?

The CHAIRMAN. Why not take "future" out? Let's take "future" out and add "and of the use of support provided" after "operations".

I think that is very important. That will make a great difference on the floor, also.

Without objection, that change is made.

NUMBER OF REQUIREMENTS IN INTERIM AID BILL ELIMINATED

I want to be sure we understand that we have eliminated from these requirements as written in this bill, a number of the requirements that were written in the interim aid bill regarding publicity and identification and so forth, and labeling.

Is there a sound reason why provisions of that character, which I apprehend will be offered on the floor, should not apply to this act?

Mr. Ambassador, will you answer that?

Ambassador DOUGLAS. I think there is, Mr. Chairman. The number of commodities to be provided under this act is so much larger than the number of commodities provided under the Relief Act that administratively it would be practically impossible to identify each commodity as coming from the United States. There are somewhere in the vicinity, of 1,500 commodities in one form or another, probably some in the parts that will be provided under this act. In that respect it differs completely from the relief legislation which the Congress has previously enacted.

The CHAIRMAN. Furthermore, if there were any labeling to be done this time, the emphasis should be in a different place, and the label should say "This is the result of mutual cooperation between the United States and the 16 countries."

Is the committee agreed? I do not want to take that responsibility to myself that those labeling provisions and the kindred, what we might call policing provisions—no, that is not a fair definition; the labeling provisions and the persistent identification of the American source of these goods is not applicable to this bill as it was in the interim aid bill? And does the committee agree that we should eliminate these?

Senator THOMAS of Utah. We have asked that they purchase elsewhere, wherever they can.

Senator SMITH. We are the source, though.

Senator GEORGE. I think there is the strongest sort of reason for not putting them in, Mr. Chairman. I agree they should not go in there. Primarily in this case, in this present instant case, we are setting up a more or less continuing organization here over a period of years, providing pretty amply for supervision. Our hands are on it over there as well as over here, and that seems to me to be all that ought to be necessary.

The CHAIRMAN. That is my view. I wanted to be sure the committee agreed.

Senator SMITH. There will be automatic publicity with regard to it if we are on the job.

Senator GEORGE. If we are on the job there will be automatic publicity. It speaks for itself.

ADDITION TO BILATERAL AGREEMENT PROVISION

The CHAIRMAN. Now I want to refer to one of the provisions we have already adopted in respect to the bilateral agreement, and I am referring to page 30, No. 1.

It now reads:

> (1) promoting industrial and agricultural production in order to enable the participating country to become independent of abnormal outside economic assistance:

There is a substantial desire among many of our colleagues to emphasize wherever possible the importance of dealing with this matter on a project basis. We have already put in a little window dressing to that effect in one place, and it would be very helpful on the floor if we add, at this point, the following:

> and for submitting for the approval of the Administrator the specific projects designed to carry out such purposes including wherever possible projects for the increased production of coal, steel, transportation facilities, and food.

I have discussed the matter with the Ambassador, and he thinks that there is no objection to this language. It is purely advisory, but does put some emphasis on the major necessities which are in the minds of many of our colleagues, and also emphasizes this idea wherever possible of dealing with specific projects. We have already carried this idea into another section of the bill. If there is no objection, I would like to add this at this point.

Senator HATCH. Mr. Chairman, before you agree to that, it strikes me offhand that instead of saying "and" which would carry the implication that this is in addition to these three top lines, it would be better to say "including" these things, which would be a part of this overall program.

The CHAIRMAN. Very good. Including the submission.

Senator HATCH. Yes.

The CHAIRMAN. All right. Without objection, this will be approved in that form.

Now, I think we can go to the front of the bill.

Senator SMITH. Mr. Chairman, may I ask one question before we do that?

The CHAIRMAN. Yes.

OTHER COUNTRIES' ROLE

Senator SMITH. At what point in our deliberations do we get to this question of where other countries furnish commodities, of their extending credits, as distinguished from our furnishing the dollars?

Take, for example, the purchase of Argentine wheat, where we have been criticized for paying top prices to the Argentine to carry out the interim aid program. Is that under the $6.8 billion discussion tomorrow?

The CHAIRMAN. Oh, no. We will do that today. Let's get through the text of the bill, and then she is open to any questions. Let's get the structure of the bill first.

This is about all that is left, except we still have to settle the maritime question and, of course, we have to settle the $6,800 million question.

"FINDINGS AND DECLARATION OF POLICY"

Now, we are on page 2, in line 21. This is "Findings and Declaration of Policy."

> Recognizing the interdependence of the United States and of Europe, and recognizing that economic disruption—

I was a little stymied when I read the first few words, because I do not know whether I want to flatly recognize the interdependence in quite such a blunt and unlimited language as that. However, I will read it.

> Recognizing the interdependence of the United States and of Europe, and recognizing that economic disruption following in the wake of war is not contained by national frontiers, the Congress finds that the existing economic situation in Europe endangers the establishment of a lasting peace, the general welfare and national interest of the United States, and the attainment of the objectives of the United Nations. The restoration or maintenance in European countries of principles of individual liberty, free institutions, and genuine independence rests largely upon the establishment of sound economic conditions, stable international economic relationships, and the achievement by the countries of Europe of a working economy independent of abnormal outside assistance. The accomplishment of these objectives calls for a program of European recovery based on a strong production effort, the expansion of foreign trade, the creation and maintenance of internal financial stability, and the development of economic cooperation, including all possible steps to establish and maintain equitable rates of exchange and to bring about the progressive elimination of trade barriers and of the obstacles to the free movement of persons within Europe. Mindful of the advantages which the United States has enjoyed through the existence of a large domestic market with no internal trade barriers, and believing that similar advantages can accrue to the countries of Europe, it is the hope of the people of the United States that these countries through a joint organization will exert sustained common efforts which will speedily achieve that economic cooperation in Europe which is essential for lasting peace and prosperity. Accordingly, it is declared to be the policy of the people of the United States to sustain and strengthen principles of individual liberty, free institutions, and genuine independence in Europe through assistance to those countries of Europe which participate in a joint recovery program based upon self-help and mutual cooperation. It is further declared to be the policy of the United States that the continuity of assistance provided by the United States should, at all times, be dependent upon the continuity of cooperation among the countries participating in the program.

Senator Thomas of Utah. Mr. Chairman, I think that in your first two lines you can overcome that fear which you felt by just saying "interdependence" by transferring the word "economic" in line 22 to line 21, "Recognizing the economic interdependence of the United States and Europe, and recognizing that disruption following in the wake * * *."

The Chairman. That is better.

Senator Thomas of Utah. Then you will not be faced immediately with the notion that we are going to have a perpetual political alliance or something of that kind with Western Europe all the time.

The Chairman. I do not see why we have to use the word "interdependence."

Senator Barkley. I have in mind the elimination of the word "interdependence" altogether and using instead "Recognizing the intimate economic relationship * * *."

The Chairman. I think that is much better. I do not like the word "interdependence".

Think of what Patrick Henry would say!

Senator George. You have that over here in another place.

The Chairman. You have something over here that has to come out on your account, and I agree.

PHRASE DELETED

Senator George. If you ever expect Russia or any of her group to come into this program, even sympathetically, at all, you cannot throw right into their teeth that you have to permit the free movement of peoples all through that area. That is one of the things they are not going to stand for. I suspect that one of the real troubles with Russia is what we did to Greece.

[Discussion was continued off the record.]

The Chairman. The subject you now raise was debated for 2 hours yesterday, and the decision was in favor of the deletion of any such phrase as that at another point in the bill.

Senator George. Of course, it is stated here in a bit different way.

The Chairman. It is the same net result.

Senator George. Yes.

The Chairman. And I think it is unnecessary.

Without objection, the sentence in line 15 will end with a period after the word "barrier" and the words "and of the obstacles to the free movement of persons within Europe" will be eliminated.

Senator Smith. You would not add the words "within Europe" after "barrier"?

The Chairman. Oh, yes; excuse me. We will cut out the words "and of the obstacles to the free movement of persons".

Without objection that change will be made.

SENATOR BARKLEY'S SUGGESTION

Now, let us go back to the suggestion that Senator Barkley has made, and see what we can do about that. Will you repeat that, Senator Barkley?

Senator BARKLEY. The way I have had it in my mind is "Recognizing the intimate economic and other relationships between the United States and the nations of Europe".

I would put the "nations of Europe" instead of just "Europe". That is my idea.

The CHAIRMAN.

> Recognizing the intimate economic and other relationships between the United States and the Nations of Europe * * *.

That certainly is a great improvement.

Senator THOMAS of Utah. Then take "economic" out before "disruption".

Senator BARKLEY. I think you might eliminate the word "economic" in line 22. It is more than economic disruptions, really that has happened over there, and "disruptions" includes any kind of disruption that has happened.

The CHAIRMAN. I think that is a great improvement. Have you any objection to that, Mr. Ambassador?

Ambassador DOUGLAS. No, sir: "Recognizing the intimate economic and other relationships between the United States and the nations of Europe * * *".

Senator SMITH. Then, wouldn't you take the word "economic" out of line 24?

Say "the Congress finds that the existing situation in Europe * * *.". Take "economic" out there, too. We spoke of other dangers as well.

The CHAIRMAN. You are quite right.

Ambassador DOUGLAS. May I raise a rather fundamental question?

The CHAIRMAN. Yes, indeed.

PROHIBITION OF EXTENDING RELIEF FOR POLITICAL PURPOSE

Ambassador DOUGLAS. Perhaps you have been bothered with me about this language in the declaration of policy.

As I recall it, and you can check me on this, there is something in the charter of the United Nations which prohibits a country from extending relief for a political purpose. Is the language in this preamble such as to make us susceptible to a charge before the United Nations that we are undertaking this program for a political purpose?

[Discussion was continued off the record.]

The CHAIRMAN. If you can show me any language of that sort in here, I would like to see it. I do not recall it.

Ambassador DOUGLAS. If not in the charter of the United Nations, in a resolution that was passed and agreed to by the Assembly?

I wish, Mr. Surrey, you would check that and get the specific reference.

The CHAIRMAN. Dr. Wilcox says you are probably talking about a resolution adopted at the First General Assembly in London.

Ambassador DOUGLAS. That is correct.

The CHAIRMAN. All right. Let us see what it is about.

Senator SMITH. In what connection was that? Was that in criticism of our giving aid in a political way?

Ambassador DOUGLAS. No. I think, as I recollect it, it was a resolution offered by the Soviet and agreed to at the first meeting of the General Assembly.

If that is the case, is there language in here which might make us susceptible or liable to a charge?

Senator THOMAS of Utah. I think there is the other thing, if you read on. Of course, you can get any kind of a charge.

Ambassador DOUGLAS. Yes.

DEPENDENCE ON ABNORMAL OUTSIDE ASSISTANCE IMPLIED?

Senator THOMAS. But we are emphasizing, beginning with line 3 on page 3, the stable international independence and the rest of it "genuine independence rests largely upon the establishment of sound economic conditions, stable international economic relationships, and the achievement by the countries of Europe of a working economy independent of abnormal outside assistance."

The CHAIRMAN. I think that is a tremendous sentence. That is the whole story.

Ambassador DOUGLAS. Yes.

Senator SMITH. It implies dependence, though, on some kind of abnormal outside assistance. Are you going to leave that implication? You want to see them get on their own feet.

Senator THOMAS of Utah. If you changed that assistance to the word Senator Barkley used in his line, "outside relationship * * *."

Senator SMITH. I am bothered by it leaving the implication that there is some normal outside assistance that we would or do justify, and we want to get them away from that.

Ambassador DOUGLAS. There is normal assistance which has continued over the years. It has taken the form of capital movement.

Senator SMITH. That is not assistance. That is ordinary national relationships.

Senator THOMAS of Utah. That is normal national intercourse.

Ambassador DOUGLAS. And what we are undertaking here is abnormal.

The CHAIRMAN. I think we are talking about two different things. The use of the word "abnormal" in connection with this enterprise indicates that there might be a normal enterprise of the same character. Why do you have that word "abnormal" in there? You have it in another place, and it bothered me yesterday.

Mr. NITZE. We thought Austria, for instance, might need Export-Import Bank loans after the period of June 30, 1952, and that she would not possibly be completely on her own feet.

The CHAIRMAN. That still simply might be an exception that proves the rule.

I would not think that the rule had to be changed to meet an occasional contingency. It seems to me the identification of this program as being "abnormal" carries the corollary that there is such a thing as "normal" assistance of a kindred nature.

Ambassador DOUGLAS. You could do it this way, could you not: "And the achievement by the countries of Europe of a working economy dependent only on ordinary commercial and financial transactions?"

Would that not do it?

Senator SMITH. I would not object to using the word "normal" there if you are talking about international economic intercourse, or something of that sort. But I have had the feeling here we are sort of recognizing that there is going to be a continual assistance of some sort that is normal, and I don't think that we should recognize that.

USE OF "ASSISTANCE" TO DESCRIBE TRADE AND FINANCIAL RELATIONSHIPS

Senator BARKLEY. That raises the question of whether ordinary trade relationships and ordinary financial relationships that go on between countries are to be described as "assistance."

Senator SMITH. That is just what I mean.

The CHAIRMAN. Precisely, that is the point.

Ambassador DOUGLAS. Could you say "on normal or on ordinary commercial and financial transactions"?

Senator BARKLEY. The word "usual" would be better there.

Ambassador DOUGLAS. "On established commercial and financial transactions."

Senator BARKLEY. We have to change that whole phrase. I don't like the words "outside assistance" there, which is supposed not to be necessary after this period is over. That is really a misnomer, because it is not that.

Senator SMITH. Why can't we leave out the word "abnormal"?

Senator BARKLEY. That is what we are doing during this period, but when they reach the economy we are talking about they are not supposed to need it.

Senator SMITH. Why can't you say "and the achievement by the countries of Europe of a working economy independent of outside assistance"?

You don't need to go into trade relationships at all. Assistance cannot be construed as ordinary trade relationships.

Senator HATCH. Do you dislike the word "normal" economy? That is what you really want, "normal economy."

Senator SMITH. "To have a normal working economy independent of outside assistance."

Senator HATCH. That is what you want.

Senator SMITH. All right. Why not use your thought there, "achievement by the countries of Europe of a normal working economy independent of outside assistance"?

Ambassador DOUGLAS. "Dependent on normal commercial and financial transactions." That is really what you are aiming at.

Senator SMITH. "A normal international economy."

Senator GEORGE. I don't quite like that "abnormal" but I thought the purpose of putting it in there, the emphasis I got out of it, was that this is an abnormal thing we are doing, and we don't propose to do it all the time, and we think other people should get themselves in a position where they do not need it.

Senator SMITH. Then why not put both in: "achievement by the countries of Europe of a normal economy independent of abnormal outside assistance."?

Senator BARKLEY. I still say "unusual" would be better than "abnormal."

Senator THOMAS of Utah. You see "normal" back in the other place, "achievement by the countries of Europe of a normal economy independent of unusual outside aid."

Senator SMITH. That rather expresses, I think, what I am getting at.

The CHAIRMAN. Will you say that again, Senator Thomas?

Senator THOMAS of Utah. "And the achievement by the countries of Europe of a normal economy independent of unusual outside aid."

Senator GEORGE. "Extraordinary outside aid." I think that is a little better.

Senator THOMAS of Utah. "Extraordinary" is still better than "unusual."

The CHAIRMAN. "Achievement by the countries of Europe of a normal economy independent of extraordinary outside assistance."

Without objection, that change will be made.

Now here is your resolution, Mr. Douglas.

Senator GEORGE. Wait a minute, Mr. Chairman. Over here on page 4 you have that same thing. You have "independent of outside abnormal economic assistance." That is the purpose of this act.

The CHAIRMAN. To become independent of extraordinary outside assistance.

Senator GEORGE. Becoming independent of the necessity for taking it.

The CHAIRMAN. The words "abnormal" in line 15 should become "extraordinary" followed by "economic assistance."

Senator GEORGE. That will be all right.

USE OF RELIEF SUPPLIES AS POLITICAL WEAPON

The CHAIRMAN. Now, Mr. Douglas, the resolution you are referring to, passed in London, the only possible applicable phrase in it is this: "Reaffirming the principle that at no time should relief supplies be used as a political weapon, and that no discrimination should be made in the distribution of relief supplies because of race, creed or political belief," and so forth.

Ambassador DOUGLAS. I guess that is it.

The CHAIRMAN. Do we collide with that?

Ambassador DOUGLAS. I do not think so.

Senator THOMAS of Utah. We do not collide if this is open for the adherence of persons or countries outside of the 16, and it is, isn't it?

The CHAIRMAN. Is that plain?

Senator GEORGE. I am not sure that we do not collide with it when you consider the different ideologies and economic and social and political systems.

Senator BARKLEY. This is not strictly a relief program, and that refers specifically to relief.

Ambassador DOUGLAS. And the distribution of relief.

DECLARATION IN PREAMBLE

Senator GEORGE. In this preamble here, the "Findings and Declaration of Policy" sort of in the nature of a preamble, we go on to say a good deal:

> The restoration or maintenance in European countries of principles of individual liberty, free institutions, and genuine independence rests largely upon the establishment of sound economic conditions, stable international economic relationships, and the achievement by the countries of Europe of a working economy independent of abnormal outside assistance, and so forth.

Senator HATCH. And you say further, beginning in line 24, "accordingly, it is declared to be the policy of the people of the United States to sustain and strengthen the principles of individual liberty."

Senator GEORGE. That is right. We are laying it down.

Senator SMITH. But you will recall when we met with some of those distinguished leaders in Bulgaria and Romania, they talked about these principles in glowing terms, as though they were the ones who were bringing this about, so we need not worry about running counter to their profession, anyway.

Senator HATCH. The speech you made to the people in Bulgaria they agreed with, except finally. They felt that you could carry this theory of individual freedom too far, that the people had to be led.

Senator BARKLEY. This proposes to sustain and maintain these things by economic aid. All our emphasis in this thing is economic. There is some other. Even that part which goes for relief is economic.

So the mere declaration in the preamble of what we hope to accomplish by this economic aid does not seem to me to collide too much with that resolution.

Ambassador DOUGLAS. I think it is all right.

Senator BARKLEY. We are not proposing here in this preamble to do anything except furnish economic aid.

Ambassador DOUGLAS. And this is open, subject of course to the participating countries, to any other country that may be invited to join and that accepts the invitation.

Senator THOMAS of Utah. I think each nation makes its own definition of what it considers a free institution, and you will discover that such a nation as Yugoslavia today talks more about its freedom from something that it was protesting against than probably anything else.

Senator SMITH. That is what I mean when I say these birds all protect freedom.

Senator GEORGE. Russia is strong on democracy.

Senator THOMAS of Utah. They all talk about democracy. I have been with the labor people in Russia. They say they haven't outlawed strikes, but they have outlawed the need for strikes.

Senator BARKLEY. The Russian Constitution is filled from beginning to end with expressions of freedom and democracy, so they are certainly not antagonistic to what we propose to profess here.

Ambassodor DOUGLAS. Somebody may raise the question on the floor.

Senator HATCH. It is the plain truth. That is what we mean to do, what we want to do. Why not say so?

Senator GEORGE. It is all right. You won't get away from the charge, of course, that Russia has already made and is repeatedly making, that this is the part of an imperialistic scheme. You can't get away from that.

Senator SMITH. I think it is a pretty well-drawn statement.

Ambassador DOUGLAS. I agree with it wholly.

"SAVING" CLAUSE SUGGESTED

The CHAIRMAN. I just miss the expressed thought in here which I think would be a great saving clause, that this is open to anybody who wants to come in and can qualify, and I was just wondering whether, on page 3, in the sentence beginning in line 9, you could not say "The accomplishment of these objectives calls for a program of European recovery" and then introduce some phrase "open to all," or something like that. Could you not at that point toss in a sort of basket clause?

Senator THOMAS of Utah. Can't we do it even stronger than that, so that it stands out by itself, by using the characteristic thing we do in some of our laws: "Nothing in this Act shall bar, for instance, other nations from coming in who meet the specifications."

Senator BARKLEY. As a matter of fact, the law itself does not name the nations.

The CHAIRMAN. Yes, it does, in section 3, but the section has been rewritten. You would not get anything out of that.

Senator BARKLEY. I do not know whether they were identified.

You might put in that identifying clause a provision, a phrase or sentence that would make it open to any other countries that accept the conditions under which aid is given to this group. That would seem to me to be an appropriate place to say something about it if you want to do it.

Senator SMITH. Your section 3 really includes any nation in Europe which adheres to and remains adherent to a joint program for European recovery.

The CHAIRMAN. You are right, Alben. We do not identify them. We identify all Europe as eligible. But is Russia in Europe?

Senator GEORGE. Partly.

Senator SMITH. Russia is in Europe and Asia, both. It is partly in Europe. We have covered that.

Senator BARKLEY. When I was in school the geography used to have a designation "Russia in Europe," "Russia in Asia."

The CHAIRMAN. Still I think that at this point, after all, this is your banner headline.

Senator THOMAS of Utah. I think so, too.

Senator HATCH. Would it do any good to add the express words "all European countries," in line 20 down there, when you say "the countries of Europe"? Say "all European countries."

The CHAIRMAN [reading]:

> Mindful of the advantages which the United States has enjoyed through the existence of a large domestic market with no internal trade barriers, and believing that similar advantages can accrue to the countries of Europe . . .

Senator HATCH. "Believing that similar advantages can accrue to all European countries, it is the hope of the people of the United States that these countries through a joint organization will exert sustained common efforts * * *"

We hope they will all join.

The CHAIRMAN. That does not quite cover the point, because that merely invites them into Bevin's Western Union. It does not invite them into this regime. God help us if they ever accepted our invitation!

Senator HATCH. Those other lines will really exert "sustained common efforts which will speedily achieve that economic cooperation in Europe which is essential for lasting peace and prosperity."

Senator BARKLEY. Here is your language in section 3:

> Any country (including the United Kingdom of Great Britain and Northern Ireland, Iceland, Ireland, and any of the zones of occupation of Germany) wholly or partly in Europe . . .

That certainly includes Russia and Turkey.

Senator SMITH. That has been completely rewritten.

PURPOSE OF PREAMBLE

Senator GEORGE. Mr. Chairman, I am not greatly worried about this preamble, because I have always had a very definite contrary view to those who believed in preambles in legislation. I do not think it has a part here at all, except to enable you to interpret a law, and this thing we are doing does not need any interpretation. It just needs administration as best you can do it.

The CHAIRMAN. That is true.

Senator GEORGE. I understand everybody is going to insist on it, I suppose.

The CHAIRMAN. If we are going to do it, won't it be wise to have just that one saving clause in here somewhere?

Senator GEORGE. You have recognized the independence of all these States. We have recognized the intimate relationship existing between all these States, and recognized the devastating effects of the war throughout Europe, and we find a situation now existing which justifies extraordinary efforts on our part to alleviate it.

Then we go ahead and indulge in our——

The CHAIRMAN. What harm would it do if you put in this fiddle-faddle?

Senator GEORGE. I did not say it did any harm.

ELIGIBILITY FOR PARTICIPATION

The CHAIRMAN. I am about to suggest some fiddle-faddle: "The accomplishment of these objectives calls for a program of European recovery open to all nations desiring to cooperate."

Senator GEORGE. That is all right. But I am afraid there won't be too many of them cooperate, because if they come in the $6,800 million will look like chickenfeed by the time about eight more got in, and then these that are already in will say, "You haven't left us enough to do us any good."

That language seems to do it, and that thought is all right, because the Marshall Plan was addressed to all of them, and there was the hope that Russia would come in.

Senator BARKLEY. Under your rewritten section 3, which has just been handed to me, you have two subsections, the first of which is limited to the countries that signed the agreement in Paris.

The CHAIRMAN. That is right.

Senator BARKLEY. "(b) Includes all other countries, wholly or partly in Europe."

The CHAIRMAN. That is right.

Senator BARKLEY. Which would carry the implication that any of them that want to come in are free to do it.

The CHAIRMAN. That is right. And that is the reason why I think the general overall statement ought to, at some point——

Senator GEORGE (continuing). Correspond with that?

The CHAIRMAN (continuing). Just touch the same idea.

Ambassador DOUGLAS. I wonder if perhaps it isn't included in the sentence beginning in line 24:

> Accordingly, it is declared to be the policy of the people of the United States to sustain and strengthen principles of individual liberty, free institutions, and genuine independence in Europe through assistance to those countries of Europe which participate in a joint recovery program based upon self-help and mutual cooperation.

The CHAIRMAN. No, because you have a list of specifications preceding their eligibility which rules out the whole of Eastern Europe, and I would rather have them rule themselves out as a result of a general specification.

Ambassador DOUGLAS. If they are prepared to accept the specifications, they can participate.

Mr. GROSS. "To any country of Europe which participates."

Senator THOMAS of Utah. I still think that the approach to this is an additional sentence, Senator Vandenberg, which carries with it what we are talking about, that "Nothing in this act shall preclude, or shall be construed to bar, cooperation of any country not so far cooperating if they adhere to the provisions of the act".

Senator SMITH. I would rather put it in a positive way: "It is the purpose of the act to include countries not now included."

I would prefer to say that. I like the positive statement, if we are going to do it.

I don't see way the chairman's suggestion on line 10 isn't the line, and then if you put down on line 22, I think it is—no, line 10—"accrue to all the countries of Europe", it sort of reemphasizes what the chairman suggested to go in line 10.

Frankly, I do not think it is necessary to have it in to determine what this means, but I think if it highlights it, it is valuable.

Then I would not object to going ahead further with Senator Thomas' suggestion, saying that it is the purpose of this act to include as rapidly as possible * * *".

The CHAIRMAN. I do not want to get too hospitable.

Senator THOMAS of Utah. You do want Czechoslovakia to come in, if she wishes.

The CHAIRMAN. That is right.

Senator THOMAS of Utah. You do want quite a number of the fringe countries.

The CHAIRMAN. I want a textual answer to the Henry Wallace's so-and-sos who say this is a closed corporation.

Senator THOMAS of Utah. You want to be able to say that this act is set up for constructive purposes and is not aimed at the destruction of something, don't you?

The CHAIRMAN. Yes, sir.

DOOR LEFT OPEN FOR PARTICIPATION OF OTHER COUNTRIES

Senator BARKLEY. Why couldn't you put right here in the beginning, on page 2, beginning with line 21, which we doctored awhile ago, "Recognizing the intimate economic and other relationships between the United States and all the nations of Europe", instead of just "the nations"?

"All" is a little more emphatic, and all that follows that then ties itself in this with that. That may not be quite far enough, Mr. Chairman, to meet your suggestion.

The CHAIRMAN. I still think you haven't anything you can just point to.

I haven't any pride of opinion about this, but it seems to me that in line 10 there are half a dozen words that you can put in after the word "recover"—page 3, line 10.

The accomplishment of these objectives calls for a program of European recovery open to all nations desiring to cooperate.

Senator GEORGE. That is all right. I don't see a thing in the world objectionable to that, if that is what we mean.

Senator HATCH. I think that is what you want. You have left the door open.

The CHAIRMAN. Without objection, that will be in.

Ambassador DOUGLAS. "All European nations"?

The CHAIRMAN. All right, "open to all European nations desiring to cooperate".

Senator BARKLEY. Let's see, now. "The accomplishment of these objectives calls for a program of European recovery open to all such nations."

You don't have to repeat the word "European"—"all such nations willing to cooperate."

Ambassador DOUGLAS. That raises the question of Spain. Spain doubtless will be willing to cooperate. Whether the other participating nations want Spain in this tea party at the moment, I do not know.

Senator BARKLEY. If we are going to open this to all of them, we have to include Spain.

EFFECT OF NATION DROPPING OUT

Senator HATCH. The last sentence, where it says "The continuity of assistance provided by the United States should be at all times dependent upon the continuity of cooperation among the nations participating in the program". Suppose one nation drops out?

The CHAIRMAN. Then she ceases to have any assistance, that is all.

Senator BARKLEY. One nation dropping out would not vitiate the whole program.

Senator HATCH. That is a very foolish question which came to my mind last night.

Are you going to vitiate the whole program if one nation drops out?

The CHAIRMAN. No.

Ambassador DOUGLAS. That language was not designed for that purpose.

The CHAIRMAN. I think that language is the guts of the bill so far as its passage is concerned.

Senator SMITH. If three nations stayed in the show under this, we could still stay.

USE OF "JOIN" OR "COOPERATE"

Senator GEORGE. I do not know whether your language there is quite accurate, looking at it again, in line three:

"The accomplishment of these objectives calls for a program of European recovery * * * ". That is the thing that is going to be open now to all nations desiring to cooperate. I suppose it is. I guess that is all right.

Senator SMITH. Is the word "join" better than "cooperate"?

The CHAIRMAN. Oh, no; because they are going to cooperate, and not just join.

Senator GEORGE. They have to cooperate.

The CHAIRMAN. Let's put it in that form for the time being.

Senator GEORGE. "Open to all European nations desiring to cooperate?"

The CHAIRMAN. Yes.

USE OF "PROGRAM" OR "PLAN"

Senator THOMAS of Utah. If you change "program" to "plan", Mr. Chairman, in line 9, that would be a stronger word there, I think.

Senator GEORGE. That is what bothers me a bit, that the program is open. I suppose it means "plan" there.

Senator THOMAS of Utah. I think that the word "plan" is a better word there than "program". That includes the whole scheme, you see, if you use "plan".

Senator GEORGE. The accomplishment of these objectives calls for a plan.

The CHAIRMAN. Is there any objection to changing "program" to "plan"?

Senator GEORGE. It seems to me it makes it a little bit stronger.

The CHAIRMAN. All right, the change is made.

ELIGIBILITY OF SPAIN

Ambassador DOUGLAS. What about Spain?

Senator GEORGE. What about Spain? She is in Europe, isn't she?

Ambassador DOUGLAS. There are two sides to the coin. One is our assistance, and the other is the extension of the invitation by participating countries.

Senator GEORGE. We did not extend an invitation to Spain?

Ambassador DOUGLAS. We did nothing. Marshall made his speech. Bevin, Bidault, and Molotov met. Molotov went home. Bevin and Bidault then extended the invitation to all European countries.

Senator GEORGE. Nobody wrote Spain a special note?

Ambassador DOUGLAS. Bevin and Bidault did not invite Spain. They invited every nation except Spain.

Senator THOMAS of Utah. Weren't they barred by action of the United Nations, not even sentimentally?

Ambassador DOUGLAS. There was an action taken by the United Nations which might be so construed.

There are two sides of the coin. One is the assistance which we are prepared to give these nations, and the other side is the extent to which the participating countries extend an invitation.

Senator BARKLEY. All the other countries that refused were invited and Spain was not invited?

Ambassador DOUGLAS. That is right.

Senator BARKLEY. By this language, we opened it to Spain, and that raises a question of whether we want to deny it to Spain. It is our aid. We may have to change our position in regard to Spain some of these days.

Ambassador DOUGLAS. I agree we may, but the participating countries are the ones that really form the program, and to the conference at which the program was originally formulated Spain was not invited. Do we want to place ourselves in the position where we are, in effect, going beyond the action of Western European countries themselves?

Senator SMITH. And where will we be if Spain says, "Grand, we will come it?"

Suppose Spain says, "We are delighted." What would happen? Would there be an explosion among the participating countries?

Ambassador DOUGLAS. I don't know whether there would be or not.

Senator BARKLEY. That would require those other countries to come in on the multilateral agreement with them.

Ambassador DOUGLAS. That is right.

Senator THOMAS of Utah. We could not very well bar them if they decided to forgive Spain and bring her in.

Ambassador DOUGLAS. I am not suggesting we bar them. I am merely pointing out that the Western European countries have to be considered in the matter of making eligible any additional countries.

Senator THOMAS of Utah. Of course, we hope ultimately for good relations with Spain, the same as with every other country.

Senator GEORGE. You will have to look at section 3 on page 5 again. Of course, it is obvious that while we could invite Spain in if we wished to, we would not want to do so, regardless of the effect on this other bunch of countries.

Senator THOMAS of Utah. She is already invited under section 3.

Senator GEORGE. If we want to modify it, I would not know how to do it. We couldn't say, "except Spain".

Senator THOMAS of Utah. No.

Senator GEORGE. We couldn't do that.

Senator BARKLEY. That does raise a delicate problem. We wouldn't want to suggest to Bevin and Bidault to write a note and say, "We are sorry. We overlooked you on the other invitation and you are now invited," but this is a wholly European invitation. We didn't invite anybody.

Ambassador DOUGLAS. This is a European enterprise initiated by European countries on the suggestion of Marshall.

Senator THOMAS of Utah. Everybody knows that if the two-world idea becomes more intensified we will work very, very hard for Spanish cooperation.

PARIS CONFERENCE DID NOT INVITE SPAIN

Senator GEORGE. Did this Paris conference have anything to say about Spain?

Abassador DOUGLAS. It did not invite Spain.

Senator GEORGE. I know it did not invite Spain. In their deliberations was it ever a matter of discussion so far as you know?

Ambassador DOUGLAS. It was a matter of discussion between Bevin and Bidault at the time they extended the invitations.

Senator GEORGE. They decided against it?

Ambassador DOUGLAS. They decided they would not then extend an invitation to Spain. It was a temporary thing.

Senator BARKLEY. They did that after the United Nations had taken its action putting her beyond the pale and all the Ambassadors, including our own, were withdrawn.

Ambassador DOUGLAS. Yes, although diplomatic relations were not served.

Senator BARKLEY. Since that they have modified their attitude and opened the frontier, but none of them has sent any more Ambassadors, as I understand.

Ambassador DOUGLAS. That is right.

Senator GEORGE. I have not any objection myself to opening this invitation to Spain. That is personal. I realize what the policy has been.

Senator BARKLEY. Here is the thing about it.

Senator GEORGE. I have never been so much disturbed about Spain.

Senator BARKLEY. If she should apply, she would have to enter into a multilateral agreement, and if the other European nations would not enter into a multilateral agreement with her, she could not get in anyhow.

Senator GEORGE. I imagine that would be another strong point of opposition that would be called to our attention.

Dr. WILCOX. Spain is barred by the Assembly from participating in any of the organizations of the United Nations.

Mr. NITZE. There are other members in the 16 that are not members of the United Nations organizations.

[Discussion was continued off the record.]

Senator SMITH. Wasn't that action in Paris because they hoped they would not have a break with Russia?

Ambassador DOUGLAS. No.

WHETHER SPAIN IS ELIGIBLE

The CHAIRMAN. The fact remains that we confront a condition, not in theory, in writing this language, and we cannot fly in the face of a situation as it is.

Ambassador DOUGLAS. I wonder whether you are not amply protected in section 3 by the language "provided such country adheres to, and for so long as it remains adherent to, a joint program." To become a party to a joint program, Spain or any country not now one of the participating countries must be acceptable to those who are participating countries. There can be no joint program unless the present participating countries, or many of them, agree to the admission of an additional country to the program.

Senator SMITH. Then we are frankly saying we are dealing with an exclusive club.

Senator THOMAS of Utah. We are, but we are not closing the membership.

Ambassador DOUGLAS. But it is their club. We do not choose the membership.

Senator SMITH. We do recognize a club that determines its own membership, and we are dealing with that.

Senator GEORGE. And that has the power, and may exercise it, to exclude somebody.

Senator SMITH. Then, instead of putting the words in on page 3, why not put a statement at the end to the effect that it is our purpose and expectation that from time to time other nations of Europe will join in the program herein outlined, or something like that?

Ambassador DOUGLAS. I still wonder whether the language on line 3 of page 4, "Those countries of Europe which participate in a joint recovery program based upon self-help and mutual cooperation" aren't sufficient.

Senator GEORGE. It might, but Spain might come back and say to us, "We are eligible under this Act if you let us come in."

Suppose they say, "No"? They didn't invite Spain. That was an affirmative act on their part. Here Spain is willing to take an affirmative act.

I think the world is frightfully made, somehow or other, Mr. Chairman.

The CHAIRMAN. If it is made at all.

Senator SMITH. What the Ambassador would like to do would be to open the door and put the bug on the participating nations.

Senator GEORGE. I think this does that. In the preamble you can use the words Senator Vandenberg has suggested, because when you get over here you then begin to declare the purposes and write the law, and section 3 really determines who is a participating nation. We said that broadly everybody was entitled to come in in Europe. Then we have some conditions attached. One of them is ability to join in a joint program, and to continue to adhere to that program. Now I understand that under this resolution of the United Nations they could not do that. They would not be permitted to do that.

The CHAIRMAN. I don't think the action of the United Nations is involved.

Senator GEORGE. I don't know; that is the charter.

The CHAIRMAN. No, it is not the charter. It is a resolution of the London Assembly.

Senator GEORGE. Is it not in the charter?

The CHAIRMAN. No, sir.

I am a little stymied at this point.

Senator THOMAS of Utah. I am not, Mr. Chairman.

Senator GEORGE. That is the best you can do with it, is to let it stand as it is in 3, unless there are some other changes that ought to be made, and put in your words that you wanted there. So far as we are concerned, we are indicating—well, not exactly, either—that Spain is eligible, but we are indicating that she must become a party to this multilateral agreement.

Senator THOMAS of Utah. And we are not asking Bevin and Bidault to change their minds and invite her. I do not think we are doing anything like that.

In fact, Mr. Chairman, I do not see in international relationships that there is any difference at all between a state that has not been invited and a state that has been invited and declines for future consideration. I think they both occupy exactly the same position, unless some definite action has been taken wherein it says that we decline to invite this state now and forever more, or some such word as that.

I think you are up against the fact that the United Nations itself is hoping to be universal at some time, and we have made the declaration that the more universal trade is in Europe, the better it is off. I think you have got to face it on those principles and trust.

"DESIRING TO COOPERATE" CHANGED TO "WHICH COOPERATE"

Ambassador DOUGLAS. Mr. Chairman, could you get over the difficulty by some such language as this:

"Open to all countries which cooperate in such plan"?

Senator THOMAS of Utah. That is there.

Senator GEORGE. That is back to the preamble: "Open to all European nations desiring to cooperate."

Ambassador DOUGLAS. Instead of "desiring to cooperate," say "which cooperate."

The CHAIRMAN. I think that is much better.

Ambassador DOUGLAS. Wouldn't that get over your idea?

The CHAIRMAN. Yes, to an extent, so it would read, "The accomplishment of these objective calls for a plan of European recovery open to all European nations which cooperate in such plan."

Senator BARKLEY. If they cannot get in, they cannot cooperate.

The CHAIRMAN. All right. We will leave it in that form.

BUILDING U.N. INTO EFFECTIVE WORLD PEACE ORGANIZATION

Now, Dr. Wilcox calls my attention to three ideas that were left out of this draft that were suggested from time to time by various witnesses in the hearings.

First, some reference to the building of the United Nations into an effective organization for world peace; in other words, to do a little more. Have we mentioned the United States?

Senator GEORGE. Yes. I think we have gone enough into that.

GERMANY IS ELEMENT IN EUROPEAN RECOVERY

The CHAIRMAN. How about this question, which constantly came up in the hearings and which I do not find here at all?

That is any emphasis on the fact that Germany is an important element in European recovery, and pretty nearly indispensable to it.

Senator BARKLEY. In the rewriting of section 3, it is there.

The CHAIRMAN. I am talking now about making a speech about European recovery.

Senator GEORGE. You have more than that, Mr. Chairman. You have this thing that we have omitted, unless you dealt with it while I was away on some momentary absence from the committee.

You have to say who is going to have charge of these zones of occupation in Germany.

INCLUSION OF GERMANY

The CHAIRMAN. Oh, yes. I am now addressing myself as to whether or not in this speech we are making we should say something about Western Germany.

Senator GEORGE. I think we certainly should. I do not think you can write Western Germany out of Europe, or Eastern Germany, even, if she ever gets in a position to come in.

Senator BARKLEY. If they had a government in Germany now, there is no question but that she would be included without even being mentioned, provided she had been invited and met with them in Paris.

Senator GEORGE. She is included, Senator Barkley, in the definition we have made. We have especially included the three occupied zones in Germany, and even Trieste, and we have not said how this administration can be carried into execution in those occupied zones, which is a very troublesome question.

Senator BARKLEY. Can we say in this bill, or do we have to say, what the relationship should be between the Administrator and whatever authority there is in Germany?

The CHAIRMAN. Yes, that is one of the open sections.

Senator GEORGE. We have not come to that. We are continuing to occupy. We may do it through the Army, and may do it through the State Department.

The CHAIRMAN. The only question I am raising at the moment is whether or not our speech is complete, since we all recognize the fact that Western Germany is the key, finally, to the whole show. Yet we have not said a word about it.

Senator BARKLEY. You were talking about speech under the guise of a preamble, were you?

The CHAIRMAN. Yes, sir.

Senator BARKLEY. It includes all Europe, and Germany is in it.

Senator HATCH. You have not singled out any other country.

Senator BARKLEY. If you spell it out as to Germany, you are doing what you have not done with regard to any of the rest of them.

Senator GEORGE. I think where we bring in all these zones that can come in now, and do not exclude any part of Germany, you can emphasize that. The plan is built on the final inclusion of Germany, the rebuilding of Germany, just the same as any other part of Europe, and we recognize it as being vital.

Senator THOMAS of Utah. I think we do it, Senator Vandenberg, in lines 1, 2, 3, and 4 on page 4. I think you have your idea there. Germany is not spelled out but surely no one can read that and think that Germany is left out of the picture.

Senator BARKLEY. Senator Hatch has just made a suggestion which seems to have merit, that you can spell it out more in detail in your report when you report this bill. You can emphasize that fact.

Senator THOMAS of Utah. This long sentence, "Accordingly, it is declared to be the policy of the people of the United States to sustain and strengthen principles of individual liberty, free institutions, and genuine independence in Europe through assistance to those countries of Europe which participate in a joint recovery program based upon self-help and mutual cooperation" includes Germany.

The CHAIRMAN. I am not raising the question that there is any danger that Germany is not included. I think it is. But I am raising the question that the whole trend of our hearings, and I think of our thinking, underscored the *sine qua non* factor, namely, that this program is not worth the paper it is written on unless you can do something about Western Germany.

Senator THOMAS of Utah. On the theory that the central economy of Germany is the economy that keeps Europe hanging together in normal times, I don't know whether you should mention it any more.

The CHAIRMAN. Mr. Ambassador, what have you to say about that?

Ambassador DOUGLAS. I do not think it is necessary to mention it, Mr. Chairman. I think the definition of the participating countries is clear.

The CHAIRMAN. That is true. It is clear that they are included, but it is not clear that we think you might as well tear up your bill unless you are going to go ahead and do something in Western Germany.

VANTAGE POINTS FOR VIEWING UNDERTAKING

Ambassador DOUGLAS. There are three points of vantage from which one can view this whole undertaking. One is from the point of vantage of Germany, and one can say, with considerable validity, I think, rightfully, unless Germany recovers Western Europe is in a perilous position.

One can look at it from another point of view and say with great effectiveness, that unless Britain recovers some of the authority which has been stripped from her by the war, Western Europe will still be in a perilous position.

And one can look at it from the point of vantage of Italy and France, that if either one of those countries falls, Europe will be in a perilous position.

The CHAIRMAN. That is true, but I think you are begging the question, because in Germany we are responsible for the initiative in going places, and we have not adequately implemented our initiative up to date.

GERMANY DISTINGUISHED FROM OTHER COUNTRIES

Senator SMITH. I think Germany is distinguishable from the other countries you mention, too, because Germany does not have a government of her own.

Senator BARKLEY. Here is another thing. We all know the psychology of the people around Germany who have been invaded two or three times in the last generation or three-quarters of a century.

In the absence of any mention of these countries, if we single Germany out to emphasize our aid to Germany, will that not play into the hands of those who seek to convince countries other than Germany that what we are doing is to try to give some sort of priority to German restoration as compared to them? We found that situation, Senator.

Senator SMITH. We found that, but I think that what Senator Vandenberg is driving at is that Germany must be brought into this self-help mutual cooperation idea, and not be built up separately.

Senator BARKLEY. Is it wise to run that risk in order to have something in the bill to make a speech about?

The CHAIRMAN. Let's eliminate it from consideration here, and when we get to the German section, let's see if we can do something about it.

EFFECTUATING PURPOSE OF ACT

Now let us go on to page 4, line 10:

(b) It is the purpose of this act to effectuate the policy set forth in subsection (a) of this section by furnishing material and financial assistance to the participating countries in such a manner as to aid them, through their own individual and concerted efforts, to become independent of abnormal outside economic assistance within the period of operations under this act, by—

(1) promoting industrial and agricultural production in the participating countries;

(2) furthering the restoration or maintenance of the soundness of European currencies, budgets, and finances; and

(3) facilitating and stimulating the growth of international trade of participating countries with one another and with other countries by appropriate measures including reduction of barriers which may hamper such trade.

Any comments?

Senator BARKLEY. Somewhere here, Mr. Chairman, we adopted an amendment to this same language, "promoting industrial and agricultural production." You put something in there about transportation. I was wondering whether you wanted to harmonize this language with what you did there, if necessary.

The CHAIRMAN. I do not think so, because the other spells out what is to be put in the bilateral treaty, and this is the general purpose.

Senator BARKLEY. That language is all right, so far as I can see.

The CHAIRMAN. All right.

Without objection, that goes.

Senator GEORGE. Have you any suggestion on this language?

Ambassador DOUGLAS. I think this is all right.

PROCEDURE

The CHAIRMAN. Now, Dr. Wilcox, where do you go next?

Dr. WILCOX. You have the little paragraph Senator George spoke of on page 14 with respect to Germany, and you also have the termination clause at the end of the bill.

Senator GEORGE. It may be a little paragraph, but it is a stubborn little fellow.

PROGRAM'S LENGTH

The CHAIRMAN. Let me ask this general question: Where is there in this bill any identification of the fact that this is a 4¼-year program? Is there any indication of it?

Ambassador DOUGLAS. It is in the authorization section, I think.

Mr. GROSS. That is on page 27, line 22.

Ambassador DOUGLAS. "There are hereby authorized to appropriate to the President, from time to time through June 30, 1952. . . ."

The CHAIRMAN. All right. We have not come to that yet. That is the big $64 or $68 question.

Now, we are on page 14, line 16:

(d) With respect to any of the zones of occupation of Germany, the President shall make appropriate administrative arrangements for the conduct of operations under this act, in order to enable the Administrator to carry out his responsibility to assure the accomplishment of the purposes of this act.

SETTING UP SPECIAL MISSIONS

Senator GEORGE. Before you get to that, Mr. Chairman, this has some connection and enables us to understand the situation a little bit better, I think, and over on page 13 section 9 (a) reads: "There shall be established in each participating country, except any of the zones of occupation of Germany, a special mission. . . ."

Now, there is no special mission set up in Germany, and nothing done here with respect to Germany until you get to the section that you have just read.

What about that free State of Trieste? What about it, Senator? How is that going to be administered?

Senator THOMAS of Utah. I think that I would, instead of saying outright that there shall be established in each participating country such a mission, I would make that progressive: "As each country or territorial entity is ready, there shall be established . . ."

This looks, from ordinary reading, as though the first thing they would do would be to set up 16 missions. I do not think that should be done until the country is ready to cooperate and is organized for cooperation, so that if this is made progressive you can include these other zones as they become organized and ready for it, Senator George.

Senator GEORGE. Yes, that might be.

Senator THOMAS of Utah. I think it would be very unwise to set up a mission for Trieste until you have a condition there ready for it, for instance, using the extreme, and that holds for the zones in Germany. As soon as we think we are ready, then is the time to set up a mission there.

The CHAIRMAN. The question is broader than that, is it not?

Senator THOMAS of Utah. The Administrator under this act can immediately make his map and he can have 16 nations with 16 missions right off. We don't want to have a mission if a country does not cooperate, does not come in, and some of the countries are not going to come in.

The CHAIRMAN. You might want a mission to facilitate their cooperation and their coming in, and to help them write the basis of their agreement with us.

Senator THOMAS of Utah. There has to be some kind of action on the part of a country before we set up something, hasn't there?

The CHAIRMAN. No, I think the fact that they signed CEEC invites the mission.

Senator THOMAS of Utah. Then you will have to do what Senator George suggests. You have to provide for those that have not signed as entities admission for them.

The CHAIRMAN. That is right.

Senator THOMAS of Utah. I still go back and think that if this is made progressive, with some such expression as "whenever the zone is ready"—those are my words and not some constitutional words, but that is what I mean.

"Whenever the zone is ready for cooperating in this plan, there shall be established a mission."

You have your preliminary arrangements.

Senator BARKLEY. You would say, "As the need therefor shall arise, there shall be established * * *". That gives you your progressive idea.

Senator GEORGE. You might say "As conditions are fulfilled in each participating country * * *."

Senator BARKLEY. I can agree with Senator Vandenberg that you have to have somebody working with these countries in setting up their machinery.

Senator GEORGE. That part of it struck me. Of course, over here on the next page one question brings up the question then of what we will do.

Senator BARKLEY. If you didn't go into any of these countries with official representatives until they worked out their own method of cooperating, you might find yourself up against the plan that they had worked out without any help from us.

The CHAIRMAN. I think the necessity of a mission is more emphatic in the first 5 minutes than it is in the last 5 minutes by a good deal.

Ambassador DOUGLAS. So long as these areas are zones of occupation.

AREAS UNDER INTERNATIONAL CONTROL

Senator GEORGE. We haven't anybody there who can come in. We ourselves are the only ones who control. We broadened this out beyond these zones. We brought in Trieste. Didn't we bring in some trusteeships, if any exist over there?

Ambassador Douglas. "Areas under international control."

Senator BARKLEY. That is the new section 3.

Senator SMITH. We anticipated a possible internationalization of the Ruhr. That was the suggestion you made.

Senator GEORGE. We have to do something specifically with respect to those areas that have no established government and that cannot participate. They cannot come in. They cannot agree. There is nobody to make them agree, except ourselves in the case of the German zones of occupation. And I should think that would be true of these other international areas.

Senator THOMAS of Utah. I don't see why we could not use Benelux, for instance, as an example, and have just one zone for those three countries and still make it work. That would depend on those three countries.

Ambassador DOUGLAS. It would depend upon the relationships among those three countries.

Doesn't (d) take care of the zones of occupation? That is in subsection (9), page 14.

Senator GEORGE. Yes, sir; that is one we skipped over. We never finally resolved that.

Ambassador DOUGLAS. Doesn't that take care of it as well as the problem insofar as it is limited to zones of occupation—and I think we should add Trieste—as well as possible.

Senator GEORGE. That is what I was talking about. If we are going to have some other comparable areas, we had better name some provision for them. I think it does, Mr. Chairman.

When we reached this, I asked that we sleep over it, because it is a very difficult position here that we are about to get into. It will be very difficult, it will have difficulty for the President, through the State

Department, or War or whatever occupying authority is set up in the zones of Germany under our control, if this administrator, who otherwise might be compelled under the act, to go in there and extend aid and assistance undertakes the work of rehabilitating the area.

It seems to me we have this situation with respect to these zones of occupation. Suppose the same thing applies to Trieste. I don't know. There is a governor down there, isn't there?

Ambassador DOUGLAS. No; there is not a governor. He has not been appointed, and therefore, there are zones of occupation.

Senator GEORGE. With respect to the zones of occupation of Germany or Trieste or any other like areas, it seems to me the President must be the dominant authority in that whole area, and that the administrator himself cannot go in there except under the direction of the President.

I do not see any other way that you can do it.

Senator BARKLEY. Suppose that during the life of the program they do get a government in Trieste.

Senator GEORGE. I mean so long as this continues. Of course, Senator Barkley, if they became eligible, that is a different thing. I do not see any other way we can do it, Mr. Chairman. It is not what I had in mind. It isn't the way I wanted to approach it. But if we are going to occupy Germany, as an illustration, and that is the immediate matter, why then the President must be supreme in that area, and this administrator, while he has the power to come in, must come in and must operate all activities. Everything in that zone must necessarily be carried out under the direction of the President. I don't see any other way we can do it.

ESTABLISHMENT OF SPECIAL ECONOMIC MISSIONS IN GERMANY

Dr. WILCOX. Mr. Chairman, the drafting committee discussed this point at some length, and I would like to ask Senator George if he interprets section 9 to mean that the establishment of special economic missions in Germany would be impossible. You see, there are those words in line 8, "Except any of the zones of occupation in Germany," and then you go over to the next page.

Senator GEORGE. I was reading them both together. It does seem it would make it impossible.

Dr. WILCOX. Suppose the President would later want to establish economic missions in Germany. Should that be prohibited?

Senator GEORGE. I don't think so. I think the administrator can go in there under the directive of the President at all times.

Dr. WILCOX. Even with the language of line 8 as it stands?

Senator GEORGE. I think you would have to modify that, or qualify it in some way, so as to show that those missions might be set up if the President so determines.

Dr. WILCOX. I think the question is whether the committee wants to exclude in this legislation the possibility of the President and the administrator and Secretary of State establishing special economic missions. The language would exclude that as it is now drawn.

Senator GEORGE. It does exclude it. I think we want to leave it open so the President can do it, but in order to avoid any possible conflict in an area in which we are supreme in command and occupation, I think we must leave that under the President, and all activity carried on in that area, looking even to the relief, or the people, or rehabilitation of their industries, must be under the President's directive so long as this occupation status continues. I see no other way out.

Ambassador DOUGLAS. And when the zones of occupation disappear and a government of Germany is established, then Germany will become a participating nation.

Senator GEORGE. Oh, yes; certainly. That is different altogether. That is all right.

MACHINERY SET UP FOR HANDLING TRIESTE

Maybe that would be true in the case of Trieste, but I do not remember the machinery that is set up for the handling of Trieste. I have a very faint recollection of it.

The CHAIRMAN. Then haven't you got to put some language at the end of your sentence in line 21, "until such time * * *", and so forth?

Ambassador DOUGLAS. It would seem to me first, Mr. Chairman, that in line 17, after the words "Germany and of the Free Territory of Trieste" there should be inserted "notwithstanding the provisions of subsection (a) of this section, the President shall make appropriate * * *".

Senator SMITH. You can say "including the establishment" and so on.

Mr. GROSS. I think you get at it more simply by changing the language of the preceding page.

The CHAIRMAN. What is that?

Mr. GROSS. In line 8 of page 13, if you say "subject to the provisions of subsection (d) of this section", then you can spell out exactly what you want to do in subsection (a).

The CHAIRMAN. And you mean to strike out "except any of the zones of occupation". Why doesn't that answer the question?

Senator SMITH. It does not answer the question of progressive establishment.

The CHAIRMAN. Let's get this one, first.

"There shall be established in each participating country, subject to the provisions of subsection (3) of this act." Wouldn't that let you in it if the President wanted subsequently to put in a special mission?

TREATMENT OF GERMANY AND TRIESTE

Senator GEORGE. Yes; I think so. I would like to hear the others' views on it, because this is so close to the center of this thing in my thinking, and many people in the country are going to think that some different treatment of Germany is essential to get recovery of Europe.

I think there should be the fullest discussion around this table, because it is going to give us trouble.

The CHAIRMAN. Let's make this one correction, anyway, at the moment, so we can get that behind us.

We will reopen section 9 to strike out, in line 8, the phrase "except any of the zones of occupation of Germany" and insert the language——

Ambassador DOUGLAS. "Except subject to the provisions of subsection (d) of this section."

Senator BARKLEY. I still believe the words might better be "except"—No; I guess that is all right. "Except as provided in subsection (b)" is what I had in mind.

The CHAIRMAN. All right. Have you got that, Mr. Rice? OK.

Senator GEORGE. Are you going to put Trieste in there, too?

The CHAIRMAN. Not there. We are just correcting this.

Now we go back to page 14, certainly we must put in, in line 17, "in the occupied zones of Germany and the Free Territory of Trieste"?

Mr. RICE. In the definition, Senator, we said the Free Territory of Trieste or either of its zones. Do you want to say the same thing?

Ambassador DOUGLAS. I think it has to be in this particular instance, either of the zones of the Free Territory of Trieste—"any of the zones of occupation of Germany and of the Free Territory of Trieste."

I think that is all right. When the zones of occupation cease to exist by the appointment of a Governor, then the Free Territory of Trieste falls into a different category.

Mr. GROSS. It doesn't become a "Free Territory of Trieste" until the Governor is appointed, so it should be, "and of Trieste."

OCCUPIED ZONES' STATUS WHEN GOVERNMENT ESTABLISHED

The CHAIRMAN. Now, can't you add a sentence to this section. I just totally agree with what Senator George just said about overriding importance of this matter in the minds of millions of our people, including me. Could you not add a sentence which you really need procedurally anyway, to the effect that whenever there is a government established in any of those occupied zones, they revert to their status among the other members of the cooperating organization?

Senator BARKLEY. They would revert to the enjoyment of such rights as other nations.

The CHAIRMAN. Take them out from under this Presidential monopoly and put them on the same basis as the rest of the people.

Senator SMITH. That doesn't imply they are between sea and sky until that time, does it?

The CHAIRMAN. Yes, they are. Until that time they are entirely at the mercy of whatever orders the President wants to make.

Senator SMITH. But they are included in the plan, or any plan the President sets up?

The CHAIRMAN. Oh, yes.

Senator THOMAS OF UTAH. What you want to say then is, "pending the establishment of governments in these places." That can be worked out—"pending the establishment of governments in these places, the President shall . . .".

Senator BARKLEY. Let me ask you this: Take Trieste. Trieste will be a government under the United Nations, with a Governor, and it will cease to be occupied territory. As a government it could not be invited by these other countries to participate. The same would apply to Germany, too, I guess, because they could not be invited, and were not. So they come into the same difficulty you find in Spain in, because of not having invited and not having signed an agreement with those

European countries after they cease to be occupied and become governments of their own.

Ambassador DOUGLAS. There would be that obstacle. I doubt very much that it would be a real obstacle, because after all, the military governments in the zones of occupation in Germany were invited by the participating countries to submit a calculation of their statements, and the calculations of estimates and requirements for Germany are included in the whole balance-of-payments calculation made by the participating countries.

Senator BARKLEY. I understand that. Does that include Trieste?

Ambassador DOUGLAS. No, because it is such a small area.

Senator BARKLEY. For a moment it raised the question in my mind, when they resume a normal government, which they are looking forward to, they resume the same status of all these other nations, the same as if they had not been occupied but had been an independent country.

Ambassador DOUGLAS. Either the invitation or the action of the military governments during the period of occupation would be a legacy of the German Government.

Senator BARKLEY. Maybe that is nothing to worry about.

PROCEDURES SAME FOR OCCUPIED ZONES EXCEPTING SPECIAL MISSIONS

Mr. GROSS. Under this bill, Senator, these areas are for all purposes considered as participating countries except for this one special problem of the establishment of a special mission. That is the only difference in the bill. And with respect to that, might it not meet your point to add to line 17, on page 14, the words "and during the period of occupation," so that we not only identify the area, but also the time for which the special relationship exists?

The CHAIRMAN. I think that is very good. I think that does what I am talking about. Where does that go?

Mr. GROSS. In line 17, after the inserted words "and of Trieste."

The CHAIRMAN. What are the new words?

Mr. GROSS. "And during the period of occupation".

The CHAIRMAN. I think that does it. Without objection, that change will be made.

Senator HATCH. Mr. Ambassador, I am trying to construe this paragraph: Is it contemplated the administrator will make a separate agreement with our Government in Western Germany, whether it is under the State Department or military department? What is the practical way that that will be worked out?

Senator SMITH. That is up to the President.

Ambassador DOUGLAS. That has to do only with the establishment of an economic mission, and the reason Germany was exempted, or special arrangements were made in the language for the establishment of economic missions in Germany, was because we are in our zone the sovereign of Germany.

Do we want to have two economic administrations in Germany, one under the powers of the government of occupation, and another one under the authority of the administrator, thus creating a confusion of authority within Germany? That was why section (d) was written.

Now, as to your question, Senator Hatch, we would be making an agreement with ourselves if there were no fusion of zones. If there were a fusion of zones, then we would be making an agreement with the bizonal authorities, and if France joined the bizonal, the present bizonal arrangements, the agreement will be made with the trizonal authority.

Senator SMITH. Then it would be the same procedure as with the other nations except for the special mission.

Ambassador DOUGLAS. That is right.

Senator SMITH. Wasn't that what troubled Senator George when he saw difficulty in having the administrator deal with another part of our own government in this section?

Senator GEORGE. No.

Senator SMITH. I am not troubled by that particularly.

HOW ACT CAN FUNCTION IN OCCUPIED AREAS

Senator GEORGE. It is much broader than that, Senator.

It is a question of how this act is going to be made to function in these occupied areas. With respect to those areas, I can see nothing else myself. I hoped there might be an expression of view around the table to see whether I was thinking right on it or not, but with respect to these areas I can see nothing the Administrator can do, although he may have textual authority to do it. He can't even go in there. He shouldn't be allowed to go in. He shouldn't do anything there at all except under direction of the occupying authority. And that would be the President of the United States. After all, whether we did it through the State Department or Army or somebody else, is another question.

Senator SMITH. Then you would broaden (d) to include everything under this act?

Senator GEORGE. Actually, although textually the Administrator is operating within the zone, practically I don't see how he can do it, how it would be wise to even start out with it, except by the President himself, under directive sending him in. Then his machinery is all there. It would be all set up, and the President may put him in there, and that isn't a satisfactory solution to the problem.

[The discussion was continued off the record.]

ECONOMIC ZONES: SEPARATE, BIZONAL, TRIZONAL

Senator BARKLEY. Let me ask you about the whole of Western Germany. You mentioned a little about if the bizonal arrangement went through and was in existence, agreement would be made with the bizonal authority; and if France comes in, it would be a trizonal authority. But suppose they do not do it, and they are all still separate economic zones. We could only deal with our zone. If Western Germany is to be restored, it has to be all the zones, it seems to me. How would we deal with the French and the British zones if they are still maintained as separate economic zones.

Ambassador DOUGLAS. The British zone, in effect, has been merged with ours.

Senator BARKLEY. It has been for certain purposes. Has it for this purpose or not?

Ambassador DOUGLAS. It has for this purpose.

Senator BARKLEY. It has not been merged with the French. Suppose it stays unmerged. How will we do anything with the French zone? What would be the mechanics?

Ambassador DOUGLAS. The requirements for the French zone of occupation are included in the calculation of requirements for Western Europe.

Senator BARKLEY. I know that. But who would sign any agreement?

Ambassador DOUGLAS. As to who signs the agreement, I presume it would be the French occupational authority.

Senator BARKLEY. It seems to me we have to guard against a hiatus in there wherein we would be helping to improve our own zone of Western Germany, but the other two zones would not get any of this assistance. If there is an open door or loose end to it, we had better take care of it.

Ambassador DOUGLAS. So far as the British and American zones are concerned, for the purposes of this act the bizonal merger, I think, provides an authority which can sign.

Senator BARKLEY. And any agreement would be signed by the bizonal authority with the same capacity, including everything that a Government could sign if it existed?

Ambassador DOUGLAS. I think that is right, sir.

DEFINITION OF PARTICIPATING COUNTRIES

Senator HATCH. I want to ask a question Mr. Rice has suggested here, Mr. Ambassador. In this list of participating countries, you use the expression, "any area under international administration." You said that the State Department was very anxious to have that in. Should similar language be in (d), and are there other areas?

Senator SMITH. Where was that put in?

Mr. RICE. In the definition of participating countries.

Ambassador DOUGLAS. I do not think it is necessary, because participating countries are defined in section 3, and it includes among other things an area under international control. There is no exception in section 9 to the establishment of an economic cooperation administrative mission in such an area. The only exception to the establishment of a mission in section 9 is in the zones of occupation of Germany.

Senator HATCH. But you included Trieste.

Ambassador DOUGLAS. And Trieste. The minute Trieste becomes the Free Territory of Trieste, it then becomes a participating nation under the definition of section 3.

Senator HATCH. Maybe I can make it clear.

The CHAIRMAN. What are they?

Ambasador DOUGLAS. There are none now, but you remember Senator Thomas referred to the possibility that the Ruhr might be placed under international control.

The CHAIRMAN. Looking ahead to the possibility of the internationalization of the Ruhr.

Ambassador DOUGLAS. Should that take place, the Ruhr would be within the definition specified and defined in section 3, a participating country.

Senator HATCH. Under that, its admission could be separate.

The CHAIRMAN. We will recess until 2 o'clock.

"ABNORMAL" MODIFIED TO "EXTRAORDINARY"

Ambassador DOUGLAS. May I bring up one question before we do, Senator?

We have used the word "extraordinary" instead of "abnormal outside assistance" in a number of instances throughout the bill. I suggest that that word "abnormal" be modified to "extraordinary" wherever it is presently used.

The CHAIRMAN. OK.

LIMITATION TO PROJECTS UNDERTAKEN BY AID FURNISHED UNDER ACT

Ambassador DOUGLAS. Then, with regard to the suggestion you made under section (c) (1), page 30, after the word "assistance,"

including a submission for the approval of the Administrator of specific projects designed to carry out such purposes, including wherever possible projects for the increased production of coal, steel, transportation facilities and food.

When we were discussing that before the committee met, I suggested it should be limited to the projects undertaken by the aid furnished under this act.

The CHAIRMAN. Yes. How do you want to change it?

Ambassador DOUGLAS. "Undertaken by assistance furnished under this act and designed to carry out * * *."

The CHAIRMAN. We are recessed until 2 o'clock.

(Whereupon, at 12:25 p.m., a recess was taken until 2 p.m. of the same day.)

AFTER RECESS

The hearing was resumed at 2 p.m., Senator Arthur H. Vandenberg, chairman, presiding.

CHANGING WORD "COLONIES" SUGGESTED

Senator THOMAS of Utah. If it is agreeable with the State Department, and I think it is, I would like for sentimental reasons, and for reasons that we have been striving to bring about, to get the word "colonies" out of this bill, and if "including its colonies and dependencies" could be changed to read, if the State Department sees no objection, to "including its dependent territories"——

Senator SMITH. You mean by that that we don't believe in the theory of colonies any more?

Senator THOMAS of Utah. Well, the whole effort of the ILO since the meeting in 1944—and England has joined with us, and France, for the most part—is based upon the theory that there are all sorts of things in territories, but it is to get rid of a word which has always stood for the exploitation of people. I don't want to do it if they are not ready to do it, but if they are ready, I would like to do it. So, if we can leave it with the understanding that if the State Department sees no reason for not changing it, it will be changed, or the other way, I don't care. I have made my point. I do know that declaration has been made, not only by the ILO and the United Nations, but all territories will be administered for the benefit of the people who live in them, and the idea of the declaration was to do away with the exploitation of populations, and the word "colony" is so closely connected with this theory of exploitation that I think it would be mighty fine to get rid of the word in a law like this.

Senator SMITH. What do you say, then, "dependent territories"?

Senator THOMAS of Utah. Yes. It reads here: "its colonies and dependencies." Let it read: "its dependent territories" or "its dependencies." That is purely sentimental, Mr. Chairman. I realize you are not going to change exploitation by a declaration made by anybody. It is like the things that Senator George was talking about. These changes will not come by law, but at the same time the nations of the world have gone on and made declarations, and they are attempting to overcome the evils of exploitation, and I think that it is a good word just to get out of this law.

The CHAIRMAN. What do you have to say, Mr. Ambassador?

Ambassador DOUGLAS. I think we should take a good look at the use of the word to see whether we run into any legal difficulties, by definition.

Senator THOMAS of Utah. I want the State Department to be sure. But if they feel all right about it——

Ambassador DOUGLAS. If there is really no legal distinction, if you prefer it that way, it could be done.

Senator THOMAS of Utah. I leave it entirely to them, Mr. Chairman. I bring it up so that we can make a good speech on this the next time we meet.

The CHAIRMAN. OK.

TERMINATION SECTION

Now where is that termination section. Page 36.

Senator SMITH. Did we get through with page 14, paragraph (d), the zones of Germany?

The CHAIRMAN. Yes, I think so.

Page 36, line 19. I kind of would like to wait until Senator George gets here before we take that up.

Is there any possible argument over the separability clause on page 40?

Senator SMITH. Isn't that the regular clause we always stick in?

The CHAIRMAN. I assume so.

Senator HATCH. On that termination, there is one thing we can be debating.

Page 36 seems to be rather awkwardly constructed, beginning where it says "none of the functions authorized under such provisions of this act may be exercised under the authoity of this act."

Senator BARKLEY. That is a good way to repeal it in advance.

Senator HATCH. It is just a question of language.

The CHAIRMAN. Well, let's read it and see what it says.

SEC. 18. After June 30, 1952, or after the date of the passage of a concurrent resolution by the two Houses of Congerss before such date, which declares that the powers conferred on the Administrator by or pursuant to subsection (a) of section 11 of this act are no longer necessary for the accomplishment of the purposes of this act, whichever shall first occur, none of the functions authorized under such provisions of this act may be exercised under authority of this act.

It really says what it means, I guess, at that.

Senator SMITH. Why not just say "may be exercised"?

Senator BARKLEY. It could be better written, but I think I understand it.

Senator THOMAS of Utah. That means that the President can't stop this Act, but Congress can.

The CHAIRMAN. That is correct.

Provided that: (a) during the twelve months following such date commodities and services with respect to which the Administrator had, prior to such date, authorized procurement for, shipment to or delivery in a participating country may be transferred to such country, and funds appropriated under authority of this Act may be obligated during such 12-month period for the necessary expenses of procurement, shipment, delivery, and other activities essential to such transfer;

(b) at such time as the President shall find appropriate after such date, and prior to the expiration of the twenty-four months following such date, the powers, duties and authority of the Administrator under this Act may be transferred to such other departments, agencies, or establishments of the Government as the President shall specify, and the relevant funds, records, and personnel of the Administration may be transferred to the departments, agencies or establishments to which the related functions are transferred; and

(c) funds appropriated under the authority of this Act shall remain available not to exceed twenty-four months following such date, for the necessary expenses of liquidating operations under this Act, for such time as the Congress from time to time, in the Acts appropriating such funds, may authorize.

POSSIBILITY OF BILL BEING VETOED

Senator THOMAS of Utah. I would like to say that if the same guy that got the President to veto the science bill is asked to pass on this bill for its constitutionality——

Senator SMITH. He will write another dissenting opinion.

Senator THOMAS of Utah. He has to veto this. We are definitely interfering with the President's control of our foreign relations.

Senator SMITH. This does not require foreign policy, so much, as it does a cleanup operation, does it?

Senator THOMAS of Utah. If there is any meaning in the need of the Administrator reporting all the time to the Secretary of State, Congress has definitely taken the authority itself here to upset a foreign policy that is, of course, no bigger than the right of appropriation, which is always with them, and that sort of thing.

But if the fellow who passes on it is, Senator Smith, as technical as the man was that got him to veto that bill, this bill will be vetoed.

Senator SMITH. I agree with you.

ADMINISTRATOR'S AUTHORITY

The CHAIRMAN. The State Department is the author of this contribution. I want to know what it means, in plain language. Will anybody volunteer?

Ambassador DOUGLAS. After June 30, the Administrator may not exercise any of the functions specified in section 11. That is after June 30, 1952, except that during the 12 months following June 30, 1952, and in respect of the procurement which he has authorized prior to that date, he may obligate the funds appropriated.

Second, when the President finds, after that date, June 30, 1952—the President may, within 24 months after June 30, 1952, or earlier if he so considers wise, transfer the authority of the Administrator to some other agencies of the Government.

Now, as to this last, (c) darned if I know what it does mean:

(c) funds appropriated under the authority of this Act shall remain available not to exceed twenty-four months following such date, for the necessary expenses of liquidating operations under this Act, for such time as the Congress from time to time, in the Acts appropriating such funds, may authorize.

Is there something omitted?

Mr. GROSS. I do not think so. That was intended to get to the Administrator, or to whatever agency the President might have transferred the authority to liquidate the operation, the authority to expend funds under this act for liquidating purposes, which must be completed within 24 months after June 30, 1952.

Ambassador DOUGLAS. Then what is "for such time as the Congress from time to time, in the acts appropriating such funds, may authorize"?

Mr. GROSS. Funds here authorized to be appropriated remain available for liquidating purposes for such time as the Congress may authorize within the 24-month period.

Ambassador DOUGLAS. Then why don't we say:

Not to exceed 24 months, for the necessary expenses of liquidation under this Act, unless the Congress shall determine that they are not available within a shorter period of time?

Mr. GROSS. That is what is intended.

The CHAIRMAN. What is intended?

Ambassador DOUGLAS.

The funds appropriated under this Act shall be available for the liquidation of the operations of the Act for a period of 24 months unless the Congress shall determine that prior to the expiration of the 24 months the funds shall not be available.

Senator HATCH. A shorter time.

Ambassador DOUGLAS. That is right.

Mr. SURREY. You might clarify that by saying, in line 23, after striking the words "not to exceed 24 months following such date" at the end of 25, "for such time but not to exceed 24 months, following such date as the Congress from time to time * * *.".

The CHAIRMAN. I could understand that. Did you follow that, Mr. Rice?

Mr. RICE. I do not believe I do yet.

Mr. SURREY. In lines 23 and 24, take out the words "not to exceed 24 months following such date." In line 25, put a comma after "time" at the end of the line, and insert "but not to exceed 24 months following such date."

Then it goes on as is.

Senator SMITH. You just take that "but not to exceed 24 months" out and put it at the end of the page.

The CHAIRMAN. In other words, you leave it entirely to Congress to fix the period that it is available, is that right?

Mr. GROSS. Within the 24-month period.

Ambassador DOUGLAS. "Shall not be available after the expiration of the 24 months unless, of course, the Congress appropriates for it."

Senator SMITH. Does that mean Congress can make an appropriation after June 30, 1952, for liquidating operations?

Ambassador DOUGLAS. No.

Senator SMITH. Does it mean the funds appropriated before that time?

Ambassador DOUGLAS. There will be no authorization for the appropriation of funds for that purpose after that time. It is not contemplated that there shall be an authorization for the appropriation for that purpose. I think it is securely written.

TIME FOR LIQUIDATING PROGRAM

The CHAIRMAN. Why, in respect to the guts of the thing, do you have to have 12 months and 24 months to wind this thing up? It seems to me that is an awfully long time.

Ambassador DOUGLAS. There may be, Senator, during the 12 months following June 30, 1952, certain procurement orders that won't be liquidated for a period of 12 months.

Senator SMITH. I can see the 12 months. I am not so sure or clear about the 24 months.

The CHAIRMAN. I don't know; it just annoys me to talk about extending a 4-year act 2 more years for the purpose of liquidating it. It just looks like reaching for too much time.

Senator GEORGE. What is the point, Mr. Chairman? Where are you?

The CHAIRMAN. We are on page 36, under the termination of the program. They want 12 months after the termination date, 1952, to liquidate, and then they want 12 more months beyond the first 12 months to use the funds appropriated unless Congress cuts down the second 12 months.

Ambassador DOUGLAS. They use the funds during the 12-month period for the purpose of liquidating the approved procurements that have been authorized prior to June 30, 1952. The 24-month period, or any time shorter than that, or within the 24-month period, the President may transfer to the appropriate agency of the Government, or agencies, the responsibilities and authority of the Administrator.

The use of the funds covered under subsection (c) is limited entirely to the expenses incident to the liquidation of the operations. It has nothing to do with the liquidation of obligations entered into for the procurement of commodities or services.

I presume that you would like to cut down the period.

The CHAIRMAN. It just looks like a needless inflammation.

Dr. WILCOX. This point was discussed in the drafting committee meeting, and the language of the old bill we felt was not at all adequate, because it gave the Administrator certain powers up through 1955 and then certain additional powers to spend the funds obligated up through 1957, which made it look like about a 9-year program, so it was cut back to, in effect, a 2-year liquidation, which is considerably less than the one in the original bill. It still does not give an answer to your question.

Mr. GROSS. The reason for that, Senator, was based largely upon the experience under the Lend-Lease Act. Of course, that is quite a different thing, and as you well know, some of the liquidation operations are still going on. The 12-months' authorization to obligate was intended to assure what we thought a reasonable amount of time to cover commodities which had been put into procurement prior to June 30, 1952, but which might have a fairly long leadtime for procurement, particularly if they are specification type equipment, for example. One year, our supply people think, is a good practical compromise. They had originally pressed for this 3-year extension that Dr. Wilcox talked about.

Some period is necessary. It might be 6 months. But I think they want to feel sure that there must be some necessary cleanup period, provided always that procurement had been authorized prior to that time.

The CHAIRMAN. I don't object to the 12 months as much as I do to the 24. You finally have a crescendo here.

ACCOUNTING REQUIREMENTS

Ambassador DOUGLAS. Why can't the duties of the Administrator be transferred to some other agency or department at the expiration of 12 months?

Mr. GROSS. They can be. The primary problem under this 24 months' period for a purely liquidating operation was suggested to us primarily on the basis of accounting requirements. The primary essential of the liquidating operation will be accounting, post orders, and collecting, or making expenditures. There again our original bill provided for a 5-year overall period within which liquidation was to have been completed. We have cut that down to 2 here. It is primarily from the accounting standpoint.

Ambassador DOUGLAS. Why can't the accounting responsibility be transferred to a department?

Mr. GROSS. That could be done. The accounting could be transferred.

TWENTY-FOUR MONTHS CUT TO TWELVE MONTHS

The CHAIRMAN. I would rather cut these 24's down to 12, and if you are troubled when you get to June 1953, you can ask for help at that time.

Without objection, the 24 months will be made 12 in all instances.

Has anybody anything else to say about termination?

Senator GEORGE. When does it terminate?

The CHAIRMAN. June 30, 1952.

Senator THOMAS of Utah. Is that in either section?

Senator SMITH. It must be in the $64 section.

Dr. WILCOX. In line 19, at the bottom.

The CHAIRMAN. Any comment? Senator George?

Senator GEORGE. No, sir.

The CHAIRMAN. Now, is there any question about the separability clause on page 40?

Without objection that is agreed to.

PROCEDURAL CONSIDERATIONS

Now, as I understand it, that leaves us with the maritime problem and the $6,800 million. Does it leave anything else, Dr. Wilcox?

Dr. WILCOX. No, I think those are all.

Senator SMITH. I have just one or two questions.

The CHAIRMAN. I just wanted to get oriented. We can't very well proceed with the maritime thing until tomorrow morning, because

Senator Lodge has a very deep interest in it, and I don't want to take up the $6,800 million until tomorrow, because I think we want the fullest possible membership present. But I would like to put you on notice that at 10 o'clock tomorrow morning I would like to settle maritime and the $6,800 million. I think that completes, with those two exceptions, the first overall reading of the bill for amendments.

Now, Senator Smith, you have something at some point or other that you wish to add?

EXTENDING CREDITS

Senator SMITH. I have some questions. The first question I want to ask is a point that Mr. Hoover raised in his comments, where he said that where money was to be spent in other countries, instead of our spending it, attempts should be made to get credits extended by those countries, and that might drastically reduce the total amount of commitments we had to make.

I would like to ask the Ambassador, to make a specific case, whether in getting grains, for example, from the Argentine, there is any reason why the Argentine should not extend the credit rather than expect us to pay dollars for Argentine wheat or meat or anything else that the Argentine might be furnishing, or any other country in a similar position to Canada.

Ambassador DOUGLAS. In the case of Canada, she has overextended herself and she is suffering as a result. Her supply of dollars is running short. She is accordingly imposing restrictions on imports from the United States in order to conserve dollars. That really throws a further burden upon Canada. If she can carry it at all, she will be able to do so only by further restricting imports from the United States.

I should think it would be an unwise and inadvisable thing to do. Moreover, Canada is making a fairly substantial contribution even under this program, because of her agreement to sell wheat to the United Kingdom for substantially under the world market price.

You see, these calculations were based upon certain prices, the calculations of dollar deficiencies. Now, to the extent to which Canada sells commodities for less than the prevailing world price, she is making a contribution to the program.

As to the Argentine, she, too, is short of dollars. She does extend credit. I cannot tell you precisely how much, although I have a paper on it somewhere.

Senator SMITH. The Argentine does not need any dollars to send her own wheat to these countries.

Ambassador DOUGLAS. No, but she needs dollars to buy from the United States.

Senator SMITH. Then you are including her, in a sense, in the recovery program.

Ambassador DOUGLAS. To the extent to which we spend dollars in the Argentine, surely. She may use those dollars for any purpose that she sees fit.

Senator SMITH. You mean to the extent to which we spend dollars in the Argentine for the things we want? That is the question Mr. Hoover raises. He points out that there is a total of some $3 billion, if I recall it—I wish I had brought his statement with me—in credits that might be advanced by these other countries, instead of our putting up the money. I am trying to get clear in my own mind how we answer his argument. If the Argentine is called upon to contribute a certain amount of wheat——

Ambassador DOUGLAS. She is imposing restrictions on imports from Western Europe now. She would be paid in soft currencies and she doesn't want soft currencies. All countries are doing precisely the same thing.

Senator SMITH. Here is the thing I was referring to:

> The program of supplies apparently calls for a large part of $3,500 million of Western Hemisphere goods to be purchased with American money from Canada, Argentina and other Western Hemisphere States. Of this amount under $200 million represents capital goods, the rest being mostly agricultural products. As the latter represents surplus production of the other Western Hemisphere countries, it would appear that they should be anxious to sell and, no doubt, to cooperate in creating world stability. It would seem, therefore, that these States should extend credit to the 16 countries for such goods. A partial guarantee, or advance against such credits by the United States to the Export-Import Bank is the most that we should be asked to give.

What is the weakness in that argument?

NEED FOR DOLLARS

Ambassador DOUGLAS. Canada needs dollars, and Canada does not get dollars by extending credit in sterling to the United Kingdom or France, or lire to Italy, and it does not relieve the Canadian position at all. It aggravates it. Canada has traditionally had a surplus on account of her trade with the United Kingdom which she has been able to convert into dollars when sterling was a convertible currency, and with the dollars which she received by converting sterling, she used to settle her deficit account with the United States. But it is of no use to Canada to extend credit to the United Kingdom and France and other European countries, and receive their local currency on credit, unless she can convert those currencies when received into dollars.

Accordingly, she will be compelled to impose further and further restrictions upon the importation of American goods from the United States.

The same thing is true of the Argentine.

BUYING WITH DOLLARS SUGGESTED

Senator WILEY. May I interject there? I know that I am getting on dangerous ground when I suggest this. I suggested it in the hearings. The world needs dollars. Canada needs dollars. All the nations we are going to help need dollars. But some of those nations, according to the best information I can get from the so-called "military geniuses" have certain assets that would not injure them which we could buy—landing fields, or whatever is necessary as we view the world tomorrow. That would give them dollars. We would buy outright, as we have bought through the years from these people. With regard to Canada, something was said in one of our hearings that in the next war Newfoundland fields would be very valuable. I am not a military man, but if we were to buy outright, they would get dollars.

Now, it seems to me it is just common horse sense, that if they want dollars, and they have got something that we need, we can give them dollars, and in doing that we can build a bank against the future.

Irrespective of what has been said, the whole argument everywhere by church groups and everyone else is that what we are doing here is to make Europe adequate so she can withstand the impact of communism. You hear people talking about the next war. That is why I suggest we must not have another Pearl Harbor. If, in the minds of our best military geniuses, point X belongs to a certain country, we do not want to take it away from her. We want to have those rights that will be perpetual enough to utilize them if and when an emergency arises. There are certain fields. We sent hundreds of millions of dollars and spent it in Africa, and certainly we need to develop our flying forces, and the way to do it is to make them world conscious, so that they can fly the world. Now, suppose the need here, for the sake of illustration, is $6 billion. I do not know what the answer will be. We can well afford to spend $1 billion as guarantee against the future if, in the judgment of men like Marshall and others, those things are imperatively necessary in the next war, and not be so sensitive to injuring people, because if they are one with us in spirit, as we hope they will be, they will join with us, if we put the cards on the table and say "We think this is necessary."

That is what I tried to interject in the previous hearings, but Mr. Marshall apparently thought that was not the thing to do. We mustn't ruffle any of these people that we are going to give $6 billion. I can't see it, and it has to take a lot of force to persuade me that I am totally wrong in this thing.

I am frank to say that I have time and time again, on the floor of the Senate, looked a year or two ahead at the state of things, and afterwards found I was justified.

Here we are going to ask the American people to appropriate a lot of money, and I say my mail is tremendously against this, as they understand it. They may not understand it. Why can't we do something, if they feel that this is imperatively necessary for the world of tomorrow, in which we are going to be engaged as the leading Nation on earth? Why can't we step out and see if there isn't some way we can bargain with them and give them dollars for something, and thus reduce the amount that goes into this overall picture? That is along the line that Hoover suggested with relation to commodities.

Senator George. Senator Wiley, that sounds right good to me, but that would not exactly be the Marshall plan. That would be another plan, wouldn't it, if we were going to help them by buying something from them and paying them money?

Senator Wiley. At least it is a practical realistic approach to a world situation.

Senator George. Yes, it is. It would be helpful to them if they had anything that we wanted to buy. But that isn't the case here.

BUYING SOMETHING NECESSARY TO UNITED STATES IN FUTURE

Senator Wiley. Let me get this straight. I wouldn't write this into this. I am saying that they who have negotiated this arrangement, and those who are handling our foreign affairs, in conjunction with the best brained brass hats we have, speak of coming events casting their shadows before. They want dollars. If we can get rid of $1 billion for something that we can see is imperatively necessary 5, 10, or 15 years from now, that reduces the amount needed here. They have got those dollars. Canada has those dollars that she needs, that interfere with our trade across the boundary.

It seems to me sufficient consideration has not been given to that. All the time we are considering reaching out and throwing out at these people funds that belong to the people of the United States, and when I see what is going on, and I see Senators of the United States going into my own State and talking as they do about the Marshall plan, and see Congressmen, I cannot but believe that if we are going to be statesmen in the practical sense—this is Lincoln's birthday—we ought to be able to fit into this program without going into the act itself the ability to get dollars for things that we imperatively need in the future.

That is the way it looks to me, because you are going to have a fight on the floor of the Senate, you are going to have a fight on the floor of the House, and it is going to be over how much money you are going to appropriate here.

Senator GEORGE. We are not disagreeing with anything on Earth you say but it looks to me like that would be another program.

(Discussion was continued off the record.)

Senator SMITH. We would probably do it separately from this plan, as a deal on its own hook. I would not want to see us use the difficult situation these people are in to say "We want something you have, and we know you don't want to give it to us."

Senator GEORGE. I may be wrong. I could not see the point of Mr. Hoover's argument. Your's is a little different from Senator Wiley's. Senator Wiley's is undoubtedly all right. If we want anything, and if someone else has it, and will sell it to us, and we want to appropriate the money for them to do it, all right, fine. But heaven knows this Administrator here wouldn't have anything to do with that. He will have all he can do under this, if he is going to have anything to do at all.

CREDIT FOR ARGENTINE WHEAT

Senator SMITH. I think that is a different question than the one of raising the point of why should not the Argentine, if she has surplus wheat, give a credit to these countries for that wheat, rather than have us pay her dollars for it?

Senator GEORGE. How are we going to make them do it? I wish they would come in and do it.

Senator SMITH. There is a hope that the other nations of the world will see the importance of rehabilitation of Europe.

Senator GEORGE. I wish Argentine would say:

> You have obligated yourself to $6,800,000,000. We will relieve you of so much of that by selling them wheat. We will take their currency.

We have no way of making them do that.

Senator SMITH. Suppose we adopt the negotiating principle of saying, "We guarantee to a certain extent these credits"?

Senator GEORGE. That might induce them to do it, if we said we would guarantee to a certain extent, to *x* percentage.

Senator SMITH. We would be that much to the good.

Senator GEORGE. They might do it then.

Senator SMITH. What is the reason we have not asked them fairly strenuously to join with us in this relief program to the end that those countries that have surplus agricultural products will pitch in and give credits without expecting us to pay them dollars?

Ambassador DOUGLAS. Let's take the case of Argentine first. We have spoken of Canada. I have doubts that we can expect Canada to do anything further.

Senator SMITH. Let's assume that the Canada book is closed.

Ambassador DOUGLAS. The Argentine has been selling materials to the United Kingdom. They are being liquidated by selling the Argentine railroads. I do not see what you can accomplish guaranteeing the sale from the Argentine to the United Kingdom in dollars. You have to put up the dollars. You might just as well do it in the first instance.

Senator SMITH. What I cannot see is why they need dollars for Argentine wheat. It is the wheat they want. They do not want the dollars.

Ambassador DOUGLAS. The Argentine wants the dollars.

Senator WILEY. The Argentine needs the dollars.

Ambassador DOUGLAS. To buy from us.

Senator SMITH. I am wondering if we have explored that adequately and have gotten to the bedrock basis that they have to have dollars.

Senator WILEY. The facts are in relation to Argentine wheat that the Argentine Government has been buying wheat from its farmer at a low price and has been charging Europeans about $5 a bushel.

Now, what I am thinking about in relation to the Hoover proposition is that if the State Department sees the picture as a world picture, and we are the great leader in world power, and we have got Pan America and we have helped the South American countries, if, in order to make available more money for the very project we are talking about, the Argentine, which has a surplus of wheat could agree, or would agree, it seems to me that is up to the State Department to find out definitely, whether or not they would not join in at least doing considerable if there was no loss to them, and they got some dollars. Suppose the wheat cost them $1.35 from the farmer, and they sell it to us for $2, if we want wheat. Thus we save the additional amount to go into the project to make sure that there is a sufficiency there.

ASKING FOR COOPERATION FROM SOUTH AMERICA

I think something like that should be explored before you start to go into an overall sum that is going to precipitate one fine fight. And I cannot see why, because we feel we are the leader in the world, we cannot reach out and ask these others to cooperate with us on this great world-saving plan, in order that Communism will not reach the shores of the Atlantic in Europe. That is the very basis of the whole thing, otherwise, we would feel that Europe could work out of her own troubles as she has in the past through the years in suffering and sweat and tears.

Now we say, "If you do not go in, you just have a breeding ground for Communism and Communism will take over."

There are those who say you are only accelerating the march of communism by the very thing we are doing.

I cannot understand why any country in South America which was with us in the war, and which has received from us tremendous sums of money during the war, should not attempt to collaborate on the basis I have suggested, where we could get wheat or whatever is necessary so they could get dollars, but not get them at the tremendously high prices they have been getting.

[Discussion was continued off the record.]

BILL PROVIDES FOR PURCHASING ESSENTIAL MATERIALS

Senator HATCH. Senator Wiley's original suggestion about the purchase in these countries, while the bill does not go as far as he wants it to, I am sure it does provide for those essential materials of which we are short, that we may purchase from those nations directly and use the funds for that purpose.

Ambassador DOUGLAS. And beyond that, Senator, the administrator may make loans which will be repaid by the delivery of strategic raw materials.

Senator SMITH. That is in our stockpiling provisions here. I think that is covered.

COUNTRIES WITH SURPLUS AGRICULTURAL PRODUCTS EXTENDING CREDIT

I am not necessarily pressing this. I am trying to get an answer to what seems on first blush to be a difficult point to answer, why another country who has a surplus of agricultural products should not extend credit as we are.

Mr. NITZE. On the question of surplus agricultural products, it seems to me Cuba is a good example. After all, Cuba's sugar production is surplus to Cuba's own requirements. The Cubans cannot eat all the sugar they grow. That is true not only of the sugar they sell to other countries, but also of the sugar they sell to us. That is the traditional way in which Cuba lives, to grow more sugar than she needs herself, and she cannot possibly continue to buy from the United States 90 percent of her total imports—she can't possibly live at all—without those imports from the United States, so she has to sell her surplus agricultural production, and it seems to me that that was really the basic fallacy in Mr. Hoover's argument.

Mr. Hoover argues that just because this agricultural production of theirs is surplus to their own internal requirements, therefore they can sell it on credit.

Cuba could not sell all its sugar on credit without very quickly being in a position where it would need relief from us. You would bust Cuba overnight if you did that.

The same thing is true to a lesser extent if you did that with these other countries. Argentina is not as wholly dependent on imports from the United States as Cuba is. But it is dependent for a number of things which are essential for her to keep up the agricultural production she now has on imports from the United States, so there is a limit to the extent to which Argentina can sell her agricultural products to Europe without receiving some dollars on them.

We have included in our estimates a continuation of credits to Argentine, but we thought the amount included was the maximum which it was safe to count on.

Senator SMITH. That was really the point of my question, whether we had explored that as fully as we could, and gotten relief from that end in financing the whole thing to the maximum extent possible, or whether all these countries thought the United States is a great, rich country with plenty of dollars, and we might as well get these dollars by selling these products we have at an excessively high rate. Certainly, when Argentine wheat was selling at $5 I got letters from all over the place, asking why I let the thing go on. There is no defense to the Argentine making us pay $5 for wheat that we are sending abroad. They at least should go as far as they can go in helping the world recovery program.

Mr. NITZE. The difficulty with the negotiations is that we are not in a position at this moment to speak with any degree of firmness. We are not certain as to what type of bill the Congress will pass, so that you cannot go down there and talk across the table to Mr. Peron and say, "Here we will do this if you will do that."

All you can do is to kind of explore in advance what might be possible thereafter. And Mr. Peron has said that he will supply, or will sell wheat and other agricultural products at prices no higher than the world price, provided he is assured of getting the petroleum and various types of transportation equipment to get wheat to the ports.

Now, it is difficult to explore that in sufficient detail, so that we know we can make available the things he wants.

The CHAIRMAN. And you are also embarrassed with Mr. Peron due to the fact that our own American exporters charge him three or four prices for many things he wants?

Mr. NITZE. That is partly our own fault because he has not placed his orders far enough in advance.

Ambassador DOUGLAS. But certainly as to price which the Argentine Government charges, every effort will be made to bring that price down to the world price.

Senator SMITH. I don't want to press the point; I just want to raise it, because it seemed to me it was a point well worth exploring fully, if some of these countries could not do a little credit advancing themselves, and that we don't go further than guarantee part of those credits rather than putting up all the money ourselves.

SHORTAGE OF DOLLARS

Ambassador DOUGLAS. They are short of dollars now, Senator. The Argentine has imposed restrictions on imports. She cannot convert other European currencies into dollars as she did before the war, so she therefore suffers from a shortage of dollars. She is not, therefore, able to buy all the things she needs from the United States.

In an extreme form, Cuba is a very good case in point.

One fallacy in Mr. Hoover's argument and proposal is that these countries do not have dollars and they need dollars to live.

Senator SMITH. Just to live. There is no other place where they can get dollars.

Ambassador DOUGLAS. Not to get dollars, no.

Mr. NITZE. Our estimates did include substantially increased exports from Europe to the Latin American countries.

Senator SMITH. That is what I wanted to get at. If we can defend ourselves by saying we have gone to the limit in exploring those possibilities——

Mr. NITZE. The World Bank people thought we had gone too far in estimating increased exports from those countries.

Senator SMITH. I will not pursue the question further, Mr. Chairman.

I would like to ask one more question which I said yesterday I would bring up.

PROTECTION FOR MOVIE AND PUBLICATION INDUSTRIES

On page 22 we are making provision to guarantee persons a certain number of dollars for soft currencies they get abroad if they put into effect certain obligations in the way of business and so on, that are in line with the program, and the question has been presented to me from a number of different sources as to whether that includes such things as copyrighted articles.

Take our movie industry, our publication industry, and things of that sort.

I wondered whether the language on page 22 could be construed to include anything of that sort, looked upon as an incentive project or something else, that the Administrator could consider as an approved project, or whether we should have special legislation endeavoring to protect these particular industries.

I am advised, possibly because of my connection with the so-called "Voice of America" program, that great good is being done by our publications abroad by the circulation of American books to have America better understood, by such periodicals as The Reader's Digest, which is now translated into many languages, and they are getting to the end of their string, all of them, because they are getting soft currency which they cannot translate.

Is this program in the language that would protect those people by getting reasonable exchanges from soft currencies into dollars?

Senator WILEY. What language are you referring to?

Senator SMITH. I am referring to page 22.

The CHAIRMAN. I would not think so, at all.

Senator SMITH. I don't think it protects them at all.

The CHAIRMAN. I would not think it should.

Senator SMITH. That is what I want to get at, whether we have any interest in any private industries abroad. I am just raising the question as a matter of policy, whether we should try and include other industries abroad that may be doing a service in part of this overall plan.

The CHAIRMAN. I think we discussed it the other days, whether or not the scientific publications and so forth came within the purview of the act, and decided they did not.

Senator SMITH. I thought the scientific publications did, under scientific information.

The CHAIRMAN. Oh, yes, in that case, but I means as projects for recovery. They just do not fit into the recovery program.

Ambassador DOUGLAS. I would not think it was intended that they would be included, the type of project you have in mind.

Senator SMITH. I am just raising the question. I was asked to present the proposition, and I see the other side of it. I think from the standpoint of our interpreting America they are valuable. I think American publications, the project to translate the Paris Herald-Tribune into other languages, and so on—and the New York Herald-Tribune people want to know if there is any chance of their getting a translation of their foreign soft currency into American dollars.

I have discussed this with Mr. Lovett, and I think possibly it should be dealt with in different legislation than this.

The CHAIRMAN. I think you might well have the same kind of convertibility guarantee within limits with respect to the "Voice of America" program in regard to those publications abroad.

Senator SMITH. But not under this legislation?

The CHAIRMAN. I would not think it had anything to do in the world with this.

Senator SMITH. I am inclined to agree with you on that.

The CHAIRMAN. But I think your hand is strengthened by the fact that you here have a precedent and a formula which might well be applied to the type of thing you are talking about in respect to the "Voice of America."

Senator WILEY. They don't want bases or basic information in this program.

The CHAIRMAN. This is not an information program.

Senator SMITH. Of course, the argument is made that the incentive undertakings to steam up production are desirable, and they might classify the movies, for example, in that field. I admit it is pretty farfetched. But that was the argument that was made to me in the conference with some of the movie people. Mr. Johnston was talking it over with me the other day. I will say to you frankly, I told them I did not feel it came in the purview of the spirit of this proposal, and I am perfectly willing to drop it at this point if that is the feeling of the committee.

ADOPTION OF NAME OF ECA

There is another thing, Mr. Chairman, that we suggested earlier in the discussion, whether the name of this program was the name that we wanted to adopt: Economic Cooperation Administration. I have no objection to it, and I rather think it is all right. It does not get the name "European" in it anywhere.

Is that the best name we can select for the name of this thing?

We have been calling it "ERP" in popular language. Now we call it "ECA."

The CHAIRMAN. One thing you get away from is ERP.

Senator SMITH. That may be completely desirable, and I have no objection to it. I am just raising a question whether we are satisfied with the Economic Cooperation Administration, which might apply to anything—domestic, foreign, or anything else.

Ambassador DOUGLAS. I hadn't thought about the title, Senator. You raised the question the other day.

Senator SMITH. It is all the way through the bill. We refer to it constantly.

85-743—73——15

Ambassador DOUGLAS. I suppose the word "cooperation" was used in order that the cooperative effort of European countries might be emphasized.

Senator SMITH. I am merely raising the question because it was sort of passed over. I do not think I have a better suggestion unless you say "European Recovery Administration."

Mr. GROSS. China and other countries may be added to it.

Ambassador DOUGLAS. Not among the participating countries.

Mr. NITZE. We are also worried about a possible conflict between a continuing organization of European countries, which we have thought of as the European organization, with the American administration which we set up, and there should not be confusion between those two entities. The European recovery program is, after all, the entire program, including what they do in mutual and self-help, as well as U.S. assistance.

The CHAIRMAN. I should think the Economic Reconstruction Act was better than Economic Cooperation. Then it is the ERA.

Ambassador DOUGLAS. I like reconstruction better than recovery, because it is reconstruction, but that is a matter of purely personal taste.

Senator SMITH. You would use the word "Administration" probably, Mr. Chairman, because that is used all the way through. Are you suggesting Economic Reconstruction Administration?

The CHAIRMAN. I was just expressing a personal plea for the Economic Reconstruction Act of 1948.

Senator SMITH. I prefer it.

Senator BARKLEY. Will the elimination of any reference to Europe in the title of the thing lead to confusion here at home in regard to some other domestic reconstruction agency or agencies in existence, for instance the RFC? Then we come along later with China's program.

The CHAIRMAN. I do not think the word "European" is in it anywhere.

Senator GEORGE. Not in the title.

Senator WILEY. If it is ERA it is a new era we are indulging in, I'll tell you.

The CHAIRMAN. We hope!

Senator SMITH. A more appropriate name would be the European Reconstruction Act of 1948, but if the State Department is afraid that will bring about confusion with the European program——

Mr. GROSS. The administrator, of course, may obtain jurisdiction over other area programs, including China.

Senator SMITH. You can't bring him in under this act.

Senator GEORGE. Have you finished, Senator Smith?

GETTING TOP EXECUTIVES FOR PROGRAM

Senator SMITH. Just in raising that point; I have one more thought I want to get out of my system, and then I will be entirely through.

That thought is what I discussed the other day, the question of whether we can have it somewhere up here that it is legal and proper for corporations, for example, that employ high-priced people, to pay the difference in salary between what a fellow gets here and what his normal salary is, or at least part of it, in order to induce high-priced people to take these jobs. I think that is worth considering.

Mr. Rice advises me that he does not think there is anything in the law that prevents that at the present time.

Mr. RICE. There is no law. We made a search of it.

Senator SMITH. The Selective Service Act had something to the effect that that could be done.

Mr. RICE. That was put in out of an excess of caution. Before that went into the act the Attorney General had ruled that they could get the difference without violating the statute.

Senator SMITH. Even before the act was passed?

Mr. RICE. Yes.

Senator SMITH. Why did they put it in the act?

Mr. RICE. Excessive caution.

Senator SMITH. It is sort of holding up a little suggestion to employers that they could well let their top men go and make a contribution to this by paying part of their compensation. There is danger in it, because they might be accused of putting someone into a job where it was of interest to the company to do so. Putting a General Motors man in there, naturally he wants to sell General Motors cars to this rehabilitation business. I can see that danger.

But we could put something in here to indicate we are suggesting the cooperation of employers to let their topflight men go, which would be well worth sticking in, and if the committee thinks the principle is sound, I will be glad to work on an amendment with Mr. Rice, even though it is not necessary to leave that little suggestion in the bill.

The CHAIRMAN. That is a two-edged sword, Senator.

Senator SMITH. Would you rather not put it in?

Senator HATCH. I was just going to observe that this whole program is characterized by one Mr. Henry Wallace as a Wall Street program. Every time you insert any language like that in the bill, you are going to invite that kind of criticism.

Senator SMITH. The language will be broad enough so it would not necessarily mean the very wealthy corporations. You want to get topflight executives to deal with this if you can.

The CHAIRMAN. It seems to me there is a certain inconsistency about writing a provision of that sort into the law. If we have the resources to proceed with this program, we ought to have the resources to pay the bill to administer it. The idea that we have to pass the hat in order to administer the disposition of $6,800 million would suggest to me that we had better not distribute $6 billion.

Senator SMITH. You have in here virtually a limitation to the Foreign Service compensation, and I thought in that connection it might be indicated.

The CHAIRMAN. So long as there is no prohibition against the thing you are talking about, I think that is the best you could hope for. I think we might put a pretty sad target up for prejudicial attack if you were suggesting that we were going to run this thing on a subsidy basis, which would be the prejudicial way in which it would be interpreted.

Senator SMITH. Oh, you are quite right. It would be attacked that way.

Well, I just raise the question. If the committee does not think it is desirable, I won't press the point. It is just a question of judgment.

The CHAIRMAN. I think the thing you are talking about has to be done by these corporations if we are going to get anywhere at all.

Senator SMITH. I am sure it has to be done. You won't get topflight men if you don't do it. Whether you want to indicate that that is expected in the bill is just a question of judgment.

NAME OF PROGRAM

That is all I had, except again to suggest that the name could be improved upon. I prefer European Reconstruction Act, or something of that sort, to Economic Cooperation Act, and if you want me to, I will move a change to something of that sort, so we can get an expression on it.

Senator BARKLEY. Don't you think we had better get a concrete name before you move to change it? I agree with you about it. I don't like the word "Cooperative," and even if you changed it only to "Reconstruction" I would like it better, but in view of other programs we may be confronted with, I am not so awfully sure that the word "European" ought not be in there to identify it.

Senator SMITH. I have that in mind. I would like to see "European Reconstruction Administration."

Senator BARKLEY. You have an Economic Reconstruction Administration here, and then you come along with the Chinese situation. You have to identify that. You can't call that an Economic Reconstruction Administration. You have to give it some other name so as to separate it from this one.

Senator SMITH. You could not bring the Chinese under this act the way we have worded it now. You would have to have separate legislation.

The CHAIRMAN. Why couldn't you? It says "The Act shall be cited as the Economic Cooperation Act."

Senator SMITH. How about the definition of participating countries?

The CHAIRMAN. I was talking about any collision in titles. There would be no collision in titles.

Suppose we think that over until we get down to the final shot at this thing, when we have it reprinted. That is one question we will bring up.

ROLE OF ROVING AMBASSADOR

Senator GEORGE. Let me ask one question now. Is this special Ambassador, this roving Ambassador, the head man for the European group, allowed to talk with anybody, in any one of the nations over there, except an organization of those nations, under this act? He can talk to a group of them, but can he talk to country X, Y, and Z directly?

Ambassador DOUGLAS. He may, but generally with the Ambassador who is accredited to that particular country.

Senator GEORGE. I understand that. I mean with respect, of course, to anything he has to do in the act.

On page 10, if you notice that language, my attention is called to this, Mr. Chairman, by a very thoughtful man who has been reading the Brookings recommendations, and he said that he thought it was a great mistake if the Brookings recommendation confined the roving

Ambassador to conference with any established organization set up by these participating countries, and that he would not be in position to be of very much direct help at least in helping, say, France, or anyone else, any other nation over there, to work out some of its problems.

[Discussion was continued off the record.]

Senator GEORGE. I just want to find out if his interpretation is correct. He had not seen this text, but he has seen, of course, the Brookings text.

Senator WILEY. You have the following sentence:

And shall discharge in Europe such additional responsibilities as may be assigned to him with the approval of the President in furtherance of the purposes of this Act.

Senator GEORGE. I know that that is some additional thing the President may give him, Senator.

Ambassador DOUGLAS. This is section 10?

Senator WILEY. No; seven.

Senator GEORGE. "He shall be the chief U.S. representative to any European organization of participating countries." In other words, he is not the chief representative of the United States even with respect to this recovery program, except through some European continuing organization.

Ambassador DOUGLAS. And he shall discharge such other duties as the President may give him.

Senator GEORGE. Yes; and then he, of course, has the completest liberty and fullest contact with the heads of the missions.

Ambassador DOUGLAS. That is right.

Senator GEORGE. The missions that are sent to each country.

Ambassador DOUGLAS. And with the Ambassador in each country.

Senator GEORGE. Well, this would not preclude a conference, if he wished to sit down and talk over the problems of France or Belgium?

Ambassador DOUGLAS. It would not preclude him from doing it, Senator. He should do it after establishing the relationship with the Ambassador in a country.

Senator GEORGE. Oh, I understand that.

Ambassador DOUGLAS. This would not preclude it.

Senator GEORGE. He is going to be a very important person in Europe.

Ambassador DOUGLAS. Very.

AUTHORITY OF ROVING AMBASSADOR

Senator GEORGE. He is the field man that represents everything that we are trying to do here—I mean the head man in the field. And they have to have somebody for these heads of missions, of course, to look to, and as I understand this scheme that we are setting up here now, they have direct contact with this roving Ambassador, fullest contact to iron out their differences. In other words he is supreme, so far as they are concerned, unless there is some difference, of course, that arises that is to be resolved in some other way.

Ambassador DOUGLAS. Yes. The chiefs of the missions report back to the Administrator.

Senator GEORGE. That impression, I think, grew out of the Brookings report, and the Brookings report rather confined his duties to the organization of these European nations and not to any one of them.

Ambassador DOUGLAS. That is right, although he may, as you know, consult with and call upon the Ambassador for any help, and he may himself go to any country and, with the Ambassador or the head of the economic mission or both, carry on any discussions with the responsible heads of the government in that country.

Senator GEORGE. I would think he would. I just wanted to be sure that we had not put anything in here that precluded it.

Ambassador DOUGLAS. There is nothing that precludes it.

Senator GEORGE. What condition did we leave Spain in? I am a bit interested in that. I want to find out.

Dr. WILCOX. You did adopt this language with respect to the Administrator, which fitted at the end of page 10.

Senator GEORGE. I did not think he wanted to be sitting down there just occasionally meeting with an organization. Maybe it wouldn't meet more than once a year.

I don't see anything in here that cuts down his power. Has he any authority on earth to ask these nations to meet in conference, these 16 countries? Has he any power of suggesting to them in any way that they shall meet?

Ambassador DOUGLAS. That would be done, I presume, Senator, through diplomatic channels.

SPAIN

Senator GEORGE. What did we do with Spain?

Ambassador DOUGLAS. We left the door open to Spain if the participating countries agree that Spain should be invited to join.

The CHAIRMAN. I would think that that was the net of it.

Senator SMITH. I think our language there is accomplished on page 3, line 9, "* * * calls for a program of European recovery open to all European nations which cooperate in such plan," and we figured that "which cooperate" would mean that Spain would have to be yanked in by the other countries.

Senator BARKLEY. They would have to agree to let Spain yank herself in.

Senator SMITH. She can't cooperate unless she is included.

Senator GEORGE. My attention has been called to the fact that Spain needs some things very, very badly, and some things very vital to our commerce, particularly our commerce in the South. She needs cotton. She is a great textile manufacturing country, and she hasn't the dollars and can't buy cotton. She can't get cotton, and she could supply and would supply very much textile goods to neighboring countries. France now seems to be restoring her trade relationships with Spain, if they could get anything to operate on, but it is open to her if she can get in and participate.

Ambassador DOUGLAS. Yes; that is my understanding.

The CHAIRMAN. That is my understanding, and I thought we agreed that that was as far as we could go.

Senator GEORGE. I think it is.

Senator SMITH. We couldn't say Spain has to be admitted. We couldn't do that.

GIVING PREFERENCE TO AGRICULTURAL PRODUCTS IN SURPLUS

Senator BARKLEY. If that is disposed of, there is one matter I would like to bring before the committee for consideration. I will try to work out an amendment by tomorrow. This applies, or it might apply, to cotton , also. It applies particularly to tobacco.

Out of this program there is to be a very considerable allotment of tobacco to Europe for the purpose of incentives and strengthening the morale of the people. Cigarettes and tobacco have become almost a medium of exchange over there, as we all know. The tastes for tobacco and the products of tobacco have changed as a result of the war. For instance, in Germany prior to the war their taste largely was for Turkish cigarettes but now they have acquired a taste for American blended cigarettes, and they prefer them very much and they want them.

The CHAIRMAN. And they are particularly interested in Paducah tobacco!

Senator BARKLEY. Paducah tobacco doesn't go into cigarettes. It goes into chewing and smoking.

But there are large surpluses of different types. Senator George has Flue-cured in Georgia; North and South Carolina have Flue-cured. In Virginia there is some dark, and Kentucky burley and dark fired tobacco, all of which they naturally want to secure a market for in Europe.

Way back yonder, before World War No. 1, 85 percent of our dark fired tobacco was exported and we used only 15 percent in this country. Tobacco and tobacco products pay into the Treasury $1.2 billion annually as revenue. That is about $1,000 per acre for all the tobacco that is used in the manufacturing of cigarettes and smoking tobaccos in this country, and that is collected from all parts of the tobacco growing sections. I am using tobacco as an outstanding example of what I am coming to.

It occurred to me that somewhere in this bill there ought to be a provision that in the distribution of agricultural products obtained from the United States, as grants to the recipient nations, the distribution should be, so far as practicable, in proportion to the surplus of each type and kind that is in existence, so that all types of this particular or any other product in the same situation would be treated fairly, and not any one type be given preference over the other.

The CHAIRMAN. I think you have another tobacco problem, Senator. Senator Robertson, of Virginia, was speaking about it yesterday. He very strongly objects to the fact that with this heavy tobacco surplus in this country there should be any purchases of tobacco under this program anywhere except in the United States, and there are very substantial tobacco purchases in other countries.

A SURPLUS OF TOBACCO

Senator BARKLEY. There are substantial surpluses of tobacco. The Commodity Credit Corporation has had for a long time a lot of tobacco on which they advanced money for export purposes. Various tobacco cooperatives have surplus tobacco on their hands.

Senator GEORGE. What Senator Robertson wanted was that where the authority is given to purchase any goods or any commodities outside of the United States, he wanted to put in an exception that that would not apply to tobacco.

Senator BARKLEY. I am not seeking to use the word "tobacco" in the language we might put in. It might apply to many agricultural products. But what I was seeking merely to get the committee to consider at this time was the propriety of providing that in the distribution of these agricultural products, preference should be given at least to those where there is a surplus.

Senator GEORGE. There certainly ought to be an equitable distribution.

Senator BARKLEY. I want you to think that over. I may have some language tomorrow.

The CHAIRMAN. Do you mean that if, let us say, there is a surplus of prunes and grapefruit and there is no surplus of wheat, that you put your emphasis on prunes and grapefruit?

Senator BARKLEY. I do not mean you should send prunes and grapefruit in lieu of wheat that might be sent in there if there was a surplus, but where you are sending those things to countries that want them you have to integrate that also with the wants of the country.

For instance, Great Britain has always used a flue-cured tobacco. Their taste has not changed. I would not want to force some other type of tobacco on to them merely because there was a surplus. You have to integrate whatever you do with the desires, tastes, and needs of the country to which it goes.

Then, Great Britain raises $2 million in annual income for the support of the government out of tobacco. Italy obtains about 30 percent of her national income for governmental purposes out of the sale of tobacco. There used to be a governmental monopoly, called the Italian regi, which bought tobacco in America and sold it to her people at enormous profits, and it was a very fruitful source of revenue to the Government. The same was true in many other European countries. Spain was one of them.

WHY SPEND MONEY FOR TOBACCO

The CHAIRMAN. Senator Connally suggested that inasmuch as this was a relief bill, we ought to put our emphasis upon edible tobacco.

So far as the tobacco item is concerned, I think the chief complaint I have had, more than against any one thing is this question: Why do you spend a quarter of a billion dollars for tobacco in order to save the lives of these Europeans and keep them sustained?

Senator GEORGE. Keep them from going Communist.

Senator BARKLEY. It is an incentive payment. The purpose of it is to keep up the morale of the people in the factories and mines.

The CHAIRMAN. I understand.

Senator SMITH. That is what the movie people say.

Senator BARKLEY. I would like to present some concrete language. Maybe Senator Robertson and I can get up something that will not be out of harmony.

The CHAIRMAN. Senator Robertson is on rather dangerous ground. I hope you won't collaborate too closely with him.

Senator BARKLEY. I did not know he made that suggestion.

The CHAIRMAN. He wants to cut out all tobacco procurement from Turkey or Cuba.

Senator BARKLEY. I doubt the wisdom of that. Some of those countries prefer Turkish tobacco, and even in Germany they want a certain type of tobacco to blend with our tobacco to make blended cigarettes which they prefer very much in preference to the wholly Turkish cigarette.

The CHAIRMAN. We will be very glad to hear your amendment when you arrive with it.

We are all through, now, except just one or two questions, unless there are questions other members of the committee want to raise.

LETTER SHOWING DIVISION BETWEEN GRANTS

Mr. Ambassador, is there any way that we can get this letter before we complete this work, showing the division between grants and so forth?

Ambassador DOUGLAS. I sent it up to you last night, sir.

The CHAIRMAN. I haven't seen it. I wonder where it went. Maybe it is over in my other office.

Ambassador DOUGLAS. It referred to the correspondence which you had with the Secretary of the Treasury, which recited that the National Advisory Council had had some apprehensions about preparing that sort of table; that you, however, felt that it was necessary, and accordingly the table was being submitted; that you understood the reasons, if it could be avoided, for avoiding giving it publicity, but if it was necessary, that you understood it was tentative and not conclusive.

Then it recited the categories: Turkey, Switzerland, and Portugal to receive aid entirely in loans, with parentheses indicating that the classification of Turkey in that group was purely tentative and that upon further investigation it might have to be changed.

Second, those receiving no aid at all. Switzerland, Turkey, and Portugal, with that qualification.

Those which would receive all their support in the form of credits, loans: Sweden, Ireland, and one other country.

Those that would receive their aid in grants exclusively: Austria and Greece.

Those that would receive the support in grants and loans:

The CHAIRMAN. That is the rest of them.

Ambassador DOUGLAS. With this language, that it is impossible to determine now the percentage of grants to loans to countries in that category; that it was the intention, however, so to administer the act that the largest percentage of proportion of loans to grants consistent with the ability to repay would be made.

The CHAIRMAN. That is a very satisfactory answer, if I can get it and put it in the record before we vote.

DOMESTIC AVAILABILITY OF SUPPLIES INVOLVED

I think there is no place in this bill where we have made any reference, even by way of a gesture, to the fact that this bill has to be geared into some elemental consideration of a domestic availability of supplies involved. Is there anything in this bill that even mentions that subject?

Ambassador DOUGLAS. I think not.

The CHAIRMAN. I think that is a very grave omission. I don't care whether it means anything or not; well, I do care. But what I am saying is that there must be some directive in this bill to the Administrator to pay some attention to the relative short supply in our own country, I would think.

Senator GEORGE. Was there anything in the amendment Senator Lodge had?

Ambassador DOUGLAS. That was confined to petroleum. I don't know whether that would quite cover it. In the discussion yesterday you will recollect that someone raised the question as to whether or not the Administrator should have the power to allocate. During that discussion the point was made that there should be purely American agencies of Government that should have the authority to allocate that portion of American production for export, and the reason was advanced for that point of view that an American agency is concerned with the internal American economy.

Senator GEORGE. I thought it was agreed that definitely the Secretary of Agriculture would allocate foodstuffs, and that export licenses could be granted only by the Secretary of Commerce.

Ambassador DOUGLAS. That is right.

Senator GEORGE. So that that actually does give somebody power to consider that.

The CHAIRMAN. Sure, but we have not said anything about it, and we have in all our previous legislation. I do not think we have mentioned it anywhere in the bill.

Senator GEORGE. Except in the amendment Senator Lodge had.

The CHAIRMAN. Dr. Wilcox says he has another amendment, so perhaps we could leave this until in the morning.

Senator GEORGE. Maybe it was the other amendment that he had, that they must take into consideration the available supply.

The CHAIRMAN. I think that is very essential, and Dr. Wilcox advises me the Senator from Massachusetts has an amendment of that sort.

REASONABLE PROFIT BASIS SUGGESTED FOR U.S. CONCERNS

Senator WILEY. Mr. Chairman, I have something here that I want to get in the record because of the thing you are suggesting right now. You are going to have real competitive strife here between those who sell abroad because of the large profits involved. That goes to the question of procurement, and that is going to raise prices in America.

I have been given this suggestion that, instead of simply giving the cash to European countries, why can we not get all the firms who furnish materials, food, clothing, and what not—and that goes for tobacco also—to agree upon the idea that what they furnish will be furnished at cost, or at a reasonable profit? What is furnished by U.S. concerns, have them cooperate on a nonprofit or reasonable profit basis.

Now, as I say, this is a manufacturer who has written to me, and the thing we have to think about at home is this terrific impact. You take farm machinery. You have the example there, as mentioned in regard to South America selling wheat at $5 a bushel, and it is inherent in human nature to get all you can. But we are basing this program on two ideas; first, it is a humanitarian effort to help our brothers in need, and if that is so, we have to take extra care that the American taxpayer does not pay a terrific amount of money out to the American citizens who make a profit because of the needs of these Europeans.

I am just throwing this idea in because I have this in front of me. It was sent to me. He said I need not acknowledge it, but it just gives that aid idea, because he recognizes the terrific impact because of shortages.

Take steel. I personally have been trying to get a little farm machinery for months. Immediately the farm machinery goes to Europe, the European buyer comes over here and he is paying out dollars that he did not have to sweat for. They are our dollars. Prices go up. That keeps the farmer here from getting farm machinery.

The same thing is true in relation to shoes, in relation to clothing. So in our hearings I have probably been a little overemphatic on this question of procurement, but if we are truly trying to help our brothers over there we have to see to it that we do not simply skimp on the people over here by permitting people who sell over here to take us for a ride.

SENATOR LODGE'S AMENDMENT

The CHAIRMAN. We will have that subject up the first thing in the morning, when we receive Senator Lodge's amendment. The Senator is offering an amendment, as I understand it, dealing with the general necessity of consulting our own short supply in all aspects.

Senator HATCH. It is rather odd that we have in there a provision about taking into consideration the requirements for domestic use in commercial exports of the European countries when we are buying the stockpiling material.

Ambassador DOUGLAS. Critical material.

The CHAIRMAN. I do not think there is a word in the bill on this other subject, and we would be hopped on from alpha to omega if we didn't have a little something we could do on the subject.

I think, gentlemen, until tomorrow morning, that concludes the prayer meeting!

(Whereupon, at 3:50 p.m., a recess was taken until the following day, Friday, February 13, 1948, at 10 a.m.)

EUROPEAN RECOVERY PROGRAM

FRIDAY, FEBRUARY 13, 1948

UNITED STATES SENATE,
COMMITTEE ON FOREIGN RELATIONS,
Washington, D.C.

The committee met, pursuant to adjournment, in the committee hearing room, U.S. Capitol, at 10 a.m., Senator Arthur H. Vandenberg, chairman, presiding.

Present: Senators Vandenberg, Capper, Wiley, Smith, Lodge, George, Thomas of Utah, Barkley, and Hatch.

Present also: The Honorable Lewis W. Douglas, Ambassador to Great Britain; Mr. Paul Nitze, Deputy Director, Office of International Trade Policy, Department of State; Mr. Ernest Gross, Legal Adviser, Department of State; Mr. Stephen E. Rice, Legislative Counsel, U.S. Senate.

The CHAIRMAN. The committee will come to order.

AMENDMENT ADOPTED YESTERDAY

The first thing I wanted to ask: Yesterday, at my request and suggestion, we adopted an amendment inserting on page 30, subsection (1), the following language:

> Including the submission for the approval of the Administrator of specific projects undertaken by aid furnished under this Act and designed to carry out such purposes, including wherever possible projects for the increased production of coal, steel, transportation facilities, and food.

The language in which this was adopted seems to be subject to misinterpretation, as evidenced by at least one publication here in Washington this morning.

The State Department has reexamined the language and prefers the substitution of the following language, which is completely agreeable with me, inasmuch as my only purpose at this point is to set up a suggestive target. Their substitute language reads as follows:

> * * * and submitting for the approval of the Administrator or upon his request, whenever he deems it in furtherance of the purposes of this Act, specific projects proposed by such country, to be undertaken in substantial part with assistance furnished under this Act including, wherever practicable, projects for increased production of coal, steel, transportation facilities, and food.

In other words, what the new language does is to identify this more definitely and specifically as a purely permissive suggestion; and yet it saves the point I wanted to make, because I know there is large interest in saying something in this act which underscores the fact that our basic interest is in things, coal, steel, transportation facilities, and food, and a definite interest in the possibility of working out the act on a basis of projects, specific projects.

Senator LODGE. Is that added to subparagraph (1)?

The CHAIRMAN. Yes. And it was adopted yesterday.

Senator LODGE. Do I understand that yesterday you did away with all conditions precedent in this bill?

The CHAIRMAN. Will you let me just settle this first?

Senator LODGE. Yes.

The CHAIRMAN. Is there any objection?

Senator GEORGE. No objection, Mr. Chairman. I thought that is what we did.

The CHAIRMAN. That is what I thought.

Senator THOMAS of Utah. How was it interpreted by the publication?

The CHAIRMAN. That we had put this exclusively on a project-to-project basis. That is not what it said.

Senator BARKLEY. But you cannot ever tell, by what we say, how it is going to be interpreted by the press.

The CHAIRMAN. The new language is clear? Without objection, the new language will be substituted for the old.

All right, Senator Lodge.

WAS WHOLE CONCEPT OF CONDITIONS PRECEDENT ELIMINATED?

Senator LODGE. I wanted to ask you whether yesterday the whole concept of conditions precedent was eliminated?

The CHAIRMAN. No, indeed.

Senator LODGE. Because the language that was given to me as having been adopted, on page 29, subsection (b), eliminates the idea of the condition precedent.

The CHAIRMAN. Oh, no; it does not. I am sorry.

Where is the language?

Senator GEORGE. We tried to make it all inclusive. The language adopted reads as follows:

> The provision of assistance under this Act results from the multi-lateral pledges of the participating countries to use all their efforts to accomplish the joint recovery program based upon self-help and mutual cooperation as incorporated in the Report of the Committee on European Economic Cooperation, signed in Paris on September 22, 1947, and is contingent upon continuous effort of the participating countries to accomplish such a joint program through multilateral undertakings, and is contingent upon the establishment of a continuing organization for that purpose.

That does not eliminate conditions precedent.

Senator LODGE. But I meant insofar as these eight points on pages 31 and 32 are concerned. Where is the language? Will you show me?

The CHAIRMAN. "In addition to continued mutual cooperation of the participating countries,"—I am still reading from this first amendment—"each such country shall conclude an agreement with the United States in order for such country to be eligible to receive assistance under this act." It is a condition precedent, clearly. "Such agreements shall provide * * *" and so forth.

Senator LODGE. You think that is the same thing as a condition precedent?

The CHAIRMAN. Why, mostly emphatically. I do not think there is the slightest doubt about it.

Senator GEORGE. Yes, it seems to me that that covers it, Senator Lodge.

The CHAIRMAN. What is your next question, Senator?

Senator LODGE. Well, I have been in contact with Representative Herter.

AMENDMENT DRAFTED BY SENATOR LODGE

The CHAIRMAN. Excuse me. Before you go into those, I understand you have an amendment dealing with gearing this thing into domestic resources in some way.

Senator LODGE. Yes.

The CHAIRMAN. Well, I think it is very important that something of that sort should go in, and we left it open pending your return.

Senator LODGE. I have an amendment which I have drafted. I have some copies here which I shall distribute.

On page 4, Section 2(b), "Purposes of Act," on line 16, after the word "Act," insert the following new language: "and without doing violence to the vital needs of the people of the United States."

I think if we adopt that, we ought to put some language in the report in which we would say:

> The violence to the vital needs of America would result, for example, if the Administrator permitted exports under E.R.P. without reference to domestic prices. It is not enough to consider whether the export is being made out of surplus. Consideration must also be given to the effect on prices.

Or some language to that effect.

The CHAIRMAN. I do not think the language you proposed in the bill itself is enough or adequate, Senator.

Senator LODGE. I am willing to go much further.

The CHAIRMAN. And I think it is a little rhetorical.

Senator LODGE. Too vague, perhaps.

Senator BARKLEY. That raises a question as to what legal interpretation should be put on the words "doing violence." I know what you are driving at, but I doubt if that is the phraseology.

The CHAIRMAN. Do we not have some phraseology in a previous law on this subject which admonishes the Administrator that he has to consult the domestic situation?

Senator LODGE. The point I am trying to get at is: to give a warning signal to the Administrator that the vital needs of the people of the United States are an ever-present underlying factor, and if there is one thing the Kremlin would like more than anything else, it is the destruction of the United States by economic need.

The CHAIRMAN. All right. I do not think you have gone far enough.

Ambassador DOUGLAS. Page 24, a new section, which would read essentially as follows:

> In providing for the procurement in the United States of commodities under this Act, the Administrator shall take into account (a) the drain upon the resources of the United States, and (b) the impact of such procurement upon the domestic price level.

The CHAIRMAN. Is that what you want?

MEANING OF TERM "TAKE INTO ACCOUNT"

Senator LODGE. I think that is weaker than mine. It has that term "take into account," which to me does not seem to give them a very positive directive.

The CHAIRMAN. You want some "violence" in this, do you?

Senator LODGE. I want a thrust in some direction. I do not just want it "taken into account."

Senator GEORGE. Suppose you said, "shall give consideration" or "is required."

Senator LODGE. Well, I think that is weaker than mine.

The CHAIRMAN. I do not think so.

Senator GEORGE. You say "shall take into account"?

Ambassador DOUGLAS. "Shall take into account."

Senator LODGE. "Take into account" means that he reads the New York Times and sees what the prices are and says, "Now, if I send this, it will have this effect on price." And if he does that, he has done all the law requires, has he not?

The CHAIRMAN. The language in the interim aid measure is that the President shall consider (a) the drain upon natural resources and (b) the necessary affect upon domestic prices.

Senator LODGE. A lot of people think it is a good thing to have high prices, and that could be interpreted the other way, could it not?

There are some people who have been beginning to come over to the Marshall plan in the last few days, because they think it will have the effect of raising prices—some members of this party.

The CHAIRMAN. I confess that if I were the Administrator, I do not know what I would do when I had done "violence to the vital needs of the people of the United States."

U.S. PEOPLE SHOULD BE ASSURED OF VITAL NEEDS

Senator LODGE. Well, it is not lawyer's language, of course. But what is needed is something carrying out the thought "so that the American people can go on, assured of the food and heat and the shelter and the clothing and other things that they need." That is what is needed. It does not mean bowling alleys and nightclubs, but it means that their homes and places of work shall be heated, and that they will have enough to eat and adequate clothing, so that they can maintain their economic lives and not have prices so high that they cannot subsist.

The CHAIRMAN. Well, you do not mean that they shall be protected against every element of sacrifice.

Senator LODGE. I certainly do not; no. That is what I say. I do not want to protect them as to their bowling alleys and nightclubs. But I say they ought to have enough heat to maintain healthful living, enough fuel so that their factories can operate and so that the transportation systems can operate, and adequate clothing and food. That is what I say: the vital needs. That is why I used that term.

POWER TO ALLOCATE COMMODITIES FOR EXPORT

Ambassador DOUGLAS. Under the administration of the act, the Department of Agriculture, which is a purely American agency, allocates the amount of food which will be available for export as compared with the amount of food which shall be available for domestic consumption. The Department of Commerce allocates the amount of coal or indicates to the Committee of the Economic Commission for Europe the amount of coal that shall be available for export from the United States. The Department of Commerce and the Department of Interior together determine the amount of petroleum products from the United States which shall be available for export. The Department of Commerce determines, through its export control, the amount of steel which can be available for export.

The power to allocate all of those commodities for export, regardless of how they may be procured, rests in purely American agencies. And the Administrator, unless the President overrides one of the Departments in the determination of the amount allocable for export, cannot provide for the procurement of anything in excess of the amount which has been allocated for export by these purely American agencies.

I should think that language along these lines would give as much protection as is appropriate in the circumstances to the American internal economic situation.

GIVING DISCRETION TO ADMINISTRATOR

Senator LODGE. Of course, we are being held responsible for the whole situation, and I think the Congress has to hold some one man responsible in the executive branch. I think the thing has got to be put on to the Administrator, even though he will necessarily have to delegate parts of it to different officials of the Government.

Senator WILEY. Why not put some language in there that will make it a hermaphrodite for both of them?

The CHAIRMAN. I should think that could be done.

Senator BARKLEY. Why not change it from "doing violence" to "without unduly affecting the vital needs"? You cannot put a straightjacket on him. He has to have discretion. Your language, as well as the Ambassador's, does give him the discretion. It points up a responsibility upon him, though, to keep in mind the domestic economy. But you just cannot spell out what he can do. All you can do is to warn him that he has to consider it. The language you used is a discretionary language.

Senator SMITH. Suppose you say "without impairing the economic stability of the United States."

Senator LODGE. I like that better than Senator Barkley's language.

The CHAIRMAN. What is the suggestion?

Senator SMITH. "And without impairing the economic stability of the United States"; in view of Cabot's words there.

Senator LODGE. Or take out that term "without doing violence," and say "without impairing the economic needs."

Senator BARKLEY. There is bound to be some impairment.

Senator LODGE. "Without vitally impairing"?

Senator SMITH. "Without vitally impairing the economic stability of the United States."

Senator LODGE. You are quite right. There has to be some impairment, but nobody wants to have this country ruined by the Marshall plan.

Senator THOMAS of Utah. How would it be to put an "oration" in the purposes of the act.

85–743—73——16

Senator WILEY. A philippic.

The CHAIRMAN. It will have to be more than that.

Senator THOMAS of Utah. I do not think it will be an oration, really; I think it will be just as strong as the rest that is there.

Senator SMITH. Why not put it up in the statement of policy. How about putting it on page 4, right after line 4: "Provided, that no assistance of the participating countries herein contemplated shall vitally impair the economic stability of the United States," just as a proviso there.

Senator THOMAS of Utah. I had in mind something more wordy than that, because I got my idea from here, and from there, and from there.

The CHAIRMAN. What is it you are suggesting, Senator Smith?

Senator SMITH. I had originally made the suggestion of substituting in Cabot Lodge's proposal here for the words "without doing violence," simply "without vitally impairing the economic stability of the United States"; and I suggested winding up that sentence with that.

Senator BARKLEY. Would the word "unduly" be better than "vitally"?

The CHAIRMAN. I want to do both; I want to put it in the purposes, and then I want this section also.

Senator LODGE. I think it is a good idea to put it in the section also.

The CHAIRMAN. So let us see if we can first cover it and then we will come back to you, Senator.

Is there any objection to the suggestion made by Senator Smith as to changing the language proposed by the Senator from Massachusetts, the suggestion being that this language would then read—Will you read it, Senator?

Senator SMITH. And without "vitally" or "unduly" or "seriously" "impairing the economic stability of the United States"; one of the three.

Senator GEORGE. Where do you propose to put that?

Senator SMITH. After the word "Act", on line 16, page 4.

Senator HATCH. "Seriously" or "vitally"? Just how would you have it read?

Senator GEORGE. In those last two lines, you are dealing with the independence of these European nations or of extraordinary outside economic assistance within the period of operations under this act. You do not want to limit that.

INSERTING PROVISO AFTER STATEMENT OF POLICY

Senator SMITH. I think it belongs better, Mr. Chairman, up on line 4, in our statement of policy. I think there should be a proviso after "program based upon self-help and mutual cooperation".

> Provided that no assistance of the participating countries herein contemplated shall vitally impair the economic stability of the United States.

I think that is where it belongs—in your statement of policy.

The CHAIRMAN. That is where I would like to have it, in the first instance.

Senator SMITH. I would like to have it there, but I have no objection to putting another check in here.

The CHAIRMAN. What has the committee to say about that?

Senator GEORGE. You put it over here in your purposes, but that is all right over there, because you have to deal with it later on.

Senator WILEY. I like the Ambassador's suggestion.

The CHAIRMAN. I would like to do that, also.

Senator WILEY. But I would like to combine the two of them. I would like to say:

In providing for the procurement in the United State of commodities under this Act, the Administrator shall take into account (a) the drain upon the resources of the United States, (b) the impact of such procurement upon the domestic price level, (c) the vital needs of the American people.

The CHAIRMAN. That is all right, when we get around to it. I want it also in the front, in the statement of purposes. I think we should have a reference to it there.

Senator SMITH. Mr. Chairman, I suggest that on page 4, line 4, after the word "cooperation," there should be inserted the following proviso:

Provided, That no assistance to the participating countries herein contemplated shall seriously impair the economic stability of the United States.

The CHAIRMAN. I think that is a good statement.

Senator BARKLEY. Do you prefer the word "seriously" to "unduly"?

Senator SMITH. I am taking the suggestion from the Ambassador here, who felt that might be a better word.

The CHAIRMAN. Without objection.

Senator WILEY. What are you doing now?

The CHAIRMAN. That is a good idea. We will find out.

Senator SMITH. Page 4, line 4, after the words "self-help and mutual cooperation":

Provided, That no assistance to the participating countries herein contemplated shall seriously impair the economic stability of the United States.

The CHAIRMAN. All right.

Now, so much for that. If there is no objection, that will be put in there.

AMENDMENT PROPOSED BY AMBASSADOR DOUGLAS

Now we will go back, over into the body of the bill, to the amendment proposed by the Ambassador.

Senator GEORGE. That is a new section on 24?

The CHAIRMAN. That is a new section on 24.

Can you add, Mr. Ambassador, one final fling along the lines suggested by the Senator from Wisconsin at that point? I do not think you can overdo this part.

Senator LODGE. I do not either.

Senator SMITH. This is one of the best selling points we have as to our colleagues.

The CHAIRMAN. A bill without it——

Senator LODGE. You cannot do it without it.

Senator WILEY. Make sure you do not sell them a pig in a poke, too

The CHAIRMAN. You will do well if you can make sure of that.

Senator SMITH. That would be a subsection (c) (3).

The CHAIRMAN. What do you have to say, Mr. Ambassador?

Ambassador DOUGLAS. I think that is all right, sir.

The CHAIRMAN. Read it the way you are now suggesting.

Ambassador DOUGLAS [reading]:

In providing for the procurement in the United States of commodities under this Act, the Administrator shall take into account (a) the drain upon the resources of the United States, (b) the impact of such procurement upon the domestic price level, and (c) the vital needs of the American people.

AUTHORITY REGARDING PRICE LEVELS

Senator LODGE. I just would like to ask whether that could not be interpreted as authorizing the Administrator to move prices up or down.

Senator WILEY. He is not fixing prices.

Senator LODGE. I know he is not fixing prices. I am talking about some fellow up there who is looking for something to say. The words "take fully into account the price level" are such that you do not say whether he is for or against a certain type of price level. He does not take sides in the thing.

Ambassador DOUGLAS. Well, I wonder whether over a four and a quarter year period you can bind anybody to the sort of price level that he or anybody may want. It is apt to fluctuate a good deal during that period.

Senator LODGE. Are you not opposed to a bad price level?

Ambassador DOUGLAS. I am always opposed to sin.

Senator LODGE. That is just it. The trouble with this amendment is that you are not opposed to sin.

Senator WILEY. You mean economic, or moral sin?

Senator LODGE. Both. I think that is a weakness. You ought to be opposed to a destructive price level or an unsound price level.

The CHAIRMAN. The language in the interim Aid Act is: "The effect of the necessary procurement on domestic prices."

That is still open to your fear, I suppose.

Senator LODGE. That is a much smaller proposition. The fellow doing all this buying is going to have a tremendous influence on economics in this country, and we are having a lot of blood on the floor now because some people do not like the way the Secretary of Agriculture has been buying grain. Of course, a lot of people do like it.

The CHAIRMAN. You certainly do not want to say that he shall undertake to keep prices down.

Senator LODGE. No; I certainly do not think you ought to say that: although, at this particular moment in history I do not think it would do any harm.

Senator WILEY. You have the general phrase "vital needs."

Senator LODGE. It always depends upon where you live. I realize that. If you are growing beef, you feel differently than if you are eating beef.

I say he ought to be in favor of a price level that keeps all elements of the community in balance, or something like that. When you say "take fully into account the price level," it makes it look as if he is some sort of an arbiter of prices.

Senator BARKLEY. Suppose you eliminate "price level" and substitute "economic conditions," or something like that. How about "effect upon economic conditions"?

The CHAIRMAN. How would it read if you left out your second one entirely?

Ambassador DOUGLAS. That will take into account (a) the drain upon the resources of the United States and (c) the vital needs of the American people.

BALANCING ELEMENTS OF ECONOMY

Senator LODGE. What you are trying to do is to keep all elements of the economy in balance. That is what you are trying to do.

Ambassador DOUGLAS. But is it appropriate to use an economic recovery program for such a purpose?

Senator LODGE. Of course, it is not. That is what I mean. Your language makes it look as if you are. It makes you look as if you are going to be the swing man in the price level.

Senator GEORGE. What is the last sentence you have there?

Ambassador DOUGLAS. "Shall take into account (a) the drain upon the resources of the United States and (c) the vital needs of the American people."

Senator GEORGE. That is all you have?

Ambassador DOUGLAS. Leaving out reference to the domestic price level.

Senator GEORGE. And what is that language that you left out?

Ambassador DOUGLAS. "The impact of such procurement upon the domestic price level."

Senator WILEY. I think that is important.

The CHAIRMAN. Suppose you say "the impact upon the domestic economy" instead of the price level.

Senator WILEY. That is all right.

The CHAIRMAN. Then you would be satisfied?

Senator LODGE. I think that is much better.

The CHAIRMAN. That is near enough to consent to suit me.

You do not mind that, Mr. Ambassador?

Ambassador DOUGLAS. There are so many things that have impact upon the domestic economy.

The CHAIRMAN. With this, I can tell 19 different Senators on the floor, who are worried about something, "Why, there it is, right there."

Senator LODGE. A mother hubbard, that covers everything and touches nothing.

The CHAIRMAN. That is all this is: An elastic clause which indicates great anxiety about the domestic impact.

Senator WILEY. A white wash; bushwa, we call it out in Wisconsin

The CHAIRMAN. I thought you were in favor of this.

Senator GEORGE. I do not think that hurts anything.

Senator THOMAS of Utah. That means, then, Mr. Chairman, that we will do nothing with page 4?

The CHAIRMAN. We have already adopted the language, as I understand it, of Senator Smith.

Senator THOMAS of Utah. That is up in the preamble?

The CHAIRMAN. Yes.

Senator THOMAS of Utah. Then we do nothing with (b)?

Senator LODGE. 2(b)? No. I withdraw my amendment.

The CHAIRMAN. That is withdrawn; and without objection, the language as finally read by our distinguished visitor will be approved.

Now, Senator Lodge, what is your next "itch"?

Senator LODGE. I wanted to ask you about the sentence on page 3 which begins on line 16 and runs down to line 24. That sentence, as I think I have told you, is a concoction and a composition of phrases which the 16 nations themselves used at Paris.

USE OF "CONSOLIDATION" IN PLACE OF "COOPERATION" SUGGESTED

But I wrote those words before Bevin made his speech, and I wondered whether on line 23, instead of the words "economic cooperation in Europe" you would like to put in the words "consolidation of Europe." Because those are the words that he used in his speech all the time.

Senator BARKLEY. That would carry with it political consolidation.

Senator LODGE. But it is out of his mouth.

Senator BARKLEY. I do not care whose mouth it is out of. I do not think we can impose upon them political union. I would like to see it come about, of course.

Senator LODGE. This just says:

It is the hope of the people of the United States that there countries through a joint organization will exert sustained common efforts which will speedily achieve that economic cooperation in Europe which is essential for lasting peace and prosperity.

It is just a hope.

I think that is a pretty good phrase. It is in Bevin's words, and I just thought there might be a little psychology in putting it in there.

Ambassador DOUGLAS. Those are Bevin's words, but not the words of the 16 participating countries. The 16 countries used the word "cooperation," and however much all of us might like to see Western Europe consolidated, to employ in this legislation that it is in a sense related to the provision of our (a), to employ the legislating, I think might be a very dangerous thing to do.

The CHAIRMAN. I think it might ruin you in Scandinavia.

Senator LODGE. Let us drop it, then.

The CHAIRMAN. All right. Next?

STATEMENT OF PURPOSE

Senator LODGE. This is something I think Ambassador Douglas would agree to. It is in the title:

To promote the general welfare, national interest, and foreign policy of the United States through necessary economic and financial assistance to foreign countries which undertake to cooperate with each other and with the United States * * *

The CHAIRMAN. What have you to say to that, Mr. Ambassador?

Ambassador DOUGLAS. "Cooperate with each other"?

Senator LODGE. "And with the United States." After all, that is what you are doing.

The CHAIRMAN. I am a little doubtful about that, Cabot. That seems to involve the interpretation that our purpose here is to tie ourselves into a bloc.

Senator LODGE. All right. I just bring it up as a suggestion.

Senator BARKLEY. I think the words "each other" are to be "one another."

"Each other" generally applies to two countries, while "one another" applies to a larger number.

The CHAIRMAN. All right. What is next?

Senator LODGE. How about Senator Barkley's suggestion?

The CHAIRMAN. Senator, did you wish to pursue the subject?

Senator BARKLEY. I think it is better to use "one another" when you are dealing with a large number of entities.

The CHAIRMAN. "Love one another." I remember that from Sunday school.

Senator WILEY. You have forgotten all the rest, though.

The CHAIRMAN. Oh, you are mistaken.

How is that, Mr. Ambassador?

Ambassador DOUGLAS. That is all right, yes.

Senator BARKLEY. Of course, there are both indications here. They have to cooperate with each other and with one another.

Senator GEORGE. They have to cooperate. And they will cooperate.

The CHAIRMAN. I do not think we need spend too much time on this, do we?

All right, Senator Lodge.

SUGGESTIONS FROM THE HERTER COMMITTEE

Senator LODGE. Then there is one matter that I talked to you about that I wanted to take up later, and then I have this business of Representative Herter.

The CHAIRMAN. All right. Senator Lodge has talked to Congressman Herter about this matter. Without any suggestion that Congressman Herter's comments are in any degree binding upon us, I think it is very important in so far as possible, if there are any suggestions from Congressman Herter which fit into our scheme of things, that they should be recognized, because he is, in my opinion, the important figure in this legislation in the House. And I think the committee would be glad to know what Congressman Herter would suggest.

Senator LODGE. There are nine suggestions here, and I may say that he got in touch with me last Saturday. I talked with Dr. Wilcox, who felt as I did that the chairman and the members of this committee would be willing for him to see a copy of this committee print in confidence. So I furnished it to him.

Senator SMITH. The suggestions are on this committee print, then?

Senator BARKLEY. Where are they? Are they in italics, or something, so that they can be identified?

Senator LODGE. I am going to read them to you. What I am going to read relates to this committee print.

The first is on page 4. He suggests adding a fourth objective, on the encouragement of private initiative.

The CHAIRMAN. Where are you? In the "Purposes of the Act"?

Senator LODGE. In the Purposes of the Act.

The CHAIRMAN. Has he any suggestion?

Senator LODGE. He has a suggestion on page 3 of his own bill, which I shall read:

> Encouragement of private initiative to assume, as conditions permit, the emergency activities which have devolved upon governments as a result of the economic devastation caused by the war.

That is out of his own bill.

The CHAIRMAN. What possible objection can there be to that?

MEANING OF "EMERGENCY CONDITIONS"

Senator HATCH. Well, I just wonder what he means by "emergency conditions." Does he mean the socialization, the nationalization?

Senator LODGE. I suppose he means the physical reconstruction of things that were damaged by military action and the steps that you have to take when you have tremendous shortages due to the war, and which are no longer necessary once normal plenty returns.

Senator GEORGE. Cabot, will you read it again? I did not get it.

Senator LODGE. Yes.

> Encouragement of private initiative to assume, as conditions permit, the emergency activities which have devolved on governments as the result of the economic devastation caused by the war.

Senator GEORGE. That just means, in plain language that we will encourage them to set up private enterprise systems, wherever they can?

Senator LODGE. When possible; when, as, and if possible.

The CHAIRMAN. That is all it means.

Senator BARKLEY. I think the idea is all right. I think he has more language there than he needs.

Senator GEORGE. I do not have any objection to it, Mr. Chairman, but there are three things and only three things, and the more we dilute them the worse we get.

The first thing we have here is to get some production out of these countries. I think possibly we have the cart before the horse there, but it does not make any difference how they come. The first is production, the next is putting their own house in order, and stabilizing their currencies, and the third is to break down those hampering restrictions that just simply keep them from being anything over there or doing anything, or accomplishing anything.

Senator LODGE. This is a step in that direction.

Senator GEORGE. Yes, I do not see any objection to it if you think it would accomplish anything by putting it in. But those are the three main points, and if we cannot approach this thing we have just about lost.

Senator SMITH. This is a plug for private enterprise.

Senator GEORGE. Yes, this looks towards private enterprise when it becomes possible.

Senator LODGE. When, as, and if it becomes possible. It is not forcing anything on anybody, as I see it.

Senator THOMAS of Utah. And the words "as conditions permit" are used?

Senator LODGE. Yes. I will read that again. I think that point is clear:

> Encouragement of private initiative to assume, as conditions permit, the emergency activities which have devalued on governments as the result of economic devastation caused by the war.

Senator GEORGE. I certainly have no objection to it, except that I do point out the danger of diluting these three essential things. It seems to me we get them weaker by adding to them.

The CHAIRMAN. I completely agree with that, Senator George. If there is not some better place to put it.

Senator LODGE. We could make it a part of these three paragraphs and not make it a separate paragraph.

The CHAIRMAN. No, I would not want to do that. These three statements are as Senator George said. This is it, right here.

Let us assume that we all agree that something of that sort should be written somewhere in this bill, and we will ask Mr. Rice and company, and Mr. Wilcox, et al., to see what they can do about it.

Ambassador DOUGLAS. I agree with the objective completely.

Senator GEORGE. Yes, I do, too.

Ambassador DOUGLAS. But I wonder whether it is a wise thing to write it into the bill.

Senator HATCH. I wanted to ask you, Mr. Ambassador, are these provisions going to be scrutinized by these participating countries?

DOUBT ABOUT THE LANGUAGE

Ambassador DOUGLAS. They are going to be scrutinized with a microscope. And those in the western participating countries that are opposed to it will use every bit of language in the legislation as an instrument to stir up opposition within the participating countries and and outside of the participating countries. And that is really the fundamental doubt that I have. It is not an opposition, but it is a doubt, a question in my mind, as to the wisdom of writing this language into the legislation itself.

The CHAIRMAN. Well, I think that is an additional valid objection to writing it into the great major purposes. But let us see if the staff can suggest something that can be put in elsewhere.

Senator THOMAS of Utah. May I suggest that the staff think about putting it in the policy?

The CHAIRMAN. All right, they will look it over.

Next?

AUTHORITY FOR CONTRACT SERVICES

Senator LODGE. On page 14, there is just a question that he asks, and I think we have answered it. It is regarding section 10. Herter says:

> Should there not be specific authority for contract services?

I think we have put that in.

The CHAIRMAN. That is in.

Senator LODGE. That is what I thought.

DEFRAYMENT OF LIABILITIES

The next is on page 22, lines 21 and 22, the language:

> And any liabilities accruing under such guaranties shall be defrayed out of funds so appropriated.

Herter says the language is not clear. Does this mean the liabilities can be deferred beyond the original 5-percent limitation?

The CHAIRMAN. Mr. Ambassador?

Ambassador DOUGLAS. That was certainly not the intention. Let me see whether there is the possibility of construing this language in such a way that it is ambiguous.

Senator GEORGE. You can say "accruing under such guaranties shall be defrayed out of funds so appropriated, subject to the limitations of this provision." That limits you to 5 percent.

The CHAIRMAN. Without objection, that language will be added at that point.

All right, Senator Lodge.

QUESTION OF OFFSHORE PURCHASES

Senator LODGE. On page 23, he refers to subsection (c), beginning at line 5: "The Administrator may provide assistance for any participating country, in the form and under the procedures authorized in subsections (a) and (b), respectively, of this section," and so forth.

Herter says,

> Will the Administrator give country *x* dollars with which country X will buy commodities offshore, or will the Administrator take the dollars and buy the commodity and transfer it to country X?

Herter believes it is bad practice to give countries dollars with which to go and compete in foreign markets.

The CHAIRMAN. What is your comment, Mr. Ambassador?

Ambassador DOUGLAS. With respect to offshore purchases, no country could buy unless the purposes of the purchase have been approved by the Administrator and the appropriate method of payment has been established, whether through one of the letters of credit to which reference is made, or letter of commitment, or otherwise.

The CHAIRMAN. You mean country X would not get the dollars until the transaction was completely identified and approved?

Ambassador DOUGLAS. That is right.

The CHAIRMAN. Does that answer Herter?

Senator LODGE. It seems to me it is probably preferable for a country to use its existing purchasing procedure rather than for the United States to set up an organization to buy offshore.

The British, for instance, in the Argentine would go ahead and place the order and set up the specifications and see that everything was the way they wanted it, to meet their needs; and then, after all that had been done, and only then, they would get the dollars. It seems to me that takes care of that.

But this is going to be an interesting thing to the House, and I wonder if we could make it clear that that is the way it would work. Because that is a great talking point.

The CHAIRMAN. I think the way this thing works is the key to a sympathetic understanding of the bill; and that is what I have personally requested the Ambassador, to see if he can put down on two or three sheets of paper, a résumé of the prices, in language that the man on the street can understand.

Senator LODGE. When he does it, I hope he will have this point in mind, because this is a point that is very interesting.

The CHAIRMAN. All right.

FIXED CRITERION FOR A LOAN OR DRAFT

Senator LODGE. Then, at the bottom of the page, beginning at line 20: "and the determination whether or not a participating country should be required to make payment for any assistance furnished to such country in furtherance of the purposes of this act," and so forth.

Herter makes this comment: "There should be some fixed criterion for the determination of a loan or draft."

That is one of his big points:

> Otherwise, the Administrator will be on the spot. Country X complains that a grant was given country Y, but that country X is being forced to accept a loan.

And he points to page 12 on his own bill:

> The arrangements between the authority and any foreign country for furnishing commodities, articles, machinery, and equipment to such country shall provide for payment of full consideration therfor. The character of the consideration shall be that which the authority deems to be the best obtainable in the light of the economic situation of the foreign country concerned, the relationship of the goods being furnished to the overall plan of reconstruction and rehabilitation, and the objectives set forth in section 10 of this Act.

Section 10 covers the broad objectives.

The CHAIRMAN. Does he think that is going to take the administrator out of an argument between country A and country B?

Senator LODGE. I think this is "loose as a goose" too. But he keeps coming back to me on how important it is to have a definite stand on loans and grants.

The CHAIRMAN. You will recall the testimony before the committee. There was a long discussion of a quest for criteria to determine the difference between loans, grants, and so forth. And we were told after all of the suggestions had been sifted out—and I think this was approved by the Harriman Commission—they finally came to the conclusion that capacity to pay was the only real rule on which you could ultimately rely.

Senator LODGE. In spite of the invidious distinctions, as it were?

The CHAIRMAN. Yes.

Is that not true, Mr. Ambassador?

Ambassador DOUGLAS. I do not know of any other criteria that could be applied.

The CHAIRMAN. I would not think Congressman Herter's criteria are any more specific than the ones we have.

EMPHASIS ON LOANS RATHER THAN GRANTS

Senator GEORGE. I think he has one good idea. It has always been my idea that we ought to put some emphasis on loans, here, rather than on grants. I do not believe in giving away all this money. I believe we can make loans, to be repaid in kind, or covered by some arrangements.

I do think the character of the aid they are getting is a material factor in determining whether it is a grant or a loan. If it is a capital asset, it has a bearing on it, and it ought to have a bearing on it. It would have, anywhere in the world, except in dealing with us.

The CHAIRMAN. Of course, that is Senator Hickenlooper's persistent point.

Senator LODGE. Herter makes that point, too.

Senator GEORGE. Herter has that in there in that statement. His statement may be pretty involved, but he has the two main things in there. He has the character of the assistance. The nature and character of the assistance ought to go far in determining whether it is a mere grant or a loan. It is not the sole point; it is just one.

Finally, the ability to repay at all for any sort of an asset is, maybe, the controlling consideration; and the Administrator would so consider it, perhaps. He would have to, maybe, fall back on that.

The CHAIRMAN. What would you say, Mr. Ambassador, in line 24, on page 23, to making it read as follows:

And the terms of such payment, if required, shall depend upon the character of the assistance and upon the capacity of such country * * *

I think that would be very helpful.

Ambassador DOUGLAS. That, I should say, was the intention, which I think the Department of State had as to what the Administrator, whoever he might be, would follow. That is to say, with very, very, very few exceptions, capital equipment would be provided as a result of the extension of credit. Foodstuffs, fertilizers, and commodities of that order might be furnished in the form of grants.

Raw materials might be furnished in the form of grants. But there would be no restriction upon the authority of the Administrator to demand a loan or to enable countries to purchase even commodities of that order, foodstuffs, fuel, and raw materials, as the result of the extension of credit, whether ability to pay justified the extension of the loan.

The CHAIRMAN. I understand that your answer is "Yes"?

Ambassador DOUGLAS. I think it is all right, yes.

The CHAIRMAN. Does that not help your point, Senator?

SOME GRANTS NEEDED

Senator GEORGE. Yes, I think it does. I think the answer is yes. And yet, there may have to be grants to assist some country, even in acquiring a capital asset.

The CHAIRMAN. Yes.

Ambassador DOUGLAS. Yes. Take for example the case of Austria.

Senator GEORGE. That is not the controlling or the only thing considered by any means.

The CHAIRMAN. Obviously, the character of the assistance has something to do with the character of the transaction.

Senator GEORGE. Yes, obviously it has. We ought to say so.

And I do not have any doubt that the Administrator would, if he is a good Administrator, take that into consideration.

The CHAIRMAN. Is there any objection?

Ambassador DOUGLAS. Would you read the language?

The CHAIRMAN. Line 24: "shall depend upon the character of the assistance and upon the capacity of such country", and so forth.

Ambassador DOUGLAS. Is it the character of the assistance, or the purpose of the assistance?

Senator GEORGE. Nature and purpose.

The CHAIRMAN. Do you want to say "nature and purpose"?

Ambassador DOUGLAS. I should think so; nature and purpose, or character and purpose.

The CHAIRMAN. The character and purpose of the assistance?

Senator LODGE. How about this phrase of Herter's: "the relationship to the overall plan of reconstruction and rehabilitation"?

The CHAIRMAN. I think that is involved in the character of the assistance.

Senator GEORGE. That is the same idea that he has, and he uses different language.

The CHAIRMAN. This simplifies it.

Ambassador DOUGLAS. I have always felt that where capital equipment was involved, the burden of proof should lie heavily upon he who extended it or made it possible to purchase it as a result of a grant.

The CHAIRMAN. Without objection, this language will be added at this point.

What is the next one, Senator?

Senator LODGE. The next one is on page 27, subsection (c), line 22.

The CHAIRMAN. We have not taken that up yet, Senator, that subsection (c). We are leaving that until this afternoon at 2 p.m.

WHO HAS TITLES TO SPECIAL ACCOUNTS

Senator LODGE. I have two points on that.

The next one goes on to page 32. He has three thoughts on this language on page 32. At line 2, as to the words "such special account," Herter asks the question:

"Who has title to these; the United States, or the foreign country?"

Senator BARKLEY. What line is that?

Senator LODGE. Line 2, the words "such special account." Herter asks who has title, the United States, or the foreign country.

Ambassador DOUGLAS. The foreign country.

Senator LODGE. Then he goes to line 9, the words "as may be agreed to," and he says:

> The agreements concluded with Italy and France under the Interim Aid Act have restricted the use of local currencies to (1) local costs, (2) retirement of debt, and (3) the retirement of currency. This is too narrow. Better use can be made of local currencies. Is it the State Department idea that the Administrator will continue the same pattern? Why not have provisions like those in the Herter bill, pages 14, 15, and 16?

That is section 2 of the Herter bill, entitled "Use of Foreign Currencies Received."

And just glancing at it, I see four users. Shall I read them?

The CHAIRMAN. Yes.

Senator LODGE [reading]:

> (1) To purchase and sell securities and otherwise to invest in enterprises and projects which will contribute to such recovery or develop new sources of wealth; (2) to purchase in such country, at the request of the Secretary of National Defense, strategic and critical materials for stockpiling in the United States, and to develop natural resources for future stockpiling; (3) to promote enterprises of mutual interest to the United States and such foreign country; (4) to aid in furnishing technical assistance to such foreign country to further its reconstruction efforts.

In other words, he advocates a much broader, more active use of these currencies.

Senator SMITH. He contemplates those funds will belong to the United States instead of these foreign countries. It is a different theory.

Senator LODGE. I do not know that he quite goes that far.

The CHAIRMAN. I do not know that that makes any difference, Senator Smith. Because under our language their use is a matter of our authority as well as theirs.

Senator LODGE. You have the Herter bill in front of you?

The CHAIRMAN. Yes.

Senator LODGE. That is page 14, section 24.

The CHAIRMAN. But I am referring to our own bill, which already says that the use can only be for such purposes as may be agreed to between such country and the Government.

Therefore, Herter is spelling out the use. I do not think that has any particular bearing on who owns the money.

Senator LODGE. Well, he is under the impression that under our bill, the uses are going to be restricted to the three limited purposes listed in the Interim Aid Act.

The CHAIRMAN. Well, unfortunately, they are not.

Senator LODGE. Unfortunately?

The CHAIRMAN. Yes, sir. And have not been.

Senator LODGE. You should like to see them limited?

The CHAIRMAN. Well, I think they might use these local currencies for some purposes that would not interest me.

Senator LODGE. Yes, sir.

The CHAIRMAN. Yes.

SIX PURPOSES FOR THE SPECIAL ACCOUNT

Ambassador DOUGLAS. There are six purposes to which it is intended this special account of local currency counterparts can be put by agreement.

Senator GEORGE. Where are those six purposes enumerated?

Ambassador DOUGLAS. They are not enumerated in this legislation.

Senator LODGE. On page 49 of this book.

Ambassador DOUGLAS. That is right.

(a) use, in whole or in part, to assist in measures of financial reform and currency stabilization;

(b) use for retirement of national debt so as to promote the most rapid achievement of internal financial stability;

(c) use for local currency costs incident to the exploration for and development of additional production of raw materials in probable long term short supply in the United States.

Senator LODGE. Is that in here?

Ambassador DOUGLAS. Yes.

Senator LODGE. Oh, yes.

Ambassador DOUGLAS. Another purpose is to supplement the dollar loans of the International Bank through the use of local currency counterpart by making some of the local currency available to the International bank, and then any other uses to which, by mutual agreement, they may be put.

Senator THOMAS of Utah. How will that become operative under this law? Will the Administrator be guided by what was adopted there?

Ambassador DOUGLAS. He will be guided by this language, and will arrive at an understanding and agreement with each one of the individual countries as to the use of these local currency counterparts.

Senator LODGE. This language is just a forecast that you have read. There is nothing binding about it.

The CHAIRMAN. It would not make any difference if it was, because the sixth clause is a basket clause which covers anything on earth, so that the other five could mean nothing.

Senator LODGE. Our bill is just unlimited, then?

The CHAIRMAN. I disagree with it. I think I should make this statement. Local currencies have been used in at least one instance under the interim aid bill, to help balance budgets, and I do not think it has any legitimate use for that purpose.

Ambassador DOUGLAS. May I correct what I told you yesterday?

[Discussion was off the record.]

USE OF COUNTERPART FUNDS

Ambassador DOUGLAS. My very strong feeling is that the local currency counterpart should not be converted into current receipts of Government, so that they can spent them for any purpose they may see fit. It is a highly inflationary thing.

Senator WILEY. May I ask a question, what is the difference, when it comes? Don't they just have printing press currency over there anyway?

Ambassador DOUGLAS. There is this great distinction, Senator. Obviously, these countries—first of all, they commit themselves to bring their financial houses into order, and that is one of the most important things that they can do. Unless they do, much of the aid we provide will be dissipated and lost.

Senator WILEY. Correct.

Ambassador DOUGLAS. They commit themselves, however, to do it.

Now, if in the process of doing it they have to operate on a budgetary deficit for a while, and some of them will, Senator, because they will not be promptly able to bring their budgets into balance—France has made long steps forward toward that end——

The CHAIRMAN. Very courageous steps.

Ambassador DOUGLAS (continuing). And very courageous, but it will take her 12 to 18 months to achieve an equilibrium between her expeditures and her income.

Now then, if the local currency counterpart can be covered in as a current income to the extent to which it brings the French budget into balance, the French Government will not have to borrow. The operation, therefore, is concealed because it is not a public transaction. If, however, the local currency counterpart is not covered in as current income and expended for any purpose, and the French Government, during the period in which it is unable to bring its budget into balance has to borrow, then the transaction is public and open, and on it the light of publicity is focused, and there is a great distinction between a concealed operation, on the one hand, and the public operation on the other.

The CHAIRMAN. I think there is another great distinction, Mr. Ambassador.

Ambassador DOUGLAS. There are a great many distinctions. If the local currency counterpart is covered into current income, then when the time comes that the local currency counterpart is no longer available, the budget of these countries will be as out of balance as it was at the beginning.

The CHAIRMAN. Therefore, if I may interject, if local currencies are permitted to be used for ordinary budget balancing purposes, we have provided these countries with the means to defeat the very objectives to which we are trying to hold them accountable.

Ambassador DOUGLAS. Precisely, Senator. That is precisely correct.

There was one situation, Greece, in which it was to the advantage of the country, as I understand it, that the local currency counterpart be covered into current income. A public transaction would have further aggravated the apprehension in Greece about the validity of the drachma. But I know of no other country in Europe in which that condition prevails.

The CHAIRMAN. How does this issue come to us at the moment? Let's get along with this so far as this bill is concerned.

Senator SMITH. I might say, in backing up Senator Lodge in bringing this up, a number of the Members of the House have talked to me, and they think it is terribly important to spell this out. We are going to have much difficulty in spelling this out if there is not some such use of these funds.

The CHAIRMAN. Suppose we let them spell it out. Then we have something we can yield to in conference.

Senator LODGE. He emphasizes two points which I have mentioned. One is the question of who has the title to these currencies, the United States or the foreign country; and secondly, these three words in line 9 "as may be agreed to" which he would like to have those agreements written so as to cover these points on pages 14 and 15.

Senator SMITH. Of his bill.

Senator LODGE. Yes.

(1) To purchase and sell securities and otherwise to invest in enterprises and projects which contribute to recovery and develop new sources of wealth.

(2) to purchase in such country at the request of the Secretary of National Defense, strategic and critical materials for stockpiling in the United States, and to develop natural resources for future stockpiling;

(3) to promote enterprises of mutual interest to the United States and such foreign countries; and

(4) to aid in furnishing technical assistance to such foreign country to further its reconstruction efforts.

I gather these are the points that are embraced in this here.

Ambassador DOUGLAS. They are not all in there.

Senator LODGE. But that ours is loose and open, and as I understand our bill, they can do almost anything with it as it now stands, and he wants to spell it out.

Senator HATCH. Under the first clause of his bill, can't they do almost anything?

The CHAIRMAN. Suppose we tell Mr. Herter that in this instance it is impossible for us to canvass his details, and to know whether they are adequate, and that we will leave this to him for his bargaining position when we finally converge.

Ambassador DOUGLAS. Senator, there is one point I would like to make, if I may. Doubtless the committee already has it in mind.

POTENTIAL MAGNITUDE OF COUNTERPART FUNDS

The accumulation of the local currency counterpart may, in some countries, be very great. In one country, Italy, for example, the calculation was made of the accumulation of the local currency counterpart just for the sake of the argument on the basis of all grants to Italy.

Italy will not receive all grants. But if all grants are made to Italy, then the local currency counterpart in Italy will be just slightly, within 15 months, under the total circulating medium, and it will be four times the nongovernmental deposits.

That gives you an idea of the magnitude of this problem and of the terrific financial power that anybody who operates this local currency special account has. In effect, if we use it for any purpose, it constitutes another Central Bank. We can inflate, deflate, do almost anything that we choose to the internal economy of one of these countries. And whether we exercise the power or whether we do not exercise the power, whatever happened in the country would be laid upon our doorstep. It is a very delicate matter, and it is one that has to be handled with a great deal of wisdom and prudence; and to recite, it seems to me, the specific purposes to which the local currency counterpart may be put in the legislation might get us into a pack of trouble.

The CHAIRMAN. The only question in my mind, Mr. Ambassador, at that point is whether or not the statement you have made, emphasizing the magnitude of this responsibility, justifies us in leaving this authority exclusively in the hands of the Administrator.

I wonder whether he should not be required to consult with the National Advisory Council upon this question.

Ambassador DOUGLAS. I would certainly see no objection whatsoever. It is a terrific responsibility.

Senator LODGE. I should think he would like to.

Ambassador DOUGLAS. I should think he would like to get as much advice as possible on any question.

The CHAIRMAN. Where could that go? Where is the delegation of power to the Administrator on this subject?

Senator SMITH. Page 32, line 9, "purposes as may be agreed to between such country and the Government of the United States."

Ambassador DOUGLAS. Say "after consultation with the National Advisory Council."

PHRASE "GOVERNMENT OF THE UNITED STATES"

Mr. GROSS. We used the phrase "the Government of the United States," instead of "the Administrator," just with that in mind.

Senator HATCH. What would that require?

The CHAIRMAN. Who is the Government of the United States?

Mr. GROSS. That, we think, would require the approval of the National Advisory Council under the Bretton Woods agreement. It gives them the power to coordinate all financial transactions.

Senator HATCH. You say you think it does. Are you sure of that?

The CHAIRMAN. I don't think that is enough, anyway.

Mr. GROSS. That was our construction of the Bretton Woods agreement.

Ambassador DOUGLAS. Would it not be preferable to say in (9) (a), "shall, after consultation with the National Advisory Council, be held or used only for such purposes as may be agreed to between such country and the Administrator"?

Senator GEORGE. Is the Secretary of the Treasury on the National Advisory Council?

Ambassador DOUGLAS. He is chairman of it.

85-743—73——17

The CHAIRMAN. I think that is agreeable. Have you that, Mr. Rice?
Mr. RICE. Yes, sir.

The CHAIRMAN. Without objection, that change will be made, and that is our answer to Mr. Herter at that point, plus the fact that we will meet him at Philippi.

Senator BARKLEY. You don't want to encourage him to make Philippi too hard when we get there.

Senator THOMAS of Utah. May I ask this question, because it is not plain: Is the Advisory Council to be consulted? It won't be in existence after June 30, 1952, will it?

USE OF LOCAL CURRENCY

Ambassador DOUGLAS. There will be no local currency counterpart after June 30, 1952.

Senator THOMAS of Utah. Will it be used by then? Then why do we have this item about the balance, if there will be none left?

Ambassador DOUGLAS. I beg your pardon; I misunderstood your question. I would be surprised if there were not a balance in some of the countries, and it was because it was anticipated there would be a balance in this set of local special currency counterpart accounts that this provision was written in requiring protection by the Congress.

Senator THOMAS of Utah. That means that the agreement must undoubtedly be made between the two countries, and if it takes the form of a treaty, be consented to up here.

The CHAIRMAN. "Subject to approval by act or Joint Resolution of the Congress."

Senator THOMAS of Utah. That means that when the windup day comes, whatever balance they have, we here will have something to say about how it is used. Am I reading that right?

Ambassador DOUGLAS. That is right, sir.

Senator GEORGE. That is only the unexpended, unencumbered balance.

Senator THOMAS of Utah. That may be decided in a century from now, is that right?

The CHAIRMAN. Are you anticipating a filibuster?

Senator THOMAS of Utah. No. Everything is all finished up, and everything is completed, but you have this money left, and the disposal of this money will be left to the two governments after consultation with each other.

Ambassador DOUGLAS. That is right.

Senator THOMAS of Utah. Through some formal action, is that not right?

Ambassador DOUGLAS. That is right.

Senator THOMAS of Utah. There is no time limit on that, because this money may be held for quite a time if it gets into a loan situation.

Ambassador DOUGLAS. That is right.

Senator THOMAS of Utah. Then you do not need any reference to the Council for the second part at all?

Ambassador DOUGLAS. No; I would not think so.

THE TERMINABLE DATE

Senator LODGE. Herter's next point is on line 12, the words "June 30, 1952."

He asks, "Should the terminable date be restricted to 1952? Might it not be advisable to use local currency thereafter?"

Ambassador DOUGLAS. They can be used, subject to the approval of Congress.

The CHAIRMAN. Yes. That is for us to decide.

Senator LODGE. Page 33, line 16: He suggests striking out the words "provide for" and inserting the word "complete," which he says makes the meaning more accurate.

The CHAIRMAN. "Provided, that notwithstanding the provisions of the subsection, the Administrator may, through June 30, 1948, complete the transfer of food. . . ."

Is there any objection to that? Without objection that change is made.

Mr. GROSS. It is not clear, Senator, what that refers to. This is a new operation. This sets a new program in motion under this interim authority. It does not complete any operations already begun. This is that interim authority after the passage of this bill which permits this Administrator to go ahead with procurement under this bill. It might meet Congressman Herter's point to say, "provide for and complete."

The CHAIRMAN. Very well. We have done that for him, without objection.

MR. HERTER'S LAST POINT

Senator LODGE. The last point is on page 34, and I think I know what the answer to it is. At the end of that paragraph that begins on line 1 and ends on line 8, Mr. Herter says, "This looks like only European countries will do any follow-up." I think we have covered that point and we know that the United States is going to do its own follow-up under other portions of the bill.

The CHAIRMAN. I think so.

Senator LODGE. That concludes Representative Herter.

The CHAIRMAN. I think you can report to Mr. Herter that his suggestions were gratefully received and, in the main, have been met.

Senator LODGE. Yes.

QUESTION OF THE MARITIME PROVISION

The CHAIRMAN. Now I would like to go to the question of the maritime provision which is where?

Ambassador DOUGLAS. Page 19, I think it is.

The CHAIRMAN. At the top of page 19. I don't think I need to read the relevant language. You are all familiar with it. The question is, what are you going to do about it?

Ambassador DOUGLAS. New language has been prepared, Senator.

Senator GEORGE. What is that? The Administrator may do what?

The CHAIRMAN. This is where he charters or sells ships.

Senator GEORGE. The Administrator is given that authority, is that right?

Ambassador DOUGLAS. That is right.

Senator SMITH. What is the new language?

A LETTER FROM SECRETARY FORRESTAL

The CHAIRMAN. Before you go into the new language, I would like to read a letter that I have received from the Secretary of Defense, Mr.

Forrestal, on this subject. This is the result of Senator Lodge's question. This is the response, Senator, to your request:

In my testimony before your committee to which you referred in the letter you sent me today I said, "our purpose and object is totally and exclusively to prevent another war by the creation of the political and economic and social equilibrium which is requisite to the maintenance of peace."

The providing of shipping is the major part of the means by which we hope to accomplish this purpose and object. As you know, I feel strongly that peace and security cannot be viewed merely in terms of great military power or wealth in the hands of the United States alone, and this is as true of shipping as it is of any other element of power or wealth.

In your letter you have adverted to a suggestion that we transfer or sell 500 vessels, and have asked me these specific questions:

"What impact, if any, would the sale of transfer of these ships as contemplated in the administration's program have upon the national security interests of the United States?

"Would it be advisable from a national security viewpoint to sell or transfer any such vessels?"

Those are the questions he is now asked to answer.

Let me state my own understanding of the suggestion referred to in your letter. My understanding is this, that the figure of 500 vessels is a ceiling figure, designed to provide the Administrator with a desirable amount of flexibility; that within this ceiling figure of 500 it is proposed to transfer title to not more than 200 vessels; that it is proposed to charter not more than 300 vessels, thereby making the ceiling figure of 500, as previously mentioned, and that all of the vessels under discussion or dry cargo vessels.

It is also my understanding, as set out at some length in the report of the Harriman committee, that the charter or transfer of title of these vessels is to take the place of any extensive shipbuilding programs in the European countries themselves, programs which would necessarily use up new steel, labor and critical materials that can better be used for other purposes.

It is not my aim to give you the impression that the charter or transfer of title of 500 vessels, or of any lesser number, will be completed without impact on our own military strength. There will be undoubtedly some effect, but it is my opinion that we stand to gain more by such charter or transfer from an overall national security standpoint than we stand to lose. In this connection, in a recent memorandum to me the general subject of shipping, the joint chiefs of staff said, "It is recognized that considerations other than military may make it desirable to dispose of some ships to foreign governments or noncitizens in furtherance of national policy. It is entirely possible that a greater ultimate military advantage might in fact be achieved by such use of some reserve tonnage now than would result by holding it idle for possible future use under war emergency conditions."

Obviously there might be changing circumstances as the European recovery program progresses, and it would therefore be my suggestion, in which the Secretary of State concurs, that the act provides that the Administrator, prior to the transfer of title to any vessel, shall consult with the Secretary of Defense with regard to the impact on national security of the proposed transfer.

This whole matter in my opinion, is closely related to the maintenance by this country of a healthy domestic shipbuilding industry. It is decidedly in the interest of national security that we maintain our own shipbuilding capacity, and with that end in view, I suggest that your committee consider the correlation between the transfer of the relatively slow American ships now in the laid-up fleet, and the construction in this country and for our own use of faster and more modern vessels, perhaps through transfer to an appropriation available for shipbuilding purposes of proceeds derived from the sales of any vessels disposed of under the European recovery program.

JAMES FORRESTAL.

Senator LODGE. That is a very interesting letter.

Senator GEORGE. He wants to get the money to build some ships.

Senator SMITH. To build some better ships.

Senator GEORGE. What is your new language now? You said you had some new language. There is a good deal in what he says.

Senator BARKLEY. This involves only these three lines in subparagraph (4); does it not?

Ambassador DOUGLAS. It is on pages 26 and 27, too.

The CHAIRMAN. This language on page 19 is the authority to charter. The language on page 26 is the authority to sell.

The following substitute is proposed by whom?

Ambassador DOUGLAS. That is language that was drafted in the Department, sir.

The CHAIRMAN. This is a substitute for (4)?

SUBSTITUTE LANGUAGE BY THE BUREAU OF THE BUDGET

Ambassador DOUGLAS. I am told also the Bureau of the Budget.

The CHAIRMAN [reading]:

(4) (a) Placing in operating condition, and, for periods not extending beyond December 31, 1952, chartering, with the approval of the President, any merchant vessel owned by the United States Government, to a participating country. If a vessel of the United States is so chartered, its documents as a vessel of the United States shall be surrendered and it shall, during the charter period, be considered as a foreign vessel for the purposes of the navigation and vessel-inspection laws of the United States.

(b) Notwithstanding the provisions of any other law, selling, after consultation with the Secretary of Defense and with the approval of the President, any merchant vessel owned by the United States Government to a participating country or to a citizen thereof, and such sale shall be effected by utilizing the services and facilities of the Maritime Commission, provided that any such sale of any war-built vessel, as defined in the Merchant Ship Sales Act of 1946 (60 Stat. 41), as amended, shall be at the purchase price and in accordance with the financial terms specified in such Act for sales of such vessels to United States citizens.

(5) Transfer of any commodity or service, which transfer shall be signified by delivery of the custody and right of possession and use of such commodity, or otherwise making available any such commodity, or by rendering a service, to a participating country or to any agency or organization representing a participating country.

In plain language, what is it you have done?

ORIGINAL LANGUAGE MODIFIED

Ambassador DOUGLAS. We have merely modified the original language so as to make it clear that the Administrator may first place in operating condition a vessel which is in the inactive fleet.

Second, if he charters a vessel, it must be only with the approval of the President.

Third, the certification as to the excess of its current requirements by the U.S. Maritime Commission has been deleted.

Fourth, the language makes it clear that the documentation of the vessel shall make it a foreign vessel for the purposes of navigation and inspection laws.

The CHAIRMAN. What have you done with this language with respect to the basis of the controversy which revolves about it?

Ambassador DOUGLAS. Not a thing, sir.

The CHAIRMAN. You have simply perfected the existing language?

Ambassador DOUGLAS. As to sale, the Secretary of Defense must be conferred with.

The CHAIRMAN. That still does not touch the basic question that has been raised.

Senator BARKLEY. Is this supposed to be a consolidation of the statements on pages 19, 26, and 27?

Ambassador DOUGLAS. Yes.

A CHALLENGE BY ORGANIZED LABOR

The CHAIRMAN. Then we confront the fundamental challenge that has been raised by all branches of organized labor, which has otherwise given us complete support for this legislation, the complaint that this is a blow at the employment of American seamen. The committee will remember, for I think all members of the committee received, Senator Overton's letter.

Senator LODGE. Will you read that, Mr. Chairman? I have forgotten it.

The CHAIRMAN. This is his letter:

I desire to direct your attention to the menace to American shipping contained in the European Recovery Program, to transfer 500 American vessels to foreign-flag control and operation. I am convinced that this feature of the plan is unnecessary, undesirable, and seriously detrimental to the American Merchant Marine:

1. Over 1,000 surplus United States ships have already been sold to foreigners at prices far below present construction costs. On account of construction programs now being carried on the Marshall Plan nations in 1950 will have merchant fleets of 10,000,000 tons more than pre-war, when this competition with American vessels was virtually destructive.

2. Our present reserve fleet of about 2,000 vessels is not a surplus. It is a stockpile to be maintained solely for wartime and emergency use. This fleet properly maintained will be available for 20 years or longer.

3. The transfer to foreigners of 500 additional vessels will reduce this essential reserve by 25 per cent.

4. The transfer will throw out of employment 20 to 25 thousand American officers and seamen presently manning these vessels, necessitating in many instances the payment of unemployment compensation.

5. The manning of the 500 ships with low-paid foreign crews may result in a dollar freight saving of about $200,000.000 which saving must be reduced by the loss of recapture by the United States of ninety percent of the profits presently being made by vessels' American charterers in accordance with charter provisions, and by the loss of income tax presently being paid on the remaining 10 per cent of the profits.

If allowance is made for these two factors, the saving will be reduced to only a small percentage of the estimated figure.

The Harriman Report states 'the limited financial savings are not sufficient to justify the drain on United States resources for national defense which such transfers would involve.'

6. The transfer will create for decades low-cost foreign competition which will be a continuing threat to the maintenance of an adequate American Merchant Marine and will jeopardize the half billion dollars presently invested in American shipping.

7. The Maritime Commission affirms this. In transmitting its recent report to Congress, its Chairman stated, 'The Commission believes that the sale, charter, loan, or outright grant to participating nations of any United States vessels in addition to the large number already approved for sale to them would be contrary to the best interests of the American Merchant Marine.'

I hope that you will view this matter as I do, and will vote against this provision of the Marshall Plan.

A CONTRADICTION WITHIN THE EXECUTIVE BRANCH

Senator LODGE. Is the Maritime Commission part of the executive branch? How do we have this apparent contradiction between the

Maritime Commission and the recommendation which the executive branch makes to us? I thought that the recommendations we had in this draft bill represented the composite views of the executive branch, and that all agencies had been consulted and approved. Why is there this conflict?

The CHAIRMAN. I would not know the answer to that.

[Discussion was continued off the record.]

The CHAIRMAN. I suppose the answer is that the Maritime Commission has sufficient autonomy so that it does not have to submit every letter it writes to the Bureau of the Budget to find out whether the thing is OK. Isn't that true?

[Discussion was continued off the record.]

Mr. GROSS. Unlike most other agencies, the members of the Commission are only subject to removal from office for malfeasance.

[Discussion was continued off the record.]

The CHAIRMAN. Very well, gentlemen. Here you are.

Senator LODGE. Did the Maritime Commission testify?

Senator THOMAS of Utah. This part of the Maritime Act was not the part that was handed over to my committee to handle, Senator Vandenberg.

Senator LODGE. Did we take testimony from the Maritime Commission on this matter?

The CHAIRMAN. No; we did not.

Senator LODGE. Did anybody? I think it is very pertinent to know why they think this, and why they are at complete loggerheads with the President on this matter.

CONTROVERSY OVER MARITIME LAW

Senator THOMAS of Utah. I think, Mr. Chairman, there is only one consideration for us to deal with here, and that is the simple consideration of its effect. This is one of the things that will affect our economy, the very thing that we have said. If it will upset the feeling of practically all of labor that is related to shipping and the rest of it, I think it is one of the most unwise things that we can do, to let the controversy come into the picture.

Now, if they need a ship, the Maritime Commission has the authority, and the Administrator can go to it; can't he?

Ambassador DOUGLAS. No, sir. If the resolution which the Senate passed at its session last week, at which eight Members were present, is agreed to by the Congress, no ships can be sold to any foreigner.

Senator THOMAS of Utah. You mean that is something which has happened which affects the basic law of the Maritime Commission?

Ambassador DOUGLAS. There are two features of this proposed language. The one has to do with the chartering of vessels for a limited period of time, December 31, of 1952. It is contemplated that 300, or not more than 300, vessels will be so chartered. Moreover, the vessels which will be chartered will be taken out of the inactive fleet. If vessels are not chartered, then the cost to the United States of the European recovery program will be increased by $100 million during the course of the 15 months. But that isn't all.

If there is no authority in this bill to charter, the American shipping interests will doubtless do precisely what they did after the enactment of UNRRA, increase their rates, and if they increase their rates to a level, 1½ or halfway between the present level and the rates which they charged after the enactment of the UNRRA legislation by the Congress, the cost to the United States will be $184 million in addition.

The CHAIRMAN. In addition to the $100 million?

Ambassador DOUGLAS. In addition to the $100 million.

It is the only club the administrator has over the shipping interests, and to deny him that power to hold down transoceanic freight rates, I think is a great mistake.

Now, as to the sale, that is a wholly different proposition, for it contemplates that more than 200 vessels will be sold out of the inactive fleet. They won't be taken away from American operators. They will be sold out of the reserve fleet, tied up. And if ships are not sold, then the cost to the United States will be increased by $54 million during the period of 15 months. If no ships are chartered, and no ships are sold during the entire four and a quarter years, the total cost to the United States will be increased thereby in the amount of between $600 million and $650 million.

The reason for chartering is not only the reason which I have given.

Senator HATCH. Does that figure include advanced shipping costs?

Ambassador DOUGLAS. That is a net saving; yes.

Senator BARKLEY. You mean that increase you speak of is based on present rates, or would it include any increase?

Ambassador DOUGLAS. The $100 million is based on the present rate.

The CHAIRMAN. I think we can at least partially simplify this problem at once. It seems perfectly obvious to me that it is impossible for us to report to the Senate a bill that involves sale, because the Senate has passed a bill which prohibits any sales, and I do not understand how we would be in any position to report a bill which violates the decision of the Senate made within the last 2 or 3 weeks on that subject. So I think that necessarily we are confined to a discussion of charter.

CHARTER OF U.S. SHIPS

Ambassador DOUGLAS. Let me deal with the charter first.

If no ships are chartered, or 200 ships are not chartered, the cost to the United States at the present level of maritime freight rates will be increased by $100 million. The reason is that at present foreign countries have to pay dollars to defray the freight cost. The foreign countries do not carry that amount of freight in ships flying their flags. American ships do carry that amount of freight, and the freight cost has to be defrayed, therefore, in dollars.

If the ships are transferred, then the foreign countries will be able to pay the freight rates and the cost of transoceanic shipment in their own currencies, of which most of them have no deficiency.

Senator THOMAS of Utah. Isn't the mere fact that a foreign country, in buying goods over here—surely it can control how the goods are to be shipped. And isn't that a deterrent to the raising of prices on the part of our own ships?

Ambassador DOUGLAS. It has to employ its fleet, Senator, to bring raw materials from all over the world and to make exports to places located all over the world. It is not now, and I think cannot be expected to be, able to employ all of its fleet to carry cargo from the United States to the foreign destination.

The CHAIRMAN. I suggest that we suspend our discussion. The Senate meets at 12 o'clock, and I suggest that we recess until 2 o'clock, when I would like to settle this, and then I would like to settle this afternoon the question of the amount, if we can.

The committee is in recess until 2 o'clock.

(Whereupon, at 11:55 a.m., a recess was taken until 2 p.m. of the same day.)

AFTER RECESS

The hearing was resumed at 2 p.m., Senator Arthur H. Vandenberg, chairman, presiding.

Senator VANDENBERG. The committee will come to order, and the Ambassador will repeat his statement.

COTTON AND TOBACCO NOT PURCHASED OUTSIDE OF THE UNITED STATES

Ambassador DOUGLAS. It is not contemplated under the program that any cotton or tobacco will be purchased outside of the United States from any funds, whether in the form of credits or cash, extended to any of the European countries by the United States.

The CHAIRMAN. What do these figures mean, then, that we read, showing diverse and sundry offshore purchases on both cotton and tobacco?

Ambassador DOUGLAS. Cotton and tobacco may be bought in other parts of the world out of the resources of any one of these individual countries. It would not be appropriate for us, would it, to say to any one of these countries: you cannot buy cotton from Turkey, one of your habitual and traditional sources, or tobacco, grown in Canada.

Senator GEORGE. Brazil? India?

Ambassador DOUGLAS. Yes, it would not be appropriate for us to say to any one of these countries, "Out of your own resources you cannot buy tobacco from a source that has been one of your traditional sources of supply."

The CHAIRMAN. But how about your other statement, which is important.

I have before me one of several million mimeographed issues by the State Department on this related subject, dated February 7, headed ERP offshore procurement, reading:

The following breakdown on off-shore procurement under the European Recovery Program was submitted to the Senate Foreign Relations Committee today.

Illustrative distribution by commodities of U.S. funds for off-shore procurement (in millions of dollars at July 1, 1947 prices).

Then it says:

Tobacco, 20.7; cotton, 165.4.

How do you explain that?

Ambassador DOUGLAS. That is moribund, that statement that you have. It is obsolete.

Senator HATCH. Let us have a new one, then.

Ambassador DOUGLAS. There is one of February the 13th, in which you will not find tobacco or cotton.

Senator HATCH. I was just trying to anticipate, Mr. Ambassador.

The CHAIRMAN. I think it is very important that you ask it, and I was wondering what to say to Senator Robertson, who could not understand why we should buy Cuban tobacco when we have a lot of American tobacco.

Ambassador DOUGLAS. The answer is that that is obsolete and has been replaced by one of February 13, 1948.

Senator HATCH. I suggest that that be read into the record.

Senator SMITH. Does this show the offshore purchases?

Ambassador DOUGLAS. Yes; the contemplated offshore purchases.

The Administrator, of course, has to make all the determinations.

The CHAIRMAN. I do not think it is necessary to take the time to read it. Let us put it in the record, however, and let us pass it around.

[The statement referred to is not printed.]

The CHAIRMAN. What is calculated to be the life of this particular statistic?

Ambassador DOUGLAS. I have not had any mortality figures on State Department statistics calculated recently, and therefore, I do not know whether they follow the businessman's table, or some different one.

But if I were insuring the paper, I would set a pretty high premium.

IMPONDERABLES WHICH CANNOT BE SURVEYED

The CHAIRMAN. I think this perfectly beautifully demonstrates the fact that we are playing with imponderables here which simply cannot be surveyed.

Ambassador DOUGLAS. Well, they can be surveyed within limits. And the program is going to be subject to change as conditions change and factors change.

The CHAIRMAN. This relieves me very much.

What are your issuing days down there at the Department? I want to be sure that I get each succeeding bulletin.

Ambassador DOUGLAS. Nothing is issued during the day. It is only at night. [Laughter.]

The CHAIRMAN. When nobody is looking?

Ambassador DOUGLAS. Under cover of darkness.

The CHAIRMAN. Dr. Wilcox, mark that "current".

$620.2 MILLION OF "OTHER IMPORTS"

Senator GEORGE. You have very big item down here at the bottom, "Other imports, $620.2 millions."

Ambassador DOUGLAS. Yes; that is right.

Senator GEORGE. Various imported raw materials. That might include cotton.

Ambassador DOUGLAS. But cotton is not on the list.

Senator GEORGE. No; cotton is not on the list.

Ambassador DOUGLAS. There are skins and some chemicals, nonferrous metals, zinc, zinc concentrates, copper from Chile, and so on.

Senator LODGE. Does this include the foreign things, that are not offshore?

Ambassador DOUGLAS. Foreign commodities?

Senator LODGE. Canada is not offshore, and Mexico?

Ambassador DOUGLAS. Yes; Canada is offshore.

Senator SMITH. Anything outside of this country.

Ambassador DOUGLAS. Anything outside of the frontier of the United States.

Senator LODGE. In maritime parlance it would be something that is at sea.

The CHAIRMAN. Can we go back to work? This has been a very illuminating exhibit, and it is gratefully received.

Ambassador DOUGLAS. Senator, the billion dollar figure to which you referred included all of the value of the imports of cotton, into all of the participating countries, to all sources.

Senator HATCH. Including our own?

Ambassador DOUGLAS. Yes. Of the billion dollars, $438 million and some odd hundred thousand dollars will be purchased in the United States.

The figures are obviously subject to variation, but that figure to which you referred covered the value of their total imports of cotton from all sources.

BACK TO THE MARITIME PROBLEM

The CHAIRMAN. Now let us get back to the maritime problem.

I said this morning that Congress had passed recently a law preventing sale. I found that they also prevented charter. And I want to read into the record this one sentence, which was passed by the Senate on February 5, 1948:

> Notwithstanding the provisions of subsection (a), no contract of sale under section 6 of the Merchant Ship Sale's Act of 1946 shall be made after March 1, 1948, and nothing contained in this or any other act shall be deemed to authorize the U.S. Maritime Commission to charter any war-built vessel as defined in the Merchant Ship Sale's Act of 946 to any person who is not a citizen of the United States, as defined in the Merchant Ship Sale's Act of 1946.

Now, I just do not see how we can report a bill which flies in the fact of the action of the Senate 1 week ago.

Senator HATCH. Senator Barkley did not hear that statement. Would you repeat it?

The CHAIRMAN. I made a statement this morning that the Senate had passed recently a prohibition against the sale of these ships. I find that the prohibition is against not only the sale but the charter, and is categorical; take effects March 1, 1948; and was passed by the Senate on February 5, 1948, within just a week.

Now, how can we, or, putting it affirmatively, can we, defend a recommendation which squarely defies this decision?

Senator BARKLEY. Well, that raises, of course, theoretically, on the surface, the fact that any action of the Senate is supposed to be a commitment and might in a sense bind us at least in the immediate future.

But it still raises a question: How well did the Senate understand what it was doing? How many were present? How much discussion was involved in it?

I do not recall it, myself.

The CHAIRMAN. Of course, if those tests are to be applied to legislation—[Laughter.]

Senator BARKLEY. I realize that that opens a very invidious question as to the validity of any action taken by the Senate that has not yet become law. I would have no idea of what the House will do about it. I do not know how the thing got through. I am not on the Committee on Interstate Commerce.

The CHAIRMAN. Plus the fact that the so-called Small Business Committee made an investigation of this subject, and this was passed as a result of disclosure of a very heated objection to any further ship sales or charters.

Senator BARKLEY. The question, I guess, in view of what you have said, is whether we are justified in reversing, or recommending a reversal of, the recent action of the Senate, based upon—I do not know what.

I do not recall that there was any debate on the floor about it. I do not know how many were present. It has been suggested that only eight Members were present. I do not know whether that is true, or not.

I do know one or two instances in which at the last minute, just before adjournment, somebody has brought something in and said it was the unanimous report of the committee, and it went through. I do not know whether that happened in this case, or not.

But I think we ought to consider, and we are compelled to consider, in spite of that, what is the wise thing to do. The Senate might reverse itself if it knew the facts. I do not know whether they knew them, or not.

NEED FOR ORGANIZED LABOR TO SUPPORT ERP

Senator HATCH. I want to ask a question. My primary concern with this bill, as I am sure that of everyone else is, is the complete program, the European recovery program; without damage or injury, of course, to our own interests, the interests of our country. I think it is very impotant that organized labor has come out so strongly in support of the Marshall plan. I think they have done a magnificent job. I would not want to endanger that support that we have.

Now, I want to ask the Ambassador: How important is this European recovery program? It does not make any difference to me what we did yesterday. Frequently I do something yesterday that is wrong, and perhaps I can right it today. That is not the point.

How important is this to the recovery program as a whole?

Senator BARKLEY. I would like to join in that question, because I was about to come to it. I appreciate very much the attitude that all the labor organizations have taken on this bill, Green and Murray and all of them. They have made a magnificent contribution. I think William Green's statement before our committee was one of the best that has been made: to the extent that the chairman complimented him on the constructive position which he took.

I do not know whether, if we went contrary to their recommendations in this shipping matter, they would become luke warm in support of the whole program, or not. I have not canvassed that situation.

I appreciate that. I think it is important that we have a united background of support from all different kinds of angles of this country, none more important than labor as a whole.

I therefore join in the question Senator Hatch has asked the Ambassador: Taking all these things into consideration, including the $650 million additional cost out of the Treasury, which might even amount to a billion if freight rates are increased by the elimination of this provision, I would like to get his reaction to that situation.

There are two alternatives here that we are up against.

The CHAIRMAN. Is that 5 years?

Ambassador DOUGLAS. Four and a quarter years.

Senator BARKLEY. But for the first 15 months, $154 million.

Ambassador DOUGLAS. And that $154 million may be something of an exaggeration, Senator, because the calculation was based upon freight rates as they were in July of 1947. Since then, those freight rates have fallen somewhat.

So that probably the net cost, were the chartering provision and the sale provision to be deleted from the bill, based on present freight rates, would be somewhere around $120 million to $129 million.

A CLUB FOR USE OVER THE SHIPPING INTERESTS

One of the principal advantages of the chartering provision is that it gives the Administrator a club which he can use over the shipping interests to prevent them from doing exactly what they did after UNRRA was passed. Should they repeat now the performance which they then gave, the cost to the United States would be much more than $125 million on the chartering account alone, but would run to about $300 million.

Senator HATCH. I wonder if a separate bill might not be introduced covering this. Let it go to the committee. Let it hang there as a club. And if these shipping interests do raise their rates—I am just trying to think out loud now, as a practical means of meeting the situation.

Ambassador DOUGLAS. A bill that is in unanimated suspense is not very much of a club, because there would be the same opposition to the passage of that bill by the shipping interests.

Senator HATCH. It is a better club if there were a sincere effort to hold hearings and tell these gentlemen, "If you raise your rates, this bill is going to pass."

Ambassador DOUGLAS. But there is another consideration, Senator. The first is that if the chartering of these vessels is not now undertaken, then I think in all equity and fairness an official amount of steel should be made available to these European countries in order that they may augment their ship construction program.

Now, steel is in short supply. Shipping is not in short supply. We have approximately 15 million tons in the reserve fleet today.

Senator WILEY. It is rotting, too.

Ambassador DOUGLAS. And much of it is rotting.

ALTERNATIVE ACTION

Senator LODGE. Is there not some other way, that we can prevent the shipowners from profiteering?

Is there not some other kind of action we can take besides turning these vessels over to the foreign governments?

Ambassador DOUGLAS. There is no other action we can take that will save dollars.

Senator LODGE. No, but leaving that out, and as to the question of keeping shipowners from profiteering, I should think we could handle that in some other way; could we not?

Senator BARKLEY. You could feel reasonably sure if you heard that the Maritime Commission would not approve these increases. But I do not know how you could be assured of that.

Senator LODGE. Write something into the bill that the rates shall not exceed a certain amount, or a percentage above a certain amount, or something like that.

Ambassador DOUGLAS. The Maritime Commission does not have the interocean rate. They control the rate indirectly, through their control of tonnage, and that is really the effect of this chartering provision, because it is a control of tonnage, and it therefore is reflected in freight rates.

One further consideration: The Maritime Commission itself has calculated over a long period of time that 11½ million tons in active service is adequate to, and fully satisfies, the U.S. maritime needs.

And over a long period of time—I am not talking about the immediate period, because there is something like 20 million tons presently in service—about 11½ million tons is all that can be effectively and efficiently used.

SHRINKING TO PEACETIME SIZE

Every industry that become blown up during the war has been faced with the problem of shrinking back to peacetime magnitude. In the case of the aviation industry, for example, the number of men employed was far, far in excess of any number which had previously been employed in this country, and far in excess of the number presently employed in the industry.

We had about 7½ million tons, as I recollect the figure, of shipping before the war, and it rose as a result of our perfectly miraculous shipbuilding construction program to some 54 million tons during the war. Now, 54 million tons, dry cargo and tankage, cannot be effectively used. About 11½ million tons over a long period of time, is what the Maritime Commission calculates is necessary.

I think that 11½ million tons is a fairly reasonable figure. It was confirmed, approximately, by a study made by the Harvard School of Business Administration as to our postwar merchant marine needs, and it was confirmed in another study that was made for me a couple of years ago by one of the ablest men in the shipping business.

So at one time or another this industry is going to face a problem of shrinking back. And I know of no better time in which it can face that problem than the present; when, if anything, we have overemployment rather than underemployment, in the United States.

UNEMPLOYMENT OF SEAMEN DOUBTED

Reference has been made by some of the representatives of labor organizations to the unemployed in this industry. It is doubtful, actually, that there is any unemployment at all. The figures that were used, as I understand the testimony of others, reflecting the number of unemployed, are figures derived from seamen who are on the register. Whenever a seaman has completed his voyage, he is considered for statistical purposes to be unemployed, and his name goes on the register. The number on that register range from 25,000 to 50,000.

It therefore constitutes a pool, into which seamen are constantly going and out of which seamen are constantly withdrawing.

The number of seamen employed in the American Merchant Marine is obviously less than it was during the war, but the tonnage employed has not shrunk yet to what the Maritime Commission calculates to be the long-term needs of the United States.

Senator LODGE. If we make these ships available, we will not get them back, will we?

Ambassador DOUGLAS. Yes; we will get them back. Under this language they cannot be chartered for any period beyond 1952.

Senator LODGE. Do you think we will get them back, then?

Ambassador DOUGLAS. Looking at our historical experience, we chartered some 2 million tons to the British in 1942, and all of that tonnage except the tonnage which the British purchased from us, and the tonnage that was lost through maritime marine accident or casualties in connection with the submarine warfare, were returned to the United States; except for 40, which are in the process of being returned.

The CHAIRMAN. I further understand, Ambassador, that the Waterman Steamship Co., to which you rather favorably referred, is quoted in this record as stating that they heartily endorse the proposal that would deny the Maritime Commission the authority to charter or sell war-built vessels to any person not a citizen of the United States, because it was felt that proposals to charter vessels to foreign nations would be extremely detrimental to the American merchant marine.

Ambassador DOUGLAS. I was not referring to Waterman as endorsing or not endorsing.

The CHAIRMAN. But I thought you indicated that the opinion was worth listening to.

Ambassador DOUGLAS. An opinion from Mr. Roberts is worth listening to. I do not know who signed that recommendation.

The CHAIRMAN. I would like to leave something in. The question I raised upstairs is simply one of comity. I just wonder if we are not building up trouble for ourselves.

SALE OF 200 VESSELS

Senator GEORGE. And may I ask how many there are to be sold? How many you want authority here to sell?

The CHAIRMAN. 200.

Ambassador DOUGLAS. The sales part of it would apply to not more than 200.

Senator GEORGE. I am speaking of the outright sales now.

Ambassador DOUGLAS. Not more than 200.

Senator GEORGE. Maybe we could separate them in one way.

Ambassador DOUGLAS. I was wondering if it would be worth considering only the chartering provision suggested; deleting the provisions in regard to the sale of ships and relying upon the Congress to extend the Ship Sale's Act of 1946.

Senator GEORGE. Well, if we chartered and limited the number that could be chartered, would that not serve the purpose?

Ambassador DOUGLAS. Yes.

Senator BARKLEY. There is nothing in the bill that limits the number, either of sale or charter.

Ambassador DOUGLAS. No, sir.

Senator BARKLEY. So that while that may be a moral commitment, it is not a legal commitment as to the sale or charter. On the surface it looks like out of 2,000 ships tied up, 500, as a ceiling is a modest number. And if they are tied up and are going to continue to be tied up, they are not employing any seamen. All they are doing is employing somebody to watch them and take care of them.

The CHAIRMAN. If you employ the ceiling as to chartering, it would be only 300.

Senator BARKLEY. Which is a still smaller proportion of the total 2,000.

Senator GEORGE. I was much impressed at the statements made before the committee in regard to this matter; but then beyond all that, we are going to have a very difficult job getting this through the Senate with 500 ships.

The CHAIRMAN. There are 300.

Senator GEORGE. Or 300. I think you are going to have a very difficult job; and without regard to the merits of it. There are a lot of interests here, some conflicting, all united in the fight against any chartering or sale of these vessels.

AN AMENDMENT PROPOSED BY THE CIO MARITIME COMMITTEE

The CHAIRMAN. And we shall also confront an amendment which has not even been suggested here, which is going to be proposed by the CIO Maritime Committee, limiting to 50 percent by weight and value the commodities that can be transported in vessels other than U.S. vessels.

Senator GEORGE. Yes.

Senator BARKLEY. Is that going to be proposed here, or on the floor?

The CHAIRMAN. On the floor.

Senator THOMAS of Utah. You think that will actually be introduced?

The CHAIRMAN. I am so advised. It is a part of their program.

Senator LODGE. What percentage is it planned to send out?

Ambassador DOUGLAS. It is an impossible thing to determine, Senator, because the foreign fleets are employed all over the world; and to the extent to which they divert the ships from present employment to the North Atlantic, to the same extent here is a deficiency in the raw materials which they received, derived from other parts of the world, in soft currency areas of the world.

So if they are to divert tonnage from one employment to another employment, which is necessary, then substitute tonnage has to be provided on account of the diversion.

More than that, there is just a calculation, the obtaining of the information, so that one can calculate whether more than 50 percent is being shipped in an American-flag or foreign-flag ship, that would present an administrative problem of considerable magnitude.

Ships leave port, and they have all kinds of cargo in them, dead weight and space cargo, purchased in a variety of different ways by a variety of different people to serve a variety of different purposes. And how one would distinguish—one could, but how one with reasonable administrative ease could distinguish between that amount which was purchased as a result of funds extended by the United States and that which was purchased from other resources of the country, that which was for this program and that which was not for this program, would be a terrific problem.

200 SHIPS FOR CHARTER

The CHAIRMAN. If you had 200 ships available for charter, would that not be a substantial leverage in this rate business.

Ambassador DOUGLAS. Yes.

Senator BARKLEY. You mean 200, or 300?

The CHAIRMAN. 200.

Senator BARKLEY. Reduce the number of charter from 300 to 200.

The CHAIRMAN. And cut out the sales.

Senator HATCH. That would be the club.

The CHAIRMAN. That is the club. And that is the basis upon which it would have to be defended.

Senator BARKLEY. It would have to be more than a club. It would be assumed that they would be operated.

Ambassador DOUGLAS. You see, there is not enough of them. They lost terrifically during the war. They rebuilt or purchased a tonnage which tends to restore their fleets, but there is not enough tonnage to meet the requirements.

We are going through the same experience in shipping after this war as we went through after the last war, except in an aggravated form. First, because of very much greater tonnage that was lost during the last war than in World War No. I, and second, because the turn-around is longer now than it was.

The CHAIRMAN. Is there available American tonnage, existing operating American tonnage, to carry this?

Ambassador DOUGLAS. Oh, yes; there is. You see, there are almost 14 million tons in the reserve fleet. But if American operators operate the ships under American-flag, then the cost to us to pay the dollar freight will be larger.

Senator SMITH. You would have to add that to your present estimate.

Ambassador DOUGLAS. That is right.

Senator BARKLEY. Your 14 million tons include these 2,000 ships that are tied up?

1,369 SHIPS IN THE INACTIVE FLEET

Ambassador DOUGLAS. The record I have indicates there are 1,369 ships tied up in the inactive fleet.

Senator BARKLEY. Then 2,000 is an incorrect number?

Ambassador DOUGLAS. Yes. It was 2,000 at one time. We have sold to foreign countries 1,000 ships and to U.S. private companies 600 ships, for a total of 1,600.

Senator BARKLEY. Well, it must have been 3,000.

Ambassador DOUGLAS. Well, I do not know that we ever had 30 million tons tied up, Senator.

Senator BARKLEY. I am talking about the number of ships. It might have been 3,000 ships.

Ambassador DOUGLAS. Yes. They were sold and not out of the reserve fleet, but perhaps when they were turned back into the fleet.

Senator BARKLEY. By whatever process you reached 1,400 ships tied up instead of 2,000?

Ambassador DOUGLAS. That is right.

The CHAIRMAN. For instance, would you contemplate chartering tankers?

Ambassador DOUGLAS. No, I do not think there are any tankers contemplated to be chartered.

Senator LODGE. There is a pretty widespread feeling around the country that one of the reasons there has not been so much is because of the tankers chartered to foreign countries.

Senator GEORGE. This is a matter as to dry-cargo ships that they are proposing here.

The CHAIRMAN. Does it say so?

Senator GEORGE. I think so. I got that impression from the testimony.

The CHAIRMAN. Are these dry-cargo ships?

Ambassador DOUGLAS. Yes; there are dry cargo.

Senator WILEY. How many tankers?

Ambassador DOUGLAS. There are 319 tankers that have been sold since the war.

Senator WILEY. What have we left?

Ambassador DOUGLAS. Our tonnage in tankers is 516.

Senator BARKLEY. 516 ships?

Ambassador DOUGLAS. Tankers. And then we have 100 tankers in the reserve fleet.

The CHAIRMAN. Well, what would happen if we said there were 200 ships provided American charters were not applying for them?

Ambassador DOUGLAS. That is all right, because American charters will not apply.

CRITICISM OF THE MARITIME COMMISSION

The CHAIRMAN. I now recall that one of the great arguments that resulted in the passage of this thing a week ago was the fact that the Maritime Commission was accused of having sold a lot of these ships in spite of the fact that there were American buyers seeking them. The proposition was, among other things, that if there is an American operator who wants to operate one of these things, he ought to have the priority. And I wondered if we would not just get a little less sales resistance if that provision were there.

Ambassador DOUGLAS. I think that charge was made against the Maritime Commission on account of the sale of tankers, Senator, particularly, but not on account of the sale of dry cargo vessels.

Senator BARKLEY. When I was at home before we met in extra session, I had a telegram from Senator Wherry, asking me to protest against the sale of certain ships by the Maritime Commission. He was speaking for the Small Business Committee. I did not know enough about what was really going on to wire the Commission, or anybody else, and I did not. But it was largely on account of the sale of tankers, as I recall it, that this protest was made; on the ground that those tankers were needed to transport fuel oil, and so forth, into certain sections of the country that needed it.

I do not think it applied to dry cargo ships.

The CHAIRMAN. I received the same telegram, Senator, and inquired into the situation, and it proved to be this: That at the time last June when the Maritime Commission offered these tankers, there were no American operators seeking them; and on that basis the Commission started to make commitments for delivery in the fall. And by the time they were around to the point of delivery, there were American bidders for every one of the tankers.

The question arose as to whether or not the right of an American to have priority was a continuing priority which continued up to the point where the delivery had been made, or something of that sort.

Senator BARKLEY. Yes; it was quite an involved subject, and I did not want to get involved without more information than I had at the time.

The CHAIRMAN. Well, gentlemen, what would you like to do about this? We have to move along.

Senator LODGE. Can we not do something with your idea of confining it to ships for which American operators have expressed no demand?

The CHAIRMAN. Well, I submit that to the Ambassador. It would be one of the major attacks that resulted in the passage of this proscription.

TROUBLE ON THE FLOOR PREDICTED FOR THE BILL

Senator LODGE. As Senator George says, leaving out the question of shipping, this bill is not sure of an easy time on the floor of the Senate.

The CHAIRMAN. I doubt whether this will live, even if we change it.

Senator LODGE. As to this labor thing, labor is all right on this bill now, but if you got labor sore on some angle of it, that might be just enough to have the vote go the wrong way in the Senate, from a practical political standpoint.

The CHAIRMAN. Well, if we are going to put anything in, it just occurred to me that if we put something of the sort indicated in, it would indicate our sympathy with their point of view, and we would just frankly leave it open to survey.

Senator LODGE. And make it clear we are doing it for the purpose of preventing the American people from being gouged.

Senator BARKLEY. It is a question of a half a million, or more, which might amount to a million or more in the long run, of taxes out of the Treasury. It is a question between that and the chartering or selling of these 500 ships.

If we are willing to pay the price, maybe we should, but if we continue we will have to pay the price out of the Treasury, which will be in addition to what we appropriate or authorize here.

Because the amount of money involved in the program does not contemplate this extra $650 million as freight, as I understand it. That is in addition.

The CHAIRMAN. That is right.

Senator WILEY. Outside of that, Senator Barkley, you claim this is a reconstruction bill. You set out to try to reinvigorate Europe. You not only would save the taxpayers' money, but you would provide an avenue of employment for Europeans to take this stuff back and forth. It would mean that they would get these dollars that they need so badly. It would add to the economic health; and we always say, when you add to the economic health you add to the moral and political health.

And it seems to me that is an element you have to consider here, too.

I read some place that, taking for instance the German ports and other ports, there are thousands of sailors with nothing to do, and I, for one, certainly would not want to strike down any particular segment of our society, but I feel with the Ambassador here that if we are going into a world program we have to see all the angles and all the facets and look into those things that benefit the morale of the people, which we expect to build up so that they can withstand the impact of communism.

One way to do that is certainly to give them employment where you can, especially if you save the taxpayers of this country money.

The CHAIRMAN. You are dead right about that.

Senator BARKLEY. If we assume these ships are going to remain tied up as they are, nobody will be employed. That is a certainty. It does not give employment to anybody except a few caretakers, to keep all these 1,300 or 1,400 ships tied up in rivers or harbors.

EMPLOYMENT OF AMERICAN SEAMAN

Now, that raises in my mind the question whether the prospect of additional employment of American sailors by prohibiting the sale or even the charter of these ships to some other country is sufficient to offset the more than half a billion dollars of increased expense involved in hauling whatever we send over there in our own ships and in no other ships.

I suppose that to the extent that they have tonnage they could haul it themselves.

Senator GEORGE. I think the employment feature enters into it, Senator, in this way: If these ships go out under foreign flags and can operate on the competitive basis to a very much greater advantage than the American ships, the American ships lose tonnage, lose business, and do not extend their operations at all.

Senator BARKLEY. If they hauled other freight besides that involved in this program, that would be true. But if they are limited to hauling the things we sent under this program, it would not impinge.

Senator BARKLEY. We could lease them or charter them or sell them.

Senator LODGE. I think they recognize that these useless, tieup ships would never furnish employment to American seamen; but they think if they were operated by foreigners, with their costs and everything else, it might take business away.

Senator BARKLEY. That might be a justifiable theory.

The CHAIRMAN. We confront a theory here which is: That based on this question, can we hope to save some useful and justified section of this provision by amending it in some fashion as indicated, rather than taking a chance on leaving the entire thing in the bill and probably losing it all.

Senator HATCH. I do not think that is quite correct, Mr. Chairman. I do not think we will lose it all.

The CHAIRMAN. I mean lose all of this provision.

Senator HATCH. Oh, yes.

Senator SMITH. You would not necessarily lose the bill.

Senator HATCH. No; I do not think it would mean that.

Senator BARKLEY. And this is not vital to the success of the program, but is just a question of dollars and cents, really, out of the Treasury.

Ambassador DOUGLAS. Plus steel.

Senator GEORGE. Yes; that is quite important. I can see the importance of it.

Ambassador DOUGLAS. Just to keep the record straight: If I understood Mr. Curran's testimony correctly—I think it was Mr. Curran's—he said the Harriman committee had opposed the transfer of vessels.

The CHAIRMAN. That was from Senator Overton's letter.

Ambassador DOUGLAS. I with great reluctance called his attention to the exact language of the Harriman committee in which it advocates the transfer of vessels.

The CHAIRMAN. Mr. Forrestal quoted them as advocating it. We have had the Harriman committee quoted both ways in the communications we have had before us.

Senator LODGE. Do you not think we have to be very sure of what we are doing? We fought, bled, and died to build up this merchant marine during the war; and I agree with the Ambassador that there is going to be some shrinkage. We cannot hope to keep it up to the pitch it was at during the war.

IMPAIRING THE MERCHANT MARINE

But I certainly think it would be a great pity if it were to be diminished. And I think the unions have one good argument, that in doing this you are impairing the merchant marine of this country; even though they would not use these ships if they could get them. I think you have to admit that they are right about that.

Ambassador DOUGLAS. I think they were wrong about it.

Senator LODGE. Well, why are they?

Ambassador DOUGLAS. Because a ship is in better condition when it is in operation than it is in the inactive fleet, tied up. It does not damage our merchant marine to charter a vessel for 3 or 4 years.

Senator LODGE. Let us say there is a useless ship down here in Chesapeake Bay, one that is not being used, and we are not going to use it, and that ship is made available to the Dutch, for instance, and the Dutch fix it up and put a crew in it and run it. Then, because of their low wages and their low rates, and everything else, there is just that much more business that they are going to take away, which would otherwise go to an American ship. It seems to me that is bound to be the sequence.

Ambassador DOUGLAS. Well, Senator, if not giving the Dutch the ship has the effect of increasing the exports of steel, in order that these European countries may build up their fleets, you will be confronted with exactly the same sort of a situation, only much aggravated, when that fleet is built up.

Senator LODGE. That is a different subject.

Ambassador DOUGLAS. If we are concerned here only with the damage to the American merchant marine, we ought to be in a prohibition against them as to the reconstruction of their merchant marine. Because they can operate ships cheaper than we can, and their newly constructed ships will be of higher speed and will be more efficient.

So it is only a question of time, it seems to me, if these European countries do recover, when the American merchant marine is going to be confronted with precisely that kind of competition.

Senator LODGE. If you follow that through to its logical conclusion, then the American merchant marine is going to disappear all at once.

Ambassador DOUGLAS. No.

Senator LODGE. It is going to get very low.

Ambassador DOUGLAS. No; because we subsidize our merchant marine.

I was going to say, alternatively: until the American Congress is willing to grant a larger subsidy in order to maintain 10 million tons in the service. If it does that, however, it again impinges upon the earning power capacity of these countries to earn dollars. I do not see how the American merchant marine can be damaged, though, by chartering.

The CHAIRMAN. I do not believe we can settle the fundamental question here. I think we confront solely the question of whether or not we want to attempt to find a middle-ground.

SUGGESTED CHANGE IN SUBSECTION (4)

Now, the suggestion made is that subsection (4) read substantially as follows:

> Chartering any merchant vessel owned by the United States which the U.S. Maritime Commission certifies as excess to its current requirements: provided that not more than 200 such ships shall be thus charterer and only when there is no request for American charter.

Or words to that effect.

Ambassador DOUGLAS. Senator, I think that quite irrespective of what the committee decides, the substitute language, with amendments, would be better than the language of the original bill.

The CHAIRMAN. All right.

Ambassador DOUGLAS (reading):

> Placing in operating condition and, for periods not extending beyond December 1, 1952, chartering with the approval of the Senate any dry cargo merchant vessel.

And I would like to insert: "In the inactive fleet, owned by the U.S. Government."

The CHAIRMAN. All right.

And where do you get the other ideas in?

Ambassador DOUGLAS. Last idea that you suggested as an amendment to the language would place the American operators in a position where they could apply for the total number of the 1,369 vessels in the inactive fleet, and because the application for the charter was pending the Administrator would be barred from chartering, but the applicants might not press their application.

The CHAIRMAN. So you do not think that is feasible?

Ambassador DOUGLAS. Well, I think it would be a trick which the operators can use. That is why I inserted "in the inactive fleet owned by the U.S. Government."

Then add the other limitations of 200 vessels.

The CHAIRMAN. I have no feeling about the matter, one way or the other. I just think we have to find some practical basis on which we can go to the floor with this thing.

Ambassador DOUGLAS. Something along those lines, I think, would strengthen your case. First of all, limiting it to dry cargo, and secondly, limiting it to the inactive fleet, and thirdly, if the committee so desires, a limitation upon the number.

Senator LODGE. What is the second?

Ambassador DOUGLAS. First, limit the chartering power to dry cargo vessels, and second, to vessels in the inactive fleet, and third, to some number.

Senator SMITH. Would that not refer to American charter applications? You say "the inactive fleet". That would mean that they have not been applied for.

Ambassador DOUGLAS. That is, not in current operation.

The CHAIRMAN. Well, what does the committee say to that?

Senator BARKLEY. I did not hear that suggestion.

The CHAIRMAN. The suggestion is that we strike out "sale" and permit "charter" with three limitations: (1) that it be dry cargo ships; (2) that it be in the inactive fleet; (3) that not more than 200 such ships be chartered.

Senator BARKLEY. That sounds like a reasonable adjustment between the two extremes.

Senator SMITH. That would be defensible.

Senator BARKLEY. We would have to take a chance on defending that on the floor, and we might get it eliminated, but we cannot help that.

Senator GEORGE. I think we could defend that better than we could the other, Senator Barkley.

Senator BARKLEY. Yes, I think we could defend that from any standpoint.

Senator HATCH. Mr. Ambassador, suppose that went through that way. Do you think that would give you sufficient protection against undue raises in the freight rates?

Ambassador DOUGLAS. I should think so. That would increase the costs somewhere in the vicinity of 30 millions.

Senator WILEY. There is another valid provision, I think, Mr. Chairman: That we in our foreign trade, built up now due to what some person has called economically feverish conditions, with $55 or $60 million a year we are giving away, so as to speak, know there will be enough pressure from European conditions to continue this thing, and not only the 1, 2, 3 or 4 years.

PRESSURE OF 13 MILLION TONS

Now, then, we have another pressure built up. That is our own group here. If we build up a tremendous merchant marine, more than the 13 million tons that the Maritime Commission has estimated as adequate, we will have that pressure too continued beyond the limit.

And it seems to me that those pressures plus the emotional pressure and then the pressure that comes from Russia, must be considered and then if we commence to get some other artifical pressures or economic pressures from our own group, this will carry over into 10 or 15 years.

And I, for one, cannot help but see that there must be a terminus some place. And I do not want to create any artificial pressure.

Senator GEORGE. The pressure you would get from this end of the line might be very effective, too.

Senator WILEY. You must have noticed, as we have talked it over here, how effective it is. We are fearful of this, and fearful of that.

Senator GEORGE. I mean what we may get hereafter.

The CHAIRMAN. Shall we proceed on the suggested basis?

Ambassador DOUGLAS. You would not make it 300; would you, Senator?

The CHAIRMAN. I would rather make it 200.

Senator WILEY. You can always come down. That is the way to argue up there.

A VOTE ON 200 OR 300 LIMIT

The CHAIRMAN. I do not know. I would like to start at a point where we can pretty well defend ourselves. It makes no difference to me, though, whether it is 200 or 300; except that I prefer 200.

Those in favor of 300 will hold up their hands.

(Senators Wiley, Smith, Barkley, and Hatch raised hands.)

Senator BARKLEY. Voting for this on the bargaining basis.

Senator GEORGE. I vote Tom Connally for it.

The CHAIRMAN. I vote Hickenlooper against it, but I see I will have to go out and get some more recruits.

Well, Mr. Rice, you prepare that on the basis of this language submitted by the Department for 300 ships.

Senator GEORGE. I think you should follow this suggested amendment. I think it is so much better than the original language. We had not adopted that; had we?

The CHAIRMAN. We are using the new form.

Senator GEORGE. I think that is undoubtedly better.

The CHAIRMAN. And the sales section goes out.

Now, before we take up the authorization of appropriations, there is just one brief question I want to submit to the committee, and they will be very much interested in the information involved.

You will recall that we have been insisting for some time, without much success, until February 11, that we have a breakdown relative to categories in which countries will find themselves in respect to gifts, loans, and so forth.

BREAKING DOWN CATEGORIES OF GIFTS, LOANS, ETC.

I now have the following letter from Ambassador Douglas, writing to the Department of State:

> I refer to your letter of January 28 to the Secretary of the Treasury and to his letter to you of February 2, relative to your request for a country-by-country analysis of the tentative estimate of the Division of ERP assistance between grants and loans.
>
> In his letter of February 2, Secretary Snyder stated that the members of the National Advisory Council were convinced that it would be undesirable to make public, prior to the inauguration of the program, an analysis of grants and loans between countries.
>
> The Department of State concurs in that view and in the reasons therefor as outlined by Secretary Snyder.
>
> However, I understand that you feel that some estimate must be given in the interest of obtaining successful action on the program by the Congress. I am therefore enclosing herewith a paper setting forth a preliminary and tentative classification of countries, showing divisions between loans and grants and proposed aid under ERP. The basis of this classification is taken from estimates prepared by the staff of the National Advisory Council and referred to in Secretary Snyder's letter to you of February 2.

For reasons which you understand so well, it would be preferable to avoid giving publicity to the paper. If, however, it is necessary to do so, I hope that the preliminary and tentative nature of the classification will be emphasized.
The classification is as follows:

It is headed "Preliminary and Tentative Classification of Countries," showing division between loans and grants and proposed U.S. aid under ERP.

The first category:

Cash payment basis, Portugal, Turkey (although Turkey is tentatively placed in the cash category, it may prove necessary and more appropriate to make ERP aid available on a loan basis).

But for the purpose of this summary, the cash payment countries are Portugal, Switzerland, and Turkey.

Second category, 100-percent loan basis: Iceland, Ireland, Sweden.

Third category, 100-percent grant basis: Austria and Greece.

Fourth category, part loan-part grant: Belgium, Denmark, France, Italy, Luxembourg, Norway, United Kingdom.

(It is not practical at this time to estimate with any precision what percentage of the proposed U.S. aid to these countries be in the form of grants and what would be in the form of loans. To each of these countries it is the intention to extend loans in as large a proportion to grants as is consistent with their individual ability to repay.) Aid to Germany out of a congressional appropriation for ERP would result in a claim against that country. The terms and methods of ultimate settlement of the claim would depend on future negotiations.

Now, the question I submit to the committee is this——

Senator SMITH. Where does that put Italy in, in that?

The CHAIRMAN. Part loan, part grant.

QUESTION ABOUT RELEASE OF TENTATIVE CLASSIFICATION

The question is one of releasing this information. I fully understand the preference that there should be no such published classification. I particularly understand and agree that it would be impossible to attempt to identify the part loan and part grant countries by percentages, if for no other reason than that a percentage thus indicated might be taken as a commitment when perhaps in practice we could get a larger percentage in the loan area. But the question is whether we shall make public this general tentative classification, with the distinct warning and understanding in connection with it that it is purely tentative.

My own feeling about it is underscored by a very bitter article in this morning's Times-Herald by George Sokolsky in which he just rips the daylights out of the so-called Marshall plan because Portugal and Switzerland are going to be the beneficiaries of our aid.

I have heard questions time and again raised about Portugal and Switzerland and Iceland and Ireland and Sweden which just reflect almost unanswerably upon the validity of this undertaking, and I wonder if it is fair to American public opinion as it is thinking of this matter, to leave it in the dark regarding these categories.

I particularly wonder whether, since obviously Congress has got to have this information when we get into the debates, this information should not be released in spite of the very persuasive arguments which are made against the release, and what I am submitting to you is the question of whether or not the committee thinks this information should be released.

Senator GEORGE. Mr. Chairman, if I may be permitted to speak, I would think we ought not to release this information under any circumstances. I should think so far as we could go would be to indicate approximately the approportion of the appropriations that might got for grants and for loans and mixed, and that would be just a guess, and I think the answer to all the arguments to which you refer, and I respect the very great desire of the American people to satisfy their curiosity about it, and the only real answer to that is, if there are any of these countries who, as a matter of fact, can be shown not to be entitled to participate here as a grantee, that then we may rely upon the Administrator, to whom we have given pretty broad powers, to see that that is done, and if anyone can convince us, he certainly should be able to convince the Administrator, that Portugal and certain other countries are able to pay their way.

I think that is just my early impression about it, that we had better not release this. I think this would get us into far more trouble than the criticism that we get, because some of the countries included in this group of 16 nations of course can pay their way. There is no doubt about that.

But if we can be convinced of that, and the American people can be confused because of that fact, it certainly looks like we ought to be able to rely on the Administrator to have judgment and discernment enough to say, "With respect to your application here, it must be a loan."

The CHAIRMAN. I quite agree with that, Senator. I do not believe I have made myself plain.

Senator GEOGRE. Yes, I understand the force of it.

The CHAIRMAN. Let me ask you this: What would you say if you were asked on the floor of the Senate, "Why is it necessary for us to make either loans or grants to Portugal or Switzerland, each of which is notoriously just as sound, on an economic basis, as we are?"

What would be your answer?

RESTRICTION ON AID TO SWITZERLAND AND PORTUGAL

Senator GEORGE. My answer would be, Mr. Chairman, that if I were Administrator, I would not make grants to them, based upon facts that I know, and that I assume the Administrator would certainly be much better than I would be in handling this program, and therefore we could rely on him. I would say frankly that I would not think of a loan being made to Switzerland or to Portugal based upon my information about their own condition. Of course, I have not investigated very carefully. But if I wouldn't make the loan, I assume certainly that the Administrator wouldn't make it.

Senator LODGE. Why couldn't Senator Vandenberg say, "It is my understanding that Portugal and Switzerland are not going to receive any money out of it?"

Senator GEORGE. I should say that. I should say that while the bill does not preclude them—I'm very strong for this bill on the theory that we have an administrator here with some power to act, and of course, if we do not get a good man, a good strong man to head it up, then we are sunk anyway. We are just in bad shape.

The CHAIRMAN. The position stated by the Senator from Georgia is the very deeply held conviction of the Secretary of the Treasury and of the National Advisory Council, and I suspect also of the State Department. Is that correct, Mr. Ambassador?

Ambassador DOUGLAS. Yes. It is a little exaggeration, Senator. We recognize the needs in informing the Congress as to the facts and we are apprehensive.

Senator GEORGE. That is all right. It is just a question of whether we make public what you give us, or enter it of record so that the Congress may know.

The CHAIRMAN. I do not believe I quite understand you, Senator. Do you mean that I would be entitled to say that it is my understanding that Portugal and Switzerland are to be dealt with on a cash basis, and that Iceland, Ireland, and Sweden are to be dealt with on a 100 percent loan basis, and so forth?

Senator GEORGE. I think you might say that if you wished to. You could certainly say this, that the judgment of the committee was, based upon all the known facts, that certainly these countries would fall in the category of borrowers, and other would not, and some would be mixed. I think you could certainly go that far and make it very strong.

But for us to publish it here as part of our committee deliberations seems to me to lead us to a lot of embarrassment. I would rather not do it if we can help it.

Senator BARKLEY. In that connection, Mr. Chairman, supplementing what Senator George has said, if we give this out, the inevitable interpretation of it will be that this is the frozen status of all these countries, not only now but during the whole period. It may be that during the period there might be a shift in the situation in one or more of the countries. They might require different treatment.

The CHAIRMAN. That would be made plain, of course.

Senator GEORGE. That is part of an answer. But I think definitely at this time that you could say the sense of the committee was that we recognize fully that certain of these countries would obtain aid through a loan, otherwise through the grant.

FEAR OF PREJUDICING THE BILL

The CHAIRMAN. The only thing I am trying to overcome is the needless and unjustified added public resistance to the plan as a whole, and when I read repeatedly assaults upon the whole Marshall plan, based upon the simple thesis that when Portugal and Switzerland became beneficiaries of American generosity we sure have turned Santa Claus with capital letters, it immediately prejudices the whole situation in a fashion almost impossible to overtake.

Senator GEORGE. Mr. Chairman, I realize that, but let me make this further suggestion to you: We want Switzerland and some other strong countries in Western Europe in so as to aid and strengthen the morale of the weaker countries.

The CHAIRMAN. Most emphatically.

Senator GEORGE. We are not predetermining what country will get a loan and what country will get something else, except through the administrative machinery which we have labored to set up, and that we cannot assume, and would not undertake to assume, that sometime during the course of the program, as Senator Barkley suggested, you may not have change in condition that would justify, of course, some change in the program.

Above everything else, these countries, strong enough to help themselves, add great, great moral force to the whole group, and while these countries are able to pay, they need things and will need things, and need certain considerations that must necessarily come largely through this European relief program. So I think you have a good answer.

I don't worry about that.

Senator BARKLEY. If I may follow that suggestion, Senator, with just this idea, this is an integrated program over there.

Senator GEORGE. That is right.

Senator BARKLEY. We have to have the support of the economically strong nations, and think in order to get their cooperation in helping their neighbors over there we have got to avoid saying to them in advance that we are just including them for window-dressing purposes. We are not really going to do anything, even if they need it. I doubt the wisdom of that, I am afraid the publication of this category might create that impression, although it is not intended.

The CHAIRMAN. What did you want to say, Senator Wiley? I apologize. I interrupted you.

Senator WILEY. That is all right.

My first reaction was favorable, because I have read in papers and magazines what purported to be almost a correct statement of what each of these countries was to get. As I remember, Britain was to get something like $2.5 billion or $3 billion. In other countries it was laid out. Now I find that that evidence is incorrect.

I think the public is entitled to be informed that such information is incorrect.

SWITZERLAND, PORTUGAL, AND SWEDEN

Now, Mr. Chairman, the other subject, these countries that you speak of like Switzerland, Portugal, and Sweden, characterized as countries in good economic condition, bring us directly to the point as to the amount that you are going to finally suggest should go into this bill.

A lot of those countries, even little Norway, floated a loan sometime ago here in the United States. But perhaps if we are going to loan them money, let it be through one of our banking institutions, either private banking or let it be the International Bank, and thus you will reduce the overhead of this amount that is involved, and that is a big issue in this country.

But I think first the people should be told definitely along the line as suggested by Senator George, that there is no definite commitment, that these sums that have been shot out over the country were mere false propaganda; that probably, thirdly, there has to be discretion in the administrator with a number of the countries that were our allies. If you remember the testimony, it was developed clearly that there was to be included in here some $500 million or $700 million for Germany, and then there was included another $500 million in the Army appropriation, as I remember, making about $1,200 million that would go into Germany. I do not know whether that figure is disputed now or not, in view of that statement, or whether that still is fixed as developed in the testimony.

Ambassador DOUGLAS. It is about $805 million. The Army has changed its request from $822 million to $805 million. There are about $400 million included for recovery in the European recovery program.

Senator WILEY. Then there was included in the Army request for food——

Ambassador DOUGLAS. $822 million.

Senator WILEY. And there was also in the Marshall plan——

Ambassador DOUGLAS. About $400 million.

Senator WILEY. That is a fixed amount you can release. But for everything else you can say that the plan has not been laid out, that there are no definite amounts. But I am getting back again to the question of when you come to debate the question of what the total amount should be. You have an absolute out in suggesting that these countries have credit with the banks or they have credit in this country for loans. Switzerland could float a loan in this country overnight, and get dollars if she wants dollars.

I do not know about Portugal. I am satisfied that Sweden could.

Senator HATCH. Sweden is in pretty tough shape herself.

Senator WILEY. Especially in relation to dollars. I know something about her economic condition. I am talking about the total overall amount.

Coming back to that proposition, I simply feel that we are consistent with the efficient handling of this program, in feeling that all the information that could be given along the line suggested by both the chairman, Senator George and Senator Barkley should be given to the public, so that once and for all they will know that we are not trying to hide stuff they ought to know.

Senator LODGE. I hope very much that that list is not going to be released from the committee in one piece like that. I think it is much better to let the information dribble out on the floor in response to questions you may get about Portugal or Switzerland. I think if you were to put it all out now as an official release, it would have a very unhappy effect abroad. Some countries would think they were being treated less well than others, and of course, from a political standpoint at home, while it is true you would be answering George Sokolsky, there are an awful lot of people in this country who would not at all appreciate the idea of Ireland being treated as well as England.

The CHAIRMAN. I would be answering the entire American press, who have hounded me for 4 weeks for information.

I am not going to say a thing.

Senator BARKLEY. Can't you say that a certain number of countries will be eligible for loans only, without identifying them; that others will be eligible for grants, without identifying them; that in view of the changing situation, it is impossible, over a 4-year period, to identify any country that would be entitled to either loans or grants exclusively?

Senator LODGE. All this is a forecast, anyway.

The CHAIRMAN. And, of course, I am not talking about a 4-year period. I am talking about the contemplation under the appropriation here pending. But I would not think of doing it in the face of opposition that has been expressed here.

Senator HATCH. I want to say something in support of you, just a moment, if I may.

CANDOR WITH THE PUBLIC

It has been repeatedly charged, not only in the press but by Senators, that we were not candid, that we were not candid with the American public, we were concealing things, and that the State Department was not candid and that it has been concealing things, and that has been quite a burden to you, sir.

The CHAIRMAN. Yes, sir.

Senator HATCH. You have not concealed things, and neither has the State Department. I have never seen a more frank, honest exposition than has been made. I am like you. In the light of the statements that have been made here, I do not think we should release them. But certainly, sir, I hope you can have an opportunity on the floor to make a very strong statement that you do have this information and you do have these facts, and nothing is concealed from anyone.

The CHAIRMAN. Thank you, Senator. I would not, however, feel free to state even on the floor that I understand these countries have been put in categories, because it apparently is the overwhelming opinion of the committee that that would be invidious, dangerous in some way. My personal reaction is that it leaves us behind the eight ball in respect to a very fundamental fact, and when you are trying to sell the American people a difficult program, and you leave them with the opportunity to just stop listening to anything else you have got to say when they cannot get a satisfactory answer to their first question, which is, "Why do you have to loan American money to Portugal and Switzerland when they are just as well off and just as sound as we are?" I can only say, "Well, abacadabra."

Senator LODGE. Why can't you answer that question and stop right there?

The CHAIRMAN. How do you answer it?

Senator LODGE. Say it is not contemplated to give any money to Portugual and Switzerland.

Senator BARKLEY. If you say that, and it is understood that that is true, what inducement have they got to join up in this European program?

The CHAIRMAN. They understand they are not going to get any money.

Senator BARKLEY. They have their own people to satisfy, as well as we have ourselves.

The CHAIRMAN. They are cooperators, not beneficiaries; that is all.

Senator LODGE. Can't you say that?

The CHAIRMAN. No.

Ambassador DOUGLAS. They are interested in remaining in the program because as the surrounding area improves, it is reflected in their own internal economy.

The CHAIRMAN. And they know that, too.

[Discussion was continued off the record.]

Ambassador DOUGLAS. We have already put out certain information.

The CHAIRMAN. Is this this week's issue?

Ambassador DOUGLAS. This is dated January 19.

Senator WILEY. I expect those were the figures that were published giving to each country so much.

The CHAIRMAN. That is 'way out of date.

Ambassador DOUGLAS. These were the figures published on the 19th of January.

Portugal, Switzerland, and Turkey were, by indication, placed in a category of countries that would receive no grants, and would therefore be on a cash basis.

Senator HATCH. Is that a public release?

Mr. NITZE. It is in this green book you have before you.

The CHAIRMAN. Where?

Senator WILEY. It shows I read material and some of the rest of them don't.

TURKEY OBJECTS TO RECEIVING NO GRANTS

Ambassador DOUGLAS. Turkey has objected violently to being placed in that category, and that is why it was noted in the communication to Senator Vandenberg that the position of Turkey might have to be changed.

Senator BARKLEY. If, in view of that statement made a month ago George Sokolsky writes a letter a month later, what good would it do to pacify him? He will write another article.

The CHAIRMAN. I am not thinking of him, Senator, except that he is a type. I am thinking about the demand that every member of this Senate press gallery who has been following these proceedings daily is making as to what the answer is.

AMERICAN PUBLIC ENTITLED TO KNOW WHAT IT CAN

Senator GEORGE. The American people, Mr. Chairman, really are entitled to know anything that they can know. But in the nature of things these allocations as between these different countries are so essentially tentative and unstable, subject to all sorts of changes, that it just seems to me that this is one of the things that, while we could inquire, trying to get the best information we can in order to look at it and evaluate the whole thing, at the same time I say what I tried to say in the beginning, that if and when applications are made or allocations are made, it is obvious that these certain countries are not entitled to a loan, or do not want a loan, and they would not be given a gift.

Ambassador DOUGLAS. The real category in which it is impossible to make any clear definition of the difference between loans and grants is the last category. I am not certain that there is much objection to the disclosure of the information with regard to Switzerland and Portugal.

Senator GEORGE. But suppose Switzerland were to say that she thought maybe it was best, on reflection, not to enter into any multilateral agreements, or have anything more to do with this thing.

Ambassador DOUGLAS. She might.

Senator GEORGE. Even if Turkey were to walk out it would be a very great deal of aid and assistance to our friends back of the curtain, would it not?

Ambassador DOUGLAS. If Turkey should walk out, it would be very critical.

Senator GEORGE. Let them stay in, and if they need grants, then they can make application for grants, and we can turn them down if they are not entitled to them.

The CHAIRMAN. I will be guided accordingly.

Senator GEORGE. I hate to disagree with you.

The CHAIRMAN. The truth of the matter is that I agree with you to the extent that when this letter was being written, they were going so far as to split the grants as between those that were going to get 50 percent or more, and I told them to take that out, just in order to avoid invidiousness, if there is such a word.

But I will just have to say, "Well, this is highly classified information which the Bureau of the Budget has said cannot be released."

Ambassador DOUGLAS. While Senator Barkley is out, I think there are one or two questions of substantive amendments that have been agreed to.

AUTHORIZATION OF FUNDS

The CHAIRMAN. I will take those up later. I want to get at this other thing, and see where our minds run. We are now going to discuss, secretly page 27, at the bottom.

(c) There are hereby authorized to be appropriated to the President, from time to time through June 30, 1952, out of any money in the Treasury not otherwise appropriated, such sums as may be necessary to carry out the provisions and accomplish the purposes of this Act: *Provided, however,* That for carrying out the provisions and accomplishing the purposes of this Act from the date of enactment of this Act through June 30, 1949, there are hereby authorized to be so appropriated not to exceed $6,800,000,000.

For the benefit of the committee, if it is of any use, I would like to make a suggestion—well, I would like to have Senator Barkley here.

If you have something you want to talk about, Mr. Ambassador, during the absence of the minority leader, proceed.

Ambassador DOUGLAS. There are two or three matters of substance which counsel would like to bring up, if he may. May he explain them to you? He has not gone over them with me?

SUGGESTED CHANGES BY THE STATE DEPARTMENT

Mr. GROSS. The first one arises out of an addition to the committee print. On page 19 there is added a provision with reference to the project problem which reads:

The allocations of commodities or services designed to carry out the purposes of this Act to specific projects which have been submitted to the Administrator where the participating countries have been approved by him.

The CHAIRMAN. I thought that was your amendment that I took this morning.

Mr. GROSS. It appears in the act in two places. The one you discussed this morning is in the bilateral agreement, the undertaking of the country to submit for approval. There are two difficulties we see with this; first, the use of "allocations" which implies allocating powers, which are not intended; and second, is the placement in the bill, which is now listed among the functions of the Administrator, which include procurement, transportation and the like.

This really is a statement of a new purpose, in a fashion, so we would prefer to change the language, but leave the thought, by adding to page 8 of the committee print, in the portion dealing with the functions of the Administrator, an insertion which would make one of the functions, the second listed function, read:

The Administrator, under the direction of the President, shall formulate programs of United States assistance under this Act, including approval of specific projects which have been submitted to him by the participating countries.

The CHAIRMAN. Is that the only change you want to make?

Mr. GROSS. On that subject, that is the only change, and it is a change in substance only because of the deletion of the word "allocation."

The CHAIRMAN. I do not see any objection to that. Without objection, that will be done.

THE SUBJECT OF APPROPRIATION

Now, Senator Barkley, We were starting to discuss the appropriation.

Senator BARKLEY. Thank you very much.

The CHAIRMAN. There is undoubtedly a wide divergence of opinion on the subject, probably even in the committee. Obviously, there is a very wide divergence of opinion on the floor and in the House. And it seems quite clear to me that something is going to happen to this figure.

My preoccupation has been to try to find a formula and which would show a reduction without impairing in any single degree the validity or the potential of the act itself, and yet, would be on a basis which we could hope to defend against the general assaults which are calculated to be made upon any figure which we report.

The suggestion I am going to make is as follows: I give it to you with no conclusion attachment on my own part, but for whatever it is worth, and then I should like very briefly to tell you why I think it is advisable.

APPROPRIATION FOR 12 RATHER THAN 15 MONTHS

My suggestion is that instead of appropriating for 15 months, we appropriate for 12 months, and that we use the figure, instead of $6,800 million, which is the official calculation of ERP for 15 months, that we use the 12 months' figure which, on the timetable and worksheets of the authors of ERP is the comparable figure as of April 1, instead of July 1, and that comparable figure is $5,300 million.

Senator GEORGE. How much, Mr. Chairman?

The CHAIRMAN. $5,300 million for 12 months, instead of $6,800 million for 15 months.

Senator SMITH. To April 30?

The CHAIRMAN. No, April 1.

Ambassador DOUGLAS. It should be $5,350 million, because of the action of the committee on the sale of ships.

The CHAIRMAN. I do not care about that.

85-743—73——19

REASONS FOR CUTTING BACK TO 12 MONTHS

Now, I want to submit that there are a number of very sound reasons for cutting this back to a 12-month appropriation, instead of 15.

If it is a 12-month appropriation, it brings this whole subject immediately in review when the next Congress meets. It is the new Congress and the new administration, whatever it is, either the present one or some other, which will have to be responsible for the fate of this great adventure hereafter.

No. 1, I think it is very important and useful that the timetable upon which we operate should produce this review and decision as early as possible in 1949.

Second, by reviewing the situation early in January in 1949, you are in the presence of reality instead of in the presence of speculation, as we are today. Being in the presence of reality, you know infinitely more then what you are talking about than you do today, because today you are entirely surrounded by imponderables, and I think the earliest possible moment when this program can be reviewed, in the light of realities, is the most logical and available time for the next review of the entire enterprise.

By January 1, you will have the benefit of the recommendations of the business management which you have created for this organization, and one of the great weaknesses in our dealing with figures at the moment is that we are dealing with estimates in which this business management that we are going to hold responsible for these results has had no chance to make any contribution whatever. We have no benefit of their point of view. That will be available January 1.

On January 1, we shall have available the report of the watchdog congressional committee, which by that time will be infinitely better informed regarding the operations of this enterprise than any Members of Congress are today.

By that time you will know what the crop has been in not only the United States but abroad next year, a factor which has a large effect upon the amount of money you actually need.

By that time you will know to what extent France and Italy are moving forward toward stability.

By that time you will know the extent to which the Soviet operation is undertaking its sabotage and subversion.

Still more important, if it is realized and recognized that this program is really coming under its most important and critical review the first of next year, it will put infinitely greater pressure upon the participating countries to make every possible progress by way of self-help between now and then.

In other words, it seems to me that entirely aside from the amount of money involved, there is every reason in the world why we should precipitate this fundamental review of the entire problem at the earliest possible reasonable date.

Furthermore, by proceeding in this fashion, we are able to reduce from $6,800 million to $5,300 million the amount of appropriation presently required without impairing by a penny the prospectus upon which ERP is built.

In other words, by achieving a reduction in the appropriation by this method, it is impossible for anybody to say that we have run out on

ERP in any fashion, or that we have cut its throat, or that we have maimed it in any degree. There is a reason for a reduction of this character. It is a reason which will be obvious; it is not an assault upon ERP either at home or abroad, which is the vital thing to be protected in connection with any result of this figure.

I think that is my story, and I should be very glad to hear any alternative suggestions that any members of the committee have to offer.

$5,300 MILLION FOR THE FIRST 12 MONTHS

Senator GEORGE. Mr. Chairman, let me ask you one question. I did not quite get it. This $5,300 million would be for the first 12 months of operation under the act?

The CHAIRMAN. That is right. That is the way it would actually operate. That is precisely what their own worksheet shows as being required.

Senator GEORGE. We might get it passed by the deadline date, or what we have talked about, April 1, or a little bit later, but it would be for the first 12 months.

Senator BARKLEY. There are two things that occur to me in connection with your suggestion and what you have had to say. I think there are strong arguments in favor of putting it upon a yearly basis, although we are beginning the program presumably at an odd time. It is not the beginning of a fiscal year. And I am assuming that at some time during the period of 4¼ years there will have to be a 15-month provision somewhere in that period.

The CHAIRMAN. I would expect that would be the second year, Senator, in my thinking.

Senator BARKLEY. I had thought that in view of the necessity for having a 15-month period somewhere in the total period, that it would probably be better to have it at the beginning. Then it would level off at the end of the fiscal year 1949 in such a way that we could pursue it from then on on a purely fiscal year basis.

But that may not be a vital consideration so far as my own viewpoint is about your suggestion.

There is another thing about it. Of course, what it amounts to is an apparent reduction without a reduction. We are reducing the total amount because we are reducing the time during which it is applicable. This bill provides for a 4¼-year period, a 4¼-year authorization.

Suppose we pass the bill with the 4¼ authorization. With this $5,300 million for the first 12 months, which would end on April 1, 1949, and in view of this overall provision for an authorization for 4¼ years, would the Appropriations Committee be authorized to appropriate only the $5,300 million, but extend the period to the 15-month period, so as to make it coincide with the end of a fiscal year, so as actually to reduce the amount for the 15-month period to $5,300 million, in view of the fact that we are undertaking to limit that $5,300 million to the 12-month period beginning the 1st day of April?

The CHAIRMAN. I do not think there is any way you can control the Appropriations Committee at that point.

Senator BARKLEY. If that be true, while I do not think there is anything we can put in the bill that would limit them in doing that, certainly if we do this, we ought to say in the report that after exhaustive consideration, the committee has come to the conclusion that this $5,-

300 million is essential for the 12-month period, so that if the Appropriations Committee, in making the appropriation, should undertake to extend the period without increasing the amount, they would have at least a barrier in the argument of our committee against doing that sort of thing. I am not assuming they would, but they could do that.

The CHAIRMAN. I am quite agreeable to that, Senator, and I realize that this appropriation is at the mercy of any sort of an assault that the Appropriations Committee wants to make on it, either in figures or device or any other thing, and I fully expect attacks of that sort to be made.

I would just like to put ourselves in the position where I think we can most forcefully defend the figure we recommended, and for my money I can make an argument, as I have briefly outlined here, for a reduction in the timetable which, as a byproduct, produces the reduction in the amount. I can make an argument for the new timetable, which I think is irresistible, and if we have to defend figures against attacks that are subversive and fatal, I would like to make the defense, so far as I am concerned, at a point where we have all of this collateral argument in favor of the formula we submit.

NEED FOR A UNANIMOUS COMMITTEE REPORT

Senator BARKLEY. I appreciate that. I think I should be frank and say that I had reached, and have reached, a conclusion in my own mind that for the 15-month period, the $6,800 million was the proper sum. I think all the arguments that have been submitted sustain that figure. And I was prepared and would be prepared if the committee voted for that figure, and for the 15 months, to go to the utmost of my ability in defending that figure. But this question arises in my mind, and I am sure the committee will want to consider it: I think it is very essential that we get a unanimous report from this committee on whatever we do; that we go out there united and prepared to defend our bill from every standpoint and from every attack.

Is there any assurance that can be given that we would have to make the same defense of the $5,300 million that we would have to make for the $6,800 million? Are any of those who are in the twilight zone of considering this bill who might go one way or the other, for or against it, upon whom we might count to help us in putting over the reduced amount and the reduced period, if a fight is actually made upon it, which I assume will be made by somebody?

What is your reaction to that situation? I know you can't give assurances as to anybody's vote.

The CHAIRMAN. I have no assurance that I could give you in regard to anybody except Senator Hickenlooper, who phoned me from the coast last night that he thinks this is the advisable arrangement to make.

I have no doubt that any figure we report is going to be attacked, and I do not know what the result of the attack will be. It might take the precise form you have indicated, and I would not even suggest that that attack would not occur. I can only say that Senator Millikin and Senator Bridges have a proposal which they will present, either here or on the floor, dealing with throwing a greater portion of whatever we appropriate into fiscal 1948, and taking it out of fiscal 1949, because they feel that with the accumulated grand total of nearly $10 billion which is going to be required of us in connection with foreign commitments, you simply cannot load that entire $10 billion on fiscal 1949. I prefer to have them present that suggestion for themselves.

Senator BARKLEY. Without knowing the motivating power behind it, that is probably a new bookkeeping maneuver in connection with a tax reduction.

The CHAIRMAN. I would not have the slightest doubt that that is what it is.

Senator BARKLEY. Whatever may be the objective, of course it would be offered and you have to settle that. That is somewhat beside the point here.

The CHAIRMAN. Except that I am about to bring it back to the point: You are entirely correct that whatever the motive, it is in net result just a bookkeeping maneuver; therefore, it is not of vital concern in dollars and cents to the Treasury.

I think that Senator Millikin and Senator Bridges, both of them in highly key positions in connection with this legislation, are primarily interested in this bookkeeping device that you are talking about.

Senator BARKLEY. I would not be surprised if that were so, and I suppose if the situation were reversed, I would have a deeper understanding of it than I even do now.

Senator LODGE. You understand it pretty well right now don't you?

The CHAIRMAN. What I was about to say, and I would not for a moment attempt to commit either one of them, because they were very specific in declining any commitment, I simply want to suggest that they were highly hospitable to $5,300 million for 12 months on the theory that they are going to get their bookkeeping device.

Senator BARKLEY. Just one other remark in that connection about your assumption. We might as well assume, all of us, that there will be an attack on whatever amount will be reported. But the effectiveness of that attack will depend a good deal upon who makes it and who supports it after it is made, and I would feel myself, as an individual member of this committee and of the Senate, happier about your suggestion about a reduction of the amount and the time, if we had some reasonable ground for expecting that influential and key men in the Senate would be reconciled to that and would help us put it through against any attack from any source.

The CHAIRMAN. I can give you no such assurances.

Senator BARKLEY. I do not suppose you could, but you can understand why it worries me a little bit.

The CHAIRMAN. I can understand why it worries me, too.

Senator BARKLEY. If I have to help you make an all-out flight for whatever amount we can report, and have to make the same fight for $5,300 million, I would have to make for $6,800 million, my own preference would be to fight for the $6,800 million, but I appreciate fully the force of your suggestion and the reason for it; and if we can get a unanimous report of this committee on that basis, I think it is entitled to serious consideration.

NOT A "TAKE IT OR LEAVE IT" PROPOSAL

The CHAIRMAN. I want everyone to understand the spirit in which the suggestion is made. This is not a "take it or leave it" proposal on my part.

Senator BARKLEY. Let me ask you this: Do you think, if we should report this suggestion by the unanimous action of the committee, that the chances are more favorable for us to be able to retain that figure in the final action of the Senate, than even if we made a unanimous report on the 15-month period with the $6,800 million?

The CHAIRMAN. I can only answer for myself. As one who would carry some responsibility for defending the bill on the floor of the Senate, knowing that an effort to reduce it will be made, I would feel infinitely stronger if I could point to a reduction which already has been made on a basis that has so many collateral reasons to defend it.

Senator HATCH. Mr. Chairman, are we not going to have the advantage of these suggestions? They are not going to be offered to the committee, but they are just to come up cold on the floor?

The CHAIRMAN. Which do you mean?

Senator HATCH. I was thinking of the bookkeeping one.

The CHAIRMAN. Senator Millikin is out of town. He will be back Tuesday, and if we can finish today, we are going over until Tuesday, and I have invited Senator Millikin to come to the committee to present his own proposition.

Senator HATCH. I think it is only fair to the committee that any Senator who has ideas should give us the benefit of them.

The CHAIRMAN. His idea has nothing to do with the amount. It has solely to do with a device to bring forward into fiscal 1948 a substantial portion of the burden.

Senator BARKLEY. As a matter of fact, it will be charged to fiscal 1948 whether it is spent or not.

The CHAIRMAN. That is exactly it.

Senator HATCH. I read this morning in the papers that a certain prominent Senator stated the amount must be reduced and cut down to specific projects. The Administrator would be so limited in funds that he could only approve certain projects which are economically sound.

If they have ideas like that, don't you think we should have the benefit of them?

The CHAIRMAN. Sure, but I haven't got any such.

Senator BARKLEY. You have to discount statements made in speeches by candidates.

Senator GEORGE. I have not conferred with Senator Millikin. I have not discussed it with him. He said something to me one day about it. It might be that that would turn out to be the very best thing that could happen to this appropriation, to throw as much in fiscal 1948 as you can, because if the stock market and every sort of market kept on acting awfully bad for the next several months, you might not be able to carry this burden in the 1949 program.

The CHAIRMAN. I think they have some pretty sound reasons for this.

Senator GEORGE. It might turn out that that would be the most helpful thing, to put as much on now as you can possibly do, because they can figure on a fairly safe surplus at the moment. But to figure on it for another year in advance is quite a different thing.

Senator BARKLEY. Of course, it ties in with the possibility of tax reduction, which might affect the revenues for 1949.

Senator GEORGE. Irrespective of the tax reduction, Senator Barkley, I think there might be some merit in it.

Senator BARKLEY. I think this. If the thing could be geared, and all the machinery set up so that as large a proportion of it would be spent wisely in 1948 as possible, it might start a stimulation of the recovery over there that would be very effective. I can appreciate that that might happen, although we have very limited time.

The CHAIRMAN. That has not anything to do with it. I think perhaps you have misunderstood me. This throwing a substantial portion of this appropriation forward into 1948 is not geared to the expenditures at all. It is a purely arbitrary device.

Senator BARKLEY. I understood that. I said if it could be, if the expenditure could be, speeded up so as to get things going over there, it might have a very great influence on what we would have to do in fiscal 1950 or 1949, even.

OTHER OPINIONS SOUGHT

The CHAIRMAN. I do not want my suggestion to dominate this discussion. I want to hear from the rest of you.

Senator George?

Senator GEORGE. Mr. Chairman, I haven't thought about it. I had figured we would have to face this issue. I am not at all sure that you are coming out with an appropriation of $6,800 million even if we passed it in the Senate to start with.

The CHAIRMAN. No, indeed.

Senator GEORGE. Because you have the House, and I am not at all sure it would pass the Senate at $6,800 million.

I had myself reached the conclusion to resolve it in this way, regardless of the amount actually authorized for this first period, whether it was 12 or 15 months: That since we had done the best that we could to set up a strong administrative agency, that our only real assurance of economy, both in the application and in the final outcome, rested in the hand of that Administrator anyhow; that if we did not appropriate enough, he would come back for additional appropriations and, if things were moving fairly well, we would have to do it, and if they weren't the Administrator, if he was a strong man, would not come back for them.

I don't know; there may be a certain advantage in appropriating for the first 12 months under this program. That does reduce a figure which might open us to some attack by unfriendly people in the country. They will say, "Well, they don't think they will ever have any other appropriation, so they have cut it down to that."

Then, on the contrary, there will be plenty of people who will say that even $5,300 million is too much.

I am appreciative of the fact, Mr. Chairman, that you have to carry a terrific burden in this fight, and if you think that splitting it in this way is helpful, I will be disposed to go along, because I can see no very strong reason against it or any valid reason. I do not know what the State Department's viewpoint might be.

The CHAIRMAN. Well, Mr. Ambassador?

Senator BARKLEY. Let me ask you this question: Have you conferred with House Members about this suggestion at all?

The CHAIRMAN. No. I didn't dare, because I think they are so cut-minded that I thought I would be rebuffed.

Dr. Wilcox calls my attention, Senator Barkley, to the fact that Congressman Herter said something in his press conference a day or two ago, which looked in this direction.

Senator GEORGE. He did. I have forgotten his exact language. He did say something that indicated he thought something like this should be done.

The CHAIRMAN. And he is the man you have to put your blue chips on in the House in connection with this bill.

Senator LODGE. Of course, he wants this figure to include China. He has expounded that already.

Senator SMITH. You mean this bill ought to include China?

Senator LODGE. This bill should include it, and he also wants to make a change in here; instead of saying, "to the President," it should be appropriated to "the Administrator."

Those are his two suggestions in this paragraph.

The CHAIRMAN. Well, gentlemen?

Senator LODGE. May I ask a question?

The CHAIRMAN. Yes.

PRICE ASSUMPTIONS IN THE $6.8 BILLION

Senator LODGE. In arriving at the $6.8 billion, what assumptions were made regarding prices?

The CHAIRMAN. Mr. Ambassador?

Ambassador DOUGLAS. The figure was first calculated on a basis of prices of July of 1947, adjusted subsequently to the price level as it was in October. Between October and December 31, the price level had risen so that the purchasing power of $6.8 billion had been reduced some $400 million. Meantime, prices have fallen. But the estimate of $6.8 billion is still $148 million shy, or rather the purchasing power of the $6.8 billion as of the price level today has been reduced by $148 million.

If, however, we are able successfully to bring down the price of wheat in the Argentine to world prices as a result of negotiations with the Argentine, then the purchasing power of the $6.8 billion would be increased by approximately $136 million so that the $148 million lost in purchasing power of the $6.8 billion, as of the present price level, would be just about absorbed by successful negotiation with the Argentine.

The $6.8 billion would then be approximately as of present price levels, and the adjustment of the Argentine wheat price, just about right.

Senator LODGE. Of course, that is a question that is sure to come up on the floor.

Ambassador DOUGLAS. Those are the facts.

Senator BARKLEY. That situation is bound to be a fluctuating situation over the 4-year period, and each year as we look into the thing and provide an appropriation we can take into consideration a price level, but we cannot possibly take it into consideration for a full 4-year period now.

Ambassador DOUGLAS. It is difficult enough for 12 months.

The CHAIRMAN. It is difficult enough for 1 week.

Ambassador DOUGLAS. In view of the present developments, yes.

There is one other consideration, Senator, that may be asked: Why should not the amount be reduced because of an anticipated greater harvest in Europe and in this country than at the time the program was formulated? That kind of question rests upon a fallacious assumption, because the crops in Europe were estimated at the time the $6 billion figure was calculated at almost precisely what it appears to be the harvest will be in the year 1948.

That is to say, it now looks as though the harvest in Europe would be about 85 percent of their pre-war level, and it was on that basis that the $6 billion was calculated.

ANOTHER REASON FOR THE JANUARY REVIEW

The CHAIRMAN. I would like to interrupt you just to say that that is another reason in my thinking for this January review. It seems to me that we should strive for the earliest reasonable time when we can review the program in the light of reality. If next January the price fluctuation has been such as to make this $5.3 billion worth $6 billion instead of $5.3 billion, it can be taken into account in respect to the appropriation which is made for the subsequent year.

I think there is every argument on earth for the earliest possible realistic review of the business that we are in.

Senator LODGE. That is what appeals to me about your proposal, Mr. Chairman. I would be in favor of it, if for no other reason than that you want it, and that you have to carry the load, but apart from that fact, I think it makes a lot of sense, because the management of this Marshall plan will have been in office long enough to really know what they are talking about, and January would be just the right time to start to take another look at this thing, even if you left out the fact that that is when the administration comes into office, and so forth.

So far as I am concerned, I am in favor of your plan.

Senator BARKLEY. Of course, the look-in that you speak of would not be as of January 1. It would be during the whole period prior to the actual appropriation. It might run into April or May, which would give you a longer period of insight into the thing.

Senator SMITH. Your figure, Mr. Chairman, would run to March 30, would it not?

The CHAIRMAN. Yes, sir.

Senator SMITH. And you would have to have in mind that for fiscal 1948 there would be 3 months that nothing was done about?

The CHAIRMAN. That is correct.

Senator BARKLEY. What would be the effect if by March 31 the appropriation for the following year had not been enacted, and there would be no authority to contract so as to prevent a hiatus there between March 31 and whatever time the new appropriation is made?

Senator SMITH. That was involved in my last question.

The CHAIRMAN. My first answer is, that you must remember that the appropriation process hereafter will not require a preview authorization. In other words, you have only one operation hereafter, instead of two. And I would think that every reasonable presumption would be that the Appropriations Committees could certainly act in 3 months upon this question.

Senator BARKLEY. Ordinarily they don't, though, in appropriations, annual appropriations. They don't usually get through the House by April 1.

EFFECT ON RFC

Now, what would be the effect of this provision, which I think we still have about the RFC having some money to advance? That is in here. What would be the effect if that were not all spent by the RFC prior to the effective date of the appropriation for the 12 months, if any balance were left over, so that it might be used during April or May of next year in the event the appropriation did not come along until that time? Would it be available?

The CHAIRMAN. I would not think so.

Senator SMITH. According to this, the RFC is refunded out of the $5.3 billion?

Senator GEORGE. It is just an advance.

Senator BARKLEY. They take over before we get ready.

Senator THOMAS of Utah. I think Senator Barkley has an idea there, that it could be remedied, although it is so far in the future, by giving the Administrator the right to ask RFC again for relief between the two times.

Senator BARKLEY. I take it for granted that if the program is going along well, and if it were very obvious next March that we were not going to get a new appropriation ready for April 1, chances would be fairly good that a deficiency or interim appropriation might be obtained to tide over that period.

The CHAIRMAN. That is my theory.

Senator GEORGE. I think, Senator Barkley, that this appropriation will kind of stand by itself. It will not come along in an ordinary general appropriation bill. This is so big within itself.

Senator BARKLEY. It will be a deficiency bill.

Senator GEORGE. It will be a separate bill from the other appropriation bills.

Senator BARKLEY. Those are just questions that bother me.

The CHAIRMAN. They are very serious questions.

Senator GEORGE. Mr. Ambassador, would you mind saying, if you are prepared to say, whether splitting up the appropriation in this way, by cutting time off, would seriously interfere in any wise with the workability of the program?

COMMENTS OF AMBASSADOR DOUGLAS

Ambassador DOUGLAS. I do not think it would seriously interfere with the workability of the program, Senator. The question is solely a legislative one, under which of the two alternative procedures, that is to say an authorization of $6,800 million for 15 months or $5,300 million for 12 months——

The CHAIRMAN. $5,300 million.

Ambassador DOUGLAS. The question is solely which of those two alternative procedures will be less subject to attack in so far as the amount is concerned.

Senator HATCH. If that appropriation should be cut down to $4 billion it would seriously interfere.

The CHAIRMAN. You might better have it cut from $5 billion to $4 billion for 12 months than for 15.

Ambassador DOUGLAS. Or if, having authorized for 4¼ years, and if, having specifically made an authorization for 12 months, the Appropriation Committee would extend the authorization for the 12 months' period, to a period longer than the 12 months, or for a 15 months' period, then the program would be seriously hampered.

The CHAIRMAN. In the same way that the program will be seriously impaired if the $6,800 million is reduced.

Ambassador DOUGLAS. Yes, sir. So it seems to me to be solely a question of tactics in the legislative branch: Which of the two alternative procedures will be less liable to successful attack.

Senator GEORGE. If that is the situation, I think undoubtedly Senator Vandenberg's suggestion will be far more helpful to us, because I have frankly visualized this program as coming up with about $4 billion for the first 12 months, and we face that possibility yet, as you can understand, of course, with two Houses and two other committees.

Ambassador DOUGLAS. We have four hurdles to jump.

I do not mean to put this idea forward as any absolute alternative, Senator George, but if the figure is substantially cut, it will have an adverse effect upon the whole program.

The CHAIRMAN. Obviously.

Senator GEORGE. Of course that is obvious. If it does not interfere with the program to split it, at the same rate for 12 months, rather than carry it on for 15 months, I think that will be helpful in getting this bill through the Senate.

Ambassador DOUGLAS. And holding the line on the amount.

Senator GEORGE. That is what I mean. I think so. There is a tremendous lot of force in the argument that Senator Vandenberg suggests that we need actual experience, we need an administrator who can come back here and tell us, and we need to know some things that will happen within the next 12 months, or within the next 9 months, that we just do not know now.

Senator WILEY. I want to ask one or two questions, and I want to express my views on this matter.

MORE INFORMATION NEEDED

First, I think the record is rather meagre. I think we should have the Treasury up here to put into the record the American picture of possibilities—not a lot of newspaper gossip as to what we are going to be able to do; what they actually will, so far as possible, estimate the income of America for taxable purposes, and what we get in our taxes. I think that is important.

Mr. Chairman, your statement almost convinces me to be a sinner, it is so dynamic and so logical, yet we have, as I understand, no assurance as to who the administrator is going to be. I think that information, if it could be gotten, should come before us first, an economic analysis of America's potential power from the standpoint of national income to handle this project. That is No. 1.

Second, the administrator. He can make us the laughing stock of the world, or he can put into this thing what we hope will be there—the vision and power to make a dynamic force for world rebuilding.

Then there is the third thing. You are talking about the impact of members who feel that this sum of $5,300 million is too much.

We heard the testimony, a lot of it being conjecture. But it seems to me that it is vitally important, besides knowing the administrator and having the figures, that we also have complete assurance that so far as we humanly can, there is going to be no further bungling; and third, that there may be a possibility of reducing this amount and still make available this amount by utilizing, as I suggested an hour or so ago, funds still available in agencies that we virtually are the owners of, because it is our dollars that is making them what they are.

$9 TO $10 BILLION FOR FOREIGN AID

You made a statement here that you figured that $10 billion was going into foreign aid.

The CHAIRMAN. Between $9 and $10 billion was the figure.

Ambassador DOUGLAS. $9,333 million is the figure.

Senator WILEY. So it is not $5,300 million, it is about $10 billion, and that requires some explanation. That requires again, the question of ascertaining our own resources. And I think the record should be clear as day on that. We should have what constitutes those other items, where they are coming from, and if it is virtually out of the American Treasury through some subsidiary organization that we have founded or built, the American people will say, "$9 billion?", "$10 billion?"

And again, whether we can afford to do it from every angle.

It seems to me to present a really crucial issue. But over and above that, if we do not get an administrator who has that ability to see through, and who will do that procurement job, not the job contemplated by the Maritime Union, or contemplated by business interests that are right now looking for big profits; if we do not have an administrator that can do that, this thing will be a fizzle.

It will be just an attempt to perform and so I would like to have this additional information, if I could, before I am to vote on this amount. I am seriously concerned because my constituents are concerned, and I am just human.

The CHAIRMAN. I would like to say to the able Senator from Wisconsin with respect to his first question that I think when we have the Harriman report and the Krug report, on the resources that are available for our foreign obligations, we have done everything humanly possible to survey the situation with the maximum expertness which we could possibly mobilize for the purpose.

I made precisely the same speech that the Senator from Wisconsin is making at the very first meeting at the White House when this subject was broached, and I think it was primarily in response to my demand that the Harriman commission was appointed. It seems to me that the record is very clear that we never had a commission in the life of this Government which did a more devoted job and a more conclusive one than the 19 civilian members of the Harriman commission did. And I would think that if you waited until doomsday, Senator, you could not hope to do anything except perhaps multiply confusion by seeking to rebuild report on report after you have the Harriman report and the Krug report as a basis

ECONOMIC RATHER THAN MATERIAL RESOURCES

Senator WILEY. I probably did not make myself plain. I had more in mind the economic resources than merely the material resources. I have spent some time on the Harriman report. But right now we are facing up against the proposition of a tax reduction, of appropriations for a number of organizations, and that picture is not before us. That is all I have—the economic statement of what the Treasury thinks the income is going to be with reasonable certainty, and what the outgo will be.

Senator BARKLEY. The Joint Committee under the Reorganization Act, based upon present taxes, is to report immediately on the amount of revenue expected in the Treasury, based on the present tax laws. Of course, that will have to be modified by whatever Congress does in the way of tax reduction, if it does anything. But that is about as accurate a report as you can get, based upon present tax laws.

Senator WILEY. Is that out?

Senator BARKLEY. It was supposed to be filed by the 15th, and I understand it will be.

TREASURY SURPLUS FOR 1948

The CHAIRMAN. I understand the Treasury reports a surplus of between $7 and $8 billion for fiscal 1948. Is that correct?

Senator BARKLEY. Yes. The report of the Joint Committee is based on the figures of the Joint Committee on Taxation and Revenue, is it not, Senator George?

Senator GEORGE. Yes.

Senator BARKLEY. So that it is as accurate as we could get.

Senator GEORGE. It is based upon their estimate of income at present rates. But your June 30 surplus is practically fixed. It is not entirely so; it is practically so.

Senator BARKELEY. The estimates revenues are around $47 billion.

Senator GEORGE. That is for the next fiscal year, for fiscal 1949, and that obviously, is an estimate, based upon estimated national income and prevailing and existing rates of taxation.

Senator WILEY. And in figuring the outgo, did they put into the statement an estimated amount for the ERP?

Senator GEORGE. I think all foreign expenditures with the exception of about $300 million, or something like that, were included in the budget.

The CHAIRMAN. I think that is true.

Dr. WILCOX. I think it is $250 million.

Senator GEORGE. They are in there in some way, if you know how to dig them out.

The CHAIRMAN. I asked that specific question, Senator, and the answer was that everything that could be contemplated is in the budget with the exception of about $250 million.

Senator GEORGE. Which arose by virtue of an increase in the amount to go to China.

The CHAIRMAN. That is correct.

Senator GEORGE. That is as I understand it.

Senator HATCH. Is it still your idea to have a final decision on this this afternoon?

The CHAIRMAN. Suit yourselves. The difficulty we confront is a physical one. While this bill is not going to the floor of the Senate for debate until March 1, I promised Senator Millikin that I would complete the work of this committee in time for him to start next week at his Finance Committee, and three members of this committee will have to be released for that purpose.

Senator WILEY. Isn't he coming before us on Tuesday?

The CHAIRMAN. I hope so, in connection with his suggestion regarding the bookkeeping device.

THE CHAIRMAN MUST CARRY THE BURDEN

Senator HATCH. I have no desire to delay, but I am frankly puzzled about the strategy. I feel much like Senator Lodge said awhile ago. The chairman says this is his decided judgment and his best opinion; he has the burden to carry and all that, and I would certainly say, yes.

The CHAIRMAN. Thank you very much and I appreciate what all of you have said along that line, but I do not want this question decided on that basis. I am prepared to defend whatever action this committee takes, and I want this question settled on a basis of the considered judgment of this committee. I do not want it said 2 months from today, if something happens to this appropriation finally, as it well may—there well may be a very serious accident—I do not want somebody to finally trace this thing back and say, "Well, on Friday afternoon we let the Chairman of the Foreign Relations Committee do as he pleased, and now look at the damned thing."

Senator BARKLEY. There is nobody going to do that on this committee.

Senator HATCH. The figure of $6,800 million we have agreed is the correct figure, because we are only reducing it proportionally as we are the time.

The CHAIRMAN. That is correct.

Senator HATCH. Now, is it better, because I know a fight is going to be made either on the floor or in the Appropriations Committee, and perhaps from both sources—what is the best procedure for us to adopt to get what we think is an adequate sum to carry out the program? That is the thing that puzzles me.

The CHAIRMAN. And when you get down to the bare bones of the rollcall up here, I venture to say that there are 25 Senators in the Senate, and certainly 200 Members of the House who have got to vote for something less than $6,800 million, and you have got to give them something less than that to vote for.

Senator GEORGE. They will certainly vote all the way from $4 up to $5 billion and maybe down to $3 billion.

The CHAIRMAN. I am trying to give them something less than that to vote for which can be defended on every soap box as a complete concurrence with the formula of ERP.

Senator HATCH. I want that carried out, and I want the appropriations to back that up.

Senator LODGE. I am for it, not just because you are for it. I think it is a damned good idea, anyway.

Senator BARKLEY. That helps the situation, doesn't it?

Senator GEORGE. There is one very important fact, so far as your legislative program goes.

The smaller the vote against this program in the Senate, the much surer it is to sail through the House at a fair figure. If you get a great big vote against it here, on the amount or anything else, you will have a terrible struggle in the House and in your Appropriations Committees.

Senator BARKLEY. With reference to the timetable mentioned by the chairman, I think it should be said that Senator Millikin had tentatively fixed an earlier date for beginning hearings on the tax bill.

Senator GEORGE. The 23d, Senator.

Senator BARKLEY. I know, but he had fixed an earlier date than that. He had not announced it, but after conferring with the chairman, I went to Senator Millikin and I urged him not to do it until the 23d. He had figured on the 16th, I think.

Senator GEORGE. You have a lot of appointments there, some preliminary things.

NEED TO DISPOSE OF THE BILL SOON

Senator BARKLEY. So if we can get this out of the way, and it means more than just voting on this thing this afternoon—we have to come in here Tuesday with a reprint of it, and we will probably occupy some time Tuesday getting into shape; we ought to get it reported as soon as reasonably possible, in view of the kind of report we must make, so that the country and the Senate can discuss it and study it before we take it up on March 1.

So, personally, I think we might be wise in disposing of this as soon as possible.

SENATOR CONNALLY'S POSITION

Senator GEORGE. I am inclined to think so, if we can; I am prepared to support the chairman's suggestion, and I do so for Senator Connally, of course, with the right reserved to him, when he comes, if we have not finally reported the bill, that he might be heard about it and might modify his position. Senator Connally has simply authorized me to vote for $6,800 billion but he said he did not know whether there might be some other proposal that he would like better. He did go that far.

NEED FOR A SECOND APPROPRIATION SOON

The CHAIRMAN. I can only say this about Senator Connally. In one of the final hearings I said to some witness, after I had developed the thought that the really important moment in the life of this adventure was when we make the second appropriation because that is the first time we will really know what we are talking about, that if this thing is showing the vitality and dependability that we hope by that time, there will be no question about adequate appropriations. If the world has gone to hell by that time, it may be even more necessary to make appropriations, or maybe not. But it seems to me that the decision which is overriding, of overriding vitality in respect to the degree with which we proceed with this thing, is the decision that is going to be made the second time, and not the first time, and that is another reason why I think the quicker we can make the second decision the better.

I think there are so many reasons for making this second decision as soon as possible, in the light of experience and reality, that you can make an argument for the formula which I suggested that you just cannot make against some abstract motion to cut $6,800 billion to $4 billion.

Ambassador DOUGLAS. The presupposition is that the Appropriations Committee will not appropriate that specific sum which is authorized for a period longer than the 12-month period. Should the Appropriations Committee do so, then you would not be, and Congress would not be, required to look at what transpired, the performance, the situation in Europe, and the future in January of 1949.

The CHAIRMAN. That is correct. But there are no presuppositions that go with this thing, Mr. Ambassador.

Senator BARKLEY. Would the Congress itself, and would the Appropriations Committee, in the exercise of reasonable judgment, feel morally bound by an act limited to 12 months, with an authorized appropriation for $5 billion, to such an extent that they would not feel justified in breaking faith with that moral obligation by extending the time beyond 12 months without an extension of the appropriation, also?

The CHAIRMAN. I do not know. Anything can happen, Senator.

Senator BARKLEY. Yes, I realize that. We have to take men as they are, and I think most of them have a sense of responsibility. We have to assume that.

The CHAIRMAN. It can be argued against this $5,300 million that we have not cut the $6,800 million a nickel.

Senator BARKLEY. That is right, and there is where we are between the devil and the deep sea. Those who are opposed to anything will say that we have not cut it a penny, and that is true. Those who are for the whole program will say that we have chiseled it down under the guise of a reduction in the time, so we have got to bear the responsibility of criticism from both sides on that.

Senator SMITH. The newspapers will probably say that you have cut the appropriation when you get the figure of $5,300 million, and they won't think about the 12 months unless you make that pretty clear.

Senator BARKLEY. That is a responsibility, if we do it, that we have to bear. We have to make that clear.

The CHAIRMAN. If you would rather think this over, I am quite willing. Senator Thomas, you haven't said a word.

Senator THOMAS of Utah. Well, Mr. Chairman, there is no need. If you sit here long enough, everybody says what you are going to say anyway.

But I do not want to say this, I am perfectly happy to go along on the 12-months appropriation. The important thing for the success of this act is in the first part of your paragraph that we are discussing, and that is some way or other to get continuity into this business. We are appropriating from time to time until January 30, 1952.

The CHAIRMAN. Yes, sir.

Senator THOMAS of Utah. We are going to have an awful lot of oratory on that, by the fellow who says that this Congress can't bind another Congress, and so on and so forth. You have heard it so much.

But anybody who has studied the history of Congress knows that every Congress is bound or has bound future Congresses.

IMPORTANCE OF CONTINUITY

But to me, and it is not sentimental and it is not just to fit in with what has been said, but it comes as a result of a long study on another proposition which I started back in 1930, before I got here, on the problem of shocking our country out of depression with a works program, the whole success of that program hinged and depended upon getting continuity of understanding into it, and that we failed to get in 1933, so it cost us more in the long run. We did an awful lot of experimenting; we didn't get industry geared to a program, and if we do not get the people of Europe thinking about the year after next right now, this program is going to bog down every year that it occurs. So that I hope when Senator Vandenberg pleads for his appropriation, he will emphasize with all the zeal he has, and with all the understanding he has, the importance of putting the continuity in this program in the first part of this paragraph.

That may be neglected, Mr. Chairman, because somebody will want to dodge that issue of inviting some oratory about not being able to bind future Congresses. But I think that if we get over to the country the idea of continuity—we held hearings after I came down here on it, and we became convinced that we had made mistakes, after 3 or 4 years. But we do not want to wait 3 or 4 years in this program to prove to ourselves that we made mistakes.

The CHAIRMAN. The best proof that I agree with you is the fact that these identical words in italics, in line 23, were put in at my instance.

Senator THOMAS of Utah. I think, sir, that if you are going to say anything to the press, if we decide on cutting this, that you ought to suggest to them that they read the whole paragraph.

The CHAIRMAN. Oh, yes.

Senator BARKLEY. After the discussion has gone around the table, I am prepared to move myself, that we accept the proposition of 1 year with $5,350 million.

The CHAIRMAN. Make it $5,300 million. That is the relative figure to $6,800 million.

Senator BARKLEY. All right. I make it $5,300 million and I think that it will be wholesome if we have a vote on it, if it shows a unanimous vote, that there is no partisanship, no division here along political lines on this agreement. I am ready to defend it against all comers, so far as I am concerned.

Senator THOMAS of Utah. I second the motion.

REQUEST FOR A VOTE POSTPONEMENT

Senator WILEY. Well, Mr. Chairman, I had hoped that the matter would go over to Tuesday, the vote. I am frank to say that the 1 year, the way you have set it up, and the arguments that have been made, have been very, very persuasive, but I have been thinking in terms of dollars in the amount of 10 billion, and I have been thinking in terms of what its effect it would be in relation to our own economy here from the standpoint of prices and inflation, and I personally would appreciate it if you could let the matter go over until Tuesday. I want

85-743—73——20

to give it real earnest consideration. I reiterate what I said twice before. Senator George mentioned the figure. I hope that somehow or other we could recapture, without taking money out from the program one might say, funds from some of these organizations that would make this a smaller amount. I want to give a little thought to that. And so I am just as sincere in my desire to do what I think is the right thing, in view of our own country and Europe, as are any of you.

Senator GEORGE. Of course, Mr. Chairman, if Senator Wiley or anyone wants to have the matter go over, it is certainly agreeable with me, but if it does go over, I rather think it might be wise not to disclose the exact proposal that we have in mind.

The CHAIRMAN. That is the problem that we will confront.

Senator BARKLEY. I would not want to insist on a vote tonight if any Senator feels that in justice to himself it ought to go over, but there is that difficulty which Senator George mentioned.

The CHAIRMAN. I was going to ask you about that. There is no way in the world that you can prevent this from going out, and the question is whether I should not very frankly tell the press, just for myself, what proposition I have submitted.

The difficulty with that is that, of course, by Tuesday everybody who is opposed to the bill as a whole, will have found marvelous reasons why this particular thing—and the better it is the more marvelous their reasons will be why it is lousy—should be tossed out the window. So that we do confront some difficulty with that phase of the problem, and I don't quite know what to do about it.

Senator WILEY. Was it understood that you were going to decide definitely today the amount and the item, as well as the final bill, or anything?

The CHAIRMAN. There was no understanding, Senator Wiley, except the general suggestion that we were going to finish up our preliminary tentative survey of the bill tonight, and have a clean print for the consideration of the full committee next Tuesday.

Senator SMITH. You are not planning to meet on Monday?

The CHAIRMAN. No; because I want to wait until Senator Hickenlooper is back.

Senator WILEY. Will Senator Connally be back then, too?

Senator GEORGE. He will be here Monday, I think.

The CHAIRMAN. I will have to make some explanation to the press as to what has happened, and I suppose the net result will be plenty of conjectures as to how we are split between the ears and so forth, which is part of life.

Senator GEORGE. You can very well say that this was still open, but somebody will get hold of it and publish it.

The CHAIRMAN. My phone will start ringing about 6:30.

Senator GEORGE. Would you be prepared to vote Senator Capper?

The CHAIRMAN. I would be prepared to vote Senator White and Senator Hickenlooper.

Senator WILEY. You had better see if Capper is in. I do not want to be a stumbling block.

The CHAIRMAN. I want to respect anything, Senator Wiley, that you feel serious about.

Senator WILEY. I feel very seriously about it, but I have tried enough lawsuits to know that any jury, if it is going to agree, has to take into consideration the judgment of the other associate members. Still Senator Capper is not here. You have not got his vote. Senator Connally is not here. Of course, that can be voted by proxy, I take it. You cannot in our committee. You do not have your full committee.

The CHAIRMAN. I am not arguing with you about this. I think we can vote the full committee, including Senator Capper, by getting hold of him on the phone.

Senator GEORGE. I can vote Senator Connally on this. I am sure he would vote for it.

Senator WILEY. See if Senator Capper is in, will you?

Senator BARKLEY. I am authorized to vote Senator Wagner.

Ambassador DOUGLAS. I presume if the committee takes the action to reduce the period of time and the amount to $5,300 million the report will be very strong on the point of the period of time.

The CHAIRMAN. Oh, certainly, but you haven't any guarantee whatever that you are not going to have your throat cut from ear-to-ear on this thing regardless of what we do here.

Ambassador DOUGLAS. I have a reasonable expectancy.

(Discussion was continued off the record.)

The CHAIRMAN. What is the wish of the committee? The Senator from Kentucky has made the motion. Senator Wiley has indicated, if I understand him, that he is prepared to let the thing go to a vote under the circumstances. Is that correct, Senator Wiley?

MATHEMATICS OF THE CHANGE

Senator WILEY. Would you mind waiting just a moment? I am trying to get some mathematics here.

The figure that you gave of $9,333 million of foreign aid consisted of European recovery, $6,800 million. That has been reduced to $1,500 million, apparently, in the bill, so that makes the [illegible]lance of the foreign aid $7,833 million, including $1,400 million f[illegible]overnment relief in occupied areas; Philippine war damage; reh[illegible]tation and veterans' benefits $133 million; and other foreign aid, including China, $750 million.

If my mathematics is right, that make a total of $7,833 million.

Senator SMITH. To what date for the whole business?

Senator WILEY. I am just taking the sheet in front of me.

Ambassador DOUGLAS. This is to cover expenditures and obligations in the fiscal year 1948 and 1949.

Senator BARKLEY. That will be the period ending June 30, 1949.

Senator SMITH. That is counting this as $6,800 million.

Senator BARKLEY. Senator Wiley, you knocked $1½ billion off.

Senator WILEY. Not according to the talk around the table, but it gives a little different complexion and, Mr. Chairman, if everyone else feels that he has arrived at a position where he can say "Aye" to your seductive influence, I can also.

The CHAIRMAN. The clerk will call the roll.

The CLERK. Mr. Capper.

The CHAIRMAN. Aye.

The CLERK. Mr. White.

The CHAIRMAN. Aye.

The CLERK. Mr. Wiley.

Senator WILEY. Aye.
The CLERK. Mr. Smith.
Senator SMITH. Aye.
The CLERK. Mr. Hickenlooper.
The CHAIRMAN. Aye.
The CLERK. Mr. Lodge.
Senator LODGE. Aye.
The CLERK. Mr. Connally.
Senator GEORGE. Aye.
The CLERK. Mr. George.
Senator GEORGE. Aye.
The CLERK. Mr. Wagner.
Senator BARKLEY. Aye
The CLERK. Mr. Thomas.
Senator THOMAS of Utah. Aye.
The CLERK. Mr. Barkley.
Senator BARKLEY. Aye.
The CLERK. Mr. Hatch.
Senator HATCH. Aye.
The CLERK. Mr. Chairman.
The CHAIRMAN. Aye.
The CLERK. Yes, 13; no, none.
The CHAIRMAN. Now, are there some tag ends here that have got to cleaned up before we can print?

AN AMENDMENT ON AGRICULTURE PRODUCTS

Senator BARKLEY. Mr. Chairman, I wanted to offer—and maybe I had better do it now; I discussed it yesterday—an amendment which has been prepared by Mr. Rice, which relates to the procurement of agricultural prod[illegible] in the United States, without mentioning any particular prod[illegible] [illegible]eads as follows, and would come on page 18, after line 18:

> *Provided further*, That in the procurement of any agricultural commodity under this Act for transfer by grant to participating countries the Administrator shall, in so far as practicable, provide for the procurement of an amount of each class or type of such commodity which bears the same proportion to the total amount of such commodities as shall be procured as the available United States supply of such type or class bears to the available United States supply of such commodity.

That is intended to direct him to purchase, out of surpluses of agricultural products, the type and class which he is supposed to purchase for use as grants to these participating recipient countries. It would emphasize the desire to exhaust surpluses where they exist.

That might have a bearing on the cotton situation. It might have a bearing—it would have a bearing—on the tobacco situation, and it might have a bearing on probably half a dozen other agricultural products. And it seems to me that inasmuch as we are providing for certain grants in this bill that there ought to be emphasis put on the use of surpluses.

Senator WILEY. In the hands of the Government?
Senator BARKLEY. Any surpluses that would exist.
Senator WILEY. Would it include that?
Senator BARKLEY. It would include that, yes.

A PRACTICAL ILLUSTRATION: TOBACCO

Senator LODGE. Could you give a practical illustration?

Senator BARKLEY. I can give you an illustration in a commodity that I am more familiar with than any other. That is tobacco.

There is to be used, as part of this program, for incentive purposes, the purchase of certain quantities of tobacco to go into Germany and these other countries for the manufacture of cigarettes, smoking and chewing tobacco, which they need and which they require, to stimulate their morale in working. Prior to this last war many of those countries preferred a Turkish type of cigarette and of tobacco, but they have been educated to the use of a blended type of tobacco, both in cigarettes and cigars and in smoking and it is, of course, hoped, to be perfectly frank about it, that due to that change in taste, there will be hereafter a market for American tobacco, and if there is any other commodity that comes in the same category, that it would be a stimulation to our markets over there; that long after this program is over there would be an increased market for our product.

Years ago there was an enormous amount of tobacco exported to Europe. The Government raises about $1,200 million in revenue now out of tobacco taxes. Great Britain raises about $2,000 million in revenue for her Government out of tobacco. Italy raises about 30 percent of her total Government income out of tobacco.

In view of the enormous tax levied on tobacco and tobacco products, it is felt that wherever they purchase this commodity, and I think it is $250 million to be used for that purpose over the period, that they use the surplus that is in existence, part of which is in the hands of the Government through the Commodity Credit Corporation, where they made loans to facilitate the export of the product to foreign countries; that where they have to buy tobacco, they buy that surplus; that where they buy that product they buy the surplus before they go out into the market and by types of which there is no surplus.

This would be an example of how it would work. Let's say the Administrator buys 50 pounds of tobacco of all types. There are 63 types of tobacco in the United States, maybe close to 70 now. They have undergone a regrading process. But out of the total number of types the available supply of type 21, which is a dark-fired tobacco which used to be used in Europe very extensively, is 5 pounds. The Administrator in buying it would buy five one-hundredths of 5 pounds, or 2½ pounds out of 50 pounds. That may be a complicated explanation, but the simplified object of it is to concentrate the purchase of this commodity on surplus types that are in existence and have been surplus for a long time.

I am frank to say that the tobacco growers of my State and other States are interested in this thing. They feel that if we are going to buy tobacco, which seems to be essential and which is part of the programs for incentive purposes in Europe, that preference ought to be given to these types that are in surplus.

Senator LODGE. These are not necessarily the types for which there is the greatest demand in Europe?

Senator BARKLEY. It would not be expected that any type would be imposed upon them that they did not want. In Great Britain they have always upon the Flue-cured tobacco, grown in North Carolina and some parts of Virginia. Their taste has undergone no change as a result of the war. They still want that type. They would get it. It so happens there is not the surplus of that that there is in these other types. It would not be expected that any type would be imposed upon any country against its own wishes, and the fact of the business is the Administrator, up to now, over in Germany, for instance, has consulted the industry in Germany and in Austria, and under the interim aid program in France and Italy, under which about 10 million pounds have been sent over, in order to stimulate those people to work by reason of the fact that they cannot get something to smoke and something that they desire to smoke. It is a psychological situation which exists in this country, as well as over there.

Senator LODGE. This will not cost the U.S.Treasury any more?

The CHAIRMAN. What have you to say about this, Mr. Ambassador?

WRITING THE LANGUAGE IN THE REPORT

Ambassador DOUGLAS. I was going to ask the Senator whether it would be satisfactory to him if language to this effect were written into the report.

Senator BARKLEY. This is what happened in the interim bill. It was written into the report. But unfortunately only one type of tobacco has been sent over there under the interim bill, and the report did not seem to have much effect.

Senator GEORGE. What Senator Barkley is aiming at undoubtedly ought to be done.

Senator BARKLEY. It is very flexible.

EQUITABLE DISTRIBUTION OF FARM COMMODITIES

Senator GEORGE. All he is seeking to do is to have an equitable distribution in the purchase of various farm commodities as between different types—an equitable distribution of purchases when made.

Senator WILEY. It is a direction? Is it mandatory?

Senator GEORGE. You have the same thing in cotton. You have various grades of cotton. Some mills can't use certain grades; some can use any grade.

Senator BARKLEY. But everything being equal, and it being practical and in harmony with the needs of the particular country, there ought to be emphasis on the sale of surpluses.

Senator GEORGE. I do not think you can quarrel with the purpose of it. The only thing in the world is whether or not they could administer it. You see, they go out to buy cotton or tobacco. They will probably buy in running bale lots, and they will take all kinds of grades and staples.

Senator BARKLEY. The Administrator will take into consideration the needs of each country.

Senator GEORGE. He ought to do that anyway, without anything being in the law.

Senator BARKLEY. This amendment has been made necessary, apparently, because there has been discrimination in the administration of the interim aid bill.

Senator LODGE. Couldn't this result in the piling up of a lot of stuff overseas that nobody wanted to use?

Senator BARKLEY. No, because they would send it overseas unless they wanted it.

Senator LODGE. I know under UNRRA, when you go to Athens, you see all these American olives there. They wouldn't eat them.

TYPES OF TOBACCO

Senator BARKLEY. There are all types of tobacco. Some of them want smoking tobacco, some cigarette, some cigar tobacco, and snuff. Some of them have their own factories in which they want to produce these things, which gives employment to people. But there is an incentive. This is really an incentive program anyhow, in a sense, so far as these things may be looked upon as luxuries and not absolute necessities. But to the fellow who uses them and has been in the habit of using them, and whose morale is stimulated by being able to get them, it is a necessity in a real sense.

Senator GEORGE. Mr. Duke gave away millions and millions of packages of cigarettes at the end of the First World War, in order to stimulate the trade, and it made him.

Senator HATCH. Would this be agreeable: "* * * shall, insofar as practicable, in consideration of the requirements of participating countries * * *" I think it would make clear what you have said.

Senator BARKLEY. I have no objection to the language.

Senator GEORGE. That would be all right. The one objection that could arise would be in the distribution of the product after it arrives there. It arrives in bulk, say, or in large shipments; but in the case of tobacco, pretty nearly any country will use the tobacco furnished them, of types and so forth. There may be some where they have a built-up trade, like England has, with the Herbert Tarryton and Pall Mall, where they use the Flue-cured tobacco with very little Turkish.

Senator HATCH. Senator Gorge, did you hear the suggestion I made?

Senator GEORGE. Yes. That is all right. I do not believe that is going to be troublesome at all, and I don't know that it will be too troublesome for the Administrator to say that he is shipping you over so many hogshead of tobacco; some is the burley type, some is the bright-leaf type, and some is the Maryland type and something else: now distribute this to the needs of the country according to the needs and useage in the countries who have made application for it.

Ambassador DOUGLAS. It seems to me that that is going to be difficult administratively.

Senator GEORGE. It would be a little difficult at that end, and here in procuring it it might be slightly difficult, but not too difficult.

Senator BARKLEY. Take in this particular product. Here is an agricultural product that is taxed heavier than any other product or any combination of products. The amount of tax that goes into the Treasury amounts to $1,000 an acre on every acre of tobacco manufactured into cigarettes. All sections that grow it have to bear this burden, not only of the taxation that you put upon them but the taxation out of which we are getting this money that we are sending over. It seems that to require that some preference be given to existing surpluses in this country is not an unreasonable request.

Senator GEORGE. I don't believe there would be any great difficulties indicated in the case of tobacco. It comes in hogsheads and it is packed that way for all purposes. If there has been any discrimination in it, in the purchase, Senator Barkley, I will join you in trying to put something in here.

COTTON

Now, so far as cotton goes, it does not so much matter with cotton, because if they can take *x* number of bales of cotton out of this country, our mills are equipped to use almost any sort of cotton, so while they prefer certain grades of staple length and so forth, when you reduce the water in the pail then you have a better market for what you have left, anyway.

Senator BARKLEY. This would help facilitate the disposition of tobacco that is in the hands of the Commodity Credit Corporation and in the hands of farmers' cooperatives which are holding it under the Government's price support program, so it would relieve, really, the Government of a burden.

Senator WILEY. Get it out, but don't complicate the administration.

Senator GEORGE. I do not think it would seriously complicate it, when you consider how it is packed for shipment abroad. It is all packed in a certain way and has to be.

Senator BARKLEY. It is all packed and labeled and sent over in hogsheads. They won't have to go into the hogsheads.

The CHAIRMAN. Are you agreed on this thing?

Senator BARKLEY. Senator Hatch's language is agreeable to me. He might read it.

Senator HATCH. I am not insisting on it. It was just in accordance with what Senator Barkley said. Add after the word "practicable" the following: "in consideration of the requirements of the participating country, provide for the procurement . . .".

Senator LODGE. That is what I have in mind.

I have two questions, and I think you have answered them both. The first is, is it going to cost any more?

Senator GEORGE. No; I don't think so.

Senator LODGE. Second, I don't want to pile up a lot of damned stuff all over the world that nobody wants.

COMMODITIES SHIPPED ONLY TO NEEDING COUNTRIES

Senator BARKLEY. They would only ship it over as the countries need it and require it, and that would probably be determined by the agency in Europe, in the various countries.

Senator WILEY. Is there any chance, Senator Barkley, in a lot of things such as you speak about, that are in surplus, that we can get a little inside price and save a little money? Then it means so much more available to do the job.

Senator BARKLEY. This only applies to where this is being sent as grants. It does not apply at all to where it is being sold.

Senator GEORGE. You have a good deal of tobacco in the Connecticut valley, and they might not buy any tobacco unless they did have this provision. That is a wrapper tobacco.

The CHAIRMAN. Without objection, the amendment will be adopted.

THE CCC AMENDMENT

Now I want to ask you about the famous CCC amendment; that is, the amendment that is in the interim aid bill. You will remember that that is the one that was most enthusiastically received of all parts of the bill upon the Senate floor reading as follows:

> Notwithstanding any other provision of law, any commodity heretofore or hereafter acquired by any agency of the Government under any price-support programs shall, to the extent that such commodity is determined by the President to be appropriate for such purpose and in excess of domestic requirements, be utilized in providing aid under this Act or any other Act providing for assistance and relief to foreign countries, and shall be disposed of by such agency for such purpose at such price as may be determined by such agency, which price may be the equivalent of the domestic market price of a quantity of wheat having a caloric value equal to that of the quantity of the commodity so disposed of. Any such agency shall report to the Congress on, ———— or as soon as practicable thereafter, the amount of losses incurred by it as the result of the disposition of commodities hereunder and the Secretary of the Treasury is authorized and directed to cancel notes of such agency held by him in an amount equal to the amount of such losses.

This is simply the provision which permitted the substitution of other foods on a caloric basis when they are held by the CCC and are in surplus. You remember this. Everybody was for it. It provides a way to use CCC commodity surpluses which otherwise might be a loss. I think it would be very smart to put it in the bill. Is there any objection that you know of, Mr. Nitze?

OBJECTION BY THE DEPARTMENT OF AGRICULTURE

Mr. Nitze. I think there is some objection on the part of the Department of Agriculture to the provision. The losses which the Commodity Credit Corporation might take might be very substantial in a program of this magnitude. As I remember it, the Appropriations Committee, in connection with foreign aid——

The Chairman. We will leave that to be offered on the floor.

Is there anything else?

THE QUESTION OF LOANS

Senator Wiley. I would like to get into the record, if I may, to see if the judgment of the experts here is any different from what it was at the hearing. You remember that it was testified there that they estimated that the amount of loans would range from 20 to 40 percent of the amount appropriated. In view of the recent developments in Europe, where they claim that there has been quite an upsurge in the economic stability of France and other countries, that they are getting now close to the top of prewar level in manufacturing and so forth, I was wondering if there was any further testimony that could be gotten into the record on that spot. In other words, if they said 30 percent, you would have $1,500 million in loans out of your $5,300 million, and the rest would be grants.

The Chairman. I do not think there are any new figures, Senator Wiley, and the figures of 20 to 40 percent we have been repeatedly warned are very tentative.

Senator WILEY. I realize that.

The CHAIRMAN. The maximum emphasis is going to be put upon loans.

Senator LODGE. There is a lot in the record, is there not, when it comes to furnishing money for hydroelectric machinery and that stuff, which will be a loan? It is correct to believe that that will be self-liquidating when it comes to power development and major works?

The CHAIRMAN. You mean loans that will be paid back? Yes, I do not think there is any doubt about that.

Senator WILEY. He is in favor of those loans.

The CHAIRMAN. Yes, sir.

Is there anything else?

Senator GEORGE. Mr. Chairman, why don't we grant you the authority of the committee and the experts to make any needful changes here in order to correct errors that are obvious errors, or supply omissions or anything from our substance, because you bring it back to us anyhow.

PRINT OF BILL AVAILABLE MONDAY

The CHAIRMAN. Without objection, that will be done. We will have a print of the bill available Monday morning, is that correct?

Dr. WILCOX. That is correct.

The CHAIRMAN. It will be circulated to your offices on Monday morning, and the committee will meet Tuesday at 10 o'clock.

Ambassador DOUGLAS. On your amendment, Senator Barkley, I was wondering whether you would be willing to use the language "shall consider," rather than "shall, inso far as possible."

Senator BARKLEY. I would rather not have it that way. I will talk to you about it.

The CHAIRMAN. All right. I am authorized to correct anything that needs correction. I will attend to that.

I am very grateful to all of you, I will tell you that, for standing by. We have just got nicely started.

Senator LODGE. I want to thank the staff and the State Department for having been so accommodating.

(Whereupon, at 5:30 p.m., a recess was taken until Tuesday, February 17, 1948, at 10 a.m.)

EUROPEAN RECOVERY PROGRAM

TUESDAY, FEBRUARY 17, 1948

UNITED STATES SENATE,
COMMITTEE ON FOREIGN RELATIONS,
Washington, D.C.

The committee met, pursuant to adjournment, in the committee hearing room, U.S. Capitol, at 10 a.m., Senator Arthur H. Vandenberg, chairman, presiding.

Present: Senators Vandenberg, Capper, Wiley, Smith, Hickenlooper, Lodge, Connally, George, Thomas of Utah, and Barkley.

Also present: Senator Millikin; the Honorable Lewis W. Douglas, Ambassador to Great Britain; Mr. Paul Nitze, Deputy Director, Office of International Trade Policy, Department of State; Mr. Ernest Gross, legal adviser, Department of State; Mr. Stephen E. Rice, legislative counsel, U.S. Senate.

The CHAIRMAN. Gentlemen, Senator Millikin, the chairman of the Senate Finance Committee, is here to present a requested amendment. Senator Millikin, we will be very glad to hear from you.

FISCAL PICTURE

Senator MILLIKIN. Senator Vandenberg and gentlemen, it is very clear to me that when you get through with this bill, and when the additional requests come in for other foreign aid, such as for China and for Korea and Greece and Turkey, and possibly something for South America before we are finished, we are going to have an enormous burden in 1 fiscal year on account of foreign affairs. In addition to that, there is a very strong sentiment in the Senate for tax reduction. There is a very strong sentiment in the Senate for increasing the appropriation for our Air Forces, and when you consider all of those things it is apparent that if we go out full strength on all of these things, we are getting into a very dubious fiscal picture; that if we do not, then each project commences to cannibalize the other.

So far as your project here is concerned, there might be some opinion that other things are, let us say, equally important, and in the consideration of this matter the proponents for the other projects will be carrying figures in their minds in connection with your figures.

What I am driving at, in a word, is that I am thinking of some kind of plan that will keep this plan from cannibalizing other legitimate projects, and to keep other legitimate projects from cannibalizing this plan.

In this fiscal year, we will have a surplus estimated by the Treasury Act at 7½ billion; estimated by the Joint Committee on Internal Revenue Taxation at some $8 billion. In the next fiscal year, we will have a surplus estimated by the Treasury at $4,800 million, and estimated by the Joint Internal Revenue Committee of some $2,800 million in addition.

Senator CONNALLY. In addition to the $4 billion?

Senator MILLIKIN. In addition to the $4 billion; in other words, $7 billion plus.

But taking any of the figures that you wish, or compromise between them, and when you figure what the impact will be of this plan and of other plans in the Senate, you are imposing an extraordinarily heavy burden upon 1 fiscal year; to wit, the fiscal year 1949.

My suggestion, in brief, is that since we have the assurance of a very large surplus in 1948—to wit, $7½ billion under one set of figures and more than $8 billion under another—that fiscal 1948 should bear a part of the burden.

The technique for accomplishing it which I suggest is that in this bill, you direct an authorization and appropriation for fiscal 1948 of *x* amount of dollars to be taken out of the surplus of fiscal 1948 and put into a trust fund available for expenditure under whatever your mechanics may be for expenditure in fiscal 1949. There is ample precedent for that kind of procedure. The law provides, for example, that in connection with social security, the Congress appropriates each year an amount equivalent to the receipts which are received from payroll taxes, and that is appropriated out of the Treasury to the trust fund in social security, and it becomes an expenditure when that transfer is made by the Treasury to the trust fund.

Senator BARKLEY. In that case, Congress required the enactment of a law covering the transfer of that specific figure.

Senator MILLIKIN. I am coming to that.

Then the managing director of the trust fund, who is the Secretary of the Treasury, may invest the funds so credited to that trust fund in a stated list of Government securities, so as a matter of practice the trust fund then purchases a special type of bond from the Treasury, with the result that the amount remains in the Treasury available for debt retirement or for other purposes.

When we passed the terminal leave bonds, when we authorized that, we did not provide for any accounting procedure, so the Treasury counted that an expenditure when the bonds were issued, rather than when they were paid, which meets the same principle.

In connection with Government corporations, whenever we set up a Government corporation and either buy capital stock or make loans or advances to it, that becomes an expenditure when made, not when the money is ultimately spent.

Those three precedents occur to me as warranting this kind of procedure.

MAKING AVAILABLE THIS YEAR'S SURPLUS DOLLARS

Personally, I would suggest that from $3 to 4 billion of the surplus of this year be made available for that purpose. That would leave, so far as I know, sufficient revenue for the Treasury to retire indebtedness in accordance with at least the viewpoint of the Senate, and considerably more because the Treasury retires indebtedness out of its general fund, part of which is accumulated in the way that I mentioned in connection with social security.

That, in a word, is what I have to suggest. When I was a young fellow, I worked in a grocery store, and we had about five bins of 17½-cent coffee. One was called Maid of Aran, one Hiawatha, and one something else, and they were all there, and the ladies used to come in and get into hair-pulling contests over which was the best grade of coffee, and we filled them all out of the same sack.

We have to meet these expenses out of the same sack. You have got the money in fiscal 1948. I am simply suggesting that we use a part of it to meet the extraordinary financial burden of fiscal 1949.

The CHAIRMAN. Have you a proposed text of an amendment to accomplish that purpose? I would not expect you to come unarmed.

Senator CONNALLY. Which brand of coffee is this?

Senator MILLIKIN. This is rough, and I would like the privilege of cleaning it up. It is on the assumption of an earlier committee print. I do not know what you have before you now. At some appropriate place——

Senator BARKLEY. If any.

Senator MILLIKIN [continuing]. Insert this proposed subsection:

> In order to reserve some part of the surplus of fiscal year 1948 for the payments under European Recovery Program to be made in fiscal 1949, there is hereby created on the books of the Treasury of the United States a trust fund to be known as the Foreign Economic Cooperation Trust Fund.

The name is not important.

> The Secretary of the Treasury shall be the sole trustee of the trust fund. Notwithstanding any other provision of law, an amount of —————— billion dollars appropriated pursuant to the authorization contained in this Act for expenditures to be made in the fiscal year 1949 shall, when appropriated, be transferred immediately to the trust fund, and shall thereupon be considered as expended during the fiscal year 1948 for the purpose of reporting government expenditures. The first expenditures made under this Act in the fiscal year 1949 shall be charged against the trust fund until the credit balance in such fund is exhausted. The provisions of the subsection shall not be construed as affecting the application of any provision of law which would otherwise govern the obligation of amounts so appropriated or the auditing or submission of accounts of transactions with respect to such amounts.

The CHAIRMAN. When you refer to the first expenditure in fiscal 1949, you probably mean it would start with the first expenditure after this act.

Senator CONNALLY. He said that. He said, "The first expenditures under this act."

Senator MILLIKIN. "Appropriated pursuant to the authorization contained in this act for expenditures to be made in the fiscal year 1949 shall, when appropriated * * *."

The CHAIRMAN. You mean the first expenditures made after the passage of this act, because the expenditures start ahead of fiscal 1949. That is the point I am making.

Senator MILLIKIN. This is drawn so that the expenditures of fiscal 1949 contemplated by your act shall come out of the trust fund set up in fiscal 1948.

The CHAIRMAN. OK.

AMOUNT TO BE TAKEN FROM FISCAL 1948 SURPLUS

Now, I understand that the figure you suggest should be inserted is what?

Senator MILLIKIN. Some place between $3 and $4 billion, and the reason I have not suggested an exact figure is because I do not know what the exact plans of the Treasury are so far as debt retirement and its other fiscal operations are concerned, nor do I know exactly how much you gentlemen intend to take out of fiscal 1948. If I knew those two things, I could give you an exact figure, but I estimate it some place between $3 and $4 billion, because taking that out of your surplus for 1948, you would have obviously a reasonable amount for debt retirement and some margin for taking care of anything that might yet happen in fiscal 1948.

Senator SMITH. And the difference between that amount and the total would be in fiscal 1949. If we took $4 billion out of fiscal 1948, then under our figures of $5,300 million, there would be $1,300 million for 1949.

Senator MILLIKIN. Whatever part of your plan here is to come out of fiscal 1949, the first expenditures would come out of this trust fund created in 1948 for use in 1949 until the amount of the trust fund has been exhausted.

AUTHORIZATION DIVIDED IN TWO PARTS

Senator SMITH. I understand that. But if I get your meaning correctly, you want us to divide our overall authorization into two parts, one part being fiscal 1948, which may be somewhere between $3 and $4 billion, and the other part being fiscal 1949, which is the difference. Is that correct?

Senator MILLIKIN. That is not exactly correct. I am simply suggesting that once you have completed whatever your plan may be here, you will have expenditures for fiscal 1949. I am suggesting that a certain amount of surplus in fiscal 1948 be put in trust to take care of your expenditures in fiscal 1949.

The CHAIRMAN. The net of it is what Senator Smith is indicating.

Senator BARKLEY. What it really does, then, assuming that we agree on the $5,300 million, and it begins on the 1st of April, is to provide that four-fifths of this entire sum shall be construed to have been expended within the 3 months from the 1st of April to the 1st of July, when it will not have been spent for this purpose, and maybe none of it will. What is the reason for this?

Senator MILLIKIN. The reason, as I have said before, if you do not do this, you are taking this and all the other claims against the revenue for 1949, and you are bogging down your fiscal situation for 1949, and from the standpoint of this plan I think that your plan will meet the attack of everyone who believes that other things are perhaps equally important.

Senator BARKLEY. You say we bog down the fiscal system. Of course, if this $7 billion plus revenue, this surplus, exists on July 1, whatever is not devoted to debt retirement will go over into the next fiscal year and be available in that year.

Senator MILLIKIN. This is a method of assuring that some part of the surplus will actually go over. That is exactly the purpose of it.

Senator BARKLEY. On the books, not much of it will go over.

Senator MILLIKIN. There is no assurance that the surplus of fiscal 1948 would go over into fiscal 1949 unless you take some affirmative action on it.

Senator BARKLEY. It would go over unless all of it were voted to debt retirement.

Senator MILLIKIN. Or for other expenditures that might be authorized for fiscal 1948.

Senator LODGE. What would happen to these funds that you plan to set up in trust, if you did not set them up in trust?

Senator MILLIKIN. If you did not set them up in trust the funds which would otherwise be set up in trust will follow whatever course the Treasury may dictate between now and the end of fiscal 1948. Let's assume that they would use the whole fund for debt retirement.

Senator LODGE. Can they do it?

Senator MILLIKIN. They can do it, and they then would have no surplus to carry over into fiscal 1949.

A DEVICE TO CREATE A BIGGER 1949 SURPLUS

Senator BARKLEY. As a matter of fact, Senator—just all of us letting our hair down—this is a device to create a bigger surplus for 1949 as a basis for a larger tax reduction; is it not?

Senator MILLIKIN. That is one of the purposes. That clearly is one of the purposes. It is also to create a larger surplus for ERP. It is also to create larger surpluses for any other projects that may be in the Senate that are considered important.

Senator BARKLEY. That is a little unusual procedure, in order to create a larger surplus in a given year than actually exists.

Senator MILLIKIN. I come back to the point that it is all out of the same bag, and we are piling up an extraordinary number of projects—this, plus your supplementals which the President is about to come in for, for other foreign aid, plus the suggestion which I made that when you finish with your next hemispheric conference you will undoubtedly have some more help to give to South America, plus all of these other things. I believe that this is a practical way to aid you in the solution of this immediate problem, and I would be less than candid if I did not say that I hope also it would aid us in our tax reduction program.

Senator CONNALLY. What effect, if any, do you think this would have on the bitter enders that are against the whole plan? Would they not attack it as a sort of artificial device?

Senator MILLIKIN. I can see at once that it would mitigate any argument that they might make that we cannot afford it.

Senator BARKLEY. I ask you if your mitigation process applies to you as chairman of the Committee on Finance, if this committee should adopt this amendment.

Will it have a mitigating effect upon your attitude?

Senator MILLIKIN. If this committee should adopt this amendment, I think that lots of ice in my system would warm and melt.

Senator BARKLEY. Almost thou persuadest me!

Senator CONNALLY. He didn't say all of it; he said lots of it.

Senator BARKLEY. It is hard for me to think of you as having ice in your veins anyway.

Senator MILLIKIN. Thank you, Senator.

The CHAIRMAN. I think we might supplement what Senator Millikin said in response to Senator Barkley's last question, which is a very practical question.

Joining Senator Millikin in this request is Senator Bridges, the chairman of the Senate Appropriations Committee, and he feels very deeply as Senator Millikin does about the desirability and necessity of this move, and while I certainly am not authorized to make the remotest kind of commitment for him in connection with the net result, I think it might melt some of the ice in his veins too, if I might use Senator Millikin's metaphor.

Senator MILLIKIN. I think it is perfectly obvious, gentlemen, that it will certainly soften the complaints of those who have other things in mind and other projects in which they are interested, that this project is hogging up all of the surplus of the next fiscal year. I don't see how it can help but have that effect.

[Discussion was continued off the record.]

EARMARKING SURPLUS FOR NEXT YEAR'S EXPENDITURE

Senator HICKENLOOPER. I take it your philosophy is about this, that if you were running a business that was to have a rather substantial expenditure next year and you were running a surplus now, you would sort of earmark part of that surplus now to take care of that substantial expenditure next year.

Senator MILLIKIN. Exactly. I have quite a few pennies in this pocket; I have some larger money in this. If I haven't enough in either pocket, I reach into one pocket to put it into the other. I think everybody with very good sense does the same thing.

Senator CONNALLY. Part of this, of course, is to prevent the Treasury, if it should be so disposed, from making other use of the surplus.

Senator MILLIKIN. It would have the effect, to the amount of the sum that you insert, of limiting the freedom of the Treasury.

Senator BARKLEY. The Treasury has no freedom except as Congress appropriates the money, except to retire the debt.

Senator MILLIKIN. That is right.

I am a little bit off my alley now, but I do not believe that the Treasury is quite as keen, under the present circumstances, for this enormously rapid retirement of debt as it has been in the past.

I think that most everyone concludes now that any device to contract credit is a highly explosive thing, and perhaps the Treasury might not feel as violently opposed to something of this kind as it would have, say, 6 months ago, or a year ago.

The CHAIRMAN. I would like to hear Senator George's comment on this matter. He is the ranking member of the Senate Finance Committee on the minority side.

THE TREASURY WOULD HAVE OBJECTIONS

Senator GEORGE. Mr. Chairman, I should imagine the Treasury would have certain objections to it. They might be budgetary, or they might regard it as a complicating factor in their fiscal policy. Basically, I would not be influenced by that view to oppose Senator Millikin's suggestion. That is, personally, I would have no objection to it. I can see that there is a certain advantage in saying that here is a definite plan and almost fixed balance for this present fiscal year; it cannot vary much from $7.5 billion already estimated. It may be increased slightly. It might be decreased by some other charges against it. So that out of that, if we want to take $3 billion and make it an expenditure against the 1948 surplus, but carry it over as a trust item under the control of the Secretary for the purpose of the administration of this act, I cannot see any special objection to it. I would not be disposed to offer any objection. If the Treasury wished to formally state its position, of course, it should have a right to do so. I do not know the Treasury's position. I have not talked with the Treasury about it. I would think the Treasury would have some objection, based upon budgetary considerations and especially the arrangement of their fiscal programs for 1949 and, maybe 1950, for the year after 1949. But I do not see that it basically alters your essential facts.

The CHAIRMAN. We confront some problems as well as the Treasury in connection with this legislation.

Senator GEORGE. Yes, sir. I think we do, and I think we confront more and more every morning. If we do not hurry up and get through with this I will be against it. You had better let us get through.

The CHAIRMAN. Senator Connally, what have you to say?

Senator CONNALLY. I do not think I would object to it. I have not heard the Treasury's objection. I assume they would have some objection, because it is a variance from their customary processes and ordinary methods, and they do not like to have that happen.

Senator GEORGE. May I ask, Mr. Chairman, a question? Senator Millikin, would you desire that it go in the bill, or would you be satisfied and content with committee action on it and the privilege to offer it on the floor?

Senator MILLIKIN. I would like to have it in the bill as committee action. I think it would be most helpful from the standpoint of the bill.

Senator GEORGE. I believe it would be somewhat helpful so far as the practical consideration of this bill on the floor is concerned. I can see how it might.

Senator MILLIKIN. If I may suggest, I think you have done some very wise things: first, in getting rid of your ultimate amount; second, in condensing this first period of expenditure to a year. All of those things are operating in the same direction that this proposed amendment operates in.

The CHAIRMAN. Senator Connally, do you have something further you want to say?

Senator CONNALLY. Yes. Of course, basically it is just changing the money from one pocket to another. This surplus of 1948 will be here to go over to 1949 unless it is applied to debt retirement.

Senator MILLIKIN. That is right; but we have no way, Senator, of knowing that it would be applied.

Senator CONNALLY. That is true. The attitude of the Treasury would determine that situation. I do not apprehend, though, that they would make any large application of this surplus to debt retirement, because they are looking forward to 1949 with apprehension just as we are. They don't know whether fiscal 1949 is going to turn out well or not.

Senator MILLIKIN. If they have no objection, Senator—I mean, if they intend to pass over part of the surplus under their own plans—then this amendment should not meet with objection. But this amendment, I suggest, is the one way that you can assure that.

85-743—73——21

Senator CONNALLY. I would not make any objection to it here until I hear whether the Treasury agrees with it. But my view is that it is to your advantage to offer this as an amendment on the floor. It would not be the Millikin amendment if you stick it in here.

Senator MILLIKIN. I am not interested in the Millikin amendment at all. I am not interested in that at all.

Senator CONNALLY. We want to put the finger on the man who has done it.

CANNIBALIZING THE BILL ON THE FLOOR

Senator MILLIKIN. I believe it would serve the purpose of this bill and all of the incidental purposes better if it were in this bill, rather than something that would have the appearance of being forced from the floor after a lot of fellows sitting on the floor might commence to cannibalize on your bill on the theory that there was not enough surplus for other purposes.

Senator CONNALLY. You have distinguished yourself by putting that word into common usage, that "cannibalize." It is an achievement.

The CHAIRMAN. You suspect we are going to confront some cannibals?

Senator MILLIKIN. I think that this is one way to dull the sharp edges of their teeth.

The CHAIRMAN. Would the committee be willing to put the amendment in the bill as it is reported to the floor?

Senator BARKLEY. I am not going to object to this, and if it is going in I do not see any objection to its going into the bill. We are going to have to fight over it on the floor unless somebody moves to strike it out. But I want to have it understood that I am not objecting with my eyes wide open. I know why it is here; I know what it is intended to do, and it may do it.

Senator MILLIKIN. Yes.

WOULD THIS PERMIT DEBT REDUCTION?

Senator SMITH. Senator Millikin, are you prepared to say whether this would still permit some debt reduction?

Senator MILLIKIN. This would permit of debt reduction.

Senator SMITH. We are not destroying that?

Senator MILLIKIN. What you are doing, as Senator Connally has pointed out, you are increasing your surplus for 1949 at the expense of 1948.

Senator SMITH. That is the way I figure it.

Senator MILLIKIN. So your increased surplus for 1949 remains available for all expenditure purposes and for debt reduction.

BOOKKEEPING DEVICE

The CHAIRMAN. In the last analysis, it does not affect the net arithmetic in the slightest. This is a bookkeeping device for obvious purposes.

Senator GEORGE. And, Senator Millikin, you say you would be willing to leave this $3 billion as against 1948? That leaves you $4,500 million of your surplus and, if no economies are effected at all, you could have $3 billion on your debt.

Senator CONNALLY. I would like to ask Mr. Douglas to speak on this. He may know the Treasury's attitude. I do not mean that I follow the Treasury, but I do think we should know the Treasury's attitude before acting.

OPPOSITION EXPRESSED BY MR. LOVETT

Ambassador DOUGLAS. Mr. Chairman, I discussed this matter with the Secretary of the Treasury and was joined in the discussion by Mr. Lovett before the Secretary left Washington last week. He expressed, I should say very candidly, opposition to the proposal. His opposition was based upon his assumption that the transfer of expenditures from the fiscal year 1949 to the fiscal year 1948 would perhaps have the effect of increasing the magnitude of any tax reduction legislation which the Congress might enact. As a result he was fearful that it would create fiscal difficulties for the Government in the fiscal year 1949 and also in the fiscal year 1950.

The CHAIRMAN. You mean difficulties as a result of excessive tax reduction?

Ambassador DOUGLAS. That is right. I think the committee should know what his view, at least generally stated, is.

Senator MILLIKIN. I may say, Mr. Chairman, that while it is too early to talk about figures, I am quite sure that any bill that comes out of the Senate Finance Committee will be a bill that can be soundly supported. We have no desire to get the Government into fiscal difficulties, and speaking of the Millikin amendment, I certainly do not want to sponsor a bill that will ultimately hang around my neck responsibility for putting the Government in the red. I shall be as solicitous about that as the Secretary of the Treasury himself would be.

Ambassador DOUGLAS. If this amendment sheds the warm sun of Arizona on the ices that are pendant from certain parts of the legislative edifice, there are advantages. I say that, looking at the problem solely from the point of view of the European recovery legislation.

Senator BARKLEY. In other words, if the warm sunshine of Arizona that would be there in 1949 could be moved up to 1948 so as to affect this ice, it might be an advantage. There is no bookkeeping involved in that sunshine whatever.

Ambassador DOUGLAS. No. That is a perennial, continuous, and enjoyable phenomenon in the State from which I come.

[Discussion was continued off the record.]

SECRETARY LOVETT'S VIEWS SOUGHT

The CHAIRMAN. Suppose we act on the amendment, advise the Secretary of the action, tell him that we have understood that in general terms he has objections and that we invite him to state his position in writing, to be included in the committee record and in the report on this particular amendment. Would that be satisfactory?

Senator CONNALLY. It is satisfactory to me. I do not know about the others.

Senator GEORGE. That is all right. Tell him to send it to the chairman, and the chairman will put it in the record.

The CHAIRMAN. On that basis, those in favor of the amendment will hold up their hands. Those opposed. The amendment is adopted.

Senator MILLIKIN. Thank you, Mr. Chairman; thank you, gentlemen.

Senator HICKENLOOPER. Did you fix the amount?

The CHAIRMAN. Yes; at $3 billion.

Now, gentlemen, you have the completed print as we finished it up to last Friday.

Ambassador DOUGLAS. I might as a technical matter make a suggestion. Perhaps the language could be reviewed to be sure it does not impose any restraints on the Administrator in the expenditure of the funds.

The CHAIRMAN. It will be understood that the language will be reviewed.

TITLE OF THE ACT QUESTIONED

Senator SMITH. Mr. Chairman, I would just like to raise one question, and that is as to the title of the act and whether we want to call this "Economic Cooperation Act." All the way through we refer to it in those terms. Or do we want to change it to something like "European Reconstruction Act"?

Senator LODGE. Or "Foreign Aid Act."

Senator CONNALLY. Don't say "Foreign"; that means everybody. Why don't we limit it?

Senator LODGE. Limit it to Europe?

Senator CONNALLY. It is limited to Europe, so why don't we say "European?"

Senator LODGE. Iceland is not in Europe, except by definition of this bill.

Senator GEORGE. And the colonies of the European States may be out of Europe.

Senator CONNALLY. I don't care; it is not important.

Senator BARKLEY. What is the name that is finally suggested?

Senator SMITH. I had in mind something like "European Reconstruction Act."

Senator CONNALLY. Don't say "Reconstruction"; they will want us to rebuild every cathedral in Europe.

Senator LODGE. I don't like the word "European" very much, because I think the bill is going to have a big impact outside of Europe.

The CHAIRMAN. I was very much in favor of changing the title at first. The more I have thought about it, the more I have concluded that perhaps we have got the best title right here. In the first place, it underscores the fact that this is an economic adventure; in the second place it underscores the fact that it is based on cooperation, and cooperation is the key to this thing or there isn't any key.

Senator Smith, I rather think that when you get all through thinking about it, adding up the liabilities and assets, that perhaps you cannot do better than "Economic Cooperation Act."

Senator SMITH. I am not pressing it too hard. The reason I bring it up is because I meant to bring it up as unfinished business before, and did not. I think there is a lot to what you say. I am not entirely happy with "Economic Cooperation."

The CHAIRMAN. So long as we get away from "ERP" I do not care very much what we fly to.

Unless there is some motion to be made——

Senator SMITH. I do not think I will make any motion.

Senator HICKENLOOPER. Mr. Chairman, at the proper time—and I apologize for being here this morning and not having been here for some time before—there are five or six questions that I would like to ask about. I have not anything in particular to offer.

The CHAIRMAN. Suppose we just run down the committee for any amendments, for comments. Senator Connally?

ON FINANCIAL AND MONETARY MEASURES

Senator CONNALLY. Mr. Chairman, I apologize. I was not here last week. I want to call attention to page 28, paragraph 2, "taking financial and monetary measures necessary to stabilize its currency, establish or maintain a valid rate of exchange, and generally to restore or maintain confidence in its monetary system;".

That paragraph is devoted largely just to the purely monetary and financial. I would like to insert, in line 13, after the word "exchange", these words: "to balance its governmental budget".

I know it will be contended that it is implicit, but I think spelling out sometimes is better than leaving it to be implied. Mr. Douglas thinks that is covered. I think at this point it is a good point to confuse our enemies with, because if there is any hint at all that they run behind with their government expenses, they are going to replenish them out of these funds, exactly. At first, you remember that when France made up its estimates at Paris it had items in there about paying a debt owed Great Britain, and some other items of purely their own governmental operations. If these governments can't put enough taxes on to maintain their ordinary governmental running expenses, I do not think that we ought to subsidize them.

Senator HICKENLOOPER. I think the fact is, Senator, that some money and some assistance heretofore has gone into that very thing. I think there is precedent, and I am very much in favor of your suggestion.

Senator CONNALLY. I do not know the facts, but you know how the temptation of those facts runs; if they can reach out and get a hunk of money and dispose of it for their own governmental expenses, they are going to do it.

The CHAIRMAN. What are you proposing, Senator?

Senator CONNALLY. Just to add "to balance its governmental budget".

It seems to me that is a reasonable requirement.

Senator HICKENLOOPER. I would like to raise a question in connection with what you are raising too, eventually.

Senator CONNALLY. I know the Ambassador thinks this is implicit, but I do not think it is implicit. This refers to stabilizing its currency. After you get the money, what are you going to do with it? I want to put it in there explicitly, and I think it will help the appeal to the Senate to know we are not intending to go in there and subsidize the ordinary governmental expenses of their clerks. France, they say, is overloaded with governmental employees.

Senator LODGE. Of course the French have two budgets, so they always balance their budget, because they have the extraordinary one and the normal one. In the sense that you used these words is what we mean by these words, not what they mean.

Senator HICKENLOOPER. With regard to the whole section, if you turn back to page 27, preliminary to Nos. 1, 2, and 3, it says, "Such agreement shall provide for the adherence of such country to the purposes of this act and shall, where applicable, make appropriate provision, among others, for—"

THE WORD "SHALL" OR "MAY"

I refer to the word "shall." I merely raise the question. Shall that be the word "shall" or "may"? "Shall" is pretty mandatory.

Senator CONNALLY. That is one of the requirements they have to subscribe to.

Senator GEORGE. We were deliberately seeking to make it mandatory.

Senator HICKENLOOPER. Does it impose an extraordinary burden on us to stabilize their currencies there? Can they say, "Well, we need another $5 billion to stabilize our currency"?

Senator GEORGE. They will say it anyway, Senator. You do not need to worry about that.

Senator HICKENLOOPER. I believe they will.

Senator GEORGE. Don't worry about that.

Senator CONNALLY. I think the "shall" ought to stay there. Unless they are going to cooperate with this act, good night, we are out.

Senator GEORGE. We were trying to make this mandatory.

Senator HICKENLOOPER. I beg your pardon. The "shall" refers to those countries.

The CHAIRMAN. How about Senator Connally's suggestion, Mr. Ambassador?

Ambassador DOUGLAS. I think the balancing of the budget is implicit in the general definition of terms of the bilateral contract. I would suggest that using that phrase specifically was using language that was perhaps too strong in the legislation.

Senator CONNALLY. If it is not in the legislation it won't be in the bilateral agreement.

Ambassador DOUGLAS. I think it will be.

Senator CONNALLY. Then why not put it in the legislation?

Ambassador DOUGLAS. There is a difference between putting language that is inflexible in legislation——

Senator CONNALLY. That is exactly what I mean.

Ambassador DOUGLAS. I would point out to you that no country can restore or maintain confidence in its monetary system unless its budgetary position is under control.

Senator CONNALLY. My point is this, that making a sound monetary system is all right. I am for that. But after you get the money, what are you going to do with it? Unless you have a budget balanced you are going to spend it for things you do not need to spend it for.

Ambassador DOUGLAS. That question, it seems to me, goes to the handling of the local currency counterpart.

MAKING THEM BALANCE THEIR BUDGET

Senator CONNALLY. What is your objection? Don't you think we ought to make them balance their budgets?

Ambassador DOUGLAS. I do think we ought to make them balance their budgets as rapidly as we can, and I think the bilateral contracts will refer to the balancing of the budgets, but Senator, in one or two of the countries, in all candor, it would be impossible to bring the budget into balance within a period of the 12 months contemplated under this specific authorization. No matter how desperately a government tried and how determined it was, it would be politically impossible for it to do it.

Senator LODGE. Mr. Ambassador, wouldn't line 22 on page 27 take care of that—those words "where applicable"?

The CHAIRMAN. I was wondering if Senator Connally would feel his amendment was ruined if it read "to balance its governmental budget as soon as possible"?

Senator CONNALLY. That takes most of the life out of it.

Senator BARKLEY. I think it was testified the other day by Mr. Douglas that one or two countries will require from 12 to 18 months to balance their budgets—and were we to write a mandatory provision in here, they would not be able to receive any of the benefits of this act during the 12 months while they were trying to balance their budgets and, not receiving any of the benefits of the act, it might be more difficult for them to balance their budgets.

The CHAIRMAN. It seems to me the virtue of Senator Connally's amendment is that it identifies balancing the budget as one of the objectives. If you have to have a little elasticity, and apparently you do, Senator, I think you can do both things with this language.

Senator GEORGE. The purposes of the act—page 4—are to further "the restoration or maintenance of the soundness of European currencies, budgets, and finances." That is just the purpose of the act, and you want to put this over here?

Senator CONNALLY. I want that in the agreements. I want to make them promise to do that.

I read that last night and marked it here. That is one of our purposes. Well, if it one of our purposes, why not carry it forward and make it one of their purposes as well as ours?

Senator GEORGE. I was just calling attention to it.

Senator CONNALLY. I am not taking issue with you.

The CHAIRMAN. Senator, are you willing to amend your suggestion so that it will read "to balance the governmental budget as soon as possible"?

Senator THOMAS of Utah. I have another idea that I would like to try on you to see if it works: "* * * exchange, and generally to restore a balanced budget and maintain confidence in its monetary system."

It is the restoration of a balanced budget that is your aim.

Senator CONNALLY. That is all right, but the "generally * * *."

Senator THOMAS of Utah. You can cut the "generally" out, but if you put it in this provision, in this part of the paragraph, instead of after "exchange," you have a reason for a balanced budget in the maintenance of the monetary system, in that the monetary system depends upon it.

Senator CONNALLY. I think the two are separate. I think you can have sound money and have an unbalanced budget. We have done that for years.

Senator THOMAS of Utah. The way some countries balance their budgets all the time is to depreciate their currencies.

Senator CONNALLY. We are keeping them from doing that.

Senator THOMAS of Utah. You have that in here, "to stabilize their currencies."

Senator CONNALLY. We have that in here. They promised to do that, but they do not promise explicitly to do this.

Senator THOMAS of Utah. I think this says what it means.

Senator HICKENLOOPER. I think it works two ways, on the countries and on the Administrator both.

The CHAIRMAN. So do I.

INFLEXIBILITY A SOURCE OF EUROPEAN OPPOSITION

Ambassador DOUGLAS. No one has a stronger conviction about a balanced budget than have I. I think if you are too inflexible about this specific matter you will hand another peg on which the organized and unscrupulous groups in Europe may hand their opposition to the plan generally; particularly I think that may be true if it is inserted into the legislation.

Senator HICKENLOOPER. Mr. Ambassador, I wish you would consider that qualification "as soon as possible" in there, and discuss it from that standpoint: "to balance its budget as soon as possible."

The CHAIRMAN. What is the objection to that?

Senator THOMAS of Utah. Some countries have balanced budgets.

Senator LODGE. Why, on page 27, I repeat, do not those two words "where applicable" give you another caveat on that?

Ambassador DOUGLAS. It does give one a caveat. That "where applicable" was intended particularly to apply to the strategic materials section.

Senator LODGE. It could apply to this.

Ambassador DOUGLAS. It could apply to all of them.

What do you think of this: "taking financial and monetary measures necessary to stabilize its currency, establish or maintain a valid rate of exchange, to take determined steps aimed at bringing their budgets into balance as soon as practicable, and generally to restore or maintain confidence in its monetary system"?

Senator CONNALLY. It probably would be, since I have looked at it, better to insert it at the end of that paragraph than to stick it in where you are talking about purely a stabilization of the currency.

Ambassador DOUGLAS. In my view, sir, whether it be correct or wrong, one of the conditions precedent to restoration and maintenance of confidence in the monetary systems of most of these European countries is clear and unmistakable evidence that determined steps are being taken to bring the respective budgets into balance. I do not believe that any one of these European countries can restore or maintain confidence in its monetary system unless the evidence of their determination to bring the budget into balance is unmistakable and uncontrovertible.

Senator CONNALLY. Some sort of amendment like this, it seems to me, is necessary in order to arm the Administrator, in order that he can bring pressure on them by saying, "Why, here it is in the act." If it is just his act alone, there will be all sorts of pressure not to do it, to get us to relax and all that. But this will arm him with something to make him do it. A lot of them are not going to do it unless you make them.

Ambassador DOUGLAS. Will that language be agreeable to you, "* * * to take determined steps aimed at bringing their budgets into balance as soon as practicable * * *"?

Senator CONNALLY. I prefer my language, with the addition of Senator Vandenberg's suggestion, "if need be."

Senator SMITH. I think "as soon as practicable" will be better.

Senator CONNALLY. I accept that.

The CHAIRMAN. The question is on the amendment, reading "to balance its governmental budget as soon as practicable." Those in favor will say "aye." Those opposed, "no." The "ayes" have it. The amendment is in.

Anything else, Senator Connally?

Senator CONNALLY. No.

The CHAIRMAN. Senator George?

Senator GEORGE. I had one, but the State Department says it might raise some question about the Bureau of the Budget.

Ambassador DOUGLAS. No, sir; the Comptroller General.

Senator GEORGE. It is kind of watered down in this language. I am kind of like Senator Connally. I am getting to the point where I want to say what I feel about some of this stuff, in spots.

AMENDMENT ON AUTHORIZING THROUGH 1952

I had suggested, in talks with Senator Connally and Senator Thomas, an amendment on page 25 preceding your appropriation for these subsequent years. I had an amendment in mind in line 14. We are authorizing continuance of this act through June 30, 1952, which is a rather contentious point, or may be so if legislation is to clear both Houses of Congress, and I had in mind an amendment at that point. I admit that what I wanted to put in is implicit in the whole act, but what I had suggested was that preceding the word "There" in line 14 of page 25 I had in mind inserting this phrase: "Conditioned upon the continuing observance of the terms of this act by the countries receiving assistance thereunder, there are hereby authorized to be appropriated * * *", so that we would not be subsequently bound to appropriate if there had not been any real effort here to do anything. There is a lot of talk that they are not doing anything in Greece, that some of our committees who have visited Greece are ready to say that there is a disposition to rather regard that as a provincial assignment that might be good for a hundred years and we will have to keep financing it.

The State Department has suggested that it might be put in a different form, but it would involve the rewriting of the whole section, and I do not want to do that. Unless it could be put in just as a phrase I do not want to do it, so I will not offer it.

Senator SMITH. Don't the words "to carry out the provisions and accomplish the purposes of this act" really imply everything you are asking for?

Senator GEORGE. No, sir; they do not imply it. That is not my purpose at all. My purpose is to say that there won't be any appropriations hereafter made unless the conditions of this act are being met by the participating countries.

The CHAIRMAN. I think we have said it.

Senator GEORGE. It is implicit, but it is not spelled out in this act.

Senator HICKENLOOPER. Can you make a qualified authorization? Doesn't the authorization have to be a firm authorization, and put your qualification in somewhere else?

Senator GEORGE. We can make it a conditional authorization.

Ambassador DOUGLAS. But it raises a lot of administrative questions.

STATE DEPARTMENT OPINION

Senator GEORGE. The State Department is of the opinion that it will raise a lot of questions with the Comptroller General and will raise administrative difficulties. I do not want to do that. That was not what I had in mind. Originally I had the idea that I would agree to no appropriation over 5 years. I will be perfectly frank with you. It has always been my view that I would stick in one stack of chips at a time and look how the game was going before I put in another stack.

The CHAIRMAN. Is that not exactly what we are doing? That is what I want.

Senator GEORGE. No, sir; that is not what you are doing at all.

You are doing it by implication, and that is the only way you are doing it. We are appropriating outright $5,300 million. We are authorizing whatever appropriation is necessary through June 30, 1952, and I wanted to say explicitly—and I would if it were left with me say—that it is expressly conditioned upon the observance of the terms of this act by countries receiving support thereunder.

The CHAIRMAN. Why don't you put it in the authorization section?

Senator SMITH. It is stated on page 3 of the declaration of policy, just as clearly as it can be. We say:

> It is further declared to be the policy of the United States that the continuity of assistance provided by the United States should, at all times, be dependent upon the continuity of cooperation among the countries participating in the program.

Senator GEORGE. I know, Senator, but here is where we are authorizing this. I have said it is implicit.

PROVISION FOR TERMINATION IMPLICIT IN THE BILL

Ambassador DOUGLAS. I think it runs through the bill, Senator. If they don't cooperate there is no request for an appropriation for the countries that do not cooperate. If any countries fail to meet their undertakings and to honor their pledges, they fall out of the countries that are eligible for assistance, and therefore any appropriations sought would thereby be reduced. Finally, there is the provision for termination of assistance in the act.

Senator GEORGE. I grant you that it is implicit in the act. We have tried to make it that way. But here we are binding ourselves over a period of years to authorize at least whatever appropriation is necessary. It won't be binding on the committees and on the Congress. They can put it up or down or do as they please about it. I grant that.

The CHAIRMAN. Would it not meet your purpose and still avoid the difficulties that have been suggested if, in line 18, after the word "act", you inserted "as defined in section 2"? Then it reads; "There are hereby authorized to be appropriated. * * * such sums as may be necessary to carry out the provisions and accomplish the purposes of this act as defined in section 2," and in section 2 it says that continuity is a condition of performance, is a condition precedent.

Senator GEORGE. I think it would rather be a limitation. I would rather leave the whole act operate on it.

Senator CONNALLY. "* * * conditioned upon continued performance by the recipient country" is what you want.

Senator GEORGE. No; I think the Comptroller General might raise some question about that.

The CHAIRMAN. Suppose you said, in line 18, "* * * * and accomplish the purposes defined in this act."

Senator GEORGE. I think it is implicit in the act. I would not want to put it in here if it was not implicit; but I did want to couple it up with this obligation. This is an authorization extending through June 30, 1952.

Senator SMITH. How do you suggest the amendment—"conditioned upon the performance"?

Senator GEORGE. I said, "conditioned upon the performance or observance of the terms of the act by the participating countries." You would have to be careful not to say that if one fell out you do not want to make an appropriation for the others.

Ambassador DOUGLAS. You would have to be very careful.

Senator GEORGE. Here is a continuing appropriation, committing ourselves. We are authorizing, over a period of years, an appropriation, and I wanted it perfectly clear that as a condition precedent they were expressly basing it upon the acquiescence and participation and observance by these terms.

The CHAIRMAN. Is it not possible to put some language in there without fouling the nest?

Ambassador DOUGLAS. We have tried to draft some in the Department. I think it is preferable without it.

Senator GEORGE. The State Department has drafted this language, and I will read it. It involves rewriting the whole section. That, in itself, is not an insuperable point.

Ambassador DOUGLAS. And it departs from the normal, customary, and usual language used by the Congress in authorizing appropriations.

Senator HICKENLOOPER. I will just make this suggestion for your thinking: page 3, line 15, which is about the only limitation that I can find in the act. I am concerned about this very same proposition that Senator George is. Line 15, that last sentence: "It is further declared to be the policy of the United States that"—I would prefer to cut out the word "the"—"continuity of assistance provided by the United States should, at all time, be dependent upon the continuity of cooperation among the countries participating in the program" and then something of this nature: "as determined by the Congress from time to time in connection with any proposed future appropriations that may be considered."

Senator CONNALLY. By that language in the bill, "among the countries participating" we mean the individual countries must be participating. We do not want to make it applicable to all of them. If some of them comply, they are in; if others do not comply, they are out. We used the words "cooperation among," which might seem to imply that they all had to cooperate.

Senator HICKENLOOPER. I was hopeful—and I read this reprint very superficially—that a much more vigorous statement of the fact that Congress would periodically from time to time make up its own mind as to whether or not appropriations would be made would be included.

A SIMILAR AMENDMENT PLACED ON PAGE 25

Senator CONNALLY. Why can't you meet that with some amendment similar to Senator George's? My view would be that on page 25, after the word "act," as suggested by the chairman, you say "conditioned, however, upon the performance by individual countries or recipient countries under this act."

Senator HICKENLOOPER. I was merely trying to get away from the qualification of the appropriation business on the fiscal bookkeeping of the Treasury.

Senator BARKLEY. Of course, every authorization or bill that provides for a program of any kind is limited to the terms of the bill. Congress can't go beyond it. It may stop short of it; it may stop short of the purposes of the act in the appropriation.

While, of course, you have to relate this authorization, it is easier to do that if we can get the right language in here that will do it. I do not see how anybody can interpret this act as a whole as taking away from Congress the right to look into this act not only every year but every 6 months, and it is proposed, I believe, to have a congressional watchdog.

Senator CONNALLY. Bloodhound, not watchdog.

Senator BARKLEY. A congressional watchdog of some sort to see that that is done day by day.

STATE DEPARTMENT SUGGESTION

Senator GEORGE. The State Department has suggested that this section might be rewritten as follows:

"In order to carry out the provisions of this act with respect to those countries which adhere to the purposes of this act and remain eligible to receive assistance thereunder, there are hereby authorized to be appropriated to the President, from time to time * * * ," and then the same as the other reprint.

Ambassador DOUGLAS. The balance of the language is exactly the same. The first three lines are new.

Senator GEORGE. And are intended to cover what I had in mind in such a way as might not involve any controversy with the Comptroller General.

Ambassador DOUGLAS. And it makes the distinction between the countries as a group and those that continue to remain eligible.

Senator GEORGE. That is right, because you have two problems.

I won't insist on the amendment. I very strongly agree with the view.

Ambassador DOUGLAS. If the committee would like to insert something in the authorization section, I would suggest that the language Senator George just read would cover it.

Senator GEORGE. It would cover what I have in mind.

WEST GERMANY A PARTICIPATING COUNTRY

The CHAIRMAN. Is Western Germany included in that language?

Ambassador DOUGLAS. Western Germany is a participating country.

Senator CONNALLY. If it is in the bill it is there.

Senator GEORGE. "* * * with respect to those countries which adhere to the purpose of this act and remain eligible to receive assistance thereunder * * *."

Senator SMITH. I would make it "participating countries," because then it comes under the definition in section 3.

The CHAIRMAN. Mr. Ambassador, your staff is nodding "yes" behind you.

Ambassador DOUGLAS. I do not think it makes any difference.

Senator SMITH. It brings Germany in under the definition in section 3 if we use the term "participating countries," and that might be desirable.

The CHAIRMAN. I think you have to have participating countries, because Germany is not a country that adheres.

Ambassador DOUGLAS. She remains eligible.

The CHAIRMAN. There is no objection to saying "to those participating countries," is there?

Ambassador DOUGLAS. No.

The CHAIRMAN. Does it meet with your approval?

Senator GEORGE. I think it does.

The CHAIRMAN. Is there objection? Without objection the section is amended.

SENATOR CONNALLY'S AMENDMENT HELPFUL

Senator CONNALLY. May I ask Senator Lodge a question?

A while ago, when you were discussing my amendment, you started to say something about two or three countries in Europe that had done something.

Senator LODGE. I said that on balancing the budgets in France and maybe others, they have a trick system of two sets of books, a double budget, so that they can say they are in balance in one way, and in another way they are not.

I think your language is very helpful.

Senator CONNALLY. Do you not think this language is helpful?

Senator LODGE. I think your language is definitely helpful.

The CHAIRMAN. Anything else, Senator George?

Senator GEORGE. No, sir.

Senator HICKENLOOPER. On this point, I merely want for the record to express myself as having been hopeful that much more vigorous language as to examination and step-by-step proceedings could be written into the bill.

Senator CONNALLY. You have the watchdog and the bloodhounds, which means a lot of free trips to Europe.

Senator HICKENLOOPER. I am not objecting to this procedure.

The CHAIRMAN. Senator Smith, is there anything in here that you want to talk about?

"EXTRAORDINARY" SUBSTITUTED FOR "ABNORMAL"

Senator SMITH. I have something on page 2 that appears in a number of places which I still raise a question about. On line 12 we use the word "extraordinary" outside assistance. That word was substituted originally for the word "abnormal." I still raise the question as to why you have to have any qualifying word there at all. Why shouldn't Europe of a "healthy economy independent of outside assistance"? I am just raising the question of whether we should not cut out the word "extraordinary" where it appears all through the bill, in connection with the words "outside assistance."

Ambassador DOUGLAS. I remember when the word "abnormal" was suggested to the committee the word "extraordinary" was substituted for the word "abnormal," and the point was, what was meant by "outside assistance" is that there are certain types of outside assistance that have been traditional, that have been implicit in the ordinary commercial and financial transactions. Many of these countries carry on those transactions with other parts of the world.

Senator SMITH. What do you mean by "assistance"?

Ambassador DOUGLAS. The extension of credit, and that is where the word "extraordinary" was put in, to make a distinction between that which was ordinary, customary, usual, as between nationals of one of these participating countries and a foreign country, or as between one of the participating countries itself and a foreign country. This is abnormal and extraordinary.

Senator SMITH. This means that we are going to be attacked on the point that even though this aims to make these countries self-supporting, we are still contemplating keeping up some sort of assistance to them, and you do not mean assistance to them in that sense. You mean the extraordinary credits and whatnot that appear as aids in relief that might apply.

It seems to me that we ought to give them a chance, and we are hoping they will be clear of any need of further aid after this period is over. I am troubled by using the word "assistance" as something we expect to give them indefinitely, according to what might be construed here.

Ambassador DOUGLAS. The purpose of the act is to place them in such a healthy economic position that they will not require outside assistance other than that which they have traditionally and customarily had. Some of these countries have, whether for better or for worse, floated loans in the American capital market. They have floated, some of them, loans in the capital markets of other countries, participating as well as nonparticipating. And the use of the word "extraordinary" was to draw the distinction.

Senator CONNALLY. All these loans would float, would they?

The CHAIRMAN. Do you call that assistance?

Ambassador DOUGLAS. That is assistance.

Senator GEORGE. I thought Dewey was emphasizing that here we were engaged in an extraordinary enterprise in helping these countries, and our purpose was to get them to where they would not need that.

Senator BARKLEY. There isn't anything in the bill anywhere that we are morally obligated to do anything beyond the extraordinary aid.

Senator SMITH. But we do not render the European countries, by this, independent of outside assistance. We leave the implication that some kind of assistance will still have to go on in these countries. I thought we wanted to make it clear, as clear as we could, that the thing to do was to make them self-sustaining. In our early days we got assistance in the form of loans, but you would not call that any sort of eleemosynary aid to us.

Senator GEORGE. It is not used in that sense at all.

The CHAIRMAN. Let us make it plain in the report that what we are talking about in connection with this is this type of aid.

Senator SMITH. That is all right, so long as we make it clear we are not thinking of continued aid in this bill.

Senator CONNALLY. This bill is limited in time.

The CHAIRMAN. Anything else, Senator Smith?

Senator SMITH. That is all.

The CHAIRMAN. Senator Barkley?

SURPLUS AGRICULTURAL PRODUCTS

Senator BARKLEY. I believe I ought to call the attention of the committee to the suggested change which the committee adopted on my motion the other day with regard to surplus agricultural products. The change suggested by the State Department is not satisfactory to me. It is on page 22. The suggested change wholly nullifies the purpose of the amendment, to begin with, which was to point up the Administrator to the fact that in the purchase of these agricultural products, depending upon the desire and requirements of the country, the administration was to use surpluses in this country as they exist. I had a very simple amendment to that effect which was diluted by the drafting service, but I think it was fairly intended to accomplish the purpose with about twice as much language as was necessary. Anyhow it was adopted, but it still carried the implication that so far as practicable, and in consonance with the requirements of the country, in the purchase of agricultural products they should purchase surpluses.

The way they have written it out is that the amount purchased have relationship to the quantity of each type and each class that is in existence and available.

The very estimable gentleman from the State Department came over to see me this morning with a redraft of that which states that "In the procurement within the United States of agricultural commodities in surplus supply in the United States * * *," and that is not what I intend at all.

Those agricultural interests that suggested the amendment wanted to see to it that in this process we work off some of the surplus that is already in existence and incidentally create, probably, a future market for some of our American products if the European countries have a taste for them. But this amendment suggested by the State Department merely says that in the purchase of supplies they should do this. It does not require the Administrator whatever to give any preference to surpluses. Therefore that redraft is not satisfactory to me. I do not want to close the door to further language, and I would rather leave it as it is and let us see about it before we take the bill up, and if they suggest something that is satisfactory, I will be perfectly willing to make the change.

TROUBLE WITH THE AMENDMENT EXPECTED

Senator GEORGE. Let me call your attention to this. We will have trouble on this amendment as it is, because of what it says, that "the Administrator shall, insofar as practicable and in consideration of the requirements of the participating countries, purchase an amount of each class or type of such commodity which bears the same proportion to the total amount of such commodity to be procured as the available U.S. supply of such type or class bears to the available U.S. supply of such commodity."

Well now, you have got a great many things in this country that have never been exported. They are types of things that have been produced, but they have not been exported at all. And we may have them in big quantities, and under this the Administrator could go out and he would be required to buy something now and send it over just because there was a quantity of it here available to him.

Take the case of naval stores. You have gum naval stores and you have naval stores produced by the titration process and you have a naval product similar chemically to the naval stores, or identical with it, obtained from a chemical process. You have three sources of supply. Some of those have not been exported, but there has been a heavy export of the gum resins, or rosins.

You have the same situation in tobacco. About one-half of our flue-cured tobacco is exported, and that is historically true. But you have other types of tobacco that are available in this market which have never had any considerable export.

I have no quarrel with the purpose of the amendment, but it looks to me like we will run into a lot of trouble. We will have people here meeting us on the floor and it will make it almost impossible to pass this amendment.

Senator BARKLEY. I did not draw this amendment. I turned to the drafting service a very simple amendment which referred to agricultural products under this program, that where they were used in grants, the surpluses should be used.

Senator GEORGE. And in the purchase of those surpluses they would not discriminate against types.

Senator BARKLEY. When it got back to me we were at the end of the bill and I did not have time to argue it.

Senator CONNALLY. You are thinking about surpluses. Doesn't that imply that not necessarily only the surplus, but the surplus should be first drawn upon, if that is sound?

Senator BARKLEY. That is what I was undertaking, and I illustrated it by the situation in tobacco, which I will be frank to say was responsible for the amendment in the first place.

The CHAIRMAN. The language you now recite, which you originally offered, it seems to me would be devoid of most of the objections that attach to this thing.

A VARIETY OF COMPLICATIONS SEEN

Ambassador DOUGLAS. I think it would lead into a great variety of complications, Mr. Chairman. Let's take, for example, the case of beef. We have horse meat, and that is now going abroad. We would have to purchase a proportionate amount of beef and ham, in an amount which bears the same proportion that the horse meat bears to the total production, and the poor Administrator would be driven mad. If there are any surpluses going abroad at all it is a very, very difficult thing to do.

The CHAIRMAN. Just stop right there. Let me ask Senator Barkley if he disagrees with that analysis. Would it not do in the meat situation exactly what the Ambassador says?

Senator BARKLEY. I do not know about horse meat. I did not know we were engaged in exporting that as a food.

The CHAIRMAN. If you did export horse meat, would you not also have to export beef and ham?

Senator BARKLEY. If the surplus of horse meat is food, I think probably that is true, but I do not think there is anybody who contends that there is any surplus of horse meat in this country available as a food.

Ambassador DOUGLAS. But it is a type. They eat in Europe. We export horse meat.

Senator CONNALLY. I think I ate horse meat in France once.

Senator BARKLEY. I ate some in Moscow, but it was not shipped from the United States.

Ambassador DOUGLAS. First, Senator, I think it ought to be limited to incentive goods. That would cover tobacco and exclude some other things.

Senator GEORGE. This, as written, does not apply to surplus at all. It says, "the Administrator, in procuring these products."

DRAFTING SERVICE "DEHYDRATED" THE AMENDMENT

Senator BARKLEY. That is not what I intended, and that is why I had in my own mind the question of whether the language as drawn up and brought in here did what I was seeking to do. You never know when you give an amendment to the drafting service what it is going to look like or provide for when you get it back. They dehydrate it and debunk it and boil it down and thin it out until you don't recognize it; and I am not criticizing the drafting service, but they have a habit of spelling out things in mysterious hieroglyphics so that you don't know your own thought when it comes back.

Senator GEORGE. I think you will agree that this will not do the way it is written. I thought you were dealing with only a surplus commodity to be given away.

Senator BARKLEY. That is right.

Senator GEORGE. And this says that in the procurement of any agricultural commodity you must buy the same amount.

Senator BARKLEY. I want to go back to my original language.

Ambassador DOUGLAS. I was wondering, Mr. Chairman, whether it would be agreeable to resolve this question by perhaps Senator Barkley and Senator George and somebody from the State Department and the Department of Agriculture getting together and seeing if they cannot draft language which covers, insofar as it can be covered.

Senator GEORGE. I think Senator Barkley can take it up with the Agriculture Department.

LANGUAGE TO BE REWRITTEN

The CHAIRMAN. It is perfectly obvious that we cannot straighten this thing out here, and we do want to reach a conclusion today. Suppose it is understood that before the bill is reported this language will be rewritten in consultation between Senator Barkley and the staff?

Senator Barkley, is that satisfactory?

Senator BARKLEY. To leave it as it is?

The CHAIRMAN. With the understanding that you will consult with the staff, and with the understanding that it will be changed.

Senator GEORGE. I wish you could do it before you report it.

The CHAIRMAN. That is what I want to do. There is not any question of reporting the bill until the latter part of next week, but I would like to get the bill out of this committee today. Debate opens the 1st of March.

Senator CONNALLY. I think you ought to allow a certain time for Senator Barkley to file his amendment.

Senator BARKLEY. When I turned it over to the drafting committee it was a very simple amendment.

Senator GEORGE. All people who grow farm products are disturbed about this. They say, "Here, we have a historic basis for exports, and others don't have any at all."

Senator BARKLEY. I do not want to disturb that. I think I illustrated it by saying Great Britain has always taken flue-cured tobacco and the war has not changed their taste. I don't want to interfere with that.

The CHAIRMAN. We will leave it that way. Is there anything else?

Senator BARKLEY. No.

The CHAIRMAN. Senator Hickenlooper?

Senator HICKENLOOPER. I have five or six questions I would like to ask. If somebody else has something, I would just as soon wait.

The CHAIRMAN. Go ahead.

Senator HICKENLOOPER. My first question was on page 3, but that has been covered by Senator George's statement on the question of spelling out the requirements.

THE RIGHT TO PROMULGATE RULES

I want to ask a question on page 7, line 16, that provision giving the head of any department or agency, or establishment of the Government, the right to promulgate rules and regulations. Does that in any way cut down the latitude or the responsibility of the Administrator for this thing?

The CHAIRMAN. No, Senator. That was a subject of great and lengthy consideration, and the only power he can delegate, that a department head can delegate, is in connection with the performance of functions. It has nothing to do with the preparation of rules and regulations. He cannot delegate the right to make rules and regulations.

Senator HICKENLOOPER. I am concerned with the responsibility being on the Administrator, and I would not want somebody to be able to run out from under him and make a lot of regulations and rules that would foul him up.

The CHAIRMAN. For instance, the Secretary of Agriculture makes the rules and regulations pursuant to the orders of the Administrator.

Senator GEORGE. Lines 22 and 23, Senator, I think make that clear.

The CHAIRMAN. We sought to do the same thing you want done.

Senator HICKENLOOPER. I am not objecting.

Senator CONNALLY. The head of the agency, as I understand it, can only make regulations for the subordinates within the functions of the department that is operating.

Senator SMITH. Governing his functions.

Senator HICKENLOOPER. I am reassured on that. That is all right.

Now, on page 12, line 20, beginning with "The Chief of the U.S. diplomatic mission will be responsible for assuring that the operations of the special mission are consistent with the foreign-policy objective of the United States * * *". I raise the question of whether or not that does not put the Administrator and he mission squarely back under he direction of the Secretary of State, rather than making them collateral.

The CHAIRMAN. That is only the chief of the diplomatic mission.

CONTROL BY THE DIPLOMATIC MISSION

Senator HICKENLOOPER. The point I am raising is that the Chief of the U.S. diplomatic mission will be responsible for assuring that the operations of the special mission—and the special mission is under the Administrator. That is the Administrator's special mission. I merely raise the question if we have not, in this bill, tossed the special mission right back under the control of the State Department there, because it puts the responsibility on the Chief of the U.S. diplomatic mission.

Senator CONNALLY. All that that does, Senator Hickenlooper, is to provide that the chief of the U.S. diplomatic mission sees that the operations of the special mission keep within the limits of our foreign policy in such country. I don't see what you want with him over there, if he is not to do that.

Senator HICKENLOOPER. It is only a question of the words "will be responsible for assuring" that this fellow does it. There is a qualification in the back end of the paragraph there.

The CHAIRMAN. Exactly. Then you spell it out in the tail end of the paragraph, and it is again the old atomic energy formula.

Senator HICKENLOOPER. That's right. I recognized the language. I am merely raising the question, and not an objection.

MEANING OF "MAY EMPLOY PERSONS"

At the bottom of page 13 I raise the question before the committee as to whether or not that is desirable. It says "may employ persons." Does that give him *carte blanche* to employ persons, or should it be qualified so that he may employ citizens?

Senator CONNALLY. There is a place that makes a specific provision about foreigners. Wouldn't that exclude everything else? I am just asking you; don't you think so?

Senator HICKENLOOPER. I do not think it would, myself. I think he can hire any foreigners under this (1).

Senator LODGE. That is line 14, page 14.

Senator HICKENLOOPER. In paragraph (b) there is a provision on the employment of citizens of other countries.

Senator LODGE. Subsection (1) does authorize foreigners to be employed for service in this country.

Senator HICKENLOOPER. My view is that it authorizes the employment of any person, which would be foreigners or anybody else, and I raise the question as to whether you want to limit that subsection (1) at the bottom of page 13 to citizens of the country, and rely on subsection (b) for the employment of foreigners.

The CHAIRMAN. This is only personnel outside of the United States, Senator.

Senator HICKENLOOPER. That is right. I am not laboring the point. I merely want to raise it because I think that under (1), outside the United States, they can hire all the foreign personnel they want in addition to these.

Senator CONNALLY. They will have to hire a lot of foreign personnel in subordinate jobs.

Senator HICKENLOOPER. Section (b), line 14, page 14, has a provision in there regarding "clerks and employees" who are foreigners.

Senator SMITH. Section (c) provides for your checkup.

Ambassador DOUGLAS. I do not want to prejudge any action of the Administrator. If 10(a)(1) does authorize him to employ foreigners, Senator, it might be to the very great advantage of the Administrator.

Senator HICKENLOOPER. I wanted to raise that point. I am not going to object to it.

Ambassador DOUGLAS. He might want to select an Englishman with regard to something going on in France, somebody who knows by bitter experience, for example, the tricks—and there are millions of them; no, that is an exaggeration—in foreign exchange.

Senator HICKENLOOPER. I am not raising the objection, necessarily. I just want to know what the position on that would be, because if they hire a bunch of foreigners over there, I want to be sure we have canvassed that point. If that is deemed desirable, to me I believe he is authorized to employ foreigners.

Ambassador DOUGLAS. I would think that he was. The question, however, is whether a foreigner would be eligible to receive the privileges, emoluments, and compensation of a member of the Foreign Service. He could not be covered into the Foreign Service. I think that is clear. He might be employed outside the Foreign Service.

The CHAIRMAN. All right, Senator Hickenlooper. What next?

Senator CONNALLY. While we are on that point I have a point I want to raise, if you will pardon me.

Senator HICKENLOOPER. Go ahead.

Senator CONNALLY. In that paragraph (1), subsection (1), "employ persons who shall receive compensation at any of the rates provided for the Foreign Service." We have a clause in here that they cannot employ but 60 people at $10,000 and not to exceed 15 at some more. But under the Foreign Service Act there are a lot of fellows that draw very high salaries—$17,500, and some of them $25,000. Is there any conflict between this clause and that?

Ambassador DOUGLAS. No. One refers to the employment of people within the continental limits of the United States, and the other refers to the employment of people outside the United States.

Senator CONNALLY. Do you mean that under this they could employ three or four fellows and pay them $17,000?

Ambassador DOUGLAS. They could.

EMPLOYMENT UNDER THE FOREIGN SERVICE RESERVE

Senator HICKENLOOPER. Can they do that, Mr. Ambassador, under the Foreign Service Reserve?

Ambassador DOUGLAS. Yes.

Senator HICKENLOOPER. This does not require them to be members of the Foreign Service Reserve.

Ambassador DOUGLAS. They may be outside or inside, at the will and wish of the Administrator.

Senator HICKENLOOPER. This says "at rates provided for the Foreign Service Reserve and Staff." They do not have to be in the Reserve.

Ambassador DOUGLAS. They may, if the Administrator wants them to be, covered into the Foreign Service Reserve and staff.

Senator CONNALLY. According to your statement, there is no limitation to the number he can employ at $17,500.

Senator HICKENLOOPER. And they can be foreigners, as I view it. Under No. (1) they do not go into the Reserve. They are only paid according to the standards of the Reserve.

Senator GEORGE. It fixes a standard of payment. They do not have to pay them up to that top salary.

Senator HICKENLOOPER. Section (2) says they may be covered into the Reserve.

Senator CONNALLY. Irrespective of the Reserve, under this law he can appoint all he wants at this high rate.

THE ADMINISTRATOR ASSUMED A PRUDENT MAN

Ambassador DOUGLAS. He can. But first it is to be assumed that the Administrator will be a prudent man, and I think in the discussion of the committee it was adequately disclosed that you had to have some adequate compensation for competent people serving overseas.

Senator CONNALLY. This limitation of 60 applies to domestic people.

Ambassador DOUGLAS. That's right.

Senator HICKENLOOPER. I haven't any suggestion for the correction of it.

Senator CONNALLY. You will have to refer that to the bloodhounds. They take a lot of fellows right here from Washington and take them over there and put them in these $17,500 jobs. I have some of them ticketed already.

Senator HICKENLOOPER. Do you mean you have some horses in the race?

Senator CONNALLY. You know what happens. You know they put pressure on fellows, and the Administrator is a human being and he will just take them all.

Senator HICKENLOOPER. May I pass on, then?

The CHAIRMAN. May I just ask Senator Connally to carry on with the meeting? I will go up and open the Senate, and I will be right back. I would like to finish the bill. There is going to be nothing on the floor of the Senate this noon.

Senator HICKENLOOPER. This next suggestion you will be interested in.

I want to raise a suggestion in connection with line 20, page 14, the section that refers to investigation by the Federal Bureau of Investigation. It is the "provided, however" at the top of page 15 that I want to call attention to: That all of these employees shall be investigated by the Federal Bureau of Investigation:

Provided, however, That they may assume their posts and perform their functions after preliminary investigation and clearance by the Administrator or the Secretary of State, as the case may be.

Senator CONNALLY. That means pending confirmation.

Senator HICKENLOOPER. It doesn't say so.

Senator CONNALLY. That is my construction, that they can appoint them and they can go to work, subject to investigation and later confirmation.

Senator HICKENLOOPER. I would like to suggest that this be added: "subject, however, to final decision as to continued employment after completion of such examination."

In another committee you are on we have been up against that same situation, on so-called emergency employment and so on, in which a fellow gets in the job and then somebody says "We have no provision for firing him. We have had the investigation. So what?" And once they get in, I would like to see this, if possible, clarified, so that that employment and preliminary examination will be clearly stated as only temporary, so that there will be no question under the civil service laws or anything else.

I think that is what it means, but it does not say so.

Ambassador DOUGLAS. There is no objection whatsoever to any language like that.

Senator GEORGE. What do you suggest, Senator?

Senator HICKENLOOPER. This is rather rough: "Provided, however, that they may temporarily"—I would like to put that word "temporarily" in there—"assume their posts and perform their functions after preliminary investigation and clearance by the Administrator or Secretary of State, as the case may be, subject, however, to final decision as to continued employment after completion of such examination or investigation."

Senator CONNALLY. All in favor of the amendment. Opposed. It is carried.

Senator GEORGE. We had a lot of trouble with that, trying to get it fixed some way or other.

Senator HICKENLOOPER. Section (3), on page 18.

Senator CONNALLY. A lot of them are going to holler about this 14-year extension.

Senator HICKENLOOPER. There will be some objection to that.

Senator GEORGE. That guaranty goes only to convertibility of currency.

Senator HICKENLOOPER. And it is only 5 percent.

Ambassador DOUGLAS. Only as to convertibility and only as to principal amount invested, actual dollars invested, and then only if the enterprise is profitable.

Senator HICKENLOOPER. I have a mark at the bottom of page 19. It begins on line 23. May I examine it for a moment?

MEANING OF "CONVERTIBILITY"

Senator CONNALLY. When you say "convertibility," do you mean the convertibility of their money into ours?

Ambassador DOUGLAS. Yes.

Senator HICKENLOOPER. I think the question I wanted to raise on section (c), page 19, line 23, is that it goes two ways. It emphasizes loans and grants to these countries, or the governments of these countries, and does not sufficiently emphasize the repayment, but I haven't anything to suggest. It is not as vigorous as I would like to see it, but I shall pass over that.

Senator GEORGE. I would acquiesce in that. I believed in them paying for more things, but I was in the minority. The members of this committee are very liberal.

Senator LODGE. I was in the minority with you.

Senator HICKENLOOPER. I want to suggest at this time that even if I vote for this bill I shall reserve the right to support on the floor a more vigorous amendment if it is proper. I do not want to foreclose myself.

I had this matter of Senator Barkley's agricultural amendment. Senator Barkley is gone.

Senator GEORGE. That won't do. He will have to rewrite this, or else this will defeat the whole bill, almost. These people who have agricultural products will never consent to this. I am afraid we can't write anything that will be very satisfactory.

Senator LODGE. We ought to have that part of the bill cleaned up before we bring it on the floor. Don't you think so?

Senator HICKENLOOPER. I think perhaps all you can do on that agricultural thing, the limit, is probably an admonition, a strong admonition.

[Discussion was had off the record.]

The CHAIRMAN. Now where are we?

Senator HICKENLOOPER. I am going through the last struggles here.

UTILIZING DEPARTMENTS AND AGENCIES OF THE GOVERNMENTS

I call attention, on the last page, page 38, to the last two words in line 3 and lines 4 and 5, "the committee is authorized, with the consent of the head of the department or agency concerned, to utilize the services, information, facilities and personnel of the departments and agencies of the Government." That is in the Atomic Energy Act, with the exception of the words "with the consent of the head of the department or agency concerned." I suggest that if this committee is to function at all, you can not circumvent its latitude by having it subject to the consent of the department or head that you are trying to dig into.

Senator CONNALLY. How about the functioning of the department?

Senator GEORGE. Is that the bloodhound committee? I rather agree with you.

The CHAIRMAN. I would not think it ought to be there.

Senator HICKENLOOPER. We have the same general provision. We have in the Joint Committee on Atomic Energy this language, practically lifted out of that act, but the thing that I am calling to your attention is that you can not use the information and the services or the facilities and the personnel, under this language, without the specific consent of the head of the department involved, and you just nullify yourself. If you want to specify the use of the services and the facilities of this agency and give your committee the authority to demand information, then I think you have to take out the words "with the consent of the head of the department or agency concerned."

Senator CONNALLY. On the other hand, suppose you go into a department and take the key man out of it. Won't it hamper the department very seriously?

Senator HICKENLOOPER. From a practical standpoint, Senator, I do not believe that you will take any personnel to any great degree. In the Joint Committee on Atomic Energy we have the same power, except that we do not have to ask anybody for it. We have been given the legislative right to utilize these services. We have not abused it. We have had some occasion to request the FBI to do some work for us, and we have had one or two occasions——

[Further discussion was continued off the record.]

Senator HICKENLOOPER. Either take the whole thing out and not refer to the utilization of that, and just go into the general powers of the committee, or say that it shall have power to investigate and go into this thing; or, if you want to leave that sentence in, then take out the words "with the consent of the head of the department or agency concerned."

I think that will rise up to smite this Joint Committee.

Senator CONNALLY. I think you had better take it all out.

The CHAIRMAN. Is it agreeable to take it all out?

Senator HICKENLOOPER. It would be much more agreeable to take it all out, rather than to leave it with those words in there.

Senator CONNALLY. There won't be any difficulty. If they request this, they will get it. I think you had better take it all out.

Senator HICKENLOOPER. I believe there is ample authority in (b) on page 36, line 22.

The CHAIRMAN. Without objection, the last sentence is eliminated.

Is there any thing else, Senator Hickenlooper?

Senator HICKENLOOPER. No; except the general philosophy.

The CHAIRMAN. Senator Thomas?

Senator THOMAS of Utah. No.

ROLL CALLED ON BILL

The CHAIRMAN. Clerk, call the roll on the passage of the bill, subject to the Barkley amendment.

The Ambassador to England is anxious to leave at 12:15 and catch a plane for London, and I would like to have him present when he hears the rollcall.

The CLERK. Mr. Capper.

The CHAIRMAN. Aye.

The CLERK. Mr. White.

The CHAIRMAN. Aye.

The CLERK. Mr. Wiley.

The CHAIRMAN. Aye.

The CLERK. Mr. Smith.

Senator SMITH. Aye.

The CLERK. Mr. Hickenlooper.

Senator HICKENLOOPER. Aye.
The CLERK. Mr. Lodge.
Senator LODGE. Aye.
The CLERK. Mr. Connally.
Senator CONNALLY. Aye.
The CLERK. Mr. George.
Senator GEORGE. Aye.
The CLERK. Mr. Wagner.
Senator THOMAS of Utah. Aye.
The CLERK. Mr. Thomas.
Senator THOMAS of Utah. Aye.
The CLERK. Mr. Barkley.
The CHAIRMAN. Aye.
The CLERK. Mr. Hatch.
Senator THOMAS of Utah. Aye.
The CLERK. Mr. Chairman.
The CHAIRMAN. Aye.

Senator HICKENLOOPER. Mr. Chairman, do I understand that we are going to look into the question on page 13, line 23, section (1), in that employment of persons to be paid on the basis of the Foreign Service Reserve? Were you going to look into that, Senator Connally.

Senator CONNALLY. No; I raised the point, but they say you can hire 1 million over there if you want to.

The CHAIRMAN. We can take another look at it, Senator.

Senator SMITH. Do I assume the Millikin amendment is going to be incorporated in an appropriate place in the bill?

The CHAIRMAN. You not only assume it, but it is there.

Senator SMITH. I don't know just where it went in, but I assume it is probably around page 25.

The CHAIRMAN. I wouldn't know about the page.

[Discussion was had off the record.]

APPRECIATION OF COOPERATION EXPRESSED

The CHAIRMAN. Mr. Ambassador, I would like to express my very great debt to you for the very spendid cooperation you have given the committee throughout this very perplexing task. We are very indebted to you. I would like to make the same expression of gratitude to the members of the committee. I think we have had marvelous cooperation. I hope the end justifies the effort.

Senator SMITH. Mr. Chairman, if it is time for the orchids, I would like to extend a bunch of orchids to the chairman.

Senator CONNALLY. I want to join in the statement you make about the Ambassador. He has been very helpful.

The CHAIRMAN. He certainly has.

Senator GEORGE. Yes, you have.

Senator CONNALLY. With regard to the chairman's services, I have already privately told him how I think he performed. I think the whole committee deserves applause. This has been a sensitive, touchy spot, and the country hasn't yet reacted, but they are reacting.

Senator GEORGE. This is the most important step taken in foreign policy in this whole Government. We did the same thing under lend-lease, but we did it definitely in anticipation of war.

Ambassador DOUGLAS. I would like to express my appreciation to you personally as chairman of the committee, and to the members of the committe, for the courteous treatment that I have received at your hands, and may I also express my very profound respect for the way in which this distinguished committee of the Senate has approached a most perplexing and tricky problem and has resolved it and drawn the thorns. It has been a great experience for me, Senator.

Senator CONNALLY. I move the veil of secrecy on this statement be removed.

The CHAIRMAN. The committee is in recess.

[Whereupon, at 12:15 p.m., the hearing was concluded.]

NOMINATIONS AND GENERAL COMMITTEE BUSINESS

TUESDAY, FEBRUARY 24, 1948

UNITED STATES SENATE,
COMMITTEE ON FOREIGN RELATIONS,
Washington, D.C.

The committee met, pursuant to call, at 10 a.m., in the committee hearing room, U.S. Capitol, Senator Arthur H. Vandenberg, chairman, presiding.

Present: Senators Vandenberg, George, and Thomas of Utah.

The CHAIRMAN. The record will show that a quorum of the committee is present.

* * * * * * *

[The first 4 pages of transcript dealing with routine nominations have been deleted.]

* * * * * * *

PARLIAMENTARY STATUS OF CHINA BILL

The CHAIRMAN. We talked about the China thing before you came in, Senator Thomas. We are in a little perplexity in connection with it. The House is quite likely to add China as a part II to the European bill. If it does, and the bill comes back here, the first question is, could we send it straight to conference without giving the Senate an independent crack at the China bill? And, leaving that question open, whether they send it back as part of the European bill or send it back independently, Senator George and I were thinking that it is highly desirable that our committee should start to make a record in executive session on the subject, at least, so that we are not totally without background when we make the decision as to what will be done when the House acts.

Senator THOMAS of Utah. Of course if the House passes it and the bill that it is in goes to conference, there is no question about that; is there?

The CHAIRMAN. No; but it would not be necessary for us to go straight to conference with the bill. We could refer the House bill to this committee and leave the request for a conference on the desk.

Senator THOMAS of Utah. In other words, what is in your mind, if I understand it, Mr. Chairman, is that we are not going to introduce a bill in the Senate.

The CHAIRMAN. That is right. We will wait and see what the House does.

Senator GEORGE. It is too important, Senator, and probably unfair, for the Senate to take it into conference and only have it reported back as a part of a conference report, without some separate consideration by this committee.

Senator THOMAS of Utah. Of course there is a parliamentary situation about that to think about, and then there is the bill itself to think about.

The CHAIRMAN. Most definitely.

Senator THOMAS of Utah. As for the Chinese problem, well, it is just trite to say it, but if Europe is hard, China is so much more difficult, so much bigger in every one of its aspects if we are ultimately going to do anything.

The CHAIRMAN. It is so big that it is pretty close to imponderable so far as we are concerned.

PROBLEM OF JURISDICTION OF TAIWAN

Senator THOMAS of Utah. It is close to imponderable, and we are losing track of the fact that we are wholly and completely responsible for one of the three of our biggest enemies. We occupy the territory completely, we are running the government for them—the Japanese—and when you take a slice like Formosa alone, we have something that is coming up to smite us for the rest of all time. Why we got into the position we did in regard to Formosa, and gave a part of Japanese territory right back to China without anybody saying anything about it, allowing what has gone on over there, is something that no one can understand. If there has been one man killed in some of these places we have been disturbed about, there have been a hundred or probably a thousand killed, and it was all so unnecessary. I just cannot understand how, under the rules of conquest or international law or any sort of scheme that I can think of, without having a soldier take part in a battle or anything like that, a great big division of a territory could be handed over as it was handed over.

The Kurile Islands is another problem, but that is a different problem. There in that situation was a sort of quid pro quo, I imagine, in Kurile, so far as the conference table was concerned. But here is an island that China herself could not administer throughout hundreds of years. They had only one successful Governor in the whole history of China, and because he was so successful they let him wear a button on his cap which was equivalent to the Confucian button or the Imperial button—just one. And when Japan got Formosa, it was handed over by Li Hung Chang with the complete understanding that here is something that we can't do anything with, and the best way to treat your enemy is to give your enemy something that he won't be able to do anything with either.

There is the one thing that I just don't know what we are going to do about, and the only hope is that—and it is a hope—nobody seems to care and that nobody will know anything about it, and probably in the economy of time it will wear itself out, like our occupation of Okinawa and the property that is there, and the rest of it.

The CHAIRMAN. How do these comments you are now making gear your opinion into the recommended China bill that we have?

Senator THOMAS of Utah. Not very directly or not very logically, Mr. Chairman, excepting that I imagine that your European relief and recovery is a bill which is consistently in theory with the hope that someday we are going to have a world of peace and some treaties defining the peace. I do not see that out of your Chinese bill.

The CHAIRMAN. No.

Senator THOMAS of Utah. In the first place, China's whole position is one that in law you cannot work out very, very consistently. Did China defeat Japan? We took extraterritoriality away from China. We renounced it so that Chiang Kai-shek could sit at the China Conference as a sort of equal with the others. But that is the last strictly legal thing we have done in relation to China that I know about, and I just don't know about the Chinese Government as an entity. Chiang Kai-shek has never been a universal ruler over China. He has always had civil war of some kind, and we have recognized his government, to be sure, but whether recognition of a government constitutes the Government's right to rule any territory that government decides to rule is still another question in international law, I assume.

We recognized Russia in 1933 and started relations with her. That doesn't mean that anything Stalin wants to do in the way of holding territory is OK with us. It doesn't even mean that we recognize the governmental status of Russia at that time.

I don't know whether China is so hard that we are just forgetting about it and acting entirely sentimentally, or whether the problem of Japan is fast being made the same way.

The CHAIRMAN. This bill is purely on a sentimental basis.

Senator THOMAS of Utah. Yes; and the theory that Chiang Kai-shek is something of a saint, and therefore * * *

[Discussion was continued off the record.]

The CHAIRMAN. The question is, do you, with your knowledge of that background, favor the presentation of a bill which contemplates practically nothing except current relief? What do you say to that?

ADMINISTRATION OF RELIEF QUESTIONED

Senator THOMAS of Utah. If the administrator, Senator Vandenberg, understands what he is doing, he can take $100 million or he can take $200 million of that and he can set up a fund which will stabilize China's money, but he has to hold on to it. The best illustration of what money means in China, and anywhere in the world for that matter, is that when a Chinese farmer made some profit with this year's crop and he knew next year's crop wasn't going to come around, he would put his profit in little silver balls. You have seen those things that the people wear for their buttons on their summer clothes throughout the Orient. Then he would bury it in an adobe brick in his house. Next year, when the fire came, or something, and the house was completely destroyed, he would go around in the ashes and find these silver pieces and start life over again. That is something that we can't even do in our country, and that accounts for the stability of China through all these ages.

If our money goes out, you and I haven't got anything. We have some bonds that are no good and we have something that depends upon somebody's trust, and if the trustee goes out we are out. The Chinaman could always survive.

Now he has been deprived of that little bit of survival through the way in which his own people have administered for him. If, therefore, we pass this bill and you have a wise administrator and the man will withstand the lobbyist who needs enough money to pay off the soldiers another time, or something of that kind, you may be able to do more with such a loan than we imagine. It may be one of the most successful. But if you do just what has been done, of course we are not going to get any of that money to the people, and the people don't expect it.

The CHAIRMAN. That is an argument for rewriting the bill.

Senator THOMAS of Utah. I am not trying to argue. I am just stating the facts about a very, very bad condition.

The CHAIRMAN. That leads to the conclusion that the thing to do is to rewrite the bill.

Senator THOMAS of Utah. It was at that point that when we were writing the bill I wanted the administration to be so big and so broad that if a situation with regard to either China or Japan arose—we got it there so far as Indonesia is concerned, working through Holland—we could move into these other spheres.

The CHAIRMAN. I think we had better have a preliminary talk with the Secretary of State promptly, don't you?

Senator THOMAS of Utah. Yes, I think so.

[Discussion was continued off the record.]

CHINA TOO BIG A BITE FOR RUSSIA

The CHAIRMAN. What chance has Japan got if China goes Communist? Suppose the Iron Curtain drops on China. What chance has Japan got except to climb under the curtain?

Senator THOMAS of Utah. It has all the chance in the world, because a communistic China is just too big a bite for Russia. You must realize this, Senator Vandenberg, that the reason our country is not going to go Communist is because practically every kid in the country has a savings bank account and practically every father has an insurance account, and practically every mother is interested in something of that kind. Now, private property became an institution in China very much longer ago than we have had private property in the West, and all of the problems revert around the private property problem in China. That isn't the case in Russia. Everything belonged to the Tsar. It would be the case in England if England tried to go communistic.

Now start your Russian wave. The communism that you will have at the end of a generation will be so very, very different from the communism that you have in Russia that there will be no comparison, and Chinese communism would probably absorb the other. The Chinaman just knows that that which is his is his, and he just hangs on to it. That is the trouble with the Chinese in trying to divide the land in the north. They have an idea that they know won't work anywhere outside of Manchuria. There we have some chance, because there is some available land, large estates. But in China proper you may not have a communistic State. You may have a single will: you may have a dictator, because they are used to that sort of thing. Politically it may be the type of thing that is run by spies, which is the real evil of Japan. But so far as the independent Chinaman is concerned, you know what has always happened whenever you have tried any of these western tricks on them. They just don't budge.

The CHAIRMAN. Suppose we try to get the Secretary of State Thursday morning at 10 o'clock. If we can't do that, try it Saturday morning at 10 o'clock. And if we can't do that, we will have to skip next week, I am afraid.

Senator THOMAS of Utah. I don't know whether what I have said is the right thing or the wrong thing. I have not talked with anybody.

The CHAIRMAN. It is very interesting, Senator.

Senator THOMAS of Utah. I never know what the State Department is doing on these things, even when they do them.

(Whereupon, at 10:50 a.m., the hearing was adjourned.)

CHINA AID ACT OF 1948

THURSDAY, FEBRUARY 26, 1948

UNITED STATES SENATE,
COMMITTEE ON FOREIGN RELATIONS,
Washington, D.C.

The committee met, pursuant to call, in the committee hearing room, U.S. Capitol, at 10 a.m., Senator Arthur H. Vandenberg, chairman, presiding.

Present: Senators Vandenberg (chairman), Capper, Wiley, Hickenlooper, Lodge, Connally, George, Thomas of Utah, and Hatch.

Also present: Hon. George C. Marshall, Secretary of State, accompanied by Mr. Willard Thorpe, Assistant Secretary; Mr. W. Walton Butterworth, Director, Office of Far Eastern Affairs; Philip Sprouse, Assistant, Office of Far Eastern Affairs; Charles Bohlen, Counsellor; and Hubert F. Havlik, Chief, Division of Investment and Economic Development, Department of State.

The CHAIRMAN. The committee will come to order. The purpose of the meeting is to make the record, and I think we can start.

I have asked Secretary Marshall to come down this morning and present the China bill, which has been recommended by the Department. We will be very glad to hear you, Mr. Secretary.

STATEMENT OF HON. GEORGE C. MARSHALL, SECRETARY OF STATE

Secretary MARSHALL. Mr. Chairman and gentlemen: If it is permissible and agreeable, I will first read a statement I have already made over on the House side in the open hearing, and then I would like to go into the more intimate details in executive session.

CIVIL WAR HINDERS ECONOMIC PLANNING

In consideration of a program of assistance to China, it should be recognized that for the main part the solution of China's problems is largely one for the Chinese themselves. The great difficulty in determining a basis and procedure to justify a program of assistance lies in the conditions which exist in China, military as well as economic.

Thus far, the principal deterrent to the solution of Chinese economic problems is the civil war which has drained the Chinese Government's internal and foreign exchange resources, continued the destruction of property and the constant disruption of economic life, and has prevented recovery. The Communist forces have brought about the terrible destruction to wreck the economy of China. This is their announced purpose—to force an economic collapse.

The Chinese Government is in dire need of assistance in its present serious economic difficulties. However, the political, economic and

85-743—73——23

financial conditions in China are so unstable and so uncertain that it is impossible to develop a practical, effective, long-term overall program for economic recovery. Nevertheless, it is desirable that the U.S. Government render assistance to China in her present critical situation in order to help retard the present rapid rate of economic deterioration and thus provide a breathing space in which the Chinese Government could initiate important steps toward more stable economic conditions.

While there are a multitude of factors in China that are involved in the consideration of such a program, the following appear of first importance:

PRESENT INTERNAL CONDITIONS

China is a country of vast area and population. Through communications north of the Yangtze River are almost nonexistent except by coastal shipping. Local governments are often so corrupt that they are undependable for assistance in the administration of relief measures. The political control by long-entrenched groups is a great difficulty to be overcome in the restoration of China to economic stability. The conduct by the Government of the civil war now in progress, particularly in view of the geographic disadvantages—exposed and lengthy communications, and the inherent difficulties in dealing with guerrilla warfare—demands a high order of aggressive leadership in all major echelons of command, which is lacking. The civil war imposes a burden on the national budget of 70 percent or more, and the financing is now carried on by means of issuance of paper money. Industrial production is low and transportation facilities are poor, the lack of adequate transportation affecting particularly the movement of foodstuffs. The results are an extreme, really a fantastic, inflation of currency, and the inevitable speculation in commodities as well as hoarding.

AID WOULD BE LIMITED

In considering the measures to be taken by the United States to assist China, it is very necessary, I think, to have in mind that a proposal at the present time cannot be predicated upon a definite termination for the necessity of such assistance as in the case of the European recovery program. Provision of a currency stabilization fund would, in the opinion of our monetary experts, require large sums which would be largely dissipated under the present conditions of war financing and civil disruption. In view of this situation, the program should not involve the virtual underwriting of the future of the Chinese economy. The United States should not by its action be put in the position of being charged with a direct responsibility for the conduct of the Chinese Government and its political, economic, and military affairs.

The proposed program of aid for China would provide economic assistance in the amount of $570 million for the period ending June 30, 1949. Of this amount, $510 million would cover minimum imports of essential civilian type of commodities, chiefly foodstuffs and raw materials, and $60 million would be for key reconstruction projects. The program concentrates on those commodities believed to be of maximum aid to Chinese civilian economy and those which will insure the greatest aid per dollar spent.

While the total import needs of China cannot be accurately estimated, in view of the generally disturbed and, in certain regions, chaotic conditions of production and trade, the need for the commodities listed can be demonstrated, we feel, with reasonable assurance. The program will therefore meet the most essential commodity requirements. China will need other imports, of course, including civilian-type commodities not included in the program, and military supplies. In addition, China has certain international financial obligations.

CHINESE FINANCIAL RESOURCES

To meet these additional needs for foreign exchange, China will have available certain financial resources of her own. These include proceeds from exports, miscellaneous receipts from such sources as overseas remittances, the sale of surplus property, and foreign government and philanthropic expenditures in China; and finally, to be called upon if necessary, China's reserves of gold and foreign exchange, which are estimated as totaling the equivalent of $274 million as of January 1, 1948. This amount would be increased to the extent the Chinese are able to bring about an improvement in their net foreign exchange receipts. On the other hand, the amount will be reduced to the extent that reserves must be used, for lack of other available funds, to make necessary payments after January 1, 1948.

U.S. ORGAN TO ADMINISTER AID

It is proposed, in the program submitted, that it would be administered by the agency or establishment of the Government created by law for the purpose of administering programs of assistance to foreign countries, or, pending the establishment of such agency, temporarily by the Department of State in cooperation with the other agencies of the Government directly concerned. The conditions under which assistance is to be extended should be spelled out in an agreement with the Chinese Government, which would be based on the same considerations underlying the conditions for assistance to European countries but of necessity adjusted to the different conditions in China.

The CHAIRMAN. Before you go into your additional discussion, may I ask you just one question to get oriented, Mr. Secretary? Do I understand from the legislation you have submitted that it is your contemplation that this program shall be administered by the instrumentality set up under the European Recovery Act?

Secretary MARSHALL. Yes, sir.

TOTAL FIGURE IN QUESTION

The CHAIRMAN. And will you tell me why the program has jumped from the $350 million which you originally discussed to $570 million?

Secretary MARSHALL. Well, Mr. Chairman, I do not think it is quite fair to say I discussed it. You questioned the total amount——

The CHAIRMAN. I agree with that.

Secretary MARSHALL. And Mr. Thorpe whispered an amount into my ear which he got by multiplying some figure by the number of months involved. I endeavored politely to protest at the time.

The CHAIRMAN. I know very well. I am not holding you to it.

Secretary MARSHALL. And I might say we got into a great many embarrassments, particularly with the Budget Bureau.

The CHAIRMAN. The answer to my question is that the initial figure was purely a casual illustrative figure, precipitated by the committee itself, and this is the first figure that represents actual calculations.

[Discussion was continued off the record.]

The CHAIRMAN. Now go ahead with your own statement. I know you have some more things you want to say, Mr. Secretary.

[Discussion was off the record.]

Senator WILEY. What is the reasonable value of the actual aid we have given China, not what they have paid for it? There must be a reasonable basis for evaluation. The second question involved is, on what basis has the aid been going out? I thought we took back the $500 million that we voted. How did they pay the 1 cent on the dollar? Where did they get the money? In your judgment, how much in reasonable value have we actually been giving here in the last 12 months?

Secretary MARSHALL. I would have to go back into the new series of calculations. I gave you the figure from V–J Day exclusive of surplus property, and that was $1,400 million plus. That was exclusive of all the surplus property. Now are you speaking of the surplus property value?

Senator WILEY. Yes.

Secretary MARSHALL. I would have to have that all dug out for you.

Senator WILEY. We have been doing pretty well by her. It must run into billions, if you take a reasonable value.

The CHAIRMAN. Is that all under cover?

Secretary MARSHALL. We have not featured it. We have just gone ahead without making any public announcements of any kind.

The CHAIRMAN. Is it something that has to be top secret?

[Discussion was continued off the record.]

The CHAIRMAN. Mr. Secretary, this document, a committee print of the House Committee on Foreign Affairs, seems to put down in black and white pretty much what you have said.*

Mr. BUTTERWORTH. You listed in the public hearings the items in this list.

Senator WILEY. Are the figures there?

SUPPLEMENTARY MILITARY PROGRAM

The CHAIRMAN. I would like to ask Mr. Bohlen one more question about the House reaction, because it is pretty important to me. Would you think, Mr. Bohlen, that the effect was sufficiently impressive to slow down the demand of those House Members who insist upon a military program in supplement to what is here proposed?

Mr. BOHLEN. Mr. Chairman, that, of course, is a very hard thing to estimate. I would say the immediate effect upon the committee was just that, because I had had a 2-hour talk with Dr. Judd the day before, and I felt that his questioning of the Secretary in the executive hearing would indicate that many of his stronger feelings had been met by the Secretary's answers, because he did not go into many points

*See: House Committee on Foreign Affairs, *Text of Proposed China Aid Bill and Background Information on Economic Assistance Program for China (submitted by the Department of State)*, February 20, 1948, 80th Congress, Second Session (1948).

that he said were facts after Secretary Marshall's testimony. Judging from his questioning, as compared to his attitude the day before, it was, I think insofar as the committee went, the information that was revealed at the executive session really took a great deal of the heat off the drive for a special military program for China as a means of handling the Chinese situation.

Secretary MARSHALL. I might add—I recall now—that he made the statement that he felt that there was much more that could be said then than even I had said. In some respects I had understated the complication.

The CHAIRMAN. Has Senator Bridges been apprised of this situation, do you know, Mr. Bohlen?

Mr. BOHLEN. He has not. It has only been before the House Foreign Affairs Committee.

The CHAIRMAN. Mr. Secretary, what your story comes down to is pretty much this: that you would agree without reservation that it is necessary for us to make a gesture, and you want to pretty much stop at the point of relief which involves no responsibility.

Secretary MARSHALL. That's it. I say it goes a little beyond that, in that it makes it possible for them to do for themselves things in the way of military assistance because it will release money that they could use for that purpose if they want to do it.

DESCRIPTION OF AID PROGRAM

The CHAIRMAN. Will you describe for the committee just in a word what is involved in the program you recommend, and how it would work?

Secretary MARSHALL. We have selected certain commodities, certain foodstuffs, certain raw materials, that we think are urgently needed there and that also lend themselves to being followed through in their disposal to an extent which permits a reasonable assurance that they will not be misused. Will you recite the list item by item?

Mr. THORPE. The cereals—wheat and rice—cotton, petroleum, and petroleum products, fertilizer, tobacco, metals, pharmaceuticals, coal, and replacement articles for existing capital equipment. Those total $510 million.

Secretary MARSHALL. That is the commodity end of it, and that is a fair approximation of what we think would be their imports during a period including what they have already purchased that is in the pipeline as of February, and it carries it up to June 30, 1949.

Now, in addition to that there is a $60 million item for certain construction. There the choice of the projects is left open, but what has actually occurred is that there have been engineering surveys, three or four of which we consider of general importance to the country, not just a localized desirability. The first of those is the Hankow-Canton Railroad, which is being run on a shoestring—lack of rolling stock, lack of rails. They have had to remove sidings, they have had to take the steel out of branch lines to get the machinery going, the plant running, and that has a very great importance to the whole economy of China south of the Yangtze River, so that is a single item, we think, of general importance to the economy of China and of a character that will not be dissipated. It has a permanency that any decent railroad construction would have.

The CHAIRMAN. How are you proposing to handle that?

Secretary MARSHALL. As to the exact details, you will have to come in on that, Thorpe.

Mr. THORPE. Yes, sir.

MANNER OF TRANSACTION

The CHAIRMAN. Is this a grant or a loan? Who gets the money, and how is it worked?

Mr. THORPE. This is the same formula as in the European recovery program, in that the administrator would determine whether it was to be a grant or loan. I must say that having in mind the situation in China, the emphasis on the program will be on the grant side, of course, but the administrator has this choice to make and will determine the projects. If it is a loan, it will be handled through the Export-Import Bank. It follows the procedural pattern of the recovery program.

Secretary MARSHALL. But the possibility of loans is pretty slender.

The CHAIRMAN. I would think so. But I am particularly interested in knowing how you carry on the transaction. Does this money go to the Chinese Government and do they build the railroad?

PROPOSED RECONSTRUCTION PROJECTS

Mr. THORPE. No; this would be a transaction similar to the ordinary Export-Import Bank transaction, in which the project would have to be spelled out, contracts would be entered into by the Chinese Government which would be approved by the administrator or by the Export-Import Bank, whoever was handling it, and the payments would be paid by the U.S. Government to the contractors upon specific performance.

Secretary MARSHALL. In this particular instance a recognized firm of American engineers had already made a survey of the railroad and I acted on it in February of 1946 and endeavored to get that and two other projects which had also been surveyed by American engineers.

Senator WILEY. Does the Government own the railroad?

Secretary MARSHALL. Yes; it is a Government line.

But I could not get the Export-Import Bank to take over the project. I thought that that one had a fair basis for their arranging the terms of a loan where there was a reasonable possibility of the return of the money if they had a certain control over the railroad receipts.

There was another one which I thought was very important. It had to do with the port of Tanglu or Taku, which is in north China, and is the entrance into the Tientsin-Peiping region. There the railroads have been cut from the north and south since the Japanese took over and they have continued to be cut, so that the only communication except by air with north China is by ship. Well, the passage over the Taku bar used to be an 18-foot clearance. Now it is down to 12, due to lack of dredging and things. But the Japanese had a very effective arrangement there all designed and partly started which would permit the easy transit of barges and small ships during the winter months as well as the summer, to come into the river up to Tientsin.

I thought the completion of that was very important, because the general economy of north China hinged on that.

Again there was another item with relation to coal mines. They needed the coal so badly, and everything in the Yellow River Valley at that time, in the summer of 1946, and in the Yangtze Valley, was dependent on the coal from the Tangshan collieries north of Tientsin, between there and the Manchurian border, and at Chinwangiao, the mines that ex-President Hoover started. The coal from there had to go for 85 miles by rail up to Chinwangiao, be loaded there, and come all the way to Shanghai or Tsingtao in order to provide coal for the railroads and the factories and for the warmth of the people.

Of course, that was a long, roundabout procedure and easily open to interference by the Communists on the rail route up to Chinwangiao, so I was anxious to get the coal mines that they had recovered from the Communists into efficient operation; and the fourth item that I thought had a relation to the general economy of China, which will come up under this, is the electrical power that is needed in the Shanghai district for running a great many of the industrial plants.

POWER SHORTAGE SERIOUS

Their power shortage there is very serious. I thought we probably could cure it in the summer of 1946 and in the fall by buying an airplane carrier and certain generating machinery. There had been a special generating plant available, but the Chinese Government fooled along until it was purchased, I think, by the Swedes. So then we went into the question of purchasing a carrier that was going to be declared surplus and using that to generate power, and we got into some technical difficulties which I do not understand but which made that out of the question. I regarded it as so very important to the economy of China and to the stability of the Government, to get electric power into the Shanghai district, because there is where they have their largest industrial setup, and therefore the greatest hazard of mob violence and things of that sort, where the factories cannot operate.

There are a number of different projects that have been considered. I thought those stood forth, among others, as affecting the general economy of China in a very definite fashion.

The CHAIRMAN. Before you leave the power project, who owns the power project now? Is that a Government operation?

Mr. THORPE. That is private ownership.

The CHAIRMAN. Haven't they any borrowing capacity?

Mr. BUTTERWORTH. They—the American Foreign Power—own the principal electric power and distributing unit, but there is also a French one and there are several Chinese ones, and they are negotiating to form an amalgamated company to participate with the Export-Import Bank on a loan to create new power units.

The CHAIRMAN. Doesn't that, then, lead to the suggestion that this particular project could be taken over by the Export-Import Bank?

Mr. BUTTERWORTH. I don't think they could find the private capital that would go along with that.

Secretary MARSHALL. I don't quite understand your reply.

Mr. BUTTERWORTH. They would not be able to have the means of repayment in dollars unless they got it from the Chinese Government.

Senator LODGE. Is the enumeration you made the reconstruction projects you have planned to take place under this bill?

Secretary MARSHALL. These are ones of which careful surveys have been made and that I myself have an intimate knowledge of, and that I thought had a general application to the economy of China quite different from the other projects that might be brought up.

Senator LODGE. Is there enough law and order in China so that if these projects could be built they could be operated?

Secretary MARSHALL. The railroad is operating now. It is very limited by the lack of cars and engines and things of that sort. There is no interruption to the railroad except physical interruption of poor maintenance and lack of facilities. Shanghai is always dependent on their keeping reasonable order. The affairs up at Taku I think should not be normally menaced, unless the Communists sweep in there and are able to put off heavy charges and blow up what has been done, but they have never held that region, and whether they will get it or not later I don't know.

The coal mine thing presents the greatest hazard. A particular mine that the Government had control of when I left they have lost.

RECONSTRUCTION AND COMMODITIES

Senator LODGE. Of this $570 million, how much is going into reconstruction?

Secretary MARSHALL. $60 million.

Senator LODGE. And the rest into more or less expandable items?

Secretary MARSHALL. Yes, sir.

The CHAIRMAN. The rest goes into commodities substantially paralleling the commodities involved in the European recovery program. How do you answer the question as to the impact on the domestic economy of this additional load?

Mr. THORPE. That has been studied rather carefully, Mr. Chairman. A lot of this is not additional load. It is load which already exists and is in the world allocations. For instance, the wheat and rice are included in here on the basis which they normally allocated to China as their share in the world allocation. The cotton we have had studied carefully by the Department of Agriculture and they feel that this is the appropriate amount of cotton. The petroleum in very large part will not come from the United States but comes from either the East Indies or from the Persian Gulf.

Senator LODGE. Is the East Indies petroleum back in production?

Mr. THORPE. It is coming back in production, yes, so that it has been studied in terms of availability, and we do not believe that it has any serious threat or competition with the European recovery program.

Senator HICKENLOOPER. Are we getting any oil out of the Persian Gulf now? Is any oil coming out of the Persian Gulf now?

Mr. THORPE. I believe so.

Secretary MARSHALL. Abadan is running fuel supplies.

HOW TO IMPLEMENT AGREEMENTS

Senator BARKLEY. Secretary Marshall, a while ago you referred to the fact that the Chinese are inclined to step aside and let somebody else do it if they indicate a willingness to do it, and that willingness might be indicated by the amount of supplies. Have we approached a point in all these military efforts that you have recited here where the Chinese Government has attempted to step aside and let us do it?

Secretary MARSHALL. You say "approached a point now." The pressure has been on to have us do a great many things in connection with it, and they have been very hopeful that we would be forced by public opinion and these various statements and all that have been made into taking such action. Their reaction is one where they are very glad to let you carry a responsibility if you will step in to do it. When you make a recommendation you get agreement, but you don't get any action. It is not very difficult to get agreements, but it is very difficult to get agreements implemented. There is a very strong tendency, as was expressed frankly by any number of their recalcitrant governmental what you call the hard-boiled element of extreme conservatism and persistence in trying to maintain the undiminished power of a one-party government of the Kuomintang, that we would have to do it: "Abide with us, and the United States will have to come in and take over this responsibility." That was very openly expressed, and they tried to crowd me into that over there at the time, when I was insisting that they take quite a different course than they were endeavoring to do.

CHINESE REQUEST FOR MILITARY AID

Senator BARKLEY. Has the Chinese Government made a specific request in connection with this legislation for additional military aid?

Secretary MARSHALL. Just what are the terms, Butterworth?

Mr. BUTTERWORTH. Over a period of time they have made a whole series of requests of varying natures, and of very large dimensions.

Secretary MARSHALL. They have come to me orally time after time, and the tendency is to do it orally as much as they can, and it is quite hard to pin them down to a formal approach, but there have been formal requests for a great many things, and also allegations that we had not fully met our commitments.

LANGUAGE OF THE BILL

The CHAIRMAN. The language of the bill you have suggested is almost a precise paraphrase of the language of the bill that we reported in respect to the European relief, is it not, in connection with most of its terms?

Mr. THORPE. It is a bill which falls in between the Interim Aid bill and the European Recovery Act, and as far as possible we have used the terminology and the approach in the European Recovery Program. But there are some things that necessarily become different as between China and the European situation.

The CHAIRMAN. They also become rather transparent when you read them, and sound almost silly. The idea of asking the Chinese to make a contract with you to "initiate, insofar as practicable, financial, monetary, budgetary, and administrative measures with a view to creating more stable currency conditions, and with a view to increasing China's ability to achieve a self-sustaining economy;".

That is just window dressing, is it not?

Mr. THORPE. No. There are a number of things that we very much hope that they will do, for example, in the tightening up of their tax procedures, their customs collections, facing more definitely the foreign exchange control market as against the black market in foreign exchange.

The CHAIRMAN. In other words, there is some reality to this?

Mr. THORPE. That is right.

Senator CONNALLY. May I ask a question?

The CHAIRMAN. Yes.

HELP NEEDED TO CONQUER COMMUNISTS

Senator CONNALLY. General, if I did not misunderstand you earlier, it seems to be your opinion that, left alone, the Chinese Government, the Nationalists, will never conquer the Communists?

Secretary MARSHALL. Following their present procedure, following their present indifference to basic things that we think they should do with relation to the common people of China; following, when I say "present procedure," their method of handling their military campaigns, they stand almost no show, in my opinion, of conquering the Communists. They might be able to stay the Communist march to the north of the Yangtze River and hold themselves certain points there; they might in Manchuria be able to, say, establish in effect a point of resistance with Mukden as the outlying part and going back to the ports.

They have been in a serious situation something like this several times during the summer of 1946. The Communists were clear down to the Yangtze right across from Shanghai, and the Communists had Shantung.

[Discussion was continued off the record.]

IMPORTANCE OF CHINESE SITUATION TO JAPANESE SITUATION

The CHAIRMAN. There is one thing you have not mentioned. Is there any importance to be attached to the impact of what happens in China on what happens in Japan?

Secretary MARSHALL. The whole eastern coast of China is important to our situation in Japan. At the same time you consider that, you have to consider whether in, you might say, redeeming the coast of Asia we get ourselves in such a seriously weakened position that we defeat ourselves by that procedure.

The original purpose when we got into this thing was to see if we could not get a stabilization of conditions out in China so that the fighting would cease and they would get ahead with their economic recovery. That is what we were struggling for, to try to obtain and to get a government that would get a reasonable support of the people. That, of course, proved an unworkable business.

[Discussion was continued off the record.]

SOURCE OF COMMUNIST SUPPORT

Senator BARKLEY. Where are the Communists getting money to support their armies?

Secretary MARSHALL. They do not have to have much money. They do not pay the fellows much. They have a rich agricultural country and in the main they have succeeded in having the peasant class more or less with them, and on many occasions they use the army to work in the fields. Maybe you can give a little better explanation than I have given on that.

Mr. SPROUSE. I think for one thing they go in and organize these areas. Usually they liquidate the landowners. They are ruthless in that sense, and they give the land to those people who have no land. Since the majority of the Chinese peasants are "have-nots" you in some sense get the support of the peasants for the Chinese Communist movement.

They say they don't use forcible recruitment, but of course they do recruit the peasants into their armies. But they are supposed to give favored treatment to the families of these peasants, so in that sense you might say they live off the land. They have no urban areas under their control in China proper so they don't have the economic and financial problems that the Central Government has.

WAR IS CHINESE RESPONSIBILITY

Senator CONNALLY. General, let me ask you one other question: You said a while ago that at present there is no prospect of the Nationalist Government conquering the Communists. Is it your further idea that if we encourage or try to stimulate the National Government that it will more or less pass the buck and say, "Go ahead and do it yourself"?

Secretary MARSHALL. No, Senator. What I meant was that in our method of doing it we must be very careful not to be generally underwriting the Chinese economy, and in particular underwriting the Chinese military effort. It would be my hope from this, and the action that has just been taken by the Generalissimo in the change of his commanders, that with the munitions they get, the improvement in the economic arrangements for the time being at least, these would be such that they can check or halt the Communist movement, and if they did that, for example, in China proper the situation as to occupation would be not unlike that of January or February 1946. They were down to Kiangsu; they were clear down to the river there.

Mr. SPROUSE. Just north of Shanghai.

Secretary MARSHALL. And down to Anhwei. They had the Yellow River Valley, they had more of Shantung, which is the eastern peninsula, than they have now, and they came down to just to the north of Hankow. That was the situation in January and February of 1946. That is where they have come back to at the present time, with the threat of having a better military force than the Government has, but they are about at the same place.

Now, on the Government side, in Manchuria the Government is back about where it was in February of 1946, with a feeble hold on Mukden. It hasn't gotten to the north of that, largely through the Russian actions. Theirs was a negative figure of defeating the Government's effort at moving with facility, and permitting the Communists to filter in with rapidity.

The question is, Can the Government hold this and improve their position? With these new commanders, and if they get busy with the thing they must do, which is to get down to the people, they have a chance to restrict, and then you can begin to figure out to what degree to go back. They have not lost Peiping, they have not lost Tientsin. They have pretty much lost control of the Tientsin-Chinwangiao Railroad.

Mr. SPROUSE. It is cut in a number of places.

CHIANG'S LEADERSHIP QUESTIONED

Senator CONNALLY. Has Chiang led in any of these field operations in person?

Secretary MARSHALL. No, Senator Connally. He has gone up time after time to put things back on their feet, but the trouble with the Chinese was that he needed a commander up there. Of course, his hold on lots of these people is very, very tenuous, and as they have political power as well as military power, it is not easy. It is very easy to say, "You shall relieve all these ineffective commanders," but it is much harder to do.

However, I never could see why in Manchuria he had to keep a man like that up there.

Senator CONNALLY. Has he done anything to clean out the political bunch that is around him in his Government, rather than the military commanders?

FORMOSA

Secretary MARSHALL. In the echelons below very little has been done.

I did not mention Formosa. That in a sense has been one of the most disheartening things of the whole business. Formosa is a very rich island. The Japanese had it very well set up in what it could produce, and the Chinese went in there and conducted the most discreditable civil government and military power until the Formosans virtually would have welcomed the Japanese back to control the thing. That probably was one of the worst examples of the whole business, because Formosa had no Communist threat at all. They just had a chance to do a good government job, and instead of that they did a rotten job, and the military inflictions on the community were inexcusable, and the thing broke out into a revolution. We have been trying to get him to relieve that fellow over there all the time, and finally when the thing came to a complete breakdown it was done, but these men always have considerable political power.

The CHAIRMAN. Is there any statement that has been made on the record as to why the Wedemeyer report has not been made public?

Secretary MARSHALL. No.

[Discussion was had off the record.]

POSSIBILITY OF RUSSIAN INFLUENCE

Senator LODGE. You spoke of the liability it would be to the United States to take over the whole responsibility in China. What advantage or disadvantage would it be for the Russians? Would they get something out of it if they were not resisted there at all?

Secretary MARSHALL. If they do not resist?

Senator LODGE. If we do not resist them and Chiang is not helped, and they can come in and do whatever they want to, would they get much out of it?

Secretary MARSHALL. If they can dominate Manchuria in that it has a government wholly sympathetic to them, and north China also, that gives them a great economic advantage, in that eastern Siberia is very dependent on the production possibilities and raw materials of Manchuria, and it would be a long time before they could set up anything in eastern Siberia commensurate with what they could get out of Manchuria.

The Russian procedure there has disturbed me quite a little bit for the reason that except for those performances in Dairen, which I do not see what they are trying to do, what they get out of it—except for that they have been very meticulous in their other procedures in Manchuria. I am convinced that under the treaty, the Sino-Soviet Treaty, they have a perfect right to come in and take over that railroad and put troops all the way along. The Chinese, under the treaty, have the obligation to guard the railroad, and they have been unable to do it for one reason or another. They have never been able to get a through line. Under the terms of the treaty the Russians are entitled to 50 percent of the rail employees. They have withdrawn them all a long time back, and yet the railroad is not open and the Chinese Government has not kept its part of the treaty contract, and my reaction would be that the Soviets would justify themselves with ease in putting troops in to do what the Chinese Government is unable to do, and that you could not contest them very much in relation to that.

They have not done those things. They have just let it go in this choke-up. You might say well, they wouldn't do that because that would interfere with the Communist group in Manchuria, but they did not interfere with the Communist group when they were on the railroad.

Senator LODGE. The reason I asked the question is because of the statements you read in the paper by Mr. Judd and Ambassador Bullitt and others that unless we do this, Russia will take over the whole of China and our position in Japan will be gone and Russia will make a tremendous military asset for herself out of China. I was just wondering whether China wasn't such a confused situation that almost anybody, Russia included, would have trouble getting much good out of it.

Secretary MARSHALL. I do not think the Russians themselves could go very far south into China, because they will get themselves into difficulties which they are anxious to avoid. I think they can get most of the things they want by a Chinese-Communist infiltration in control of a region.

[Discussion was continued off the record.]

Secretary MARSHALL. I have been very much disturbed with the quietness with which the Russians have acted there, because it seemed to me that they were building up a case where they could ignore their booty looting of Manchuria, because they would put that on the basis of war booty. They stand on that, and you can say whatever you want to about the outrageous procedure, but they could come up before the United Nations with quite a case, because they could say they had gotten out of Manchuria and hadn't done this; that we, on the contrary, had done this and that, and the Chinese Government had been unable to keep the railroad clear. They had a perfect right under the treaty to do this and that.

I don't know, but I have been fearful of some such procedure as that. Or, it may be that they are busy in the West and they are not ready to turn to the East, and they are perfectly willing for us to make a muddle of it.

CHINA AID DIFFERENT FROM EUROPEAN

Senator LODGE. This whole program rests on an entirely different footing, does it not, from the ERP program? It is a 1-year commitment with a very much more limited objective, isn't that true?

Secretary MARSHALL. Yes, sir. The ERP commitment was built up on a very careful calculation of what the ERP would do for itself in this 4¼-year period, and if it all worked out as it was calculated the thing ended on a zero basis. Of course you have no hope for that in China. The best you can do is to try to give them a further chance to do something themselves to purify the situation.

I do not know how familiar you are with this, but there has been a great deal of pressure in China brought to bear on me personally, and while I was out there, in increasing volume in the late summer and fall and early winter of 1946 not to do anything at all because they maintain—I am talking about bankers, manufacturers, so-called Chinese liberals—that all we were doing was protracting the life of a government which must fall.

Well, now, in all of these discussions they never brought up who was to head this new government, and one or two suggestions were made that were so out of the question that they did not even back them themselves. They were very insistent, though, that what we were doing was simply strengthening what they call the CC Clique, the Ch'en Li-fu organization, who were jubilant themselves that they had the thing in hand and we were, as I say, merely prolonging the agony. Of course that still comes to us in a very heavy volume. You can get part of that by reading the editorials in the Shanghai papers that come right out there in China.

One of the reasons that these men, and particularly the so-called liberal group, have taken that stand so decidedly is the Government procedure, which involves assassinations of people who have stated their views, largely intellectuals and others, who were hounded so much.

[Discussion was continued off the record.]

The CHAIRMAN. May I interrupt just long enough to ask the committee this question? We have to go to the floor at 12 o'clock. I would like very much to have a meeting of the committee Saturday morning, if possible, to find out just what we want to do in procedure in connection with this bill. Would it be possible for the committee to meet at 10:30 Saturday morning? How about it?

Senator GEORGE. I can meet.

Senator BARKLEY. I can meet. I prefer not to meet on Saturday, but I can meet if that is the only convenient time.

The CHAIRMAN. The difficulty is that next week we have to release you and Senator Connally and Senator George to Senator Millikin, so I do want to find out where we are at before that, and I do not see how I can do it unless we meet Saturday morning.

CHINA AID UNDER ERP MANAGEMENT

Senator CONNALLY. May I ask the General one question on that point? General, do you want this to be put under the ERP management?

Secretary MARSHALL. Yes.

Senator CONNALLY. Do you think that would work? Isn't this problem in China so different from the European that you would have to have practically two organizations to run it?

Secretary MARSHALL. I think you will have to have one man under the administrator that heads the China part of the program, but the business procedures and all are not entirely unlike.

FOREIGN AID STATISTICS

Senator WILEY. I want to get a little information about these figures again.

According to the economic text of the committee print, there is a statement that since V–J Day about $1,400 million has been authorized for aid, and that is approximately half of the U.S. Government economic, financial, and military aid since 1937. I think you said that that did not include certain items.

Secretary MARSHALL. It did not include the surplus property.

Senator WILEY. And included in that was about some $60 or $70 million worth of ships?

Secretary MARSHALL. Ninety-seven ships.

Senator WILEY. Which had a lend-lease invoice value of $67 million.

What I am getting at is that I would like to have that broken down so that he who runs can understand, can see, and can comprehend. You have $1,400 million since V–J Day; then you have plus that the invoice value of all this surplus stuff. Then, if there is some other assistance, I would like to have that incorporated in there. There may be other items that we don't understand. And now you are asking for $570 million additional, and you have got on the isles of the Pacific an accumulated reservoir of supplies, surplus goods and munitions, and in this $570 million you are not contemplating that any of that be used for these other surplus goods, but I presume you do contemplate the utilization of some of these surplus munitions and goods in further assistance. If so, to what extent and under what authority, and so forth?

I think that whole picture is one that we should comprehend. Have I made myself clear?

Secretary MARSHALL. Yes.

IS FEAR OF RUSSIA JUSTIFIABLE?

Senator WILEY. Then there is this other phase of it that I think is troubling every American, and I heard it so dynamically stated yesterday morning by one whom I consider one of America's great thinkers, at a breakfast group. He said when he opened up the newspaper and saw what had happened to the land of Benes immediately everything went black. Then immediately he settled back and said, well, the thought came to him: "Here is Russia, fearful, afraid of neighbors. She has gone through 500 years of impact from outside. So she is reaching in here and taking over this country, feeling that this is an outer barrier from these attacks."

"Now," he says, "she has her problems—60 or 70 nationalities within her borders. Is she overextending herself to where she gets, even in

Czechoslovakia, into a situation where she won't be able to assimilate what she is trying to chew?"

That brought up this thought—I think Senator Lodge brought it into the picture, telling about some of our friends and others in the House who say, "Well, if you don't go to war and lick the Russian attempt to take over China, Russia will take over 500 million Chinese and make them into great soldiers on behalf of the Communist movement."

I am asking you whether or not you do not think that there is a great deal of fear in this picture that is not realizable in the sense that Russia can't assimilate all these folks? They won't be assimilated anyway. What is your judgment on that picture?

Then you brought in this other element of Japan. I think we should have you back here to get your analysis of that.

I have heard it said that the Japanese people are starving because of the Russian control of the fish supply, and that creates a tremendous situation in Japan and may result ultimately, I suppose, in Russia taking over Japan.

I think in all these things we are novices, and we need the judgment of you people with the world outlook. I assume that you have that.

Secretary MARSHALL. I am making an attempt at it.

Senator WILEY. I am seriously concerned, but at the same time I am seriously concerned with our being precipitated into conditions like in Palestine, where we can't chew what we have assumed.

Secretary MARSHALL. Senator, I am trying to do my best to see that we act where there is some chance of popular result of action, and that we carefully avoid procedures which will draw us into things which will be tremendously, I think, to our disadvantage, and weaken us in the future.

[Discussion was continued off the record.]

Senator WILEY. Mr. Chairman, on Saturday next, when we hold a meeting under Mr. Vandenberg, is it the understanding that the Secretary is to come back?

Senator CONNALLY. I do not think so. As I understand Chairman Vandenberg, he wanted merely to have an executive meeting to determine procedure, as to how we approach the subject.

HELPING CHIANG CARRY ON

Senator WILEY. I understand this, that the bill simply provides for $570 million. That is just a drop in the bucket, and it is to provide a little food and a little medicine. But certainly over and above that there must be the thought that we are going to continue feeding them some of this surplus ammunition and stuff to help Chiang carry on. I would like to have a further talk with the Secretary here and get his ideas as to what would happen to China if the Communists did take over. What would actually happen there so far as we are concerned, so far as the world is concerned, having in mind what you said of the different factions among the Communists, and having in mind that many a greedy animal has choked itself to death by trying to eat too much.

What is the impact on us? We put in half a billion dollars here now; next year another half a billion. Are we helping ourselves? Are we helping Chiang's cause?

Secretary MARSHALL. This is not a commitment for another half a billion dollars a year from now.

Senator WILEY. I realize that. Is it your humble opinion that this is the thing to do in the light of the present circumstances?

Secretary MARSHALL. You virtually destroy that government if you do not do this now.

CANNOT REVERSE TREND OF CENTURIES

Senator HICKENLOOPER. I would like to make this observation, Mr. Chairman. I presume there is merit in the necessity for this half billion dollars, and it probably will accomplish a commensurate purpose. But you have an economy that for 2,000 years has been in a rumpus and they have had war lords running this section, they have had government standards of various types, and they have had periods of quiet and they have had general periods of turmoil.

The only thing that concerns me is, do we hope, or have we any delusions that in the course of 15 or 20 years we can reorient the mind that has been operating in China for 3,000 years, that has had nothing but turmoil, starvation, confusion, and that situation there? Are we deluding ourselves that we can reorient that thing and establish an orderly government in a vast area over there that is as big as the United States and has 400 million people in it? Or should we look at it realistically and say, "Well, there are certain things we can do in the immediate moment that will be more helpful in our long-range policy than if we fail to do them, and we should do them modestly, without getting ourselves tangled up too much in them."

Secretary MARSHALL. That is about it. But I must say this, that we had a situation in 1946 that bade fair to allow a great many political compromises to be made and to allow a rather liberal group, who were educated men, mostly outside of China, to give a lead to the Government along the lines which we thought not only reduced the turbulence but would be introductory toward its gradual assimilation of the character of government that we think can endure successfully. Of course, that was ripped to pieces by the action, largely, in my opinion, of the dyed-in-the-wool political fellow who wasn't going to resign any political power of any kind. Power was also financial, because his political position was also his governmental position, and, therefore, there was a good chance of making quite a step.

You are exactly right, that you cannot overcome the trend of centuries.

Senator HICKENLOOPER. I got out of law school in 1922 and a fellow offered me a job in China because Sun Yat Sen was going to set up an orderly government there and resources were going to be fine. They are still squabbling.

Secretary MARSHALL. Had it not been for the Japanese War, with the progress they had made up to 1930 I think they would have achieved a pretty wholesome situation. Tremendous progress was made. But as they got into the war and as these fellows got older in

85-743—73——24

their positions and corroded in their selfishness, in their enthusiasm for power, you got around to this present situation.

Senator HICKENLOOPER. I think it is apparent, too, that the completely new position that the Soviet occupies in Europe and Asia, the strengthening in the organization and control, the unity of the Soviet setup, puts a different present picture on it than has existed for a long time.

Senator CONNALLY. Thank you, General. We appreciate your coming up very much.

(Whereupon, at 12:10 p.m., the hearing was adjourned, to reconvene on Saturday, Feb. 28, 1948, at 10:30 a.m.)

GENERAL COMMITTEE BUSINESS

SATURDAY, FEBRUARY 28, 1948

United States Senate,
Committee on Foreign Relations,
Washington, D.C.

The committee met at 10:30 a.m., pursuant to call, in the committee hearing room, U.S. Capitol, Senator Arthur H. Vandenberg, chairman, presiding.

Present: Senators Vandenberg (chairman), Capper, Wiley, Hickenlooper, Lodge, George, Thomas of Utah, Barkley, and Hatch.

CHINA PART II OF EUROPE BILL

The Chairman. Gentlemen, we confront something of a jigsaw puzzle here, and I want to find out what is in your minds about it. I have been trying to get some word from the House as to how they propose to proceed with these three bills. We may get word in the next half hour, because Mr. Eaton is meeting, as I understand it, with the Speaker and the majority leader now. My guess is that the House, at least, will put China on this bill as part II when they get it. There is quite a group over there, headed by Mr. Herter, that wants to wrap all three of them up in one bill. If they try to do that I do not see how we can get through with this thing before summer. I can see some sense in putting China on, because the language of the bill is almost a duplicate of our bill on Europe, except it has to leave out, of course, the cooperative features.

But suppose they put China on this bill as part II and, after we have passed Europe by itself I certainly do not want to put China on it here. I think we are underway with Europe and we do not want to stop. Suppose they put China on. Then the bill comes back and, of course, the natural sequence is to go to conference. But I do not believe we can take an amendment like China just straight to conference and bypass the whole Senate, can we, on China?

Senator Thomas of Utah. Is that not what you did before?

The Chairman. It was only $18 million. It was not really worth talking about.

Senator George. I would not think we could. I would think you would have to bring it back here to this committee, unless somebody in the Senate puts it on as an amendment. I do not know that they will. I haven't heard anything of that kind happening, but it might happen.

If it does come back here as title II of the bill and the Senate has not acted on it, it does seem to me you would be compelled to move that the bill go to the committee for consideration of that additional feature, and we would have to report it back and give the Senate some opportunity to approve it.

The CHAIRMAN. In any event we have to anticipate the fact that we have to take some action on the thing in the next 3 or 4 weeks.

Senator GEORGE. Why could we not report it as a separate bill?

The CHAIRMAN. The only reason we cannot go to work on it right away is the fact that we agreed with Senator Millikin to let you and Senator Barkley and Senator Connally off for 10 days for the tax bill hearings.

EXECUTIVE HEARINGS ON CHINA

Senator BARKLEY. To what extent do you think it is necessary to hold hearings on the China bill?

The CHAIRMAN. I do not think it is necessary to hold public hearings at all.

Senator BARKLEY. That is what I figured.

Senator LODGE. I think we ought to have some private hearings, though.

Senator GEORGE. I do not care anything about public hearings on it, but I do think we have to have hearings. I think it is very important. It is a step over there that, if we once take it in this way, we are going to have to keep up, of course.

Senator HATCH. You are not on the Finance Committee yourself, Mr. Chairman?

The CHAIRMAN. No.

Senator HATCH. Why could you not hold hearings by a subcommittee while they are in session?

The CHAIRMAN. I do not know whether that will be satisfactory or not.

Senator GEORGE. I think Senator Connally would want to be here at the hearings, anyway. You might get along without Barkley and myself.

Senator HATCH. The idea would be just to take the evidence.

The CHAIRMAN. You mean as a referee making the record.

Senator HATCH. And then let the others have the benefit of that record.

The CHAIRMAN. I swear I don't know what to do about it.

Senator HATCH. Does that make sense, Senator Barkley?

Senator BARKLEY. Yes; although you know what happens. Nobody ever reads the hearings held by a subcommittee.

CHINA AID AS SEPARATE BILL

Senator GEORGE. I think it is too important. I think you had better act on it as a separate bill or else, if not put on in the Senate by way of an amendment, that you will bring the bill back here before sending it to conference, and then we could send it to conference. I suppose the parliamentary situation would permit of some expression of opinion, some expression of view by the Senate for our guidance in the conference. I imagine there will be no special opposition to the China aid as the State Department has recommended it, but there may be a disposition to enlarge it, to expand it.

Senator BARKLEY. If we voted it out as a separate bill here, and it were not put on in the Senate but were put on in the House, and it came back to the Senate and we sent it immediately to conference to take up that amendment, the Senate might agree to it or it might agree to it with a modification, which would put it in conference. In either way I imagine the Senate would want to act on it—not just discuss it and send it to conference.

The CHAIRMAN. That is just the point. You think the Senate has to have an independent crack at the China end of this?

Senator GEORGE. I do not see why you could not proceed by subcommittee next week and have the subcommittee consist of all the available members. Senator Connally will probably want to be here and we would like to be here, but in the interest of time——

The CHAIRMAN. When you look at the timetable, we are going to start in the Senate on March 1st with Europe. I would think we would get certainly out of the Senate by March 15th. I don't believe there is more than 2 weeks' debate up here, and I don't know that there is 2 weeks' debate.

Senator GEORGE. That depends on how it gets going. I doubt if there is 2 weeks' debate myself, in view of the latest developments in Europe. But one cannot know.

The CHAIRMAN. Let's assume that, for the sake of argument, we got out of the Senate on March 15th with the European program. Meanwhile the House will, by March 15th, have reported whatever it is going to report, I think, so that when we get through here on the floor we will know what they are working on, and at that time, if we are set up for it, we can do what is necessary. But I think we ought to get ready for it, and the thing that puzzles me is how we can get ready for it with this Finance Committee intervening, and it has to intervene because that was the agreement with the chairman.

Senator GEORGE. Yes; and a whole lot of hearings have been set and a whole lot of witnesses have been invited to come in.

The CHAIRMAN. How long will that run?

Senator GEORGE. About a full week. Senator Millikin has had to regard requests, you know, coming in, whether what they say has any pertinency to the Knutson bill or not, and they want to come in. Beginning on Tuesday, he expects to hold daily sessions, forenoon and afternoon, but on Monday just to go until 12.

NO DISAGREEMENT ON PRESENT FORM

Senator BARKLEY. If we are to proceed here on the Senate bill along the lines of the State Department's recommendation a subcommittee, it seems to me, might well proceed with that. But if there were any effort made to expand it into a military proposition, I think we probably all would like to hear any hearing on that phase of it.

Senator GEORGE. And that would mean a long debate in the Senate, of course.

The CHAIRMAN. In the form it is in, I agree with Senator George that I rather think it will, barring this argument about expansion into military aid, sort of slide through, because you have settled almost everything in advance. There is no argument about administration because you have already threshed out administration and settled it in the European show, inasmuch as this bill puts this thing under the same management. Practically all of the applicable provisions of the European bill are already in here. Those have all been liquidated and settled. You are pretty much down to the amount. I think everybody agrees it is just a gesture, in a sense. It is a pretty expensive one, but nevertheless it is probably unavoidable, psychologically, and I would think that it was a rather logical appendage to the European bill if the House wants to act that way. And to complete the logic I would think that we would reduce the $570 million from a 15 months' basis to a 12 months' basis, so that it, along with all the rest of this show, pursuant to our theory of the thing, comes under review next January.

If you took a fifth off $570 million you would take $114 million off, and you would be down to about a $450 million bill instead of $570 million.

Now, as to the Greek thing, I do not see how there is any logic in tying the Greek thing into this bill at all, because the Greek thing is totally different. It is simply the amendment of another law and an increase in the appropriation.

REDUCE TIME PERIOD TO 12 MONTHS

Senator BARKLEY. Getting back to the China thing, in view of the fact that we reduced the European bill to 12 months why did the State Department recommend 15 months for the China aid?

The CHAIRMAN. I do not know; maybe so they could give us a chance to put our trademark on the bill by reducing it.

Senator LODGE. Mr. Chairman, I would not be prepared to approve any China figure on the scant knowledge I have on it.

The CHAIRMAN. We have no knowledge as of today.

Senator LODGE. I would want to study that figure, break it all down, and see what goes into it before I would approve it.

The CHAIRMAN. I quite agree with that, but I am saying that abstractly I think we should reduce it from 15 to 12. Even on that basis you would be down from $570 million to $450 million.

Senator Lodge. I certainly agree with that. I think we might be able to go further.

The CHAIRMAN. That may well be.

REPORT GREECE-TURKEY ISSUE SEPARATELY

Then the question is the Greek-Turkish thing. That is a rather simple decision. I do not mean that it is not difficult, but I mean there isn't much to wrangle about in respect to detail. You either do or you don't.

Senator BARKLEY. That amount is based on a proportionate figure, based on the present appropriation, the appropriation under which they are now operating, is it not?

The CHAIRMAN. I do not know on what it is based.

Senator BARKLEY. I thought it was a proportionate amount for the months involved.

The CHAIRMAN. It might be more logical for us, inasmuch as we are going to start on the floor with Europe on Monday, and we can not make up our minds finally as to what will be done about China until the House acts, for us to immediately take up Greece-Turkey and get that out of the way, and report that to the floor of the Senate.

Senator LODGE. Here in the committee?

The CHAIRMAN. Yes.

Senator LODGE. Speaking just for myself, Mr. Chairman, I do not have any desire for public hearings on the China or the Greece or the Turkey, but I do feel the need for executive hearings.

The CHAIRMAN. Oh, quite O.K. Yes; indeed.

MILITARY ASSISTANCE TO GREECE AND TURKEY

Senator LODGE. And insofar as the Greek and Turkish thing is concerned, I would like to have General Livesey called, who was the head of our mission there and who is on his way back now, or is back. He has been there for over a year.

We constantly hear these talks from eminent people in the State Department and others that we are going to have to send troops there and all that, and I think it would be very interesting for this committee to hear what he has to say candidly about the military situation there.

Senator HATCH. Is Griswold coming back here?

Senator LODGE. I guess he is.

Senator BARKLEY. He is not coming back now. As I understand it, he is coming back at the end of the fiscal year if he is coming back at all.

The CHAIRMAN. And you know Livesey is coming back here.

Senator LODGE. I know he has left Greece. Wherever he is, they could get him here inside of a few days.

The CHAIRMAN. How would you feel, Senator George, about the Greece-Turkey thing? Do you think we dare go ahead with that with a subcommittee? I do not like that idea.

Senator GEORGE. I do not think you can do that. I think this Greece-Turkey thing is a troublesome situation. We are now asked to increase the appropriation for the Greek-Turkish loan, but obviously the increased appropriation will be applicable only to military aid and military supplies and the maintenance of military personnel over there, and you have a dual administration right there staring you in the face. You have a military mission and military activity, and then you have the European Administrator administering funds to Greece and Turkey, and there you are. It is a very troublesome thing, as it is written here. I don't know; it may be in the original bill.

They may send anybody over there, any officer or employee of the Government. I suppose that would mean armed forces, if you need them.

Senator LODGE. Does that mean troops?

The CHAIRMAN. I would not think so.

Senator GEORGE. It does not restrict it: *

> By detailing to the United States Missions to Greece or Turkey under this Act, or to the Governments of these countries in implementation of the purposes of this Act, any persons in the employ of the United States Government; and, while so detailed, any such person shall be considered, for the purpose of preserving his rights and privileges,

And so forth——

The CHAIRMAN. Then you get over on page 3, line 3:

*For the draft of this Greek-Turkish Aid Bill see p. 745.

By detailing to the United States Missions to Greece or Turkey under this Act, or to the Governments of those countries in implementation of the purposes of this Act, a limited number of members of the military services of the United States to assist those countries, in an advisory capacity only;

Senator LODGE. I think it ought to be clarified at the top of page 2, to put in "subject to the limitations of section 2," or something like that.

The CHAIRMAN. I think this very clearly stops short of anything like combat troops.

Senator LODGE. I think section 2 does, but I think the first part at the top of page 2 raises the question in people's minds, and we can put something in there.

Senator BARKLEY. Does that not refer to a different type of personnel?

Senator LODGE. I think it does. I think it certainly is meant to.

The CHAIRMAN. "Any person in the employ of the Government," and the Army is in the employ of the Government.

Senator GEORGE. Yes, sir—what there is of it.

The CHAIRMAN. It does not say what it means, if it means what it says on page 3.

Senator GEORGE. It is difficult to figure this out. You know, you have made provision for support and supplies and rehabilitation under this European bill for this same territory, for Greece and Turkey. Now you are going to do something else, and this increase here is applicable, in the nature of things, and can be applicable, only to increased military facilities of some sort—training or what not.

The CHAIRMAN. I think that is so.

AMBASSADOR TO GREECE ILL

Senator LODGE. I think Senator George raises a very, very important point. Look at these rumors you hear about MacVeagh, the Ambassador there. I hear he is being sent to Portugal. He is a very, very high-class fellow.

Senator BARKLEY. He has not been in Greece practically since the operation started.

Senator LODGE. He was there last summer.

Senator BARKLEY. Unfortunately he lost his wife, and then he got sick.

Senator LODGE. He was there until the death of his wife. Then he came here and had an operation.

GREEK ARMY SCATTERED

Senator GEORGE. I am greatly disturbed about this whole thing, because I don't see that we are making a lot of progress toward the objective that we started out toward here.

The CHAIRMAN. Except that, by golly, they still aren't in Greece!

Senator WILEY. No, but the Greeks are eating on us and sleeping on us and taking it as easy as can be, and they won't do any fighting.

The CHAIRMAN. I do not know that that is right or not.

Senator LODGE. There is some truth in that. The army has no striking power. Every time a Greek Congressman wants to get a company or battalion for his hometown he gets it, so the army is scattered all over and has no striking power. The Greek soldier is all right as an individual, but when I was there last summer General Livesay said it wasn't going to do any good to increase the Greek Army and give them more equipment if they were going to be scattered from hell to breakfast when they couldn't take over an area and really have any hitting power.

THREAT FROM STALIN

Senator WILEY. I would like to know several things, Mr. Chairman. Before we get into the Greek thing, before we get into China, I would like to have General Marshall back here again. I would like to have him give us the picture, the real picture, as he sees the world situation. Here is Stalin, now, going to take over little Finland. He is going to pull another Czechoslovakia. And here we are, piddling around on whether or not we are going to send troops, yet we are sending our money—$5 or $6 billion of it—over there, so that when it just gets all fixed up he can go in and take it all over.

I don't know. I think the American people should be told definitely just what the situation is, and Stalin should be told. You say you are not ready for war. What the hell! It is coming on you so fast that Stalin is outplaying Hitler at his best take. He is taking more land than Hitler ever took, and he is going right on. The question is, are we going to just let him go on doing this, or are we going to get out?

The CHAIRMAN. Do you mean get out of his way?

POLICY RE-THINKING NEEDED

Senator WILEY. Yes, sir; either get out of his way or stop him, because meanwhile you are just letting him strengthen himself, go all the way, have his own way. He has taken all the bait and taken every trap, and now, in your suggestion by Senator George about China, you are just opening up $570 million more, and the evidence showed the other day that there was $1,400 million given her since V–J Day plus all the surplus, and God knows how much that is, and we don't know how much more beside the $570 million we are going to give in these surplus goods that are out there.

I don't know under what authority we are doing it. And if we are going to do something in Greece, Marshall said definitely that the Chinese—and we know that the Greeks—are perfectly willing to let us do all the fighting and provide everything, and they haven't gone anywhere, so to speak. There are more guerrillas there now than ever were, and I think our policy should be brought up for reevaluation before this committee. We ought to know definitely just where we are going from here before we go ahead and vote $6 or $7 billion and put our necks into a noose that means we are going to continue it and we are going to continue it in this way so that every year Stalin can bite off three or four more hunks.

The CHAIRMAN. Stalin hasn't bitten off anything that we have put any sort of stake in up to date.

Senator LODGE. Don't we attach a lot of importance to Czechoslovakia, though?

The CHAIRMAN. Yes, but she always was in the orbit and nobody ever pretended otherwise.

"EFFECTIVE SHOW OF FORCE" SUGGESTED

Senator LODGE. Don't you think the time is coming when we have to give very serious consideration to the matter of making a really effective show of force somewhere?

The CHAIRMAN. I haven't any doubt in the world that what you say is true and what Senator Wiley says is true. Neither have I any doubt in the world that we are doing one of two things with our European recovery program, and either one of them is necessary. The first is, if we are successful we are saving the situation. Second, if we are not successful, at least we are buying time, which seems to be what our chief activity internationally always is.

Senator LODGE. We are buying time. Are we making any use of the time we are buying?

The CHAIRMAN. The question you ask and the question Senator Wiley asks are questions that have to be answered. But certainly meanwhile we have got to give time, whatever we use it for.

I quite agree with both of you that we ought to use it usefully, but we have sure got to buy it.

UNIVERSAL MILITARY TRAINING

Senator HATCH. Did Secretary Marshall make his statement about universal military training while you were here? You had gone, I think. He told us that that was going to be his answer to Czechoslovakia.

Senator GEORGE. He said that was the greatest thing we could do, to have universal military training promptly. He said it was the greatest step that we could take.

FINLAND THREATENED

The CHAIRMAN. Certainly the greatest thing we can do at the moment is to pass the European bill with the least possible delay and with the least possible emasculation. With Finland going, how you can expect those little Scandinavian countries to stand up unless they have got a shot in the arm of some sort from us is just beyond possibility. And, whether it works or not, by golly in my book that is one investment that ought to be made in an awful hurry.

Senator BARKLEY. In Czechoslovakia, when we were over there in September they were deluding themselves, those that were not on the inside of the Communist fight, with the belief and the claim that while they were under Russian domination in their international relationships, internally they were as independent as we in any other country. I had a feeling that the timetable would run out in 6 months, that Russia was not going to be satisfied with just controlling the international affairs of Czechoslovakia. Well, it took them 5 months to do it, but they have complete control of internal Czechoslovakia, as they have of Yugoslavia and Bulgaria.

The same situation is true in Finland. There is nothing they can do. They are right under the guns. The Soviet has bases there within 10 miles of Helsinki. They won't even let a Finn go through.

EUROPE INTIMIDATED BY RUSSIAN EXPANSION

The more they creep toward the West the more they are going to intimidate Sweden, Norway, Denmark, and all the rest of them. In France they have the jitters right now.

The CHAIRMAN. The farther they creep the closer they get to a new exposure.

Senator GEORGE. They will probably move on Italy first.

The CHAIRMAN. That seems to be the expectation.

Senator GEORGE. And they may not have a lot of trouble there when they do move.

[Discussion was continued off the record.]

REJUVENATE SELECTIVE SERVICE

Senator LODGE. What I can't get through my head is, if the situation is as bad as it seems to be, why we ought not to go to selective service and really get an army that is in shape to do something, instead of this universal military training that won't give us a single man for service and that will take 80,000 men out of our Regular Army for instructors. I can't get it through my head. It seems to me what we want is a readiness. General Eisenhower says the next war will be decided in the first 60 days. That argues for an Army, Navy, and Air Force that are immediately ready.

The CHAIRMAN. I do not see how U.M.T. is the answer except, Senator George, that he meant psychologically.

Senator GEORGE. Psychologically is what he meant.

Senator LODGE. The British have 90,000 troops in Palestine. We couldn't put 90,000 troops in the field without selective service.

Senator GEORGE. We certainly could not.

Senator LODGE. And if we are buying time, one of the uses to which time ought to be put is to make the American people realize that selective services once again may be one of things we have to face. That hurts, but——

Senator GEORGE. They will have to face more than that, too, it seems to me.

Senator LODGE. But they ought to at least start facing that.

Senator GEORGE. That is one big step, but then there are others.

Senator LODGE. That is a very painful thing.

Senator GEORGE. It is a very painful thing.

ERP BILL PSYCHOLOGICALLY IMPORTANT

The CHAIRMAN. All of that is the reason why I think the European Recovery bill, the way we have presented it, is almost impregnable, because we have precipitated a real showdown next January on the realities and, by God, we will know all about the realities by next January, and to fiddle around in the meantime over an authorization, as to whether you shall take $1.25 billion or $1.50 billion of it, when you can recoup yourself even on your next fiscal year's appropriation because you are in control of the last quarter and you can put her up or put her down to balance the books in the face of reality, is beyond me, Just why we should at the moment, when the important thing is the psychology, argue between $1.25 billion and $1.50 billion, just passes my understanding.

Senator LODGE. The only reason is that the people do not realize how grave the situation is.

Senator GEORGE. They realize how grave it is, Senator Lodge, but they do not see how we are meeting it.

The CHAIRMAN. There is not a man upon the floor who does not know how grave it is, to some extent.

Senator GEORGE. I think the gravity is pretty well understood by the man out in the field, but he does not see how these efforts are coordinating and how they are really reaching it. It is pretty difficult. Here we start off with the European programs and here comes China, and now here are Greece and Turkey down here. All that is more or less confusing and we run a grave risk.

STOP SPREAD OF COMMUNISM

I don't want to be too pessimistic about it, but I think we ought to know it, ought to feel it, and ought to understand it to appreciate it. I have seen a complete revulsion of feeling in the United States on this question of aid. Somebody has got to be able to present this picture. I don't mean in our committee or in the Senate. The Government has got to be able to show what we are trying to do and that every single effort we are making moves in the direction of unifying for defensive purposes at least the movement that is going on on the other side of the Iron Curtain.

Every time we bring in anything new it may have some connection with it, but it is not apparent. It is not apparent to the man and woman, busy as they are making a living, carrying on their home affairs.

The CHAIRMAN. I am going to try to say exactly what you are talking about next Monday noon.

Senator GEORGE. If we can't sell it to the American people as one entire program to prevent the spread of communism down to the point where it actually becomes a present and immediate threat to us, although we might not have war before 1954 or 1955 but we will have war of one type or another if they take all of Europe—it is a bit distracting at least to people who are sympathetic with the main program to have the Greek and Turkish thing thrown back here now at this time in a separate proposal, and then the Chinese.

UNITED STATES MUST PRESENT UNITED FRONT

The CHAIRMAN. I think the greatest hazard to American peace is Henry Wallace. I mean that literally, and I mean it for this reason. I have, as I have said repeatedly, faced Mr. Molotov a couple of hundred days last year, and I have seen his reaction to things, and when he confronts what he thinks is a united America which has drawn the line and said "That is it," he thinks it over and usually he backs up. But if he has the slightest encouragement to think that the representatives of the United States who were talking to him haven't got a united country behind them, he just has a holiday, and I know of no reason, sitting over in the Politburo in Moscow, when he sees Henry Wallace carry a congressional district, why he should not just laugh and say, "All I have to do is wait."

Then he looks across the country and he sees polls in which sometimes Wallace outruns Truman somewhat. That is the deadliest thing, in my book, that can happen to the United States.

Senator LODGE. Don't you think that the Russians are going to go so far before next November that they are just going to blow Wallace right up out of the air?

The CHAIRMAN. I do not know whether he will be discredited or not.

Senator GEORGE. I do not know whether it is going to blow that way or not.

POPULAR CONCERN OVER WASTAGE

Senator HICKENLOOPER. Mr. Chairman, one reason I was late is because I have had a superintendent of schools from a small Iowa community in my office for the last three-quarters of an hour. I have known him for a number of years. I have had a dozen Iowa superintendents in my office in the last few days, and probably all of you have. They have been attending this meeting in Atlantic City.

We do not go for a lot of fancy superintendents of schools. We have had, unfortunately, one or two who have damaged our school system out there, but most of them are pretty sensible, well-trained fellows, and they are in pretty close touch with the people, because we have nothing but small towns in our State.

I have been screaming in my inefficient way about the administration of this thing, as most of you have, as the chairman has, as everybody has. I think there is no dispute about the importance of administration.

I am utterly convinced that in my own State the people first feel that we have an obligation in our own interest to attempt to get Europe to rehabilitate itself as the greatest hedge against Communism and everything else. But there is a tremendous fear out there. I have had school superintendents who were Democrats and those who were Republicans in my office in the last 10 days. They are not talking politics. They are talking the practicality of this situation. And the one fear in our mind is that we will get a politician to run the thing and we will have a repetition of UNRRA. They go back to the wastage and to the dollars that have been thrown over the dam, and they say, "We don't care"—I have had any number of them say,

> Our people don't care whether it is $5 billion or $10 billion that we spend. There is no limit on the amount we spend if we get business-like, sound, sensible results out of this thing; if we stimulate Europe and don't get into another giant WPA where the money will be thrown to the birds and go over the dam.

They are worried about the administration of this thing, and if the President sends up the name of an Administrator and an assistant of whom the American people say,

> Well, they are two-fisted guys that will run this show and do a business-like job of it, and they won't two-step in a political or diplomatic way about the thing but they will really get the money to where it is going,

The people in our State, who have been erroneously accused of being isolationists—they never have been—will vigorously support a program of real reconstruction in Europe, but not a program of a gargantuan WPA over there. If they get the idea that this money in a short time is being wasted and being thrown around inefficiently and with a bunch of altruism instead of practical recovery programs, they are going to kick a lot on it. If it is run in a sound way and with acceptable administration, they are going to support it very definitely.

The CHAIRMAN. I think your analysis is correct.

Senator HICKENLOOPER. It is purely administration, so far as I can find it, and not the amount of dollars. I have had any number of people say,

> We don't care whether it is $10 billion or $5 billion. If it has to be $10 billion to get Europe back on its feet in a self-supporting way, we will go for that. But if it doesn't do that, then $5 billion is too much.

BACKGROUND INFORMATION NEEDED

Senator LODGE. Did you see the poll Senator Young took in North Dakota? He sent out 20,000 mimeographed questionnaires. It was overwhelmingly in favor of this proposition.

Senator BARKLEY. I agree with Senator George and the rest of you. Somewhere along the line we have fallen down on letting the American people know exactly the background for all this. The newspapers did not and cannot carry a connected account of all this aid and what it means. You can't read the papers. If you read them every day you don't get a connected story about it. You get sketchy accounts of what happened here and what somebody said there.

I had an experience a week or two ago that rather amazed me. I was asked to address a student body at the University of Kentucky, about 7,000 students, and they had me to lunch with the faculty beforehand. After we finished the meal they asked me to explain the Marshall plan. Well, that is a big task, to do that from our viewpoint, and with all the knowledge we have about it. In the meantime Dr. McVey, who had been president of the university for a long time but had retired and is now president emeritus, had gone out and made a number of speeches over the State on "The Marshall Plan As I Understand It," and they said they were sure that he didn't understand it, from what he said about it, although he was for it and in good faith attempting to give information to the people.

Well, I went on about half an hour or three-quarters without interruption to try to give them the background of what we were all trying to do, and it was discouraging to see the lack of information that these professors had on the thing. When it was over they said that they understood the Marshall plan better than they had before, and so forth and so forth, but if those professors of political science and history and the whole faculty gathered there together do not understand all we know about this and are trying to educate the American people in it, how is the average man in the street, the worker, the farmer, the merchant, the lawyer, going to understand it?

We can't do it. We can't go out over the country and speak about it and tell them what we think about it. But the Government, and I mean not only the executive but the legislative department, all together, has fallen down in letting the American people know exactly what this is all about and why it is.

The CHAIRMAN. I don't know whether they have fallen down or not. In net result they have fallen down.

Senator BARKLEY. That is what I mean.

The CHAIRMAN. I can testify that I have been up to midnight for 3 weeks writing the speech that I am going to deliver Monday noon, and it was the most difficult thing to get all of these factors correlated in the place where they belong. I never had such a jigsaw puzzle in my life.

Senator BARKLEY. That is a fact. There is no doubt about that. That fact confronts all of us.

The CHAIRMAN. And as a result I have to talk an hour and a half to tell my story.

Senator BARKLEY. That is not too long.

The CHAIRMAN. But you can't talk to the country an hour and a half.

Senator BARKLEY. I think there has been a lag there. Who is responsible for it I do not know. I agree with Senator Hickenlooper: If the American people understand it and know the implications, they are for it. I have tried it out on all kinds of audiences.

ADVANCE KNOWLEDGE OF ADMINISTRATOR

The CHAIRMAN. I had a letter from Chris Herter the day before yesterday, and he is underwriting precisely the same point that Senator Hickenlooper and you were referring to, and he wanted to know if it was not possible, in some way, for the President to indicate in advance who is going to be this administrator, so that it could achieve the purpose that the Senator is talking about.

Senator HICKENLOOPER. That would be highly desirable, but I think it is utterly impractical.

The CHAIRMAN. I wrote him and said it was highly desirable but utterly impractical, because all you would do would be to hang up one more target for those who are looking for excuses instead of reasons to throw back against you.

Senator HICKENLOOPER. I would not go to the President and say, "Who in hell are you going to appoint?" I don't think we should. Of course, it would be desirable if we knew.

The CHAIRMAN. For what it is worth, I am going to put that on the line.

Senator BARKLEY. I agree with you about that, yet there are all sorts of rumors floating around about who is going to be appointed.

[Discussion was continued off the record.]

EUROPE LOOKS TO AMERICA

Senator HICKENLOOPER. Senators Barkley and Hatch, you remember last fall, wherever we went, one of the questions that inevitably came up was, "When is America going to save us from this thing?" The question from the people we talked to was, "When is America going to save us from this thing?"

Senator GEORGE. That is absolutely fatal to anything we do, if that is going to be their attitude.

Senator BARKLEY. That is the attitude of the people of the countries under Russian domination now—Finland and Poland and Rumania. They were hoping and praying that we would be in war with Russia and rescue them from Russian domination.

Senator GEORGE. They would like to see us go to war. I want to talk more about peace. I want to see if we can't do something to stop the war.

Senator HICKENLOOPER. I am not suggesting a war. I do not know how you can reach this. I am disappointed in Czechoslovakia, that they have capitulated as easily as they did. The Czechs I know are not that kind of people. But there is a foundation there of support.

Senator GEORGE. They were almost entirely surrounded, Senator, by fringes of this curtain that extended out to them and all around them. Germany is getting in the same hole—even Germany.

EUROPEAN ALLIANCE

The CHAIRMAN. Senator George, in response to your question, your earlier question, the charter says, in article 51, "Nothing in the present charter shall impair the inherent right of individual or collective self-defense, if an armed attack occurs against a member of the organization, until the Security Council has taken the measures necessary to maintain international peace and security."

Then chapter VIII, following with article 52, specifically authorizes regional arrangements for these purposes.

Senator GEORGE. Something similar to what we did in South America.

The CHAIRMAN. Precisely the same thing we did at Rio.

Senator GEORGE. If we had that sort of organization over there, if there were some strong man in Europe who could head it up, then our aid would begin to count, if he were big enough to do it.

Senator HATCH. Wasn't that in effect what Churchill said in his speech at Fulton?

Senator GEORGE. Yes; but more than that.

Senator LODGE. He proposed a common citizenship with France.

Senator HATCH. In his speech in Fulton he proposed an outright alliance.

The CHAIRMAN. You apply the Rio formula to the Committee of European Economic Cooperation countries and you have it.

Senator HICKENLOOPER. How are you going to reach a situation like Czechoslovakia, where there was no armed attack, at least outwardly so far as anybody sees—no armed attack by an outside enemy? Would this formula apply to Czechoslovakia?

The CHAIRMAN. Oh, no; but it would apply, certainly, to what is going to happen probably one of these days in some of the CEEC countries.

Senator THOMAS of Utah. The Finns can't resist. The majority in the Finnish Parliament are Communists.

[Discussion was continued off the record.]

The CHAIRMAN. You want to hear General Livesey?

Senator LODGE. On the Greek and Turkish thing.

The Chairman. Whom else do we want?

Senator HATCH. I don't know how much you think of the ladies' judgment, but Mrs. Gifford Pinchot spent 6 months in Greece.

The CHAIRMAN. She would not interest me any. I do not mean to be invidious, but if we are going out after private citizens we will be here a long time.

Senator LODGE. You do not want any private citizens?

The CHAIRMAN. Not unless there is some awfully good reason.

Senator HICKENLOOPER. Is Griswold coming back?

The CHAIRMAN. I don't know.

Senator BARKLEY. He is reported in the press to be contemplating coming back at the end of the year, which is the first of July—not just coming over on a visit, but to quit. So the papers have said. I don't know whether there is anything to that or not.

The CHAIRMAN. Suppose we say, for the time being, that we will schedule executive hearings on China, Greece, and Turkey starting Wednesday, March 10th, with the expectation of being able to take the bills immediately to the floor when the European bill is concluded. Would that be all right?

Senator LODGE. And confining it to official witnesses, because if we are going to have private people, I have two that I want to have heard, but I do not want to have them heard unless we are going to have a policy of hearing private people.

The CHAIRMAN. Yes; official witnesses.

Senator GEORGE. I would think that would be about the best you can do with this situation.

Senator HATCH. If you pass these bills separately, a Greece-Turkey bill, and it goes to the House and then they wrap them all up in one package and the Senate has already acted on them——

The CHAIRMAN. That would not be any trouble.

Senator HATCH. Then you could come to conference.

The CHAIRMAN. Exactly; then you go straight to conference and you can straighten them out.

Senator HATCH. That would be the quickest way to handle it.

The CHAIRMAN. Yes.

If there is no objection, we will tentatively proceed on that theory.

Senator GEORGE. You are not going to give out any statement to the public?

The CHAIRMAN. I think I have to give out a statement that we will start March 10th on these hearings, and that is all.

Senator LODGE. Will Dr. Wilcox see to it that General Livesey is notified that we expect him?

The CHAIRMAN. You look that up, Dr. Wilcox.

Senator LODGE. I want to know what is happening about Ambassador MacVeagh and Governor Griswold. I have an idea that Ambassador MacVeagh, who is a great expert on Greece—he is not a fellow Republican or personal friend of mine—is being pushed around, and I would like to know what is happening.

REPORT ON ERP

Dr. WILCOX. You have before you a copy of the report on the European recovery program. I would like to say that it has been set to be released for the Sunday morning press. During the hearings the staff was requested from time to time to be sure and put something in the report along particular lines. I suppose there were 50 or 60 of those requests.

I think most of them are in. We had to meet a deadline last night at 8 o'clock, and when we got out of here at 9:30 to get this to the Government Printing Office we were pretty dizzy, and I would not guarantee that everything is in, but we did our best with the pressure we were working under to get all the points in, and we tried to represent the attitude of the committee as well as we could under the circumstances.

Senator GEORGE. May I ask if you have anything in the report indicating that established channels, agencies, and so forth, will be used as far as possible and, as Douglas said in the hearing, to the greatest extent possible in the procurement of supplies?

Dr. WILCOX. That is under part 2, on the administration of the program, and also under the section on the manner of procurement.

Senator GEORGE. We did not put anything in our bill on that, and I thought there would be something in the bill on that, perhaps. It will be very simple to put it in, but if the report covers it I would like to know that, because I have had innumerable inquiries on that one point.

Dr. WILCOX. It covers it, Senator. We tried to make that very explicit.

The CHAIRMAN. I just want to suggest that I have made no plans for continuity of debate. I hope you will all feel not only free to come into the thing from start to finish, but I hope you will all give yourselves whatever assignments you think you ought to take in connection with speaking on this subject. I shall do the best I can to make a sum total presentation Monday noon. It will take me about an hour and a half. But beyond that there is plenty of work to be done by everybody else, and particularly if there is hostile cross-examination I shall need all the assistance that is available.

Senator GEORGE. You are not going to submit to examination until you finish your main speech?

The CHAIRMAN. No, sir.

Senator GEORGE. You should not do that under any circumstances.

(Discussion was continued off the record, and at 12 noon the hearing was adjourned.)

ASSISTANCE TO GREECE AND TURKEY

MONDAY, MARCH 15, 1948

United States Senate,
Committee on Foreign Relations,
Washington, D.C.

The committee met, pursuant to call, at 10 a.m., in the committee hearing room, U.S. Capitol, Senator Arthur H. Vandenberg, chairman, presiding.

Present: Senators Vandenberg (chairman), Capper, Wiley, Smith, Lodge, Connally, George, Thomas of Utah, Barkley, and Hatch.

Also present: Hon. George C. Marshall, Secretary of State, accompanied by Maj. Gen. Horace L. McBride, Maj. Gen. A. M. Harper, and Mr. George C. McGhee, Coordinator for Aid to Greece and Turkey, Department of State.

The Chairman. The committee will come to order.

The bill before the committee this morning is the proposal to amend the Greek-Turkey bill by the addition of $275 million. Secretary of State Marshall.

Mr. Secretary, we will be glad to hear from you.

STATEMENT OF HON. GEORGE C. MARSHALL, SECRETARY OF STATE

Secretary Marshall. Mr. Chairman, you have before you a request for the provision of further American military aid to Greece and Turkey in the amount of $275 million through the period ending June 30, 1949. The proposed legislation would supplement, with respect to these two countries, the European recovery program to which Congress is currently giving its consideration and which envisages only economic assistance to participating states. It would also extend the act of May 22, 1947, for aid to Greece and Turkey, voted by Congress in response to the President's message of March 12, 1947.

American aid already granted Greece and Turkey under this legislation has been of great importance in helping to preserve their freedom and independence during the past critical year. In the case of Greece, however, attainment of our objectives of economic rehabilitation and pacification has been prevented in part by the intensification of guerrilla warfare, supported from neighboring countries.

SOVIET VETO IN UNITED NATIONS

In July and August 1947, Soviet vetoes prevented action by the U.N. Security Council on the majority report of its Balkan Investigating Commission that Yugoslavia, Albania, and Bulgaria were supporting guerrilla warfare in Greece. These three neighboring countries have subsequently flouted the resolution of the U.N. General Assembly of October 21, 1947, calling upon them to do nothing which could furnish aid or assistance to the guerrillas and to cooperate with Greece in the settlement of their disputes by peaceful means. A U.N. Special Committee on the Balkans was set up by the Assembly to observe compliance with its recommendations and to be available to assist in their implementation. Yugoslavia, Albania, and Bulgaria have not only refused to permit this committee to enter their territory but have rejected repeated invitations by the committee to enter into negotiations for the peaceful conciliation of their differences with Greece. The Soviet Union and Poland have failed to accept the places on the committee which are still reserved for them. Greece, on the other hand, has given the committee full cooperation and facilities and has expressed its willingness to comply with the Assembly's recommendations.

INCREASED GUERRILLA ACTIVITY

On December 24, 1947, establishment of a Greek junta under the guerrilla leader Markos was announced over the Belgrade radio and on Christmas Day a large-scale guerrilla attack was launched against the Greek border town of Konitsa which, the U.N. Committee reported, was logistically supported from Albania. Propaganda in favor of Markos and against the Greek Government and the United States is carried on ceaselessly by the government-controlled press and radio in the Communist-dominated countries of Eastern Europe, and intensive campaigns are conducted, obviously with official sanction, to collect money and supplies for the guerrillas in Greece.

As a consequence of foreign aid, the guerrillas have been able to improve their armament as well as their military organization and tactical planning, and they have more than doubled their numbers, chiefly by forced recruiting, since the inception of the American aid program.

The results for Greece have been to pile still more ruins upon those left by the last war and to drive over 450,000 people from their rural homes in the districts where the guerrillas operate to seek refuge in the cities of northern Greece. It is significant that these people have not joined the guerrillas. They have fled from what the President described in his second report to Congress on assistance to Greece and Turkey as "determined and ruthless destruction intended to render people homeless and drive them from the soil; to force them into overcrowded urban centers where they have become charges of an already overburdened state; and to create for them conditions of misery and hardship in the hope that this will make them susceptible to political agitation." The latest example of the ruthlessness of the Greek guerrillas in connivance with foreign powers is the planned removal of 12,000 or more Greek children to the countries of Eastern Europe, recently announced over the Belgrade, Sofia, Bucharest, and Markos radios. The true purpose of this plan can easily be seen behind the fiction of humanitarianism, and the Greek Government has justly denounced it as comparable to the practices of Nazi Germany.

STRENGTHENING OF GREEK ARMED FORCES NEEDED

Intensification of guerrilla activity has made necessary the strengthening of the Greek Armed Forces and the creation of local national guard units to take over from the mobile army the protection of threatened towns, villages, and lines of communications. This has required the diversion by the Greek Government of increasing amounts of money and supplies needed for economic rehabilitation. It has also obliged the American Aid Mission to divert to military purposes some $23 million of the American funds originally intended for the Greek economy. In all, $172 million, or about 57 percent of the total of $250 million programed for Greece under the 1947 act, is being expended for military purposes.

SIGNS OF HOPE

Serious as it is, the Greek situation is not without hope. Unfavorable worldwide and local economic factors which have contributed to retard recovery now show signs of improvement. Important administrative, financial, and fiscal reforms and many reconstruction projects undertaken in Greece with the help of the American mission are beginning to make their effects felt. On the political side, the Greek Government has commendably resisted temptations to meet the crisis by departures from democratic principles and recourse to totalitarian methods, and has carried on as a coalition under the leadership of the chief of the Liberal Party and with the support of a large majority of the freely elected Greek Parliament. Greater military progress may also be expected through intensified operations against the guerrillas by the Greek forces in the numbers and with the equipment presently authorized and now proposed and with the advice of the American military officers who have reached the field.

The danger remains that the Communist-dominated countries of Europe will increase their pressure on Greece just as they have in other directions in Europe. It is the boast of the totalitarian leaders that democracies are incapable of timely and decisive action.

CONSEQUENCES OF FAILURE

Should we fail to continue our efforts, the consequences would be swift and tragic and they would not be confined to Greece. The recent report on Greece of the subcommittee of the House of Representatives Select Committee on Foreign Aid states:

> Should the United States now withdraw its support from Greece, which would almost certainly result in the establishment of a Communist Government, the Communist parties throughout Europe would undoubtedly utilize the opportunity to point out to those who are now valiantly resisting Communist infiltration in other countries the uncertainty of relying on United States help. The effects of such withdrawal would greatly weaken the determination of the constitutional forces resisting Communism elsewhere.

TURKEY

Turkey is confronted by the same threat as Greece, but not in so active a manner. Turkey is economically and militarily stronger than Greece and was thus able, with foreign diplomatic support, to resist

Soviet pressure for the cession of the strategic eastern Province of Kars and Ardahan and for control of the Straits. Thereafter, in the latter half of 1946, the guerrilla movement began in war-ravaged Greece, an easier route for Communist expansion toward the Mediterranean, the Near East, and Africa. To remain relatively safe from aggression, Turkey must remain strong; but she cannot do so indefinitely on her own meager resources. The maintenance of the large army rendered necessary by the situation imposes a special and heavy financial burden.

While the proposed program for military aid to Turkey and Greece involves no moral or other commitment for its continuation beyond the fiscal year 1949, no assurance can be given that additional aid will not be required so long as the active Communist threat to these two countries exists. This was recognized in the President's message to Congress of March 12, 1947, in which he said that he would not hesitate to go before Congress again if further funds or further authority should be needed. This matter, the President then said, was one involving the foreign policy and national security of the United States in a fateful hour.

SITUATION MORE SERIOUS THAN A YEAR AGO

The hour is far more fateful now than it was 1 year ago. By intimidation, fraud, and terror, Communist regimes have been imposed upon Hungary and Czechoslovakia. Totalitarian control has been tightened in other countries of Eastern Europe, and these states have been linked together in a network of alliances. Other European peoples face a similar threat of being drawn against their will into the Communist orbit.

In this situation, the United States must avoid hasty action which could lead to the dissipation of our resources, or fear which would lead to sterile inaction. With calm determination we must pursue the policy confirmed last May by the Congress.

QUESTIONS ON THE PROGRAM

I think it is possible, Mr. Chairman, that I might touch on several things that came up in the House hearing and that have arisen since that will save some questioning later.

The CHAIRMAN. Before you do that, I may ask you, Mr. Secretary, if there is anything about the statement you have made thus far that would preclude our giving it out as a public matter?

Secretary MARSHALL. No, sir. That is permissible.

PROSPECTS FOR IMPROVEMENT

These questions have been asked me: Why, in the light of our previous recommendations regarding the military situation in Greece, there has been so little success, and what are the prospects for improvement? The fact of the matter was, when our people arrived there they found that what was happening was the appeal of each village for protection, and the natural reaction of the political leaders to give the villages that protection, so that the guerrilla forces could select a particular village with reasonable assurance that the troops of the permanent army, the mobile army, were largely chained to the defense of other villages. Each village insisted on holding the guard that it then had, which consisted of troops of the permanent army, and the front involves something over 600 miles, so it was plainly evident that the guerrillas could always be in the majority unless there was some freedom of action on the part of the permanent forces. When there was a Communist threat, the authorities of the village would appeal directly to Athens against the removal of any troops from that village to concentrate to meet this Communist threat, so the first thing that had to be done to remedy that situation was to create what we might call a home guard, 100 battalions, and about 60 of those, I believe, are already formed and armed. They are supported by the Greek Government. The total is to be 100. That means that these villages have a battalion in the village.

Senator CONNALLY. Of what strength?

Secretary MARSHALL. About 500, and they are armed, so that that has released the troops of the permanent army so that they can act with decision and in strength against any action of the guerrillas.

[Discussion was continued off the record.]

GUERRILLA STRENGTH

Senator SMITH. The figure that I got, that I recall, and my colleagues can correct that if I am wrong, was that the guerrillas were approximately 20,000 last October and the Greek Army was about 100,000. Possibly both have increased a little bit since then.

Secretary MARSHALL. The guerrilla strength may have been as you have just stated. I thought it was a shade smaller than that. But the strength of the army was about 120,000 and it is now 132,000. The effectiveness of the army is not measured in the increase from 120,000 to 132,000 nearly so much as in the fact that the army has now become a more compact available mobile unit, and its training has been improving right along.

General Van Fleet was selected to represent this Government in advisory assistance to the Greek Government and particularly the Greek Army—specifically the Greek Army—in their operations against the guerrilla forces because it was felt that he, better than most military leaders that we could provide at the time, understood the business of aggressive fighting. The army had been suffering from this stalemate where they had to defend villages and were prevented from having freedom to act in strength against any guerrilla threat, and that had had an effect on their morale.

Now, with the freedom from village guardianship, leaving that to the home guards, the morale situation has naturally improved, and the effectiveness of the army has naturally improved, but the aggressive leadership that is now being brought into the situation I think is far more effective than even the additional materiel that we hope will be provided and is being provided at the present time.

Senator SMITH. Do you mean, Mr. Secretary, aggressive leadership on our part?

Secretary MARSHALL. On their part.

U.S. MILITARY FORCES IN GREECE

Senator SMITH. It was stated on the floor the other day by a member of the Senate that we knew that we had American troops fighting in Greece.

Secretary MARSHALL. That is not correct. I think the total strength of our personnel, military personnel, in Greece, is about 250 people, almost all of whom are involved in more or less executive administrative tasks.

Senator SMITH. That is clearly what we understood when we were there, and I was amazed at this statement from one of our colleagues who said he knew the facts, that there were American fighters on the frontline in Greece.

The CHAIRMAN. I am getting that statement now from the record, because I think we have to have a categorical reply on the record just as soon as we locate it.

Senator BARKLEY. Let me ask you this, General, I realize what you said, that the effectiveness of the army is not necessarily reflected in the comparative size. But we are asked, and will be asked even more when this matter comes up, why it is that 132,000 Greek soldiers can't destroy and defeat 22,000 or 24,000 guerrillas. That is not an easy question to answer.

FIGHTING ON A MOUNTAINOUS BORDER

Secretary MARSHALL. I would not quite say that, Senator Barkley. Where you can concentrate as you desire, secretly in a mountainous country against a force which has to meet threats over a 600-mile front, the 20-odd thousand guerrilla force has a potential effectiveness far and away beyond its comparative strength with the opposing forces. We were involved in very much the same situation on the Mexican border in 1916. We had 1,200 miles of border and we finally concentrated by putting all the National Guard down there, a great many troops, and it was largely the result of a foray by Villa with a very small force, but the trouble was he could select virtually any point on that border he wanted for that assault, and if we were not there in reasonable strength to meet it he would be successful, as he was momentarily at Columbus, N. Mex.

Here you have 600 miles or more of mountains, with all the trails, roads, and passes, and all the little villages and farms to terrorize, so that a force of the size of the guerrillas has a capacity far and away beyond its comparative strength with that of the other side.

Senator BARKLEY. Is that guerrilla force in a body, or is it deployed along that 600 miles of border?

Secretary MARSHALL. It works both ways. As a rule—I think I am correct, but the General here can correct me if I am not—just where they are at any particular time is a matter of secrecy, and their appearance is sudden and with all the elements of surprise. Is that correct?

General HARPER. That is correct.

Secretary MARSHALL. That, of course, gives a great advantage, and particularly the fact that this force—I believe it has been proven—can retire into a neighboring state for rehabilitation and for protection and for a gathering for another effort. That is quite a pertinent factor.

GREEK HOME GUARD

Senator LODGE. Mr. Secretary, how long has this home guard been established, or is it in the process of being established now?

General HARPER. Since about the middle of December.

Senator LODGE. Then, do you expect that the professional Greek Army will be an effective unified striking force when this spring offensive takes place?

General HARPER. That is a difficult question to answer, completely. We expect it will be positively improved over what it has been.

Senator LODGE. Do you think that this home guard will be able to maintain order and security in these local communities?

General HARPER. To a degree.

Senator LODGE. Are they well trained?

General HARPER. They are not as well trained by any means as we should desire. Their physical vigor is a question of individuals. They are reservists who have been called back to duty. Therefore, unfortunately, it consists of men who have in great measure families and children at home.

Senator LODGE. Will they result in the pressure being taken off the Greek Congressmen, the demand that the Greek Army be subdivided into small units? Will it have that effect?

General HARPER. It will tend to do so. The degree of success that we will have still has to be proven.

Senator LODGE. So at least we can say it is a step in the right direction?

General HARPER. Positively so.

[Discussion was continued off the record.]

U.S. "TROOPS" IN GREECE

The CHAIRMAN. Before you leave that subject, I would like to get this on the record. A Member of the Senate in the debate on March 12 made the following statement: "I may say to the Senator from Massachusetts that as a member of the Armed Services Committee I have reason to know that not only do we have troops up in front unarmed, but the number is being increased."

What is your comment?

Secretary MARSHALL. Mr. Chairman, I would say that the expression "troops" is quite misleading. There was an increase from the original number of military personnel who went to Greece which was——

Mr. MCGHEE. Originally they had slightly over 100.

Secretary MARSHALL (continuing). Slightly over 100, and that has now been built up to 252.

Mr. MCGHEE. The maximum will be around 300.

Secretary MARSHALL. Eventually we will reach the figure of 300.

As I said before, practically all of those individuals are involved in administrative or executive roles or as advisers to Greek military officials, and they are not troops in any sense of the word.

FUNCTION OF AMERICAN MILITARY REPRESENTATIVES

The CHAIRMAN. Will you state for the record precisely what function is served by any American military representatives "up in front"?

Secretary MARSHALL. Those that are, to use that language, "up in front," have been doing, I think, two things: Looking over the situation in order to keep us informed as to just what conditions actually are, and offering advisory assistance to the leaders of Greek units on the divisional level. That does not prohibit their helping by their advice subordinate leaders, and I think the General just referred to the fact that we hope to have some advisers with these home guard battalions.

Senator CONNALLY. He meant regular Greek officers.

Secretary MARSHALL. He meant young regular officers—some advisers with Greek regular battalions.

The CHAIRMAN. Does that mean that we have no American military units of any nature in actual combat?

Secretary MARSHALL. That is correct, sir. We have no combat unit in Greece.

The CHAIRMAN. So that the ordinary use of the word "troops" would not apply to any representatives of the Army that are even up in front?

Secretary MARSHALL. That is correct, sir. What we have could, I think, properly be described as a mission, a helpful mission.

The CHAIRMAN. That is essentially a mission of officers?

Secretary MARSHALL. Yes, sir.

Senator BARKLEY. They are in uniform?

Secretary MARSHALL. Yes, sir.

Senator CONNALLY. You, of course, probably have some enlisted men or noncommissioned officers, of course?

Secretary MARSHALL. Some noncommissioned officers.

Senator THOMAS of Utah. May we have a breakdown of the 252 Americans, to see just what they look like, actually?

Secretary Marshall. I will have that submitted to complete my statement.

[Discussion was continued off the record.]

Senator HATCH. I was going to say, when Senator Vandenberg developed his point, I got the very necessary implication, if not the direct charge, that we have—he used the term "combat troops"; I was going to say "fighting men."

[Discussion was continued off the record.]

Secretary MARSHALL. We have no fighting men in Greece from our Army in the sense that they are occupied in fighting. We have some very splendid officers there in an advisory capacity.

[Discussion was continued off the record.]

U.S. OFFICERS ACT IN AN ADVISORY CAPACITY

Secretary MARSHALL. Our agreement with the Greek Government provides for our officers acting only in an advisory capacity.

There are several questions coming up, but it might help if I read General Van Fleet's statement after his reconnaissance of the front, if that is agreeable.

The CHAIRMAN. Very good.

GENERAL VAN FLEET'S STATEMENT

Secretary MARSHALL (reading).

We have had an opportunity to visit five divisions throughout northern and eastern Greece, some battalions of the National Guard, schools and training centers, gendarmerie, and units of the Royal Hellenic Air Force. We also visited many wounded and prisoner bandits. We saw the results of the very good job the British Military Mission is doing, the tremendous amount of materiel which had been given by Great Britain to Greece. American equipment which will continue to arrive weekly will greatly encourage the Greek Army, and this encouragement already has been felt.

My impression is that the Greek soldier is a magnificent fighter. He is proud, brave and determined. His morale is excellent. More important perhaps is that the morale of the people of northern and eastern Greece is also wonderful. All the Nation, to the last man, is behind the Army, which, with continuing American aid, will finish its job this year. The will of the Greek Nation for freedom, order and everlasting peace is so strong that I can not see any other force able to overcome this will.

I saw a great number of bandits taken prisoner. They are well cared for and well fed by the Army which captured them. Among them there are some fine-looking lads who have been forced by bandits to fight with them, and it is possible that many of these young men will return back to the National ranks.

The other type of bandit is a very poor human type. They are men of low mentality, degenerate, with no sense of honor, without any morality. It is against this type of bandit that the Greek Nation fights, and surely all of us wish to see Greece get rid of them. I come back from this inspection trip very optimistic, and I think this terror will end this year.

We are sorry that there must be fighting and more bloodshed in this cruelly tried country. My advice to the misguided bandits is to surrender immediately. To the others it is to get out of Greece and stay out forever, otherwise be killed. I am sure that with continuously increasing American aid the Greek Army will finish its job and be victorious this summer.

Senator SMITH. What was the date of that?

The CHAIRMAN. That is a statement by General Van Fleet?

Secretary MARSHALL. That was made on March 9.

WHO IS GENERAL VAN FLEET?

The CHAIRMAN. Will you state in just a few sentences just who General Van Fleet is, by way of indicating his experience and reliability?

Secretary MARSHALL. General Van Fleet commanded a regiment in the landing on the Normandy Beaches. When I arrived there, I think 4 days after the initial landing, one of the first statements made to me in the summary of the situation, while we were still on the beach, was that there was a colonel over to the right of us commanding a regiment who should be commanding a division, and his name was Van Fleet.

A little later he was given a brigade—I think in about a week or two—and a little later he was given a division, and commanded it in the sweep across France. He commanded it in the fighting at Metz; he then carried his division into the fighting in the Bulge in December and January of 1944–45. He then carried that division across the Remagen Bridge and, once on the other side, he was given command of the corps that defended the bridgehead, and with that corps he a few weeks later played a conspicuous part in the reduction of the Ruhr encirclement, where some 300,000 Germans were eliminated.

He then, continuing as a corps commander, was involved in the advance to the southeast, toward the Czechoslovakian border, so in a period of 7 months—I think 7 months—he had risen from commanding a regiment of some 3,000 men to commanding a corps of some 200,000 or more men. It was one of the most conspicuous demonstrations of great leadership that we had during the war, and with all that he is a very quiet, unobtrusive man. He has nothing to say for himself at all, but he is effective regarding his job and his mission.

The CHAIRMAN. And he is the head of our military mission in Greece?

Secretary MARSHALL. He is now the head of our military mission in Greece, with the authority of this Government and of the Greek Government to act as our principal adviser in the development of an effective Greek military effort to reduce this guerrilla threat. He, of course, is a part of Governor Griswold's mission.

Senator LODGE. Does he believe that the Greek Army, using only its own personnel, can take care of this thing next year?

Secretary MARSHALL. That is his statement here.

Senator LODGE. And there is no evidence of the need of sending in any non-Greek troops at all?

Secretary MARSHALL. He says nothing of that sort.

The CHAIRMAN. As the public record stands, it is quite clear, on the basis of General Van Fleet's statement publicly, that the answer to your question is reasonably satisfactory.

Senator LODGE. He expresses the belief that the Greek Army can do it by itself.

[Discussion was continued off the record.]

ECONOMIC SITUATION

Secretary MARSHALL. As regards the economic situation in Greece, there has not yet been an opportunity under our program to assist to get full benefit, but we are encouraged by the fact that in January the situation leveled off. In other words, the deterioration which had continued up through December ceased and, to use the expression again, the situation rather leveled off. At that time, as I understand it, although Mr. McGhee can give you the exact details, the budget was practically in balance. In other words, their taxes would meet their expenses. I think the deficit was calculated as only about $10 million gold, and the budget was something over $200 million gold. That is a great improvement over the previous situation. And from that I hope an improvement can be started which will be very important.

As to the work that has been carried on of a purely nonmilitary nature by the Griswold mission, the beneficial results from that would come now, rather than last fall or last winter. The Corinth Canal has been cleared for commerce; certain harbors have been rehabilitated; about 800 miles of road have been rebuilt, which were very important to the general economy, and quite a bit of that nature has been done. Of course, in some places close to the front they have had the unfortunate experience of putting in a bridge and finishing it at night, and having it destroyed before morning by the Communist forces.

I might add that the technique displayed by the Communist Party and its representatives everywhere is to always increase the burden on the state. Turkey, which I will refer to later, is under the heavy burden of having to maintain a very large military force, which it cannot afford to maintain without some measure of relief. It is only necessary to maintain that because of the threats against Turkey. The Greek Government is forced to maintain these hundred battalions of the Home Guards and to make good on the destruction that is done and to care for some 450,000 refugees. All of that takes it out of the Greek exchequer, which is part of the scheme of maneuver of the Communist movement. The strikes in France, the strikes in Italy but notably in France, had as their most serious effect, so long as they were finally avoided, the increased burden on the French treasury which would almost defeat our interim aid program.

Everywhere you find the same procedure, and that is now threatened in Italy. As to Italy——

Senator SMITH. Could I ask just one question about Greece before we get to Italy?

WIDENED AUTHORITY OF MILITARY ADVISERS

I understood Mr. McGhee to say a minute ago that since our new policy in Greece—I am interested in that, because when I was in Greece in October I was told by our military advisers there that they had to be careful about giving any military advice because of instruction from here. Did we widen our authority to them so far as giving military aid instructions which they had not had before?

Secretary MARSHALL. Yes.

Senator SMITH. Could we have, in just a word, the extent of that widened authority? How far have we gone? When I was there in October, they were criticizing the handling of the Greek forces. They said, "If we could tell them what to do we would help them enormously."

Mr. McGHEE. The public statement made at the time of the change in policy was that we would give military advice, operational advice. Previously we had groups there only to determine the logistic requirements of the Greek Army, to see that the right stuff got there and that the Greeks were taught how to use it. We broadened that to give them military advice.

IF ITALY GOES COMMUNIST

The CHAIRMAN. What happens under ERP, and what happens under this bill, if Italy goes Communist? You can answer off the record at the moment, and then call the Department together and have a mass meeting and answer it on the record for the debate.

(Discussion was continued off the record.)

The CHAIRMAN. Now I wish this for the record. I do not ask you to do it now, but please do it in the next 24 hours if you can. On the record I want an answer to two questions, and I want the answers available for use on the Senate floor.

The first question is, if the Communists take control of Italy, what is the effect upon our European recovery program?

Second, if the Communists take over in Italy, what is the effect upon the Greece and Turkey situation and your request for an increased appropriation in connection with it? Will you give me an answer on the record to those two questions?

Senator LODGE. By that phrase "take over" do you mean to get a majority of the votes, or have certain Ministers in the Cabinet?

The CHAIRMAN. Enough so they control the Government.

Senator GEORGE. The developments there within the last 2 days, Mr. Secretary—I know, of course, the State Department should have the best information that can be gotten about it—look very much like the Communists are moving to solidify elements at least of the Socialist groups with them, for the purpose of this April 18 election. And it looks like they may be making some headway, for the time being.

Secretary MARSHALL. I think they are. That is the thing that troubles us so much, and we want to get whatever action that can be used to bolster up the other parties and discourage the Socialists from going over to the side of the Communists.

[Discussion was continued off the record.]

Senator CONNALLY. I want to say that these questions that the chairman has handed you are pretty ticklish questions, to say now, in advance, if and when it is gone. I don't know myself what we would do.

The CHAIRMAN. They are going to be very ticklish questions for the chairman of the committee to confront on the floor of the Senate, and I want to know what his answer is.

Senator CONNALLY. What I am afraid of is the effect on the public and reaction, not here alone but all over the world, as to the fact that we are going to do so and so, here and when. Those are going to be things that have to be determined on the record at the moment when the contingency arises.

Secretary MARSHALL. I do not think I would tie up the Government or the State Department in great detail.

The CHAIRMAN. I would not expect you to. If the answer is that you can't answer, that is the answer.

Secretary MARSHALL. I think something can be said.

EFFECT ON ERP

The CHAIRMAN. Certainly something can be said about what happens to ERP, and it would be very helpful if it was said, I would think.

Senator CONNALLY. On the other hand, if you say we are going to discontinue it, which I assume we would under those circumstances, would not the propaganda machines open up on the ground that now they are trying to browbeat you into voting that way?

Secretary MARSHALL. There is that particular aspect, yes; but I was thinking of the overall aspect.

The CHAIRMAN. Will some witness be available to tell us how you reached the figure of $275 million?

Secretary MARSHALL. Yes, sir. Mr. McGhee, here, is Governor Griswold's immediate representative, and he is in the State Department, and he is familiar with every detail of that.

The CHAIRMAN. Before we go to him, let's see if there are any questions of you. We obviously will have to have another day on this. I thought perhaps we could get through with you this morning and have your associates come back on Wednesday morning.

POLITICAL CONDITIONS IN GREECE

Senator HATCH. We have been discussing almost altogether the military situation in Greece. We are constantly confronted on the floor with criticism of the political conditions in Greece, the contest between the right and the left, and maintaining the rightist Government, against the Liberal forces.

Mr. McGHEE. I think we can tell you that the coalition between the Liberals and the Conservatives, the Populists and the Liberals, is working very well. As you know, quite a lot through the influence of Governor Griswold, Ambassador MacVeagh, and Mr. Henderson in Greece, there was composed a coalition Government who, together, represent the vast majority of the people of Greece. The Liberal, Mr. Sophoulis, was made Premier, and the Populist, Mr. Tsaldaris, Vice Premier,

There was a period during which the coalition did not appear to be working.

Senator HATCH. There was complete division of authority, I have heard. No one has a say. One Minister would overrule others. Did that occur?

Mr. McGHEE. On the face of it there was the division of authority. It is true, of course, that the Cabinet was split between the Liberals and the Populists, and it was true that the Populist Ministers followed Mr. Tsaldaris and the Liberals had a tendency to follow Mr. Sophoulis. However, we have recently been advised that that coalition is working very well; that there is no division in the Cabinet, and we have every reason to believe that the coalition is a satisfactory form of government.

Of course, under the leadership of Mr. Sophoulis, the Liberal, it does avoid the accusation that it is a monarchical-fascist government, which was leveled at the old Government.

Senator HATCH. Then you are satisfied that the political situation is improving?

Mr. McGHEE. Yes, sir. We do not pretend that it is perfect. Obviously a coalition government is by its nature a weak government. It would be much stronger if all the Ministers were of the same political party. However, you can't have both. You can't have a broad-base government, which we feel we have, and as strong a government as you would like. However, discipline within the Government I think has been improved, and our people actually are discussing that with the Government.

[Discussion was continued off the record.]

WEAKNESS FROM DISORGANIZATION

Mr. McGHEE. A lot of the weaknesses in the Greek Government flow from the disorganization created during the war. They greatly overstaffed themselves. Most of their good men were taken away. The improvement of that situation is a long and difficult process, and the Mission is working directly with the Ministers concerned. There has already been some reorganization of the Ministries. There has been the removal of some 8,000, and there will eventually be the removal of 15,000, civil servants from the rolls. The basic thing has been the weakness of the structure rather than the failure of the two party leaders to cooperate.

[Discussion was continued off the record.]

THE BRITISH IN GREECE

The CHAIRMAN. Before you leave, will you describe the present status of the British in Greece, and what is contemplated by way of further British cooperation in Greece?

Secretary MARSHALL. The first intention of the British Government with relation to Greece following our entry into the situation out there was to withdraw their small military combat force of about 5,000 men and, in due time, their advisory personnel who were engaged in purely training functions. Later the British Government reconsidered that, at our urging, and agreed to leave their small military combat force in Greece and to continue on with their personnel in instruction along the lines that they had been engaged in.

The CHAIRMAN. How big was that combat group?

Secretary MARSHALL. 5,000.

Mr. McGHEE. That is correct.

Secretary MARSHALL. With the introduction of our military personnel into the picture, along the lines of advice on operations, tactics, and strategy, we had to find a basis of procedure which would not result in confusion among the British and ourselves and the Greek forces. That has been satisfactorily arranged and the whole procedure is going ahead in a harmonious fashion. The British are doing and have been doing a very valuable work there in their training activities. Most of the equipment of the Greek troops is British equipment, which, of course, the British military personnel are much more familiar with than ourselves, and much better adapted to as instructors, so that has been harmonized and we have no trouble.

The CHAIRMAN. Are the 5,000 British troops still there?

Secretary MARSHALL. They are still there.

The CHAIRMAN. Do they engage at all in combat?

Secretary MARSHALL. They have not up to the present time.

[Discussion was continued off the record.]

Secretary MARSHALL. In 1944 the British military forces joined with the forces of the Greek Government in fighting the Communists in the region of Athens, successfully driving the Communists out. Since then there has been no active military participation. This force is now stationed at Salonika.

The CHAIRMAN. And it is expected to remain?

Secretary MARSHALL. And it is expected to remain.

The CHAIRMAN. Are there any other questions to be asked of the Secretary?

THE GREEK ARMY

Senator CONNALLY. Just one question. With regard to the Greek Army, this 120,000 or 132,000 that you described, have they headquarters somewhere up in northern Greece where they are mobilized, or are they scattered out all over the country?

General HARPER. They have two corps headquarters, one at Salonika and one at Katerine. The main headquarters is in Athens. In addition to that they have eight divisions in the field.

Senator CONNALLY. Do they operate under the jurisdiction of these two corps commanders?

General HARPER. They operate under the corps commanders; yes, sir.

Senator CONNALLY. The reason I asked the question was, it seemed to me it would be necessary to keep a large force concentrated somewhere there so they could send out from it detachments or other organizations to combat these guerrillas that run in and take a village.

General HARPER. In great measure they are deployed throughout Greece; as the Secretary has explained, due to the striking capacity of the guerrillas to strike anywhere, they have to be distributed. It is hoped that when we have all these National Guard battalions formed that they can concentrate the Greek Army. I think the committee will see the effects of that, shall we say, in the middle of April, when it is hoped that we will see an offensive operation on the part of the Greek Army.

Senator GEORGE. How large are the divisions, General?

General HARPER. They are about 8,000. There are two types of divisions, mountain division and heavy division. The mountain division approaches around 8,000, and the heavy division about 9,700.

The CHAIRMAN. We will ask General Harper and General McBride to come back along with Mr. McGhee on Wednesday morning at 10 o'clock. We will continue on into the details of this matter. I just want to release the Secretary today, if possible.

THE JEWISH-ARAB SITUATION

Senator WILEY. I do not see how we can get a clear understanding of this situation unless we ask the Secretary something about this Jewish-Arab situation, and also in relation to American investments in oil lands out there, and that whole layout in the Near East. Just what is the situation? Where does Russia fit into that situation between the Arabs and the Jews, and where do we fit in? What can we expect there at any time?

Secretary MARSHALL. That is a rather brief question, Senator.

Senator WILEY. They are pretty close to one another right up there.

Secretary MARSHALL. The Palestine problem is a very serious one, as you all realize.

[Discussion was continued off the record.]

The CHAIRMAN. I have to go to the floor. I will ask Senator Connally to continue the meeting until we are through with the Secretary, and I will ask the committee to come back at 10 o'clock Wednesday morning; also General Harper, General McBride, and Mr. McGee. There is no meeting tomorrow.

[Discussion was continued off the record.]

MONEY SPENT IN GREECE AND TURKEY

Senator CONNALLY. Have you the information as to how much of the $300 million appropriated for Greece has been spent?

Secretary MARSHALL. I think it is all allocated.

Mr. MCGHEE. Actually by the end of this month all except about $8 million will actually have been spent.

Senator GEORGE. What about Turkey?

Mr. McGhee. All of the $100 million for Turkey has been given to the Department of the Army and the Navy for expenditure. It is true, though, that all of the supplies which have been ordered and are now en route will not reach Turkey until approximately September. All will have been shipped, it is now calculated, in July.

SUPPLIES USE BY THE GUERRILLAS

Senator Connally. What proof have you, if any, or what information have you, that actual supplies for these guerrillas have been coming out of Yugoslavia and Albania?

Secretary Marshall. The type of supplies and equipment found on the dead and wounded.

Mr. McGhee. We have evidence that in the battle of Konitsa artillery shells and other equipment had to come across the border. There was no other way the equipment could have arrived at this place.

Senator Barkley. Is that Russian equipment?

Mr. McGhee. No, sir.

Senator Lodge. Where was it made?

Mr. McGhee. In part it is captured German equipment. In part it is U.S. equipment that was distributed in the Balkans to the underground forces. General Harper can give more details on that.

Senator Lodge. You know it must have come through Yugoslavia and Albania?

Mr. McGhee. Yes, sir.

Secretary Marshall. Wasn't that the finding of the Commission?

Mr. McGhee. That is right.

[Discussion was continued off the record.]

Senator Connally. Are there any other questions by any member of the Senate committee?

Thank you very much, General, for your very enlightening statement. You have no objection to giving the press a copy of your statement?

Secretary Marshall. No, sir.

[Whereupon, at 12 noon, the hearing was adjourned, to reconvene at 10 a.m. Wednesday, March 17, 1948.]

ASSISTANCE TO GREECE AND TURKEY

WEDNESDAY, MARCH 17, 1948

UNITED STATES SENATE,
COMMITTEE ON FOREIGN RELATIONS,
Washington, D.C.

The committee met, pursuant to adjournment, at 10 a.m. in the committee hearing room, U.S. Capitol, Senator Arthur H. Vandenberg, chairman, presiding.

Present: Senators Vandenberg (chairman), Wiley, Lodge, Connally, George, Thomas of Utah, Barkley, and Hatch.

Also present: Maj. Gen. Horace L. McBride, Maj. Gen. A. M. Harper, Lt. Col. Charles I. Davis, and Mr. George C. McGhee, Coordinator for Aid to Greece and Turkey, Department of State.

The CHAIRMAN. The committee will come to order. We can start in on the record.

Mr. McGhee, are you in a position to speak for the State Department regarding the meaning of this bill, and so forth?

Mr. MCGHEE. Yes, sir.

The CHAIRMAN. Will you take a seat at the table?

Do you wish to make a statement of your own first?

Mr. MCGHEE. Yes, Mr. Chairman; I have a statement here, if it please your committee.

The CHAIRMAN. Go right ahead.

STATEMENT OF GEORGE C. McGHEE, COORDINATOR FOR AID TO GREECE AND TURKEY, DEPARTMENT OF STATE

Mr. MCGHEE. Secretary Marshall has discussed the broad political considerations involved in continuation of the program of military assistance to Greece and Turkey. My purpose is to review in greater detail operations to date under the Greek and Turkish economic as well as military programs, and to discuss plans for utilization of the new $275 million appropriation which has been requested.

PROGRESS IN GREECE

The progress thus far made in Greece is not as great as originally was expected, primarily as a result of the continued assistance which Greece's northern neighbors have given to the guerrilla forces. Secretary Marshall has said that the most important success has been the continued existence of Greece as a free nation, which would not have been possible in the absence of the aid program. More specifically, accomplishments under the program have been that the supplies needed to maintain the Greek state, which otherwise could not have been obtained, have been provided; work has gone ahead in reconstructing Greece's badly needed transportation facilities which were destroyed during the war; significant progress has been made in rehabilitation of Greek agriculture; basic economic and governmental reforms which are necessary for Greek recovery have been instituted; and the Greek National Army has been strengthened both in manpower and materiel, and a National Defense Corps has been established.

The American Mission for Aid to Greece consists of the American civilians and 237 American military personnel under the leadership of former Nebraska Gov. Dwight P. Griswold. In carrying out its vast responsibilities, the mission has worked closely with the Greek Government, which has shown every disposition to cooperate in undertaking the basic reforms needed to place the Greek economy on a sound basis. It has not always been easy to assure implementation of measures agreed to be essential, however, largely because of the fact that the Greek Government structure was greatly weakened as a result of the war and occupation and continued insecurity since liberation. As part of the mission's program, concerted efforts are being made to improve the Greek Government machinery.

Intensive guerrilla activity has made it necessary to transfer some $23 million from economic to military programs, and rehabilitation has suffered accordingly. Thus, while it originally was contemplated that about half of the $300 million earmarked for Greece would be spent for economic purposes, the revised program now provides only $127 million. Further, continued insecurity has retarded production and trade and has led to a serious condition of inflation, aggravated by enlarged military expenditures and the drain upon the Greek budget necessitated by caring for some 450,000 refugees who have concentrated in urban areas.

The sum of $84,450,000 has been earmarked from Greek aid funds to finance the civilian imports program, and an additional $37,900,000 under Public Law 84 funds has been provided for this purpose. American-procured Greek imports financed through February 29, 1948, from these funds include 317,000 long tons of wheat and flour, 20,000 tons of milk, 11,000 tons of pulses, 121,000 tons of petroleum products, and 55,000 tons of coal. These supplies have not only sustained the life of the Greek people but have enabled the Greek economy to make the maximum contribution toward self-sufficiency.

The reconstruction program, originally scheduled at $48 million, has been reduced to $25 million. Substantial progress has been made under the amended program in the repair of vital Greek transportation and other facilities destroyed during the war.

The CHAIRMAN. You are referring now to the previous program?

Mr. MCGHEE. That's right. This is a report of what happened under the previous program.

Clearance of the Corinth Canal, which saves 200 miles in passage from the Aegean to the Adriatic Seas, is scheduled for completion by the first of June. Reconstruction of the port of Salonika and repair of the docks at Piraeus are expected to be completed in July. By the first of May, construction and development work on five airfields needed for both military and civilian transport in Greece will be completed. It is expected that by August 31, 800 miles of highways will have been restored to prewar condition. Present estimates are that by March 1 more than 19,000 families will have been rehoused under the mission's program.

Twelve million dollars of aid funds have been set aside for agricultural rehabilitation, and it is expected that, by April 1, 9,000 acres of new land will have been drained and 60,000 acres restored to drainage through the repair and maintenance of existing works.

Senator WILEY. Where is that located?

Mr. McGHEE. Mostly in the north and northeast, in Macedonia.

Senator WILEY. Is that where the guerrillas are?

Mr. McGHEE. This program is in guerrilla territory, but these plains have been rehabilitated and are now in agricultural production.

AGRICULTURAL PRODUCTION

Senator WILEY. What percentage of increase in agricultural production do you estimate?

Mr. McGHEE. I am not sure that I can say that. Greek agriculture is now running about 90 percent of prewar. The immediate objective is to restore it to full 100 percent, and then to increase it.

Senator WILEY. Is that sufficient to take care of the requirements, the food requirements?

Mr. McGHEE. No, sir. Greece has never sustained itself, principally in wheat. Right now Greece needs to import some 400,000 tons of wheat a year. They are actually cultivating some 30-degree slopes in an effort to attain maximum production, and have a $7.50 per bushel, measured in drachmas, price internally to stimulate production. In other products, of course, Greece has an exportable surplus, and exports agricultural products.

Senator WILEY. What is that, now?

Mr. McGHEE. Their principal exports are olive oil and tobacco.

Senator WILEY. I mean in dollars. What does it amount to? You said they have an exportable surplus. Do you mean by that a surplus of exports over their imports?

Mr. McGHEE. No, sir; and exportable surplus of their needs in these commodities. It amounts this year to about $67 million; totally they have an import deficit, a balance of exchange deficit. This ran before the war some $30 or $40 million a year as a deficit. The deficit is much greater now.

The CHAIRMAN. Go ahead.

Mr. McGHEE. Irrigation projects will by April 1st make it possible to cultivate 33,500 acres of land not now in use. To improve the distribution and utilization of agricultural produce, there will be constructed 16 food-processing plants.

A COMPREHENSIVE ECONOMIC PROGRAM

Greece now has, for the first time since liberation, a comprehensive economic program. Of great significance is the fact that there is now, at least on paper, a nearly balanced internal budget. This has been made possible by the adoption of new stringent tax laws and improvements in the machinery for revenue collection; and by substantial reductions in Greek Government expenses, including the removal from the public payrolls of some 15,000 civil service employees. Extensive banking and credit reforms are being instituted. In order to alleviate the hardship on the Greek export trade imposed by overvaluation of the drachma, an exchange certificate plan has been put into operation. This plan provides greater monetary incentive to exporters without incurring the disadvantages which would accompany an outright devaluation of the currency. The Greek distribution system is being drastically reorganized in order to attain more effective utilization of supplies, and by June 30, 1948, all UNRRA stocks will have been disposed of. Trade between Greece and Germany, which constituted the largest single segment of prewar Greek commerce, has to some extent been revived. A Foreign Trade Administration, headed by an American, has been created, which must approve all applications for import licenses based on essentiality to the Greek economy.

U.S. MILITARY ASSISTANCE

On the military side, with American assistance it has been possible to increase the size of the Greek National Army from 120,000 to 132,000 men and to create a National Defense Corps which ultimately will total 50,000 men. Thus, while the guerrilla situation has as yet shown no improvement, the Greek forces are now in a much better position to cope with the problem. Over $100 million worth of American equipment and maintenance supplies have already been furnished these forces, and additional materiel, including mountain artillery and heavy machineguns, are scheduled to be provided under this year's program. The formation and equipment of the National Defense Corps battalions and improvements in the Greek National Army will for the most part have been accomplished by early spring, and the effect of these measures should be reflected in more successful operations of the Greek armed forces during the spring and summer of 1948. The extent of success, however, is of course dependent upon whether the dimensions of the military task are appreciably increased by developments which cannot be foreseen at this time.

THE TURKISH PROGRAM

The special problem of the Turkish program, which consisted of $100 million for military assistance, necessitates a long planning period in order to assure the best use of the funds in increasing the effectiveness of the Turkish armed forces. A military survey group was sent to Turkey to develop a specific list of requirements and to establish a program based on this list in the light of fund and supply availabilities. The final program was completed in December 1947 and since that date procurement has been actively prosecuted. As a result of the normal procurement lags, superimposed upon the rather protracted planning period, the first important shipments to Turkey could not be made until the early months of 1948, and consequently some of the supplies will not be ready for shipment until after the end of the fiscal year. It is estimated, however, that the bulk of the shipments will be ready at U.S. ports before the end of July 1948, and if the capacity of Turkish ports and internal transport permit, as is now believed to be the case, by the end of September 1948 nearly all program cargoes under the present program will have been received in Turkey.

PRESENT FUNDS SOON EXHAUSTED

At the current rate of commitments, virtually all funds in the present programs for Greece and Turkey will be exhausted by March 31, 1948, although deliveries will continue through part of the next fiscal year. It is necessary that funds from the proposed supplementary appropriation be authorized for use at the earliest practicable date in order to initiate procurement for military requirements during the next fiscal year, as well as to meet urgent military needs for Greece during the remainder of the present fiscal year over and above those for which funds are now available. It is for that reason that the Department has requested the Congress to incorporate in the bill extending Public Law 75 authority for the advance by the Reconstruction Finance Corporation of $50 million, to be reimbursed to the Corporation after enactment of the related appropriation bill.*

As it has been stated, the additional funds requested under Public Law 75 are for military purposes only. Both Greece and Turkey are included in the proposed European recovery program now before the Congress, and it is assumed that any additional economic requirements for those countries will be met under that program.

DIVISION OF FUNDS BETWEEN GREECE AND TURKEY

The CHAIRMAN. Will you at that point divide the additional $275 million between Greece and Turkey?

Mr. McGHEE. Our planning is for $200 million to Greece and $75 million to Turkey. It is hoped no commitment will be made for these amounts, and that the Executive will be permitted to allocate in the light of the urgencies of the two countries. The planning study made for Greece contemplates $186 million from Western Hemisphere sources. It provides for no balance-of-payments deficit of funds going to Turkey. This, however, is subject to revision now, and later by the Administrator.

ITEMIZATION REQUESTED

Senator LODGE. Do you have an itemization of the $200 million.

Mr. McGHEE. Yes, sir; we have a detailed itemization which is contained in a secret document which has been furnished to the committee.

Senator LODGE. I don't want to know the secret, but what can you tell me that isn't a secret?

Mr. McGHEE. We will tell you everything, Senator Lodge.

Senator LODGE. I don't want to have it in confidence. What can you say for the record as to the breakdown of that $200 million.

Mr. McGHEE. If it suits the committee, could you wait until General Harper and General McBride testify? They are here representing the American missions in Greece and Turkey, for that purpose, and I think can go into those details in a more authoritative manner than I can. We have detailed breakdowns on the $275 million which are based on careful study, and of course they are all for military expenditures.

The CHAIRMAN. Well now, your money for relief in Greece under the original Greek-Turkey Act is all gone?

---

*Public Law 75, "An Act to provide assistance for Greece and Turkey is printed on p. 766.

Mr. McGhee. All of it will be gone by March 31. As a matter of fact, Governor Griswold advises that his present programs actually extend him $17,500,000 beyond existing funds, so he is cutting back now on his programs.

The Chairman. And there is no relief contemplated in the new addition?

Mr. McGhee. This $275 million includes no funds for economic purposes.

The Chairman. Therefore, all economic relief in Greece after April 1, will be under the European Recovery Program?

Mr. McGhee. That is correct, sir.

ADMINISTRATION UNDER ERP

The Chairman. How will the management of the Economic Recovery Program dovetail and gear into Governor Griswold's machinery and the military machinery?

Mr. McGhee. These questions, sir, remain to be worked out in detail after the ERP legislation is passed and the Administrator is appointed. There is now contained in Governor Griswold's Mission all of the economic activities in which ERP will want to engage. As a matter of fact, there is a wider range of activities in Governor Griswold's Mission than will be in existence in any other of the ERP countries. With the new source of funds, and with the new legal responsibilities, it is quite true that whoever administers this economic program in Greece must look to the ERP Administrator. Our experience has shown, however, that it is extremely important to integrate the economic and military aid programs in Greece. The two are directly related. You can't permit an increase in the Army without an immediate economic impact. You can't sustain the military effort without sustaining the Greek economy. You can have a collapse of the Greek economy through inflation or other financial factors.

What we would seek, sir, if it is not possible to name the same man ERP Administrator and Public Law 75 Administrator, is an extremely close degree of coordination, closer, we feel, than will probably be required in any other European country.

The Chairman. All right.

Mr. McGhee. The requirements of Greece and Turkey for economic assistance from the United States under the European Recovery Program differ considerably. The havoc wrought upon the Greek economy by the war and subsequent turmoil renders it necessary that Greece continue to receive substantial aid to meet her international balance-of-payments deficit during the period covered by the program. In Turkey, while the war did not result in destruction of production facilities, the cutting off of normal sources of imports and the necessity for maintaining a large standing army have had serious effect upon the country's domestic economy. Industrial and transportation equipment suffered from disuse and undermaintenance; agricultural production was hampered by the diversion of manpower and animals to the Army; and stocks of consumer goods were drastically reduced. If Turkey is required to spend substantial amounts on military equipment beyond the American aid program, a gold and dollar drain might be created which would prejudice her participation in the European recovery program on a cash basis.

Senator WILEY. Where is that Army stationed in Turkey?

Mr. MCGHEE. I would like to refer that to General McBride.

General MCBRIDE. They are employed in battle positions right now. They have an Army in the east, an Army in the west, and an Army in reserve in the center, ready for action.

The CHAIRMAN. If the Senator permits, we will get to those questions when the other witnesses appear.

Mr. MCGHEE. The sum of $275 million requested under Public Law 75 is considered to be the minimum amount which will be needed during the period April 1, 1948, to June 30, 1949, to accomplish the objectives of the program. The amount has been established as a result of careful appraisal by the Department of State and the Department of National Defense of the military requirements for Greece and Turkey developed by the respective aid missions in these countries.

The tentative breakdown of the military programs, which was made for purposes of planning and for presentation to the Congress, has not been officially communicated to the Greek and Turkish Governments, nor is it intended that any commitment will be made to those countries as to the amounts which they will receive. It is important that the President be vested with authority to allocate the funds as between the two countries and the various services in the light of the relative urgency of requirements as the program develops. To accomplish this objective it is necessary that the funds be made available in total and not earmarked by country and otherwise.

I would like to discuss briefly two changes in Public Law 75 which have been incorporated in the new draft bill prepared by the Department of State for the purpose of improving the administration of the program:

FBI INVESTIGATION

Section I(2) of Public Law 75 provides that no civilian personnel shall be assigned to Greece or Turkey to administer the purposes of the act until such personnel have been investigated by the Federal Bureau of Investigation. In programs such as these time is an extremely important factor, and in many cases time lost in investigations has been costly; urgent work in the field has been delayed, and qualified applicants have accepted positions elsewhere during the course of their investigations. It is hoped, therefore, than in extending the Greek and Turkish programs the Congress will see fit to authorize the appointment of personnel subject to subsequent investigations by the Federal Bureau of Investigation, provided that such personnel may assume their positions and perform their functions after preliminary investigation and clearance by the Department of State. I understand that similar provision is incorporated in proposed legislation for the European recovery program.

The CHAIRMAN. Is that included in your draft bill?

Mr. MCGHEE. Yes, sir.

Senator LODGE. Why should they need that now that your program has gotten going?

Mr. MCGHEE. Senator, we face the problem of replacement of existing personnel—not in a large number, but a considerable number will come home after this initial year's commitment, and at that time we would encounter the usual 6 to 7 weeks' delay which has been our experience if we waited for the investigations. We feel there is no appreciable risk in the people going over.

Senator LODGE. I don't think there is, but why can't you organize the thing so you could put the investigation on in anticipation?

Mr. McGHEE. I wish it were possible. You know it is very difficult to get personnel. When we get a request for a mission we have to negotiate for several weeks with the individuals concerned, and if they have to wait 6 or 7 weeks they may accept another job during the period they are waiting.

Senator LODGE. Are these people with the Government or people privately employed?

Mr. McGHEE. Both. We have sought people privately employed, and by and large most of our people are privately employed. Then when a fellow gets over, he discovers he needs an assistant, and then you have to wait 6 or 7 weeks for the assistant.

Senator LODGE. If you planned, you would know he would need an assistant before he left.

Mr. McGHEE. I wish we could. The limitations of planning are very great. The picture moves swiftly. People wait until the last minute to decide that they are going to go home. The difficulties of getting personnel are very great.

The CHAIRMAN. Go ahead.

SECOND AMENDMENT IN PUBLIC LAW 75 PROPOSED

Mr. McGHEE. Section I(2) of Public Law 75 also provides that the provisions of the act of May 25, 1948 (52 Stat. 442), as amended, applicable to personnel detailed pursuant to that act shall apply to persons in the employ of the Government of the United States detailed to Greece and Turkey in connection with the aid program. Public Law 402 (80th Cong., second sess.) approved January 27, 1948, expressly repealed the act of May 25, 1948. An amendment of Public Law 75 will be required to meet this situation, and in proposing the legislative change there has been incorporated wording to meet an administrative problem which has been encountered in the establishment of allowances for military and naval officers attached to the American Mission for Aid to Greece. Under the proposed amendment such officers, as well as civilian personnel employed by the mission, may be paid identical travel and subsistence allowances, the amounts to be determined by the President notwithstanding pertinent regulations of the U.S. Armed Forces.

With the exception of the foregoing modifications, it is planned that administration of the funds requested will continue substantially as for those previously approved under Public Law 75 for military purposes. With the enactment of the European recovery program, however, consideration may be given to a change in the organization of the American representation in Greece in order to provide greater coordination of the several American programs in that country.

The CHAIRMAN. Well, Mr. McGhee, I think that is a very good statement, and in many aspects it is very encouraging to me. I want to ask you one or two fundamental questions.

A 15-MONTH PROGRAM

Your amendment contemplates a 15-month program?

Mr. McGhee. The funds requested, Mr. Chairman, will be spent over the period of 15 months. The extension of it, of course, is just for the additional fiscal year. Most of the funds requested will be spent during the fiscal year 1949. A few of the funds would be committed during fiscal 1948. The program, though, is estimated to carry through fiscal 1949.

The Chairman. What I am getting at is, supposing Congress decided to handle this in its fiscal aspect on the same basis as ERP and made the increased appropriation to April 1, instead of to July 1. Would it be a pro rata calculation?

Mr. McGhee. No, sir. There will at the outset of this program be a greater expenditure than would be pro rata, for the reason that we are very anxious to get into the guerrilla war in Greece some material that is vitally needed, and we will move in requisitioning a considerable amount of that material and equipment the moment we have these increased funds. There would be a saving, obviously, and it would be feasible to do it. The saving would not be pro rata.

Could we have a quick estimate of that amount?

Colonel Davis. Beginning the first of April?

Mr. McGhee. That's right.

Colonel Davis. About $10 million to $15 million a month.

The Chairman. For 3 months, that is $30 million to $45 million.

Colonel Davis. That is right off the bat, sir.

The Chairman. I don't know that the committee would be interested in it. I wanted to get the comparable figure.

SIZE OF U.S. MILITARY MISSION IN GREECE

It is particularly important to us, I think, that we nail down beyond any chance for argument the precise size and type of the personnel which goes to Greece at the present time and under the contemplated bill.

I have this memorandum from the State Department this morning. I think the figure is slightly different from those you have used, although not appreciably so. I would like to know if this is a fair statement:

> There are at present 242 U.S. military, including 26 civilians and 41 U.S. naval personnel, or a total of 283, attached to the military sections of the American Mission for Aid to Greece.

That is a total of 283.

> Of the military personnel, 136 men, including 73 commissioned officers and 63 enlisted men (all noncommissioned officers) are engaged in giving military advice to operational units of the Greek forces.

That is a total of 136 men—73 commissioned officers and 63 enlisted men.

> The number of these military advisers is expected to be increased to a full strength of approximately 170, including 90 officers and 80 enlisted men.

Is that correct?

Mr. McGhee. That statement is essentially correct.

General Harper. That is correct.

The Chairman. Is there any point in the activities of these 170 men where they are engaged with combat troops?

AN ADVISORY CAPACITY

Mr. McGhee. They are in an advisory capacity with various echelons of combat troops, yes, sir.

The Chairman. Down to what level?

Mr. McGhee. They are down to the division level, although they may in individual cases advise at lower echelons.

The Chairman. None of them, however—what do you mean by "advise"? Is that advice at headquarters or does it carry on into the field?

Mr. McGhee. It carries on into the field, sir. It is military advice, operational advice.

The Chairman. Do the advisers move into the field with troops?

Mr. McGhee. Yes, sir.

The Chairman. What is the answer, then; what is the authetic and final answer to the critic who says that we are putting——

Senator Lodge. He said we had combat troops in Greece, which is not true.

The Chairman. Is that a correct answer, that Senator Lodge has just indicated?

Mr. McGhee. That is absolutely correct. The missions of these men are not for combat. Our agreement with the Greek Government provides only for advisory services.

Senator Lodge. An officer there as an instructor or observer isn't in a position of a combat officer, and he is liable to get shot at.

[Discussion was continued off the record.]

The Chairman. Perhaps I should have waited with my question, but I wanted to identify these data with your statement on the same subject.

Mr. McGhee. People are arriving and departing, but the figures you gave are substantially correct.

Senator Lodge. Your figure of 136 military advisors, subtracted from 242, leaves 106. Who are they?

Mr. McGhee. They were part of the original mission. Our original function in Greece was to supply the Greek Army. We had people to determine the requirements, supervise unloading, and to teach the Greeks how to use the equipment.

Senator Barkley. Is this number of people referred to there in that memorandum entirely separate and apart from the number who are under Griswold?

Mr. McGhee. All of these, sir, constitute the military portion of Governor Griswold's mission. They are part of his mission. They are separate from the civilian personnel.

Senator Barkley. He has others in his mission?

Mr. McGee. That is correct.

Senator Barkley. How many of them are there?

Mr. McGhee. The figure, I think, is 183 civilians in the mission.

Senator Barkley. So that 183 plus the 283 is the whole contingent?

Mr. McGhee. There are in addition, sir, some Corps of Engineer personnel who are engaged in implementation of the construction program, and certain personnel employed by American contractors who are over and above the mission personnel.

Senator Barkley. They are privately employed?

Mr. McGhee. Yes, sir.

Senator Barkley. The Army Engineers aren't.

Mr. McGhee. The Army Engineers have established a Grecian district in Athens. They are not under Governor Griswold.

Senator Barkley. They are also separate from these you mentioned a while ago?

Mr. McGhee. Yes, sir.

Senator Barkley. How many of them?

Mr. McGhee. There are approximately 254 Americans employed by contractors, and somewhere around 125 Corps of Engineer personnel.

The Chairman. I just want to ask one or two other fundamental questions.

WASTE INCREASE

The greatest propaganda publicity in this country about waste abroad has been attached to what has happened in Greece heretofore. Have you caught up with all of those errors and mistakes, and are you going to quit making them, and are you responsible for them?

Mr. McGhee. Mr. Chairman, one of the greatest burdens this mission has had to suffer is that people have generally attributed to the mission some of the mistakes that it has discovered and has been attempting to correct.

The Chairman. I think that is true.

Mr. McGhee. There was the time that the mission announced that they had discovered $75 million worth of UNRRA supplies in warehouses. That was no new discovery. Everybody knew the stuff was there. The initial cost of that equipment was probably not in excess of $50 million. But we get letters from people in the Department every day who honestly think that is Public Law 75 material.

Senator Wiley. Did you take it over?

Mr. McGhee. No, sir. It was taken over by UNRRA, and the last thing I want to do is to be an apologist for UNRRA. We were not in a position to control the allocation of UNRRA goods. The UNRRA machinery itself, although they had a large number of personnel in Greece, was in a very weak position viz-a-viz the Greek Government. They could not enforce any agreements they had with the Greek Government.

Senator Wiley. What became of the $50 million?

Mr. McGhee. As soon as it was discovered by the mission, we took our best men and created a Division of Distribution under Governor Griswold. We abolished the old Ministry of Supply and got the Greek Government to create a new Ministry of Distribution, and the mission has now scheduled these UNRRA goods so that they say all will be distributed by June.

Senator Wiley. Of what did it consist, mostly?

Mr. McGhee. Everything in the world; a lot of things the Greek Government doesn't want or need; a lot of supplies which for various reasons which I could explain, and which make sense really only in

Greece because it is such a complicated picture, but the various ministries in charge had not distributed the stuff. In a lot of cases the material was destined for parts of Greece that have since been cut off by the guerrillas. In a lot of cases the ministries had held on to the supplies because they were their only source of income, and they wanted to dole them out. In other cases they were holding out for higher prices. In a lot of cases the ministry concerned didn't have the drachma to actually pay for transporting the stuff or, in the case of machinery, for installing it. In many cases there weren't transportation facilities to take the stuff where it was to be utilized.

THE UNRRA PROGRAM

However, the total UNRRA program was a large program. It was some $475 million and the program had only terminated at the period when we came in, so it is not a disproportionate amount of the total supplies that were brought in, if this amount was only $50 million when it was discovered by the mission in October.

I assure you, sir, that there has been no report, even, of the stoppage of the distribution of supplies under this program. There was a subsequent report about food spoilage. We have tracked them all down, and they all pertain to UNRRA supplies, and the mission is making vigorous efforts to see that even UNRRA evils are taken care of.

Senator GEORGE. Who has charge of those supplies now?

Mr. McGHEE. The Greek Government owns the supplies, and previously the distribution was among the various Greek ministries who were concerned with the particular thing involved. There has now been coordinated in the Ministry of Distribution this express authority for the distribution of these supplies to the Greek economy, and there has been developed a program which will assure a fair distribution over Greece in June of this year of all those supplies. Our mission has been very careful not to bring in anything where there were UNRRA supplies that could take up that purpose.

We had, for instance, a large program for canning plants. We discovered a great many there that UNRRA had brought in and had not distributed. We canceled our program. We used the pressure of not bringing anything in until these canning plants had been set up and gotten into operation, and 16 of them have now been installed which had been setting there in warehouses.

Senator WILEY. What do you mean by canning plants?

Mr. McGHEE. To process foods. There is a great surplus of certain foods in Greece, but due to lack of refrigeration and preservation facilities it cannot be preserved for future use. We have established community canning projects where the people can bring their fruits and vegetables and have them canned on a cooperative basis.

LANGUAGE CHANGES IN THE LAW

The CHAIRMAN. One thing more from the head of the table. Will you take the text of this bill and point out to us the precise language which changes existing law?

Mr. McGHEE. Yes, sir; I will attempt to do that. I am not any authority on legislative law.

The basic thing, of course, is the extension of the amount.

The CHAIRMAN. Let's start at the front of the bill and show me the language which is different in this bill from the existing law.

Mr. McGHEE. Yes, sir. All of this language amends existing law. This language does not repeat any existing law.

The CHAIRMAN. You say subsection 2 is all new language?

Mr. McGHEE. Yes, sir.

The CHAIRMAN. Is that your understanding, Dr. Wilcox?

Dr. WILCOX. Essentially that is true. Section 2, paragraph 3, is modified by adding the words "to the United States missions to Greece or Turkey under this Act, or to the governments of those countries in implementation of the purposes of this Act." That language is to be found both at the beginning of paragraph 2 of section 1 and of section 2, paragraph 3.

Mr. McGHEE. That is correct.

Dr. WILCOX. There was some question as to why that added clause was put into the bill at both these points—whether that had any real effect upon the number of men to be detailed.

Mr. McGHEE. No; I would like to explain the purposes of that, sir. This is a technical point. It arises out of our efforts to preserve the civil service rights of Americans in the employ of this Government who go to Greece either in the mission or in the employ of the Greek Government. We relied for the preservation of these rights upon this act which was subsequently repealed, so it was necessary to introduce new legislation in order to preserve the rights.

In introducing the legislation we changed the wording in the manner Dr. Wilcox has mentioned, in order to indicate that the preservation of these rights applies both to people detailed to the government concerned and enter into the employ of the government, and to include also those who are members of American missions who are assisting the government. That is the only intent, sir. It is to take care of the repeal of this law on which we depended in our original act, and to further clarify the language of that law so that we can be sure that the people who are members of the American missions, and not just those detailed to the governments, are covered.

In doing so, we are sought to take care of another technicality which has arisen, in that the GAO tells us that our right to give the same allowances to military personnel as to civilian personnel was questionable under the law. We have been doing that because we have been feeling that it is fair to the military people to get the same allowances as the civilian personnel. We seek to clearly establish that right, which will assure that what has been done in the past will in fact be legalized.

The CHAIRMAN. Is that all this act does, except to change the amount of the appropriation?

Mr. McGHEE. That is correct. We have inserted, of course, the $50 million RFC loan which previously was $100 million and the FBI change. That is all the changes.

The CHAIRMAN. Where is the FBI change?

Dr. WILCOX. At the bottom of page 2.

Mr. McGHEE. These are all, in fact, technical points, sir, except the increase. Basically we do not seek to change this act.

The CHAIRMAN. So that the passage of this suggestion of yours, aside from increasing the amount $275 million, and aside from referring to a $50 million temporary advance from RFC, does nothing except to correct the personnel status as you have indicated?

Mr. McGhee. That is correct, sir. Of course, we have expressed in our presentation to you the intent of applying this money for military purposes only.

Senator Connally. Mr. McGhee, have you been over there personally, in Greece?

Mr. McGhee. Yes, sir; I was there for a brief period, approximately 3 weeks, 4 months ago, Senator Connally.

ORIGINAL INTENTION OF PROGRAM

Senator Connally. I notice you say that under the program you originally intended to spend a great deal of money, about half of the $300 million, for the economic program. The revised program now provides only $127 million.

Mr. McGhee. That is correct.

Senator Connally. Is that out of the $300 million or out of this?

Mr. McGhee. This all refers to last year's program.

The Chairman. So you are still giving some of this $100 million that you are giving them here, or $200 million.

Mr. McGhee. The $200 million will go entirely for military expenses. We rely on the ERP.

Senator Connally. That whittles that down.

Now, you said a good many supplies went to maintain the Greek state. Do you mean the running expenses of the Greek Government?

Mr. McGhee. No, sir; that probably is loose language. It means the Greek nation.

Senator Connally. I got the idea that you meant you had to subsidize the Greek Government to keep it in operation.

A BASIC PART OF THE PROGRAM

Mr. McGhee. No. sir; one basic part of our program is that our funds were spent for supplies to be purchased abroad. The Greek Government never sees any of this money.

Senator Connally. You said something about levying new taxes. My understanding is that when we went in there, Greece had a very poor taxation system.

Mr. McGhee. That is correct.

Senator Connally. A lot of rich fellows were escaping taxation. Have you corrected that?

Mr. McGhee. We think we have. The basic problem was that there has been no legal requirement for people in business in Greece to keep books as we do in this country, and there was no evidence upon which to base an increase tax system, as we have in this country. There has been introduced in Parliament, and we expect to have passed any day, a law requiring that by April 1 all business concerns must keep books.

TAX REFORMS

Even before that can take place, largely due to our pressure, new tax reforms were introduced which increased taxes 40 percent.

Senator Lodge. What kind of taxes?

Mr. McGhee. One has to use the best taxes one can get, in the absence of any basis for a direct income tax. The most profitable of these taxes have been taxes against people who have made windfall profits, taxes against importers who have made windfall profits, taxes against people who made profits out of the loans that they had made before the currency suffered inflation; increased taxes against the shipowners, which was a law recently passed and which will for the first time assure that the Greek shipowners will pay a fair share of their profits to the Greek Government.

They now pay a tax of 40 percent on their earnings, and it is not the earnings that they say are their earnings; it is a tax on earnings based on what that type of ship will earn in the world market according to Lloyd's register.

There is a tax on nightclubs. Nightclubs have since been abolished in Greece. But basically the attempt has been made to impose the tax on people who have the capacity to pay.

THE CORINTH CANAL

Senator Connally. Mr. McGhee, how much did you spend on clearing the Corinth Canal?

What did that cost?

Mr. McGhee. We originally estimated it might cost us $2 million. We now estimate that it will cost us some $700,000.

Senator Connally. That is not a large amount, but that does not contribute so much to the domestic economy of Greece. That is, it does not contribute except to Greece's getting out in the Adriatic, does it?

Mr. McGhee. It serves two functions, sir. Ships in their national trade will go through and will pay revenue to the Greek state in foreign currencies, which will be very useful. In addition any ship going from Athens to the western coast of Greece will be saved the 200-mile trip around the Peloponnesus. And Patras—which is an important port in the Gulf of Corinth—is a very short distance—only 50 or 60 miles—from Athens directly, whereas if you have to go around the Peloponnesus it is a very great distance.

PETROLEUM PRODUCTS

Senator Connally. What did you do with the 121,000 tons of petroleum products?

Mr. McGhee. That has first priority to supply the Greek military machine. They have a number of trucks, a tremendous number of trucks, engaged in transport. That is for both military and civilian use. The civilian use is the normal civilian use in a backward country. There are relatively few automobiles in Greece, and during most of the period of our aid mission, gasoline has been eliminated for pleasure purposes. Only government employees, doctors, and people of that sort can get gasoline for automobiles. Greece has almost been out of gasoline and petroleum products several times since we have been there.

AIR FIELDS

Senator Connally. You are building and developing five airfields?

Mr. McGhee. That is correct.

85-743—73——27

Senator CONNALLY. You say they are needed for both military and civilian transport in Greece?

Mr. McGHEE. Mostly for the military.

Senator CONNALLY. Why should we spend any money giving them civilian transport facilities for airplanes, when you can walk across Greece?

Mr. McGHEE. Greece needs at least one international airport. That pays for itself, of course.

Senator CONNALLY. All of this new money, then, would be for the military?

Mr. McGHEE. That is correct.

Senator CONNALLY. And we are going to increase the personnel somewhat?

Mr. McGHEE. No, sir. We anticipate on reducing the personnel.

Senator CONNALLY. The military personnel?

Mr. McGHEE. No, sir. That will go up to the levels the Chairman has read, and will level out.

Senator CONNALLY. We will increase that somewhat?

Mr. McGHEE. On the civilian side we hope to decrease.

Senator CONNALLY. I hope you increase your military and get busy over there.

A TIE-IN WITH ERP

How do you plan now to tie this in with ERP? You said there was some hope that the ERP man and the mission head would be the same man. You will get your eggs pretty badly scrambled if you don't look out in that sort of thing.

Mr. McGHEE. As I started to say, this is our objective. It depends on the final form of the ERP legislation and upon negotiations with the Administrator. I am advised by our lawyers that nothing under the present wording precludes that, and we would seek to justify that on this basis, which I have explained, that we have found by experience the necessity for extremely close coordination between the military and the economic efforts, and hitherto, of course, this has all been under the control of Governor Griswold. We feel that it is necessary that the two be conducted as one program.

GREEK RECOVERY

Senator CONNALLY. How long do you figure it is going to take to complete this plan to crush the guerrillas and establish the Greeks on a high plane of prosperity and happiness?

Mr. McGHEE. Sir, we do not seek to establish the Greeks on a high level of prosperity and happiness. I think the answer on the economic side is really a part of the economic recovery program. That program is a 4-year program, and Greece is one of the 16 countries. It is unlikely that Greece will recover ahead of general European recovery, because her recovery really depends upon general European recovery. Before the war she sold most of her products to European countries, and some 40 percent to Germany. She bought most of her things from European countries, some 27 percent from Germany.

I think since Greece did not have a complicated industrial setup, which means you have vast numbers of workers who are dislocated if you don't have the raw materials, that Greece in many ways has a simpler problem in recovery, at least to her prewar level, bad as it was, than do other European countries in achieving their prewar levels.

IMPROVEMENT IN THE GREEK GOVERNMENT

Senator CONNALLY. Has there been any improvement in the Government over there? They have had a coalition sort of government. At first, you had a great deal of difficulty, one Minister going in one direction, another Minister going in a different direction. Has that been improved any?

Mr. McGHEE. Originally there was this difficulty you mentioned. I don't pretend it is working to everyone's complete satisfaction. There are certain inherent difficulties in a coalition movement. Sophoulis is the Prime Minister and Tsaldaris is the Foreign Minister and Deputy Prime Minister. We have been recently advised that the coalition is now working very well together. A month ago I would not have told you that, because there was a fairly difficult situation, and our chargé called on the Greek Government and advised them of the concern we felt.

Senator CONNALLY. Why don't you tell them "To hell with you; if you don't get busy and work together we will withdraw"?

Mr. McGHEE. I assure you Governor Griswold tells them something like that, or stronger than that, about every week in the year.

Senator CONNALLY. They don't do anything about it?

Mr. McGHEE. You can see some improvement, and the fact that this coalition now appears to be working is heartening. We don't pretend it is as good as it can be. It is one of the things we have to put up with if we want to have a coalition government.

Senator CONNALLY. In Greek political life there are a whole flock of factions and groups over there. Every little group has a leader, and they are butting in and raising the devil about something.

Mr. McGHEE. That is correct.

Senator CONNALLY. It looks to me like they ought to have a strong pronouncement: "You fellows here want to get ahead with this program. You had better cooperate. If you don't, we are through."

Mr. McGHEE. Of course, they can analyze the world situation in many ways as well as or better than we, and they know what a difficult position it would create for us if Greece fell to the Communists. This no doubt gives them a little more assurance in their dealings with us, and this probably cannot be avoided. But I agree completely with you that those administering our aid do, and I assure you Governor Griswold does, and those who have been close to him and have seen his operation, use to the maximum that bargaining power of our aid.

[Discussion was continued off the record.]

The CHAIRMAN. Are there any other questions of Mr. McGhee?

Senator WILEY. Yes; I wanted to ask one question.

You have given us the additional amounts that you are asking for aid to Greece and Turkey. Now we have got, as you have already testified, quite a good-sized mission to Greece, and I presume we have quite a good-sized mission to Turkey.

Mr. McGHEE. Not so large, of course, sir.

PAYING FOR THE MISSIONS

Senator WILEY. I want to know whether that mission is paid out of the sums you are asking for.

Mr. McGHEE. The mission is paid out of these funds. Last year the Appropriations Committee of the House limited the amount to be spent for administrative purposes under this act to $4,500,000, of which no more than $300,000 could be spent in Washington, and we have lived under that limitation.

Senator WILEY. I suppose the military are not paid out of it?

Mr. McGHEE. The military are not paid out of that sum. The military are paid out of the total sum of Public Law 75.

Last year we did have some post-UNRRA funds, which will not be available this year. That was $39 million.

SOURCES FOR GREEK AID

Senator WILEY. You had $39 million more than was appropriated for aid last year? Is there any other source of revenue for Greek aid in any way?

Mr. McGHEE. The only other source would be through surplus property credits, but the supplies available against such credits are just about eliminated, so it is unlikely that there will be any substantial amounts going to Greece further under the existing credits. There is a $25 million credit which has not yet been exhausted, but there are no supplies available in Germany, available against that credit.

Senator WILEY. At what do you estimate the reservoir of UNRRA supplies on hand?

Mr. McGHEE. I would judge that the original cost value of the supplies remaining would probably be around $35 million. This, of course, has in many cases very small current utility value. A lot of these stocks are in a bad state of repair. Many of them do not fit into the program. They are really things which are surplus to the basic requirements of Greece, which is what we are considering.

Senator WILEY. Then you have outlined, so far as you know, any what you might call revenue sources for aid for Greece?

Mr. McGHEE. That is correct; out of Greece's own earnings in the world markets.

Senator WILEY. Or where we are holding the bag.

Mr. McGHEE. That is correct, sir.

Senator CONNALLY. Mr. McGhee, under this bill the President could switch money from Greece to Turkey or Turkey back to Greece?

Mr. McGHEE. That is correct.

Senator CONNALLY. Up to the limit of the appropriation?

Mr. McGHEE. We feel that is desirable. The situation can change greatly in each country. Previously we had some flexibility in that we could shift from the economic to the military, and we did do that. Under this we would not have that type of flexibility. This is solely a military expenditure.

Senator CONNALLY. With regard to this $200 million, will that be for equipment, supplies, ammunition, and food for the army?

Mr. McGHEE. General Harper will give you that breakdown, Senator, but it is basically for the subsistence of the Greek Army, plus the supplies they need.

U.S. SHIPS FOR GREECE

Senator WILEY. I saw in the papers last night, or heard somewhere, that the President had transferred to Italy some 200 ships. Well, are we going to transfer ships to Greece?

Mr. McGHEE. We have transferred under this program six gunboats to Greece. There is no plan for the transfer of further ships to Greece. There are, under the program, plans for the transfer of four submarines to Turkey. That is included in the military breakdown.

The CHAIRMAN. All right; thank you, Mr. McGhee.

Senator WILEY. I just want to ask Mr. McGhee, in the transfer of these ships and the transfer of these gunboats, that is over and above this money, again?

Mr. McGHEE. No, sir; it is included in the money, and the cost of these, according to the policy of this Government, is charged against this program.

Senator WILEY. Do you know on what basis they figure?

Mr. McGHEE. The basis varies. The basis in general, I would say, under this type of goods, runs from 10 to 20 percent of original cost.

Senator WILEY. In actual money, approximately what would it be? We are disposing of these gunboats or submarines or whatnot. How much would the total amount be that would reduce this total amount in paying the bill, $5 or $10 million?

Mr. McGHEE. The value of the submarines, which for instance are the only ships or surface vessels to be transferred this year, as I recall, is what, $4 million?

General McBRIDE. About $4 million. We don't have the six gunboats figure. We can find that for you.

Senator WILEY. Was there any other property transferred?

Mr. McGHEE. No, sir.

Senator WILEY. Any airplanes?

Mr. McGHEE. Oh, yes; but they are all charged against this program. The original act requires that anything charged to Greece or Turkey be charged against this program.

Senator WILEY. Then the idea is, if we appropriate this money, the Army and Navy will sell the goods and they get the money?

Mr. McGHEE. That's correct. The money goes to them in compensation for what is provided on the same basis that these supplies would be sold to any country to which it is our policy to sell. There are no cut-rate prices given on equipment going under this program which would not be given to any other country to whom we sell such supplies.

Senator WILEY. But the results of the sale mean that this amount of money is transferred, then, to the Army and Navy for them to go ahead and spend?

Mr. McGHEE. No, sir. Normally the Army and Navy take the money and, of course, requisition and purchase supplies to replace things that are taken away.

Senator BARKLEY. Does any of it go into the general fund of the Treasury?

Mr. McGHEE. To my knowledge none has.

Colonel DAVIS. I might clarify that a little bit. We have a certain criterion of requirements for the Army from which we determine the supplies that may be applied against these programs that are excess to our requirements, to the actually foreseeable requirements of the Army. If those supplies that are needed for these two programs are excess to our requirements, they go into this program at the disposal price that we would dispose of these supplies for to any other purchaser. Now, if we receive, under a deal like that, $10 million for that amount of property, that goes into the miscellaneous receipts of the Treasury. If the requirement is sufficiently great for these two programs that we need to take things out of our stocks that we have to replace, then that money is retained in the Army fund and is used to replace the items on our shelves that we have to have.

Senator WILEY. Does that apply to the Navy in the same way?

Colonel DAVIS. So far as I know, in general that is correct.

Mr. MCGHEE. The $4 million would go into the general receipts.

Colonel DAVIS. If those ships that were provided were excess to the Navy's requirements, I am under the impression that that is covered into the miscellaneous receipts of the Treasury. But if we provide an item that we have to replace for use of the Active Army, we keep that money and go out and make our purchases for their replacement.

Senator CONNALLY. That is very satisfactory.

[Statements by General Harper and General McBride, and all of the discussion incident thereto, were off the record.*]

The CHAIRMAN. Is there anything else? Thank you very much, General. We are obliged to you, Mr. McGhee, and to all of you for your helpfulness. I think you have made a pretty good case. In fact, that is an understatement.

I would like to meet on Friday morning at 10 o'clock and write up this bill and have it over with. Senator Lodge had a witness.

THE CHINA AID BILL

Senator GEORGE. We are not going to do anything about China in this bill?

The CHAIRMAN. No. Then we will go right to China after we do this.

Senator, you suggested that you had a witness who knows whereof he speaks. I wonder if he would not be more eligible for the Appropriations Committee than he would for us, under the general concept that we confront.

Senator LODGE. All right; whatever you say.

The CHAIRMAN. At any event, let's try and all be here at 10 o'clock Friday morning to finish up this bill. I am skipping Thursday because there is a Republican conference tomorrow, and I thought perhaps, Senator, you still needed a free day.

Senator BARKLEY. I will take it.

The CHAIRMAN. We will recess until Friday.

[Whereupon, at 11:45 a.m., a recess was taken until Friday, March 19, 1948, at 10 a.m.]

---

*For the prepared statements by Generals Harper and McBride see pp. 740, 743.

ASSISTANCE TO GREECE AND TURKEY

FRIDAY, MARCH 19, 1948

UNITED STATES SENATE,
COMMITTEE ON FOREIGN RELATIONS,
Washington, D.C.

The committee met, pursuant to adjournment, at 10 a.m., in the committee hearing room, U.S. Capitol, Senator Arthur H. Vandenberg, chairman, presiding.

Present: Senators Vandenberg (chairman), Capper, Smith, Hickenlooper, Lodge, Connally, George, Thomas of Utah, Barkley, and Hatch.

THE HOUSE BILL

The CHAIRMAN. I want to talk first about what we are up against on this procedure. As I understand it, the House Foreign Affairs Committee is under promise to the House Steering Committee to report a bill. When? *

Dr. WILCOX. Tomorrow or this afternoon.

The CHAIRMAN. The bill will have three parts—ERP, Greece, and Turkey, and China. They propose to bring it up on the floor Monday, under a rule, and they expect to pass all three of them in one batch by the middle of next week. So we get our bill back not only with the ERP amendments, but also with these two new sections.

Obviously we cannot send that to conference and deprive the Senate of an independent, free right to deal with these two new sections. So it seems to me that this procedure over there, against which I will say I very earnestly protested time and time again because I think it is unfair and unsound, but in which I think they rather enjoyed putting us behind the eight ball—in view of that situation, I would like to tie up Greece, and Turkey, and China together if we can do that by the middle of next week, or at least get them each out right away, so that we can get independent action on them.

Then, when we have independent action on them, we can take the bill off the table and send the whole thing to conference. I don't know any other way to proceed if the Senate is to have a fair crack at the thing.

Senator HICKENLOOPER. I understand our child has gone out into the world and is now coming back with three offspring.

Senator LODGE. This bill comes back from the House. Then what does it do, go on the table?

The CHAIRMAN. It stays on the table until we have acted in the Senate on Greece, and Turkey, and China. Then we have the Senate's

---

*Because of its length, the bill as reported by the House Foreign Affairs Committee is not printed.

independent judgment on those two things. Then we can take the bill off the table and send it to conference without ever sending our Greek, Turkey, or China bill to the House, because we have the Senate's mandate.

Senator LODGE. You mean send the Greek-Turkish bill then to conference?

The CHAIRMAN. You send the amended House bill to conference, which takes in ERP, China, and Greece, and Turkey.

Senator BARKLEY. Mr. Chairman, we have made legitimate these bastards that were sent over here by a process of post mortem insemination.

Senator GEORGE. We could consider the amendments that the House puts in the bill. That is the orderly way to do it.

AN INDEPENDENT SENATE JUDGMENT

The CHAIRMAN. But we can not, Senator George, can we, deal with Greece, Turkey, and China as amendments to the House bill until we have had an independent Senate judgment on those two things?

Senator GEORGE. We would have to take the independent judgment on those amendments to the House bill.

Senator BARKLEY. You can take action on those two amendments.

Senator GEORGE. And in the meantime we—this committee—is able and ready to advise the Senate what conclusions we have reached. Maybe we will report separate bills. We can say we have reported bills appropriating so much to Greece and Turkey and so much to China. We can act on those amendments to that bill. We might recommend their amendments.

Senator HICKENLOOPER. I was going to ask that. From a parliamentary standpoint, do we have a right to amend their amendments that they put on a bill?

Senator BARKLEY. You can agree to the House amendments with any amendment they want to put on in the Senate.

The CHAIRMAN. That is virtually what I was trying to say.

Senator GEORGE. That is what you would reach by the other process anyway. Of course, I think you are entirely right in saying we are obliged to let the Senate say what they want to do about Greece, Turkey, and China. They haven't said anything except about Europe.

FEAR OF RENEWED ERP DEBATE

The CHAIRMAN. The only reason I hate to have the debate in the Senate, the Greek-Turkey debate and the China debate on amendments to ERP, is that I am afraid it will open up all the old ERP debate again.

Senator GEORGE. It could.

The CHAIRMAN. And I thought we could short circuit that phase of it.

Senator GEORGE. You can short circuit it by your separate bills, but after all, do you reckon anybody would want to open up ERP now?

The CHAIRMAN. I would not trust some of these gentlemen.

Senator BARKLEY. Suppose the House bill comes over with the amendments. Suppose we take up our bills independently for China,

Greece, and Turkey, and even pass them. You still have to act in the Senate on the House amendments. You have either to agree or disagree to them.

The CHAIRMAN. No; you haven't. You can send the thing to conference.

Senator BARKLEY. But you have to disagree with the amendments in sending it to conference.

The CHAIRMAN. That is just a formality.

Senator BARKLEY. But if we have in the meantime passed our China, Greece, and Turkey bills, you would be a little inconsistent in disagreeing with the House amendments unless they were so different from ours that you had to disagree with them anyhow.

The CHAIRMAN. I think that is a technicality.

Senator GEORGE. You can proceed as you wish.

The CHAIRMAN. I want to proceed in the best way.

Senator GEORGE. If you are fearful that ERP will be opened up and somebody will discover that we have made a serious mistake there, then the thing to do is, when the House bill comes there, hold it on the table and proceed with your separate bills and act on them, and then formally put in what we put in by way of amendment to the House bill, and then go to bat. We change it purposely in some minor detail, if nothing else.

The CHAIRMAN. And then send the whole thing to conference.

Senator HICKENLOOPER. We can amend their amendments by substituting what we pass.

Senator GEORGE. Whatever we do.

Senator SMITH. We have to leave the package tied up, then?

The CHAIRMAN. Oh, sure.

Senator GEORGE. That would leave one package.

NEED FOR A PROMPT "VERDICT"

The CHAIRMAN. In any event it is perfectly obvious, I think, that we have to shove along and get a Greek-Turkish verdict out of here and a China verdict out of here pretty promptly.

Senator GEORGE. Are there to be other hearings on the Greek-Turkish end of it?

The CHAIRMAN. I would not think there was any further necessity. I think we confront a perfectly obvious unavoidable squeeze play.

Senator GEORGE. Then we have to go into the China matter.

The CHAIRMAN. That's right. The first thing I would like to do this morning is to wind up this Greek matter, if we have reached the point where we can act. I don't know of any further testimony that is required under the circumstances. If any members of the committee want any, I will be glad to produce it, but I would like to have everyone remember the pressure of this time table as a result of what the House is doing.

Senator CONNALLY. The House has lumped them all together.

The CHAIRMAN. Yes.

Senator CONNALLY. They have not finished, have they?

The CHAIRMAN. They are supposed to this afternoon or tomorrow.

Senator CONNALLY. What is your idea of how we should handle this?

The CHAIRMAN. We have just gone over that.

Senator CONNALLY. I beg your pardon. Don't repeat it.

The CHAIRMAN. Just briefly, we will get our bill back with Greece, Turkey and China included in one package.

Senator CONNALLY. We will get our bill back with the House substitute, I suppose.

The CHAIRMAN. We will leave that on the table until the Senate can act for itself on its own Greece-Turkey and on its own China bills, so that the Senate will have had an independent opportunity to pass upon those two things. Then we will substitute those two things when we have finished with them in the Senate, and I hope it won't take very long for those sections of the House bill, and wrap the whole thing up and send it to conference.

Senator CONNALLY. You mean, in effect, take up their bill and consolidate it before it goes to conference?

The CHAIRMAN. That's right, but not to consolidate it before the Senate has had a chance to take its own independent action on these.

Senator CONNALLY. We could either do that on separate bills or we could do it on the House bill.

The CHAIRMAN. We just went through that discussion, too. The chief difficulty with that is that if we take it up on the basis of the amendments to the House bill, that puts ERP again on the floor of the Senate and I just want to avoid that.

Senator CONNALLY. I want to avoid it too.

Senator BARKLEY. What is your program if we get this Turkish-Greek bill out today, as to when you will take it up, before the House bill comes back?

The CHAIRMAN. Yes, sure; but there will be no chance to take it up until next week.

Senator BARKLEY. I understand; but if we pass the tax bill today, which we might do, we can take it up Monday.

The CHAIRMAN. Yes.

Senator GEORGE. Technically, when you offer amendments in the form of our separate Greek-Turkish-China thing to the House bill—technically—that opens up the whole ERP bill for anything anybody wants to say on the floor of the Senate anyway, but probably they would not be encouraged to open it up. They might not think of that, and might go on and say they wanted to say something on Greece and Turkey and China.

Senator CONNALLY. Their action practically eliminates everything except China, Greece, and Turkey. They agree to the amount, and don't alter any of the provisions.

The CHAIRMAN. They will make a lot of changes.

THE CHINA BILL

Senator THOMAS of Utah. Mr. Chairman, in the China proposition what if that bill comes over here with an entirely different theory than the one that we have so far been thinking about? What if it comes over as a military bill, a straightout bill as Bullitt wants to sustain Chiang Kai-shek and to bring peace by force in China? Take our bill as we have it and that bill. There is so much difference between the two in policy, in action and in hope and aspiration and everything else that I just don't see how you can help but get the whole idea of military mixed up in the Greek proposition.

The CHAIRMAN. Senator Barkley?

Senator BARKLEY. Suppose we pass a China bill of our own, sans military provisions, and then they send theirs over here with that in there. Will you be justified in sending that bill to conference by the mere substitution of ours, so that only the conferees, so far as the Senate is concerned, would have any voice in the military features of the China proposition?

HOUSE COOLING OFF ABOUT CHINA

The CHAIRMAN. No; by the time we have reached China on the floor of the Senate, which probably could not be until the end of next week, we will know what the House is going to do on China. My understanding is that they are cooling off a little in their maximum ardor in respect to the military phase of the bill and are down to some sort of an earmarking of $100 million of this $570 million to be used for the purchase of military supplies. Douglas is watching it very carefully to see that it is worded so that we assume no military responsibility. It is more on the line of the fashion in which we are dealing with the military phase of the Greek problem. And I think that, if that is the way they write their bill, we should have a vote in the Senate on that subject.

Senator BARKLEY. My guess is that there is less heat on the floor of the House altogether on the military end of the China proposal than there is in the committee, with certain members who have been pushing with a sharp stick ever since this thing came up about military aid to China. I think it is liable to thin out on the floor, although I may be mistaken.

THE "WAIL" OF CHIANG KAI-SHEK

Senator CONNALLY. Did you read that wail of Chiang Kai-shek in the papers today?

Senator GEORGE. Chiang Kai-shek has a complete confession of his own failure in the paper this morning.

Mr. Chairman, before we move on, we could, when the House bill comes over, take the Greek bill and go to conference on it, and insist on the House people putting these other things in separate bills, if we wanted to do that. That would mean some delay, I guess.

The CHAIRMAN. That is just a deadlock. It would mean a long delay.

Senator GEORGE. That is the honest way to do it.

Senator CONNALLY. It is confusing to put them all in one bill.

PROTESTS AGAINST THE HOUSE PACKAGE

The CHAIRMAN. I want to say again, for the record, that I have three times gone over to the House leadership and just as insistently as I could I have protested against this package game, but without success.

Senator GEORGE. There is another question I want to raise. Might we not want the bill, as they send it over here, to come back into the committee so that we might in an orderly way prepare an amendment that would cover Greece, Turkey, and China to the House bill, and go to the floor on that? As you say, that opens up the other end of it, the European end of it.

The CHAIRMAN. There is another disadvantage to that. That postpones any Senate action until after the House has acted, and what I am trying to do is clear the track as far as possible.

Senator GEORGE. You want to go ahead with the Greece-Turkey think before they act? Then you are going to have to have an amendment putting them in as separate titles to this bill.

The CHAIRMAN. That is correct.

Senator GEORGE. And provide for the administrator.

Senator CONNALLY. You are going to find the House being very positive. It is going to have its back lifted to make the Senate do something it wants to do.

Senator LODGE. Don't you think you might lose time? Supposing you have a bill over here which had a military underwriting of China in it. There are some members of this body, and I think I am one of them, who, if you had to vote on that whole omnibus, would vote against it, and you might save time by going back on that.

MONEY FOR CHIANG WASTED

Senator GEORGE. I think I would, too. As much as I sympathize with China, I am afraid that that $575 million is a complete waste of money if it is going to Chiang. It is a waste; that is all there is to it.

Senator CONNALLY. $575 million for the whole of China is just giving the beggar at the corner a dime.

Senator LODGE. I do not even enthuse about treating it like Greece. I understood you to say that Douglas said it would be all right, and he was going to treat China like Greece.

The CHAIRMAN. No; that was my observation. Douglas' statement is that he recognizes the necessity for some kind of a gesture of this sort in the House, and the thing he wants to protect against is to be very sure that it involves no military commitment on our part.

Senator LODGE. What do you say about Greece?

The CHAIRMAN. I said I thought the House committee was going to handle the China military end on the Greek pattern.

Senator LODGE. I wouldn't like that, Mr. Chairman, at all.

The CHAIRMAN. We can cross that bridge when we come to it.

Senator LODGE. We have a military commitment in Greece. It is true we are not going to send troops—probably we are not.

Senator CONNALLY. Don't make any commitment on that.

Senator LODGE. I don't have the power to make a commitment, but Greece is obviously a very unfortunate place to try to send troops to. I don't think they would ever do it. But China is so damned big that the objections that hold true in the case of Greece don't hold true in the case of China.

The CHAIRMAN. I think that is true, but I don't think there is any advantage in raising that issue this morning, because we don't know in what form we are going to confront the issue.

Senator GEORGE. I think, in view of the fact that you have to have universal military training and the renewal of the Draft act, it will probably tend to cool off some of the gentlemen in the House.

The CHAIRMAN. We shall see; I hope so.

Senator LODGE. The reason I raise it is because it does involve a question of procedure. If you have something like that wrapped up with your ERP you have a much longer delay than if you follow what Senator George suggested and treat the thing separately.

CHINA BOTHERS SENATOR CONNALLY

Senator CONNALLY. China bothers me a great deal. I doubt if you are going to do them any good unless you do give them military aid, yet I have no enthusiasm for it.

Senator LODGE. Senator, the day we send troops to China or to Russia, this country is through. There just isn't enough manpower in this country to protect China by manpower.

Senator CONNALLY. I will vote for it, I suppose, but I think it is a waste of money because I don't think it will do any good.

Senator LODGE. I will be willing to vote to send them some money, but I'll be damned if I want to send them manpower. We can print money, but there is no method of producing manpower apart from the method Senator Barkley discussed earlier.

THE PARLIAMENTARY STANDPOINT

Senator SMITH. Senator George, can I ask you from the parliamentary standpoint how you visualize the procedure? Do I understand now that they are going to put their full package business on as amendments to our Senate bill which they are considering?

Senator GEORGE. That's right.

Senator SMITH. Then if we deal with these separately, we will put these in as amendments to their amendments and go into conference on that?

Senator GEORGE. We would offer whatever we do on the Greece, Turkey, and China matters as substitutes for their sections 1, 2, and 3, or whatever they are. That will be a substitute, and that will go to conference.

Senator SMITH. Then is their approach to Greece and Turkey similar to our approach?

Dr. WILCOX. Yes; they have put them all together in this one omnibus bill.

Senator SMITH. Do they deal with Greece and Turkey the way we do here, with $275 million and these other clarifying provisions? Is it about the same thing?

Dr. WILCOX. That is my understanding.

Senator BARKLEY. They have not really written it yet.

Senator SMITH. We expect to hear from it by Monday or Tuesday?

Senator GEORGE. I understand we may hear from it tonight.

Dr. WILCOX. Their omnibus bill does include language on Greece and Turkey identical with the language that we have in our bill here.

Senator SMITH. Then there will be no amendment for us to make to their amendment, if we pass it this way.

Senator CONNALLY. But you could strike it out and say we do not want it all in one bill.

Senator SMITH. What does happen, Mr. Chairman, if we do not like this idea of one package and we want to defeat the one-package idea? Will we defeat the whole show? Will they stand pat?

The CHAIRMAN. I do not think we can decide any of these questions until we see what their bill is.

Senator SMITH. I think that is true.

The CHAIRMAN. Whatever it is, we have to have our initial action from the Foreign Relations Committee on Greece and Turkey and China, so that it seems to me that at the moment we can concentrate on writing up our phase of the Greece-Turkey bill and our phase of the China bill, and then we will have them ready to handle in whatever fashion the parliamentary situation permits.

Senator GEORGE. Report them as separate bills?

The CHAIRMAN. Yes.

Senator CONNALLY. In order to get those into conference we would have to pass them.

Senator GEORGE. We would have to attach them as substitutes to their bill.

Senator LODGE. We are going to have more hearings on China?

The CHAIRMAN. I have the first witness out here. I thought we would get rid of the Greek-Turkey bill in 30 minutes and start on China right today.

Senator BARKLEY. The Turkish-Greek thing is fairly simple. We can report that again and get that behind us.

Senator CONNALLY. Then it is another step that we have already taken. The policies are all the same.

OBJECTIONS TO THE LANGUAGE

The CHAIRMAN. In the first place, let me say again that I have been objecting to all this language in the act down to line 14 on page 3. All of this long rigamarole here is for the purpose of correcting a technicality in the law regarding the relative status of civilian and military employees, and it looks to me that as a matter of rather important psychology when we go to the floor and say "All this bill does is to put another $275 billion on the Greek show," it is a darned funny thing that we have to take four pages of type to do it.

Senator THOMAS of Utah. Mr. Chairman, this is still assumed to be a temporary matter, isn't it?

The CHAIRMAN. Yes.

Senator THOMAS of Utah. It may not be a temporary matter, as we all know.

The CHAIRMAN. That is right.

Senator THOMAS of Utah. Then why should we feel that it is necessary to settle these differences of administration between a man in uniform and a man out of uniform?

The CHAIRMAN. Apparently it is very unfair to the civilians, and they are going to be under the orders of the General Accounting Office charged $2 apiece per day for something or other.

Senator LODGE. Can't we make a separate bill out of that and report it to the calendar as a separate bill?

The CHAIRMAN. I told them to go over to the House with it.

Senator HICKENLOOPER. I think one of the important phases of this bill from the boys over at the other end of the Avenue is contained in lines 13 and 14 of page 2. Those two little lines in there seem very significant to me.

The CHAIRMAN. That is just a sample of the kind of collateral questions that are going to be raised by this language.

Senator CONNALLY. Why should we meddle with that at all? Let them go on and pay them as they have been paying them all the time.

Senator LODGE. We can make a different bill. We don't have to report this with the parts struck out in italics, do we? We can make a clean bill, can't we?

Senator BARKLEY. I doubt the wisdom of bringing in a separate bill on that little chickenfeed stuff.

Senator LODGE. I move we strike out everything to and including line 13 on page 3.

Senator GEORGE. I suppose there is some real valid reason why they would like to have this. As I understood it, they cannot do what they want to do with some of their military personnel over there who are doing civilian work, doing administrative jobs; and vice versa, they can't do something for the civilians that they would like to do. Is there a lot of trouble, do you think, to explain that to the Senate? Of course, I would rather just have a plain bill. You have to keep section 3 in.

Senator LODGE. Yes.

WHY THE SECTION IS NEEDED

Dr. WILCOX. May I say, Mr. Chairman, with respect to this, the State Department points out that the General Accounting Office has caused a great deal of trouble with respect to travel allowance and with respect to reemployment rights and so on, and all the military, public health, and naval personnel would, unless some legislative provision is enacted, have to kick back $2 a day from the time they had been assigned, and they feel that since the original Greek-Turkish bill provided that the personnel would operate under the act of 1938. Now that that act has since been repealed and as a result there is no provision to take care of these personnel who are operating in Greece and Turkey; that void has to be covered by some legislative enactment, and they thought this would be the appropriate place to do it.

We asked them if they could not abbreviate the provisions of this law, if they could not eliminate all of this. They, of course, can, if the committee does not want to enact the protecting clauses that they think are so essential.

Senator SMITH. In that connection won't we have to have similar legislation to this to protect similar personnel in ERP?

Senator CONNALLY. If you are going to put this in at all it ought to be in at the end of the bill. As it is now, it looks like that is the main thing in the bill.

The CHAIRMAN. You read three pages before you ever reach the thing we are talking about.

Senator GEORGE. What we need to do is to put section 3 as No. 1. That is your first section, and then put this other thing in. It looks to me like maybe we had just as well do it. We will have to do it sooner or later.

Dr. WILCOX. I asked the Department again this morning whether, in the light of the Chairman's strong protest, they could not devise some three or four lines that would meet his objections, and they said they would make another attempt and see what could be done.

Senator LODGE. If the House is reporting out this enormous encyclopedic omnibus book, with forty or fifty pages in it, why can't all this technical detail dealing with military and civilian employment and which is of really secondary importance be tucked away in there where it won't attract so much attention and would not appear to be something of major importance—which it is not. If we put these technical matters in this bill, it will raise many questions and waste a lot of time. If you put it in a bill of 40 or 50 pages, it will not attract undue attention—just the amount it deserves.

Senator CONNALLY. You are going to get messed up with the House. I am in favor of letting them do their messing and we do ours.

Senator LODGE. Let's have them take on this as part of their mess.

Senator GEORGE. Do you want to strike it out of this bill?

The CHAIRMAN. I think we are asking for trouble. I think Senator Connally's suggestion substantially cushions the impact of the thing.

Senator CONNALLY. You are going to find that a lot of these members up there are more concerned about what some employee is going to get in the way of allowances than he is about what Greeks and Turks are going to get.

Senator LODGE. A lot of those flyspeck fellows up there will love this stuff.

The CHAIRMAN. Suppose we do this: Suppose we make section 3 section 1, and tentatively put this other language below section 3, with a final injunction to our staff and to the State Department to cut her down to the absolute minimum. You cannot tell me, since this whole subject is raised by a simple repeal act, that there is not some way that you can exempt this show from the repeal act in a couple of sentences.

Senator LODGE. Very reluctantly I withdraw my motion to strike it all out. I still think we ought to strike it all out.

Senator SMITH. Wouldn't you make subsection (b) of section 3 the first thing that stands out in the reader's mind? Then your reconstruction finance thing is minor to the main thing.

Senator CONNALLY. It is minor, but it is the first step.

Senator GEORGE. That is all right. I think Senator Smith is probably right. The other is the main thing.

A 12-MONTH BASIS

The CHAIRMAN. The only suggestion I have to offer, and I have no particular predilection, is that we have written ERP on a 12-month basis, and I think there is a good deal of sense in writing all these bills on a 12-month basis, so that the whole subject passes in review at once next January. What would the committee think of putting this bill on a 12-month basis instead of 15? That would mean that we amend by deleting $400 million and inserting in lieu thereof $45 million less than that figure.

Senator CONNALLY. I think we made a mistake in amending the old act. I don't see why in the devil they didn't make it a clean bill and say that in addition to the amounts appropriated under so and so, we would appropriate so and so.

Senator LODGE. Why can't we do it that way? Why do we have to amend this bill?

The CHAIRMAN. Isn't that what, in net effect, happens here?

Senator LODGE. This $675 million is bad psychology. We are not appropriating $675 million.

$675 MILLION A BAD FIGURE

The CHAIRMAN. I agree with that completely. That is a bad figure.

Senator LODGE. It is terrific.

Senator GEORGE. Mr. Chairman, I think it very well to cut it down so as to bring it under review, but I do think this, that in all human probability if they are going to do anything for Turkey you have to let Turkey have what little money they are getting under this, because they must make commitments in advance if they are going to get ready for any possible push. I don't think there is going to be any war over there at all, but at the same time I suppose we are getting ready for eventualities, and maybe if we cut down Greece here they could not do very much if they were scaled down on a 12 months' basis.

Senator LODGE. They have already been scaled down from $103 million to $75 million.

Senator CONNALLY. Under this bill the President can allocate. He can switch some of the Greek money to Turkey, or some of the Turkish money to Greece. But if you cut it down, he can't switch as much.

Senator LODGE. I wonder whether we ought not to give them the $103 million they asked for. They have had no justification for the cut, and Turkey certainly is the best bet we have over there now.

MONEY WASTED IN GREECE

Senator GEORGE. I think we are wasting money in Greece. If it were to be done over again I don't know that I would vote any money for Greece. I have no enthusiasm to increase a lot of this money to Greece, because so long as we furnish the money to Greece in these amounts they are going to pretty well live off of us.

Senator CONNALLY. That may be true. But Greece is so close to Turkey that it would imperil Turkey.

Senator GEORGE. They are not going to get Greece alone. They will have to take Italy or Turkey with it. I haven't any enthusiasm at all, nor any confidence, in what we are doing in Greece.

Senator BARKLEY. On the question of cutting down to a 12 months' basis, I have a feeling that the situation over there, in as much as we are in it, is a little different from ERP.

The CHAIRMAN. I think that is so.

Senator BARKLEY. It is military, and that isn't in ERP. And if we know we are going to have to add this on ultimately for another 3 months, or for another 12, as the case may be, the psychology would be bad for us to reduce it right now, when the amount is so small.

The CHAIRMAN. All right; I agree.

INCREASE BY $275 MILLION

What do you say to Senator Lodge's suggestion? Why can we not have that last sentence rewritten so that it does what we are doing, namely, increases the appropriation by $275 million and get both this $400 million and the $675 million out of there?

85-743—73——28

Senator CONNALLY. I would not want to increase it to $103 million. Why don't you say $100 million?

Senator LODGE. That is a separate question, Senator Connally. They asked for $103 million.

Senator CONNALLY. I know they did. I think it is better to round it out.

The CHAIRMAN. What do you say about that? Is there any objection to that?

Senator GEORGE. It is a little clumsy to draw.

Senator SMITH. You would not amend the old bill under those conditions?

Senator GEORGE. When you start to doing that, it is going to be somewhat clumsily put together—amend it by deleting $400 million and inserting in lieu thereof $675 million, and by inserting after the word "repaid" the following: There are two amounts there.

Senator LODGE. Do you think that is rather clumsy as it stands?

Senator GEORGE. No. I say if we do not amend the present act, we have a sort of a clumsy provision—hereby appropriating an additional sum for Greece and Turkey of $275 million. I agree with you that the psychology of the thing would be better.

Senator LODGE. It would be easier for the average person to understand, it seems to me.

Senator SMITH. What you would have to do is extend the operation of this previous act for this additional 12 or 15 months' period, and make the additional appropriation therefor. It would be an extension of the act. This act is supposed to die.

Senator GEORGE. I do not understand that the original act dies. Just the appropriation expires. We have to have another appropriation.

The CHAIRMAN. You have a sentence on page 3 which says "No interest shall be charged on advances made by the Treasury to the RFC."

Senator CONNALLY. That is to the RFC; that is not from the RFC back to this fund.

The CHAIRMAN. Suppose we put the question in this form, that the committee approves reporting the bill with the increased appropriation of $275 million, and that the method of writing up the bill shall be subject to a further consultation with our legislative counsel and with the State Department.

Senator CONNALLY. That is all right, except I would suggest that instead of amending this $400 million that we simply say that there is hereby authorized to be appropriated, and so forth and so on, $275 million additional.

The CHAIRMAN. That is exactly what I was after.

Senator SMITH. For the purposes of carrying out this act.

Senator CONNALLY. And leave out the $400 million. When you stick in $400 million, every time you are reminding the fellow that is going to vote, "Here, we have given them $400 million and we are going to chuck them another $275 million more."

The CHAIRMAN. And then the $675 million sticks up after that, and nowhere in the bill does it say anything about what we are doing, which is authorizing $275 million. That figure is not in the bill.

Senator BARKLEY. Of course that provision, I think, is bad form, but it follows the practice that we have engaged in for years, where there is an increase in an authorization for an agency like the RFC.

We have frequently increased the lending authority by striking out the previous lending authority and substituting a new one. So this is not the only time in which this has happened.

Senator CONNALLY. It is the only time we are struggling with it.

The CHAIRMAN. If the committee is willing, let's take a vote.

Senator CONNALLY. It is going to be a good drafting job to fix that up in the right way.

The CHAIRMAN. And probably the net result ought to be submitted back to the committee again.

Senator GEORGE. You have the same thing on your $50 million advance by the RFC. You have to do that over again, too.

The CHAIRMAN. Yes. You give them the authority to advance an additional $50 million to carry out the provisions of this amended act.

Senator HICKENLOOPER. You have your reference in there "without interest," which undoubtedly would apply to the entire $675 million overall, and if you change it to $275 million the "without interest" would not apply.

The CHAIRMAN. Suppose we take our vote on the general principle that we are approving the increase of $275 million and we are refering the bill back to our staff and to legislative counsel and the State Department for suggested redrafting, and the redraft will be submitted to the committee for its approval.

Senator CONNALLY. And we will start with section 3.

The CHAIRMAN. Call the roll on the motion.

The CLERK. Mr. Capper?

Senator CAPPER. Aye.

The CLERK. Mr. White?

The CHAIRMAN. He votes "aye."

The CLERK. Mr. Wiley? [absent] Mr. Smith?

Senator SMITH. Aye.

The CLERK. Mr. Hickenlooper?

Senator HICKENLOOPER. Aye.

The CLERK. Mr. Lodge?

Senator LODGE. Aye.

The CLERK. Mr. Connally?

Senator CONNALLY. Aye.

The CLERK. Mr. George?

Senator GEORGE. I vote "aye," Mr. Chairman, but we are wasting money on Greece.

The CLERK. Mr. Wagner?

Senator BARKLEY. He would vote "aye."

The CLERK. Mr. Thomas?

Senator THOMAS, of Utah. Aye.

The CLERK. Mr. Barkley?

Senator BARKLEY. Aye.

The CLERK. Mr. Hatch?

Senator BARKLEY. He was called out. Vote him "aye."

The CLERK. Mr. Chairman?

The CHAIRMAN. Aye. Phone Mr. Wiley.

[Senator Wiley voted "aye."]

The CLERK. Ayes, 13; noes, 0.

Senator CONNALLY. I sympathize with China, but I swear, it looks to me like it is just hopeless.

[Whereupon, at 11 a.m., the hearing was adjourned.]

ASSISTANCE TO GREECE AND TURKEY

SATURDAY, MARCH 20, 1948

UNITED STATES SENATE,
COMMITTEE ON FOREIGN RELATIONS,
Washington, D.C.

The committee met pursuant to adjournment, in the committee hearing room, United States Capitol, at 10 a.m., Senator Arthur A. Vandenberg, chairman, presiding.

Present: Senators Vandenberg (chairman), Capper, Wiley, Smith, Hickenlooper, Lodge, Connally, George, Thomas of Utah, and Hatch.

The CHAIRMAN. This is the one-sheet form in which the Greek-Turkish bill is wound up. I think it is such a tremendous improvement, and I think it is all right:

A BILL To amend the Act approved May 22, 1947, entitled "An Act to provide for Assistance to Greece and Turkey"

Be it enacted by the Senate and House of Representatives of the United States of America in Congress assembled, That in addition to the amounts authorized to be appropriated under subsection (b) of section 4 of the Act of May 22, 1947 (61 Stat. 103), there are hereby authorized to be appropriated not to exceed $275,000,000 to carry out the provisions of such Act, as amended.

SEC. 2. (a) Subsection (a) of section 4 of such Act of May 22, 1947, is hereby amended by adding at the end thereof the following: "The Reconstruction Finance Corporation is authorized and directed to make additional advances, not to exceed in the aggregate $50,000,000, to carry out the provisions of this Act, as amended, in such manner and in such amounts as the President shall determine. No interest shall be charged on advances made by the Treasury to the Reconstruction Finance Corporation for this purpose."

(b) Subsection (b) of section 4 of the said Act is hereby amended by inserting after the word "repaid" the following: "without interest".

SEC. 3. Subsections 2 and 3 of section 1 of such Act of May 22, 1947 are hereby amended to permit detailing of persons referred to in such subsections to the United States Missions to Greece and Turkey as well as to the governments of those countries. Section 302 of the Act of January 27, 1948 (Public Law 402, Eightieth Congress) and section 10(c) of the Economic Cooperation Act of 1948 (relating to investigations of personnel by the Federal Bureau of Investigation) shall be applicable to any person so detailed pursuant to subsection 2 of such Act of 1947: *Provided,* That any military or civilian personnel detailed under section 1 of such Act of 1947 may receive such station allowances or additional allowances as the President may prescribe (and payments of such allowances heretofore made are hereby validated).

Senator THOMAS of Utah. Did you get it on one sheet by using a bigger sheet?

The CHAIRMAN. This will be printed on one sheet.

Furthermore, we have it arranged with some degree of relative importance. The first section is the same, except that we used the figure we are talking about, instead of a lot of figures we aren't talking about. The second section is verbatim.

Senator LODGE. That's good; I think that is swell; that is the way they all ought to be written.

The CHAIRMAN. We are told it is adequate in all aspects.

Senator GEORGE. OK; let's pass it up.

The CHAIRMAN. All right—with thanks.

[Whereupon the hearing was adjourned.]

ASSISTANCE TO CHINA*

SATURDAY, MARCH 20, 1948

UNITED STATES SENATE,
COMMITTEE ON FOREIGN RELATIONS,
Washington, D.C.

The committee met, pursuant to adjournment, at 10 a.m. in the committee hearing room, U.S. Capitol, Senator Arthur Vandenberg, chairman, presiding.

Present: Senators Vandenberg (chairman), Capper, Wiley, Smith, Hickenlooper, Lodge, Connally, George, Thomas of Utah, and Hatch.

Also present: Mr. Willard L. Thorpe, Assistant Secretary of State for Economic Affairs; Mr. W. Walton Butterworth, Chief, Division of Far Eastern Affairs; Dr. H. F. Havlik, Chief, Division of Investment and Economic Development; Mr. M. H. Walker, Assistant Chief, Division of Investment and Economic Development; Mr. Philip Sprouse, Office of Far Eastern Affairs; and Mr. Robert Eichholz, Office of the Legal Adviser, Department of State.

The CHAIRMAN. Where do we go from here on China?

THREE CHEERS FOR THE NATIONALISTS

I think it is perfectly obvious that we cannot make any sort of a case for a China bill comparable with the case that we have made for the other one. I think it is perfectly obvious that this is essentially three cheers for the Nationalist Government in the hope that it can get somewhere in the face of Communist opposition. What efforts does the committee want to make to go into further details in respect to the economic background, and so forth, of the figures? I suppose if there is any information available further it ought to be presented, but I have such a feeling of a sort of frustration in connection with the whole act that I do not know where to start or where to end.

Senator LODGE. I do not want to prolong the agony, Mr. Chairman, but I think there are a few questions that I would like to get answers to which I know will be asked on the floor, and we have to have some kind of answers for them.

The CHAIRMAN. Go ahead.

NUMBER OF PEOPLE HELPED

Senator LODGE. How many people will be helped by these programs for cereals, metal, tobacco, and everything else? What is the number of people that it is planned to reach?

***Printed as a separate transcript from the executive session held on the same day relating to Greece and Turkey.**

Mr. THORPE. The only thing I can specifically define in terms of numbers of people would be with respect to the cereals. My understanding is that those cereals will go primarily to the largest cities along the coast, and reach somewhere in the neighborhood of 11 or 12 million people directly. That is, our cereals will be feeding that many people in these cities where rationing systems are being applied. Actually, of course, as I indicated yesterday, the effect of taking care of that many people relieves pressures for quite unspecified numbers of people back in the interior.

Senator LODGE. That is the cereals. How about the fertilizers? How many farmers are going to get fertilizer, and what areas are they going to be in? And while you are thinking of that, where are these metals going to come from—this copper?

Dr. HAVLIK. From this country.

Senator LODGE. They are all coming from this country? Isn't there metal out there somewhere? Aren't there mines out in the Far East?

Dr. HAVLIK. These represent the quantities which the Chinese have been importing in addition to their regular supplies that they have had at home.

Senator LODGE. Is there any machinery, machine tools, or anything like that, included?

Dr. HAVLIK. There are spare parts, repair parts——

Senator LODGE. For trucks?

Dr. HAVLIK. For trucks, automotive equipment for everything across the board. Machine tools as such we do not contemplate, except they might possibly enter a reconstruction project.

Senator LODGE. The reason I asked the question is that there are a lot of people on the Senate floor who scrutinize all these propositions from the standpoint of the goods going through the recipient nation to Russia, and with all politeness and everything else I think there has been enough sent to justify them for having that suspicion.

Dr. HAVLIK. There is no program for machine tools in this.

Senator LODGE. What are you sending under this program that could be construed as being a munition of war?

MUNITIONS

Dr. HAVLIK. It depends upon how broadly you construe it, but this is not a munitions of war program. The stuff itself isn't.

Senator LODGE. I know that, but if you read Senator Ferguson's thesis, you will realize he is looking for munitions of war all the time, and you see metals and you see brass and copper, and right away you think of copper being in short supply in this country. Of course, our copper resources are wearing out, and that whole train of thought is started and you have to have a really substantial argument for it.

Mr. THORPE. I think on those items it is a fact that this represents more or less the usual amount that has been going in recent months, and so far as the military items are concerned, the only thing that I think could possibly be stretched to that would be the aviation gasoline. Something like 12 percent of the petroleum that goes in here is aviation gasoline, or becomes aviation gasoline.

Senator SMITH. Mr. Thorpe, I notice in the paper this morning that of this $570 million, the House broke it down into $150 million for military aid and the balance of $420 million for these other things. Can you comment on that, on what the background there is and what is your attitude on that?

Mr. THORPE. What apparently happened was that the House Committee wanted to give an indication of support in the form of military aid, and what they have done is to take the $570 million and they have said, "We will rearrange that. We will only provide $420 million for the civilian items, and $150 million for military items." I haven't any idea where they propose to cut, because, just taking the simple items of cereals, cotton, and petroleum, you run more than the $420 million which they have allowed.

Senator LODGE. You haven't seen the House bill?

Mr. THORPE. No, I haven't seen the House bill. We have a copy of it here, but I don't think that defines. In fact, one of the real problems is that military items and civilian items have a shadowy area in between for definition.

Senator LODGE. Is it your understanding that it is items of military supply?

CHINA BILL SAME AS GREEK-TURKISH BILL

The CHAIRMAN. I will answer that for you. They have taken the military $150 million and put it over into the Greek-Turkish bill as an amendment, so that it applies in China to everything that it applies to in Greece-Turkey. Isn't that a fact?

Mr. BUTTERWORTH. That is my understanding. Everything that is in the Greek-Turkish military bill is to be supplied to China.

Senator LODGE. I can't buy that; I'm sorry.

The CHAIRMAN. I am not trying to sell it to you, brother. I am telling you what the facts are. I don't want you to shoot me on sight just for being a herald of the morning.

Senator SMITH. Does that mean in their part covering Greece and Turkey they have added China for $150 million?

Mr. THORPE. That's right, and it includes the same procedures of supply, of advice, of, shall I say, substantial participation in their operations.

The CHAIRMAN. And, of course, it carries the same implication inevitably that the Greek-Turkish bill has carried, and it is quite impossible.

Senator LODGE. It is completely impossible.

Senator WILEY. Both ends of the table agree. Now that is settled.

Senator LODGE. Take these eight or nine commodities, now. What will reach the little man down below? Are they going to get hung up with certain officials grabbing them off?

Mr. THORPE. That has been one of the concerns. I think under the early days of UNRRA operation that happened, and steadily the situation has been improved as they have set up controls and observation.

Senator LODGE. In China?

Mr. THORPE. In China, from the point of view of preventing their getting into speculative channels. We feel quite confident that the interim aid which is now going is actually moving right along and finally into consumption channels, and not getting diverted into speculative channels.

FIFTEEN U.S. SUPERVISORS

Senator LODGE. How many people have you over there now to give you this information on whether the little man is actually getting the help or not?

Mr. WALKER. There are about 15.

Mr. THORPE. About 15 people.

Senator LODGE. Do they travel around and make spot checks?

Mr. WALKER. The only thing that is going forward now is cereals, and that is very effective.

RATION SYSTEMS

Mr. THORPE. I might say that we have been responsible for getting ration systems set up in these cities. It has been our man out there who has been saying, "If American stuff is coming in, it has to be distributed more equitably," and they have started their rationing. We held up on our interim aid cereals until they put in a rationing system in the big cities, and it has been really our planning and suggestion and insistence that has gotten rationing in. Of course, the cereals are the main items going in at the present time.

WHY THE COMMUNISTS ARE POPULAR

Senator LODGE. What do the Communists do in China that makes them so popular?

Mr. BUTTERWORTH. I think their popularity in general arises out of two factors. One is that in China, if there were no Communists and if Russia was as quiet as she was in the twenties and thirties, China would be going through revolutionary change as she tries to slough off some of the cocoon of semimedievalism and adjust herself to the conditions of a modern world. For example, over the centuries the Chinese genius for government has been directed toward a highly decentralized form of government, interfering very little with the lives of the people. And now, through no fault of her own, she finds herself catapulted into the 20th century, which places a premium on the highly centralized form of government with a great measure of interference. An she can't make that adjustment overnight.

Second, I think the Chinese Communists have pursued a revolutionary policy, and the outside support that they have garnered as the opposition, the only effective opposition party to the Kuomintang and their land policies, is probably more responsible than any other one factor for their general support. And you can see that reflected in a practical way in the military operations in terms of their intelligence. It is literally, I should say, a thousand times better than the Nationalist Government's in such areas as Manchuria. The countryside favors the Communists, supplies them with information, and in every way helps them because of the support that they have gotten both directly because of their ruthless but effective land policy, and indirectly because of the ills which the Kuomintang Government has brought upon itself.

In saying that about the Kuomintang I would like to also add that they did a remarkable job in the late twenties and the early thirties. They had real revolutionary reformist zeal and they had a great deal of esprit, and they performed remarkably at that time.

Senator SMITH. That was the Sun Yat-sen leadership?

Mr. BUTTERWORTH. And Chiang Kai-shek from 1927 on, after he threw the Russians out. China made great progress at that time, but they seem to have been unable to revivify their party and their instrument of government and to reinvigorate their administration.

AN ASSET TO RUSSIA

Senator LODGE. How much of an asset can China be to Russia?

Mr. BUTTERWORTH. That is a large question.

Senator LODGE. I know it is, but we have got to think about it.

Senator THOMAS of Utah. Will you let me butt in on that question? I think you will find that Russia will leave China alone unless some of our troops, or some Japanese troops or some other country's troops, come into China. There is no reason for her from a military, social, economic, or any other standpoint to interfere there. But Russia will naturally block the coming of any other foreign country into its sphere, and I use "sphere" both legally, properly, and improperly—into a sphere with which she has had great trouble in the past in maintaining anything like a proper control. She has been driven out twice. She probably feels that that part of the Pacific is an outlet which she must at least not let someone who is antagonistic to her come near. If we make no military mistakes over there, Russia will be busy with her knitting in other parts of the world, because she has got plenty on her side of the line that she has got to do which is actually new to the present Russian Government.

The CHAIRMAN. Are you not also saying, Senator, that she will be satisfied with the existing situation so long as her proxies are making satisfactory progress?

CHINESE COMMUNISTS AS PROXIES

Senator THOMAS of Utah. I think we make too much of the notion that the Chinese Communists are actual proxies of the world revolution notion, because it is very, very sure that if the Communists become completely successful in China it will not be successful in accordance with the Russian notion of what communism is. The Communists are dividing the land up and are reinstituting or making more vivid and more sure private property all the way along the line, and the one reason why the Chinese flock to the Communists and do not go the other way is that the Communist soldiers spend half of their time growing food stuffs in the fields, and that, of course, is something that comes to them from long time. We did it here in America ourselves when we started capturing the West. We always planted corn for the next winter as our people moved on, and that is the way Ghengis Khan fought, and Kubla Khan, and it is the way everybody fights in the Orient. You haven't had great supply lines even for the Japanese troops. They have learned how to live on the people. They don't supply their own soldiers in the same way in which we supply our soldiers.

I go back into ancient history, Mr. Butterworth, instead of just the moment. But this movement in China, as has been pointed out, is not something that has been born out of even the Nationalist Government in China. It is very old. The real Chinese revolution is connected up with an idea, just as the Indian revolution and the Russian revolution were.

JUSTIFICATION FOR BUTTING IN

Senator WILEY. What is our justification for butting in, if what you say is true?

Senator THOMAS of Utah. Well, we have been butting in since 1844, making treaties and taking care of our own missionary interests, taking care of our businessmen, taking care of our exports. I doubt very much whether it is butting in. But in the great massive revolutions, the like of which we can't even imagine because of the number of people and the extent of the territory and the factors connected with revolution, even in the revolution in Japan, you see, there was something that no one could believe could actually take place as fast as it did. It took place as fast as it did because you had there a single language and a highly developed nationalistic state. They did not call it that, but that is what it was.

You see, you had 200 or 300 years of military unification in Japan. These things you haven't got in China.

Senator LODGE. Mr. Butterworth, do you subscribe generally to what Senator Thomas has said?

Mr. BUTTERWORTH. Yes, I do.

Senator LODGE. In other words, even if there weren't a Bolshevik Government in Russia, Chinese history leads us to believe that there would be a succession of revolutions in that country because there always have been?

Is that true?

Mr. BUTTERWORTH. Yes. I think so. I put it slightly differently. I would say that at the present time the Kremlin would not like to see a united China, even if that China was a so-called Communist China.

SOVIET TERRITORIAL AMBITIONS

Senator LODGE. What do you think her territorial ambitions are in China?

Mr. BUTTERWORTH. I think so far as exploiting the assets are concerned they are largely limited to Manchuria.

Senator THOMAS of Utah. And to protect her interests in Mongolia.

Mr. BUTTERWORTH. As the Senator has said, they have a huge and potentially rich territory in Siberia, and they want to develop that. I would not expect that they would send a great deal of industrial equipment to Manchuria, for example, as long as their own Siberian cities need that.

Senator THOMAS of Utah. I will just bet anything that even the equipment that has been taken from Manchuria is probably on side tracks now, on loaded cars, and that it has not moved into the industrial part of Russia. I don't know whether that is a fact, but that would be my guess, judging from the way in which they work.

Mr. BUTTERWORTH. Certainly, and they obviously had that very well thought out beforehand, because when they went into northern Korea they took very little, so far as we can gather, of the industrial equipment, but when they went into Manchuria they looted it in a very widespread and very systematic way, because by that time they had learned from their Berlin experience that you could not take these highly specialized machines and pile them into box cars and shoot them out without great care, otherwise you just ended up with a great industrial junk pile.

Senator LODGE. Your conclusion is, at the present time you are not at all sure that the Russians do want to absorb China, first; and second, you are not at all sure that the steps of military aid, so-called, would result in achieving that?

PROBLEM NOT SOLVED BY MILITARY AID

Mr. BUTTERWORTH. I don't think the problem in China is one that is going to be solved by military aid, because military aid is not going to create support as such for the National Government. It is not going to help solve its own social and economic and political problems, which is necessary in order to create that support, and also for the morale of the Army as well.

Senator LODGE. China isn't having an invasion. China isn't being subjected to a foreign invasion. And therefore military aid would not be effective in preventing the absorption of China by Soviet Russia. Is that true?

Mr. BUTTERWORTH. That is true, unless we wanted to make an all-out war.

Senator LODGE. I think that is a good way to have a suicide.

Mr. Chairman, don't you think we ought to hear what the General Staff has to say on the whole program of extending military aid to China?

The CHAIRMAN. Yes, except as to the extent with which we can find a formula which was reasonably innocuous in its conditions.

HOUSE BILL UNSATISFACTORY

We face here a fact, not a theory, and I suppose we might as well get it out of the way. The House is hell bent on writing military aid for China in this bill, and they are sure going to write it in. The form in which they have written it in, in my opinion as in yours, is completely impossible, because they have attached it to the Greek-Turkish bill, which carries all of the implications that are involved in the Greek-Turkish situation, which are entirely unsatisfactory to any of us.

By putting it in the Greek-Turkish bill they bring into play all of the terms of the Greek-Turkish bill which are essentially, so far as personnel is concerned, military missions and so forth. Well, that is already taken care of in China, and there is another bill pending in the Armed Services Committee now to formalize the whole thing. This in my mind is the purely practical parliamentary question of how we could write a gesture of military sympathy into this text to accommodate the viewpoint which we face under an almost unlivable condition that the House has created in a parliamentary sense in connection with the whole legislation. We cannot allow this problem, if we can help it, to indefinitely postpone ERP and Greek-Turkish aid and everything else, and yet it could very easily do that.

Senator LODGE. Mr. Chairman, every time since I have been on this committee we are always told about how adamant the House is and how strong the House is. When it was the information program it was Rankin and Hoffman and whoever that other fellow was. Now we have these China fellows who won't give in if you won't do this or that. I am getting awfully tired of it, frankly. I hope somebody is going to tell them over there some time that we are not going to give in unless they do so and so.

Senator HATCH. I don't think you should confine it to this committee. You heard the arguments made on the tax bill repeatedly.

The CHAIRMAN. The only thing that concerns me about it is that we don't get into a stalemate which stymies the entire program. I think that would be a tragic mistake.

Senator LODGE. I do, too. I want to avoid that as much as you do.

The CHAIRMAN. And I do not think this is the particular moment to stand on our rights and force this issue you are talking about, although I completely sympathize with your point of view.

Senator LODGE. I don't want to be called legalistic or anything like that, but it would be a tragic thing if we were ever to commit this country to sending an army to China. Better not have the ERP, in my opinion. If we have to wrap ERP with sending an army to China, then we are lost.

The CHAIRMAN. I agree with that completely.

A $570 MILLION BET ON CHIANG

Senator SMITH. Why aren't we, in this whole thing, simply making a $570 million bet on Chiang's outfit for another year? That is really what the House wants. Why couldn't we even consider what Senator Connally suggested yesterday, the possibility of a loan to China in that amount, and let Chiang do what he wants with it? He is the fellow we think is the best bet in China today to possibly bring about order. I think all the flurries around about Russia are entirely wrong. We are not going to send any military force to China, but we are sympathetic in this country with Chiang's outfit, and we are just betting that for another year he will have a chance. We are giving him $500 million to survive.

I would like to ask Mr. Thorpe whether that is the size of it or not.

Senator CONNALLY. Let me intervene just before Mr. Thorpe gets into that.

It seems to me that the more we monkey with this Chinese thing and send a mission over there and all that, the more danger there is that Russia will come in. She isn't going to stand for our approaching a military situation, and I agree with Senator Lodge that we can't send an army over there because that means that we are in a war; that is all there is to it.

Senator LODGE. And there is no end to it.

Senator CONNALLY. I am very doubtful about the whole program, to tell you the truth. I would like to see old Chiang win out, but he has had about—how long has he been in power?

A YEAR'S LEEWAY

Senator SMITH. We just want to give him another year's leeway.

Senator CONNALLY. He has had a good many years to win out, and he hasn't won out yet. With those preliminary remarks, however, I welcome Mr. Thorpe's solution.

CIVILIAN ASSISTANCE

Mr. THORPE. All I want to say is that I think it is a fair way of putting it that this is a bet on the Generalissimo, giving him this opportunity. And the program is very deliberately set up to be one that can be described as civilian assistance and not in any way hinting that the United States is getting itself involved in commitments in the military area, because we have discovered from the Greek-Turkish situation, for example, where we started in with a program which was a combination of military and economic, that actually what happened was that the military requirements increased and increased. Less and less was accomplished on the economic side. There were relief requirements that developed from the refugees, and so forth. And actually the developments under the Greek-Turkish situation have been—I don't know that I should say—different from what were anticipated, but certainly when the program was started it was thought that here was a limited amount of military assistance which would do the trick.

Now, if Greece has done that, the Chinese situation has just the possibilities of being endless if we get ourselves committed to it in a military way.

On the other hand, this program is the kind of program we would certainly do in China if we had China in a situation of a substantially satisfactory government. This is the kind of assistance that we would give them to help them over their present economic situation.

I think the question is whether, because of the civil war, we will not give them this kind of aid—commodity assistance—to keep their economy going or not.

HOUSE AS IMPONDERABLE AS CHINA

The CHAIRMAN. Well, Mr. Secretary, you have found out in the Greek-Turkish program that relief is of secondary effectiveness so long as there is inadequate military defense. And I suppose that is the theory, the basic theory, upon which those who are insisting upon military aid for China are proceeding. And this feeling is not alone in the House. I come back to the fact that we have just got to coldbloodedly here deal with the fact that we confront a condition and not a theory, and half of it is parliamentary and half of it is Chinese, and I think the House is about as imponderable as China is in dealing with it.

I was about to say, though, that it is not confined to the House. We have some key men in the Senate, and the chairman of the

Senate Appropriations Committee is one of them. This is sine qua non so far as he is concerned.

Senator GEORGE. He is for China, is he?

The CHAIRMAN. And military aid.

Senator LODGE. What is the opposite of sine qua non? That's what I am.

The CHAIRMAN. What do you say to this. I am just thinking out loud now, and I think I am exploring an idea that Senator Connally brought out. Maybe I am libeling him by suggesting that he originally proposed something of the sort.

Suppose, without any reference to military aid, recognizing the fact that whatever went into military aid there would never be repaid—what about taking $100 million of this sum and making it a loan to the Nationalist Government of China?

Senator THOMAS of Utah. Why not take the same amount that they have set?

Senator CONNALLY. I don't know whether we would put it in the act or not, but I would certainly want some assurances when we hand this out that we were going to supervise somewhat its expenditure, and not just give it to him to put in his pocket and give Soong the other half of it.

Mr. THORPE. That is just the trouble.

Senator GEORGE. Then you are in a war.

DIFFICULTY OF MILITARY ASSISTANCE

Mr. BUTTERWORTH. That is the crux of the difficulty of extending military assistance. Then logically the question can be posed to you, are you going to follow this equipment up to see that it is properly used? When you embark on that, you find yourself inevitably drawn into plans and operations, and in a country like China you will find that the Chinese communication system isn't suitable, so you have to bring in large numbers of engineers to establish your own communications system with the various units. That is the avenue. You can see the vista down the end of it very clearly.

Senator LODGE. I see it.

The CHAIRMAN. Mr. Butterworth, didn't you say we already have a large staff of military aides in China?

Mr. BUTTERWORTH. Yes; but they are, under their directive, confined to operations south of the Yangtze, and to training troops. They are not allowed to participate in plans and operations and, of course, we are not supplying—the U.S. Government is not supplying—equipment and munitions that that group has to follow to their end use. But if you get a military clause, then I think it will be logically posed as to whether or not the group that is there should not followup and see that that equipment is used in a 100 percent effective way.

The CHAIRMAN. What do you say to the offhand curbstone suggestion that I threw out?

Mr. BUTTERWORTH. I should say it was infinitely preferable to the action of the House.

The CHAIRMAN. I am sure it is preferable. Is that as far as you care to go?

THE PARLIAMENTARY SITUATION

Senator THOMAS of Utah. If you are going to think of the parliamentary situation, and are going to divide your ground up in that way, you ought to make the sum not just $100 million, but the equivalent of the amount that is going for military aid in the House bill. Then, when you get into conference, maybe you can tone down the military part and turn it into a loan. You won't have the amount to quarrel over, but you will have the wording of the way you handle it.

The CHAIRMAN. So just what would you do?

Senator THOMAS of Utah. I think it was $150 million, you see. If you made the loan, instead of $100 million, $150 million, then probably that is the Senate's counter to the House's proposal on their own plane. I am just thinking of the parliamentary situation and nothing else.

Senator SMITH. And you would make a grant of the balance? The $420 million would be a grant of these commodities?

Senator THOMAS of Utah. That relieves you of just one parliamentary argument, whether you can cutout the military provisions of the House proposal.

Senator CONNALLY. How would it do to loan them $150 million and then, if he squanders it and throws it away, we wash our hands of it and say, "Well, now, the hell with you"?

Senator HATCH. We won't.

Senator CONNALLY. Who won't?

Senator HATCH. If he squanders it away the same group will be back.

Senator WILEY. Of course.

Senator CONNALLY. And we will say, "Here, you wasted this money and fattened your crowd around you." That is what Marshall says has been going on with these crooks that are hanging around Chiang Kai-shek that he can't shake because they carried Ward No. 3 'way back yonder when he started out.

How do you feel about keeping this China bill away from ERP? I am opposed to this.

The CHAIRMAN. So am I. But the House has been opposite. We can create a stalemate and postpone ERP until it is too late. They have us behind the 8-ball now so far as the time table is concerned. I don't believe this is the time when we can stand on an issue if there is any way around it.

MISTAKE TO COUPLE ERP WITH CHINA AID

Senator CONNALLY. I think it is a fatal mistake to couple ERP with this Chinese business. They ought to stand on their own legs. The problems involved are wholly different and our approaches are different. I just don't believe that we ought to—I don't even like the Administrator being under ERP. I heard the arguments here the other day for it, but those, in brief, are my views.

The CHAIRMAN. I agree with that completely, Senator, but I just don't see how, under the circumstances, we can take that position.

Senator WILEY. Mr. Chairman, what is the judgment of the military big shots as to the value of our aiding China under these circumstances if conditions in Europe should become more critical—if we should have some overt act, and so forth? What is the implication of this whole thing from a military viewpoint?

THE SECRETARY OF STATE OPPOSES MILITARY AID

The CHAIRMAN. I think the situation is very clear, that the Secretary of State is unalterably opposed to military aid to China. Is that correct?

Mr. THORPE. That is correct.

Senator CONNALLY. How can we afford to do it if he is that way? He knows more about China than we do, or he ought to. He stayed out there a year, didn't he?

(Discussion was continued off the record.)

The CHAIRMAN. General Marshall presents a picture of what seems to be—and I do not use that invidiously—a very substantial military cooperation through the diversion of surplus property. That is immediately rebutted by the advocates of China aid by saying that the terms of such aid are such that China can't comply with them, and it costs more money than China has, in spite of the fact that it sold for one cent on the dollar, and, if he had a loan to use substantially as he sees fit, we would have financed his purchase of surplus materials, and I think you can defend that.

Senator LODGE. Equipment?

The CHAIRMAN. Yes.

Senator LODGE. That is all right, but that isn't aid. That is equipment. Military aid involves personnel, it involves instruction, it involves organization, and it involves training.

The CHAIRMAN. I am talking about a loan that does not confine itself to anything and is not defined for any purpose. I am talking about letting him have $100 million to do with as he sees fit, which is a cuckoo, I will admit.

RUSSIAN SUPPORT FOR CHIANG

Senator CONNALLY. At present Russia is committed, or is supposed to be, to recognizing and supporting Chiang's government. She is just looking for an excuse, no doubt, or a pretext, to break away from that policy. We are going to give it to her if we don't mind ourselves in this bill. That is worth considering. I don't think $100 million or $200 million or $300 million or $500 million or $600 million is going to save China.

The CHAIRMAN. Certainly not.

Senator CONNALLY. I have almost lost hope about China so far as Mr. Chiang is concerned. I do not believe that all this opposition to him is necessarily, strictly speaking, Communist. I think they are fighting the government that is in. They are just opposed to his long regime and they don't think they are getting their reforms, and they are not getting their land and they are not getting this and not getting that and the other.

Senator LODGE. It is the regular ins versus the outs.

Senator CONNALLY. And they think somewhat like General Marshall, that they have a group in there that are pretty bad. It is a sort of Republican insurrection like we have had here in the last 10 years under the Democratic administration.

The CHAIRMAN. It sounds more like the Democratic revolution in the South.

U.S. STAKES IN CHINA

Senator GEORGE. What commitments have we already got in any part of China? Have we any commitments in any part of China? What is our stake in China, as China exists today?

Senator CONNALLY. Rump steak!

Mr. BUTTERWORTH. We have comparatively small capital investments in China, and over the amount over 50 percent of it is in missionary and other philanthropic enterprises. So that, unlike the British and the French, we have not capital interests there. Our own interests in China of a commercial nature that are of any importance are the current trade interests, but, of course, since we have been assisting China to acquire the means to do their purchasing from the United States, it is not exactly a normal commercial operation.

Senator GEORGE. I suppose Great Britain and France are not doing very much about China, are they?

Mr. BUTTERWORTH. No.

The CHAIRMAN. What is the specific answer to that question? I think it is important. Are the British doing anything?

Mr. BUTTERWORTH. They are simply holding on to Hong Kong and trading in south China and operating such mines as they still have.

Senator GEORGE. Are the French doing anything?

Mr. BUTTERWORTH. Very little.

Senator CONNALLY. The British have Kowloon, over on the mainland.

The CHAIRMAN. Well, gentlemen, there you are. I have no predilection or preconceptions.

Senator HATCH. Is the situation such that we have to tie this China bill on this?

The CHAIRMAN. I think it is unless you are prepared to have an indefinite postponement of the balance of the bill.

WILL THE HOUSE BE REASONABLE?

Senator GEORGE. Why do you think that? Don't you suppose the House will be reasonable about it, if we just said we have to take more time on China? I don't know. Of course you have, as you say, some people in the Senate that are going to want to do something. You don't think we could make any progress?

The CHAIRMAN. We can try, Senator. All I know is that I made a personal appeal three times to the Republican House leadership, and Senator Lodge was with me on one occasion. I laid it down just as strongly as I knew how to lay it down.

Senator GEORGE. I don't know what to say about it. I am just not willing to go along with it myself at this time, I know that. I just don't see any point in it, and I don't see any commonsense in it.

Let me ask about this cotton. What are you going to do with the cotton? Where is it going?

TEXTILE MILLS IN CHINA

Mr. THORPE. There are textile mills in China which are operating.

Senator GEORGE. How close are they to the Reds?

Mr. THORPE. They are primarily in the Shanghai area. They are, I should say, in a relatively sheltered area.

Senator GEORGE. What are we going to do with the cotton when we take it over there? Are we going to control the distribution of the textiles that are manufactured from it?

Mr. THORPE. There is at the present time a little organization which we have set up which involves some representatives of the textile industry and the Chinese Government and our people which actually deals with the allocation of cotton to the various mills. Of course, some of the mills are Government-owned mills and some of them are privately owned mills.

Senator GEORGE. Are we going to sell that product in China, or are we going to ship it back here?

Mr. THORPE. That product is sold in China.

Senator GEORGE. It is going to be kept there?

Mr. THORPE. Yes, sir.

Senator GEORGE. It is not going to be sent here?

Mr. THORPE. No, sir.

Senator GEORGE. Where is it bought?

Mr. THORPE. The cotton is bought in the United States. We have reviewed that with the Department of Agriculture and have their assurance that this can be met without putting a strain on our cotton situation.

FERTILIZER

Senator GEORGE. What about the fertilizer here, $30 million worth of fertilizer? What is that? Is that nitrogen, nitrates?

Mr. WALKER. $18 million is nitrogenous fertilizers, and $12 million phosphates.

Senator GEORGE. Eighteen and twelve?

Mr. BUTTERWORTH. That is to go mainly to Formosa.

Mr. WALKER. There are no nitrogenous fertilizers going until the next fiscal year.

Mr. BUTTERWORTH. It is for the sugar industry in Formosa which the Japanese built up and which is based on artificial fertilizer.

Mr. THORPE. We might also say fertilizer is under international allocation, and this is all within the allocation which China would receive.

Senator GEORGE. And already you have shortages in the United States, and have had shortages in the United States. This international game will play you out, finally. There has to be some end to it somewhere and, so far as I am concerned, Mr. Chairman, I want to be excused on China at this time. I might do something later on.

Senator CONNALLY. I don't think we are ready to act on China.

Senator GEORGE. Let's keep this bill here on China.

Senator LODGE. Senator George, may I ask you a question? Regardless of whether this committee acts on a bill, aren't we going to confront the question of China because the House has put it in? We are going to have to meet it.

Senator GEORGE. We could go into conference and say we are not going to consider that and say take it out. I don't know whether we would succeed in that, and I don't know whether we would get by the Senate without it being put in. It might be added on the floor of the Senate.

The CHAIRMAN. There are two schools of thought in the Senate.

Senator GEORGE. There are more than two.

TWO SCHOOLS OF THOUGHT

The CHAIRMAN. I mean two positive schools of thought. I know there are 96 schools of thought in the Senate.

For instance, Senator Flanders, who has followed the rest of this relief program just as faithfully as can be, writes me a letter and says, "Now listen: I want you to know that when you get along to China, that is where I get off the train."

Senator GEORGE. He is not for it?

The CHAIRMAN. No. And then you have the chairman of the Appropriations Committee, who says "Don't bring any bill in here without China and military aid in it."

(Discussion was off the record.)

Senator HATCH. I want to ask the chairman if, as a result of his conversation with the House men, he thinks they might compromise on a loan.

NO ERP WITHOUT CHINA

The CHAIRMAN. I have not discussed that with them at all, but I think we could. My impression of the House attitude is that they have somewhat sobered recently. But one of their leaders who is in a position to speak with some authority said he didn't think he could pass ERP without China hooked on to it—that he just couldn't pass ERP.

Senator HATCH. That is what I am thinking about—ERP.

Senator CONNALLY. I think he is wrong. I think you can whip the House on ERP. The pressure for passage of ERP would be so strong the House couldn't stand out, I don't believe, on the sole issue of China. I don't think we are ready, yet, to act on China. I know I am in a devil of a fix on it. I don't know what to do. But the loan has one advantage over this other. It is not a commitment. It is not a commitment to military help. We just loan them the money, and if Chiang throws it away and wastes it, it is just gone.

Senator GEORGE. I don't know whether you could justify a straight loan. I would rather do it that way, if you could do it. The American people can ask a whole lot of pertinent questions about a loan to China.

Senator CONNALLY. They have asked so many now that I can't answer that adding one more won't make any difference.

Senator HATCH. Suppose you made a direct loan. How much would be used for military purposes and how much would go to lining the pockets of Chiang's crowd?

Mr. BUTTERWORTH. In all honesty I think you would have to have the gift of prophecy to answer that. Also, you must consider what will happen in the political period when this loan is made. You may very well have changes. The situation in China is a deteriorating situation, very rapidly.

HOW MUCH DOWN THE RATHOLE?

Senator Hickenlooper. You do not have to have the gift of prophecy, just the gift of history. How much of what we have given in the past has gone down the rathole? Better than 50 percent, even when the Japs were at their throats.

Mr. Butterworth. The record is certainly bad, and you have to say this for the Chinese, that they are in a state of hyperinflation. I saw Germany in that state after the last war, and a good many of the signs that I saw in Germany then I recognize in China. You have the speculative atmosphere, everybody looking after himself, everybody trying to get what he can in a deteriorating situation to protect himself, and in a country like China, which has the strong family system, everyone is looking after his own tribe.

Senator Hickenlooper. Mr. Chairman, that gets you down to the point that if China is in the state of collapse that Chiang indicated a couple of days ago, if they are that near the brink and you toss another $570 million in there, won't the scrounging around to get theirs be more ahead of the catastrophe than it has been in the past?

RESISTING COMMUNIST AGGRESSION

The Chairman. That is all true, Senator. There is one other factor, though, that we have not mentioned, that I do not think can be overlooked because it crops out in all the thinking of the country, and in most of the newspaper comment, and it is this basic abstraction that we are undertaking to resist Communist aggression, and we are ignoring one area completely and letting it completely disintegrate without even a gesture of assistance.

Senator Hickenlooper. Mr. Chairman, I have stated before, time and again, that I hope we can do for China whatever is practicable and helpful, but I hate to approach it under any subterfuge.

Senator Lodge. Anybody who opens up a war on all 360° of the circle is just crazy.

The Chairman. I am not talking about that, Senator, at all.

Senator Lodge. That is what they advocate. They want us to make our diplomatic, political, and economic effort all the way around the world at once.

The Chairman. Let's turn it around. One House of this Congress having gone as far as it has in connection with China, suppose the whole thing failed and we didn't do anything. Wouldn't that inevitably be the end of the Nationalist Government in China forthwith?

Mr. Butterworth. Certainly.

RESPONSIBILITY FOR NATIONALIST FALL

The Chairman. Do we want that responsibility?

Mr. Butterworth. No. And that is the primary reason that I believe led General Marshall to bring in this program.

Senator Wiley. At the same time we have to be sure we don't get our nose under the military tent so it is just one step further in.

The Chairman. We just all agree on that, Senator, and that is why I think Senator Connally's original idea, about a loan, without any reference in this bill to military assistance, is the answer, if there is one.

Senator LODGE. We still confront the military phase in the House bill.

The CHAIRMAN. Oh, yes. I am not afraid of that. I think we can get that out.

Senator LODGE. You do?

The CHAIRMAN. Yes.

Senator CONNALLY. How much money, since the World War, have we given to China?

Mr. THORPE. One billion and a half, with a few items not included that we haven't any valuation on, since the end of the war.

Senator WILEY. Since the end of the war.

CHIANG GOING DOWN GRADUALLY

Senator CONNALLY. Has she shown any improvement with the money we gave her? Hasn't Chiang been going down gradually ever since he got this money?

Mr. THORPE. The Chinese situation is worse today than it has been at any time since the end of the war.

Senator WILEY. What is the value of the goods? Are you putting it on a dollar basis or the actual basis when you say a billion and a half?

Mr. THORPE. Those are the items that I was not including—the surplus sales are not included.

Senator WILEY. That is what I thought you said last time, so you have to add to that that tremendous amount of surplus that has gone in there on the basis of 1 to 100 percent.

Senator CONNALLY. I don't put much value on that, because the Army would probably have destroyed a lot of that stuff. They have been doing that all over the world with surplus materials.

Senator WILEY. They cost the taxpayers something, and we want to know what China has got.

Senator GEORGE. Have we a lot of surplus property now in China?

Mr. THORPE. We have sold all the property in China to the Chinese.

Senator GEORGE. We have sold all we had there?

Senator LODGE. There was a lot on the islands.

Mr. THORPE. Which has been sold to them, but which has not yet all moved to China.

A 12 MONTHS' BASIS

The CHAIRMAN. It seems to me our problem is to see how cheaply we can avoid the calamity to which I just recently referred; that we dare not take the responsibility for the collapse of the Nationalist Government in China. Our very practical problem is, what is the cheapest way in which we can meet that situation, because it is a condition and not a theory. In the first place, without any deterioration in the impact of what we do, we can certainly put this program on a 12 months' basis instead of 15. That cuts the $570 million to $450 million.

Mr. THORPE. On a broken-down calculation, it is $105 million that would come off.

The CHAIRMAN. Well, all right.

Senator CONNALLY. What is the advantage of the 12 months? Don't you create a vacuum in there for 3 months that we would have to appropriate for in a separate bill?

The CHAIRMAN. No; because this runs to April, and we are reviewing ERP and everything else the first of January. The advantage of it at this moment is that it is a reason to save $115 million of this investment that we do not want to make.

Senator CONNALLY. I think we ought to make it the fiscal year, myself.

Senator WILEY. What about this argument that you make that we don't want to face the responsibility of seeing Chiang go to hell? Here, we are going to have the same thing if we let him linger on for 12 months. There are other imponderables in the picture. The same argument will be thrown at us: "You had better give us this amount or we will go to hell."

Senator HICKENLOOPER. Maybe hell will be more attractive at the end of 12 months.

Senator HATCH. You will have your European Recovery Program 12 months past, and you will know better what the world situation is than we do today. We may all be going to hell by that time.

The CHAIRMAN. The nearest text I could throw out for debate would be to cut this bill to $450 million and put $100 million of it in a loan and $350 million of it on the program recommended by the Department.

Senator CONNALLY. Aren't we avoiding a military commitment there, but yet when we say we spend $350 million for civilian aid what are you going to do with the other $100 million?

Doesn't that raise the impression or the implication that the $100 million is to be used for military purposes?

A MILITARY COMMITMENT NOT MADE

The CHAIRMAN. If they want to raise it, but I don't think we have made any commitment of a military nature when we do that.

Senator LODGE. What do you do with the $150 million?

The CHAIRMAN. It is a loan to the Chinese Government.

Senator CONNALLY. To do what it pleases with it. He is so busy dividing up the graft that he doesn't pay much attention to the army in the field.

The CHAIRMAN. The word "military" doesn't appear in the bill.

Senator SMITH. That would throw the House thing out, then. Do you think you can convince them to do that? That strikes me as the right approach.

Senator LODGE. Does that contain any implication that anybody could possibly find that it involves sending one single man, one single American military personnel?

The CHAIRMAN. Not one, because, assuming that the House agreed, we have deliberately taken this factor out of the Greek-Turkish bill, where they put it, where the implication does exist, and we have put it over here without any strings tied to it, so that we have affirmatively retreated from the kind of obligation that would have been involved in having it in the Greek-Turkish bill.

Senator LODGE. Could they consider this as implying any military personnel on our part?

Mr. BUTTERWORTH. I don't think they could, as the chairman has stated it.

OBJECTION TO A LOAN

Mr. THORPE. May I make one suggestion, as a technical matter. I think there will be a number of people who will question whether it makes sense to talk in terms of a loan in this situation, and there is another way of setting it up, namely, that $100 million will be earmarked for advances to the Government of China by the Treasury, the terms of which will be arranged at a later date in accordance with the use to which the funds are put, or something of that sort, at least escaping from the specific notion of a loan and leaving it for a later time as to whether it is to be a grant or just what.

Senator SMITH. What is your objection to a loan?

Mr. BUTTERWORTH. I think you get back, then, into the problem of the end use of this stuff, and the responsibility for its use.

The CHAIRMAN. I am afraid you do.

Mr. THORPE. Not responsibility. If they used it, for instance, for some capital purpose, eventually—if you are thinking it is going into military, then I think it ought to be written off as a grant.

Senator LODGE. Why couldn't you spell out "military equipment" and use those words? That is all Bullitt and those fellows signed their names to.

Senator CONNALLY. If Chiang is worth a damn he will use it for that. His Government is about to sink. If he has any sense at all he will use it for military purposes without our saying so.

The CHAIRMAN. Senator, if he has $100 million to use for his own critical necessities, why aren't you even further away from any military identifications?

Senator LODGE. I think you are. But I am just saying, you are going to have a little trouble maybe explaining this thing, that's all.

The CHAIRMAN. I would take a chance on that.

Senator CONNALLY. Furnishing war materials is taking part in the war almost as much as if you are sending troops. There is no doubt about that. You are arming their men and supporting them.

Senator LODGE. When you send them gasoline and wheat you are doing that.

Senator CONNALLY. Not in the same sense.

The CHAIRMAN. There isn't one word of commitment of one single American soldier in the formula I am talking about.

Senator LODGE. Or officer.

Senator SMITH. Or Mission.

Senator LODGE. Or man in uniform.

Senator HATCH. There is this criticism you will have to meet that Mr. Thorpe suggested. When you call it a loan, everybody knows it is not a loan. It is not going to be repaid.

The CHAIRMAN. I would just as soon call it a grant.

Senator CONNALLY. None of this will be repaid, for that matter. The $500 million is gone.

The CHAIRMAN. Senator George, does this get any closer to your point of view?

Senator GEORGE. I don't know. I don't understand it at all. I don't see any answer to it, myself. You want to just give, or make a straight loan or grant of, $100 million and cut down these supplies to China by that amount?

The CHAIRMAN. Yes, sir, so your bill is $450 million total.

Senator GEORGE. And you want to do away with the House bill; that is, that provision in the House bill?

The CHAIRMAN. Yes, sir.

Senator GEORGE. Where they just add China into the Greek program?

The CHAIRMAN. Yes, sir. I want to take them smack all out of the Turkish bill.

Senator GEORGE. That puts them under the Administrator and everything else?

The CHAIRMAN. That is correct.

Senator GEORGE. We already have a mission in China training people down there some place, and I suppose Chiang would send the money down there to them, or part of it.

A GESTURE

Senator CONNALLY. This whole thing is a gesture. My idea of suggesting the loan was that we are making the gesture and we are not committing ourselves to military aid, because military aid means war.

Senator LODGE. Is there anybody in China besides Chiang and the Communists? Isn't there anybody who makes any sense who isn't hopelessly reactionary or Communist?

Mr. BUTTERWORTH. Yes; there are quite a few people in China, but if you mean by that, has there appeared on the scene some alternative figure to the generalissimo, the answer to that is "No."

THE COMMUNIST-REACTIONARY DILEMMA

Senator LODGE. I hate to see us on the horns of this dilemma all over the world, that because we don't like Communists, we have to deal with reactionaries all over the world.

The CHAIRMAN. Is this true, Mr. Butterworth? Here is a note from a member of the staff: "China has not defaulted on any loan from the United States."

Dr. HAVLIK. Since V–J Day this is correct.

Mr. BUTTERWORTH. She is in default on a great many prewar obligations.

Dr. HAVLIK. There is a moratorium on that, generally speaking.

The CHAIRMAN. That is a pretty good answer to a loan. It is better than most of your excuses for the rest of the bill.

A $500 MILLION LOAN IN 1942

Mr. BUTTERWORTH. There is this to be said, that in 1942 the Treasury made a loan of $500 million and that has been an important nest egg which has made possible a lot of financing by the Chinese Government of such obligations as this.

Senator GEORGE. Didn't we get that loan back?

Mr. THORPE. There are two different $500 millions.

Senator GEORGE. There were two $500 million; yes.

Mr. THORPE. He is talking of the early one, in 1942.

Senator GEORGE. One $500 million was to stabilize their currency.

Mr. THORPE. That is the one he is speaking about.

Mr. BUTTERWORTH. This was made about at the time of the fall of Singapore, as I recall it.

Senator CONNALLY. That is still outstanding.

Mr. BUTTERWORTH. But it hasn't fallen due.

Senator GEORGE. If you want to do anything about it, I guess the best thing to do is what you suggest. It is going to be hard to justify a loan or a grant of money to the Nationalist Government in China because there are a lot of people in the United States who don't think a lot of that Government.

Senator CONNALLY. Won't the gift be just as bad?

Senator GEORGE. It might; but the other is food. They say you are helping them to live and you are giving them some food to live on—wheat; fertilizer to make some crops; and so on.

The CHAIRMAN. But we have not met our parliamentary difficulty, Senator, unless we can get this $100 million off by itself.

Senator GEORGE. As I say, maybe that is the best way you can do it, but we will have difficulty in justifying it.

Senator CONNALLY. Is it your idea to put the loan in and tell the House we are not going to put up with their version: "You take ours or leave it?"

The CHAIRMAN. Then we go to conference and say "This is ours, and we stand on it."

Senator CONNALLY. It is all very confusing to me—perplexing, pusillanimous.

Senator GEORGE. It is an adventure in chaos.

Senator CONNALLY. It is a straightout gamble, just giving it to them and letting it go.

AMERICANS SYMPATHETIC WITH CHINA

The CHAIRMAN. I think the American people generally are deeply sympathetic with China.

Senator GEORGE. That's right.

The CHAIRMAN. And her resistance against communism even more than Europe's against communism.

Senator GEORGE. They are sympathetic. There is one way to save China from Russian communism, and that is to send an army up on the Manchurian border big enough to stop it. Otherwise you are not ever going to stop communism in China.

I wish you would get me up a map from the State Department showing me how far they have got now.

Mr. BUTTERWORTH. I have it, and I have the information about the percentages.

Senator CONNALLY. Let me ask you this, before you get to the percentages. Hasn't there been a comparable movement of resistance and of war lords against the central government in China for 50 years? Haven't we had that there, and won't we always have it there?

Mr. BUTTERWORTH. Ever since the fall of the dynasty in 1911 they have had separatist movements of some kind.

Senator GEORGE. You say you have the percentages of the population?

Mr. BUTTERWORTH. Yes; they are on this memorandum.

The CHAIRMAN. We have to do something; that is perfectly obvious. What do you have to say about the pending suggestion and, if you don't like that one, what suggestion have you to offer?

THE MONEY NOT TO BE EARMARKED

Senator HICKENLOOPER. I think to give them the money and not earmark it is the only way you can do. Otherwise you are tied up with the military and it would be, as Senator George says, more than an adventure in chaos if we got into that in a military way. It would be complete chaos.

COMMENT BY SENATOR WILEY

Senator WILEY. Mr. Chairman, may I ask a question of Senator Thomas?

Yesterday Mrs. Wiley came home and she told about a very prominent Chinaman who was over here who was introduced to and addressed the congressional women. He was introduced by Madam Koo, and she told me of what a dynamic speaker he was. She said he outlined this fact, because he was questioned, that down through the years the upper classes in China have kept the lower classes down. The rich people have simply not given the ordinary Chinaman a fair opportunity, and he gave the impression—and it has been stated here—that the revolutionary movements that have obtained are a push upward by the lower class for somewhat of economic equality, like ownership of land, like being able to live as they should live, and so forth.

Well now, it has been stated here that Communists are doing as they have done in other places. They are dividing up the land and giving the common man a fairer shake. It was also stated at one of the last meetings we had that the Communists were also enforcing ruthless conduct upon the ordinary chap; that if he didn't do as they said they would shoot him, and so forth. That was one reason why the farmers and the lower people in the villages were with the Communists.

This is the point I am getting at: If it is true that the common people have in their hearts a feeling for this revolutionary Communist movement, what are we doing about the future of America? If we are going to back up the opposition and that opposition is going down, where do we come out? Heretofore China has been friendly toward us. But if the new dominant group takes over and we have created in them a sense of opposition and of hatred toward us, then it seems to me that we are doing the very thing we say we are afraid of having accomplished if Russia takes over.

I would like to get your reaction to that. I am seriously concerned when Senator George says it is an adventure in chaos. If we get one-sixth of the people of the globe, or about one-fifth in China, feeling that we of this hemisphere are opposing their desire for more light, for more development, then we are injuring the future of our children and grandchildren, and to me that is a serious question—that we proceed rightly. It isn't the exact dollars involved. It is a question of whether maybe we proceeded wrongly heretofore. If we have, we had better straighten our course and correct it.

Do you see what I am driving at?

Senator LODGE. Isn't that the dilemma we are in all around the world, and that Wallace in his crookedness says we are in a world revolution, which is true, but he does not say that Stalin is an unfit man to be the leader of the people who are reaching for the light.

RUSSIAN DOMINATION

Senator WILEY. Now we have this situation. You have the admission here that the Communists in China will not be dominated by the Russian Communists. Do you see what I am getting at? The statement is that the Communists in China will not be dominated by the Russians unless we force Russia into this picture.

Senator LODGE. If I didn't think that the Communists in China were going to be dominated by the Russians, I would not vote for a nickle, because I think Chiang is utterly incapable of governing mainland China. I would let them have their revolution. I would just as soon let them have one here; I would just as soon have one here. I hope we will have one next November.

Senator HICKENLOOPER. Senator Thomas, may I ask you this question along that very line? It no doubt is true that what we might refer to as the responsible or more intelligent Chinese want China for China. But here Chiang has been in operation now for 15 or 18 years. I have a feeling that the Chinese that advance that theory want China for their own personal looting purposes within China, so that outsiders don't interfere with that, or put bad ideas in the minds of the masses of the Chinese people.

CORRUPTION, LOOT, AND GRAFT

The reason I am afraid for this thing is that Chiang has been in charge of this revolutionary movement and whatever orderly government there is in China for 15 or 18 years, and he still hasn't cleaned out the corrupt war lords that are in his own machine. He is still operating on the basis of loot and graft. I don't say that he is personally, necessarily, but he is not only tolerating that but he is living on that thing, and he hasn't cleaned his own house. Unless he has done so within the last 2 weeks, he has not made a substantial removal or changed that looting system and graft system of China even under the altruism under which he is alleged to be operating. That is the thing that discourages me about China.

Senator THOMAS of Utah. That is true, of course. It is a squeeze thing, and you can't expect those things to be changed because they just simply won't come out. But you can keep things from being worse from an international standpoint.

Senator HICKENLOOPER. I agree with that.

I want to change the complexion of the government by peaceful means.

CHINESE DON'T WANT FOREIGN CONTROL

Senator THOMAS of Utah. Everywhere you go and find Chinese, they do not want any kind of foreign control. They have been fighting to get rid of the foreigners in China for a very, very long time. Now, the trouble with the present situation, the thing that might happen, would be that you bring about a situation whereby we have to go in, which invites another country. Then you are back just exactly about 75 years in Chinese history, where the fight against the extraterritorial control came in.

We have gotten rid of that as a result of a lot of factors, so that you have got China united in just one idea, and it is the first time she has been united, and that is that there will be a China, a China controlled by the Chinese. Back in Chiang Kai-shek's thinking, and in all of his ideas, is that great big idea. You may say it is mystical in its nature, because everything of that kind is mystical. But if you go back and study Machiavelli, you will find that he is working along a good old theory, that you don't want the kind of aid which makes it necessary for you to turn against the aider and drive him out after he has saved you from one situation. The Chinese is thoroughly sick of that, and in an international way we don't want to do anything which will put backward the coming of China as a national entity in the world. That can come.

You can go in and you can accept the French way of getting along or, worse still, the Portuguese way of getting along, or the Japanese way of getting along. It was all on an exploitation basis.

Senator HICKENLOOPER. Hasn't that exploitation in the last 50 or 75 years, let's say, by the outside nations that have come in and exploited, brought more progressive development to China than they had in a thousand years beforehand?

Senator THOMAS of Utah. Sure. Everything that has been done that way has contributed toward it. You can say the same thing of Japan. The foreign influence on Japan ultimately brought her destruction.

A DEADLOCK WITH THE HOUSE

Senator LODGE. Mr. Chairman, if you don't report a bill on China, and if the Senate has not had a chance to pass on its own China bill, then don't we absolutely certainly confront a deadlock?

The CHAIRMAN. I think so.

Senator LODGE. That would make it impossible to get anything done before the middle of April.

A PARLIAMENTARY NECESSITY

The CHAIRMAN. I think we confront a condition, not a theory, and I don't think it makes much difference what China is or what China is going to be. This is a problem in psychology, in the first place, and it is a problem of parliamentary necessities in the second place.

Senator LODGE. And political skulduggery in the third place.

The CHAIRMAN. I don't think this country would stand for our turning our backs on China, and that is what we have done if we don't do something about China. And I am sure Congress wouldn't let you turn your back on China. So you can't turn your back. You have to do something. And your problem is, What can we do?

Senator CONNALLY. Can't we justify treating China separately?

The CHAIRMAN. Yes, you can justify it, Senator; but in the course of your justification the Italian elections will have occurred and we won't have passed ERP.

Senator LODGE. We are going, in the Senate, to have a separate bill anyway.

Senator CONNALLY. I am not in favor of lying down to the House.

Senator LODGE. I am not either.

Senator CONNALLY. This is our field and our function.

Senator SMITH. But won't you block the whole thing to stand pat? I agree with the chairman, that we have to do something on this China thing, and do it promptly.

Senator CONNALLY. We can do it, but we don't have to gum it up with this ERP and all this other stuff.

Senator HICKENLOOPER. Listening in on this discussion and in my own mind, it appears to me that this amounts to this, that we may be searching around for what is the least thing we can do for China as a gesture, and as a practical thing to save ERP. It is not so much China as it is the European Recovery Program and how can we get out of the mess?

The CHAIRMAN. Plus the fact that the country, in my opinion, will not permit you to leave out China.

Senator HICKENLOOPER. That is part of why you have to do it.

Senator GEORGE. Plus the fact that we have to legislate in conjunction with the House under the Constitution, whether we like it or not.

We can introduce our bill in the Senate from this committee, and that will be notice to the country that we are going to do something about it.

Senator LODGE. You do favor our reporting on a bill, don't you?

Senator CONNALLY. Oh, yes.

THE TIME SCHEDULE

The CHAIRMAN. Here is the time schedule we confront. It is my understanding that the House will pass the joint bill next week before they take their Easter recess. We are going to take up Greece and Turkey on the floor on Tuesday. I don't know how much opposition we will get on that. I think it would be substantially reduced from the other one. I would like to follow it immediately with our China bill. Then, when the House bill comes over we can send it to conference, because we have had the independent expression of the Senate on both of these additional issues, and we can enter a full conference on the whole subject and we will see what we do in conference. But we haven't released ourselves to a complete freedom to do whatever the necessities of the ultimate situation are.

Senator LODGE. Speaking just for myself, I am glad to support that kind of plan. The only one thing where I don't want to compromise is on the question of sending American military aid to China.

The CHAIRMAN. I don't want to compromise there either.

Senator CONNALLY. What would you think, Mr. Chairman—of course it is a little beside the point—we have a military mission over there. Why shouldn't we have a civilian mission over there to feel out a lot of this situation and see what is going on in China. These military fellows approach the thing merely from a military angle, most of them. Some of them don't. It looks to me like we can very wisely send over three or four big men to look into the whole situation in China, economic wise and otherwise.

Mr. BUTTERWORTH. The bill does contemplate, you see, that we do send a civilian mission in connection with the administration of these commodities, so that we will follow them through and, in the process of doing so, we have to give a lot of advice to the Chinese about the operation.

Senator CONNALLY. That, of course, is more or less confined simply to how many biscuits you are going to give this Chinaman and how many to that. I am talking about a big mission to survey the whole Chinese situation. China, to me, is just an imponderable. It is just impossible. It is almost hopeless. If she can't work out with 450 million people her destiny, she is in one hell of a fix!

The CHAIRMAN. This is $1 apiece for them.

CHINA A SORE SPOT FOR YEARS

Senator CONNALLY. I have been struggling for China ever since I have been here, for 30 years. We used to have bills in the House and in the Senate about China. She has been a sore spot for years and years and she is always going to be a sore spot. I don't care what you do now, China is going to be on our necks as long as any of us are around here.

I don't know what to do about it. I think presently that that loan business is the best way.

Senator THOMAS of Utah. I am ready to experiment with Senator Vandenberg's suggestion.

Senator CONNALLY. You mean introduce an independent China bill?

Senator THOMAS of Utah. The way he has suggested it there.

Senator SMITH. Would it be possible for us to pass this bill as you suggest, for $450 million on a 12 months' basis, and leave your loan proposition to trading in conference?

The CHAIRMAN. No, I don't think you can get by without a great deal of difficulty.

Senator SMITH. You will have to state on the floor, then, that our loan is military aid.

The CHAIRMAN. No; your loan is at the option of the government which we recognize, the government which has asked us for aid, and for such purposes as its exigencies require. Anybody can draw his own conclusions from that.

Senator SMITH. Couldn't we get our colleagues who have had this military aid in mind to sit down, and have them understand so that we don't have to debate that on the floor? They are the chief ones who have been raising the point.

Senator LODGE. In the interest of international amity it is much better if we don't discuss that in the open. If we have to discuss it, it can be discussed in such a way as to make them look pretty weak.

Senator CONNALLY. It will have to be discussed. These fellows that want military aid are going to blah-blah unless the chairman can choke them off.

The CHAIRMAN. I am willing to take on a lot of things, but I don't think that is one of them.

Senator George, I am around to you again.

Senator GEORGE. I will go along with your suggestion on it, if you want to do it. I frankly don't think it is worthwhile to do a thing in the world about this situation.

The CHAIRMAN. Do you think we can afford to do nothing?

SAYING "NO"

Senator GEORGE. Yes. I think this: I think if we had a State Department who could say "No" so loud that it would be heard from Maine to the Gulf of Mexico about five times we would be in a lot better state. This thing has been sloughed on you. I appreciate that; I understand that. The House people have done it. And if you don't think we can say "No," we just don't say "No."

The CHAIRMAN. I don't think we can say "No" at the moment.

Senator SMITH. We can't say "No" on aid to China. I think we can say "No" on military operations in China, very definitely.

Senator LODGE. You can't say "No" on aid to China if you want to save ERP. I can say "No" on aid to China by itself. I am being put under pressure.

Senator HATCH. Everybody is being blackmailed into this.

Senator SMITH. We all admit that without a struggle.

The CHAIRMAN. Do you want to think this over until Monday?

Senator LODGE. I am being put under pressure, and I am ready to be on it, now.

Senator SMITH. Do you agree we can't just say "Nothing doing" on China?

Senator CONNALLY. I know there is a lot of sentiment for it, and most of that sentiment is for military aid, although not by saying so. What are we giving them any money at all for, except to strengthen their forces?

Senator SMITH. A lot of people think this is a Communist issue in China, and it isn't quite the same picture, as I gather it from the State Department reports.

Senator CONNALLY. If Mr. Chiang Kai-shek had everything he wanted in the way of supplies and all that, you would not have this bill here.

[Discussion was continued off the record.]

Senator CONNALLY. Why wouldn't it be a good idea to wait until Monday? Let's get Marshall up here on this thing. Let's get him here in person.

Senator GEORGE. If we could do any relief work in China; if what we could give there would relieve the Chinese people if it were adequate to do it, if it were even partially adequate to do a genuine relief job, that would be another story. And that is as far as I think we can wisely get into this picture. I think we are just inviting the Russians to come in the moment we begin to go into this picture. They will say, "Yes, this is a part of the Marshall Plan. Now they have extended it to the Far East, and they are confronting us there."

The CHAIRMAN. Certainly if we put China in the Greek-Turkey bill that is what Russia will say.

Senator LODGE. That is just folly.

The CHAIRMAN. It is total folly.

Senator GEORGE. I don't think we should do it now, but I do think if you can separate the thing, if you can say this is legitimate aid to China, although it is very inadequate—for this immense number of people it is practically nothing—that is all right. We can spend all this money over there without having a whole lot of Americans over there.

They will be missions, civil or military or both, or mixtures. And then, sooner or later, Russia will resent this thing, as sure as there is a Kingdom, if she is not already overextended, which she may be. But she will extend herself still further so long as she can keep up this expansion. She won't begin to crumble as long as her expansionism can keep going.

The CHAIRMAN. I don't want to ask the committee to vote on this suggestion this morning.

Senator GEORGE. I am perfectly willing to go along with you on it, because that is the best you can do about it. I know that. That takes it out of this Greek-Turkish thing. That is certainly a desirable thing.

The CHAIRMAN. And it takes it out of the military.

Senator GEORGE. It does immediately, Mr. Chairman; I grant you that. But I don't see any end to all our activities except military activity anyhow, so far as I am concerned.

COMBINING WITH ERP

Senator CONNALLY. I think Senator George made one very vital point. If we combine these as the House wants to do, they are going to say that "this is part of the ERP, and we are against it."

Senator LODGE. That is a very valid argument.

Senator CONNALLY. I think if we are going to deal with China at all we ought to deal with China in a separate bill.

The CHAIRMAN. I think the fact that the Senate does deal with it in a separate bill adds something to it.

Senator LODGE. Can we say in a report the argument that Senator George makes, that it ought to rest on its own footing?

The CHAIRMAN. There is no trouble on the timetable about waiting until Monday for a decision.

Senator GEORGE. I don't think you need wait, unless you want to get a military view of it. I was just reading the excerpts from Wedemeyer's report. He doesn't think there is very much to a relief program unless it be a real military program of supplies in a pretty big way.

Senator CONNALLY. If we make this loan to Chiang——

Senator GEORGE. He can use it for war purposes, necessarily. I would and everybody else would.

WEDEMEYER'S TESTIMONY

Senator LODGE. Has Wedemeyer's testimony been printed?

The CHAIRMAN. We have galley proofs now available for all members of the committee of the House testimony.

SUSPICION OF MILITARY PARTICIPATION

Senator GEORGE. I think we should go just as far as we can to avoid any suspicion of military participation of any kind, and furnish the other just as supplies and let it go.

Senator WILEY. Well now, Mr. Chairman, Senator George's statement as to what he thought the symptoms in China really mean is very fundamental. If I could be convinced that that is true, then I feel that it is a serious mistake to continue our aid to China. I think we are meddling, we are violating our original fundamental foreign policy 'way down to George Washington, which probably in the next 5 years we will return to if we keep on meddling all over the world. On the other hand, I would like to be thoroughly convinced of that.

Senator GEORGE. Senator, it is just my own feeling about it.

Senator WILEY. I have somewhat the same feeling.

Senator GEORGE. I have no proof of it. I don't know anything about China.

The CHAIRMAN. I certainly would not quarrel with the conclusions, but I don't think that that affects the problem that we confront at the moment.

Senator WILEY. The second thing, Mr. Chairman, is this question of military judgment, the question of what the effect of losing face in the Orient will be, whether it will be so interpreted—what affect, with MacArthur in Japan, will this have? Do we need to maintain face in China, in this world conflict of ideologies that may burst out here, may burst out there? Will it seek to contain the Russians on two fronts by keeping a big force, or is it sufficient to have MacArthur in Japan only to keep a force in Siberia?

Those are military matters that it seems to me we have to consider in the overall picture from the standpoint of foreign relations. I have no objection to reporting this bill out today. But your regular meeting is Tuesday, is it not?

The CHAIRMAN. We cannot wait much longer.

Senator WILEY. On Tuesday let's have Marshall down again, and someone else. Report this out, if you want to, today, so far as I am concerned. But I would like to get this overall picture. Forrestal has appeared before the Armed Services Committee, and here we are, sitting around dealing with foreign relations, and 50 percent of those foreign relations are the question of evaluating the military situation in the world. We haven't got it, and I am frank to say that I think we should have it, Mr. Chairman.

A GENERAL VIEW OF GOVERNMENT POLICY

The CHAIRMAN. Let me say this to you: Entirely aside from this legislation, I think the time has come when we must do precisely what you are suggesting, and as soon as we can clear the track I should like very much to have the Secretary of State come down here and tell us what this Government's policy is in connection with a lot of things that are going on. And we will just plan on doing that at the very first available moment.

Senator WILEY. It is very plain from the release that came in here this morning, indicating that we have joined France and Britain now, that we are playing on the Italian card table. We are saying now that we think we ought to turn over Trieste to Italy because they can't agree on a governor. That is the sum and substance of it. In other words, we are up to our necks all over in this international poker game, and heretofore we have been shown that we have been plain asses in dealing because we don't know how totally the world has been contracted. It is awfully small.

Here is China. The people have been sold that Chiang is our great friend, and his gang have got to be supported. It might be interesting to find out how much propaganda money has been spent on that. We have had two elements in Manchuria fighting it out there. One-fifth of the globe is involved. It is a matter of population, and I think it is mighty important from the standpoint of foreign relations and foreign policy to do that which will not create in one-fifth of the globe hatred toward these people—not so much in this generation as in the generations to come, when perhaps they may reach a higher state of civilization and be more adapted from many viewpoints, and probably develop some latent ingenuity like it took us 100 years to develop. Those are the things that to me are fundamental, and my responsibility, I sense, would be rather heavy in that direction, because the seed we sow today develops the fruit tomorrow, and that is why I would like to have all the facts.

Senator SMITH. You mean by that you do not think we should act today? Is that your general point?

Senator WILEY. This is just stepping out in one direction. The Chairman has his ideas.

Senator SMITH. Oh, yes. I think this is a special case that should be dealt with right away.

Senator WILEY. This may be whipped into better shape in conference.

The CHAIRMAN. This is a pure curbstone idea this morning, so far as I am concerned. I have no devotion to the thing.

Senator CONNALLY. Marshall was before the House. I have been reading some of his testimony there. He does not look on this thing with any satisfaction at all. He realizes it is chaos and perplexity. I don't want to insist, and I am ready to vote today if you want to vote. I would like to wait for Marshall, because he has been out there. I am prepared to vote for the loan and a separate bill, and cut it loose from the ERP.

The CHAIRMAN. We did have Marshall, and we had a long examination of him.

Senator CONNALLY. I don't suppose he has changed his mind. He doesn't change it often.

Mr. THORPE. I think Mr. Butterworth and I, who have been in touch with Secretary Marshall, can say that there is no indication, unless his trip to the West Coast has changed his mind, of any shift in his attitude from what it was when he appeared before the committee.

Senator CONNALLY. I assume he has the same ideas. Of course, he changed his mind after he went out to China. He went out there with a definite attitude and he had to change it because of conditions that he found existed in China.

The CHAIRMAN. What does the committee wish to do?

Senator SMITH. Is your proposal before us now for action—$100 million loan and $350 million grant?

The CHAIRMAN. We would cut the pattern back to 12 months, similar to ERP. That is a figure of $450 million, and we would put $100 million of it in a loan to the Government of China.

Senator GEORGE. And the other in supplies.

The CHAIRMAN. The other under the supplies.

Senator WILEY. I take it, Mr. Chairman, before I arrived, testimony was given as to the items of supplies? In substance, what were they?

The CHAIRMAN. They are in the booklet.

Senator WILEY. Was there a judgment given by Mr. Thorpe or Mr. Butterworth as to their impact upon our own local supply and whether it made any particular impact?

Mr. THORPE. All these have been studied in relation to our local supply. I would say that if anything, this does not represent increases going to China over what has been going into China, and in cases where there are particular agencies concerned, like the Department of Agriculture, we have worked with them to make sure that this was within the availabilities as calculated.

The CHAIRMAN. I would be quite happy to have the Secretary return and meet with us in a final meeting Monday morning to discuss this formula with him.

Senator HATCH. And in the meantime, Mr. Chairman, could not the staff redraft it and put this suggestion into shape so that we could look at it, and submit it so the Secretary can see it?

The CHAIRMAN. I have no disposition to push for a vote today, if there is the slightest inclination otherwise.

Mr. THORPE. May I make one comment, Mr. Chairman. I do not want to quarrel over amounts, but on the basis on which all the calculations were presented, which would come to $570 million, if you do reduce it to 12 months it should be $465 million instead of $450 million. It may be than you prefer to have a rounded figure.

The CHAIRMAN. We are in conference on the figures, and that is one of our necessities to get a rational device to get into conference.

Mr. THORPE. All I was saying was that instead of the $450 million you suggested, $465 million would be consistent with the background information and analysis we have presented.

PARALLELING WITH ERP

Senator CONNALLY. We are trying to avoid paralleling this with ERP. It looks to me like it would be a very good idea to leave it 15 months, because if you are going to parallel with ERP the Russians will say, oh, yes; this is part of the ERP and we are not for it. That may be a minor point and no doubt is, but I think that a 15 months' period will be better than a 12.

The CHAIRMAN. Inasmuch as my only comment is that this is by common consent a pretty doubtful venture, I should think if there was any one adventure that could be cut back to the earliest possible review date, this is the one.

Senator CONNALLY. This is an authorization. The Appropriations Committee will make the appropriation.

The CHAIRMAN. Do you think we had better go over to Monday?

Senator CONNALLY. I am not going to insist on it, but I think we ought to think about it a little more than we have.

I am firm, though, that we ought to have a separate bill, and we ought not to surrender to the House on tying all this up in one basket. China is a different proposition from Europe. The motives are different. We are dealing with contracts and agreements with 16 countries in Europe that differentiate this program from China. In China it is just a handout.

Senator SMITH. I agree with you, if we can do it.

The CHAIRMAN. Does the committee wish to vote today, or does it wish to wait until Monday? Those in favor of voting today will hold up their hands.

All right. The committee will recess until 10 o'clock Monday, and we will settle this thing Monday morning.

[Whereupon, at 12:05 p.m., the hearing was adjourned, to reconvene on Monday, March 22, 1948, at 10 a.m.]

ASSISTANCE TO CHINA

MONDAY, MARCH 22, 1948

UNITED STATES SENATE,
COMMITTEE ON FOREIGN RELATIONS,
Washington, D.C.

The committee met, pursuant to adjournment, in the committee hearing room, U.S. Capitol, at 10 a.m., Senator Arthur H. Vandenberg, chairman, presiding.

Present: Senators Vandenberg (chairman), Capper, Wiley, Smith, Hickenlooper, Lodge, Connally, George, Thomas of Utah, and Hatch.

The CHAIRMAN. Ambassador Douglas phoned me a little while ago and said that the Secretary would come up this morning if we felt it was indispensable, but that he would greatly appreciate it if his visit could be postponed until later in the week because of the accumulation of responsibilities which he confronts on his return, and with which we are somewhat familiar. He said he would be glad to come on Wednesday morning and talk with us about the whole situation. I told him I would let him know whether it would be satisfactory to the committee to wait until Wednesday. If we insist upon his coming, he will come this morning.

STATEMENT BY AMBASSADOR DOUGLAS

Now, on the pending business, Ambassador Douglas made the following statement: He said that the Secretary had been advised of the tentative program upon which we were working last Saturday; that his entire predilection is to make sure that we make no military commitments to China, and that nothing that we do can be read as an obligation on our part to follow through with military aid; that he thinks the form in which we are proposing or did propose tentatively on Saturday to act is satisfactory.

Under those circumstances, I want to send him word right away whether we want to insist on his coming this morning, or whether we can wait until Wednesday.

Senator CONNALLY. You said "as determined Saturday." Was that the plain relief bill, or including the loan?

The CHAIRMAN. Including the loan.

Senator CONNALLY. Will that be satisfactory to him?

The CHAIRMAN. Yes; with the statement that I am making, that he wants to be very sure that there is no sort of military commitment to follow through on our initiative in respect to military activities in China. He thinks that that is, for the sake of the record, on the basis of the formula of what we were discussing.

[Discussion was continued off the record.]

MONEY FOR MILITARY PURPOSES

Senator GEORGE. I don't see how China is going to use any money for military purposes.

The CHAIRMAN. Will you first tell me what word to send to the Secretary?

Senator GEORGE. I think there is no need for dragging him up here. I think everybody understands General Marshall's attitude. We do not want to get involved in this matter in a military way. I don't think we should bring him up.

The CHAIRMAN. Suppose Dr. Wilcox, you phone his office that it will not be necessary for him to come this morning; that we will be very glad to hear him on Wednesday morning to discuss the whole general picture.

Senator CONNALLY. These fellows that want military aid to China and want it spelled out claim that all the military people except Marshall are the other way—all the military people, like Chennault, Wedemeyer, and so on.

Senator LODGE. But they don't agree on what they mean by the phrase "military aid." I have been lobbyed this weekend to no end. Everybody has been calling me up on the China thing.

Senator CONNALLY. I asked Bullitt this morning, "Do you want to send any troops?"

"Oh, no, no, no, no, no!"

Senator SMITH. Bullitt, of course, is the great proponent of it.

STATEMENT BY GEN. LOWELL W. ROOKS

Senator LODGE. There are a lot of others. Here is General Rooks. I read his testimony in the House yesterday. He says this:

> I feel that to be of assistance this country, upon invitation of the Chinese Government, if that is forthcoming, should assist with military supplies, munitions of all kinds, as rapidly as they can be gotten there; and further, there should be no hesitancy in introducing into China and making available to the Chinese Government American forces to the extent deemed necessary in training, organizing, equipping, and advising in the over-all strategy and tactics of their campaign.

That is Gen. Lowell W. Rooks, formerly head of UNRRA, and he is a Regular Army officer.

Senator CONNALLY. Mark him off.

Senator LODGE. I am marking him off anyway, but I cite this to show that this idea you and I have about troops isn't the same as some others have.

Senator WILEY. They are cockeyed.

Senator LODGE. You bet they are. I would like to ask General Marshall what does he suggest we put in this bill to be sure it isn't a military bill.

The CHAIRMAN. I think he is satisfied so long as we omit all reference to military supplies and leave the expenditure of this $100 million to the option of the Chinese National Government, the Government which we recognize; that there is no commitment of any nature, because if it is used for military supplies it is at their option and not ours.

Senator LODGE. And this is on the understanding that we get China out from under the Greek-Turkish bill, where the House put it.

The CHAIRMAN. That was mentioned. Obviously I would think that it ought to come out from under there.

Senator GEORGE. They have a separate title in here on that.

Senator CONNALLY. It seems to me that we ought to stand pat on that. Just tell them, you have got to take that out of there.

CONTROVERSY BETWEEN BULLITT AND MARSHALL

Senator SMITH. As I understand, this is an issue between Bullitt and Marshall, and we are taking Marshall's side of that controversy, and the House is taking Bullitt's side.

I have a résumé of his testimony. He has a four-point program. He wants to send MacArthur there to help run the show for Chiang Kai-shek.

Senator CONNALLY. That crowd is for bullets, and we are not.

Senator LODGE. If you send MacArthur there as an adviser he can't advise unless he sets up signal communications all over the area. When you set up signal communications over an area like that, it means signal troops. You can't get away from it.

Senator GEORGE. I am sorry we have given military aid to Greece. I am not for military aid here. If it is going to get you in trouble anywhere in the world it will get you in trouble in Greece and Turkey.

Senator WILEY. We have troops ready to land in Italy today.

Senator GEORGE. They will set up a counteroffensive to any economic and military programs we put in motion over there. You and I know it. It is just an open invitation to them to do it.

HOUSE COMMITTEE REPORT

The CHAIRMAN. The House committee report winds up and summarizes the thing in one sentence:

> Not all witnesses were in agreement that military aid should be given to China, but nearly all were agreed that without military-type aid, economic aid would be a most dubious venture. For these reasons the provision was made for aid to China at a cost not to exceed $150,000,000 of the same character as aid to Greece and Turkey under Title 3. This amount does not appear large*

Senator GEORGE. There is this to be said. If China is to get any military supplies, she has got to get them through the United States. She has got to get them here. Now, that is all there is to it. There is no other source of supplies open to her. We armed them over there with our arms, outfitted them, and trained several divisions of them, or are supposed to have. And she is not going to be able to take the $100 million that we have to have, that we let her have in cash, to get any supplies unless she gets them here. If they take to buying planes from us they have to get American pilots to fly them over there. When they get over there, they are over there. There isn't any other way for them to do it.

Senator SMITH. Does that mean that you oppose the $100 million loan? I see your point. But do you go that far?

Senator GEORGE. I don't see how any money loan is going to do them any good.

Senator CONNALLY. They can spend the money here for military supplies.

---

*See: House Committee on Foreign Affairs, *Report on Foreign Assistance of 1948*, House Report No. 1585, 80th Congress, second session (1948). This 106-page document is too long to reproduce in the appendix of this hearing.

Senator GEORGE. How could they do it except our Government permitted it and handled it for them? I don't want to get into military aid, but we have gotten into military aid in Greece and Turkey and Italy.

Senator LODGE. Senator, you think, don't you, that it is a very different thing; military aid to Greece and Turkey is a very different thing?

YALTA AGREEMENT A CRIME

Senator GEORGE. Yes. I think you get into a war, though, quicker in Greece, and Turkey, and Italy than you will in China, because I think it will take a century for anybody to bring any order out of China, and Russia is not going to be greatly concerned unless they moved into Manchuria, into the area we gave Russia under the Yalta agreement. I have some sympathy for China, because we just about gutted the empire at the Yalta agreement. That was probably the crime of the century. They are helpless, wholly helpless from now on out, if Russia ever wants to take them. And there you go.

I think, Senator Lodge, it is quite different from Greece and Turkey, because I think maybe Greece and Turkey will do a little better fighting over there, and I think that anything we give to China is probably just a complete waste, just a venture into outer darkness. We don't know what we are doing and we can't do any good by it, but I am just speculating in my own mind. And it is difficult. If we are going to say there shall not be any military aid at all, what is the use of making any $100 million loan to them?

[Discussion was continued off the record.]

NEED TO DO SOMETHING

The CHAIRMAN. Let's just briefly sum up the situation in which we find ourselves, and the problem we confront which led to a tentative conclusion last Saturday. We obviously have got to do something about China, because if we failed to do it, it would be the end of any chance whatever for the Nationalist Government in China, in my opinion.

Senator LODGE. Not only that, but the end of ERP.

The CHAIRMAN. I am coming to that.

And I do not believe we want to take the responsibility for that upon ourselves, because it certainly does not reflect our attitude nor the attitude of the American people.

There is a very large sector of American public opinion, and I guess I am part of it, that has not agreed with American foreign policy in its demand for a Communist coalition in China, and which does feel that consistency requires us to do something about the China situation in connection with our general attitude toward the world's problem today.

Secondly, I am sure there is a feeling in Congress which makes it unavoidably necessary to deal with the China situation in connection with this current legislation. I very much doubt whether we could hope to get ERP through, even remotely, in time to be psychologically effective if we fail to take some cognizance of this demand for Chinese legislation.

A CONDITION, NOT A THEORY

So we confront a condition and not a theory. We are all agreed that we want to avoid military commitments in China which create any sort of precendent or underwrite any sort of obligation with respect to American troops in China or in respect to our acceptance of any sort of a military commitment in connection with the Chinese situation.

To accomplish all of these purposes, we had pretty generally come to the conclusion on Saturday that Senator Connally's idea about setting aside a loan or a grant to the Chinese Government to be used at their option, avoiding any reference to military commitments in our bill, was the best way to meet the emergency which we cannot ignore or avoid.

So it seems to me that we are right back where we were Saturday, and unless somebody has a better formula, I think we ought to proceed to formalize what was our informal decision Saturday.

The staff has put together a text on one sheet of paper which I would like to read to you.

Senator Connally. A statement or a bill?

The Chairman. A bill.

Senator George. On China?

The Chairman. On China.

$570 MILLION WILL DO NO GOOD

Senator Connally. I'll tell you how I feel about it. I am going along with this thing, but I think the whole Chinese project of $570 million isn't going to make a bit of difference on what is happening in China. I doubt if it will do any good, but if it will, I am for it.

The Chairman. To take the reverse of that, don't you think it would make an awful difference over there if we slammed the door?

Senator Connally. It probably would, psychologically. We don't call it military aid, but if they didn't need military aid we wouldn't be giving them this money. That is what we are doing it for, to help them whip the Communists.

Senator Wiley. Of course.

That is the very heart of the matter. The military aid they need is American troops, and we don't want to be sucked into that. If what Senator Thomas says is correct, they have captured 3 million stands of small arms. We have noticed every now and then that big dumps of ammunition are blown up. And again it is a question of administration.

Senator Connally. They claim they haven't any ammunition and they haven't any way to make it.

Senator George. They haven't any cartridges at all to shoot in their guns, is what they claim.

The Chairman. Let's take a look at this and we will see where we are.

Senator George. This is the whole of what we propose to do, now?

The Chairman. That's right.

THE ENACTING CLAUSES

After the enacting clause:

SEC. 2. It is the purpose of this Act to provide immediate aid to China to relieve human suffering, to assist in retarding economic deterioration, and to afford the people of China an opportunity to initiate measures of self-help necessary to rebuilding the bases for more stable economic conditions, such aid to be provided under the applicable provisions of the Economic Cooperation Act of 1948 which are consistent with the purposes of this Act.

In other words, at that point we are covering in anything that is consistent.

Senator GEORGE. Anything that suits their case.

The CHAIRMAN. "It is not the purpose of this act that China, in order to receive aid hereunder, shall adhere to a joint program for European recovery." That is the only point at which we have to separate the same two.

Senator SMITH. Why not change line 2 to say "to assist in aiding economic rehabilitation" instead of the negative statement, "to assist in retarding economic deterioration"?

The CHAIRMAN. We will come back to that.

SEC. 3. (a) In order to carry out the purposes of this Act, there is hereby authorized to be appropriated for aid to China a sum not to exceed $363,000,000, to remain available for obligation for the period of one year following the date of enactment of this Act.

(b) There is also hereby authorized to be appropriated to the President a sum not to exceed $100,000,000 for the additional aid to China through grants or on such other terms as the President may determine to be appropriate, to remain available for obligation for the period of one year following the date of enactment of this Act.

SEC. 4. An agreement shall be entered into between China and the United States containing those undertakings by China which the Secretary of State, after consultation with the Administrator for Economic Cooperation, may deem necessary to carry out the purposes of this Act and to improve commercial relations with China.

SEC. 5. Notwithstanding the provisions of any other law, The Reconstruction Finance Corporation is authorized and directed, until such time as an appropriation is made pursuant to section 3 (a), to make advances, not to exceed in the aggregate $50,000,000, to carry out the provisions of this Act (other than section 3(b)), in such manner and in such amounts as the President shall determine. From appropriations authorized under section 3(a), there shall be repaid without interest to The Reconstruction Finance Corporation the advances made by it under the authority contained herein. No interest shall be charged on advances made by the Treasury to The Reconstruction Finance Corporation in implementation of this subsection.

Senator CONNALLY. This $50 million is the RFC advance. You say "other than section 3(b)." That is the $100 million-loan section.

The CHAIRMAN. Yes.

Senator CONNALLY. What do you mean by that?

The CHAIRMAN. Why do you exempt that?

Dr. WILCOX. This $100 million is a sum apart, and it is not to be considered as part of this act. It is $100 million that is completely extra from the $350 million and the $50 million applies to the $350 million and not to the $100 million, which is the loan which the committee decided it wanted to extend.

LANGUAGE CONFUSING

Senator CONNALLY. The language may be the best you can do, but I think it is a little confusing.

The CHAIRMAN. I think it is unfortunate to have it in at all. So long as we are doing the thing, it ought to be done. That is just $50 million on account of the whole bill. I don't know why you have to divide it up.

Senator SMITH. They will probably want that in a hurry, too.

The CHAIRMAN. Sure. If it is any use to them, they ought to have that when they want it. I would rather take out "(other than section 3(b))."

The CHAIRMAN. That $50 million is available to the President.

Senator CONNALLY. "In such manner and in such amounts"——

Senator SMITH. Then in the second line below that, you change that from "appropriations authorized under section 3(a)" to "appropriations authorized hereunder."

The CHAIRMAN. Yes. You will have to change the next one, also.

Senator THOMAS of Utah. It is assumed, under the loan provision, that China may at some time pay back part of this $100 million.

The CHAIRMAN. It is assumed.

Senator THOMAS of Utah. It is a loan, with the understanding that they ought to live up to their obligations?

The CHAIRMAN. Yes, and I think it would be very interesting to have the record to justify the statement made Saturday, that China has not defaulted on a loan from the United States. That is an almost unbelievable statement.

Senator HATCH. Don't you think "loans" should be included—"grants or loans?"

A LOAN SHOULD BE SPECIFIED

Senator CONNALLY. There is nothing in this bill about a loan.

Senator HICKENLOOPER. It says "grants."

Senator HATCH. I think a loan ought to be specified.

The CHAIRMAN. I think so, too: "through grants or loans on such terms as the President may determine."

Senator GEORGE. I suppose the President will let them have it for military purposes.

The CHAIRMAN. If that is their object. That does not commit us.

Senator CONNALLY. We are appropriating it to the President.

Senator HATCH. Do you have to appropriate to the President? I am thinking about blank checks and arguments that are going to be made.

The CHAIRMAN. I would like very much to eliminate it if it could be done.

Dr. WILCOX. The only thing is, it is consistent with other language used in appropriation acts. That is the only thing.

Senator HATCH. That just sticks up like a sore thumb.

The CHAIRMAN. It certainly does.

Senator CONNALLY. Why don't you strike out "to the President"?

Senator GEORGE. You haven't got the President in 3 (a) up there.

Senator SMITH. How are you going to get the terms worked out, then? Who will determine the terms of the loan?

Senator GEORGE. "In order to carry out the purposes of this act there is hereby authorized to be appropriated to the President for aid to China——". You have got to get it out of the Treasury.

Senator CONNALLY. If we put in "the President" and they use it to buy some arms, people will be saying, "Oh, I told you so." Then they have discovered what we are up to.

Senator SMITH. You mean they have made that surprising discovery?

Senator WILEY. You have a lot of it over on the islands of the Pacific that you want to get rid of at 1 cent on the dollar.

The CHAIRMAN. Let's give them the money to pick up that stuff.

Senator WILEY. Don't give them the money, because they will pick it up and keep the money, too.

Senator CONNALLY. We have them in a place where we can demand an accounting.

The CHAIRMAN. Do we need that in there?

Dr. WILCOX. I don't think we do. The main reason it was done was because it was in all the other bills.

Senator GEORGE. You have to appropriate to some agency or to the President. The Treasury couldn't pay out money just to China.

Dr. WILCOX. Appropriate to the Administrator?

The CHAIRMAN. That wouldn't do. I think it has to be appropriated to the President.

Senator GEORGE. The Comptroller General would put the Secretary of the Treasury in jail if it was not appropriated to somebody.

"ASSIST IN ECONOMIC REHABILITATION"

Senator SMITH. Now, instead of saying "assist in retarding economic deterioration", I say "to assist in economic rehabilitation."

The CHAIRMAN. Much better.

Senator GEORGE. Are we committing ourselves to rehabilitate the whole of China?

Senator SMITH. "To assist in economic rehabilitation."

Senator GEORGE. This is just the first installment.

Senator WILEY. Twelve months from now you will have it on your hands again.

The CHAIRMAN. That is no worse than "in retarding economic deterioration."

The report from the Legal Division of the Department of State is that you do not need to put in "appropriate to the President" if you do not want to. It then remains for the Appropriations Committee.

Senator GEORGE. They will have to appropriate it to somebody.

Senator CONNALLY. If you are going to appropriate to anybody, you had better appropriate to the President.

The CHAIRMAN. I think so.

Senator CONNALLY. He has to do it.

Senator HATCH. It provides in (b) that the President has to say so: "or on such other terms as the President may determine to be appropriate." That is in here. In effect that, as I construed it, was an appropriation to the President, and I objected to pointing it out there so plainly.

Senator SMITH. What you mean, Senator Hatch, is that you can just say "There is also authorized to be appropriated a sum not to exceed * * *." Is that your thought?

The CHAIRMAN. Senator Connally?

Senator CONNALLY. The House has $150 million in there.

The CHAIRMAN. Yes. But if you take your pro rata off of that, it is down to $120 million even in the House. We can meet that with the House and split it if we have to.

Senator THOMAS of Utah. Then you changed the $150 million in section 5 to $50 million, didn't you?

The CHAIRMAN. Right.

THE WORD "LOANS"

Then that word "loans" ought to go in as you suggested: "through additional aids to China through grants or loans."

Senator SMITH. What would be the objection to making this a straight loan proposition? If we want to remit the thing later, we can do it. Why not differentiate it by making it a straight loan, without talking about grants?

Is that impractical?

Senator THOMAS of Utah. The loan idea does put the responsibility on them a little bit more than the grant idea. You grant it for certain things that you will see ahead of them, but if you lend it to them, if they spend it in a way that we do not want them to spend it, it is our fault for giving them a loan, but we are not responsible for what they did with it.

The CHAIRMAN. I would rather have it just "loans" so far as I am concerned.

Senator CONNALLY. It avoids the suspicion that we are doing it for some particular military reason.

The CHAIRMAN. That's right.

Senator SMITH. Paragraph (a) is a grant for rehabilitation. (b) is a loan. I think that is what you intended.

The CHAIRMAN. I think that is better. I think that again dilutes any possibility of responsibility.

Suppose it read "for additional aid to China through loans on such terms as the President may deem advisable?"

Senator GEORGE. "As the President may determine to be appropriate" or "deem advisable."

Senator CONNALLY. I don't like that word "advisable." That suggests that he knows what they are going to do with it.

Senator SMITH. What was the clause Dr. Wilcox gave us in there?

The CHAIRMAN. "Without regard to the provisions of the Economic Cooperation Act of 1948."

Senator CONNALLY. I don't like the idea of tying it into ERP at all. It seems to me it ought to be an independent thing.

Senator SMITH. I think so, too.

The CHAIRMAN. We are going just as far as we can go to make it an independent bill, and then it is up to us in conference.

Senator CONNALLY. This bill will never get to conference.

The CHAIRMAN. Oh, yes. When we get to conference we have the House bill with its parts 1, 2, 3, and so on. We have legislated on part 1; we have legislated on part 2; we have legislated on part 3. Technically these two bills are not before the conference.

Senator CONNALLY. Exactly.

The CHAIRMAN. But the Senate's position with respect to parts 2 and 3 is legislated independently.

Senator THOMAS of Utah. If you ask for the conference, you can specifically ask that that be put in, can't you?

Senator CONNALLY. No. You can't confer on anything that has not passed both of the Houses.

Senator GEORGE. You will have to move to strike out title 4 and, if we approve this, insert in lieu thereof this.

Senator SMITH. And you will have to move to strike China out of the Greek-Turkish part in title 3.

Senator GEORGE. Yes. That will be word striking; but here you will have to move to strike out all of title 4 unless you want to keep in this language that they have evidently worked on over there a month?

The CHAIRMAN. Do you mean that speech?

Senator GEORGE. Yes. It is a good speech.

Senator CONNALLY. Why not strike all of their bill out and substitute ours?

Senator GEORGE. You can strike out all after the enacting clause and substitute our own just by adding this to it. You can do it either way.

Senator SMITH. You have the Bullitt-Marshall row right here between the Senate and the House committees.

QUESTION OF LOANS OR GRANTS

The CHAIRMAN. On this question of loans or grants, we now get the viewpoint of the Treasury, which objects to the use of the word "loans," and it is suggested that we leave out both the words "loans" and "grants," so that it reads, "There is also hereby authorized to be appropriated to the President a sum not to exceed $100 million for additional aid to China on such terms as the President may determine to be appropriate."

Dr. WILCOX. I'm sorry; I didn't make my point clear. If you want to leave the word "loans" in, they would prefer that you put the word "grants" in. They didn't like to put the word "loans" in the bill, because they say there is not the slightest ghost of a chance of our getting paid back.

Senator GEORGE. I think maybe you had better just say "grants"—"for grants on such terms as the President may deem appropriate" and let it go. Leave the word "loans" out. The loan did sound a little like it was their business, but they will have to get the money from us and they will have to make a case every time they come up here to get the money.

Senator SMITH. The question of paying back isn't up. That question won't come up until it comes time to pay, and then we can make a gracious gesture.

Dr. WILCOX. They were consulted on the language, and they had pretty strenuous objections to this language.

Senator GEORGE. They do not want to have to carry them as loans.

The CHAIRMAN. They don't want the word "loans" further depreciated in its status.

"OH, WHAT TANGLED WEBS WE WEAVE . . ."

Senator HATCH. I don't want to be critical, but I cannot help but think, as I read this paragraph, that this committee is against military aid to China almost unanimously. Well, we are including $100 million here which you know will be used for military aid. We are talking about loans which we know will not be paid. And I was just thinking, sitting here, that somewhere in the report we should place, "Oh, what tangled webs we weave, when first we practice to deceive."

The CHAIRMAN. So far as the chairman is concerned, he is not included in your classification of those who are opposed to helping the Chinese with military supplies at their option, and on their order, and on their responsibility, because I think that if we facilitate them in obtaining all of the surplus supplies that are left out there, we have done a perfectly legitimate thing and a highly helpful thing.

Senator HATCH. I withdraw my statement. I think we are doing just what we have to under the circumstances.

The CHAIRMAN. And it is what we are doing now in a halfhearted sort of way.

Senator HATCH. I cannot help but dislike this way of legislation, as everybody else does.

The CHAIRMAN. Why, sure.

Senator CONNALLY. There is nothing violative of international law for us to sell them arms or get them to them on a credit. We have done that in all the wars until we passed the arms embargo, you know. We went ahead and sold arms to the warring nations in Europe before we got into the war.

That doesn't make any difference to Russia. She doesn't look at international law or anything else. She looks at the politburo.

Senator HICKENLOOPER. Isn't what we are resisting getting ourselves committed for continuous future military aid? So far as I am concerned, I would just as soon they spend the whole $450 million for guns and ammunition if it does not commit us, if we don't get our foot in the door to the point where we have to keep on in spite of ourselves.

The CHAIRMAN. I think we have avoided that, and I think we can say something about it in the report.

PHRASE "MILITARY AID"

Senator LODGE. I would like to say something about that. I think this committee ought to completely clarify this question, and not deal with this loose phrase, "military aid," which is so tremendously dangerous.

The House report, on page 55, is half-baked and superficial. It is bureaucratic in the way it approaches this thing, and it is very dangerous to have a confusion of this kind on such a phrase, and it is very dangerous for the idea to get out that China and Greece and Turkey are on the same footing. You heard General Harper the other day make his statement, which I know is the statement of every professional soldier I have ever talked to, that it would be folly to send troops to Greece. Greece is so small, and he said that the question of sending troops to Greece is never going to seriously come up.

Then you have the testimony of General McBride, who says that the Turks are so aggressive and have such a fine spirit that you never need to send American troops there. We are sending equipment to those people so they can hold an airbase themselves. That is an entirely different thing. I am looking at it not from the legalistic standpoint but from the standpoint of American manpower. If we have another war, we will lose it unless we conserve our manpower. If we start throwing it around and trying to beat them on the ground and hammer their heads against a wall all over the world, this country is going to be ended, and it is inexcusable, I think, for a responsible body to write the kind of stuff that appears here on page 55.

85-743—73——31

I think we ought to have in our report a very clear statement of exactly what we mean, and I think what we mean is, giving them supplies of a military character and continuing the training activities that are going on there now, and getting an absolutely accurate definition of what those training activities are, and no more. Because this is getting your nose under the tent in a great big way, and they didn't know what they were doing when they did this.

Senator CONNALLY. We are disagreeing with that.

Senator LODGE. I think we ought to state it in the report in a very clear way, and I think we ought to get this word "Chinese" out of the language on page 101 of the House bill. I think that is very important.

The CHAIRMAN. That is a problem of conference.

Senator LODGE. And I don't think the thoughtful people who are red hot about this China thing would object to taking it out of the Greek-Turkish classification.

The CHAIRMAN. Senator Lodge, in your definition do you exclude military advice, such as is now being given?

Senator LODGE. I exclude military advice at the lower levels. I certainly do. If you start trying to put liaison people in all units, the way we did, for instance, when the French army and the U.S. army were serving together during the war, you have a big job on your hands. This is a matter of personal experience. We had people down as low as a battalion. You must then have your own signal communications and quartermaster units—a veritable army. We were then at war; we did have the army.

Senator CONNALLY. We can't do that in China. It would take all our Army to do that.

Senator LODGE. But that is what this testimony of General Rooks here leads to, very clearly. And all I say is, we ought to think this thing out and get it in sharp focus and not have it fuzzy and vague, and not toss around a phrase like "military aid" without knowing what its implications are if the Russians jump into Norway, which so many people think they will do, and we have a war and she swarms over France and we get back into England and North Africa, we are going to be under the temptation of fighting an orthodox war, and we will be licked, whereas if we wait, we may win it.

The CHAIRMAN. I am trying to be sure that I understand what you mean by "clarification." What is it that we are doing in Greece and Turkey which you want to exclude from what we do in China?

Senator LODGE. In Greece and Turkey there is not the possibility of there being done what there is the possibility of there being done in China. I put it the other way around. If they limit themselves entirely to what is done in Greece and Turkey, insofar as the details are concerned I would have no objection. What I object to is applying the principle of Greece and Turkey to China, because the country is so big. It is a very different principle. In Turkey you have a country where the people are full of spirit and they can stand on their own feet and you don't need to tell the Turks how to run maneuvers or how to do all those things. They know how to do all those things. In Greece you have a little bit of a country, a little bit of a sandy peninsula there, and they are two entirely different places.

What I want to avoid in China is anything which is liable to lead us to sending troops.

ALL IN AGREEMENT

The CHAIRMAN. We are all in agreement on that.

Senator GEORGE. We are all in agreement on that. In the first place, they have more troops than we have, or could have more—several million more.

Senator LODGE. Of course they could.

Senator GEORGE. Yes; sure. We don't need to send any troops over there.

Senator LODGE. But if you did what Bullitt says—and he is shocked when you tell it to him——

Senator GEORGE. We would have certain types of military men over there.

Senator CONNALLY. I said, "Do you want to send troops over there?"

Bullitt says, "Oh, no; not a soldier." He is not my mentor; I'll say that.

IMPLICATIONS OF THE BILL

Senator LODGE. I see that. But what he wants to do means we will have to send troops. He doesn't see that because he doesn't know enough about the military, because a man like Mark Clark or MacArthur cannot take over that situation and give competent advice, or what General Rooks calls here "organizing tactics" unless he has people in all the units, and if he is going to have people in all the units he is going to have to fed them, gas them, have radio and telephone communication, and that means signal troops and quartermasters, and who in hell is going to do all that? You run right into troops, which you don't do in Turkey and Greece.

Senator CONNALLY. I do not think this bill implies that. They have to have some top advisers. They already have them over there. They can't go on down to the lower units.

Senator LODGE. I don't object to the fellow who goes in and talks with Chiang every morning. We have had that, and it hasn't done a damned bit of good. But that isn't what Bullitt really wants, and that isn't what this fellow Rooks wants, if you read his testimony.

Senator SMITH. Do you think this bill implies that we are giving what Bullitt wants, the way it is drafted now?

Senator LODGE. I think if we let this bill go here, with the language on page 101, title 3, that is certainly what that means. That is why we are going to take that language out in conference. That is the point I am making. If the conference report comes back with this in it, it is going to be one hell of a tough vote for me.

Senator CONNALLY. Mr. Chairman, that will have to come up in conference. We can't solve that here, as I see it. I want to renew my objection to putting this under ERP. Here is what you say: "such aid to be provided under the applicable provisions of the Economic Cooperation Act of 1948 which are consistent with the purposes of this act."

Well, that doesn't mean a thing to me except maybe to get into an argument with ERP. I don't see any good that that does. I prefer an independent act regarding China.

Senator GEORGE. You would have to set up an independent agency then.

Senator CONNALLY. The President has the authority to do that.

The CHAIRMAN. Don't you think the point is pretty sound that this procurement ought to all be under one authority regarding the procurement in order to ration it properly?

Senator CONNALLY. There is some force of argument there. That is true.

The CHAIRMAN. Then there is the practical situation that I submit to your good judgment, that the more we tear this apart——

Senator GEORGE. The harder it will be to put it back.

The CHAIRMAN. The harder it will be to get it together again.

PROBLEM OF GRANTS AND LOANS

What is the committee's decision with respect to this problem of grants and loans?

Senator GEORGE. I would just say "grants."

Senator CONNALLY. I would, too.

Senator GEORGE. Grants on such terms as the President wishes to impose to make the money available, and then leave it up to the President.

Senator CONNALLY. We don't get any loan back, anyway.

Senator GEORGE. There is no use in making loans. You have to go through all kinds of functions to get the thing ironed out if you make a loan.

Senator CONNALLY. The only reason I suggested a loan was to avoid the responsibility of buying war supplies ourselves and turning them over to China. A grant is just as good, though.

Senator GEORGE. Surely the President won't do that as long as Secretary Marshall is over there, because he is not in favor of that at all.

Senator CONNALLY. He is in favor of giving them arms.

Senator GEORGE. He might be, but he will say, "If they want to buy some, let them have the money to pay for them."

The CHAIRMAN. Then we have the word "grants" back and "loans" is out.

Senator SMITH. What is the difference, then, between (a) and (b)?

The CHAIRMAN. The difference is that (a) is economic aid under the terms of the Economic Cooperation Act, where applicable, and (b) is without limitation.

Senator GEORGE. It is just an additional appropriation to be granted to China.

The CHAIRMAN. There is a very substantial difference.

Senator CONNALLY. Do you want to leave in "or on such other terms"?

Senator GEORGE. No; "through grants on such terms."

Tell him in the report that this is the money that we are just going to give away, on the orders of the Chinese. Whatever they want to do with it, let them do it. They cannot get military supplies, though, gentlemen, except from us.

The CHAIRMAN. That is true.

Senator GEORGE. And that is all right.

The CHAIRMAN. I think they are entitled to get them through us at their option.

Senator GEORGE. They have to have something to shoot in all those guns. They have guns over there enough to run a war, a big war, for a long time, but they haven't got anything to shoot in them.

Senator SMITH. Then, Mr. Chairman, just to clarify my own thinking, your section 3(a), that $363 million, is to be provided under the provisions of the Economic Cooperation Act of 1948, and 3(b) is freed from that, under such terms as the President may determine.

A DEPUTY FOR CHINA

Senator GEORGE. Can't the Administrator appoint a deputy for China, if he wants to?

The CHAIRMAN. Oh, yes.

Senator GEORGE. Has he that authority? If he has not, he should be given special authority. It is absolutely necessary that this procurement all be done through one agency or through one governmental office. They will have to and should use, and under our bill will be required to use, private channels.

Senator CONNALLY. A lot of these purchases may be made in Asia.

Senator GEORGE. They may be, but most of them will be made over here. War has been making purchases for China and Japan already, and are now, and they get things all mixed up every time they make a purchase.

The CHAIRMAN. Well, I guess this is the best we can do under difficult circumstances.

Senator GEORGE. I move we report this one sheet here.

The CHAIRMAN. The Senator from Georgia moves that we report the bill. The clerk will call the roll.

"TO ASSIST IN ECONOMIC REHABILITATION"

Dr. WILCOX. May I ask one question? I understand when I was out of the room line 2 was changed to read "to assist in economic rehabilitation." The language that is there was chosen very carefully by the State Department because of their concern not to make a forthright commitment to get involved in putting China too far back on her feet. The committee may not agree with the State Department, but I think the Department is entitled to have its position known. They were very careful to discard the words "economic rehabilitation" and to put in this term, so as to make perfectly clear that the committee does not take on that burden.

Senator SMITH. I see that. But then you are making a sharp distinction with the ERP program.

Senator THOMAS of Utah. Would they object if you left out "to assist in retarding economic deterioration" and simply said, "to relieve human suffering and to afford the people of China an opportunity to initiate measures of self-help"?

The CHAIRMAN. Let's take all that phrase out.

Senator GEORGE. That is all right. I have no objection to that.

The CHAIRMAN. That shortens up the bill again.

Senator GEORGE. I do not want to get us too far committed here.

Senator SMITH. I see the point of that.

Senator GEORGE. There would be an implication there, and everybody will come back here next year and say we promised to do that.

Senator HATCH. I want to ask one question.

The CHAIRMAN. Yes?

Senator HATCH. That is as to section 3, the appropriation of $363 million. Apparently it is for economic recovery. Is it limited to that? Or couldn't it be used for almost any purpose—the $363 million also?

The CHAIRMAN. No. It is to be used under the applicable provisions of the Economic Cooperation Act of 1948.

Senator HATCH. Section 3 says, "In order to carry out the purposes of this act, there is hereby authorized to be appropriated for aid to China a sum not to exceed $363 million, to remain available for obligation for the period of 1 year following the date of enactment of this act."

Is that tied to what you have just said, or is that an outside appropriation?

The CHAIRMAN. Section 2 says, "It is the purpose of this Act * * *" and so forth, "such aid to be provided under the applicable provisions of the Economic Cooperation Act of 1948."

You might, if there is the remotest danger of what you say, strike out the words "for aid to China" so it reads, "In order to carry out the purposes of this act there is hereby authorized to be appropriated a sum not to exceed $363 million." I think it is clear.

Senator GEORGE. I doubt if we were very wise in striking out this phrase up here in section 2, "to assist in retarding economic deterioration." I am rather inclined to the view that the State Department and the Administrator may want to do some things over there to strengthen that economy a little bit, to stop inflation, and that they would hardly be able to do them if they were confined to relieving human suffering and to efforts to afford the people of China an opportunity to initiate measures of self-help necessary to rebuilding the bases for more stable economic conditions. I expect that phrase ought to go in. But if you want it out, it is all right with me.

The CHAIRMAN. It is all right with me to put it in, too.

Senator GEORGE. I think it has a purpose. I think there would be some things they could do there.

Senator HATCH. I want to revert again to my former question, to point out one thing that prompted it. The purposes of the act are "to provide immediate aid to China to relieve human suffering, to assist in retarding economic deterioration, and to afford the people of China an opportunity to initiate measures of self-help necessary to rebuilding the bases for more stable economic conditions."

Under that last clause, it appears to me anything can be instituted.

The CHAIRMAN. You have stopped short of the full quotation, Senator: "such aid to be provided under the applicable provisions of the Economic Cooperation Act of 1948."

Senator HATCH. Which are consistent. They can construe those purposes to mean military aid. The other would not be consistent with it. That may be very technical.

The CHAIRMAN. I think it is pretty technical.

Senator GEORGE. I do not think, Senator Hatch, they can construe it that way.

Senator WILEY. Why don't you wait until January to get on your bench?

Senator HATCH. I am thinking about what is coming up on the floor when this bill comes up.

The CHAIRMAN. Can we get back to the phrase Senator George is speaking about?

Senator CONNALLY. It is a better argument to people who are going to criticize this program to put it in, because we are not doing anything except to help them retard their deterioration, which everybody knows is going on.

CHECKING THE DOWNWARD DRIFT

Senator GEORGE. Trying to check their downward drift.

Senator CONNALLY. Everybody knows those influences are in operation, and if we can aid them in checking them, so much to the good.

Senator GEORGE. I think almost every time they go to spend any money over there, there is somebody down here in the General Accounting Office who will raise a question about it and say, "Well, you haven't any right." Suppose they let them have enough money to build a few miles of railroad or bridges that have been blown up.

Senator SMITH. Wouldn't the expression "rebuilding the bases for more stable economic conditions" cover it?

A MOUTH-FILLING PHRASE

Senator CONNALLY. That is a mouth-filling phrase that doesn't mean a thing.

Senator GEORGE. It is pretty general.

The CHAIRMAN. My only objection to the language stricken out is that it is such a gloomy prospectus.

Senator SMITH. That is what bothered me when I read it. It is just a negative thought.

Senator LODGE. It is a challenge to them to work harder next year.

The CHAIRMAN. What is your feeling, Senator Lodge, as a result of your comment about this phrase? Do you want it in or out?

Senator LODGE. I would rather have the gloomy phrase and leave it to the Chinese to show that we are wrong.

The CHAIRMAN. Senator Smith?

Senator SMITH. I have no objection.

The CHAIRMAN. All right; it is back in.

Now, Senator George's motion.

Senator LODGE. Mr. Chairman, I would just like, before we vote, to read the last sentence of the House report on the China business:

HOUSE REPORT MISLEADING

The two types of aid are not separated by any watertight partition, but they are sufficiently distinct in character so that they are separated from aid to Europe into the recovery type of aid covered by Title 1, which includes Greece and Turkey, and by the primarily military type of aid, covered by Title 3, specifically for Greece and Turkey. The distinction is essentially the same as the distinction between the Truman Doctrine and the Marshall Plan, or between a fence and a corn field. It is equally as valid for China as for Europe.

I don't think I have read more dangerous and misleading over-simplification than that, and I just ask whether it isn't the sense of this committee that in our report on our China bill we make it clear exactly what we have in mind by "military aid", to-wit, making supplies available to them.

Senator CONNALLY. We don't mention military aid. Why should we drag it into the report?

Senator GEORGE. You could mention it in the report, Senator Lodge. You could say that in distributing this $100 million or the other sums here, if China should request military supplies, then we could put in exactly our position, and say that it is simply confined to the furnishing of such supplies as they themselves may desire to purchase.

Senator LODGE. That is a very far cry from this language here.

Senator GEORGE. That is a terrible statement here. You are right about that.

Senator LODGE. I wanted to bring that point up.

The CHAIRMAN. I think we can say something as Senator George has suggested.

Senator GEORGE. If any part of it is used at the election of China, then our position is specifically stated, that we are not furnishing military aid, we are simply furnishing supplies which they desire to get here, and which may be available to them.

The CHAIRMAN. And such advice as is now being furnished under whatever the other law is.

Senator LODGE. And state what it is.

Senator GEORGE. And restrict our activities.

The CHAIRMAN. That can be done.

Senator SMITH. That will be in the report?

The CHAIRMAN. Personally, I would prefer to leave it all out, because I think we are just deliberately bypassing the question of military aid, and I don't know why we bypassed it in the bill and then came back to it in the report. Yet there is something to be said for your point.

CHINA GIVEN $100 MILLION

Senator CONNALLY. My theory in suggesting the loan immediately was to let China do as she pleased. We are not doing that. We are giving her $100 million.

Senator LODGE. My thought was that if this language in the House report stood unchallenged——

Senator GEORGE. It will be a part of the report on this general legislation from the other branch of Congress.

Senator CONNALLY. We will meet that in the conference.

Senator GEORGE. We cannot disagree with their report.

Senator CONNALLY. But we can disagree with the bill upon which the report is founded. We are disagreeing with the whole bill, and when we go to conference we can fight those things out in conference.

THE HOUSE REPORT

Senator LODGE. I don't know how much significance ought to be attached to a House report.

Senator CONNALLY. What can you do about it? They have a right to say it and they have said it, and there is nothing to be done about it, as I see it, except to say "No, we are not for your bill."

Senator THOMAS of Utah. To carry out Senator Connally's idea about this $100 million, I don't know why we can't leave out section (b) entirely, and just simply say that not to exceed $363 million, and

$100 million to the Government of China to use as it sees fit, be provided. Those are not legal words, but that is what you are driving at.

The CHAIRMAN. I think that is what we have done.

Senator THOMAS of Utah. I think that is what you have done. I can't see anything the matter with the bill itself.

Senator GEORGE. I can see Senator Lodge's trouble about it. He just doesn't like the report, and I don't myself.

Senator THOMAS of Utah. I don't like the House report. I don't like its theory.

Senator LODGE. What do you do when you don't like a House report? Do you just ignore it?

Senator CONNALLY. I am in favor of keeping (b), but I think in "on such other terms as the President may determine to be appropriate" you are putting the President on the spot as to how this $100 million is going to be used. If they use it for arms, somebody is going to say: "Yeah, the President did it." It isn't the President who does it; it is the Government that does it.

I think it would be better to say aid to China through grants, and leave out all that about the President.

Senator SMITH. No conditions, no terms, no nothing.

Senator CONNALLY. No conditions, no terms, no nothing. If you want to help them, and that is what we are trying to do, do that.

EXACT LANGUAGE NOT MATERIAL

Senator WILEY. I have refrained from entering into this discussion, and I want to make my point clear. The exact language is not material to me. Why I favor to a large extent Senator Lodge's position is this: We have a report here which virtually says that the policy of one branch of this government is that we shall go into China. If that policy is to be the policy of this government, to me it means that we will go into an adventure that will simply waste our resources and throw away, to a large extent, a lot of our freedoms. So whatever you say in this bill along the line you have discussed to me is not so significant if we meet head on the challenge of the House. And the country has to know our position, otherwise this report is going to be the voice of the people, the voice from the lower House.

I want to be here on Wednesday. I want to know about the Jewish situation; I want to know about the Chinese situation. We heard on the radio last night that our forces in the Mediterranean are alerted, that they are ready to send our Marines into Italy at a moment's notice, or on 24 hours' notice. We have got to get this whole picture, because if we are going to decimate our strength by trying to handle all the political problems on the globe, we will have very little political freedom left of our own.

So I think the big challenging thing here is to be definite and certain and make it sure in your report, if you don't make it in your bill, that it is the consensus of opinion of this committee, anyway, that we are not for putting our troops, our strength, or our forces into China. I know that we have revoked the provisions as to exporting arms and we are not violating any international law if we sell them directly by this government.

[Discussion was continued off the record.]

OVERALL PICTURE DANGEROUS

Senator WILEY. The overall picture here is a dangerous picture. You are going to let the statement go out that both committees, the Foreign Relations and the Foreign Affairs Committees, believe that China is our baby and we have to protect and send our resources over there. To me that is the dangerous thing, and that is what I want to avoid.

The CHAIRMAN. I think we all agree with that.

Senator WILEY. But we have to be outspoken on it.

The CHAIRMAN. I was about to add one additional thought. Senator Lodge, you are in agreement with the House that China ought to be treated in this aspect the same as Greece and Turkey. The difference is that you don't want to do in Greece and Turkey, by way of active military enlistments, any more than you do in China. Isn't it true that you want both of them treated alike?

Senaor LODGE. I think if you put China in the category of Greece and Turkey you are going to have to send troops, whereas you are not going to have to send them to Greece and Turkey.

The CHAIRMAN. You mean because of the physical problem involved?

Senator LODGE. You cannot generalize about military situations. Each is different from the other.

The CHAIRMAN. Let us do this: We will not have to report this bill for 2 or 3 days. Let us have the staff work upon a section in the report to be submitted to the committee, and see if we can agree upon language to accomplish the objective.

TWO THOUGHTS FOR THE STATEMENT

Senator LODGE. And I would like to make a suggestion to the staff that that statement have two thoughts in it: First, that we favor making military supplies available; and secondly, that we have no objection to continuing the particular kind of advice that they are getting now, and get from the Department of the Army or from the State Department exactly what that is and the law under which it is being done.

Those are two thoughts that ought to go into that report.

The CHAIRMAN. I suggest that you sit in with the staff in working on this thing.

Senator LODGE. I will.

Senator CONNALLY. I don't know about all that argumentation in here.

Senator LODGE. We can write something and submit it to you.

SECTION 3

Senator CONNALLY. Mr. Chairman, section 3 doesn't suit me, and I'll tell you why. We say it is a grant—additional aid to China through grants—and then say on such terms, such other terms as the President may determine. You tie the hands of the grants. It is not a grant at all. It is on such other terms as the President may prescribe.

Senator SMITH. You think it gives us a responsibility that we ought not to take?

Senator CONNALLY. It puts the responsibility on the President. The whole theory of the loan was to give them money and let them do what they wanted to do with it.

Senator SMITH. What is the usual language when you want to make a loan to a foreign government? Do you tie conditions to it?

Senator CONNALLY. If you do, it is not a grant any more.

The CHAIRMAN. I would think that somebody had to control the negotiation of this loan.

Senator CONNALLY. If you do, it is not a grant any more.

The CHAIRMAN. I do not think that follows.

Senator WILEY. You can attach conditions to a gift.

Senator CONNALLY. If they spend this, then, for arms, which they probably will do if they have any sense, they will accuse us of having covered up and of having this in mind.

The CHAIRMAN. Suppose you said: "on such financial terms as the President may determine to be appropriate."

Senator GEORGE. I think that is probably the best you can do with it. You don't need any "or" in there. You can say: "grants on such terms as the President may determine to be appropriate."

Senator CONNALLY. Do you have to leave that in?

Senator GEORGE. Yes. He might not have the $100 million right quick. The President has to protect the Treasury. He has to take a look and see how we stand down there.

Senator WILEY. He has to protect a few Chinamen, too, otherwise it will be dissipated.

Senator CONNALLY. Why not cut out "to be appropriate?"

The CHAIRMAN. I think that is an improvement.

Senator SMITH. You are leaving in "without regard to the provisions of the ERP"?

The CHAIRMAN. By doing that I think you eliminate any suggestion that he is going to pass upon the character of the investment.

Senator GEORGE. Let's do it that way: "through grants on such terms as the President may determine."

The CHAIRMAN. Senator George moves that the bill be reported. The clerk will call the roll.

Senator CONNALLY. Hadn't we better meet again and look over the report, and see what we are going to report?

The CHAIRMAN. Yes; we will do that.

Senator HATCH. You are all convinced that this does not include military aid except as the Chinese themselves purchase it?

Senator GEORGE. We are not providing military aid. We are furnishing money.

Senator HATCH. Senator Barkley wanted to vote "aye" but against the bill if it contains a provision for military aid.

The CHAIRMAN. I think it can be said categorically that it does not. I think you can say that in the report on this bill we have made provisions for certain things, and just cut it off there, so that you have a positive, definite limitation of what we are doing under the China provision.

Senator CONNALLY. You can also justify 3(b) by saying you could not anticipate all the needs China might have, and we furnish this aid all right up here under ERP, but we thought that it would be well to give them $100 million to do with as they pleased in carrying out the program.

Senator SMITH. For things that ERP might not cover. That is the theory.

Senator CONNALLY. Yes. They might buy a lot of stuff out there in their own area.

Senator LODGE. I may be awfully dense, but it seems to me that this $100 million is military aid if they choose to buy cartridge belts with it.

The CHAIRMAN. It is so intended—at their option and on their responsibility.

Senator LODGE. Then it depends on whom you are talking to.

Senator CONNALLY. They will understand it if they get the $100 million.

The CHAIRMAN. All right, Mr. Clerk.

The CLERK. Mr. Capper.

Senator CAPPER. Aye.

The CLERK. Mr. White.

The CHAIRMAN. Aye.

The CLERK. Mr. Wiley.

Senator WILEY. Aye.

The CLERK. Mr. Smith.

Senator SMITH. Aye.

The CLERK. Mr. Hickenlooper.

The CHAIRMAN. Aye.

The CLERK. Mr. Lodge.

Senator LODGE. Aye.

The CLERK. Mr. Connally.

Senator CONNALLY. Aye.

The CLERK. Mr. George.

Senator GEORGE. Aye.

The CLERK. Mr. Wagner.

Senator THOMAS of Utah. Aye.

The CLERK. Mr. Thomas.

Senator THOMAS of Utah. Aye.

The CLERK. Mr. Barkley.

Senator HATCH. Aye.

The CLERK. Mr. Hatch.

Senator HATCH. Aye.

The CLERK. Mr. Chairman.

The CHAIRMAN. Aye.

The CLERK. Thirteen yeas, no nays.

The CHAIRMAN. We will submit this report, or at least this section of the report, to the committee, so we will be sure we know exactly what we are saying.

Senator CONNALLY. If they can get the whole report up it will be better.

The CHAIRMAN. I think that is advisable, and we will meet Wednesday at 10 for a free-for-all with the Secretary of State.

All right, gentlemen. I guess that is the best we can reluctantly do.

We have the nomination of North Winship, of Georgia, to be Minister to South Africa.

Senator GEORGE. He is the oldest man in the diplomatic service. He is General Winship's brother.

The CHAIRMAN. He has been in the service for two pages.

Without objection, the nomination is confirmed.

Senator LODGE. He is a good man.

The CHAIRMAN. Here are some routine nominations, consuls from class 3 to 2. They will take the usual procedure.

[Whereupon, at 11:35 a.m., the hearing was adjourned, to reconvene on Wednesday, March 24, 1948, at 10 a.m.]

UNITED NATIONS INTERNATIONAL CHILDREN'S EMERGENCY FUND

THURSDAY, MARCH 25, 1948

UNITED STATES SENATE,
COMMITTEE ON FOREIGN RELATIONS,
Washington, D.C.

The committee met, pursuant to call, at 10 a.m., in the committee hearing room, U.S. Capitol, Senator Arthur H. Vandenberg, chairman, presiding.

Present: Senators Vandenberg (chairman), Capper, Wiley, Smith, Connally, Thomas of Utah, and Hatch.

WHAT TO DO ABOUT THE CHILDREN'S FUND

The CHAIRMAN. Senator Smith has a problem. He has a special problem, an extra problem. It is all his. There is one title in the bill to which we have not paid any attention, and that is an authorization up to $60 million for the children's fund.

Senator CONNALLY. Oh, yes.

The CHAIRMAN. I turn that over to Senator Smith, to address himself to it.

Senator SMITH. I feel I am in a difficult situation at the moment.

Senator CONNALLY. There is nothing in the bill about it; is there?

The CHAIRMAN. There is in the House bill.

Senator CONNALLY. Are we passing the House bill?

The CHAIRMAN. We are getting ready to meet the House bill in conference.

Senator SMITH. The question is whether we ought to report out a bill here, the bill which I introduced in the Senate, or whether you want to leave it in the House bill and pick it up in conference. The chairman suggested to me that that might put him in an embarrassing situation when we get to conference if we haven't done anything about it.*

[Discussion was continued off the record.]

Senator CONNALLY. If we start making appropriations to the children's fund and they want another appropriation for some other fund and so forth and so on, we will never get anywhere.

Senator SMITH. I am not quarrelling with that, because, as I told the chairman yesterday, I agree with the chairman it is the wrong way to finance it. The United Nations should have an overall budget and include whatever is necessary, and then we take our share and do not quibble over the items.

*For a copy of this bill see p. 772.

THE ORGANIZATION SETUP UNDER INTERIM AID

The practical situation is that we began last year under the interim aid bill. They got a start. Their organization is set up. It is a question of continuing this until the end of the next calendar year with an authorized appropriation of $60 million provided it is matched on certain conditions, and whether we want to bypass that and let them go and leave them out on a limb, or what we can possibly suggest as an alternative. My difficulty is in leaving them in a condition where they can't operate. You will recall, Senator Connally, on the floor when Senator Pepper offered his amendment to stick in $300 million for children's feeding. The chairman asked me to reply to it because I had been studying the thing, and I said distinctly then that I opposed that; as much as I believed in the children's feeding bill, it should not be attached to that bill, and Mr. Pate requested that it be not attached because they had another method, and this is another method.

REPORT FROM THE STATE DEPARTMENT

The Chairman. We have a report from the Department on this thing. Let's see what it says.

Senator Smith. I just read that. I think their suggestion is very good.

The Chairman.

In view of the international character of the Fund the Department is of the opinion that any United States contribution to the Fund should be made only on the basis of matching those of other contributors. Since over $20,000,000 of the $40,000,000 originally authorized as a United States contribution still remains available to match contributions of other governments and since the extent of additional contributions by other governments is somewhat uncertain, the Department is unable to determine whether or to what extent additional funds would be used. However, the Department perceives no objection to the enactment of an authorization for an additional contribution of $60,000,000 on a matching basis.

It is noted that a new formula for matching is proposed. Section 1 of Public Law 84, 80th Congress, as amended by Section 16 of Public Law 389, 80th Congress, provides that the United States may not contribute more than 57 per centum of the aggregate amount contributed to the Fund "by all governments, including the United States". This has been interpreted both by officials of the Fund and by the Department of State to refer only to contributions to the Fund made by governments for the benefit of persons outside the territory of the contributing governments themselves, and not to include goods or services furnished by such governments to their own citizens under arrangements worked out with the Fund. The proposed new formula prohibits any United States contribution in excess of 50 per cent of the Fund's total resources and is intended to prohibit any United States contribution unless other governments have made contributions amounting to 20 per cent of the total resources of the Fund contributed after May 31, 1947, "for use in the world program for the special care and feeding of children under the supervision of the Fund". The quoted phrase is somewhat ambiguous but presumably refers to contributions for the benefit of persons outside the borders of the contributing country. The remaining 30 per cent of the total resources of the Fund presumably would consist of supplies and services furnished by various governments for use within their own borders in programs administered by the Fund.

This formula changes the 57–43 ratio on contributions to a ratio of approximately $70 from the United States for every $30 contributed by other countries for persons outside their own borders. The Department perceives no objection to increasing the ratio of the United States contributions to this extent. It does not, however, seem advisable to include supplies and services furnished by the recipient countries to their own children as part of their contributions for the United States to match. The furnishing of food and services for its own children to the greatest extent possible is a normal function and obligation of any country. It would be very difficult, furthermore, to determine, value and account for the exact contribution which a country makes toward the provision of food and services for its own children.

It is suggested that the language of the Bill be changed by the following amendments: Strike out the material in lines 10 through 13 on page 2 and insert in lieu thereof, "(1) 70 per cent of the total resources contributed after May 31, 1947, by all governments for programs carried out under the supervision of such Fund. Provided: that in computing the amount of resources contributed by any government there shall not be included contributions for the benefit of persons located within the territory of such contributing government; or". Also strike out Section 3 of the Bill."

CHILDREN'S FUND OPERATES IN SATELLITE COUNTRIES

By the way, I was told yesterday that this Children's Fund operates in some of the satellite states. Is that correct?

Senator SMITH. Yes, it does. It operates behind the Curtain. I really ought to ask Pate to come over and explain that to us. It operates today in Poland and it operates——

Dr. WILCOX. I think in all the satellite states.

Senator CONNALLY. Those that are members of the United Nations, or all of them, whether they are members or not?

Dr. WILCOX. I think all of them.

Senator SMITH. I think all of them. The whole theory is, I think, that of giving aid to children who are undernourished. It is a children's proposition without regard to race, creed, color, nationality, or anything else. I raised the question with them whether in the satellite countries it would not be to Russia's interest to see that the children are nourished, whether they would not have a backfire if they did not nourish the children. Assuming that to be true, they feel there will be a problem of milk supplies and they feel we should not necessarily cut off children just because they happen to be in so-called enemy or satellite countries.

The CHAIRMAN. That has a very fine humane impulse behind it. On the other hand, I don't know how you can do anything except build up this rival aggressive competitive enemy that we confront, when we go in and help them at the point of greatest emotional appeal. I suppose it is a hard-boiled, hard-hearted thing to say that we ought not to help the children of Bulgaria, but the moment you help the children of Bulgaria you have certainly relieved the Bulgarian Government of an obligation at a point where it might be most impressive to Bulgarians that their own Government wasn't worth a damn.

VETO THE BILL OR COOPERATE

Senator SMITH. That is the very point I have raised with the group. They said, course they are willing to accept any conditions we lay down. They still make the appeal—and the Quakers are behind it—that we ought not distinguish. I just bring it up so that the committee will see the problem we have, whether we want to put the veto on the whole movement or quit the whole job, or whether we want to try to cooperate with them in working out some program.

85-743—73——32

Senator CONNALLY. My objection to your proposal is that it throws out the United Nations organizations. If we are going to say "Well, we want to do something for this Children's Fund", fine. We are going to give them more than we are required to, more than the plan envisages. Then, after you do that, you find something else.

"Oh, here is a great organization. We ought to do something special." Well, it will be an endless leg-pulling arrangement, that's all there is to it.

COMMUNITY CHEST—AN ANALOGY

The CHAIRMAN. Well, Senator, an exact analogy is a Community Chest. You provide a Community Chest for the purpose of making adequate provision, and then protecting the public against extra-adequate solicitation, and if you ever allowed one agency in a Community Chest to carry on outside solicitation for funds, your Community Chest would die in 20 minutes.

Senator CONNALLY. That is what I am trying to say, that it throws the arrangement out of balance. Here you have all these activities under the UNO. Let them go on. If they are not right, let UNO change them and set up a new system. But to pick one of them out and say, "Well, we are going to give you special consideration now," is wrong, and we will never get it back down once you start. They are going to gig us. We are already paying the bulk of the contributions to UNO.

Senator SMITH. Let me correct you there, Senator. This State Department memorandum says that "the Fund should be able to start winding up operations by the end of 1949," and turn over to the UNO health organization those activities.

The CHAIRMAN. You will forgive me for not being particularly impressed by promises and prospectuses for terminating the Children's Fund, ever, having faced the history of its inception.

THE MORNING WHEN IT ALL STARTED

Do you remember, Senator, the morning when all this started in a meeting of the American delegation in the Pennsylvania Hotel, when it was called to our attention that La Guardia had $550,000 left, and that was going to be the Children's Fund?

Senator CONNALLY. That's right. They were going to give it to them.

The CHAIRMAN. Mrs. Roosevelt was greatly interested, and I immediately raised the question: What in the world was the sense of talking about $550,000 to look out for the children of the world? It was stated the only thing contemplated was to create a staff of special instructors in the field of child hygiene to teach them how to look after this whole children's field. I said that morning that I ventured to prophesy that "in 1 year your $550,000 will have grown to a $100 million demand," and here we are.

Not only that; they have ambitious schemes for carrying on from child nutrition into child education. Why, they have the most ambitious program in the world, haven't they, Senator?

Senator SMITH. We have scotched that. I told them we could not go outside the nutrition end of it. I think that part of it they have given up. You are quite right; that was in the picture. Miss Lenroot has been trying to develop a worldwide child physical education program, feeding, and everything else, which is natural, because she is enthusiastic about the subject. I don't know whether Senator Thomas knows anything about that or not.

PRESIDENT HOOVER'S REPORT

I would like to read this. This is Hoover's report when he came back in the spring of 1946 on this children's situation. He said:

> There are somewhere from 20 to 30 million physically subnormal children on the continent of Europe, and millions more in Asia. After the First World War, we gave restorative food to 10 million undernourished children. I deplore that this special aid for children has had no counterpart after this war and suggest the redemption of these children be organized at once. The job could be done with $300 or $400 million—a charge beyond any organized private charity but not a great sum from the world as a whole.

In December 1946, the first General Assembly of the United Nations established the International Children's Emergency Fund, not as a specialized agency of a permanent continuing character, but as a committee of the Secretariat for the duration of the emergency. Then the Department goes on to say they figure this thing can be wound up by the end of 1949, and whatever health activities may be recommended for children will be dumped into the World Health Organization.

I am simply presenting the case as best I can for them. I am not sure that I should not ask Mr. Pate, who is in my office now, to come in and tell you what it is all about, to see whether we are justified in cutting it off.

CHILDREN IN THE UNITED STATES "SUBNORMAL" ALSO

Senator CONNALLY. There are a lot of children in the United States within your classification there that are subnormal and all that sort of business because they don't get enough to eat.

Senator SMITH. This was a special job we did after the First World War. I was in that with Hoover at that time. Possibly we should not have done it, because it created a lot of little Nazis. There is no doubt about that. I do not feel we can carry our prejudices quite that far.

Senator CONNALLY. I am not against your fund, but I do not think we ought to take it out of its setting in the United Nations.

Senator SMITH. Could we, in your judgment, offer any other alternative to the solution of this, without shutting down on the whole thing right now? What do you think?

The CHAIRMAN. Senator, I think I have completely changed my mind about the best method of handling this thing. We are going to confront this separate title for $60 million in the House bill, and without any doubt we will have to do something about it. I feel about this the same as I do about the proposition that interests Senator Thomas in respect to one of the useful activities in connection with the China fund. I think that in conference, we are going to be forced to ask the House to recede from so many things that I would just as soon have two or three of these particularly appealing things to agree with them on in some degree when we get into conference. We can't expect them to recede on everything and we recede on nothing. And I am perfectly sure that in conference we can do something along the line you have in mind, Senator Thomas, which is in the House bill.

Senator THOMAS of Utah. Yes.

CHILDREN'S FUND TO GO TO CONFERENCE RATHER THAN FLOOR

The CHAIRMAN. I am perfectly sure that we not only can, but must do something about the children's fund. So instead of taking the children's fund to the floor for independent action, I think we had better let the children's fund go into the conference to be settled.

Senator SMITH. Frankly, Mr. Chairman, that was my thought yesterday in discussing the matter with you. If I reported the bill out and had to defend this bill, every question you legitimately raise might be raised on the floor, and we will get a great deal of confusion on the subject, and I think we can handle it better in conference than by trying to get a separate bill passed in the Senate.

Senator CONNALLY. It is in the House bill? Then it is before the conference.

Senator SMITH. It will be perfectly satisfactory to me. I introduced the bill at the request of these people so we would have it before us, and could decide what machinery could be used in order to deal with it in order not to discourage them and cut them off at the base from doing anything.

Senator CONNALLY. These governments that we are talking about, have money to have armies. Why don't they have money to feed their children? It is their responsibility.

Senator SMITH. I will be honest with the committee. I find difficulty in justifying the continuance of this certainly beyond this year, because, taking the satellite countries, it would be the most shortsighted policy for Russia and those countries not to take care of their children. So far as the participating countries go, you have the $5.3 billion, which contemplates relief, and it seems to me that would normally include the problem of nutrition to start there.

Senator CONNALLY. It ought to start there.

Senator SMITH. It may be, while this is pending, that we can give them a year's lease on life for what they ask for. They have the Quakers and others working and all steamed up and helping the children's program. I am sympathetic with finding a formula in conference to carry this on perhaps for another year, with the idea that they can wind it up then and turn the health aspects over to the World Health Organization.

FUNDS DURING THE LAST 10 MONTHS

The CHAIRMAN. Do you know how much the Children's Fund has had to disburse during the last 10 months or a year?

Senator SMITH. They had from us $15 million.

The CHAIRMAN. The total.

Senator SMITH. They have had about $40 million.

The CHAIRMAN. In the last 10 months Poland got $5 million from this Fund, and Yugoslavia $4.3 million. Bulgaria got $1,083,000; Albania, $256,000. But take this Yugoslavia figure, which sticks out like a sore thumb. They have money enough to maintain armies to harass us with major hazards, and if they have money enough to do that they have money enough to look out for their children.

Senator CONNALLY. They have an army reputedly of 600,000 men in Yugoslavia, a little bit of a country.

The CHAIRMAN. I just do not think that that is right. That is 1,300,000 children in Poland and Yugoslavia out of a total of 3,250,000 children all told to be looked after.

Senator SMITH. There is no doubt about the Polish work. Pate himself was there. He has been in Poland for a number of years.

The CHAIRMAN. If it is agreeable with you, Senator Smith, suppose we leave it for conference.

Senator SMITH. It is all right with me. I feel that is the wisest procedure. I want to make it clear that I am trying to present the case of these people and not leave it in the air.

DEALING WITH THE HOUSE BILL

Senator CONNALLY. What you do is, when the House bill comes over, you disagree to it and appoint conferees and so on, so there will be nothing before the conference except—do you want to substitute our bill for their bill?

The CHAIRMAN. I am going to substitute for their particular titles that we have passed on separately. That is, they have a title on Greece-Turkey. We will substitute our title. They have a title on China. We will substitute our China title. Then the amended bill we will send to conference, and the whole thing, then, is in conference, including anything in their bill which is not in our bill.

Senator CONNALLY. Are you talking of taking and splitting it up and substituting for each one, or substituting the whole bill?

The CHAIRMAN. I don't know; whatever Charlie Watkins figures out down there.

Senator CONNALLY. It seems to me it would be better to substitute the whole bill. Then we can switch around. If you split it up, you are more or less confined.

The CHAIRMAN. We will get all of our bill and all of their bill in conference, and I think, Senator Thomas, that that is the best way to handle your suggestion.

Senator THOMAS of Utah. I think it is, and it will handle itself very well that way, because it is merely a percentage of the appropriation going for this. It isn't any added sum, or anything of that kind, and the House words are all right.

Senator SMITH. It says:

> Not less than 5 percent nor more than 10 percent of the funds made available for the purposes of this title are to be used for the purposes of carrying out section 404.

Senator THOMAS of Utah. The reason I am so much in favor of it is that here is one bit of work that isn't experimental, Senator Connally. It has been going on now since the last war. We know about what they will do, and the only way to bring any kind of recovery anywhere is to find something that is stable and functioning, and build on that. Here we have one institution that is working in China and which has the support of the people everywhere, and it, too, is the type of thing which was used in the beginning of Chiang Kai-shek's administration before his adherents got old and therefore conservative, for the greatest mass educational plan that has ever been tried anywhere.

Of course, China lends itself to that because the Chinese language is a picture language and you can have as many people in your class as can see. You don't have to teach them individually, as we do, with the alphabet. And if we are careful in conference about it and consider it, I am happy.

KEEPING UNITY

I think, Mr. Chairman, the one thing we have to think about all the time is keeping this unity business going, or we are going to go smash on a number of lines, and I don't want anything to come out of the committee, so long as we are sending things out, except with 13 for and none against. That is an extremely pretty picture. But at the same time, if we are going to meet this complex situation in the House, let's take that which is the best thing the House has to offer rather than something which isn't so good. That is my feeling on these things. I don't know about the Children's Fund, but I think that the argument would hold for that. If you have an institution that is functioning, we should go along with it.

Senator SMITH. That was my reason for bringing it up. It is badly set up, but there is something functioning there. A lot of people are enthusiastically working on it, developing a worthwhile project, and I hate to see it cut off. I think that handling it in conference is the right way to do it. I won't urge the reporting of the bill. I think this is the right procedure.

Senator WILEY. May I ask, Mr. Chairman, what we are discussing now?

QUESTION OF LEGISLATING INDEPENDENTLY OR GOING TO CONFERENCE

The CHAIRMAN. The House has an appropriation for the Children's Fund. The question was whether we should attempt to legislate independently on that ahead of the conference, and we have decided to let that go to conference without attempting to legislate upstairs. And Senator Thomas was interested in a provision in the House bill which earmarks a small percentage of the Chinese Relief Fund for a special educational purpose, and we have decided not to attempt to legislate independently on that in the Senate, but to let that go to conference. They are both very worthy enterprises.

Among other things, my point of view was that since we were going to be forced to make the House recede on an awful lot of things they had done, it would be better to leave a couple of things in the House bill that we could at least partially accede to.

Senator WILEY. You want to horse trade, I see.

The CHAIRMAN. That is what a conference is.

[Discussion then continued on other matters until 11:15 a.m., whereupon the committee recessed. This discussion is not printed.]

NOMINATION OF PAUL G. HOFFMAN, AS DIRECTOR OF THE ECONOMIC COOPERATION ADMINISTRATION

WEDNESDAY, APRIL 7, 1948

United States Senate,
Committee on Foreign Relations,
Washington, D.C.

The committee met, pursuant to call, at 10 a.m. in the committee hearing room, U.S. Capitol, Senator Arthur H. Vandenberg, chairman, presiding.

Present: Senators Vandenberg, Capper, White, Wiley, Smith, Hickenlooper, Lodge, Thomas of Utah, and Barkley.

Also present: The Honorable Robert M. Lovett, Under Secretary of State.

The Chairman. The committee will come to order.

The committee has before it the nomination of Mr. Paul G. Hoffman, president of the Studebaker Corp. of South Bend, Ind., to be Administrator for Economic Cooperation. I asked Mr. Hoffman to drop down this morning and say "hello" to the committee and answer any questions that any member of the committee might want to ask.

CHOICE OF MR. HOFFMAN COMMENDED

The clerk has just handed me this editorial from the Washington Times Herald, and I rather think I would like to read some of it into the record as perhaps a thesis for our brief hearing this morning, because it seems to me that it emphasizes some pretty important points from our point of view, and I think it is particularly significant that it should come from one of the really bitter critics of the entire ERP (European recovery program) enterprise.

This is what this critic has to say:

> It seems to us that Mr. Hoffman is about as good a choice as the President could have made under the circumstances.

That is high praise from this particular newspaper. But this is the interesting point:

> The Hoffman career began with the Studebaker automobile concern in 1911, when the present president of that company started work as an auto salesman in Los Angeles. Mr. Hoffman was the founder and chief spark plug of the well-known Committee for Economic Development.
>
> It was his public comments on the Marshall plan which gave him the inside track for the ERP directorship. Hoffman took a cautious and businesslike view of the whole affair, in strong contrast to emotionalists who wanted the United States to give its shirt away.
>
> For one thing, Hoffman has insisted from the start that the economic revival of Germany is a must if the rest of Western Europe is to be put back on its

feet. That seems only common sense, since prewar Germany was the biggest workshop and raw material processor in Europe.

For another thing, Hoffman has said frequently that American resources are not limitless, that we've got to put our own economic stability first, and that we must not shovel out more of our real wealth than we can afford.

I read the next paragraph in a quieter mood:

He has also opposed the State Department's ambitions to run the ERP show from General Marshall's office. Hoffman's position has been that the ERP director should have full power to handle the job on his own, and that he should merely cooperate closely with the State Department.

He has taken a hard-boiled attitude on the matter of repayments by our ERP beneficiaries where possible; as when he remarked on one occasion that "true loans must some day be repaid, principal and interest, in goods and services," and on another that "loans should be truly loans, currency transactions should be currency transactions, and gifts should be gifts."

All this adds up to a picture of a man who can run the ERP as economically and efficiently as can be hoped—if he will stick to his present ideas and not let himself be kidded or sidetracked by politicians, bureaucrats, log rollers or world savers.

I think that is a rather nice summary of the situation.

IMPORTANCE AND ACCEPTABILITY OF APPOINTMENT

I want to simply say this to the committee on my own account regarding this appointment, because it is a very great responsibility we have this morning in this connection. I think this is the most important single appointment in the last 10 years that has been made in the Government.

During the last 3 or 4 months, ever since this legislation has been pending, I have necessarily had almost daily contacts with representatives of one group after another reflecting, I should say, the cross-sectional viewpoint of the United States. In every instance these anxious citizens always wound up their interview by inquiring who was going to be the Administrator, and they all emphasized the importance of this assignment, as we all have in our own minds also. I always declined to make any suggestions myself, but sought to draw out from these various groups any names that they could propose for our consideration. And the thing that struck me very forcefully was the fact that half of the time they were themselves proposing Mr. Hoffman, and the other half of the time, when they were proposing someone else and then I would subsequently inquire about this man or that, when I reached Mr. Hoffman's name I never found a single complaint against him.

I think he comes, for my money, as close to representing what will be an acceptable choice to the country as could have been made, and personally I am very happy to put on the record my own feeling that he is fully qualified for the assignment, and that he has been highly and patriotically unselfish in telling the President that he is willing to serve.

In spite of whatever prejudice that statement may create in the committee against him, I throw Mr. Hoffman to the wolves, and you are welcome to tear him apart.

Senator THOMAS of Utah. Mr. Chairman, after you make the Washington Times Herald the platform on which you stand, don't you think we had better suspend until we get an editorial from the Chicago Tribune? Then we will know where we are at.

The CHAIRMAN. I think it is very significant.

If any members of the committee want to ask Mr. Hoffman any questions, I am sure he will be glad to answer them.

Mr. Hoffman, I think it would be well if you just briefly sketched for the record your own experience, so that it will be in the record.

STATEMENT OF PAUL G. HOFFMAN

Mr. HOFFMAN. Thank you.

The CHAIRMAN. I would like to have you particularly indicate the various advisory positions you have occupied in connection with the Government.

Mr. HOFFMAN. Well, sir, first may I say that I am distressed but honored that I am being considered.

Senator WILEY. Did you say "distressed"?

Mr. HOFFMAN. I would have been very happy if you were considering someone else very seriously. But nevertheless it is a challenge, and certainly anyone who is as eager as I am to contribute what he can to peace in the world could not turn down an opportunity of this kind.

That does not mean that I will make good on the opportunity. I mean, I just could not turn down any hope to live up in part to what Senator Vandenberg has had to say.

WITNESS' EXPERIENCE

So far as my business record is concerned, it is very simple. I started in the automobile business in 1909 in Chicago in a shop of one of the companies there, and then went to Los Angeles in 1911 as salesman for Studebaker, and I have been with Studebaker ever since except during the world war period of World War I, when I was in the Army.

The CHAIRMAN. Will you describe what your Army service was?

Mr. HOFFMAN. I was a first lieutenant in the Field Artillery but was, at the end of about a year's service, detailed and put in charge of transportation at Camp Jackson, S.C., which was more or less of a business job, running transportation down there.

I have, so far as any public office is concerned, never held any. I worked for the Army during their first consideration of some of their business problems, and I was chairman of, I think, the first Army Committee on Contract Termination at the time Mr. Patterson was Under Secretary. I was more or less directly under him at that time, and spent quite a little time there. I have done odd jobs now and then when I have been asked to by the Government, just having gotten back from Japan and Korea yesterday morning. At the request of the Army we spent some 3 weeks on that trip, trying to find out what might be done to promote recovery in Japan and Korea, and that report was made yesterday to Secretary Royall. The members of the mission hope it will prove somewhat helpful.

Senator WILEY. That was a Government mission you were on?

Mr. HOFFMAN. Yes, sir.

That, Mr. Senator, is as far as the record goes on any official connection.

The CHAIRMAN. You were a member of the Harriman Commission?

Mr. HOFFMAN. I was a member of the Harriman committee. I think the most important committee of which I have been a member was the Harriman committee. That did give me, I think, a considerable background so far as European recovery is concerned. I think when I first took membership on that committee I was quite skeptical as to whether we could contribute to European recovery in such a manner that it would not perhaps put our own economy in some danger. After serving on the committee for some length of time, I concluded that it was very essential that we do what we could to help the European countries to help themselves, and I concluded that if the program were sensibly carried forward, it should not imperil our economy.

CARE NEEDED IN CARRYING FORWARD PROGRAM

But I want to make it clear I never have subscribed to the idea that we can contribute even a million, let alone several billion, dollars to the European recovery program without involving our country in sacrifice, and the people of our country. It is going to put a strain on us. And I think we have got to be very careful as to how the program is carried forward, because it isn't so much the overall strain as it is the strain in particular places. That is, if we should ship out of the country certain types of material and do it unwisely, it might put our whole situation here in some jeopardy. So I think there has to be a most careful consideration of what goes out of the country in the way of goods, particularly to make sure that we are not putting our own situation in some peril.

ENABLING LEGISLATION

I should have come before you letter perfect on this enabling act. I have read it, and I am not flattering when I say that I think it is a very clear piece of legislation. By next Sunday night I will be able to take an examination on it sentence by sentence, because that, of course, it is my job, to find out exactly how you want this undertaking carried forward. I have read it twice, but I wouldn't want to be examined this morning, because I didn't have any copy of it until I got back here, and I have had to read it in between minutes since yesterday morning at 8 o'clock.

I have read, of course, earlier drafts, and I might say that I am delighted that numerous changes were made, because some of the earlier drafts I think left much to be desired. But this latest draft of the enabling legislation it seems to me charts a very clear course for the Administrator, and if he stays on that course I think this job can be taken care of and I think that granted, shall I say, luck—I don't know—I believe we can help the Europeans help themselves.

APPROACH TO BUILDING UP PRODUCTION IN EUROPE

I found myself very unhappy with the ideas that were rather freely expressed at one time that we were under some moral obligation to feed the European people and take care of them. We can't undertake the moral obligation of feeding all the people in the world. I don't think that is a feasible approach to it. And on the other hand, it seemed to me one had to approach it in a very tough manner and find out what the chances were to build up production in Europe. That was the approach we made in the Harriman committee: What is the real chance to get production built up?

I asked the Department of Commerce to give me an estimate as to what the national income of Europe was in 1947—a very rough figure. No one knows. But they came up with a figure of about $100 billion for the 275 million people, against our $200 billion for 145 million people. Those 275 million people, taken as a whole, are good people. They are people that have been productive in the past. They never have had the same situation so far as mechanization and horsepower that we have had. I don't know the exact figures, but today we have 4 horsepower behind every worker, and that is what makes the worker highly productive. That situation has not prevailed in Europe. Still the European people have been a productive people.

It all went down to this, that when I got through making the best guesses that I could make on the European situation, it looked to me reasonable to believe that in a 4-year period, if a program were properly administered, we could build up that production in Europe by about one-third; that that was a sound goal, and it would still leave $135 billion for 275 million people against our $200 billion for 145 million.

It is not a goal up in the clouds. It is, you might say, altogether perhaps too low an objective to strive for. But it is an attainable objective, and I think the difference between the Europe that is immunized from communism by a fairly decent standard of living and a Europe that is ripe for communism by too much poverty is the $35 billion. In other words, that one-third, it seems to me, is an extremely important one-third. You put a third on top of what they now have for Europe and I think you have a great immunity.

I conceive of this job primarily as a job in which the Administrator and his staff should keep their eyes right on one goal, and that is increasing production. At the same time I want to be sure that the economies are sound from a fiscal monetary standpoint.

I do not see it as a job where the Administrator shall be called upon for political considerations or military decisions, or even consultation. I think if they keep their eyes on the ball of production and bring a reasonably stable economy to Europe, other divisions of the Government can handle the other portion of it.

That is a brief statement, Senator Vandenberg, of the approach.

As I say, to sum it all up, I came out of the weeks of, I think, concentrated study of the Harriman committee with the conclusion that the odds favor success in this undertaking, but I would be the last one to say that you can guarantee anything. I do not care how conscientiously the job is carried forward and how competently, it still is a gamble, but I think I wrote you, Senator, a little note, and I told you that one of the things that impressed me deeply was a statement made by Will Rogers, the fact that America has never lost a war and never won a peace. It is high time we won a peace, and I think the European recovery program, which is, I think, the phrase, although China is included and that is a little bit awkward—I do not know just how to phrase that—but this recovery program does give an opportunity to strike a real blow for peace, and that is the spirit in which, if I were confirmed, I would approach the task. I certainly need all the help that I can get from anywhere, because I would expect, if the job is competently administered, that the Administrator would have no friends in Europe when he got through, because I think that you have to anticipate that, because what he thinks is good for Europe may not be what Europe thinks it wants.

BRITISH WAR LOAN QUESTIONED

Perhaps I should not bring this in, but I was disturbed by the British war loan when it was made. I took part in it with a great deal of misgivings, because it seemed to me we failed to attach the conditions to it that should have been attached in order to make it operate to the best advantage of the British people. I was told that that was not a possibility, that that went against the amenities of the situation.

APPROACH TO OBJECT OF PROMOTING RECOVERY

I know nothing about amenities. I have been in business all my life. But nevertheless I would certainly want to see this job approached in every country from the standpoint of not what they want, because what they want politically may be something that would not contribute toward their recovery, and the acid test is, it does or it doesn't. If it does, they ought to get the help, and if it doesn't, they ought to be turned down.

You are going to have to turn down a good many people in governments on things by which they set great store. The question is, Will it promote recovery? If it won't promote recovery and build up production, these dollars and these goods should not go for that purpose. If it is to be a political objective, that is somebody else's decision. If it is a humanitarian objective, that is somebody else's decision. This idea is a recovery program. But that is aside from the point.

I came back from Japan convinced that if we want to stop spending and spending and spending for relief we had better do some investing for recovery, and I feel the same way about Europe. We are a humane people and we do spend billions for relief. We spent it for UNRRA—United Nations Relief and Rehabilitation Agency. That kind of appeal always seems to get a good response. Well, for my money the place to spend money is to try and help these people help themselves so they can get on a self-supporting basis. As I say, that would be the yardstick that would be applied so far as I am personally concerned to any expenditure.

POSSIBLE VALUE FOR DOLLARS SPENT

But don't let anybody think that anybody can supervise the spending of $6 billion and not have considerable waste. I think this ought to be said, that if we go into a war and you can get 80 cents on the dollar for your money you are a miracle man. Whether we got 80 cents on the dollar in the last war I don't know. My guess is we didn't. I can see too many evidences of waste around the world. That isn't said critically, because you have to win the war and that means you have to go ahead and spend and hope you are spending sensibly.

I think this is a program where we are spending to win a peace, and I think there has to be a certain recognition that even with the best setup we can conceive—and that is going to take time to bring that into being; you can't do it overnight—I want to tell you that if this Recovery Administration, this European Recovery Administration, is held to an account and is held to the expenditure of every dollar wisely, it cannot make good.

I think we can do this: I think we can get 90 cents on the dollar fighting for peace as against maybe 70 cents fighting a war. I believe that maybe—and it is a maybe—this program, which might total us—well, the Harriman committee, you know, as a committee, felt certain of only one thing when they got through, and that was there should be no overall dollar figure, that the group didn't live or the man didn't live that could project a program through 4 years; that if you saw 1 year ahead you were having almost infinite wisdom, let alone 4 years. The program might cost $12 billion, it might cost $16 billion, it might cost $17 billion. None knows. The only thing you want to do is to start out and try to get 100 cents on the dollar in the way of value in the form of recovery in these countries, because we have a great stake in that, and you ought to hope that you will be wise enough and smart enough so that you can get 90 cents on the dollar.

That is about what I think is possible, but not 100 cents.

I hope, if I should be confirmed and there is some silly expenditure of $88 that comes to light, that the whole program might not be criticized, because things will slip through. We will make mistakes. There will be million dollar mistakes and $10 million mistakes. But the effort will be on the overall to get 90 cents in value out of $1 fighting for peace as against 65 cents, maybe, or 70 cents that you have to accept when you are fighting a war.

The CHAIRMAN. I think if you got 90 cents you would break all records.

Senator LODGE. In peace or war.

COUNCIL FOR ECONOMIC DEVELOPMENT'S PROGRAM

Senator SMITH. I would like to ask Mr. Hoffman this question: In your qualifications you did not say a word about the so-called CED—Council for Economic Development. The reason I raise that is because that gives us a picture of your study of conditions in this country and your qualifications to know the relations of our economy to this whole picture.

Mr. HOFFMAN. I am very glad to. I thought Senator Vandenberg wanted to know what I had done in the way of official activities.

CED, of course, was organized, as some of you may know, late in 1942 out of a concern that is somewhat forgotten now, but a good many people in the administration and out were very much concerned about the question of employment after the war. In fact, I remember quite vividly I was on the platform with one of our very well-known labor leaders in Philadelphia in 1943 when he gave a new high in the way of what unemployment would be after the war. He said "up to 35 million." Up to that time 19 million had been the highest figure given as to what unemployment would be.

But everybody was concerned about the unemployment situation, and as that job unfolded it seemed to have two phases. First of all was the very practical problems of getting employers out of their attitude of looking toward the postwar period with distress. In other words, I think the current thinking at that time was that come victory, we were going to see a depression that was going to make the depression of the thirties look like a picnic, and therefore the proper attitude was one of trying to build up some reserves. And we had to substitute for that a program that called for very bold planning on the part of individual businesses, and that would never give the economy a chance to drop down even for a minute. We said, "If we have our plans for conversion ready, and if they are bold plans, we can make this shift and we won't need to have any lag in employment." That was a much greater undertaking, on the surface, than it actually was, because when we began to check we found there were only 200,000 concerns in America that employed eight people or more at that time, so the problem was getting 200,000 employers insterested in trying to develop plans for their own businesses.

That was one phase of the program. We had 70,000 men on our committee at one time, so we had practically everybody that was an employer on the committee. And as they began to go out and talk to other people about making plans they began to make them for themselves. I remember Walter Fuller, after he had made one speech, said, "I find I ought to go home and make a plan for the Curtis Publishing Co." and I think all of us had that same reaction.

I don't mean to say for a moment that CED was solely responsible, but I do think that the bold business planning that took place during the war was responsible for one thing, and that was no lag, because you know that experts in and out of Government were very freely predicting 8 million unemployed by Christmas of 1945, and there never was any unemployment.

CED STUDIES AND PROGRAM

I saw President Truman in August, and we had spent some $70,000 making the check of industry in two ways, one on an industry basis and the other on a community basis. In other words, we had cross-checked as to what was going to happen to employment in the fall of 1945, and on the basis of a cross-check it came out within 1 percent. In other words, one study showed 25 percent above prewar and the other 26 percent and, as you know, there was no unemployment. That was one phase of it. It just didn't happen.

Another phase was, we went out to the business and tried to get him to plan boldly. They said, "What's the use of planning boldly, because if you succeed, whatever you make in the way of profits is taken away from us, and how can we possibly succeed under present conditions," which I think is a rather general plea and attitude of most of us, whatever line of activity we find ourselves in.

We then undertook to make studies of various phases of Government activity that had some impact on business, and tried to come up with recommendations that might give a favorable environment to business expansion, and we had the advantage of having freedom of action and money, and we had employed, I think, the top-flight economist in America to initially make the study, and then we have done something that up to now we do not think has been done on a large scale.

After the economist finished with his study we asked him to sit down, if he will, with a group of businessmen and specialists in that field, the tax field, labor field, or whatever it is. The economist or social scientist, after he has prepared his first draft around a table like this, where about 15 or 20 men take it up paragraph by paragraph—I think Dr. Harold Groves, in his first tax study for the committee, came with what would have been a completed draft of his book on the impact of taxes on unemployment, and after he was cracked at by the businessmen and by the other tax economists he wrote his book over. He wrote his book three times, and it was finally published after it had been through three drastic revisions.

I think it is fair to say that most economists, writing by themselves and depending on theory, are apt to come out with a very sound study when it comes to the broad principles involved, but oftentimes do not take into account some of the practical aspects of the problem. On the other hand businessmen, when they make a study, are very apt to have a very narrow viewpoint on what is needed, and forget the broad questions because they do not know the broad principles, and they will come out with a program that looks good for next week but isn't so good for the next 10 years. So we tried to bring together the theoretical knowledge of the economist and the practical knowledge of the experts and businessmen, and I think on the whole the studies that have come out have reflected this new technique and new approach and have stood the test pretty well. Looking back on the studies we did over 4 years ago, they are still pretty good.

WITNESS'S EDUCATION FROM CED

Senator SMITH. My thought, Mr. Hoffman, in asking the question, was that it indicates to me that you have access to these hard-boiled business brains in this whole picture of European recovery, and also have in mind the needs of our economy at home in relating the two together; that this experience has been of great value in giving you first the knowledge of the real people and how to relate them to the so-called theorists when they have to be called in as experts from that angle.

Mr. HOFFMAN. I hope that all the money that has been spent by my friends in financing CED has not been lost on me so far as education is concerned. I have been subjected to a lot of knowledge in the field of economics and in the problems of our domestic economy. I can't tell you, Senator, how much of that took.

Senator BARKLEY. You made yourself vulnerable.

WITNESS' KNOWLEDGE OF COUNTRIES' CONDITIONS

Senator LODGE. Have you been abroad much, Mr. Hoffman?

Mr. HOFFMAN. I would not for one moment claim any knowledge, any more than very superficial knowledge, of the European scene. The closest I have been to China is Korea. So if the necessary qualification is expert knowledge of conditions in the 16 countries, Germany, and China, I don't have it.

Senator LODGE. Not so far as I am concerned. I just wondered.

Mr. HOFFMAN. I have been abroad many times. But you know, when you go abroad on business—I never have made the kind of study you would have to make of an economy, and I, for example, would consider at the moment that I have a workable knowledge of the situation in Japan and a workable knowledge of the situation in Korea. We spent 2 or 3 hard weeks, night and day, studying that. That doesn't make one an expert, but it gives you somewhat of a working knowledge. But I have enough of a working knowledge so I wouldn't trust myself. If I were going to reach decisions on Japan and Korea, I would want much more knowledge than I have now.

I think this job is going to call for extensive use of technicians. I hold that men like Ed Mason, Calvin Hoover, and Richard Bissell have a great contribution to make to the knowledge you need of a given economy before you can determine what is necessary to promote recovery of that economy, along with the practical knowledge that you get from business group.

The CHAIRMAN. I think you are entitled to ask any citizen of the United States to do anything you want to ask him to do. I think you have a right to demand it.

Mr. HOFFMAN. My first demand, sir, was of a friend of mine who makes about $100,000 a year, to come down here for $15,000. I got his promise. That is all I have accomplished so far.

Senator LODGE. That is a good beginning.

The CHAIRMAN. Are there any other questions that any members of the committee want to ask Mr. Hoffman?

QUESTION OF TRADE BETWEEN EAST AND WEST EUROPE

Senator SMITH. Can I ask just one more, Mr. Chairman?

The question of the trade between the East and West of Europe came up frequently on the floor of the Senate, and a great hullabaloo was had over that thing. I noticed in the paper, in an interview you had yesterday, that you were entirely sold on the idea of continuing the East and West trade, and that is one of the approaches.

Mr. HOFFMAN. That question was asked, and my answer was, "I have no knowledge of that." I said I would just assume that if the trade were restricted to nonmilitary items—it was a question of food flowing from one place, and other items that were nonmilitary in character flowing back—that that would come almost willy-nilly. You could not stop it. Trade flows. But I passed no opinion on that, because you have to make a study of that to decide what should go and what should not go. I would say that my present view, at least, is that certain types of trade would be perfectly feasible.

Senator LODGE. For the record you do want to say, do you not, that you would be opposed to sending munitions and articles of military character on to a country not in harmony with us politically?

Mr. HOFFMAN. A most careful screening of any items of trade between the United States, and Western European country, and any other country that was not in harmony with our beliefs, is necessary.

COMMENDATION OF STATE DEPARTMENT

The CHAIRMAN. Senator Wiley wants to say something. I just want to interject this comment before I forget it.

Under Secretary Lovett is here. There has been a lot of pretty mean things said about the State Department in the course of diverse and sundry debates, and I have participated in some of it myself. But I know of no more unselfish service that has been rendered in connection with the development of this whole plan than has been rendered by Mr. Lovett and his associates in the State Department, with a complete willingness and an earnest desire on their own parts to be severed from these responsibilities so that this enterprise can proceed on a basis of economic autonomy and independence. And I think the State Department in general, and Mr. Lovett in particular, are entitled to have that statement said unequivocally, and they have some orchids coming in connection with it.

Senator Wiley?

COMMENDATION OF WITNESS

Senator WILEY. Mr. Chairman, I want to compliment our distinguished friend here, and I want to ask him a few questions also.

First, I like the twinkle in your eye. You are going to have a hell of a job, and without a little sense of humor you won't be able to meet it.

Senator BARKLEY. Pay particular attention to the gleam, also.

Senator WILEY. I assume you not only have the gleam but you have a song in your heart, and you will be able to outsing the Europeans who are liable to take most of us for a ride every time they have the opportunity.

I am glad to hear your statement that you will keep your eyes open and that you realize that the job there is not defined by the way they define it.

My contact with Europe is very superficial. I have had some experience. And I need not express to you the feeling that there are many Europeans who felt that much of our own activity was not creating in them the spirit of self-help, that it was creating in them the spirit of dependence, reliance on others, and not begetting in them the initiative, the rebirth of spirit which is so necessary in order for Europe to come back. I realize that.

I am glad to see that as a business man with your background you realize, too, apparently, from your statement, that the matter of procurement is a tremendous thing. We have very selfish interests in this country, too. They are preparing to take us for a ride. You have lawyers in Washington by groups representing folks, writing letters out to business interests, telling them "We can do the job for you." In other words, brother, if you get 90 cents you are a miracle man. But when you are awake to that situation in our own land, and see to it that we get a dollar's worth of value and then you get it on a boat and you get it over there and you get those European gangsters over there again, you have one hell of a job. But I think you are worthy of it, and I think you are going to be adequate to it. I say so.

GERMAN SITUATION

I want to ask you about Germany. I came back from Germany. So far as I know, I have no German blood in my veins. I made some statements months ago that I felt that Germany was the hub of the recovery of Europe. But I also recognize that in the last few days the Krupp group has been found not guilty of certain charges by our courts, and there is again a great fear being rebuilt in this country that we are laying the foundation for another building up of a German war potential and industry. I felt that we had to have a rejuvenated industrial life in Germany.

I would like to get your reaction to that. How is that going to be handled? The military is still in there. The Department was to be in there, but they have turned it back to the military, apparently permanently. You have some job there to see to it that those folks who are so scared of Stalin, who may try to reinvigorate a German opportunity or a rebuilding of essentials as a German war potential. That is right down your alley, because you are trying to get these 55 or 60 million Germans reinvigorated industrially to produce those things that are nonwar potentials.

I would like to get your idea about that German situation.

Mr. HOFFMAN. Senator, I wish I could be precise about the German situation. I can't be, because after all, I got back from Japan yesterday at 8 o'clock, and I wouldn't want to try to lay out any program for Germany. I think I can say this with some assurance, that I think a substantial increase in German industrial production can be permitted without that in any way being allowed to become a menace from the standpoint of war-making capacity. That, however, is the type of project that you have to study and decide just what could be permitted.

But I think one thing we ought to do is to keep control for a very long period of time of certain of the fundamental aspects of the German industrial situation. If you control power and one or two other elements of an economy you do not need to be too much concerned about their going into war making quickly. One thing people forget, and that is this: The Germans could have been stopped at any time if there had been a determination to stop them before World War II. We are, I think, without doing any bragging, the most skilled industrialists in the world, but we were not turning out war production here in any volume until some 16 or 18 months after we got started, and you could not put Germany back into war production short of 16 to 18 months in the kind of weapons that we now know about. What kind of weapons the next war will be fought with I don't know. I think, generally speaking, we protect ourselves against the last war, not against the next war. But you do still have a period of preparation, and if we keep enough control—and this is outside of the province, in my opinion, of the recovery administrator, to keep enough military control over certain elements of the economy—even from the standpoint of observation you could move in quickly and destroy any approaching activity along war-making lines.

That is a very inadequate answer, and I hope maybe a few months later to give a better answer.

Senator WILEY. Just one other question from me.

Mr. HOFFMAN. In Japan, for example, I did make some study over there. They can't go to war for a long, long time. I make that statement categorically. The Japanese can't go to war again for a long, long time. Sure, 50 years from now. But there has been an excellent job of demilitarizing a country from the standpoint of industry and from the standpoint of the whole situation.

Senator WILEY. Of course, I would not want to disagree openly with you, but we are living in an age of miracles, and the next conflict—pray God it never comes—is not going to be something that will have to be prepared for as we prepared for others wars. Of course, at any time someone may find a shortcut to something diabolical that could be utilized without an expenditure of great armies and great physical effort. But that is something for us to keep alert to.

SECURITY FOR LOANS

Just one other question, Mr. Chairman.

I am very much interested along the line you have discussed here in seeing to it, not that we should not do charity where charity is needed, and not that we should not feed the hungry; not that we should not respond as people who have been blessed by the Lord with many things. But I am interested in seeing that those who can and should will receive loans which will be secured by reasonable means, such as a businessman knows how to secure loans, and that a larger percentage than the minimum of 20 percent be so secured, and that we would probably nearer reach the 40 percent.

Let me tell you that in the highest echelon in the British Government I have heard folks say, "For God's sake don't give us any more money. We don't want it." That is what was said time and time again. When I spoke to the Labor Government about that they said, "Well, that is all politics." But other men of big stature said that to me. So what about this loan proposition?

Mr. HOFFMAN. I could not answer that without a good deal more study than I have made, except as a general principle.

Senator WILEY. That is all I want.

Mr. HOFFMAN. I think the most dangerous thing to do to build up a country is to give them something. If they can stand a loan, all right. I think speaking generally—and that is the only way I can speak, Senator—gifts are a very bad idea. But I think also that loans that are not good loans are really worse. In other words, we should not put on a loan basis what is really a gift. That is really far worse, in my opinion, than going out and making clear that the gift is a gift.

Does that answer your question at all?

Senator WILEY. With this exception. This program, as I understand it, contemplates not simply dealings with governments, but dealings with citizens of governments who are going to get into industrial projects, building light plants and so on, and I would rather have their security than the governments' security. I would rather see the collateral, whatever it would be, stocks or bonds, back of that loan, from a light plant built to serve village X or town X, or some other industrial plant. Do you see what I am getting at? We have built up a precedent in Europe by our loans to governments which amount to gifts. So I would rather have the dealing with the citizen.

Mr. HOFFMAN. I frankly don't know the answer to all the aspects of that, except to say that generally we want to keep this whole thing, in my opinion, on just as businesslike a basis as we can, and the important thing is not to kid ourselves. In other words, if it really is a gift, for heaven's sake let's say it is a gift. If it really is a loan that we can get back let's make it a loan and let's put it on a businesslike basis. I think that would be one aspect that has real possibilities, that where we can not expect repayment in our own currency, it will be possible many times to trustee local currencies and direct the way they are used for the broad purposes of the recovery program.

I think, while I have not had a chance to think this thing through, I do see real opportunities to multiply the value of the dollars in that way. In other words I think that, speaking generally, if we give governments things and they sell those things, that money ought to be trusteed, and that money ought to be spent at the discretion of that particular government and ourselves and spent in a way, or invested in a way, to multiply the value of the dollars.

That is going to take a good deal of thinking in each particular case as to how best to work out the program in a given country, but those are the broad general principles under which I think it should operate.

The CHAIRMAN. All right, Mr. Hoffman. Thank you very much, sir.

Senator HICKENLOOPER. I would like to ask Mr. Hoffman some questions. I was trying to defer to the other members here.

The CHAIRMAN. Go ahead, Senator Hickenlooper.

LACK OF PLAN OF OPERATION

Senator HICKENLOOPER. Perhaps I should preface whatever questions I have by stating my general attitude. One of my great fears and misgivings with this whole program is that nobody has a plan of operation. Nobody knows what they are going to do with the money over there, and the past experience of our manipulation of our funds has been that we have been hell bent to funnel money into Europe willy-nilly without either demanding results or knowing what results we can expect to get. I think that is probably one of the great weaknesses of this plan, except that by dollars in some way we are going to stimulate this production.

EXTENT OF ADMINISTRATOR'S CONTROL OVER PERSONNEL

I go a step further than that and assume in my own mind—and I have had nothing to change my mind on that—that the 100 percent future of this plan depends on the Administrator. If you get good administration of this plan you can write the bill in 100 words. If you get bad administration, you could not get legislation in 100,000 words that could possibly succeed. So I am personally committed to the idea that not only does the Administrator have complete responsibility for the success of this plan, but he has some tremendous obligations in connection with it, and one thing that I am concerned with is, how much freedom or latitude have you been definitely assured in the selection of your assistants, or how much control is going to be exercised over you in the personnel that you set up, or have you been handed a ready-made organization at this time?

Mr. HOFFMAN. No, sir; I have not, and it was clearly understood in the talks I had with the President that I had complete control insofar as the selection of personnel was concerned, and I don't think anyone should take this responsibility unless such assurance were given.

Senator HICKENLOOPER. And you are undertaking it on that basis?

Mr. HOFFMAN. If I am confirmed, I am undertaking it on that basis.

Senator HICKENLOOPER. I would like to have a few bets on that and give some odds on your confirmation.

Mr. HOFFMAN. Certainly I would never have thought of taking the job if there had been a string attached to it that I was to take so and so and so and so. I never asked the question before that was assured me.

Senator HICKENLOOPER. I therefore assume that you are going to accept the responsibility for the selection of your personnel and the organization, and I trust you will not yield to any undue influence.

Mr. HOFFMAN. If a good organization does not ensue, it will be entirely my responsibility.

The CHAIRMAN. You do not need to pay any attention to Senators who ask you for anything, either.

Senator LODGE. You may get a few letters from some of us in this room, too.

Senator BARKLEY. I do not want to discount my letters in advance. It is a lot easier to write a letter than to explain to a fellow that you can't write one.

Senator HICKENLOOPER. I think without doubt there will be numerous constituents who will want to be placed, but I hope you will use your judgment.

Senator LODGE. Some of them may be good, too.

ADMINISTRATOR'S FREEDOM TO OUTLINE COMPLAINTS

Senator HICKENLOOPER. What would your attitude, Mr. Hoffman, be if you got into this thing for, let's take an arbitrary figure of 6 months, 7 or 8 months, or a year, and run afoul of many handicaps in your administration of this thing as you think it should be administered? Would you feel free to outline those complaints to this committee or to any other proper committee, irrespective of, for instance, administration pressures to the contrary to keep hush-hush about some of these things? Can we go into this with the idea that its progress or development under all circumstances can be fairly and vigorously presented and, if things are going wrong, we can know about it?

I do not necessarily mean this committee, but any one who is responsible.

Mr. HOFFMAN. I think the objectives of the program are too important to allow any personalities or to allow any what I would call amenities in the situation to control. In other words, this program has to succeed, in my opinion, if it is possible to succeed, and if I found that the situation was one in which I felt I could not be effective, I would want to either resign or have the situation changed so I thought I might become effective.

Senator HICKENLOOPER. I have a feeling often that resignations that occur in government do not accomplish the purpose, necessarily, unless the reasons for the resignations and the things that led up to them are fairly well understood so that they can be corrected. I am not anticipating your resignation.

The CHAIRMAN. No one has mentioned it, but I think it is directly in line with your question: I remind Mr. Hoffman that there is a joint congressional committee to be appointed for the purpose of constant liaison between your administration and the Congress.

Senator HICHENLOOPER. I had that committee in mind. I was thinking about that body.

The CHAIRMAN. I think that committee comes squarely into the situation that Senator Hickenlooper is talking about, and I would hope, and I am sure I am expressing the opinion of the Congress as a whole, that you would be totally frank with your comments to our committee and you would feel free to disclose all of your troubles to them. if you have any of a nature that you cannot control yourself.

Mr. HOFFMAN. I certainly would, sir.

ERP SOLUTION TO FINANCING ACTIVITIES OPPOSED TO PROGRAM

Senator HICKENLOOPER. Let's assume a situation of this kind. I would like to get your reaction to it. Let's assume that our friends the British are presently engaged in shipping jet engines of a very superior grade to the Russians. I assume for the sake of this question that some of their factories are shipping over 50 percent of these advanced jet engines now to the Russians, and that some of their factories are shipping a very substantial percent of their radionic equipment, which could be used mostly in war activities, to the Russians at this time.

What kind of solution could we have to that situation under the ERP?

Mr. HOFFMAN. I would feel that that was something I would want to refer to the State Department. I mean to say that if, during the course of the recovery program, a given country, perhaps not as a result of any financing of that particular industry, began engaging in an activity of that kind, I would feel that that certainly should be flagged, but I would say that went to the very high level, the very highest levels, as to what ought to be done about it.

Senator HICKENLOOPER. But this European recovery program money might either directly or almost directly be going into the financing of factories of this kind. In other words, we might find ourselves in the position of taking this money and financing such activities which, at least so far as I am concerned, would be directly opposed to the program.

Mr. HOFFMAN. Of course it should be stopped. How to stop them I could not answer this morning. If you asked me for a completely extemporaneous answer, if that situation developed I would certainly expect to communicate with the Secretary of State and would suggest that it was important enough to be discussed with the President and a solution worked out. That is the way I would go about it, not having any knowledge of government.

Senator HICKENLOOPER. The reason I might be concerned about this hypothetical question is, if such a situation does exist, the situation has not yet been worked out.

Senator LODGE. Hasn't that happened in the case of these firearms to Belgium?

Senator HICKENLOOPER. I don't know.

I don't like to be too mysterious, but I think I have accurate information that jet engines are being shipped to Russia now. Information has been given on this subject, but nothing has been done about it—and electronic equipment, and so on—on the theory that the British manufacturers have to live. That is the answer. They have to live.

Mr. HOFFMAN. I think those of us who saw what happened as a result of shipping scrap iron prior to World War II certainly should be alive to the dangers of that type of activity.

DEFERRED CREDITS ON U.S. PURCHASES SUGGESTED

Senator HICKENLOOPER. Without doubt we are going to have to make purchases offshore of many of these things. And I realize that it is easier to write a check on the U.S. Treasury than it is to negotiate, perhaps, an agreement that may not be fully acceptable to some other countries at the outset, but it would seem to me that if this is a recovery program to which other countries are at least giving lip service, there isn't any reason why grain purchases from the Argentine, and coffee purchases from Brazil that may go into this, should not carry their share of the obligation on it, rather than just have an American Government check written on that, which will come back here in dollars and put pressure on our economy.

It seems to me that it is perfectly sound to say that the Argentine should bear a certain portion, a substantial portion, of the amount of that purchase, for instance of wheat as an illustration, or meat, and that they could well be asked to take deferred credits on this country so they won't pressure us with their dollars immediately in our own country for manufactured goods.

I have the feeling that that has not received very favorable consideration here simply because—I don't know why, but one reason perhaps is that it is easier to write a check than it is to negotiate. But if we bought $1 billion worth of wheat from the Argentine, there is no reason why the Argentine should not carry credits on that in whatever way they want to arrange it with Europe for 35 or 40 percent. We can guarantee the rest of it on, let's say, 10-year credits, so they can come back over the next 10 years here when your economy may need it and be spent, rather than to get a billion dollars this year with orders that cannot be filled and that just increase the demand on our own economy.

That is just an extremely rough suggestion.

Mr. HOFFMAN. It is a very interesting idea.

Senator HICKENLOOPER. Of course, the rule is to just write a check on the Treasury for all these things. But we are coming to the time when our economy, I think, has to look to itself a little bit, not only from the standpoint of spending money but from the standpoint of pressures on our economy, and I think undoubtedly there are many other countries in the world that can make a contribution. The Argentine has only one place to sell its meat and its wheat, and that is Europe, so it would seem to me they would be very interested at least in doing that before they would refuse an outlet for their stuff.

Brazil has one place to sell coffee in bulk, and that is here, and as a secondary market it has Europe. So I think we should talk quite seriously to those fellows about the disposal of their products, their surpluses. And I think we could probably induce them to carry a part of this load and to defer some of these credits, which would be helpful. Maybe it is not feasible. I don't know.

Mr. HOFFMAN. I don't know either, but it is an interesting question. So far as I am concerned, I would hope that we could drive the hardest possible bargain in anything we had to buy outside of this country. I presume that would impinge somewhat on State Department activities. There would have to be consultations, but speaking generally, there is a very interesting idea there, I think.

DRIVING BARGAINS WITH OTHERS SUGGESTED

Senator HICKENLOOPER. It seems to me that we are driving a hard bargain with the American people because we are forcing this expenditure on the American people whether they like it or not. I think a great many of them feel that we have to do it. But we are driving a bargain with the American people, and I don't know what they would do if they voted on it. We, I think, might well explore the idea of driving some good bargains with some of these other people who otherwise will make tremendous profits out of it and contribute nothing to the program.

Mr. HOFFMAN. Let me answer that in an oblique manner. I think unless the American people see every evidence that this money is being spent wisely the program will not be continued, and therefore a very great obligation rests upon the Administrator to see that we come as close to getting value received as we can. Just because I think the program should go forward, unless it is administered in that manner I think the people might some day revolt.

Senator HICKENLOOPER. I certainly do not envy you your job, I will tell you that. It is a tough job. But I still can't avoid the idea that Government administration too often tends to slip into the line of least resistance, and this may very easily get into a glorified WPA (Works Progress Administration) unless it is very carefully and vigorously watched.

Mr. HOFFMAN. I am very glad to have your warning, sir.

Senator HICKENLOOPER. I don't know that it is a warning.

Mr. HOFFMAN. I think it is.

Senator HICKENLOOPER. I don't have any idea that you feel any less that way than I do.

Mr. HOFFMAN. I feel that if there is even a trace of WPA in this operation the whole recovery program is put in jeopardy, so that's that.

DIVISION OF U.S. MONEY TO PAY INTERNATIONAL

Senator HICKENLOOPER. Just one other question that I would like to get your views on. Some of the money that we have given, notably to France, and perhaps to Britain and to some of the other countries, I am informed has been used to pay off some portion of their international debts within Europe. In other words, we have given money for relief purposes and otherwise, and the governments have taken a portion of that money and applied it to their international credits, perhaps even in South America.

I realize a statewide currency is one of the basic essentials in Europe. They have to have some medium of exchange to operate on. But I merely suggest that those practices are probably not down the line of what my hopes, at least, are for this program, that this is a recovery program and not a debt-paying program or credit arranging program, except in such fields as the administration or the Administrator feels he must go into in order to stabilize currency.

Mr. HOFFMAN. I would think that made a lot of sense.

Senator HICKENLOOPER. It has been done to balance their budgets in some kind of rigged manner.

Mr. HOFFMAN. Thinking of it, I would only take a given situation and analyze it and see whether there are special circumstances that, from the standpoint of the stabilizing of currency, make some departure from what is sound principle necessary. We should not give any country money to pay off debts.

Senator HICKENLOOPER. I do not think the money that has been used was given for that purpose, but it was diverted for that purpose and I hope that nothing in this program goes along that line.

I do not think I have anything more.

The CHAIRMAN. Thank you, Mr. Hoffman. We will excuse you. We are indebted to you.

Mr. HOFFMAN. Thank you very much.

Senator LODGE. We will be seeing you.

The CHAIRMAN. And how.

ROLLCALL VOTE

While we are still at it, I think this is important enough to call the roll, if the committee is ready to vote on Mr. Hoffman. I suggest that the Clerk call the roll.

Dr. WILCOX. Mr. Capper.

The CHAIRMAN. Aye.

Dr. WILCOX. Mr. White.

The CHAIRMAN. Aye.

Dr. WILCOX. Mr. Wiley.

The CHAIRMAN. Aye.

Dr. WILCOX. Mr. Smith.

Senator SMITH. Aye.

Dr. WILCOX. Mr. Hickenlooper.

Senator HICKENLOOPER. Aye.

Dr. WILCOX. Mr. Lodge.

Senator LODGE. Aye.

Dr. WILCOX. Mr. Connally.

Senator BARKLEY. Aye.

Dr. WILCOX. Mr. George.

Senator BARKLEY. Aye.

Dr. WILCOX. Mr. Wagner.

Senator THOMAS of Utah. Aye.

Dr. WILCOX. Mr. Thomas.

Senator THOMAS of Utah. Aye.

Dr. WILCOX. Mr. Barkley.

Senator BARKLEY. Aye.

Dr. WILCOX. Mr. Hatch.

Senator BARKLEY. Aye.

Dr. WILCOX. Mr. Chairman.

The CHAIRMAN. Aye.

Mr. Hoffman is confirmed, and I will report the nomination today. I wonder if it would be rushing the performance to ask for consideration.

Senator BARKLEY. I think it could be done, Mr. Chairman.

Senator THOMAS of Utah. If you want a motion from the committee, I move that the nomination be reported today and that the President even be notified on it.

The CHAIRMAN. Without objection that motion will be entered and the order made.

[The meeting adjourned at 11:30 a.m.]

APPENDIX I

DOCUMENTS RELATING TO S. 2202

LEGISLATIVE CHRONOLOGY OF S. 2202

TO PROMOTE WORLD PEACE AND THE GENERAL WELFARE, NATIONAL INTEREST, AND FOREIGN POLICY OF THE UNITED STATES THROUGH ECONOMIC, FINANCIAL, AND OTHER MEASURES NECESSARY TO THE MAINTENANCE OF CONDITIONS ABROAD IN WHICH FREE INSTITUTIONS MAY SURVIVE AND CONSISTENT WITH THE MAINTENANCE OF THE STRENGTH AND STABILITY OF THE UNITED STATES

Senate Action

Introduced by Mr. Vandenberg on February 23, 1948.
Referred to Committee on February 23, 1948.
Public Hearings held on January 8–10, 12–16, 19–24, 26–31, February 2–5, 1948.
Executive Session Hearings held on February 9–13, 17, 1948.
Ordered Reported (Vote 13–0) on February 17, 1948.
Reported (S. Rept. 935) on February 26, 1948.
Passed (Vote 69–17) on March 13, 1948.
Conference Committee appointed on April 1, 1948 (Messrs. Vandenberg, Capper, Wiley, Connally, and George).
Conference Report (H. Rept. 1655) agreed to on April 2, 1948.

House Action

Referred to Committee on March 15, 1948.
Executive Meetings held on March 16, 17, 18, 19, 20.
Ordered Reported favorably on March 19, 1948.
Reported (H. Rept. 1585) on March 20, 1948.
Rule Granted by Rules Committee on March 22, 1948 (H. Res. 505—H. Rept. 1587).
Passed with amendments (Vote 329–74) on March 31, 1948.
Conference Asked With Senate on April 1, 1948 (Conferees: Messrs. Eaton, Vorys, Mundt, Bloom, and Kee).
Conference Report (H. Rept. 1655) agreed to (Vote 318–75) on April 2, 1948.
Signed by President on April 3, 1948 (Public Law 472).

MEMORANDUM OF CONVERSATION

Date: November 4, 1947.
Participants: Senator Vandenberg, Under Secretary of State Lovett, and Francis O. Wilcox.

Following are the main points which arose in Senator Vandenberg's conversation with Mr. Lovett relating to the Marshall plan:

(1) Mr. Lovett said the State Department proposed to bring up legislation relating to interim aid first. This would be followed by the Marshall plan which would be presented to the Committee by November 10. It is the State Department's hope that the interim program can be approved by Congress before the end of November. The Marshall plan, according to their schedule, would be approved by March 31.

(2) Mr. Lovett used as one of his main arguments the fact that Senator Vandenberg had suggested at the White House that a vote for the interim aid program should not be considered as a commitment on the part of any Member of the Congress for the Marshall plan.

(3) He stressed the fact that the stop-gap program would be handled by existing State Department machinery for relief. It would not, therefore, be necessary to go into the problem of administration in connection with the interim program. That whole question would be ironed out during our study of the Marshall plan proper.

(4) He said that the Department has a plan for China and he suggested that he come back to discuss the problem in detail with Senator Vandenberg. The Secretary, he says, is handling China policy. He expressed a grave doubt whether any sort of Marshall plan could be put into operation satisfactorily in China.

(5) As far as the Middle East and Latin America are concerned, Mr. Lovett thought that these areas could be handled by increasing the funds available for the Export-Import Bank.

(6) He emphasized the fact that any four-year program for Europe was not feasible since it is impossible to forecast exact conditions, prices and other variables. He, therefore, thought that a 15-month program to start with would be adequate. This would give the next Congress the chance to act on the matter before the end of the fiscal year June 30, 1949. By limiting our aid at the outset to 15 months, United States control over the program might be more effectively exercised.

(7) As to the basic method of extending aid, Mr. Lovett thought that we ought to think in terms of grants-in-aid up to the amount involved in fuel, food and fertilizer—that is to say something over 60 percent. Presumably, the other would be extended in the form of loans. He thought the total amount involved would be somewhere between 16 and 20 billions with from six to seven billions set aside for the first year.

(8) He argued that some sort of trusteeship might be set up to supervise the expenditure of local currency funds in the 16 European countries which would accumulate from the sale of United States goods abroad. This trusteeship system would give guidance with respect to the use of the funds for further reconstruction purposes and would avoid the accusation that the United States is trying to dominate the situation.

(9) He stressed the point that dollars were being required by too many states and that it was essential to stabilize the currency of the 16 nations as the basis for further reconstruction. He did not see why it was necessary for all states to insist upon payment for their goods in dollars.

(10) He pointed out that near agreement had been reached between the Bureau of the Budget and the State Department relating to the administration of the program. He said that the arguments advanced for the corporation were not valid and that the Department felt it would be advisable to have a small organization set up either inside or outside the Department to handle the program. In any event, they were agreed that the control of American foreign policy ought to remain clearly in the hands of the Secretary of State.

(11) He pointed out that the United States intended to conclude a multilateral treaty with the 16 nations and later 16 bilateral treaties which would lay down the conditions to be imposed with respect to the program.

(12) He also pointed out that the interim program would not be confined solely to fuel, food, and fertilizer. The program also calls for certain other materials which would seem to be necessary to keep the factories in Italy and France going and give the people their employment.

November 4, 1947.

MEMORANDUM

To: Senator Connally.
From: Francis O. Wilcox.
Subject: Administration of the Marshall Plan.

You suggested that I set down on paper a summary of the ideas circulating in the government about the administration of the Marshall plan. At the present time there is a fairly wide divergence of opinion between the State Department, the Harriman Committee, and the Bureau of the Budget. I understand they hope to resolve this difference of opinion very soon so that they may present a program to the Congress on which they can be united.

The central issue in the controversy is the role that the Department of State should play in the administration of the program. Everyone is agreed that the Marshall plan will constitute a very important part of our foreign policy during the next four years. If then the Department of State is not to administer the program directly, satisfactory arrangements must be made to coordinate at least the policy aspects of the program with the foreign policy of the United States. It follows, therefore, that great care must be taken to avoid an arrangement which would result in conflict between the Secretary of State and any other agency which may be set up to administer the program.

One of the points on which there is general agreement is the desirability of retaining a considerable amount of flexibility in the program. This would seem to be necessary in view of the fact that changing conditions in Europe and the changing supply picture in the United States will make long-range planning well nigh impossible. As a result of these factors the administration of the program becomes exceedingly important.

I. Functions to be Carried Out with Respect to the Marshall Plan

There are, of course, a number of important functions which must be carried out and for which suitable administrative arrangements must be made. In brief these include the following:

(1) The determination of policy and program within the framework laid down by the law passed by Congress. This would include the determination of availability of supplies and their allocation to various countries. It would also include such difficult questions as to whether or not aid might be withheld from particular countries.

(2) The exercise of any necessary domestic controls required for the successful execution of the program.

(3) The overall management of the program, including the administration of funds, the review and clearance of requisitions, procurement, storage, shipping, etc.

(4) The negotiation of agreements with various European countries relating to the program.

(5) The administration in Europe of the program, including such matters as the proper identification of supplies, the control of local currency proceeds, etc.

(6) The encouragement abroad of maximum self-help through participation in a continuing organization of the 16 European countries and in other international agencies.

II. The Harriman Committee Report

The Harriman Committee's preliminary report stresses the importance of a strong and flexible administrative organization. In order to accomplish this, the Committee will probably recommend that a new organization be set up in the government. This organization would be *outside* of the Department of State and its head would be appointed by the President and confirmed by the Senate. The report does not state whether the agency would be a corporate organization or whether it would be comparable to the old Foreign Economic Administration. Questions of policy involving the economic foreign policy of the United States would be settled by a Board made up of the heads of the interested agencies. The new organization itself, however, would be performing what would seem to be primarily an operating job.

The danger which some people fear in this kind of an organization is that it would tend to enter into conflicts with the Department of State over our foreign policy inasmuch as it is always very difficult to draw any sharp line of distinction between policy on the one hand and operations on the other. The report recommends that the Secretary of State should be empowered to make specific recommendations to the new organization on operating matters where operations might have an effect on foreign policy; but, if the director of the new agency reports directly to the President and not to the Secretary of State, trouble might arise. Likewise, it should be noted that the deputy to the administrator in charge of European operations would report directly to the new organization from Europe and presumably would not go through State Department channels. This arrangement, too, might lead to possible conflict both in the field and at home.

III. Bureau of the Budget Position

I understand the Bureau of the Budget believes that no new executive agency is needed at this time, but that interdepartmental machinery now in existence is adequate to meet the situation. They seem to think that the program might best be handled by an Under Secretary of State for European recovery aided by an Assistant Secretary. They believe that the Department has done a good job with respect to the relief program and the Greek-Turkish program and that just as good a job can be done *in* the Department with respect to the Marshall plan. They feel that the Secretary of State, who is responsible for the foreign policy of the United States, should be in control so that our country can speak with one voice abroad. Above all, they do not want to create a new organization which would move in the direction of setting up staffs comparable to those now found in certain divisions of the Departments of State, Treasury, Agriculture and Commerce. A new agency, they claim, would result in a great deal of fumbling around and a great deal of lost motion due to recruiting and occupational problems.

IV. State Department Position

Unofficially the State Department position seems to be half-way between the Bureau of the Budget and the Harriman Committee. Their idea seems to be that a new European cooperative administration should be set up to take care of primary administrative responsibility for the program. The head of the organization would report to the President but would operate in accordance with foreign policy guidance from the Department of State. The State Department accordingly would participate actively with the new agency in the formulation and execution of the program and its concurrence would be required for important decisions relating to allocation.

Meanwhile, State Department emphasizes that the new agency could be a small one and that many of the functions to be performed with respect to procurement, allocation, transportation, etc., could be carried on by the Departments of Commerce and Agriculture, the Office of Defense Transportation, the Treasury Department, and other United States agencies.

Abroad there would be established a special United States representative for the program with ambassadorial rank. He would be assisted by a small staff and would report to the Secretary of State and through him to the director of the new agency. Directives going to the field would be prepared jointly by members of the State Department staff and the staff of the new agency. A small mission would be created in each of the 16 countries whose members would be recruited jointly by the new agency and the State Department and placed within the foreign service. Thus, the State Department would turn most of the work over to the new agency, but would still retain control for policy purposes.

December 31, 1947.

Hon. George C. Marshall,
Secretary of State,
Washington, D.C.

My Dear Mr. Secretary: I ask for your Department's reaction to the following suggestion in connection with Section 9, Paragraph (c), of the proposed ERP legislation. This now reads:

"There are hereby authorized to be appropriated to the President from time to time, out of any money in the Treasury not otherwise appropriated, such amounts, not to exceed $17,000,000,000, as may be necessary to carry out the provisions and accomplish the purposes of this Act etc."

I suggest the elimination of the words "not to exceed $17,000,000,000" so that the Paragraph will read: "There are hereby authorized to be appropriated to the President from time to time, out of any money in the Treasury not otherwise appropriated, such sums as may be necessary to carry out the provisions and accomplish the purposes of this Act etc."

My reasons are as follows: (1) It is common practice for Congress to make authorizations in the proposed language when the obligations are continuing and particularly when they reach from one Congress into another.

(2) By proposing to limit actual appropriations to one year, the Bill correctly concedes that one Congress cannot bind another. A four-year authorization is equally futile, in specific amount. It does not even possess the virtue of a "ceiling" because any future Congress which might wish to exceed the present "ceiling"

will be just as ready to increase the "ceiling" as it will be to appropriate the funds. The effective test each year is the Congressional appropriation—and there is no other. Therefore a general, continuing authorization serves every practical purpose from any viewpoint. It just as definitely recognizes a contemplated continuity as if expressed in figures.

(3) But to express this principle in figures (namely, $17,000,000,000) in the legislation itself may invite a specific reliance abroad which is impossible under our Constitutional procedure. Furthermore, it can only be an educated guess of highly doubtful validity when we thus attempt to assess events for the next four years at home or abroad, and when the entire ERP enterprise is at the mercy of good or bad contingencies.

(4) The Committee on Foreign Relations can and should refer, in its report, to the historic basis of the negotiations upon which ERP is based. It can and should identify the final estimates of which it takes judicial notice when it acts. But I draw a sharp distinction between these elements of a working prospectus and the statutory identification of an actual figure to which the Committee would have to give exhaustive study before it could give it legislative sanction.

I shall be glad to have a memorandum indicating your Department's reaction to this proposal.

With warm personal regards and best wishes,

sincerely,

ARTHUR H. VANDENBERG,
U.S. Senate.

THE UNDER SECRETARY OF STATE,
Washington, January 2, 1948.

Hon. ARTHUR H. VANDENBERG,
U.S. Senate.

MY DEAR SENATOR VANDENBERG: In the absence of Secretary Marshall, your letter of December 31 on the subject of Section 9, Paragraph (c), of the proposed ERP legislation has been referred to me for action.

Your suggestion that the words "not to exceed $17,000,000,000" be eliminated from the Paragraph in question has been given careful consideration. The Paragraph, after the elimination of this language, would read as follows:

> "There are hereby authorized to be appropriated to the President from time to time, out of any money in the Treasury not otherwise appropriated, such sums as may be necessary to carry out the provisions and accomplish the purposes of this Act, etc."

The Department of State has consulted the President and the Executive agencies represented on the Interdepartmental Committee, as well as those agencies having a direct interest or responsibility in this matter, and I am glad to report that we are in agreement with the suggestion you make. It appears to conform to the basic principles on which the legislation is requested.

This Department will, therefore, take the necessary steps prior to appearance before the Committees of Congress to change the Section under discussion in conformity with the proposal made in your letter of December thirty-first.

With kind personal regards, I am

Very sincerely yours,

(Signed) ROBERT A. LOVETT.

JANUARY 7, 1948.

MEMORANDUM

To: Senator Connally.
From: The committee staff.
Subject: Preliminary comments on ERP draft legislation.

On the assumption that the draft legislation as presented by the State Department would be used as a basis for the Committee's consideration of the ERP, the Committee staff has prepared a brief commentary directed at certain provisions of the bill. No attempt has been made to examine many of the broad issues involved in the Marshall Plan. Nor have we attempted to indicate the proper course of action or the "answers." The present memo is designed rather to direct attention to certain sections of the bill which may need revision or further study. No doubt many additional points will be brought out during the hearings.

1. Sec. 2(a): Relationship of ERP to Asia and Latin America

The bill properly recognizes the interdependence of the United States and Europe. In so doing, however, is there an implication that the United States is not also interested in Latin America and Asia? The provision (2)(a) was inserted because of the State Department's view—which it will defend strongly at the hearings—that European recovery is in effect the key to world recovery. In view of the coming Bogota conference and in view of our concern with a recovery program for China, should it be made clear that the United States, in proceeding with ERP, is not exhibiting a lack of concern for other regions of the world?

2. Sec. 3: Is Iceland a Part of Europe?

In Section 3 Iceland is included as one of the countries "wholly or partly in Europe" to be considered as participating countries within the meaning of the Act. In view of the reluctance of the United States to define the Western Hemisphere in the past—particularly in drawing up any definition which might exclude Iceland—is it desirable for the United States in this legislation to recognize Iceland as a part of Europe?

3. Sec. 3: Are Trusteeship Areas Included?

Section 3 provides that any of the countries of Europe, including their "colonies and dependencies", may be participating countries. Does the term "colonies and dependencies" include the trusteeship areas of the participating states?

4. Sec. 3: Revision of Estimates If New States Participate

This section makes clear that any country wholly or partly in Europe can be a participating country so long as it remains an adherent to the joint program for European recovery. The door is thus left open for the Soviet Union and its satellite states and possibly other European states as well to participate in the enterprise. What procedure is contemplated for the revision of the estimates with respect to requirements in cases new states are admitted? Will it be necessary to ask for additional appropriations?

5. Sec. 4(a): Authority of Secretary of State

This section provides that "all those functions of the Administrator which affect the conduct of the foreign policy of the United States shall be performed subject to the direction and control of the Secretary of State." It is, of course, appropriate to protect the proper responsibility of the Secretary of State in the conduct of foreign policy. The language, however, would seem to be all inclusive and might be interpreted to mean even those functions which *indirectly* affect the conduct of foreign policy. Should this provision be modified?

6. Sec. 4(c): Operation of Program Without Administrator

This section would permit the President to carry out the program through existing agencies pending the appointment of the Administrator. Such an arrangement would seem to be desirable in that it would permit the President to launch the program without undue delay. The section, however, might be subject to criticism by opponents of the bill since it would seem to permit the President to go on with the program for an *indefinite* period without setting up the new agency contemplated. Would it be advisable to put a time limit on the President's authority in this connection?

7. Sec. 4(d): Salary of Consultants

Under the terms of this section certain officials of the new Administration can be paid salaries above the $10,000 ceiling. This would seem to be desirable in view of the necessity of recruiting experts in many fields without delay. On the other hand, the bill provides for an unlimited number of consultants and experts at a rate not to exceed $50 per day which can total more than $15,000 per year. Should there be some limitation on the number of such consultants to be hired or on the Period of time during the year when they can receive the $50 per diem?

8. Sec. 5: Responsibility of U.S. Representative in Europe

This section provides for a United States Special Representative in Europe. The headquarters of the Representative would presumably be the seat of the central European organization. The bill, however, does not make clear to whom the United States Representative would be responsible or what his relations with the embassies (and ambassadors) in various countries would be. Moreover, it leaves open the question as to whether instructions would be issued to him by the Secretary of State or the Administrator or both.

9. Sec. 6(a): Responsibility of Personnel Abroad

Closely related to the foregoing is Section 6(a) which contemplates the use, by the new Administrator, of personnel who would be placed in the Foreign Service Reserve of the Foreign Service staff. Many of these would probably be attached to various embassies. To whom would they be ultimately responsible—the head of mission in each country or the United States Special Representative?

10. Sec. 6(d): FBI Clearance

United States citizens employed by the new organization are to be investigated by the FBI. The bill also provides that such individuals may take their posts following a preliminary clearance by the State Department. Some such provision would seem desirable in view of the six-months' time normally required for FBI clearances. On the other hand, double investigations would be undesirable in that the same people would be approached at different times by different agencies with respect to the loyalty of the same individual. Moreover, this procedure would entail an undesirable waste of time. Could not some arrangement be worked out to meet the clearance requirements and yet not hold up the operation of the Administration?

11. Secs. 6–7: Hiring of Field Staff

Under Sections 6 and 7 it is apparent that the new Administrator would not possess the authority himself to hire any of his staff operating outside the United States. Presumably, all such people would be appointed by the Secretary of State and inducted into the Foreign Service Reserve or the Foreign Service staff group through the Board of the Foreign Service. No doubt the Administrator could recruit individuals and recommend them to the State Department for approval. In any event, the legislation would leave one with the impression that the authority of the Department of State over the hiring of the personnel of the ECA is quite complete. Should this authority of the State Department be limited and should the Administrator's role in the hiring of his personnel be more clearly spelled out?

12. SEC. 7(a)(1): UNLIMITED OFFSHORE PROCUREMENT

Public Law 84 and the Foreign Aid Act of 1947 imposed limitations upon the amount of money which could be spent for offshore procurement. This bill apparently includes no such limitation but would authorize the procurement of any or even all the commodities required from other countries. In view of the changes in the world economy which have taken place recently and in view of the nature of this program, is any limitation with respect to offshore procurement desirable?

13. SEC. 7(a)(2): MEANING OF LANGUAGE "ANY OTHER SERVICES"

Under the language of 7(a)(2) the Administrator may perform "any other services with respect to a participating country which he determines to be required for accomplishing the purposes of this Act". Opponents to the bill will certainly raise questions about the breadth of this language. Can the words "any other services" legitimately be interpreted to mean services short of military assistance or might the President and the Administrator possess the authority under the Act to go so far as to send armed troops to any of the participating countries? Should this language be clarified?

14. SEC. 7(a)(3): NATURE OF TECHNICAL INFORMATION AND ASSISTANCE

Section 7 contains general authority for the "procurement of and furnishing technical information and assistance". Does this grant of authority contemplate an increased export from this country of American technical books, films and magazines and possibly field training programs to increase European production?

15. SEC. 7(b)(1): SIMPLIFICATION OF ACCOUNTING PROCEDURES

This section provides that commodities or services procured outside the United States may be accounted for on such certification as the Administrator may prescribe to assure expenditure in furtherance of the purposes of the Act and that such certification shall be binding on the accounting offices of the United States. Under this language the strict procedures of the General Accounting Office may be avoided and the Administrator could set up a simpler accounting system in order to keep track of expenditures. Would such a simplification of procedures seem desirable in view of the nature of the program and the difficulty of certifying in the normal way purchases made in foreign countries?

16. SEC 7(c)(1): GRANTS OR LOANS

According to the draft legislation the Administrator may provide assistance for participating countries in the form of grants or loans. What proportion of the total amount will be utilized in the form of grants and what proportion in the form of loans? On what basis will the Administrator determine the manner in which assistance will be extended? Presumably a state will be called upon to repay the assistance granted if it is financially able to do so. Does this mean that some states like Denmark, which may have ample supplies in the way of fuel, food and fertilizers, may nevertheless be granted assistance in the form of dollar exchange so that they can buy needed industrial equipment?

17. SEC. 7(c)(1): THE AMINISTRATOR AND THE NATIONAL ADVISORY COUNCIL

In determining whether assistance shall be in the form of grants or loans the Administrator is to act in consultation with the National Advisory Council. This function will have an extremely important bearing upon our foreign policy. Is it to be assumed that the Administrator can ignore the recommendations of the National Advisory Council? Would the Administrator, the NAC, or the Secretary of State make the final determination?

18. SEC. 7(c)(1): ADMINISTRATOR AS MEMBER OF NATIONAL ADVISORY COUNCIL

Section 7 makes clear that the Administrator must cooperate closely with the National Advisory Council on International Monetary and Financial Problems. Since the European Recovery Program will to a very large extent constitute American foreign policy during the next four years, should not the Administrator be designated as a member of the NAC?

19. Secs. 7(a)(5)–8(d): Sale and Transfer of U.S. Merchant Vessels

These two sections of the bill provide for the transfer and the sale of United States merchant vessels, the latter to be done in accordance with the terms of of the Merchant Ship Sales Act of 1946. So far considerable criticism has arisen with respect to this apparent desire of the framers of the Marshall Plan to encourage the shipment of commodities made available under the bill in vessels under foreign registry. Should any limitation be placed upon the number of vessels sold or transferred? Should any limitation be placed upon the quantity of goods to be shipped in vessels under foreign registry? Should steps be taken to protect the Merchant Marine and American seamen against the competition of cheaper foreign shipping? Is the procedure set up in the Act of 1946 sound now in view of recent developments?

20. Secs. 9(e)–10(b)(6): Unexpended Balances of Local Currency Funds

The bill provides for the merging of the unexpended balances in the local currency funds under the Interim Aid Act and the Relief Bill with the local currency funds set up under the proposed ERP legislation. The unexpended balances in such funds are to be used for such purposes as may be agreed to between the participating countries and the United States. Previously, legislation relating to this subject called for the approval of Congress with respect to the final utilization of such funds. Should this Act call for similar congressional authority or is it to be assumed that the nature of the present program is such that an executive agreement will suffice?

21. Sec. 10(b)(5): Provision Relating to Stockpiling

During the hearings on interim aid considerable interest was expressed by members of the Committee about the possibility of securing under the long-range program strategic materials for stockpiling purposes. The language of Section 10 certainly makes this possible, but it may not be sufficiently mandatory in character to accomplish the purposes the Committee has in mind. Should the language be strengthened?

22. Sec. 13: Termination of the Program

While the program is scheduled to run until June 30, 1952, the Administrator is given authority to carry on under certain conditions until June 30, 1955. Similarly, funds made available under agreements concluded before July 1, 1952 may be available for expenditure through June 30, 1957. To some people this will look as though the State Department intends to create a seven-year, even a nine-year, instead of a four-year program. The experience of Lend Lease clearly demonstrates that additional time is needed for liquidation purposes and certainly long-range planning like that contemplated in the present bill cannot be terminated abruptly. Is the program open to legitimate objection because of these provisions relating to its termination?

23. Sec. 7(b)(3): Guaranties to Private Investors

Under the terms of the bill the Administrator may make certain guaranties to individuals or corporations investing in projects approved by the Administrator and the participating country. This would be done in order to stimulate European recovery through private investment. It is not clear, however, just what would be guarantied. Would the guaranty cover the principal invested in each case? Would it cover normal business risks in case the investment dropped in value over a period of years? Would such guaranties apply only to U.S. citizens or to businesses owned and operated by U.S. citizens? The total liabilities assumed under such guaranties shall not exceed five percent of the funds appropriated. Is this figure adequate?

"Working Sheet" of European Recovery Program Legislation

This committee print is described by the Chairman during the February 9 executive session as a "working sheet" which was "put together by the staff of the committee in collaboration with the experts from the State Department in an effort, first, to put down in black and white the administrative phases as recommended by the Brookings Institution, and then to put into type some of the major suggestions that arose in the course of the hearings." The Department of State submitted its original draft of the bill to the Foreign Relations Committee on January 7, 1948. The changes in that draft are in italics and the striken part is in lined type. This document, which is reproduced by off-set printing, contains marginal notes apparently made at the time the bill was discussed. The first two pages of this draft are missing from the Foreign Relations Committee's files.

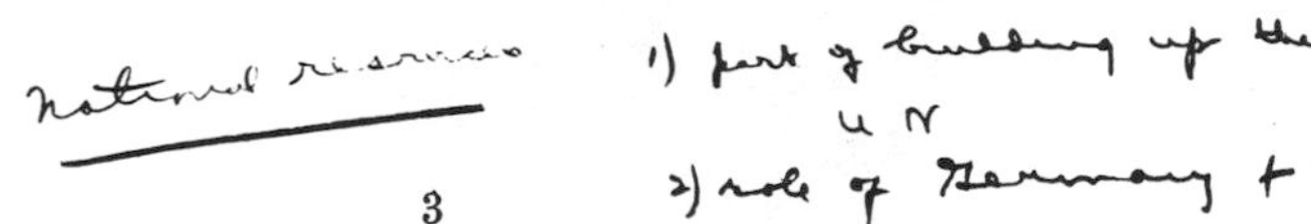

peace, the general welfare and national interest of the United States, and the attainment of the objectives of the United Nations. The restoration or maintenance in European countries of principles of individual liberty, free institutions, and genuine independence rests largely upon the establishment of sound economic conditions, stable international economic relationships, and the achievement by the countries of Europe of a ~~working~~ economy independent of ~~abnormal~~ outside assistance. The accomplishment of these objectives calls for a program of European recovery based upon a strong production effort, the expansion of foreign trade, the creation and maintenance of internal financial stability, and the development of economic cooperation, including all possible steps to establish and maintain equitable rates of exchange and to bring about the progressive elimination of trade barriers ~~and of the obstacles to the free movement of persons~~ within Europe. Mindful of the advantages which the United States has enjoyed through the existence of a large domestic market with no internal trade barriers, and believing that similar advantages can accrue to the countries of Europe, it is the hope of the people of the United States that these countries through a joint organization will exert sustained common efforts which will speedily achieve that economic cooperation in Europe which is essential for lasting peace and prosperity. Accordingly, it is declared to be the policy of the people of the United States to sustain and strengthen principles of individual liberty, free institutions, and genuine independence in Europe through assistance to those countries of Europe which participate in a joint recovery program based upon self-help and mutual cooperation. It is further declared to be the policy of the United States that the continuity of assistance provided by the United States should, at all times, be dependent upon the continuity of cooperation among the countries participating in the program.

PURPOSES OF ACT

(b) It is the purpose of this Act to effectuate the policy set forth in subsection (a) of this section by furnishing material and financial assistance to the participating countries in such a manner as to aid them, through their own individual and concerted efforts, to become independent of abnormal outside economic assistance within the period of operations under this Act, by—

(1) promoting industrial and agricultural production in the participating countries;

(2) furthering the restoration or maintenance of the soundness of European currencies, budgets, and finances; and

(3) facilitating and stimulating the growth of international trade of participating countries with one another and with other countries by appropriate measures

including reduction of barriers which may hamper such trade.

PARTICIPATING COUNTRIES

Sec. 3. Any country (including the United Kingdom of Great Britain and Northern Ireland, ~~Eire,~~ Iceland, *Ireland*, and any of the zones of occupation of Germany) wholly or partly in Europe, including its colonies and dependencies, is a participating country within the meaning of this Act ~~while it remains an adherent to~~ *provided it adheres to, and for so long as it remains an adherent to,* a joint program for European recovery designed to accomplish the purposes of this Act.

ESTABLISHMENT OF ECONOMIC COOPERATION ADMINISTRATION

Sec. 4. (a) There is hereby established, with its principal office in the District of Columbia, an agency of the Government which shall be known as the Economic Cooperation Administration, hereinafter referred to as the Administration. The Administration shall be headed by an Administrator for Economic Cooperation, hereinafter referred to as the Administrator, who shall be appointed by the President, by and with the advice and consent of the Senate, and who shall receive compensation at the rate of $20,000 per annum. *The Administrator shall be responsible to the*

President and shall have a status in the executive branch of the Government comparable to that of the head of an executive department. Except as otherwise provided in this Act, the administration of the provisions of this Act is hereby vested in the Administrator *and his functions shall be performed under ~~the direction and~~ control of the President.* ~~All those functions of the Administrator which affect the conduct of the foreign policy of the United States shall be performed subject to the direction and control of the Secretary of State.~~

(b) There shall be in the Administration a Deputy Administrator for Economic Cooperation who shall be appointed by the President, by and with the advice and consent of the Senate, and shall receive compensation at the rate of $17,500 per annum. The Deputy Administrator for Economic Cooperation shall perform such functions as the Administrator shall designate, and shall be Acting Administrator for Economic Cooperation during the absence or disability of the Administrator or in the event of a vacancy in the office of Administrator.

(c) The President is authorized, pending the appointment and qualification of the first Administrator or Deputy Administrator for Economic Cooperation appointed hereunder, to provide for the performance of the functions of the Administrator under this Act through such departments, agencies, or establishments of the United States Government as he may direct.

(d) Any department, agency, or establishment of the Government (including, whenever used in this Act, any corporation which is an instrumentality of the United States) performing functions under this Act is authorized to employ, for duty within the continental limits of the United States, such personnel as may be necessary to carry out the provisions and purposes of this Act, and funds available pursuant to section ~~9~~ *13* of this Act shall be available for personal services in the District of Columbia and elsewhere without regard to section 14 (a) of the Federal Employees Pay Act of 1946 (60 Stat. 219). Personnel, not to exceed sixty, of the Administration may be compensated without regard to the provisions of the Classification Act of 1923, as amended, of whom not more than ten may be compensated at a rate in excess of $10,000 per annum, but not in excess of $15,000 per annum. Experts and consultants, as authorized by section 15 of the Act of August 2, 1946 (5 U. S. C. 55a), may be employed by the Administration, and may be compensated at rates for individuals not in excess of $50 per diem.

(e) The head of any department, agency, or establishment of the Government performing functions under this Act may, from time to time, promulgate such rules and regulations as may be necessary and proper to carry out his functions under this Act, and he may delegate to such officers of his department, agency, or establishment as he may designate the authority to perform any of his functions under this Act.

GENERAL FUNCTIONS OF ADMINISTRATOR

SEC. 5. (a) The Administrator, under the direction of the President, shall—

(1) review and appraise the requirements of participating countries for assistance under the terms of this Act;

(2) formulate programs of United States assistance under this Act for such countries;

(3) provide for the efficient execution of any such programs as may be placed in operation; and

(4) terminate provision of assistance or take other remedial action as provided in section 15 of this Act.

(b) In order to strengthen and make more effective the conduct of the foreign relations of the United States—

(1) the Administrator and the Secretary of State shall keep each other fully and currently informed on all matters, including prospective action, arising within the scope of their respective duties which are relevant to the conduct of the duties of the other;

(2) whenever the Secretary of State believes that any action, proposed action, or failure to act on the part

of the Administrator is inconsistent with the foreign-policy objectives of the United States, he shall consult with the Administrator and, if differences of view are not adjusted by consultation, the matter shall be referred to the President for final decision.

NATIONAL ADVISORY COUNCIL

SEC. 6. Section 4 (a) of the Bretton Woods Agreement Act (59 Stat. 512, 513) is hereby amended to read as follows:

"SEC. 4. (a) In order to coordinate the policies and operations of the representatives of the United States on the Fund and the Bank and of all agencies of the Government which make or participate in making foreign loans or which engage in foreign financial, exchange or monetary transactions, there is hereby established the National Advisory Council on International Monetary and Financial Problems (hereinafter referred to as the 'Council'), consisting of the Secretary of Treasury as Chairman, the Secretary of State, the Secretary of Commerce, the Chairman of the Board of Governors of the Federal Reserve System, the Chairman of the Board of Trustees of the Export-Import Bank of Washington, and during such period as the Economic Cooperation Administration shall continue to exist, the Administrator for Economic Cooperation."

UNITED STATES SPECIAL REPRESENTATIVE ABROAD

SEC. ~~5~~ *7*. There shall be a United States Special Representative in Europe who shall (a) be appointed by the President, by and with the advice and consent of the Senate, (b) be entitled to receive the same compensation and allowances as a chief of mission, class 1, within the meaning of the Act of August 13, 1946 (60 Stat. 999), and (c) have the rank of ambassador extraordinary and plenipotentiary. He shall be the chief United States representative to any European organization of participating countries which may be established by the participating countries to further a joint program for European recovery, and shall discharge in Europe such additional responsibilities as may be assigned to him with the approval of the President in furtherance of the purposes of this Act. He may also be designated as the United States representative on the Economic Commission for Europe.

~~SEC. 6. (a) For the purpose of performing functions under this Act outside the continental limits of the United States, the Secretary of State may (1) appoint or assign persons to any class in the Foreign Service Reserve for the duration of operations under this Act without regard to that provision of the Act of August 13, 1946 (60 Stat. 1000), which limits appointments to periods of not more than four years: *Provided,* That with respect to the appointment or assignment of persons to perform functions within~~

85-743 O - 73 - 35

~~the responsibility of the Administrator, the Secretary of State shall make such appointments or assignments in consultation with the Administrator; and (2) by regulations prescribed by him, provide for the appointment, for the duration of operations under this Act, of Foreign Service staff officers and employees, and alien clerks and employees. A person, whether or not such person is a war-service or temporary employee, thus appointed as staff officer or employee from any Government agency without break in service and with the consent of the head of the agency concerned shall, upon the termination of the appointment as staff officer or employee, be entitled to the same rights as those provided for Foreign Service Reserve Officers in section 528 of the Act of August 13, 1946 (60 Stat. 1010).~~

~~(b) The provisions of the Act of August 13, 1946 (60 Stat. 999), shall, except as provided in this section, apply fully to all persons appointed or assigned pursuant to the authority contained in this section.~~

~~(c) A representative of the Administration, designated by the Administrator, shall be a member of the Board of the Foreign Service, and section 211 (a) of the Foreign Service Act of 1946 (60 Stat. 1001), is hereby amended accordingly.~~

~~(d) Civilian personnel who are citizens of the United States appointed pursuant to this section to perform func-~~

~~tions under this Act shall be appointed subject to investigation by the Federal Bureau of Investigation: *Provided, however,* That they may assume their posts and perform their functions after preliminary investigation and clearance by the Department of State.~~

PUBLIC ADVISORY BOARD

SEC. 8. (a) There is hereby created a Public Advisory Board, hereinafter referred to as the Board, which shall advise and consult with the Administrator with respect to general or basic policy matters arising in connection with the Administrator's discharge of his responsibilities. The Board shall consist of the Administrator, who shall be Chairman, and not to exceed twelve additional members to be appointed by the President, by and with the advice and consent of the Senate, and who shall be selected from among citizens of the United States of broad and varied experience in matters affecting the public interest, other than officers and employees of the United States (including any agency or instrumentality of the United States) who, as such, regularly receive compensation for current services. Members of the Board other than the Administrator shall receive, out of funds made available for the purposes of this Act, a per diem allowance of $50 ~~per day~~ for each day spent in actual meetings of the Board or at conferences held upon the call of the

Administrator, plus necessary travel and other expenses incurred while so engaged.

(b) The Administrator may appoint such other advisory committees as he may determine to be necessary or desirable to effectuate the purposes of this Act.

SPECIAL ECA MISSIONS

SEC. 9. (a) There shall be established in each participating country, except any of the zones of occupation of Germany, a special mission for economic cooperation under the direction of a chief who shall be responsible for the performance within such country of operations under this Act. The chief shall be appointed by the Administrator, shall receive his instructions from the Administrator, and shall report to the Administrator on the performance of the duties assigned to him. The chief of the special mission shall take rank immediately after the chief of the United States diplomatic mission in such country.

(b) The chief of the special mission shall keep the chief of the United States diplomatic mission fully and currently informed on all matters, including prospective action, arising within the scope of the operations of the special mission and the chief of the diplomatic mission shall keep the chief of the special mission fully and currently informed on all matters relative to the conduct of the duties of the chief of the special

mission. The chief of the United States diplomatic mission will be responsible for assuring that the operations of the special mission are consistent with the foreign-policy objectives of the United States in such country and to that end whenever the chief of the United States diplomatic mission believes that any action, proposed action, or failure to act on the part of the special mission is inconsistent with such foreign-policy objectives, he shall so advise the chief of the special mission. If differences of view are not adjusted by consultation, the matter shall be referred to the Secretary of State and the Administrator for decision.

(c) The Secretary of State shall provide such office space, facilities, and other administrative services for the special mission in each participating country as may be agreed between the Secretary of State and the Administrator.

(d) With respect to any of the zones of occupation of Germany, the President shall make appropriate administrative arrangements for the conduct of operations under this Act, in order to enable the Administrator to carry out his responsibility to assure the accomplishment of the purposes of this Act.

PERSONNEL OUTSIDE UNITED STATES

SEC. 10. (a) For the purpose of performing functions under this Act outside the continental limits of the United States the Administrator may—

(1) without regard to the provisions of the Classification Act of 1923, as amended, employ personnel who shall receive compensation at any of the rates provided for Foreign Service Reserve officers under section 414 of the Foreign Service Act of 1946 (60 Stat. 999, 1003), or any of the rates provided for Foreign Service Staff officers and employees by section 415 of the Foreign Service Act of 1946 (60 Stat. 999, 1003). Personnel so appointed shall be entitled to receive the allowances and benefits authorized by title IX of the Foreign Service Act of 1946 (60 Stat. 999, 1025), and established under authority of title IX; and

(2) recommend persons to be appointed or assigned to any class in the Foreign Service Reserve, and the Secretary of State may appoint or assign such persons to any class in the Foreign Service Reserve, for the duration of operations under this Act, without regard to that provision of the Foreign Service Act of 1946 (60 Stat. 999, 1009) which limits appointments to periods of not more than four years; or recommend persons to be appointed as Foreign Service Staff officers and employees and the Secretary of State may appoint, for the duration of operations under this Act, such persons as Foreign Service Staff officers and employees, and a person so appointed from any Government agency

without break in service and with the consent of the head of the agency concerned shall, upon the termination of such appointment, be entitled to the same rights as those provided for Foreign Service Reserve officers in section 528 of the Foreign Service Act of 1946 (60 Stat. 1003, 1010). Transfers of Foreign Service officers, Foreign Service Reserve officers, and Foreign Service Staff officers and employees appointed or assigned pursuant to this subsection and promotions of Foreign Service Reserve officers and Foreign Service Staff officers and employees appointed or assigned pursuant to this subsection may be effected by the Secretary of State upon the recommendation of the Administrator. The provisions of the Foreign Service Act of 1946 (60 Stat. 999) shall, except as otherwise provided herein, apply fully to all persons appointed or assigned to the Foreign Service system pursuant to the authority contained in this subsection.

(b) For the purpose of performing functions under this Act outside the continental limits of the United States, the Secretary of State may, at the request of the Administrator, appoint, for the duration of operations under this Act, alien clerks and employees in accordance with applicable provisions of the Foreign Service Act of 1946 (60 Stat. 999).

(c) Section 211 (a) of the Foreign Service Act of 1946 (60 Stat. 999, 1001) is hereby amended to read as follows:

"Sec. 211. (a) The Board of the Foreign Service shall be composed of the Assistant Secretary of State in charge of the administration of the Department who shall be Chairman; two other Assistant Secretaries of State designated by the Secretary to serve on the Board; the Director General; and one representative each, occupying positions with comparable responsibilities, from the Departments of Agriculture, Commerce, and Labor, and from the Economic Cooperation Administration during such period as it shall continue to exist designated, respectively, by the heads of each such department or agency of the Government. The Secretary may request the head of any other Government department to designate a representative, occupying a position with comparable responsibilities, to attend meetings of the Board whenever matters affecting the interest of such department are under consideration."

(d) Civilian personnel who are citizens of the United States appointed pursuant to this section to perform functions under this Act shall be appointed subject to investigation by the Federal Bureau of Investigation: Provided, however, That they may assume their posts and perform their functions *after preliminary investigation and clearance by the Administrator or the Secretary of State, as the case may be.*

NATURE AND METHOD OF ASSISTANCE

SEC. ~~7~~ *11.* (a) The Administrator may, from time to time, furnish assistance to any participating country by providing for the performance of any of the functions set forth in paragraphs (1) through (5) of this subsection when he deems it to be in furtherance of the purposes of this Act, and upon the terms and conditions set forth in this Act and such additional terms and conditions consistent with the provisions of this Act as he may determine to be necessary and proper.

(1) Procurement from any source, including Government stocks, of any commodity which he determines to be required for the furtherance of the purposes of this Act, and the term commodity as used in this Act shall mean any material, article, merchant vessel, supply, or goods necessary for the purposes of this Act.

(2) Processing, storing, transporting, and repairing any commodities, or performing any other services with respect to a participating country which he determines to be required for accomplishing the purposes of this Act.

(3) Procurement of and furnishing technical information and assistance.

(4) Chartering any merchant vessel owned by the United States which the United States Maritime Commission certifies as excess to its current requirements.

(5) Transfer of any commodity or service, which transfer shall be signified by delivery of the custody and right of possession and use of such commodity, or otherwise making available any such commodity, or by rendering a service, to a participating country or to any agency or organization representing a participating country: *Provided,* That merchant vessels, except as provided in subsection (d) of section ~~8~~ *12,* may not be transferred under authority of this Act otherwise than by charter: *And provided further,* That if a vessel of the United States is chartered under the provisions of this Act its documents as a vessel of the United States shall be surrendered and it shall, during the charter period, be considered as a foreign vessel for the purposes of the navigation and vessel-inspection laws of the United States.

(b) The Administrator may provide for the performance of any of the functions described in subsection (a) of this section—

~~(1) by making funds available in the form of advances or reimbursements to any participating country, or to any agency or organization representing a par-~~

~~ticipating country. Expenditures of advances made, or for which reimbursements are made, under authority of this paragraph for commodities or services procured outside the continental limits of the United States may be accounted for exclusively on such certification as the Administrator may prescribe to assure expenditure in furtherance of the purposes of this Act and such certification shall be binding on the accounting officers of the Government;~~

(1) by establishing accounts against which, under regulations prescribed by the Administrator—

(i) leters of commitment may be issued in connection with supply programs approved by the Administrator (and such letters of commitment, when issued, shall constitute obligations of applicable appropriations); and

(ii) withdrawals may be made by participating countries, or agencies or organizations representing participating countries, upon presentation of contracts, invoices, or other documentation specified by the Administrator.

Such accounts may be established on the books of the Administration, or any other department, agency, or establishment of the Government specified by the Administrator, or, on terms and conditions approved by the

Secretary of the Treasury, in banking institutions in the United States. Expenditures of funds which have been made available through accounts so established shall be accounted for on standard documentation required for expenditures of Government funds: Provided, That such expenditures for commodities or services procured outside the continental limits of the United States under authority of this paragraph may be accounted for exclusively on such certification as the Administrator may prescribe to assure expenditure in furtherance of the purposes of this Act, and such certification shall be binding on the accounting officers of the Government.

(2) by utilizing the services and facilities of any department, agency, or establishment of the Government as ~~he~~ *the President* shall direct, *or* with the consent of the head of such department, agency, or establishment, or, in ~~his~~ *the President's* discretion, by acting in cooperation with the United Nations or with other international organizations or with agencies of the participating countries, and funds allocated pursuant to this section to any department, agency, or establishment of the Government shall be established in separate appropriation accounts on the books of the Treasury;

(3) by making, under rules and regulations to be

prescribed by the Administrator, guaranties to any person of investments in connection with projects approved by the Administrator and the participating country concerned as furthering the purposes of this Act, which guaranties shall terminate not later than fourteen years from the date of enactment of this Act: *Provided*, That—

(i) the guaranty to any person shall not exceed the amount of dollars invested by such person in the project with the approval thereof by the Administrator and shall be limited to the transfer into United States dollars of other currencies or credits in such currencies received by such person as income from the approved investment, as repayment or return thereof, in whole or in part, or as compensation for the sale or disposition of all or any part thereof;

(ii) the total liabilities assumed under such guaranties shall not exceed 5 per centum of the total funds appropriated for the purposes of this Act *and any liabilities accruing under such guaranties shall be defrayed out of funds so appropriated*; and

(iii) as used in this paragraph, the term "person" means a citizen of the United States or any corporation, partnership, or other association created under the law of the United States or of any State or Territory and substantially beneficially owned by citizens of the United States.

(c) (i) The Administrator may provide assistance for any participating country, in the form and under the procedures authorized in subsections (a) and (b), respectively, of this section, through grants or upon payment in cash or on credit terms or on such other terms of payment as he may find appropriate, *including payment by the transfer to the United States under such terms and in such quantities as may be agreed to between the Government of the United States and the participating country of materials which are required by the United States as a result of deficiencies or potential deficiencies in its own ~~natural~~ resources.* In determining whether such assistance shall be through grants or upon terms of payment, and in determining the terms of payment, he shall act in consultation with the National Advisory Council on International Monetary and Financial Problems, and the determination whether or not a participating country should be required to make payment for any assistance furnished to such country in furtherance of the purposes of this Act, and the terms of such payment, if required, shall depend upon the capacity of such country to make such payments without jeopardizing the accomplishment of the purposes of this Act.

(ii) When it is determined that assistance should be extended under the provisions of this Act on credit terms, the Administrator shall allocate funds for the purpose to the Export-Import Bank of Washington, which shall, notwithstanding the provisions of the Export-Import Bank Act of 1945 (59 Stat. 526), as amended, make and administer the credit as directed, and on terms specified, by the Administrator in consultation with the said National Advisory Council. The Administrator shall make advances to or reimburse the Export-Import Bank of Washington for necessary administrative expenses in connection with such credits. The bank shall deposit into the Treasury of the United States as miscellaneous receipts amounts received by the bank in repayment of principal and interest of any such credits. Credits made by Export-Import Bank of Washington with funds so allocated to it by the Administrator shall not be considered in determining whether the bank has outstanding at any one time loans and guaranties to the extent of the limitation imposed by section 7 of the Export-Import Bank Act of 1945 (59 Stat. 529), as amended.

PROCUREMENT FROM GOVERNMENT AGENCIES

SEC. ~~8~~ *12.* (a) The Administrator, in the exercise of any authority conferred under section ~~7~~ *11* of this

Act, may procure (i) commodities owned by any department, agency, or establishment of the Government if the owning agency determines that such commodities are available for such procurement, and (ii) services from any department, agency, or establishment of the Government which the owning agency determines to be available for such procurement. The Administrator shall reimburse or pay, at replacement cost or, if required by law, at actual cost, or at such other price authorized by law agreed by the Administrator and the owning agency, out of funds available for the purposes of this Act, the owning or disposal agency, as the case may be, for such commodities or services. The amount of any reimbursement or payment to an owning agency for commodities or services so employed shall be credited to current applicable appropriations, funds, or accounts from which there may be procured replacements of similar commodities or such services and facilities: *Provided,* That where such appropriations, funds, or accounts are not reimbursable except by reason of the foregoing provision and when the head of the owning agency determines that replacement of any commodity employed under authority of this section is not necessary, any funds received in payment therefor shall be covered into the Treasury as miscellaneous receipts.

(b) Any commodity procured out of funds made available for the purposes of this Act may, in lieu of being transferred to a participating country, be disposed of for any other purpose authorized by law, whenever in the judgment of the Administrator the interests of the United States will best be served thereby. Funds realized from such disposal shall, upon approval of the Bureau of the Budget, revert to the respective appropriation or appropriations out of which funds were expended for the procurement of such commodity.

(c) The Administrator, in furtherance of the purposes of paragraph (5) of subsection (b) of section ~~10~~ *14*, and in agreement with a participating country, may promote, by means of funds made available for the purposes of this Act, an increase in the production in such participating country of materials which are required by the United States as a result of deficiencies or potential deficiencies in the natural resources of the United States.

(d) Whenever the Administrator shall determine that sale to a participating country, or to a citizen thereof, of any merchant vessel would be in furtherance of the purposes of this Act, and whenever the President shall so direct, the United States Maritime Commission shall effect such sale at the purchase price and under the terms specified in the Merchant Ship Sales Act of 1946 (60 Stat. 41), as amended,

85-743 O - 73 - 36

or other applicable law, and upon such additional terms and conditions as the Administrator may specify.

AUTHORIZATION OF APPROPRIATIONS

SEC. ~~9~~ *13.* (a) Notwithstanding the provisions of any other law, the Reconstruction Finance Corporation is authorized and directed, until such time as an appropriation shall be made pursuant to subsection (c) of this section, to make advances not to exceed in the aggregate ~~$500,000,000~~ *$1,000,000,000* to carry out the provisions of this Act, in such manner, at such time and in such amounts as the President shall determine, and no interest shall be charged on advances made by the Treasury to the Reconstruction Finance Corporation for this purpose. The Reconstruction Finance Corporation shall be repaid without interest from appropriations authorized under this Act for advances made by it hereunder.

(b) Such part as the President may determine of the unobligated and unexpended balances of appropriations or other funds available for the purposes of the Foreign Aid Act of 1947 shall be available for the purpose of carrying out the purposes of this Act.

(c) There are hereby authorized to be appropriated to the President, from time to time *through June 30, 1952,* out of any money in the Treasury not otherwise appropriated, such sums as may be necessary to carry out the provisions and accomplish the purposes of this Act: *Provided, however,* That for carrying out the provisions and accomplishing the purposes of this Act from the date of enactment of this Act through June 30, 1949, there are hereby authorized to be so appropriated not to exceed $6,800,000,000.

(d) Funds made available for the purposes of this Act shall be available for incurring and defraying all necessary expenses incident to carrying out the provisions of this Act, including ~~[illegible]~~ administrative expenses and expenses for compensation, allowances and travel of personnel, including Foreign Service personnel whose services are utilized primarily for the purposes of this Act, and, without regard to the provisions of any other law, for motor vehicles, typewriters, and printing and binding.

(e) The unexpended portions of any deposits which may have been made by any participating country pursuant to section 6 of the joint resolution providing for relief assistance to the people of countries devastated by war (Public Law 84, Eightieth Congress) and section 5 (b) of the Foreign Aid Act of 1947 (Public Law 389, Eightieth Congress) may be merged with the deposits to be made by such participating country in accordance with section ~~10~~ *14* (b) (6) of this Act, and shall be held or used under the same terms and conditions as are provided in section ~~10~~ *14* (b) (6) of this Act.

BILATERAL AND MULTILATERAL AGREEMENTS

SEC. ~~10~~ *14.* (a) The Secretary of State, after consultation with the Administrator, is authorized to conclude, with individual participating countries or any number of such countries or with an organization representing any such countries, agreements in furtherance of the purposes of this Act.

~~(b) As a condition precedent to the performance for any participating country of any of the functions authorized under this Act, such participating country shall conclude an agreement with the United States, which shall signify the adherence of such country to the purposes of this Act and, where applicable, shall make appropriate provision for—~~

(b) As a condition precedent to the performance for any participating country of any of the functions authorized under this Act, such country shall conclude an agreement with the United States providing for the adherence of such country to the purposes of this Act and containing commitments by such country to make reciprocal multilateral pledges to all of the participating countries, including, among others, undertakings by each country to participate in a joint program for European recovery based on self-help and mutual cooperation in which each country undertakes, among other things—

(1) to use all its efforts to develop its production to reach agreed targets;

(2) to apply all necessary measures leading to the rapid achievement of internal financial, monetary, and economic stability;

(3) to cooperate in all possible steps to reduce barriers to the expansion of trade;

(4) to remove progressively obstacles to the free movement of persons within Europe; and

(5) to set up by mutual agreement a joint organization to review progress achieved in the execution of the program and to insure to the fullest extent possible by joint action, the realization of the economic conditions necessary to the effective achievement of the general objectives to which each country has pledged itself.

(c) In addition to the provisions to be included pursuant to subsection (b) of this section, such agreement with the United States shall also, where applicable, make appropriate provision for—

(1) promoting industrial and agricultural production in order to enable the participating country to become independent of abnormal outside economic assistance;

(2) taking financial and monetary measures necessary to stabilize its currency, establish or maintain a proper rate of exchange, and generally to restore or maintain confidence in its monetary system;

(3) cooperating with other participating countries in facilitating and stimulating an increasing interchange of goods and services among the participating countries and with other countries and cooperating to reduce barriers to trade among themselves and with other countries;

(4) making efficient use, within the framework of a joint program for European recovery, of the resources of such participating country, including any commodities, facilities, or services furnished under this Act;

(5) facilitating the sale to the United States for stock-piling purposes, for such period of time as may be agreed to and upon reasonable terms and in reasonable quantities, of materials which are required by the United States as a result of deficiencies or potential deficiencies in its own natural resources, and which may be available in such participating country after due regard for reasonable requirements for domestic use and commercial export of such country;

(6) placing in a special account a deposit in the currency of such country, in commensurate amounts and under such terms and conditions as may be agreed to between such country and the Government of the United States, when any commodity or service is made available through any means authorized under this Act, and

is not furnished to the participating country on terms of payment. Such special account, together with the unexpended portions of any deposits which may have been made by such country pursuant to section 6 of the joint resolution providing for relief assistance to the people of countries devastated by war (Public Law 84, Eightieth Congress) and section 5 (b) of the Foreign Aid Act of 1947, shall be held or used only for such purposes as may be agreed to between such country and the Government of the United States, *and under agreement that any unencumbered balance remaining in such account on June 30, 1952, will be disposed of within such country for such purposes as may, subject to approval by Act or joint resolution of the Congress, be agreed to between such country and the Government of the United States*;

(7) publishing in such country and transmitting to the United States, not less frequently than every calendar quarter after the date of the agreement, of full statements of operations under the agreement, including a report of the use of funds, commodities and services received under this Act; and

(8) furnishing promptly, upon request of the United States, any relevant information which would be

of assistance to the United States in determining the nature and scope of ~~future~~ operations under this Act.

~~(c)~~ *(d)* Notwithstanding the provision of subsection (b) *or (c)* of this section, the Administrator, during the three months after the date of enactment of this Act, may perform with respect to any participating country any of the functions authorized under this Act which he may determine to be essential in furtherance of the purposes of this Act, provided that such country (i) has signified its adherence to the purposes of this Act and its intention to conclude an agreement pursuant to ~~subsection (b)~~ *subsections (b) and (c)* of this section, and (ii) he finds that such country is complying with the applicable provisions of subsection (b) *or (c)* of this section*: Provided, That, notwithstanding the provisions of this subsection, the Administrator may, through June 30, 1948,* ~~provide~~ *for the transfer of food, medical supplies, fibers, fuel, petroleum and petroleum products, fertilizer, pesticides, and seed to any country of Europe which participated in the Committee of European Economic Cooperation and which undertook pledges to the other participants therein, when the Administrator determines that the transfer of any such supplies to any such country is essential in order to make it possible to carry out the purposes of this Act by alleviating conditions of hunger and cold and by preventing serious economic retrogression.*

(e) The Administrator shall encourage the joint organization of the participating countries referred to in subsection (b) of section 14 of this Act to ensure that each participating country makes efficient use of the resources of such country, including any commodities, facilities, or services furnished under this Act, by observing and reviewing such use through an effective follow-up system approved by the joint organization.

TERMINATION OF ASSISTANCE

SEC. 15. The Administrator, in determining the form and measure of assistance provided under this Act to any participating country, shall take into account the extent to which such country is complying with its undertakings embodied in its pledges to other participating countries and in its agreement concluded with the United States under ~~this~~ section. The Administrator shall terminate the provision of assistance under this Act to any participating country whenever he determines that (1) such country is not adhering to its agreement concluded under ~~this~~ section, and that in the circumstances remedial action other than termination will not more effectively promote the purposes of this Act or (2) because of changed conditions, assistance is no longer consistent with the national interest of the United States.

EXEMPTION FROM CONTRACT AND ACCOUNTING LAWS

SEC. ~~11~~ *16*. When the President determines it to be in

furtherance of the purposes of this Act, the functions authorized under this Act may be performed without regard to such provisions of law regulating the making, performance, amendment, or modification of contracts and the expenditure of Government funds as the President may specify.

UNITED NATIONS

SEC. ~~12~~ *17.* (a) The President is authorized to request the cooperation of or the use of the services and facilities of the United Nations, its organs and specialized agencies or other international organizations, in carrying out the purposes of this Act, and may make payments, by advancements or reimbursements, for such purpose, out of funds made available for the purposes of this Act, as may be necessary therefor to the extent that special compensation is usually required for such services and facilities.

(b) The President shall ~~transmit~~ to the Secretary General of the United Nations copies of reports to Congress on the operations conducted under this Act.

(c) Any agreements concluded between the United States and participating countries or groups of such countries in implementation of the purposes of this Act shall be registered with the United Nations if such registration is required by the Charter of the United Nations.

~~SEC. 13. After June 30, 1952, or after the passage of a concurrent resolution by the two Houses before June 30,~~

~~1952, which declares that the powers conferred by or pursuant to section 7 of this Act are no longer necessary for the purposes of this Act, the Administrator shall not exercise any of the powers conferred by or pursuant to such section 7, except that through June 30, 1955, any of such powers may be exercised to the extent necessary to carry out an agreement with a participating country concluded before July 1, 1952, or before the passage of such concurrent resolution, whichever is the earlier, and funds made available for the purpose of this Act required to carry out any such agreement shall be deemed obligated as of the date of such agreement, and shall be available for expenditure to carry out such obligations through June 30, 1957, and funds made available for the purpose of this Act shall be available for the expenses of liquidating operations under this Act for such time as the Congress from time to time, in the Acts appropriating such funds, may authorize.~~

TERMINATION OF PROGRAM

SEC. 18. After June 30, 1952, or after the date of the passage of a concurrent resolution by the two Houses of Congress before such date, which declares that the powers conferred on the Administrator by or pursuant to subsection (a) of section 11 of this Act are no longer necessary for the accomplishment of the purposes of this Act, whichever shall first occur, none of the functions authorized under such pro-

visions of this Act may be exercised under authority of this Act: Provided, That

(a) during the twelve months following such date commodities and services with respect to which the Administrator had, prior to such date, authorized procurement for, shipment to or delivery in a participating country may be transferred to such country, and funds appropriated under authority of this Act may be obligated during such twelve-month period for the necessary expenses of procurement, shipment, delivery, and other activities essential to such transfer;

(b) at such time as the President shall find appropriate after such date, and prior to the expiration of the twenty-four months following such date, the powers, duties, and authority of the Administrator under this Act may be transferred to such other departments, agencies, or establishments of the Government as the President shall specify, and the relevant funds, records, and personnel of the Administration may be transferred to the departments, agencies, or establishments to which the related functions are transferred; and

(c) funds appropriated under the authority of this Act shall remain available not to exceed twenty-four months following such date, for the necessary expenses of liquidating operations under this Act, for such time

as the Congress from time to time, in the Acts appropriating such funds, may authorize.

REPORTS TO CONGRESS

SEC. ~~14~~ *19*. The President from time to time, but not less frequently than once every calendar quarter through June 30, 1952, and once every year thereafter, until ~~all funds made available for the purposes of this Act have been expended~~, shall transmit to the Congress a report of operations under this Act. Reports provided for under this section shall be transmitted to the Secretary of the Senate or the Clerk of the House of Representatives, as the case may be, if the Senate or the House of Representatives, as the case may be, is not in session.

JOINT CONGRESSIONAL COMMITTEE

SEC. 20. (a) There is hereby established a joint congressional committee to be known as the Joint Committee on Foreign Economic Cooperation (hereinafter referred to as the committee), and to be composed of seven Members of the Senate to be appointed by the President of the Senate, and seven Members of the House of Representatives to be appointed by the Speaker of the House. A vacancy in the membership of the committee shall be filled in the same manner as the original selection. The President of the Senate and the Speaker of the House, acting jointly, shall appoint a chair-

man and a vice chairman from among the members of the committee.

(b) It shall be the function of the committee to make a continuous study of the programs of United States economic assistance to foreign countries, and to review the progress achieved in the execution and administration of such programs. ~~The committee shall aid, to the extent it deems advisable, the several standing committees of the Congress having~~ legislative jurisdiction over any part of the programs of United States economic assistance to foreign countries; and it shall make a report to the Senate and the House of Representatives from time to time concerning the results of its studies, together with such recommendations as it may deem desirable. The Administrator shall consult with the committee from time to time with respect to his activities under this Act.

(c) The committee, or any duly authorized subcommittee thereof, is authorized to hold such hearings, to sit and act at such times and places, to require by subpena or otherwise the attendance of such witnesses and the production of such books, papers, and documents, to administer such oaths, to take such testimony, to procure such printing and binding, and to make such expenditures as it deems advisable. The cost of stenographic services to report such hearings shall not be in excess of 25 cents per hundred words. The pro-

visions of sections 102 to 104, inclusive, of the Revised Statutes shall apply in case of any failure of any witness to comply with any subpena or to testify when summoned under authority of this subsection.

(d) The committee is authorized to appoint and fix the compensation of such experts, consultants, technicians, and clerical and stenographic assistants as it deems necessary and advisable. The committee is authorized, with the consent of the head of the department or agency concerned, to utilize the services, information, facilities, and personnel of the departments and agencies of the Government.

(e) There are hereby authorized to be appropriated such sums as may be necessary to carry out the provisions of this section, to be disbursed by the Secretary of the Senate on vouchers signed by the chairman.

SEPARABILITY CLAUSE

SEC. ~~15~~ *21.* If any provision of this Act or the application of such provision to any circumstances or persons shall be held invalid, the validity of the remainder of the Act and the applicability of such provision to other circumstances or persons shall not be affected thereby.

Calendar No. 978

80th CONGRESS
2d Session

S. 2202

[Report No. 935]

IN THE SENATE OF THE UNITED STATES

February 23 (legislative day, February 2), 1948

Mr. Vandenberg (for himself and Mr. Connally) introduced the following bill; which was read twice and referred to the Committee on Foreign Relations

February 26 (legislative day, February 2), 1948

Reported by Mr. Vandenberg, without amendment

A BILL

To promote the general welfare, national interest, and foreign policy of the United States through necessary economic and financial assistance to foreign countries which undertake to cooperate with each other in the establishment and maintenance of economic conditions essential to a peaceful and prosperous world.

Be it enacted by the Senate and House of Representatives of the United States of America in Congress assembled, That this Act may be cited as "The Economic Cooperation Act of 1948".

FINDINGS AND DECLARATION OF POLICY

Sec. 2. (a) Recognizing the intimate economic and other relationships between the United States and the nations of

Europe, and recognizing that disruption following in the wake of war is not contained by national frontiers, the Congress finds that the existing situation in Europe endangers the establishment of a lasting peace, the general welfare and national interest of the United States, and the attainment of the objectives of the United Nations. The restoration or maintenance in European countries of principles of individual liberty, free institutions, and genuine independence rests largely upon the establishment of sound economic conditions, stable international economic relationships, and the achievement by the countries of Europe of a healthy economy independent of extraordinary outside assistance. The accomplishment of these objectives calls for a plan of European recovery, open to all such nations which cooperate in such plan, based upon a strong production effort, the expansion of foreign trade, the creation and maintenance of internal financial stability, and the development of economic cooperation, including all possible steps to establish and maintain equitable rates of exchange and to bring about the progressive elimination of trade barriers. Mindful of the advantages which the United States has enjoyed through the existence of a large domestic market with no internal trade barriers, and believing that similar advantages can accrue to the countries of Europe, it is the hope of the people of the United States that these countries through a joint organization will

85-743 O - 73 - 37

exert sustained common efforts which will speedily achieve that economic cooperation in Europe which is essential for lasting peace and prosperity. Accordingly, it is declared to be the policy of the people of the United States to sustain and strengthen principles of individual liberty, free institutions, and genuine independence in Europe through assistance to those countries of Europe which participate in a joint recovery program based upon self-help and mutual cooperation: *Provided,* That no assistance to the participating countries herein contemplated shall seriously impair the economic stability of the United States. It is further declared to be the policy of the United States that continuity of assistance provided by the United States should, at all times, be dependent upon continuity of cooperation among countries participating in the program.

PURPOSES OF ACT

(b) It is the purpose of this Act to effectuate the policy set forth in subsection (a) of this section by furnishing material and financial assistance to the participating countries in such a manner as to aid them, through their own individual and concerted efforts, to become independent of extraordinary outside economic assistance within the period of operations under this Act, by—

(1) promoting industrial and agricultural production in the participating countries;

(2) furthering the restoration or maintenance of the soundness of European currencies, budgets, and finances; and

(3) facilitating and stimulating the growth of international trade of participating countries with one another and with other countries by appropriate measures including reduction of barriers which may hamper such trade.

PARTICIPATING COUNTRIES

SEC. 3. As used in this Act, the term "participating country" means—

(a) any country, together with dependent areas under its administration, which signed the report of the Committee of European Economic Cooperation at Paris on September 22, 1947; and

(b) any other country (including any of the zones of occupation of Germany, any areas under international administration or control, and the Free Territory of Trieste or either of its zones) wholly or partly in Europe, together with dependent areas under its administration;

provided such country adheres to, and for so long as it remains an adherent to, a joint program for European recovery designed to accomplish the purposes of this Act.

ESTABLISHMENT OF ECONOMIC COOPERATION ADMINISTRATION

SEC. 4. (a) There is hereby established, with its principal office in the District of Columbia, an agency of the Government which shall be known as the Economic Cooperation Administration, hereinafter referred to as the Administration. The Administration shall be headed by an Administrator for Economic Cooperation, hereinafter referred to as the Administrator, who shall be appointed by the President, by and with the advice and consent of the Senate, and who shall receive compensation at the rate of $20,000 per annum. The Administrator shall be responsible to the President and shall have a status in the executive branch of the Government comparable to that of the head of an executive department. Except as otherwise provided in this Act, the administration of the provisions of this Act is hereby vested in the Administrator and his functions shall be performed under the control of the President.

(b) There shall be in the Administration a Deputy Administrator for Economic Cooperation who shall be appointed by the President, by and with the advice and consent of the Senate, and shall receive compensation at the rate of $17,500 per annum. The Deputy Administrator for Economic Cooperation shall perform such functions as the

Administrator shall designate, and shall be Acting Administrator for Economic Cooperation during the absence or disability of the Administrator or in the event of a vacancy in the office of Administrator.

(c) The President is authorized, pending the appointment and qualification of the first Administrator or Deputy Administrator for Economic Cooperation appointed hereunder, to provide, for a period of not to exceed thirty days after the date of enactment of this Act, for the performance of the functions of the Administrator under this Act through such departments, agencies, or establishments of the United States Government as he may direct. In the event the President nominates an Administrator or Deputy Administrator prior to the expiration of such thirty-day period, the authority conferred upon the President by this subsection shall be extended beyond such thirty-day period but only until an Administrator or Deputy Administrator qualifies and takes office.

(d) Any department, agency, or establishment of the Government (including, whenever used in this Act, any corporation which is an instrumentality of the United States) performing functions under this Act is authorized to employ, for duty within the continental limits of the United States, such personnel as may be necessary to carry out the provisions and purposes of this Act, and funds available pursuant to section 14 of this Act shall be available for personal services in the District of Columbia and elsewhere without regard to section 14 (a) of the Federal Employees Pay Act of 1946 (60 Stat. 219). Of such personnel employed by the Administration, not to exceed sixty may be compensated without regard to the provisions of the Classification Act of 1923, as amended, of whom not more than ten may be compensated at a rate in excess of $10,000 per annum, but not in excess of $15,000 per annum. Experts and consultants or organizations thereof, as authorized by section 15 of the Act of August 2, 1946 (U. S. C., title 5, sec. 55a), may be employed by the Administration, and individuals so employed may be compensated at rates not in excess of $50 per diem and while away from their homes or regular places of business, they may be paid actual travel expenses and not to exceed $10 per diem in lieu of subsistence and other expenses while so employed.

(e) The head of any department, agency, or establishment of the Government performing functions under this Act may, from time to time, promulgate such rules and regulations as may be necessary and proper to carry out his functions under this Act, and he may delegate authority to perform any of such functions to his subordinates, acting under his direction and under rules and regulations promulgated by him.

GENERAL FUNCTIONS OF ADMINISTRATOR

SEC. 5. (a) The Administrator, under the control of the President, shall in addition to all other functions vested in him by this Act—

(1) review and appraise the requirements of participating countries for assistance under the terms of this Act;

(2) formulate programs of United States assistance under this Act, including approval of specific projects which have been submitted to him by the participating countries;

(3) provide for the efficient execution of any such programs as may be placed in operation; and

(4) terminate provision of assistance or take other remedial action as provided in section 17 of this Act.

(b) In order to strengthen and make more effective the conduct of the foreign relations of the United States—

(1) the Administrator and the Secretary of State shall keep each other fully and currently informed on matters, including prospective action, arising within the scope of their respective duties which are pertinent to the duties of the other;

(2) whenever the Secretary of State believes that any action, proposed action, or failure to act on the part

of the Administrator is inconsistent with the foreign-policy objectives of the United States, he shall consult with the Administrator and, if differences of view are not adjusted by consultation, the matter shall be referred to the President for final decision.

NATIONAL ADVISORY COUNCIL

SEC. 6. Section 4 (a) of the Bretton Woods Agreement Act (59 Stat. 512, 513) is hereby amended to read as follows:

"SEC. 4. (a) In order to coordinate the policies and operations of the representatives of the United States on the Fund and the Bank and of all agencies of the Government which make or participate in making foreign loans or which engage in foreign financial exchange or monetary transactions, there is hereby established the National Advisory Council on International Monetary and Financial Problems (hereinafter referred to as the 'Council'), consisting of the Secretary of Treasury as Chairman, the Secretary of State, the Secretary of Commerce, the Chairman of the Board of Governors of the Federal Reserve System, the Chairman of the Board of Trustees of the Export-Import Bank of Washington, and during such period as the Economic Cooperation Administration shall continue to exist, the Administrator for Economic Cooperation."

PUBLIC ADVISORY BOARD

SEC. 7. (a) There is hereby created a Public Advisory Board, hereinafter referred to as the Board, which shall advise and consult with the Administrator with respect to general or basic policy matters arising in connection with the Administrator's discharge of his responsibilities. The Board shall consist of the Administrator, who shall be Chairman, and not to exceed twelve additional members to be appointed by the President, by and with the advice and consent of the Senate, and who shall be selected from among citizens of the United States of broad and varied experience in matters affecting the public interest, other than officers and employees of the United States (including any agency or instrumentality of the United States) who, as such, regularly receive compensation for current services. The Board shall meet at least once a month and at other times upon the call of the Administrator or when three or more members of the Board request the Administrator to call a meeting. Not more than a majority of two of the members shall be appointed to the Board from the same political party. Members of the Board, other than the Administrator, shall receive, out of funds made available for the purposes of this Act, a per diem allowance of $50 for each day spent away from their homes or regular places of business, for the purpose of attendance at meetings of the Board, or at conferences held upon the call of the Administrator, and in necessary travel, and while so engaged, they may be paid actual travel expenses and not to exceed $10 per diem in lieu of subsistence and other expenses.

(b) The Administrator may appoint such other advisory committees as he may determine to be necessary or desirable to effectuate the purposes of this Act.

UNITED STATES SPECIAL REPRESENTATIVE ABROAD

SEC. 8. There shall be a United States Special Representative in Europe who shall (a) be appointed by the President, by and with the advice and consent of the Senate, (b) be entitled to receive the same compensation and allowances as a chief of mission, class 1, within the meaning of the Act of August 13, 1946 (60 Stat. 999), and (c) have the rank of ambassador extraordinary and plenipotentiary. He shall be the chief United States representative to any organization of participating countries which may be established by such countries to further a joint program for European recovery, and shall discharge in Europe such additional responsibilities as may be assigned to him with the approval of the President in furtherance of the purposes of this Act. He may also be designated as the United States representative on the Economic Commission for Europe. He shall keep the Administrator, the Secretary of State, the chiefs of the United States diplomatic missions, and the chiefs of the special missions provided for in section 9 of this Act currently informed concerning his activities. He shall consult with the chiefs of all such missions, who shall give him such cooperation as he may require for the performance of his duties under this Act.

SPECIAL ECA MISSIONS ABROAD

SEC. 9. (a) There shall be established in each participating country, except as provided in subsection (d) of this section, a special mission for economic cooperation under the direction of a chief who shall be responsible for assuring the performance within such country of operations under this Act. The chief shall be appointed by the Administrator, shall receive his instructions from the Administrator, and shall report to the Administrator on the performance of the duties assigned to him. The chief of the special mission shall take rank immediately after the chief of the United States diplomatic mission in such country.

(b) The chief of the special mission shall keep the chief of the United States diplomatic mission fully and currently informed on matters, including prospective action, arising within the scope of the operations of the special mission and the chief of the diplomatic mission shall keep the chief of the special mission fully and currently informed on matters relative to the conduct of the duties of the chief of the special mission. The chief of the United States diplomatic mission will be responsible for assuring that the operations of the special mission are consistent with the foreign-policy objectives of the United States in such country and to that end whenever the chief of the United States diplomatic mission believes that any action, proposed action, or failure to act on the part of the special mission is inconsistent with such foreign-policy objectives, he shall so advise the chief of the special mission. If differences of view are not adjusted by consultation, the matter shall be referred to the Secretary of State and the Administrator for decision.

(c) The Secretary of State shall provide such office space, facilities, and other administrative services for the United States Special Representative in Europe and his staff, and for the special mission in each participating country, as may be agreed between the Secretary of State and the Administrator.

(d) With respect to any of the zones of occupation of Germany and of the Free Territory of Trieste, during the period of occupation, the President shall make appropriate administrative arrangements for the conduct of operations under this Act, in order to enable the Administrator to carry out his responsibility to assure the accomplishment of the purposes of this Act.

PERSONNEL OUTSIDE UNITED STATES

SEC. 10. (a) For the purpose of performing functions

under this Act outside the continental limits of the United States the Administrator may—

(1) employ persons who shall receive compensation at any of the rates provided for the Foreign Service Reserve and Staff by the Foreign Service Act of 1946 (60 Stat. 999), together with allowances and benefits established thereunder; and

(2) recommend the appointment or assignment of persons, and the Secretary of State may appoint or assign such persons, to any class in the Foreign Service Reserve or Staff for the duration of operations under this Act, and the Secretary of State may thereafter assign, transfer, or promote such persons upon the recommendation of the Administrator. Persons so appointed to the Foreign Service Staff shall be entitled to the benefits of section 528 of the Foreign Service Act of 1946.

(b) For the purpose of performing functions under this Act outside the continental limits of the United States, the Secretary of State may, at the request of the Administrator, appoint, for the duration of operations under this Act, alien clerks and employees in accordance with applicable provisions of the Foreign Service Act of 1946 (60 Stat. 999).

(c) Civilian personnel who are citizens or residents of the United States employed or appointed pursuant to this section to perform functions under this Act shall be investigated by the Federal Bureau of Investigation which shall make a report thereof to the appointing authority as soon as possible: *Provided, however,* That they may temporarily assume their posts and perform their functions after preliminary investigation and clearance by the Administrator or the Secretary of State, as the case may be, but such employment may be terminated after the receipt of the report of the Federal Bureau of Investigation.

NATURE AND METHOD OF ASSISTANCE

SEC. 11. (a) The Administrator may, from time to time, furnish assistance to any participating country by providing for the performance of any of the functions set forth in paragraphs (1) through (5) of this subsection when he deems it to be in furtherance of the purposes of this Act, and upon the terms and conditions set forth in this Act and such additional terms and conditions consistent with the provisions of this Act as he may determine to be necessary and proper.

(1) Procurement from any source, including Government stocks, of any commodity which he determines to be required for the furtherance of the purposes of this Act. As used in this Act, the term "commodity" means any commodity, material, article, merchant vessel authorized to be chartered under paragraph (4) of this

subsection, supply, or goods necessary for the purposes of this Act.

(2) Processing, storing, transporting, and repairing any commodities, or performing any other services with respect to a participating country which he determines to be required for accomplishing the purposes of this Act.

(3) Procurement of and furnishing technical information and assistance.

(4) With the approval of the President, placing in operating condition, and, for periods not extending beyond December 31, 1952, chartering to participating countries, not more than three hundred dry-cargo merchant vessels owned by the United States and not in operation at the time of charter. If a vessel of the United States is so chartered, its documents as a vessel of the United States shall be surrendered and it shall, during the charter period, be considered as a foreign vessel for the purposes of the navigation and vessel-inspection laws of the United States.

(5) Transfer of any commodity or service, which transfer shall be signified by delivery of the custody and right of possession and use of such commodity, or otherwise making available any such commodity, or by rendering a service to a participating country or to any

agency or organization representing a participating country.

(b) The Administrator may provide for the performance of any of the functions described in subsection (a) of this section—

(1) by establishing accounts against which, under regulations prescribed by the Administrator—

(i) letters of commitment may be issued in connection with supply programs approved by the Administrator (and such letters of commitment, when issued, shall constitute obligations of applicable appropriations); and

(ii) withdrawals may be made by participating countries, or agencies or organizations representing participating countries, upon presentation of contracts, invoices, or other documentation specified by the Administrator.

Such accounts may be established on the books of the Administration, or any other department, agency, or establishment of the Government specified by the Administrator, or, on terms and conditions approved by the Secretary of the Treasury, in banking institutions in the United States. Expenditures of funds which have been made available through accounts so established shall be accounted for on standard documentation required for expenditures of Government funds: *Provided,* That such expenditures for commodities or services procured outside the continental limits of the United States under authority of this section may be accounted for exclusively on such certification as the Administrator may prescribe to assure expenditure in furtherance of the purposes of this Act, and such certification shall be binding on the accounting officers of the Government.

(2) by utilizing the services and facilities of any department, agency, or establishment of the Government as the President shall direct, or with the consent of the head of such department, agency, or establishment, or, in the President's discretion, by acting in coöperation with the United Nations or with other international organizations or with agencies of the participating countries, and funds allocated pursuant to this section to any department, agency, or establishment of the Government shall be established in separate appropriation accounts on the books of the Treasury.

(3) by making, under rules and regulations to be prescribed by the Administrator, guaranties to any person of investments in connection with projects approved by the Administrator and the participating country concerned as furthering the purposes of this Act,

85-743 O - 73 - 38

which guaranties shall terminate not later than fourteen years from the date of enactment of this Act: *Provided*, That—

(i) the guaranty to any person shall not exceed the amount of dollars invested in the project by such person with the approval of the Administrator and shall be limited to the transfer into United States dollars of other currencies, or credits in such currencies, received by such person as income from the approved investment, as repayment or return thereof, in whole or in part, or as compensation for the sale or disposition of all or any part thereof;

(ii) the total liabilities assumed under such guaranties shall not exceed 5 per centum of the total funds appropriated for the purposes of this Act and any liabilities accruing under such guaranties shall be defrayed within the limits of funds so appropriated; and

(iii) as used in this paragraph, the term "person" means a citizen of the United States or any corporation, partnership, or other association created under the law of the United States or of any State or Territory and substantially beneficially owned by citizens of the United States.

(c) (1) The Administrator may provide assistance for any participating country, in the form and under the procedures authorized in subsections (a) and (b), respectively, of this section, through grants or upon payment in cash, or on credit terms, or on such other terms of payment as he may find appropriate, including payment by the transfer to the United States (under such terms and in such quantities as may be agreed to between the Administrator and the participating country) of materials which are required by the United States as a result of deficiencies or potential deficiencies in its own resources. In determining whether such assistance shall be through grants or upon terms of payment, and in determining the terms of payment, he shall act in consultation with the National Advisory Council on International Monetary and Financial Problems, and the determination whether or not a participating country should be required to make payment for any assistance furnished to such country in furtherance of the purposes of this Act, and the terms of such payment, if required, shall depend upon the character and purpose of the assistance and upon the capacity of such country to make such payments without jeopardizing the accomplishment of the purposes of this Act.

(2) When it is determined that assistance should be extended under the provisions of this Act on credit terms, the Administrator shall allocate funds for the purpose to

the Export-Import Bank of Washington, which shall, notwithstanding the provisions of the Export-Import Bank Act of 1945 (59 Stat. 526), as amended, make and administer the credit as directed, and on terms specified, by the Administrator in consultation with the National Advisory Council on International Monetary and Financial Problems. The Administrator shall make advances to, or reimburse, the Export-Import Bank of Washington for necessary administrative expenses in connection with such credits. The Bank shall deposit into the Treasury of the United States, as miscellaneous receipts, amounts received by the Bank in repayment of principal and interest on any such credits. Credits made by the Export-Import Bank of Washington with funds so allocated to it by the Administrator shall not be considered in determining whether the Bank has outstanding at any one time loans and guaranties to the extent of the limitation imposed by section 7 of the Export-Import Bank Act of 1945 (59 Stat. 529), as amended.

PROTECTION OF DOMESTIC ECONOMY

SEC. 12. (a) The Administrator shall provide for the procurement in the United States of commodities under this Act in such a way as to (1) minimize the drain upon the resources of the United States and the impact of such procurement upon the domestic economy, and (2) avoid impairing the fulfillment of vital needs of the people of the United States.

(b) The procurement of petroleum and petroleum products under this Act shall, to the maximum extent practicable, be made from petroleum sources outside the United States; and, in furnishing commodities under the provisions of this Act, the Administrator shall take fully into account the present and anticipated world shortage of petroleum and its products and the consequent undesirability of expansion in petroleum-consuming equipment where the use of alternate fuels or other sources of power is practicable.

(c) In procuring from sources within the United States any agricultural commodity not in short supply in the United States for transfer by grant to any participating country in accordance with the requirements of such country, the Administrator shall, insofar as practicable and where in furtherance of the purposes of this Act, provide for the procurement of an amount of each class or type of any such commodity in approximate proportion to the total exportable supply of such class or type of such commodity.

REIMBURSEMENT TO GOVERNMENT AGENCIES

SEC. 13. (a) The Administrator shall make reimbursement or payment, out of funds available for the purposes of this Act, for any commodity, service, or facility procured under section 11 of this Act from any department, agency, or establishment of the Government. Such reimbursement or payment shall be made to the owning or disposal agency, as the case may be, at replacement cost, or, if required by law, at actual cost, or at any other price authorized by law and agreed to between the Administrator and such agency. The amount of any reimbursement or payment to an owning agency for commodities, services, or facilities so procured shall be credited to current applicable appropriations, funds, or accounts from which there may be procured replacements of similar commodities or such services or facilities: *Provided,* That such commodities, services, or facilities may be procured from an owning agency only with the consent of such agency: *And provided further,* That where such appropriations, funds, or accounts are not reimbursable except by reason of this subsection, and when the owning agency determines that replacement of any commodity procured under authority of this section is not necessary, any funds received in payment therefor shall be covered into the Treasury as miscellaneous receipts.

(b) The Administrator, whenever in his judgment the interests of the United States will best be served thereby, may dispose of any commodity procured out of funds made available for the purposes of this Act, in lieu of transferring such commodity to a participating country, (1) by transfer of such commodity, upon reimbursement, to any department, agency, or establishment of the Government for use or disposal by such department, agency, or establishment as authorized by law, or (2) without regard to provisions of law relating to the disposal of Government-owned property, when necessary to prevent spoilage or wastage of such commodity or to conserve the usefulness thereof. Funds realized from such disposal or transfer shall revert to the respective appropriation or appropriations out of which funds were expended for the procurement of such commodity.

AUTHORIZATION OF APPROPRIATIONS

SEC. 14. (a) Notwithstanding the provisions of any other law, the Reconstruction Finance Corporation is authorized and directed, until such time as an appropriation shall be made pursuant to subsection (c) of this section, to make advances not to exceed in the aggregate $1,000,000,000 to carry out the provisions of this Act, in such manner, at such time and in such amounts as the President shall determine, and no interest shall be charged on advances made by the Treasury to the Reconstruction Finance Corporation for this purpose. The Reconstruction Finance Corporation shall be repaid without interest from appropriations authorized under this Act for advances made by it hereunder.

(b) Such part as the President may determine of the unobligated and unexpended balances of appropriations or other funds available for the purposes of the Foreign Aid Act of 1947 shall be available for the purpose of carrying out the purposes of this Act.

(c) In order to carry out the provisions of this Act with respect to those participating countries which adhere to the purposes of this Act, and remain eligible to receive assistance hereunder, there are hereby authorized to be appropriated to the President, from time to time through June 30, 1952, out of any money in the Treasury not otherwise appropriated, such sums as may be necessary to carry out the provisions and accomplish the purposes of this Act: *Provided, however,* That for carrying out the provisions and accomplishing the purposes of this Act for the period of one year following the date of enactment of this Act, there are hereby authorized to be so appropriated not to exceed $5,300,000,000.

(d) Funds made available for the purposes of this Act shall be available for incurring and defraying all necessary expenses incident to carrying out the provisions of this Act, including administrative expenses and expenses for compensation, allowances and travel of personnel, including Foreign Service personnel whose services are utilized primarily for the purposes of this Act, and, without regard to the provisions of any other law, for printing and binding, and for expenditures outside the continental limits of the

United States for the procurement of supplies and services and for other administrative purposes (other than compensation of personnel) without regard to such laws and regulations governing the obligation and expenditure of government funds, as the Administrator shall specify in the interest of the accomplishment of the purposes of this Act.

(e) The unexpended portions of any deposits which may have been made by any participating country pursuant to section 6 of the joint resolution providing for relief assistance to the people of countries devastated by war (Public Law 84, Eightieth Congress) and section 5 (b) of the Foreign Aid Act of 1947 (Public Law 389, Eightieth Congress) may be merged with the deposits to be made by such participating country in accordance with section 15 (b) (6) of this Act, and shall be held or used under the same terms and conditions as are provided in section 15 (b) (6) of this Act.

(f) In order to reserve some part of the surplus of the fiscal year 1948 for payments thereafter to be made under this Act, there is hereby created on the books of the Treasury of the United States a trust fund to be known as the Foreign Economic Cooperation Trust Fund. Notwithstanding any other provision of law, an amount of $3,000,000,000, out of sums appropriated pursuant to the authorization contained in this Act shall, when appropriated, be transferred immediately to the trust fund, and shall thereupon be considered as expended during the fiscal year 1948, for the purpose of reporting governmental expenditures. The Secretary of the Treasury shall be the sole trustee of the trust fund and is authorized and directed to pay out of the fund such amounts as the Administrator shall duly requisition. The first expenditures made out of the appropriations authorized under this Act in the fiscal year 1949 shall be made with funds requisitioned by the Administrator out of the trust fund until the fund is exhausted, at which time such fund shall cease to exist. The provisions of this subsection shall not be construed as affecting the application of any provision of law which would otherwise govern the obligation of funds so appropriated or the auditing or submission of accounts of transactions with respect to such funds.

BILATERAL AND MULTILATERAL UNDERTAKINGS

SEC. 15. (a) The Secretary of State, after consultation with the Administrator, is authorized to conclude, with individual participating countries or any number of such countries or with an organization representing any such countries, agreements in furtherance of the purposes of this Act.

(b) The provision of assistance under this Act results from the multilateral pledges of the participating countries to use all their efforts to accomplish a joint recovery program based upon self-help and mutual cooperation as embodied in the report of the Committee of European Economic Cooperation signed at Paris on September 22, 1947, and is contingent upon continuous effort of the participating countries to accomplish a joint recovery program through multilateral undertakings and the establishment of a continuing organization for this purpose. In addition to continued mutual cooperation of the participating countries in such a program, each such country shall conclude an agreement with the United States in order for such country to be eligible to receive assistance under this Act. Such agreement shall provide for the adherence of such country to the purposes of this Act and shall, where applicable, make appropriate provision, among others, for—

(1) promoting industrial and agricultural production in order to enable the participating country to become independent of extraordinary outside economic assistance; and submitting for the approval of the Administrator, upon his request and whenever he deems it in furtherance of the purposes of this Act, specific projects proposed by such country to be undertaken in substantial part with assistance furnished under this Act, which projects, whenever practicable, shall include projects for increased production of coal, steel, transportation facilities, and food;

(2) taking financial and monetary measures neces-

sary to stabilize its currency, establish or maintain a valid rate of exchange, to balance its governmental budget as soon as practicable, and generally to restore or maintain confidence in its monetary system;

(3) cooperating with other participating countries in facilitating and stimulating an increasing interchange of goods and services among the participating countries and with other countries and cooperating to reduce barriers to trade among themselves and with other countries;

(4) making efficient and practical use, within the framework of a joint program for European recovery, of the resources of such participating country, including any commodities, facilities, or services furnished under this Act, which use shall include, to the extent practicable, taking measures to locate and control, in furtherance of such program, assets, and earnings therefrom, which belong to the citizens of such country and which are situated within the United States, its Territories and possessions;

(5) facilitating the transfer to the United States by sale, exchange, barter, or otherwise for stock-piling purposes, for such period of time as may be agreed to and upon reasonable terms and in reasonable quantities, of materials which are required by the United States as a

result of deficiencies or potential deficiencies in its own resources, and which may be available in such participating country after due regard for reasonable requirements for domestic use and commercial export of such country;

(6) placing in a special account a deposit in the currency of such country, in commensurate amounts and under such terms and conditions as may be agreed to between such country and the Government of the United States, when any commodity or service is made available through any means authorized under this Act, and is not furnished to the participating country on terms of payment. Such special account, together with the unexpended portions of any deposits which may have been made by such country pursuant to section 6 of the joint resolution providing for relief assistance to the people of countries devastated by war (Public Law 84, Eightieth Congress) and section 5 (b) of the Foreign Aid Act of 1947 (Public Law 389, Eightieth Congress), shall be held or used only for such purposes as may be agreed to between such country and the Administrator in consultation with the National Advisory Council on International Monetary and Financial Problems, and under agreement that any unencumbered balance remaining in such account on June 30, 1952, will be disposed of within such country for such purposes as may, subject

to approval by Act or joint resolution of the Congress, be agreed to between such country and the Government of the United States;

(7) publishing in such country and transmitting to the United States, not less frequently than every calendar quarter after the date of the agreement, full statements of operations under the agreement, including a report of the use of funds, commodities and services received under this Act; and

(8) furnishing promptly, upon request of the United States, any relevant information which would be of assistance to the United States in determining the nature and scope of operations and the use of assistance provided under this Act.

(c) Notwithstanding the provisions of subsection (b) of this section, the Administrator, during the three months after the date of enactment of this Act, may perform with respect to any participating country any of the functions authorized under this Act which he may determine to be essential in furtherance of the purposes of this Act, if such country (1) has signified its adherence to the purposes of this Act and its intention to conclude an agreement pursuant to subsection (b) of this section, and (2) he finds that such country is complying with the applicable provisions of subsection (b) of this section:

Provided, That, notwithstanding the provisions of this subsection, the Administrator may, through June 30, 1948, provide for the transfer of food, medical supplies, fibers, fuel, petroleum and petroleum products, fertilizer, pesticides, and seed to any country of Europe which participated in the Committee of European Economic Cooperation and which undertook pledges to the other participants therein, when the Administrator determines that the transfer of any such supplies to any such country is essential in order to make it possible to carry out the purposes of this Act by alleviating conditions of hunger and cold and by preventing serious economic retrogression.

(d) The Administrator shall encourage the joint organization of the participating countries referred to in subsection (b) of this section to ensure that each participating country makes efficient use of the resources of such country, including any commodities, facilities, or services furnished under this Act, by observing and reviewing such use through an effective follow-up system approved by the joint organization.

MATERIALS REQUIRED BY THE UNITED STATES

SEC. 16. The Administrator, in furtherance of the purposes of section 15 (b) (5), and in agreement with a participating country, may promote, by means of funds made available for the purposes of this Act, an increase in the production in such participating country of materials which are required by the United States as a result of deficiencies or potential deficiencies in the resources within the United States.

TERMINATION OF ASSISTANCE

SEC. 17. The Administrator, in determining the form and measure of assistance provided under this Act to any participating country, shall take into account the extent to which such country is complying with its undertakings embodied in its pledges to other participating countries and in its agreement concluded with the United States under section 15. The Administrator shall terminate the provision of assistance under this Act to any participating country whenever he determines that (1) such country is not adhering to its agreement concluded under section 15, or is diverting from the purposes of this Act assistance provided hereunder, and that in the circumstances remedial action other than termination will not more effectively promote the purposes of this Act or (2) because of changed conditions, assistance is no longer consistent with the national interest of the United States.

EXEMPTION FROM CONTRACT AND ACCOUNTING LAWS

SEC. 18. When the President determines it to be in furtherance of the purposes of this Act, the functions authorized under this Act may be performed without regard to such provisions of law regulating the making, performance, amendment, or modification of contracts and the expenditure of Government funds as the President may specify.

EXEMPTION FROM CERTAIN FEDERAL LAWS RELATING TO EMPLOYMENT

SEC. 19. Service of an individual as a member of the Public Advisory Board (other than the Administrator) created by section 7 (a), as a member of an advisory committee appointed pursuant to section 7 (b), as an expert or consultant under section 4 (d), or as an expert, consultant, or technician under section 23 (d), shall not be considered as service or employment bringing such individual within the provisions of sections 109 or 113 of the Criminal Code (U. S. C., title 18, secs. 198 and 203), of section 190 of the Revised Statutes (U. S. C., title 5, sec. 99), or of section 19 (e) of the Contract Settlement Act of 1944, or of any other Federal law imposing restrictions, requirements, or penalties in relation to the employment of persons, the performance of services, or the payment or receipt of compensation in connection with any claim, proceeding, or matter involving the United States.

UNITED NATIONS

SEC. 20. (a) The President is authorized to request the cooperation of or the use of the services and facilities of the United Nations, its organs and specialized agencies, or other international organizations, in carrying out the purposes of this Act, and may make payments, by advancements or reimbursements, for such purpose, out of funds made available for the purposes of this Act, as may be necessary therefor, to the extent that special compensation is usually required for such services and facilities.

(b) The President shall cause to be transmitted to the Secretary General of the United Nations copies of reports to Congress on the operations conducted under this Act.

(c) Any agreements concluded between the United States and participating countries, or groups of such countries, in implementation of the purposes of this Act, shall be registered with the United Nations if such registration is required by the Charter of the United Nations.

TERMINATION OF PROGRAM

SEC. 21. (a) After June 30, 1952, or after the date of the passage of a concurrent resolution by the two Houses of Congress before such date, which declares that the powers conferred on the Administrator by or pursuant to subsection (a) of section 11 of this Act are no longer necessary for the accomplishment of the purposes of this Act, whichever shall first occur, none of the functions authorized under such provisions may be exercised; except that during the twelve months following such date commodities and services with respect to which the Administrator had, prior to such date, authorized procurement for, shipment to, or delivery in a participating country, may be transferred to such country, and funds appropriated under authority of this Act may be obligated during such twelve-month period for the necessary expenses of procurement, shipment, delivery, and other activities essential to such transfer, and shall remain available during such period for the necessary expenses of liquidating operations under this Act.

(b) At such time as the President shall find appropriate after such date, and prior to the expiration of the twelve months following such date, the powers, duties, and authority of the Administrator under this Act may be transferred to such other departments, agencies, or establishments of the Government as the President shall specify, and the relevant funds, records, and personnel of the Administration may be transferred to the departments, agencies, or establishments to which the related functions are transferred.

REPORTS TO CONGRESS

SEC. 22. The President from time to time, but not less frequently than once every calendar quarter through June 30, 1952, and once every year thereafter until all operations under this Act have been completed, shall transmit to the Congress a report of operations under this Act. Reports provided for under this section shall be transmitted to the Secretary of the Senate or the Clerk of the House of Representatives, as the case may be, if the Senate or the House of Representatives, as the case may be, is not in session.

JOINT CONGRESSIONAL COMMITTEE

SEC. 23. (a) There is hereby established a joint congressional committee to be known as the Joint Committee on Foreign Economic Cooperation (hereinafter referred to as the committee), and to be composed of seven Members of the Senate to be appointed by the President of the Senate, and seven Members of the House of Representatives to be appointed by the Speaker of the House. In each instance, not more than four members shall be members of the same political party. A vacancy in the membership of the committee shall be filled in the same manner as the original selection. The President of the Senate and the Speaker of the House, acting jointly, shall appoint a chairman and a vice chairman from among the members of the committee.

(b) It shall be the function of the committee to make a continuous study of the programs of United States economic assistance to foreign countries, and to review the progress achieved in the execution and administration of such programs. Upon request, the committee shall aid the several standing committees of the Congress having legislative jurisdiction over any part of the programs of United States economic assistance to foreign countries; and it shall make a report to the Senate and the House of Representatives, from time to time, concerning the results of its studies, together with such recommendations as it may deem desirable. The Administrator, at the request of the committee, shall consult with the committee from time to time with respect to his activities under this Act.

(c) The committee, or any duly authorized subcommittee thereof, is authorized to hold such hearings, to sit and act at such times and places, to require by subpena or otherwise the attendance of such witnesses and the production of such books, papers, and documents, to administer such oaths, to take such testimony, to procure such printing and binding, and to make such expenditures as it deems advisable. The cost of stenographic services to report such hearings shall not be in excess of 25 cents per hundred words. The provisions of sections 102 to 104, inclusive, of the Revised Statutes shall apply in case of any failure of any witness to comply with any subpena or to testify when summoned under authority of this subsection.

(d) The committee is authorized to appoint and, without regard to the Classification Act of 1923, as amended, fix the compensation of such experts, consultants, technicians, and organizations thereof, and, clerical and stenographic assistants as it deems necessary and advisable.

(e) There are hereby authorized to be appropriated

such sums as may be necessary to carry out the provisions of this section, to be disbursed by the Secretary of the Senate on vouchers signed by the chairman.

SEPARABILITY CLAUSE

SEC. 24. If any provision of this Act or the application of such provision to any circumstances or persons shall be held invalid, the validity of the remainder of the Act and the applicability of such provision to other circumstances or persons shall not be affected thereby.

Calendar No. 978

80TH CONGRESS } SENATE { REPORT
2d Session } { No. 935

EUROPEAN RECOVERY PROGRAM

REPORT

OF THE

COMMITTEE ON FOREIGN RELATIONS

ON

S. 2202

A BILL TO PROMOTE THE GENERAL WELFARE, NATIONAL INTEREST, AND FOREIGN POLICY OF THE UNITED STATES THROUGH NECESSARY ECONOMIC AND FINANCIAL ASSISTANCE TO FOREIGN COUNTRIES WHICH UNDERTAKE TO COOPERATE WITH EACH OTHER IN THE ESTABLISHMENT AND MAINTENANCE OF ECONOMIC CONDITIONS ESSENTIAL TO A PEACEFUL AND PROSPEROUS WORLD

FEBRUARY 26 (legislative day, FEBRUARY 2), 1948.—Ordered to be printed with an illustration

UNITED STATES
GOVERNMENT PRINTING OFFICE
72148 WASHINGTON : 1948

—From New York Times.

CONTENTS

Calendar No. 978

80TH CONGRESS, 2d Session — SENATE — REPORT No. 935

EUROPEAN RECOVERY PROGRAM

FEBRUARY 27 (legislative day, FEBRUARY 2), 1948.—Ordered to be printed with an illustration

Mr. VANDENBERG, from the Committee on Foreign Relations, submitted the following

REPORT

[To accompany S. 2202]

The Committee on Foreign Relations, having had under consideration a bill (S. 2202) to promote the general welfare, national interest, and foreign policy of the United States through necessary economic and financial assistance to foreign countries, unanimously report the bill favorably to the Senate, without amendment, and recommend that it do pass.

MAIN PURPOSE OF THE BILL

This bill provides for the participation of the United States in a European recovery program for approximately a 4-year period. It is a major step in the development and promotion of a peaceful and prosperous world which is the principal objective of United States foreign policy. The authorization for the first year is 5.3 billion dollars, 1 billion of which may be advanced by the Reconstruction Finance Corporation pending congressional action on appropriations. The assistance contemplated, which will involve both loans and grants, will not be confined to relief commodities; the program is designed to help European nations to help themselves to recovery in such a way as to become independent of outside assistance. A new agency, the Economic Cooperation Administration, headed by an Administrator, will be established to administer the program at home and abroad. The bill contains ample safeguards and conditions in order to insure that the money appropriated will be properly administered and wisely spent and that the domestic economy of the United States will not be impaired. Assistance extended by the United States will be contingent upon the continuous cooperation of the participating countries. Except for liquidation purposes the program will terminate on June 30, 1952.

Introduction

The American people, victorious in battle, look out upon a world disrupted by war and shaken by its aftermath. Our efforts to win back to peace have included unswerving support of the United Nations, as well as generous assistance to foreign countries in need of aid. The decision which must now be made is whether we shall continue the effort to achieve our goal: The establishment of a stable world with free political institutions and the rule of law. Events of the next few years may well decide the issue. World stability and European stability are inseparable; free institutions and genuine independence cannot perish in Europe and be secure in the rest of the world. We must therefore shape our course upon the basis of our determination whether the countries of Europe can preserve their liberties and independence if they do not achieve economic recovery.

The committee is convinced they cannot. In the light of this conviction, it has given earnest consideration to the form and scope of a program of American assistance based upon and flowing from a European recovery program of self-help and mutual aid.

Sixteen European countries have come forward with such a program, designed to achieve genuine recovery within approximately 4 years.

This report analyzes in some detail the conclusions of the committee, based upon its study, and offers the recommendations of the committee with respect to the Economic Cooperation Act of 1948.

Part I. Background Developments

1. Events Leading up to the Present Situation

During the summer of 1947, when UNRRA expired, Europe had not achieved a condition of economic and political stability. Not only did the extreme cold of last winter curtail European crops, but they were even more severely affected by the severe drought of the summer just passed. Moreover, the international monetary system was thrown out of balance by the rapidly rising cost of imports and the suspension of the convertibility of the pound sterling. These developments made it particularly difficult for the countries of Europe to secure needed supplies.

In order to alleviate immediate suffering and to pave the way for later long-range action, on November 17, 1947, President Truman called Congress into special session to deal with "the rise in prices * * * (and) * * * the crisis in western Europe." Congress met his request in December and provided funds for interim aid to France, Italy and Austria until April 1, 1948, when it was expected that the long-range program would be in operation.

The present legislation was anticipated by two addresses, one by Under Secretary of State Dean Acheson, on May 8, 1947, the second by Secretary of State George C. Marshall, on June 5, 1947, in which both indicated that the United States stood ready to consider how far she might be able to help Europe help herself on the road to recovery. On July 11, 1947, 16 western European nations on their own initiative responded to the suggestion, and met in Paris to prepare a report setting forth their needs and their willingness to cooperate in a joint recovery program. Meanwhile, United States agencies,

Members of Congress traveling abroad, and special committees appointed by the President, studied the needs of the European nations, and the impact of the contemplated assistance upon our resources and upon our domestic economy. On December 19, 1947, President Truman sent his special message to Congress on the situation in Europe, requesting relief in the amount of $17,000,000,000 for a period to run from April 1, 1948, to June 30, 1952, with a recommendation for an appropriation of $6,800,000,000 for the 15-month period running from April 1, 1948, to June 30, 1949. The President also made a number of recommendations as to administration, the types of agreements to be made, and the financial arrangements which were to be embodied in the new program.

2. THE COMMITTEE HEARINGS

The committee conducted hearings on the European recovery program from January 8 to February 5, inclusive. On January 8 Secretary of State George C. Marshall accompanied by Ambassador Lewis W. Douglas and members of the State Department staff presented the program in general terms and urged the speedy passage of the draft bill which he presented for legislative consideration. On following days Ambassador Douglas returned to analyze in detail the political, economic, and administrative problems involved in a recovery program.

On January 12 Secretary of Commerce W. Averell Harriman presented the findings of the Harriman committee, discussing in detail the impact of the program upon the United States economy and other related matters. On January 13 Secretary of Agriculture Clinton P. Anderson described the food and agricultural parts of the recommended program and pointed out what they would mean to the farmers and consumers of the United States. On the same day Secretary of the Interior Julius A. Krug presented an analysis of the findings of the Krug committee on national resources and foreign aid with particular emphasis upon the effect of the recovery program upon certain commodities in short supply.

On January 14 Secretary of the Treasury John W. Snyder discussed the principal financial aspects of the program and the measures the participating countries would be expected to take. Mr. William M. Martin, Jr. explained the possible role of the Export-Import Bank in such a program. On the same day Secretary of the Army Kenneth C. Royall discussed the role of Germany in the rehabilitation of the European economy and the relationship of the European recovery program to the national defense. The list of Government witnesses was completed on January 15 when Secretary of Defense James V. Forrestal described the relationship of the recovery program to the security interests of the United States.

During the 3 weeks that followed, nearly 100 nongovernmental witnesses appeared before the committee. Included were representatives of many of our outstanding national organizations, spokesmen of business, labor, agricultural, veterans, religious, educational, and service groups. Included also were many outstanding individuals who appeared in their capacity as private citizens, such as John Foster Dulles, Bernard Baruch, and Robert M. La Follette.

Following the conclusion of the public hearings the committee met in executive session for an additional week to continue its consideration of the European recovery program, taking as a basis for discussion the draft proposal submitted by the Department of State. On the basis of information obtained during the hearings the committee proceeded to rewrite the bill, essentially altering it in many important particulars. On February 17 the committee concluded its deliberations and voted unanimously to report the bill favorably to the Senate.

As in the case of the Foreign Aid Act, the committee was greatly impressed with the thorough documentation which was available during its examination of the European recovery program. It is probable that no legislative proposal coming before the Congress has ever been accompanied by such thoroughly prepared documentary materials. In addition to the extensive documents submitted by the Department of State, the reports of the Paris Conference of the CEEC countries, the Nourse, Krug, and Harriman reports, the handbook on the European recovery program prepared by the staffs of the Senate Foreign Relations Committee and the House Foreign Affairs Committee, the special report of the Brookings Institution, and the numerous reports of the House Select Committee on Foreign Aid were all available. Added to these reports was a great deal of material which had been produced in the course of congressional experience with foreign-aid matters prior to 1948, such as discussions relating to UNRRA, interim aid, etc.

Particular reference should be made at this point to the report submitted by the Brookings Institution. Early in its consideration of the European recovery program it became apparent to the committee that the task of providing for a satisfactory administrative organization for such an important program would be extremely difficult. Accordingly, the Chairman of the Foreign Relations Committee invited the Brookings Institution to analyze the various proposals which had been advanced and to submit its findings and recommendations. On January 22 this report was completed. It served as a basis of discussion for the members of the committee and helped them arrive at a satisfactory solution.

The committee was likewise impressed by the fact that very few opposition witnesses appeared to testify against the bill. Representatives of labor and management alike warmly endorsed its objectives. All witnesses were heard who asked to be heard. A complete list of the witnesses who testified before the committee is attached as Appendix II of this report.

3. WHY EUROPE IS IN NEED AT THIS TIME

Economic nationalism, political tensions and uncertainty, war devastation, the prolonged interruption of international trade, the loss of foreign income and dollar funds, internal financial disequilibrium, shortage of supplies from southeast Asia, the wartime movement of peoples to certain areas of western Europe, and a 10-percent increase of population have all contributed to economic break-down in Europe. Germany, a focal point in the European economy, is paralyzed. Inflation is rampant. Subversive elements are hampering recovery and engineering social chaos.

Apart from this, Europe is suffering from invisible devastation—the loss of soil fertility, the deterioration of war-strained machinery, and the lowering of individual productive capacity because of exhaustion, hunger, and the loss of technical skills.

These factors aggravate historic economic difficulties in western Europe; a region which, with relatively slender natural resources, attempts to maintain a disproportionately large population by being an industrial workshop and commercial middleman for the rest of the world. According to the International Bank, the CEEC countries with twice the population of the United States have one-half our national income.

The physical volume of goods shipped from western Europe to the rest of the world in the prewar years did not equal in value the supplies which had to be obtained from outside. The difference was made up by the so-called invisible items in the trade balance—income from overseas investments, earnings from shipping, insurance and commercial financing, and the money spent by tourists. The war has upset this balance. Furthermore, the world-wide inflation since 1939 has increased the cost of European imports much more than it has increased the price she has been able to obtain for her exports.

The difficulty involved in rebuilding an intricate working system of business, professional, and financial relationships has been a major impediment to recovery.

Eastern Europe has suffered its own war devastation and large amounts of available exports have been exacted by the Soviet Union as reparations, as payment for occupation costs, or under enforced commercial agreements, thus weakening one source of supply and trading.

The residents in the CEEC countries in 1947 were living on an emergency subsistence level averaging 2,250 calories a day instead of their prewar diet of 2,800 calories or the 3,350 calories of the average American diet.

The bill in several ways recognizes the present needs but attempts rather to provide the breathing spell wherein western Europe, on its part, will take the joint measures to meet the basic difficulties lest they become chronic.

4. EUROPEAN PROGRESS TOWARD RECOVERY

Steady progress toward economic recovery has characterized the period since the end of the war. In mid-1947, however, the recovery process began to slow down. In part, this was the result of the unprecedentedly severe winter of 1946–47, followed by spring floods and summer drought, which compelled the countries to maintain unexpectedly high food imports and to cut down on other imports. Shortages of imported materials began to appear and to limit production in important industries. In part, it was also the result of cumulative fatigue; heavy reconstruction efforts in all countries were overtaxing people who for years had not had proper rest and nourishment. And, in part, it was the result of labor unrest, in many cases politically inspired for the very purpose of retarding recovery and prolonging economic difficulties by a party which thrives on distress.

However, for 1947 as a whole, national income in the participating countries as a group had reached 91 percent of the 1938 level. Owing to the increase in population, per capita national income was only 86 percent of the 1938 level. These over-all measures conceal, of course, wide variations between countries and between different branches of the economy within each country. In eight countries, industrial production in 1947 exceeded 1938 levels, and the average for all countries except Germany was approaching the 1938 level. Coal production had recovered well in most countries; the United Kingdom nearly achieved its target of 200,000,000 tons and has been able to resume coal exports of about 200,000 tons a week; French output slightly exceeded prewar; the smaller western European producers were almost back to 1938 levels; coal production in western Germany, however, was less than two-thirds of 1938 output.

The Continent's 1947 production of steel is estimated at slightly over 35,000,000 tons, or 63 percent of its prewar output. The average was brought down by western Germany, for production in the other participating countries was equal, on the average, to 1938. The United Kingdom reached its target of 14,000,000 tons, and France reached 93 percent of its 1938 production. In the case of Belgium-Luxemburg, 1947 production surpassed 1938.

Output of hydroelectric power in 1947 exceeded 1938 by nearly 40 percent. France has been particularly successful in increasing this important source of energy.

In most countries, agricultural production was severely affected by the weather in 1947 and averaged hardly more than four-fifths of 1938 output. This was especially serious because food consumption had dropped from a prewar average of about 2,900 calories to less than 2,500 calories, and the poor crops in 1947 meant that even the current level of food intake would be difficult to maintain. Great efforts have been and are being made by the participating countries to reduce their need for imported food. British farmers are now producing about half of the country's food requirements, as compared to a third before the war. The French Government has increased its bread-grain acreage goal for 1948 from 84 percent to 95 percent of prewar and is also expanding production in French North Africa. The United Kingdom and France are initiating programs for production of groundnuts in their overseas dependencies in order to reduce their need for imported fats and oils. All countries are taking measures to increase the use of farm machinery and of fertilizer in order to raise output while economizing on labor.

Although progress toward recovery has slowed down, the momentum has not been lost. Despite real difficulties, the efforts of the peoples of western Europe give support to the conclusion that their economy will respond to a recovery program over a period of several years and that the basic objectives of the production program appear to be attainable if the will to cooperate and to produce is vigorous.

5. EUROPEAN RECOVERY TARGETS

The committee appreciates that goals and targets, which seem optimistic to many American experts, are not the same as achievements; but it is worth while to record what the CEEC countries and

western Germany hope to achieve by the end of 1951. This program does not necessarily mean a recreating of all prewar conditions, some of which were admittedly undesirable.

The CEEC countries have set themselves the following aims to be achieved by the end of 1951:

(1) Restoration of prewar bread-grain production and of an intensive livestock economy.

(2) Increase of coal production to 584,000,000 tons yearly, an increase of 30,000,000 tons above the 1938 level.

(3) Expansion of electricity output by nearly 70,000,000,000 kilowatt-hours and an increase of generating capacity by 25,000,000 kilowatts, which is two-thirds above prewar.

(4) Development of oil-refining capacity to 2½ times prewar.

(5) Increase in crude steel production to 55,000,000 tons yearly, or 20 percent above prewar.

(6) Expansion of inland transport to carry 25 percent more than prewar.

(7) Rehabilitation and restoration of the merchant fleets of the participating countries.

(8) Supply from European production of most of the capital equipment needed for these expansions.

The committee feels that the early months after the initiation of the program provide the most opportune time for putting vigorous measures into effect. Such national and cooperative action must be undertaken now, when levels of employment are high in almost all parts of the world. Certain of the production goals should be revised to enable greater concentration on the achievement of the food and coal targets and on the production for export goals. Full use must be made of existing capacity; bottlenecks must be eliminated. Schemes for the proper training of manpower can contribute greatly to the required result. There must be organizational skill and initiative. The resources of dependent territories must be better developed.

The estimates of this program presuppose a considerable reduction in the rate of capital development as compared with the CEEC statements. Essentiality must be measured in terms of the scarcity of the goods and of the urgency of the need for these goods before additional capacity is constructed. The rigor of certain estimates may be gaged to the fact that they assume exports to the Western Hemisphere in fiscal 1949 to be approximately as large in physical terms as those to the same area in 1938, even though the German contribution will be only a third as large and Austria and Italy will be below prewar performance.

So that our own visi[illegible] is not clouded, and in fairness to the participating countries, it is entirely appropriate that the committee quote from the CEEC report at this point:

> It is not only a problem of Europe and the American Continent; it is a problem of the balance of the whole world economy.

Further, while stating that in the initial period the contribution to this world problem which Europe can make by its own exertions is of prime importance, the report concludes:

> But as the 4-year period develops, the world considerations rather than those of European production itself will be decisive.

85-743 O - 73 - 40

6. MEASURES TAKEN BY THE PARTICIPATING COUNTRIES TO STRENGTHEN THEIR ECONOMIES

The committee has observed with satisfaction that since the Paris Conference last summer the participating countries have taken immediate steps to strengthen their economies and to cooperate with one another. The following examples may be cited:

1. The Financial Committee of the CEEC conference recommended the adoption of a proposal for setting off debits against credits in inter-European payments as a means of stimulating intra-European trade. The operation of a multilateral clearing arrangement was entrusted to the Bank for International Settlement. On January 19, 1948, the first inter-European clearing under the new system was announced.
2. The Study Committee of Customs Unions, established at the CEEC conference, is examining the possibility of establishing a common customs union among all the countries represented and appointed a tariff committee which is attempting to complete the preparation of a specimen common tariff.
3. In addition to the project for a general European customs union, there are several projects of more limited scope: (*a*) Denmark, Iceland, Norway, and Sweden; (*b*) France and Italy; (*c*) Greece and Turkey. The Benelux customs union entered into effect January 1, 1948.
4. Since the Paris Conference the CEEC countries have intensified their efforts to attain budgetary balance, reduce inflationary pressures in general, and restore confidence in their currency. This is strikingly illustrated by the vigorous and courageous actions taken by France and Italy in recent months.
5. A conference on manpower met in Rome and developed measures to utilize more effectively surplus manpower in such countries as Italy, to facilitate the movement of labor across international boundaries, and to improve occupational qualifications and training.
6. Five of the sixteen countries, not yet being members of the United Nations, are not members of the Economic Commission for Europe, but they have been invited to the committees of the Commission. It is planned to reestablish the prewar system for exchanging freight cars and to facilitate highway truck traffic.

In spite of these gains, it seems clear to the committee that the western European nations require an organization with wider powers and greater responsibilities than the Paris Conference. Such an organization might well have the responsibility for screening requirements and integrating production and investment programs and should be in a position to make positive proposals to its member governments for raising the productive efficiency of the western European economy. The vast potentialities of the dependent territories should be mobilized behind any program of European aid.

7. UNITED STATES ASSISTANCE TO EUROPE SINCE THE WAR

Since the end of the Second World War, the United States has extended assistance to Europe in the form of (1) repayable loans and credits, and (2) relief supplies and grants not requiring specific repayment. Most American assistance belongs to the first category.

Credits and loans.—Interest-bearing credits and loans include (1) the loan to the United Kingdom of $3,750,000,000, authorized by Congress in July 1946; (2) two Export-Import Bank reconstruction loans to France, one of $550,000,000 in September 1945, the second of $650,000,000 in June 1946; (3) sale of United States surplus property abroad and surplus merchant vessels on long-term credit, to France at a credit of $300,000,000, and to Italy at a credit of $160,000,000 for purchase of surplus property in Europe, and $42,000,000 to each for the purchase of merchant vessels; (4) lend-lease settlements and pipe-line credits. In the period from July 1, 1945, to June 30, 1947, the United States Government authorized repayable loans and credits to the Paris Conference countries of $7,353,000,000 in all.

Grants and relief.—Grants and relief include (1) UNRRA, toward which the United States contributed $2,700,000,000; (2) United States foreign-relief program, including an authorization of $332,000,000 in July 1947, and a donation of $15,000,000 to the International Children's Emergency Fund; (3) interim aid to Austria, France, and Italy, in the amount of $522,000,000, enacted in December 1947; (4) Greek-Turkish aid, to the amount of $400,000,000; (5) relief of occupied areas; (6) lend-lease aid not repayable. In the period from July 1, 1945, to June 30, 1947, the United States Government authorized assistance under the programs listed above of some $1,943,000,000, allocable to certain of the Paris Conference countries. A further $767,000,000 allocable to German relief, and $481,000,000 not allocable to specific countries in Europe but intended almost entirely for the Paris Conference countries, were authorized, making a total of $3,191,000,000, to which interim aid should be added, making the total as of December 31, 1947, $3,788,000,000.

Thus loans, credits, grants, and relief to the Paris Conference countries and Germany authorized in the period July 1, 1945, to December 31, 1947, totaled a little over $11,000,000,000.

These figures do not take into account remittances from private individuals and voluntary agencies in the United States, which in the year 1946 ran slightly more than half a billion dollars, a sum which it is estimated was equaled in 1947.

A break-down of United States loans, credits, grants, and relief contributions for the two fiscal years July 1, 1945, to June 30, 1947, is as follows:

TABLE A.—*U. S. Government loans, property credits, and grants—Amount available, utilized, and unutilized, as of June 30, 1947, by type and country*

[Millions of dollars]

Country	Amount available, July 1, 1945–June 30, 1947			Amount utilized, July 1, 1945–June 30, 1947			Unutilized balance, June 30, 1947		
	Total	Loans and property credits	Grants and other relief	Total	Loans and property credits	Grants and other relief	Total	Loans and property credits	Grants and other relief
Total	16,302	9,128	7,174	12,575	7,309	5,266	3,727	1,819	1,908
Europe	12,160	7,977	4,183	9,902	6,752	3,150	2,258	1,225	1,033
Paris Conference countries	9,331	7,388	1,943	7,828	6,414	1,414	1,503	974	529
Austria	195	11	184	140	1	139	54	9	45
Belgium and Luxemburg	210	149	61	210	149	61			
Denmark	30	30		15	15		15	15	
France	1,928	1,907	21	1,719	1,698	21	209	209	
Greece	745	121	624	329	55	274	417	67	350
Italy	926	331	595	784	223	561	142	108	34
Netherlands	303	283	20	276	256	20	27	27	
Norway	81	80	1	11	10	1	70	70	
Sweden	1		1	1		1			
Switzerland	2		2	2		2			
Turkey	141	41	100	6	6		134	34	100
United Kingdom	4,769	4,435	334	4,334	4,000	334	435	435	
Countries not at Paris Conference	2,305	546	1,759	1,866	337	1,529	439	209	230
Czechoslovakia	247	73	174	204	30	174	42	42	
Finland	106	106		71	71		35	35	
Germany	767		767	537		537	230		230
Hungary	37	37		10	10		27	27	
Poland	439	90	349	379	30	349	60	60	
U. S. S. R.	410	242	168	364	196	168	45	45	
Yugoslavia	301		301	301		301			
Europe unallocable	522	41	481	207		207	315	41	274
Canada	−6	−6		−12	−12		6	6	
Latin-American countries	495	473	22	206	184	22	289	289	
China	1,328	229	1,099	1,262	163	1,099	66	66	
Japan	606	15	591	398	7	391	208	8	200
Korea	170	25	145	48	3	45	122	22	100
Philippines	769	76	693	194	76	118	575		575
All other countries	367	332	35	169	134	35	198	198	
Unallocable	411	6	405	405		405	6	6	

TABLE B.—*United States Government loans and property credits—Amount available, utilized, and unutilized, as of June 30, 1947, by type and country*

[Millions of dollars]

Country	Amount available, July 1, 1945–June 30, 1947			Amount utilized, July 1, 1945–June 30, 1947			Unutilized balance, June 30, 1947		
	Total	Export-Import Bank and other loans	Property credits	Total	Export-Import Bank and other loans	Property credits	Total	Export-Import Bank and other loans	Property credits
Total	9, 128	6, 426	2, 703	7, 309	5, 052	2, 258	1, 819	1, 374	445
Europe	7, 977	5, 734	2, 242	6, 752	4, 776	1, 976	1, 225	958	267
Paris Conference countries	7, 388	5, 544	1, 845	6, 414	4, 689	1, 725	974	855	120
Austria	11	1	10	1	----------	1	9	1	9
Belgium and Luxemburg	149	100	49	149	100	49	----------	----------	----------
Denmark	30	20	10	15	15	----------	15	5	10
France	1, 907	1, 200	707	1, 698	998	700	209	202	7
Greece	121	25	96	55	5	50	67	20	46
Italy	331	130	202	223	24	199	108	106	2
Netherlands	283	205	78	256	197	59	27	8	19
Norway	80	50	30	10	----------	10	70	50	20
Turkey	41	28	13	6	----------	6	34	28	6
United Kingdom	4, 435	3, 785	650	4, 000	3, 350	650	435	435	----------
Countries not at Paris Conference	546	149	397	337	87	250	209	62	147
Czechoslovakia	73	23	50	30	22	8	42	----------	42
Finland	106	81	26	71	58	13	35	23	13
Hungary	37	7	30	10	----------	10	27	7	20
Poland	90	40	50	30	7	23	60	33	27
U. S. S. R.	242	----------	242	196	----------	196	45	----------	45
Europe, unallocable	41	41	----------	----------	----------	----------	41	41	----------
Canada	−6	−6	----------	−12	−12	----------	6	6	----------
Latin-American countries	473	394	79	184	149	35	289	245	44
China	229	98	131	163	60	103	66	38	28
Japan	15	----------	15	7	----------	7	8	----------	8
Korea	25	----------	25	3	----------	3	22	----------	22
Philippines	76	70	6	76	70	6	----------	----------	----------
All other countries	332	128	206	134	7	127	198	121	78
Unallocable	6	6	----------	----------	----------	----------	6	6	----------

TABLE C.—*U. S. Government grants under other relief—Amount available, utilized, and unutilized, as of June 30, 1947, by type and country*

[Millions of dollars]

Country	Amount available, July 1, 1945–June 30, 1947					Amount utilized, July 1, 1945–June 30, 1947					Unutilized balance, as of June 30, 1947			
	Total	UNRRA and post-UNRRA	Occupation program	Lend-lease	Other	Total	UNRRA and post-UNRRA	Occupation program	Lend-lease	Other	Total	UNRRA and post-UNRRA	Occupation program	Other
Total	7,174	2,642	2,014	1,151	1,365	5,266	2,310	1,484	1,151	319	1,908	332	530	1,046
Europe	4,183	1,973	1,219	420	570	3,150	1,641	989	420	99	1,033	332	230	471
Paris Conference countries	1,943	802	285	420	436	1,414	673	285	420	35	529	129		400
Austria	184	104	79			139	59	79			45	45		
Belgium and Luxemburg	61	1		60		61	1		60					
France	21	3		16	2	21	3		16	2				
Greece	624	321			303	274	271			3	350	50		300
Italy	595	359	206		30	561	325	206		30	34	34		
Netherlands	20	1		19		20	1		19					
Norway	1	1				1	1							
Sweden	1	1				1	1							
Switzerland	2	2				2	2							
Turkey	100				100						100			100
United Kingdom	334	9		325		334	9		325					
Countries not at Paris Conference	1,759	969	771		61	1,529	945	524		61	230		230	
Czechoslovakia	174	168			6	174	168			6				
Germany	767	13	754			537	13	524			230		230	
Poland	349	304			45	349	304			45				
U. S. S. R.	168	166			2	168	166			2				
Yugoslavia	301	293			8	301	293			8				
Europe unallocable	481	227	180		74	207	24	180		3	274	203		71
Latin-American countries	22			5	17	22			5	17				
China	1,099	334		644	121	1,099	334		644	121				
Japan	591		591			391		391			200		200	
Korea	145	1	144			45	1	44			100		100	
Philippines	693	10	28		655	118	10	28		80	575			575
All other countries	35	1	31	2		35	1	31	2					
Unallocable	405	324		79	2	405	324		79	2				

8. THE PARTICIPATING COUNTRIES

The 16 countries which attended the Paris Conference and signed the CEEC report are as follows: Austria, Belgium, Denmark, France, Greece, Iceland, Ireland, Italy, Luxemburg, the Netherlands, Norway, Portugal, Sweden, Switzerland, Turkey, and the United Kingdom. A number of other states were invited but did not attend: Finland, Poland, Hungary, Rumania, Bulgaria, Yugoslavia, Czechoslovakia, and Russia.

In view of the cooperative nature of the recovery program, the committee believed the door should be left open for those other countries if they choose to enter. To this end, in addition to the CEEC signatories and western Germany, the act envisages the possibility of any other country wholly or partly in Europe, including Trieste and areas under international administration and control, becoming a participating country. Such countries must, however, adhere to a joint program for European recovery. Under the terms of the act the words "participating country" include its dependent areas.

Some criticism has been voiced because certain states like Portugal and Switzerland, which are in sound economic condition, are listed among the participating countries. The fact that a state is a "participating country" does not necessarily mean that it will receive assistance from the United States. The committee stressed the fact that some of the CEEC countries will not require any direct assistance from our Government and that they should be looked upon as cooperators in the program rather than recipients of our aid. Their contribution to European recovery will be considerable. When it is remembered how closely the participating countries are bound together by ties of trade and commerce it is evident why they must all be brought into the program and why they must all work together as a team if the goal of European recovery is to be realized.

Of all the sovereign states of Europe, Spain was the only one which was not extended an invitation to attend the Paris conference. From an economic point of view Spain might be able to make a contribution to such a program. On the other hand, due to the nature of the Franco regime and due to the resolutions adopted at various international conferences, the CEEC countries at the Paris conference did not believe it appropriate or consistent with the spirit of such resolutions to invite Spain to participate at that time. Whether she eventually takes part in the program will depend upon her own willingness to assume the obligations involved, the willingness of the participating countries to admit her, and the ability of Spain to conclude a satisfactory bilateral agreement with the United States.

Part II. The Administration of the Program

A. THE ECONOMIC COOPERATION ADMINISTRATION

The committee agreed that the complex nature of the recovery program and the magnitude of the task to be performed called for the creation of a new and separate operating agency. Many of the activities contemplated partake of the character of a business enterprise. But the administration of such a program, with its wide ramifications abroad, is much more than a business venture. It involves our relations with foreign nations and is, in many of its aspects, inextricably bound up with United States foreign policies at the highest level.

The problem before the committee, therefore, was to devise an administrative arrangement which would insure the smooth and effective operation of the business aspects of the enterprise without, at the same time, impinging upon the essential authority of the Secretary of State in the conduct of foreign relations.

The committee completely agreed with the Secretary of State that it would be unwise to place the agency in the Department of State. Such a move would impose upon the Secretary responsibility for duties of an operational nature, not within the normal range of the Department's activities and might, as a result, impair the execution of its policy functions. Under the circumstances a new and separate agency seemed to be a wise alternative.

It is also apparent that the form of the new agency must be such as to insure sufficient flexibility of structure and operations. For this reason some people have argued that a part of the program, at least, might be entrusted to a new organization with corporate structure comparable, in some degree, to the Reconstruction Finance Corporation. It is argued that such an organization could be given in its charter considerable flexibility, free from the normal governmental regulations relating to procurement, personnel, and auditing. In addition, it could be authorized to enter into contracts, settle claims, and in general resort to ordinary business practices in a program that is essentially of a business character.

It should be pointed out, however, that all of these advantages claimed for the corporate form can be obtained for the noncorporate form by making provision in the act for necessary exemptions with respect to procurement, personnel, and auditing. Moreover, in view of the importance of the program and its impact upon other agencies of the Government, the committee decided that there would be a real advantage in creating a new agency as an integral part of the executive branch on a plane with the 10 Cabinet departments.

As a result of these considerations the act provides for a new and separate agency with a noncorporate form. Considerable leeway has been given the agency with respect to the hiring and payment of personnel, accounting procedures and other related matters. And every effort has been made to insure smooth working relationships between the new agency and the existing departments and agencies of the Government.

10. THE ADMINISTRATOR

Closely related to the form of the new agency is the nature of the administrative direction or supervision provided for it. The choice facing the committee lay between direction by a single administrator or by a board or commission.

Fear has been expressed in some quarters that the appointment of a single administrator might result in the concentration of too much power in the hands of one individual. The committee felt strongly, however, that in a program of such magnitude, where speed of decision and centralization of responsibility are essential, a single administrator would prove far more satisfactory than a board or commission.

The committee likewise agreed that the head of such an agency, if he is to perform his duties in an effective manner, must have a status that will place him upon a plane of equality with the heads of other departments and agencies of the Government with whom he must cooperate in developing his program. From time to time there may be unreconciled differences between these agencies. In order that such differences may be satisfactorily resolved, it is particularly essential that the Administrator of the new agency be given a position that would entitle him to have the same direct access to the President as the heads of the 10 Cabinet departments.

The bill covers these general principles in some detail. It vests the responsibilities and powers assigned the Economic Cooperation Administration in a single Administrator who is to be appointed by the President, with the advice and consent of the Senate. The Administrator will be responsible to the President, will perform his functions under the control of the President, and will have a status in the executive branch comparable to that of the head of an executive department.

In general, the Administrator will provide the central administrative direction for the program. Among other things, he will review the requirements for participating countries, formulate programs of United States assistance, provide for the execution of such programs, and terminate assistance according to the terms of the bill. The Administrator's functions will be examined in detail in other sections of this report.

Because of the nature of the program, the committee, throughout its deliberations, emphasized the fact that the Administrator would have to be given considerable authority to enable him to perform his functions effectively. Accordingly, the selection of the Administrator will have to be made with the greatest of care. He must be an able administrator, a dynamic leader, and cooperative in his approach to other agencies.

11. RELATIONS OF THE ADMINISTRATOR TO THE SECRETARY OF STATE

As has been pointed out above, the main problem facing the committee with respect the administrative aspects of the recovery program was to devise a formula which would permit the Administrator to carry out his operating functions in an effective manner without impinging upon or impairing the authority of the Secretary of State in the conduct of foreign relations. Obviously the Secretary of State is vitally concerned with all operations under the program that may affect the foreign relations and policies of the United States. But experience during the war years, when interagency quarrels hampered the war effort, clearly demonstrated that it is impossible to draw a clean line between operations and foreign policy. The committee believes that the formula of cooperation outlined in the bill will result in the kind of concerted action between the Administrator and the Secretary of State that will strengthen rather than weaken the conduct of our foreign relations.

Under the terms of the bill the Secretary of State is authorized, in consultation with the Administrator, to conclude the basic agreements with the participating countries in furtherance of the purposes of this act. On his part, the Administrator is charged with responsibility for the central administrative direction of the program, including the formulation and execution of assistance programs, methods of financing, procurement, storage, and delivery of commodities, etc.

In order to avoid possible misunderstandings, the bill provides that the Administrator and the Secretary of State shall keep each other fully and currently informed on matters, including prospective action, arising within the scope of their respective duties which are pertinent to the duties of the other. Whenever the Secretary of State believes that any action, proposed action, or failure to act on the part of the Administrator is inconsistent with our foreign policy, he shall consult with the Administrator. If the differences are not adjusted by such consultation the matter will be referred to the President for final decision.

This procedure is somewhat comparable to the formula adopted by the Congress in the Atomic Energy Act of 1946. In case of differences the Secretary of State has a temporary veto over the actions of the Administrator with the President acting as the referee. It is unlikely that few, if any, such differences will ever reach the President's desk.

With respect to personnel the position of the Administrator is clear. He will possess the authority to recruit and to appoint personnel for service both at home and abroad and such personnel will be responsible to him for the performance of their duties. If the Administrator so desires he may recommend the appointment of personnel serving abroad to any class in the Foreign Service Reserve or staff.

12. RELATIONS OF THE ECONOMIC COOPERATION ADMINISTRATION WITH OTHER AGENCIES

The committee agreed that the Administrator would not find it necessary to create a large agency in order to perform his functions under the act, but should utilize the existing facilities of departments and agencies of the Government already engaged in such activities. Thus, in developing the financial aspects of the program, the Administrator will act in consultation with the National Advisory Council. Similarly with respect to the appraisal of European requirements, the availability of commodities, procurement, and other related matters, the Administrator will lean heavily upon the Departments of Agriculture, Treasury, Commerce, Interior, Army, Labor, and other agencies.

To insure the necessary cooperation without unduly imposing upon existing agencies, the bill authorizes the Administrator to utilize the facilities and services of any department or agency of the Government as the President shall direct, or with the consent of the head of such agency. Since ultimate responsibility for the program centers in the President it is not anticipated that any difficulties will arise on this score.

In the extension of loans to the participating countries the Administrator will utilize the facilities of the Export-Import Bank. Funds will be allocated for such purposes and the bank will make and administer the credit as directed, and on terms specified, by the

Administrator in consultation with the National Advisory Council. The role of the bank is thus a purely ministerial one.

One possible source of disagreement between the Economic Cooperation Administration and other agencies lies in the allocation of scarce commodities. Differences may well arise when the Administrator, as one of the claimants for such commodities, presents the requirements for his program to the Secretary of Commerce and the Secretary of Agriculture. In view of the fact that the European recovery program represents but one part of the total domestic and world supply picture, however, the committee considered it essential, in order to protect our own domestic economy, to leave the power of allocation in neutral hands rather than bestow it upon the Administrator who, as a claimant for a particular area, might tend to give undue emphasis to the needs of his own program. In the event agreement cannot be reached with respect to scarce materials, the matter would, of course, have to be referred to the President for final settlement.

13. SPECIAL ECA MISSIONS ABROAD

The bill also provides for the establishment of satisfactory working relations between the officials of the Economic Cooperation Administration abroad and our regular diplomatic representatives in the participating countries.

In the highly complicated task of formulating, carrying out, and reviewing assistance programs, the Administrator will need special representatives with a high degree of technical competence in each of the CEEC countries. Of necessity these representatives will be in intimate contact with many departments of the participating governments and, from time to time, will have to confer with the highest officials. Under such circumstances close working relations with our regular embassies and legations are absolutely essential.

Accordingly the bill provides for the establishment in each participating country of a special mission for economic cooperation. The chief of the mission, who will be second in rank to the chief of the United States diplomatic mission, will be appointed by the Administrator and be responsible to him. So that there will be no misunderstanding about division of labor, it is made clear that the chief of the special mission is responsible, in the country where he is stationed, for assuring the performance of operations under the act.

This does not mean that he should be permitted to take action which runs counter to the foreign policy objectives of the United States. Such a possibility is safeguarded by the provision that the chief of the special mission and the chief of the diplomatic mission will keep each other currently informed of their activities. This will enable the chief of the diplomatic mission to consult with the chief of the special mission whenever the former believes that any action or failure to act on the part of the special mission is inconsistent with our foreign policy. Differences of view which cannot be reconciled in the field will be referred to the Administrator and the Secretary of State for decision.

Given men of good will, working in the general interests of the United States and world peace, the committee strongly believes that this formula, while perhaps not the best which could be devised from a theoretical point of view, will in fact prove the most satisfactory basis for operating relations.

14. UNITED STATES SPECIAL REPRESENTATIVE ABROAD

This report has already emphasized the fact that the success of the recovery program will depend in large measure upon the effective cooperation of the participating countries. Such cooperation will develop, to a very great extent, through the activity of the continuing organization which the CEEC states have agreed to set up. The committee agreed that it was imperative for the United States to be adequately represented at such an organization.

In fact this will be the chief responsibility of the United States special representative in Europe provided for in section 8 of the bill. In addition, he will probably serve as a roving ambassador, discharging such additional responsibilities with respect to the recovery program as may be assigned him with the approval of the President. The committee believed it would be unwise to define the duties of the special representative in any detail at the present time. In general, however, the committee agreed that he might perform extremely valuable services in coordinating the activities of the chiefs of the special missions in the participating countries, and handling matters which require joint negotiations with two or more states and cannot therefore be handled in the normal way.

While the exact relationship between the special representative and the Secretary of State, the Administrator, the chiefs of the special missions and the chiefs of the diplomatic missions can only be worked out in practice, the bill provides that he must keep all these individuals informed of his activities. Moreover, he is to consult with the chiefs of the special missions who must give him whatever cooperation he may require for the performance of his duties under the act.

Clearly the special representative, like the Administrator, will be a key figure in the European recovery program. On his knowledge, skill, perseverance, and diplomacy much of the success of this joint enterprise will depend. Every effort should be made to find an individual who possesses the many qualifications necessary for this difficult undertaking.

15. THE PUBLIC ADVISORY BOARD

Because of the broad range of problems involved in the recovery program, the committee believed it highly desirable to create a public advisory board to advise with the Administrator with respect to basic policy matters. Two direct benefits will flow from such an arrangement. In the first place, an advisory board made up of eminent citizens with varied experiences and representing various interests, will be able to contribute many valuable suggestions and criticisms for the use of the Administrator. He will undoubtedly wish to lean heavily upon their counsel. In the second place, if the Administrator works closely with an advisory body consisting of representatives of labor, business, agriculture, and other interested groups, public confidence in the enterprise will be greatly augmented.

As provided in the bill the Public Advisory Council will be bipartisan and will consist of not more than 12 members appointed by the President and confirmed by the Senate. As the name indicates it is to function in an advisory capacity only. The act provides that it shall meet at least once a month and at other times upon the call of the Administrator or the request of three or more of the Board members. The committee sincerely believes the Board will prove a valuable asset to the Administrator without constituting a burden upon his time.

The Administrator is also authorized to appoint such other advisory committees as he may consider necessary to carry out the purposes of the act. It is very probable, as the recovery program progresses, that the Administrator will find special advisory groups in industry, labor, agriculture, commerce, and other specialized fields of considerable assistance to him.

16. THE JOINT CONGRESSIONAL COMMITTEE

The European recovery program will be a gigantic enterprise. It will involve the cooperation and the resources of the United States. Its outcome will determine, to a very large extent, whether peace and prosperity will prevail in the western world. Its successful execution will be of continuing interest to the executive branch, the Congress, and the people of the United States for the next 4 years.

For these reasons the committee believed it would be highly desirable to establish a congressional committee to be known as the Joint Committee on Foreign Economic Cooperation. This joint committee will be bipartisan in character and will be made up of seven Members of the Senate and seven Members of the House. Its chairman and vice chairman will be appointed by the President of the Senate and the Speaker of the House acting jointly.

It will be the task of the joint committee to make a continuous study of United States foreign-aid programs and to review the progress achieved in the execution and administration of such programs. It will also, upon request, aid the standing committees of the Congress having legislative jurisdiction over the various aspects of foreign economic assistance. Finally, it will report to the Congress from time to time making such recommendations as it may deem desirable.

After careful consideration of the issues involved, the committee agreed that it would be most inadvisable to bestow legislative authority upon the joint committee. The recovery program will have many facets, both international and domestic. It will be related to foreign policy, shipping problems, export controls, farm production, stock piling, foreign trade, and financial policy—to mention only a few. To grant the joint committee legislative authority would compel it to invade the proper jurisdiction of many of the standing committees of the Congress.

The committee felt strongly, however, that the joint committee will serve as a useful mechanism to bridge the gap between the executive and legislative branches and thus help bring about that teamwork within our own Government which is essential if the program is to succeed. It is believed that the joint committee can play a very helpful role both in keeping the Congress informed and in advancing healthy criticisms and helpful suggestions for the use of the Administrator. The bill provides that the Administrator, at the request of the joint committee, shall consult with the committee from time to time with respect to his activities.

Part III. Requirements of the Program and Availabilities of Commodities

17. HOW THE REQUIREMENTS WERE SCREENED

Your committee considered with care the way in which the requirements of the participating countries were originally prepared by the Committee on European Economic Cooperation (CEEC) and the method by which they were screened by the executive branch.

Basic commodities and productive equipment which are essential to the reactivation of the European economy were subjected to careful study by committees composed of technical experts drawn from the participating countries. The CEEC established technical committees covering the fields of food and agriculture, fuel and power, iron and steel, transport, timber, and manpower. These technical committees collected exhaustive information from each of the participating countries and prepared technical reports based on an expert examination and evaluation of the materials bearing on their subject. Each of these technical reports outlines the nature of the commodity problem, establishes anticipated levels of production, estimates and justifies the amount of requirements needed to achieve the objectives of the program, and indicates the net amount of import requirements which the participating countries taken together will need from the rest of the world.

In addition to the technical committees mentioned above, the CEEC also formed a balance of payments committee to translate the net import requirements of the participating countries into financial terms and a committee of financial experts to examine ways and means of removing financial obstacles to intra-European trade.

The general report of the CEEC together with the detailed reports of the technical committees were transmitted to the United States Government on September 22, 1947.

The executive branch made a close analysis of the principal commodity requirements of the participating countries. The commodities and services selected for this detailed scrutiny were generally those which the CEEC regarded as the basic essentials for recovery and also those which involved difficult supply problems.

In these selected areas, the executive branch first examined the data presented in the CEEC reports to determine that, apart from supply considerations, the program was not based on unwarranted assumptions regarding levels of consumption or rates of new investment activity. Judgments based on expert knowledge and experience were required in each step of this process. The criteria adopted for this stage of the screening process, however, are easily explained. A requirement figure was regarded as unjustified until it could be demonstrated that the country concerned needed a commodity for its economic recovery or that it could not dispense with that commodity on any reasonable and practical standard of consumption consistent with the objective of European economic recovery. For example, on this basis the stated needs for certain types of heavy agricultural machinery were disregarded because it is believed that European farms are not large enough to permit them to be utilized effectively in promoting economic recovery.

Against these estimates of requirements as initially justified, the executive branch set its first approximation of availabilities. The primary figure in this estimate was domestic production in each of the participating countries. It was assumed that within practical limits, such as established trade relations, the surplus production of each participating country would be made available to others in the group. An examination was then made to determine the extent to which these net deficiencies between domestic production and requirements of the participating countries taken together could be obtained from the rest of the world.

If the net import deficits could not be met from world availabilities, a reexamination was made to ascertain whether or not requirements could be further scaled down or alleviated by substitute commodities without imperiling the objective of the program. The substitution of finished steel for crude and semifinished steel is an example of this procedure. In food, however, there was no choice but to cut requirements from the desirable level of food intake to the practical level dictated by supply scarcities.

In the process of making its estimates, the executive branch consulted for several weeks with technical representatives of the CEEC. In addition to the information obtained in the course of these discussions, the executive branch utilized information obtained from the participating countries' missions in the United States, our missions in the CEEC countries, the United Nations and its specialized agencies, the Krug, Nourse, and Harriman reports, from private citizens and business firms, and from the American press.

At the same time, Members and committees of the Congress were examining various aspects of the program in preparation for intensive hearings which would enable the Congress to enact sound legislation.

Admittedly, the committee had not the time, or resources, or technical competence necessary to make detailed investigations of each of the CEEC requirement figures. The committee was convinced, however, that the methods used by the executive branch in the screening process were sound, and had been applied by competent individuals in a scientific manner. The results of the screening are brought out in the following sections of the report.

18. REQUIREMENTS OF THE PARTICIPATING COUNTRIES

The committee has accepted generally the validity of the estimated requirements of the participating countries as screened and presented by the executive branch. The estimates and timetable (dating from April 1, 1948), far from being extravagant, seem to provide a tight fit in view of the far-reaching objective of economy recovery. The committee recognizes, furthermore, that in actual practice the Economic Cooperation Administration must keep its program of assistance flexible so that adjustments can be made from time to time in light of specific needs and supply considerations and subject to the general provisions of the bill.

The following table gives the exports from the Western Hemisphere of certain major commodities for the period April 1, 1948, to June 30, 1949. The financing of a substantial portion of these exports will require United States assistance under the program.

Estimated quantities of selected imports of the participating countries from the United States and other Western Hemisphere countries Apr. 1, 1948, to June 30, 1949

Commodity	Unit	From United States	From other Western Hemisphere	Total
Bread grains	Thousands of metric tons	8,195	9,165	17,360
Coarse grains	do	1,205	4,055	5,260
Fats and oils	do	182	388	570
Oilcake and meal	do	246	1,468	1,714
Sugar	do	180	2,408	2,588
Meat	do	30	1,401	1,431
Pulses	do	187	122	309
Dairy products	do	562	71	633
Eggs	do	60	95	155
Dried fruits	do	153	3	156
Fresh fruits	do	358	261	619
Coffee	do		275	275
Cocoa	do		65	65
Tobacco	do	256	42	298
Cotton	do	691	296	987
Nitrogen fertilizer	do	82	132	214
Agricultural machinery	Millions of dollars	136	22	158
Coal	Thousands of metric tons	43,250		43,250
Coal-mining machinery	Millions of dollars	82		82
Petroleum [1]	Thousands of metric tons	29,274		29,274
Timber	Thousands of cubic feet board measure	2,310	6,599	8,909
Iron ore	Thousands of metric tons		1,475	1,475
Crude and semifinished steel	do	935	431	1,366
Finished steel	do	2,069		2,069
Trucks	Thousands of units	67	11	78
Freight cars	do	20		20
Steel equipment	Millions of dollars	48		48
Timber equipment	do	17		17
Electrical equipment	do	95		95

[1] Includes imports of oil and petroleum products by participating countries from the United States and from American companies operating in the Caribbean, Middle East, and other areas outside the United States. It is expected that the proportion of these imports coming from the United States will be 20 to 30 percent in volume during the period Apr. 1, 1948, through June 30, 1949.

The principal requirements of the participating countries and western Germany for the 4 years 1948–51 from the United States as indicated in the CEEC report fall into four major categories: Food and fertilizer, 26.5 percent; coal and petroleum, 14.2 percent; iron and steel, 5.9 percent; timber, 2 percent; and equipment, 16.2 percent. This amounts to 64.8 percent of the total. The balance of the import requirements consists of a wide variety of specialty products, many of which are produced in quantity only in the United States.

The committee appreciates the fact that the executive branch has had to make reductions and substitutions in the estimates of net import requirements given in the CEEC report by determining the urgency of need of particular commodities, the size of the import requirements remaining after supplies from indigenous production are increased to practical limits and are properly utilized, and by judging the extent to which the United States can prudently and wisely undertake to meet those import requirements.

The reductions and substitutions made by the executive branch in the CEEC estimates are illustrated by the following tables:

Comparison of selected food and agricultural import requirements for 1948–49 [1] *as estimated by CEEC and by the executive branch (dependent overseas territories are not included)*

Commodity	Unit	Estimated total import requirements		Executive branch estimate as percent of CEEC estimate
		CEEC	Executive branch	
Bread grains	Thousand metric tons	17,988	14,270	79
Coarse grains	do	9,349	5,700	61
Fats and oils	do	2,968	2,464	83
Oilcake and meal	do	4,417	2,750	62
Sugar	do	3,053	3,056	100
Meat (including horse meat)	do	2,603	1,933	74
Cheese	do	279	249	89
Processed milk	do	240	346	144
Eggs	do	346	209	60
Dried fruit and nuts	do	455	493	108
Rice	do	352	140	40
Coffee (green)	do	422	435	103
Pulses	do		530	
Fresh fruits	do	2,811	2,818	100
Cocoa	do	338	276	82
Tobacco	do	247	328	133
Nitrogen fertilizer	do	297	180	61
Agricultural machinery	Million dollars	266	160	60

[1] CEEC estimated requirements for food and agricultural commodities were based on crop years, July 1 to June 30 of the following year. The first year of estimated requirements under the European recovery program was assumed by CEEC to relate to the crop year 1947–48. Requirements are larger in 1947–48 than in 1948–49 and following years. The CEEC assumed that full satisfaction of its 1947–48 requirements would result in much lower requirements in 1948–49 and later years. However, CEEC requirements for 1947–48 were in fact not met, and therefore the CEEC would probably want to revise its requirement estimates upward for 1948–49. In the table given above, the CEEC requirements relate to 1948–49 rather than to 1947–48. Since the 1948–49 CEEC requirements are lower than those for 1947–48, the extent to which the executive branch estimates of requirements differ from those of the CEEC is understated.

Comparison of certain selected import requirements from the United States for comparable 12-month periods as estimated by CEEC and by the executive branch (dependent oversea territories are not included)

Commodity	Unit	Import requirements from United States		Executive branch estimate as percent of CEEC estimate
		CEEC, calendar year 1948	Executive branch, fiscal year 1949	
Petroleum (from dollar sources)[1]	Thousand metric tons	23,766	19,542	82
Timber	Million board feet	789	789	100
Crude and semifinished steel	Thousand metric tons	2,040	748	37
Pig iron	do	182	35	19
Scrap (or pig-iron equivalent)	do	1,399		0
Finished steel, other than sheets and tin plate.[2]	do	449	1,150	256
Timber equipment [3]	Million dollars	10.1	9.8	97
Electrical equipment	do	150	95	63
Freight cars	Thousand units	47	20	43
Steel plant and equipment	Million dollars	100	48	48

[1] Total imports from dollar sources, largely outside the continental United States.

[2] Executive branch estimates of finished-steel requirements of the participating countries from the United States take account of the anticipated deficits in pig iron, crude and semifinished steel, and scrap requirements of the participating countries. To the extent that availabilities in the United States permit, the executive branch has estimated that finished steel might offset in part the deficits in pig iron, scrap, and crude and semifinished steel. Taking these selected iron and steel products on a ton-for-ton basis, the executive branch estimated that 48 percent of CEEC requirements of 4,070,000,000 metric tons of iron and steel might be met.

[3] Total timber equipment requirements in 1948, as estimated by the CEEC, are 16.4 million dollars, of which 6.3 million dollars were for dependent areas of the United Kingdom and France. In order to raise productivity in the timber-producing colonial areas, the executive branch estimated that 7.1 million dollars of timber equipment might be made available from the United States to these dependent areas in the fiscal year 1948–49.

85-743 O - 73 - 41

The program as recommended by the executive branch and accepted by the committee is based upon detailed commodity and country studies.

The committee recognizes that it is difficult to be precise either as to the cost and composition of the import requirements or as to the level of dollar earnings achieved by exports and other dollar funds which the participating countries may be able to obtain from sources other than new United States Treasury funds. The following estimates for the 15-month period April 1, 1948, to June 30, 1949, however, were presented by the executive branch, and it is the committee's judgment that these estimates have generally withstood critical examination.

European Recovery Program Committee—Recapitulation table: Illustrative composition of imports of commodities and services from Western Hemisphere and possible sources and distribution of financing, Apr. 1, 1948, to June 30, 1949 (at July 1, 1947, prices)

[In millions of dollars]

Import	Total imports	Possible sources and distribution of financing		
		Own resources	Sources other than United States funds	United States funds
Bread grains	1,600.3	138.8	336.7	1,124.8
Coarse grains	552.3	68.6	66.6	417.1
Fats and oils	378.4	29.2	76.2	273.0
Oilcake	190.7	17.4	33.3	140.0
Sugar	295.8	35.1	33.4	227.3
Meat	393.1	14.5	33.3	345.3
Dairy products	275.2			275.2
Eggs	85.3	6.7		78.6
Dried fruit	34.3	2.8		31.5
Rice	47.8	3.1		44.7
Coffee	156.6	34.1	38.3	84.2
Other foods	168.0	23.5		144.5
Subtotal	4,177.8	373.8	617.8	3,186.2
Tobacco	293.4	57.3		236.1
Cotton	790.0	214.4	42.1	533.5
Nitrogen	42.8	5.2		37.6
Phosphates	3.1	.5		2.6
Potash				
Agricultural machinery	158.7	12.6	12.9	133.2
Coal	389.3	13.5		375.8
Mining machinery	81.9	1.0	2.9	78.0
Petroleum products	651.9	330.1		321.8
Timber	333.4	185.7	16.0	131.7
Iron and steel:				
Finished	226.7	85.9	21.7	119.1
Crude and semifinished	86.2	57.4		28.8
Pig iron	1.6	.2		1.4
Scrap iron	2.0			2.0
Iron ore	8.8			8.8
Trucks	116.8	17.0	21.8	78.0
Freight cars	60.0			60.0
Steel equipment	48.1		9.1	39.0
Timber equipment	17.0	.4		16.6
Electrical equipment	95.0	5.0	6.0	84.0
Other imports	4,228.2	3,025.3	408.0	794.9
Total commodity imports	11,812.7	4,385.3	1,158.3	6,269.1
Net freight	827.0	235.5		591.5
Other dollar payments	319.4	319.4		
Total	12,959.1	4,940.2	1,158.3	6,860.6

The participating countries and western Germany, according to column 1 in the preceding table, will require imports from the Western Hemisphere amounting to $12,959,000,000. The executive branch estimates that these countries as a group will export about $4,940,000,000 of goods and services to the Western Hemisphere in the first period of 15 months. This estimate is indicated in column 2. The difference between column 1 and column 2, amounting to $8,019,000,000, indicates the approximate net deficit which the participating countries and western Germany will probably incur on current account with the the Western Hemisphere. It should be emphasized at this point that the indicated net deficit of the participating countries with the Western Hemisphere is based on the assumption that these countries will engage in a vigorous domestic productive effort and will cooperate fully in measures of self-help and of mutual assistance, and will thus reduce their requirements from the Western Hemisphere to a minimum consistent with a true recovery program.

In addition to dollar earnings obtained through exports, the participating countries will also be expected to obtain funds from such sources as the International Bank and credits advanced by Western Hemisphere countries other than the United States. The amount of these funds, expressed in terms of July 1, 1947, prices, are indicated in column 3. The difference between net imports (column 1) and export proceeds plus borrowings from sources other than net United States Treasury funds (column 2 plus column 3) appears in column 4. About $6,860,000,000, in terms of July 1, 1947, prices, will be needed to meet the uncovered import deficit of the participating countries and western Germany with the Western Hemisphere in the 15-month period.

This estimate of the uncovered deficit with the Western Hemisphere amounting to $6,860,000,000 is reconciled with the executive branch's request for an authorization of $6,800,000,000 in the following tabulation:

		Millions
Goods to be purchased in Western Hemisphere with new United States funds (at July 1, 1947, prices), column 4 of recapitulation		$6, 860
Adjustments:		
Add adjustment for price increases [1]	$482	
Deduct savings on shipping [2]	100	
		382
Adjusted cost of commodities and shipping services to be purchased in Western Hemisphere with new United States funds		7, 242
Authority to obligate funds for procurement of items to be delivered in subsequent years		200
Uncovered deficit of bizonal Germany with nonparticipating countries outside the Western Hemisphere		200
Total being requested for European recovery program and by Department of Army for Germany (GARIOA)		7, 642
Deduct appropriations being requested by Department of Army for prevention of disease and unrest in Germany (GARIOA)		822
Total requirement for first 15 months, European recovery program		6, 820
Authorization requested for European recovery program (preceding line in rounded amount)		6, 800

[1] This figure is equivalent to the adjustment for higher prices of $565,000,000.
[2] These are possible savings if additional temporary transfers of bulk-cargo carriers are made.

The preceding tables have indicated the magnitude of the import requirements and possible sources of finances upon which the participating countries as a group might be able to draw. Each of the participating countries, however, has its particular import requirements from the Western Hemisphere, its possible sources of funds to finance those import requirements, and, finally, many of the countries have the particular problem of a net import deficit which requires a solution. The following table high lights these problems on a country-by-country basis:

TABLE 1.—*Recapitulation of tables showing illustrative composition of imports of commodities and services from Western Hemisphere and possible sources and distribution of financing, Apr. 1, 1948, to June 30, 1949*

[At July 1, 1947, prices]

	Total imports [1]	Possible sources of financing		
		Dollar earnings [2]	Sources other than new United States funds	New United States funds [3]
	Mils. of dols.	*Mils. of dols.*		*Mils. of dols.*
Austria	233	39	12	182
Belgium-Luxemburg	853	334	196	323
Denmark	237	45	28	164
Finance	1,931	369	128	1,434
Greece	262	67	9	186
Iceland	23	10		13
Ireland	192	40		152
Italy	1,160	183	108	869
Netherlands	1,136	271	160	705
Norway	253	163	56	34
Portugal	144	144		
Sweden	499	423	43	33
Switzerland	535	535		
Turkey	69	69		
United Kingdom	4,311	2,133	418	1,760
Germany:				
Bizone	1,014	100		914
French zone	93	13		80
Saar	14	3		11
Total	12,959	4,941	1,158	[3] 6,860

[1] Including net dollar payments for freight and other invisibles.
[2] Including drawings of $72,000,000 by Portugal on its gold and foreign-exchange resources.
[3] This column includes funds being requested by the Department of the Army for prevention of disease and unrest in Germany. A reconciliation with the $6,800,000,000 being requested for the European recovery program is made elsewhere.

It must be emphasized, however, that the country-by-country distributions are very tentative and are not binding upon the Administrator. The amounts in column (4), which indicate the possible country distribution of new United States funds, do not necessarily represent the amount which each participating country would receive nor the terms on which such sums would be advanced by the Administrator.

It should be emphasized that the estimates given above are based on the assumption that certain of the participating countries, notably Portugal and Switzerland and possibly Turkey, will not require any financial assistance from the United States, either in the form of loans or of grants. Their participation in the program is based on their ability to assist in furthering the recovery objective and the advantages to them of general European economic recovery and not on the basis of anticipated financial assistance from the United States.

19. THE BALANCE-OF-PAYMENTS SITUATION

The standard of living and the rate of economic development in Europe depend in the final analysis upon European production and resources. In the first period the amount of proposed outside assistance represents less than 5 or 6 percent of the estimated national income of the participating countries.

The "shortage of dollars" is basically the shortage of world production and trade to get dollars. For example, the European countries cannot, without frustrating recovery, produce enough goods and services to satisfy indigenous requirements and to export at a level equivalent to their total Western Hemisphere requirements amounting in the next 15 months to $12,959,000,000.

The committee accepts the general reasoning of the program—that if the import requirements of the European countries are no less than the amount indicated above, and that if the assumed volume of exports is achieved, these countries will still be subjected to very severe strains even under the most favorable developments.

Without wishing to prejudge the figure of $822,000,000 being requested separately for Germany by the Department of the Army, the following summary, including at the time of the committee's action the adjustment for price increases, appears to be realistic:

Summary of balance of payments deficit of the participating countries with the Western Hemisphere for the period Apr. 1, 1948–June 30, 1949, and proposed sources of financing

[In millions of dollars]

	United States	Other Western Hemisphere	Total Western Hemisphere
	Mils. of dols.	*Mils. of dols.*	*Mils. of dols.*
1. Selected imports	4,239	3,346	7,585
2. Other imports	2,750	1,478	4,228
3. Total imports	6,989	4,824	11,813
4. Selected exports	295	303	598
5. Other exports	1,960	1,455	3,415
6. Total exports	2,265	1,758	4,013
7. Merchandise balance	−4,734	−3,066	−7,800
8. Freight (net)	−293	−145	−438
9. Other invisibles (net)	+263	+13	+276
10. Balance (July 1, 1947, prices), break-down available by countries	−4,764	−3,198	−7,962
11. Adjustment for higher prices	−412	−153	−565
All above figures based on July 1, 1947, prices, as was CEEC. This adjustment allows for a 7½-percent rise in United States and 5 percent in other Western Hemisphere export prices, and a 5-percent rise in European export prices. The rise in prices may well be greater than this allowance covers.			
12. Adjusted balance	−5,176	−3,351	−8,527
13. Total deficit, Western Hemisphere			8,527
14. Uncovered deficit, bizonal Germany, with nonparticipating countries outside Western Hemisphere			200
15. Total to be financed			8,727
16. To be met by sources other than new U. S. Treasury financing			−1,285

Summary of balance of payments deficit of the participating countries with the Western Hemisphere for the period Apr. 1, 1948–June 30, 1949, and proposed sources of financing—Continued

[In millions of dollars]

	United States	Other Western Hemisphere	Total Western Hemisphere
	Mils. of dols.	*Mils. of dols.*	*Mils. of dols.*
17. Total new financing by U. S. Treasury			7,442
18. Appropriations being requested by Army for prevention of disease and unrest in Germany			−822
19. Subtotal			6,620
20. Add: Funds required for obligation prior to June 30, 1949, to cover contracts for shipments in subsequent period			200
21. Total requirement for first 15 months, ERP			6,820
Rounded to			6,800

The CEEC countries did not indicate that the assistance of the United States would be essential in meeting the deficits of the participating countries with nonparticipating countries outside the Western Hemisphere. But it is appropriate for the United States Government, as an occupying authority, to take responsibility for a part of the deficit which bizonal Germany will incur with nonparticipating countries outside the Western Hemisphere. As indicated in line 14 of the above table, about $200,000,000 will be required for this purpose in the period April 1, 1948, to June 30, 1949.

20. AVAILABILITY OF COMMODITIES

The committee observed that the proposed program is based upon a realistic assessment of availabilities in this country and the rest of the world. The reductions made in the CEEC estimates by the executive branch arise in part from lower estimates as to the availability and probable future supplies of such commodities as grain, fats and oils, steel scrap, petroleum, and freight cars.

Food.—The Secretary of Agriculture testified that the amount of food required under the program could be provided after fulfilling our own domestic requirements and without upsetting the existing domestic channels of trade. In general, the total food requirements of the participating countries for the first 15-month period are well above the probable total availabilities. Food shipments from the United States are expected to be appreciably smaller than for the past 2 years. Even so, it may be necessary to delay for a few years our start in adjusting to more desirable wheat acreages.

(*a*) Bread grains: Low availabilities of bread grains will most seriously affect food consumption in the participating countries. Western Europe was a prewar food deficit area and will continue to be so even under the most favorable conditions. Food consumption targets as planned by the CEEC countries will not be achieved by 1952 unless there is a series of very favorable crop conditions in many areas of the world. If conservation measures and crop prospects are favorable in the United States, the program contemplates shipment from the United States to participating countries and their dependent overseas territories of 89,000,000 bushels of bread grains between April 1 and June 30, 1948 and 218,000,000 bushels during the fiscal year 1948–49. During the 15-month period, exports of bread grains from nonparticipating countries other than the United States constitute 61 percent of the total imports of the participating countries. The volume of exports from the other Americas and eastern Europe will be of decisive importance.

(*b*) Coarse grains: Western European nations cannot restore their livestock as rapidly as would be desirable from their viewpoint because they will not be able to import enough feed grains. Exports from the United States of coarse grains in fiscal 1948–49 would be about 45,000,000 bushels. Most, if not all, of these grains should be used for food purposes. There should be no difficulty on the part of the United States in meeting this requirement.

(*c*) Fats and oils: United States exports of fats and oils to Europe under the proposed program would be more than offset by imports into the United States. This country normally exports edible fats and imports inedibles.

(*d*) Meat: No export of the types of meat consumed in the United States are planned during the first 15 months of this program. A small amount of horse meat will be shipped.

Fertilizer.—The need for fertilizers to increase indigenous supplies of food remains acute and the world demand is greater than at any time in history. Nitrogen consumption in the United States has more than doubled in the last decade. Nitrogen fertilizer allocation recommendations are under the International Emergency Food Council. It is unlikely that more than the current rate of 70,000 tons annually, including shipments by the United States Army, could be exported from the United States to the participating countries. The present rate of exports from the United States represents about 8 percent of our total yearly commercial supply of nitrogen and 4 percent of our phosphate rock. The supply available for United States farmers would be maintained at about the present levels.

Agricultural machinery.—Farm machinery is badly needed in western Europe to increase production. The CEEC request would have taken about one-third of the estimated 1946 production of the United States. Noimally, Europe has taken about 5 percent of our production. The proposed $136,000,000 program for the 15-month period would double that percentage but increased production in this country should provide for this program and also maintain the supply at a slightly higher rate than currently to the American farmer and take care of our other regular customers abroad. Every effort must be made to see that the exact amounts and kinds of machinery furnished will be fitted to the needs of these countries and used to the best advantage.

Coal.—The United States resources are adequate to provide the quantity of western European coal import requirements, although this program will call for full and efficient use of our transportation system. The coal mining equipment requirements essential to the expansion of coal mining productivity have been carefully reviewed in consultation with American manufacturers. It is considered that these requirements can be met if production can be scheduled promptly.

Electrical equipment.—Large generating equipment, of the types in which supply problems now exist in this country, is not expected to be supplied in the initial period. Our contribution in electrical equipment is relatively small in dollar amount, but involves many items of specialized character available only from the United States.

Timber.—The volume of timber requested from this country appears to be moderate and within the limits of what we can supply, especially by exporting types not in major demand in this country.

Freight cars.—The CEEC estimated requirements for 1948 are 47,000 cars. This request did not appear to be fully justified, and in view of the large internal needs in the United States, provision was made for exports from the United States of only 20,000 cars in 1948–49. This estimate of requirements conforms with the judgment of the Harriman committee on this subject.

Tobacco.—The western European countries have traditionally been our largest tobacco export market. The shortage of dollar exchange, however, has prevented the participating countries from importing the full amount of their requirements for American tobacco. As a result of the sudden curtailment of exports, a reserve of tobacco has accumulated in the United States. Tobacco imports to the participating countries provide an outlet for excess consumer purchasing power and thereby contribute to the alleviation of inflationary pressures in the domestic economy. Furthermore, in many western European countries sales of tobacco provide an important source of revenue to the Government. Tobacco ranks as a readily available incentive, good for purposes of encouraging labor to work increased hours and on stepped-up production schedules.

Petroleum, iron and steel.—Owing to the special problems regarding the requirements and availability of petroleum and iron and steel, these commodities are considered at some length in separate sections of this report.

21. AVAILABILITY OF PETROLEUM

In order to protect the petroleum reserves of the United States, the committee provided in the bill that the procurement of petroleum and petroleum products shall to the maximum extent practicable be made from petroleum sources outside the United States. The original CEEC requests for 26,493,000 metric tons from dollar sources in the first 12 months has been reduced 18 percent by the executive branch because of the critical shortages of oil, transportation, and refining facilities. This reduction should not appreciably retard recovery in Europe, although substantial adjustments will be required in programs of emergency utilization.

Very little, if any, fuel oil will be exported from the United States. A sizable proportion of United States exports will consist of specialty products, such as lubricants, which can be obtained in volume only from the United States. In percent of United States production, shipments to participating countries will account for 1.8 percent of United States crude oil output in 1948 or about 11 percent of their import requirements. Our exports of petroleum will be more than offset by imports. Total European requirements of petroleum are to be met largely from the other Western Hemisphere areas (supplying 50 percent of the requirements in 1948) and from the Middle East (supplying 38.6 percent in 1948 and an increasingly large proportion thereafter). It is estimated that the United States exports to CEEC countries will decline from the 1938 level of 77,000,000 barrels to 35,000,000 barrels in 1948.

Your committee gave considerable attention to the possible impact of current political uncertainties in the Middle East on the security and reliability of that area as a source of supply for Europe. This and other factors led the committee to underline the danger that western Europe, which has little petroleum wealth of its own, may be overexpanding, from the viewpoint of its own welfare, the petroleum-consuming equipment where the use of alternate fuels or other sources of power are practicable. For example, the CEEC report contemplated some substitution of petroleum-burning equipment for coal-burning equipment and an over-all petroleum consumption level in 1951 double that in 1938. The estimates of the executive branch assumed that these substitutions contemplated by the CEEC would not be possible. Coal remains the basic source of energy in western Europe and in 1951 will account for about 80 percent of total energy production.

22. AVAILABILITY OF IRON AND STEEL

The estimates of the executive branch on iron and steel import requirements of the participating countries recognize that an adequate supply of steel is a prime necessity for a thriving European economy. Steel requirements for European recovery exceed prewar consumption levels, since a substantial backlog of war damage and deferred maintenance of plant and machinery must be made up as rapidly as practical. Furthermore, increased output and export of metal products are essential to the achievement of equilibrium in the European balance of payments. Taking selected iron and steel products on a ton-for-ton basis, the executive branch estimates that 48 percent of the CEEC requirements of iron and steel might be met.

Current steel output of the participating countries together with western Germany is about 70 percent of the 1938 level. The CEEC finished steel production target is set at 30,000,000 tons in 1948, or about 9,000,000 tons above the current rate. United States studies of European steel production possibilities indicate that shortages of steel-making materials, particularly imported scrap, might prevent CEEC targets from being reached in 1948. The finished steel and metal fabricating industries of the United Kingdom and Italy will be principally affected by the unavailability of imported scrap, pig iron and crude and semifinished steel.

In order to alleviate and partially offset the unfavorable effects of prospective deficits in steel-making materials, including semifinished steel, the executive branch estimated that finished steel might be exported in quantities larger than those indicated for finished steel by the CEEC report. This course of possible action was recommended after a thorough exploration of suggested alternatives.

One suggestion was that the participating countries might further reduce their programed exports of finished steel. Some reduction in programed exports of finished steel by the participating countries will undoubtedly occur, according to the executive branch estimates. Further reductions would gravely endanger the long-run position of the participating countries, which together were the major prewar exporters of steel to the rest of the world, to regain export markets and to earn vitally needed foreign exchange. Furthermore, in the world's presently disorganized markets, ability to export steel and related products to certain countries also confers on the participating countries an ability to obtain foodstuffs and raw materials on more favorable terms.

A second suggestion relates to the possibilities of expanding steel production and exports of bizone Germany. Examination of the situation, however, indicates that bottleneck factors ranging from transport to replacement-parts shortages will effectively limit output below the amount of steel-making capacity scheduled for retention in that area. The occupation authorities also have indicated that additional steel production, except for amounts already earmarked for export, will be needed to reactivate the economy of bizone Germany. However, the committee assumes that careful attention will be given to the possibility of increasing bizonal steel-ingot production.

Accordingly, the executive branch estimated that 1,150,000 metric tons of finished steel in addition to sheet and tinplate requirements might be made available from the United States to the participating countries in fiscal 1949. This country in 1947 exported about 4,000,000 tons of finished steel and about 1.2 million tons of such exports were destined to the participating countries. Although production of finished steel in the United States for the first 9 months of 1947, according to the Harriman Committee report, was equivalent to an annual rate of 62,300,000 net tons of finished steel products, exports of steel at the 1947 rate will continue to pinch the domestic economy. In view of all the circumstances, however, exports of finished steel to the participating countries in the amount estimated by the executive branch are essential to European recovery and will not significantly impair the strength and productivity of the American economy.

23. THE IMPACT OF THE RECOVERY PROGRAM UPON THE DOMESTIC ECONOMY

After extensive inquiry, the committee has come to the conclusion that, given efficient administration of the program, the American economy is able to withstand the general impact of a new foreign aid program of the size contemplated. Continued high levels of economic activity in the United States and efficient resource utilization are assumed. It is also assumed that the American people regard a European recovery program as worthy of some short-run sacrifices, chiefly in terms of some retardation in our rising standards of living. A small fraction of the strength of the American economy, properly applied and aided by the industry and straight thinking of the European people, can furnish the impetus to move the European economy off dead-center.

While it has been necessary to examine this conclusion on a commodity-by-commodity basis, and with due regard to the depletion of our resources, the great strength and inherent flexibility of our private enterprise economy must be kept in perspective.

Our gross national product in 1947 was over $230,000,000,000 of which only 8 percent was exported. The committee was impressed by the fact that the 1948 level of exports, including those contemplated in this program, will be less than in 1947.

The excess of exports over imports is the final test of the over-all inflationary impact of this program upon the United States. Assuming the full authorization of 5.3 billion dollars, this excess is expected to be at least $1,000,000,000 less than in 1947. Furthermore, the Krug report concludes:

From the standpoint of preserving both the national security and our standard of living, our economy in general is physically capable of providing the resource requirements of a considerable program of foreign aid.

The Executive Branch concludes that inflation is largely the result of factors other than exports and that depletion of our natural resources is a long-run problem which we must solve with or without a European recovery program. The foreign-aid program, not in itself the principal factor, nevertheless compels us to face certain domestic problems squarely.

Almost all the testimony points to the serious fact that the problems raised by specific commodities in relatively short supply, if not dealt with effectively, could destroy this optimistic picture. The United States is no limitless cornucopia. There is no slack in the American economy, and every shipment of scarce goods—especially food, steel, industrial and agricultural machinery, and fertilizer which Europe must have—adds to the economic danger of inflation which means a shortage of goods in relation to demand. Such critical commodities can tip the scale between stability and inflation and start a chain reaction in our economy even though the percentage of our export to western Europe to total production is relatively small. It is clear that the impact of a new foreign-aid program will depend upon the domestic measures we adopt and the skill applied in the administration of the recovery program. In its proposals regarding these critical commodities, the executive branch has proceeded with caution.

Under this bill the obligations upon the Administrator are clear. Procurement must be provided for in such a way as to (1) minimize the drain upon the resources of the United States and the impact of such procurement upon the domestic economy, and (2) avoid impairing the fulfillment of vital needs of the people of the United States. The bill provides that the Administrator, in procuring agricultural commodities within the United States will, subject to the stated conditions, provide for the procurement of an amount of each class or type of any such commodities in approximate proportion to the total exportable supply of such class or type of such commodity. In addition, the bill provides for a businesslike, highly responsible Administrator, within the executive branch, which should be able to cushion these impacts upon our domestic economy.

Part IV. Special Problems in Connection With the Program

24. METHOD OF PROCUREMENT

In considering the procedures to be followed in the procurement of commodities for transfer to participating countries, the committee adopted two basic principles: the first is that private procurement and normal channels of commerce, trade, and transportation are to be used to the maximum extent practicable; the second principle is that flexibility in the procurement procedures, subject to such controls as may be necessary to assure proper expenditure, is essential to an adequate functioning of a program of such magnitude and complexity.

It is intended that procurement through United States Government channels will be utilized normally where necessary to assure that purchases for this program will not unduly affect the price level in this country or other aspects of the domestic economy. An example of this is the procurement of wheat through the Commodity Credit Corporation. Where procurement is through private channels, the bill establishes adequate safeguards to make certain that this Government's funds have been properly expended in execution of approved programs of supply.

25. PROCUREMENT OF COMMODITIES OUTSIDE THE UNITED STATES

The bill authorizes the Administrator to provide for procurement from sources outside of the United States. This authority is required primarily to protect against inflationary tendencies which would result from concentrated buying in this country of commodities in inadequate supply in the United States. Commodities available from other Western Hemisphere countries are among those in shortest supply in the United States. The scope of the recovery program and the wide range of the supplies involved make it impractical to limit the Administrator's authority to procure outside the United States although such limitations were included in earlier foreign-aid legislation.

The program assumes that other Western Hemisphere countries will, in addition to the credits they have previously provided to the CEEC countries, help to meet the CEEC countries' deficits at least to the extent of $700,000,000 from their own resources during the first 15 months. The offshore purchases in dollars permitted under this bill will also have the effect of assisting Western Hemisphere countries to meet their urgent dollar requirements with some of their export surplus. The Administrator is in a position to make certain that procurement outside the United States is on reasonable commercial terms.

Instances may arise in which the Administrator will find it desirable to finance the procurement for one participating country of commodities which are available in another such country. This will make possible increased trade among the participating countries and will make available dollar exchange to the exporting country thereby diminishing its requirements for direct assistance from the United States.

The planned offshore purchases are largely from the Western Hemisphere. Food products comprise about 60 percent of the total. The illustrative work sheets prepared by the executive branch indicate tentatively that about $2,615,000,000 or 38 percent of the requested $6,800,000,000 (15-month period) are needed for offshore procurement, or approximately $2,000,000,000 for the 12-month period.

Further, the bill states that the procurement of petroleum and petroleum products shall to the maximum extent practicable be made from petroleum sources outside the United States. Most of the purchases in dollars, however, will be from American companies operating in the Caribbean and Middle East areas.

The committee contemplates that offshore procurement of commodities will be effected to a very large extent through the normal channels of trade.

The following table is inserted here for illustrative purposes:

Illustrative distribution by commodities of United States funds for offshore procurement

[In millions of dollars at July 1, 1947, prices]

	Value
Bread grains	389. 2
Coarse grains	301. 5
Fats and oils	172. 8
Oilcake and meal	121. 0
Sugar	179. 7
Meat	334. 5
Dairy products	40. 0
Eggs	47. 1
Dried fruit	. 6
Rice	39. 4
Coffee	82. 0
Other foods	67. 3
Subtotal	1, 775. 1
Nitrogen	21. 2
Agricultural machinery	17. 9
Petroleum	(1)
Timber	37. 3
Iron ore	8. 8
Trucks	9. 4
Timber equipment	. 1
Other imports [2]	620. 2
Total	2, 490. 0
Adjustment for price increases after July 1, 1947	125. 0
United States funds for offshore procurement	2, 615. 0

[1] Petroleum is not included in the above table inasmuch as all purchases in dollars of petroleum will be from United States companies. The petroleum to be shipped to the participating countries by United States companies will be largely from sources outside the continental United States.

[2] This item is made up of various important raw materials, such as nonferrous metals and ores, hides and skins, chemicals, wood pulp and newsprint, and of various manufactures and semimanufactures, and machinery and parts.

26. STRATEGIC MATERIALS AND STOCK PILING

Lend lease and the Second World War cut deeply into the available stocks of natural resources of the United States. This would indicate the necessity of increased imports of such strategic materials as chromite, manganese, bauxite, lead, and zinc. In principle, this country is committed to a program for stock piling strategic materials on a large scale which can be done only by expanding total world production. The dependent territories of western European countries can contribute much to the production of strategic metals and minerals.

The committee deems this matter to be of the utmost importance and believes that the proposed method of obtaining strategic materials contained in the bill is more likely to result in our obtaining a larger quantity of such materials than alternative plans which have been suggested.

Section 15, paragraph 5, provides that the bilateral agreements should facilitate—

> the transfer to the United States by sale, exchange, barter, or otherwise for stock-piling purposes, for such period of time as may be agreed to and upon reasonable terms and in reasonable quantities, of materials which are required by the United States as a result of deficiencies or potential deficiencies in its own resources, and which may be available in such participating country after due regard for reasonable requirements for domestic use and commercial export of such country.

Agreements with participating countries for the transfer of such materials may extend beyond the period of the bill and will specify the terms and quantities governing the transfer of such material.

In addition, part of the funds appropriated may be used by the Administrator of ECA to finance development of increased sources of supply. Technical information and assistance may be provided for increasing production. Local currency proceeds may be used to foster exploration development.

The Administrator under certain circumstances may require the repayment of loans under the program in the form of delivery of strategic materials. Section 11, subsection c, paragraph 1, makes explicit reference to this subject even though the Administrator would possess authority to take such action under the general language of this subsection. Ordinarily, it is contemplated that such materials will be purchased by us with dollars separately appropriated. If we require the delivery of strategic materials as a consideration for a grant, the capacity of the country to repay any loans would correspondingly be diminished. In calculating the capacity of a country to repay, its receipts from future exports of all types, including strategic materials which might be sold to us, should be taken into consideration.

27. SHIPPING AND THE RECOVERY PROGRAM

The committee carefully examined the problem of providing shipping to the participating countries. The proposal which the committee had submitted to it was for authority in the legislation to sell and charter merchant vessels to participating countries. It was proposed that 200 vessels would be sold and 300 chartered. In making its examination, the committee considered the possible adverse effect of such action on our merchant marine and merchant seamen and on our national defense. The committee also took into account the joint resolution entitled "A joint resolution to continue until March 1, 1949, the authority of the Maritime Commission to sell, charter, and operate vessels, and for other purposes" amending the Merchant Ship Sales Act of 1946 by prohibiting the sale or charter of United States war-built merchant vessels to foreign nations.

The committee decided that, in the circumstances, it would be unwise to authorize the transfer of title to American merchant ships. On the other hand, the committee felt that to prohibit the temporary transfer for a limited period of time would be uneconomic and contrary to the best interests of the American people. The legislation therefore authorizes the charter of 300 dry-cargo merchant vessels.

In making this authorization, the committee was guided by the following considerations which were not present in the Senate's consideration of the Joint Resolution referred to above. The charter of these 300 vessels, for a period not to extend beyond June 30, 1952, would permit a savings to the American taxpayer, over the 4½-year period, of approximately $240,000,000, based on July 1, 1947 freight rates. Moreover, the Maritime Commission has estimated that the size of the long-range active United States merchant fleet will be 11,400,000 deadweight tons, which estimate was concurred in by the armed services. Since the present active fleet is approximately 24,000,000 deadweight tons, it is clear that a reduction in the size of the American merchant fleet is inevitable. To require the operation of these 300 vessels by the United States would therefore have the effect of maintaining our American merchant fleet at an abnormally high level for a temporary period, and postponing, at considerable cost to the United States Government, the inevitable readjustment that must be made.

The committee inquired of the Secretary of National Defense as to whether the national security interest of the United States would be prejudiced by the sale or transfer of ships. In his reply, Secretary Forrestal stated that, in his opinion, by the charter or transfer of title ot 500 vessels, or any lesser number, we stand to "gain more by such charter or transfer, from an over-all national security standpoint, than we stand to lose."

28. USE OF LOCAL CURRENCY DEPOSITS

Each participating country is required to deposit in a special account the local currency equivalent of commodities provided to them on a grant basis. This procedure is similar to that provided by the Foreign Aid Act of 1947.

These deposits may be used only for purposes agreed to between the participating country and the Administrator, the latter acting in consultation with the National Advisory Council. The committee strongly believes that this procedure will assure the use of these deposits in a manner consistent with, and in support of, the recovery effort. While it would be unwise at this time to prescribe the specific uses which could be made of such deposits, the following might be appropriate:

(*a*) Immobilization of the local currency, in whole or in part, to assist in measures of financial reform and currency stabilization;

(*b*) Use for retiring the national debt so as to promote the most rapid achievement of financial stability;

(*c*) Use for costs incidental to the development of additional production of raw materials which will be in short supply in the United States;

(*d*) Use to defray the costs in the currency of the participating country, pursuant to arrangements approved by the International Bank, of projects mutually agreed by the United States and the participating country as contributing to European recovery;

(*e*) Use for local currency administrative expenses of the United States incident to the operation of the program.

The committee considered the advisability of providing even greater control over the use of the local currency deposits through actual ownership by the United States. It determined, however, that this would seriously weaken the program and embarrass the United States. The size of the deposits in certain countries would be so large that United States ownership of the local currency involved would give our Government responsibility for the financial policies of these countries. This would not only be contradictory to the essential nature of the program—European recovery through self-help and mutual cooperation—but it would put the United States in the untenable position of assuming a responsibility which it could not possibly discharge. The committee is certain that the requirement that the deposits be utilized in agreement with the United States avoids the serious pitfalls which would result from any greater nominal or actual control.

As in the Foreign Aid Act of 1947, any agreement covering the disposition of unencumbered balances remaining on June 30, 1952, will have to be approved by the Congress of the United States.

29. THE ROLE OF WESTERN GERMANY IN THE PROGRAM

Throughout the hearings and during its deliberations in executive session the members of the committee attached great importance to the role of western Germany in a European recovery program. For many years prior to World War II Germany was the hub of the European industrial system. Its industrial production and its technical know-how have been instrumental in making western Europe a great manufacturing and trading center. Because of the devastation brought on themselves by the war and the resultant dislocation of the German economy, Germany has lagged far behind other States in its recovery program. At the present time their production is still less than 50 percent of its prewar figure. It is apparent that Europe cannot be vigorous and healthy again so long as Germany remains sick.

This does not mean that requirements for western Germany should be given priority in the European recovery program nor does it mean that steps would be taken which would result in the resurgence of Germany as a military power in Europe. Clearly United States assistance should be applied in a way as to obtain effective results. In line with this principle the committee believed that, where the recovery of Europe as a whole could be advanced more rapidly by supplying additional essential goods and services to Germany rather than to other participating countries, then such a course would seem justifiable. At the same time every precaution must be taken to prevent the rebuilding of German economy in such a way that Germany will ever again become a threat to the peace.

Inasmuch as the United States is one of the occupying powers our responsibility with respect to German participation in the European recovery program is great. Our representatives must cooperate fully with the other participating countries in matters of mutual concern. To this end it is expected that the zones of western Germany will be represented on the continuing organization to be established by the participating countries.

During the hearings Secretary Marshall announced that the State Department plans to take over from the Department of the Army on approximately July 1, 1948, the responsibility for the administration of United States occupation policies in Germany. Meanwhile, for the first year of the recovery progrım the appropriations for those minimum essentials necessary to forestall disease and unrest will be sought by the Army. The additional funds necessary for rehabilitation and recovery are included as a part of the present authorization. These funds will be allocated by the Administrator in such a way as to insure the proper integration of the German economy into the total European recovery program.

In view of the special responsibilities of the United States as one of the occupying powers, it is recognized that the relationship between the Administrator and the officials of our Government responsible for our occupation policy in Germany will be unique.

The only government in the zones of occupation of Germany is a military government. In the case of the bizonal area of Germany, the military governments are arms of the United States and British Governments. The agreements establishing the fusion of the United States and United Kingdom zones give the United States administration in Germany ample power to assure the performance in the bizonal area of operations under this act.

The problem which the committee faced was to make certain that the Administrator would be in a position to discharge his responsibilities while at the same time assuring that the highly complex and vital administration of the occupied areas is clearly fixed in a military governor, whether he be a commanding general or a civil commissioner. The key importance of Germany to the success of the recovery program involves concentrated and energetic effort with respect to every aspect of the economic life of the area. Hence, United States administration in Germany is a single problem. The responsibilities of the military governor include, but are not limited to, operations under the bill. The Administrator will, of course, have full authority to perform, with respect to the occupied areas, all functions vested in him by section 11 (a) of the bill. However, in the light of the special problems discussed above, the committee concluded that administrative arrangements within the occupied areas for the conduct of operations under the bill should be left to the President. It is the intention of the committee that the administrative arrangements to be made by the President will assure full coordination between the Administrator and the occupation authorities in order that the Administrator may carry out his responsibilities, without impairment of the responsibility of the military government for the successful accomplishment of the occupation objectives. Similar considerations apply with respect to the zones of the Free Territory of Trieste, if either of these zones becomes a "participating country."

30. DISMANTLING OF PLANTS IN GERMANY

During the debate in the Senate on the Foreign Aid Act of 1947, the chairman of the committee promised to investigate the policies and practices being applied in Germany to the dismantling of plants under the reparations program. Accordingly, this question was examined thoroughly during the hearings on this bill.

The committee is satisfied that the policies of this Government with respect to dismantling of German plants are consistent with the European recovery program and that they do not jeopardize the vital role that western Germany is required to play under the program.

A part of the capacity scheduled for dismantling are war plants whose destruction or removal as producing units is required under the agreed program for the elimination of Germany's facilities for manufacturing war materials. The industrial capacity represented by the nonwar plants cannot be used in Germany within the period of the recovery program because of the shortages of raw materials, transport,

85-743 O - 73 - 42

manpower, and the other factors which hamper the expansion of German production. On the other hand, certain industrial capacity scheduled for removal from Germany is required by some of the participating countries in order to reach their production targets.

Except for the remnants of three plants which have already been allocated to the Soviet Union and dismantled, no deliveries of plants and equipment are being made from the United States zone to the Soviet Union.

Shipments are continuing to the member nations of the Inter-Allied Reparation Agency (in accordance with the terms of the Paris reparation agreement signed in January 1946 by all those nations, including the United States) entitled to reparation from Germany, except the Soviet Union and Poland. Most of this equipment is destined for countries expected to participate in the European recovery program, and that which has been received is already making a contribution to the industrial production of those countries. Continuation of deliveries will serve to meet some of the urgent requirements for capital equipment in connection with their programs for expanding industrial production. Much of this equipment could not be obtained elsewhere except by dollar payments and in some instances could not be obtained at all within the critical period. In addition the committee finds that to discontinue dismantling would violate our international commitments under the Paris reparation agreement.

31. EUROPEAN ATTITUDE TOWARD THE EUROPEAN RECOVERY PROGRAM

The attitude of western Europeans toward the program ranges from cautious approval to unreserved enthusiasm. With the exception of the various national Communist Parties, which have followed faithfully the Moscow party line, and other extreme left-wing elements, political parties in western Europe have supported their governments' efforts toward closer economic cooperation on the European Continent. There has been sporadic criticism in individual countries about certain details, but the program is acknowledged to be vital to European recovery.

The fears of western Europe that the Congress of the United States would act too late and grant too little assistance for real recovery have been receding in recent weeks. The fear that Congress might attach to the program unacceptable political conditions still persists and has provided ammunition for Communist propaganda. However, the committee has been gratified to note a growing realization and appreciation of the sacrifice and effort which the United States will be required to make on behalf of European recovery.

The initial response to Secretary Marshall's Harvard speech in eastern Europe was favorable. But, after Russia clarified her position, the attitude of the Communist-dominated countries changed correspondingly. However, some statements which filter through censorship express regret about nonparticipation and hope for closer east-west economic relations.

32. THE ROLE OF EASTERN EUROPE AND EAST-WEST TRADING

The Soviet Union and Communist Parties elsewhere in Europe are in a position either to make substantial contributions to European recovery or to imperil its success. Recent developments indicate that the latter course might be taken. Through the Cominform, established in October 1947, the Communist Party has waged a "cold war" on the United States and has continuously distorted American motives behind the program initiated by the European countries themselves. Communist-inspired strikes and disturbances have already taken place in a number of ERP countries and might occur again, thereby greatly impeding the production effort of western Europe.

The Soviet Union, furthermore, is in an effective position to hinder the restoration of trade between eastern and western Europe. At present the over-all volume of trade between eastern and western Europe is about 30 percent of the prewar volume. The CEEC report, however, assumes that the westward flow of cereals from eastern Europe will reach prewar levels and timber will reach 75 percent of the prewar level in 1951. The restoration of this trade, which traditionally has consisted of food supplies, timber, and coal from the east and manufactured goods from the west, is one of the basic assumptions on which the participating countries predicated their import requirements from the Western Hemisphere.

The number of bilateral trading agreements concluded or being negotiated between eastern and western Europe is encouraging. On the other hand, Russia and her satellite states likewise have entered into a number of agreements which may have the effect of retarding the normal flow of trade. This web of trade agreements, together with the Russian grain and barter arrangements, constitute the Molotov plan which has the effect of tightening Russian control over the exports of the satellite countries and diverting their products from the west, where they normally flowed, to the east.

In the light of the Molotov plan and the attitude of the Cominform toward the European recovery program, there can be no certainty that the assumed restoration of trade will actually occur. Healthy trade relations within the European Continent will greatly aid the objective of ERP and the door is left open to the participation of eastern European countries in the program. If restoration of trade between the east and west of Europe does not occur, it is the opinion of the State Department that "recovery in the west of Europe will be much slower and more difficult, but not impossible of achievement."

The committee accepts and approves the assumption concerning the desirability of restoring east-west trading. This is another clear indication which should destroy the misconception, ceaselessly propagated, that the economic cooperation bill is designed to split Europe into two economic camps.

33. ATTITUDE OF THE SOVIET UNION TOWARD THE PROGRAM

After the Soviet Union's refusal to take part in any plan of concerted action for European recovery on the grounds that such a plan "would lead to interference in the internal affairs of European countries," England and France invited other European countries to meet in Paris for the developing of a recovery program. None of the eastern European states took part in the Paris Conference, although Czechoslovakia and Poland had signified their interest before the withdrawal of the Soviet Union.

As plans for the program progressed, Russian opposition crystallized through the formulation of the Molotov plan—a tight network of trade agreements among the eastern European states—and the creation of the Cominform, a new version of the Comintern, made up of parties in eastern Europe and France and Italy. Since its formation, the Moscow-dominated Cominform has been the mouthpiece of Russian opposition to the program. This is reflected by the adoption at the first meeting of the Cominform of a declaration which states in part:

> The Truman-Marshall plan is only a constituent part, the European subsection, of a general plan for the policy of global expansion pursued by the United States in all parts of the world.

The keynote of Communist propaganda against the recovery program was sounded at that same meeting by A. A. Zdhanov, a leading member of the Politburo, when he branded the Marshall plan as aimed at "the economic enslavement of the European countries." This cry of "American imperialism" has remained the theme of Communist propaganda against the program. Equally false is the theme, disseminated in western Europe, that the United States is attempting to resurrect the military might of western Germany.

34. THE ROLE OF THE UNITED NATIONS

In giving its unanimous approval to the European recovery program the committee reiterated once more its firm adherence to the Charter of the United Nations. Since the San Francisco Conference the goals of the United States foreign policy have been identical with the principles and purposes of the Charter. The committee believed that the successful completion of the European recovery program will constitute an important step toward the attainment of the objectives of world peace and security to which the United Nations is dedicated.

While the United States alone cannot determine the extent to which existing international machinery will be utilized, it is the established policy of the United States to make the fullest possible use of the machinery of the United Nations and its affiliated agencies in any such cooperative enterprise. It should be remembered, however, that 5 of the 16 CEEC countries are not yet members of the United Nations. Nevertheless, the CEEC report underlines the principle that "whereever suitable international machinery exists, it is the desire of the participating countries that these tasks should be effectively followed up within the framework of the United Nations."

As the program evolves and stability returns to Europe it is anticipated that the International Bank for Reconstruction and Development will be of considerable assistance in extending loans to the participating countries. The International Monetary Fund should contribute toward the general goal of stabilizing currencies in the world.

The Food and Agriculture Organization will aid in restoring agricultural equilibrium to Europe and in solving problems relating to food supply. The Economic Commission for Europe may be an important instrumentality in resolving some of Europe's economic problems which have resulted from the war. Already much valuable assistance has been rendered by these and other international agencies.

The bill drafted by the committee is unmistakably clear on this point. Sections 11 and 20 authorize the President to cooperate with the United Nations and its specialized agencies and to make payments for such purposes out of the appropriations authorized. Copies of reports to Congress on the operations of the program will be transmitted to the Secretary General of the United Nations and agreements concluded under the program will be registered with the United Nations whenever such registration is required by the Charter.

PART V. UNDERTAKINGS OF THE PARTICIPATING COUNTRIES

35. OBLIGATIONS OF PARTICIPATING COUNTRIES—MULTILATERAL PLEDGES

Throughout the hearings members of the committee repeatedly stated that the European recovery program must be a joint venture based upon the principles of self-help and mutual cooperation, with each participating country fully collaborating if satisfactory results are to be achieved. Accordingly, the committee looked with considerable satisfaction upon the far-reaching pledges, including the creation of a joint organization, which the CEEC countries voluntarily assumed at their Paris meeting. It is expected that these and other undertakings will be incorporated in multilateral pledges exchanged among the participating countries. While some of these pledges are dealt with in detail in other sections of this report, because of their importance it may be well to quote here the following paragraphs of the CEEC report:

> In order to insure that the recovery programme is carried out, the sixteen participating countries pledge themselves to join together, and invite other European countries to join with them, in working to this end. This pledge is undertaken by each country with respect to its own national programme, but it also takes into account similar pledges made by the other participating countries. In particular, each country undertakes to use all its efforts:
>
> (i) to develop its production to reach the targets, especially for food and coal;
> (ii) to make the fullest and most effective use of its existing productive capacity and all available manpower;
> (iii) to modernise its equipment and transport, so that labour becomes more productive, conditions of work are improved, and standards of living of all peoples of Europe are raised;
> (iv) to apply all necessary measures leading to the rapid achievement of internal financial monetary and economic stability while maintaining in each country a high level of employment;
> (v) to cooperate with one another and with like-minded countries in all possible steps to reduce the tariffs and other barriers to the expansion of trade both between themselves and with the rest of the world, in accordance with the principles of the draft Charter for an International Trade Organisation;
> (vi) to remove progressively the obstacles to the free movement of persons within Europe;
> (vii) to organise together the means by which common resources can be developed in partnership.

The present bill (sec. 15) makes clear that the extension of aid by the United States results from the pledges accepted at Paris and is contingent upon the continued effort of the participating countries to accomplish a joint recovery program through multilateral undertakings and the establishment of a continuing organization. The committee believes that these pledges, if they are faithfully observed, will do much to bring about in Europe the economic conditions essenial for peace and prosperity.

In stressing the importance of these obligations, the committee was sensitive to the fact that the countries of western Europe are highly developed sovereign nations and would be properly resentful of any interference from the outside in their internal affairs. There can be no possible criticism on this score in as much as the undertakings were voluntarily assumed by the CEEC countries upon their own initiative and in no sense represent an attempt on the part of the United States to impose restrictions on the sovereign rights of the participating countries.

36. OBLIGATIONS OF PARTICIPATING COUNTRIES—BILATERAL AGREEMENTS

The committee has made every effort to guarantee the success of this venture in the light of its past experience with foreign aid programs. Therefore, in addition to the multilateral undertakings, special bilateral agreements will be concluded between the United States and each of the participating countries. These agreements will respect the dignity of both countries and give assurance that the assistance granted will be used to the best possible advantage. They will vary in content depending upon the nature of the assistance furnished and the conditions applicable in each particular instance. In general, however, the recipient country, in addition to adhering to the purposes of the act and exchanging the multilateral pledges referred to above, will undertake such commitments as the following in the bilateral agreements:

1. To promote industrial and agricultural production in order to become independent of extraordinary outside economic assistance;
2. To take steps to stabilize its currency, establish a valid rate of exchange, and to balance its governmental budget as soon as practicable;
3. To cooperate in stimulating an increasing interchange of goods and services with other countries and to reduce trade barriers;
4. To make efficient and practical use of its own resources and of the assistance furnished by the United States;
5. To facilitate the sale or transfer to the United States on reasonable terms and in reasonable quantities of certain materials required as a result of deficiencies in our own resources;
6. To deposit in a special account the local currency equivalent of assistance in the form of grants furnished under the agreement to be used in a manner agreed to by the two governments;
7. To publish and transmit to the United States not less frequently than every calendar quarter full statements of operations under the agreement;
8. To furnish promptly, upon request of the United States, any information relating to the operation of the program and the use of assistance furnished under this act.

It will be noted that a number of the conditions contained in the Foreign Aid Act of 1947, including the provisions relating to labeling and the limitations upon the reexportation of commodities, are omitted from the present bill. After reviewing these conditions, the committee believed that it would be unwise to include them because of the fundamental differences in the nature of the two programs.

37. TERMINATION OF ASSISTANCE

Apart from the bilateral and multilateral undertakings described above, the interests of the United States are further protected by the provision that assistance to any of the participating countries may be terminated for a variety of reasons. Whenever the Administrator determines that a recipient country is not adhering to the terms of its agreement with the United States, or is diverting assistance to purposes other than those provided in the act, he shall terminate such assistance unless, under the circumstances, remedial action other than termination will more effectively promote the purposes of the act. Moreover, the Administrator is directed to terminate assistance with any participating country whenever, because of changed conditions, such assistance is no longer consistent with the national interests of the United States.

38. TOWARD A UNION OF THE EUROPEAN STATES

While the bill provides for the economic rehabilitation of Europe, it has broader implications. Revival of the economic health of Europe combined with a development of ever-closer political and economic ties among the participating countries are the twin elements of peace and prosperity. It is therefore implicit in the program that at its end lies, not only economic cooperation in the form of customs unions and the elimination of trade and economic barriers set forth in the CEEC report, but also closer political and cultural bonds. This need has already been stressed by British, French, and other leaders.

Divided and engaged in nationalistic rivalries the participating countries will find it difficult to sustain their free institutions and independence and to increase their standard of living. The maintenance of their peace and genuine independence rests largely upon their mutual cooperation and sustained common effort.

Several of the witnesses appearing before the committee urged a unification of the European states. In rewriting the bill the committee was mindful of these many admonitions and, drawing upon the language of the CEEC report, wrote into section 2 (a) the following:

> Mindful of the advantages which the United States has enjoyed through the existence of a large domestic market with no internal trade barriers, and believing that similar advantages can accrue to the countries of Europe, it is the hope of the people of the United States that these countries through a joint organization will exert sustained common efforts which will speedily achieve that economic cooperation in Europe which is essential for lasting peace and prosperity.

PART VI. FINANCIAL ASPECT OF THE PROGRAM

39. TOTAL FOREIGN AID CONTEMPLATED

The committee believes there is no question of the ability of the United States to finance its share of the European recovery program. This determination was made after full consideration of other requests which will probably be made for appropriations for foreign aid in other parts of the world. United States assistance in this program can be accomplished without unduly affecting the American economy or neglecting other critical areas where assistance is needed. During an early stage of the hearings the committee requested the Secretary of State to submit an over-all estimate of the total amount which would be required for foreign financial assistance to cover the remainder of fiscal year 1948 and fiscal 1949. On February 6, 1948, the following estimate was submitted:

	Millions
Included in President's Budget of Appropriations:	
1. European recovery program	$6, 800
2. Government and relief in occupied areas	1, 400
3. Philippine war damage, rehabilitation and veterans' benefits	[1] 133
4. Other foreign aid (including China)	750
Total	9, 083
Additions to President's Budget of Appropriations: Other foreign aid (including China) (around)	250
Total	9, 333

[1] Appropriation request for fiscal year 1949 authorized by Public Law 370 (79th Cong.).

It is the understanding of the committee that these figures include all contemplated requests for appropriations for foreign aid with the exception of the contributions of the United States to the United Nations and other international organizations. Item No. 4, entitled "Other foreign aid," includes the China-aid program, Greek-Turkish military aid, the Army request for Japanese-Korean reconstruction, inter-American military cooperation, and Trieste aid. The request for assistance to China is $570,000,000. The amounts which will be requested for the four other programs are not known since they have not been fully cleared and screened in the executive branch. The total for the four would be slightly under $500,000,000.

40. THE PURPOSE IS RECOVERY, NOT RELIEF

This bill provides for United States assistance in a recovery program geared to the individual and collective needs of the participating countries. It is therefore a recovery bill and differs from the interim aid and earlier relief measures in that its primary concern is the recreation of a strong, productive, self-supporting western European economy. Obviously, some relief-type goods must be provided within the framework of the program, but all assistance, no matter what its form may be, will be devoted solely to European recovery.

If the measure were purely relief, certain of the participating countries would not immediately be eligible, since they have resources upon which to draw. They would, however, require assistance as their resources were exhausted. Ambassador Douglas explained the problem as follows:

> Those countries that would receive no relief would exhaust what resources they have until they reach the point of zero and thereafter would be in the paupers' line, unable to pay for imports and unable to export. In other countries imports would be diminished. The energy of the individuals to work would be diminished, their exports would decline, and the conditions would continuously deteriorate. And in order to make up the deficiency, if we were prepared to do so, we would have to appropriate even a larger sum of money and provide even more commodities than is contemplated under this program.

The State Department estimates, covering the first 15-month period based on an appropriation of 6.8 billion dollars, assigned roughly two-thirds, or 4.5 billion dollars, to relief-type goods, and one-third, or 2.3 billion dollars to recovery-type goods. In practice, the Administrator would adjust the program to conform to new developments, and there would be a steady decrease in the percentage of relief-type goods, and a steady increase in recovery-type goods. Under the heading of recovery-type items are incentive goods (such as tobacco and coffee), farm supplies and equipment, industrial raw materials, coal-mining machinery, capital equipment and parts, and components for machinery and equipment. Relief-type items are food, fuel, fertilizers, and cotton and wool fibers.

The tables below illustrate the distribution of relief-type and recovery-type items as follows:

TABLE 1.—*Illustrative distribution between relief-type and recovery-type commodities and services financed with new U. S. Treasury funds and imported by the participating countries from the Western Hemisphere, Apr. 1, 1948, to June 30, 1949*

[In millions of dollars, at July 1, 1947, prices]

	Relief-type commodities and services	Recovery-type commodities and services	Total
Totals brought forward from table 2	4,899	1,961	6,860
Plus adjustment for price increases	342	140	482
	5,241	2,101	7,342
Less:			
Savings on shipping	71	29	100
Department of Army, GARIOA	822		822
Subtotal	893	29	922
	4,348	2,072	6,420
Plus:			
Authority to obligate funds for procurement of items, chiefly capital equipment, to be delivered in subsequent years		200	200
Uncovered deficit of bizone Germany with nonparticipating countries outside the Western Hemisphere	134	66	200
Subtotal	134	266	400
Authorization requested for ECA	4,482	2,338	6,820
Above in rounded amount			6,800
Relief-type goods and services as percent of total authorization requested	66		
Recovery-type goods and services as percent of total authorization requested		34	

TABLE 2.—*Recapitulation of illustrative distribution between relief-type and recovery-type commodities and services financed with new U. S. Treasury funds and imported by the participating countries from the Western Hemisphere, Apr. 1, 1948, to June 30, 1949*

[In millions of dollars, at July 1, 1947, prices]

	Total relief-type commodities and services	Total recovery-type commodities and services	Total
Austria	118.6	63.4	182.0
Belgium-Luxemburg and dependencies	255.2	67.9	323.1
Denmark	77.8	86.3	164.1
France and dependencies	968.9	465.3	1,434.2
Greece	137.3	48.6	185.9
Iceland	7.8	4.9	12.7
Ireland	102.6	49.2	151.8
Italy	719.4	149.4	868.8
Netherlands and dependencies	311.3	393.7	705.0
Norway		34.1	34.1
Portugal and dependencies			
Sweden		32.9	32.9
Switzerland			
United Kingdom and dependencies	1,490.9	269.3	1,760.2
Western Germany:			
Bizone	630.7	283.8	914.5
French zone	71.6	8.8	80.4
Saar	7.0	3.9	10.9
Total	4,899.1	1,961.5	6,860.6

41. NATURE OF ASSISTANCE: GRANTS OR LOANS

The duration of the European recovery program and the changes which cannot now be foreseen, make it impracticable to establish now the extent of aid to be provided any participating country or to determine whether such aid is to be in the form of grants or loans. Similarly, it cannot now be determined whether certain commodities or classes of commodities should throughout the life of the program be furnished on a grant or loan basis.

The committee has, however, established the criteria for determining whether assistance should be in the form of grants or loans. This determination is to depend primarily on two factors: (1) the character and purpose of the assistance and (2) the capacity of the country concerned to make repayments without jeopardizing the accomplishment of the purposes of the bill. It is clear that grants should not be made to countries which have the capacity to pay cash or repay loans. It is equally clear that it would be unrealistic to require a participating country to contract dollar debts now if it does not have the capacity to pay without jeopardizing the purposes of the program. However, to the fullest extent practicable within the above test, payment should be made or loans used in order to finance imports of capital equipment and raw materials for use in connection with capital development, and grants should be used to finance imports of supplies of food, fuel, and fertilizer and raw materials not used for capital development.

While recognizing that a definitive answer cannot now be given to the question as to what percentage of assistance will be financed by loans and what percentage by grants, the committee believe it desirable to obtain an estimate. In response to its inquiry the National Advisory Council has estimated that roughly 20 to 40 percent of assistance will be in the form of loans, while 60 to 80 percent will be grants. Without attempting to make a determination, it is probable that in the early stages of the program the countries will be divided into four classes: (1) Countries, such as Switzerland and Portugal, which will pay cash for commodities received; (2) countries to which assistance will be furnished by loans; (3) countries, like Austria and Greece, where assistance will be entirely by grants; and (4) countries, like France and Great Britain, where assistance will be partly by loans and partly by grants.

In determining whether assistance should be furnished by grant or loan and in fixing the terms of repayment of any such loan, the committee has deemed it important to provide that the Administrator should act in consultation with the National Advisory Council. It should also be noted that the committee has made explicit that, in determining the terms of a loan, the Administrator may provide payment by the transfer to the United States of materials required as a result of deficiencies in its own resources under such terms as may be agreed to between the Administrator and the participating country.

42. COMPARISON OF ESTIMATES OF REQUIREMENTS

The committee considered the requirements of the participating countries during the first year of the recovery program as estimated by the executive branch, the Harriman committee, the International

Bank for Reconstruction and Development, and the CEEC. All of these estimates are based upon balance of payments calculations. The executive branch estimated a deficit of 6.75 billion dollars, the Harriman committee estimated 6.88 to 7.69 billion dollars, and the International Bank 7.6 billion dollars as compared with the CEEC estimate of 8.03 billion dollars.

Only the executive branch and the Harriman committee estimated the amount of new United States Treasury funds which would be required after allowing for assistance from other sources. These estimates were not on a completely comparable basis. When the necessary adjustments are made, however, both the executive branch and the Harriman committee estimates are virtually identical with the 5.3 billion dollars for the first year of the program unanimously approved by the committee.

43. REDUCTION OF AUTHORIZATION TO 5.3 BILLION DOLLARS

The great majority of witnesses appearing before the committee expressed the conviction that the 6.8 billions dollars requested by the Department of State for the first 15 months of the program should not be reduced. Due to the many imponderables involved there are sound reasons why that sum should be looked upon as a minimum rather than a maximum figure. Possible crop failures, changing price levels, political disturbances, uncertainties about production schedules and world trade—these are only a few of the intangibles which make it impossible to predict the future requirements of the program with any high degree of certainty. Given the tremendously important stakes involved, it would seem far better to have a little too much available than not enough.

The committee considered it wise, however, to reduce the amount authorized from 6.8 to 5.3 billion dollars, at the same time reducing the period covered from 15 to 12 months. Such a reduction would, in no way, impair the effectiveness of the program, since the 5.3 billion-dollar figure is, in fact, the amount necessary to carry through the 6.8 billion-dollar program for a 12-month period. At the same time, there are a number of strong arguments in favor of such a change.

In the first place, it would seem desirable that the program be reviewed by the Congress at the earliest reasonable date in 1949. By that time the people of the United States will have determined the composition of the Congress and the administration which, in the long run, will be responsible for the execution of the program. By that time, too, many of the imponderables which now exist will have been resolved. We will know far better then than now the exact impact of crops, prices, political disturbances, and production results upon the program.

In the second place, by January 1949 we will have the benefit of the recommendations of the Administrator and his staff. Such recommendations, framed in the light of 6 or 8 months' experience by those in charge of the program, will be invaluable. Moreover, by that time, the studies of the joint congressional committee proposed in the present bill will be available.

Finally, if it is generally recognized that the recovery program is coming under critical review early in 1949, it will encourage the participating countries to exert every effort to show substantial progress by way of self-help between now and then. This additional impetus, coming during the early stages of the program, may prove exceedingly helpful.

44. APPLICATION OF PORTION OF 1948 SURPLUS TO 1949 EXPENDITURES

The Joint Committee on Internal Revenue Taxation has estimated a Treasury surplus of approximately $8,000,000,000 in fiscal year 1948. The Treasury has estimated the surplus at about $7,500,000,000.

The committee felt that it would be appropriate to reserve $3,000,000,000 of this 1948 surplus for disbursements under the program in 1949 which would otherwise have been accounted for as expenditures in that fiscal year. This action will not affect the program in any way. It will merely assure that a portion of the surplus in fiscal 1948 is not used for debt retirement during that year and will increase, to that extent, the anticipated budgetary surplus for 1949.

Senator Millikin, chairman of the Senate Committee on Finance, explained to the committee that this procedure would tend to prevent this important project from cannibalizing other legitimate projects and would tend to prevent other legitimate projects from cannibalizing the recovery program during a year when there might be many demands upon the United States Treasury.

45. ADVANCE OF $1,000,000,000 BY RECONSTRUCTION FINANCE CORPORATION

In the Relief Assistance Act and the Foreign Aid Act the committee inserted a provision calling for advances by the Reconstruction Finance Corporation pending the appropriation of necessary funds by the Congress. This was considered desirable because of the urgent needs of the recipient countries.

Under the Foreign Aid Act authority to grant additional assistance to France, Austria, and Italy will expire on April 1, 1948. In view of this situation, in view of the compelling needs of other participating countries, and in order to prevent delay in carrying out the objectives of this act, the committee agreed that the same procedure should be followed. Accordingly the bill authorizes the Reconstruction Finance Corporation to make advances not to exceed $1,000,000,000 in the aggregate in such manner as the President shall determine in carrying out the program.

46. THE EUROPEAN RECOVERY PROGRAM AND THE UNITED STATES MILITARY ESTABLISHMENT

In considering the cost of the European recovery program some people ask whether the United States can afford to participate in such a program. It is just as pertinent to ask whether the United States can afford not to participate.

There are, in effect, two possible courses which the United States might follow in the pursuit of national security. On the one hand, we might cooperate fully with the other nations in an earnest attempt to establish and maintain those economic conditions in the world which are essential to international peace and prosperity. This is the purpose of our participation in the European recovery program.

If, on the other hand, the road of international cooperation is abandoned, then the United States would have no alternative but to greatly expand and strengthen its military establishments so as to be ready for any eventuality in a divided and uncertain world.

This point was emphasized by Secretary Royall and Secretary Forrestal in their testimony before the committee. Secretary Royall pointed out that if an adequate recovery program were not inaugurated the Department of the Army, in the interests of national security, would be compelled to seek an additional appropriation of at least 2¼ billion dollars for the Army and the Air Forces alone for the next fiscal year. He said that the Army would have to modernize existing equipment, purchase new types of equipment developed since the war, and resort to the draft unless some other methods of increasing voluntary enlistment could be devised. Secretary Forrestal also testified that an over-all increase of from 25 to 50 percent in defense appropriations would be necessary if there were no recovery program.

Viewed in this light the cost of the European recovery program may be compared to the premium on an insurance policy. Certainly it would be far less expensive than if the United States were to stand alone in isolation in a chaotic world. Moreover, it should be remembered that increased defense expenditures constitute, not a 4-year, but a perpetual commitment, with the amount tending to increase each year in proportion to the development of disorder and chaos in the world. The committee is convinced that the European recovery program is a calculated risk which the United States cannot afford to reject.

47. FINANCING FROM SOURCES OTHER THAN UNITED STATES GOVERNMENT FUNDS

The committee agreed that wherever feasible the balance of payments deficits of the participating countries should be financed from sources other than the United States Treasury.

The estimate of the executive branch anticipated that $1,285,000,000 of financing will be available in the first 15-month period from the following sources: $500,000,000 from the International Bank, private investments, and the remaining portion of outstanding Export-Import Bank credits; $700,000,000 from credits advanced by other countries in the Western Hemisphere; and $85,000,000 from certain of the participating countries.

The committee understands that the Harriman committee estimated the sources of other financing would amount to $1,250,000,000 in 1948; $750,000,000 from the International Bank; $450,000,000 from other countries in the Western Hemisphere; and $50,000,000 from private investment.

Mr. John J. McCloy, President of the International Bank for Reconstruction and Development, informed the committee that the executive branch's estimates of financing from other sources are high rather than low, largely because he does not believe that credits will be available from other Western Hemisphere countries in the assumed amount.

The committee believes that the United States should encourage other Western Hemisphere countries, in their interest as well as ours, to finance from their resources as much as possible of the import deficit of the participating countries. The committee took this factor into account in formulating its decision on the authorization of purchases from sources outside the United States. A reasonable expectation, therefore, is that the other Western Hemisphere countries might be able to finance about $700,000,000 of the deficit of the participating countries in the first 15 months of the program. To rely on any larger amount would be unrealistic in view of the present dollar exchange difficulties of Canada and certain other American countries.

48. THE ROLE OF THE INTERNATIONAL BANK

Many people have inquired about the legitimate role of the International Bank for Reconstruction and Development in the European recovery program. Since this agency was created for the express purpose of assisting in reconstruction and development projects in the postwar world, why should it not assume a major share of the burden of the program?

Mr. John J. McCloy, president of the bank, appeared before the committee during the hearings and answered that question very categorically. Up to the present time the Bank has made four loans: $250,000,000 to France, $195,000,000 to the Netherlands, $40,000,000 to Denmark, and $12,000,000 to Luxemburg. But there are many additional applications for loans and it must be kept in mind that the bank must serve 46 States and not just 16. Moreover, as Mr. McCloy pointed out, the bank has less than $500,000,000 to lend at the present time. Finally, because of the express limitations of its charter, the bank can lend only to those countries with long range reconstruction and development programs and whose credit standing indicates that repayment prospects are good.

It follows that the bank cannot be counted on as one of the major resources available during the initial period of the program. The committee believed, however, that it could best be tied into later stages when more stable economic conditions exist in Europe and when long range development projects can be more properly financed on the basis of hard loans. Following is an outline of the bank's capital stock and the dollars available for lending:

International Bank for Reconstruction and Development—Outline of capital stock and dollars available for lending

Capital stock:		
Authorized (100,000 shares)		$10, 000, 000, 000
Subscribed (82,631 shares)		8, 263, 100, 000
Paid in—		
2 percent in gold or United States dollars		165, 262, 000
18 percent in currencies of the 46 members		1, 487, 358, 000
Total paid in		1, 652, 620, 000
80 percent subject to call on the United States to meet obligations of the bank	$2, 540, 000, 000	
80 percent subject to call on other member countries to meet obligations of the bank	4, 070, 480, 000	
		6, 610, 480, 000
Total		8, 263, 100, 000

International Bank for Reconstruction and Development—Outline of capital stock and dollars available for lending—Continued

Dollars available for lending:	
2 percent in gold or United States dollars	$165, 262, 000
18 percent of United States subscription	571, 500, 000
Available dollar capital	736, 762, 000
Proceeds of sale of bonds (July 15, 1947)	250, 000, 000
Total dollars available for lending	986, 762, 000
Loans agreed to	497, 000, 000
Balance of dollars available for loans	489, 762, 000

49. ROLE OF PRIVATE ENTERPRISE

As a result of the economic conditions brought on by the war, private enterprise has not been in a position to provide substantial assistance to the devastated countries of Europe. One incontrovertible fact is that the magnitude of the problem is such as to make it unrealistic to expect that recovery can be effected at this time through assistance rendered primarily by private enterprise. There is no doubt, however, that as the recovery program progresses, private enterprise will be able to play an increasingly important role. In fact, the committee is convinced that an essential element of this program will be the encouragement by the Administrator of private enterprise to contribute through its initiative and capital in the reconstruction and development of Europe.

Even today, however, American business interests are prepared to assume business risks abroad, provided they have assurance that they will be able to transfer foreign currency proceeds into dollars. Accordingly, authorization is given the Administrator to make guaranties for the transfer into dollars of local currency proceeds realized from newly made investments, including loans, approved by both the participating country and the Administrator. This authorization, which is limited to 5 percent of the funds appropriated, does not provide for the underwriting of normal business risks; it deals only with guaranties of transferability from local currencies to dollars. These guaranties are to be made only with respect to projects which further the recovery program.

The committee also agreed that American business enterprise and technical know-how should prove of great value to the Administrator in a consultative capacity. To this end, a provision has been inserted in the bill authorizing the Administrator to employ not only consultants but organizations of consultants to assist him in this program.

50. PRIVATE VOLUNTARY AMERICAN RELIEF TO FOREIGN COUNTRIES

The committee noted with satisfaction that between July 1, 1945, and June 1947, private gifts and grants-in-aid amounted to $1,451,000,000.

It is desirable that private aid continue and that all voluntary agencies engaged in foreign aid should register with the Advisory Committee on Voluntary Aid.

This program, however, is essentially a recovery program. The private relief has an elasticity that governmental programs do not have. Frequently it covers needs not otherwise met such as special diets for invalids and the rehabilitation of displaced persons. The committee has been impressed by the repeated testimony which demonstrated that individual American participation in European aid elicits many responses of good will.

51. THE USE OF FOREIGN-OWNED UNITED STATES ASSETS

The committee deemed it desirable that the participating countries, to the extent practicable, should take measures to locate and control the assets held by their citizens in this country and the earnings from these assets so that the dollar incomes would be available to foreign governments to further the purposes of this act. This does not mean that the foreign governments must seize or liquidate private assets held by their citizens. It is not considered desirable to require the liquidation of such assets and thus deprive European countries of reserves which they may need either to achieve economic stability or to meet inevitable emergency requirements for which the program does not fully provide.

In view of the cost of this program to the American taxpayer, it is the intent of the committee that all idle, hoarded, or unproductive assets should be put to use. The precise form of use will necessarily vary according to the circumstances of the particular country and the nature of the assets.

As of the middle of 1947, the CEEC countries held $7,094,000,000 in United States assets. The total long-term assets amounted to $4,930,000,000; about $2,200,000,000 of this represents stocks and bonds, the bulk of which are probably of a readily marketable character. Short-term assets amount to $2,164,000,000. In the present crisis, many foreign countries have already drawn their reserves below what ordinarily would be regarded as a prudent level. Depletion of these reserves delays and jeopardizes the restoration of international convertibility of currencies and expanded international trade and investments.

It is important to distinguish between blocked assets and free assets. During the course of the hearings, the Secretary of the Treasury started to free $1,100,000,000 of blocked assets to help the recipient countries to obtain control of them. These assets have been concealed contrary to the laws and national interests of the countries concerned. The recipient countries can perhaps count on obtaining in the next 12 months a part of the 400 million dollars estimated to be held directly in the United States for resident nationals of these countries. The largest portion of the 400 million dollars of directly held assets, namely, 100 to 150 million dollars, is owned by French citizens, and the French Government is making every effort to mobilize these resources.

Two other related matters may be mentioned here: The pledging of foreign-owned assets and gold reserves. (*a*) The pledging of foreign-owned assets in the United States as collateral for loans is not without precedent. However, this would normally involve the nationalization or seizure of such assets by governments—a step which is contrary to the philosophy of the bill. (*b*) The CEEC countries held about $6,568,000,000 in gold reserves as of June 30, 1947. There have been serious drains on these reserves since that date. Most of the participating countries have already drawn their gold reserves below levels necessary to provide adequate working capital for their international trade or adequate backing to maintain sound currencies. It may be noted during 1947 the net increase in United States gold holdings was close to $1,900,000,000, a factor which has aggravated the exchange position of other countries.

52. THE EXTENT OF PRIVATE GOLD HOARDING

The committee properly took account of the fact that concealed private gold hoardings do not work for the recovery of the European countries. Popular discussions have mentioned such hoardings to the extent of $3,000,000,000 for France alone. The Secretary of the Treasury testified that the actual amount of private gold hoarding is unknown, but that it may be inferred from existing evidence that the actual figure is of much smaller dimensions than $3,000,000,000. In fact, statistics on gold production and gold reserves would indicate that there has not been an increase in gold hoarding since the outbreak of the war, and that the private holdings in all of western Europe at that time was considerably less than $1,000,000,000. The recovery program, by working toward the stabilization of European currencies, will provide the conditions which will bring gold out of hoarding and into the hands of the monetary authorities.

53. DURATION OF THE PROGRAM

The committee felt strongly that authorization for this program should extend through June 30, 1952, approximately 4 years, so that the maximum results could be achieved from the pledges and undertakings of the participating countries. This assurance of the United States should enable the participating countries to demonstrate their intent to take courageous and wise measures of self-help and mutual cooperation. Many of the recovery benefits of this program will only just begin to appear in the first 12 months' period.

After June 30, 1952, or after the date of the passage of a concurrent resolution by the two Houses of Congress before that date, the Administrator is allowed a period of 12 months to wind up operations. The committee rejected an earlier proposal which would have allowed 3 years for liquidating operations.

It should be pointed out that the termination provisions will not invalidate agreements for the transfer of materials to the United States under the program, or the guarantees to private investors made by the Administrator in connection with approved projects. Such agreements and guaranties are explained in other sections of this report.

PART VII. RECOMMENDATIONS OF THE COMMITTEE

54. CONCLUSION

On February the 13 the committee concluded its deliberations and unanimously voted to report the bill to the Senate for favorable action.

The committee believes that the program proposed is a sound one, that it will impose no dangerous strain upon the economy of the

85-743 O - 73 - 43

United States, and that it will be adequate to provide the margin for success in an effort which must be essentially and primarily European.

This kind of assistance, in peacetime, is without precedent in the history of mankind. This assistance is not, and cannot be, a permanent feature of American foreign policy. For Americans, the approval of this act represents a major decision. If Europeans fully understand this decision, they will realize that the United States is making adjustments almost as severe as they are likely to call upon each other to make. Above the details of the legislation, the debates, the statistics, and the work sheets, it is the expression of a great ideal of common welfare and peace. This ideal must become the common currency among the peoples of the world.

56

APPENDIXES

Appendix I

Section by Section Analysis of the Economic Cooperation Act of 1948

Section 1: Section 1 contains the short title of the bill.

Section 2 (a): After setting forth the congressional findings, this subsection states the policy of the bill.

Section 2 (b): The stated purpose of the bill is to effectuate the policy set forth in section 2 (a).

Section 3: This section defines the term "participating country."

The term "dependent areas under its administration," as used in this section, is intended to refer to all colonies and dependencies of a participating country and to trust territories administered by a participating country under the international trusteeship system of the United Nations. Action under the bill in respect of all such areas would have to be consistent with the principles set forth in article 73 of the Charter of the United Nations and, as regards trust territories, consistent also with the terms of the relevant trusteeship agreement.

Section 4 (a): This subsection establishes the Economic Cooperation Administration and the office of the Administrator.

Section 4 (b): This subsection establishes the office of the Deputy Administrator for Economic Cooperation.

Section 4 (c): This subsection assures the possibility of commencement of operations as soon as possible after the bill's passage, even though it may not have been possible for the first Administrator or Deputy Administrator to take office. The President is authorized, in such event and for a period of not more than 30 days after the date of enactment of the bill, to provide for the performance of the functions of the Administrator through such agencies of the Government as he may determine. However, if the President nominates an Administrator or Deputy Administrator during such 30-day period, the authority of the President to provide for the performance of the Administrator's functions through other agencies of the Government will continue until the Administrator or Deputy Administrator takes office.

Section 4 (d): This subsection authorizes the Administration, or any other department, agency, or establishment of the Government performing functions under the bill, to employ personnel for duty within the continental limits of the United States. Employment of personnel for service in the District of Columbia and elsewhere in the United States under this authority is not subject to the personnel ceilings imposed by section 14 (a) of the Federal Employees Pay Act of 1946. The Administrator is given authority to compensate not more than

60 of the persons performing duties within the United States without regard to the provisions of the Classification Act of 1923, and to compensate not more than 10 of these persons at rates up to $15,000 per year. In addition, this subsection authorizes the employment by the Administration of experts and consultants, or organizations of experts or consultants, such as engineering and accounting firms, and individuals so employed may be compensated at rates up to $50 per day. The number of experts and consultants who may be compensated up to the amount specified in this subsection is not limited. Payments to organizations employed by the Administration under this subsection may be made at such rates and in such manner as the Administrator may authorize in contracts with such organizations.

Section 4 (e): This section, which authorizes the Administrator or the head of any other department, agency, or establishment of the Government performing functions under the bill, to promulgate necessary rules and regulations and to delegate authority to his subordinates to perform his functions under the bill, is consistent with standard administrative procedures. The subsection is not intended to permit the delegation of rule-making power to subordinates.

Section 5 (a): This subsection enumerates certain functions to be performed by the Administrator. The authority of the Administrator to formulate programs of United States assistance under the bill includes authority to approve specific projects which may be proposed to him by a participating country, to be undertaken by such country in substantial part with assistance furnished under the bill. This authority is designed to implement the undertaking provided for in section 15 (b) (1) of the bill.

The authority reposed in the Administrator to provide for the efficient execution of programs refers to the effective performance on the part of agencies of the United States Government with respect to services rendered by such agencies, under approved programs, in procurement, storage, transportation, or other handling necessary to insure the transfer of commodities in conformity with the programs.

Section 5 (b): This subsection prescribes arrangements under which the Administrator and the Secretary of State will concert their respective activities so as to strengthen and make more effective the conduct of the foreign relations of the United States. To this end effective working relations should be established between the Administration and the Department of State.

Section 6: Under this section the Administrator is made a member of the National Advisory Council on International Monetary and Financial Problems during the existence of the Administration.

Section 7 (a): This subsection creates a Public Advisory Board, to advise and consult with the Administrator with respect to general or basic policy matters arising in connection with the Administrator's discharge of his responsibilities.

Section 7 (b): This subsection authorizes the Administrator to establish other advisory committees. Members of such committees may receive compensation in accordance with the provisions of section 4 (d) relating to experts and consultants employed by the Administration.

Section 8: This section provides for a United States special representative in Europe.

Section 9 (a): This subsection provides for the establishment of special ECA missions abroad. The chief of a special mission is to be second in rank to the Ambassador, Minister, or chargé d'affaires ad interim, as the case may be, in charge of the United States diplomatic mission.

Section 9 (b): This subsection assures proper coordination between the chief of the special mission and the chief of the United States diplomatic mission.

Section 9 (c): In order to assure that the United States special representative in Europe and his staff, as well as the ECA mission in each participating country, will receive office space, facilities, and other administrative services, the Secretary of State and the Administrator are authorized to make appropriate agreements to this end.

Section 9 (d): In view of the special circumstances existing in the zones of occupation of Germany, this subsection provides that in place of the establishment of special ECA missions, the President shall make appropriate administrative arrangements with respect to the zones of occupation of Germany in order to enable the Administrator to carry out his responsibility to assure the accomplishment of the purposes of this act. Similar arrangements may be provided for the zones of the Free Territory of Trieste if either of the zones of the Free Territory of Trieste becomes a participating country as defined in section 3.

Section 10 (a): Under this subsection two alternative procedures are made available to the Administrator for the employment of personnel for the purpose of performing functions under this bill outside the continental limits of the United States. Under the first of the procedures, such personnel will be outside the Foreign Service system but will receive compensation, allowances, and benefits comparable to those provided for Foreign Service reserve and Foreign Service staff officers and employees.

Under the second procedure, the Administrator may recommend to the Secretary of State persons to be appointed or assigned as Foreign Service reserve officers or as Foreign Service staff officers and employees for the purpose of performing operations under the bill outside the continental limits of the United States. Foreign Service staff officers and employees appointed from other Government agencies pursuant to this procedure may be given the same reemployment rights as are provided for Foreign Service reserve officers by section 528 of the Foreign Service Act of 1946. The assignment to a post abroad or the transfer from one post abroad to another and the promotion of persons appointed to the Foreign Service reserve or staff under this section are to be made by the Secretary upon the recommendation of the Administrator.

Thus, the pay scale of all persons appointed pursuant to this subsection will range from $720 to $13,500, exclusive of allowances for quarters, cost of living, and representation.

It is contemplated that the two procedures outlined above are to be mutually exclusive. It is left to the judgment of the Administrator with respect to each appointment, whether such appointment should be within or outside the Foreign Service system. Under existing legislation there is nothing to prevent the Secretary of State, at the request of the Administrator, from assigning officers in the Foreign Service system to perform functions under this bill. In such event such officers could be paid out of funds made available in accordance with section 14 (d) of this bill.

Section 10 (b): This subsection provides for the appointment of alien clerks and employees for duty outside the continental limits of the United States.

Section 10 (c): This subsection deals with the investigation of citizens or residents of the United States who are appointed pursuant to section 10 for the performance of functions under the bill.

Section 11: This section prescribes the forms and procedures by which the Administrator may provide assistance to a participating country, and the methods of furnishing such assistance. Under the authority of this section, and with the funds authorized under section 14, the Administrator will be able to launch immediately into operations which will relieve the drain on the dollar assets of the participating countries. These assets are now being drained at a rate which will, shortly after April 1, leave several participating countries without any dollar assets available, as a practical matter, for purchasing essential commodities in dollar areas. These countries, however, will then have under contract or on hand in the United States a substantial quantity of commodities for delivery in the ensuing months. These undelivered commodities comprise the "pipe line" of supply to the countries concerned. Those commodities in the "pipe line" which are eligible for provision under this bill, may be financed by the Administrator out of funds made available under the bill, as part of the assistance to be provided thereunder. As in the case of the Foreign Aid Act of 1947, under which the same type of operation was authorized, the "pipe line" at any moment will embrace commodities not theretofore landed in the territory of a participating country. The language of the present bill will permit the Administrator to arrange for this important aspect of assistance.

Section 11 (a): This subsection authorizes the Administrator to furnish assistance to any participating country, in the forms prescribed. He may provide for procurement of any commodity which he determines to be required for the furtherance of the purposes of the bill. The authority to procure "from any source" provided in paragraph 1 includes the authority to procure "offshore," that is, from outside the territory of the United States.

The term "commodity" is broadly defined, except that the reference to merchant vessels is limited to vessels chartered under the authority set forth in paragraph 4 of this subsection. The Administrator is authorized to furnish technical information or technical personnel for instruction purposes to a participating country, as well as other forms of technical information and assistance.

Merchant vessels chartered under authority of this subsection under such terms and conditions as the Administration may determine while being operated by a participating country, will not be subject to laws designed to control the operation of United States vessels.

The provision authorizing transfer of any commodity or service is intended to authorize the actual delivery of a commodity into the custody of a participating country, or the rendering of a service for such country. These acts represent the actual rendering of the assistance authorized under the program. By defining transfer as the act of delivery or of rendering a service, a standard is established for measuring the amount of assistance actually provided for a participating country. This measure is important in connection with fiscal operations and in the preparation of reports on operations under the bill. The paragraph authorizes transfer not only to a participating country itself, but to any agency or organization representing such country. Under this authority, commodities, for example, could be delivered directly to business firms designated by the participating country as its agent to receive such commodities or to an organization representing a group of such countries.

Section 11 (b): This subsection prescribes the method under which the Administrator may provide the types of assistance authorized under section 11 (a).

Paragraph (1) of section 11 (b) authorizes the Administrator, for the purpose of facilitating procurement, to establish accounts on the books of the Administration, or of any other department, agency, or establishment of the Government, or, on terms and conditions approved by the Secretary of the Treasury, in United States banking institutions (including their overseas branches). In addition to authorizing Government procurement through procedures specified herein, the paragraph will enable the Administrator to permit utilization of normal trade channels, with adequate safeguards to assure proper expenditure for approved purposes.

Under subparagraph (i) a letter of commitment could be issued by the Administrator to participating countries, in order to facilitate their contracting with suppliers, or could be issued to suppliers. The letter of commitment would embody a commitment on the part of the Administrator to make payment for the furnishing of specified commodities, upon presentation of the letter of commitment, together with contracts, invoices, bills of lading, or other supporting documents enumerated therein sufficient to demonstrate that the funds are being properly spent for approved purposes. The utilization of this procedure, in effect, would enable a participating country to institute essential approved procurement without the necessity for borrowing, or immobilizing its scarce dollar reserves by furnishing an irrevocable letter of credit to a supplier. Such borrowing, or the furnishing of an irrevocable letter of credit, has frequently been required of foreign countries making contracts in the United States in order to relieve the supplier of credit risk. A letter of commitment, which would create an obligation against appropriations made under authority of the bill, would normally be used by a supplier in the place of an irrevocable letter of credit and on the same basis as a United States Government contract to purchase, and the supplier could use the letter of commitment for his own credit arrangements in the same way as he could use a United States Government contract.

Subparagraph (ii) of this subsection authorizes the Administrator to permit withdrawals, against an established account, by a participating country. The Administrator would specify the documents which must be submitted to effect withdrawals, in order to assure full compliance with the terms and conditions of the supply program.

The foregoing procedures will permit the Administrator, acting within prudent limits, to authorize advances for the making of payments by or on behalf of participating countries, and to authorize reimbursement to such countries for payments already made by them for approved commodities. Such payment or reimbursement can be effected without requiring the submission of all documents which are ordinarily prerequisite to the expenditure of United States Government funds. This will make possible procurement in a businesslike manner, through normal channels of trade, subject to adequate safeguards established by the Administrator to demonstrate that all expenditures are within the approved program and in accordance with the terms and conditions established by the Administrator for such expenditures. The safeguards will enable him to make certain that amounts authorized to be withdrawn will not exceed the needs of participating countries to make current dollar payments for approved supply items. In addition, the Administrator will be in a position to assure that the timing and method of procurement is consistent with the best interests of the domestic economy of the United States. However, this subsection requires, with respect to procurement within the United States, the eventual submission of all standard documents necessary for auditing purposes. Experience has shown that, with respect to procurement outside the United States, particularly through normal trade channels, it is frequently impossible to obtain all the standard documentation required for auditing of accounts. Hence, the Administrator is authorized to prescribe the documents required in support of expenditures for offshore procurement.

Paragraph (2) of subsection (b) permits the utilization by the administrator of any department, agency or establishment of the Government in connection with provisions of assistance under the bill. This authority includes procurement through regular Government procurement agencies. Funds allocated to any such agency out of funds appropriated under authority of the bill will be established in separate appropriation accounts in the Treasury. The paragraph also authorizes the provision of assistance through action and cooperation with the United Nations, with other international organizations or with agencies of the participating countries.

Paragraph (3) authorizes the Administrator to make guaranties for the transfer into dollars of local currency proceeds from projects abroad, under conditions and subject to the limitations contained in the paragraph. The approval of the Administrator will be expressed through the guaranty contract with the American investor. The approval power will not stop with the writing of the guaranty contract itself. Regulations will be promulgated by the Administrator to assure a follow-up to determine that the agreed amount of dollars have actually been invested, that the resulting investment is reasonably related to the recovery purposes for which the guaranty was extended, and that the local currency proceeds tendered for transfer into dollars are justifiably attributable to the guaranty investment. The term "investment" includes loan, as well as so-called equity, investments.

It is expected that upon the termination of the administration in 1953, a statute would be enacted providing for the liquidation of the transfer guaranty in the period following 1953, and would designate or provide for the funds to be used for this purpose.

(c) This subsection specifies the financial terms pursuant to which the Administrator may provide assistance to a participating country.

The provision for consultation between the Administrator and the National Advisory Council in this subsection (as well as in subsec. (2) of this section and par. (6) of sec. 15 (b)) contemplates that if, after such consultation, differences of view remain, the matter in disagreement will be referred to the President for final decision. When it is determined that it is appropriate to provide assistance to a participating country on a loan basis, the Administrator will allocate funds for this purpose to the Export-Import Bank of Washington which will make and administer the credit as directed and on terms specified by the Administrator in consultation with the National Advisory Council.

Section 12 (a): This provision is designed to assure the protection of the domestic economy.

Section 12 (b): This subsection provides an added measure to assure the protection of the domestic economy by avoiding unnecessary drains upon petroleum and petroleum products of the United States.

Section 12 (c): Under this subsection the Administrator in the procurement of agricultural commodities within the United States for transfer by grant to any participating country will procure an amount of each class or type of each such commodity approximately proportionate to the total exportable surplus of such class or type of such commodity. The application of this subsection is qualified by the following conditions: (1) The agricultural commodities must not be in short supply in the United States; (2) the class or type must be within the requirements of the participating country for which the procurement is being provided; (3) the procurement of a proportionate amount of each class or type must be administratively practicable; and (4) such procurement should not hinder, but should be in furtherance of the purposes of the act.

Section 13 (a): From time to time assistance for the participating countries will take the form of commodities that are normally procured by United States Government departments, agencies, and establishments for their own purposes. Similarly, assistance will sometimes be provided in the form of services that can readily be rendered by such departments, agencies, or establishments. Under this subsection whenever such commodities or services, or facilities, are made available to participating countries, the departments, agencies, or establishments from which such commodities, services, or facilities are obtained will be reimbursed out of funds appropriated under this bill. This subsection also prescribes the procedures under which such reimbursement will be effected.

Section 13 (b): Cases will arise in the course of operations under this bill when commodities procured under a program of assistance to the participating countries (1) can fill some more urgent need of the United States Government; (2) are determined no longer to be appropriate for transfer under the original program; or (3) are in danger of spoilage or wastage, or must be disposed of in order to conserve their usefulness. In such cases, under this subsection, the Administrator may dispose of such commodities in the best interests of the Government of the United States, in accordance with the procedures set forth in this subsection.

Section 14 (a): This subsection authorizes an advance from the Reconstruction Finance Corporation of $1,000,000,000 in order to permit operations pending enactment of an appropriation act. In authorizing this advance this subsection provides a procedure, standard in laws of this character, to permit immediate start of operations once the authorizing legislation is enacted. In view of the urgent need of making assistance available to the participating countries and to keep the pipe lines flowing, the committee has considered the sum of $1,000,000,000 essential for that purpose pending consideration and enactment of an appropriation act.

Section 14 (b): This subsection is a precautionary measure, the purpose of which is to assure that any unused balances of funds under the Foreign Aid Act of 1947 shall be available for carrying out the purposes of this bill.

Section 14 (c): This subsection contains the standard authorization for appropriations. The introductory language, referring to those participating countries which adhere to the purposes of the bill and remain eligible to receive assistance thereunder, merely restates and reflects the conditions precedent to the receipt of assistance which are set forth in other provisions of the bill. The language is not intended to impose a new condition, and the tests for eligibility are provided elsewhere in the bill, as well as the methods of determining eligibility. While this subsection authorizes appropriations without any specific limitation as to amount, for the period believed essential for the execution the recovery program, it limits the amount which may be appropriated for the period of 1 year following the date of enactment of this bill to $5,300,000,000. This will permit a congressional review of operations under the bill early in the next session of Congress, without jeopardizing the accomplishment of the purposes of the bill.

Section 14 (d): This subsection gives general authority to use the funds made available under this bill for all the various incidental expenses that will be found essential to effective operations. It specifically authorizes the use of such funds for administrative expenses and compensation of various classes of personnel and permits the disregard of certain laws that would unduly hamper the type of operations that will be necessary in an unusual program of this type.

Section 14 (e): This subsection authorizes the merger of local-currency deposits made under the Relief Assistance Act and the Foreign Aid Act of 1947 with similar local-currency deposits to be made under this bill. Such local-currency deposits if so merged, would then be held for use in accordance with the terms and conditions specified in paragraph (6) of subsection 15 (b) of this bill. This section, when enacted into law, will provide the congressional approval required by the Relief Assistance Act and the Foreign Aid Act of 1947 for the deposit of the unexpended balances remaining in the local-currency accounts established under such act. Thus uniformity in the ultimate disposition of all these balances will be assured in accordance with the policies established in this bill.

Section 14 (f): This subsection establishes a foreign economic trust fund consisting of $3,000,000,000 of the funds appropriated for the first 12 months of operations under the bill, and requires that expenditures made for carrying out this bill during such period will first be met out of such trust fund. When the $3,000,000,000 placed in the trust fund has been exhausted by these expenditures, future expenditures will be made out of appropriation accounts in the customary manner. From the point of view of the Administrator's operations under the act, the trust fund will be utilized in exactly the same manner as ordinary appropriation accounts. The only difference which will result from the creation of a trust fund is the recording of the expenditure of the $3,000,000,000 as part of the budgetary expenditures of the fiscal year ending June 30, 1948.

Section 15 (a): This subsection authorizes the Secretary of State, after consultation with the Administrator, to conclude such agreements as may be necessary in furtherance of the purposes of this bill.

Section 15 (b): This subsection provides that in addition to the multilateral reciprocal pledges to be given among themselves, each participating country to be eligible to receive assistance under this bill, will be required to conclude an executive agreement with the United States. Inasmuch as the purpose of the bill, as stated in section 2 (b), is to effectuate the policy set forth in section 2 (a) of the bill, this portion of the bilateral agreement will, in effect, constitute an undertaking by each participating country to adhere to the policies of the bill governing the objectives in Europe of the program. In addition, subsection (b) enumerates certain provisions which will, where applicable, be embodied in the bilateral agreement between each participating country and the United States.

The first of these provisions embodies an undertaking by the country concerned to promote industrial and agricultural production in order to enable such country to become independent of extraordinary outside economic assistance. It also makes clear that the Administrator has authority to approve specific projects which may be proposed by a participating country to be undertaken in substantial part with assistance provided under the bill and is designed to further the purposes of the bill.

Paragraph (5) of section 15 (b) is designed to make available to the United States in accordance with the terms of the paragraph, materials required by the United States as a result of deficiencies or potential deficiencies in its own resources. Agreements with participating countries for the transfer of such materials may extend beyond the period of the bill and will specify the terms and quantities governing the transfer of such materials.

In addition to providing for reports to the United States by each participating country on operations under the agreement, paragraph (7) also assures that adequate publicity will be given within each participating country by the government of such country to United States assistance furnished under the bill.

Section 15 (c): Detailed and comprehensive agreements such as are contemplated under subsection (b) may well require some time to conclude, particularly since the constitutional systems of some participating countries require that agreements of this character be submitted to their legislatures for ratification. Accordingly, subsection (c) authorizes the Administrator, for a period of 3 months after the date of enactment of this bill, to provide assistance to any participating country in accordance with the terms of the bill whenever such country has signified its adherence to the purpose of the bill and its intention to conclude an agreement in accordance with subsection (b) of this section and provided that the Administrator finds that such country is complying with those provisions of subsection (b) as he may determine to be applicable. In order to assure that conditions of hunger and cold will be alleviated and economic retrogression will be avoided, the Administrator is further authorized through June 30, 1948, to provide for the transfer of stated essential subsistence items even though it has not been possible within that period to complete the interim arrangements contemplated by this subsection.

Section 15 (d): The follow-up system contemplated in this subsection will supplement that provided for the Administrator by the special missions established under section 9 of the bill.

Section 16: This section is designed to make possible the use of funds appropriated under authority of this bill to increase the production in participating countries of materials required by the United States as a result of deficiencies or potential deficiencies in its own resources.

Section 17: This section authorizes the Administrator in certain circumstances to terminate assistance to any participating country. In certain cases, viewed in the light of the nature or circumstance of a violation, certain corrective or preventive action by the Administrator, or by other agencies of the Government may be more appropriate than termination of assistance. Accordingly, under this section, the Administrator may provide for, or recommend to the President or to the appropriate agency of the Government, the taking of such action.

Section 18: This provision is necessary in order to provide flexibility in connection with the procurement and shipment of commodities and other similar operations under the bill. Among the laws concerning which it can be expected that this authority will be exercised by the President are:

1. R. S. 3648—Advances of Public Money; Prohibition Against. This law generally prohibits advance payments out of public funds for articles or services prior to receipt of such articles or services.
2. R. S. 3709—Advertising for Purchases and Contracts. This law requires generally advertising for all Government purchases.
3. R. S. 3710—Opening of Bids. This law provides that all persons bidding on Government contracts must be given an opportunity to be present at the opening of bids.
4. 47 Stat. 1520—American Materials Required for Public Use. This law, known as the Buy American Act, requires the purchase of raw and finished material produced in the United States if they are intended for United States public use.

The general authority for exemption from laws such as those referred to above will also permit waiver in cases where a law specifically requires a finding to be made by the heads of various departments before operations may be carried on with regard thereto. Such requirements could delay operations to an extent which would be harmful in an urgent program of this type. In order to assure that the power of waiver will be employed only where essential, the bill provides that the President must specify which laws are to be waived.

Section 19: The purpose of this section is to make it possible for persons to serve on the Public Advisory Board or on any [other] advisory committee established under the authority of section 7 (b), or as a consultant to assist the Administrator in carrying out this bill, despite the participation of such a person in activities, as part of his regular business operations, which would bring him within the prohibition of certain existing Federal laws. Under existing legislation it is unlawful, for example, for a person to act as attorney or agent in the prosecution of a claim against the Government while such person is serving as an official or employee of the Government. This type of legislation is necessary and proper in connection with ordinary operations of the Government. However, it is extremely desirable in connection with the European recovery program to permit the employment of experienced lawyers and businessmen. Legislation of the type waived by section 19 would unduly restrict the participation of such persons in the program. This was demonstrated during the war when similar exemptions were permitted in order to enable greater participation of businessmen in connection with wartime programs.

Section 20: This section deals with the utilization of the services and facilities of the United Nations, its specialized agencies, and other international organizations and provides for the procedures to be followed in order to keep the United Nations informed of operations under this bill.

Section 21 (a): This subsection provides that operations under the bill are to be terminated on June 30, 1952, or prior thereto if the two Houses of Congress shall pass a resolution declaring that such operations should be terminated. The operations to which this provision applies are those set forth in section 11 (a), namely, the various methods by which assistance may be rendered to the participating countries. An exception to the terms of the provision will permit the completion of commitments made by the Administrator prior to June 30, 1952. Hence, if the Administrator has authorized the procurement of a commodity prior to June 30, 1952, but shipment or delivery to the participating country has not been effected prior to that date, these functions may be performed after that date to the extent necessary to carry out such commitment. This subsection also permits contracts to be made after June 30, 1952, to the extent necessary to carry out these commitments. For example, the Administrator may use funds appropriated under this bill for payment of freight on commodities shipped during the 12-month period following June 30, 1952, if such commodities are procured under a commitment entered into by the Administrator prior to that date. It is believed that, by limiting the period during which these operations may be continued to 12 months, this bill provides assurance that operations will be completely terminated at the earliest date consistent with the effective carrying out of the purposes of the bill.

Section 21 (b): Under this subsection, the liquidating activities under this program, at such time after June 30, 1952, as the President may find appropriate, may be transferred to such departments, agencies, or establishments of the Government as the President finds appropriate.

Section 22: Section 22, by providing that the President must at least once every calendar quarter until June 1952, and once every year thereafter until all operations under this bill have been completed, transmit to Congress a report of operations under this bill, assures that the Congress will be kept currently informed of such operations.

Section 23: This section provides for the establishment of a joint congressional committee. It is to be noted that the authorization in section 23 (d) to appropriate funds for use by the joint commission is separate from, and in addition to, the authorization to appropriate funds in section 14.

Section 24: This section contains the usual separability provision.

Appendix II

Witnesses appearing before the committee

Date of appearance	Name	Affiliation
January. 8	George C. Marshall	Secretary of State.
Jan. 9, 10, 12	Lewis W. Douglas	Ambassador to Great Britain.
Jan. 12	W. Averell Harriman	Secretary of Commerce.
Jan. 13	Clinton P. Anderson	Secretary of Agriculture.
	Julius A. Krug	Secretary of the Interior.
Jan. 14	John W. Snyder	Secretary of the Treasury.
	William McChesney Martin, Jr.	Chairman of the Board of Directors of the Export-Import Bank.
	Kenneth C. Royall	Secretary of the Army.
Jan. 15	James V. Forrestal	Secretary of Defense.
Jan. 16	John J. McCloy	President, International Bank for Reconstruction and Development.
Jan. 19	Bernard Baruch	
Jan. 20	John Foster Dulles	Attorney.
	Eugene Meyer	Chairman of the board, Washington Post.
	Charles R. Hook	President, American Rolling Mills Co.
	George F. Zook	President, American Council on Education.
	Guy I. Burch	Director, Population Reference Bureau.
	Kathryn H. Stone (Mrs.)	First vice president, League of Women Voters.
Jan. 21	James F. O'Neil	National commander, The American Legion.
	Ray H. Branaman	Commander in chief, Veterans of Foreign Wars.
	Oren Root, Jr.	National planning committee, American Veterans' Committee.
	Ray Sawyer	National legislative director, American Veterans of World War II.
	Henry Hazlitt	Financial editor, Newsweek.
Jan. 22	William J. Donovan	Donovan, Leisure, Newton & Irvine.
	Harvey W. Brown	President, International Association of Machinists.
	Margaret F. Stone (Mrs.)	Chairman of legislation, National Women's Trade Union League of America.
	Luther Gulick	Member, National Planning Association; president, Institute of Public Administration.
	Ralph McGill	Editor, The Atlanta Constitution.
	Robert P. Patterson	Chairman, Committee for the Marshall plan.
	Henry J. Taylor	Commentator and author.
Jan. 23	Curtis Calder	Chairman, international relations committee, National Association of Manufacturers.
	William Green	President, American Federation of Labor.
	Calvin B. Hoover	Professor, Duke University.
	Paul Hoffman	Chairman, Committee for Economic Development.
Jan. 24	Merwin K. Hart	President, National Economic Council.
	Paul A. Porter	Member of the national board, Americans for Democratic Action.
	Herbert Lehman	The American Jewish Committee.
	J. L. Blair Buck (Mrs.)	President, General Federation of Women's Clubs.
	Donald R. Burgess (Mrs.)	President, Maryland State Division, American Association of University Women.
	Mildred B. Northrop	Women's Action Committee for Lasting Peace.
Jan. 26	H. J. Heinz	H. J. Heinz Co.
	R. W. Gifford	Chairman of the board, Borg-Warner International Corp.
	James G. Patton	President, National Farmers' Union.
	Arthur Schutzer	Executive secretary, American Labor Party.
	Clark W. Eichelberger	American Association for the United Nations.
Jan. 27	George C. Tenney	Acting editor, the Electrical World.
	Robert Moses (Statement presented by Frederick A. Collins)	Department of parks, New York City.
	Norman Thomas	Chairman, Postwar World Council.
	Walter White	Secretary, National Association for the Advancement of Colored People.
	Carlton Koepge	Engineer.
	Bernard Weitzer	National legislative representative, Jewish War Veterans of the United States of America.
	Joseph Willen (Mrs.)	National Council of Jewish Women.
Jan. 28	Robert M. La Follette, Jr.	President's Committee on Foreign Aid.
Jan. 29	Arnold J. Wilson	President, Illinois Manufacturers' Association; president, General Time Instruments Corp.
	John Ben Shepperd	President, United States Junior Chamber of Commerce.

Witnesses appearing before the committee—Continued

Date of appearance	Name	Affiliation
Jan. 29	William Brooks	North American Grain Export Association, National Grain Trade Council.
	Robert F. Loree	Chairman, National Foreign Trade Council.
	Marvin J. Coles	Foreign Freight Forwarders Association.
	James H. Sheldon	Member of the advisory council, Society for the Prevention of World War III.
	Jean I. Pajus	Economic adviser, Society for the Prevention of World War III.
	Frazier Bailey	President, National Federation of American Shipping.
	Norman Littell	Attorney.
	Kathryn Lee Marshall (Mrs.)	National legislative secretary, Women's International League for Peace and Freedom.
	Willford King	Chairman, Committee for Constitutional Government.
	A. O. Tittman	
Jan. 30	Allan B. Kline	President, American Farm Bureau Federation.
	J. T. Sanders	Legislative counsel, the National Grange.
	J. D. Zellerbach	President, Crown Zellerbach Corp.
	Carlton Barrett	President, Tate-Jones & Co., Inc.
	James M. Reed	Secretary, foreign-service division, American Friends Committee on National Legislation.
	Joseph G. Dubuque	Professor, University of Maryland.
Jan. 31	Charles P. Taft	President, Federal Council of Churches of Christ in America.
	Robert M. La Follette, Jr.	Member of the President's Committee on Foreign Aid.
	Lewis H. Brown	President, Johns-Manville Co.
	William Batt, Sr.	Chairman, Philadelphia branch of the Stimson committee; director of the United Nations Council.
	J. R. Gormley	Port agent, Pacific Coast Marine, Firemen, Oilers, Water Tenders, and Wipers Association.
	Robert Rosamond	
Feb. 2	Joseph Scott	Attorney.
	Martin L. Sweeney	
	Russell B. Brown	General counsel, Independent Petroleum Association of America.
	L. H. Pasqualicchio	National deputy, Order Sons of Italy in America.
	John B. Trevor	American Coalition of Patriotic Societies.
	Ely Culbertson	Citizens Committee for United Nations Reform.
	Harry Lundeberg	President, Seafarers International Union of North America; secretary-treasurer, Sailors Union of the Pacific (AFL).
Feb. 3	James B. Carey	Secretary-treasurer, Congress of Industrial Organizations.
	Joseph Curran	President, National Maritime Union.
	Ronald Bridges	Council for Social Action of the Congregational Christian Churches of the United States.
	Paul M. Mulliken	Secretary, National Retail Farm Equipment Association.
	Agnes Waters (Mrs.)	
Feb. 4	Earl O. Shreve	President, United States Chamber of Commerce.
	David A. Bunn	Legislative representative, Committee for Effective Citizenship, National Inter-Collegiate Christian Council.
	True D. Morse	President, Doane Agricultural Service, Inc.
	George P. Murdock	Professor, Yale University.
	Carl A. Schmidt	
Feb. 5	Walter P. Reuther	International president, United Automobile, Aircraft and Agricultural Implement Workers (CIO).
	Hamilton Fish	
	Benjamin A. Javits	Attorney.

APPENDIX II

DOCUMENTS RELATING TO S. 2393

LEGISLATIVE CHRONOLOGY OF S. 2393

TO PROMOTE THE GENERAL WELFARE, NATIONAL INTEREST AND FOREIGN POLICY OF THE UNITED STATES BY PROVIDING AID TO CHINA

Senate Action

Introduced by Mr. Vandenberg and referred to Committee on March 25, 1948.
Hearings held in executive session on February 24, 26, 28, March 20, 22, 1948.
Ordered reported (vote 13–0) on March 25, 1948.
Reported (S. Rept. 1026) on March 25, 1948.
Passed on March 30, 1948.

House Action

Referred to Committee.
(See S. 2202 as amended).

85-743 O - 73 - 44

[COMMITTEE PRINT]

FEBRUARY 20, 1948

DRAFT, CHINA AID BILL

STAFF NOTE.—This is the draft bill submitted by the Department of State to the Senate Foreign Relations Committee and the House Foreign Affairs Committee on February 18, 1948. It is printed herewith for the use of the Foreign Relations Committee and the Senate in its consideration of the China aid program.

80TH CONGRESS
2D SESSION

S.

IN THE SENATE OF THE UNITED STATES

FEBRUARY , 1948

Mr. ______ introduced the following bill; which was read twice and referred to the Committee on Foreign Relations

---

A BILL

To promote the general welfare, national interest, and foreign policy of the United States by providing aid to China.

Be it enacted by the Senate and House of Representatives of the United States of America in Congress assembled, That this Act may be cited as the "China Aid Act of 1948".

SEC. 2. It is the purpose of this Act to provide immediate aid to China to relieve human suffering, to assist in retarding economic deterioration, and to afford the people of China an opportunity to initiate measures of self-help necessary to rebuild the bases for more stable economic conditions.

SEC. 3. (a) The President may, whenever he finds it in furtherance of the purposes of this Act and upon the terms and conditions set forth in this Act and upon such additional terms and conditions, consistent with the provisions of this Act, as he may determine to be necessary and proper—

(1) procure, or provide for the procurement of, from any source, including Government stocks, the following commodities landed in China after the date of enactment of this Act: *Provided,* That the procurement of petroleum and petroleum products and other commodities in short supply in the United States shall, to the maximum extent practicable, be made from sources outside of the United States, its Territories, and possessions:

(i) cereals, fertilizer, petroleum and petroleum products, tobacco, cotton, metals, coal, pharmaceuticals, and replacement articles for existing capital equipment;

(ii) materials and equipment needed in connection with projects, approved by the President, to restore or develop within China transportation facilities, sources of fuel and power, export industries and such other projects as the President may approve; and

(iii) such other commodities as the President finds are necessary for the accomplishment of the purposes of this Act;

(2) transport and store, or provide for transportation and storage of, such commodities;

(3) transfer such commodities to China;

(4) detail to assist and advise the Government of China, in implementation of the purposes of this Act, any persons in the employ of the United States; and the provisions of the Act of January 27, 1948 (Public Law 402, Eightieth Congress), applicable to personnel assigned for service to the government of another country pursuant to such Act, shall be applicable to personnel detailed pursuant to this paragraph;

(5) promote, in furtherance of the purposes of subsection (j) of section 5 and in agreement with the Government of China, an increase in the production in China of materials which are required by the United States as a result of deficiencies or potential deficiencies in the natural resources of the United States.

(b) The President, acting through such departments, agencies, or establishments of the Government (including, whenever used in this Act, any corporation which is an instrumentality of the United States) as he shall direct, may perform any of the functions specified in subsection (a) of this section—

(1) by allocation of funds herein authorized, for payments or reimbursements to any such department, agency, or establishment; or

(2) by establishing in the United States accounts against which withdrawals may be made, in connection with supply programs approved by the President, upon presentation of contracts, invoices, or other documentation specified by him.

SEC. 4. (a) The President may provide assistance for China in the form and under the procedures authorized in section 3, without payment or by means of loans under the procedures provided for in subsection (b) of this section. The National Advisory Council on International Monetary and Financial Problems shall advise the President in determining whether such assistance shall be without payment or by means of loans, and in determining the terms of any such loans. The determination whether or not China should be required to make payment, whether in money or other valuable consideration, for any assistance furnished to it in furtherance of the purposes of this Act, and the terms of such payment, if required, shall depend upon its capacity to make such payment without jeopardizing the accomplishment of the purposes of this Act: *Provided*, That where it is determined that China can be required to make payment only for a part of the assistance furnished it under this Act, such payment shall, to the extent practicable, first be required for commodities specified in subparagraph (ii) of paragraph (1) of subsection (a) of section 3.

(b) When it is determined that assistance should be extended under the provisions of this Act by means of loans, the President shall allocate funds for the purpose to the Export-Import Bank of Washington, which shall, notwithstanding the provisions of the Export-Import Bank Act of 1945 (59 Stat. 526), as amended, make and administer the loan as directed, and on terms specified, by the President. The Export-Import Bank may be reimbursed for necessary administrative expenses in connection with such loans. The bank shall deposit into the Treasury of the United States as miscellaneous receipts amounts received by the bank in repayment of principal and interest of any such loans. Loans made by Export-Import Bank of Washington with funds so allocated to it by the President shall not be considered in determining whether the bank has outstanding at any one time loans and guaranties to the extent of the limitation imposed by section 7 of the Export-Import Bank Act of 1945 (59 Stat. 529), as amended.

SEC. 5. Before any aid is made available to China under the authority of this Act, an agreement shall be entered into, subject to the limitations and provisions of this Act, between China and the United States containing an undertaking by China, together with such other undertakings as the President may deem necessary to carry out the purposes of this Act and to improve commercial relations with China—

(a) to make efficient use of any commodities made available under the authority of this Act, and to provide for the distribution of such commodities at such prices and under such terms and conditions as are in furtherance of the purposes of this Act;

(b) to initiate, insofar as practicable, financial, monetary, budgetary, and administrative measures with a view to creating more stable currency conditions, and with a view to increasing China's ability to achieve a self-sustaining economy;

(c) to place in a special account a deposit in Chinese currency in commensurate amounts and under such terms and conditions as may be agreed to between the Government of China and the Government of the United States, when any commodity or service is made available through any means authorized under this Act, and is not furnished to China on terms of payment.

Such special account, together with the unexpended portions of any deposits which may have been made by China pursuant to section 6 of the joint resolution providing for relief assistance to the people of countries devastated by war (Public Law 84, Eightieth Congress) shall be held or used only for such purposes as may be agreed to between the Government of China and the Government of the United States, and any unencumbered balance remaining in such account on June 30, 1949, shall be disposed of within China for such purposes as may, subject to approval by act or joint resolution of the Congress, be agreed between China and the Government of the United States;

(d) to publish in China and transmit to the United States, not less frequently than every calendar quarter after the date of the agreement, full statements of operations of the Government of China under the agreement, including a report of the use of funds, commodities, and services received under this Act;

(e) to furnish promptly, upon request of the United States, any relevant information which would be of assistance to the United States in determining the nature and scope of future operations under this Act;

(f) to give full and continuous publicity by all available media (including government radio) within

China, so as to inform the ultimate consumers, as to the purpose, source, character, and amounts of commodities made available under the authority of this Act;

(g) not to export or permit removal from China of commodities made available under the authority of this Act, except to the extent agreed upon by the Government of the United States;

(h) to make all possible efforts to secure the maximum production and distribution of locally produced commodities, and not to permit any measures to be taken involving sale, distribution, or use of any commodities of the character covered in this Act which would reduce the locally produced supply of such commodities or which would reduce the utilization of foreign sources of supply other than the United States;

(i) to permit representatives of the Government of the United States, including such committees of the Congress as may be authorized by their respective Houses, and representatives of the press and radio of the United States, to observe and report on the distribution and utilization of the commodities made available under this Act and the special account provided for in subsection (e) of this section;

(j) to facilitate the sale, to the United States for stock-piling purposes, for such period of time as may be agreed to and upon reasonable terms and in reasonable quantities, of materials which are required by the United States as a result of deficiencies or potential deficiencies in its own natural resources, and which may be available in China after due regard for reasonable Chinese requirements for domestic use and commercial export.

SEC. 6. The President shall promptly terminate the provision of aid under this Act (a) whenever he determines that China is not adhering to the terms of its agreement entered into in accordance with section 5 of this Act; or (b) whenever he finds, by reason of changed conditions, that the provision of aid under this Act is no longer consistent with the national interests of the United States.

SEC. 7. All commodities made available under the authority of this Act or the containers of such commodities shall, to the extent practicable and desirable, be marked, stamped, branded, or labeled in a conspicuous place as legibly, indelibly, and permanently as the nature of such commodities or containers will permit, in such manner as to indicate to the people of China that such commodities have been furnished or made available by the United States of America.

SEC. 8. (a) The President may, from time to time, promulgate such rules and regulations as he may find necessary and proper to carry out any of the provisions of this Act.

(b) The President may delegate to the Secretary of State any of the powers or authority conferred on him under the provisions of this Act, other than the determinations provided for in section 9 hereof.

(c) Whenever there shall be created by law a new agency or establishment of the Government for the purpose of administering programs of assistance to foreign countries, the President may transfer to such new agency or establishment, or delegate to the head thereof, such of the powers and authority conferred on the President under this Act as he shall prescribe, and, in the event of such transfer or delegation, the provisions of the Act creating such new agency or establishment which pertain to the appointment, assignment, and compensation of personnel performing functions under such Act outside the continental limits of the United States shall apply to the persons performing functions under this Act outside the continental limits of the United States.

(d) Civilian personnel who are citizens of the United States appointed to perform functions under this Act outside the continental limits of the United States shall be appointed subject to investigation by the Federal Bureau of Investigation: *Provided, however,* That they may assume their posts and perform their functions after preliminary investigation and clearance by the Department of State.

SEC. 9. When the President determines it to be in furtherance of the purposes of this Act, the functions authorized under this Act may be performed without regard to such provisions of law regulating the making, performance, amendment, or modification of contracts and the expenditure of Government funds as the President may specify.

SEC. 10. (a) Notwithstanding the provisions of any other law, the Reconstruction Finance Corporation is authorized and directed, until such time as an appropriation shall be made pursuant to subsection (b) of this section, to make advances not to exceed in the aggregate $150,000,000 to carry out the provisions of this Act, in such manner, at such time and in such amounts as the President shall determine, and no interest shall be charged on advances made by the Treasury to the Reconstruction Finance Corporation for this purpose. The Reconstruction Finance Corporation shall be repaid without interest from appropriations authorized under this Act for advances made by it hereunder.

(b) There are hereby authorized to be appropriated to the President from time to time, out of any money in the Treasury not otherwise appropriated, such amounts not to exceed $570,000,000 as may be necessary to carry out the provisions and accomplish the purposes of this Act.

(c) Funds made available for the purposes of this Act shall be available for incurring and defraying all necessary expenses incident to carrying out the provisions of this Act, including administrative expenses and expenses in the District of Columbia and elsewhere for compensation, allowances, and travel of personnel, including Foreign Service personnel whose services are utilized primarily for the purposes of this Act, and without regard to section 14 (a) of the Federal Employees Pay Act of 1946 (60 Stat. 219). Expenditures may be made outside the continental limits of the United States for procurement of supplies and services and for other administrative purposes (other than compensation of personnel) without regard to such laws and regulations governing the obligation and expenditure of Government funds as the President shall specify in the interest of the accomplishment of the purposes of this Act.

(d) Funds authorized under this Act, when allocated to any department, agency, or establishment of the Government, shall be available for obligation and expenditures in accordance with the laws governing obligations and expenditures of such department, agency, or establishment, or organizational unit thereof, concerned.

(e) The President, whenever in his judgment the interests of the United States will best be served thereby, may dispose of any commodity procured out of funds made available for the purposes of this Act, in lieu of transferring such commodity to China, (1) by transfer of such commodity upon reimbursement to any department, agency, or establishment of the Government for use or disposal by such department, agency, or establishment as authorized by law, or (2) without regard to provisions of law relating to the disposal of Government-owned property, when necessary to prevent spoilage or wastage of such commodity or to conserve the usefulness thereof. Funds realized from such disposal or transfer shall revert to the respective appropriation or appropriations out of which funds were expended for the procurement of such commodity.

SEC. 11. (a) The President is authorized to request the cooperation of or the use of the services and facilities of the United Nations, its organs and specialized agencies or other international organizations, in carrying out the purposes of this Act, and may make payments by advancements or reimbursements, for such purpose, out of funds made available for the purposes of this Act, to the extent that special compensation is usually required for such services and facilities.

(b) The President shall transmit to the Secretary General of the United Nations copies of reports to Congress on the operations conducted under this Act.

(c) Any agreement concluded between the United States and China in implementation of the purposes of this Act shall be registered with the United Nations if such registration is required by the Charter of the United Nations.

SEC. 12. The President, from time to time, but not less frequently than once every calendar quarter, and until the end of the quarterly period after all operations under the authority of this Act have been completed, shall transmit to the Congress a report of operations under this Act. All information received pursuant to undertakings provided for by section 5 (e) of this Act shall, as soon as may be practicable after the receipt thereof, be reported to the Congress. Reports provided for under this section shall be transmitted to the Secretary of the Senate or the Clerk of the House of Representatives, if the Senate or the House of Representatives, as the case may be, is not in session.

SEC. 13. After June 30, 1949, or after the passage of a concurrent resolution by the two Houses before such date, which declares that the powers conferred by or pursuant to sections 3 and 4 of this Act are no longer necessary for the accomplishment of the purposes of this Act, whichever shall first occur, none of the functions authorized under such provisions of this Act may be exercised under authority of this Act: *Provided*, That, during the twelve months following such date commodities which were, on such date, in process of procurement for shipment to or delivery in China may be transferred to China, and funds appropriated under authority of this Act may be obligated during such twelve-month period for the necessary expenses of procurement, shipment, delivery, and other activities essential to such transfer, and shall remain available during such period for the necessary expenses of liquidating operations under this Act.

SEC. 14. Section 2 of the Foreign Aid Act of 1947 (Public Law 389, Eightieth Congress) is amended by striking out therefrom the word "China" and the comma immediately following.

SEC. 15. If any provision of this Act or the application of such provision to any circumstances or persons shall be held invalid, the validity of the remainder of the Act and the applicability of such provision to other circumstances or persons shall not be affected thereby.

Calendar No. 1068

80TH CONGRESS
2D SESSION

S. 2393

[Report No. 1026]

IN THE SENATE OF THE UNITED STATES

MARCH 25 (legislative day, MARCH 15), 1948

Mr. VANDENBERG, from the Committee on Foreign Relations, reported the following bill; which was read twice and ordered to be placed on the calendar

---

A BILL

To promote the general welfare, national interest, and foreign policy of the United States by providing aid to China.

Be it enacted by the Senate and House of Representatives of the United States of America in Congress assembled, That this Act may be cited as the "China Aid Act of 1948".

SEC. 2. It is the purpose of this Act to provide immediate aid to China to relieve human suffering, to assist in retarding economic deterioration, and to afford the people of China an opportunity to initiate measures of self-help necessary to rebuilding the bases for more stable economic conditions, such aid to be provided under the applicable provisions of the Economic Cooperation Act of 1948 which are consistent with the purposes of this Act. It is not the

85-743 O - 73 - 45

purpose of this Act that China, in order to receive aid hereunder, shall adhere to a joint program for European recovery.

SEC. 3. (a) In order to carry out the purposes of this Act, there is hereby authorized to be appropriated to the President for aid to China a sum not to exceed $363,000,000 to remain available for obligation for the period of one year following the date of enactment of this Act.

(b) There is also hereby authorized to be appropriated to the President a sum not to exceed $100,000,000 for additional aid to China through grants, on such terms as the President may determine and without regard to the provisions of the Economic Cooperation Act of 1948, to remain available for obligation for the period of one year following the date of enactment of this Act.

SEC. 4. An agreement shall be entered into between China and the United States containing those undertakings by China which the Secretary of State, after consultation with the Administrator for Economic Cooperation, may deem necessary to carry out the purposes of this Act and to improve commercial relations with China.

SEC. 5. Notwithstanding the provisions of any other law, the Reconstruction Finance Corporation is authorized and directed, until such time as an appropriation is made pursuant to section 3, to make advances, not to exceed in the aggregate $50,000,000, to carry out the provisions of this Act in such manner and in such amounts as the President shall determine. From appropriations authorized under section 3, there shall be repaid without interest to the Reconstruction Finance Corporation the advances made by it under the authority contained herein. No interest shall be charged on advances made by the Treasury to the Reconstruction Finance Corporation in implementation of this subsection.

Calendar No. 1068

80TH CONGRESS
2d Session

SENATE

REPORT
No. 1026

AID TO CHINA

REPORT

OF THE

COMMITTEE ON FOREIGN RELATIONS

ON

S. 2393

A BILL TO PROMOTE THE GENERAL WELFARE, NATIONAL INTEREST, AND FOREIGN POLICY OF THE UNITED STATES BY PROVIDING AID TO CHINA

MARCH 25 (legislative day, MARCH 15), 1948.—Ordered to be printed with an illustration

UNITED STATES
GOVERNMENT PRINTING OFFICE
WASHINGTON : 1948

TABLE OF CONTENTS

Calendar No. 1068

80TH CONGRESS 2d Session } SENATE { REPORT No. 1026

AID TO CHINA

MARCH 25 (legislative day, MARCH 15), 1948.—Ordered to be printed with an illustration

Mr. VANDENBERG, from the Committee on Foreign Relations, submitted the following

REPORT

[To accompany S. 2393]

The Committee on Foreign Relations, having had under consideration the subject of extending assistance to China, unanimously report to the Senate a bill (S. 2393) to promote the general welfare, national interest, and foreign policy of the United States by providing aid to China, and recommend that it do pass.

1. MAIN PURPOSE OF THE BILL

The bill provides for a program of assistance to China by authorizing the appropriation of $463,000,000 for a period of 1 year. $363,000,000 of this amount will be administered under the applicable provisions of the Economic Cooperation Act of 1948, although it is not contemplated that China will adhere to a joint program for European recovery. A sum not to exceed $100,000,000 will be authorized through grants, on such terms as the President may determine. The Reconstruction Finance Corporation is authorized to advance $50,000,000 to carry out the purposes of the act.

2. MESSAGE FROM THE PRESIDENT ON AID TO CHINA

MESSAGE FROM THE PRESIDENT OF THE UNITED STATES TRANSMITTING RECOMMENDATION THAT THE CONGRESS AUTHORIZE A PROGRAM FOR AID TO CHINA IN THE AMOUNT OF $570,000,000 TO PROVIDE ASSISTANCE UNTIL JUNE 30, 1949

To the Congress of the United States:

On several occasions I have stated that a primary objective of the United States is to bring about, throughout the world, the conditions of a just and lasting peace. This is a cause to which the American people are deeply devoted.

Since VJ-day we have expended great effort and large sums of money on the relief and rehabilitation of war-torn countries to aid in restoring workable economic systems which are essential to the maintenance of peace. A principle which has guided our efforts to assist these war-torn countries has been that of helping their peoples to help themselves. The Congress is now giving careful consideration to a most vital and far-reaching proposal to further this purpose—the program for aid to European recovery.

I now request the Congress to consider the type of further assistance which this country should provide to China.

A genuine friendship has existed between the American people and the people of China over many years. This friendship has been accompanied by a long record of commercial and cultural association and close cooperation between our two countries. Americans have developed a deep respect for the Chinese people and sympathy for the many trials and difficulties which they have endured.

The United States has long recognized the importance of a stable Chinese nation to lasting peace in the Pacific and the entire world. The vast size and population of China make her an important factor in world affairs. China is a land with rich tradition and culture and a large and energetic population. It has always been our desire to see a strong, progressive China making a full contribution to the strength of the family of nations.

With this end in view, we have supported the National Government of China since it first came to power 20 years ago. China and the United States were allies in the war against Japan, and as an ally we supported China's valiant war efforts against the Japanese. Since the Japanese surrender we have provided a great deal of additional assistance. Military aid was given the Chinese Government, not only to help defeat the Japanese invaders but also to assist in reoccupying Japanese-held areas. The United States contributed the major share of the extensive aid received by China under the program of the United Nations Relief and Rehabilitation Administration. We made available to the Chinese Government at minimum cost large quantities of surplus goods and equipment of value to China's economy. We are currently extending further aid to China under our foreign-relief program.

Nevertheless, the Chinese Government and people are still laboring under the double and interrelated burden of civil war and a rapidly deteriorating economy. The strains placed upon the country by 8 years of war and the Japanese occupation and blockade have been increased by internal strife at the very time that reconstruction efforts should be under way. The wartime damage to transport and productive facilities has been greatly accentuated by the continued obstruction and destruction of vital communications by the Communist forces.

The civil warfare has further impeded recovery by forcing upon the Government heavy expenditures which greatly exceed revenues. Continual issuances of currency to meet these expenditures have produced drastic inflation, with its attendant disruption of normal commercial operations. Under these circumstances, China's foreign-exchange holdings have been so reduced that it will soon be impossible for China to meet the cost of essential imports. Without such imports, industrial activity would diminish and the rate of economic deterioration would be sharply increased.

The continued deterioration of the Chinese economy is a source of deep concern to the United States. Ever since the return of General Marshall from China, the problem of assistance to the Chinese has been under continuous study. We have hoped for conditions in China that would make possible the effective and constructive use of American assistance in reconstruction and rehabilitation. Conditions have not developed as we had hoped, and we can only do what is feasible under circumstances as they exist.

We can assist in retarding the current economic deterioration and thus give the Chinese Government a further opportunity to initiate the measures necessary to the establishment of more stable economic conditions. But it is, and has been, clear that only the Chinese Government itself can undertake the vital measures necessary to provide the framework within which efforts toward peace and true economic recovery may be effective.

In determining the character and dimensions of the program which might be suited to this purpose, we have had to take into account a number of diverse and conflicting factors, including the other demands on our national resources at this time, the availability of specific commodities, the dimensions and complexities of the problems facing the Chinese Government, and the extent to which these problems could be promptly and effectively alleviated by foreign aid. United States assistance to China, like that provided to any other nation, must be adapted to its particular requirements and capacities.

In the light of these factors, I recommend that the Congress authorize a program for aid to China in the amount of $570,000,000 to provide assistance until June 30, 1949.

The program should make provision for the financing, through loans or grants, of essential imports into China in the amount of $510,000,000. This estimate is based upon prices as of January 1, 1948, since it is impossible at present to predict what effect current price changes may have on the program. Revised dollar estimates can be presented in connection with the request for appropriations if necessary. The essential imports include cereals, cotton, petroleum, fertilizer, tobacco, pharmaceuticals, coal, and repair parts for existing capital equipment. The quantities provided for under this program are within the limits of available supplies. The financing of these essential commodity imports by the United States would permit the Chinese Government to devote its limited dollar resources to the most urgent of its other needs.

The program should also provide $60,000,000 for a few selected reconstruction projects to be initiated prior to June 30, 1949. There is an urgent need for the restoration of essential transportation facilities, fuel and power operations, and export industries. This work could be undertaken in areas sheltered from military operations and could help in improving the supply and distribution of essential commodities.

As in the case of aid to European recovery, the conduct of this program of aid should be made subject to an agreement between China and the United States setting forth the conditions and procedures for administering the aid. The agreement should include assurances that the Chinese Government will take such economic, financial, and other measures as are practicable, looking toward the ultimate goal of economic stability and recovery. The United States would, of course, reserve the right to terminate aid if it is determined that the assistance provided is not being handled in accordance with the agreement or that the policies of the Chinese Government are inconsistent with the objective of using the aid to help achieve a self-supporting economy.

Pending establishment of the agency which is to be set up for the administration of the European recovery program, the assistance to China should be carried forward under the existing machinery now administering the foreign-relief programs. Legislation authorizing the Chinese program should make possible transfer of the administration of the Chinese program to the agency administering our aid to European recovery. The need for authority in the administering agency to make adjustments in the program from time to time will be as great here as in the European recovery program.

The proposed program of aid to China represents what I believe to be the best course this Government can follow, in the light of all the circumstances. Nothing which this country provides by way of assistance can, even in a small measure, be a substitute for the necessary action that can be taken only by the Chinese Government. Yet this program can accomplish the important purpose of giving the Chinese Government a respite from rapid economic deterioration, during which it can move to establish more stable economic conditions. Without this respite the ability of the Chinese Government to establish such conditions at all, would be doubtful. The achievement of even this limited objective is of such importance as to justify the proposed program of aid.

I recommend, therefore, that this program be given prompt and favorable consideration by the Congress.

HARRY S. TRUMAN.

THE WHITE HOUSE, *February 18, 1948.*

3. COMMITTEE HEARINGS

The committee held executive hearings on aid to China on February 26, March 19 and 20, 1948. During the course of the hearings the committee heard the views of Hon. George C. Marshall, Secretary of State; Hon. Willard L. Thorp, Assistant Secretary of State; W Walton Butterworth, Director, Office of Far Eastern Affairs, and their assistants. On March 22, after a lengthy discussion of the policy questions involved, the committee drafted the present bill, which it approved by a unaminous vote of 13 to 0.

Since the committee had before it the printed testimony on aid to China, given by private witnesses to the House Foreign Affairs Committee, it was considered unnecessary to hold public hearings.

4. Text of the Committee Bill

A BILL To promote the general welfare, national interest, and foreign policy of the United States by providing aid to China

Be it enacted by the Senate and House of Representatives of the United States of America in Congress assembled, That this Act may be cited as the "China Aid Act of 1948".

Sec. 2. It is the purpose of this Act to provide immediate aid to China to relieve human suffering, to assist in retarding economic deterioration, and to afford the people of China an opportunity to initiate measures of self-help necessary to rebuilding the bases for more stable economic conditions, such aid to be provided under the applicable provisions of the Economic Cooperation Act of 1948 which are consistent with the purposes of this Act. It is not the purpose of this Act that China, in order to receive aid hereunder, shall adhere to a joint program for European recovery.

Sec. 3. (a) In order to carry out the purposes of this Act, there is hereby authorized to be appropriated to the President for aid to China a sum not to exceed $363,000,000 to remain available for obligation for the period of one year following the date of enactment of this Act.

(b) There is also hereby authorized to be appropriated to the President a sum not to exceed $100,000,000 for additional aid to China through grants, on such terms as the President may determine and without regard to the provisions of the Economic Cooperation Act of 1948, to remain available for obligation for the period of one year following the date of enactment of this Act.

Sec. 4. An agreement shall be entered into between China and the United States containing those undertakings by China which the Secretary of State, after consultation with the Administrator for Economic Cooperation, may deem necessary to carry out the purposes of this Act and to improve commercial relations with China.

Sec. 5. Notwithstanding the provisions of any other law, the Reconstruction Finance Corporation is authorized and directed, until such time as an appropriation is made pursuant to section 3, to make advances, not to exceed in the aggregate $50,000,000, to carry out the provisions of this Act in such manner and in such amounts as the President shall determine. From appropriations authorized under section 3, there shall be repaid without interest to the Reconstruction Finance Corporation the advances made by it under the authority contained herein. No interest shall be charged on advances made by the Treasury to the Reconstruction Finance Corporation in implementation of this subsection.

5. The Situation in China

The political, social, financial, and military situation in China is so well known that it need not be discussed in detail in this report. China occupies a central position in east Asia and contains both two-thirds of its area and its population. The Chinese people make up one-fifth of the world's population. Her economy is primarily agricultural. The future of east Asia as a whole is closely bound up with developments in China.

Because of the traditional friendship between our peoples, China's difficulties produce in the United States a profoundly sympathetic response [which is often accompanied by a sense of frustration, in that aid extended by the United States has too infrequently given rise to measures of self-help on the part of the Chinese themselves, which must be taken if our aid is to be effective.]

There are favorable factors. China could be reasonably self-sufficient in food and raw materials resources. There is a large and valuable labor pool. Among the politically conscious people there is sentiment in favor of democratic government. There is a great record in, and respect for, the constructive values of civilization.

[The unfavorable factors presently outweigh the favorable.] China's economy and prospects are marred by an 8-year war with Japan, and a civil war that also includes the usual Communist tactics of disruption, destruction, and sabotage. Inefficiency, corruption, and bureaucratic maladies become even more devastating in a period of dislocation and inflation. Ineptitude in military leadership and corruption among army commanders has contributed largely to the lowered morale of the Chinese Government troops. The country never developed a favorable balance of trade, and the unfavorable balance obviously grew worse in the past few years. An important psychological factor is the lack of popular confidence in the Chinese Government.

It is hardly necessary to repeat that China faces colossally difficult and complicated tasks and that, accordingly, the further constructive and cooperative role of the United States is not easy to determine and is, perforce, beset with grave and honest doubts.

(A) POLITICAL CIRCUMSTANCES

The Kuomintang has been in control of the National Government since 1928. It has taken the initial steps toward democracy through the promulgation of the constitution and the election of a national assembly, while the Chinese Communist aims are directed toward a totalitarian government. The Chinese Communist propaganda has been bitterly anti-American and follows the Moscow line regarding all American policies. There appears to be some hope that there exists in China the social and political elements and ideals which could widen and increase the political appeal and leadership of a nationalist government—to combat the hard core of a disruptive, alien-orientated communism in open rebellion.

In the Sino-Soviet Treaty of August 1945 the U.S.S.R. undertook to support only the National Government, which was recognized by all the powers as the legal Government of China. The U.S.S.R. has not provided the assistance to the National Government with "material resources" called for in that treaty. Instead, the U. S. S. R. removed large quantities of industrial equipment from the factories of Manchuria, perhaps to the extent of $2,000,000,000. (See appendix C.)

(B) ECONOMIC CRISIS

China's economy has deteriorated steadily since the defeat of Japan. The destruction of communications has isolated the resources from the centers of consumption and the ports. The food deficit of 2,000,000 tons for the coming year is largely a result of the civil war. The cost of civil war has caused mounting Government deficits. The inflationary stampede impedes production and distribution and stimulates speculation and hoarding. The note issue increased more than eight times during 1947. In mid-March the black-market rate for United States dollars was slightly more than 450,000 Chinese dollars to 1 United States dollar. Seventy percent of the Government's expenditures has gone for military purposes. Revenue has covered less than one-third of the total Government expenditures.

Private Chinese holdings of gold, foreign exchange, and long-term assets in all foreign currencies may amount to $500,000,000, but the Chinese Government finds it increasingly difficult to mobilize these resources. Cash remittances to China by Chinese residents abroad have sharply declined. China has so drained her official foreign-exchange holdings that she will soon be unable to procure essential imports needed for the continuation of her basic civilian economy.

Valuable resources, such as coal and the foodstuffs of the rural areas, are under Communist control. The announced purpose of the Chinese Communist is to engineer economic collapse in China.

(C) POPULATION AND AREA UNDER CHINESE COMMUNIST CONTROL

As of March 15, 1948, according to a rough estimate, the Chinese Communists controlled 25 percent of the total area of China and 33 percent of the total population, or about 150,000,000.

Due to the fluid nature of military operations and the loosely defined areas of Chinese Government and Chinese Communist control in many disputed areas, where there is constant shifting of control, it is impossible to present more than a rough estimate.

The strength of the Chinese Communist armed forces is estimated as follows: 1,150,000 regulars and 2,000,000 local militia. The Chinese Government some 6 months ago publicly announced 3,800,000 as the strength of its armed forces.

6. Previous Aid to China

The Department of State has submitted to the committee the following estimates of previous American aid to China:

U. S. Government economic, financial, and military aid to China since 1937

[In millions of United States dollars]

Pre-VJ-day:		
Export-Import Bank credits		120. 0
1942 congressional credit		500. 0
Lend-lease		849. 4
Subtotal		1, 469. 4
Post-VJ-day:		
Lend-lease:		
Military		728. 0
Civilian pipe-line credit		49. 6
Naval aid		17. 7
Surplus and excess property credits:		
Office of Foreign Liquidation Commissioner dockyard credit	4. 0	
West China credit	20. 0	
Maritime Commission credit authorization	16. 5	
		40. 5
Export-Import Bank credits		82. 8
UNRRA:		
United States 72-percent contribution applied to China program (FAS plus 25 percent for shipping and insurance)		465. 8
Contribution to Board of Trustees for UNRRA equipment and funds		4. 7
United States foreign relief program		45. 7
United Nations International Children's Emergency Fund		2. 1
Subtotal		1, 436. 9
Total		2, 905. 8

Since figures for certain surplus-property sales were not included in the above total, the State Department subsequently furnished the

committee with the following supplemental figures in a letter to the chairman, dated March 19:

Type of surplus	Procurement cost	Sales price or value realized
Civilian-type surplus property in China, India, and 17 Pacific islands	$824,000,000	$175,000,000
Rifle ammunition	6,566,589	656,658
TNT	275,000	99,000
Air Force equipment	9,449,850	935,312
Naval vessels	70,589,298	(gift)
Transport aircraft	34,800,000	750,000
Ammunition	4,441,337	44,413
Air Force equipment	25,292,365	4,426,163
Total	975,414,439	181,911,546

The State Department emphasizes that it is impossible to draw up a total for the surplus-property transactions since in some cases the surplus stocks are still in the process of being transferred and the full value of the property will not be known until the transfers have been completed. The above figures, therefore, are only estimates in some cases.

The committee agreed that the extent of such aid underscores once more the fundamental and traditional interest of the United States in the welfare of China.

7. The Program Proposed by the Department of State

Under the present circumstances, it is not possible to develop a practical, effective, long-term, over-all program for China's economic recovery, predicated upon outside assistance from the United States. We cannot underwrite the destiny of China.

Of necessity, this China-aid program differs in several fundamentals from the European-recovery program so recently endorsed by the Senate. Some of the basic ingredients for recovery and cooperative effort, which in a short time might respond to American aid, do not exist in the project for China.

The committee feels that the United States should not be put in the position of being held responsible for the conduct of the Chinese Government and its political, economic, and military affairs. It is believed that this aid program, designed to meet the most essential commodity requirements, would relieve human suffering and give the hard-working people of China a chance to arrest the rate of economic deterioration in China, and to afford the Chinese Government another opportunity to undertake a vigorous program of self-help. An aid program such as proposed by the Department of State, under the present realities, may not arouse much hopeful enthusiasm among Americans, though the committee believes it is sufficient to encourage the constructive, democratic elements in China.

The Department's proposal called for economic assistance in the amount of $570,000,000 for a period of about 15 months, ending June 30, 1949. Of this amount, $510,000,000 would cover minimum imports of essential civilian type of commodities, chiefly foodstuffs and raw materials, and $60,000,000 for key reconstruction projects. This aid would free Chinese resources to finance other necessary imports and military supplies.

The detailed estimates and justifications are not commitments to China, but they do reasonably illustrate the magnitude of the program. The program must have just as much flexibility and careful administration as that provided for in the Economic Cooperation Act. The testimony of the executive branch affirms that aid of the size contemplated has taken into account both requirements and availabilities and that such aid can be furnished without jeopardizing the European recovery program or the American domestic economy.

Probable list of imports, with values expressed on a cost, insurance, and freight basis (prices as of Jan. 1, 1948)

Item	Value
1. Cereals (wheat and rice)	$130, 000, 000
2. Cotton	150, 000, 000
3. Petroleum and petroleum products	110, 000, 000
4. Fertilizer	30, 000, 000
5. Tobacco	28, 000, 000
6. Metals	24, 000, 000
7. Pharmaceuticals	5, 000, 000
8. Coal	3, 000, 000
9. Replacement articles for existing capital equipment	30, 000, 000
Total	510, 000, 000

This represents:

225,000 tons of wheat equivalent.

451,300 tons of rice.

750,000 bales of cotton.

25,198,000 barrels of petroleum and petroleum products to come principally from Eastern Hemisphere sources, except possibly lubricating oils and greases.

40,000 short tons of soluble phosphatic fertilizer from North America.

42,100 short tons of nitrogenous fertilizer, North and South America supplying 32,100 short tons, Europe supplying 10,000 short tons.

84,500,000 pounds of United States tobacco.

17,588 metric tons of lead, zinc, aluminum, brass, and copper.

115,373 metric tons of iron and steel (no scrap).

Replacement articles of existing capital equipment are also required. The total amount of each item is relatively small and offers no serious problem of availability.

8. Committee Action

After a careful consideration of the program submitted by the Department of State the committee took the following action:

(1) It gave general approval to the program of the Department but shortened and completely rewrote the Department's proposed bill.

(2) It reduced the request for $570,000,000 for a 15 months' period to $363,000,000 for a 12 months' period.

(3) It added a grant of $100,000,000 for whatever purpose decided upon by the Chinese Government.

(4) It took appropriate steps to correlate the China aid program to the applicable provisions of S. 2202 (Economic Cooperation Act of 1948), thus assuring that the China program would have the advantages of the management and safeguards provided in S. 2202. In doing

this, the bill is clear that China, in order to receive aid, does not have to adhere to a joint program for European recovery.

9. How the Program Will Be Administered

It is clear that the China program must be carefully coordinated with the European recovery program. Many of the problems are similar and central direction for the two programs would avoid unnecessary waste and duplication, resulting in more effective operations both in Europe and in China. For this reason, the committee agreed that the assistance provided for in this bill should be extended under the applicable provisions of the Economic Cooperation Act of 1948.

This means that economic aid for China will be placed under the same Administrator who will be in charge of the European recovery program. There will be a United States mission in China of much the same character as those provided for participating countries in Europe. Likewise, the program will be based upon a bilateral agreement between China and the United States similar in character to those made between the United States and European countries.

It will of course be left to the Administrator to determine which of the provisions of the Economic Cooperation Act of 1948 are applicable to China. Appendix A of this report indicates in general terms those provisions which would seem to be pertinent.

10. $100,000,000 Grant Authorized

In section 3 (b) of the bill the committee has provided an authorization for a grant not to exceed $100,000,000 for additional aid to China on the administrative terms which the President deems appropriate.

In view of the Chinese requirements for military supplies, it may be assumed that the Chinese Government, on its own option and responsibility, would seek this grant for such supplies. With intelligent planning, and careful conservation and efficient utilization the Chinese Government could achieve much with this sum. The flow to China of military supplies, surplus to our own requirements, is continuing under contracts concluded with the Chinese Government.

The committee does not intend that the Administrator of the Economic Cooperation Act should be held responsible for this part of the bill. It is assumed that the President will make use of the advice of the appropriate agencies of this Government.

11. The Problem of Extending Military Aid to China

During recent months there has been a great deal of discussion, both in and out of the Congress, about the desirability of extending military aid to China. The committee considered this question at some length with particular emphasis on the impact of such assistance upon our total foreign policy.

With the passage of the present bill our military assistance to China will be of two main types. In the first place, $100,000,000 of the total amount appropriated will be extended in the form of grants to be used by the Chinese Government without any of the conditions and controls which will prevail with respect to the expenditure of the remaining $363,000,000. Presumably, therefore, this amount can be used for the procurement of military supplies and equipment if the National Government so desires. The committee agreed, however, that the broad language of section 3 (b) of the present bill should not be interpreted to include the use of any of the armed forces of the United States for combat duties in China.

In the second place, under existing legislation, the United States Government will continue to furnish military advisers to the recognized government of China. At the present time the Army advisory group stationed there consists of 572 officers and 921 enlisted men. This figure includes military police and weather and air transport personnel not directly connected with the work of the advisory group.

United States military personnel in China do not participate in combat. Nor do they command Chinese troops. They are serving in an advisory capacity only. Combat units of American troops are definitely not involved.

For many years the United States has been deeply interested in the maintenance of the integrity and independence of China—which is clearly one of the essential elements of peace in the Far East. Today that independence and integrity are threatened by civil strife. If no aid is given now by the United States, the inference appears to be clear that we face either the possibility of China becoming a communist-dominated satellite state or a civil war of increased length and intensity.

China is a maze of imponderables. It is impossible to know the quantity and type of aid necessary for the restoration of a stable and independent China. The committee is convinced, however, that the assistance contemplated in this bill should appreciably strengthen the position of the national government without, at the same time, involving the United States in any additional commitments of a military nature.

Congress should not undertake either to determine the actual apportionment of available military forces as between different theaters or areas, or to make specific and detailed military commitments which may affect such allocation in the future. Apportionment of specific military forces is emphatically a matter for the responsible military authorities to determine.

12. Reconstruction Projects

The Department's proposed program provided for $60,000,000 in initiating key reconstruction projects prior to June 30, 1949. [The justifications mention that substantial loans for certain of these projects and others have been requested by the Chinese Government from the Export-Import Bank. But these requests have not been met because the bank is unable to find reasonable assurances of repayment.] The actual selection of projects, determination of priority of construction, and allocation will remain a matter for the determination of the Administrator of the program. The following projects have been under study and would appear to the committee to be of the kind urgently needed in China: electrical power project for Shanghai, rehabilitation of Hankow-Canton-Kowloon Railroad, and the reopening of western Kiangse and Hsiangtan coal mines.

It is possible that the Administrator may find that a larger proportion of the $363,000,000 might well be applied to initiating recovery projects which the Chinese could be expected to continue without outside assistance. With such projects, the United States would seem to be in a better position to observe the end uses made of United States funds, and to encourage private enterprise. For example, the improvement of agricultural production and rural conditions and land reforms through the adoption of such recommendations of the China-United States Agricultural Missions as are suitable for early introduction, and within a reasonable share of the funds provided, seems to have appealed both to Chinese and American experts. The agricultural economy of China is very different from that of western Europe and it should be so treated. Every effort should be made to encourage the free movement of foodstuffs from rural districts to urban areas.

13. The Problem of Stabilization of Currency

There has been public discussion on the alternative of advancing silver, in lieu of comparable amounts of commodities, so that, granted certain measures, China might return to a hard-money basis as a step in the stabilization required. One report has stated that this need not be a tremendous loan because in 1947 the total amount of currency circulating in China only amounted to the equivalent of between 250 and 350 million dollars. Another figure mentioned has been 600,000,000 ounces of silver as a loan from the United States upon which to base a regulated currency.

Secretary Marshall states, however:

> Provision of a currency stabilization fund would, in the opinion of our monetary experts, require large sums which would be largely dissipated under the present conditions of war financing and civil disruption.

It is understood that a further report on this subject is being forwarded to the committee.

14. Repayment of Loans by China

It is the understanding of the committee that the Chinese Government has never defaulted on any loan from the United States Government. Final determination of the terms of repayment of the United States Government $500,000,000 credit of 1942 and other Chinese wartime obligations will be made in a settlement of war accounts between China and the United States. The Export-Import Bank's earmarking of $500,000,000 authorization for loans to China, at the request of Secretary Marshall, lapsed on June 30, 1947. After the expiration of the earmarking, the Chinese made applications for substantial credits, but none was extended by the bank because of inability to find reasonable assurances of repayment.

The committee was impressed by the record of the Chinese Government with respect to the repayment of its loans from the United States. It is only fair to point out, however, that in view of the financial situation of the National Government it is probable that the great proportion of the assistance contemplated in this bill will have to be advanced in the form of grants.

15. Will United States Aid Benefit the Common People?

Ambassador Stuart, on February 19, 1948, stated that the China aid program "was designed to benefit the common people." The

85-743 O - 73 - 46

committee repeats that the Administrator is under obligation to see that this actually takes place—in the rural districts as well as in the relatively few urban centers. The end use of American dollars in China is a primary obligation on the Administrator and the Chinese Government.

16. American Business Interests in China

American business in China is at a standstill. American commercial interests have complained of discriminatory measures which deny them general equality of commercial opportunity. By removing obstacles to export movements and insuring nondiscriminatory treatment of United States commercial interests, the Chinese Government would greatly encourage the traditional free enterprise of China and so much to attract foreign trade and investment. It would appear to the committee that the Chinese Government would find it advantageous in many ways to take constructive action along these lines.

17. Bilateral Agreement With China

The committee intends to give broad authority to the Secretary of State, after consultation with the Administrator for economic cooperation, to enter into an agreement with China which would contain undertakings by China which would assure the American taxpayer, insofar as is possible, that his money is being effectively used for the purposes of this act and for the people of China. While recognizing that certain details might need to be modified or added to fit the proposed program, the committee took cognizance of the agreement signed at Nanking on October 27, 1947, pursuant to Public Law 84, Eightieth Congress. The text of this agreement is reprinted in appendix B.

18. Chinese Measures and Pledges of Self-Help

Outside aid can be effective only if the Chinese Government itself is able and willing to set its course definitely in a direction calculated to give China strength and stability. A government committed to serving the interest of all its people is less vulnerable to designing alien influences. Consequently, the committee, in its favorable action on aid for China, was considerably impressed by the statement of General Chang Chun, president of the Executive Yuan of the Republic of China, released for publication in Nanking, January 28, 1948:

> As a result of her suffering and losses during more than 8 years of war and the subsequent Communist rebellion, China is now facing unprecedented economic difficulties. In order to overcome these difficulties, the Chinese Government, in the light of the long history of Chinese-American friendship, has requested economic and technical assistance from the United States. It was with gratification that the Chinese Government noted the inclusion of China in the interim-aid bill and the announced intention of the United States Government to take early action during the present session of the Congress to provide substantial aid for China. The Chinese Government fully recognizes that in order to secure the maximum benefit from external aid an adequate and practicable program of domestic measures of self-help is needed. This program should at the beginning lay stress on financial and economic measures of immediate importance which will be followed or accompanied by certain other reforms in the fields of general administration and military reorganization.

The main financial and economic reform measures which the Chinese Government intends to undertake are:

(1) Control and readjustment of Government expenditures both in Chinese national currency and foreign currencies so as to realize all practicable economies.

(2) Improvement of the national, provincial, and local tax systems and the administration thereof with the dual object of increasing the yield and placing the tax burden upon economic groups that are best able to pay.

(3) With a view to insuring greater efficiency in the performance of their duties, the treatment of civil servants as well as officers and men will be gradually raised. Simultaneously, a program will be enforced for the gradual reduction of Government personnel.

(4) Strengthening and extension of control over the supply of essential commodities of daily necessity with a view to checking speculation and the abnormal rise of prices.

(5) In order to insure the maximum effectiveness of external aid, every effort will be made toward laying the basis for a more stable monetary system.

(6) Banking and credit systems to be reformed through the centralization of control in the Central Bank of China and the maintenance of a counterinflationary policy.

(7) Promotion of exports through removal of obstacles to export movements.

(8) Improvement of import control; but as soon as conditions permit, the emergency control measures shall be modified.

(9) Improvement of agricultural production and rural conditions and land reforms through the adoption of such recommendations of the China-United States Agricultural Mission as are suitable for early introduction.

(10) Rehabilitation of communications and essential industries as far as conditions permit in order to increase production and reduce dependence upon abnormal imports.

[The appendixes of this report have been deleted and are identical to the appendixes of the amended report on Aid to China that follows.]

Calendar No. 1068

80TH CONGRESS
2d Session

SENATE

REPORT
No. 1026

AID TO CHINA

AMENDED REPORT

OF THE

COMMITTEE ON FOREIGN RELATIONS

ON

S. 2393

A BILL TO PROMOTE THE GENERAL WELFARE, NATIONAL INTEREST, AND FOREIGN POLICY OF THE UNITED STATES BY PRCVIDING AID TO CHINA

MARCH 25 (legislative day, MARCH 15), 1948.—Ordered to be printed with an illustration

UNITED STATES
GOVERNMENT PRINTING OFFICE
★ 73553 WASHINGTON : 1948

TABLE OF CONTENTS

Calendar No. 1068

80TH CONGRESS } SENATE { REPORT
2d Session } { No. 1026

AID TO CHINA

MARCH 25 (legislative day, MARCH 15), 1948.—Ordered to be printed with an illustration

Mr. VANDENBERG, from the Committee on Foreign Relations, submitted the following

AMENDED REPORT

[To accompany S. 2393]

The Committee on Foreign Relations, having had under consideration the subject of extending assistance to China, unanimously report to the Senate a bill (S. 2393) to promote the general welfare, national interest, and foreign policy of the United States by providing aid to China, and recommend that it do pass.

1. MAIN PURPOSE OF THE BILL

The bill provides for a program of assistance to China by authorizing the appropriation of $463,000,000 for a period of 1 year. $363,000,000 of this amount will be administered under the applicable provisions of the Economic Cooperation Act of 1948, although it is not contemplated that China will adhere to a joint program for European recovery. A sum not to exceed $100,000,000 will be authorized through grants, on such terms as the President may determine. The Reconstruction Finance Corporation is authorized to advance $50,000,000 to carry out the purposes of the act.

2. MESSAGE FROM THE PRESIDENT ON AID TO CHINA

MESSAGE FROM THE PRESIDENT OF THE UNITED STATES TRANSMITTING RECOMMENDATION THAT THE CONGRESS AUTHORIZE A PROGRAM FOR AID TO CHINA IN THE AMOUNT OF $570,000,000 TO PROVIDE ASSISTANCE UNTIL JUNE 30, 1949

To the Congress of the United States:

On several occasions I have stated that a primary objective of the United States is to bring about, throughout the world, the conditions of a just and lasting peace. This is a cause to which the American people are deeply devoted.

Since VJ-day we have expended great effort and large sums of money on the relief and rehabilitation of war-torn countries to aid in restoring workable economic systems which are essential to the maintenance of peace. A principle which has guided our efforts to assist these war-torn countries has been that of helping their peoples to help themselves. The Congress is now giving careful consideration to a most vital and far-reaching proposal to further this purpose—the program for aid to European recovery.

I now request the Congress to consider the type of further assistance which this country should provide to China.

A genuine friendship has existed between the American people and the people of China over many years. This friendship has been accompanied by a long record of commercial and cultural association and close cooperation between our two countries. Americans have developed a deep respect for the Chinese people and sympathy for the many trials and difficulties which they have endured.

The United States has long recognized the importance of a stable Chinese nation to lasting peace in the Pacific and the entire world. The vast size and population of China make her an important factor in world affairs. China is a land with rich tradition and culture and a large and energetic population. It has always been our desire to see a strong, progressive China making a full contribution to the strength of the family of nations.

With this end in view, we have supported the National Government of China since it first came to power 20 years ago. China and the United States were allies in the war against Japan, and as an ally we supported China's valiant war efforts against the Japanese. Since the Japanese surrender we have provided a great deal of additional assistance. Military aid was given the Chinese Government, not only to help defeat the Japanese invaders but also to assist in reoccupying Japanese-held areas. The United States contributed the major share of the extensive aid received by China under the program of the United Nations Relief and Rehabilitation Administration. We made available to the Chinese Government at minimum cost large quantities of surplus goods and equipment of value to China's economy. We are currently extending further aid to China under our foreign-relief program.

Nevertheless, the Chinese Government and people are still laboring under the double and interrelated burden of civil war and a rapidly deteriorating economy. The strains placed upon the country by 8 years of war and the Japanese occupation and blockade have been increased by internal strife at the very time that reconstruction efforts should be under way. The wartime damage to transport and productive facilities has been greatly accentuated by the continued obstruction and destruction of vital communications by the Communist forces.

The civil warfare has further impeded recovery by forcing upon the Government heavy expenditures which greatly exceed revenues. Continual issuances of currency to meet these expenditures have produced drastic inflation, with its attendant disruption of normal commercial operations. Under these circumstances, China's foreign-exchange holdings have been so reduced that it will soon be impossible for China to meet the cost of essential imports. Without such imports, industrial activity would diminish and the rate of economic deterioration would be sharply increased.

The continued deterioration of the Chinese economy is a source of deep concern to the United States. Ever since the return of General Marshall from China, the problem of assistance to the Chinese has been under continuous study. We have hoped for conditions in China that would make possible the effective and constructive use of American assistance in reconstruction and rehabilitation. Conditions have not developed as we had hoped, and we can only do what is feasible under circumstances as they exist.

We can assist in retarding the current economic deterioration and thus give the Chinese Government a further opportunity to initiate the measures necessary to the establishment of more stable economic conditions. But it is, and has been, clear that only the Chinese Government itself can undertake the vital measures necessary to provide the framework within which efforts toward peace and true economic recovery may be effective.

In determining the character and dimensions of the program which might be suited to this purpose, we have had to take into account a number of diverse and conflicting factors, including the other demands on our national resources at this time, the availability of specific commodities, the dimensions and complexities of the problems facing the Chinese Government, and the extent to which these problems could be promptly and effectively alleviated by foreign aid. United States assistance to China, like that provided to any other nation, must be adapted to its particular requirements and capacities.

In the light of these factors, I recommend that the Congress authorize a program for aid to China in the amount of $570,000,000 to provide assistance until June 30, 1949.

The program should make provision for the financing, through loans or grants, of essential imports into China in the amount of $510,000,000. This estimate is based upon prices as of January 1, 1948, since it is impossible at present to predict what effect current price changes may have on the program. Revised dollar estimates can be presented in connection with the request for appropriations if necessary. The essential imports include cereals, cotton, petroleum, fertilizer, tobacco, pharmaceuticals, coal, and repair parts for existing capital equipment. The quantities provided for under this program are within the limits of available supplies. The financing of these essential commodity imports by the United States would permit the Chinese Government to devote its limited dollar resources to the most urgent of its other needs.

The program should also provide $60,000,000 for a few selected reconstruction projects to be initiated prior to June 30, 1949. There is an urgent need for the restoration of essential transportation facilities, fuel and power operations, and export industries. This work could be undertaken in areas sheltered from military operations and could help in improving the supply and distribution of essential commodities.

As in the case of aid to European recovery, the conduct of this program of aid should be made subject to an agreement between China and the United States setting forth the conditions and procedures for administering the aid. The agreement should include assurances that the Chinese Government will take such economic, financial, and other measures as are practicable, looking toward the ultimate goal of economic stability and recovery. The United States would, of course, reserve the right to terminate aid if it is determined that the assistance provided is not being handled in accordance with the agreement or that the policies of the Chinese Government are inconsistent with the objective of using the aid to help achieve a self-supporting economy.

Pending establishment of the agency which is to be set up for the administration of the European recovery program, the assistance to China should be carried forward under the existing machinery now administering the foreign-relief programs. Legislation authorizing the Chinese program should make possible transfer of the administration of the Chinese program to the agency administering our aid to European recovery. The need for authority in the administering agency to make adjustments in the program from time to time will be as great here as in the European recovery program.

The proposed program of aid to China represents what I believe to be the best course this Government can follow, in the light of all the circumstances. Nothing which this country provides by way of assistance can, even in a small measure, be a substitute for the necessary action that can be taken only by the Chinese Government. Yet this program can accomplish the important purpose of giving the Chinese Government a respite from rapid economic deterioration, during which it can move to establish more stable economic conditions. Without this respite the ability of the Chinese Government to establish such conditions at all, would be doubtful. The achievement of even this limited objective is of such importance as to justify the proposed program of aid.

I recommend, therefore, that this program be given prompt and favorable consideration by the Congress.

HARRY S. TRUMAN.

THE WHITE HOUSE, *February 18, 1948.*

3. COMMITTEE HEARINGS

The committee held executive hearings on aid to China on February 26, March 19 and 20, 1948. During the course of the hearings the committee heard the views of Hon. George C. Marshall, Secretary of State; Hon. Willard L. Thorp, Assistant Secretary of State; W. Walton Butterworth, Director, Office of Far Eastern Affairs, and their assistants. On March 22, after a lengthy discussion of the policy questions involved, the committee drafted the present bill, which it approved by a unaminous vote of 13 to 0.

Since the committee had before it the printed testimony on aid to China, given by private witnesses to the House Foreign Affairs Committee, it was considered unnecessary to hold public hearings.

4. Text of the Committee Bill

A BILL To promote the general welfare, national interest, and foreign policy of the United States by providing aid to China

Be it enacted by the Senate and House of Representatives of the United States of America in Congress assembled, That this Act may be cited as the "China Aid Act of 1948".

SEC. 2. It is the purpose of this Act to provide immediate aid to China to relieve human suffering, to assist in retarding economic deterioration, and to afford the people of China an opportunity to initiate measures of self-help necessary to rebuilding the bases for more stable economic conditions, such aid to be provided under the applicable provisions of the Economic Cooperation Act of 1948 which are consistent with the purposes of this Act. It is not the purpose of this Act that China, in order to receive aid hereunder, shall adhere to a joint program for European recovery.

SEC. 3. (a) In order to carry out the purposes of this Act, there is hereby authorized to be appropriated to the President for aid to China a sum not to exceed $363,000,000 to remain available for obligation for the period of one year following the date of enactment of this Act.

(b) There is also hereby authorized to be appropriated to the President a sum not to exceed $100,000,000 for additional aid to China through grants, on such terms as the President may determine and without regard to the provisions of the Economic Cooperation Act of 1948, to remain available for obligation for the period of one year following the date of enactment of this Act.

SEC. 4. An agreement shall be entered into between China and the United States containing those undertakings by China which the Secretary of State, after consultation with the Administrator for Economic Cooperation, may deem necessary to carry out the purposes of this Act and to improve commercial relations with China.

SEC. 5. Notwithstanding the provisions of any other law, the Reconstruction Finance Corporation is authorized and directed, until such time as an appropriation is made pursuant to section 3, to make advances, not to exceed in the aggregate $50,000,000, to carry out the provisions of this Act in such manner and in such amounts as the President shall determine. From appropriations authorized under section 3, there shall be repaid without interest to the Reconstruction Finance Corporation the advances made by it under the authority contained herein. No interest shall be charged on advances made by the Treasury to the Reconstruction Finance Corporation in implementation of this subsection.

5. The Situation in China

The political, social, financial, and military situation in China is so well known that it need not be discussed in detail in this report. China occupies a central position in east Asia and contains both two-thirds of its area and its population. The Chinese people make up one-fifth of the world's population. Her economy is primarily agricultural. The future of east Asia as a whole is closely bound up with developments in China.

Because of the traditional friendship between our peoples, China's difficulties produce in the United States a profoundly sympathetic response, particularly at this critical moment when China is an important part of a common front against aggressive Communism.

There are favorable factors. China could be reasonably self-sufficient in food and raw materials resources. There is a large and valuable labor pool. Among the politically conscious people there is powerful sentiment in favor of democratic government. There is a great record in, and respect for, the constructive values of civilization.

On the other hand, China's economy has been damaged by an 8-year war with Japan, and a civil war that also includes the usual Communist tactics of disruption, destruction, and sabotage. The country never developed a favorable balance of trade, and the unfavorable balance obviously grew worse in the past few years. China faces colossally difficult and complicated tasks and the further constructive and cooperative role of the United States is not easy to determine. But the present proposal is clearly justified by the current facts and the self-help proposals already courageously made by the Nationalist Government (see sec. 18) warrant our cooperation.

(A) POLITICAL CIRCUMSTANCES

The Kuomintang has been in control of the National Government since 1928. It has taken the initial steps toward democracy through the promulgation of the constitution and the election of a national assembly, while the Chinese Communist aims are directed toward a totalitarian government. The Chinese Communist propaganda has been bitterly anti-American and follows the Moscow line regarding all American policies. There exists in China the social and political elements and ideals which can combat the hard core of a disruptive, alien-orientated communism in open rebellion.

In the Sino-Soviet Treaty of August 1945 the U. S. S. R. undertook to support only the National Government, which was recognized by all the powers as the legal Government of China. The U. S. S. R. has not provided the assistance to the National Government with "material resources" called for in that treaty. Instead, the U. S. S. R. removed large quantities of industrial equipment from the factories of Manchuria, perhaps to the extent of $2,000,000,000. (See appendix C.)

(B) ECONOMIC CRISIS

China's economy has deteriorated steadily since the defeat of Japan. The destruction of communications has isolated the resources from the centers of consumption and the ports. The food deficit of 2,000,000 tons for the coming year is largely a result of the civil war. The cost of civil war has caused mounting Government deficits. The inflationary stampede impedes production and distribution and stimulates speculation and hoarding. The note issue increased more than eight times during 1947. In mid-March the black-market rate for United States dollars was slightly more than 450,000 Chinese dollars to 1 United States dollar. Seventy percent of the Government's expenditures has gone for military purposes. Revenue has covered less than one-third of the total Government expenditures.

Private Chinese holdings of gold, foreign exchange, and long-term assets in all foreign currencies may amount to $500,000,000, but the Chinese Government finds it increasingly difficult to mobilize these resources. Cash remittances to China by Chinese residents abroad have sharply declined. China has so drained her official foreign-exchange holdings that she will soon be unable to procure essential imports needed for the continuation of her basic civilian economy.

Valuable resources, such as coal and the foodstuffs of the rural areas, are under Communist control. The announced purpose of the Chinese

Communist is to engineer economic collapse in China. It is the purpose of this bill to help prevent any such calamity. It is a vote of confidence in China, and her people, and their long, heroic resistance to aggressors at home and abroad.

(C) POPULATION AND AREA UNDER CHINESE COMMUNIST CONTROL

As of March 15, 1948, according to a rough estimate, the Chinese Communists controlled 25 percent of the total area of China and 33 percent of the total population, or about 150,000,000.

Due to the fluid nature of military operations and the loosely defined areas of Chinese Government and Chinese Communist control in many disputed areas, where there is constant shifting of control, it is impossible to present more than a rough estimate.

The strength of the Chinese Communist armed forces is estimated as follows: 1,150,000 regulars and 2,000,000 local militia. The Chinese Government some 6 months ago publicly announced 3,800,000 as the strength of its armed forces.

6. Previous Aid to China

The Department of State has submitted to the committee the following estimates of previous American aid to China:

U. S. Government economic, financial, and military aid to China since 1937

[In millions of United States dollars]

Pre-VJ-day:		
Export-Import Bank credits		120. 0
1942 congressional credit		500. 0
Lend-lease		849. 4
Subtotal		1, 469. 4
Post-VJ-day:		
Lend-lease:		
Military		728. 0
Civilian pipe-line credit		49. 6
Naval aid		17. 7
Surplus and excess property credits:		
Office of Foreign Liquidation Commissioner dockyard credit	4. 0	
West China credit	20. 0	
Maritime Commission credit authorization	16. 5	
		40. 5
Export-Import Bank credits		82. 8
UNRRA:		
United States 72-percent contribution applied to China program (FAS plus 25 percent for shipping and insurance)		465. 8
Contribution to Board of Trustees for UNRRA equipment and funds		4. 7
United States foreign relief program		45. 7
United Nations International Children's Emergency Fund		. 2. 1
Subtotal		1, 436. 9
Total		2, 905. 8

Since figures for certain surplus-property sales were not included in the above total, the State Department subsequently furnished the committee with the following supplemental figures in a letter to the chairman, dated March 19:

Type of surplus	Procurement cost	Sales price or value realized
Civilian-type surplus property in China, India, and 17 Pacific islands	$824,000,000	$175,000,000
Rifle ammunition	6,566,589	656,658
TNT	275,000	99,000
Air Force equipment	9,449,850	935,312
Naval vessels	70,589,298	(gift)
Transport aircraft	34,800,000	750,000
Ammunition	4,441,337	44,413
Air Force equipment	25,292,365	4,426,163
Total	975,414,439	181,911,546

The State Department emphasizes that it is impossible to draw up a total for the surplus-property transactions since in some cases the surplus stocks are still in the process of being transferred and the full value of the property will not be known until the transfers have been completed. The above figures, therefore, are only estimates in some cases.

The committee agreed that the extent of such aid underscores once more the fundamental and traditional interest of the United States in the welfare of China.

7. The Program Proposed by the Department of State

Under the present circumstances, it is difficult to develop a practical, effective, long-term, over-all program for China's economic recovery, predicated upon outside assistance from the United States. We must deal with developments as they unfold. As in all foreign-aid programs, we must make it plain that our commitments are confined to the terms of this legislation.

Of necessity, this China-aid program differs in several fundamentals from the European-recovery program so recently endorsed by the Senate. Some of the basic ingredients for recovery and cooperative effort, which in a short time might respond to American aid, do not exist in the project for China. But it is believed that this aid program, designed to meet the most essential requirements, would relieve human suffering and give the hard-working people of China a chance to arrest the rate of economic deterioration in China, and to afford the Chinese Government further opportunity to undertake a vigorous program of self-help. The committee believes it is sufficient to encourage the constructive, democratic elements in China to "carry on."

The Department's proposal called for economic assistance in the amount of $570,000,000 for a period of about 15 months, ending June 30, 1949. Of this amount, $510,000,000 would cover minimum imports of essential civilian type of commodities, chiefly foodstuffs and raw materials, and $60,000,000 for key reconstruction projects. This aid would free Chinese resources to finance other necessary imports and military supplies.

The detailed estimates and justifications are not commitments to China, but they do reasonably illustrate the magnitude of the program. The program must have just as much flexibility and careful administration as that provided for in the Economic Cooperation Act. The testimony of the executive branch affirms that aid of the size contemplated has taken into account both requirements and availabilities and that such aid can be furnished without jeopardizing the European recovery program or the American domestic economy.

Probable list of imports, with values expressed on a cost, insurance, and freight basis (prices as of Jan. 1, 1948)

Item	Value
1. Cereals (wheat and rice)	$130, 000, 000
2. Cotton	150, 000, 000
3. Petroleum and petroleum products	110, 000, 000
4. Fertilizer	30, 000, 000
5. Tobacco	28, 000, 000
6. Metals	24, 000, 000
7. Pharmaceuticals	5, 000, 000
8. Coal	3, 000, 000
9. Replacement articles for existing capital equipment	30, 000, 000
Total	510, 000, 000

This represents:

225,000 tons of wheat equivalent.

451,300 tons of rice.

750,000 bales of cotton.

25,198,000 barrels of petroleum and petroleum products to come principally from Eastern Hemisphere sources, except possibly lubricating oils and greases.

40,000 short tons of soluble phosphatic fertilizer from North America.

42,100 short tons of nitrogenous fertilizer, North and South America supplying 32,100 short tons, Europe supplying 10,000 short tons.

84,500,000 pounds of United States tobacco.

17,588 metric tons of lead, zinc, aluminum, brass, and copper.

115,373 metric tons of iron and steel (no scrap).

Replacement articles of existing capital equipment are also required. The total amount of each item is relatively small and offers no serious problem of availability.

8. Committee Action

After a careful consideration of the program submitted by the Department of State the committee took the following action:

(1) It gave general approval to the program of the Department but shortened and completely rewrote the Department's proposed bill.

(2) It reduced the request for $570,000,000 for a 15 months' period to $363,000,000 for a 12 months' period.

(3) It added a grant of $100,000,000 for whatever purpose decided upon by the Chinese Government.

(4) It took appropriate steps to correlate the China aid program to the applicable provisions of S. 2202 (Economic Cooperation Act of 1948), thus assuring that the China program would have the advantages of the management and safeguards provided in S. 2202. In doing

this, the bill is clear that China, in order to receive aid, does not have to adhere to a joint program for European recovery.

9. How the Program Will Be Administered

It is clear that the China program must be carefully coordinated with the European recovery program. Many of the problems are similar and central direction for the two programs would avoid unnecessary waste and duplication, resulting in more effective operations both in Europe and in China. For this reason, the committee agreed that the assistance provided for in this bill should be extended under the applicable provisions of the Economic Cooperation Act of 1948.

This means that economic aid for China will be placed under the same Administrator who will be in charge of the European recovery program. There will be a United States mission in China of much the same character as those provided for participating countries in Europe. Likewise, the program will be based upon a bilateral agreement between China and the United States similar in character to those made between the United States and European countries.

It will of course be left to the Administrator to determine which of the provisions of the Economic Cooperation Act of 1948 are applicable to China. Appendix A of this report indicates in general terms those provisions which would seem to be pertinent.

10. $100,000,000 Grant Authorized

In section 3 (b) of the bill the committee has provided an authorization for a grant not to exceed $100,000,000 for additional aid to China on the administrative terms which the President deems appropriate.

In view of the Chinese requirements for military supplies, it may be assumed that the Chinese Government, on its own option and responsibility, would seek this grant for such supplies. With intelligent planning, and careful conservation and efficient utilization the Chinese Government could achieve much with this sum. The flow to China of military supplies, surplus to our own requirements, is continuing under contracts concluded with the Chinese Government.

The committee does not intend that the Administrator of the Economic Cooperation Act should be held responsible for this part of the bill. It is assumed that the President will make use of the advice of the appropriate agencies of this Government.

11. The Problem of Extending Military Aid to China

During recent months there has been a great deal of discussion, both in and out of the Congress, about the desirability of extending military aid to China. The committee considered this question at some length with particular emphasis on the impact of such assistance upon our total foreign policy.

With the passage of the present bill our military assistance to China will be of two main types. In the first place, $100,000,000 of the total amount appropriated will be extended in the form of grants to be used by the Chinese Government without any of the conditions and controls which will prevail with respect to the expenditure of the remaining $363,000,000. Presumably, therefore, this amount can be used for the procurement of military supplies and equipment if the National Government so desires. The committee agreed, however, that the broad language of section 3 (b) of the present bill should not be interpreted to include the use of any of the armed forces of the United States for combat duties in China.

In the second place, under existing legislation, the United States Government will continue to furnish military advisers to the recognized government of China. At the present time the Army advisory group stationed there consists of 572 officers and 921 enlisted men. This figure includes military police and weather and air transport personnel not directly connected with the work of the advisory group.

United States military personnel in China do not participate in combat. Nor do they command Chinese troops. They are serving in an advisory capacity only. Combat units of American troops are definitely not involved.

For many years the United States has been deeply interested in the maintenance of the integrity and independence of China—which is clearly one of the essential elements of peace in the Far East. Today that independence and integrity are threatened by civil strife. If no aid is given now by the United States, the inference appears to be clear that we face either the possibility of China becoming a communist-dominated satellite state or a civil war of increased length and intensity.

China is a maze of imponderables. It is impossible to know the quantity and type of aid necessary for the restoration of a stable and independent China. The committee is convinced, however, that the assistance contemplated in this bill should appreciably strengthen the position of the National Government without, at the same time, involving the United States in any additional commitments of a military nature.

Congress should not undertake either to determine the actual apportionment of available military forces as between different theaters or areas, or to make specific and detailed military commitments which may affect such allocation in the future. Apportionment of specific military forces is emphatically a matter for the responsible military authorities to determine.

12. Reconstruction Projects

The Department's proposed program provided for $60,000,000 in initiating key reconstruction projects prior to June 30, 1949, which it has been impossible for China to finance through existing channels. The actual selection of projects, determination of priority of construction, and allocation will remain a matter for the determination of the Administrator of the program. The following projects have been under study and would appear to the committee to be of the kind urgently needed in China: electrical power project for Shanghai, rehabilitation of Hankow-Canton-Kowloon Railroad, and the reopening of western Kiangse and Hsiangtan coal mines.

It is possible that the Administrator may find that a larger proportion of the $363,000,000 might well be applied to initiating recovery projects which the Chinese could be expected to continue without outside assistance. With such projects, the United States would seem to be in a better position to observe the end uses made of United States funds, and to encourage private enterprise. For example, the improvement of agricultural production and rural conditions and land reforms through the adoption of such recommendations of the China-United States Agricultural Missions as are suitable for early introduction, and within a reasonable share of the funds provided, seems to have appealed both to Chinese and American experts. The agricultural economy of China is very different from that of western Europe and it should be so treated. Every effort should be made to encourage the free movement of foodstuffs from rural districts to urban areas.

13. The Problem of Stabilization of Currency

There has been public discussion on the alternative of advancing silver, in lieu of comparable amounts of commodities, so that, granted certain measures, China might return to a hard-money basis as a step in the stabilization required. One report has stated that this need not be a tremendous loan because in 1947 the total amount of currency circulating in China only amounted to the equivalent of between 250 and 350 million dollars. Another figure mentioned has been 600,000,000 ounces of silver as a loan from the United States upon which to base a regulated currency.

Secretary Marshall states, however:

> Provision of a currency stabilization fund would, in the opinion of our monetary experts, require large sums which would be largely dissipated under the present conditions of war financing and civil disruption.

It is understood that a further report on this subject is being forwarded to the committee.

14. Repayment of Loans by China

It is the understanding of the committee that the Chinese Government has never defaulted on any loan from the United States Government. Final determination of the terms of repayment of the United States Government $500,000,000 credit of 1942 and other Chinese wartime obligations will be made in a settlement of war accounts between China and the United States. The Export-Import Bank's earmarking of $500,000,000 authorization for loans to China, at the request of Secretary Marshall, lapsed on June 30, 1947. After the expiration of the earmarking, the Chinese made applications for substantial credits, but none was extended by the bank.

The committee was impressed by the record of the Chinese Government with respect to the repayment of its loans from the United States. It is only fair to point out, however, that in view of the financial situation of the National Government it is probable that the great proportion of the assistance contemplated in this bill will have to be advanced in the form of grants.

15.. Will United States Aid Benefit the Common People?

Ambassador Stuart, on February 19, 1948, stated that the China aid program "was designed to benefit the common people." The committee repeats that the Administrator is under obligation to see that this actually takes place—in the rural districts as well as in the relatively few urban centers. The end use of American dollars in China is a primary obligation on the Administrator and the Chinese Government.

16. American Business Interests in China

American business in China is at a standstill. American commercial interests have complained of discriminatory measures which deny them general equality of commercial opportunity. By removing obstacles to export movements and insuring nondiscriminatory treatment of United States commercial interests, the Chinese Government would greatly encourage the traditional free enterprise of China and so much to attract foreign trade and investment. It would appear to the committee that the Chinese Government would find it advantageous in many ways to take constructive action along these lines.

17. Bilateral Agreement With China

The committee intends to give broad authority to the Secretary of State, after consultation with the Administrator for economic cooperation, to enter into an agreement with China which would contain undertakings by China which would assure the American taxpayer, insofar as is possible, that his money is being effectively used for the purposes of this act and for the people of China. While recognizing that certain details might need to be modified or added to fit the proposed program, the committee took cognizance of the agreement signed at Nanking on October 27, 1947, pursuant to Public Law 84, Eightieth Congress. The text of this agreement is reprinted in appendix B.

18. Chinese Measures and Pledges of Self-Help

Outside aid can be effective if the Chinese Government itself sets its course definitely in a direction calculated to give China strength and stability. Consequently, the committee, in its favorable action on aid for China, was considerably impressed by the statement of General Chang Chun, president of the Executive Yuan of the Republic of China, released for publication in Nanking, January 28, 1948.

As a result of her suffering and losses during more than 8 years of war and the subsequent Communist rebellion, China is now facing unprecedented economic difficulties. In order to overcome these difficulties, the Chinese Government, in the light of the long history of Chinese-American friendship, has requested economic and technical assistance from the United States. It was with gratification that the Chinese Government noted the inclusion of China in the interim-aid bill and the announced intention of the United States Government to take early action during the present session of the Congress to provide substantial aid for China. The Chinese Government fully recognizes that in order to secure the maximum benefit from external aid an adequate and practicable program of domestic measures of self-help is needed. This program should at the beginning lay stress on financial and economic measures of immediate importance which will be followed or accompanied by certain other reforms in the fields of general administration and military reorganization.

The main financial and economic reform measures which the Chinese Government intends to undertake are:

(1) Control and readjustment of Government expenditures both in Chinese national currency and foreign currencies so as to realize all practicable economies.

(2) Improvement of the national, provincial, and local tax systems and the administration thereof with the dual object of increasing the yield and placing the tax burden upon economic groups that are best able to pay.

(3) With a view to insuring greater efficiency in the performance of their duties, the treatment of civil servants as well as officers and men will be gradually raised. Simultaneously, a program will be enforced for the gradual reduction of Government personnel.

(4) Strengthening and extension of control over the supply of essential commodities of daily necessity with a view to checking speculation and the abnormal rise of prices.

(5) In order to insure the maximum effectiveness of external aid, every effort will be made toward laying the basis for a more stable monetary system.

(6) Banking and credit systems to be reformed through the centralization of control in the Central Bank of China and the maintenance of a counterinflationary policy.

(7) Promotion of exports through removal of obstacles to export movements.

(8) Improvement of import control; but as soon as conditions permit, the emergency control measures shall be modified.

(9) Improvement of agricultural production and rural conditions and land reforms through the adoption of such recommendations of the China-United States Agricultural Mission as are suitable for early introduction.

(10) Rehabilitation of communications and essential industries as far as conditions permit in order to increase production and reduce dependence upon abnormal imports.

19. Conclusion

In the judgment of the committee, the Nationalist Government of China, led for 20 years through tremendous difficulties by the selfless patriotism of Generalissimo Chiang Kai-shek, represents our common contest against threats to international peace and security and against Communist aggression, and deserves support within our resources as proposed in this act. Further, the aid authorized by this act is tangible proof of American interest in the independence and integrity of China, in the welfare of the Chinese people, and in stabilized peace in the Far East.

APPENDIXES

Appendix A

Analysis of the China Aid Bill and Relevant Provisions of the Economic Cooperation Act of 1948

Section 2: This section sets forth the purposes of the bill and the form in which the major portion of the contemplated aid to China is to be provided. The purposes of the bill are stated to be the provision of aid to China to relieve human suffering, to assist in retarding economic deterioration, and to afford the people of China an opportunity to initiate measures of self-help necessary to rebuilding the bases for more stable economic conditions. This section also states that such aid is to be provided under the applicable provision of the Economic Cooperation Act of 1948 which are consistent with the purposes of the bill, and that it is not the purpose of the bill that China shall adhere to a joint program for European recovery in order to receive aid under the bill. This means that, in general, aid will be provided for China under the bill in the same manner and to the same extent as assistance is provided for participating countries under those provisions of the Economic Cooperation Act of 1948 which are relevant to the purposes of the bill and to conditions in China. Thus, the provisions of the Economic Cooperation Act will be applied to China without reference to the purposes of that act, but solely with reference to the purposes of the bill.

There follows an outline demonstrating how the various provisions of S. 2202, as recently passed by the Senate, might properly be applied to aid to China in the light of presently indicated conditions in China:

OUTLINE OF PROVISIONS OF S. 2202

Sections 1, 2, and 3 relate solely to conditions in Europe and to a joint program for European recovery and would therefore not be applicable.

Section 4 would be applicable, except that the Administrator for Economic Cooperation would not have authority, for the purposes of the present bill, to compensate additional personnel, other than experts and consultants, without regard to the provisions of the Classification Act of 1923, as amended.

Section 5 would be applicable, but the authority in the Administrator to terminate provision of aid under section 18 would be subject to the modification of section 18 discussed below.

Sections 6 and 7 relating to the National Advisory Council on International Monetary and Fiscal Problems and to the Public Advisory Board would be applicable.

The functions of the United States Special Representative in Europe, provided for in section 8, relate to the coordination of cooperative efforts of participating countries and of the operations of the United States special missions in the participating countries. It would therefore be inappropriate to establish such a representative in China since no coordination between several countries receiving assistance is contemplated by the present bill. This section would therefore be inapplicable.

Those provisions of section 9 which relate to the special missions for economic cooperation; namely, subsections (a), (b), and (c), would be applicable, but excluding reference to the United States Special Representative in Europe.

Section 10, relating to overseas personnel, would be applicable.

Section 11 would be applicable. As in the case of assistance to participating countries, commodities and services which had not been landed in China on the date of enactment of the present bill could be made available to China under the provisions of the present bill. With reference to the guaranties provided under paragraph (b) (3), the 5 percent limitation contained in subparagraph (ii) of that paragraph would, of course, be interpreted to refer to 5 percent of the funds appropriated under section 3 (a) of the present bill.

Section 12, relating to the protection of the domestic economy, and section 13, relating to reimbursement to Government agencies, would both be applicable.

Subsections (a), (b), (c), and (f) of section 14 relate solely to the availability of funds for carrying out the purposes of the Economic Cooperation Act of 1948, and they would therefore not be applicable to the present bill. Subsections (d) and (e) of section 14 would, however, properly be applicable to the present bill.

Subsections (a), (b), (d), and (e) of section 15 relate primarily to conditions in Europe and to the cooperation by participating countries in a joint program for European recovery. They would therefore not be applicable except to the extent discussed in the analysis below of section 4 of the present bill. As to subsection (c) of section 15, the Administrator might, in the absence of a finally concluded bilateral agreement and during the 3 months after the date of enactment of the bill, perform functions for China under the present bill if China had signified its adherence to the purposes of the present bill and had signified its intention of concluding an agreement under section 4 of the present bill, and if the Administrator found that China was in fact complying with the intent of such agreement. The proviso of subsection 15 (c) which permits the relatively unconditional transfer through June 30, 1948, of certain limited classes of commodities to countries which signed the report of the Committee of European Economic Cooperation would not be applicable to China since that proviso is grounded on the evidence of adherence to United States policy inherent in the fact of signing such report.

Section 16, relating to assistance from other countries and section 17, covering other duties of the Administrator, would be applicable.

Section 18 would be applicable, except for the provision relating to the pledges between participating countries. Section 18 should, of course, be applied to termination of assistance to China with reference to the agreement concluded under section 4 of the present bill, since no agreement will be concluded with China under section 15 of the Economic Cooperation Act of 1948.

Section 19 (relating to exemption from contract and accounting laws), section 20 (relating to exemption from certain Federal employment laws), and section 21 (relating to the United Nations) would be applicable.

In view of the prohibitions against obligation after the period of 1 year following the date of enactment of the present bill contained in section 3 of the present bill, subsection (a) of section 22 would not be applicable. Subsection (b) of section 22 would be applicable at such time during the 12 months following June 30, 1952, as the President might find it appropriate to transfer the powers, duties, and authority of the Administrator for Economic Cooperation under the Economic Cooperation Act of 1948 to another Government agency.

Section 23 relating to reports to Congress would be applicable as if the date June 30, 1952, therein referred to were June 30, 1949.

Section 24 (relating to a joint congressional committee) and section 25 (containing the standard separability clause) would be applicable.

Section 3: Subsection (a) of section 3 of the China Aid Act authorizes the appropriation to the President of not to exceed $363,000,000 to remain available for obligation for 1 year following the date of enactment of the bill, in order to carry out the purposes of the bill under the applicable provisions of the Economic Recovery Act which are consistent with such purposes.

Subsection (b) of section 3 authorizes an additional appropriation to the President of not to exceed $100,000,000 to remain available for obligation for 1 year following the date of enactment of the bill, in order to carry out the purposes of the bill and without regard to the provisions of the Economic Recovery Act of 1948. Funds appropriated under this subsection may be expended for aid to China through grants in furtherance of the purposes of the bill, on such administrative terms as the President may determine to be appropriate for the furtherance of such purposes.

Section 4: This section provides for the conclusion of an agreement with China containing those undertakings by China which the Secretary of State, after consultation with the Administrator for Economic Cooperation, may deem necessary to carry out the provisions of the bill and to improve commercial relations with China (including measures to afford equality of opportunity to American enterprises).

It is contemplated that in negotiating that part of the agreement which will relate to aid made available to China with funds appropriated under subsection (a) of section 3 of the present bill, the executive branch will be guided by, but not limited to, such of the provisions of the paragraphs of subsection 15 (b) of the Economic Cooperation Act of 1948 as can appropriately be made applicable to China. For example, it is anticipated that the matters covered by paragraphs (5) through (8) of subsection 15 (b) of S. 2202, as passed by the Senate, could be made applicable to China with only clerical modifications in the language of such paragraphs. As to the matters covered by paragraphs (1) through (4) of that act, varying degress of modification, verging in some instances on complete revision, might be appropriate in the light of circumstances in China.

Section 5: This section authorizes advances by the RFC, not to exceed in the aggregate $50,000,000, to carry out the provisions of the bill until funds are appropriated under subsection 3 of the bill.

Appendix B

Agreement Between the United States of America and the Republic of China Concerning United States Relief Assistance to the Chinese People

Whereas, it is the desire of the U. S. of America to provide relief assistance to the Chinese people to prevent suffering and to permit them to continue effectively their efforts toward recovery; and

Whereas, the Chinese Government has requested the U. S. Government for relief assistance and has presented information which convinces the Government of the U. S. that the Chinese Government urgently needs assistance in obtaining the basic essentials of life for the people of China; and

Whereas, the U. S. Congress has by Public Law 84, 80th Congress, May 31, 1947, authorized the provision of relief assistance to the people of those countries which in the determination of the President, need such assistance and have given satisfactory assurance covering the relief program as required by the act of Congress; and

Whereas, the Chinese Government and the U. S. Government desire to define certain conditions and understandings concerning the handling and distribution of the U. S. relief supplies and to establish the general lines of their cooperation in meeting the relief needs of the Chinese people;

The Government of the Republic of China, represented by Dr. Liu Shih Shun, political Vice Minister for Foreign Affairs in charge of the Ministry of Foreign Affairs, and the Government of the U. S. A., represented by Ambassador J. Leighton Stuart, have agreed as follows:

ARTICLE I. FURNISHING OF SUPPLIES

(A) The program of assistance to be furnished shall consist of such types and quantities of supplies, and procurement storage transportation and shipping services related thereto, as may be determined from time to time by the U. S. Government after consultation with the Chinese Government in accordance with Public Law 84, 80th Congress, May 31, 1947, and any acts amendatory or supplementary thereto. Such supplies shall be confined to certain basic essentials of life, namely food, medical supplies, processed and unprocessed material for clothing, fertilizers, pesticides, fuel, and seeds.

(B) Subject to the provisions of Article III, the U. S. Government will make no request and will have no claim for payment for U. S. relief supplies and services furnished under this agreement.

(C) The U. S. Government agencies will provide for the procurement, storage, transportation and shipment to China of U. S. relief supplies except to the extent that the U. S. Government may authorize other means for the performance of these services in accordance with the procedures stipulated by the U. S. Government. All U. S. relief supplies shall be procured in the U. S. except when specific approval of procurement outside the U. S. is given by the U. S. Government.

(D) The Chinese Government will from time to time submit in advance to the U. S. Government its proposed programs for relief import requirements. These programs shall be subject to screening and approval by the U. S. Government and procurement will be authorized only for items contained in the approved programs.

(E) Transfers of U. S. relief supplies shall be made under arrangements to be determined by the U. S. Government in consultation with the Chinese Government. The U. S. Government whenever it deems it desirable may retain possession of any U. S. relief supplies, or may recover possession of such supplies transferred, up to the city or local community where such supplies are made available to the ultimate consumers.

ARTICLE II. DISTRIBUTION OF SUPPLIES IN CHINA

(A) All U. S. relief supplies shall be distributed in accordance with the terms of this agreement by the Chinese Government and by established voluntary agencies in China which are agreed upon between the two governments. Representatives of the USA shall have direct supervision and control of supplies made available by the U. S. Government under this agreement.

(B) All U. S. relief supply imports shall be free of fiscal charges including customs duties up to the point where they are sold for local currency as provided by Article III of this agreement unless when because of price practices, it is advisable to include customs charges or government taxes in prices fixed, in which case the amount thus collected on U. S. relief supply imports will accrue to the special account referred to in Article III. All U. S. relief supply imports given freely to indigents, institutions and others, and those turned over to voluntary agencies for distribution shall be free of fiscal charges including customs duties.

(C) The Chinese Government will designate a high-ranking official who shall have the responsibility of liaison between the Chinese Government and the U. S. representatives responsible for the relief program.

(D) U. S. relief supplies and similar supplies produced locally or imported from outside sources shall be distributed by the Chinese Government and voluntary agencies without discrimination as to race, creed, or political belief, and the Chinese Government shall not permit the diversion of any such supplies to nonessential uses or for export or removal from the country while need therefor for relief purposes continues. The Chinese Government shall not permit the diversion of U. S. relief supplies or an excessive amount of supplies similar to U. S. relief supplies which are produced locally or imported from outside sources in the maintenance of armed forces.

(E) The Chinese Government will take appropriate steps regarding the distribution of U. S. relief supplies and similar supplies produced locally and imported from outside sources designed to assure a fair and equitable share of the supplies to all classes of the people.

(F) A distribution and price-control system shall be inaugurated in such major urban centers of China as circumstances permit with the intent of insuring that all classes of the population, irrespective of their purchasing power, shall receive a fair share of the imported or indigenously produced relief supplies. In permitting U. S. relief supplies made available under this agreement to be utilized in support of Chinese efforts to improve consumption and price controls, it is understood that the U. S. Government undertakes no responsibility for the success of these urban programs.

ARTICLE III. UTILIZATION OF FUNDS ACCRUING FROM SALES OF U. S. SUPPLIES

(A) The prices at which U. S. relief supplies will be sold in China shall be agreed upon between the Chinese Government and the U. S. Government.

(B) When U. S. relief supplies are sold for local currency the amount of such local currency shall be deposited by the Chinese Government in a special account in the name of the Chinese Government.

(C) Until June 30, 1948, such funds shall be disposed of only with the approval of the duly authorized representative of the U. S. Government for relief and work relief within China, including local currency expenses of the USA incident to the furnishing of relief. Any unencumbered balance remaining in such account on June 30, 1948, shall be disposed of within China for such purposes as the U. S. Government pursuant to act or joint resolution of Congress may determine.

(D) The Chinese Government will, upon request, advance funds against proceeds from the sale of U. S. relief supplies to the U. S. representatives, to meet local currency expenses incident to the furnishing of relief, including the operation of the U. S. relief mission in China and certain urgent relief projects being undertaken by Chinese Government organs and voluntary agencies.

(E) While it is not intended that the funds accruing from sales of U. S. relief supplies normally shall be used to defray the local expenses of the Chinese Government in handling transporting internally, and distributing the U. S. relief supplies, including local currency cost of discharging cargo and other port charges, the U. S. representatives will consider with the Chinese Government the use of the funds to cover the unusual costs which would place an undue burden on the Chinese Government.

(F) The Chinese Government will each month make available to the U. S. representatives reports on collections, balances, and expenditures from the fund.

(G) The Chinese Government will assign officials to confer and plan with the U. S. representatives regarding the disposition of funds accruing from sales to assure a prompt and proper use of such funds.

ARTICLE IV. EFFECTIVE PRODUCTION, FOOD COLLECTIONS, AND USE OF RESOURCES TO REDUCE RELIEF NEEDS

(A) The Chinese Government will exert all possible efforts to secure the maximum production and collection of locally produced supplies needed for relief purposes.

(B) The Chinese Government will undertake not to permit any measures to be taken involving delivery, sale, or granting of any articles of the character covered in this agreement which would reduce the locally produced supply of such articles and thereby increase the burden of relief.

(C) The Chinese Government will furnish regularly current information to the U. S. representatives regarding plans and progress in achieving this objective.

(D) The Chinese Government affirms that it has taken and is taking insofar as possible the economic measures necessary to reduce its relief needs and to provide for its own future reconstruction.

ARTICLE V. U. S. REPRESENTATIVES

(A) The U. S. Government will send to China the representatives required to discharge responsibilities of the U. S. Government under this agreement and the Public Law 84, 80th Congress, May 31, 1947. The Chinese Government will permit and facilitate the movement of the U. S. representatives to, in, or from China.

(B) The Chinese Government will permit and facilitate in every way the freedom of the U. S. representatives to supervise the distribution of U. S. relief supplies and to travel, inspect, and report in connection with any matters relating to this agreement and will cooperate fully with them in carrying out all of the provisions of this agreement. The Chinese Government will furnish the necessary auto transportation to permit the U. S. representatives to travel freely throughout China and without delay.

(C) The U. S. representatives and the property of the mission and of its personnel shall enjoy in China the same privileges and immunities as are enjoyed by the personnel of the U. S. Embassy in China and the property of the Embassy and of its personnel.

ARTICLE VI. FREEDOM OF THE U. S. PRESS AND RADIO REPRESENTATIVES TO OBSERVE AND REPORT

The Chinese Government will permit representatives of the U. S. press and radio to observe freely and report fully without censorship regarding the distribution and utilization of relief supplies and the use of funds accruing from sale of U. S. relief supplies.

ARTICLE VII. REPORTS, STATISTICS, AND INFORMATION

(A) The Chinese Government will maintain adequate statistical and other records and will consult with the U. S. representatives, upon their request, with regard to the maintenance of such records.

(B) The Chinese Government will furnish promptly upon request of the U. S. representatives available information concerning the production, U. S. distribution, importation, and exportation of any supplies which affect the relief needs of the people.

(C) In case U. S. representatives report apparent abuses or violations of this agreement the Chinese Government will investigate and report and promptly take such remedial action as is necessary to correct such abuses or violations as are found to exist.

ARTICLE VIII. PUBLICITY REGARDING U. S. ASSISTANCE

(A) The Chinese Government will permit and arrange full and continuous publicity regarding the purpose, source, character, scope, amounts, and progress of the U. S. relief program in China including the utilization of funds accruing from sales of U. S. relief supplies for the benefit of the people.

(B) All U. S. relief supplies and any articles processed from such supplies, or containers of such supplies or articles, shall, to the extent practicable, be marked, stamped, branded, or labelled in a conspicuous place in such a manner as to indicate to the ultimate consumer that such supplies or articles have been furnished by the U. S. A for relief assistance, or if such supplies, articles or containers are incapable of being so marked, stamped, branded, or labelled, all practicable steps will be taken by the Chinese Government to inform the ultimate consumer thereof that such supplies or articles have been furnished by the U. S. for relief assistance.

ARTICLE IX. TERMINATION OF RELIEF ASSISTANCE

The U. S. Government will terminate any or all of its relief assistance at any time whenever it determines (one) by reason of changed conditions, the provision of relief assistance of the character authorized by Public Law 84, 80th Congress, May 31, 1947, is no longer necessary; (two) any provisions of this agreement are not being carried out; (three) U. S. relief supplies, or an excessive amount of similar supplies produced locally or imported from outside sources, are being used to assist in the maintenance of armed forces in China; or (four) U. S. relief supplies or similar supplies produced locally or imported from outside sources are being exported or removed from China. The U. S. Government may stop or alter its program of assistance whenever in its determination other circumstances warrant such action.

The Chinese Government reserves the right to terminate this agreement whenever it deems such relief assistance as is provided in this agreement is no longer necessary.

ARTICLE X. DATE OF AGREEMENT

This agreement shall take effect as from this day's date. It shall continue in force until a date to be agreed upon by the two governments.

Done in duplicate in the English and Chinese languages at Nanking this 27th day of October 1947, corresponding to the 27th day of the tenth month of the thirty-sixth year of the Republic of China.

For the Government of the United States of America:

J. LEIGHTON STUART.

For the Government of the Republic of China:

DR. LIU SHIH SHUN.

APPENDIX C

U. S. S. R. NOTE TO CHINA RELATING TO THE TREATY OF FRIENDSHIP AND ALLIANCE

AUGUST 14, 1945.

YOUR EXCELLENCY: With reference to the treaty of friendship and alliance signed today between the Republic of China and the U. S. S. R., I have the honor to put on record the understanding between the high contracting parties as follows:

1. In accordance with the spirit of the afore-mentioned treaty, and in order to put into effect its aims and purposes, the Government of the U. S. S. R. agrees to render to China moral support and aid in military supplies and other material resources, such support and aid to be entirely given to the National Government as the Central Government of China.

2. In the course of conversations regarding Dairen and Port Arthur and regarding the joint operation of the Chinese Changchun Railway, the Government of the U. S. S. R. regarded the three eastern Provinces as part of China and reaffirmed its respect for China's full sovereignty over the three eastern Provinces and recognize their territorial and administrative integrity.

3. As for the recent developments in Sinkiang the Soviet Government confirms that, as stated in article V of the treaty of friendship and alliance, it has no intention of interfering in the internal affairs of China.

If Your Excellency will be so good as to confirm that the understanding is correct as set forth in the preceding paragraphs, the present note and Your Excellency's reply thereto will constitute a part of the afore-mentioned treaty of friendship and alliance.

I take this opportunity to offer Your Excellency the assurances of my highest consideration.

V. M. MOLOTOV.

CHINA: COMMUNIST CONTROLLED AREAS, 19 MARCH 1948

APPENDIX III

DOCUMENTS RELATING TO S. 2358

Legislative Chronology of S. 2358

To Amend the Act Approved May 22, 1947, Entitled "An Act To Provide for Assistance to Greece and Turkey"

Senate Action

Introduced by Mr. Vandenberg and referred to Committee on March 22, 1948.
Hearings held in executive session on February 28, March 15, 17, 19, 20, 1948.
Ordered reported (vote 13–0) on March 19, 1948.
Reported (S. Rept. 1017) on March 22, 1948.
Passed on March 23, 1948.

House Action

Referred to Committee on March 24, 1948.
(See S. 2202 as amended.)

SECRET

Statement by Maj. Gen. A. M. Harper on the Current Military Problem in Greece Before the Senate Foreign Relations Committee

March 17, 1948

1. Gentlemen, the problem of Greece is not simple. Rather it is very complex; from the view of its form of government, its customs and traditions, its feeble economy, its prostrate finances and, in turn, the persistent ideological and bandit war now being prosecuted within her borders under the overall guidance and assistance from without. But from the general confusion, and frustration of the situation one fact alone appears crystal clear: In the national interest the military program must be continued. In turn, it may be positively stated, based on experience, that without the military program the economic program cannot be successfully executed. Further, in any solution of the problem of Greece time and patience are essential.

2. The mission and objective of the military program has been and continues to be as follows:

> The attainment of internal security for Greece at the earliest practicable date.

With this principle as the guide it thus became necessary to analyze the problem anew in the light of recent developments, assess its magnitude and arrive at a logical military solution with minimum means. Such a study developed on overall program for the three armed services of Greece totalling $248,000,000. This program was transmitted to the Department of National Defense. However, the exigencies of our national obligations lead to the early conclusion that a program in excess of $200,000,000 was inconsistent with the total contemplated for the overall general world program. Thus a program severely curtailed to the latter figure has been developed as an austerity program and is submitted herewith.

3. It is felt that a statement on the accomplishments or value of the program to date is indicated.

The Congress and the American people should not be unduly concerned that the program in Greece has not yet produced all the results desired. The general conception is that the Greek armed forces, consisting essentially of an army of 120,000 men, should be capable of an expeditious elimination of the bandit menace to the security of Greece. This is felt to be a very natural conclusion and merits an explanation or rebuttal. Some facts to this end are set forth below.

a. Greece has been engaged in a National War, in the hands of occupation enemy forces or a guerrilla war for five years prior to her recent liberation by the allies. During this period her armed forces were completely destroyed, her economy reduced to a level which could not support the nation, and her currency twice seriously depreciated. The moral, physical, political and psychological impact on the Greek people was, thus, terrific, and continued existing lack of security, both military and economic, does not tend to induce a strong national pride and determination.

b. Politically the Greek people have always been devoted to the democratic process. In general, however, her governmental system does not tend to produce strong governments. From the military point of view a weakness is manifested in that there is in fact no Commander-in-Chief. Rather the civil government is directly responsible for military operations and controls.

c. The guerrillas have refuge along a 500 mile border, a border which physically has not been closed despite the effort of the United Nations. Continued substantial assistance to the guerrillas from foreign countries has enhanced their strength. The guerrilla's ability to move freely across the border gives him much initiative and makes him very elusive.

d. He has an ideal habitat for his activities in the rugged, difficult mountain chains which characterize vast areas of Greece. If threatened he disperses or goes over the border. Due to his ruthlessness his intelligence system is very effective. He is well led and cunning, he evades encirclement and fixed battle. The Germans, during their occupation, are said to have stated that it took 25 German soldiers for each bandit. The bandit strength in Greece on Febraury 1 was estimated as 24,000. The last estimate I got was 26,500. They are effectively armed.

e. The bandits have held the initiative due to the terrain and the border situation. Thus, moving at night they strike villages suddenly, murder and despoil and are gone as suddenly. This practice has forced the Greek army in great measure, to adopt a dispersed role throughout the extended areas of Greece in a justified effort to protect its villages. The NDC battalions are being formed in order to free the National Army from this static role and thus make them available for offensive operations. This dispersion of the Greek army and the sudden striking tactics of the guerrillas has made it exceedingly difficult for the formation of an active reserve and similarly it has made it almost impossible for the Greek army units to be relieved from field duty for rest and acutely needed further training and combat indoctrination. In this attainment alone the guerrillas have been cunningly successful.

f. Further, the Greek army has lacked an aggressive combat spirit. The Greek soldier has a tendency to engage in long range fire fights in the hope that the guerrillas will disperse. This characteristic is not to be assumed as a Greek one alone. All army officers of modern armies know that this is normal and typical of all recruit forces and untried troops. To eliminate it, they must have strong aggressive leaders, effective control and extended field training. The latter the guerrillas will not allow them to do. The former, it is hoped in some measure can be accomplished by the presence among them of the 80 American officers now being provided. The 100 NDC battalions now being formed should solve the latter problem.

4. In balance, however, it is far from the truth to state that our military program in Greece has been unfruitful of results. Rather, it has accomplished the following extremely essential results.

a. The government and people of Greece are still politically free and psychologically oriented to the west.

b. The rich farm lands of the major Grecian valleys are kept reasonably cleared of bandits and are under successful cultivation, thus assisting materially in the internal economy of Greece. The Greek armed forces have been successful in preventing the establishment by the so-called "Free Greek government" of a capital and have prevented the guerrillas from occupying any major urban center or port. A Greek national military force in being has been created from nothing. It is young; all ranks require more training but its future should be bright, as the Greek is basically fine material. He is both strong and intelligent. This basic material will be molded into an aggressive force.

5. The following is a brief statement in explanation of the breakdown and utilization of the funds for the recommended program of $200,000,000.

Ground	$170, 084, 018
Air	14, 642, 637
Navy	12, 000, 000
Administration	3, 273, 345
Total	200, 000, 000

A. THE GROUND PROGRAM—TOTAL EAR MARK, $170,084,018

With this sum it is expected, in addition to projecting the present program, that certain deficiencies in equipment of the NDC battalions and the Greek National Army, notably mountain artillery, vehicles and automatic weapons will be partially rectified. Similarly, the acute need of a raise in the present ceiling of 132,000 for the army is accomplished in degree by providing an increase of 8,000. This is a compromise from the 18,000 recommended as essential by the military mission and approved by the Chief of the Mission. This increased ceiling is essential in an effort to implement a more balanced force and also bring combat units closer to T/O strength. The increase in dollars over the projection of the present program is for Ground—approximately $14,000,000.

B. THE AIR PROGRAM

Total ear mark recommended program	$14, 642, 637
Ear mark old program	10, 605, 000
Available for improvements	4, 037, 637

The air force is a very valuable element of the Greek armed forces. As presently organized it is, however, inadequate for its task. It requires two more fighter squadrons, in addition to its present 2½, as well as certain material and logistical improvements briefly as follows:

78 planes and spares	$546,000
Ammunition and armament	160,250
Training	35,000
Vehicles	62,000
Communications	36,000
Clothing	45,000
Operation and POL	1,250,000
Ground handling equipment	12,500
Maintenance	50,000
Medical	34,400
Quanset huts	134,400
4 Control towers	12,000
Hard standings	300,000
Gun emplacements	192,000
Lighting	60,000
Ammunition revetments and taxiways	72,000
Rations of 300 more men	74,075
Total	3,075,265
25 percent handling	750,387
Total	3,826,012
Price adjustment	211,625
Total	4,037,637

C. THE NAVAL PROGRAM—EAR MARK, $12,000,000

The sum of $12,000,000 has been requested for logistic support of the Greek navy through June 1949. This amount is considered the minimum required for the continuance of the current naval program and does not envision an increase in either manpower or ships. The ships of the Greek navy quite properly, consist only of escort vessels, minesweepers, amphibious craft and auxiliaries, to a total of 110 vessels. The personnel required to man this navy to eighty percent of war complement is 13,500 including one thousand officers. The greater part of the fund will be spent for fuel, ammunition, spare parts and shop equipment necessary for the overhaul and refit of ships. The missions and roles being executed by the Greek navy are as follows:

I. Support the Greek National Army in the anti-guerrilla campaign by providing transport, amphibious-assault craft, and naval-gunfire support.

II. Sweep mines in Greek waters in order to permit resumption of seaborne commerce and in order to fulfill Greece's part of the international task of postwar mine clearance.

III. Guard coastal waterways, intercept, capture or destroy armed caiques used by the guerrilla forces to implement infiltration tactics.

IV. Transport prisoners to designated islands for safe keeping and then patrol such islands and other areas where surveillance is required.

As long as the Greek navy is in a position to maintain control of the seas around Greece and her insular possessions, denying free movement to guerrilla or other forces, the civil strife may be kept confirmed to the mainland. If, however, the navy should lose control of Hellenic waters the bandits undoubtedly would find ways and means of subjugating one island after another. The navy, therefore, may be looked upon as one of the most stabilizing factors in the current struggle to preserve the political and territorial integrity of the Greek nation.

6. This program, to a total cost of $200,000,000 required to carry the Greek military plan to June 30, 1949, or to an unknown earlier cut off date, in the event of success, is urgently recommended as wise, essential and in the national interest. This is a conservative program in which no consideration has been given to the natural national aspiration of the Greek government for a large and prideful future armed forces establishment. This improved program is for the sole purpose of accomplishing the elimination of organized banditry in Greece as positively and as early as possible. The eventualities in Greece are unpredictable. The program logically provides for meeting the situation we face today.

There are now out with the Greek armed forces some 150 American officers and men. It is proposed that we give the Greek nation and its armed forces the material, psychological inspiration and the competent American advice to assist toward success. Anything less than the whole program will again smack of two little and too late. The difference between adequacy and failure in dollars is slight, politically it is immense.

TOP SECRET

Statement of Maj. Gen. Horace L. McBride on Continuing Aid to Turkey

Turkey stands in a unique position in Eurasia today. Strategically located in a key position in the Middle East and the Arab world, she is the one country on the periphery of Soviet Russia which presents a united and firm national front against Soviet expansion. Her determination to stand up against Soviet pressure and the ability of the western democracies to support her will prove to be a test case for all Middle East countries. Loss of Turkey to Russia might well result in Russian domination of the Middle East.

The objectives of assistance to Turkey are:

First: To stiffen the Turkish will and ability to resist to the end that the Turks continue a firm national posture against Soviet pressure.

Second: To improve the Turkish military potential so that in event of war either in the form of attack on Turkey, or development of hostilities in adjacent areas, the Turks will resist with force any Soviet aggression and will have the maximum possible military capacity to conduct a holding and delaying action in their own country.

In Turkey we have an asset of inestimable value for the maintenance of peace and stability in the Middle East. Turkey exerts a profound influence on other countries in that region, especially the Arab states and Iran. These countries have watched the Turkish Republic pull itself forward since the catastrophe of World War I and gain and maintain its sovereignty and independence against foreign aggression. Turkey stands firm in its determination to resist any aggression against its independence and territorial integrity. The Turks are a tough, courageous people. The Turk soldier has proven himself a determined stubborn fighter. The Turk Armed Forces will fight any aggressor, no matter what the odds or chances for victory, and they will be backed by a united citizenry. They will fight with or without allies, with or without additional arms and equipment. Such spirit is rare today, and it is to our national interest that we encourage their spirit and strengthen their ability to resist.

The strength of the Turkish Armed Forces lies in the spirit and determination of its soldiers. A Turk is proud to serve his country. Although he is drafted into the military service, for a period of three years, he serves with pride and distinction. He receives few privileges and lives a Spartan existence. He is issued but a single uniform and his maximum pay as a private soldier amounts to $3.00 a year. The Turk Army is armed with weapons and equipment that can be generally classed as archaic and obsolete. They have a collection of weapons of all countries and all makes. They have equipment produced in Russia, Austria, England, France, and U.S., in fact, from almost every country that has ever manufactured munitions. Their supply and maintenance problems are practically insurmountable. In spite of these discouraging conditions, the Turk still maintains his determination to resist to the end any aggressor who has designs on his national security.

The $100,000,000.00 aid program authorized by Public Law 75, 80th Congress, will be of materiel assistance to the Turks in improving their defensive capabilities. In our own interests, however, we should go further. Money spent in modernizing the equipment and training of the Turkish Armed Forces can be considered as directly strengthening the security of the United States. It is difficult to conceive of any region in the world today where we can so effectively strengthen the determination to resist aggression at so little cost.

Improved equipment and training in the Turkish Armed Forces will so strengthen their defensive capabilities that any aggressor will have reason to pause before undertaking an offensive action against Turkey. Such an operation would require a major effort to be assured of an early success. Any operation designed to by-pass Turkey and directed against the oil fields of Iraq or Arabia, or through the Balkans toward the Mediterranean, would expose the lines of

85-743 O - 73 - 48

communication to attack from Turkish bases. This would necessitate holding reserves in considerable strength to meet possible attacks by forces based in Turkey.

In the event that efforts to maintain peace fail and we become involved in another war, Turkey could provide her allies with bases of vital importance from which to launch attacks against strategic objectives in the Balkans or Russia. This is predicated of course on the timely strengthening of Turkish Armed Forces to permit them a chance to hold this strategic area until their potential allies could arrive and utilize this area as a base of operations.

It is recommended that aid to Turkey be continued through Fiscal Year 1949. The urgent need for expansion of the present program is clearly indicated if our past expenditures are to be made effective and the Turkish Armed Forces are to become reasonably effective combat units in a modern war. Our objectives are not to provide modern equipment for a fully mobilized Turkish defense force. We hope to provide Turkey with a small, modern, and well balanced defensive force which they can maintain with their own resources at the conclusion of our assistance. The Ground Force Program will give Turkey a well equipped, mobile, striking force which can be augmented by additional units equipped from local resources to meet their special defensive requirements. The Air Force program provides for the establishment of a tactical Air Force designed primarily to improve the capabilities of the ground arm to defend and delay. The very modest Navy program will give the Turks a few modern defensive craft with supporting shore establishments to protect their coastal shipping and patrol their coastal waters.

The sum of money proposed for the 1949 program is less than that considered to be necessary to accomplish our objectives. The Department of National Defense has recommended $103,000,000.00 as the amount required to reach the objective set for 1949. In view of budgetary requirements this has been reduced to $75,000,-000.00. Although this is considerably less than estimated needs, this sum can be advantageously used and will permit definite and constructive work to be done in modernizing a portion of the Turk Army.

Detailed studies have been prepared showing the proposed use of these funds. These studies are available to your Committee.

[COMMITTEE PRINT]

FEBRUARY 28, 1948

DRAFT, BILL AMENDING ACT FOR ASSISTANCE TO GREECE AND TURKEY

STAFF NOTE.—This is the draft bill submitted by the Department of State to the Senate Foreign Relations Committee and the House Foreign Affairs Committee on February 26, 1948. It is printed herewith for the use of the Foreign Relations Committee and the Senate in its consideration of the Greek-Turkish aid program.

80TH CONGRESS
2D SESSION

S.

IN THE SENATE OF THE UNITED STATES

MARCH , 1948

Mr. -------- introduced the following bill; which was read twice and referred to the Committee on Foreign Relations

---

A BILL

To amend the Act approved May 22, 1947, entitled "An Act to provide for assistance to Greece and Turkey".

Be it enacted by the Senate and House of Representatives of the United States of America in Congress assembled, That paragraph (2) of section 1 of the Act entitled "An Act to provide assistance to Greece and Turkey", approved May 22, 1947 (61 Stat. 103), be, and the same is hereby, amended to read as follows:

"(2) by detailing to the United States Missions to Greece or Turkey under this Act,' or to the Govern ments of those countries in implementation of the purposes of this Act, any persons in the employ of the Government of the United States; and, while so detailed, any such person shall be considered, for the purpose of preserving his rights and privileges as such, an officer or employee of the Government of the United States and of the department or agency from which detailed. Traveling expenses of such personnel to and from the place of detail shall be paid by the Government of the United States. Such personnel, and personnel detailed pursuant to paragraph 3 of this section, may receive such station allowances or additional allowances as the President may prescribe; and payments of such allowances heretofore made are hereby validated.

"Civilian personnel who are citizens of the United States detailed or appointed pursuant to this Act to perform functions under this Act outside the continental limits of the United States shall be investigated by the Federal Bureau of Investigation, which shall make a report thereof to the detailing or appointing authority as soon as possible: *Provided, however,* That they may assume their posts and perform their functions after preliminary investigation and clearance by the Department of State."

SEC. 2. Paragraph (3) of section 1 of said Act is hereby amended to read as follows:

"(3) by detailing to the United States Missions to Greece or Turkey under this Act, or to the Governments of those countries in implementation of the purposes of this Act, a limited number of members of the military services of the United States to assist those countries, in an advisory capacity only; and the provisions of the Act of May 19, 1926 (44 Stat. 565), as amended, applicable to personnel detailed pursuant to such Act, as amended, shall, except as otherwise provided herein, be applicable to personnel detailed pursuant to this paragraph."

SEC. 3. (a) Subsection (a) of section 4 of said Act is hereby amended by adding at the end thereof the following: "The Reconstruction Finance Corporation is authorized and directed to make additional advances, not to exceed in the aggregate $50,000,000, to carry out the provisions of this Act in such manner and in such amounts as the President shall determine. No interest shall be charged on advances made by the Treasury to the Reconstruction Finance Corporation for this purpose."

(b) Subsection (b) of section 4 of said Act is hereby

amended by deleting "$400,000,000" and inserting in lieu thereof "$675,000,000", and by inserting after the word "repaid" the following: ", without interest,".

Calendar No. 1060

80TH CONGRESS } SENATE { REPORT
2d Session } { No. 1017

AID TO GREECE AND TURKEY

REPORT

OF THE

COMMITTEE ON FOREIGN RELATIONS

ON

S. 2358

A BILL TO AMEND THE ACT APPROVED MAY 22, 1947, ENTITLED "AN ACT TO PROVIDE FOR ASSISTANCE TO GREECE AND TURKEY"

MARCH 22 (legislative day, MARCH 15), 1948.—Ordered to be printed with illustrations

UNITED STATES
GOVERNMENT PRINTING OFFICE
73-338 WASHINGTON : 1948

10940
GREECE AND TURKEY
IN RELATION TO THE SURROUNDING COUNTRIES
U. S. S. R.
AUSTRIA
HUNGARY
RUMANIA
YUGOSLAVIA
BULGARIA
BLACK SEA
ITALY
Istanbul
BOSPORUS
ARDAHAN-KARS AREA
ALB.
Kavalla
Salonika
ANKARA
IRAN
Larisa
DARDANELLES
Yanina
Volos
TURKEY
GREECE
AEGEAN SEA
Ismir
IONIAN SEA
Patras
ATHENS
Tripolis
Iskanderun
SYRIA
MEDITERRANEAN SEA
LEBANON
IRAQ
TUNISIA
PALESTINE
TRANS-JORDAN
SAUDI ARABIA
The international boundaries shown on this map do not necessarily correspond in all cases to the boundaries recognized by the U. S. Government.
LIBYA
EGYPT
10940 3-48

CONTENTS

80TH CONGRESS *2d Session*	SENATE	REPORT No. 1017

AID TO GREECE AND TURKEY

MARCH 22 (legislative day, MARCH 15), 1948.—Ordered to be printed, with an illustration

Mr. VANDENBERG, from the Committee on Foreign Relations, submitted the following

REPORT

[To accompany S. 2358]

The Committee on Foreign Relations, having had under consideration the subject of amending the act of May 22, 1947, providing for assistance to Greece and Turkey, unanimously report a bill (S. 2358) to amend said act to the Senate and recommend that it do pass.

1. MAIN PURPOSE OF THE BILL

The main purpose of this bill is to amend the act to provide assistance to Greece and Turkey by authorizing the appropriation of an additional $275,000,000 for the period ending June 30, 1949. The additional sum requested will be used entirely for military assistance. The Reconstruction Finance Corporation is authorized to advance an amount not to exceed $50,000,000 to carry out the provisions of the act. The bill also clarifies the status of United States personnel in Greece and Turkey, whose position was left uncertain following the repeal of the act of May 25, 1938.

PART I. THE REQUEST FOR FUNDS AND THE HEARINGS

2. SECRETARY MARSHALL'S LETTER TO THE CONGRESS

On February 28, 1948, Secretary of State George C. Marshall sent to the President Pro Tempore of the Senate and the Speaker of the House a draft bill providing for the continuation of assistance to Greece and Turkey. Since the letter which accompanied the draft bill sets forth in succinct terms the reasons for continued aid, it is reproduced here for the information of the Senate.

FEBRUARY 28, 1948.

When the Nazis were still unconquered and Japanese power in the Pacific had not yet been broken, the cooperation that had been engendered among the peoples of the world by their realization of mutual danger led us to hope, that following the successful termination of hostilities, we could expect a period in which the community of nations would work together with good-will and understanding for the common objective of universal peace. Many of the countries which had undergone the ravages of enemy occupation, or which had made sacrifices for the allied cause according to their capabilities, looked forward to the opportunity of pursuing, in peace, their national rehabilitation and democratic development. Unfortunately, events have not justified these hopes.

Greece and Turkey were among those countries which had hoped to be able to face their problems of postwar readjustment with the assurance that, as long as their policies did not encroach upon the rightful interests of other countries, they would be free and even encouraged to reestablish their national life on a peacetime footing, thereby contributing to the early return of normal international relationships. However, hostilities had barely ceased before a concerted campaign against both Greece and Turkey was inaugurated in neighboring countries. The purpose of this campaign was clearly to undermine the territorial integrity and political independence of Greece and Turkey which would deprive the peoples of these countries of the very liberties which they had struggled so hard during the war years to retain.

Turkey has been under constant pressure to grant military bases in the Straits to a foreign power and to cede to that same power Turkish territory in the Kars-Ardahan region. The northern neighbors of Greece have furnished moral and material support to the Greek communist guerrillas who are attempting to overthrow the legal Greek Government and establish the dictatorship of a foreign-inspired minority. This support is being continued in the face of a resolution adopted by the General Assembly of the United Nations last October.

In the circumstances it has been necessary for Turkey, in the interest of her national security, to maintain a large military establishment which constitutes a severe drain on her economy but which cannot be further reduced without destroying the confidence of the Turkish people in their ability to resist aggression. The conditions are even more critical in Greece, where, as the result of enemy destruction, no extensive rehabilitation was possible within the meager resources of the shattered Greek economy which the Germans left behind as a heritage when they withdrew.

The Congress is well aware, I am sure, that, since the liberation of Greece in 1944, several friendly countries have assisted in efforts to restore Greek economic stability, and that large sums have been expended to this end by the British Government, by UNRRA, and by the United States. These efforts have not been unavailing. Without them, I am convinced, Greece would not today be a sovereign nation. They have not, however, accomplished what might have been hoped, primarily because of the hostile forces determined to deprive Greece of her sovereignty have, with foreign assistance, intensified their efforts to spread chaos and disintegration.

The importance of assisting Greece and Turkey to maintain their status as free and sovereign nations, not only as it affects the security of the United States, but also as it relates to the orderly evolution of international peace within the framework of the United Nations, was recognized last year when the Congress approved the request of the President for authorization, under Public Law 75, to extend aid in the sum of $400,000,000 to these two countries. As a result of that Congressional decision, both Greece and Turkey have been strengthened by the knowledge that the United States was willing to help them resist pressure from beyond their borders. Both have been successful in their efforts to retain their territorial integrity and political independence.

The President, in his second quarterly report on Assistance to Greece and Turkey submitted to the Congress on February 16, reviewed the progress made under this program and stated that additional aid would be sought. I am now requesting the Congress to amend Public Law 75, authorizing the appropriation of an additional $275,000,000 to allow the United States to continue financial assistance to Greece and Turkey and a draft bill which will accomplish this purpose is attached. I am advised by the Director of the Budget that the proposed legislation is in accordance with the program of the President. The funds requested are intended for military assistance required by Greece and Turkey, and are exclusive of any economic assistance which will be provided under the European Recovery Program, if that program is authorized by the Congress. The urgency of prompt action by the Congress is emphasized by the necessity for maintaining unbroken the supply lines from this country which support the

Greek armed forces now in the field combating the guerrillas. Additional funds are required for the Greek program by April 1 if this flow is to be maintained.

The totalitarian groups whose aggressive aims have thus far been frustrated by the continued existence of a free Greece and a free Turkey are convinced that time will play into their hands; their leaders state with assurance that the United States will soon tire of giving aid to far-off Mediterranean countries, and that eventually they will be able to take over by default. It is my belief, however, that the Congress and the American people are unwilling to abandon the Greek and Turkish people at a time when a foundation is being laid which will enable them to stand their own ground without outside aid. It is in my judgment definitely in our self-interest as a nation and consistent with the principles of the United Nations Charter, to help these free people retain their freedom. A world in which it is possible for indirect aggression to deprive nations of their inherent right to pursue their peaceful national existence would be a world completely devoid of the ideals which the American people have so recently fought to preserve.

Faithfully yours,

G. C. Marshall.

3. TEXT OF THE COMMITTEE'S BILL

A BILL To amend the Act approved May 22, 1947, entitled "An Act to provide for assistance to Greece and Turkey"

Be it enacted by the Senate and House of Representatives of the United States of America in Congress assembled, That in addition to the amounts authorized to be appropriated under subsection (b) of section 4 of the Act of May 22, 1947 (61 Stat. 103), there are hereby authorized to be appropriated not to exceed $275,000,000 to carry out the provisions of such Act, as amended.

Sec. 2. (a) Subsection (a) of section 4 of such Act of May 22, 1947, is hereby amended by adding at the end thereof the following: "The Reconstruction Finance Corporation is authorized and directed to make additional advances, not to exceed in the aggregate $50,000,000, to carry out the provisions of this Act, as amended, in such manner and in such amounts as the President shall determine. No interest shall be charged on advances made by the Treasury to the Reconstruction Finance Corporation for this purpose."

(b) Subsection (b) of section 4 of the said Act is hereby amended by inserting after the word "repaid" the following: "without interest".

Sec. 3. Subsections 2 and 3 of section 1 of such Act of May 22, 1947, are hereby amended to permit detailing of persons referred to in such subsections to the United States Missions to Greece and Turkey as well as to the governments of those countries. Section 302 of the Act of January 27, 1948 (Public Law 402, Eightieth Congress) and section 10(c) of the Economic Cooperation Act of 1948 (relating to investigations of personnel by the Federal Bureau of Investigation) shall be applicable to any person so detailed pursuant to such subsection 2 of such Act of 1947: *Provided*, That any military or civilian personnel detailed under section 1 of such Act of 1947 may receive such station allowances or additional allowances as the President may prescribe (and payments of such allowances heretofore made are hereby validated).

4. COMMITTEE HEARINGS

The committee met in closed session on March 15 to hear Secretary of State George C. Marshall on the general problem of assistance to Greece and Turkey. It met again on March 17 to hear George C. McGhee, Coordinator for Aid to Greece and Turkey, and Maj. Gens. Horace L. McBride and A. M. Harper, who have been serving as advisers in the field. On March 19, after a careful consideration of the basic issues involved, the committee wrote up the bill which it now presents for the Senate's approval.

In view of the extensive hearings held in 1947 on this question the committee did not believe it necessary to hold additional public hearings at this time. The testimony of Secretary Marshall and Mr. McGhee given in executive session is included as a part of this report, however, for the information of the Senate.

Part II. The Background

5. THE ORIGINAL BILL PROVIDING ASSISTANCE TO GREECE AND TURKEY

The committee report on the original Greek-Turkish assistance bill described the serious economic situation in Greece, the destruction wrought by communism and occupation by the enemy, the chaos and uncertainty caused by the guerrillas, and the great need of Greece for assistance from the United States if stability was to be restored. The immediate occasion for the consideration of the first bill was the announcement by the British Government on February 24, 1947, that it was unable to provide further aid to Greece. This was followed on March 3, 1947, by a request for assistance addressed to the United States by the Greek Government. On March 12, 1947, President Truman appeared before the Congress in joint session and urged assistance in the amount of $400,000,000 for aid to Greece and Turkey, for the period ending June 30, 1948.

On May 22, 1947, the act to provide assistance to Greece and Turkey, incorporating the request of the President, became law. It authorized the President, when he deemed it in the interest of the United States, to extend financial and other assistance to the two countries. For this purpose an appropriation not to exceed $400,000,000 was authorized. In general, the assistance contemplated took the following forms: (1) Financial aid such as loans, grants, and credits; (2) persons in the employ of the United States Government; (3) military personnel for advisory purposes only; (4) articles, services, and information; and (5) instruction and training of personnel in Greece and Turkey. Consistent with the sovereign independence of Greece and Turkey, the bill provided adequate safeguards against the improper utilization of the assistance rendered.

6. ASSISTANCE RECEIVED BY GREECE AS POSTWAR AID SINCE LIBERATION DAY

Foreign assistance received by Greece from outside sources since the war is as follows:

	Made available (in millions of dollars)
Direct U.S. Government credits and grants: [1]	
Greek-Turkish aid program	300
Post-UNRRA relief (Public Law 84)	40
OFLC credits [2]	80
Maritime Commission credits [3]	45
Export-Import Bank loan	14
Total	479
International aid program:	
UNRRA [4]	354
Pre-UNRRA civilian supply [5]	28
Total	382
British assistance:	
Sterling loan	40
Military and other [6]	200
Total	240

Other: [7]	Made available (in millions of dollars)
Canadian post-UNRRA relief	4
New York Federal Reserve loan [8]	6
Private relief organizations	17
Total	31
Grand total	1,132

[1] Does not include lend-lease of $81,000,000.
[2] Utilization to Dec. 31, 1947: $46,000,000. Office of Foreign Liquidation Commissioner.
[3] Utilization to Jan. 31, 1948: $41,000,000.
[4] United States share: approximately $252,000,000.
[5] From United States, United Kingdom, and Canadian military forces.
[6] Incomplete; does not include some military subsidies in 1945 and 1947.
[7] Source: Treasury Department.
[8] Gold-secured; about $2,000,000 of original amount of $10,000,000 has been repaid and equivalent in gold security released.

7. BRITISH ASSISTANCE TO GREECE

The British assistance to Greece consists of advisory training missions and a contingent of troops. The advisory missions consist of a military, a naval, and an air mission. In addition there is also a police and prisons mission. These have been active in Greece since 1944, from which time until May 22, 1947, British assistance was substantial. The work of the British military missions both in organization and training complements the work of the United States military mission. Since December 1944, when they helped quell a communist-inspired insurrection, the British troops have not been actively engaged in military operations. It should be noted that first under the Caserta agreement of September 1944, and under all subsequent agreements of the Greek Government, British troops have been stationed in Greece upon the invitation and with the affirmation of the Greek Government.

8. RECENT DEVELOPMENTS WITH RESPECT TO GREECE AND TURKEY

Greece

Since the passage of the Greek-Turkish bill, Greece has been subjected to increased political pressures. The guerrilla warfare has been intensified and the guerrillas have increased in numbers. On December 24, 1947, they proclaimed a "Free Government" under the leadership of Markos Vafiades, which, although it has been unable to secure a seat in any community in Greece, still remains an external menace to the established government. Several identical Balkan treaties of alliance have been signed among the neighbors of Greece and the communiqués issued with them indicate that they were "especially pointed at Greece." In addition, societies have been organized in the neighboring countries to assist the Greek guerrillas.

Disturbed by the Greek developments, the United Nations Organization set up a Special Committee on the Balkans to investigate the situation in Greece. The Committee found that Yugoslavia, Albania, and Bulgaria were engaged in giving assistance to the guerrillas and harboring them. In its report of January 2, 1948, the Committee said:

> Without any doubt * * * the guerrillas were supplied with ammunition from across the frontier—

and that—

a constant supply of ammunition is arriving from Albania.

When the Free Government was established, the Committee on the Balkans warned on December 29, 1947, that either direct or indirect assistance by any state to this insurrectionary movement would constitute—

a grave threat * * * to * * * international peace and security.

On this occasion Under Secretary of State Lovett warned the Russian satellite states against recognizing the so-called free government.

Turkey

Turkey's problem, while distinct and different from the Greek, arises from the same causes, namely, direct and indirect pressures brought to bear by Soviet Russia. While Turkey suffered economically as a consequence of the war, her domestic economy and internal security remained intact. She would have been well on the way to prosperity were it not that the pressures from abroad force her to maintain a comparatively large standing army for security purposes. Two pressures in particular should be noted. In March 1945 Russia demanded a change in the 1936 Montreux Convention, which would give the U.S.S.R. joint control with Turkey over the straits. The Turkish Government, supported by the United States and Great Britain, rejected this demand. The second pressure was also applied in 1945, when the Soviet Government demanded the territories of Kars and Ardahan in eastern Turkey. These Soviet pressures continue without let-up to the present moment.

The committee was impressed with the splendid morale of the Turkish people and military personnel. It also noted with satisfaction the measures adopted by Turkey to help herself, and the use she is making of the assistance supplied by the United States.

Part III. The Present Situation

9. ECONOMIC BACKGROUND AND SITUATION IN GREECE

As noted in the committee's report on the original bill to provide assistance to Greece and Turkey, the Greek economy was completely disorganized by the war. Economic collapse during the past year has been avoided only through American financial assistance and technical guidance. The aim of the guerrilla warfare is and has been to disrupt the national security and to produce thereby seriously adverse economic conditions. As a result of the guerrilla activities 450,000 refugees are now grouped in the larger urban centers of northern Greece, where they are a heavy relief burden. Foreign trade has stagnated. Inflationary pressures continue. The disastrous drought last summer has cut the annual crop of bread grains to two-thirds of normal. Adverse political conditions make industrialists reluctant to invest in unproductive enterprises. Merchants market their goods only when they are assured that profits can be converted into other tangible goods.

The committee recognizes that it will be difficult to overcome many of these difficulties without security in Greece. As the President pointed out in his second report to the Congress on assistance to Greece and Turkey, "until the military threat to Greece has been removed there is no possibility of Greek economic recovery."

10. FISCAL SITUATION IN GREECE SINCE WORLD WAR II

Since the day of her liberation Greece has passed through two inflations. The Greek public has no confidence in its own currency, the sale of Government bonds is impossible, Government budgets have not been balanced, expenditures have exceeded anticipated receipts, refugees constitute a terrifically heavy charge, exports are disappointingly low, and there is an absence of a strong central authority to maintain proper control over expenditures. The committee was informed that as a result of corrective measures recommended by the mission the inflation tended to level out in January and the budget was approaching a balance as the fight against inflation was beginning to produce effective results. In spite of these hopeful signs the American aid mission finds itself confronted with a difficult fiscal problem the nature of which was described in the Report on Greece by the House Select Committee on Foreign Aid (p. 8):

> Even with the unprecedented domestic revenue measures mentioned above, 40 percent of the Greek budget revenues are still derived from foreign-aid sources, nearly all of which have been supplied by this country, both through UNRRA and through direct aid. A subsidy of this magnitude cannot be maintained. In addition, the United States is providing $172,000,000 in military equipment and supplies, $25,000,000 in reconstruction equipment and supplies, as well as $84,000,000 in consumer goods with which to finance the internal costs of reconstruction, and $12,000,000 in agricultural equipment. Administration, public health, and training programs account for the other $7,000,000. None of these expenditures appear within the Greek budget.

11. RATE OF PROGRESS ON ROAD TO STABILITY

Because of the lack of security and the other serious handicaps confronting the Government, progress toward recovery in Greece has been discouragingly slow. The committee noted, however, that a number of reforms have been adopted with the aim of correcting the economic and fiscal situation.

These reforms include the following: (1) Efforts are being made to stabilize the cost of living and to relate wages to the cost of living. (2) Success is attending efforts to bring the budget into reasonable balance. (3) The deficit in the new budget has been reduced from 1,900 billion drachmas to 207 billion drachmas. (4) About 15,000 Government employees are to be discharged, of whom approximately 8,000 have already been removed from the pay rolls. This represents a saving of 25 percent in civil-service salaries. (5) By raising taxes and levying new taxes, increases in revenue are anticipated to the amount of 42 percent. (6) Plans are on foot to install a centralized Government budget control. (7) Industrial production at the end of 1947 had risen to 75 percent of prewar production. (8) A program has been adopted to revive the Greek export trade including vital trade with the United States-United Kingdom zones in Germany. (9) An exchange certificate plan has been adopted to encourage Greek exports and thus increase the amount of foreign exchange available to Greece. (10) Restrictions have been placed on the use of credit and to centralize control of bank credits in the Bank of Greece. (11) An import program has been developed in order to meet the needs of industry and the civilian economy on an austerity basis. (12) The reconstruction program as it relates to transportation and communication, industrial, mining, agriculture, and other fields is progressing.

The prospects for a good harvest are encouraging. Long-term projects for Greek self-sufficiency also look promising. The production of foodstuffs is increasing.

12. STATUS OF PREVIOUS $400,000,000 APPROPRIATION

Greece

The original $400,000,000 program of assistance to Greece and Turkey called for the expenditure of $300,000,000 for Greece, 50 percent of which was to be for military purposes. The expansion of the Greek national army, however, has required a diversion of $14,000,000 from the economic to the military program. How the $300,000,000 allotted to Greece has been apportioned is shown by the accompanying chart.

As illustrated by the accompanying chart a total of nearly $172,000,000 has been allocated for military purposes to Greece. This sum may be broken down as follows:

Ground Force	$149, 500, 000
Air Force	9, 500, 000
Navy	12, 850, 000
Total	171, 850, 000

Turkey

The $100,000,000 for Turkey was apportioned as follows:

Ground Force	$48, 500, 000
Air Force	26, 750, 000
Naval Force	14, 750, 000
Arsenal improvement	5, 000, 000
Highway improvement	5, 000, 000
Total	100, 000, 000

The funds thus provided have gone toward the purchase of heavy defensive ordnance, vehicles, other army equipment, airplanes, and naval supplies. Turkey possesses an excellent army imbued with a high morale, but its equipment is heterogeneous and obsolete. The $100,000,000 allocated is being used largely for the modernization of equipment.

85-743 O - 73 - 49

APPORTIONMENT OF GREEK AID FUNDS

Effect of Military and Economic Situation on Distribution of Aid Funds

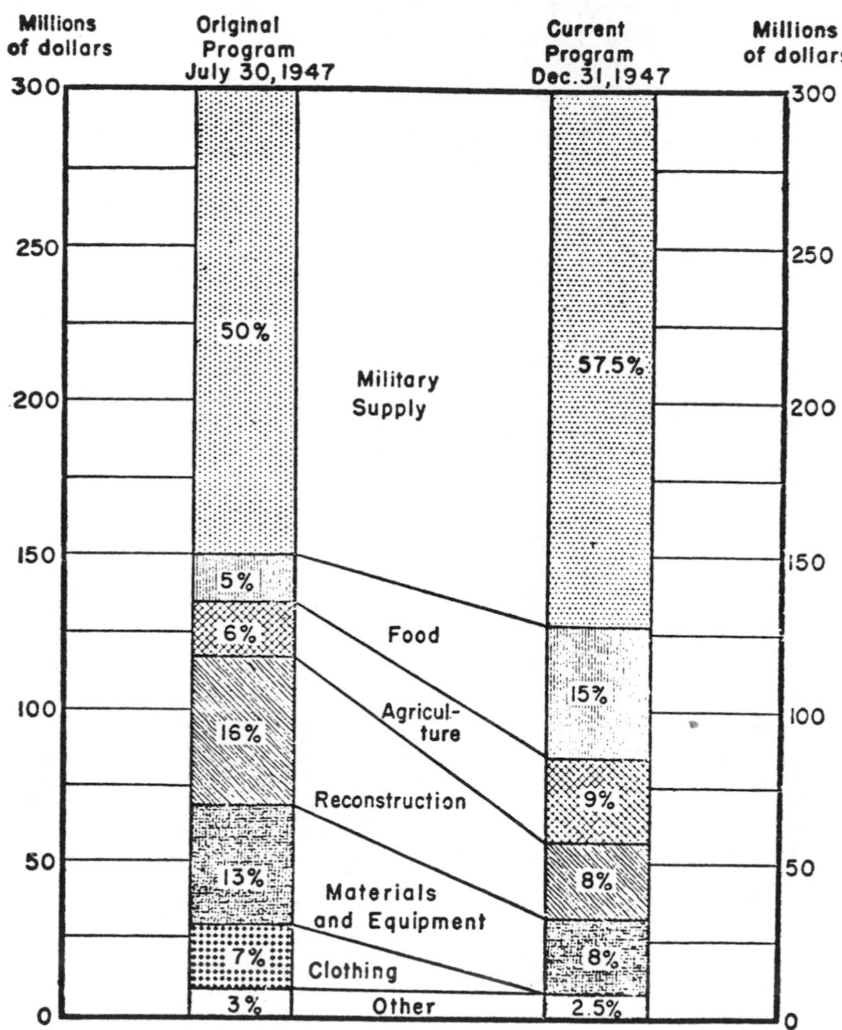

CS/G 2652

Part IV. Further Military Assistance

13. MILITARY SITUATION IN GREECE

The first requirement of the assistance program is the destruction of guerrilla bands. The guerrillas have increased in number from 14,000 in May 1947 to 20,000 in December 1947, and they are now estimated at a probable 26,500. Only a fraction are Communists, a small part brigands and criminals, and a large proportion Creek conscripts pressed into the guerrilla services under systematic terrorization. Only military action will restore stability and permit economic development. As stated, the aim of the guerrilla forces is the dislocation of the rural population in northern Greece, which will produce an increased number of refugees who must seek assistance in the larger urban communities. Thus by swelling the population of the northern cities beyond the capacity of their permanent and temporary housing facilities, the guerrillas hope to create chaos and misery. Their forces operate over an area of hundreds of miles, possess the advantage of surprise, and have been able to develop heavy local superiority at most points chosen for attack. Upon the approach of Government reinforcements, the attackers are able to retreat into the mountains, or in some cases across the northern frontier, and evade pursuit.

14. THE NATURE OF UNITED STATES MILITARY ASSISTANCE

The total strength of the regular Greek National Army, when the mission began its work, was 120,000 men. It is now 132,000 men. This is the mobile force used to combat the guerrillas. In addition, the national guard is being increased from 21,000 to 50,000 men to protect the villages and communities. The regular army is being equipped further with mountain artillery and automatic arms. The United States military group operating in Greece prior to December 7, 1947, instructed the Greek regular forces in how to use the equipment supplied by the United States, determined which supplies were needed, and saw to it that supplies reached their destination. Since December 7, 1947, the members of the American military mission have also given military advice.

During the Senate debates on the European-recovery program the question was raised as to whether American troops are actually engaged in fighting the guerrillas in Greece. Committee members inquired into this matter further during the hearings and were categorically told that there are no units of American combat troops in Greece. Staff members of our mission have extended military advice to the Greek Army staff down to the divisional level. But they have not actively engaged in fighting at the front.

This point is emphasized in the President's report on assistance to Greece and Turkey. In referring to the Greek request to strengthen our military mission there the report states:

> These United States military advisers will neither participate in combat nor command Greek troops.

15. NUMBER AND SERVICE OF AMERICAN PERSONNEL

Greece

On December 31, 1947, the American mission in Greece consisted of 286 people; 142 for economic aid, 8 for foreign relief, and 136 in the military group. Of the latter figure, 95 belonged to the Army and 41 belonged to the Navy group.

There are at present 242 United States military (including 26 civilians) and 41 United States naval personnel, or a total of 283, attached to the military sections of the American mission for aid to Greece.

Of the military personnel, 136 men, including 73 commissioned officers and 63 enlisted men (all noncommissioned officers), are engaged in giving military advice to operational units of the Greek forces. The number of these military advisers is expected to be increased to a full strength of approximately 170, including 90 officers and 80 enlisted men.

The present civilian personnel consists of 183 members, most of them specialists able to assist in matters concerning public finance, civil government, industry, labor, public health, relief and welfare, public information, taxation, engineering, construction, budget, etc.

Turkey

The mission to Turkey is smaller than that sent to Greece. Of the 251 authorized, 182 have been assigned. There are 76 officers, 55 enlisted men, and 51 civilians; 71 belong to the Army group, 34 to the Air Force group, and 13 to the Navy group.

16. PROPOSED PROGRAM OF FURTHER MILITARY ASSISTANCE

The $275,000,000 requested in the bill amending the act for assistance to Greece and Turkey is solely for military purposes. The Departments of State and of Defense believe it essential, if maximum benefits are to be derived from the expendiutre, that a complete freedom of transfer of funds from Greece to Turkey, or from Turkey to Greece, as may be required, shall be provided for. Therefore, based on detailed estimates, they request authorization of a single sum of $275,000,000, without allocation. The committee is of the opinion that the request is reasonable and should be granted.

The anticipated utilization of the $275,000,000 is as follows:

Ground Force	$202, 357, 363
Air Force	50, 642, 637
Navy	22, 000, 000
Total	275, 000, 000

It should be noted that the program covers the period of fiscal 1949, for both Greece and Turkey, as well as the requirements in the last quarter of fiscal year 1948, to meet Greek military needs over and above those for which funds are now available.

17. ADVANCE BY RECONSTRUCTION FINANCE CORPORATION

The original $400,000,000 appropriated for assistance to Greece and Turkey will have been used up or earmarked by March 31, 1948. Since it is anticipated that approximately 3 months will elapse before the necessary appropriations can be made and take effect, during which time an expenditure of from $15,000,000 to $20,000,000 a month will be required, it is important to provide an advance in order to permit uninterrupted procurement of material essential to continuation of the program. In addition, about $20,000,000 is needed for immediate procurement of material to be used in impending Greek operations. The bill, therefore, provides that the Reconstruction Finance Corporation shall make available at the discretion of the President up to $50,000,000 to carry out the provisions of the act, in order that there shall be no delay or discontinuity.

18. AMENDMENTS RELATING TO PERSONNEL

The present bill also provides for several technical changes in the original legislation in order to clarify the status of United States personnel in Greece and Turkey. Briefly summarized these changes are as follows:

1. Section 3 provides that personnel may be detailed to the United States mission in the country concerned, or to the Governments of Greece and Turkey. This clarifies the provision made in Public Law 75 (80th Cong.) which simply authorized the detail of personnel "to assist those countries."

2. A second change liberalizes the provision in the Greek-Turkish bill relating to loyalty clearance of personnel. The original bill provided that no civilian personnel should be assigned to Greece and Turkey until such personnel had been investigated by the Federal Bureau of Investigation. Because of the time factor involved the committee believed it would be preferable to permit personnel to assume their posts after preliminary clearance by the Department of State with a subsequent investigation by the FBI. This is, in substance, the provision of the Economic Cooperation Act of 1948 as approved by the Senate.

3. Public Law 75 also stipulates that the provisions of the act of May 25, 1938, as amended, shall be applicable to personnel detailed to Greece and Turkey in connection with the aid program. Public Law 402 (80th Cong.) expressly repealed the act of May 25, 1938, however, and the committee believed it desirable to make a specific reference to the relevant section of Public Law 402 in order to protect the status of our governmental personnel in Greece and Turkey.

4. Finally, the committee thought it advisable to place civilian and military personnel in Greece and Turkey on the same plane with respect to travel and subsistence allowances. Specific language was incorporated in section 3 of the bill to accomplish this purpose.

19. ADMINISTRATION OF THE PROGRAM IN THE FIELD

Since the inception of the Greek-Turkish program certain criticisms have been directed at the United States mission in Greece. For the most part they have concerned two aspects of the program: (1) The distribution of supplies; and (2) the relationship between the American Ambassador and the chief of the special mission in Greece.

The committee noted, however, that most of these criticisms have arisen with respect to situations over which the United States had no control. The recent discovery of large quantities of UNRRA supplies in Greek warehouses is a case in point. Clearly the failure to distribute UNRRA supplies should be attributed to the inadequacy of UNRRA machinery and to the local political situation in Greece rather than to any error on the part of our mission. As soon as the mission began its work it made arrangements for the equitable and immediate distribution of available supplies. Similarly, where perishable goods were deteriorating due to the break-down of governmental machinery, the mission took steps to insure that the distribution was immediately effected. In short, the mission has been instrumental in seeing to it that not only its aid money but prior contributions have been wisely spent.

The committee also inquired into the differences which are reported to have arisen between the head of the Greek aid mission and the chief of the diplomatic mission of the United States in Greece. The committee is satisfied, however, that the relatively minor differences which initially existed were quickly resolved with the result that the relations between the two have been harmonious and satisfactory both to the State Department and to the missions themselves.

20. THE RELATIONSHIP OF THE EUROPEAN RECOVERY PROGRAM

At the present time the Congress is considering a European recovery program, which will extend economic assistance to 16 European countries including Greece and Turkey. According to the terms of the Economic Cooperation Act of 1948 the program will be under the supervision of a special economic mission in these countries. Clearly the activities of the special missions for economic cooperation must be closely related to the military and economic activities being carried on by existing American missions there.

While the committee expressed a deep interest in this general problem, it is obvious that the details must await the establishment of the Economic Cooperation Administration. Whatever administrative arrangements are finally worked out, the committee agreed that the two progams must be closely integrated with lines of responsibility clearly fixed so that American aid can be extended with maximum effectiveness and efficiency.

PART V. CONCLUSION

21. RECOMMENDATION OF THE COMMITTEE

On March 19 the committee completed its deliberations on the bill and by a unanimous vote of 13 to 0 agreed to report it to the Senate for favorable action.

In making its decision the committee agreed that a very strong case had been made in the hearings for the extension of additional aid to Greece and Turkey. Assistance granted by the United States during the past critical year has been indispensable to these two countries in their valiant efforts against disheartening odds to preserve their freedom and their independence. But the objective is only half won. As a result of the constantly increasing totalitarian pressure in Europe the need for assistance in 1948 is even more imperative than it was in 1947.

The committee is convinced that it is recommending the only course of action, under the circumstances, which is consistent with our own national security and world peace. The withdrawal of American aid at this time would be a catastrophic blow to the forces of freedom and independence. It would result in the expansion of totalitarianism in Europe and would be painfully discouraging to those nations who believe in the vitality of democracy and who still have hope for tomorrow.

The committee hopes the Senate will act without delay upon this important measure. That is the best kind of an answer to those who charge that the democracies are incapable of timely and decisive action.

APPENDIXES

Appendix A

[Public Law 75—80th Congress]

[Chapter 81—1st Session]

[S. 938]

AN ACT To provide for assistance to Greece and Turkey

Whereas the Governments of Greece and Turkey have sought from the Government of the United States immediate financial and other assistance which is necessary for the maintenance of their national integrity and their survival as free nations; and

Whereas the national integrity and survival of these nations are of importance to the security of the United States and of all freedom-loving peoples and depend upon the receipt at this time of assistance; and

Whereas the Security Council of the United Nations has recognized the seriousness of the unsettled conditions prevailing on the border between Greece on the one hand and Albania, Bulgaria, and Yugoslavia on the other, and, if the present emergency is met, may subsequently assume full responsibility for this phase of the problem as a result of the investigation which its commission is currently conducting; and

Whereas the Food and Agriculture Organization mission for Greece recognized the necessity that Greece receive financial and economic assistance and recommended that Greece request such assistance from the appropriate agencies of the United Nations and from the Governments of the United States and the United Kingdom; and

Whereas the United Nations is not now in a position to furnish to Greece and Turkey the financial and economic assistance which is immediately required; and

Whereas the furnishing of such assistance to Greece and Turkey by the United States will contribute to the freedom and independence of all members of the United Nations in conformity with the principles and purposes of the Charter: Now, therefore,

Be it enacted by the Senate and House of Representatives of the United States of America in Congress assembled, That, notwithstanding the provisions of any other law, the President may from time to time when he deems it in the interest of the United States furnish assistance to Greece and Turkey, upon request of their governments, and upon terms and conditions determined by him—

(1) by rendering financial aid in the form of loans, credits, grants, or otherwise, to those countries;

(2) by detailing to assist those countries any persons in the employ of the Government of the United States; and the provisions of the Act of May 25, 1938 (52 Stat. 442), as amended, applicable to personnel detailed pursuant to such Act, as amended, shall be applicable to personnel detailed pursuant to this paragraph: *Provided, however,* That no civilian personnel shall be assigned to Greece or Turkey to administer the purposes of this Act until such personnel have been investigated by the Federal Bureau of Investigation;

(3) by detailing a limited number of members of the military services of the United States to assist those countries, in an advisory capacity only; and the provisions of the Act of May 19, 1926 (44 Stat. 565), as amended, applicable to personnel detailed pursuant to such Act, as amended, shall be applicable to personnel detailed pursuant to this paragraph;

(4) by providing for (A) the transfer to, and the procurement for by manufacture or otherwise and the transfer to, those countries of any articles, services, and information, and (B) the instruction and training of personnel of those countries; and

(5) by incurring and defraying necessary expenses, including administrative expenses and expenses for compensation of personnel, in connection with the carrying out of the provisions of this Act.

SEC. 2. (a) Sums from advances by the Reconstruction Finance Corporation under section 4(a) and from the appropriations made under authority of section 4(b) may be allocated for any of the purposes of this Act to any department, agency, or independent establishment of the Government. Any amount so allocated shall be available as advancement or reimbursement, and shall be credited, at the option of the department, agency, or independent establishment concerned, to appropriate appropriations, funds or accounts existing or established for the purpose.

(b) Whenever the President requires payment in advance by the Government of Greece or of Turkey for assistance to be furnished to such countries in accordance with this Act, such payments when made shall be credited to such countries in accounts established for the purpose. Sums from such accounts shall be allocated to the departments, agencies, or independent establishments of the Government which furnish the assistance for which payment is received, in the same manner, and shall be available and credited in the same manner, as allocations made under subsection (a) of this section. Any portion of such allocation not used as reimbursement shall remain available until expended.

(c) Whenever any portion of an allocation under subsection (a) or subsection (b) is used as reimbursement, the amount of reimbursement shall be available for entering into contracts and other uses during the fiscal year in which the reimbursement is received and the ensuing fiscal year. Where the head of any department, agency, or independent establishment of the Government determines that replacement of any article transferred pursuant to paragraph (4)(A) of section 1 is not necessary, any funds received in payment therefor shall be covered into the Treasury as miscellaneous receipts.

(d)(1) Payment in advance by the Government of Greece or of Turkey shall be required by the President for any articles or services furnished to such country under paragraph (4)(A) of section 1 if they are not paid for from funds advanced by the Reconstruction Finance Corporation under section 4(a) or from funds appropriated under authority of section 4(b).

(2) No department, agency, or independent establishment of the Government shall furnish any articles or services under paragraph (4)(A) of section 1 to either Greece or Turkey, unless it receives advancements or reimbursements therefor out of allocations under subsection (a) or (b) of this section.

SEC. 3. As a condition precedent to the receipt of any assistance pursuant to this Act, the government requesting such assistance shall agree (a) to permit free access of United States Government officials for the purpose of observing whether such assistance is utilized effectively and in accordance with the undertakings of the recipient government; (b) to permit representatives of the press and radio of the United States to observe freely and to report fully regarding the utilization of such assistance; (c) not to transfer, without the consent of the President of the United States, title to or possession of any article or information transferred pursuant to this Act nor to permit, without such consent, the use of any such article or the use or disclosure of any such information by or to anyone not an officer, employee, or agent of the recipient government; (d) to make such provisions as may be required by the President of the United States for the security of any article, service, or information received pursuant to this Act; (e) not to use any part of the proceeds of any loan, credit, grant, or other form of aid rendered pursuant to this Act for the making of any payment on account of the principal or interest on any loan made to such government by any other foreign government; and (f) to give full and continuous publicity within such country as to the purpose, source, character, scope, amounts, and progress of United States economic assistance carried on therein pursuant to this Act.

SEC. 4. (a) Notwithstanding the provisions of any other law, the Reconstruction Finance Corporation is authorized and directed, until such time as an appropriation shall be made pursuant to subsection (b) of this section, to make advances, not to exceed in the aggregate $100,000,000, to carry out the provisions of this Act, in such manner and in such amounts as the President shall determine.

(b) There is hereby authorized to be appropriated to the President not to exceed $400,000,000 to carry out the provisions of this Act. From appropriations made under this authority there shall be repaid to the Reconstruction Finance Corporation the advances made by it under subsection (a) of this section.

SEC. 5. The President may, from time to time, prescribe such rules and regulations as may be necessary and proper to carry out any of the provisions of this Act; and he may exercise any power or authority conferred upon him pursuant to this Act through such department, agency, independent establishment, or officer of the Government as he shall direct.

The President is directed to withdraw any or all aid authorized herein under any of the following circumstances:

(1) If requested by the Government of Greece or Turkey, respectively, representing a majority of the people of either such nation;

(2) If the Security Council finds (with respect to which finding the United States waives the exercise of any veto) or the General Assembly finds that action taken or assistance furnished by the United Nations makes the continuance of such assistance unnecessary or undesirable;

(3) If the President finds that any purposes of the Act have been substantially accomplished by the action of any other inter-governmental organizations or finds that the purposes of the Act are incapable of satisfactory accomplishment; and

(4) If the President finds that any of the assurances given pursuant to section 3 are not being carried out.

SEC. 6. Assistance to any country under this Act may, unless sooner terminated by the President, be terminated by concurrent resolution by the two Houses of the Congress.

SEC. 7. The President shall submit to the Congress quarterly reports of expenditures and activities, which shall include uses of funds by the recipient governments, under authority of this Act.

SEC. 8. The chief of any mission to any country receiving assistance under this Act shall be appointed by the President, by and with the advice and consent of the Senate, and shall perform such functions relating to the administration of this Act as the President shall prescribe.

Approved May 22, 1947.

APPENDIX B

TABLE I.—STATUS OF APPROPRIATION FOR ASSISTANCE TO GREECE AND TURKEY AS OF JAN. 31, 1948

Agency and program	Allocations [1] to disbursing agencies	Allotments by disbursing agencies to programs	Obligations	Expenditures
Department of State:				
Greek program	$49,200,000	$32,525,000.00	$21,728,876.54	$21,359,678.73
Turkish program	5,000,000	359.00		
Departmental administrative expenses	300,000	154,000.00	126,851.80	122,293.62
Total	54,500,000	32,679,359.00	21,855,728.34	21,481,972.35
Department of the Army: [2]				
Greek program	132,000,000	88,823,425.64	51,043,857.71	14,376,732.66
Turkish program	76,237,500	22,924,612.86	10,413,399.68	284,601.47
Total	208,237,500	111,748,038.50	61,457,257.39	14,661,333.53
Department of the Navy:				
Greek program	17,460,000	9,926,111.86	4,447,713.36	2,072,165.11
Turkish program	14,012,500	5,165,446.12	2,333,309.87	1,605,810.17
Total	31,472,500	15,091,557.98	6,781,023.23	3,677,975.28
Treasury Department:				
Greek program	19,040,000	14,490,597.77	5,939,850.53	3,309,826.87
Turkish program				
Total	19,040,000	14,490,597.77	5,939,850.53	3,309,826.87

TABLE I.—STATUS OF APPROPRIATION FOR ASSISTANCE TO GREECE AND TURKEY AS OF JAN. 31, 1948—Continued

Agency and program	Allocations[1] to disbursing agencies	Allotments by disbursing agencies to programs	Obligations	Expenditures
Department of Agriculture:				
Greek program	26,014,650	19,325,619.11	19,317,748.25	1,555,058.70
Turkish program				
Total	26,014,650	19,325,619.11	19,317,748.25	1,555,058.70
Federal Security Agency:				
Greek program	100,000	44,600.00	9,902.19	3,201.92
Turkish program				
Total	100,000	44,600.00	9,902.19	3,201.92
Federal Works Agency:				
Greek program				
Turkish program	3,750,000	3,750,000.00	1,510,469.93	18,254.01
Total	3,750,000	3,750,000.00	1,510,469.93	18,254.01
Total for all agencies:				
Greek program	243,814,650	165,135,354.38	102,487,948.58	42,676,663.39
Turkish program	99,000,000	31,840,417.98	14,257,179.48	1,908,665.65
Departmental administrative expenses	300,000	154,000.00	126,851.80	122,293.62
Total	343,114,650	197,129,772.36	116,871,979.88	44,707,622.66
Unallocated funds	56,885,350			
Appropriated by Congress	400,000,000			

[1] This column represents funds allocated to disbursing agencies by allocation letters to the United States Treasury Department through Feb. 15, 1948.

[2] Figures shown under the Department of the Army are for the period ended Dec. 31, 1947.

NOTE.—Allotments, obligations, and expenditures are based on reports submitted by the agencies.

APPENDIX IV

DOCUMENTS RELATING TO S. 2331

LEGISLATIVE CHRONOLOGY OF S. 2331

TO PROVIDE FOR THE SPECIAL CARE AND FEEDING OF CHILDREN BY AUTHORIZING ADDITIONAL MONEYS FOR THE INTERNATIONAL CHILDREN'S EMERGENCY FUND OF THE UNITED NATIONS

Senate Action

Introduced by Mr. Smith and referred to committee on March 16, 1948.
Hearing held in executive session on March 25, 1948.
(See S. 2202 as amended.)

80TH CONGRESS
2D SESSION

S. 2331

IN THE SENATE OF THE UNITED STATES

MARCH 16 (legislative day, MARCH 15), 1948

Mr. SMITH introduced the following bill; which was read twice and referred to the Committee on Foreign Relations

A BILL

To provide for the special care and feeding of children by authorizing additional moneys for the International Children's Emergency Fund of the United Nations.

Be it enacted by the Senate and House of Representatives of the United States of America in Congress assembled, That the President is hereby authorized and directed any time after the date of the enactment of this Act and before July 1, 1949, to make contributions (a) from sums appropriated to carry out the purposes of this Act and (b) from funds made available pursuant to the proviso in the first paragraph of the first section of the joint resolution of May 31, 1947 (Public Law 84, Eightieth Congress), as amended, to the International Children's Emergency Fund of the United Nations for the special care and feeding of children.

SEC. 2. No contribution shall be made pursuant to this Act or such joint resolution of May 31, 1947, which would cause the sum of (a) the aggregate amount contributed pursuant to this Act and (b) the aggregate amount contributed by the United States pursuant to such joint resolution of May 31, 1947, to exceed whichever of the following sums is the lesser:

(1) 50 per centum of the total resources contributed after May 31, 1947, by all governments for programs carried out under the supervision of such fund; or

(2) $100,000,000.

SEC. 3. No contribution shall be made pursuant to this Act or such joint resolution of May 31, 1947, unless, at the time of such contribution, governments other than the United States Government have provided for use in the world program for the special care and feeding of children under the supervision of the fund at least 20 per centum of the total resources contributed for such use after May 31, 1947.

SEC. 4. Funds made available pursuant to such joint resolution of May 31, 1947, shall remain available through June 30, 1949.

SEC. 5. There is hereby authorized to be appropriated to carry out the purposes of this Act for the fiscal year ending June 30, 1949, the sum of $60,000,000.

ADDRESS OFFICIAL COMMUNICATIONS TO
THE SECRETARY OF STATE
WASHINGTON 25, D. C.

DEPARTMENT OF STATE
WASHINGTON

In reply refer to
E

March 24, 1948

My dear Senator Vandenberg:

In your letter of March 17, 1948, to the Secretary of State you requested comments on S. 2331 introduced on March 16, 1948, by Senator Smith "to provide for the special care and feeding of children by authorizing additional moneys for the International Children's Emergency Fund of the United Nations".

In view of the international character of the Fund the Department is of the opinion that any United States contribution to the Fund should be made only on the basis of matching those of other contributors. Since over $20,000,000 of the $40,000,000 originally authorized as a United States contribution, still remains available to match contributions of other governments and since the extent of additional contributions by other governments is somewhat uncertain, the Department is unable to determine whether or to what extent additional funds would be used. However, the Department perceives no objection to the enactment of an authorization for an additional contribution of $60,000,000 on a matching basis.

It is noted that a new formula for matching is proposed. Section 1 of Public Law 84, 80th Congress, as amended by Section 16 of Public Law 389, 80th Congress, provides that the United States may not contribute more than 57 per centum of the aggregate amount contributed to the Fund "by all governments, including the United States". This has been interpreted both by officials of the Fund and by the Department of State to refer only to contributions to the Fund made by governments for the benefit of persons outside the territory of the contributing governments themselves, and not to include goods or services furnished by such governments to their own citizens under arrangements worked out with the Fund. The proposed new formula prohibits any

The Honorable
Arthur H. Vandenberg, Chairman,
Committee on Foreign Relations,
United States Senate.

85-743 O - 73 - 50

any United States contribution in excess of 50 per cent of the Fund's total resources.and is intended to prohibit any United States contribution unless other governments have made contributions amounting to 20 per cent of the total resources of the Fund contributed after May 31, 1947, "for use in the world program for the special care and feeding of children under the supervision of the Fund". The quoted phrase is somewhat ambiguous but presumably refers to contributions for the benefit of persons outside the borders of the contributing country. The remaining 30 per cent of the total resources of the Fund presumably would consist of supplies and services furnished by various governments for use within their own borders in programs administered by the Fund.

This formula changes the 57-43 ratio on contributions to a ratio of approximately $70 from the United States for every $30 contributed by other countries for persons outside their own borders. The Department perceives no objection to increasing the ratio of United States contributions to this extent. It does not, however, seem advisable to include supplies and services furnished by the recipient countries to their own children as part of their contributions for the United States to match. The furnishing of food and services for its own children to the greatest extent possible is a normal function and obligation of any country. It would be very difficult, furthermore, to determine, value and account for the exact contribution which a country makes toward the provision of food and services for its own children.

It is suggested that the language of the Bill be changed by the following amendments: Strike out the material in lines 10 through 13 on page 2 and insert in lieu thereof, "(1) 70 per cent of the total resources contributed after May 31, 1947, by all governments for programs carried out under the supervision of such Fund, Provided; that in computing the amount of resources contributed by any government there shall not be included contributions for the benefit of persons located within the territory of such contributing government; or". Also strike out Section 3 of the Bill.

Because of the urgency of the matter this letter has not been cleared with the Bureau of the Budget, to which a copy is being sent.

Sincerely yours,

For the Secretary of State:

Charles E. Bohlen

Charles E. Bohlen
Counselor

ADDRESS OFFICIAL COMMUNICATIONS TO
THE SECRETARY OF STATE
WASHINGTON 25, D. C.

DEPARTMENT OF STATE
WASHINGTON

April 1, 1948

In reply refer to
E

My dear Senator Vandenberg:

In my letter to you dated March 24, 1948, in connection with S. 2331, a Bill to make further provision for the special care and feeding of children, there was a suggestion for a change in the language of the Bill as introduced. Through inadvertence, three words of the proposed amended language were misplaced, and, for the sake of clarity, it is suggested that a few additional words be inserted. Therefore it would be appreciated if you will consider the next to last paragraph of that letter amended to read as follows:

> It is suggested that the language of the Bill be changed by the following amendments: Strike out the material in lines 10 through 13 on page 2 and insert in lieu thereof, "(1) 70 per cent of the total resources contributed after May 31, 1947, by all governments including the United States for programs carried out under the supervision of such Fund, <u>Provided</u>: that in computing the amount of resources contributed there shall not be included contributions by any government for the benefit of persons located within the territory of such contributing government; or". Also strike out Section 3 of the Bill. (Sec. 205 of Title II of House Bill)

This matter has been discussed informally with Mr. Wilcox of your staff, and your cooperation in this matter is appreciated.

Sincerely yours,

For the Acting Secretary of State:

Charles E. Bohlen
Charles E. Bohlen
Counselor

The Honorable
Arthur H. Vandenberg, Chairman,
Committee on Foreign Relations,
United States Senate.

APPENDIX V

[Public Law 472—80th Congress]
[Chapter 169—2d Session]
[S. 2202]

AN ACT

To promote world peace and the general welfare, national interest, and foreign policy of the United States through economic, financial, and other measures necessary to the maintenance of conditions abroad in which free institutions may survive and consistent with the maintenance of the strength and stability of the United States.

Be it enacted by the Senate and House of Representatives of the United States of America in Congress assembled, That this Act may be cited as the "Foreign Assistance Act of 1948".

TITLE I

Sec. 101. This title may be cited as the "Economic Cooperation Act of 1948".

FINDINGS AND DECLARATION OF POLICY

Sec. 102. (a) Recognizing the intimate economic and other relationships between the United States and the nations of Europe, and recognizing that disruption following in the wake of war is not contained by national frontiers, the Congress finds that the existing situation in Europe endangers the establishment of a lasting peace, the general welfare and national interest of the United States, and the attainment of the objectives of the United Nations. The restoration or maintenance in European countries of principles of individual liberty, free institutions, and genuine independence rests largely upon the establishment of sound economic conditions, stable international economic relationships, and the achievement by the countries of Europe of a healthy economy independent of extraordinary outside assistance. The accomplishment of these objectives calls for a plan of European recovery, open to all such nations which cooperate in such plan, based upon a strong production effort, the expansion of foreign trade, the creation and maintenance of internal financial stability, and the development of economic cooperation, including all possible steps to establish and maintain equitable rates of exchange and to bring about the progressive elimination of trade barriers. Mindful of the advantages which the United States has enjoyed through the existence of a large domestic market with no internal trade barriers, and believing that similar advantages can accrue to the countries of Europe, it is declared to be the policy of the people of the United States to encourage these countries through a joint organization to exert sustained common efforts as set forth in the report of the Committee of European Economic Cooperation signed at Paris on September 22, 1947, which will speedily achieve that economic cooperation in Europe which is essential for lasting peace and prosperity. It is further declared to be the policy of the people of the United States to sustain and strengthen principles of individual liberty, free institutions, and genuine independence in Europe through assistance to those countries of Europe which participate in a joint recovery program based upon self-help and mutual cooperation: *Provided*, That no assistance to the participating countries herein contemplated shall seriously impair the economic stability of the United States. It is further declared to be the policy of the United States that continuity of assistance provided by the United States should, at all times, be dependent upon continuity of cooperation among countries participating in the program.

PURPOSES OF TITLE

(b) It is the purpose of this title to effectuate the policy set forth in subsection (a) of this section by furnishing material and financial assistance to the participating countries in such a manner as to aid them, through their own individual and concerted efforts, to become independent of extraordinary outside economic assistance within the period of operations under this title, by—

(1) promoting industrial and agricultural production in the participating countries;

(2) furthering the restoration or maintenance of the soundness of European currencies, budgets, and finances; and

(3) facilitating and stimulating the growth of international trade of participating countries with one another and with other countries by appropriate measures including reduction of barriers which may hamper such trade.

PARTICIPATING COUNTRIES

SEC. 103. (a) As used in this title, the term "participating country" means—

(1) any country, together with dependent areas under its administration, which signed the report of the Committee of European Economic Cooperation at Paris on September 22, 1947; and

(2) any other country (including any of the zones of occupation of Germany, any areas under international administration or control, and the Free Territory of Trieste or either of its zones) wholly or partly in Europe, together with dependent areas under its administration;

provided such country adheres to, and for so long as it remains an adherent to, a joint program for European recovery designed to accomplish the purposes of this title.

(b) Until such time as the Free Territory of Trieste or either of its zones becomes eligible for assistance under this title as a participating country, assistance to the Free Territory of Trieste, or either of its zones, is hereby authorized under the Foreign Aid Act of 1947 until June 30, 1949, and the said Foreign Aid Act of 1947 is hereby amended accordingly, and not to exceed $20,000,000 out of funds authorized to be advanced by the Reconstruction Finance Corporation under subsection (a) of section 114 of this title, or under subsection (d) of section 11 of the Foreign Aid Act of 1947 notwithstanding any appropriation heretofore made under such Act, may be utilized for the purposes of this subsection: *Provided*, That section 11 (b) of the Foreign Aid Act of 1947 shall not apply in respect of the Free Territory of Trieste or either of its zones: *And provided further*, That the provisions of section 115 (b) (6) of this title shall apply to local currency deposited pursuant to section 5 (b) of that Act.

ESTABLISHMENT OF ECONOMIC COOPERATION ADMINISTRATION

SEC. 104. (a) There is hereby established, with its principal office in the District of Columbia, an agency of the Government which shall be known as the Economic Cooperation Administration, hereinafter referred to as the Administration. The Administration shall be headed by an Administrator for Economic Cooperation, hereinafter referred to as the Administrator, who shall be appointed by the President, by and with the advice and consent of the Senate, and who shall receive compensation at the rate of $20,000 per annum. The Administrator shall be responsible to the President and shall have a status in the executive branch of the Government comparable to that of the head of an executive department. Except as otherwise provided in this title, the administration of the provisions of this title is hereby vested in the Administrator and his functions shall be performed under the control of the President.

(b) There shall be in the Administration a Deputy Administrator for Economic Cooperation who shall be appointed by the President, by and with the advice and consent of the Senate, and shall receive compensation at the rate of $17,500 per annum. The Deputy Administrator for Economic Cooperation shall perform such functions as the Administrator shall designate, and shall be Acting Administrator for Economic Cooperation during the absence or disability of the Administrator or in the event of a vacancy in the office of Administrator.

(c) The President is authorized, pending the appointment and qualification of the first Administrator or Deputy Administrator for Economic Cooperation appointed hereunder, to provide, for a period of not to exceed thirty days after the date of enactment of this Act, for the performance of the functions of the Administrator under this title through such departments, agencies, or establishments of the United States Government as he may direct. In the event the President nominates an Administrator or Deputy Administrator prior to the expiration of such thirty-day period, the authority conferred upon the President by this subsection shall be extended beyond such thirty-day period but only until an Administrator or Deputy Administrator qualifies and takes office.

(d) (1) The Administrator, with the approval of the President, is hereby authorized and empowered to create a corporation with such powers as the Administrator may deem necessary or appropriate for the accomplishment of the purposes of this title.

(2) If a corporation is created under this section—

(i) it shall have the power to sue and be sued, to acquire, hold, and dispose of property, to use its revenues, to determine the character of any necessity for its obligations and expenditures and the manner in which they shall be incurred, allowed and paid, and to exercise such other powers as may be necessary or appropriate to carry out the purposes of the corporation;

(ii) its powers shall be set out in a charter which shall be valid only when certified copies thereof are filed with the Secretary of the Senate and the Clerk of the House of Representatives and published in the Federal Register, and all amendments to such charter shall be valid only when similarly filed and published;

(iii) it shall not have succession beyond June 30, 1952, except for purposes of liquidation, unless its life is extended beyond such date pursuant to Act of Congress; and

(iv) it shall be subject to the Government Corporation Control Act to the same extent as wholly owned Government corporations listed in section 101 of such Act.

(3) All capital stock of the corporation shall be of one class, be issued for cash only, and be subscribed for by the Administrator. Payment for such capital stock shall be made from funds available for the purposes of this title.

(e) Any department, agency, or establishment of the Government (including, whenever used in this title, any corporation which is an instrumentality of the United States) performing functions under this title is authorized to employ, for duty within the continental limits of the United States, such personnel as may be necessary to carry out the provisions and purposes of this title, and funds available pursuant to section 114 of this title shall be available for personal services in the District of Columbia and elsewhere without regard to section 14 (a) of the Federal Employees Pay Act of 1946 (60 Stat. 219). Of such personnel employed by the Administration, not to exceed one hundred may be compensated without regard to the provisions of the Classification Act of 1923, as amended, of whom not more than twenty-five may be compensated at a rate in excess of $10,000 per annum, but not in excess of $15,000 per annum. Experts and consultants or organizations thereof, as authorized by section 15 of the Act of August 2, 1946 (U. S. C., title 5, sec. 55a), may be employed by the Administration, and individuals so employed may be compensated at rates not in excess of $50 per diem and while away from their homes or regular places of business, they may be paid actual travel expenses and not to exceed $10 per diem in lieu of subsistence and other expenses while so employed.

(f) The Administrator may, from time to time, promulgate such rules and regulations as may be necessary and proper to carry out his functions under this title, and he may delegate authority to perform any of such functions to his subordinates, acting under his direction and under rules and regulations promulgated by him.

GENERAL FUNCTIONS OF ADMINISTRATOR

SEC. 105. (a) The Administrator, under the control of the President, shall in addition to all other functions vested in him by this title—

(1) review and appraise the requirements of participating countries for assistance under the terms of this title;

(2) formulate programs of United States assistance under this title, including approval of specific projects which have been submitted to him by the participating countries;

(3) provide for the efficient execution of any such programs as may be placed in operation; and

(4) terminate provision of assistance or take other remedial action as provided in section 118 of this title.

(b) In order to strengthen and make more effective the conduct of the foreign relations of the United States—

(1) the Administrator and the Secretary of State shall keep each other fully and currently informed on matters, including prospective action, arising within the scope of their respective duties which are pertinent to the duties of the other;

(2) whenever the Secretary of State believes that any action, proposed action, or failure to act on the part of the Administrator is inconsistent with the foreign-policy objectives of the United States, he shall consult with the Administrator and, if differences of view are not adjusted by consultation, the matter shall be referred to the President for final decision;

(3) whenever the Administrator believes that any action, proposed action, or failure to act on the part of the Secretary of State in performing functions under this title is inconsistent with the purposes and provisions of this title, he shall consult with the Secretary of State and, if differences of view are not adjusted by consultation, the matter shall be referred to the President for final decision.

(c) The Administrator and the department, agency, or officer in the executive branch of the Government exercising the authority granted to the President by section 6 of the Act of July 2, 1940 (54 Stat. 714), as amended, shall keep each other fully and currently informed on matters, including prospective action, arising within the scope of their respective duties which are pertinent to the duties of the other. Whenever the Administrator believes that any action, proposed action, or failure to act on the part of such department, agency, or officer in performing functions under this title is inconsistent with the purposes and provisions of this title, he shall consult with such department, agency, or officer and, if differences of view are not adjusted by consultation, the matter shall be referred to the President for final decision.

NATIONAL ADVISORY COUNCIL

Sec. 106. Section 4 (a) of the Bretton Woods Agreements Act (59 Stat. 512, 513) is hereby amended to read as follows:

"Sec. 4. (a) In order to coordinate the policies and operations of the representatives of the United States on the Fund and the Bank and of all agencies of the Government which make or participate in making foreign loans or which engage in foreign financial, exchange or monetary transactions, there is hereby established the National Advisory Council on International Monetary and Financial Problems (hereinafter referred to as the 'Council'), consisting of the Secretary of the Treasury, as Chairman, the Secretary of State, the Secretary of Commerce, the Chairman of the Board of Governors of the Federal Reserve System, the Chairman of the Board of Directors of the Export-Import Bank of Washington, and during such period as the Economic Cooperation Administration shall continue to exist, the Administrator for Economic Cooperation."

PUBLIC ADVISORY BOARD

Sec. 107. (a) There is hereby created a Public Advisory Board, hereinafter referred to as the Board, which shall advise and consult with the Administrator with respect to general or basic policy matters arising in connection with the Administrator's discharge of his responsibilities. The Board shall consist of the Administrator, who shall be Chairman, and not to exceed twelve additional members to be appointed by the President, by and with the advice and consent of the Senate, and who shall be selected from among citizens of the United States of broad and varied experience in matters affecting the public interest, other than officers and employees of the United States (including any agency or instrumentality of the United States) who, as such, regularly receive compensation for current services. The Board shall meet at least once a month and at other times upon the call of the Administrator or when three or more members of the Board request the Administrator to call a meeting. Not more than a majority of two of the members shall be appointed to the Board from the same political party. Members of the Board, other than the Administrator, shall receive, out of funds made available for the purposes of this title, a per diem allowance of $50 for each day spent away from their homes or regular places of business, for the purpose of attendance at meetings of the Board, or at conferences held upon the call of the Administrator, and in necessary travel, and while so engaged, they may be paid actual travel expenses and not to exceed $10 per diem in lieu of subsistence and other expenses.

(b) The Administrator may appoint such other advisory committees as he may determine to be necessary or desirable to effectuate the purposes of this title.

UNITED STATES SPECIAL REPRESENTATIVE ABROAD

SEC. 108. There shall be a United States Special Representative in Europe who shall (a) be appointed by the President, by and with the advice and consent of the Senate, (b) be entitled to receive the same compensation and allowances as a chief of mission, class 1, within the meaning of the Act of August 13, 1946 (60 Stat. 999), and (c) have the rank of ambassador extraordinary and plenipotentiary. He shall be the representative of the Administrator, and shall also be the chief representative of the United States Government to any organization of participating countries which may be established by such countries to further a joint program for European recovery, and shall discharge in Europe such additional responsibilities as may be assigned to him with the approval of the President in furtherance of the purposes of this title. He may also be designated as the United States representative on the Economic Commission for Europe. He shall receive his instructions from the Administrator and such instructions shall be prepared and transmitted to him in accordance with procedures agreed to between the Administrator and the Secretary of State in order to assure appropriate coordination as provided by subsection (b) of section 105 of this title. He shall coordinate the activities of the chiefs of special missions provided for in section 109 of this title. He shall keep the Administrator, the Secretary of State, the chiefs of the United States diplomatic missions, and the chiefs of the special missions provided for in section 109 of this title currently informed concerning his activities. He shall consult with the chiefs of all such missions, who shall give him such cooperation as he may require for the performance of his duties under this title.

SPECIAL ECA MISSIONS ABROAD

SEC. 109. (a) There shall be established for each participating country, except as provided in subsection (d) of this section, a special mission for economic cooperation under the direction of a chief who shall be responsible for assuring the performance within such country of operations under this title. The chief shall be appointed by the Administrator, shall receive his instructions from the Administrator, and shall report to the Administrator on the performance of the duties assigned to him. The chief of the special mission shall take rank immediately after the chief of the United States diplomatic mission in such country.

(b) The chief of the special mission shall keep the chief of the United States diplomatic mission fully and currently informed on matters, including prospective action, arising within the scope of the operations of the special mission and the chief of the diplomatic mission shall keep the chief of the special mission fully and currently informed on matters relative to the conduct of the duties of the chief of the special mission. The chief of the United States diplomatic mission will be responsible for assuring that the operations of the special mission are consistent with the foreign-policy objectives of the United States in such country and to that end whenever the chief of the United States diplomatic mission believes that any action, proposed action, or failure to act on the part of the special mission is inconsistent with such foreign-policy objectives, he shall so advise the chief of the special mission and the United States Special Representative in Europe. If differences of view are not adjusted by consultation, the matter shall be referred to the Secretary of State and the Administrator for decision.

(c) The Secretary of State shall provide such office space, facilities, and other administrative services for the United States Special Representative in Europe and his staff, and for the special mission in each participating country, as may be agreed between the Secretary of State and the Administrator.

(d) With respect to any of the zones of occupation of Germany and of the Free Territory of Trieste, during the period of occupation, the President shall make appropriate administrative arrangements for the conduct of operations under this title, in order to enable the Administrator to carry out his responsibility to assure the accomplishment of the purposes of this title.

PERSONNEL OUTSIDE UNITED STATES

SEC. 110. (a) For the purpose of performing functions under this title outside the continental limits of the United States the Administrator may—

(1) employ persons who shall receive compensation at any of the rates provided for the Foreign Service Reserve and Staff by the Foreign Service Act of 1946 (60 Stat. 999), together with allowances and benefits established thereunder; and

(2) recommend the appointment or assignment of persons, and the Secretary of State may appoint or assign such persons, to any class in the Foreign Service Reserve or Staff for the duration of operations under this title, and the Secretary of State may

assign, transfer, or promote such persons upon the recommendation of the Administrator. Persons so appointed to the Foreign Service Staff shall be entitled to the benefits of section 528 of the Foreign Service Act of 1946.

(b) For the purpose of performing functions under this title outside the continental limits of the United States, the Secretary of State may, at the request of the Administrator, appoint, for the duration of operations under this title, alien clerks and employees in accordance with applicable provisions of the Foreign Service Act of 1946 (60 Stat. 999).

(c) No citizen or resident of the United States may be employed, or if already employed, may be assigned to duties by the Secretary of State or the Administrator under this title for a period to exceed three months unless such individual has been investigated as to loyalty and security by the Federal Bureau of Investigation and a report thereon has been made to the Secretary of State and the Administrator, and until the Secretary of State or the Administrator has certified in writing (and filed copies thereof with the Senate Committee on Foreign Relations and the House Committee on Foreign Affairs) that, after full consideration of such report, he believes such individual is loyal to the United States, its Constitution, and form of government, and is not now and has never been a member of any organization advocating contrary views. This subsection shall not apply in the case of any officer appointed by the President by and with the advice and consent of the Senate.

NATURE AND METHOD OF ASSISTANCE

SEC. 111. (a) The Administrator may, from time to time, furnish assistance to any participating country by providing for the performance of any of the functions set forth in paragraphs (1) through (5) of this subsection when he deems it to be in furtherance of the purposes of this title, and upon the terms and conditions set forth in this title and such additional terms and conditions consistent with the provisions of this title as he may determine to be necessary and proper.

(1) Procurement from any source, including Government stocks on the same basis as procurement by Government agencies under Public Law 375 (Seventy-ninth Congress) for their own use, of any commodity which he determines to be required for the furtherance of the purposes of this title. As used in this title, the term "commodity" means any commodity, material, article, supply, or goods necessary for the purposes of this title.

(2) Processing, storing, transporting, and repairing any commodities, or performing any other services with respect to a participating country which he determines to be required for accomplishing the purposes of this title. The Administrator shall, in providing for the procurement of commodities under authority of this title, take such steps as may be necessary to assure, so far as is practicable, that at least 50 per centum of the gross tonnage of commodities, procured within the United States out of funds made available under this title and transported abroad on ocean vessels, is so transported on United States flag vessels to the extent such vessels are available at market rates.

(3) Procurement of and furnishing technical information and assistance.

(4) Transfer of any commodity or service, which transfer shall be signified by delivery of the custody and right of possession and use of such commodity, or otherwise making available any such commodity, or by rendering a service to a participating country or to any agency or organization representing a participating country.

(5) The allocation of commodities or services to specific projects designed to carry out the purposes of this title, which have been submitted to the Administrator by participating countries and have been approved by him.

(b) In order to facilitate and maximize the use of private channels of trade, subject to adequate safeguards to assure that all expenditures in connection with such procurement are within approved programs in accordance with terms and conditions established by the Administrator, he may provide for the performance of any of the functions described in subsection (a) of this section—

(1) by establishing accounts against which, under regulations prescribed by the Administrator—

(i) letters of commitment may be issued in connection with supply programs approved by the Administrator (and such letters of commitment, when issued, shall constitute obligations of the United States and monies due or to become due thereunder shall be assignable under the Assignment of Claims Act of 1940 and shall constitute obligations of applicable appropriations); and

(ii) withdrawals may be made by participating countries, or agencies or organizations representing participating countries or by other persons or organizations, upon presentation of contracts, invoices, or other documentation specified by the Administrator under arrangements prescribed by the Administrator to assure the use of such withdrawals for purposes approved by the Administrator.

Such accounts may be established on the books of the Administration, or any other department, agency, or establishment of the Government specified by the Administrator, or, on terms and conditions approved by the Secretary of the Treasury, in banking institutions in the United States. Expenditures of funds which have been made available through accounts so established shall be accounted for on standard documentation required for expenditures of Government funds: *Provided*, That such expenditures for commodities or services procured outside the continental limits of the United States under authority of this section may be accounted for exclusively on such certification as the Administrator may prescribe in regulations promulgated by him with the approval of the Comptroller General of the United States to assure expenditure in furtherance of the purposes of this title.

(2) by utilizing the services and facilities of any department, agency, or establishment of the Government as the President shall direct, or with the consent of the head of such department, agency, or establishment, or, in the President's discretion, by acting in cooperation with the United Nations or with other international

organizations or with agencies of the participating countries, and funds allocated pursuant to this section to any department, agency, or establishment of the Government shall be established in separate appropriation accounts on the books of the Treasury.

(3) by making, under rules and regulations to be prescribed by the Administrator, guaranties to any person of investments in connection with projects approved by the Administrator and the participating country concerned as furthering the purposes of this title (including guaranties of investments in enterprises producing or distributing informational media: *Provided*, That the amount of such guaranties in the first year after the date of the enactment of this Act does not exceed $15,000,000), which guaranties shall terminate not later than fourteen years from the date of enactment of this Act: *Provided*, That—

(i) the guaranty to any person shall not exceed the amount of dollars invested in the project by such person with the approval of the Administrator and shall be limited to the transfer into United States dollars of other currencies, or credits in such currencies, received by such person as income from the approved investment, as repayment or return thereof, in whole or in part, or as compensation for the sale or disposition of all or any part thereof: *Provided*, That, when any payment is made to any person under authority of this paragraph, such currencies, or credits in such currencies, shall become the property of the United States Government;

(ii) the Administrator may charge a fee in an amount determined by him not exceeding 1 per centum per annum of the amount of each guaranty, and all fees collected hereunder shall be available for expenditure in discharge of liabilities under guaranties made under this paragraph until such time as all such liabilities have been discharged or have expired, or until all such fees have been expended in accordance with the provisions of this paragraph; and

(iii) as used in this paragraph, the term "person" means a citizen of the United States or any corporation, partnership, or other association created under the law of the United States or of any State or Territory and substantially beneficially owned by citizens of the United States.

The total amount of the guaranties made under this paragraph (3) shall not exceed $300,000,000, and as such guaranties are made the authority to realize funds from the sale of notes for the purpose of allocating funds to the Export-Import Bank of Washington under paragraph (2) of subsection (c) of this section shall be accordingly reduced. Any payments made to discharge liabilities under guaranties issued under paragraph (3) of this subsection shall be paid out of fees collected under subparagraph (ii) of paragraph (3) of this subsection as long as such fees are available, and thereafter shall be paid out of funds realized from the sale of notes which shall be issued under authority of paragraph (2) of subsection (c) of this section when necessary to discharge liabilities under any such guaranty.

(c) (1) The Administrator may provide assistance for any participating country, in the form and under the procedures authorized in subsections (a) and (b), respectively, of this section, through grants or upon payment in cash, or on credit terms, or on such other terms of payment as he may find appropriate, including payment by the transfer to the United States (under such terms and in such quantities as may be agreed to between the Administrator and the participating country) of materials which are required by the United States as a result of deficiencies or potential deficiencies in its own resources. In determining whether such assistance shall be through grants or upon terms of payment, and in determining the terms of payment, he shall act in consultation with the National Advisory Council on International Monetary and Financial Problems, and the determination whether or not a participating country should be required to make payment for any assistance furnished to such country in furtherance of the purposes of this title, and the terms of such payment, if required, shall depend upon the character and purpose of the assistance and upon whether there is reasonable assurance of repayment considering the capacity of such country to make such payments without jeopardizing the accomplishment of the purposes of this title.

(2) When it is determined that assistance should be extended under the provisions of this title on credit terms, the Administrator shall allocate funds for the purpose to the Export-Import Bank of Washington, which shall, notwithstanding the provisions of the Export-Import Bank Act of 1945 (59 Stat. 526), as amended, make and administer the credit on terms specified by the Administrator in consultation with the National Advisory Council on International Monetary and Financial Problems. The Administrator is authorized to issue notes from time to time for purchase by the Secretary of the Treasury in an amount not exceeding in the aggregate $1,000,000,000 (i) for the purpose of allocating funds to the Export-Import Bank of Washington under this paragraph during the period of one year following the date of enactment of this Act and (ii) for the purpose of carrying out the provisions of paragraph (3) of subsection (b) of this section until all liabilities arising under guaranties made pursuant to such paragraph (3) have expired or have been discharged. Such notes shall be redeemable at the option of the Administrator before maturity in such manner as may be stipulated in such notes and shall have such maturity as may be determined by the Administrator with the approval of the Secretary of the Treasury. Each such note shall bear interest at a rate determined by the Secretary of the Treasury, taking into consideration the current average rate on outstanding marketable obligations of the United States as of the last day of the month preceding the issuance of the note. Payment under this paragraph of the purchase price of such notes and repayments thereof by the Administrator shall be treated as public-debt transactions of the United States. In allocating funds to the Export-Import Bank of Washington under this paragraph, the Administrator shall first utilize such funds realized from the sale of notes authorized by this paragraph as he determines to be available for this purpose, and when such funds are exhausted, or after the end of one year from the date of enactment of this Act, whichever is earlier, he shall utilize any funds appropriated under this title. The Administrator shall make advances to, or reimburse,

the Export-Import Bank of Washington for necessary administrative expenses in connection with such credits. Credits made by the Export-Import Bank of Washington with funds so allocated to it by the Administrator shall not be considered in determining whether the Bank has outstanding at any one time loans and guaranties to the extent of the limitation imposed by section 7 of the Export-Import Bank Act of 1945 (59 Stat. 529), as amended. Amounts received in repayment of principal and interest on any credits made under this paragraph shall be deposited into miscellaneous receipts of the Treasury: *Provided*, That, to the extent required for such purpose, amounts received in repayment of principal and interest on any credits made out of funds realized from the sale of notes authorized under this paragraph shall be deposited into the Treasury for the purpose of the retirement of such notes.

PROTECTION OF DOMESTIC ECONOMY

SEC. 112. (a) The Administrator shall provide for the procurement in the United States of commodities under this title in such a way as to (1) minimize the drain upon the resources of the United States and the impact of such procurement upon the domestic economy, and (2) avoid impairing the fulfillment of vital needs of the people of the United States.

(b) The procurement of petroleum and petroleum products under this title shall, to the maximum extent practicable, be made from petroleum sources outside the United States; and, in furnishing commodities under the provisions of this title, the Administrator shall take fully into account the present and anticipated world shortage of petroleum and its products and the consequent undesirability of expansion in petroleum-consuming equipment where the use of alternate fuels or other sources of power is practicable.

(c) In order to assure the conservation of domestic grain supplies and the retention in the United States of byproduct feeds necessary to the maintenance of the agricultural economy of the United States, the amounts of wheat and wheat flour produced in the United States to be transferred by grant to the participating countries shall be so determined that the total quantity of United States wheat used to produce the wheat flour procured in the United States for transfer by grant to such countries under this title shall not be less than 25 per centum of the aggregate of the unprocessed wheat and wheat in the form of flour procured in the United States for transfer by grant to such countries under this title.

(d) The term "surplus agricultural commodity" as used in this section is defined as any agricultural commodity, or product thereof, produced in the United States which is determined by the Secretary of Agriculture to be in excess of domestic requirements. In providing for the procurement of any such surplus agricultural commodity for transfer by grant to any participating country in accordance with the requirements of such country, the Administrator shall, insofar as practicable and where in furtherance of the purposes of this title, give effect to the following:

(1) The Administrator shall authorize the procurement of any such surplus agricultural commodity only within the United States: *Provided*, That this restriction shall not be applicable (i) to any agri-

cultural commodity, or product thereof, located in one participating country, and intended for transfer to another participating country, if the Administrator, in consultation with the Secretary of Agriculture, determines that such procurement and transfer is in furtherance of the purposes of this title, and would not create a burdensome surplus in the United States or seriously prejudice the position of domestic producers of such surplus agricultural commodities, or (ii) if, and to the extent that any such surplus agricultural commodity is not available in the United States in sufficient quantities to supply the requirements of the participating countries under this title.

(2) In providing for the procurement of any such surplus agricultural commodity, the Administrator shall, insofar as practicable and applicable, and after giving due consideration to the excess of any such commodity over domestic requirements, and to the historic reliance of United States producers of any such surplus agricultural commodity upon markets in the participating countries, provide for the procurement of each class or type of any such surplus agricultural commodity in the approximate proportion that the Secretary of Agriculture determines such classes or types bear to the total amount of excess of such surplus agricultural commodity over domestic requirements.

(e) Whenever the Secretary of Agriculture determines that any quantity of any surplus agricultural commodity, heretofore or hereafter acquired by Commodity Credit Corporation in the administration of its price-support programs, is available for use in furnishing assistance to foreign countries, he shall so advise all departments, agencies, and establishments of the Government administering laws providing for the furnishing of assistance or relief to foreign countries (including occupied or liberated countries or areas of such countries). Thereafter the department, agency, or establishment administering any such law shall, to the maximum extent practicable, consistent with the provisions and in furtherance of the purposes of such law, and where for transfer by grant and in accordance with the requirements of such foreign country, procure or provide for the procurement of such quantity of such surplus agricultural commodity. The sales price paid as reimbursement to Commodity Credit Corporation for any such surplus agricultural commodity shall be in such amount as Commodity Credit Corporation determines will fully reimburse it for the cost to it of such surplus agricultural commodity at the time and place such surplus agricultural commodity is delivered by it, but in no event shall the sales price be higher than the domestic market price at such time and place of delivery as determined by the Secretary of Agriculture, and the Secretary of Agriculture may pay not to exceed 50 per centum of such sales price as authorized by subsection (f) of this section.

(f) Subject to the provisions of this section, but notwithstanding any other provision of law, in order to encourage utilization of surplus agricultural commodities pursuant to this or any other Act providing for assistance or relief to foreign countries, the Secretary of Agriculture, in carrying out the purposes of clause (1), section 32, Public Law 320, Seventy-fourth Congress, as amended, may make payments, including payments to any government agency procuring or selling such surplus agricultural commodities, in an amount not to exceed 50 per centum of the sales price (basis free along ship or free on board vessel, United States ports), as determined by the Secretary of Agriculture, of such surplus agricultural commodities. The rescission of the remainder of section 32 funds by the Act of July 30, 1947 (Public Law 266, Eightieth Congress), is hereby canceled and such funds are hereby made available for the purposes of section 32 for the fiscal year ending June 30, 1948.

(g) No export shall be authorized pursuant to authority conferred by section 6 of the Act of July 2, 1940 (54 Stat. 714), including any amendment thereto, of any commodity from the United States to any country wholly or partly in Europe which is not a participating country, if the department, agency, or officer in the executive branch of the Government exercising the authority granted to the President by section 6 of the Act of July 2, 1940, as amended, determines that the supply of such commodity is insufficient (or would be insufficient if such export were permitted) to fulfill the requirements of participating countries under this title as determined by the Administrator: *Provided*, *however*, That such export may be authorized if such department, agency, or officer determines that such export is otherwise in the national interest of the United States.

(h) In providing for the performance of any of the functions described in subsection (a) of section 111, the Administrator shall, to the maximum extent consistent with the accomplishment of the purposes of this title, utilize private channels of trade.

REIMBURSEMENT TO GOVERNMENT AGENCIES

SEC. 113. (a) The Administrator shall make reimbursement or payment, out of funds available for the purposes of this title, for any commodity, service, or facility procured under section 111 of this title from any department, agency, or establishment of the Government. Such reimbursement or payment shall be made to the owning or disposal agency, as the case may be, at replacement cost, or, if required by law, at actual cost, or at any other price authorized by law and agreed to between the Administrator and such agency. The amount of any reimbursement or payment to an owning agency for commodities, services, or facilities so procured shall be credited to current applicable appropriations, funds, or accounts from which there may be procured replacements of similar commodities or such services or facilities: *Provided*, That such commodities, services, or facilities may be procured from an owning agency only with the consent of such agency: *And provided further*, That where such appropriations, funds, or accounts are not reimbursable except by reason of this subsection, and when the owning agency determines that replacement of any commodity procured under authority of this section is not necessary, any funds received in payment therefor shall be covered into the Treasury as miscellaneous receipts.

(b) The Administrator, whenever in his judgment the interests of the United States will best be served thereby, may dispose of any commodity procured out of funds made available for the purposes of this title, in lieu of transferring such commodity to a participating country, (1) by transfer of such commodity, upon reimbursement, to any department, agency, or establishment of the Government for use or disposal by such department, agency, or establishment as authorized by law, or (2) without regard to provisions of law relating to the disposal of Government-owned property, when necessary to prevent spoilage or wastage of such commodity or to conserve the usefulness thereof. Funds realized from such disposal or transfer shall revert to the respective appropriation or appropriations out of which funds were expended for the procurement of such commodity.

AUTHORIZATION OF APPROPRIATIONS

SEC. 114. (a) Notwithstanding the provisions of any other law, the Reconstruction Finance Corporation is authorized and directed, until such time as an appropriation shall be made pursuant to subsection (c) of this section, to make advances not to exceed in the aggregate $1,000,000,000 to carry out the provisions of this title, in such manner, at such time, and in such amounts as the President shall determine, and no interest shall be charged on advances made by the Treasury to the Reconstruction Finance Corporation for this purpose. The Reconstruction Finance Corporation shall be repaid without interest for advances made by it hereunder, from funds made available for the purposes of this title.

(b) Such part as the President may determine of the unobligated and unexpended balances of appropriations or other funds available for the purposes of the Foreign Aid Act of 1947 shall be available for the purpose of carrying out the purposes of this title.

(c) In order to carry out the provisions of this title with respect to those participating countries which adhere to the purposes of this title, and remain eligible to receive assistance hereunder, such funds shall be available as are hereafter authorized and appropriated to the President from time to time through June 30, 1952, to carry out the provisions and accomplish the purposes of this title: *Provided, however*, That for carrying out the provisions and accomplishing the purposes of this title for the period of one year following the date of enactment of this Act, there are hereby authorized to be so appropriated not to exceed $4,300,000,000. Nothing in this title is intended nor shall it be construed as an express or implied commitment to provide any specific assistance, whether of funds, commodities, or services, to any country or countries. The authorization in this title is limited to the period of twelve months in order that subsequent Congresses may pass on any subsequent authorizations.

(d) Funds made available for the purposes of this title shall be available for incurring and defraying all necessary expenses incident to carrying out the provisions of this title, including administrative expenses and expenses for compensation, allowances and travel of personnel, including Foreign Service personnel whose services are utilized primarily for the purposes of this title, and, without regard to the provisions of any other law, for printing and binding, and for expenditures outside the continental limits of the United States for the procurement of supplies and services and for other administrative purposes (other than compensation of personnel) without regard to such laws and regulations governing the obligation and expenditure of government funds, as the Administrator shall specify in the interest of the accomplishment of the purposes of this title.

(e) The unencumbered portions of any deposits which may have been made by any participating country pursuant to section 6 of the joint resolution providing for relief assistance to the people of countries devastated by war (Public Law 84, Eightieth Congress) and section 5 (b) of the Foreign Aid Act of 1947 (Public Law 389, Eightieth Congress) may be merged with the deposits to be made by such participating country in accordance with section 115 (b) (6) of this title, and shall be held or used under the same terms and conditions as are provided in section 115 (b) (6) of this title.

(f) In order to reserve some part of the surplus of the fiscal year 1948 for payments thereafter to be made under this title, there is hereby created on the books of the Treasury of the United States a trust fund to be known as the Foreign Economic Cooperation Trust Fund. Notwithstanding any other provision of law, an amount of $3,000,000,000, out of sums appropriated pursuant to the authorization contained in this title shall, when appropriated, be transferred immediately to the trust fund, and shall thereupon be considered as expended during the fiscal year 1948, for the purpose of reporting governmental expenditures. The Secretary of the Treasury shall be the sole trustee of the trust fund and is authorized and directed to pay out of the fund such amounts as the Administrator shall duly requisition. The first expenditures made out of the appropriations authorized under this title in the fiscal year 1949 shall be made with funds requisitioned by the Administrator out of the trust fund until the fund is exhausted, at which time such fund shall cease to exist. The provisions of this subsection shall not be construed as affecting the application of any provision of law which would otherwise govern the obligation of funds so appropriated or the auditing or submission of accounts of transactions with respect to such funds.

BILATERAL AND MULTILATERAL UNDERTAKINGS

SEC. 115. (a) The Secretary of State, after consultation with the Administrator, is authorized to conclude, with individual participating countries or any number of such countries or with an organization representing any such countries, agreements in furtherance of the purposes of this title. The Secretary of State, before an Administrator or Deputy Administrator shall have qualified and taken office, is authorized to negotiate and conclude such temporary agreements in implementation of subsection (b) of this section as he may deem necessary in furtherance of the purposes of this title: *Provided*, That when an Administrator or Deputy Administrator shall have qualified and taken office, the Secretary of State shall conclude the basic agreements required by subsection (b) of this section only after consultation with the Administrator or Deputy Administrator, as the case may be.

(b) The provision of assistance under this title results from the multilateral pledges of the participating countries to use all their efforts to accomplish a joint recovery program based upon self-help and mutual cooperation as embodied in the report of the Committee of European Economic Cooperation signed at Paris on September 22, 1947, and is contingent upon continuous effort of the participating countries to accomplish a joint recovery program through multilateral undertakings and the establishment of a continuing organization for this purpose. In addition to continued mutual cooperation of the participating countries in such a program, each such country shall conclude an agreement with the United States in order for such country to be eligible to receive assistance under this title. Such agreement shall provide for the adherence of such country to the purposes of this title and shall, where applicable, make appropriate provision, among others, for—

(1) promoting industrial and agricultural production in order to enable the participating country to become independent of extraordinary outside economic assistance; and submitting for the approval of the Administrator, upon his request and whenever he deems it in furtherance of the purposes of this title, specific projects proposed by such country to be undertaken in substantial part with assistance furnished under this title, which projects, whenever practicable, shall include projects for increased production of coal, steel, transportation facilities, and food;

(2) taking financial and monetary measures necessary to stabilize its currency, establish or maintain a valid rate of exchange, to balance its governmental budget as soon as practicable, and generally to restore or maintain confidence in its monetary system;

(3) cooperating with other participating countries in facilitating and stimulating an increasing interchange of goods and services among the participating countries and with other countries and cooperating to reduce barriers to trade among themselves and with other countries;

(4) making efficient and practical use, within the framework of a joint program for European recovery, of the resources of such participating country, including any commodities, facilities, or services furnished under this title, which use shall include, to the extent practicable, taking measures to locate and identify and put into appropriate use, in furtherance of such program, assets, and earnings therefrom, which belong to the citizens of such country and which are situated within the United States, its Territories and possessions;

(5) facilitating the transfer to the United States by sale, exchange, barter, or otherwise for stock-piling or other purposes, for such period of time as may be agreed to and upon reasonable terms and in reasonable quantities, of materials which are required by the United States as a result of deficiencies or potential deficiencies in its own resources, and which may be available in such participating country after due regard for reasonable requirements for domestic use and commercial export of such country;

(6) placing in a special account a deposit in the currency of such country, in commensurate amounts and under such terms and conditions as may be agreed to between such country and the Government of the United States, when any commodity or service is made available through any means authorized under this title, and is furnished to the participating country on a grant basis. Such special account, together with the unencumbered portions of any deposits which may have been made by such country pursuant to section 6 of the joint resolution providing for relief assistance to the people of countries devastated by war (Public Law 84, Eightieth Congress) and section 5 (b) of the Foreign Aid Act of 1947 (Public Law 389, Eightieth Congress), shall be held or used within such country for such purposes as

may be agreed to between such country and the Administrator in consultation with the National Advisory Council on International Monetary and Financial Problems, and the Public Advisory Board provided for in section 107 (a) for purposes of internal monetary and financial stabilization, for the stimulation of productive activity and the exploration for and development of new sources of wealth, or for such other expenditures as may be consistent with the purposes of this title, including local currency administrative expenditures of the United States incident to operations under this title, and under agreement that any unencumbered balance remaining in such account on June 30, 1952, shall be disposed of within such country for such purposes as may, subject to approval by Act or joint resolution of the Congress, be agreed to between such country and the Government of the United States;

(7) publishing in such country and transmitting to the United States, not less frequently than every calendar quarter after the date of the agreement, full statements of operations under the agreement, including a report of the use of funds, commodities, and services received under this title;

(8) furnishing promptly, upon request of the United States, any relevant information which would be of assistance to the United States in determining the nature and scope of operations and the use of assistance provided under this title;

(9) recognizing the principle of equity in respect to the drain upon the natural resources of the United States and of the recipient countries, by agreeing to negotiate (a) a future schedule of minimum availabilities to the United States for future purchase and delivery of a fair share of materials which are required by the United States as a result of deficiencies or potential deficiencies in its own resources at world market prices so as to protect the access of United States industry to an equitable share of such materials either in percentages of production or in absolute quantities from the participating countries, and (b) suitable protection for the right of access for any person as defined in paragraph (iii) of subparagraph (3) of section 111 (b) in the development of such materials on terms of treatment equivalent to those afforded to the nationals of the country concerned, and (c) an agreed schedule of increased production of such materials where practicable in such participating countries and for delivery of an agreed percentage of such increased production to be transferred to the United States on a long-term basis in consideration of assistance furnished by the Administrator to such countries under this title; and

(10) submitting for the decision of the International Court of Justice or of any arbitral tribunal mutually agreed upon any case espoused by the United States Government involving compensation of a national of the United States for governmental measures affecting his property rights, including contracts with or concessions from such country.

(c) Notwithstanding the provisions of subsection (b) of this section, the Administrator, during the three months after the date of enactment of this Act, may perform with respect to any participating country any of the functions authorized under this title which he may determine to be essential in furtherance of the purposes of this title, if (1) such country has signified its adherence to the purposes of this title and its intention to conclude an agreement pursuant to subsection (b) of this section, and (2) he finds that such country is complying with the applicable provisions of subsection (b) of this section: *Provided*, That, notwithstanding the provisions of this subsection, the Administrator may, through June 30, 1948, provide for the transfer of food, medical supplies, fibers, fuel, petroleum and petroleum products, fertilizer, pesticides, and seed to any country of Europe which participated in the Committee of European Economic Cooperation and which undertook pledges to the other participants therein, when the Administrator determines that the transfer of any such supplies to any such country is essential in order to make it possible to carry out the purposes of this title by alleviating conditions of hunger and cold and by preventing serious economic retrogression.

(d) The Administrator shall encourage the joint organization of the participating countries referred to in subsection (b) of this section to ensure that each participating country makes efficient use of the resources of such country, including any commodities, facilities, or services furnished under this title, by observing and reviewing such use through an effective follow-up system approved by the joint organization.

(e) The Administrator shall encourage arrangements among the participating countries in conjunction with the International Refugee Organization looking toward the largest practicable utilization of manpower available in any of the participating countries in furtherance of the accomplishment of the purposes of this title.

(f) The Administrator will request the Secretary of State to obtain the agreement of those countries concerned that such capital equipment as is scheduled for removal as reparations from the three western zones of Germany be retained in Germany if such retention will most effectively serve the purposes of the European recovery program.

(g) It is the understanding of the Congress that, in accordance with agreements now in effect, prisoners of war remaining in participating countries shall, if they so freely elect, be repatriated prior to January 1, 1949.

WESTERN HEMISPHERE COUNTRIES

Sec. 116. The President shall take appropriate steps to encourage all countries in the Western Hemisphere to make available to participating countries such assistance as they may be able to furnish.

OTHER DUTIES OF THE ADMINISTRATOR

Sec. 117. (a) The Administrator, in furtherance of the purposes of section 115 (b) (5), and in agreement with a participating country, shall, whenever practicable, promote, by means of funds made available for the purposes of this title, an increase in the production in such participating country of materials which are required by the United States as a result of deficiencies or potential deficiencies in the resources within the United States.

(b) The Administrator, in cooperation with the Secretary of Commerce, shall facilitate and encourage, through private and public travel, transport, and other agencies, the promotion and development of travel by citizens of the United States to and within participating countries.

(c) In order to further the efficient use of United States voluntary contributions for relief in participating countries receiving assistance under this title in the form of grants or any of the zones of occupation of Germany for which assistance is provided under this title and the Free Territory of Trieste or either of its zones, funds made available for the purposes of this title shall be used insofar as practicable by the Administrator, under rules and regulations prescribed by him, to pay ocean freight charges from a United States port to a designated foreign port of entry (1) of supplies donated to, or purchased by, United States voluntary nonprofit relief agencies registered with and recommended by the Advisory Committee on Voluntary Foreign Aid for operations in Europe, or (2) of relief packages conforming to such specified size, weight, and contents, as the Administrator may prescribe originating in the United States and consigned to an individual residing in a participating country receiving assistance under this title in the form of grants or any of the zones of occupation of Germany for which assistance is provided under this title and the Free Territory of Trieste or either of its zones. Where practicable the Administrator is directed to make an agreement with such country for the use of a portion of the deposit of local currency placed in a special account pursuant to paragraph 6 of subsection (b) of section 115 of this title, for the purpose of defraying the transportation cost of such supplies and relief packages from the port of entry of such country to the designated shipping point of consignee. The Secretary of State, after consultation with the Administrator, shall make agreements where practicable with the participating countries for the free entry of such supplies and relief packages.

(d) The Administrator is directed to refuse delivery insofar as practicable to participating countries of commodities which go into the production of any commodity for delivery to any nonparticipating European country which commodity would be refused export licenses to those countries by the United States in the interest of national security. Whenever the Administrator believes that the issuance of a license for the export of any commodity to any country wholly or partly in Europe which is not a participating country is inconsistent with the purposes and provisions of this title, he shall so advise the department, agency, or officer in the executive branch of the Government exercising the authority with respect to such commodity granted to the President by section 6 of the Act of July 2, 1940 (54 Stat. 714), as amended, and, if differences of view are not adjusted by consultation, the matter shall be referred to the President for final decision.

TERMINATION OF ASSISTANCE

SEC. 118. The Administrator, in determining the form and measure of assistance provided under this title to any participating country, shall take into account the extent to which such country is complying with its undertakings embodied in its pledges to other participating countries and in its agreement concluded with the United States under section 115. The Administrator shall terminate the provision of assistance under this title to any participating country whenever he determines that (1) such country is not adhering to its agreement concluded under section 115, or is diverting from the purposes of this title assistance provided hereunder, and that in the circumstances remedial action other than termination will not more effectively promote the purposes of this title or (2) because of changed conditions, assistance is no longer consistent with the national interest of the United States. Termination of assistance to any country under this section shall include the termination of deliveries of all supplies scheduled under the aid program for such country and not yet delivered.

EXEMPTION FROM CONTRACT AND ACCOUNTING LAWS

SEC. 119. When the President determines it to be in furtherance of the purposes of this title, the functions authorized under this title may be performed without regard to such provisions of law regulating the making, performance, amendment, or modification of contracts and the expenditure of Government funds as the President may specify.

EXEMPTION FROM CERTAIN FEDERAL LAWS RELATING TO EMPLOYMENT

SEC. 120. Service of an individual as a member of the Public Advisory Board (other than the Administrator) created by section 107 (a), as a member of an advisory committee appointed pursuant to section 107 (b), as an expert or consultant under section 104 (e), or as an expert, consultant, or technician under section 124 (d), shall not be considered as service or employment bringing such individual within the provisions of section 109 or 113 of the Criminal Code (U. S. C., title 18, secs. 198 and 203), of section 190 of the Revised Statutes (U. S. C., title 5, sec. 99), or of section 19 (e) of the Contract Settlement Act of 1944, or of any other Federal law imposing restrictions, requirements, or penalties in relation to the employment of persons, the performance of services, or the payment or receipt of compensation in connection with any claim, proceeding, or matter involving the United States.

UNITED NATIONS

SEC. 121. (a) The President is authorized to request the cooperation of or the use of the services and facilities of the United Nations, its organs and specialized agencies, or other international organizations, in carrying out the purposes of this title, and may make payments, by advancements or reimbursements, for such purposes, out of funds made available for the purposes of this title, as may be necessary therefor, to the extent that special compensation is usually required for such services and facilities. Nothing in this title shall be construed to authorize the Administrator to delegate to or otherwise confer upon any international or foreign organization or agency any of his authority to decide the method of furnishing assistance under this title to any participating country or the amount thereof.

(b) The President shall cause to be transmitted to the Secretary General of the United Nations copies of reports to Congress on the operations conducted under this title.

(c) Any agreements concluded between the United States and participating countries, or groups of such countries, in implementation of the purposes of this title, shall be registered with the United Nations if such registration is required by the Charter of the United Nations.

TERMINATION OF PROGRAM

SEC. 122. (a) After June 30, 1952, or after the date of the passage of a concurrent resolution by the two Houses of Congress before such date, which declares that the powers conferred on the Administrator by or pursuant to subsection (a) of section 111 of this title are no longer necessary for the accomplishment of the purposes of this title, whichever shall first occur, none of the functions authorized under such provisions may be exercised; except that during the twelve months following such date commodities and services with respect to which the Administrator had, prior to such date, authorized procurement for, shipment to, or delivery in a participating country, may be transferred to such country, and funds appropriated under authority of this title may be obligated during such twelve-month period for the necessary expenses of procurement, shipment, delivery, and other activities essential to such transfer, and shall remain available during such period for the necessary expenses of liquidating operations under this title.

(b) At such time as the President shall find appropriate after such date, and prior to the expiration of the twelve months following such date, the powers, duties, and authority of the Administrator under this title may be transferred to such other departments, agencies, or establishments of the Government as the President shall specify, and the relevant funds, records, and personnel of the Administration may be transferred to the departments, agencies, or establishments to which the related functions are transferred.

REPORTS TO CONGRESS

SEC. 123. The President from time to time, but not less frequently than once every calendar quarter through June 30, 1952, and once every year thereafter until all operations under this title have been completed, shall transmit to the Congress a report of operations under this title, including the text of bilateral and multilateral agreements entered into in carrying out the provisions of this title. Reports provided for under this section shall be transmitted to the Secretary of the Senate or the Clerk of the House of Representatives, as the case may be, if the Senate or the House of Representatives, as the case may be, is not in session.

JOINT CONGRESSIONAL COMMITTEE

SEC. 124. (a) There is hereby established a joint congressional committee to be known as the Joint Committee on Foreign Economic Cooperation (hereinafter referred to as the committee), to be composed of ten members as follows:

(1) Three members who are members of the Committee on Foreign Relations of the Senate, two from the majority and one from the minority party, to be appointed by the chairman of the committee; two members who are members of the Committee on Appropriations of the Senate, one from the majority and one

from the minority party, to be appointed by the chairman of the committee; and

(2) Three members who are members of the Committee on Foreign Affairs of the House, two from the majority and one from the minority party, to be appointed by the chairman of the committee; and two members who are members of the Committee on Appropriations of the House, one from the majority and one from the minority party, to be appointed by the chairman of the committee.

A vacancy in the membership of the committee shall be filled in the same manner as the original selection. The committee shall elect a chairman from among its members.

(b) It shall be the function of the committee to make a continuous study of the programs of United States economic assistance to foreign countries, and to review the progress achieved in the execution and administration of such programs. Upon request, the committee shall aid the several standing committees of the Congress having legislative jurisdiction over any part of the programs of United States economic assistance to foreign countries; and it shall make a report to the Senate and the House of Representatives, from time to time, concerning the results of its studies, together with such recommendations as it may deem desirable. The Administrator, at the request of the committee, shall consult with the committee from time to time with respect to his activities under this Act.

(c) The committee, or any duly authorized subcommittee thereof, is authorized to hold such hearings, to sit and act at such times and places, to require by subpena or otherwise the attendance of such witnesses and the production of such books, papers, and documents, to administer such oaths, to take such testimony, to procure such printing and binding, and to make such expenditures as it deems advisable. The cost of stenographic services to report such hearings shall not be in excess of 25 cents per hundred words. The provisions of sections 102 to 104, inclusive, of the Revised Statutes shall apply in case of any failure of any witness to comply with any subpena or to testify when summoned under authority of this subsection.

(d) The committee is authorized to appoint and, without regard to the Classification Act of 1923, as amended, fix the compensation of such experts, consultants, technicians, and organizations thereof, and clerical and stenographic assistants as it deems necessary and advisable.

(e) There are hereby authorized to be appropriated such sums as may be necessary to carry out the provisions of this section, to be disbursed by the Secretary of the Senate on vouchers signed by the chairman.

SEPARABILITY CLAUSE

SEC. 125. If any provision of this Act or the application of such provision to any circumstances or persons shall be held invalid, the validity of the remainder of the Act and the applicability of such provision to other circumstances or persons shall not be affected thereby.

TITLE II

SEC. 201. This title may be cited as the "International Children's Emergency Fund Assistance Act of 1948".

SEC. 202. It is the purpose of this title to provide for the special care and feeding of children by authorizing additional moneys for the International Children's Emergency Fund of the United Nations.

SEC. 203. The President is hereby authorized and directed any time after the date of the enactment of this Act and before July 1, 1949, to make contributions (a) from sums appropriated to carry out the purposes of this title and (b) from sums appropriated to carry out the general purposes of the proviso in the first paragraph of the first section of the joint resolution of May 31, 1947 (Public Law 84, Eightieth Congress), as amended, to the International Children's Emergency Fund of the United Nations for the special care and feeding of children.

SEC. 204. No contribution shall be made pursuant to this title or such joint resolution of May 31, 1947, which would cause the sum of (a) the aggregate amount contributed pursuant to this title and (b) the aggregate amount contributed by the United States pursuant to such joint resolution of May 31, 1947, to exceed whichever of the following sums is the lesser:

(1) 72 per centum of the total resources contributed after May 31, 1947, by all governments, including the United States, for programs carried out under the supervision of such Fund: *Provided*, That in computing the amount of resources contributed there shall not be included contributions by any government for the benefit of persons located within the territory of such contributing government; or

(2) $100,000,000.

SEC. 205. Funds appropriated for the purposes of such joint resolution of May 31, 1947, shall remain available through June 30, 1949.

SEC. 206. There is hereby authorized to be appropriated to carry out the purposes of this title for the fiscal year ending June 30, 1949, the sum of $60,000,000.

TITLE III

SEC. 301. This title may be cited as the "Greek-Turkish Assistance Act of 1948".

SEC. 302. In addition to the amounts authorized to be appropriated under subsection (b) of section 4 of the Act of May 22, 1947 (61 Stat. 103), there are hereby authorized to be appropriated not to exceed $275,000,000 to carry out the provisions of such Act, as amended.

SEC. 303. (a) Subsection (a) of section 4 of such Act of May 22, 1947, is hereby amended by adding at the end thereof the following: "The Reconstruction Finance Corporation is authorized and directed to make additional advances, not to exceed in the aggregate $50,000,000, to carry out the provisions of this Act, as amended, in such manner and in such amounts as the President shall determine. No interest shall be charged on advances made by the Treasury to the Reconstruction Finance Corporation for this purpose."

(b) Subsection (b) of section 4 of the said Act is hereby amended by inserting after the word "repaid" the following: "without interest".

SEC. 304. Subsections (2) and (3) of section 1 of such Act of May 22, 1947, are hereby amended to permit detailing of persons referred to in such subsections to the United States Missions to Greece and Turkey as well as to the governments of those countries. Section 302 of the Act of January 27, 1948 (Public Law 402, Eightieth Congress), and section 110 (c) of the Economic Cooperation Act of 1948 (relating to investigations of personnel by the Federal Bureau of Investigation) shall be applicable to any person so detailed pursuant to such subsection (2) of such Act of 1947: *Provided*, That any military or civilian personnel detailed under section 1 of such Act of 1947 may receive such station allowances or additional allowances as the President may prescribe (and payments of such allowances heretofore made are hereby validated).

TITLE IV

SEC. 401. This title may be cited as the "China Aid Act of 1948".

SEC. 402. Recognizing the intimate economic and other relationships between the United States and China, and recognizing that disruption following in the wake of war is not contained by national frontiers, the Congress finds that the existing situation in China endangers the establishment of a lasting peace, the general welfare and national interest of the United States, and the attainment of the objectives of the United Nations. It is the sense of the Congress that the further evolution in China of principles of individual liberty, free institutions, and genuine independence rests largely upon the continuing development of a strong and democratic national government as the basis for the establishment of sound economic conditions and for stable international economic relationships. Mindful of the advantages which the United States has enjoyed through the existence of a large domestic market with no internal trade barriers, and believing that similar advantages can accrue to China, it is declared to be the policy of the people of the United States to encourage the Republic of China and its people to exert sustained common efforts which will speedily achieve the internal peace and economic stability in China which are essential for lasting peace and prosperity in the world. It is further declared to be the policy of the people of the United States to encourage the Republic of China in its efforts to maintain the genuine independence and the administrative integrity of China, and to sustain and strengthen principles of individual liberty and free institutions in China through a program of assistance based on self-help and cooperation: *Provided*, That no assistance to China herein contemplated shall seriously impair the economic stability of the United States. It is further declared to be the policy of the United States that assistance provided by the United States under this title should at all times be dependent upon cooperation by the Republic of China and its people in furthering the program: *Provided further*, That assistance furnished under this title shall not be construed as an express or implied assumption by the United States of any responsibility for policies, acts, or undertakings of the Republic of China or for conditions which may prevail in China at any time.

SEC. 403. Aid provided under this title shall be provided under the applicable provisions of the Economic Cooperation Act of 1948 which are consistent with the purposes of this title. It is not the purpose of this title that China, in order to receive aid hereunder, shall adhere to a joint program for European recovery.

SEC. 404. (a) In order to carry out the purposes of this title, there is hereby authorized to be appropriated to the President for aid to China a sum not to exceed $338,000,000 to remain available for obligation for the period of one year following the date of enactment of this Act.

(b) There is also hereby authorized to be appropriated to the President a sum not to exceed $125,000,000 for additional aid to China through grants, on such terms as the President may determine and without regard to the provisions of the Economic Cooperation Act of 1948, to remain available for obligation for the period of one year following the date of enactment of this Act.

SEC. 405. An agreement shall be entered into between China and the United States containing those undertakings by China which the Secretary of State, after consultation with the Administrator for Economic Cooperation, may deem necessary to carry out the purposes of this title and to improve commercial relations with China.

SEC. 406. Notwithstanding the provisions of any other law, the Reconstruction Finance Corporation is authorized and directed, until such time as an appropriation is made pursuant to section 404, to make advances, not to exceed in the aggregate $50,000,000, to carry out the provisions of this title in such manner and in such amounts as the President shall determine. From appropriations authorized under section 404, there shall be repaid without interest to the Reconstruction Finance Corporation the advances made by it under the authority contained herein. No interest shall be charged on advances made by the Treasury to the Reconstruction Finance Corporation in implementation of this section.

SEC. 407. (a) The Secretary of State, after consultation with the Administrator, is hereby authorized to conclude an agreement with China establishing a Joint Commission on Rural Reconstruction in China, to be composed of two citizens of the United States appointed by the President of the United States and three citizens of China appointed by the President of China. Such Commission shall, subject to the direction and control of the Administrator, formulate and carry out a program for reconstruction in rural areas of China, which shall include such research and training activities as may be necessary or appropriate for such reconstruction: *Provided*, That assistance furnished under this section shall not be construed as an express or implied assumption by the United States of any responsibility for making any further contributions to carry out the purposes of this section.

(b) Insofar as practicable, an amount equal to not more than 10 per centum of the funds made available under subsection (a) of section 404 shall be used to carry out the purposes of subsection (a) of this section. Such amount may be in United States dollars, proceeds in Chinese currency from the sale of commodities made available to China with funds authorized under subsection (a) of section 404, or both.

Approved April 3, 1948.

○